CONTINUUM ENCYCLOPEDIA OF
POPULAR MUSIC OF THE WORLD

VOLUME II:
PERFORMANCE AND PRODUCTION

Editorial Board

www.continuumpopmusic.com

CONTINUUM ENCYCLOPEDIA OF
POPULAR MUSIC
OF THE WORLD

VOLUME II:
PERFORMANCE AND PRODUCTION

EDITED BY
JOHN SHEPHERD, DAVID HORN,
DAVE LAING, PAUL OLIVER AND PETER WICKE

continuum
LONDON • NEW YORK

First published 2003 by
Continuum
The Tower Building, 11 York Road, London SE1 7NX
370 Lexington Avenue, New York, NY 10017–6503

The publishers thank the following for permission to use copyright material:

'Vigilante Man', by Woody Guthrie. © 1961 Ludlow Music Inc., U.S.A., assigned to TRO ESSEX MUSIC LIMITED of Suite 2.07, Plaza 535 Kings Road, London SW10 0SZ. International Copyright Secured. All Rights Reserved. Used by Permission.

'Fernando', by Stig Anderson, Benny Andersson and Bjorn Ulvaeses. Reproduced by kind permission of Bocu Music Ltd, 1 Wyndhan Yard, London W1H 2QF.

'She's Nineteen Years Old', written by McKinley Morganfield. © 1958 Watertoons (admin Bug Music Inc.).

'A Foggy Day (In London Town)', music and lyrics by George Gershwin and Ira Gershwin. © 1937 (renewed 1964) George Gershwin Music and Ira Gershwin Music, USA Warner/Chappell Music Ltd, London W6 8BS. Reproduced by Permission of International Music Publications Ltd. All Rights Reserved.

British Library Cataloguing-in-Publication Data
A catalogue record for this book is available from the British Library
ISBN 0–8264–6322–3

Library of Congress Cataloguing-in-Publication Data
Continuum encyclopedia of popular music of the world/
edited by John Shepherd . . . [et al.].
    p. cm.
Includes bibliographical references and index.
    ISBN 0–8264–6321–5--ISBN 0–8264–6322–3 (v.2)
    1. Popular music--Encyclopedias. I. Shepherd, John, 1947–
    ML102.P66C66 2003
    781.63'09--dc21

                        2002074146

Typeset by Wyvern 21 Ltd, Bristol
Printed and bound in Great Britain by Bookcraft Ltd, Midsomer Norton, Bath

Contents

Contents

Introduction

The *Continuum Encyclopedia of Popular Music of the World* had its genesis in the International Association for the Study of Popular Music (IASPM) in the mid-1980s.

IASPM was established in the early 1980s as a response to the increasing number of scholars publishing in the field of popular music. These scholars needed an organization through which to share and comment on their work, through which to advocate the legitimacy and desirability of work on popular music, and through which to advocate the inclusion of popular music studies in the academy.

Early in the life of IASPM, there was a recognition of the need for a comprehensive and reliable reference work on popular music that would serve the needs of scholars, researchers, students, and information and media professionals, as well as the general public.

The *Continuum Encyclopedia of Popular Music of the World* was planned as a response to that need. The first volume to be produced from the *Encyclopedia* project was *Popular Music Studies: A Select International Bibliography*, published in 1997.

The title of this, the second volume of the *Encyclopedia* proper, is *Performance and Production*. It was preceded by Volume I, *Media, Industry and Society*, and will be followed by volumes on locations, genres and personalities.

Because no model existed for this kind of comprehensive, scholarly reference work on popular music, extensive research was undertaken to develop a systematic, subject-based taxonomy for such a new field of study. It is for this reason that, rather than alphabetically, the entries in these volumes are organized in terms of sections and subsections that reflect the logic of this taxonomy. Subject areas that, in an alphabetical sequence, would have been scattered arbitrarily throughout the volumes are in this way brought together and organized coherently to constitute an unprecedented body of knowledge. Because the volumes are organized in this way, it is important for the reader to consult both the Table of Contents and the pages setting out the Arrangement of the Material at the beginning of each volume. However, each volume has its own index that makes it easy to locate discussions of specific terms within a range of entries.

It is in part the subject-based character of these volumes that makes them distinctive among popular music reference works. The scholarly character of these volumes is apparent also in the comprehensive end matter that is provided for most entries: bibliographies, discographies, sheet music listings, filmographies, and listings of visual recordings. The volumes draw on the expertise of the world's leading popular music scholars, and are additionally distinctive in covering the popular music of the whole world rather than specific regions of it.

This volume contains a major section of the *Continuum Encyclopedia of Popular Music of the World*: 'Musical Practises.' It is subdivided into four principal parts: 'Performers and Performing,' 'Musical Production and Transmission,' 'Musical Instruments' and 'Musical Form and Practise.' The first part contains entries on types of performing groups and individuals (for example, Accordion Band and Cabaret Singer), as well as on a wide variety of performance techniques. The second part, 'Musical Production and Transmission,' contains entries on different kinds of personnel (for example, Disc Jockey), as well as on interpretive and technological processes (for example, Orchestration and Double-Tracking) and technologies (for instance, Sampler). The third part contains the volume's entries on musical instruments – not only those that have played a major role in the history of popular music, but also those that, at first blush, might seem to have had a less intimate relation with that history. The final part contains entries on various aspects of musical form – harmony, melody, rhythm and timbre – as well as on other dimensions of music and its practise (such as Arrangement, Lyrics and Stage Act).

One observation needs to be made about the end matter of each entry. For reasons of historical documentation, the sheet music listings, discographical references and discographies customarily contain the first publication details of songs and recordings. However, to assist readers in hearing this music where possible, reference is also sometimes made to reissues of older recordings on compact disc. The reissues listed are those that were available at the time the entry was signed off for publication. The period during which entries for this volume were signed off stretched from March 1998 to June 2002. Reissues listed in the discographical references and discographies of these entries may as a consequence no longer be available. However, the likelihood is that these particular recordings have been reissued elsewhere since that time.

The distinction between discographical references and discographies is an important one. If a particular piece of music is referred to in an entry, there will also be a reference to it in the entry's end matter, either in the sheet music listing or in the discographical references (and sometimes both). Discographies, on the other hand, provide a list of representative recordings of relevance to the entry in general. It must be stressed that these discographies are solely representative, and are not intended to be comprehensive. A distinction is drawn in discographical references and discographies between dates of recording and dates of issue where these differ. Dates of recording are in roman type; dates of issue are italicized.

Details of all films and visual recordings (videos) referred to in an entry are provided in a filmography or visual recordings listing at the end of the entry. Items in

filmographies contain references to those responsible for the films' music.

The definition of popular music is an issue that continues to be debated and is of clear importance to the scope of the *Encyclopedia*. The Editorial Board has resisted the temptation to offer a precise definition of the term 'popular music' in its instructions to contributors, recognizing that the terms 'popular,' 'classical' and 'folk' are discursive in character, and changing products of historical, social, political and cultural forces rather than terms that designate easily distinguishable musics. The question of where 'the popular' ends and 'the folk' begins has proved particularly difficult. The advice given to contributors has been that music created and disseminated in rural situations in an exclusively oral-aural fashion with little currency outside its location of origin does *not* constitute a prime focus for these volumes. However, it does not follow from this that such music should not be discussed if it is commonly accepted as 'popular,' or if it forms an important source for later styles or genres commonly accepted as 'popular.' While the principal emphasis of the *Encyclopedia* is on the urban, the commodified and the mass disseminated rather than on the rural, the oral-aural and the restrictedly local, therefore, this emphasis is far from exclusive. The principal test for including music as 'popular' has been whether it has been so regarded by communities of practitioners or users. The tendency has therefore been to be inclusive rather than exclusive. As a consequence, 'classical' music is included if its use has been popular in character.

The *Encyclopedia* is global in scope. However, it is important to emphasize that this volume on its own is not comprehensively global, although the intention of the Editorial Board has been to include internationally important material on a world basis. Information relating to musical practises that is, by contrast, of purely or mainly national, regional or local importance will be included in subsequent volumes on Locations, whose coverage is, indeed, comprehensively global.

Ottawa, Canada
September 2002

Acknowledgments

The Editorial Board's first debt of gratitude is to Philip Tagg, Professor of Music at the University of Montréal, who, over a two-year period in the early 1990s at the Institute of Popular Music, University of Liverpool, developed a detailed taxonomy of popular music, its practise and its study. This taxonomy served as a basic model for developing the structure of the *Encyclopedia* as well as its major sections and headword lists. Thanks are also due to the University of Göteborg (Sweden) for agreeing to second Philip from its Department of Musicology to the Institute of Popular Music at the University of Liverpool during the first of these two years.

A special word of thanks is due to Alyn Shipton, whose vision and dedication in the formative period of the *Encyclopedia* were vital to the development and long-term viability of an ambitious publishing project.

Thanks are also due to the University of Liverpool, the University of Exeter, the University of Göteborg (Sweden), and especially Carleton University (Ottawa), all of which have made significant financial contributions, as well as contributions in kind, in support of this project. In this context, special thanks go to Professor Graeme Davis, Vice-Chancellor of the University of Liverpool when the project began; Dr. John ApSimon, Dean of Graduate Studies and Research (1991–96) and subsequently Acting Vice-President (Academic) (1996–97) and Vice-President (Research and External) (1997–2000), Carleton University; Professor Janice Yalden, Dean of Arts (1988–92), Carleton University; Dr. Stuart Adam, Dean of Arts (1992–97) and subsequently Vice-President (Academic) and Provost, Carleton University; Dr. Roger Blockley, Dean of Graduate Studies and Research, Carleton University; Dr. Aviva Freedman, Dean of Arts and Social Sciences, Carleton University; and Dr. Feridun Hamdullahpur, Vice-President

(Research), Carleton University. In addition, thanks are due to Ocean Group, plc, to BMI and to the British Academy for their financial assistance in the earlier stages of the project's development at the University of Liverpool.

So many individuals have made important contributions to the development of the *Encyclopedia* since work on it began 12 years ago. Regrettably, it is impossible to mention them all. However, the Editorial Board is especially grateful to Carole Pegg, who at Exeter conducted an important initial study on the feasibility of developing an encyclopedia on world popular music; and to Jean-Pierre Sévigny at Carleton for his extensive work on the *Encyclopedia*'s headword lists and lists of contributors. The Editorial Board is grateful also to Mick Gidley then at the University of Exeter and to Paul Wells, Director of the Center for Popular Music at Middle Tennessee State University, both of whom contributed significantly to the early development of the *Encyclopedia*; to Paul Hansen, who lent administrative assistance to the project at the University of Liverpool; to Andy Linehan, Curator of Popular Music, British Library National Sound Archive, for his invaluable assistance with discographical information; and to Steve Cork at the British Library for his enormous help with sheet music information. Thanks are also due to Mona-Lynn Courteau, Janet Hilts, Megan Jerome and Sundar Subramanian, senior students in Carleton's B.Mus. program, and Joy Gugelar, a master's student in Carleton's School of Journalism and Communication, for their excellent work as research assistants. Many of the contributors to this volume of the *Encyclopedia* also often gave willingly of their time and expertise in addition to writing their entries, and the Editorial Board would like to extend thanks to them.

The Editorial Board wishes to thank Janet Joyce and Veronica Higgs at the Continuum International Publishing Group in London for their unwavering support through the long and sometimes difficult process that led to the completion of the first two volumes of the *Encyclopedia*. Veronica's expertise and calm guidance have been very much appreciated by both the Editorial Board and the editorial team at Carleton. Without Janet's conviction and determination, this project would never have come to fruition. The Editorial Board would also like to welcome Joanne Allcock of the Continuum International Publishing Group to the project, and to thank her for her important contribution during the final production stages of this volume.

Finally, the Editorial Board wishes to place on record its sincere appreciation for the work undertaken at Carleton University by the editorial team: Jennifer Wilson (chief editor), Jennie Strickland (project manager), Jennifer Rae-Brown, Karen Barber, Janet Shorten and Emily Wilson. Very special thanks are due to Jennifer Wilson, who has been with the project since 1996. The very high editorial standards evidenced in the entries that follow are due entirely to her professionalism, patience and total commitment to the project, as well as to her wonderful ability to lead the work of her colleagues.

List of Contributors

Pedro R. Abraham, Jr. is Associate Professor, Department of Art Studies, University of the Philippines.

Thomas A. Adler is a folklorist living in Lexington, Kentucky.

Lara Allen is a Research Fellow, University of the Witwatersrand, South Africa.

Gage Averill is Professor of Ethnomusicology, New York University.

Ian Babb is a graduate of the B.Mus. program, McGill University, Canada.

David Badagnani is a Ph.D. candidate and adjunct faculty in ethnomusicology, School of Music, Kent State University, Ohio.

Richard Baillargeon is a freelance writer living in Quebec City, Canada.

Jerome 'Butch' Baldassari is Adjunct Associate Professor of Mandolin, Vanderbilt University, Nashville, Tennessee.

Jon Bates is a musician, journalist and lecturer in music technology in the United Kingdom.

Theodore S. Beardsley, Jr. is President of the Hispanic Society of America.

Simon Bottom is a Ph.D. candidate, Institute of Popular Music, University of Liverpool.

Rob Bowman is Associate Professor, Department of Music, York University, Canada.

David Brackett is Assistant Professor of Music, State University of New York at Binghamton.

Roy C. Brewer is a freelance musician and independent researcher living in Eugene, Oregon.

Mike Brocken is a broadcaster for the BBC and proprietor of Mayfield Records, UK.

David Buckley works as a freelance writer and humanities tutor in Munich, Germany.

William L. Cahn lives in Bloomfield, New York, and is a member of the percussion group Nexus.

Raoul Camus is Professor Emeritus of Music, Queensborough Community College, City University of New York.

Petr Cancura is a recent graduate of the B.Mus. program, Carleton University, Canada.

Chris Clark works at the British Library National Sound Archive.

Jonathan Clark is an historian of mariachi music and founder of the Mariachi Workshop, San José State University, California.

Omar Corrado is Professor of Latin American Music, University of Buenos Aires, Argentina.

Stephen Cottrell is Lecturer in Music, Goldsmiths College, University of London.

Mona-Lynn Courteau is a graduate of the B.Mus. program, Carleton University, Canada.

Tony Cummings is the editor of England's contemporary Christian music magazine, *Cross Rhythms*.

Philippe Donnier lives and works in Córdoba, Spain.

Charles Doutrelepont is Associate Professor of French, Carleton University, Canada.

Ralph T. Dudgeon is Professor of Music, Cortland College, State University of New York.

Wayne Eagles is a performance instructor in jazz/rock guitar, Carleton University, Canada.

Peter Ellis lives and works in Bendigo, Victoria, Australia.

David Evans is Professor of Music, Rudi E. Scheidt School of Music, University of Memphis.

Franco Fabbri is a musician and musicologist working for RAI-Radio Tre, Italy.

Jan Fairley is a Fellow, Institute of Popular Music, University of Liverpool.

Gerry Farrell is Senior Lecturer in Music, City University, London.

Steven Feld is Professor of Music and Anthropology, Columbia University, New York.

Robert D. Ferlingere is the compiler and publisher of *A Discography of Rhythm & Blues and Rock 'n' Roll Vocal Groups, 1945 to 1965*.

Kim Field is a musician and writer living in Seattle, Washington.

Umberto Fiori is a musician, poet and translator who lives and works in Milan.

Ken Garner is Senior Lecturer in Media and Journalism, Glasgow Caledonian University.

David Gibson is the editor of *Saxophone Journal*.

Bryan Gillingham is Professor of Music, Carleton University, Canada.

Abigail Gilmore is Lecturer in Cultural Studies, Staffordshire University, UK.

Richard Graham is a music historian and educator in Memphis, Tennessee.

Terence Gunderson teaches percussion and jazz history at Casper College, Wyoming.

Armin Hadamer is a Ph.D. candidate in German cultural studies, University of Maryland.

Stan Hawkins is Associate Professor of Music, Oslo University, Norway.

Trevor Herbert is Professor of Music, The Open University, UK.

David Horn is Senior Fellow, Institute of Popular Music, University of Liverpool.

Hasse Huss is a Ph.D. candidate, Department of Social Anthropology, Stockholm University, Sweden.

Megan Jerome is a recent graduate of the B.Mus. program, Carleton University, Canada.

Bruce Johnson is Associate Professor of English, University of New South Wales, Australia.

Steve Jones is Professor of Communication, University of Illinois, Chicago.

Laurence D. Kaptain is Professor of Music, University of Missouri-Kansas City.

Keir Keightley is Assistant Professor, Faculty of Information and Media Studies, University of Western Ontario, Canada.

Elaine Keillor is Professor of Music, Carleton University, Canada.

Serge Lacasse is Assistant Professor of Music, University of Western Ontario, Canada.

Dave Laing is Reader, Centre for Communication and Information Studies, School of Communication and Creative Industries, University of Westminster, London.

John W. Landon is Professor Emeritus, College of Social Work, University of Kentucky.

Mark Langer is Associate Professor of Film Studies, Carleton University, Canada.

James P. Leary is Professor of Folklore and Scandinavian Studies, University of Wisconsin-Madison.

Marion Leonard is Lecturer, Institute of Popular Music, University of Liverpool.

Claire Levy is Associate Professor of Musicology, Institute of Art Studies, Bulgarian Academy of Sciences.

Iain MacInnes is a music producer with BBC Scotland.

William Mahar is Professor of Humanities and Music, Pennsylvania State University at Harrisburg.

Marie-Laure Manigand is Assistant Curator of the International Music Collection, British Library National Sound Archive.

Peter Martin is Dean of Undergraduate Studies, Faculty of Social Sciences and Law, University of Manchester.

Rick Mattingly is Publications Editor of the Percussive Arts Society and an instructor at Bellarmine University, Louisville, Kentucky.

Fred E. Maus is Associate Professor of Music, University of Virginia.

Richard Middleton is Professor of Music, University of Newcastle Upon Tyne, UK.

Andre Millard is Professor of History and Director of American Studies, University of Alabama at Birmingham.

Terry E. Miller is Co-Director, Center for the Study of World Musics, Kent State University, Ohio.

Tôru Mitsui is Professor of Music and English, Kanazawa University, Japan.

Tom Morgan is Associate Professor of Music and Director of Percussion Studies, Washburn University, Kansas.

Michael Morse is a bassist, composer and teacher living in Toronto, Canada.

Kazadi wa Mukuna is Co-Director, Center for the Study of World Musics, Kent State University, Ohio.

Karl Neuenfeldt is Senior Lecturer in Music, Central Queensland University, Australia.

Hiroshi Ogawa is Professor of Sociology, Kansai University, Japan.

Paul Oliver is Director of the International Centre for Vernacular Architecture, Oxford Brookes University.

Arthur W. J. G. Ord-Hume is Director and Senior Archivist, The Library of Mechanical Music and Horology, Guildford, UK.

Barbara Owen is Librarian of the A.G.O. Organ Library, Boston University.

Panayotis Panopoulos teaches in the Department of Social Anthropology, the University of the Aegean, Greece.

Carole Pegg is a freelance researcher and lecturer based in the Faculty of Music, University of Cambridge.

Richard A. Peterson is Professor of Sociology, Vanderbilt University, Nashville, Tennessee.

John Potter is Lecturer, Department of Music, University of York, UK.

César Quezada lives and works in Santiago, Chile.

Randy Raine-Reusch lives in Vancouver and is a composer, instrumentalist and recording artist specializing in new and experimental music for world instruments.

Corey D. Ramey is the owner of CDRAMEY.com and lives in Tennessee.

Guthrie P. Ramsey, Jr. is Assistant Professor of Music, University of Pennsylvania.

N. Scott Robinson teaches world music and culture at Kent State University, Ohio.

Owe Ronström is Assistant Professor of Ethnology, Gotland University, Sweden.

Neil V. Rosenberg is Professor of Folklore, Memorial University of Newfoundland, Canada.

Tony Russell is a music historian living in London.

Sergio Sauvalle lives and works in Santiago, Chile.

Ann Allen Savoy is Executive Producer, Vanguard Records, Santa Monica, California.

T.M. Scruggs is Assistant Professor of Ethnomusicology, University of Iowa.

Ferenc Sebö is a musician who lives and works in Budapest, Hungary.

Chris Sedwell is a graduate of the M.Phil. program, Institute of Popular Music, University of Liverpool.

Bhesham Sharma is Lecturer, Institute of Popular Music, University of Liverpool.

Daniel Sheehy is at the Smithsonian Institution, Washington, DC.

John Shepherd is Professor of Music and Sociology, Carleton University, Canada.

Alyn Shipton teaches jazz history at Oxford Brookes University.

Helena Simonett is Adjunct Professor of Music, Blair School of Music, Vanderbilt University, Nashville, Tennessee.

Graeme Smith is a popular music writer and Research Fellow, Youth Research Centre, University of Melbourne, Australia.

Jeffrey L. Snedeker is Professor of Music, Central Washington University, Ellensburg, Washington.

Neil Sorrell is Senior Lecturer in Music, University of York, UK.

Andrew Spencer is Professor of Music, Central Michigan University.

Alexander Stewart is Assistant Professor of Music, University of Vermont.

Henry Stobart is Lecturer in Ethnomusicology, Royal Holloway College, University of London.

Jonty Stockdale is Director of Studies, Leeds College of Music, UK.

Robert Strachan is Visiting Lecturer, Institute of Popular Music, University of Liverpool.

James A. Strain is Associate Professor of Percussion, Northern Michigan University.

Will Straw is Associate Professor, Department of Art History and Communication Studies, McGill University, Canada.

Stephen Stuempfle is Chief Curator, Historical Museum of Southern Florida, Miami.

Philip Tagg is Professor of Music, University of Montréal, Canada.

Garry Tamlyn is Deputy Director and Head of Popular Music, Queensland Conservatorium, Griffith University, Australia.

Paul Théberge holds the Canada Research Chair in Music, Carleton University, Canada.

Janet Topp Fargion is Curator of the International Music Collection, British Library National Sound Archive.

Rodrigo Torres is Professor of Music, Universidad de Chile.

Edwin Ricardo Pitre Vásquez lives and works in São Paulo, Brazil.

Jonathan Wacker is Assistant Professor of Percussion, School of Music, East Carolina University, North Carolina.

Steve Waksman is Assistant Professor of Music and American Studies, Smith College, Massachusetts.

Robert Walser is Professor of Musicology, University of California, Los Angeles.

Chris Washburne is Assistant Professor of Music and Director of the Louis Armstrong Jazz Performance Program, Columbia University, New York.

Paul F. Wells is Director of the Center for Popular Music and Associate Professor of Music, Middle Tennessee State University.

Peter Wicke is Director of the Center for Popular Music Research, The Humboldt University, Berlin, Germany.

Christopher Wiltshire is a freelance musician living in Sheffield, UK.

Tim Wise is a Ph.D. candidate, Institute of Popular Music, University of Liverpool.

Abbreviations

A&R	artist and repertoire
AACM	Association for the Advancement of Creative Musicians
ABA	American Bandmasters Association
ABC	American Broadcasting Company
ABC	Audit Bureau of Circulations (UK)
ABC	Australian Broadcasting Corporation
ACB	Association of Concert Bands
ACTRA	Alliance of Canadian Cinema, Television and Radio Artists
A/D	analog/digital
ADAMI	Société civile pour l'administration des droits des artists et musiciens interprètes
ADC	analog-to-digital converter
ADR	alternative dispute resolution
ADT	artificial double tracking
AES	Audio Engineering Society
AFM	American Federation of Musicians
AFN	American Forces Network
AFRS	Armed Forces Radio Service
AFRTS	Armed Forces Radio and Television Service
AFTRA	American Federation of Television and Radio Artists
AGVA	American Guild of Variety Artists
AIR	All India Radio
AKM	Staatlich Genehmigte Gesellschaft der Autoren, Komponisten und Musikverlager (Austria)
AM	amplitude modulation
AMC	American Music Conference
amp	amplifier
AOL	America Online
AOR	album-oriented rock
APRA	Australian Performing Right Association
ARC	American Record Company
ARIA	Australian Record Industry Association

ARSC	Association for Recorded Sound Collections
ARTISJUS	Bureau Hongrois pour la Protection des Droits d'Auteur
ASBDA	American School Band Directors Association
ASCAP	American Society of Composers, Authors and Publishers
AT&T	American Telephone and Telegraph Company
ATBB	alto, tenor, bass, bass
ATV	Associated Television Ltd.
AV	audiovisual
BAPMAF	Bokoor African Popular Music Archives Foundation
BARD	British Association of Record Dealers
BASBWE	British Association of Symphonic Bands and Wind Ensembles
BBC	British Broadcasting Corporation
BDS	Broadcast Data Systems
BECTU	Broadcasting, Entertainment, Cinematograph and Theatre Union (UK)
BESLA	Black Entertainment and Sports Lawyers Association
BET	Black Entertainment Television
BIB	Board for International Broadcasting
BID	Berlin Independents Days
BIEM	International Bureau of Societies Administering the Rights of Mechanical Recording and Reproduction [Bureau International des Sociétés gerant les Droits d'Enregistrement et de Reproduction Mécanique]
BIPE	Bureau d'aide à l'Insertion Professionnelle des Étudiants
BMG	Bertelsmann Music Group/Bertelsmann Musik Gesellschaft
BMI	Broadcast Music Inc.
BMRB	British Market Research Bureau
BPI	British Phonographic Industry
BPM	beats per minute
BUMA	Het Bureau voor Muziek-Auteursrecht (The Netherlands)
BVMG	Buena Vista Music Group
CAA	Creative Artists' Association
CASH	Composers and Authors Society of Hong Kong
CB	citizens' band
CBC	Canadian Broadcasting Corporation
CBDNA	College Band Directors National Association
CBS	Columbia Broadcasting System
CCM	Contemporary Christian music
CD	compact disc
CDC	Carnival Development Committee (Trinidad and Tobago)
CD-R	CD-Recordable
CD-ROM	compact disc read-only memory
CEA	Centre Européen d'Achats
CEDDI	Centre Européen de Distribution International
CEO	chief executive officer
CHA	Copyright Holders' Association (Chinese Taipei)
CHR	Contemporary Hit Radio
CIA	Central Intelligence Agency
CIEM	Confédération Internationale des Editeurs de Musique

CIMI	Comité International pour la Musique Instrumentale
CINARS	Commerce international des arts de la scène/International Exchange for the Performing Arts
CIRPA	Canadian Independent Record Production Association
CISAC	Confédération Internationale des Sociétés d'Auteurs et Compositeurs
CMA	Chinese Musicians' Association
CMA	Country Music Association
CMEA	Council for Mutual Economic Assistance
CMF	Country Music Foundation
CND	Campaign for Nuclear Disarmament
COMPASS	Composers and Authors Society of Singapore
CPA	Concert Promoters Association (UK)
CPU	central processing unit
D/A	digital/analog
DAB	digital audio broadcasting
DAC	digital-to-analog converter
DAT	digital audio tape
dB	decibel
DCC	digital compact cassette
demo	demonstration
DEMS	Development Education Media Services Foundation (the Philippines)
DGG	Deutsche Grammophon Gesellschaft
DIN	Deutsche Industrie Normen
DJ	disc jockey
DLT	digital linear tape
DSP	digital signal processing
DTP	desktop publishing
DVD	digital versatile disc/digital video disc
ECAD	Escritório Central de Arrecadação e Distribuição
EMI	Electrical and Musical Industries Ltd.
EP	extended play
EPROM	electrically programmable read-only memory
EQ	equalizer
FACTOR	Foundation to Assist Canadian Talent on Records
FBI	Federal Bureau of Investigation
FCC	Federal Communications Commission (US)
FEN	Far East Network
FFRR	full frequency range recording
FIA	International Federation of Actors
FIM	International Federation of Musicians
FLADEM	Federation of Latin American Publishers
FM	frequency modulation
fps	frames per second
FRC	Federal Radio Commission
FSK	frequency shift keying
FSLN	Frente Sandinista de Liberación Nacional
G&W	Gulf & Western
GATT	General Agreement on Tariffs and Trade

GDM	Gesamtverband Deutscher Musikfachgeschäfte/Association of German Retailers
GDR	German Democratic Republic
GEMA	Gesellschaft für Musikälische Aufführungs- und Mechanische Vervielfältigungsrechte (Germany)
GESAC	Groupement Européen des Sociétés d'Auteurs et Compositeurs
GMA	Gospel Music Association
GTL	Gramophone and Typewriter Ltd.
hi-fi	high fidelity
HMV	His Master's Voice
Hz	hertz
IAEL	International Association of Entertainment Lawyers
IASA	International Association of Sound and Audio-visual Archives
IASPM	International Association for the Study of Popular Music
IATSE	International Alliance of Theatrical Stage Employees
IBB	International Broadcasting Bureau
IBOC	in-band on-channel
IC	integrated circuit
ICAMD	International Centre for African Music and Dance
ICM	International Creative Management
IFPI	International Federation of the Phonographic Industry
IGEB	Die Internationale Gesellschaft zur Erforschung und Förderung der Blasmusik [The International Society for the Promotion and Investigation of Band Music]
IJF	International Jazz Federation
ILMC	International Live Music Conference
ILO	International Labour Organization
IMF	International Managers Forum
IMMS	International Military Music Society
INS	Immigration and Naturalization Service (US)
IPR	Intellectual Property Rights
ips	inches per second
IRA	Irish Republican Army
ISP	Internet service provider
ITB	International Talent Booking
JASPM	Japanese Association for the Study of Popular Music
JASRAC	Japanese Society for Rights of Authors, Composers and Publishers
JFM	Jamaica Federation of Musicians & Affiliated Artistes
KCI	Yayasan Karya Cipta Indonesia
kHz	kilohertz
LD	laser disc
LFE	low-frequency effects
LP	long-playing record
MBI	Music Business International
MC	Master of Ceremonies (rapping)
MCA	Music Corporation of America
MCPS	Mechanical Copyright Protection Society

MD	minidisc
MGM	Metro-Goldwyn-Mayer
MIA	Music Industries Association (UK)
MIAC	Music Industry Advisory Council (Australia)
MIDEM	Marché d'Industrie de Disque et d'Editions Musicale
MIDI	musical instrument digital interface
MMF	Music Managers Forum
MNW	Music NetWork
MoD	music on demand
MOR	middle-of-the-road [music]
MP3	MPEG Layer III
MPB	música popular brasileira
MPEG	Moving Picture Experts Group
MPGA	Music Producers Guild of the Americas
MTC	MIDI time code
MTV	Music Television
MU	Musicians Union (UK)
MUJ	Musicians' Union of Japan
NAB	National Association of Broadcasters (US)
NACPA	North American Concert Promoters Association
NACWPI	National Association of College Wind and Percussion Instructors
NAIRD	National Association of Independent Record Distributors and Manufacturers
NAMM	National Association of Music Merchants (US)
NARAS	National Academy of Recording Arts and Sciences
NARD	National Association of Rudimental Drummers
NARM	National Association of Recording Merchandisers (US)
NAS	National Academy of Songwriters (US)
NBA	National Band Association
NBC	National Broadcasting Company
NCBA	National Catholic Bandmasters' Association
NVGD	Nederlandse Vereniging van Grammofoonplaten Detailhandelaren (The Netherlands)
OWI	Office of War Information
PANAFEST	Pan African Festival
PAs	personal appearances
PAS	Percussive Arts Society
PC	personal computer
PCM	pulse code modulation
PMRC	Parents Music Resource Center
PPD	published price to dealer
PPI	Philips Phonographische Industrie
PPL	Phonographic Performance Ltd.
ppq	pulses per quarter-note
PRS	Performing Right Society
PVC	polyvinyl chloride
R&B	rhythm and blues
R&D	research and development

RAM	random access memory
RAO	Russian Authors Organization
RCA	Radio Corporation of America
R-DAT	rotary head-DAT
RFE	Radio Free Europe
RIAA	Recording Industry Association of America
RIAJ	Recording Industry Association of Japan
RKO	Radio-Keith-Orpheum
RL	Radio Liberty
rpm	revolutions per minute
SABAM	Société Belge des Auteurs, Compositeurs et Editeurs
SACEM	Société des Auteurs, Compositeurs et Editeurs de Musique
SACM	Sociedad de Autores y Compositores de Música (Mexico)
SADAIC	Sociedad Argentina de Autores y Compositores de Música
SAG	Screen Actors Guild (US)
SAMRO	South African Music Rights Organisation
SCD	Sociedad Chilena del Derecho de Autor
SCMS	Serial Copy Management System
SCSI	small computer systems interface
SDMI	Secure Digital Music Initiative
SESAC	Society of European Stage Authors and Composers
SGAE	Sociedad General de Autores y Editores (Spain)
SIAE	Società Italiana degli Autori ed Editori
SME	Sony Music Entertainment
SMEJ	Sony Music Entertainment Japan
SMPA	Swiss Music Promoters Association
SMPTE	Society of Motion Picture and Television Engineers
SNAM	Syndicat National des Artistes Musiciens de France
SNCC	Student Non-Violent Co-ordinating Committee
SNEP	Syndicat National de l'Edition Phonographique (France)
SPARS	Society of Professional Audio Recording Services
SPEBSQSA	Society for the Preservation and Encouragement of Barber Shop Quartet Singing in America, Inc.
SPEDIDAM	Société de perception et de distribution des droits des artist-interprètes
SPN	Stichting Popmuziek Nederland
STEED	send tape echo echo delay
STIM	Svenska Tonsättares Internationella Musikbyra (Sweden)
TOBA	Theater Owners Booking Agency
TRO	The Richmond Organization
U&I	Utilities and Industries Corporation
UA	United Artists
UMG	Universal Music Group
UNESCO	United Nations Educational, Scientific and Cultural Organization
USIA	United States Information Agency
VAAP	Vsesojuznoje Agentstvo po Avtorskim Pravam
VCR	video cassette recorder
VDU	visual display unit

VHF	very high frequency
VJ	video jockey
VOA	Voice of America
VPL	Video Performance Ltd.
VTR	videotape recorder
VUT	Verband Unabhängiger Tonträgerprodzenten
WASBE	World Association for Symphonic Bands and Ensembles
WBDNA	Women Band Directors National Association
WCI	Warner Classics International
WEA	Warner-Elektra-Atlantic
WIPO	World Intellectual Property Organization
WMG	Warner Music Group
WMI	Warner Music International
WOMAD	World of Music, Arts and Dance
WOMEX	Worldwide Music Expo
WPA	Work Projects Administration
WTO	World Trade Organization
ZAIKS	Stowarzyszenie Autorow (Poland)

Pitch Notation

The system used is based on Helmholtz's model: middle c is c, with octaves above as c^1, c^2, c^3, etc., and octaves below as C, C^1, C^2, etc.

Chords and Chordal Progressions

These can be expressed in absolute or relative terms. Absolute (specific) chords and chordal progressions are expressed according to common read sheet practise; for example: C for the C major triad; D^{-7-5} for a D-major triad with a diminished fifth and minor seventh. Harmonies relating to any tonal center are expressed using roman numerals; for example: I vi ii^7 V^7, I-III-VII IV.

Arrangement of the Material

Part I
Performers and Performing

Part 1
Performers and Performing

1. Groups

Accordion Band

The term 'accordion band' can describe a number of ensemble types. The first category is ensembles comprised entirely or mainly of accordions. The term can be applied more loosely to a second category of ensembles that contain one accordion or a small number of accordions in conjunction with other instruments providing rhythmic or harmonic support for or with other melodic or lead instruments.

In the twentieth century, most accordion ensembles of the first category used piano accordions. Although accordions with a piano keyboard had first appeared around the 1850s, it was not until the 1890s that the modern piano accordion with Stradella bass and reed ranks with couplers was developed, largely by Italian manufacturers. The early twentieth century saw the emergence of popular theatrical players who demonstrated publicly the power and musical versatility of the instrument. By the late 1920s, its popularity was burgeoning in both amateur and professional use, in Europe, Britain and the United States, and subsequently throughout the world.

Both professional and amateur developments were stimulated by the marketing activities of the dominant manufacturing company Hohner, based in Trossingen in southwest Germany. In the late 1920s, it sponsored a model 'accordion orchestra' that toured European cities, promoting the company's instruments. This initiative, along with published sheet music arrangements of popular classics and the accreditation of accordion teachers, met with a favorable response and resulted in the formation of numerous amateur accordion ensembles. Although the Nazis disapproved of these ensembles because of the accordion's association with popular music, the bands continued to exist in continental Europe and in Britain.

Such bands are usually associated with accordion clubs, which flourish within a global network. Focusing on enthusiasm for and love of the instrument, these clubs may include players from a wide range of musical genres, playing styles and accordion types, from light classical to folk. As is common in musical movements outside the boundaries of high-art aesthetic authority, soloists and members of accordion bands and orchestras who belong to such clubs organize a musical world around competitions, self-promoted concert programs and tours, newsletters, Web sites and magazines.

Within professional entertainment music, the accordion boom and promotions of the 1930s also brought forth popular professional accordion bands in the United Kingdom. These were dance bands, playing current popular hits and light music, becoming more swing-influenced through the 1930s. The preeminent band, billed and recording as 'Primo Scala's Accordion Band,' was organized by Harry Bidgood (1898–1957), a successful band leader and musical director. His band recorded widely in the 1930s and 1940s, and was popular in dance halls and nightclubs. Members of Primo Scala's Accordion Band dressed like gypsies in an attempt to convey a sense of the exotic, exemplifying the 'continental' association of the accordion, although the repertoire consisted predominantly of dance band 'evergreens' and medleys. Similar ensembles were common in prewar Germany.

An unrelated type of accordion band is the Orange accordion marching band of Protestant Northern Ireland. These ensembles, of up to about 30 players, usually using chromatic single-action accordions favored by Irish traditional music players, are modeled on other street marching bands, such as fife and drum and pipe bands. These bands are associated with Orange lodges and play a combination of Irish tunes, often with strong sectarian associations, Protestant hymns and popular Irish songs. They are a central part of the highly politicized street marching associated with community conflict in the province. Similar ensembles, with no sectarian association or repertoire, also exist as community bands in provincial towns in the Republic of Ireland.

As well as being used in accordion bands, accordions of many kinds are included in popular music ensembles throughout the world. In addition to this front-line use, in the prewar period and into the 1950s the piano accordion was widely used as a relatively anonymous accompanying instrument in larger dance bands. As a studio recording instrument, it was a convenient sweetener in orchestration, exploiting the chorus effect of detuned tremolo reeds and the close chord voicings it conveniently produces.

Bibliography

Whitehouse, Edmund. 1998. 'The Accordion Bands.' *This England* (Winter): 46–48. http://www.accordions.com/index/art/bands.shtml

Discography

Great Days of the Accordion Bands. Empress 828. *2000*: USA.

GRAEME SMITH with MIKE BROCKEN

Backup Singers

Backup singers or backing vocalists provide vocal accompaniment for the featured singer in a band or a singing group, either in live performance or on record. Arrangements that counterposed backup singers to a lead voice may have originated in choral music, but the practise became institutionalized in US popular music in the era of big bands and close harmony vocal groups. One of the most important vocal backup groups was the Pied Pipers. Formed in 1937, the group backed Frank Sinatra and Johnny Mercer on hit recordings. At the same time, the leading close harmony group the Ink Spots had Bill Kenny as lead tenor and other members providing backup vocals. In later years, various groups such as the Sweet Inspirations specialized in providing backup vocals, while some backing singers, notably Luther Vandross, became recording stars in their own right.

Discography

Dorsey, Tommy, and His Orchestra with Frank Sinatra and the Pied Pipers. 'I'll Never Smile Again.' RCA-Victor 26628. 1940: USA.

Ink Spots, The. 'If I Didn't Care.' *Anthology*. MCA 11728. 1939; *1998*: USA.

Pied Pipers, The. *Good Deal Macneal 1944–1946*. Hep Jazz HEP 33. *1986*: UK.

Sweet Inspirations, The. *What the World Needs Now Is Love*. Atlantic SD-8201. *1969*: USA.

Vandross, Luther. *Never Too Much*. Epic EK-37451. *1981*: USA.

DAVE LAING

Ballroom Orchestra

The literal meaning of the term 'ballroom orchestra' – an orchestral ensemble performing music for dancing in a ballroom – is frequently nuanced to refer to the provision of music for a distinct set of couple dances, among which the 'modern' waltz, fox trot and quickstep are prominent. In its heyday, in the years between World Wars I and II, the ballroom orchestra offered social dancers in many parts of the world a music that represented an opportunity to combine a respectable leisure activity with a display of elegance, couching its product in a style whose strictly applied conventions ensured the absence of any danger of physical or moral abandonment.

Though relatively uncomplicated in its musical identity by this time, both the ballroom orchestra and ballroom dancing had passed through rather more intricate formative stages. Orchestras were virtually essential to the ballrooms of the aristocracy, but the origins of the concept of a 'ballroom orchestra' lie rather in the gradual emergence of public ballrooms in the nineteenth century and of an associated repertoire of dance music, including quadrilles, galops and – especially – Viennese waltzes. Publishers began to produce music for ensembles specializing in the provision of such music in public venues. In the United States, for example, Philadelphia publisher J.W. Pepper published 'J.W. Pepper's Ball-Room Quadrille Journal' in 1880, and in Boston 'White's Ball Room Orchestra' appeared in several installments in the 1880s.

In the craze for social dancing that erupted in the United States in the first years of the twentieth century, the public – and the musicians – rejected much of this music in favor of new dances derived in significant measure from the African-American subculture (the turkey trot, for example) and from a combination of Hispanic and African-American sources (as in the case of the tango). To those trained in more mannered and regularized dancing – whether or not they sympathized with the moral outrage that contemporary dance frequently engendered – the new dances often seemed ungainly or over-erotic, or both. In this situation, new trendsetters emerged, chief among whom were Irene and Vernon Castle. Sometimes credited with being the first modern ballroom dancers, the Castles specialized in exhibition dancing, in which they 'substituted a hectic elegance for the easy rough and tumble of the animal dances' (Stearns and Stearns 1994, 97), reinforcing their impact by setting up an instruction studio and producing an instruction manual, *Modern Dancing*. As the Stearns put it, 'dancing became much safer with the Castles' (1994, 97). The Castles' connections (through Irene Castle) to US high society also strengthened the perception that this particular approach to dancing had social status.

The Castles' repertoire included a prominent place for an updated, and slowed-down, waltz, but probably their most lasting specific contribution to popular dance lay in their role in popularization of the fox trot. Like those of the animal dances, the fox trot's origins were close to the African-American subculture, and like them it underwent a process of regularization and sophistication. Unlike the animal dances, however, it never lost its allure, and went on to become a dance that epitomized the ballroom orchestra repertoire. Featured by vaudevillian Harry Fox around 1914, the fox trot became a staple of the Castles' performances, thanks in no small measure to the efforts of their musical director, orchestra leader James Reese Europe. From his own roots in African-American culture, Europe had already provided the Castles with an up-tempo one-step, influenced by ragtime and the animal dance rhythms; now he provided a slower, partly syncopated music for their flowing version of the latest dance phenomenon.

The repertoire of the dance orchestra at this time was very varied and, in the case of Europe, included ragtime-derived pieces. As dancing continued to develop in the 1920s, many dance orchestras responded to the influence of jazz, and the term 'ballroom orchestra' showed the first signs of being reserved to describe an ensemble providing music for more formal – and generally also more restrained – dancing styles. These styles did not remain static, however; a notable new addition was the quickstep, added to the repertoire in the early 1920s as a faster version of the fox trot.

The distinction between dance and ballroom orchestra was not a hard-and-fast one – most jazz-influenced dance bands played for dances where some type of formal dancing was encouraged – but rather involved a gradual shifting of emphasis. This process was assisted by the emergence of orchestra leaders who explicitly espoused a more restrained style built around a set of couple dances, each with its conventions and each danced in 'closed hold.'

Thus, beginning in the 1920s, the term 'ballroom orchestra' came to denote a large group of musicians (although an orchestra could be made up of as few as six), combining, for example, strings, woodwind, brass and percussion, playing music for a more formal style of dancing. Both ballroom music and ballroom dancing were considered socially and fashionably 'refined,' and a knowledge of the formal techniques associated with ballroom dancing (for example, control, deportment, accuracy of steps) was necessary for all who aspired to have the epithet applied to them. As part of the process, many of the innumerable dance halls that opened during the first half of the twentieth century described themselves as 'ballrooms' in order to acquire an air of social significance. Dance floors in some halls (such as the Grafton Rooms in Liverpool) were 'sprung,' and this helped to increase their 'ballroom' status.

Ballroom orchestras specialized in 'strict-tempo' numbers, indicating to the dancers specific steps, a regularized pattern and accurate timing. Some orchestras were criticized for being too regimented. Ballroom orchestras were also renowned for not playing much 'hot' (i.e., jazz) music.

In the United Kingdom, where ballroom dancing became particularly popular, certain ballroom orchestra leaders acquired considerable celebrity, perhaps the most illustrious being Victor Silvester (1900–78). Originally a dance instructor, and then a world-champion dancer (1922), Silvester traveled the country's ballrooms for over 40 years, performing sweet strict-tempo music, and he also made hundreds of recordings for EMI (he had record sales of at least 60 million). Fifty-seven editions of his book *Modern Ballroom Dancing* were published. Another well-known ballroom orchestra leader was Sidney Thompson, who continued to produce recordings of strict-tempo instruction throughout the post-World War II era. Annunzio Mantovani (1905–80), better known for his 'cascading strings,' was also conductor of a strict-tempo orchestra at the Hotel Metropole, as well as leader of the orchestra at the Monseigneur Restaurant.

One of the most interesting UK ballroom orchestra leaders was Josephine Bradley. Ms. Bradley was a champion ballroom dancer who launched her own orchestra in the 1930s. She would lead not only the orchestra, but also the dancers, and would partner amateur and professional dancers during the evening's entertainment. Like Silvester and Thompson, Bradley was regarded as a 'straight' dancing teacher, but, after a visit to the Feldman Swing Club in 1943, she 'converted' to jive dancing – a change that caused something of a furor. Jive-style dancing was often regarded as rather lower class and, as a dancer of the time remarked, 'not a pursuit of the academic classes' (Charles Lowe, quoted in Jenkins 1994, 22), whereas ballroom dancing was seen as elegant and 'acceptable.'

Despite the advent of rock 'n' roll in the mid-1950s, ballroom orchestras continued to exist, as ballroom dancing was still considered a necessary social skill. In the 1950s, Victor Silvester was able to transfer his hugely popular radio program, *Dancing Club*, to television, where it ran for many years. He also broadcast a dancing request program on the BBC World Service.

By the 1980s, the old-style ballroom orchestra had all but disappeared, but strict-tempo dancing itself survived. The orchestras that serviced the dancers (and that still sometimes added the suffix 'ballroom orchestra' to their names – for example, the Columbia Ballroom Orchestra) tended to be far more eclectic, playing a wide variety of dance music for competitive dancers and allocating time for modern, 'old-tyme,' Latin and strict-tempo dancing in one evening's entertainment/competition. By this time, the social stratification that contributed to the distinctiveness of the ballroom orchestra in its heyday had lost much of its significance, and ballroom dancing had come to be considered as one performance genre among many.

Bibliography

Castle, Vernon, and Castle, Irene. 1914. *Modern Dancing.* New York: The World Syndicate Co.

Jenkins, Tricia. 1994. *Let's Go Dancing.* Liverpool: Institute of Popular Music.

Silvester, Victor. 1927. *Modern Ballroom Dancing.* London: H. Jenkins. (Reprint, North Pomfret, VT: Trafalgar Square Publishing, 1993.)

Silvester, Victor. 1950. *Dancing for the Millions: A Concise Guide to Modern Ballroom Dancing.* London: Odhams Press.

Silvester, Victor. 1974. *Modern Ballroom Dancing: History and Practice.* London: Barrie & Jenkins.

Spaeth, Sigmund. 1948. *A History of Popular Music in America.* New York: Random House.

Stearns, Marshall, and Stearns, Jean. 1994. *Jazz Dance: The Story of American Vernacular Dance.* New York: Da Capo Press.

Sheet Music

'J.W. Pepper's Ball-Room Quadrille Journal.' 1880. Philadelphia: J.W. Pepper.

'White's Ball Room Orchestra No. 3.' 1880. Boston, MA: Jean White.

DAVID HORN and MIKE BROCKEN

Band

'Band' is a widely used term for instrumental or instrumental-plus-vocal ensembles in many styles and genres of popular music. In the typology of ensemble titles, bands are generally less formally structured or smaller than 'orchestras' and more formal and often larger than 'groups.'

The English word 'band' is paralleled in other languages by '*banda*' (Spanish) and '*bande*' (French). Outside the Anglophone nations, ensembles have sometimes used the English term as part of their name. In Francophone Africa in the 1970s, the English spelling was used in Mali by the Super Rail Band and in Senegal by the Star Band de Dakar. In his study of Haitian popular music, Averill (1997, 103) notes that, in the 1970s, ensembles often chose names that included the English word 'band.'

In Europe, bands were in existence from the thirteenth century, when men employed by a city as watchmen also formed instrumental bands to perform at ceremonial events. In England, these ensembles were called 'waits.'

Bands can be categorized by their titles in the following way: those named after their instrumentation; those named for their occupational origin or function; those derived from their geographical origin; those that incorporate a musical style in their title; those named after the individual who conducts or leads them; and those identified by the gender, ethnicity or demographics of their members.

The earliest band genre defined by its type of instrumentation was that of the wind bands of medieval Europe. These involved shawms, trombones and bombards, and they played for ceremonial and ritual events. Subsequently, there have been brass bands in Europe and in the colonies of European nations, fife and drum bands, flute bands (in, for example, Northern Ireland) and accordion bands. Trinidad is the source of steel bands, which play drums or 'steel pans' made from oil drums. In the southern United States, string bands, jug bands and washboard bands emerged in the early twentieth century.

Among the most widespread of the bands defined by their occupational function were the military bands that appeared in Europe in the sixteenth and seventeenth centuries, with instrumentation based on drums, wind and brass instruments. Many brass bands of the nineteenth and twentieth centuries in Britain and elsewhere were based in workplaces such as coal mines and factories. More recent types of functional bands are church bands, dance bands, wedding bands, theater bands (sometimes called pit bands after the space in front of the stage where they are located), show bands and the marching bands to be found at North American colleges and universities.

Town or civic bands were set up in many parts of Europe, North America and elsewhere. In parts of Southern Europe and Latin America, nineteenth-century municipal bands could have up to 80 players. The town bands of the United States were employed to perform at civic functions and to give concerts, often free of charge and in the open air. Charles Ives paid homage to the town bands of early twentieth-century New England in his *Three Places in New England* (1931).

Bands identified with musical styles or genres have been an important feature of popular music over the last century. Even though the Original Dixieland Jazz Band was preceded by New Orleans marching bands like the Excelsior and the Eureka, and most historians contest the claims of its title, the naming of the band was paradigmatic. In North American popular music, the Dixieland and other jazz bands were followed by hillbilly bands, western swing bands, big bands (the name connoting jazz-related dance music), R&B bands, Cajun bands and numerous others.

Bands named after their leader could be found in the United States of the late nineteenth century when John Philip Sousa was the country's most famous bandsman. Irving Berlin played on this trend in his well-known song 'Alexander's Ragtime Band' (1911). The foregrounding of a conductor or band leader became a general feature of later forms of instrumental dance music. In some instances, a leader would have several bands with the same instrumentation that were sent out to perform under his name.

All-female bands were often identified as such in North America and Britain through names like the International Sweethearts of Rhythm and Ivy Benson's All-Girl Orchestra. Other types of bands defined by ethnicity include the numerous 'Gypsy bands' of Eastern Europe in the twentieth century and the distinctly inauthentic Geraldo's Gaucho Tango Orchestra, a group of English musicians based in London in the 1930s.

Warner (1996) argues that, in rock music, following the adoption of the name 'the Band' by the ensemble associated with Bob Dylan, 'the term . . . was used to differentiate the serious rock cliques from the more ephemeral, chart-oriented pop groups' (274). Subsequently, most commentators on the proliferating types of rock music referred to ensembles as 'bands.'

Bibliography

Averill, Gage. 1997. *A Day for the Hunter, A Day for the Prey: Popular Music and Power in Haiti*. Chicago: University of Chicago Press.

Warner, Simon. 1996. *Rockspeak!: The Language of Rock and Pop*. London: Blandford.

Sheet Music

Berlin, Irving, comp. and lyr. 1911. 'Alexander's Ragtime Band.' New York: Ted Snyder Co. Music Publishers.

Discographical Reference

Ives, Charles. *Three Places in New England (Orchestral Set No. 1), for Orchestra, Kv 30*. London 443776. *1993*: UK.

DAVE LAING

Banda

'*Banda*' (Eng. 'band') is a generic term for a variety of ensembles consisting of brass, woodwind and percussion instruments found throughout Spain's former colonies. In the mid-1800s, civilian bands were introduced into every overseas European colony, where they took root and flourished in their new environment.

The so-called *bandas populares* (popular bands) or *bandas de viento* (wind bands) were a ubiquitous feature of Mexico's musical life in the later nineteenth century and thrived in both rural and urban areas. The instrumentation of the early popular bands was quite varied. After the Mexican Revolution (1910–20), the lineup in regional bands became increasingly standardized. Distinct types developed in different regions and acquired their own vernacular vocabulary: for example, *tambora* (a double-headed bass drum) in the state of Sinaloa, but *tamborazo* ('drum beat') in Zacatecas.

The *banda sinaloense* ('Sinaloan *banda*' or simply '*banda*') dates back to the military bands of European colonists and to the brass music of German immigrants to Mexico's Pacific coast in the mid-nineteenth century. After the consolidation of *bandas* in the early twentieth century, band membership in Sinaloa averaged nine to 12 musicians, playing clarinets, cornets or trumpets, trombones with valves, saxhorns (commonly called *armonía* or *charcheta*), tuba, snare drum (*tarola*), and *tambora* with attached cymbals. While the brass and reed instruments were imported from Europe, the drums were manufactured locally.

Bandas performed at various outdoor celebrations – bullfights, cockfights, horse races, parades, saint's days, weddings and funerals. Like the military bands at that time, *bandas populares* played an eclectic mix of marches, operatic selections and popular pieces. In the 1920s, *orquestas* (orchestras with stringed instruments) throughout Mexico began to respond to music from the United States by replacing the traditional double bass with the tuba, integrating a percussion set, and adding instruments such as saxophone and banjo. This new formation became known as 'jazz band' ('*banda jazz*'), a term used throughout Spanish Latin America. Inspired by these new trends in popular music, Sinaloan *bandas* also began to play the new upper-class ballroom dances: the fox trot, the charleston and the tango. *Banda*'s main appeal was, and has continued to be, its danceable music, which includes an ample variety of rhythms ranging from the local *son, guaracha*, polka, waltz and schottische to fox trot, *danzón*, bolero, cha-cha, mambo and *cumbia* later in the twentieth century.

Unaffected by the developing radio, film and recording industries of the early 1930s, which revolutionized Mexico's musical world, *banda* musicians continued to play in their traditional surroundings; they also found ample work in the *cantinas* (bars and brothels) of the lower-class urban neighborhoods. Some of those who had moved to the cities of Mazatlán and Culiacán eventually became involved in the 1950s and 1960s with the newer technological media – radio and recordings. To broaden the appeal of the bands, a few leaders with entrepreneurial spirit began to modify the makeup of the traditional *banda* by incorporating such new elements as Cuban percussion instruments (bongo drums, maracas and *cencerros* (cowbells)), slide trombones and saxophones. These commercially oriented *bandas*, known as *banda-orquestas*, performed a more cosmopolitan repertoire of mainstream dance music and popular international pieces (big-band mambo). They aspired to a more polished and precise playing style, and note-reading skills became more important for professional musicians.

In the mid-1980s, a modernized, synthesized version of the acoustic *banda sinaloense* emerged: *tecnobanda* ('technobanda' or just '*banda*'). While *tecnobanda* retained the trumpets, trombones and percussion, with the possible addition of saxophones, the characteristic *tambora* and the clarinets were eliminated, and the traditional tuba and *charchetas* (horns) replaced with electric bass and synthesizer. Because of these changes in instrumentation, a typical *tecnobanda* consisted of seven to 11 musicians only (compared to 14 to 17 musicians of a traditional *banda*). With deep roots in regional Mexican music, *tecnobanda* was highly innovative, and the integration of a vocalist allowed it to develop a new and independent repertoire. *Tecnobanda* and its associated dance style, *quebradita*, spread in the late 1980s from Guadalajara to Los Angeles, where it gained great popularity among immigrants as well as among US-born youths of Mexican heritage. *Billboard*, the US popular music magazine, declared 1993 'the *banda* year.' After its success in the United States, *tecnobanda* reemerged in Mexico and was eventually embraced by Mexico City and its culture industries.

The accelerating processes of globalization, including mass mediation and transmigration, contributed to *banda*'s growing acceptance and popularity in the United States in the 1990s. Current transnational Sinaloan *bandas* have come to include many of *tecnobanda*'s innovations, in particular a lead vocalist. Embracing the international Latin repertoire of *baladas* and *cumbias*, *bandas* have been able to enter the arena of commercial popular music.

Bibliography

Flores Gastélum, Manuel. 1980. *Historia de la Música Popular en Sinaloa* [A History of Popular Music in Sinaloa]. Culiacán: Dirección de Investigación y Fomento de Cultura Regional.

Simonett, Helena. 2001. *Banda: Mexican Musical Life Across Borders*. Middletown, CT: Wesleyan University Press.

Discography

Banda El Recodo de Cruz Lizárraga. *Histórico: Banda El Recodo en Vivo* (2 CDs). Fonovisa TFT2-2219. *1997*: Mexico.

Banda La Costeña de Don Ramón López Alvarado. *Secreto de Amor*. Fonovisa FPCD-9604. *1997*: USA.

Bandas Sinaloenses: 'Música Tambora.' The First Recordings of Tambora Music from the Mexican State of Sinaloa (1952–1965). Arhoolie CD-7048. *2001*: USA.

Las 30 Bandas del Siglo (3 CDs). Fonovisa FTCD-80705. *1997*: USA.

HELENA SIMONETT

Barbershop Quartet

A barbershop quartet is an a cappella vocal group comprising tenor, lead, baritone and bass voices, which performs in a style featuring a flexible tempo, a preponderance of dominant seventh chords, ringing harmonics, characteristic arranging devices and a focus on the popular songs of an earlier period in North American history (very loosely, 1890–1930).

Barbershop harmony has its roots in vernacular close harmony traditions of the early nineteenth century. In the 1840s, North American quartets such as the Hutchinson Family and Ossian's Bards imitated the close harmony of touring Austrian and German groups, especially the Rainer Family (the 'Tyrolese Minstrels'). Quartet choruses based on these models were soon written into the musical performances of blackface minstrel shows by composers such as Stephen Foster, and this style of singing was popularized throughout the United States for decades by both white and African-American minstrel quartets.

A vigorous community-based, recreational style of quartet singing took root among African-American singers, who contributed distinctive stylistic mannerisms, especially the practise of 'snaking' (later, 'swiping') from one chord to another. The barbershop rubric was indeed first used in African-American communities of the late nineteenth century due to the ubiquity of recreational close harmony singing in black barbershops, which then served as popular male gathering spots. Both black and white quartets performed throughout the latter part of the nineteenth century, and their repertoires demonstrated a robust interchange of 'hearth-and-home' (or sentimental parlor) songs, novelty songs, minstrel songs, 'coon' songs, rags and spirituals. Many important African-American musicians of the twentieth century, including Scott Joplin, W.C. Handy, Willie 'the Lion' Smith and Louis Armstrong, were involved early in their lives with barbershop-style close harmony quartet singing.

From the early 1890s to the 1920s, white 'pioneer era' quartets, including the Manhansett Quartette, the Edison Male Quartet (the Haydn Quartet), the American Quartet and the Peerless Quartet, recorded many of the most popular Tin Pan Alley songs and arrangements of the period, becoming some of the most successful (and now the most forgotten) artists of the first half of the twentieth century. 'Comedy fours' performed on the vaudeville circuits and mixed comedy with barbershop arrangements. The barbershop quartet came to serve as a sonic icon for turn-of-the-century North America, a status it shared only with the ubiquitous village brass band.

Black barbershop quartets at the turn of the century, such as the Unique, Standard, Magnolia, Golden Gate, Knickerbocker, Calliope, Meadowbrook, Criterion and Twilight quartets, toured with African-American revues and also performed in black or integrated minstrel shows, but they seldom had the kind of access to recording studios enjoyed by their white counterparts. Following the success of a 1910 song, '(Mr. Jefferson Lord) Play That Barber Shop Chord,' the term 'barbershop' came to supplant other names for the style (for example, 'curbstone' or 'street-corner' harmony) among white audiences as well. Although barbershop quartets were heard often on radio (the first live radio jingle is reputed to have been in barbershop style), barbershop singing was in decline even before the Depression, overtaken by jazz, crooned ballads and 'menagerie' dances, such as the fox trot.

Facing the hardships of the Depression and an increasingly urban and modernist America, portions of the US middle class indulged in nostalgia for turn-of-the-century life and took part in various neo-Victorian revival movements, among them one for barbershop quartet singing. The revival was institutionalized first in the barbershop quartet competitions organized in New York City in 1935. The Midwestern revival, which gave birth to the Society for the Preservation and Encouragement of Barber Shop Quartet Singing in America (SPEBSQSA), was launched in Tulsa, Oklahoma in 1938 by Rupert Hall and O.C. Cash. In its first years, the barbershop revival chapter meetings were often held either in the hotels on the salesman circuit or in the lodges of Midwestern fraternal societies or businessmen's clubs.

Soon, 'Parade of Quartets' concerts had developed into national (and then international) contests for quartets and choruses. The SPEBSQSA, along with the two societies of women barbershoppers (Sweet Adelines International and Harmony Incorporated), grew to represent approximately 80,000 members at the movement's peak, with chapters in England, Sweden, The Netherlands, Australia and many other countries.

The growth phase of the barbershop movement was accompanied by an increasing reliance on written scores, professional arrangements and choruses rather than quartets. Choruses allowed for the participation of larger numbers of less skilled singers and, by the 1960s, the barbershop organizations had adopted parallel competitions for choruses and quartets. Still, significant pockets of interest in informal, oral approaches to harmonizing ('woodshedding') have continued to exist in the barbershop organizations.

Public perception of barbershopping was shaped by popular cultural representations, such as the Broadway musical *The Music Man* (1957), the resident quartet (the Dapper Dans of Disneyland) at Disneyland's 'Main Street, USA,' Norman Rockwell's famous illustration of a barbershop quartet, which graced a 1936 cover of *The Saturday Evening Post*, and appearances by quartets in Hollywood movies as well as in radio and television broadcasts hosted by Arthur Godfrey and Ed Sullivan. In terms of the sound of barbershop singing, this public perception has lagged well behind the advances in barbershop harmony of recent decades.

The Buffalo Bills, original stars of the Broadway and film versions of *The Music Man*, were perhaps barbershop's best-known stars, but the women's barbershop group, the Chordettes, went on to modest success as popular harmonizers. Other recording stars with a background in barbershop singing include the Mills Brothers, the Four Freshmen, the Jordanaires (Elvis Presley's backup singers) and the Osmond Brothers. Leading SPEBSQSA quartets have included the Suntones, the Boston Common, the Second Edition, the Vocal Majority, the Ritz and Acoustix.

The principles of barbershop harmony have become increasingly formalized over the years as a result of the adjudication criteria and centralized training developed by the barbershop societies. The lead voice sings the melody, harmonized by the two voices below and by the tenor above (however, the lead and baritone voices are allowed to cross to maintain the melody in the lead voice). Barbershoppers sing as much as possible in close harmony on adjacent chord tones, although falsetto is often employed in the tenor voice. Barbershop arrangers attempt to harmonize every note with consonant chords (even notes usually treated as non-chord tones, such as passing notes, suspensions and appoggiaturas).

The dominant seventh chord, referred to as the 'barbershop seventh,' comprises a large percentage of the chords in classic barbershop arrangements (between 35 and 60 percent is the oft-cited figure). This is in part due to the harmonic structure of turn-of-the-century songs. Borrowing from European Romantic-era composers, Tin Pan Alley tunesmiths increasingly employed secondary dominant (V^7 of V) relationships for harmonic variety, both in cadential passages and in the main chord progressions of the chorus. This practise had its most exaggerated form in ragtime progressions and in songs featuring long strings of secondary dominants, such as 'Five Foot Two, Eyes of Blue' (1925). These 'circle-of-fifths' progressions result in some of the characteristic chromatic voice leading in barbershop.

Barbershoppers aim for just intonation over tempered tunings, and they tune their chords so that the overtones produced by each of the voices overlap and fortify those produced by the other singers, producing 'ringing' chords rich in harmonics, which barbershoppers call 'extended' sound. The rhythm of barbershop arrangements is typically flexible, with the sensuous features of the chord progressions and 'selling the song' taking precedence over a fixed rhythm. Elaborate 'tags' are a feature of most arrangements, as are 'swipes' (chord changes on a single syllable usually around one or more stable notes). Staggered entrance chords ('bell chords,' 'pyramids' or 'cascades') are also common.

Bibliography

Abbott, Lynn. 1992. '"Play That Barbershop Chord": A Case for the African-American Origin of Barbershop Harmony.' *American Music* 10(3): 289–325.

Averill, Gage. 1999. 'Bell Tones and Ringing Chords: Sense and Sensation in Barbershop Harmony.' *The World of Music* 41(1): 37–51.

Averill, Gage. 2002. *Four Parts, No Waiting: A Social History of American Barbershop Harmony*. New York and London: Oxford University Press.

Close Harmony, Ballads and Funnies with Barber Shop Chords. 1925. New York: Pioneer Music.

Finson, Jon W. 1994. *The Voices That Are Gone: Themes in Nineteenth-Century American Popular Song*. New York and Oxford: Oxford University Press.

Garnett, Liz. 1999. 'Ethics and Aesthetics: The Social Theory of Barbershop Harmony.' *Popular Music* 18(1): 41–61.

Hamm, Charles. 1979. *Yesterdays: Popular Song in America*. New York: W.W. Norton & Co.

Kaplan, Max, ed. 1993. *Barbershopping: Musical and Social Harmony*. Rutherford, NJ/London: Fairleigh Dickinson University Press/Associated University Presses.

Martin, Claude Trimble ('Deac'). 1932. *A Handbook for Adeline Addicts*. Cleveland, OH: Schonberg Press.

Martin, Claude Trimble ('Deac'). 1970. *Deac Martin's Book of Musical Americana*. Englewood Cliffs, NJ: Prentice-Hall.

Spaeth, Sigmund, ed. 1925. *Barber Shop Ballads: A Book of Close Harmony*. New York: Simon & Schuster.

Stebbins, Robert A. 1996. *The Barbershop Singer: Inside the Social World of a Musical Hobby*. Toronto: University of Toronto Press.

Sheet Music

Henderson, Ray, comp., and Lewis, Sam M., & Young, Joe, lyrs. 1925. 'Five Foot Two, Eyes of Blue.' New York: Leo Feist, Inc.

Muir, Lewis, comp., and Tracey, William, & MacDonald, Ballard, lyrs. 1910. '(Mr. Jefferson Lord) Play That Barber Shop Chord.' New York: J. Fred Help Company.

Discography

Barbershop Harmony Favorites, Vols. 1–2. SPEBSQSA, Inc. *1991*: USA.

Best of Barbershop Quartets: 38 Years of Winners. SPEBSQSA, Inc. n.d.: USA.

The Heritage Hall Museum of Barbershop Harmony Presents Close Harmony Pioneers. SPEBSQSA, Inc. *1994*: USA.

Visual Recording

'Can't Stop Singing.' 1999. Georgia Public Communications Commission and PBS Home Video.

GAGE AVERILL

Big Band

The term 'big band' can be applied to any large jazz or dance orchestra, usually with a minimum of 10 players, and averaging 14, although some larger ensembles have expanded to more than twice that number. The term has remained in use as the generic definition of a large jazz ensemble but, when it is applied to define the 'big band era,' it carries a more specialized meaning, and defines the period from the mid-1920s until the early 1940s that is also known as the 'swing era.' During these two decades, big bands were among the principal performers of popular music in the United States and Europe, and there were widespread imitators in territories as diverse as the USSR and Argentina.

Although syncopated orchestras employed large numbers of players, they were offshoots of ragtime, and were not generally known as big bands. Such orchestras were based on the east coast, but the big band movement began in the West, with the arranger Ferde Grofé and drummer Art Hickman, who altered the instrumentation of the basic Dixieland jazz band to add additional saxophones, and used the brass and reeds in apposition in written 'arrangements.' Paul Whiteman built on this, employing Grofé as arranger, and is generally credited with leading the first large jazz orchestra to carry the name 'big band.' His 1921 instrumentation included two cornets, trombone, three reeds, two violins, piano, banjo, tuba and drums.

Most other big bands of the 1920s followed a similar instrumentation, although the violin rapidly fell out of use, except by improvising soloists such as Joe Venuti or Matty Malneck. Whiteman's arrangements were ponderous, and his band was slow to develop a sense of swing comparable to that of smaller recording groups until much later in the 1920s, by which time he had hired several leading jazz musicians to join the ranks of his 'symphonic jazz' orchestra. The momentum in big band development had shifted to the work of Fletcher Henderson and Duke Ellington in New York. Henderson and his arranger Don Redman began writing material that used the entire section of three reeds as if they were a single improvising soloist – with long melodic lines harmonized together, most strikingly in a 'choir' of three clarinets. Ellington developed a subtler tonal palette, and composed material that would use effectively the individual timbres of his musicians, both as soloists and in the ensemble.

In the 1930s, big bands slowly expanded, most bands having three or four trumpets, three trombones, four or five reeds, guitar, piano, bass and drums. The beat shifted from a 2/4 to a 4/4 pulse, aided by the substitution of guitar and double bass for banjo and tuba.

Clarinetist Benny Goodman is credited with launching the swing era, but his band was just one of a number of large orchestras that played the popular music of the day, and dominated recording and broadcasting for over a decade. Prominent US big band leaders included Charlie Barnet, Count Basie, Cab Calloway, Jimmy and Tommy Dorsey, Erskine Hawkins, Earl Hines, Harry James, Andy Kirk, Jimmie Lunceford, Artie Shaw, Charlie Ventura and Chick Webb, among dozens of others. In Britain, Ambrose, Ted Heath, Jack Hylton, Jack Payne and Lew Stone were the best known. Other European bands included those of Ray Ventura and Gregor Kelekian in France, the Goldener Seiben (who quickly expanded beyond their original number) in Germany, the Ramblers Orchestra and Gregoire Nakchounian in The Netherlands, Aleksander Tsfasman in the USSR and Lulle Elboj in Sweden.

Since the swing era, big bands have continued to flourish, but the economics of running a 14-piece band have meant that only those with some measure of sponsorship have existed continuously; broadcasting has been a significant element, in this regard, for such bands as the Danish Radio Jazz Orchestra, the WDR Orchestra in Germany, the big band of the Suisse Romande in Lausanne and the BBC Big Band in Britain.

Bibliography

Berendt, Joachim-Ernst. 1982 (1975). *The Jazz Book: From Ragtime to Fusion and Beyond*. Rev. ed. Westport, CT: Lawrence Hill. (First published Frankfurt am Main: Fischer Bücherei, 1953.)

McCarthy, Albert. 1971. *The Dance Band Era, 1910–1950*. Philadelphia: Chilton Book Co.

McCarthy, Albert. 1974. *Big Band Jazz*. London/New York: Barrie and Jenkins/G.P. Putnam's Sons.

Schuller, Gunther. 1989 (1968). *The Swing Era: The Development of Jazz, 1930–1945*. New York: Oxford University Press.

Simon, George T. 1981. *The Big Bands*. Rev. ed. New York: Schirmer Books. (First published New York: Macmillan, 1967.)

Stokes, W. Royal. 1994. *Swing Era – New York: The Jazz Photographs of Charles Peterson*. Philadelphia: Temple University Press.

ALYN SHIPTON

Bluegrass Band

The bluegrass band is a direct descendant of the 'old-time' US string bands (fiddle(s), guitar, banjo and/or mandolin) that were first recorded in the 1920s. All bluegrass bands owe their existence in part to Bill Monroe and His Blue Grass Boys (1939–96), particularly his influential 1946–48 band.

Like many earlier hillbilly string bands, the 1946–48 Blue Grass Boys consisted of a mandolinist (Monroe, who also had a high tenor voice), a lead vocalist and guitarist (Lester Flatt), a five-string banjoist (Earl Scruggs), a fiddler (Chubby Wise) and a bassist (Howard 'Cedric Rainwater' Watts). Yet, they created a sound that was considered unique for its day. Not only were they greatly influenced by gospel, honky-tonk and swing music, but banjoist Scruggs developed a different style of fingerpicking that became *de rigueur* for banjoists in all subsequent bluegrass bands. Indeed, his three-finger picking style – built on traditional techniques from his North Carolina roots – changed the banjo from an accompanimental instrument to an instrument of great melodic potential. Guitarist Flatt also developed a new way of playing guitar accompaniment, using bass runs rather than chords as fills to bridge the gaps between chord progressions. Furthermore, Wise's fiddle playing was greatly influenced by western swing, which was closely linked to jazz. So, although its strength was its musical simplicity, bluegrass has been viewed by some as having 'progressive tendencies' (Sandberg and Weissman 1976, 69).

It is no exaggeration to suggest that Monroe's band – vocally and instrumentally – created a model in the 1940s that bands have continued to attempt to imitate. For example, most bluegrass bands have endeavored to emulate Monroe's idiosyncratic high lead vocals and even higher tenor harmonies (which could occasionally become falsetto). Trio vocal harmonies (high lead vocals, with baritone and higher tenor harmonies) have also become commonplace, as has the use of string bass. Whereas 'old-time' string band music usually kept 2/4 time, often without a string bass, the string bass in bluegrass has tended to keep a flowing 4/4 or 'cut time' beat.

While 'traditional' bluegrass bands have adhered strictly to this 'classic' acoustic string band and harmony formula, other bluegrass bands have absorbed different influences, just as Monroe did. 'Progressive bluegrass' (from the mid-1960s) and 'newgrass' (from the early 1970s) bands incorporated repertoire and performance practises (and, occasionally, even electric instruments) from folk and rock. By the late 1970s, experiments with jazz harmonies and unusual rhythms had led to the development of a jazz-oriented instrumental offshoot of bluegrass called new acoustic music, led by mandolinist David Grisman, whose small band ensembles featured only mandolins, fiddle, guitar and bass. A decade later, banjoist Bela Fleck moved even further from bluegrass to incorporate bebop and funk in his jazz group, the Flecktones. Meanwhile, mainstream bluegrass was, in the late 1980s, dominated by neo-traditionalists like the Johnson Mountain Boys. In the early 1990s, bluegrass saw its first women stars, following the path blazed by singer and fiddler Alison Krauss who, with her band Union Station, has become one of the most successful contemporary bluegrass performers.

So, although many bluegrass bands have remained faithful to Monroe's 'classic' string band formula, there have also been experimenters such as Grisman, Fleck and many others. In fact, the bluegrass band has provided a good example of the way in which many popular music genres exist in a state of dualistic tension between the desire to broaden the repertoire and the wish to remain true to the 'roots' of the music.

Such discourses have been further complicated by the definitions of what constitutes an 'authentic' bluegrass band. These definitions entail a series of apparent contradictions. Despite bluegrass bands' commercial beginnings and experimental possibilities, they have been considered by some fans to be an 'artistic' institution and specifically 'traditional.' According to this view, crossover is therefore anathema – an engagement with undesirable mass-cultural styles of music. A rigid adher-

ence to the Monroe formula is seen as a means of preventing any despoliation of the music's integrity and traditions – as if bluegrass were a 'folk music' (that is, created in an orally based closed folk community). The very lineup of a bluegrass band, therefore, is seen by some as not only a stylistic but a cultural indicator. The choice of 'traditional' instrumentation may reinforce the hagiography of 'old-time' string band music and endorse a nostalgic vision of the culture and economic conditions that spawned the 'original' bluegrass band – Bill Monroe's Blue Grass Boys. Conversely, it may be seen as the starting point for a fresh approach to country music that weds older instruments and musical forms with newer cultural perspectives and roles, as with such performers as Krauss, Laurie Lewis and Rhonda Vincent.

Bibliography

Cantwell, Robert. 1984. *Bluegrass Breakdown: The Making of the Old Southern Sound*. Urbana, IL: University of Illinois Press.

Fenster, Mark. 1995. 'Commercial (and/or?) Folk: The Bluegrass Industry and Bluegrass Traditions.' *South Atlantic Quarterly* 94(1): 81–108.

Rosenberg, Neil V. 1985. *Bluegrass: A History*. Urbana, IL: University of Illinois Press.

Sandberg, Larry, and Weissman, Dick. 1976. *The Folk Music Sourcebook*. New York: Knopf.

Smith, Richard D. 2000. *'Can't You Hear Me Callin'': The Life of Bill Monroe, Father of Bluegrass*. Boston, MA: Little, Brown and Co.

Discography

Appalachian Stomp: Bluegrass Classics. Rhino R2 71870. *1995*: USA.

Appalachian Stomp: More Bluegrass Classics. Rhino R2 75720. *1999*: USA.

NEIL ROSENBERG and MIKE BROCKEN

Brass Band

Introduction

A brass band is an ensemble in which all or most of the participants play lip-vibrated brass instruments. Performers usually play from written music, but some Asian and South American bands play from memory or improvise. Most brass bands are amateur, and owe their origins to both art and vernacular influences. In Britain, the term 'brass band' has a very precise meaning. It refers to a form of amateur music-making with a standard instrumentation and consistent orthodoxies of performance style, repertoire and social function. The British brass band format is also found in other parts of the world, but in most countries such standardization does not exist, and widely different combinations of instruments are described as 'brass bands.'

Despite the enormous diversity of groupings to which the term is sometimes indiscriminately applied, a brass band can almost always be taken to be a popular music practise in which most of the practitioners are amateurs, and the musical values of which are different from those found in art music. This is the case even in countries – such as Britain – where the idiomatic repertoire and performance practises owe much to the art music tradition. Brass bands have never been part of an art music culture; indeed, art music brass players self-consciously avoid the term, in favor of descriptors that carry more elite resonances, such as 'brass ensemble,' 'brass octet,' 'brass quintet' and so on.

History

Brass bands originated because of major technological changes in the design, manufacture and subsequent commodification of brass instruments which took place in the nineteenth century. Before then, brass instruments were almost always played by professionals. The exceptions were those cases where brass instruments had some functional or symbolic place in a secular or sacred ritual – for example, hunt calls on horns, the sounding of prayer trumpets in Tibetan religious orders and, more exceptionally, the use of trombone choirs in religious worship in Moravian churches. Brass instruments were expensive, because they were made individually by craftsmen. And because all instruments in this family (with the exception of the trombone) were devoid of mechanical means for changing notes, the skills needed to play them were rare and highly sophisticated.

In the nineteenth century, several conditions converged to make brass instrument playing a popular activity. Technical developments – particularly the invention of piston valve instruments – changed the musical identity of brass instruments. This happened simultaneously with the development of a wider set of economic circumstances that made it possible for working-class people to own such instruments. Also, in Victorian Britain, where the brass band developed most rapidly, there was a widespread belief among the middle and upper classes that collective music-making was both morally beneficial for the working class and in accord with a broader set of ideals conducive to social cohesion. These technical, social and economic conditions prevailed in a century when there was a general trend in much of Europe and also (to an extent) the United States toward an industrial as opposed to an agricultural economic base, and toward urbanization as opposed to ruralism. The resultant demographic changes provided the essential context for new forms of amateur music-making.

Brass instruments were used in military bands in the first part of the nineteenth century. Military bands – usually mixed brass, wind and percussion bands – on both sides of the Atlantic were sustained privately by commanding officers who needed them to supply music for dancing and other diversions, as well as for more ceremonial use. An important early means by which brass instruments could be played chromatically came with the development of keyed brass in the late eighteenth and early nineteenth centuries. The keyed bugle and the ophicleide (the bass member of the keyed bugle family) continued to be used well into the nineteenth century, but the development of the *brass* band as a popular practise came in the 1840s, when valve instruments – especially those employing the designs of the Belgian inventor, Adolphe Sax – became widely disseminated. Valve instruments were invented in the 1820s, but it took more than 20 years for their potential to be realized. Given that a player was capable of producing notes in the mouthpiece (itself a relatively straightforward process), these instruments allowed the player to change the notes by depressing and releasing valves which were operated using only the three most dexterous fingers of the right hand. Furthermore, the instruments themselves were robust and durable, and could be made quickly and routinely. Their manufacture did not rely on long-established craft skills, as was the case with, for example, stringed instruments. The instruments quickly became popular commodities, and by the 1860s a large brass instrument production industry had developed. The instruments were relatively cheap, and easy payment schemes were widely available. A person of modest talent could learn basic playing techniques in a matter of weeks, and gifted players sometimes attained virtuoso ability within a few years of starting to play.

The brass band had become an important feature of popular music in Britain by 1860. There is evidence of the existence of some bands in the 1830s, but it was not until the 1840s (following the acquisition of the agency for Sax's designs by the Distin family, a troupe of entrepreneurial British brass players) that bands started to be formed throughout the country. Some grew from and took over the functions of existing village bands, but most were entirely new. Their advent was largely the result of effective mass marketing. They were supported by subscriptions and sometimes by employers. It was common for a band to use the name of the mill, factory or coal mine in which its players worked. Some have taken this to mean that brass bands usually received patronage from their members' employers, but it is doubtful whether most such employers did more than guarantee a loan for the purchase of instruments.

Brass band contests, which have remained the principal raison d'être of the British brass band movement, started in the 1840s. The Victorian contests were run commercially as open-air entertainments. The most important pioneering entrepreneur of these contests was Enderby Jackson (1827–1903) who claimed, probably justifiably, that he had invented the 'modern' brass band contest. The railway network grew quickly in Britain and made it possible for 'national' contests to be held by the 1850s. The contests were genuinely popular. They attracted audiences of thousands, and the congregation of so many players quickly led to the establishment of common orthodoxies of style and repertoire. The dominance of three brass band conductors from the north of England – John Gladney (1839–1911), Alexander Owen (1851–1920) and Edwin Swift (1843–1904) – who used broadly similar lineups of instruments, led to the establishment of a standard contesting brass band format, made up of:

   one soprano cornet (in E♭)
   eight or nine cornets (in B♭)
   one flugel horn (in B♭)
   three tenor horns (in E♭)
   two baritones (in B♭)
   two euphoniums (in B♭)
   two tenor trombones
   one bass trombone
   two basses (in E♭)
   two basses (in B♭)
   percussion

This combination of brass instruments produces a distinctive homogenous sound, because they are all, with the exception of trombones, made from predominantly conical, as opposed to cylindrical, tubing. Contesting has thus had a defining influence on the British brass band tradition. Because the rules of brass band contests, and consequently the printed music for contesting bands, dictate the instrumentation, all such bands make a similar, very distinctive sound. Twentieth-century contesting brass bands had a warm, mellow sound characterized by a gentle vibrato.

In the twentieth century, the changes to the idiom of the British brass band were comparatively slight, but the repertoire, which in the nineteenth century was almost entirely based on marches, operatic transcriptions and dance music, became much more eclectic. Some major composers wrote for brass bands (Elgar, Vaughan Williams and Hans Werner Henze, for example), but such contributions to the idiom never really altered its cultural classification. Arrangements of popular and art music have prevailed, and a group of specialist composers, adept at writing for this combination of instruments, has produced a steady supply of new repertoire. Brass band players and their audiences have never reacted warmly to radical musical languages. The most enduringly popular and performed pieces are those that

allow the players to demonstrate technical expertise and musical expression in the context of a solidly tonal sound-world – all within a highly disciplined and controlled mode of expression.

There has always been a buoyant market for brass band records in the United Kingdom. The Black Dyke Mills Band made its first commercial gramophone record in 1903. A record made by the Besses o' the Barn band was released a year later. The International Staff Band of the Salvation Army made its first recording in 1904. The BBC transmitted brass band music from its earliest days, and in 1942 appointed Harry Mortimer, one of the most notable cornet soloists of his day and a member of the brass band world's best-known dynasty, to the post of 'brass and military band supervisor.' Mortimer, who was at this time responsible to Arthur Bliss, the BBC's director of music, increased both the quantity of brass band broadcasting and its quality. He auditioned bands before giving them broadcasting time, and during his period of office there were as many as 18 programs a week – an average of 500 a year – featuring brass bands. This number decreased after the 1960s, with brass band broadcasting being shared between the national and regional broadcasting services. Radio and television contests have also had some success, but these are mainly organized by regional rather than national networks.

The British model of the brass band was replicated in parts of Australasia and, to a lesser extent, Canada. In the late twentieth century, there was a growth of this format of brass band in the United States, and more especially in continental Europe, where the contest ethos was warmly accepted.

The commodification of valve brass instruments is the principal reason why brass bands were established in other parts of the world too, but the near-manic obsession with discipline, orthodoxy and virtuosity that the contesting movement imposed on brass bands in Britain has been less marked or entirely absent elsewhere. As in Britain, brass bands developed rapidly in the United States during the nineteenth century, as a result of similar processes of commodification, and manufacturing companies such as the Indiana-based Conn Corporation produced vast quantities of instruments, using virtuoso players from the bands of Patrick Gilmore and J.P. Sousa to promote them. But the principal difference between US brass bands and those of countries in which the British model is copied is that, in the United States, the instrumentations of bands seem to follow pragmatic expediencies, and repertoires respond to local tastes rather than observe a set pattern. Consequently, in such cases the brass band idiom is more relaxed and less earnest, more interested in the need to be functional and to entertain and less concerned with personal and group efficiency. These qualities were evident in the nineteenth-century marching bands of New Orleans and other parts of the southern United States, which some writers have identified as the prototype of some forms of jazz. It is certainly true that many such bands had a preponderance of brass instruments, and some, such as the band led by Henry Allen Snr. at Algiers, Louisiana, were made up entirely of conical bore 'sax'-type instruments.

Many brass bands have developed in previously colonized countries. Brass bands abound in former colonies in Africa, South America, Asia and the Pacific, where Western brass instruments, the very same instruments that led to the engagement of the urban working classes with notated music-making in Britain, are played. However, such bands seldom copy the fixed pattern of instrumentation found in Britain. Sometimes Western playing techniques are imitated, but more often their practises bear no resemblance to the British model and are genuinely assimilated into indigenous musical values.

Social and Musical Roles

In nineteenth-century Britain, brass bands provided the first point of access for many working-class people to art music instruments. Published music for bands was simple, functional and based on opera derivatives, marches and popular songs. But contesting bands were ambitious and, in the absence of a standard instrumentation, bandmasters arranged operatic overtures and selections of art music. This became one of the main routes through which art music was disseminated and popularized. In the United States, such transcriptions made less ambitious demands on players, except for those soloists who were highlighted and exhibited for their skills.

Throughout the world, brass bands have remained an important form of communal music-making. The practical features of brass instruments are the most enduring reason for the success of brass bands. The instruments are easy to learn and play; they are durable; they do not require any part of the instrument to be routinely renewed (no reeds or strings, for example); and they are largely unaffected by extremes of temperature or humidity. It was these qualities that made brass bands the standard instrumental lineup in the Salvation Army. Indeed, brass bands became so integral to Salvationism that the Army set up its own instrument-manufacturing operation, and publishing and distribution network.

The factors that seem to be common to almost all brass bands are their links with communities, their assimilation into secular ritual, and the extent to which the repertoire is derived from some other form of music-making, whether it be art music, indigenous music, military music or dance music. The contribution of brass bands to the musical world as a whole lies in the fact that, for many working-class players and their attendant musical values (often gained through aural, rather than notated, means of learning), they have provided the point both of musical origin and of entry into professional music.

An assessment of the contribution of brass bands to popular music as a whole is difficult, because so many different kinds of music-making are covered by the one term. The British version of the species is easy to summarize. It is one of the most durable of all musical practises that originated in the Victorian era. It has continued to have its own unique, discrete and largely self-contained values. But the virtuosity of these bands is often stunningly impressive. It is remarkable that, at the end of the twentieth century, the British model was gaining support and being imitated internationally, in both Europe and the United States. This was due in no small measure to the ambitions of manufacturers of brass band instruments, who launched effective advertising campaigns aimed mainly at parents and educators.

Brass bands must be seen in their individual social contexts. They have been, and have continued to be, one of the signifying features of communities, prominent in both landscapes and soundscapes, and integral in community rituals. The relationship between bands and such communities differs according to the broad circumstances and cultural patterns in which they are found. Such relationships are often complex, posing challenges for cultural classification; but relationships are always present, and are reflected in the practises, styles and repertoires of bands.

In Britain, the sound of a brass band has become a familiar ingredient in a range of stereotypical media representations. It is not just Victoriana that is summoned up by this timbre, but also instant resonances of the working class and of the industrialized regions of the north of England. Such images – in television films and commercials – reflect assumptions about brass bands, some, but not all, of which are based on historical authenticity. Even in the late twentieth century, when lawyers, doctors, teachers and architects were as likely to be found in a brass band as coal miners or factory and mill workers, the image of the brass band was redolent with those features that reflect its tradition. Brass band players and supporters are often affronted by such cliché-ridden characterization of their 'movement.' In other parts of the world, where brass bands are oblivious of the orthodoxies of the British model, stereotypes are less easily formed and such concerns do not exist.

Bibliography

Andrews, Frank. 1997. *Brass Band Cylinder and Non-Microgroove Disc Recordings, 1903–1960*. Winchester: Piccolo Press.

Herbert, Trevor, ed. 1991. *Bands: The Brass Band Movement in the 19th and 20th Centuries*. Milton Keynes and Philadelphia: Open University Press.

Herbert, Trevor, and Sarkissian, Margaret. 1997. 'Victorian Bands and Their Dissemination in the Colonies.' *Popular Music* 16(2): 165–79.

Herbert, Trevor, and Wallace, John, eds. 1997. *The Cambridge Companion to Brass Instruments*. Cambridge: Cambridge University Press.

Russell, J.F., and Elliot, J.H. 1936. *The Brass Band Movement*. London: J.M. Dent and Sons.

Schafer, William J. 1977. *Brass Bands and New Orleans Jazz*. Baton Rouge and London: Louisiana State University Press.

Taylor, Arthur. 1979. *Brass Bands*. St. Alban's: Granada.

TREVOR HERBERT

Cajun Band

A Cajun band is a group of musicians, generally of French-speaking descent, who play Cajun music. The term 'Cajun' ('Cadien') is a pejorative form of the word 'Acadian,' the name for the French-speaking inhabitants of what are now the Canadian provinces of New Brunswick, Nova Scotia and Prince Edward Island, who were driven out by the English-speaking majority between 1750 and 1780 and settled in Louisiana. The Cajun music performed by Cajun bands can range from early fiddle duets to North American country-influenced 'honky-tonk' music sung in Cajun French.

The Cajun band has evolved in much the same way as the North American country band. The earliest Cajun bands consisted of as few as two people: two fiddle players or one fiddler and a triangle player. When a band had two fiddlers, one would play the song's melody and the other would either play backup chords or play the melody on the low strings in unison with the lead fiddler. The term for backup fiddling in Cajun French is *segoner* or 'to second.' Fiddles were adjusted to various tunings which were passed down from generation to generation. These different tunings gave a haunting or drone-like feel to the early music. The other accompanying instrument, the triangle or *tit fer*, was made from the tine of a hay rake and, when it was struck in time to the fiddler's music, its sound carried the beat to the far corners of a room, helping the dancers hear the beat when the room was noisy.

When, in the late 1800s, the diatonic accordion was introduced into Cajun music, it gradually became the lead instrument in Cajun bands. The accordion was not immediately accepted, because it came in 'odd keys,' that is to say, keys that demanded great skill from the fiddle players. In 1910, accordions in the keys of C and D were introduced in the Louisiana prairies, and fiddlers found they could accompany in these keys. The practise in the bands was for the fiddlers to tune their fiddles to the accordion in such a way that they could always play with the same positions for the left hand that they had originally used in learning the songs; for example, when a C accordion was in a band, the fiddler would tune the fiddle down to a G tuning, a full tone below standard tuning. The diatonic accordion also had a profound effect on the material played by the Cajun bands, since it has a limited tonal scale. Many of the old fiddle tunes were difficult or impossible to play on the diatonic accordion, so those tunes were replaced by melodies more adaptable to the accordion. A Cajun band at the turn of the nineteenth century would have played many styles of dances: mazurkas, contradances, square dances, two-step waltzes and standard waltzes.

With the introduction of radio, tunes from Texas and the rest of the nation were introduced into Louisiana, and the two-step and simple waltz took over the Cajun band's repertoire. The guitar entered the Cajun scene via country music and was used in much the same way as the fiddle to back up the accordion. Cajun musicians would even tune their guitars down a full tone to 'match' the accordions. In the 1920s, open chords were used as guitar accompaniment, and the band would usually consist of an accordion, a fiddle and a guitar.

The radio also introduced Texas swing music, and the Cajuns adopted this music, translating the lyrics into French and putting aside the accordion for the mandolin, dobro, banjo and any other instrument that would imitate the Texas sound. Crude amplifiers came onto the scene, often having to be hooked to car motors for electricity generation. During this era, Harry Choates recorded the hit song 'Jole Blon,' which was played on national radio. Although rural bands continued to use the accordion during this time, drums, bass and lap steel guitars were now added to the simple Cajun trio.

After World War II, veterans longed to hear the accordion music of earlier days, and the accordion again became the lead instrument in Cajun bands. As soon as amplifiers became available, they were always used for each instrument so that the music could be heard in noisy dance halls. By the early 1950s, the instrumentation of the Cajun dance hall band was the same as is used in modern Cajun bands. Although the bass and steel guitar are now amplified and the accordion uses an accordion pickup, the music has not changed drastically since the 1950s. Sometimes, western-style twin fiddles are employed in the band and the repertoire sounds like a Cajun French version of Nashville, but the traditional sound of Cajun music still comes through, ever unique and powerful.

Bibliography

Ancelet, Barry Jean. 1999. *Cajun and Creole Music Makers/ Musiciens cadiens et créoles.* Jackson, MS: University Press of Mississippi. (Originally published as *The Makers of Cajun Music/Musiciens cadiens et créoles.* Austin, TX: University of Texas Press, 1984.)

Broven, John. 1983. *South to Louisiana: The Music of the Cajun Bayous.* Gretna, LA: Pelican Pub. Co.

Daigle, Pierre V. 1977. *Tears, Love, and Laughter: The Story of the Acadians.* Church Point, LA: Acadian Pub. Enterprise.

Gumbo Ya-Ya: A Collection of Louisiana Folk Tales. Gretna, LA: Pelican Pub. Co.

Post, Lauren C. 1990. *Cajun Sketches from the Prairies of Southwest Louisiana.* Baton Rouge, LA: Louisiana State University Press.

Savoy, Ann Allen, ed. 1984. *Cajun Music: A Reflection of a People.* Eunice, LA: Bluebird Press.

Discographical Reference

Choates, Harry. 'Jole Blon.' *J'ai été au bal (I Went to the Dance), Vol. 1.* Arhoolie CD-331. 1946; *1992*: USA.

Discography

Abshire, Nathan, and His Pine Grove Boys. *French Blues.* Arhoolie 373. *1993*: USA.

Ardoin, Amédé. *Amédé Ardoin – Pioneer of Louisiana French Blues 1930–34: 'I'm Never Comin' Back'.* Arhoolie 7007. *1995*: USA.

Cajun and Creole Music, 1934/1937. Rounder 611842. *1999*: USA.

Cajun and Creole Music II, 1934/1937. Rounder 611843. *1999*: USA.

Cajun Dance Party: Fais Do-Do. Columbia/Legacy CK 46784. *1994*: USA.

Cajun String Bands: The 1930s. Arhoolie 7014. *1997*: USA.

Gran Prairie: A Cajun Music Anthology, Vol. 3 – The Historic Victor-Bluebird Sessions, 1935–1940. Country Music Foundation 18. *1994*: USA.

Le Gran Mamou: A Cajun Music Anthology, Vol. 1 – The Historic Victor-Bluebird Sessions, 1928–1941. Country Music Foundation 13. *1990*: USA.

LeJeune, Iry. *Iry LeJeune: The Definitive Collection.* Ace 428. *1994*: USA.

McGee, Dennis. *The Complete Early Recordings of Dennis McGee.* Yazoo 2012. *1994*: USA.

Raise Your Window: A Cajun Music Anthology, Vol. 2 – The Historic Victor-Bluebird Sessions, 1928–1941. Country Music Foundation 17. *1994*: USA.

Roger, Aldus. *Aldus Roger: A Cajun Legend.* La Louisianne 1007. *1995*: USA.

ANN ALLEN SAVOY

Catch Clubs

Catch clubs, popular in seventeenth- and eighteenth-century Britain, were male-only social organizations for the singing of catches.

The 'catch' – in musical terms, a canon or round – was known at all levels of society during Elizabethan times, always in the context of revelry, womanizing, jocularity and/or drunkenness (see Shakespeare's *Twelfth Night*, Act 2, Scene 3). However, membership of the seventeenth-century clubs was very much restricted to the upper echelons of society. Their genesis was related to the Puritan domination of British political and religious life (1649–60), when private music meetings began to flourish, particularly in English cathedral cities. Church musicians, denied their usual musical practises, turned from anthems and psalms to lighter fare. Charging sixpence for admission, William Ellis, formerly organist at St. John's College in Oxford, opened his doors during the 1650s to a group of male friends for sessions of drinking and vocalizing. Although some of the catches were of an inoffensive nature, many of those composed by Ellis were highly licentious, an element that was heightened by the attendant puns caused by the canonic style.

Lavatorial humor continued to characterize the vocal activities in the catch clubs of the Restoration period (from 1660), and Samuel Pepys frequented clubs in London. His diaries mention 'Playfords (sic) new Ketch-book that hath a great many new fooleries in it' (Latham and Matthews 1971, 205). Dean Henry Aldrich continued the Oxford tradition, inviting members of the cathedral choir to his rooms in Christ Church, where he instituted rules for performance and attendance – penalties included exclusion from the following meeting. In 1685, his catches appeared in John Playford's *Musical Companion*, alongside similar works by Blow and Purcell. The latter produced a host of catches, many with sexually explicit texts (probably by the composer or his friends). Playford dedicated his 1667 edition of *The Musical Companion* to his friends in the 'Music-Society meeting in the Old Jury, London,' and the popularity of these publications suggests that there were many such meetings throughout the land (precise documentation is sparse). In the 1702 edition, his son, Henry, stated that the collection of pieces was 'chiefly for the encouragement of Musical Societies which will be speedily set up in all the chief Cities and Towns in England,' as well as in 'the kingdoms of Great Britain and Ireland' – a catch club had been established by the men of Dublin's Christ Church and St. Patrick's cathedrals as early as 1679.

Despite the often scatological nature of catches, eighteenth-century clerics wholeheartedly supported the clubs. In 1757, Dr. William Hayes, organist at Worcester Cathedral and later professor of music at Oxford, declared 'how much (catch-singing) contributed to the *Improvement* of the younger Practitioners, enabling them to sing readily at sight ... and thereby, not a little, to (contribute) to the just execution of *Church-Music*' (Robinson and Hall 1989, 13).

The Noblemen and Gentlemen's Catch Club, formed in 1761, is the earliest club with extant minutes. Rules specified that the penalty for being 'deficient in his part' or for one who 'actually sings out of time or tune' involved drinking a glass of wine. Coffee, tea 'or any other such heterogeneous beverages' were banned, as was conversation on political or religious subjects.

Gradually, the terms 'catch' and 'catch club' became diluted, making way for the more refined glee club. By the middle of the nineteenth century, many organizations that retained the title (such as the Canterbury Catch Club) were virtually orchestral societies with some vocal items – madrigals, part-songs and glees – included in their concerts.

Bibliography

Latham, R., and Matthews, W. 1971. *The Diaries of Samuel Pepys*, Vol. 1. London: Harper Collins.

Playford, John. 1673. *The Musical Companion*. London: Printed by W. Godbid.

Robinson, B.W., and Hall, R.F. 1989. *The Aldrich Book of Catches*. London: Novello.

Wiltshire, C. 1993. *The British Male Voice Choir: A History and Contemporary Assessment*. Ph.D. thesis, Goldsmith College, University of London.

CHRISTOPHER WILTSHIRE

Chorus Line

A chorus line is a group of singer-dancers, typically between eight and 16 in number, who are regularly choreographed in a line or lines across the stage as part of a musical stage entertainment. Although best known for its performances as a unit, often in unison, the chorus line frequently provided the performers for the smaller roles or contributions required by the show. Predominantly female for much of its history, the chorus line has been associated by spectators with the display and glamorization of the female body; for professionals, however, it has equally long associations with the workaday world of theatrical 'hoofing,' its opportunities and (especially) its insecurities. The linear arrangement itself – originally used at important points to maximize display – has eventually joined a select group of theatrical devices that epitomize the traditional desire to entertain.

The emergence of the chorus line as a regular feature of musico-theatrical entertainment appears to have required a conjuncture of several factors at its source. Partly as a result of the growing tendency of mid-nineteenth-century popular theater to parody the more solemn manifestations of established traditions, including that of the chorus of singers and dancers, there was a willingness to treat the idea of the chorus with flexibility. The period was also characterized by changes (hotly disputed) in attitudes toward the display of the female body on stage; by the 1860s, theatrical entrepreneurs recognized the consequent box-office value not just of having an all-female chorus, but of dressing its members in short skirts and tights. Although the practise of revealing the female form on stage was by no means new, in the 1840s and 1850s such exposure had been limited to what was called 'living statuary.' By the 1860s, it was being firmly linked to movement, partly to walkarounds derived from the minstrel show, but more especially to high-stepping march-like movements carried out to martial music. Precision 'marching' in line by the French *chorines* was a major attraction in the groundbreaking popular US spectacle *The Black Crook*, which ran for an unprecedented 16 months in New York in 1866–67.

One of the first appearances of a formation recognizable as a chorus line was in the burlesque shows put on in New York in the late 1860s/early 1870s by Lydia Thompson and Her British Blondes. Here, song and dance were united in a raucous variation on the 'leg show.' By 1873, the show had settled on a particular form of ending in which the Blondes lined up across the stage and sang a number that called for a high kick at the end of every verse. The residual French influence in the form of the cancan was apparent to observer Olive Logan, who asked rhetorically and with heavy sarcasm of potential chorus girls, 'Can you sing brassy songs, and dance the cancan, and wink at men, and give utterance to disgusting half-words, which mean whole actions?' (Toll 1976, 218–19).

By the time of the emergence of the revue in the 1880s and 1890s, the line of chorus girls had become standard; it had also become more accepted. In the series of quick-paced, visually spectacular *Follies* produced annually in New York by Florenz Ziegfeld between 1907 and 1925 and inspired by the French Folies Bergère, the line was used as a key element in Ziegfeld's project of 'glorifying the American girl.' Always elegantly and sometimes scantily dressed, and going through up to 10 different costumes a night, the Ziegfeld Girl, 'with her expressive but controlled sexuality ... was a living display for middle-class consumer culture' (Allen 1991, 245).

In the all-black shows of the second and third decades of the twentieth century, it was the dancing of the male and female chorus that tended to draw most attention. The pattern was set by *Darktown Follies* (1913), which 'exploded in a variety of dancing,' including the Texas Tommy, in which the chorus danced as couples, then broke vigorously away (Stearns and Stearns 1994, 127, 129), and a circle dance, in which the entire company formed a line and, in the words of one participant, 'did a sort of sliding walk with their hands on the hips of the person in front of them' (ibid., 125). In the Prohibition era, the all-female chorus lines, carefully coordinated by size and skin color, became a major attraction at Harlem nightspots, such as the Cotton Club and Connie's Inn, which catered for a white audience. Conscious of the prevailing sentiments of their white clientele regarding the attractiveness of African-American womanhood, the clubs insisted even more strictly than the stage shows on a policy of employing only light-skinned women (the so-called 'high yallers').

According to one historian, the black chorus line in these clubs was distinguished by 'its rhythmic, exhilarating energy level. Having grown up exposed to such popular dance forms as the cakewalk, buck dancing, and ballin' the jack, the dancers were well prepared for the fast turns, high jumps, and kicks demanded by their black choreographers' (Bogle 1980, 38). The chorus lines also had a reputation for opportunism, appropriating from specialist dance acts whatever novel dance steps caught their fancy (Emery 1988, 346).

In 1934, the Cotton Club experimented successfully with an all-male chorus line (Haskins 1985, 99–101), but, by the late 1930s, with the revue in decline and burlesque reduced to a strip show, and with increasing costs acting as a deterrent to production numbers, the opportunities for all types of chorus line had decreased. Movies of the 1930s continued to feature them in some form (although, in the films of Busby Berkeley, the dancing of the chorus-line girls declined in favor of their contribution to grandiose *tableaux vivants*), but, by the 1940s, in both the stage musical and the film musical, the increasing use of the chorus to illustrate and embody the idea of 'community' and its individual members meant that there was less interest in the functions of 'pure' entertainment and display that the chorus line represented.

The television variety show, which rekindled the fortunes of many entertainers in the 1950s and 1960s, also brought the chorus line back before the public. Meanwhile, the nightclub context, which had never disappeared, provided the setting for the musical *Sweet Charity* (1966), whose depiction of life at the 'bump and grind' end of chorus-line life combined the musical's interest in communities with the theater's longer-standing affection for song-and-dance display. With an increased

interest in dance and the flair of choreographers such as Bob Fosse and Michael Bennett, the dancing chorus line became one option among many for musical theater choreographers. In *A Chorus Line* (1975), the line itself finally became the subject. Centering on the itinerant performers who roam from show to show without much success, *A Chorus Line* uses the phenomenon of the (male and female) chorus line to explore issues of individuality and conformity; and like *Sweet Charity*, it ties together the entertainment and the community traditions (Gottfried 1979).

Bibliography

Allen, Robert C. 1991. *Horrible Prettiness: Burlesque in American Culture*. Chapel Hill, NC: University of North Carolina Press.

Bogle, Donald. 1980. *Brown Sugar: Eighty Years of America's Black Female Superstars*. New York: Harmony Books.

Emery, Lynne Fauley. 1988. *Black Dance from 1619 to Today*. 2nd rev. ed. London: Dance Books. (First published Palo Alto, CA: National Press Books, 1972.)

Erenberg, Lewis. 1981. *Stepping Out: New York Nightlife and the Transformation of American Culture, 1890–1930*. Westport, CT: Greenwood Press.

Gottfried, Martin. 1979. *Broadway Musicals*. New York: Abrams.

Haskins, Jim. 1985 (1977). *The Cotton Club*. London: Robson Books.

Parker, David, and Parker, Julia. 1975. *The Natural History of the Chorus Girl*. Newton Abbot: David & Charles.

Stearns, Marshall, and Stearns, Jean. 1994 (1968). *Jazz Dance: The Story of American Vernacular Dance*. New York: Da Capo.

Toll, Robert C. 1976. *On with the Show: The First Century of Show Business in America*. New York: Oxford University Press.

Filmography

A Chorus Line, dir. Richard Attenborough. 1985. USA. 118 mins. Musical Drama. Original music by Marvin Hamlisch, Edward Kleban.

Sweet Charity, dir. Bob Fosse. 1969. USA. 148 mins. Musical Drama. Original music by Cy Coleman, Dorothy Fields, Joseph E. Gershenson.

DAVID HORN

Combo

'Combo' is a term most often used in jazz, and primarily in swing-related forms of that music, to describe a group of instrumentalists. It derives from 'combination' (in other words, a combination of instruments or instrumentalists) and gained currency particularly with respect to recording or broadcasting groups in which the number of personnel fluctuated, making the use of a numerical description, such as 'quartet' or 'quintet,' for example, inappropriate. Some authorities suggest that, in general, a combo has between eight and 10 members, but abiding characteristics are the informality of the material played and the absence of formal arrangements.

Bibliography

Levet, Jean-Paul. 1992. *Talkin' That Talk: Le Langage du blues et du jazz* [Talkin' That Talk: The Language of Blues and Jazz]. Paris: Hatier.

ALYN SHIPTON

Country Music Band

The country music band has evolved over the years along with the many changes in the music itself. The only constant throughout the twentieth century was that country music bands tended to feature stringed instruments rather than brass, reeds or woodwinds. Various names have been applied to country music aggregations over the years, including 'Old-time,' 'Hillbilly,' 'Western' and 'Nashville sound,' but these appellations say more about the image of the performers than about the sound of their music. The evolving constitution of the country music band is best understood by an examination of the several distinct forms that emerged over the years.

In 1920, there were numerous musical aggregations that played on weekends and special occasions. They were generally led by a fiddle, other instruments being added as circumstances allowed; the most structured groups were composed of family members. After 1924, radio stations across the South and Southwest featured fiddle players, but the reels and breakdowns so captivating in live performance proved monotonous heard on radio.

The string band evolved to give texture and to maintain listener interest. The lead fiddle was augmented by other instruments, most often including guitar, banjo, harmonica, mandolin and dobro, with vocals provided by instrumentalists. Early innovators in the form included the Skillet Lickers, Dixie Mountaineers and Georgia Wildcats.

Harmonizing duets proliferated in the 1930s. These generally had a guitar and one other instrument, but simulated a four-voiced band by also singing in close harmony. The most successful of these were sibling groups, not necessarily because they got along, but due to the fact that, before turning professional, they had spent years singing together. Exemplars included the Delmore Brothers, the Monroe Brothers, the Blue Sky Boys and the Girls of the Golden West.

Western swing bands developed in the 1930s in the oil boomtowns of Oklahoma and Texas, playing for couple dancers who wanted to hear the latest swing numbers played on strings. The innovators, Milton Brown and Bob Wills, augmented the string band with an electric steel guitar, vocalist, piano, bass, drums and sometimes a brass section. The larger aggregations depended on written arrangements.

Especially following the great success of Jimmie Rodgers in the late 1920s, vocalists came to the fore in country music bands, as they did a decade later in pop music bands. To give prominence to the story being told by the band-leading vocalist, all the other musical elements were simplified and routinized, with instrumental fills complementing the vocals by evoking earlier iconic songs in the same subgenre. In the 1930s, the new hot string bands featured vocalists, as illustrated, for example, by Roy Acuff and the Smoky Mountain Boys.

The predominance of the singer in the country music band was further entrenched with the advent of the honky-tonk style. Like western swing, this form developed in the roadhouses outside southwestern oil boomtowns and was perfected in the boomtowns of World War II. Rather than rely on more players to increase volume, however, honky-tonk bands were leaders in the use of amplified instruments. The vocalist was featured and usually played rhythm guitar. There was sometimes a fiddle, but the lead instrument was an electric guitar usually augmented by pedal steel, bass and, later, drums. Ernest Tubb, Hank Snow and Hank Williams were early exemplars of the form, and its renaissance in the 1960s was led by George Jones, Merle Haggard and Buck Owens.

Bluegrass, the hot new form to emerge just after World War II, bucked the trends toward electrification and featured vocalist. All-acoustic, and rooted in the string band with a high-pitched duet vocal sound, it relied on fast-paced interplay between instrumentalists, with vocals adding to the effect. The style was developed by Bill Monroe and the alumni of his band. The novel fingerings of Earl Scruggs brought the banjo a prominence it had never before known, and also encouraged other instrumentalists to innovate.

In the early 1950s, what would later become rockabilly moved in the opposite direction from bluegrass. Featuring a lead vocalist, electric guitar and increasingly provocative body movements, it was grounded in a heavy rhythm provided by electric rhythm guitar, bass, drums and, often, piano. Notable exponents included Bill Haley, the young Elvis Presley, Jerry Lee Lewis and Buddy Holly. While bluegrass vocals evoked the imagery of 'olden times in the hills,' rockabilly voiced the concerns of contemporary youth.

While the predominant form has continued to be that of lead vocalist and backing band, bands that feature multiple artists have reemerged from diverse sources. Some, like the Oak Ridge Boys, have come from gospel music; others, like Alabama, have come from rock; and still others, including BR5-49, model their image on the old-time string bands.

While there have been numerous permutations and combinations in the country music band form and sound, many of them derived from pop music, the most distinctive new form of country music band to develop since 1960 is notable for its lack of fixed form. Though presaged by the variety of aggregations that backed Jimmie Rodgers' recordings, the recording studio band was perfected in the 'Nashville sound' era by record producers Owen Bradley, Chet Atkins and Billy Sherrill. On a session-by-session basis, they assembled any combination of instrumental virtuosos to get the desired sound. Their talents lay in playing, on demand, in any one of a number of different styles, and melding their contributions with those of the other players, creating fresh head arrangements in a matter of minutes. Early model session musicians included Harold Bradley, Hank Garland, the Anita Kerr Singers and Grady Martin.

Bibliography

Malone, Bill C. 1985. *Country Music U.S.A.* Austin, TX: University of Texas Press.

Peterson, Richard A. 1997. *Creating Country Music: Fabricating Authenticity*. Chicago: University of Chicago Press.

Rosenberg, Neil. 1985. *Bluegrass: A History*. Urbana, IL: University of Illinois Press.

Discography

Classic Country Music: A Smithsonian Collection. Notes by Bill C. Malone. Smithsonian RD-042. *1991*: USA.

Roots of Country. Notes by Andrew G. Hager. Curb 77865. *1996*: USA.

RICHARD A. PETERSON

Dance Band

Most instrumental ensembles outside the concert tradition have functioned primarily or partly as dance bands. In popular music studies, however, the term generally has a narrower meaning: a twentieth-century European or North American orchestra playing popular tunes as dance music for patrons of hotel ballrooms and nightclubs.

The dance band in that sense might have been anything from a trio to an orchestra of 20 pieces or more, but by the beginning of the 1920s it usually had a sectional arrangement of brass, reeds, strings and rhythm instruments. A typical instrumentation might have been three or four trumpets, two or three trombones, four or five reeds (chiefly clarinet and saxophone), four strings

(violins, violas, cello), piano, banjo (later, guitar), brass bass (later, string bass), bass and drums, although the musicians might have drawn on many other instruments, such as Latin percussion, Hawaiian guitar, accordion or harp, for coloration on particular pieces.

By the end of the 1920s, the presence or absence of a string section was often a clue to an orchestra's distance from or attachment to jazz. Leading African-American orchestras like Duke Ellington's or Fletcher Henderson's, which functioned both as dance bands and as show bands, seldom employed strings. The white orchestra led by Paul Whiteman, however, was flexible enough to execute both concert pieces like Gershwin's 'Rhapsody in Blue,' which called for a substantial string section, and popular dance tunes that required few or no strings, featuring instead cameos by jazz soloists like Bix Beiderbecke.

Whiteman's use of strings, as required, gave his music a particular appeal in parts of Europe where, as Starr (1983) remarks, 'the tradition of light orchestral music was far stronger than in America' (67). That appeal drew Leningrad musician Leopold Teplitsky to the United States in 1926, in search of records and arrangements. Back in Russia, his attempts to emulate Whiteman's mix of modern dance music and 'concert jazz' met with popular success and critical disdain (Starr 1983, 66–69).

Whiteman's fame was assisted by the movie *King of Jazz* (1930). His contemporaries in the United States and Europe, although on the whole less fortunate in securing film opportunities, were profitably active in the other rapidly growing media of the 1920s, radio and recording. Hookups from hotel ballrooms or nightclubs allowed direct live broadcasting of dance bands in their milieu. They also enshrined the mutually beneficial relationship of orchestra and venue, which was further enhanced when a band secured a recording contract that explicitly acknowledged its primary employer. In London, Roy Fox and, later, Lew Stone were billed on the labels of their Decca recordings 'at the Monseigneur Restaurant,' and Ambrose and His Orchestra likewise 'at the May Fair Hotel'; the Savoy Orpheans and the Savoy Havana Band were under the aegis of the Savoy Hotel, while smaller, more intimate venues, like the Kit-Cat and Embassy clubs, lent their fashionable aura to the Kit-Cat Band and the Embassy Rhythm Eight.

In the early days of radio, the broadcasting of dance music was seen, to some extent, literally: as a way of supplying music for dancers who had no musical resources of their own. (The common scene in movies and books, in which the carpet is rolled back and the radio switched on, is not simply a fictional device for getting a pair of lovers decorously into each other's arms.) Records of dance music were envisaged as playing a similar role. Executives of the US music business, however, quickly perceived that both media served a far larger and more diverse group than would-be waltzers and frustrated fox-trotters. A significant percentage of listeners, although disbarred by age, health, temperament or religious belief from actually dancing to music, was nonetheless eager to hear it, sometimes, no doubt, creating an imaginary context for enjoying it that was free of those restrictions – to borrow the title of a popular record program on US radio in the 1940s, a make-believe ballroom.

Radio networks in the United States also realized that the effect of transmitting a dance program by a 'name' band direct from its location could be achieved more reliably and cheaply and without much loss of ambiance by the use of an in-house orchestra. Its unlocated and therefore unbranded studio broadcasts could then be offered to advertising sponsors such as the manufacturers of Ipana toothpaste or Camel cigarettes, which lent their names to the Ipana Troubadours and the variety show *Camel Caravan*. Many of the most famous US dance orchestras of the 1930s had radio sponsors, and professional dance band musicians unable to find a leader to hire them might make a living instead in the pool of New York studio musicians employed for various radio broadcasts by CBS or NBC. This informal guild, which included such players as Tommy and Jimmy Dorsey and Benny Goodman, also furnished most of the personnel needed by the New York-based record companies to make discs of popular songs and tunes.

In Britain, where the radio culture was essentially national rather than regional and where commercial sponsorship was inapplicable, the shifting of dance music from the ballroom to the radio studio was epitomized by the institution of the BBC Dance Orchestra, playing exclusively on radio under the leadership of Jack Payne and, later, Henry Hall. Other European countries, too, had their 'official' radio dance bands – for example, L'Orchestre Jazz de l'INR in Belgium. Insofar as the names of such bands spread beyond national European boundaries, radio was largely responsible. In the 1930s, for example, the BBC broadcast bands from France (Ray Ventura), Holland (the Ramblers) and Denmark (Kai Ewen) (McCarthy 1971, 132–37).

Another consequence of radio's raid on the dance halls was the rapid elevation to star status of the dance band singer. In a hotel ballroom or a *palais de danse*, the band vocalist sat to one side of the stage, an intermittently required cameo performer or character actor in the drama of the musical arrangement. On record labels, his/her contribution would be reduced to a terse 'with vocal refrain' in small print. Radio did much to dispel this anonymity and to confer personality on dance band

singers like Bing Crosby and Mildred Bailey, who rose from the ranks of the Whiteman orchestra, or Frank Sinatra, who sang with the bands of Tommy Dorsey and Harry James, enabling them to create performing and recording careers in their own right, unattached to any particular orchestra.

The ability of radio to provide dance band music on a national, and to some extent international, scale in the 1930s did not necessarily discourage local bands or local dance halls; indeed, in places it may have encouraged them. In Liverpool, for example, a sizable audience existed for local dance bands and professional, semiprofessional and amateur bands flourished, many relying heavily on the use of commercially available music, molded to their own style, rather than on making their own arrangements (Jenkins 1994). In addition to playing at the grander venues, bands provided music for local halls, and enthusiasm was such that 'even swimming pools could be drained and boarded over for dancing' (Jenkins 1994, 3).

By the mid-1930s, there was a sharp distinction, nationally and locally, between dance bands regarded as 'hot' – incorporating musicians with jazz reputations and employing material or arrangements with jazz coloration – and those judged to be 'sweet' or 'novelty.' In the United States, the big bands of, for example, Benny Goodman, Artie Shaw and Woody Herman dispensed swing music that was radically different in spirit from the cooler or more playful repertoire of bands catering to more sedate or unsophisticated tastes – those, for example, of Guy Lombardo, Jan Garber, Sammy Kaye and Kay Kyser, Horace Heidt and His Musical Knights or Shep Fields and His Rippling Rhythm. Among their spiritual counterparts in Britain might be numbered the bands of Jack Payne, Maurice Winnick and Mantovani.

Such ensembles, dismissed by US sophisticates as 'Mickey Mouse bands,' interspersed what was still, at least theoretically, dance music with humorous novelty material for which nobody would have thought to leave their seat, such as Kyser's 'Three Little Fishies' or, in Britain, Payne's 'My Brother Makes the Noises for the Talkies' or Henry Hall's 'The Teddy Bears' Picnic.' The swing ensembles of Goodman, Shaw, James, Ellington, Herman, Count Basie, Jimmie Lunceford, Charlie Barnet, Glenn Miller and other leaders, by contrast, although attracting large radio audiences, continued to perform in public, at venues like the Savoy Ballroom in New York, the Meadowbrook in Cedar Grove, New Jersey or the Palomar in Los Angeles. They performed expressly for dancers, thereby inspiring, particularly within the African-American clientele of the Savoy, a continuous creative output of new dances like the Lindy Hop, the Shag and the Truck, all of which attained national currency.

After World War II, the economics of ballroom operation and one-night-stand touring could no longer support the giant orchestras of the swing era, and even leaders as established as Basie or Goodman were forced to reduce their personnel to six or seven. In Britain, the Mecca and Locarno ballroom chains provided weekly dances to the accompaniment of big-band music in many cities during the 1950s and 1960s, but the decline of formal dance that began with rock 'n' roll and accelerated in the 1960s left these venues without a clientele, although some have been rescued by the participants and spectators of exhibition dancing and its televised championships. In the United States, where a few dance orchestras like Lester Lanin's or Peter Duchin's survived on debutante balls and such high-society jobs, nostalgia for the polite conventions of the dance floor has also reanimated some venues and orchestras.

Bibliography

Colin, Sid. 1977. *And the Bands Played On*. London: Elm Tree Books.

Jenkins, Tricia. 1994. *'Let's Go Dancing': Dance Band Memories of 1930s Liverpool*. Liverpool: Institute of Popular Music, University of Liverpool.

McCarthy, Albert. 1971. *The Dance Band Era: The Dancing Decades from Ragtime to Swing, 1910–1950*. London: Studio Vista.

Rust, Brian. 1972. *The Dance Bands*. London: Ian Allan.

Rust, Brian. 1975. *The American Dance Band Discography, 1917–1942*. New Rochelle, NY: Arlington House.

Simon, George T. 1974 (1967). *The Big Bands*. Rev. ed. New York: Macmillan.

Starr, S. Frederick. 1983. *Red and Hot: The Fate of Jazz in the Soviet Union, 1917–1980*. New York: Oxford University Press.

Towler, Edward. 1985. *British Dance Bands (1920–1949) on 12-Inch Long-Playing Records*. Harrow, Middlesex: General Gramophone Publications.

Sheet Music

Gershwin, George, comp. 1924. 'Rhapsody in Blue.' New York: New World Music Corp.

Discographical References

Hall, Henry. 'The Teddy Bears' Picnic.' Columbia DB955. 1932: UK.

Kyser, Kay. 'Three Little Fishies.' Brunswick 8358. 1939: USA.

Payne, Jack. 'My Brother Makes the Noises for the Talkies.' Columbia CB317. 1931: UK.

Whiteman, Paul, and His Orchestra. 'Rhapsody in Blue.' RCA-Victor 35822. 1927: USA.

Discography

An Anthology of Big Band Swing 1930–1955. MCA GRP 26292. *1993*: USA.

Everybody Dance!: 25 British Dance Bands of the Thirties. ASV/Living Era CD AJA 5362. 1930–40; *2000*: UK.

Shake That Thing: America's Top Bands of the 20s. ASV/Living Era CD AJA 5002. 1925–30; *1992*: UK.

Filmography

King of Jazz, dir. John Murray Anderson. 1930. USA. 93 mins. Musical. Original music by Milton Ager, George Gershwin, Billy Rose, Mabel Wayne.

TONY RUSSELL

Duo

A duo is a musical ensemble containing only two performers. Unlike in Western classical music, in which duo formats are determined by the demands of a written score, in popular music most duo formats have taken shape in less formal ways. The principal exception is areas of popular music in which the vocal duo takes the form of a vocal duet, written with two parts, usually one male and one female. Most duos in popular music consist of two singers or singer/instrumentalists, but there are some instances of two-person instrumental groups.

Male vocal harmony duos have been a significant element in country music and in soul music in the United States. 'Brother' acts were popular in country music from the 1920s to the 1940s: the Allen Brothers in the 1920s and the 1930s; the Blue Sky Boys, the Delmore Brothers, the Callahan Brothers, the Shelton Brothers and the Dixon Brothers in the 1930s; the Louvin Brothers in the 1940s; and the Everly Brothers in the 1950s. In 1960s soul music, Sam and Dave recorded numerous hits for the Stax label, while the Righteous Brothers made memorable white soul recordings. Eric B and Rakim were a leading rap duo.

Male singing duos have occasionally been in evidence in mainstream popular music since the 1920s, when Bing Crosby and Al Rinker were billed as 'Two Boys and a Piano.' In the rock era, Simon and Garfunkel were the most popular male duo. Female vocal duos are almost unknown in black American music and are found infrequently in country music, where the best-known duos have been the Judds and the Davis Sisters. The Canadian sisters Kate and Anna McGarrigle are leading figures in folk music. Salt 'n' Pepa were among the few female vocal duos in rap music.

In contrast, numerous duos combining male and female singers can be found in many areas of popular music. Such duos frequently perform duets – songs that contain a separate part for each singer. In music theater genres such as opera, operetta and stage musicals, the duet has a dramatic purpose in presenting a dialog between two characters. In the twentieth century, such pairs of singers as Nelson Eddy and Jeanette MacDonald, and Fred Astaire and Ginger Rogers became renowned for their duets in Broadway and Hollywood musicals.

The male–female vocal duo was a major feature of country music from the 1950s to the 1970s. The most renowned partnerships included Porter Wagoner and Dolly Parton, George Jones and Tammy Wynette, and Loretta Lynn and Conway Twitty. In black popular music of the 1960s, the Motown company introduced Marvin Gaye and Tammi Terrell, while Stax recorded William Bell and Judy Clay, and in Chicago Jerry Butler and Betty Everett recorded many duets. Among later soul duos have been Roberta Flack and Donny Hathaway, and Womack and Womack. Bob and Marcia were an internationally known reggae duo.

In the pop music mainstream, the mixed vocal duo has often been regarded as a novelty act. Examples are Sonny and Cher, the Israeli duo Esther and Abi Ofarim, and Peters and Lee from Britain.

Another form of duo combines vocals and instrumental playing. The partnership of pioneer electric guitarist Les Paul and vocalist Mary Ford had many hits, as did the similar R&B duos of Mickey and Sylvia, Inez and Charlie Foxx, and Ike and Tina Turner. In the pop sphere, the most commercially successful act of this type was the Carpenters, a brother-and-sister duo, followed by the Swedish duo Roxette. The British acts Soft Cell and the Communards were rare examples of all-male duos combining vocals and instrumental playing.

Instrumental duos in twentieth-century popular music were found less frequently, principally because most genres demand both a leading instrument and a rhythm section with two or more players. This rhythmic necessity meant that duos had to include a rhythm instrument, generally a guitar or a banjo. In jazz, the partnership of Eddie Lang (guitar) and Joe Venuti (violin) was well known in the 1920s, and in a later era there were also guitar and bass duets featuring such figures as Jim Hall and Pat Metheny. Later, the virtuosity of the Hammond organ enabled the formation of organ–drum duos.

The most famous duos in blues were 'Scrapper' Blackwell and Leroy Carr, who combined piano and guitar, and 'Brownie' McGhee and Sonny Terry, whose guitar–harmonica formula inspired a number of European imitators. Tom Darby and Jimmie Tarlton were pioneer country music performers playing twin guitars. Post-1945 country music favored larger groups, with the exception of the bluegrass genre in which Lester Flatt and Earl Scruggs were leading figures on guitar and banjo.

Popular music's crossovers with the classical musics of India and Europe brought to the fore the sitar–tabla duo, epitomized by Ravi Shankar and Alla Rakha, and twin pianos, as performed in the United States by Ferrante and Teicher and in Britain by Rawicz and Landauer.

The new dance music genres of the late 1980s onward introduced a new type of duo whose members produced or remixed recordings and at times performed them in person. Some examples were C+C Music Factory (US), the Chemical Brothers (UK), and Air and Daft Punk (both France).

Discography

Air. *Moon Safari*. Astralwerks 6644. *1998*: USA.

Allen Brothers, The. *Allen Brothers, Vol. 1: 1927–1930*. Document 8033. *2000*: Austria.

Bell, William. *Duets*. Stax 8584. *1968*: USA.

Blue Sky Boys, The. *Blue Sky Boys on Radio, Vol. 1*. Copper Creek 120. *1996*: USA.

Bob and Marcia. *Young Gifted & Black*. Trojan 122. *1976*: UK.

C+C Music Factory. *Super Hits*. Columbia/Legacy 63539. *2000*: USA.

Callahan Brothers, The. 'Somebody's Been Using That Thing.' *White Country Blues, 1926–1938*. Columbia/ Legacy 47466. *1993*: USA.

Carpenters, The. *Singles (1969–1981)*. A&M 490456. *2000*: USA.

Carr, Leroy, and Blackwell, 'Scrapper.' *Leroy Carr and Scrapper Blackwell (1930–1958)*. Story of the Blues 3538. *1989*: USA.

Chemical Brothers, The. *Dig Your Own Hole*. Astralwerks 6180. *1997*: USA.

Communards, The. *Red*. London 8280662. *1987*: USA.

Daft Punk. *Homework*. Virgin 42609. *1997*: USA.

Darby, Tom, and Tarlton, Jimmie. *Complete Recordings*. Bear Family 15764. *1995*: Germany.

Delmore Brothers, The. *Weary Lonesome Blues*. Old Homestead 153. *1983*: USA.

Dixie Chicks, The. *Wide Open Spaces*. Monument 68195. *1998*: USA.

Dixon Brothers, The. *Dixon Brothers, Vol. 1: 1936*. Document 8046. *2000*: Austria.

Eric B and Rakim. *Paid in Full*. 4th & Broadway 444005. *1987*: USA.

Everly Brothers, The. *All-Time Original Hits*. Rhino 75996. *1999*: USA.

Ferrante, Art, and Teicher, Louis. *Ferrante and Teicher: Greatest Hits*. Curb 77338. *1990*: USA.

Flack, Roberta, and Hathaway, Donny. *Roberta Flack and Donny Hathaway*. Atlantic 7716. *1972*: USA. Reissue: Flack, Roberta, and Hathaway, Donny. *Roberta Flack* and Donny Hathaway. WEA International 82794. *2002*: USA.

Flatt, Lester, and Scruggs, Earl. *'Tis Sweet to Be Remembered: The Essential Flatt and Scruggs*. Columbia/Legacy 64877. *1997*: USA.

Foxx, Inez and Charlie. *Mockingbird: The Best of Inez Foxx*. Stateside 6000. *1986*: USA.

Gaye, Marvin, and Terrell, Tammi. *20th Century Masters – The Millennium Collection: Marvin Gaye & Tammi Terrell*. Uptown/Universal 157600. *2000*: USA.

Jones, George, and Wynette, Tammy. *George and Tammy Super Hits*. Sony 67133. *1995*: USA.

Judds, The. *The Judds: Greatest Hits*. RCA 8318-2-R. *1988*: USA.

Louvin Brothers, The. *When I Stop Dreaming: The Best of the Louvin Brothers*. Razor & Tie 2068. *1995*: USA.

Lynn, Loretta, and Twitty, Conway. *20 Greatest Hits*. MCA MCAD-5943. *1988*: USA.

McGarrigle, Kate and Anna. *Kate & Anna McGarrigle*. Warner Brothers 2862. *1975*: USA.

Mickey and Sylvia. *Love Is Strange: A Golden Classics Edition*. Collectables 5833. *1997*: USA.

Ofarim, Esther and Abi. *2 in 3*. Philips SBL 7825. *1968*: UK.

Paul, Les, and Ford, Mary. *The Legendary Duo at Their Best*. Collectables 91. *2001*: USA.

Peters and Lee. *We Can Make It*. Philips 6308 165. *1973*: UK.

Rawicz, Marjan, and Landauer, Walter. *Warsaw Concerto*. ASV 5158. *1995*: UK.

Righteous Brothers, The. *Anthology 1962–1974*. Rhino R2-71488. *1989*: USA.

Roxette. *Don't Bore Us, Get to the Chorus: Greatest Hits*. Edel America 18205. *2000*: USA.

Salt 'n' Pepa. *The Best of Salt 'n' Pepa*. WEA International 7062. *2000*: USA.

Sam and Dave. *The Very Best of Sam & Dave*. Rhino 71871. *1995*: USA.

Shankar, Ravi. *Ragas & Talas*. Angel 67308. *2000*: USA.

Simon and Garfunkel. *The Best of Simon & Garfunkel*. Columbia/Legacy 66022. *1999*: USA.

Soft Cell. *Memorabilia: Singles*. Mercury 510178. *1991*: USA.

Sonny and Cher. *The Singles+*. KMG 8124. *2000*: USA.

Terry, Sonny, and McGhee, 'Brownie.' *Absolutely the Best*. Varese Sarabande 061071. *2000*: USA.

Turner, Ike and Tina. *Proud Mary: The Best of Ike and Tina Turner*. EMI America 95846. *1991*: USA.

Venuti, Joe, and Lang, Eddie. *Stringing the Blues*. Koch 7888. *2000*: USA.

Wagoner, Porter, and Parton, Dolly. *The Essential Porter Wagoner and Dolly Parton*. RCA 66858. *1996*: USA.

Womack and Womack. *Love Wars*. Elektra 60293. *1983*: USA.

DAVE LAING

Ensemble

The term 'ensemble' has two meanings in popular music as it does in art music. It is used to define both a group of instrumentalists and those sections of a piece of music in which all the instrumentalists involved play together. It is derived from the French term meaning 'together.'

In the former sense, within the European/North American tradition, the term is most widely used in those areas of popular music that relate to jazz or cross over into contemporary composition. It can be applied generally to groups of various sizes (up to that of a small orchestra) or it can be used as a proper noun to describe a specific collection of players.

When 'ensemble' is employed as a generic term, the ensemble is categorized by the number of players involved. Hence, the smallest ensemble, two players, is a duo and larger groups are (self-evidently) trio, quartet, quintet, sextet, septet, octet and nonet. No consistently agreed upon or applied formula exists for naming groups of more than nine players. The US arranger Marty Paich described his 10-piece band as a 'dectet,' but this usage is rare, as is Gerry Mulligan's equivalent 'tentette.' Most frequently, groups with 10 or more players are simply defined as an 'x-piece' ensemble, where x is the number of instrumentalists.

In the Western classical tradition, some ensemble names also indicate standard instrumentation – hence, the 'piano trio' consists of piano, violin and cello, and the 'string quartet' consists of two violins, viola and cello. There are far fewer generally accepted such terms in popular music – apart from the piano trio, which, in jazz, almost always consists of piano, bass and drums. Variants are often named after the instrumentalist who pioneered or popularized a particular combination of instruments, such as the Nat 'King' Cole Trio of piano, guitar and bass. The names of other individuals serve to define certain larger combinations, such as Gerry Mulligan's 'drumless' quartet of baritone saxophone, bass, drums and either trumpet or valve trombone. The Miles Davis Nonet is an equally immediately identifiable instrumentation that includes French horn, tuba and baritone saxophone, alongside a conventional jazz sextet of trumpet, alto saxophone, trombone, piano, bass and drums.

Within jazz, groups that use the word 'ensemble' as part of their title are generally those of the post-World War II period (except in Francophone countries where 'ensemble' has always denoted 'group' in a general sense). Most do so to denote some connection with the art-house world – for example, the Art Ensemble of Chicago, whose jazz performances combine exotic instruments, face paints, bizarre costumes and a strong theatrical element. In the area of contemporary composition, some groups employ the term 'ensemble' in their title – for example, the Hyperion Ensemble or the Nieuw Ensemble (the latter exemplifying the 'new complexity' of composers like Brian Ferneyhough), while other comparable ensembles avoid it – for example, Peter Maxwell Davies's Fires of London.

In its other category of usage, the term 'ensemble' is most often employed in referring to pieces of music that contrast passages of solo or small-group work with passages that have much fuller instrumentation. Hence, critics might refer to the discipline (or lack of it) in ensemble sections or 'in the ensemble,' meaning 'as a whole.'

Outside the European/North American tradition, 'ensemble' is most frequently used in the generic sense, to describe groups of instrumentalists across a huge range of genres. The term is also applied to dance groups (as it is to a lesser extent within Western music) in which the boundaries between instrumental, vocal and terpsichorean performance are movable. By and large, in world music, the term is used by outsiders seeking to categorize various types of performance groups, and it is used as a proper noun less frequently.

Within popular music, some types of ensemble have survived in a more or less traditional form; examples include Balinese gamelan and Japanese *nohgaku*, with its accompanying drummers. However, the impact of technology on traditional cultures has resulted in considerable modification both of ensemble style and of the content of the material performed, which has led, in due course, to new types of ensembles playing new styles of popular music. There are few general studies of this process, but there are some comparative papers that provide insight, in particular Malm's tabular comparison of the development of national pop and rock over three decades, from the 1960s through the 1980s, in Tanzania, Tunisia, Sweden and Trinidad (Malm 1992).

Bibliography

Berendt, Joachim-Ernst. 1982. *The Jazz Book: From Ragtime to Fusion and Beyond*. Rev. ed. Westport, CT: Lawrence Hill. (First published Frankfurt am Main: Fischer Bücherei, 1953.)

Collier, Graham. 1973. *Inside Jazz*. London: Quartet Books.

Malm, Krister. 1992. 'The Music Industry.' In *Ethnomusicology: An Introduction*, ed. Helen Myers. London: Macmillan, 349–64.

Myers, Helen. 1993. *Ethnomusicology: Historical and Regional Studies*. London: Macmillan.

ALYN SHIPTON

Fife and Drum Band

Fife and drum music is performed by a combination of one or more fifes (a short transverse flute of wood, metal or bamboo usually with six finger holes) and several side (snare) drums and/or kettledrums, sometimes with a bass drum added. It exists as folk music in a variety of European and New World cultural traditions with varied combinations of instruments and various social functions. In some of these traditions, it has interacted with the world of popular music.

This music is first reported in Europe in the late Middle Ages and Renaissance as the military music of foot soldiers, used to convey signals and regulate marching. German and Swiss mercenaries spread it throughout much of Western Europe, and it soon took hold in colonies of the New World. It was also used, however, for outdoor dances, some of them imitating military movements, and dance tunes were often played for marching and drilling. It continued to have both military and dance functions through the nineteenth century. As the nature of warfare changed in the twentieth century, the fife and drum band's military role was reduced to providing music at formal parades and settings in which a sense of the military past and its heritage was evoked. In the United States, Canada and some countries of Europe, civilian fife and drum bands were formed in the twentieth century, some of them growing out of bands associated with local militia units of the previous century. These groups serve as social clubs with a quasi-military theme and image, and they sometimes engage in historical military reenactments. The Company of Fifers and Drummers, with over 100 corps, mostly in the US mid-Atlantic and northeastern states and in eastern Canada, was formed in 1965 and maintains a newsletter, museum, archive and library. Fife and drum music is often used in films to evoke a militaristic feeling.

In the United States, Brazil, Curaçao and a number of former British colonies in the Caribbean, distinctive African-American fife and drum traditions have developed. (African-American musicians also participate in the more formal northeastern tradition.) Most of the music's militaristic associations have been abandoned or greatly transformed, as it has come to serve variously as social dance music at country picnics and in the West Indian Jonkonnu festival, as accompaniment to mummers' plays, and as serenading music at Christmas and at New Year. In all cases, it remained a type of folk music in the twentieth century, but it has largely been superseded by various types of popular music and, by the end of the century, had become nearly or entirely extinct in a number of traditions. In the United States, however, its decline as a folk music has been accompanied by an influence on popular music. A brief look at this tradition's development and influence will be instructive.

There are numerous reports of African-American musicians performing fife and drum music for militia units in the eighteenth and nineteenth centuries in the American colonies and in the United States. During the slavery period (until 1865), music was one of the few ways in which slaves could participate in military service, since they were not allowed to bear arms. Many no doubt were also attracted to this music because drumming for gatherings of slaves was frequently forbidden by law, out of fear that it might draw large crowds and incite rebellion. Drumming, which had been so important in many of the ancestral African cultures, was thus channeled into a Western military context. However, in this process black musicians began to introduce melodic, scalar, rhythmic and repertoire elements from their own musical traditions. By the 1830s, this transformation had been heightened by the growing popularity of minstrel tunes derived from or imitative of the folk music of the slaves, which were often performed by fife and drum bands for marching and dancing. Following Emancipation, African-American musicians increasingly adapted this music to their social needs and emphasized its role as accompaniment for dancing. Fraternal organizations in the rural and small-town South of the late nineteenth and early twentieth centuries sometimes supported fife and drum bands, while other bands were organized within families or local communities. The usual instrumentation was a fife (often made of bamboo cane) and two or three drums – bass, snare, and sometimes a kettledrum or second snare drum. By the middle of the twentieth century, fife and drum music was still thriving in rural areas of western Georgia, Mississippi and southwest Tennessee, and perhaps elsewhere.

The tradition in Tate and Panola counties of northwest Mississippi is the best documented. It was first recorded by folklorist Alan Lomax in 1942. Sid Hemphill's Band, whose members had been playing together since the beginning of the century, performed a march tune and three popular song tunes in the Western tradition, with the drums playing in rhythmic unison. When Lomax returned to the area in 1959, he recorded the Young family band in a quite different style, emphasizing blue notes and percussive effects on the fife, rhythmically separate drum lines, riff-based melodies, and a generally spontaneous and improvisatory approach to performance. The music accompanied individualized dancing at country picnics with a strong element of display. Further documentation was carried out in the area in subsequent

decades by George Mitchell, David Evans, William Ferris, Luther Dickinson, Robert Gordon and others, always capturing this improvisational style. It would appear, then, that during the first half of the twentieth century, undoubtedly under the influence of improvised blues and jazz music, fife and drum music in this area became more improvisational and absorbed many musical elements from the African tradition while de-emphasizing those from the European tradition. A similar Africanizing process can be observed in some other New World fife and drum traditions documented in the twentieth century.

In the 1960s, the Young family band made a number of national and international concert appearances, most notably at the Newport Folk Festival. Beginning in 1978, fife and drum bands led by Othar Turner or Napoleon Strickland played the opening music (or 'call') at the annual Delta Blues Festival in Greenville, Mississippi, to represent the 'roots' of the blues and its connections to African music. Since then, many other blues and folk festivals within and outside the mid-South region have staged this music for similar representations. By the end of the twentieth century, the only remaining folk event with fife and drum music was the annual two-day picnic sponsored by Othar Turner (b. 1907), a farmer near Senatobia, Mississippi, with music supplied by his family band. By the late 1990s, this event had become an attraction for fans of blues and rock music, musicians and musical tourists, most of them white, from around the region, the nation and abroad. Whereas, in the past, traditional fife and drum musicians had often alternated on other instruments (for example, fiddle, guitar, banjo) or blues musicians had played at the picnics between fife and drum sets, visiting blues and rock musicians had now become the dominant element, and some attempted to add the sounds of electric guitar or conga drum to that of the Turner band. By the year 2000, most of those in attendance at the picnic were coming from outside the local community.

In recent years, Turner and his musicians have made recordings in collaboration with blues-rock guitarists Luther Dickinson and Judah Bauer and with Senegalese and African-American players of the *kora* and various African drums. Earlier, around 1980, Tav Falco's Panther Burns recorded in Memphis with drummers from a fife and drum band. These attempts at fusion music, some of them designed to demonstrate historical or stylistic connections with African music, blues or rock, and all of them initiated by producers or musicians outside the folk tradition, have met with limited artistic success. More significantly, however, artists from within the Mississippi folk tradition have carried a musical sensibility formed by exposure to or participation in fife and drum bands of the mid-twentieth century into blues music. Such artists include singing drummers Joe Hicks (the Fieldstones), George Walker (the Blues Busters), Calvin Jackson (R.L. Burnside, Junior Kimbrough and Mississippi Bound), R.L. Boyce (Jessie Mae Hemphill) and Hezekiah Early (Hezekiah and the House Rockers), as well as blues singer-guitarists Fred McDowell, R.L. Burnside, Jessie Mae Hemphill and Junior Kimbrough. Specific tracks recorded by Hemphill, Burnside and Early demonstrate connections between blues and fife and drum music in repertoire items, rhythmic patterns and the tendency to treat the drumset as a collection of individual drums.

Fife and drum music in North America was only marginally a popular music in the twentieth century in respect to public concerts, radio airplay, hit records and so on, but it influenced popular blues styles of Mississippi and Memphis in the last decades of the century and gained additional popular exposure through documentary media products, tourism and various recorded musical fusions.

Bibliography

Brown, Howard May, and Frank, Jaap (with Raoul F. Camus and Susan Cifaldi). 2001. 'Fife.' In *The New Grove Dictionary of Music and Musicians*, Vol. 8, ed. Stanley Sadie. London: Macmillan, 786–88.

Evans, David. 1972. 'Black Fife and Drum Music in Mississippi.' *Mississippi Folklore Register* 6(3): 94–107.

Ferris, William. 1983. 'Othar Turner, Cane Fife Maker.' In *Afro-American Folk Art and Crafts*, ed. William Ferris. Jackson, MS: University Press of Mississippi, 173–80.

Lomax, Alan. 1993. *The Land Where the Blues Began*. New York: Pantheon.

Mitchell, George. 1971. *Blow My Blues Away*. Baton Rouge, LA: Louisiana State University Press.

Discography

Afro-American Folk Music from Tate and Panola Counties, Mississippi. Rounder 18964-1515-2. *2000*: USA.

Blues Busters. *Busted!*. High Water/HMG 6512. *1999*: USA.

Burnside, R.L. *Sound Machine Groove*. High Water/HMG 6501. *1997*: USA.

Burnside, R.L., and the Sound Machine. *Raw Electric 1979–1980*. Inside Sounds ISC-0513. *2001*: USA.

Charles W. Dickerson Field Music Incorporated. *Bits and Pieces*. Charles W. Dickerson Field Music Incorporated CWD-1002. *1967*: USA.

Falco, Tav. *Tav Falco's Panther Burns: Behind the Magnolia Curtain*. Frenzi FZ4000. *1980*: USA.

Fieldstones, The. *Memphis Blues Today!*. High Water/HMG 6505. *1997*: USA.

Hemphill, Jessie Mae. *Feelin' Good*. High Water/HMG 6502. *1997*: USA.

Hemphill, Jessie Mae. *She-Wolf*. High Water/HMG 6508. *1998*: USA.

Hezekiah and the House Rockers. High Water/HMG 6511. *1998*: USA.

Jackson, Calvin, and Mississippi Bound. *Goin' Down South*. M&M MMBCD 6. *1999*: The Netherlands.

Kimbrough, Junior. *Do the Rump!*. High Water/HMG 6503. *1997*: USA.

Sounds of the South. Atlantic 7 82496-2. *1993*: USA.

Traveling Through the Jungle: Fife and Drum Band Music from the Deep South. Testament TCD 5017. *1995*: USA.

Turner, Otha [sic], and the Afrossippi Allstars. *From Senegal to Senatobia*. Birdman BMR 025. *2000*: USA.

Turner, Otha [sic], and the Rising Star Fife and Drum Band. *Everybody Hollerin' Goat*. Birdman BMR 018. *2001*: USA.

Twenty Miles (Donovan and Judah Bauer with R.L. Boyce, Othar Turner Fife and Drum, and Spam). Fat Possum/Epitaph 80302-2. *1997*: USA.

Visual Recordings

Turner, Othar. 1972. 'Gravel Springs Fife and Drum.' Center for Southern Folklore (film and video).

Young, Ed. 1965. 'Buckdancer.' Radium Films (film).

DAVID EVANS

Gamelan

'Gamelan' is a generic term for various sets of percussion instruments found mainly on the Indonesian islands of Java and Bali, and also in Malaysia. The gamelan is also closely related to other Southeast Asian ensembles that bear different names, such as the *pi-phat* of Thailand (and Cambodia), the *hsaing-waing* of Myanmar (Burma) and the *kulintang* of the Philippines. Their common feature is a group of suspended knobbed gongs and metallophones of various sizes with plates or bars supported over resonators, to which are added drums and, often, bamboo flutes, bowed and plucked stringed instruments, and voice. The metal traditionally favored is bronze, but iron is a good substitute, as it is far cheaper and provides an easier medium from which to manufacture gamelans. In Java, most of the instruments are struck with padded mallets, while the Balinese ensembles make more use of lighter, unpadded wooden mallets. This, plus the tendency of Balinese music to be much faster, with complex interlocking patterns, contributes to the obvious differences among the main types of gamelan. Two unique tuning systems are available: the approximately equidistant pentatonic *sléndro*; and the heptatonic *pélog*, which is often reduced to a pentatonic set, differing from *sléndro* by its use of semitones.

The gamelan is ascribed mythical origins as a kind of signaling system among the gods, so even the modern ensembles are respected and considered a link with the spirit world. Gamelan music is as important to the ceremonies and entertainments of the poorest villages as to those of the city palaces. This is why, despite the tendency of the urban young to dismiss gamelan music as archaic and impeded by its long pieces, peculiar tuning systems and use of old poetry in regional languages, its propaganda value has been skillfully exploited in Indonesia since it became an independent state in 1945. A style of short, catchy tunes, with rhythms often borrowed from foreign sources – for example, the rumba – was developed into a hugely popular genre known as *lagu dolanan* ('playful melodies'). Their most important features are the simple vocal style that many of the pieces inherited from children's songs, and texts that deal with everyday topics and government exhortations. The most famous and prolific composer of such pieces was the late Ki Narto Sabdho, a *dhalang* (shadow puppeteer) and gamelan director from the Javanese city of Semarang. In the late 1970s, musicians such as Mus Mulyadi combined gamelan music with synthesizers, drum machines and other favorite instruments of global popular music, and all kinds of fusions have been tried. Several groups in the West have worked along similar lines. In 1994, on MTV Networks Europe, the Icelandic star Björk performed an arrangement of her song 'One Day' with gamelan accompaniment. A contrasting situation exists with, for example, the popular music and dance genre *jaipongan*, which emerged in West Java in the 1970s and is devoid of foreign influences.

New compositions within traditional forms and instrumentations (*kreasi baru*) are a strong feature of gamelan music throughout Java and Bali, and a more experimental approach more akin to Western avant-garde practises (*komposisi baru*) is also flourishing, though its appeal is more restricted.

Gamelans are notoriously difficult to record, largely because of balance problems. One of the most interesting outcomes of the Indonesian cassette industry, where recordings are produced and sold cheaply and sound quality is not always a priority, is the emphasis on the *pesindhèn* (solo female singer). The practise of placing her to the fore with her own microphone and singling her out for acknowledgment in the insert notes has created and reinforced her position as a star: a female singer among male instrumentalists. Certain *dhalang* have also become popular stars. Their art is based on the most ancient traditions, and the musical accompaniment is provided by the gamelan.

The special aural and visual appeal of the gamelan, as well as its versatility as a resource for conveying the deepest values of traditional Javanese and Balinese culture, for initiating educational projects involving all ages and levels of musicianship, and for exploring new sounds and compositional practises, has enhanced its status and brought it to the forefront of world music. A large body of scholarly publications on the gamelan and the use of gamelans in ethnomusicology courses in North American, European, Australasian and Japanese universities have given support to a perception of gamelan music as one of the most revered traditional musical genres in the world. The ability of gamelan music to contend with a relatively small share of the commercial market, as well as to embrace experiments in popular and avant-garde styles, is a testament to its resilience and versatility.

Bibliography

Becker, Judith. 1980. *Traditional Music in Modern Java: Gamelan in a Changing Society*. Honolulu: University Press of Hawaii.

Lindsay, Jennifer. 1992. Javanese Gamelan. 2nd ed. Singapore: Oxford University Press. (First published Kuala Lumpur: Oxford University Press, 1979.)

Sorrell, Neil. 1990. *A Guide to the Gamelan*. London: Faber & Faber.

Tenzer, Michael. 1991. *Balinese Music*. Berkeley and Singapore: Periplus Editions.

Discographical Reference

Björk. 'One Day.' *Debut*. Elektra 61468. *1993*: USA.

NEIL SORRELL

Garage Band

The 'British invasion' of beat groups in the mid-1960s inspired thousands of young North Americans to form their own amateur bands, characterized more by enthusiasm than by technical skill. The term 'garage band' referred to the typical rehearsal space used by these white, suburban high-school students. Also described as 'punk' groups, many of them recorded for local labels, playing music such as 'Wild Thing' (originally by the Troggs), 'Louie Louie' (the Kingsmen), 'Gloria' (Them) or 'Hey Joe' (the Leaves). Critic/performer Lennie Kaye made the classic selection of garage band music for his 27-song compilation, *Nuggets*.

Bibliography

Bangs, Lester. 1980. 'Protopunks: The Garage Bands.' In *The Rolling Stone Illustrated History of Rock & Roll*, ed. Jim Miller. 2nd ed. New York: Random House, 261–64.

Discographical References

Kingsmen, The. 'Louie Louie.' Wand 143. *1963*: USA.
Leaves, The. 'Hey Joe.' Mira 222. *1966*: USA.

Nuggets: Original Artyfacts from the First Psychedelic Era,
   1965–1968. Sire H-3716. *1972*: USA.
Them. 'Baby Please Don't Go'/'Gloria.' Decca F12018.
   1964: UK.
Troggs, The. 'Wild Thing.' Fontana TF 689. *1966*: UK.

DAVE LAING

Glee Clubs

Glee clubs, popular in eighteenth- and nineteenth-century Britain, were male-only social organizations for the performance of part-songs and glees.

Although the term 'glee' had existed alongside 'catch,' 'round' and 'canon' since the seventeenth century, its use in the 1700s was a means of differentiation from the more robust and bawdy repertoire of catch clubs. As unaccompanied three- or four-part compositions for male voices with alto lead, the glee, with stylized texts concerning the joys of music, nature and romantic love, appealed to the refinement of upper-middle-class Georgian and, later, Victorian gentlemen who attended glee clubs. These organizations proliferated during the second half of the eighteenth century. For example, the Anacreontic Society was founded in 1766, 'for supper and the singing of catches, glees and songs,' and met at the Crown and Anchor tavern in the Strand, London. Similar organizations throughout Britain helped to establish the glee as a uniquely English form, and jingoism played a part in the later establishment of glee clubs throughout the British Empire. The influence of the Anglican choral tradition through the use of male altos was crucial.

Some clubs began as quartets or double quartets (singing at fashionable drawing-room parties), which then expanded numerically to the point where formal organization was required. The Canterbury Catch and Glee Club flourished between 1770 and 1860 and, according to a member's report (written by a Mr. Welby in 1875 and reprinted in *The Music Student* of 1920), established a membership of 500 'Gentry, Clergy and leading Tradesmen' who could afford the annual subscription of one guinea. 'New members were proposed and balloted for. No citizen could be admitted unless a member.' In later years, the club developed into an orchestral society and the vocal aspects were demoted to post-concert late-night sessions at which the singing was 'free and easy, the mirth growing fast and furious till the small hours ... Gin punch in half pint mugs was the beverage and the mutton-pie man supplied the solids.' The conviviality was emphasized by the club motto, 'Harmony and Unanimity.'

At the Bristol Orpheus Glee Society – one of the clubs that remained purely vocal – singers sat at tables ranged around three sides of a square, with the conductor occu-pying the fourth. After an hour's singing, members repaired to the beer or coffee end of the room for refreshments financed by their two-guinea annual subscriptions. Before singing resumed, voting for new members would take place. These evenings were decidedly 'meetings' rather than rehearsals, as the club gave only one concert a year, when, because of its high standing, there was little difficulty in selling tickets for all 1,200 seats. By the middle of the nineteenth century, the club had introduced annual ladies' nights, when part-songs would be performed. Other clubs introduced similar evenings, influenced by composers writing soprano parts in their glees. The usual tavern venue was forsaken, and the event would take place at concert rooms within the local town hall. Smoking concerts proved popular, especially at clubs with instrumentalists: at one London concert, 'the conductor, the stringed instrument players and the performers upon wind instruments too when they could get a chance' combined 'the aroma of the music with the fragrance of the weed' (reported in the *Musical Times* (February 1882), 77).

Glee-writing competitions were popular, and well-known glee composers – Webbe, Cooke, Spofforth, Callcott, Stevens and Goss – used the events to establish their reputations. Glees such as Webbe's *Glorious Apollo*, Cooke's *Strike the Lyre* and Spofforth's *Hail Smiling Morn* were often adopted as 'signature tunes' by various clubs, their texts summarizing the organizations' raison d'être, namely, 'Sing we in harmony ... ,' 'glee and good humour our hours employ ... ,' 'Of harp and trumpet's harmony ... ,' 'Anthems of the opening sky ...' Singing in praise of music and indulging in the delights of Bacchus encapsulated the activities of the glee club, establishing a rationale for its direct descendant, the male voice choir.

Bibliography

Barrett, W. 1886. *English Glees and Partsongs*. London: Longmans, Green and Co.
Wiltshire, C. 1993. *The British Male Voice Choir: A History and Contemporary Assessment*. Ph.D. thesis, Goldsmiths College, University of London.

CHRISTOPHER WILTSHIRE

Group

In popular music, the term 'group' denotes an ensemble of vocalists or instrumentalists, or a combination of the two. The term has often been applied to ensembles that are smaller and less formally organized than either bands or orchestras and, in some cases, the word itself has been part of an ensemble's stage name. However, in the past two decades, 'group' and 'band' have often been used interchangeably in discussions of jazz and Western pop and rock.

In the United States, the appellation 'group' was widely used from the 1930s onward for vocal ensembles such as the Mills Brothers and the Ink Spots. Later generations of small ensembles of singers continued to be known as groups.

From the 1930s onward, small ensembles that were formed from within dance bands and jazz orchestras were often referred to as small groups. Thus, Benny Goodman formed a trio, and later a sextet, with the rhythm section of his swing orchestra to play small-group jazz.

Woody Guthrie referred to the Almanac Singers of the 1940s as 'the only group that rehearsed on stage' (Cantwell 1996, 138); subsequent folk revival ensembles such as the Weavers (US) and the Ian Campbell Folk Group (UK) were also referred to as groups, as were the skiffle groups that flourished in Britain and parts of continental Europe in the mid-1950s. In some nations that had been British colonies, the term was also widespread. In Nigeria, for instance, *fuji* ensembles like Sikiru Ayinde (Barrister) and his Fuji Group and Ayinla Kollington and his New Fuji Group chose the nomenclature.

In the 1960s, the Beatles and other English ensembles were widely known as 'beat groups,' although only a few – such as the Spencer Davis Group – included the word in their stage name. According to Warner (1996), the adoption of the term 'beat group' or 'pop group' was 'a deliberate rejection of band, which seemed to belong to the jazz, swing, dance or big band era that rock was rejecting' (286).

The international appeal of beat groups led to their imitators being called '*gruppo pop*' in Italian, '*groupes*' in French and '*gruppes*' in Spanish. In Japan, the beat style itself was known as 'group music.' The English word was also adopted in Bulgaria to describe the music of Beatles-inspired ensembles. A genre of Mexican popular music of the 1990s was called '*grupo*.'

Many groups in genres such as jazz, R&B and rap have not called themselves by that name, however. Among the alternatives have been 'quartet,' 'combo,' 'posse' and 'crew.'

Bibliography

Cantwell, Robert. 1996. *When We Were Good: The Folk Revival*. Cambridge, MA: Harvard University Press.

Warner, Simon. 1996. *Rockspeak!: The Language of Rock and Pop*. London: Blandford.

DAVE LAING

House Band

'House band' denotes the resident band at a club, theater or ballroom. The term also refers to the backing musicians used by a particular record label at the majority of its sessions. In Chicago during the 1920s, certain musicians became famous for leading the house bands that backed much better-known jazz or variety soloists. Examples include the violinists Erskine Tate, who led the band at the Vendome Theater, and Carroll Dickerson, who was the leader at the Sunset Café and the Savoy Ballroom. Often, such bands became famous through broadcasts. In London, for instance, Roy Fox's Monseigneur Restaurant house band acquired household fame through its radio relays and its discs. One of the longest lived such bands was the orchestra at Frank Sebastian's New Cotton Club at Culver City, California, led by multi-instrumentalist Les Hite throughout the 1930s.

As early as the 1920s, record companies started to use regular backing musicians for their studio sessions. A pioneer in this field was Fletcher Henderson, who spent much of the early 1920s as house accompanist (as both solo pianist and band leader) for the New York-based Black Swan Records, an offshoot of W.C. Handy's publishing company. Later, Sammy Price performed a similar role for Decca. From 1928, the US-born pianist Carroll Gibbons did this job for HMV in London, leading the label's house band, the New Mayfair Dance Orchestra, for two years and recording dozens of sessions accompanying singers as varied as Noël Coward and Paul Robeson.

The house band concept was revived in the rock world during the 1960s, especially in the field of soul music: the Stax label's house band in Memphis and Motown's house band directed by William 'Mickey' Stevenson helped to define the sound both of each label and of the entire era.

Bibliography

Charters, Samuel B., and Kunstadt, Leonard. 1981 (1962). *Jazz: A History of the New York Scene*. New York: Da Capo Press. (First published New York: Doubleday, 1962.)

Guralnick, Peter. 1986. *Sweet Soul Music: Rhythm and Blues and the Southern Dream of Freedom*. New York: Harper and Row.

Kenney, William Howland. 1993. *Chicago Jazz: A Cultural History, 1904–1930*. New York: Oxford University Press.

McCarthy, Albert. 1971. *The Dance Band Era, 1910–1950*. Philadelphia: Chilton Book Co.

McCarthy, Albert. 1974. *Big Band Jazz*. London/New York: Barrie and Jenkins/G.P. Putnam's Sons.

ALYN SHIPTON

Jazz Band

Although the term 'jazz band' encompasses each and every type of jazz ensemble, it carries a more specific meaning, in that it is the only term used to define the standard six- to eight-piece lineup of the traditional or

Dixieland jazz band. The term has its origin on the US west coast where it was in use by 1913, but it came into common usage during the period around 1916, when 'jass' or 'jazz' became the label associated with the music played by syncopated bands in Chicago led by Tom Brown and Johnny Stein. Both these musicians hailed from New Orleans, where the kind of music they played was still referred to, by the musicians themselves, as 'ragtime,' and the instrumentation they used was modeled on that of a ragtime band.

The arrival in New York of the Original Dixieland Jazz Band (a group that grew out of Johnny Stein's earlier ensemble) in 1917, and its recording activity, brought the term 'jazz band' to a widespread audience in the United States and beyond and, by 1918, the term was being used to denote any small group playing hot or improvised music. The syncopated orchestras of James Reese Europe and Will Vodery both included 'bands within a band' that, by 1918, played 'jazz' in the olio of vaudeville engagements or at dances after formal concerts. These groups were referred to as 'jazz bands' by the contemporary press, an early example of the usage applied to African-American ensembles.

Many prototypical 'jazz bands' followed the five-piece instrumentation of the Original Dixieland Jazz Band: cornet, trombone, clarinet, piano and drums. These 'fabulous fives' included the New York-based Original Memphis Five and Jimmy Durante's Original New Orleans Jazz Band.

In New Orleans and Chicago, jazz band instrumentation often included an additional reed instrument (often an alto or tenor saxophone), plus guitar or banjo and tuba or double bass. Early recording techniques make it difficult to discern the role of bass and drums, but Steve Brown, the bassist with the New Orleans Rhythm Kings, and with whom he recorded in Chicago in 1922, became the first jazz double bass virtuoso.

The New Orleans Rhythm Kings, a white ensemble, was one of a number of influential Chicago ensembles in the 1920s, the so-called 'classic jazz era.' The most influential African-American band of the same period was that of Joe 'King' Oliver, which, in 1923, consisted of two cornets (Oliver himself and Louis Armstrong), clarinet (Johnny Dodds), trombone (Honore Dutrey), piano (Lil Hardin), banjo (Johnny St Cyr or Bill Johnson) and drums (Baby Dodds). These players contributed to a substantial body of recordings that defined the 'classic' jazz band approach and repertoire. Armstrong's playing with his Hot Five and Hot Seven extended the idea of the soloist; Johnny Dodds's recordings, under his own name and with trombonist Kid Ory, in the New Orleans Wanderers and the New Orleans Bootblacks, extended the concept of ensemble playing; and 'Jelly Roll' Morton

(with his Red Hot Peppers) developed varied textures and instrumental combinations in the first jazz compositions specifically tailored for the phonograph record.

In the 1930s, the main development of jazz shifted to New York. In the late 1920s, white Chicagoans, such as Eddie Condon, had moved there to play in a rugged Dixieland style and, by the 1930s, similar New York groups were being led by trumpeters Louis Prima and Joseph 'Wingy' Manone and saxophonist Bud Freeman. Freeman's Summa Cum Laude Orchestra, which included trumpeter Max Kaminsky and valve trombonist Brad Gowans, is regarded as the apotheosis of the Chicagoan Dixieland jazz band.

However, larger swing orchestras began to predominate, despite the fact that such orchestras led by Artie Shaw, Tommy Dorsey and Bob Crosby contained smaller Dixieland-style combos within their ranks. Consequently, in 1939 cornetist Muggsy Spanier founded Spanier's Ragtimers to revive the repertoire of 'King' Oliver. This, and recording sessions organized by the French critic Hugues Panassié the previous year for clarinetist Sidney Bechet and trumpeter Tommy Ladnier, marked the beginning of a revival movement. Successive revivals ensured not only the survival of traditional jazz throughout the second half of the twentieth century, but also the preservation of the basic jazz band instrumentation.

The revival continued with the Yerba Buena Jazz Band in San Francisco in the 1940s (which emphasized its point by including two banjos). It was later succeeded there by Turk Murphy's various ensembles. In New Orleans, critics Gene Williams and Bill Russell began to record hitherto unheard veterans, such as trumpeter Bunk Johnson and clarinetist George Lewis, sparking the so-called 'New Orleans Revival.' Lewis's discs for the Climax label in 1942 and Johnson's for the Jazz Man label the same year became widely imitated by players the world over. The Preservation Hall Jazz Band of New Orleans (established in 1961) continued the brand of revivalism initiated by Johnson and Lewis, using an instrumentation of trumpet, trombone, clarinet, banjo, piano, bass and drums. In the 1940s, Kid Ory came out of retirement on the west coast to lead his Creole Jazz Band, a similar seven-piece ensemble with the guitar in place of the banjo. This in turn was similar to the lineup adopted in 1947 by Louis Armstrong, when he gave up fronting a big band and returned to leading the small group called Louis Armstrong and His All Stars, a sextet that had no guitar or banjo in its rhythm section.

The late 1940s saw jazz bands springing up in many parts of the world as part of the revivalist movement. In Australia, Graeme Bell's band reinvented the idea of jazz for dancing and toured through Czechoslovakia, France and Britain. In the United Kingdom, the revival was initiated by George Webb's Dixielanders and Humphrey Lyttelton's band; later significant British revivalists who led archetypal jazz bands included Ken Colyer, Chris Barber, Acker Bilk and Kenny Ball. Comparable groups included, among many others, the Cotton City Jazz Band in Belgium, the Cardinal Jazz Band and Papa Bue's Viking Jazz Band in Denmark, Les Haricots Rouges in France and the White Eagle Band in Berlin.

In the United States, the revival movement led to the widespread establishment of semiprofessional or amateur jazz bands across the country and, since 1974, many of these have gathered each May to perform at the Sacramento Dixieland Jubilee, a festival attended by upward of 250,000 people annually.

Despite the essentially conservative nature of this kind of music, some jazz bands have remained innovative. In the 1950s in Britain, Sandy Brown experimented, first, with Ghanaian highlife music and, later, with rock fusion in an album of material from the musical *Hair*. Chris Barber's Jazz Band became the Chris Barber Blues and Jazz Band when he added a blues-oriented electric guitarist to his personnel and toured with blues musicians such as Louis Jordan, Sonny Terry and Brownie McGhee. Barber also experimented with Balkan rhythms, rock–jazz fusion and scaled-down Ellingtonian repertoire for his eight-piece jazz band. In the United States, the Black Eagle Band has applied a consistently innovative approach to programming and repertoire, while broadly remaining within the Dixieland framework. Equally, Igor Bourco's Russian jazz band has incorporated elements of his country's traditional music, and that of Georgia, into its performances.

Although the term has continued to be most widely used to delineate the traditional style of jazz ensemble, some leaders have chosen to use the term 'jazz band' in the title of bands from other genres. An obvious example is Gerry Mulligan, who called his large groups of the 1960s his Concert Jazz Band. This tradition continued into the twenty-first century, with the Carnegie Hall Jazz Band led by trumpeter Jon Faddis.

Bibliography

Berendt, Joachim-Ernst. 1982 (1975). *The Jazz Book: From Ragtime to Fusion and Beyond*. Rev. ed. Westport, CT: Lawrence Hill. (First published Frankfurt am Main: Fischer Bücherei, 1953.)

Goggin, Jim, and Klute, Peter. 1994. *The Great Jazz Revival*. San Rafael, CA: Donna Ewald.

Lange, Horst H. 1978 (1959). *The Fabulous Fives*. 2nd ed. Chigwell, Essex: Storyville.

Levet, Jean-Paul. 1992. *Talkin' That Talk: Le Langage du blues et du jazz* [Talkin' That Talk: The Language of Blues and Jazz]. Paris: Hatier.

Panassié, Hugues. 1934. *Le Jazz Hot*. Paris: Editions R.A. Correa. (Published as *Hot Jazz: The Guide to Swing Music*, trans. Lyle and Eleanor Dowling. London: Cassell, 1936.)

Schuller, Gunther. 1986 (1968). *The History of Jazz. Vol. 1: Early Jazz, Its Roots and Musical Development*. New York: Oxford University Press.

ALYN SHIPTON

Jazz Ensemble

A jazz ensemble is a group made up of any number of jazz instrumentalists or vocalists, from a duo upward. By the late 1920s, the established form of 'classic' jazz band or ensemble was a septet: trumpet, trombone, clarinet or saxophone, guitar, piano, bass and drums. A parallel tradition of larger ensembles had begun in 1921 with Paul Whiteman's band. The typical 1930s big band included three or four trumpets, three trombones, four or five saxophones, guitar, piano, bass and drums. Smaller 1930s ensembles played small-group swing.

From the mid-1940s onward, modern jazz or bebop ensembles emerged; they used the swing rhythm section, but gradually abandoned the guitar, and employed a 'front line' of trumpet and one or more saxophones. The archetypal small bebop group was the 1945 quintet of Dizzy Gillespie and Charlie Parker, which used trumpet and alto saxophone plus rhythm section. In the late 1940s, Gil Evans and Miles Davis experimented with a nine-piece band that added French horns, trombone, tuba and baritone saxophone to the mix.

In the 1950s and early 1960s, small modern jazz groups still followed the bebop model of instrumentation, sometimes adding another saxophone or trombone, and larger bands still used the conventional big band instrumentation. One exception was the Modern Jazz Quartet (founded from the rhythm section of Dizzy Gillespie's 1946–50 big band), which used vibraphone, piano, bass and drums. Another exception was the 'pianoless' quartet of Gerry Mulligan, which used baritone saxophone, trumpet (later, trombone), bass and drums, with harmonic changes underpinned by the bass line rather than played as full chords.

At the very beginning of the 1960s, Ornette Coleman adopted the Mulligan instrumentation, but also doubled up each instrument to form an octet for his *Free Jazz* album. He later extended the boundaries of instrumentation by playing trumpet and violin himself, along with alto saxophone. His instrumental experiments were paralleled by those of the Art Ensemble of Chicago: it adopted an array of percussion and world music instruments in addition to saxophones, trumpet, bass and (eventually) drums. Similar multi-instrumental ensembles were pioneered by Anthony Braxton, who mastered an impressive array of woodwind instruments as well as piano.

The 1960s also saw the beginnings of jazz rock, in which rock instrumentation was added to the basic jazz ensemble. Electric bass guitars superseded double basses, and keyboards and electric pianos replaced or coexisted with acoustic pianos. A genuine fusion of approaches occurred, with jazz musicians like Miles Davis or Wayne Shorter and Joe Zawinul (in Weather Report) adding rock rhythm sections, and rock bands like Blood, Sweat and Tears or the Chicago Transit Authority (known as Chicago from 1970) adopting jazz horn sections.

In Britain, a different type of fusion occurred in the 1960s, with John Mayer's and Joe Harriott's Indo–Jazz Fusions bringing the sitar and tabla into the jazz ensemble, along with improvisations built around ragas.

In the 1990s, considerable experimentation with the instrumentation of the jazz ensemble took place in Europe: the Norwegian Jan Garbarek attempted fusions with Middle Eastern traditional instruments and early-music vocal or instrumental ensembles; English saxophonist John Surman worked with church organ and choir; and Austrian saxophonist Wolfgang Puschnig worked with a traditional European brass band (in *Alpine Aspects*). There was also in Europe an openness to techniques pioneered by Western art music composers like John Cage, with pianists John Wolf Brennan (in Switzerland), Keith Tippett (in England) and Benoît Delbecq (in France) using prepared piano arrangements within an improvising ensemble. On a larger scale, the French ensemble Système Friche experimented with minimalism and with unorthodox instruments, including the hurdy-gurdy. Likewise, the Dutch Clusone Trio was one of a number of ensembles that made the cello a central improvisatory instrument.

In parallel with an unprecedented level of experimentation, the end of the twentieth century saw almost all types of jazz ensemble continuing unabated, and with very few forms of instrumentation consigned to history.

Bibliography

Berendt, Joachim-Ernst. 1982 (1975). *The Jazz Book: From Ragtime to Fusion and Beyond*. Rev. ed. Westport, CT: Lawrence Hill. (First published Frankfurt am Main: Fischer Bücherei, 1953.)

Collier, Graham. 1973. *Inside Jazz*. London: Quartet.

Litweiler, John. 1984. *The Freedom Principle: Jazz After 1958*. New York: Da Capo Press.

Discographical References

Ornette Coleman Double Quartet, The. *Free Jazz (A Collective Improvisation)*. Rhino 1364. *1961*: USA.

Puschnig, Wolfgang. *Alpine Aspects*. Amadeo/PolyGram 511 204 2. *1991*: Austria.

ALYN SHIPTON

Jubilee Singers

Groups of African Americans who performed traditional spirituals and slave songs, jubilee singers were a phenomenon in black music for some 80 years. The original company, the Fisk Jubilee Singers, was formed by Fisk University students who were hoping to raise money for facilities through their singing. When Emancipation, or the 'Year of Jubilee,' occurred, the university treasurer, George L. White, organized a choir of 'colored Christian singers,' which first performed in public in 1867 and commenced its tours to raise funds in 1871. White named the company the 'Jubilee Singers' while it was performing in Ohio. After a few disappointments, the company had immense success with its concerts in the east, and subsequently on tour in Great Britain, where it performed for Queen Victoria. After three triumphant months in London, the choir had equal success in Scotland, performed for the Queen of The Netherlands and sang for eight months in Germany before returning to the United States. Proceeds from the Singers' concerts went toward completion of Fisk University's Jubilee Hall in 1875, the year in which the first students graduated. Fisk University disbanded the Jubilee Singers in 1878, but the members organized themselves as a joint-stock company and continued to perform for two years. (A Jubilee Singers group exists again at Fisk University, but it is far removed from the original.)

Theo F. Seward's notation of the 'jubilee songs,' as the repertoire of anthems and spirituals was known, is the only indication that exists of the choir's power, beauty and musical form. The songs' chorus–verse structure, with the leader singing the verse and the choir the chorus, the employment of internal refrains and the use of lowered thirds, fifths and sevenths characterized the African-American idiom. And yet, as early as 1881, a writer for the *Peoria Journal* regretted that the Fisk Jubilee Singers 'have lost the wild rhythms, the barbaric melody, the passion' that they had previously exhibited (quoted in Seroff 1980, 5). In 1882, reorganized and with different personnel, a new company toured the world for six years under the direction of F.J. Loudin, a member of the original troupe. Its members sang in England, Australia, India, Burma and Japan, their success inspiring the formation of other groups. One of these was led by Orpheus McAdoo, a former member of Loudin's company. After a brief visit to London, McAdoo's Virginia Jubilee Singers sailed for South Africa, where, despite initial racist reactions, they stayed for five years. Not without compromise, while there McAdoo recruited artists for a new 'Minstrel, Vaudeville and Concert Company,' which was formed in 1897.

Although members of the first generation of Fisk Jubilee Singers were born in slavery, some were in their mid-teens when they sang on tour. The direct inheritance of song style from slavery was soon distanced, partly by the perceived need for trained voices, and partly by the expectations of the predominantly white audiences. Following the success of the Fisk Jubilee Singers, the Hampton, Tuskegee, Wilberforce and Utica institutes formed their own choirs, generally as jubilee singers, to tour and raise funds; a few imposters claiming to seek support for black universities were also on the circuit. In 1904, Charles Williams from Holly Springs, Mississippi formed the Williams Jubilee Singers, 'The World's Greatest Harmonizing Octette.' Previous jubilee companies had often had 10 or a dozen members, or an octet making a 'double quartet,' but the increasing tendency was to reduce the size of the groups and to feature, as did Williams, a popular quartet (or quartette). Publicity material for the Williams Jubilee Singers emphasized their musical training at such universities and colleges as Rust, Drake, Livingston and Oberlin. As more jubilee companies were formed, emphasizing the formal training and musical credentials of the singers became common practise.

The earliest of the jubilee groups to record was the Fisk University Jubilee Quartet, under the direction of John Wesley Work II, who sang tenor. The well-drilled Quartet expanded the repertoire of jubilee songs by singing both popular spirituals and Stephen Foster sentimentals at their December 1909 sessions for Victor; by 1916, they had over 30 items issued on 78 rpm discs, and nine on Edison cylinders. It was not until 1919 that the first titles appeared as being performed by the Fisk University Jubilee Singers, only the Rev. James Andrew Myers being common to both the Quartet and the new Singers, who were, in fact, a quintet. On the 60 titles issued on disc between 1909 and 1926, there is little in style, format, personnel or even repertoire that can be considered indicative of the original sacred songs and unsophisticated performances whose range and passion had so moved world audiences.

A number of similarly trained choirs recorded in the mid-1920s; among them was one of several groups that recorded under the name of Eva Jessye's Dixie Jubilee Singers. With a degree in music, the leader played piano and tutored her choir in classical and operatic techniques, although she herself aspired to perform on the concert stage. Professional in approach were the Pace Jubilee Singers, managed by Charles Henry Pace, a businessman with an interest in publishing the newly developing gospel music; the sextet was lifted by the sweet-toned but impressive singing of soprano Hattie Parker. Similarly, the Elkins–Payne Jubilee Singers, led by the director of a Williams and Walker vaudeville show, William C. Elkins, indicated a commercial intent. While the voices of the Virginia Female Jubilee Singers, recorded in 1921, appear to be rooted in the earlier rural styles of harmony singing, the members of the contemporary Norfolk Jubilee Quartet, also from Virginia, were unashamedly secular in many of their close harmony recordings, issued as being performed by the Norfolk Jazz Quartet. They were as much in demand on the vaudeville stage as they were for singing at church functions. Even the Utica Institute Jubilee Singers from southern Mississippi became a popular quartet: the group toured with revue companies, broadcast regularly from New York and appeared on film and in Chautauqua companies, recording jubilee songs and even coon songs in the late 1920s.

In the 1930s, jubilee singing became far more free, and was no longer dependent on the formal musical training of the university groups. The quartets that had been developing in parallel with the jubilee choirs since the 1880s now dominated, with their harmonies, deep bass lines, chordal techniques, rhythmic complexity and melodic ornamentation. In Jefferson County, Alabama, a strong local tradition had evolved that was showcased in the dramatic and varied recordings of the Birmingham Jubilee Singers. Although they retained the jubilee connotation on the more traditional spirituals, their gospel and secular songs were issued as being performed by the Birmingham Quartet.

Jubilee singing cannot be identified as a single musical practise, but, rather, was the meeting and overlapping of two or three African-American song traditions: the arranged singing of the earliest Fisk Jubilee Singers, the trained voices of the university octets and sextets, and the harmonized but often extempore performances of the gospel/jazz quartets, all of which, under the 'jubilee' banner, acknowledged their common roots in slave songs and spirituals. With changes of emphasis – for example, in the smoothness of close harmony or the use of jazz rhythms – jubilee groups such as the Golden Gate Quartet and the Selah Jubilee Singers continued to perform and record throughout the 1940s.

Bibliography

Erlmann, Veit. 1988. 'A Feeling of Prejudice: Orpheus McAdoo and the Virginia Jubilee Singers in South Africa, 1890–1898.' *Journal of South African Studies* 14(3): 331–50.

Funk, Ray. 1986. 'Three Afro-American Singing Groups.' In *Under the Imperial Carpet: Essays in Black History,*

1780–1950, ed. Rainer Lotz and Ian Pegg. Crawley: Rabbit Press, 145–63.

Marsh, J.B.T. 1876. *The Story of the Jubilee Singers, with Their Songs*. 3rd ed. London: Hodder and Stoughton.

Marsh, J.B.T. 1903. *The Story of the Jubilee Singers, with Their Songs, with Supplement by F.J. Loudin*. London: Hodder and Stoughton.

Raichelson, Richard M. 1975. *Black Religious Folksong: A Study in Generic and Social Change*. Ph.D. thesis, University of Pennsylvania, Folklore Program.

Ricks, George Robinson. 1977. *Some Aspects of the Religious Music of the United States Negro*. New York: Arno Press.

Seroff, Doug. 1980. *Birmingham Quartet Scrapbook: A Quartet Reunion in Jefferson County*. Birmingham, AL: Birmingham City Auditorium.

Tallmadge, William H. 1980. Notes to *Jubilee to Gospel: A Selection of Commercially Recorded Black Religious Music, 1921–1953*. JEMF-108.

Discography

The following recordings have important notes by Duck Baker, David Evans, Ray Funk, Ken Romanowski, Doug Seroff and John Vanco.

Birmingham Jubilee Singers, The. *Complete Recorded Works, Vol. 1 (1926–1927) and Vol. 2 (1927–1930)* (notes and recordings). Document Records DOCD-5345 and DOCD-5346. *1995*: Austria.

Dixie Jubilee Singers/Bryant's Jubilee Quartet & Quintet. *Complete Recorded Works (1924–28)/(1931)* (notes and recordings). Document Records DOCD-5438. *1996*: Austria.

The Earliest Negro Vocal Groups, Vol. 4 (notes and recordings). Document Records DOCD-5531. *1997*: Austria.

Elkins–Payne Jubilee Singers, The. *Complete Recorded Works in Chronological Order* (notes and recordings). Document Records DOCD-5356. *1995*: Austria.

Fisk Jubilee Singers, Vol. 1 (1909–1911) and Vol. 2 (1915–1920) (notes and recordings). Document Records DOCD-5533 and DOCD-5534. *1997*: Austria.

Norfolk Jazz & Jubilee Quartets. *Complete Recorded Works, Vol. 1 (1923–1926) to Vol. 6 (1937–1940)* (notes and recordings). Document Records DOCD-5381 to DOCD-5386. *1995*: Austria.

Pace Jubilee Singers, Vol. 1 (1926–1927) and Vol. 2 (1928–1929) (notes and recordings). Document Records DOCD-5617 and DOCD-5618. *1998*: Austria.

Selah Jubilee Singers, The. *Complete Recorded Works, Vol. 1 (1939–1941) and Vol. 2 (1941–1945)* (notes and recordings). Document Records DOCD-5499 and DOCD-5500. *1996*: Austria.

Utica Institute Jubilee Singers (1927–1929) (notes and recordings). Document Records DOCD-5603. *1998*: Austria.

PAUL OLIVER

Jug Band

A jug band usually included only one jug player, who used it as a bass rhythm instrument. Earliest on record was Whistler's Jug Band, whose 1924 recording featured only one jug in the group, although a 1930 film of the band shows three jugs being played. Whistler (Buford Threlkeld) formed his band in Louisville, Kentucky, where a number of such groups played. Among them were a band led by Earl MacDonald, and several groups formed by violinist Clifford Hayes, including the Dixieland Jug Blowers. It was this group's records that inspired Will Shade to form the Memphis Jug Band. Memphis rapidly became another center, with Cannon's Jug Stompers and the South Memphis Jug Band developing an essentially blues style. Always quick to exploit a novelty, Clarence Williams made a number of jazz records with his Seven Gallon Jug Band, and Tampa Red continued the idiom into the 1930s. It was revived briefly in the 1960s by Jim Kweskin.

Bibliography

Cox, Fred, Randolph, John, and Harris, John. 1993. *The Jug Bands of Louisville*. Chigwell: Storyville Publications.

Oliver, Paul. 1990 (1965). *Conversation with the Blues*. Cambridge: Cambridge University Press.

Olsson, Bengt. 1970. *Memphis Blues and Jug Bands*. London: Studio Vista.

Discography

Clifford Hayes and the Louisville Jug Bands, Vols. 1–4. Notes by Brenda Bogert. RST Records JPCD 1501-1504. 1924–31; *1994*: Austria.

Memphis Jug Band. *Complete Recorded Works, Vols. 1–3 (1927–1930)*. Document DOCD 5021-5023. *1990*: Austria.

PAUL OLIVER

Latin Band

In general usage, the word 'Latin,' applied to music, indicates music from or inspired by the Spanish Caribbean, the islands and the coastal areas from Venezuela to southern Mexico. The term 'Latin band' implies a dance band and covers a wide range of sizes, from the 'society orchestra' down to small combos. Caribbean dance music is primarily in 2/4 or 4/4 rhythm, heavily syncopated and punctuated with a rich array of percussion instruments: claves, maracas, guiros, *cencerros*, bongos and assorted other drums. These instruments are mostly of Afro-Caribbean origin, whereas the melodic structures of the music they play are eminently European.

The local music of Santiago de Cuba was notably influential in the development of pan-Caribbean popular music. The carnival bands, itinerant trios and later sextets of Santiago exerted increasing influence on dance bands throughout the islands, especially by means of recordings from early in the twentieth century onward.

In the early decades of the twentieth century, the dance music of the middle and upper classes in the Americas was often identical to that of London or Paris and quite distinct from that of the lower classes of the Caribbean. But after World War I, the picture changed. Prohibition, which came into effect in 1919 in the United States, had a grave impact on supper clubs and nightclubs, many of which closed their doors or survived precariously as clandestine clubs known as 'speak-easies.' Tourists from the United States flocked to Montréal, the Mexican border towns and the Caribbean, with Havana being the most popular destination. US musicians increasingly found employment there, among them a young violinist named Enric Madriguera. Born in Barcelona and brought to the United States at the age of 14, he subsequently played with US dance bands, one of which took him to Havana – as a violinist and as a Spanish interpreter. By 1924, Madriguera was the conductor of the Havana Casino Orchestra during the winter season and spent the rest of the year performing with his own band on New York radio and making recordings, with other engagements in New York and Florida. Adept at performing the Cuban society dance, the elegant *danzón*, he introduced it to Americans in the United States. US music became the staple of the better clubs in Havana because the US tourists were timid about revealing their ineptness in performing the *danzón*. Madriguera was intensely interested in the dance music of the lower classes and especially the Afro-Cuban *son*, a dance form considered vulgar by the best Havana society. In order to lure North Americans to the dance floor, he evolved a discreet form of the *son*, blended with segments of pure fox trot and Charleston. It would come to be known as the rumba and would have great success in New York, London, Paris, Madrid and Berlin. The Cuban percussionists in Madriguera's orchestra employed Afro-Caribbean instruments such as claves, maracas, bongos, timbales, *cencerros* and guiros. Simultaneously, a few small bands from the Caribbean began to perform in Europe, especially in Paris.

The collapse of Wall Street in 1929 sent North Americans back home and would keep them there for most of the following decade. The dance floors of Havana were as empty as those of New York had been a few years earlier. The formerly affluent US tourists were nostalgic for their rum and rumba; both were to return. Cuban musicians began to come to the United States. One of the great all-time rumba hits was 'The Peanut Vendor' ('El Manisero'), recorded by the Havana Casino Orchestra and featured in the Hollywood film *The Cuban Love Song* (1931). 'Peanut fever' raged in the United States as well as in Europe through dozens of different recordings. Other rumba recording successes quickly followed, many of them supplied by Madriguera, who was now director of Latin music at Columbia Records. Prohibition was repealed in 1933 and, despite hard times, dance music – with Latin music now a basic component – flourished. By this time, Madriguera had serious competitors: Xavier Cugat (born in Gerona, Spain) and Carlos Molina (from Colombia), both of whom, curiously enough, had also been trained as violinists. These three came to dominate the Latin band scene in the United States. Meanwhile, the composer of 'El Manisero,' Moisés Simons, had established himself in Paris with Rico's Creole Band. And in 1933, just before the repeal of Prohibition, Cuba's distinguished pianist-composer Ernesto Lecuona took his band, the Lecuona Cuban Boys, on a tour of Europe (Spain, Italy, London and Paris), where they recorded intensively. The group was enormously popular, and its success exceeded all expectations; it extended the tour for as long as possible, returning to Havana on the last boat to depart from Holland in 1939.

Back in the United States, Latin music had become firmly established. The Latin percussion instruments were combined into a single, eccentric instrument, the drum battery, which became indispensable for swing music and equally important for Latin music that was increasingly being performed by non-Latin bands. A Latin number would become a staple in both films and Broadway musicals for several decades after Vincent Youmans included his 'Carioca' (a rumba) in the score for the movie *Flying Down to Rio* (1933) and Cole Porter's 'Begin the Beguine' (a bolero) was performed in the musical *Jubilee* (1935). Such films and musicals, together with the increasing recordings of Latin and pseudo-Latin music, would intensify international interest in Caribbean music. The British band leader known as Ambrose was sometimes billed as the 'Latin from Mayfair,' and a US hit lampoons the career of an Irish-American girl who masquerades as authentic but is only a 'Latin from Manhattan.' The ability to sing in Spanish became increasingly important for US band vocalists.

Table 1 lists chronologically the major Latin bands known internationally via recordings, live appearances and film. The creation of the 'Good Neighbor Policy' in the United States initiated the golden age for Latin bands. US films of the 1940s often included segments

1. Groups

Table 1

Decade	Performer/Band	Musical Forms
1920s	Enric Madriguera	*danzón*
	Rico's Creole Band	*son*
1930s	Don Azpiazu	rumba
	Carlos Molina	
	Lecuona Cuban Boys	
	Xavier Cugat	
	Jose María Romeu	bolero
	Ambrose	
	José Morand	
	Casino de la Playa	
1940s	Desi Arnaz	conga
	Sacasas	*guaracha*
	Brillo's Caracas Boys	
	Alfredo Mendez	
	Noro Morales	
	Chuy Reyes	
	Pérez Prado	mambo
	Machito	
	Tito Puente	
	Tito Rodriguez	
	Edmundo Ros	
1950s	Miguelito Valdés	
	Charlie Palmieri	cha-cha-cha
	José Curbelo	
1960s	Eddie Palmieri	
	Johnny Pacheco	*pachanga*
	Ray Barreto	*guaguancó*
	Johnny Colon	*bugalú*
	Carlos Santana	Latin rock
	Cal Tjader	
1970s	Willie Colon	salsa
	El Chicano	Latin disco
	Joe Bataan	Latin soul
	Cachao	*descarga*
		cumbia
1980s	Miami Sound Machine	*areito*
	Los Van Van	merengue
1990s	Son de Azucar	*songo*

featuring the Cugat and Madriguera orchestras. *Carnival in Costa Rica* (1947) was a major vehicle for the Lecuona Cuban Boys, who also toured Latin America extensively. A plethora of new groups flourished. Latin American musicians increasingly performed with US orchestras – for example, Juan Tizol played with Duke Ellington,

Chano Pozo with Dizzy Gillespie, and Machito with Stan Kenton. Indeed, in the late 1940s these musicians would develop a new jazz concert style called 'Cubop.' More recent films such as *The Mambo Kings* (1992) feature the orchestras of Machito and Tito Puente.

From the 1920s onward, a succession of Latin dances increasingly blended US and Caribbean dances – for example, the *son* plus the fox trot became the rumba, and fast rumba plus swing became the mambo. Although a number of Puerto Rican musicians were successful and influential in these developments, the scene was dominated by Cubans until the end of the 1950s. Thus, the Cuban revolution – aided and abetted by the overwhelming success of rock music – all but wiped Latin music off the orchestral and instrumental map. Attempts to popularize the Dominican merengue at this time had little success, although the Brazilian bossa nova filled the Latin dance gap, briefly, in the 1960s. For the time being, US and European youth idolized Elvis Presley and the Beatles. Open form dance choreography predominated. Meanwhile, large Puerto Rican and Cuban communities in the United States continued to supply a demand, so that, for a time, Latin bands were the staple of a self-imposed segregated society. The band type known as *charanga* (flutes, violins, piano, bass and timbales) was now enhanced by the addition of such Afro-Cuban instruments as the bongos and the conga drum. Especially popular were the *charangas* of Charlie Palmieri and Johnny Pacheco. Puerto Rican musicians now dominated, particularly in New York. Orchestras and combos proliferated and created a new sequence of dance forms that now blended elements from rock music, the major producers of this type of music being Carlos Santana and Cal Tjader. Dancers performed as often in pairs (close dancing) as in free form, the former imposing more structured rhythmic patterns. As immigration to the United States from the Dominican Republic and the coastal regions of Colombia increased, the merengue now proliferated and the *cumbia* found favor. By this time, the dances as well as the musicians were likely to be pan-Caribbean, especially in New York. Thus was salsa invented, the word itself a catchall for a general style (percussion-based) that, with free improvisation, can change tempo and rhythm at any moment. During the 1980s and 1990s, salsa finally penetrated mainstream music, the more permanent Latin bands again gaining recognition in the United States as well as abroad. At the same time, nostalgia for the music of earlier Latin bands grew considerably. A large selection from earlier recordings has continued to be provided on compact disc by Harlequin Records (Interstate Music of East Sussex, England). Radio broadcasting in Spain has actively revived the careers of earlier Latin bands. Toward the end of the twentieth century, Spanish groups combined Andalusian, Caribbean and rock music to create new hybrids such as the *rumba flamenca* and the *macarena* (a line dance), which have both remained extremely popular with Latin bands.

Such developments have continued and have shown no evidence of decline; in any event, Latin bands constituted a significant element in the music of Western society for most of the twentieth century. An elegant gala benefit, held in May 1998 on Audubon Terrace in New York City, featured the orchestra of Tito Puente and was attended by guests spanning three generations. Puente began his repertoire with a number of famous boleros, interspersed with a few rumbas and followed by several mambos and cha-cha-chas. Next came a concert segment featuring Puente on the timbales in a master performance of 'Cubop.' A healthy sequence of salsa followed, with the last segment devoted to Latin soft rock. During the earlier segments, members of the oldest generation were predominant on the dance floor. Gradually, they were joined by members of the other two generations. The evening provided a clear illustration of the current status of Latin bands and their music.

Bibliography

Alberti, Luis. 1975. *De música y orquestras bailables dominicanas* [On Dominican Music and Dance Orchestras]. Santo Domingo: Museo del Hombre Dominicano.

Beardsley, Theodore S., Jr. 1980–86. 'Rumba-Rhumba: problema internacional músico-léxico' [Rumba-Rhumba: International Musical-Lexical Problem]. *Revista Interamericana* X: 527–33.

Beardsley, Theodore S., Jr. 1992. 'Ernesto Lecuona (1895–1963): Noticias bibliodiscográficas' [Ernesto Lecuona (1895–1963): Bibliodiscographical Notes]. *Noticias de Arte* (Nov.-Dec.): 9–12.

Beardsley, Theodore S., Jr. 2001. 'Hispanic Music in the United States.' In *The Guide to United States Popular Culture*, ed. Ray B. Browne and Pat Browne. Bowling Green, OH: Bowling Green State University Popular Press, 388–89.

Bloch, Peter. 1973. *La-Le-Lo-Lai: Puerto Rican Music and Its Performers*. New York: Plus Ultra.

Collazo, Bobby. 1987. *La última noche que pasé contigo* [The Last Night I Spent with You]. San Juan: Cubanacan.

Diáz-Ayala, Cristóbal. 1981. *Música cubana* [Cuban Music]. San Juan: Cubanacan.

Figueroa, Frank M. 1994. *Encyclopedia of Latin American Music in New York*. St. Petersburg, FL: Pillar Publications.

Loza, Stephen. 1993. *Barrio Rhythm: Mexican-American Music in Los Angeles*. Urbana, IL: University of Illinois Press.

Madriguera, Enric. 1994. *Caribbean Music (1920–1941)*, ed. T.S. Beardsley, Jr. Harlequin CD 44.

Molina, Carlos. 2000. *Caribbean Music (1932–1946)*, ed. T.S. Beardsley, Jr. Harlequin CD 156.

Pérez Perazzo, Alberto. 1988. *Ritmo Afrohispano antillano* [Afro-Hispanic Rhythm of the Antilles]. Caracas: Editorial Sucre.

Polin, Bruce. 1998. *Descarga*. Flatbush, NY: Descarga. [Comprehensive (365 pp.) catalog of currently available Latin CDs, including reissues of original recordings from 1920 onward, as well as current recordings. See also www.descarga.com.]

Roberts, John Storm. 1979. *The Latin Tinge: The Impact of Latin American Music on the United States*. New York: Oxford University Press.

Santana, Sergio. 1992. *Qué es la salsa?* [What Is Salsa?]. Medellin: Ediciones Salsa y Cultura.

Valverde, Umberto, and Quintero, Rafael. 1996. *Abran paso. Historia de las orquestas femeninas de Cali* [Make Way: History of the Female Orchestras of Cali]. Cali: Editorial Universidad del Valle.

Sheet Music

Porter, Cole, comp. and lyr. 1935. 'Begin the Beguine.' New York: T.B. Harms.

Simons, Moisés, comp. and lyr. (English lyrics by L. Wolfe Gilbert and Marion Sunshine). 1930. 'The Peanut Vendor' ('El Manisero'). New York: Edward B. Marks Music.

Youmans, Vincent, comp., and Kahn, Gus, & Eliscu, Edward, lyrs. 1933. 'Carioca.' New York: T.B. Harms.

Filmography

Carnival in Costa Rica, dir. Gregory Ratoff. 1947. USA. 96 mins. Musical. Original music by Ernesto Lecuona, Harry Ruby, Sunny Skylar, Al Stillman.

The Cuban Love Song, dir. W.S. Van Dyke. 1931. USA. 80 mins. Musical/Romance. Original music by Charles Maxwell (II), Herbert Stothart.

Flying Down to Rio, dir. Thornton Freeland. 1933. USA. 89 mins. Musical. Original music by Edward Eliscu, Gus Kahn, Vincent Youmans.

The Mambo Kings, dir. Arnold Glimcher. 1992. France/USA. 100 mins. Drama. Original music by Carlos Franzetti, Robert Kraft.

THEODORE S. BEARDSLEY, JR.

Lineup

The full personnel of a band or orchestra is frequently termed the 'lineup.' Although its first use remains uncertain, it appears to have arisen from the conjunction of two sources: the presentation of the members of a band, frequently in formal attire (tuxedo, black tie) for the purpose of publicity and photography; and the similar presentation of band members to an audience. In the first instance, the musicians may be seen standing and holding their instruments, with additional instruments (such as other saxophones) at their feet, or they may be 'lined up' facing the camera, or facing the band leader. In the second instance, the musicians are customarily presented with their instruments in playing positions or, in the case of large orchestras, with the players positioned at music stands. When presented in rows, the 'front line' usually consisted of the players of wind instruments, with the drums at center rear, the piano at extreme left or right, and other musicians disposed in groups or 'sections.' Such grouping of musicians for publicity or stage presentation continued until the 1950s, when more informal, and apparently spontaneous, arrangements became popular.

For discographical purposes, the term 'lineup' has continued to be applied to a published personnel, usually in the sequence: trumpet, cornet, trombone, clarinet saxophones, other horns, piano, guitar, banjo, string bass, brass bass, drums, other percussion, vocalist. The name of a featured vocalist may precede those of the band members.

Bibliography

Keepnews, Orrin, and Grauer, Jr., Bill. 1955. *A Pictorial History of Jazz, People and Places from New Orleans to Modern Jazz*. London: Robert Hale Ltd.

Rose, Al, and Souchon, Edmond. 1967. *New Orleans Family Album*. Baton Rouge, LA: Louisiana State University Press.

Rust, Brian. 1972. *Jazz Records 1902–1942*. New York: Arlington House.

PAUL OLIVER

Male Voice Choirs

Male voice choirs are amateur male-only clubs for part-singing, formally organized with rules and a constitution, self-financed and led by a conductor who may or may not be an employee of the group.

Male choirs have a wider repertoire, a broader socio-economic membership and a longer history than any other type of secular choir. Gentlemen were organizing social singing clubs in seventeenth-century England. Catches – vocal canons distinguished by the scatological nature of their texts and attendant puns – were known to all levels of society, but the catch clubs were run by and for the upper echelons. Rules maintained standards of behavior and attendance. Penalties could include drinking beer instead of claret – imbibing alcohol was a prerequisite. A subscription was charged; the musical direction was usually in the hands of a professional.

Throughout the next century, these gentlemen's clubs flourished in Britain. Typical was the Noblemen and Gentlemen's Catch Club, formed in 1761. Gradually, the clubs' repertoire was widened in response to Georgian refinement, and the singing of glees, whose texts concentrated on nature and romantic (rather than bawdy) love, became popular. This peculiarly English form of part-song was originally for solo male voices with an alto lead (indicating the musical influence of the Established Church). Alcoholic consumption remained a feature of these glee clubs, where smoking concerts and ladies' nights were fashionable.

The philanthropy of new middle-class, largely Nonconformist, factory and mill owners in the nineteenth century was often responsible for the emergence of singing classes for working-class Britons and, taking the pattern (ATBB) and the framework of the established glee club, many choirs were developed for men. In terms of diverting men from the evils of drink, this means of controlling social behavior seemed, to mill owner and churchman alike, perfectly acceptable. Contemporaneously, education for the lower classes and the explosion of sight-singing through the work of Mainzer, Hullah and Curwen accelerated the spread of male choirs to the extent that, in urban areas, few places of employment were without such a group. This did not apply solely to industrial workplaces – banks and insurance houses (including London's stock exchange) had male choirs.

Throughout mainland Europe, a significant driving force in developing male choirs was nationalism. The defeat of Napoleon at the Battle of Leipzig in 1813 fanned the flames of musical patriotism already present in Germany through the *Liedertafel* movement. Schubert and Weber were closely involved, and meetings around Schubert's own 'singing table' often had a political, revolutionary nature. Both composers left a considerable canon of part-songs concerning freedom and equality. More significantly, they caused thousands of similarly nationalistic effusions to be produced throughout the nineteenth century. Many other Northern and Central European countries were affected by the expression of nationalism through male choirs. In Finland, for example, at a time when Swedish was still the first language, the Helsinki University (Male) Chorus established its reputation by singing in Finnish.

Many German part-songs were published in nineteenth-century Britain and, because of their directness and, most importantly, because they used a tenor rather than alto lead, the works appealed to choirs in parts of Britain where the glee had never taken root. Welsh choirs responded warmly to the patriotic texts, as they did to the programmatic works of the French composers Adolphe Adam and Laurent de Rille. Through the extensive migration to the New World, musicians such as Daniel Protheroe and Joseph Parry, familiar with the contemporary development of a male choir tradition in the coalfields of their native Wales, found themselves at the new North American universities alongside German academicians who were establishing music courses. Thus was nurtured the male choir tradition on the North American campus. The United States also developed its own unique contribution to the tradition. The idiosyncratic harmonic vocabulary and repertoire of barbershop quartets and choruses form a distinct and separate branch of male choral singing.

The network of expatriate Welshmen was only part of the exportation of male voice choir work from Britain, which had been going on since the early eighteenth century. In 1702, publisher Henry Playford exhorted gentlemen to set up clubs in 'Foreign Plantations,' as he called the developing colonies. But it was to the old nineteenth-century Empire that most of the export occurred. Bombay and Indian military towns like Pune boasted Glee and Madrigal Unions in the days of the Raj. Through Welsh influence, choirs (many of which have continued to exist) were established in the mining areas of South Africa and Patagonia. In Australasia, the Teutonic influence was also felt, with many choirs retaining the title 'Liedertafel' at least until World War I.

The first four decades of the twentieth century marked the golden age of male choir work in Europe and beyond. Composers were writing new part-songs, which conductors were prepared to produce as well as continuing with works by Mendelssohn, Brahms and earlier composers. In England, for example, Elgar, Holst, Bantock and many others provided a steady flow of compositions, which the choirs would learn through their sound knowledge of tonic sol-fa. Often, the commissions were for performance at competitive festivals, events that caught the imagination of the general public; packed audiences would be enthralled by contests between a dozen or more choirs. Indeed, the competitions were central to the development of male choral singing in Britain, and musical directors with 'star' status emerged, especially in northern towns and cities. These musicians and their choirs were highly regarded by the London music press, and this regard, combined with public acclaim, resulted in an unsurpassed degree of respectability and acceptance for male voice choirs in the musical life of the country during this period.

From the middle of the century, social revisions and changes from industry- to service-based economies produced an erosion of interest in male choirs. By the mid-1990s, the average age of individual members throughout Europe, university choirs apart, was 55. Recruitment of younger men thus became more difficult and, through a developing conservatism in approach, composers were less inclined to produce new music.

At the end of the twentieth century, male choir activities were strongest (per head of population) in Germany, The Netherlands and Scandinavia. Despite the extremely wide repertoire, the appeal to a very broad social spectrum had been through expressions of nationalism (folk songs and hymns) and spirituals from the southern US states (with their overtones of religious and political freedom). This gave the male choir movement a populist thrust, which denied it a place in the Western musical establishment and often obscured its potential as a medium of high artistic credence.

Bibliography

Barrett, W. 1886. *English Glees and Partsongs*. London: Longmans, Green and Co.

Roberts, K. 1970. *A Checklist of 20th Century Choral Music for Male Voices*. Detroit, MI: Information Coordinators.

Robinson, B.W., and Hall, R.F. 1989. *The Aldrich Book of Catches*. London: Novello.

Tortolano, W. 1973. *Original Music for Men's Voices*. Metuchen, NJ: Scarecrow Press.

Wiltshire, C. 1993. *The British Male Voice Choir: A History and Contemporary Assessment*. Ph.D. thesis, Goldsmiths College, University of London.

CHRISTOPHER WILTSHIRE

Mandolin Orchestra

The origins of the mandolin orchestra can be traced to the mandolin *circolos* (circles) that developed in Italy around the mid-1800s. Instrumentation consists of individual sections for first mandolin, second mandolin, *mandolas* (either tenor or octave), *mandocello*, guitar and bass. The term 'orchestra' refers more to the nature of the music and the number of players involved in the group than to a direct parallel with a symphonic orchestra. From its Italian roots, the concept of the mandolin orchestra spread across Europe to Spain, and was brought from Spain to the United States in 1880 by a touring *bandurria* group, the 'Spanish Students.' From that point on, mandolin orchestras and soloists enjoyed immense popularity in the United States and Europe, partly as a result of the Gibson Guitar Company's promotion of the concept of the mandolin orchestra. This popularity continued until the 1920s, when interest started to wane. This was the result of repeated performances of the repertoire and changes in musical tastes, as well as the effects of World War I.

In the late 1990s, a sort of renaissance of the mandolin orchestra was underway worldwide. Orchestras, ensembles and soloists were performing a wide array of music in the United States, Germany, France, Italy and Japan.

Bibliography

Adelstein, Samuel. 1917. *Mandolin Memories*. Reprint of the *Cadenza* issues, January–May 1901. New York: C.L. Partee Music Co.

Bauer, Walter Kaye. 1973. *Familiar Music for the Mandolin*. Carlstadt, NJ: Lewis Music Publishing Co.

Carter, Walter. 1994. *Gibson Guitars: 100 Years of an American Icon*. Los Angeles: General Publishing Group.

Ruppa, Paul. 1988. *The Mandolin in America After 1880 and the History of Mandolin Orchestras in Milwaukee, Wisconsin*. M.M. thesis, University of Wisconsin–Milwaukee.

JEROME 'BUTCH' BALDASSARI

Mariachi Group

The mariachi is Mexico's best-known folk-derived musical ensemble. The word 'mariachi,' most likely of indigenous origin, denotes a type of ensemble as well as an individual member of such a group. Since the 1950s, the standard mariachi has consisted of two trumpets, three to six violins, a *vihuela*, a classical guitar and a *guitarrón*. All players normally sing, and a folk harp is optional. A mariachi can perform alone or accompany one or more vocalists. Its instrumentation allows for great versatility, and contemporary mariachis perform a wide variety of national, international and popular genres. Mariachis are most common in Mexico and the southwestern United States, but can be found throughout the Americas and on other continents as well.

The most widely known mariachis are highly organized, well rehearsed, elegantly uniformed show groups of 11 or more musicians, each of whom has extensive musical training. Such ensembles make recordings, perform frequently on mass media, give concerts and accompany renowned vocalists. In contrast, other mariachis are informally attired pickup groups of seven or fewer musicians with little or no formal training, who often wander from bar to bar, offering their services to the clientele. Both types fill a need, and most mariachi groups fall somewhere between these two extremes. Some mariachis perform regularly at a restaurant, bar or nightclub; others gather in public squares or plazas, waiting to be hired. Virtually all play contracted engagements such as parties and weddings. Services are normally paid for by the hour or by the song. Uninitiated observers frequently assume a mariachi is playing only for tips, but this is seldom the case.

A mariachi is expected to play almost any song an audience requests, and a typical group may have well over a thousand selections in its working repertoire. Pieces are traditionally learned by ear and committed to memory; little written mariachi music is available. Even though it is often learned directly from other musicians, almost the entire contemporary mariachi repertoire can be traced to arrangements found on popular recordings.

The formal mariachi uniform – with its tightly fitting ornamented pants (or skirt), short jacket, embroidered belt, pointed boots, wide bow tie and sombrero – is a gala version of the *traje de charro* (Mexican horseman's attire), which was borrowed from Mexico's equestrian tradition.

History

String bands comprising members of the violin, harp and guitar families have been popular in rural Mexico from the colonial era to the present. Regional variants of these ensembles that evolved in Jalisco and the surrounding states of central western Mexico were the precursors of today's mariachi. The contemporary mariachi, however, is an urban phenomenon that evolved mainly in Mexico City.

The earliest mariachi known to have visited Mexico City was led by Justo Villa, and performed for President Porfirio Díaz in 1905. Two years later, that group made the first phonograph recordings of mariachi music under the name Cuarteto Coculense. In the 1920s, the groups of Concho Andrade and Cirilo Marmolejo became the first mariachis to take up permanent residence in the capital city. Both performed in Plaza Garibaldi, a downtown square that has since become the world's center of mariachi activity.

Beginning in the 1930s, the mariachi became a kind of folkloric house orchestra for Mexico's burgeoning radio, film and record industries, where its main role was that of accompanying popular *ranchera* (country style) vocalists. Mariachi Tapatío de José Marmolejo, formed in the mid-1930s, was the first mariachi to become widely popular, and Mariachi Vargas de Tecalitlán has been considered Mexico's leading mariachi since the mid-1940s. Mariachi México de Pepe Villa, the group that standardized the use of two trumpets in the mariachi, was extremely popular during the 1950s and 1960s. Other Mexican groups that were influential during the latter half of the twentieth century include mariachis Perla de Occidente, Los Mensajeros, Nuevo Tecalitlán, Oro y Plata, de América, Dos Mil and Águilas de América.

The US Mariachi Movement

Mariachi music has become deeply rooted in the United States, particularly in the southwest, and Los Angeles has in many ways become to the United States what Mexico City is to Mexico as an urban mecca of mariachi music. Mariachi Los Camperos de Nati Cano, formed in that city in 1961, was the country's pioneer group in popularizing this music among non-Hispanics. Mariachi Uclatlán, founded the same year at the University of California at Los Angeles, initiated the involvement of educational institutions in mariachi music, and many hundreds of US schools now offer mariachi performance classes. Mariachi Cobre, founded in Tucson, Arizona in 1971, was the first prominent Mexican-American mariachi. Cobre and Los Camperos are traditionalists, whereas Sol de México of Los Angeles embraces jazz and pop genres, and Campanas de América of San Antonio fuses Texas-Mexican and Caribbean styles with that of the traditional mariachi.

In 1979, the first International Mariachi Conference, held in San Antonio, Texas, gave birth to what is often referred to as a 'mariachi movement.' Since that time, mariachi festivals and conferences have proliferated, and as many as 100 such events are celebrated annually in the United States alone. Linda Ronstadt's 1987 album *Canciones de mi Padre* and subsequent tours were an outgrowth of this movement, and helped create new audiences for mariachi music throughout the world. Renewed interest in this tradition was generated in its country of origin, where annual international mariachi festivals were founded in Guadalajara in 1994 and in Mexico City in 2000. Other towns in Mexico, and in other Latin American countries, now hold mariachi festivals as well.

Although mariachi music has always been male-dominated, Mexico has had a number of all-female mariachi groups since the 1940s. Similar ensembles have existed in the United States since at least the 1970s, and mariachis of mixed gender are becoming more common virtually everywhere in the mariachi world.

Bibliography

Clark, Jonathan. 1992–98. Liner notes to *Mexico's Pioneer Mariachis*, Vols. 1–4. Arhoolie/Folklyric 7011, 7012, 7015 and 7036.

Fogelquist, Mark. 1975. *Rhythm and Form in the Contemporary 'Son Jalisciense'*. Unpublished M.A. thesis, University of California, Los Angeles.

Fogelquist, Mark. 1996. 'Mariachi Festivals and Conferences in the United States.' In *The Changing Faces of Tradition: A Report on the Folk and Traditional Arts in the United States*, ed. Elizabeth Peterson. Research Division Report No. 38. Washington, DC: National Endowment for the Arts, Office of Public Information, 18–23.

Jáuregui, Jesús. 1991. *El mariachi: el símbolo musical de México* [The Mariachi: Musical Symbol of Mexico]. México, D.F.: Banpaís, S.N.C.

Loza, Steven. 1993. *Barrio Rhythm: Mexican American Music in Los Angeles*. Chicago: University of Illinois Press.

Mendoza, Vicente T. 1956. *Panorama de la música tradicional de México* [Panorama of Traditional Mexican Music]. México, D.F.: Universidad Autónoma de México.

Ochoa Serrano, Alvaro. 2000. *Mitote, fandango y mariacheros* [Indigenous Dance, Spanish Dance and Mariachi Musicians]. Zamora, Michoacán: El Colegio de Michoacán.

Pearlman, Steven. 1988. *Mariachi Music in Los Angeles*. Ph.D. thesis, University of California, Los Angeles (University Microfilm).

Rafael, Hermes. 1983. *Origen e historia del mariachi* [Origin and History of the Mariachi]. México, D.F.: Editorial Katún, S.A.

Rafael, Hermes. 1999. *Los primeros mariachis en la Ciudad de México* [The First Mariachis in Mexico City]. México, D.F.: Privately published.

Saldívar, Gabriel. 1934. *Historia de la música en México (épocas precortesiana y colonial)* [History of Mexican Music (Pre-Conquest and Colonial Periods)]. México, D.F.: Secretaría de Educación Pública, Publicaciones del Departamento de Bellas Artes.

Sheehy, Daniel. 1997. 'Mexican Mariachi Music: Made in the U.S.A.' In *Musics of Multicultural America: A Study of Twelve Musical Communities*, ed. Kip Lornell and Anne K. Rasmussen. New York: Schirmer Books, 131–54.

Sheehy, Daniel. 1999. 'Popular Mexican Musical Traditions: The Mariachi of West Mexico and the Conjunto Jarocho of Veracruz.' In *Music in Latin American Culture: Regional Traditions*, ed. John M. Schechter. New York: Schirmer Books, 34–79.

Stevenson, Robert. 1952. *Music in Mexico: A Historical Survey*. New York: Thomas Y. Crowell Company.

Discographical Reference
Ronstadt, Linda. *Canciones de mi Padre*. Asylum 60765-2. *1987*: USA.

Discography
Cuarteto Coculense: The Very First Mariachi Recordings, 1907–08 (Mexico's Pioneer Mariachis, Vol. 4). Arhoolie/Folklyric CD 7036. *1998*: USA.

Mariachi Coculense de Cirilo Marmolejo: 1926–36 (Mexico's Pioneer Mariachis, Vol. 1). Arhoolie/Folklyric CD 7011. *1993*: USA.

Mariachi Tapatío de José Marmolejo: 'El Auténtico' (Mexico's Pioneer Mariachis, Vol. 2). Arhoolie/Folklyric CD 7012. *1994*: USA.

Mariachi Vargas de Tecalitlán (Mexico's Pioneer Mariachis, Vol. 3). Arhoolie/Folklyric CD 7015. *1992*: USA.

JONATHAN CLARK

Medicine Shows

Medicine shows were traveling entertainments used to attract crowds for the purpose of selling nostrums, tonics and cure-all medicines. Called in English, variously, mountebanks, charlatans and quack doctors, among other terms, sellers of medicines and ointments have been known for centuries to have traded in the streets, at markets and fairs, and from door to door. In the eighteenth century, mountebanks erected stalls, from which they sold tonics, and which also had enclosed tented booths, where they could extract teeth or treat ailments in some privacy. At the stall would be a zany (traditional clown of the commedia dell' arte) and a drummer or piper, to draw a crowd with laughter and music. The 'quack and his zany' became a feature of every public gathering throughout Europe, and a great many medicine shows were operating in North America, even before the Revolution.

In the United States, quacks differed little from their European predecessors, making up liniments and potions, mixing herbal tonics laced with alcohol, licorice or even morphine, and selling their nostrums to the crowds at county fairs or, simply, on street corners. At a time when there were few rural doctors and no hospital beds for hundreds of thousands of people, the persuasive patter of the traveling 'doctor' was reassuring and the medicines he sold were avidly bought. From the simple form of the clown and drummer, the medicine show began to rival the minstrel show, having entertainers in blackface accompanied by players of banjo, tambourine and bones on stage. The manufacturers of medicines, such as Ka-Ton-Ka, sold as the 'Great Indian Medicine,' or the Kickapoo Indian Medicine Company, which sold an Indian Cough Cure and Indian Worm Killer, among other purportedly 'Indian' remedies, put out large touring shows. By the 1890s, the Kickapoo Company alone had over a hundred separate units on the road. 'Quaker' and 'Oriental' healers sold pills and potions during the intermissions of traveling shows, which, in some instances, reached the scale of vaudeville entertainments.

Members of the syndicated medicine shows looked on the pitchmen with some disdain. The 'high' pitchmen worked from a wagon painted with eye-catching motifs and ornamented lettering. Others used a cart or, in later years, the back of a truck, which could accommodate a piano and a dancer or even a small string band. Held in the least regard were the 'low' pitchmen, who set up a crude platform or simply sold their nostrums on street corners to the people drawn by one or two banjo or guitar players. Medicine shows of all kinds provided opportunities for jazz, blues, hillbilly and country musicians to travel and to earn money through their playing. Occasionally the show might hire a complete band, as did Dr. Ross Byar, whose show had more than a dozen jazz musicians in the 1930s. Taken over by Doc Milton

Bartok, the 14-piece, all-black jazz band was still playing for the Bardex Show in 1948. Several famous players, like Dewey 'Pigmeat' Markham, later a stalwart of the Apollo Theater, Harlem, got their start in show business with the medicine troupes. They included Harry Houdini, Buster Keaton and Bert Williams, most of whom worked the bigger shows, such as Dr. Hill's California Concert Company or 'Colonel' Edward's Oregon Indian Medicine Company.

It was the high-pitch and low-pitch doctor shows that employed the majority of rural musicians. Among well-known hillbilly and Southern white musicians who played in them were Uncle Dave Macon, Clarence Ashley, Fiddlin' John Carson and Clayton McMichen; these were the first generation to be known by their records. Jimmie Rodgers, Hank Williams and 'Harmonica' Frank Floyd were among the next generation, who played the shows in the 1930s. Innumerable African-American songsters and blues singers played the shows, from Gus Cannon, Walter 'Furry' Lewis and Frank Stokes to 'Brownie' McGhee, Sonny Terry and 'Pink' Anderson. Even 'T-Bone' Walker and Muddy Waters served their time with the medicine companies. Fortunately, in a large number of cases, the kinds of song and music they performed were put on record. They included titles like 'In the Jailhouse Now,' 'I Got Mine,' 'Chicken You Can Roost Behind the Moon' and many others that were shared, and doubtless exchanged, by both white and black singers.

For a period in the 1940s, musicians like Rambling Tommy Scott and Charlie Monroe and his Kentucky Pardners recorded on radio for shows that were sponsored by companies producing patent medicines. Unfortunately, despite the fact that one or two attempts were made to 're-create' a medicine show on record, a show was recorded on location only once. This was justifiably called *The Last Medicine Show*, and featured the patter of the doctor, Chief Thundercloud, and Peg Leg Sam (Arthur Jackson) entertaining on harmonica, interspersed with jokes and repartee. Made by Bruce Bastin and Pete Lowry, this recording demonstrates the measure of spontaneity in performance, the mixture of songster material and blues in the repertoire, and the excited participation of the crowd from a small tobacco town. Although largely disregarded in studies of rural and small-town music and musicians, the medicine shows played an important part in the dissemination of blues and country music in the first half of the twentieth century.

Bibliography·

Holbrook, Stewart. 1959. *The Golden Age of Quackery*. New York: Macmillan.

Jenner, C. Lee. 1983. *The Vi-Ton-Ka Medicine Show*. New York: American Place Theatre.

McNamara, Brooks. 1976. *Step Right Up*. Garden City, NY: Doubleday and Company.

Oliver, Paul. 1984. *Songsters and Saints: Vocal Traditions on Race Records*. Cambridge: Cambridge University Press.

Russell, Tony. 1970. *Blacks, Whites and Blues*. London: Studio Vista.

Webber, Malcolm. 1941. *Medicine Show*. Caldwell, ID: Caxton Printers.

Discographical References

Anderson, Pink. 'I Got Mine.' *Medicine Show Man*. Prestige Bluesville 1051. *1962*: USA.

Anderson, Pink. 'In the Jailhouse Now.' *Medicine Show Man*. Prestige Bluesville 1051. *1962*: USA.

Carson, Fiddlin' John. 'I Got Mine.' *Complete Recorded Works, Vol. 1 (1923–1924)*. Document 8014. *1998*: Austria.

Chief Thundercloud and Peg Leg Sam. *The Last Medicine Show*. Flyright 507–508. *1972*: USA.

Stokes, Frank. 'Chicken You Can Roost Behind the Moon.' *The Beale Street Sheiks*. Document 5012. *1990*: Austria.

Discography

Anderson, Pink. *Medicine Show Man*. Prestige Bluesville 1051. *1962*: USA.

Peg Leg Sam. *Medicine Show Man*. Trix 3302. *1972*: USA.

Scott, Tommy. *Tommy Scott's Original Georgia Peanut Band at the Medicine Show*. Concorde 005. *1977*: USA.

Filmography

Born for Hard Luck, dir. Tom Davenport and the Curriculum in Folklore, University of North Carolina, Chapel Hill. 1988. USA. 29 mins. Biography (Documentary). Original music by Peg Leg Sam.

Free Show Tonite, dir. Paul Wagner, Steven J. Zeitlin and the Office of Folklife Programs, North Carolina Department of Cultural Resources. 1983. USA. 59 mins.

PAUL OLIVER

Minstrel Troupes

Early blackface minstrelsy in the United States consisted of solo or duo acts by white performers who blackened their faces, wore motley clothing and presented various types of physical, verbal and musical comedy. After 1843, groups of specialty performers banded together into quartets or quintets to create evening entertainment that lasted from 60 to 180 minutes. By the late 1840s, the size of the groups increased to seven and sometimes as many as 10 members and, by the 1850s, most ensembles included a core group of entertainers supported by several guest artists. Minstrel performers were usually white males, but some African Americans and women did appear in shows in the United States and England before the Civil War.

The early minstrel repertory shows focused on songs, dances, mock lectures and novelty acts, with some of the material derived from African-American urban and rural sources but often exaggerated for comic purposes. Minstrelsy was immersed in commercialized popular culture after 1845, and managers retreating from the stylized, racially based elements of the early shows incorporated a variety of music, ranging from authentic African-American banjo styles to parodies of Italian opera choruses. As a male-dominated form of entertainment, blackface comedy provided a nativist critique of European culture, reinforced class and gender stereotypes, and created complicated tropes of North American and African-American life.

Burlesque was the essence of the minstrel show throughout its entire history, a fact which complicates interpretations that characterize blackface comedy as concerned only with demeaning African Americans. Not only did the minstrel show exhibit a wide variety of musical styles, but it treated women and all 'ethnic' groups as 'outsiders' whose social behaviors and sentimental attitudes were fitting subjects for comedy. Many of the songs and lectures satirized the growing economic and class differences in US society and ridiculed nearly every new trend in popular culture.

The number of items in a typical show varied from around a dozen in 1843 to as many as two dozen or more by the late 1850s. The typical entertainment included instrumental numbers, novelty acts (acrobats, characters in animal costumes, dancers, and circus or museum oddities), short skits, opera burlesques, parodies of urban concert life, comic and sentimental songs, and ensemble dance numbers.

Blackface minstrelsy was North America's most successful cultural export before 1865, and touring ensembles performed the music and comedy throughout the United States and England. Two months after the Virginia Minstrels inaugurated the minstrel 'show' in New York on 6 February 1843, they toured England and Ireland. Various groups calling themselves Ethiopian Serenaders or Virginia Serenaders (there were at least five different groups using each of those names) had visited England by 1848. The English-born Buckley family (James, George Swayne, Frederick and Richard Bishop), known as the New Orleans Serenaders after their US performances as blackface minstrels, toured England, Scotland and Ireland for nearly two years (1846–48). By the late 1850s, Raynor and Pierce's Minstrels, one of many groups calling themselves 'Christy' Minstrels, had visited the British Isles, making the Christy name synonymous with blackface variety entertainment.

Tours allowed companies to repeat programs often rather than creating new material, saved the costs of investing in new theaters or expensive renovations and took advantage of the audience's interest in topical entertainment. As an artifact of popular culture with strong ties to other forms of musical theater, minstrelsy depended on paying audiences and aggressive marketing for its financial success. Most traveling companies hired managers, agents or both to arrange financial details, secure bookings, promote the programs and arrange travel accommodation. The profits, if any, were usually divided by shares, with the manager and the ensemble leaders getting double shares depending on the composition of the group and whether or not it had any star performers.

The major companies toured within their own regions and traveled at least three distinct, but sometimes overlapping, circuits similar to those used by other popular theater performers and touring opera ensembles. The northern, southern and western circuits provided numerous opportunities for shorter sidetrips to cities and towns along the major routes. The northern circuit, which usually included Lower Canada, commenced in New York City and took groups by rail to Philadelphia, Pittsburgh, Cleveland, Chicago, Detroit, Toronto, Buffalo, Rochester, Albany and back. The New England portion of the northern circuit began in New York, from where the ensembles moved by rail to Hartford, Providence, Worcester, Boston and Portland, reversing the circuit for the trip home. Regional groups, such as Ordway's Aeolians, often began their tours in Boston and visited cities in Maine, Rhode Island, Connecticut and New York.

The southern route used by Buckley's New Orleans Serenaders, the Christy Minstrels and other groups took them by rail from New York to Philadelphia, Baltimore, Washington and Richmond, from where they often moved deeper into the South, usually ending up in New Orleans but often diverting to Nashville and into Kentucky. The return trip from New Orleans brought the major ensembles up the Mississippi to the Ohio, and thence by railroad to New York. Nelson Kneass (1823–68), the leader and musical arranger for groups known as the Sable Harmonists and Sable Brothers and Sisters, took his ensembles by boat from town to town along the Ohio and Mississippi rivers (the western tour of the 1840s) before returning east to work with other minstrel groups. These tours, which are documented in playbills and newspapers located in various local and regional archives, reveal how popular minstrel shows had

become and how varied the typical programs were by the early 1850s.

Disputes and breakups were common during tours. The original Virginia Minstrels dissolved in July 1843, leaving Daniel Emmett (1815–1904) and Richard (Pell) Pelham (1825–76) in England. Pell remained there to form Pell's Serenaders, and featured the famous African-American dancer William Henry 'Master Juba' Lane (ca. 1825–52) around 1848. In 1850, Buckley's New Orleans Serenaders toured the western circuit, traveling through Pennsylvania and down the Ohio River to Cincinnati, Louisville and Nashville. When the Buckley family left the Serenaders in Nashville after a dispute with Samuel Sanford (1821–1905), Sanford continued the tour with virtually the same act by retaining the costumes and appropriating the names of the Buckleys.

In 1851, Sanford's New Orleans Opera Troupe embarked on its second southern tour (Baines 1967). Sanford used every public relations device available to promote his ensemble. He frequently quoted a *Baltimore Sun* review claiming that his group had performed for the 'last nine years, throughout England, Ireland, Scotland, and all the principal cities of the United States, and, for the last three years, exclusively in the cities of New York, Boston, Philadelphia, and Baltimore.' By 1853, Sanford was boasting that his New Orleans Opera Troupe had entertained 'over 200,000 persons in thirteen Southern and Western States' (Baines 1967).

Sanford's tours and those of the other traveling ensembles disseminated the basic styles and contents of the minstrel show throughout the United States and established it as the most popular form of home-grown entertainment before the Civil War. There was scarcely a region in the United States that had not seen some form of minstrelsy by the mid-1850s, when many groups traveled even farther west. The Buckleys set off for San Francisco for the 1852–53 season, performing in small towns and cities along the way, only to discover that the city already had its own resident blackface ensemble led by Thomas Maguire (1824–96). Other solo performers and companies followed the Buckleys, the most prominent being George Christy (1827–68), who appeared with Maguire's Minstrels in 1858.

By the late 1860s, Duprez and Greene's Minstrels (1858–65) had introduced uniformed personnel, increased the number of performers and promoted their appearances with large billboards. Those changes continued through the 1870s and 1880s, when economy and efficiency forced the consolidation of smaller companies (8–14 players) into larger ensembles of 50–75 performers each. Companies featuring African-American men and women, such as the Hyers Sisters Opera Buffa Company, became common by the early 1870s, when there were nearly 30 different African-American ensembles performing regionally or on tour. Sam Hague (1828–1901), the English-born blackface entertainer, acquired a company called the Georgia Slave Troupe Minstrels in 1865, changed its name to Sam Hague's Slave Troupe of Georgia Minstrels and brought the ensemble to England in 1866. A second African-American group, called the Famous Original Georgia Minstrels and organized by the African-American entertainer Charles B. 'Barney' Hicks (ca. 1840–1902), conducted four annual tours of New England, the mid-Atlantic states and Lower Canada in the late 1860s, eventually visiting Germany, England and Wales during the 1870–71 season (Southern 1996). Charles Callender (1827–97) succeeded Hicks as the manager of the Original Georgia Minstrels around 1872 and toured annually for several years before selling out in 1878 to J.H. 'Jack' Haverly (1836–1901). Callender formed other minstrel companies with black performers and introduced plantation scenes and sketches into his programs, along with spirituals and 'jubilee' choruses, which shaped the ways in which some white North Americans viewed African-American life and culture.

By the 1890s, when the myth of the 'Old South' was firmly established as a convention in US entertainment, the earlier forms of blackface minstrelsy were eclipsed by vaudeville and transformed into a series of separate acts that were 'more like high class ballad or operatic concerts than a minstrel show' (Toll 1974). By the 1920s, minstrel acts were absorbed into traveling medicine and tent shows, and the formats used by the large companies became part of amateur theatricals across the United States.

Bibliography

Baines, Jimmy Dalton. 1967. *Samuel Sanford and Negro Minstrelsy*. Ph.D. thesis, Tulane University.

Cockrell, Dale. 1997. *Demons of Disorder: Early Blackface Minstrels and Their World*. New York: Cambridge University Press.

Lahmon, W.T., Jr. 1998. *Raising Cain: Blackface Performance from Jim Crow to Hip Hop*. Cambridge: Harvard University Press.

Lott, Eric. 1993. *Love and Theft: Blackface Minstrelsy and the American Working Class*. New York: Oxford University Press.

Mahar, William J. 1998. *Behind the Burnt Cork Mask: Early Blackface Minstrelsy and Antebellum American Popular Culture*. Urbana, IL: University of Illinois Press.

Nathan, Hans. 1962. *Dan Emmett and the Rise of Early Negro Minstrelsy*. Norman, OK: University of Oklahoma Press.

Southern, Eileen. 1996. 'The Georgia Minstrels.' In *Inside the Minstrel Mask: Readings in Nineteenth-Century Black-*

face Minstrelsy, ed. Annemarie Bean, James V. Hatch and Brooks McNamara. Hanover and London: University Press of New England, 163–75. (First published as 'The Georgia Minstrels: The Early Years' in *Inter-American Music Review* 10(2) (1989): 157–67.)

Toll, Robert C. 1974. *Blacking Up: The Minstrel Show in Nineteenth-Century America*. New York: Oxford University Press.

Winans, Robert B. 1984. 'Early Minstrel Show Music, 1843–1852.' In *Musical Theatre in America: Papers and Proceedings of the Conference on the Musical Theatre in America (1981)*, ed. Glenn B. Loney. Westport, CT: Greenwood Press, 71–97.

Wittke, Carl. 1968 (1930). *Tambo and Bones: A History of the American Minstrel Stage*. New York: Greenwood Press.

WILLIAM MAHAR

Mouth Organ Bands

The international popularity of the harmonica was duplicated in Australia from the mid-nineteenth to the mid-twentieth centuries to such an extent that distinguished composer Alfred Hill described it as Australia's 'national instrument' and proposed calling it the Australian Pipes. The harmonica's portability and ease of use gave it particular appeal in the context of Australia's vast distances; its low cost and early association with non-Anglophone cultures (German immigrants and multicultural groups of workers in goldfields) also democratized it in the face of the exclusionary politics of Anglo-centric aesthetics. It thus became a significant means of music-making for groups that were aesthetically marginalized, and its association with nationalist rural mythologies was proclaimed in model names like 'Boomerang.'

From the 1920s, the instrument's power in constructing such musical communities was manifested in the emergence of mouth organ bands. With as many as 30 musicians, playing a repertoire ranging from popular to classical, these were constituted on the basis of such categories as place (for example, Victoria's Geelong West City Harmonica Band, the most successful in competition), age (school-based groups), gender (women's bands, pioneered by the Silvabelles) and trade (department stores, and transport organizations – for example, the North Sydney Tramway Harmonica Band). The development of competitive activity, centered on the annual Royal South Street Eisteddfod in Ballarat, Victoria, became formalized with the establishment of the Victorian Mouth Organ Bands Association in 1932, bringing this grass-roots music-making into an ambiguous relationship with institutionalized aesthetics, simultaneously demotic and deferential. Although Victoria's Yarraville Mouth Organ Band, established in 1933, was still active in the 1990s, its heyday was from the 1920s to the 1940s, when it played a particularly significant role in the democratization of music-making during the Great Depression.

Bibliography

Grieve, Ray. 1995. *A Band in a Waistcoat Pocket: The Story of the Harmonica in Australia*. Sydney: Currency Press.

Johnson, Bruce. 1997. 'Australia's National Instrument?' *Perfect Beat* 3(2)(January): 96–101.

Discography

Australian Harmonica History (4 cassettes; Vol. 2: Mouth Organ Soloists and Bands). RGAHH5CAS, RGAHH6CAS, RGAHH7CAS, RGAHH8CAS. *1995*: Australia. Also released as *A Band in a Waistcoat Pocket* (2-CD set). Larrikin Records LRH 390/1. *1995*: Australia.

BRUCE JOHNSON

One-Man Band

'One-man band' is the term most frequently applied to a solo musician who plays two or more instruments simultaneously. As such, the medieval players of pipe and tabor can be numbered among them. The end-blown flute or pipe was fingered by one hand while the player's other hand (usually the right) beat the tabor drum, which was suspended from the player's neck. Players of the 'whittle and dubb' (a pun on the simple walling technique of 'wattle and daub') would entertain crowds at fairs and markets, or accompany jugglers, acrobats and clowns. Known in England since the fourteenth century, pipe and tabor players were still to be heard in Brittany and the Basque country six centuries later. A popular folk instrumental ensemble was the 'Devil's violin,' 'Jingling Johnny' or, in North America, the 'Stump Fiddle,' variants of a pole topped with cymbals which clashed as it was struck on the ground. With a monochord, pans, bells and even jingles made of cola bottle caps, the novelty instrument could be enhanced with foot-pedal devices to operate cymbals or drum, a technical advance that was exploited by many one-man bands in the nineteenth century.

One of the 'London poor' interviewed by Henry Mayhew in the 1840s was a blind player of a rail of 14 bells mounted on a small carriage; the bells were struck with hammers attached by cords to foot-operated pedals, while he played the violin. Subsequently, the ingenious blind musician devised a violoncello mounted on a wheeled frame, which he played with his feet in harmony with his violin playing, and, later still, an assembly of four accordions similarly played. A mid-nineteenth-century description of 'London Outdoor Music' (1859) depicted 'an ingenious personage' who

was a 'Band in Himself,' a street entertainer dancing in thick boots to his own music. He carried a multicolored drum on his back, which he struck with drumsticks attached to his elbows, a hurdy-gurdy in his hands, pan pipes on a rack at his mouth, cymbals tied to the inside of his knees and a tree of small bells on his hat. A woman provided accompaniment on a fiddle.

Such a 'one-man band' was probably not an uncommon sight in the streets for many years. The sheet music of a 1900 cakewalk, 'Foggy Jones,' shows a seated black man playing banjo, a bass drum on his back surmounted by a smaller one, cymbals, and a harmonica in a harness. Partly because they had novelty appeal, and perhaps also because they were independent, such one-man bands were often to be found among songsters. One such was Sam Jones, a Cincinnati songster known as 'Stovepipe No. 1,' who played guitar, harmonica and a deep-toned stovepipe blown as a jug would be.

Most one-man bands, such as Daddy Stovepipe (Johnny Watson) and Weldon 'Juke Boy' Bonner, played two or three instruments, usually guitar, harmonica and, possibly, drums. Some made their own instruments – for instance, the songster Jesse 'Lone Cat' Fuller. He played guitar, harmonica, kazoo on a rack, and his own invention, the 'fotdella.' The latter was a pedal-operated string bass with a damping bar, which he played with his feet. Attached were pedal cymbals and a ratchet device which produced a washboard-like rhythm. One of the most inventive of the instrument-building performers was the white one-man band C. 'Fate' Norris of Dalton, Georgia: he created a trestle frame on which were mounted a bass fiddle and two guitars, which he played with three pedals operated by his left foot and one by his right, while he played fiddle and blew on kazoo or harmonica.

Although the phrase 'one-man band' was commonly applied to such multi-instrumentalists, the only jazz musician so described was Rahsaan Roland Kirk. He played simultaneously, by employing circular breathing, a tenor saxophone, a 'manzello' (adapted saxello) and the 'strich,' a B♭ alto sax modified to facilitate one-handed playing. To these he added a siren whistle, and he later experimented with a 'trumpophone,' 'slide-ophone,' 'black puzzle flute,' nose flute, piccolo, clavietta and harmonica, usually playing three horns at once.

In one of the few published papers on one-man bandsmen, Hal Rammel (1990) describes in detail the instruments built and played by Joe Barrick, an Oklahoman born of Choctaw parents in 1922, who played mandolin, fiddle and guitar in Western bands. In the mid-1970s, he invented a flatbed guitar to which he added a bass guitar, banjo and snare drum; he played all of these with hammers operated by his right foot and with frets moved with treadles raised by his left foot, while playing a guitar-mandolin built on a cow skull. Joe Barrick termed his composite foot-instrument a 'piatarbajo,' each component of which had its own microphone, amplifier and speaker, placed so that the sound created was of a group of separate instrumentalists.

One-man bands are still to be found as outdoor entertainers. One seen and heard by the writer at the Grand National steeplechase at Aintree, England in April 1998 was equipped similarly to the 'Band in Himself' of 140 years before.

Bibliography

Buchner, Alexander. 1971. *Folk Music Instruments.* London: Octopus Books, 121.

'London Outdoor Music.' 1859. *Illustrated London News* (1 January).

Mayhew, Henry. 1968 (1861–62). *London Labour and the London Poor*, Vol. 3. New York: Dover Publications.

Oliver, Paul. 1984. *Songsters and Saints: Vocal Traditions on Race Records.* Cambridge: Cambridge University Press.

Oster, Harry. 1991. Notes to *Jesse Fuller: Frisco Bound.* Arhoolie CD 360.

Rammel, Hal. 1990. 'Joe Barrick's One-Man Band: A History of the Piatarbajo and Other One-Man Bands.' *Musical Traditions* 8: 4–23.

Winter, J. 1980. 'Rahsaan Roland Kirk' (Interview). *Coda* 172: 10.

Sheet Music

Gearen, Joseph, comp. and lyr. 1900. 'Foggy Jones. Cakewalk or Two-Step.' Chicago: Gearen Music Company.

PAUL OLIVER

Orchestra

An orchestra can be a large ensemble of any kind. In popular music, the term has been used without much attention to consistency to describe a wide range of ensembles. Ensembles using the word in their name include ballroom orchestras (for example, the Victor Silvester Orchestra), society or syncopated orchestras (for example, Europe's Society Orchestra), dance bands (for example, the Ray Noble Orchestra and the BBC Dance Orchestra, led by Jack Payne and, later, Henry Hall), in-house studio ensembles (such as the Victor Young Orchestra, which provided many accompaniments for Bing Crosby's recordings) and big bands (for example, Fletcher Henderson and His Orchestra, Benny Goodman and His Orchestra and Duke Ellington and His Orchestra). A big band famous for its easy listening fare has been James Last and His Orchestra. Use of the word is intended to give some indication of size of ensemble; in many cases, it is also intended to suggest status and/or cultural acceptance.

The instrumentation of these ensembles has varied considerably. The presence or absence of strings could be – although not consistently so – an indicator of a cultured status and the ensemble's proximity to or distance from jazz. Thus, strings are present in many recordings made by James Reese Europe's organization of music for the renowned society dancing couple Irene and Vernon Castle. And while the Paul Whiteman Orchestra was sufficiently flexible to include strings for performances of pieces such as Gershwin's 'Rhapsody in Blue,' it drew on them far less extensively for the execution of popular dance tunes. Strings were absent from organizations such as those of Fletcher Henderson and Duke Ellington, and Artie Shaw's consistent attempts to find a role for strings in several of his big bands were only intermittently successful.

The word 'orchestra' has also been used in the world of popular music – and sometimes with a certain degree of irony – to describe small dance bands, folk ensembles of unorthodox instrumentation and rock groups such as the Electric Light Orchestra. Finally, it has been used within popular music to refer to the classical symphony orchestra, as well as to ensembles whose instrumentation has either followed – or has been significantly influenced by – that of the symphony orchestra. These organizations have played a significant role in the history of popular music and popular culture.

The term 'orchestra' did not originally attach to these kinds of organizations. It originally denoted the area between actors and audience in classical Greek theater where the singing and dancing of the chorus took place. It continued to define a space rather than the occupants of that space until the eighteenth century, when the musicians of the French theater became known as 'the orchestra.' The term then became synonymous with such large groups of musicians, which were generally based on a string ensemble. The term has continued to be widely used to define the standard instrumentation of the symphony orchestra, which has been relatively unaltered since the late nineteenth century. It consists of 32 violins (in two sections), 12 violas, 12 cellos, eight double basses, four flutes, four oboes, four clarinets, four bassoons, eight horns, four trumpets, three trombones, tuba and percussion, with the optional addition of harp and piano.

Smaller ensembles are known as 'chamber' orchestras, or named according to the predominant instruments they contain – notably 'string' orchestras. (Brass and wind groups are more often referred to as ensembles or bands than orchestras.) In the latter half of the nineteenth century, string orchestras were the focus of much popular music, notably in Vienna, where Johann Strauss the Younger (1825–99) introduced his waltzes, polkas and marches to audiences during frequent tours of Europe. He also visited the United States in 1872. The tradition of performing popular parts of the classical repertoire with a symphony orchestra remained a vital element in twentieth-century music all over the world, but particularly in the United States, where the most notable exponents included Arthur Fiedler (1894–1979), who conducted his Boston Pops Orchestra for four decades from 1930. Leopold Stokowski (1882–1977) combined a similar repertoire with pioneering performances of new music by Rachmaninoff and Stravinsky, introducing the latter's 'Rite of Spring' to a vast international audience in the soundtrack of Walt Disney's film *Fantasia* (1940).

Fantasia was a deliberate attempt to combine popular classics with animation, but, in most types of movies, film soundtracks employed the symphony orchestra as the standard form of musical accompaniment until well after World War II. Film studios in many parts of the world employed their own in-house orchestras to record soundtrack music by composers who ranged from specialists to established symphonists. Film scores by Sir William Walton (1902–83) and Dmitri Shostakovich (1906–75) have remained among their best-known works.

Gramophone records and broadcasting were equally influential in establishing the symphony orchestra in public popularity, and most large broadcasting organizations employed their own orchestras. Versatility was the key ingredient in such ensembles, although some broadcasters set up different orchestras for different purposes. The BBC in Britain was notable in this regard, with the result that, while the BBC Symphony and BBC Philharmonic orchestras, together with regional orchestras in Scotland and Wales, generally tackled new music or the great classics, the BBC Concert Orchestra and the BBC Dance Orchestra (which subsequently became the BBC Big Band) were recruited to perform at the 'popular' end of the repertoire.

Many of the orchestras set up for broadcasting and recording achieved unprecedented levels of audience, especially those directed by Arturo Toscanini (1867–1957) and Bruno Walter (1876–1962). Toscanini was guest conductor of the BBC Symphony Orchestra from 1935 to 1939, and conductor and music director of the NBC Symphony Orchestra in the United States from 1935 to 1954. Since the end of World War II, numerous conductors have propelled themselves and their orchestras to huge international popularity through a canny mix of live performance, broadcasting and recording – notably, Herbert von Karajan (1908–89), Leonard Bernstein (1918–90), André Previn (b. 1929), Seiji Ozawa (b. 1935), Michael Tilson Thomas (b. 1944), Leonard Slatkin

(b. 1944) and Sir Simon Rattle (b. 1955). John Williams (b. 1932) has been the internationally best-known orchestral composer and conductor of all. Since his first score for *I Passed for White* (1960), he has been responsible for the scores of dozens of major movies, including *Jaws*, the *Star Wars* series, the *Indiana Jones* series and many more. His scores have also formed the basis for numerous Grammy-winning albums, so that Williams has frequently won awards from both the sound recording and the movie industries for the same music.

In the 1990s, in addition to the enduring popularity of the classical and romantic repertoire, some elements of the newest and most challenging orchestral compositions by twentieth-century composers acquired a level of popular support that propelled them into the same segment of the market as pop and rock performers. These included *Tabula Rasa* by Arvo Pärt, *Protecting Veil* by John Tavener and Symphony No. 3, Op. 36 (the 'Symphony of Sorrowful Songs') by Henryk Górecki. This popular showing, and the continued success of composers like John Williams in achieving a mass market for their orchestral film scores, suggests a healthy future for the symphony orchestra and its repertoire.

Bibliography

Del Mar, Norman. 1984. *Anatomy of the Orchestra*. Berkeley, CA: University of California Press.

Morton, Brian. 1996. *The Blackwell Guide to Recorded Contemporary Music*. Oxford and Cambridge, MA: Blackwell.

Paris, Alain. 1989. *Dictionnaire des Interprètes et de l'Interprétation Musicale* [Dictionary of Performers and of Musical Performance]. 3rd ed. Paris: Robert Laffont.

Discographical References

Górecki, Henryk. *Górecki: Symphony No. 3*. Philips 442411. *1994*: The Netherlands.

Ma, Yo-Yo. *Protecting Veil/Wake Up & Die* (John Tavener, comp.). Sony 62821. *1998*: USA.

Pärt, Arvo. *Tabula Rasa*. ECM 817764-2. 1977–84; *1984*: Germany.

Whiteman, Paul, and His Orchestra. 'Rhapsody in Blue.' RCA-Victor 35822. 1927: USA.

Discography

Fantasia (Original soundtrack). Disney 60007. *1991*: USA.

Indiana Jones and the Last Crusade (Original soundtrack). Warner Brothers 2-25883. *1989*: USA.

Indiana Jones and the Temple of Doom (Original soundtrack). Import 50806. *1999*: USA.

Raiders of the Lost Ark (Original soundtrack). DCC 90. *1995*: USA.

Star Wars: The Phantom Menace (Original soundtrack). Sony 61816. *1999*: USA.

Star Wars Trilogy (Original soundtracks). RCA-Victor 09026-68748-2. *1997*: USA.

Williams, John. *Jaws*. MCA MCAD-1660. *1975*: USA.

Filmography

Fantasia, dir. James Algar, Samuel Armstrong, Ford I. Beebe, Walt Disney, Jim Handley, Albert Heath, T. Hee, Graham Heid, Wilfred Jackson, Hamilton Luske, Bianca Majolie, Sylvia Moberly-Holland, Bill Roberts, Paul Satterfield, Ben Sharpsteen and Norman Wright. 1940. USA. 116 mins. Animated Musical. Original music by Johann Sebastian Bach, Ludwig van Beethoven, Franz Schubert, Igor Stravinsky, Pyotr Tchaikovsky.

Indiana Jones and the Last Crusade, dir. Steven Spielberg. 1989. USA. 126 mins. Action. Original music by John Williams.

Indiana Jones and the Temple of Doom, dir. Steven Spielberg. 1984. USA. 118 mins. Action. Original music by John Williams.

I Passed for White, dir. Fred Wilcox. 1960. USA. 93 mins. Melodrama. Original music by Jerry Irving, John Williams.

Jaws, dir. Steven Spielberg. 1975. USA. 124 mins. Thriller. Original music by John Williams.

Raiders of the Lost Ark (aka *Indiana Jones and the Raiders of the Lost Ark* (US video title)), dir. Steven Spielberg. 1981. USA. 115 mins. Action. Original music by John Williams.

Star Wars: Episode I – The Phantom Menace, dir. George Lucas. 1999. USA. 131 mins. Science Fiction. Original music by John Williams.

Star Wars: Episode IV – A New Hope, dir. George Lucas. 1977. USA. 121 mins. Science Fiction. Original music by John Williams.

Star Wars: Episode V – The Empire Strikes Back, dir. Irvin Kershner. 1980. USA. 124 mins. Science Fiction. Original music by John Williams.

Star Wars: Episode VI – The Return of the Jedi, dir. Richard Marquand. 1983. USA. 133 mins. Science Fiction. Original music by John Williams.

ALYN SHIPTON

Palm Court Orchestra

'Palm courts' were areas in luxury hotels given over to air, space, food and relaxation, thus creating an ambiance for the 'discerning' guest. This ambiance included music provided by an 'orchestra' (occasionally only three pieces) playing light classics (Grieg, Dvořák), waltzes and tunes from operettas. Violins predominated, often accompanied by a piano and/or cello.

From the beginning of the twentieth century, practically all the most luxurious hotels, cruise ships, department store restaurants, cafés and even health spas employed palm court or 'salon' orchestras to entertain their guests while they dined or relaxed. Some of the larger hotels had two orchestras, one of which played dance music in the evenings; otherwise, the personnel in the orchestra would switch to dance music at night. At the Savoy in London, for example, Carroll Gibbons and the Boy Friends played palm court music, while Carroll Gibbons and the Savoy Hotel Orpheans played music for dancing.

One of the most famous palm court orchestra leaders of the inter-war years was Albert Sandler, who performed at the Park Hotel in London and at the Grand Hotel in Eastbourne. Other leaders of note included Leslie Jeffries, Reginald King and Alfredo Campoli. Sandler was also renowned for his BBC Sunday radio broadcasts. The BBC banned dance music on the Sabbath and so Sandler's *Music at the Palm Court* was a great attraction on Sunday evening radio. In many ways, the famous BBC 'light music' tag was created with palm court music in mind.

Prior to World War II, palm court orchestras were also popular among Europe's 'café society,' particularly in Germany. However, the genre began to fade when hotels' livelihoods were irrevocably changed by the war.

The BBC, however, continued to broadcast palm court music for many years after the war. Ray Jenkins and His Cosmopolitans and the Kursaal Orchestras were frequently featured on the BBC Home Service in the late 1940s and the 1950s. With the advent of Radio 1 in 1967, however, the light music output at the BBC underwent severe modification and, apart from the ubiquitous Max Jaffa broadcasts on Radio 2, palm court music and orchestras faded away. In the late 1990s, however, broadcaster Dennis Norden rekindled an interest in the light music genre in the United Kingdom and palm court orchestras were occasionally heard again on the BBC. In addition, the success of the film *Titanic* drew attention to palm court music, which was played on board the ill-fated vessel in the movie. While these changes were taking place, in Australia the Sydney Palm Court Orchestra (founded in 1974) continued to offer its services.

Discography

Campoli, Alfredo. *Campoli's Choice*. Flapper 9744. *1991*: UK.

Campoli, Alfredo, and His Salon Orchestra. *Alfredo Campoli & His Salon Orchestra*. Flapper 9707. *1990*: UK.

Gibbons, Carroll. *Carroll Gibbons with the Savoy Hotel Orpheans*. Flapper 9734. *1991*: UK.

Sandler, Albert, and His Orchestra. *Albert Sandler & His Orchestra.* Flapper 9732. *1990*: UK.

Filmography

Titanic, dir. James Cameron. 1997. USA. 195 mins. Historical Romance. Original music by James Horner.

MIKE BROCKEN

Pit Band

The ensemble of musicians that provides the music for a stage show from the orchestra pit is sometimes referred to as a pit band. In most theatrical presentations involving a pit band, the pit is located in front of the stage at a lower level and often has a sunken floor.

Up to the mid-nineteenth century, the term 'pit' was used in the English-speaking world to refer to the floor of a theater, which was often sunk below ground level and which was occupied by the artisan and working-class (and typically most boisterous) sections of the audience. Those who frequented it were known, derisively, as 'groundlings.' From the early eighteenth century in England, the pit also housed the orchestra, whose members had previously been seated either in a gallery or in a box. A screen or screens often separated the orchestra from the audience. As the pit was replaced by stalls for the audience, usually on a sloping or raked floor, the members of the orchestra remained its sole occupants.

The practise of employing an accompanying body of musicians, located offstage, has a long history in popular theater. From the eighteenth century onward, the numerous forms of popular theatrical entertainment that developed – whether they were based around plot and dialog or around a series of separate acts – almost invariably required an orchestra to provide accompaniment for song and dance and to play music for linking passages. Straight theater also often required the services of pit musicians to provide music – for example, for an interlude or even as an accompaniment to dramatic scenes. The practise continued into the twentieth century, where (although straight theater's use of accompanying music had in general declined) the range of theatrical styles requiring pit musicians was further extended, from the larger cinemas of the silent screen era to the staged performances of star singers.

The term 'pit band' itself arose in the United States in the early twentieth century and was current by the 1920s, at first in the context of the revue, burlesque and vaudeville stage, where its colloquial ring and its link to jazz helped maintain distinctions from the more formal operetta and musical comedy styles, for which the pit contained an 'orchestra' with a prominent string section. A pit band would normally be a small or medium-size unit dominated by wind, brass and percussion; its personnel would often be jobbing musicians, who could

be expected to be both musically literate and generally dependable (Hennessy 1994, 84). In a tradition with its own history, its director would also be the musical arranger and would contribute to the musical numbers. The term clearly had evaluative connotations for the musicians themselves: when the pit band providing music for a revue was an already constituted ensemble, it would most probably seek to have itself referred to as an orchestra. Broadly speaking, these types of distinction have remained in place, and contemporary references to the musical unit accompanying a musical comedy as a pit band are likely to be critical, playful or ironic.

Perhaps coincidentally, therefore, the term preserves something of the informality and reflects something of the hierarchy that characterized the theatrical pit. In terms of accomplishment, however, the pit band is typically a highly skilled unit, invariably professional in the professional theater, and typically consisting of freelancing musicians in the amateur theater.

Bibliography

Hennessy, Thomas. 1994. *From Jazz to Swing: African-American Jazz Musicians and Their Music, 1898–1935.* Detroit, MI: Wayne State University Press.

DAVID HORN

Polka Band

The term 'polka band,' current in North America since the 1930s, denotes an ensemble of social dance musicians descended chiefly from the European immigrant working class. The diverse instrumentation of these ensembles frequently includes an accordion or related 'squeezebox.' Their repertoire has featured not only the polka, but also the waltz, the schottische and other nineteenth-century couple dances.

The polka emerged around 1830 in a rural Germanicized Czech region near the Polish border. Buoyed by the mass production of the accordion and the standardization and proliferation of wind instruments, the polka became the rage throughout Europe, North America and imperial outposts in the mid-nineteenth century. Passé as a form of commercially successful popular music by the early twentieth century, the polka has nonetheless persisted as a widely varied and continuously evolving folk and popular genre. In the United States, Germans, Italians, Mexicans, Scandinavians and Slavs have developed distinctive polka styles and substyles. Some prominent instances at the end of the twentieth century included: the stately Bohemian sound, with its heavy bass horn sound, brass and reed antiphony, and dissonant vocal harmonies; the virtuosic Slovenian sound, with its rapid-fire accordion duets, percussive four-string banjo rhythms, and 'blatty' saxophone fills; the Polish 'honky' and 'dyno' innovations, emphasizing bright trumpet leads, swirling improvisations of concertina and clarinet, and a rhythm section of rimshot, cymbal-happy drumming, bellows-shaking piano accordion and booming electric bass; the 'Dutchman' (German) fusion of bouncing tuba syncopations with a swinging, note-filled attack on the 'German' or 'Chemnitzer' concertina; and the Mexican *conjunto* combination of hot right-hand runs on three-row button accordion, a *bajo sexto* (10-string guitar) emphasizing offbeats, and tight vocal duets.

Far removed from their old-world origins, polka bands commenced their transformations in the late 1920s, when members of local bands drawn from many ethnic groups had a chance to become professional musicians through new opportunities provided by radio stations, record labels and dance halls, and by improved roads and automobiles. Initially oriented toward a kindred audience, successful bands learned the favorite tunes of other ethnic groups while absorbing jazz and hillbilly conventions. The career of band leader Hans Wilfahrt (1893–1961) offers an example of such success. Born in the German-Bohemian enclave of New Ulm, Minnesota, Wilfahrt was first a member of a trio that played old country tunes for weddings and house parties. But, by the 1920s, he had organized a larger band, moved to cosmopolitan Minneapolis, commenced recording for OKeh, secured a regular radio show, begun barnstorming over a five-state area and expanded his playlist to include Polish, Swedish and Anglo-American tunes. His switch to Decca in the 1930s was marked by the consolidation of his trademark 'Whoopee John' persona (a grinning lederhosen-clad yodeler in a Jaeger hat), and by a profusion of new swing-inflected dance tunes, with exclusively English titles, that rivaled the popularity of his crooning colleague on the Decca label, Bing Crosby.

Since the late 1930s, crossover ensembles like Wilfahrt's have been known as 'polka bands,' a generic term ratified by the massive international popularity of the 'Beer Barrel Polka,' 1939's top jukebox hit in the United States. Like Wilfahrt's, post-1930s polka bands have augmented their core repertoire with country, pop and, eventually, rock standards. However, the 1950s onset of rock 'n' roll compelled many young people who were potential polka aficionados to reject accordions in favor of guitars. Abandoned by major record labels, polka bands retreated to the margins of popular music. Meanwhile, sweet jazz maestro Lawrence Welk's occasional saccharine polka stylings, televised from the 1950s until the 1990s, caused polka bands to acquire the 'squarest' status conferred by popular culture – an unwarranted status only improved toward the end of the twentieth century as world music consumers, prowling folk and pop cultures' borderlands, rediscovered not only the venerable appeal of accordions, ethnic roots and couple dances, but also the ongoing vitality of contemporary polka bands.

Bibliography

Dolgan, Robert. 1977. *The Polka King: The Life of Frankie Yankovic.* Cleveland, OH: Dillon/Liederbach.

Greene, Victor. 1992. *A Passion for Polka: Ethnic Old Time Music in America, 1880–1960.* Berkeley, CA: University of California Press.

Keil, Charles, Keil, Angeliki V., and Blau, Dick. 1992. *Polka Happiness.* Philadelphia: Temple University Press.

Leary, James P. 1997. 'Czech American Polka Music in Wisconsin.' In *Musics of Multicultural America: A Study of Twelve Musical Communities,* ed. Kip Lornell and Anne K. Rasmussen. New York: Schirmer Books, 25–47.

Leary, James P. 1998. 'Polka Music in a Polka State.' In *Wisconsin Folklore,* ed. James P. Leary. Madison, WI: University of Wisconsin Press, 268–83.

Leary, James P., and March, Richard. 1991. 'Dutchman Bands: Genre, Ethnicity and Pluralism in the Upper Midwest.' In *Creative Ethnicity: Symbols and Strategies in Contemporary Ethnic Life,* ed. Stephen Stern and John Allan Cicala. Logan, UT: Utah State University Press, 21–43.

Peña, Manuel. 1985. *The Texas-Mexican Conjunto: History of a Working-Class Music.* Austin, TX: University of Texas Press.

Proulx, E. Annie. 1996. *Accordion Crimes.* New York: Scribners.

Rippley, LaVern J. 1992. *The Whoopee John Wilfahrt Dance Band.* Northfield, MN: German Department, St. Olaf College.

Spottswood, Richard K. 1982. 'Commercial Ethnic Recordings in the United States.' In *Ethnic Recordings in America: A Neglected Heritage.* Washington, DC: American Folklife Center, 51–66.

Welk, Lawrence. 1971. *Wunnerful, Wunnerful!.* Englewood Cliffs, NJ: Prentice-Hall.

Discographical References

Andrews Sisters, The. 'Beer Barrel Polka.' Decca 2462. 1939: USA.

Glahe Musette Orchestra. 'Beer Barrel Polka.' Victor V-710. 1936: Germany.

Discography

Deep Polka: Dance Music from the Midwest (ed. Richard March). Smithsonian Folkways SF 40088. *1998*: USA.

Minnesota Polka: Dance Music from Four Traditions (ed. James P. Leary). Minnesota Historical Society. *1990*: USA.

Play Me a Polka: Tex-Czech Polkas (ed. Bubba Hernandez). Rounder 6029. *1994*: USA.

Yankovic, Frankie. *The Early Years: Original Recordings, 1938–1944* (3 vols.). Sunshine Records SNC 109, 110, 111. *ca. 1992*: USA.

Visual Recordings

Blank, Les, and Gosling, Maureen. 1984. 'In Heaven There Is No Beer?'. Flower Films (film).

Ciesielka, Thomas, and Candee, Rees. 1995. 'Frank Yankovic: America's Polka King.' Lakeview Productions (video).

Erickson, Dave. 1994. 'Polka from Cuca.' Ootek Productions (video).

JAMES P. LEARY

Quartet

In popular music, a quartet is an ensemble made up of four musicians, four singers or a mixture of instrumentalists and singers. Unlike in Western classical music, in which quartet formats are determined by the demands of a written score, most quartet formats in popular music have evolved in less formal ways. The principal exceptions are certain vocal genres in which songs are arranged for four specific voices.

Male vocal quartets have a long history in both secular and religious popular music in the United States. The Hutchinson Family (which for a period was composed of three males and one female) and other touring groups of the 1840s drew on European close harmony singing and in turn inspired the barbershop quartet style (Hamm 1979, 141–61). This has become highly formalized over the last century, and such quartets as the Haydn, American and Peerless were among the recording artists of the early twentieth century.

Black gospel four-part harmony singing was noted as early as 1851 in the United States (Lornell 1988, 16), and the quartet format took shape at the end of the nineteenth century and during the first half of the twentieth through such widely recorded groups as the Norfolk Jazz and Jubilee Quartets and the Golden Gate Quartet. In the post-World War II rural South, white gospel groups like the Jordanaires flourished, as did country quartets such as the Oak Ridge Boys.

In the commercial mainstream of US popular music, vocal groups have generally been less formally organized in terms of size, harmonies and repertoire. Nevertheless, there were a considerable number of male voice quartets, ranging from the Ink Spots and the Mills Brothers in the 1930s through to the Four Freshmen, the Crew-Cuts, and Dion and the Belmonts in the 1950s and the Four Seasons in the 1960s. In later decades, such vocal groups were rare, although Boyz II Men successfully revived four-part harmony in the 1990s. Female pop quartets of the 1950s and 1960s included the Chordettes (formerly a barbershop group) and the Shirelles.

Mixed male and female vocal quartets were found less frequently, although both the Mamas and the Papas and Manhattan Transfer achieved success in the 1960s and 1980s, respectively. The most successful of all, however, was ABBA, a quartet that featured two female lead singers.

Although Benny Goodman formed a quartet consisting of piano, bass, drums and his clarinet from within his orchestra in 1938, jazz quartets became widespread only in the 1950s following the demise of the big bands and the rise of bebop as a small ensemble genre. The longest lasting of these was the Modern Jazz Quartet, founded in 1952. This quartet was unusual in not containing a brass instrument: most renowned modern jazz quartets, such as those led by Ornette Coleman and John Coltrane, have featured a saxophone with piano, bass and drums.

The most ubiquitous four-musician ensembles of the latter half of the twentieth century were those deriving from the rock 'n' roll and beat group lineup of bass guitar and drums, plus two guitars (lead and rhythm) or one guitar and lead vocalist. The popularity of the Beatles, in particular, inspired thousands of imitators worldwide, and the majority of bands in subsequent generations and genres of rock adopted the same lineup.

The string quartet familiar from Western classical music (first and second violins, cello and viola) is occasionally found in popular music. Examples are the Kronos Quartet, which assumed an avant-garde role in performing works by Philip Glass and Jimi Hendrix, among others, and the Brodsky Quartet, in its collaboration with Elvis Costello.

Bibliography

Hamm, Charles. 1979. *Yesterdays: Popular Song in America*. New York: W.W. Norton.

Lornell, Kip. 1988. *Happy in the Service of the Lord: Afro-American Gospel Quartets in Memphis*. Urbana, IL: University of Illinois Press.

Discography

ABBA. *Greatest Hits*. Epic EPC 69218. *1976*: UK.

Beatles, The. *1*. Apple/Parlophone 592 9702. *2000*: UK.

Benny Goodman Quartet, The. *After You've Gone*. Bluebird 85631. *1987*: USA.

Boyz II Men. *II*. Motown 5304312. *1994*: UK.

Chordettes, The. *Mainly Rock 'n' Roll*. Ace CDCHD 934. *1990*: UK.

Coleman, Ornette. *The Shape of Jazz to Come*. Atlantic 1317. *1959*: USA.

Coltrane, John. *A Love Supreme*. Impulse!. AS-77. *1964*: USA.

Costello, Elvis, and the Brodsky Quartet. *The Juliet Letters*. Warner Brothers 9362 45180-2. *1993*: USA.

Crew-Cuts, The. 'Sh-Boom.' Mercury 456. 1954: USA.

Dion and the Belmonts. 'Where or When.' Laurie 3044. *1960*: USA.

Four Freshmen, The. *Freshmen Favorites*. Capitol T-743. *1956*: USA.

Four Seasons, The. *Sherry and 11 Others*. Vee-Jay SR 1053. *1962*: USA.

Golden Gate Jubilee Quartet, The. *Our Story*. Sony Jazz 4940532. *2001*: USA.

Ink Spots, The. *Best of the Ink Spots*. EMI CDB 792 3752. *1989*: UK.

Jordanaires, The. *Beautiful City*. RCA-Victor PM-3081. 1953: USA.

Kronos Quartet, The. *The Kronos Quartet*. Nonesuch 79111-2. *1986*: UK.

Mamas and the Papas, The. *The Mamas and the Papas*. RCA-Victor RD 7803. *1966*: UK.

Manhattan Transfer. *Live*. Atlantic K 50540. *1978*: UK.

Mills Brothers, The. *Great Hits*. MCA MCAD-31035. *1987*: UK.

Modern Jazz Quartet, The. *Lonely Woman*. Atlantic SD-1381. *1962*: USA.

Norfolk Jazz and Jubilee Quartets. Vol. 2: 1923–1925. Document DOCD-5382. *1996*: Austria.

Oak Ridge Boys, The. *Seasons*. MCA MCAD-31124. *1986*: USA.

Shirelles, The. *The Best of the Shirelles*. Ace CDCHD 356. *1998*: UK.

The Heritage Hall Museum of Barbershop Harmony Presents Close Harmony Pioneers. SPEBSQSA, Inc. *1994*: USA.

DAVE LAING

R&B and Rock 'n' Roll Vocal Groups

Rhythm and blues (R&B) vocal groups flourished in the United States in the 1940s and 1950s. The groups, male or female, usually consisted of four voices (lead tenor, tenor, baritone and bass in the case of male groups), although they sometimes had three, five or six members. Group members were overwhelmingly drawn from the African-American community, although several of these groups were racially mixed. Their singing style drew on the vocal inflections of church choirs or spiritual vocal groups, which were applied both to up-tempo, or 'jump,' R&B numbers and to pop ballads (Gillett 1996). Their records were usually released with a ballad on one side of the record and an R&B song on the flip side. These records were marketed first as 'race' records for the black population, and they were then renamed 'rhythm and blues' after *Billboard* magazine introduced an R&B chart in June 1949.

The main black vocal groups prior to the evolution of the R&B vocal group included the Mills Brothers, the Charioteers, the Five Red Caps, the Four Vagabonds (or the Vagabonds) and the Ink Spots, who 'sang white-oriented pop material ... nicely but sparingly spiced with black expressive devices' (Floyd 1995, 175). These groups had been popular with both black and white audiences.

Among the better-known pioneer R&B vocal groups were the Ravens (a quartet featuring bass lead singer Jimmy Ricks) and the Orioles (a quartet that also had a guitar-playing member and featured the sweet tenor voice of 'Sonny Til,' the stage name of Earlington Tilghman). The first records were released by these groups in July 1946 ('Bye Bye Baby Blues') and July 1948 ('It's Too Soon to Know'), respectively. Close on the heels of these pioneering groups were the Clovers (who were the biggest-selling R&B group of the 1950s), the Dominoes and the 5 Royales (who began as the Royal Sons, a spiritual group).

A typical group song was led by a solo singer – usually the lead tenor, but sometimes the bass singer – or by two vocalists singing different parts of the song. Occasionally, the song would be sung by the entire group in unison. A cappella singing – choral singing without instrumental accompaniment – was an interesting aspect of these groups' abilities, generally done at practise sessions. Songs from these sessions exist mainly on practise tapes and demo records. The majority of a cappella recordings that were released were taken from these sources and were by white vocal groups; most were released in 1965 or later.

The R&B vocal groups originated in many different parts of the United States, and their sound is generally reflective of the area from which they came. As a rule, the New York City groups were polished and smooth in their delivery, the style of the west-coast groups was rougher and cruder, and the Chicago and New Orleans groups were somewhat more bluesy (the Chicago sound usually featured a prominent guitar, whereas the New Orleans sound featured a piano).

Although there were groups consisting of members in their thirties and forties, R&B vocal groups were primarily made up of teenagers and young adults who wanted to impress their peers (especially women) with both their singing prowess and their notoriety as recording artists. These groups took their names from many sources, including birds (Ravens, Orioles, Cardinals, Sparrows), cars (Cadillacs, Four Wheels, Impalas), animals (Colts, Gazelles, Jaguars), royalty (Crowns, Kings, Pharaohs, Sultans), age groups (Schoolboys, Teenagers, Youngsters) and precious stones (Diamonds, Five Emeralds, Gems, Sapphires).

R&B vocal groups both composed songs and performed many pop standards that were given a definite rhythm and blues treatment. These records sold poorly, if at all, in the white community, which was unfamiliar with black speech inflection and word pronunciation.

The 'age' of the R&B vocal groups lasted approximately from 1946 through 1965, at which time their black audience was in the process of shifting its attention to soul music. According to Millar (1971, 5), over 15,000 black vocal groups were recorded during the 1950s. Very few R&B groups were able to adapt their style to suit the new tastes of their audience, and so the R&B vocal groups began to fade away.

Although a few R&B groups have continued to exist, they do not generally sound the same as their ancestors from the late 1940s and 1950s. One of the most notable R&B groups that changed its sound to suit its audience was the Dells, who released their first record as the El Rays in about June 1954 on the Chicago-based Checker label. The Dells had transformed their song styling from R&B to soul by 1970, and continued to perform and record in this and other styles such as disco and urban contemporary until 1986, when they disbanded. Other R&B groups of note that were also able to change their styles to coincide with the tastes of their audience were the Platters, who appealed to the teenage rock 'n' roll fans of the 1950s, and the Impressions and the O'Jays, who released many hit records in both the R&B and soul genres.

Rock 'n' roll vocal groups sang in a style derived from the R&B vocal groups but adapted to appeal to a wider, mostly white, audience eager to break away from the pop music of the previous generation. Rock 'n' roll group lyrics were often aimed more directly at a youth audience through songs like 'A Teenager in Love,' 'Why Do Fools Fall in Love?' and 'Yakety Yak.' Such groups were mostly made up of white members (many of whom were of Italian descent). Some of the more prominent rock 'n' roll vocal groups were Dion and the Belmonts, the Four Seasons (previously known as the Variatones and the Four Lovers), the Mello-Kings, Danny and the Juniors, the Elegants and the Skyliners. Some African-American groups, notably the Coasters, Frankie Lymon and the Teenagers, the Shirelles and the Drifters, appealed strongly to rock 'n' roll audiences.

In general, rock 'n' roll vocal groups received more radio airplay than R&B vocal groups due to the fact that most groups' members were white. Rock 'n' roll vocal groups chose their names from the same sources and sang the same kind of songs as R&B vocal groups.

R&B and rock 'n' roll vocal groups are sometimes described as 'doo-wop' groups. The term is used to attempt to separate these groups from mainstream R&B and rock 'n' roll vocal groups by reason of the way in which 'doo-wop' songs contain background sounds such as 'doo wop,' 'doo wah' and other nonsense syllables. Examples of doo-wop records include the Chords' 'Sh-Boom' and 'Earth Angel' by the Penguins.

Bibliography

Baptista, Todd R. 1996. *Group Harmony: Behind the Rhythm and the Blues*. New Bedford, MA: TRB Enterprises.

Engel, Edward R. 1977. *White & Still All Right!*. n.p.: Crackerjack Press.

Ferlingere, Robert D. 2000. *A Discography of Rhythm & Blues and Rock 'n' Roll Vocal Groups, 1945 to 1965*. 3rd ed. Jackson, CA: The author.

Floyd, Samuel A. 1995. *The Power of Black Music: Interpreting Its History from Africa to the United States*. New York: Oxford University Press.

Gillett, Charlie. 1996. *The Sound of the City: The Rise of Rock and Roll*. 3rd ed. London: Souvenir Press.

Gribin, Anthony J., and Schiff, Matthew M. 1992. *Doo-Wop: The Forgotten Third of Rock 'n' Roll*. Iola, WI: Krause Publications.

Gribin, Anthony J., and Schiff, Matthew M. 2000. *The Complete Book of Doo-Wop*. Iola, WI: Krause Publications.

Groia, Philip. 1973. *They All Sang on the Corner: New York City's Rhythm and Blues Vocal Groups of the 1950s*. Setauket, NY: Edmond Publishing Company.

McCutcheon, Lynn Ellis. 1971. *Rhythm and Blues: An Experience and Adventure in Its Origin and Development*. Arlington, VA: R.W. Beatty.

Millar, Bill. 1971. *The Drifters: The Rise and Fall of the Black Vocal Group*. London: Studio Vista.

Millar, Bill. 1975. *The Coasters*. London: Methuen.

Ochs, Michael. 1984. *Rock Archives: A Photographic Journey Through the First Two Decades of Rock & Roll*. Garden City, NY: Doubleday.

Pruter, Robert. 1996. *Doowop: The Chicago Scene*. Urbana, IL: University of Illinois Press.

Silvani, Lou. 1992. *Collecting Rare Records: A Guide to Take You Through the World of Rare Records*. New York: Times Square Records.

Ward, Brian. 1998. *Just My Soul Responding: Rhythm and Blues, Black Consciousness, and Race Relations*. Berkeley, CA: University of California Press.

Discographical References

Chords, The. 'Sh-Boom.' Cat 104. 1954: USA.

Coasters, The. 'Yakety Yak.' Atco 6116. *1958*: USA.

Dion and the Belmonts. 'A Teenager in Love.' Laurie 3027. *1959*: USA.

Lymon, Frankie, and the Teenagers. 'Why Do Fools Fall in Love?' Gee 1002. *1956*: USA.

Orioles, The. 'It's Too Soon to Know.' Natural 5000. 1948: USA.

Penguins, The. 'Earth Angel (Will You Be Mine).' DooTone 348. 1954: USA.

Ravens, The. 'Bye Bye Baby Blues.' King 4234. 1946: USA.

ROBERT D. FERLINGERE

Ragtime Band

A ragtime band was an ensemble constituted to play the orchestral version of ragtime as arranged in *The Red Back Book of Rags* (ca. 1912) and other early twentieth-century collections of instrumental scores. The ensemble added color and depth to piano ragtime compositions by Scott Joplin, James Scott and others, but did not fundamentally alter the nature of the music until the 1920s, when New Orleans ensembles like those of Armand J. Piron and John Robichaux introduced an element of improvisation. The instrumentation consists of a rhythm section of piano and/or guitar, double bass or tuba and drums, with a 'front line' of one or two trumpets, violin, clarinet and trombone (occasionally with a flute, additional violin and cello). The basic instrumentation was adopted as the standard model for pioneer jazz bands from the earliest years of the twentieth century. Ensemble ragtime was also played by guitar, mandolin or banjo-based string bands.

Bibliography

Berlin, Edward A. 1980. *Ragtime: A Musical and Cultural History*. Berkeley, CA: University of California Press.

Berlin, Edward A. 1994. *King of Ragtime: Scott Joplin and His Era*. New York: Oxford University Press.

Blesh, Rudi, and Janis, Harriet. 1950. *They All Played Ragtime*. New York: Alfred A. Knopf.

Hasse, John Edward, ed. 1985. *Ragtime: Its History, Composers and Music*. London: Macmillan.

The Red Back Book of Rags (Standard High-Class Rags). ca. 1912. St. Louis, MO: Stark Music Co.

Schafer, William J., and Riedel, J. 1973. *The Art of Ragtime*. Baton Rouge, LA: Louisiana State University Press.

ALYN SHIPTON

Religious Vocal Groups and Choirs

Introduction

Ensembles performing popular religious music may be divided into three broad categories: small groups, choirs and congregations. In terms of commercial popular music, the first of these has made the most significant contribution, but in terms of noncommercial, or less commercial, everyday music-making, choirs and congregations have been sites where many people have heard, learned and participated in religious music.

Historically, although many churches and religious organizations often included a regular role in their worship rituals for music provided by small groups, that role was often a secondary one to that of the choir and the congregation. In such cases, vocal groups were often formed as offshoots of religious activity. In some churches, especially in the modern era, it became more common to integrate small group music, often with instrumental backing, into worship. In both cases, groups often remained amateur – as did soloists who emerged by similar routes – but it was largely from this source that the record industry in the United States laid the foundations of the commercial recording of religious group music, as a consequence of which it was open to some groups to become professionals.

Choir music can perhaps be broken down into the following categories:

(a) Choir music as a classical musical form. In Britain, Europe and North America, larger churches and cathedrals employ choir directors to train choirs to perform repertoire ranging from the classics to hymnody. In broadcasts and recordings, such music is enjoyed for its aesthetic attractions of purity of tone and richness of harmony rather than for any spiritual message its lyrics might contain.

(b) Choir music as a religious folk form. Certain types and traditions of Christian choir music attract secular audiences, such music's religious message acting as a kind of conveyor of folk religion to a largely secularized audience. Such choir music is as diverse as the male voice choirs of the Welsh chapels and the hand-clapping, tambourine-shaking exuberance of African-American choirs.

(c) Choir music as a denominational emblem. For decades, religious groups and denominations have channeled considerable resources into particular choirs to act as flag-bearers for a denomination or movement. The Mormon Tabernacle Choir, the Westminster Cathedral Choir or the Church of God in Christ Choir may share little stylistic or theological common ground, but each is a denominational emblem.

(d) Choir music as a musical training ground. From UK pop idol Gareth Gates (trained in Bradford Cathedral Choir) to literally thousands of R&B/soul singers who began their singing in black church choirs, possibly the most important function of contemporary Christian choirs is as a training institution where the basics and nuances of vocal technique are developed.

Congregational singing is a form of collective religious vocal music with relatively few connections to the commercial, professional world. In the Protestant denominations especially, it has a rich history that is marked by theological contestation and stylistic diversity and that has been influenced by – and has itself reflected – social change. Interventions in this history by professional and commercial concerns have been made mainly by individuals in the role of hymn writers, and by publishing companies (which might include church denominations themselves), for whom hymnals and books of choruses have often been very big sellers. Congregations themselves have tended to remain resolutely amateur performers. Familiarity with congregational singing decreased in many Western countries with the decline in church attendance that marked much of the twentieth century, but in musical terms group singing in congregations has remained what it has always been: an opportunity for both trained and untrained singers to collaborate in performances for which they themselves are also the audience.

Christianity and Popular Music

Within the diversifying strands of the Christian church, there were many competing attitudes and, indeed, theologies concerning the music of Christian worship. An unchanging tradition, in church practise and music, was held as tantamount to holiness, even though these musical traditions bore no resemblance to the Davidic Jewish musical origins of early Christianity. The Roman Catholic church endeavored to hold onto music forms unchanged since the twelfth century, and the mass in Latin remained a global cultural influence in many parts of the world. In Russia, the musical traditions of Orthodoxy remained fossilized in the solemn incantations of the priesthood. And in Europe, the new music of sixteenth- and seventeenth-century hymn writers quickly became a newer, Protestant tradition. This disconnection between the music of Christian worship and the music of the masses was from time to time challenged by various religious leaders. In the nineteenth century, General William Booth, founder of the Salvation Army, took the popular brass band music and popular melodies of the day, added evangelistic lyrics and, for a decade or two at least, reconnected church music to the mainstream. In Africa and Asia, churches began to emerge that coupled indigenous folk music with lyrics and messages plucked from the Bible. The connection between folk traditions and the Christian faith continued into the twentieth century. In the 1930s, the members of the Carter Family took their Appalachian harmonies and mixture of secular and gospel material to become seminal figures in the evolution of country music, while in the 1940s Austria's von Trapp Family (later to be immortalized in the film *The Sound of Music*) toured with a popular version of folk music and Christian faith.

North America

It was in the United States, though, that the Christian faith and popular music were to merge most thoroughly.

By the twentieth century, the Christian church, with its centuries-old traditions of congregational worship, was in a pivotal position to influence most of the major streams of popular music. Since the Reformation and the development of the hymn, European hymnody had been the dominant form of music for worship and one that was brought to the Americas by the early settlers. The religious movement known as the Great Awakening, which swept the colonies from the 1730s, popularized the works of English hymn writers such as Isaac Watts and John Wesley, and, by the nineteenth century, these hymns were being absorbed into the numerous cultural traditions of the United States.

By the late nineteenth century, two musical strands in particular were evident in the North American church, and both these strands were to have a huge influence on the emergent styles of twentieth-century popular music. The first was the church music of the white rural South. At the turn of the century, there was a rapid increase in the number of new religious songs published. Hymn writers like Fanny Crosby, Homer Rodeheaver and dozens more found their hymns sung, particularly in the new Pentecostal denominations. In the Southern states, publishers of these new religious songs developed a novel way of promoting them. Through a method known as 'shape note' singing, which obviated the need to read music, the skills of harmony singing could be taught. Special schools were set up in churches and school halls to teach 'shape note' singing, and these proved extraordinarily popular. The singing schools of the rural South were in turn publicized by singing groups, which often took the names of the songbooks or publishers they promoted. So, by the 1920s, groups like the Original Stamps Quartet were very popular, touring and performing on local radio. Their music, soon to be dubbed Southern gospel, was a synthesis of the barbershop harmony of nineteenth-century popular music and the hillbilly/country music which, by the 1930s, was being popularized by groups like the Carter Family – a trio that rose from the obscurity of Maces Springs, Virginia to establish what was to become a country music dynasty.

By the 1940s, numerous groups – including the Delmore Brothers, with their soft, bluesy sound, and the Louvin Brothers, with a harmony blend that was later a huge musical influence on the Everly Brothers – were beginning to enjoy enormous popularity in the Southern states. The Blackwood Brothers were the most popular Southern gospel group of all, but there were numerous other country/Southern gospel harmonizers whose 78s, mostly released on the groups' own 'custom' labels, and flamboyant onstage performances at All-Night Sings (multi-group concerts, often staged overnight in city sports stadia) gained them a large follow-ing – groups like the Statesmen Quartet (an influential group from Atlanta, featuring the lugubrious lead voice of Jake Hess), the Harmoneers (from Knoxville) and the Crusaders (from Birmingham), whose lead singer, Bobby Strickland, was much admired by a teenage Elvis Presley. It is a matter of record that Elvis used to listen to the Blackwood Brothers' daily live radio program on WMPS and was a regular at the monthly All-Night Sings at Memphis's Ellis Auditorium. Elvis in fact auditioned for the Songfellows, an offshoot of the Blackwood Brothers, but failed the audition because of his inability to sing harmony.

It was Elvis Presley who was to cause the jaunty har-monies of Southern gospel to be catapulted from regional folk tradition to internationally popular style. He often recorded with the Jordanaires, a Southern gospel group willing to sing secular as well as gospel mat-erial. The group's crisp backups became an integral part of Elvis's sound, and when, in 1957, Elvis began to make occasional gospel recordings, it was to Southern gospel that he often turned for style and material. Major labels began recording groups like the Blackwood Brothers, the Speers and the Statesmen Quartet and, by 1968, the style was so established that the Gospel Music Association (GMA) was formed in Nashville to promote the music and hold an annual awards ceremony. Southern gospel has continued to exist in dozens of touring groups and in its own radio programs, festivals and magazines, although, with its stylized clean-cut image, it may have seemed increasingly anachronistic. Yet, against all pre-dictions, Southern gospel has found a mass market through the unlikely vehicle of video. In the mid-1990s, one of the popular figures in Southern gospel, song-writer, group leader and entrepreneur Bill Gaither, began producing a series of in-concert videos in which he brought together most of the popular Southern gospel groups, such as the Cathedrals, the Statesmen Quartet and the Stamps Quartet under the name 'Homecoming Friends.' These videos have hugely expanded the South-ern gospel audience, finding a folk religion echo in the hearts of hundreds of thousands of ordinary North Americans. But it has been another form of Christian music that has taken religious music to an unprecen-ted level in terms of record sales.

Contemporary Christian Music

Contemporary Christian music (CCM) grew out of a late-1960s religious movement in California, in which tens of thousands of hippies turned away from drugs and free love to embrace a form of Christian fundamental-ism. This phenomenon, known as the Jesus Movement, spawned dozens of groups and soloists who took ele-

ments of the pop and rock music of the day and utilized them to sing overtly evangelistic songs. Soloists like Larry Norman and Randy Stonehill and groups like Second Chapter of Acts and Love Song were soon releas-ing albums onto the religious market and, once the net-work of Christian radio stations began in the 1970s to switch from spoken-word broadcasting to a predomin-antly Christian music output, a subculture developed that grew steadily over the next two decades.

CCM is less a musical genre than a niche market where evangelical Christians, alienated by the perceived immorality and worldliness of pop and rock culture, can enjoy pop, rock, rhythm and blues (R&B) and even dance music with lyrics that either directly evangelize or at least concur with a Christian world-view. Throughout the last two decades of the twentieth century, the CCM scene expanded to surprising dimensions. Pop gospel soloists like Amy Grant, Michael W. Smith and Kathy Troccoli all entered the US pop charts, as too did Chris-tian bands as diverse as hardcore rap band P.O.D., R&B gospel duo Mary Mary, pop rock team dc Talk and R&B gospel choir-cum-rap outfit God's Property. CCM also became an international phenomenon: as far back as 1964, the Joy Strings, a British Salvation Army beat group, enjoyed a pop hit; and, in the 1990s, Christian dance groups like the World Wide Message Tribe and dba were able to get nightclub exposure, while a Chris-tian pop rock team from Littlehampton in the United Kingdom, Delirious?, enjoyed a string of minor placings in Britain's pop charts.

African-American Gospel Music

If Delirious? and dc Talk represented white evangel-icalism's hope to be a voice for God against the godless hedonism of youth culture, it was the black church's premier artist, Kirk Franklin, who pushed the record sales of Christian music to previously unscaled heights. Kirk Franklin & the Family's platinum album of 1993 in many ways completed a full circle in terms of the devel-opment of religious music. The uninhibited worship of African-American congregations was among the first forms of folk art ever recorded. In fact, in the nineteenth century, the Fisk Jubilee Singers, from one of North America's first all-black universities in Nashville, developed what was to become an international audi-ence with their smooth, sedate renditions of Negro spir-ituals. The Jubilee choirs, with their decorous presenta-tion and sentimental material, were often more attuned to the European choral tradition than to the fiery exuberance of the African-American church. It was not until the 1930s, when ex-blues singer Thomas A. Dorsey founded the National Convention of Gospel Choirs and Choruses and began writing for choirs as well as for soloists, that black American choir music began to find its creative voice. However, it was in the 1960s when song-writer, singer and choir arranger James Cleveland took black choir music to the next level of popularity. Cleveland laid claim to the first million-selling gospel album with *Peace Be Still*, recorded with the Angelic Choir of Nutley. It was when Cleveland established the Gospel Music Workshop of America that the proliferation of top-quality black choirs across the United States was given a creative focus and, when jazz-tinged chord pro-gressions and increased instrumentation began to be added to the call-and-response fervor and key-climbing frenzy of the Pentecostal choir, a unique subgenre was effectively created. In 1969, the earthily cathartic sound of gospel choir music suddenly and unexpectedly found an international audience: 'Oh Happy Day' by the Edwin Hawkins Singers had begun as a 'custom' release origin-ally credited to the Northern California State Youth Choir; picked up by a San Francisco DJ, it became an international bestseller. Choir music was a relatively late tributary of black gospel to find a large audience.

World War II marked a watershed for gospel music and ushered in what music historians have called its 'golden age.' Between 1945 and 1965, it moved out of the clapboard church and the storefront meeting onto the US radio airwaves and into prestigious concert halls. In the process, gospel music ceased to be primarily con-cerned with congregational participation in which young and old, good singers and bad, worshiped God in music; instead, it became 'performance' music – an alternative means of entertainment for North America's black churchgoers, sung by professionals.

Early postwar gospel's main thrust came from dozens of all-male vocal groups singing in a style that, regardless of the size of the group or congregation, became known as 'quartet' singing. It featured lead singers who bor-rowed from the frenetic, barely controlled excitement of the 'hard' preachers of the prewar years, backed by har-monies as silkily smooth as the old 'jubilee' groups, though with a more inventive range of voices that often included high tenor falsettos. The quartet style had first emerged in the 1930s with seminal groups like the Famous Blue Jay Singers, the Golden Gate Quartet and the Kings of Harmony Quartette (who continued to record after 1943 as the Original Kings of Harmony). In the postwar years, these and hundreds more younger groups began to make records for the dozens of inde-pendent record companies that had sprung up in most US cities. These companies often exploited the groups they recorded by paying pitiful advances and seldom any royalties, but the exposure that their records were given on the burgeoning gospel radio programs gave

dozens of groups the opportunity to turn professional and tour.

Another means of exposure for gospel singing groups was provided by the denominational conventions that had been part and parcel of religious black America since the 1920s. These celebrations/'preach-ins' often used the services of the proliferating groups of professional gospel singers, nearly all of which sang a cappella. The vocal music that many of these touring professional groups produced has remained among the most inventive of any genre. There were such groups as the Dixie Hum-mingbirds, featuring the legendary hard voice of Ira Tucker, the Swan Silvertones, whose falsetto, Claude Jeter, produced one of the most soulful sounds ever heard in music, and the Spirit of Memphis Quartet from 1928, which included a triumvirate of superb lead singers – Wilber 'Little Axe' Broadnax, Silas Steele and Jethroe Bledsoe; there were quartets who could holler and scream with larynx-lacerating abandon, such as the Sensational Nightingales; and there were quartets like the Five Blind Boys of Mississippi (otherwise known as the Jackson Harmoneers), who were neither boys nor blind but who could scream a congregation into apo-plexy, and the Soul Stirrers who, in teenage Sam Cooke, had a lead voice of pristine, soulful purity. The flashily ecstatic music of groups like these and dozens more, such as the Pilgrim Travelers, the Harmonizing Four, the Five Blind Boys of Alabama and the Swanee Quintet, with lead singers ducking and weaving around a melody and wringing every note of emotion out of a song, was a seminal contribution that laid the foundations of the later secular soul music.

By the late 1940s, the male quartets' ghetto popularity was being challenged by female groups, who sang punchy three-part harmony and featured down-home versions of the old hymns and gospel tunes. Typical of these quartets were the Angelic Gospel Singers, and the Davis Sisters, who sang using jazz-tinged harmonies of dazzling intricacy. But the most popular female group on the gospel programs was the Ward Singers, who had an entrepreneurial genius in Clara Ward and a sensa-tional lead voice in Marion Williams.

Professionalization and Secularization

Throughout the decades, religious music coped sur-prisingly well with the demands of show business, larg-ely by allowing a degree of professionalism to coexist with the amateur principles of church-based singers and musicians. The nineteenth-century para-church minis-try of US evangelist Dwight L. Moody, for example, sub-sidized part of its activities by selling materials like the hugely popular hymnal *Sacred Songs and Solos*, largely featuring songs popularized by soloist Ira Sankey. With the Fisk Jubilee Singers touring the world with their versions of African-American spirituals, and Southern gospel's Vaughan Quartet, billed as North America's 'first professional gospel singing group,' touring the Southern states from 1910, the pattern was set. Music might be an integral part of Christian ministry, but alongside the musical offerings made to God by congregations large and small, urban and rural, black and white, churchgoers' demand for sanctified forms of entertainment and edification ensured opportunities for some of the most talented and determined singers to step out from the obscurity of local church worship and take to the road.

By the 1930s, there was a growing number of professional gospel soloists and groups, both black and white. Some of these made attempts to 'cross over' to mainstream entertainment – such as the appearances in nightclubs of Sister Rosetta Tharpe and the Golden Gate Quartet. But, by and large, gospel music was performed at churches and in auditoria to audiences of churchgoers. By the 1950s, greatly helped by the regular airplay of gospel music on Christian radio stations, the professional gospel circuit – both white Southern gospel All-Night Sings and black gospel multi-artist programs – kept hundreds of gospel vocalists on the road.

The rise of the professional gospel singer brought problems for the churches. Since professional gospel artists were unaccountable to their local church, the life styles of many of them did not meet Christian standards. Drunkenness, immorality (exacerbated by gospel groupies) and drug abuse were all part of both the Southern and the black gospel circuits of the 1950s. As well, many concerts were promoted by gospel DJs and entrepreneurs notorious for shortchanging road-weary artists, ensuring that many professionals made a meager living. These factors meant that, by the early 1960s, the most talented singers in the black churches were moving not into professional gospel, but into secular R&B/soul music.

By then, gospel was being exploited by a secular record industry that wanted the passion and soul of black church music but without the encumbrance of lyrics about God. But while gospel's offspring, soul, had attracted away from the black church many of its finest singers, by the 1970s the corner had been turned. A pioneering gospel artist, Andraé Crouch, formed the Disciples and began grafting the rhythms of the 'Motown sound,' together with those of the group Earth, Wind & Fire, onto songs about Jesus. Although this shocked conservative elements within the church, the Disciples' albums sold well and found a substantial following both in the black church and among white evangelicals.

By the 1980s, 'crossover' did not necessarily mean moving from R&B to gospel. The Winans, Tramaine Hawkins (originally one of the Edwin Hawkins Singers) and the Clark Sisters were all gospel artists who had an impact on R&B with R&B-style songs about God. By the 1990s, gospel rap had developed, and even on a 'traditional' choir album one was likely to hear funk bass lines, horn sections and many of the production values of secular R&B. The wheel had clearly turned full circle.

Africa

Ever since European missionaries brought the Christian faith to the African subcontinent, African variants of gospel music have flowed from the indigenous churches. But it took the intervention in 1986 of a Western pop star to take the Zulu gospel variant *iscathamiya* and catapult it unexpectedly into mainstream popularity. The 10-member choir Ladysmith Black Mambazo met US singer-songwriter Paul Simon in a Durban recording studio, and the choir played a major part in Simon's synthesis of Western and African musical styles on his multimillion-selling *Graceland* album. The choir was instantly elevated to the status of African musical ambassadors, touring the world's concert halls and recording with such diverse artists as Stevie Wonder, Dolly Parton and George Clinton. It is Ladysmith Black Mambazo's early a cappella albums, recorded for Gallo Records from 1970, that best demonstrate the group's polyrhythmic, Zulu harmonies coupled with vivid declarations of Christian faith. In recent years, the group, still led by Joseph Shabalala, has become secularized, singing for Disney film soundtracks, television's *Sesame Street* and off-Broadway musicals. The 1997 album *Heavenly* and *The Star and the Wiseman*, a compilation, both sold a million copies. A choir of women singers from Natal, the Women of Mambazo, was formed in 2000 and was led by Nellie Shabalala, wife of Joseph Shabalala.

Bibliography

Broughton, Viv. 1996. *Too Close to Heaven: The Illustrated History of Gospel Music*. London: Midnight Books.

Cummings, Tony. 1975. *The Sound of Philadelphia*. London: Methuen.

Gaither, Bill, with Jenkins, Jerry. 1997. *Homecoming: The Story of Southern Gospel Music Through the Eyes of Its Best-Loved Performers*. Grand Rapids, MI: Zondervan.

Hayes, Cedric J., and Laughton, Robert. 1992–93. *Gospel Records, 1943–1969: A Black Music Discography*. London: Record Information Services.

Heilbut, Anthony. 1971. *The Gospel Sound: Good News and Bad Times*. New York: Simon and Schuster.

Sankey, Ira D. 1874. *Sacred Songs and Solos*. London: Morgan & Scott.

Thompson, John J. 2000. *Raised by Wolves: The Story of Christian Rock & Roll*. Toronto: ECW Press.

Discographical References

Cleveland, James, and the Angelic Choir of Nutley. *Peace Be Still*. Savoy 14076. *1962*: USA.

Edwin Hawkins Singers, The. 'Oh Happy Day.' *Oh Happy Day*. Pair 3301. *1969*: USA.

Franklin, Kirk, & the Family. *Kirk Franklin & the Family*. Sparrow G2-72119. *1993*: USA.

Joy Strings, The. 'It's an Open Secret.' Regal-Zonophone RZ 501. *1964*: UK.

Ladysmith Black Mambazo. *Heavenly*. Shanachie 64098. *1997*: USA.

Ladysmith Black Mambazo. *The Star and the Wiseman*. Wrasse Records 5652982. *1998*: UK.

Simon, Paul. *Graceland*. Warner Brothers 25447. *1986*: USA.

Filmography

The Sound of Music, dir. Robert Wise. 1965. USA. 174 mins. Musical. Original music by Oscar Hammerstein II, Irwin Kostal, Richard Rodgers.

TONY CUMMINGS

Rock Band

A rock band is a small ensemble of normally four to six musicians. It has a lineup that derives from the do-it-yourself aesthetics of the British 'Mersey sound' of the late 1950s and early 1960s. The standard lineup of that time was well suited to the needs of amateurs: lead guitar, rhythm guitar, bass guitar, drums and vocals. This lineup was made famous by British bands such as the early Beatles, the Rolling Stones, the Who, the Yardbirds, the Kinks and the Searchers. It became the core of the rock band, and has continued to constitute a kind of standard for hard and heavy metal bands such as Van Halen, AC/DC and Metallica that adhere to the roots of the rock aesthetic.

However, even in the early days the standard lineup of three guitars and drums was expanding. Keyboards were added: normally, a small portable electric organ such as the Vox Continental, an instrument that required much more musical training than the ubiquitous guitar, but that allowed for greater musical versatility. John Mayall's Bluesbreakers and Eric Burdon's Animals were among the first bands that used it in the early 1960s. Producer George Martin also played a Vox organ on early Beatles recordings.

As the musical center of gravity shifted back to the United States in the mid-1960s, the term 'rock band' was used to refer to all those groups that performed guitar-based rock 'n' roll and R&B-derived music. The core of the lineup remained the same. However, it was complemented by a broad variety of instruments. Different stylistical influences played a hand in this. While folk-rock bands added acoustic instruments or replaced the lead or rhythm guitar with an acoustic guitar (the Byrds; Fairport Convention), jazz-influenced bands expanded their lineups to include different kinds of wind instruments (Blood, Sweat and Tears; Chicago). Progressive rock bands relied heavily on keyboards (Nice; Emerson, Lake and Palmer). In addition, instruments not normally associated with rock, such as the flute (Jethro Tull), the violin (Flock; the Mahavishnu Orchestra) and the cello (the Electric Light Orchestra), found their way into the rock band. Also, a broad range of percussion instruments was added to the standard drumset.

The keyboard sections of rock bands were expanded after 1965 with the arrival of the Mellotron. The cheaper and lighter versions of the instrument built in the 1970s made a particular impact. This instrument could substitute for many other, usually stringed, instruments by virtue of its internal sound library. One of the first rock bands to integrate the Mellotron into its lineup was the British band King Crimson. Subsequently, synthesizers and sequencers became increasingly important, as these devices allowed for a more or less unlimited generation and shaping of sounds. Rock bands like Can, Tangerine Dream and Kraftwerk were built around them. During the 1970s, electronic instruments became a standard feature in the lineup of many rock bands.

However, the rock band was not just a specific kind of lineup. During the 1960s, it became the symbolic embodiment of the vision of a free and self-determined creative life within a collective context driven by values of solidarity, equality and mutual respect. Although this vision was by and large a rather nostalgic and romantic ideology, many rock bands took it quite seriously and at least tried to synthesize art and life, music and politics within the social unit of the band. In the late 1960s, the collective experience of a shared life and work was the driving force behind the music of many bands, even if this ideal clashed sooner rather than later with the hard realities of the music business.

Since the era of punk and new wave, the term 'rock band' has been used again in a more limited way to refer to a guitar-based lineup, even if the lineup includes additional instruments. This follows an overall logic in which rock came to be a generic term alongside others, instead of being regarded as a musical and cultural symbol of a generation of young people.

Bibliography

Clawson, Mary Ann. 1999. 'Masculinity and Skill Acquisition in the Adolescent Rock Band.' *Popular Music* 18(1): 99–114.

PETER WICKE

Salon Orchestra

The salon orchestra was a nineteenth-century instrumental ensemble that was an important provider of public musical entertainment.

The salon orchestra had three standard lineups that developed in the metropolitan cultures of Paris, Vienna and Berlin. These lineups were based on the piano trio (piano, violin and cello) and, less often, the string quartet. The leader was normally the first violinist, who also performed the principal melodic part. The second violin or viola played accompanying chords, while the cello added melodic embellishments and, together with the double bass, provided a bass line that anchored the harmonies. The piano alternated between accompanying and solo parts, while the percussion provided a rhythmic foundation as well as sound effects. Various wind instruments added to the melodic and harmonic textures of the music. In 1868, the Austrian conductor Margold introduced the harmonium into his orchestra. This orchestra was well known throughout Europe. The harmonium soon became indispensable as a 'filler' instrument, capable of replacing missing instruments in the lineup.

The Vienna lineup consisted of first violin, second violin, cello or double bass, and sometimes flute, piano and percussion. The somewhat larger Paris lineup consisted of first violin, second violin, cello, double bass, piano, percussion and sometimes flute, clarinet, trumpet or cornet and trombone. The most common and widespread lineup was the Berlin lineup: first and second violin, viola, cello, double bass and sometimes flute, clarinet, cornet, trombone, piano or harmonium and percussion. This lineup emerged at the end of the nineteenth century. At this time, about 200 ensembles were registered in Germany alone. These ensembles could draw from about 20,000 professional musicians active in this kind of music.

Salon orchestras provided the market for a specialized sector of the music publishing business. Their repertoire consisted mainly of classical compositions and specially arranged operatic excerpts, potpourris (mixtures of popular melodies) and so-called 'light music' – popular melodies in 'elevated,' concert-like arrangements. Good ensembles had up to a thousand *Concert-* and *Salon-Piécen* in their repertoire for the extremely popular 'wish concerts' – concerts where the audience could request the pieces to be played.

Unlike the ballroom orchestra, the salon orchestra performed in concert-like settings. Principal venues were coffeehouses and hotel lobbies, as well as seaside promenades, music pavilions in public parks and gardens and, until the emergence of the film soundtrack, early cinemas showing silent movies. With the emergence of dance cafés and film soundtracks, the salon orchestras – with a few exceptions – disappeared.

The term 'salon orchestra' has continued to be used into the twenty-first century. However, the term normally refers to an ensemble using electronic instruments playing an old-fashioned repertoire that rarely has anything in common with the repertoires performed by the nineteenth-century ensembles. Some ensembles similar to those of the nineteenth century have persisted, but their repertoires are somewhat wider in range and more eclectic than those of the nineteenth-century ensembles.

Bibliography

Keldany-Mohr, Irmgard. 1977. *Unterhaltungsmusik als soziokulturelles Phänomen des 19. Jahrhunderts: Untersuchung über den Einfluß der musikalischen Öffentlichkeit auf die Herausbildung eines neuen Musiktypes* [Entertainment Music as a Sociocultural Phenomenon: Studies About the Influence of Musical Publicity on the Emergence of a New Type of Music]. Regensburg: Bosse.

Spohr, Mathias, ed. 1999. *Geschichte und Medien der 'gehobenen Unterhaltungsmusik'* [History and Media of 'Elevated Entertainment Music']. Zürich: Chronos.

Discography

Caféhaus- u. Salonorchester der 30er und 40er Jahre. EMI Electrola 1C 134 2601263. *1982*: Germany.

PETER WICKE

Second Line

The term 'second line' has two connected meanings, both specific to African-American culture in New Orleans. The first, and major, use refers to the group of dancers who follow the band at street parades, sometimes in elaborate dress and typically adding their own rhythms on bottles and pans and with bodily percussion. The second, more metaphorical use denotes participatory, interactive performance-centered activity which the African-American community in the city uses to distinguish and define itself.

The term first appeared in print in the late 1930s (Ramsey and Smith 1939, 27), but its colloquial usage was probably current by 1900. Firsthand accounts of the second line from the earliest generation of jazz musicians to emerge from New Orleans vary in detail. Sidney Bechet emphasized the participation of children, while 'Jelly Roll' Morton recalled the second line as heading the parade (Bechet 1960; Lomax 1950). Both, however, also remembered the second line as potentially bringing participants into conflict with authority. Bechet recalled the unpredictability of the police, and Morton described the second line as offering a kind of protection, complete with 'all forms of ammunition ready to fight the foe' (Bechet 1960, 61–62; Lomax 1950, 15). One observation shared by many accounts, from different points in time, is that those who make up the second line are not members of the group immediately responsible for the particular event, but are integral to it. They form a participating audience whose support for and intercommunication with the main group (including the musicians, whose choice of rhythms they influence) are crucial factors.

Second lines are a key part of three particular types of event: parades organized by social aid and pleasure clubs; parades featuring Mardi Gras Indian 'gangs'; and funerals (sometimes themselves called 'second lines').

The history of New Orleans benevolent societies dates from the end of the eighteenth century. By the late 1860s, they had expanded from social aid to sport and leisure clubs and had taken on an important role in community life, becoming major suppliers of entertainment, including street parades, for which they hired brass bands. Some parades became daylong events. It was in this context that public, improvisational second line dancing in response to a marching band – from high-stepping to shuffling and strutting – appears to have become established as a regular community activity; and here, too, that a vital dance culture developed in which the ground was laid for the centrality of the 'dance impulse' (Schafer 1977, 43) in early New Orleans jazz. (The importance of the second line to jazz was acknowledged by the New Orleans Jazz Club in 1949 when it named its newly launched journal *The Second Line*.) By the late twentieth century, all social aid and pleasure club parades had become regulated by city ordinances, a process that included setting and monitoring the route. At the same time, the city government increasingly noted the benefits to tourism that accrued from encouraging and facilitating club parades, and the second line became a key element in the attraction. Although aware of the implications of both developments, the clubs (still important in the social life of the city) continued to plan and hold elaborate parades as community events, and second line dancing continued to provide the opportunity for a combination of personal creativity and social support.

In contrast to the clubs, the Mardi Gras (or black) Indians 'refuse to register their activities . . . or to subjugate themselves to the prevailing order, which they consider to be largely racist and hostile to their traditional culture' (Smith 1994, 45). Their parading, before and during Mardi Gras, typically uses the back streets of the working-class districts – 'where they come and go as they please' (Smith 1994, 48) – and involves second line dancing in the form of support for the individual 'tribes.' Although the history of the Indians is obscure (the oldest surviving tribe can date its foundation to 1885), some historians have seen their second line parades as supporting evidence that the Indians are urban descendants of the maroons, escaped slaves who formed renegade communities and their own trading networks and who,

over many years, 'melted' into areas of the city that were remote from the authorities' control (Smith 1994, 47).

Despite the apparent contrast in the regulatory status of the parades of the Mardi Gras Indians and those of the social aid and pleasure clubs, the two often involve many of the same people. The nature of second line participation is also basically the same, suggesting a fundamental, unifying role in African-American social life – a role that Smith, one of few non-African-American commentators to have observed Mardi Gras rituals firsthand, sees both as serving 'to cleanse and renew the spirit of the community' and as acting as a conduit for information (Smith 1994, 49).

The role of the second line at a funeral is specifically to express the community's support and empathy both in mournful respect – while the band plays a dirge, the second liners dance slowly, 'dancing and dipping to the beat, their feet seldom leaving the pavement' (Atkinson 1997, 148) – and in celebration, which typically begins with marching and dancing to the up-tempo tune 'Didn't He Ramble.'

The second line has been interpreted as offering important evidence of African survivals in African-American culture. Floyd, for example, sees the second line as connected particularly to the meanings, uses and movements of the African ring shout, which becomes straightened out ('because of the necessity of the participants to move to a remote destination') in its new context (Floyd 1995, 83). Equally important to contemporary commentators, especially within New Orleans itself, has been the continuing role of second line in contemporary cultural practise, where it has contributed in a major way to the idea of a 'performance-drenched city' (Roach, quoted in Atkinson 1997, 141) with its own distinct identity.

Bibliography

Atkinson, Connie Zeanah. 1997. *Musicmaking in New Orleans: A Reappraisal.* Unpublished Ph.D. thesis, University of Liverpool.

Bechet, Sidney. 1960. *Treat It Gentle: An Autobiography.* London: Cassell.

Floyd, Samuel A. 1995. *The Power of Black Music: Interpreting Its History from Africa to the United States.* New York: Oxford University Press.

Lomax, Alan. 1950. *Mr. Jelly Roll: The Fortunes of Jelly Roll Morton, New Orleans Creole and 'Inventor of Jazz.'* New York: Duell, Sloan & Pierce.

Malone, Jacqui. 1996. *Steppin' on the Blues: The Visible Rhythms of African American Dance.* Urbana, IL: University of Illinois Press.

Ramsey, Frederic, and Smith, Charles Edward, eds. 1939. *Jazzmen.* New York: Harcourt Brace.

Schafer, William J. 1977. *Brass Bands and New Orleans Jazz*. Baton Rouge, LA: Louisiana State University Press.

The Second Line. 1949–. New Orleans, LA: New Orleans Jazz Club.

Smith, Michael P. 1994. 'Behind the Lines: The Black Mardi Gras Indians and the New Orleans Second Line.' *Black Music Research Journal* 14(1): 43–73.

Discographical Reference

New Orleans All-Star Marching Band, The. 'Didn't He Ramble.' *New Orleans Parade*. Dixieland Jubilee DJ-518. *1972*: USA.

DAVID HORN

Silent Movie Orchestra

A silent movie orchestra provided non-recorded musical prologues and accompaniment for a cinematic image. It consisted of anything from a single instrument to an 80-piece orchestra, and could include various devices to provide wind, thunder, hoofbeats or other effects.

The provision of musical accompaniment to silent film preceded the use of cinema cameras to record the image. When Emile Reynaud's hand-drawn animated films were projected at the Musée Grevin in Paris in 1892, they were accompanied by original piano music. Although often attributed to the need to cover up the sound of the projection machinery, the use of music to accompany silent motion pictures drew on traditions of combining music and visual performance in operetta, music-hall productions, song slides and other nineteenth-century popular entertainments.

Early motion pictures were shown in a variety of venues, and their musical accompaniment depended on the place where they were presented. This ranged from a single instrument in modest storefront theaters to small orchestras in established vaudeville houses. Given that musical accompaniment for each film had to be adapted to such widely divergent circumstances, there was little standardization initially. Most early accompaniment was improvised locally, drawing on the practise of using 'melos' – snippets of mood music to accompany the action in stage melodramas. Soon afterward, musical accompaniments became slightly more standardized as film companies began to supplement film prints with 'cue sheets,' which suggested particular types of music to reinforce the narrative mood of each scene. Appropriate musical passages that portrayed these moods were published in arrangements for piano, organ or orchestra.

By the middle of the second decade of the twentieth century, even greater standardization of accompaniment had been instituted, most notably through the use of Joseph Carl Breil's scores for *The Birth of a Nation* (1915) and *Intolerance* (1916), which were distributed in ver-

sions for piano and orchestra. By the mid-1920s, film premières in large metropolitan theaters had full orchestra scores especially prepared by in-house theater conductors/composers/arrangers. Subsequently, the scores were published and distributed to theaters along with the films by film studios. The leading creators of these scores, such as Dr. Hugo Riesenfeld of New York's Strand Theater or Erno Rapee of the UFA Palast in Berlin and the Roxy in New York, were considered major stars of the period, and their orchestras were as much of an entertainment attraction as the films themselves. Indeed, much of the impetus behind the conversion to sound film was less a matter of replacing silent movie orchestras than an attempt to give a theatergoer anywhere the same sonic experience of orchestral accompaniments and musical prologues as that previously available only in the largest theaters.

Bibliography

Berg, Charles Merrell. 1976. *An Investigation of the Motives for and Realization of Music to Accompany the American Silent Film, 1896–1927*. New York: Arno Press.

Marks, Martin Miller. 1997. *Music and the Silent Film: Contexts and Case Studies, 1895–1924*. New York: Oxford University Press.

Prendergast, Roy M. 1992. *Film Music – A Neglected Art: A Critical Study of Music in Films*. 2nd ed. New York: W.W. Norton.

Filmography

The Birth of a Nation, dir. D.W. Griffith. 1915. USA. 165 mins. Historical Epic. Original music by Joseph Carl Breil, D.W. Griffith.

Intolerance, dir. D.W. Griffith. 1916. USA. 163 mins. Historical Epic. Original music by Joseph Carl Breil, Carl Davis, D.W. Griffith.

MARK LANGER

Singing Families

A singing family is a troupe of professional or semiprofessional musical entertainers whose members are drawn uniquely or predominantly from the same family. Their repertoire is typically dominated by group-based vocal numbers. As a precise descriptor, the term is used in reference to those touring nineteenth-century ensembles that were described at the time as 'singing families' and that performed in a particular style, but it may also be used in a more generic sense to include a range of twentieth-century performing groups with a family base.

The first singing family to become widely known came from the Swiss Tyrol. The Family Rainer, four brothers and a sister from a cattle-farming family in the Ziller valley, undertook several tours of Europe between 1824 and the end of the decade. By the time they arrived in

London in 1827, their considerable reputations had preceded them. Their artistic and financial success, in Britain as elsewhere in Europe, was due not so much to their identity as a family as to their repertoire of Alpine music, their appearance and (especially) their manner of performance. Composer-pianist Ignaz Moscheles remarked that the Rainers' 'freedom from affectation, the pure delivery of their characteristic songs, their dress – the genuine Tyrolean costume – all these together proved very attractive and delightful to a constantly increasing crowd of hearers' (quoted in Nathan 1946, 68–69). Yodeling (*jodeln*) was a specialty.

From 1839 to 1842, a differently constituted Rainer Family (two women and two men, probably not all blood family members) toured the United States and, after an indifferent start, achieved huge success. Once again, what the audiences perceived as a simple freshness in their style – a contrast to the dominant operatic bel canto – was a key element. Added to this was a recognition, more marked in the United States than it had been in Europe, of the 'attainability of fine results by untutored singers [and] the satisfaction in doing ensemble work in which each voice counts no less and no more than the rest' (Nathan 1946, 77). The family environment stood as the perfect context within which these results might be achieved – the family hearth was still the main place where most people experienced music – and, as a consequence, the family aspect of the singing family now became centrally important, a development that was aided by the fact that the family was beginning to be used also as a symbol of cohesion, continuity and integrity in a changing world.

The Rainers spawned a large number of US imitators (Nathan lists 17 by way of example), one of which, the Hutchinson Family from New Hampshire, was to become the singing family par excellence. Three brothers and a sister (out of 13 Hutchinson siblings) formed the original Hutchinson Family in 1842; with many changes of personnel, the group continued as professional touring performers into the 1890s. From featuring a considerable number of 'Alpine' songs in their early career, the members of the group established a mixed repertoire that drew on many sources, European and North American, and combined the comic, the sentimental and the serious. This approach, coupled with the easygoing rapport that the Hutchinsons established with their audiences and the skill and vitality with which they promoted themselves, enabled the singing family tradition as they exemplified it to help set the pattern for much popular entertainment – although one particularly noteworthy feature of their repertoire, songs advocating radical causes (most famously, abolitionism), had

to wait some time to reemerge in a twentieth-century guise.

Early press reviews of the Hutchinsons spoke of their family performance style in terms such as 'full of mountain melody' (Cockrell 1989, 140), sustaining the connection between the Rainers' Alpine home and the topography of the Hutchinsons' New Hampshire. What particularly fascinated the audiences on the Hutchinsons' tours of the United States and Europe was 'naturalness' of tone and clarity of intonation. This was the result of much hard work in the home and in the church-based singing schools (rather than a consequence of the effect of rarified air on voice production); recognizing this, many in their audiences easily made a connection between family background as a musical resource on which the Hutchinsons drew extensively and the social ideal expressed in their most characteristic sound, a close vocal blend that did not overshadow individuality.

Another significant achievement of singing families was that, within their context, a space was created for women to be professional performers in popular entertainment without having to subscribe to or follow the expectations of the theater. To this, given the Victorian ideal of womanhood, the tendency of singing families to espouse good causes made a useful contribution.

Although the vogue for this type of singing family effectively died with the nineteenth century within Anglo-American culture, it remained as a constituent part of musical practise in parts of Europe. In another part of the Tyrol, in the 1930s, the Trapp family (later immortalized in Rodgers' and Hammerstein's musical *The Sound of Music*) followed a similar career to that of the Rainers over a century earlier, turning domestic music-making *en famille* into a professional touring group which came to the United States in the late 1930s and enjoyed considerable success there. The Trapps' decision to visit the United States was not a commercial one, however, but was made in response to political changes in Austria under the Third Reich. Their repertoire, too, was somewhat different, being centered more around German compositional classics – although *jodeln* remained an option.

Strong residual effects of the singing family tradition continued to influence US popular music in the twentieth century. They can be seen both in musical idioms that have a close connection to traditional, especially rural or semirural, culture and within mainstream urban popular music. Recorded country music from the late 1920s to the 1930s in particular featured numerous groups with a family base. The Carter Family became the most celebrated, its identity as a family contributing significantly to its perceived role as an upholder of traditional values and virtues in the face of fundamental social change affecting the South. In terms of performance style, a liking for close harmonizing among family members (especially as practised by brothers such as Bill and Earl Bolick, the Blue Sky Boys, and later by the Everly Brothers) suggests the possibility of some continuity with earlier singing families. This particular link was not confined to country music, however. Coincidentally or otherwise (and without the possible role of the barbershop tradition being overlooked), close harmony also became a trademark of groups of sisters fronting 1930s jazz and dance bands, such as the trios of the Boswell Sisters and the Andrews Sisters. Another legacy of nineteenth-century singing families, the ideology of naturalness, adhered to the Andrews Sisters in particular, but in a way that the nineteenth century could not have anticipated: when they appeared in movies, the sisters invariably played themselves.

African-American music in this period – both its performers and its promoters – tended to pay less heed to the concept of the performing family ensemble either as a formative idea or as a marketing device, although one or two successful ensembles, such as the Mississippi Sheiks, had a prominent family base. However, it is notable that, in the late 1930s and the 1940s, the first African-American vocal group to achieve commercial success with a non-African-American audience, the Mills Brothers, did so as a family-based group. The three brothers, too, based their style on close harmony. All-male rhythm and blues vocal groups of the 1940s and 1950s, specialists in vocal colorings and interplay, again tended to avoid or underplay family identities, even when, as with the Flamingos, family members were involved and there was a history of family music-making. When, therefore, Motown marketed the Jackson 5 in the late 1960s as a family group, the company was in one sense running counter to the prevailing practise among African-American vocal ensembles. But, following Motown's promotion, what attracted public attention to the Jackson 5 was not family alone, but the mixture of family closeness – and its implications for musical performance in an African-American style – and teenage energy and confidence, a hitherto unexplored combination. It cannot have harmed Motown's approach that its own reputation for schooling its performers fitted well with the enduring image of the institution – the family – which had been responsible for that for generations. A decade or so later, Sly and the Family Stone in turn employed the concept of the performing family ensemble quite differently, using the idea of an extended family as a metaphor (there were no members of the same family in the group) for a commonality of purpose and ideals.

The persistence into the rock era of family-learned vocal harmonizing – and its continuing transformation – is evident in the music of the Beach Boys, although the Wilson family's more dysfunctional features, emanating especially from the brothers' father Murray, illustrate a decline in the ability of the singing family to evoke ideals of domestic harmony. But, if earlier associated ideologies of the family have waned, the idea of the family as a special laboratory of informal musical education and a symbol of a particular, even unique, form of togetherness has continued to have resonance. A good example of this is provided by the 1990s Irish band the Corrs.

Bibliography

Cockrell, Dale, ed. 1989. *Excelsior: The Journals of the Hutchinson Family, 1842–1846*. Stuyvesant, NY: Pendragon Press.

Gaines, Steven. 1986. *Heroes and Villains: The True Story of the Beach Boys*. New York: New American Library.

Nathan, Hans. 1946. 'The Tyrolese Family Rainer, and the Vogue of Singing Mountain-Troupes in Europe and America.' *Musical Quarterly* 32: 63–79.

Trapp, Maria Augusta. 1953. *The Trapp Family Singers*. London: Geoffrey Bles.

Discography

Andrews Sisters, The. *Greatest Hits: The 60th Anniversary Collection*. MCA 11727. *1998*: USA.

Beach Boys, The. *The Absolute Best*. 2 vols. Capitol C2-96795-6. *1991*: USA.

Blue Sky Boys, The. *Blue Sky Boys on Radio*. 4 vols. Copper Creek 120-121, 145-146. *1996–97*: USA.

Boswell Sisters, The. *1930–1936*. L'art Vocal 13. *1995*: USA.

Carter Family, The. *Best of the Best of the Original Carter Family*. Koch 1478. *1998*: USA.

Corrs, The. *Forgiven, Not Forgotten*. Atlantic 92612. *1996*: USA.

Everly Brothers, The. *Cadence Classics: Their 20 Greatest Hits*. Rhino R2-05258. *1986*: USA.

Flamingos, The. *The Doo Bop She Bop: The Best of the Flamingos*. Rhino R2-70967. *1990*: USA.

Jackson 5, The. *Soulsation*. 4 vols. Motown 530-489-2. *1995*: USA.

Mills Brothers, The. *The Mills Brothers, 1931–1940*. 4 vols. Giants of Jazz 53086, 53273/6/9. *1998*: USA.

Mississippi Sheiks, The. *Mississippi Sheiks Complete Recorded Works*. 4 vols. Document DOCD 5083-5084. *1991*: Austria.

Original Trapp Family Singers, The. *The Original Trapp Family Singers*. BMG/RCA-Victor 63205. *1998*: USA.

Trapp Family Singers, The. *Everywhere Christmas*. Harrison Digital Productions HDP-310. *1990*: USA.

Trapp Family Singers, The. *Folk Music of Many Lands*. Harrison Digital Productions HDP-311. *1994*: USA.

Trapp Family Singers, The. *Sacred and Early Music*. Harrison Digital Productions HDP-312. *1995*: USA.

Filmography

The Sound of Music, dir. Robert Wise. 1965. USA. 174 mins. Musical Romance. Original music by Irwin Kostal, Richard Rodgers.

DAVID HORN

Society Orchestra

The idea of 'high society' employing musicians to play for dancing is an old one. The concept of a 'society orchestra,' formed under patronage specifically to fulfill the recreational requirements of the top echelon of wealthy households, first appeared in the United States in the latter years of the nineteenth century (Blesh 1958). It came into its own for a relatively short period between 1910 and 1930, and the term was particularly associated with orchestras that specialized in providing music for the so-called 'Four Hundred': the exclusive 400 families of New York City and the US east coast.

The first orchestra to give itself the name 'society orchestra' was formed by African-American orchestra leader James Reese Europe in 1913. Europe created his society orchestra as a specialist ensemble from the members of the Clef Club, an organization that he himself had founded to promote professional opportunities for African-American musicians. The orchestra was for hire for large-scale high-society events up and down the east coast (Badger 1995, 85). At one such occasion, Europe met the dancers Irene and Vernon Castle, who were often hired to give dance performances in society homes. The encounter led to the formation of a highly influential partnership, in which Europe became the Castles' musical director and played a key role in their popularization of new dances for a wider public.

Following Europe's death in 1919, his place in society was taken by Charles Luckyeth Roberts, whose 'dinner-jacketed orchestra played for the Astors, the Warburtons, the Wanamakers, the Vanderbilts, and the Goulds at Newport, Nantucket, and Narragansett, on Fifth Avenue and in Palm Beach' (Blesh and Janis 1971, 200). Roberts was the first African-American musician to play regularly at the Everglades Club at Palm Beach, and he became a favorite of the then Prince of Wales (Blesh and Janis 1971, 202). In imitation of the US scene, London set up a Four Hundred Club.

Bibliography

Badger, Reid. 1995. *A Life in Ragtime: A Biography of James Reese Europe*. New York: Oxford University Press.

Blesh, Rudi. 1958. *Shining Trumpets: A History of Jazz*. Rev. ed. New York: Knopf.

Blesh, Rudi, and Janis, Harriet. 1971. *They All Played Ragtime*. 4th ed. New York: Oak Publications.

DAVID HORN

Spasm Band

Groups of children who played improvised instruments on the street, particularly in New Orleans in the 1920s and 1930s, have frequently been referred to by jazz writers as 'spasm bands.' The term was apparently derived from the name of the best known of such groups, the Razzy Dazzy Spasm Band, a group of white children assembled in New Orleans by Emil 'Stalebread' Lacoume, who was then aged 12. Lacoume played zither at the time, and was known to play guitar, piano and bass later on. Other members of the band were Willie 'Cajun' Bussey (harmonica); 'Chinee' (homemade half-barrel bass); Emil 'Whisky' Benrod (whistle and kazoo); and percussionist Charley Stein (kettle, rattle and cowbell). The only extant photograph of the band shows a second zither player and a homemade soapbox banjo, probably played by 'Warm Gravy.' The celebrated actress Sarah Bernhardt is reported to have given the members of the Razzy Dazzy Spasm Band gratuities when they performed before her in 1900. Lacoume was, apparently, the only member of the band to become a career musician. Though blind, he played at resorts on Lake Pontchartrain and with the Halfway House Orchestra led by Abbie Brunis. Other groups, assembled by African-American children, were heard and photographed, but the names of the performers were not noted and there is no evidence that they called themselves 'spasm bands.' Such groups have been confused with the 'second line,' but this term refers to the followers of parade bands.

Bibliography

Huber, Leonard V.N. 1971. *New Orleans: A Pictorial History from Earliest Times to the Present Day*. New York: Crown Publishers.

Rose, Al, and Souchon, Edmond. 1967. *New Orleans Family Album*. Baton Rouge, LA: Louisiana State University Press.

PAUL OLIVER

Steel Band

A steel band is an ensemble comprising steel drums or pans, instruments generally fabricated from oil or chemical barrels. Several different types of pans are included, each with its own register of notes. A lead or tenor pan is made from one barrel, while a variety of other pans consist of sets of two or more barrels. Each set is played by one musician. The total range of a typical steel band extends from around A^2 to f^2. Generally, the pans in a steel band are accompanied by a trap set and various Caribbean percussion instruments. Steel bands vary greatly in size. In Trinidad, the birthplace of pans, bands range from under 10 to as many as 100 players. In other parts of the world, most bands have fewer than 25 members, although some are considerably larger.

The global dissemination of the steel band over the latter half of the twentieth century was one of the more remarkable aspects of this musical phenomenon. What began as a form of grass-roots carnival expression in Trinidad became a type of musical ensemble that can be found in community, school and entertainment settings in countries around the world. Although there are some professional steel bands, the vast majority consist of amateur musicians. A democratic, community-based approach to music-making is, in fact, a major aspect of the steel band's appeal to both performers and audiences.

History

The immediate precursor of the steel band in Trinidad was the *tamboo bamboo* ('bamboo drum') band, in which musicians played different-size pieces of bamboo that were struck together or stamped on the ground during pre-Lenten carnival street processions. During the 1930s, *tamboo bamboo* men began beating on metal containers (such as paint and trash cans), automobile parts and other metal objects. This metallic percussion proved to be louder and more durable than bamboo; around 1940, carnival bands began to discard their bamboo altogether. During this period, it was discovered that the bottoms of metal containers could be pounded into various shapes to produce musical tones when struck with sticks. Performance on different types of early pans was modeled on the roles of the diverse instruments of the *tamboo bamboo* band, although there was also influence from military marching bands, African-derived skin drums and, perhaps, East Indian-derived *tassa* drum ensembles. The earliest steel bands essentially provided a polyrhythmic background for the singing of carnival revelers.

The creators of the steel band were primarily young African-Trinidadian men from working- or lower-class backgrounds. Steel bands were based in various urban neighborhoods and villages, and intense rivalries ensued as panmen developed their new instruments. After World War II, panmen often named their bands after movies, such as *Casablanca, Destination Tokyo, The Cross of Lorraine* and *The Desperadoes*. During carnival, the band members paraded the streets, often masquerading as sailors, and sometimes engaged in violent clashes. Panmen and their music were widely condemned by the

middle and upper classes and even by many members of the working class. However, by the late 1940s, there were some prominent civic leaders, artists and politicians who began promoting the steel band as an indigenous art form and arranged for bands to play in concert settings. Meanwhile, a steel band association was organized and middle-class youths began forming bands of their own.

By the 1950s, steel bands had become an integral part of the cultural life of the colony, performing everywhere from elite social clubs to nightclubs for sailors and tourists to weddings and christenings in working-class communities. When Trinidad and Tobago achieved independence from Britain in 1962, the steel band was already an important national symbol. During the 1960s, businesses began to sponsor steel bands, and state support for the movement grew. By the 1970s, pan instruction was being offered in a number of schools, a development that encouraged women to join bands.

The institutionalization of the steel band movement was paralleled by a transformation of the music. In the course of the 1940s, more notes were added to pans by grooving additional sections on the bottoms of containers and, by the end of the decade, the full-size oil barrel had become the most popular source of instruments. Meanwhile, the tonal quality of pans improved, and the wrapping of playing sticks with strips of rubber helped to create a mellower sound. By the early 1950s, all pans in a steel band contained sufficient notes to make conventional Western harmony possible. While steel bands played only simple melodies during the World War II period, by the early 1950s they were performing a variety of local calypsos, Latin American musical genres (such as mambos, boleros and sambas), North American popular songs and European classical selections. Steel bands have continued to maintain eclectic repertoires.

Contemporary Practise

In Trinidad (and in other countries), pans have not been fully standardized in terms of their ranges and layouts of notes. Nonetheless, there are several common types of instruments. One version of the tenor pan has 28 notes, ranging from d to f^2. A nine bass, consisting of nine barrels, has 30 notes, ranging from G^2 to c. Among the instruments with registers between those of the tenor and the nine bass are the double tenor (two barrels), the double second (two barrels), the quadraphonic (four barrels), the guitar (two or three barrels), the cello (three or four barrels), the tenor bass (four barrels) and the six bass (six barrels). Steel bands also include a 'rhythm section,' consisting of such instruments as a trap set, timbales, congas, tambourines, scrapers, cowbells and irons (often automobile brake drums struck with pieces of metal).

The most important performance occasion for steel bands in Trinidad has been the Panorama, a multi-round national competition held during the carnival season. Each band has a musical arranger who prepares a 10-minute interpretation of a current calypso, consisting of variations on the calypso's verse and chorus. Various melodic and harmonic parts are assigned to the different sections of pans and are learned phrase by phrase by the section members, usually by ear. For the biennial Steelband Music Festival, steel bands play both calypsos and 'tunes of choice,' typically European symphonic pieces. Other performance occasions include street processions during the carnival, staged concerts, a competition for small ensembles, and a range of community, school and church events. Several steel band arrangers, such as Ray Holman, Clive Bradley, Jit Samaroo, Len 'Boogsie' Sharpe and Robert Greenidge, have developed substantial reputations both in Trinidad and abroad. Among leading Trinidadian bands have been numbered Desperadoes, Renegades, Trinidad All Stars, Phase II and Exodus.

Although the steel band movement has had its largest and most vibrant manifestation in Trinidad, bands have also been active in other parts of the Anglophone West Indies and in a number of other countries around the world, including Venezuela, the United States, Canada, the United Kingdom, Switzerland, Nigeria and Japan. The dissemination of the steel band has been facilitated by migration to and from Trinidad, steel band tours, the distribution of recordings, and tourism in the Caribbean. Significant steel band scenes have existed in centers with substantial West Indian populations, such as New York, London, Toronto and Miami. In these and other cities, steel bands have performed in Trinidad-style carnivals and in various other community and civic events. Meanwhile, many non-West Indians have learned to play pans. In the United States, for example, there are numerous steel bands associated with colleges, high schools and elementary schools. Many of these ensembles have been assisted by West Indian panists. England also has well-established school steel band programs, while Switzerland boasts over a hundred community bands.

For Trinidadians at home and abroad, the steel band has remained an important symbol of national identity and a catalyst for local community solidarity. This national pride, however, has been coupled with a cosmopolitan outlook, both in steel band repertoires and in the encouragement of proficiency on pans among students and musicians of all backgrounds. Much attention has been devoted to furthering the establishment of the steel band as a new type of musical ensemble, to be utilized by musicians and composers throughout the world. Some of the key concerns have been identifying the best types of metal for pans, standardizing the notes on different pans, ensuring the availability of skilled pan tuners (fabricators of instruments), increasing musical literacy among panists, encouraging more compositions for steel bands and developing more professional opportunities for panists.

One of the steel band movement's greatest strengths has been its transnational networks. Panists around the world have remained in contact with each other through travel, correspondence and the Internet. The rapid circulation of information and ideas among panists, along with a passionate commitment to their instruments, should inspire continued innovation and growth in the steel band movement throughout the twenty-first century.

Bibliography

Allen, Ray, and Slater, Les. 1998. 'Steel Pan Grows in Brooklyn: Trinidadian Music and Cultural Identity.' In *Island Sounds in the Global City: Caribbean Popular Music and Identity in New York*, ed. Ray Allen and Lois Wilcken. New York: New York Folklore Society and Institute for Studies in American Music, Brooklyn College, 114–37.

Chatburn, Thomas. 1990. 'Trinidad All Stars: The Steel Pan Movement in Britain.' In *Black Music in Britain: Essays on the Afro-Asian Contribution to Popular Music*, ed. Paul Oliver. Milton Keynes: Open University Press, 118–36.

Goddard, George 'Sonny.' 1991. *Forty Years in the Steelbands: 1939–1979*, ed. Roy D. Thomas. London: Karia Press.

Hill, Errol. 1972. *The Trinidad Carnival: Mandate for a National Theatre*. Austin, TX: University of Texas Press.

Stuempfle, Stephen. 1995. *The Steelband Movement: The Forging of a National Art in Trinidad and Tobago*. Philadelphia: University of Pennsylvania Press.

Thomas, Jeffrey. 1992. *Forty Years of Steel: An Annotated Discography of Steel Band and Pan Recordings, 1951–1991*. Westport, CT: Greenwood Press.

Thomas, Jeffrey. 1995. 'Steel Band/Pan.' In *Encyclopedia of Percussion*, ed. John H. Beck. New York: Garland Publishing, 297–331.

Discography

Amoco Renegades Steel Orchestra. *A Panorama Saga: Tribute to Jit Samaroo*. Delos DE 4026. *1995*: USA.

Desperadoes Steel Orchestra. *The Jammer*. Delos DE 4023. *1993*: USA.

NIU Steel Band, The. *1992: The Taiwan Tour*. Northern Illinois University School of Music NITT92. *1992*: USA.

Pan Is Beautiful V: World Steelband Festival, Vols. I & II

(Classics in Steel). Trini-T Records PBV 01/88 & PBV 02/88. *1989*: Trinidad and Tobago.

Pan Odyssey: Steelbands of Trinidad and Tobago. Sanch CD 9504. *1995*: Trinidad and Tobago.

Red Stripe Ebony Steelband, The. *Best of Steeldrums*. ARC International Music EUCD1110. n.d.: UK.

Samaroo Jets, The. *Quintessence*. Delos DE 4024. *1994*: USA.

STEPHEN STUEMPFLE

Street Musician

The concept of the street musician is of one who sings and plays in the street. On occasion, the concept contrasts with those of the professional and 'legitimate' amateur musician, and, in this sense, the term 'street musician' can carry with it pejorative implications of impoverishment and an inferior status.

In all probability, there have been street musicians since streets were first built, and human beings began to sing, or to make and play the first musical instruments. The Bible records numerous instances of street musicians, such as the women who followed Miriam, the sister of Moses and Aaron, playing their timbrels as they rejoiced in the saving of the Israelites (ca. 1500 B.C.). More remarkable was the range of musical instruments employed, but most notably the harp, lyre, shawm and trumpet played in the streets by the ancient Assyrians (Engel 1929).

Streets imply settlements of sufficient size to make defined and surfaced routes desirable, and street musicians are generally associated with large villages, towns or cities with a population large enough to support them. It should be emphasized that making music in the streets is a worldwide phenomenon. Making music in this way may often be associated with religious, state or ceremonial processions, with parades of marchers, celebrants, worshippers or mourners stepping or dancing to the beat of drums, the blare of horns or the chanting of leaders. Depending on their function, such parades may be military or jazz, penitent, festive, protesting, traditional or spontaneous, and the musicians or singers may be habitually heard on set urban routes. The Easter processionals of Portugal and Spain, the marches of the Orangemen and apprentices of Northern Ireland, the parades of New Orleans or the Lord Mayor's Show in London, or the mariachi bands of Garibaldi Square in Mexico City are familiar popular spectacles involving music in the streets.

However, it is the music made by soloists, duos or small groups on street corners or in doorways that is called to mind when 'street musicians' are discussed. From the Bauls of Bengal to the gypsy bands of Romania, street musicians have a long history and a worldwide dis-

tribution. Often playing for alms or 'tips,' such musicians are frequently heard but seldom researched or recorded. Consequently, the history of street music remains to be written. How extensive and complex is the subject may be ascertained merely by examining aspects of its history in England.

Although their origins are inaccessible, the minstrels who entertained in the streets and at the hostelries and fairs of medieval towns were described by a number of diarists and writers. At a time when books were rare, and when the theater proper did not exist, 'poetry and music travelled with the minstrels and gleemen on the highway,' Jusserand (1909) wrote of entertainment in the thirteenth century. Their instruments were chiefly the *vielle* (a form of fiddle), the tambourine, the lute and the *rota* (a small harp). Although some minstrels were employed by the aristocracy and in some towns, such as Beverley in Yorkshire, even formed guilds, the majority were wayfarers, subject to the repression and contempt of the literate classes, who paid them little attention. Alternatively, like the sixteenth-century author of the *Anatomy of Abuses*, Phillip Stubbes, they were 'suche drunken sockets and bwdye parasits as range the cuntreyes, ryming and singing of vncleane, corrupt and filthie songs in tauernes, ale-houses, innes, and other publique assemblies . . . Every towne, citie, and countrey is full of these minstrelles to pype up a dance to the deuill.'

From the sixteenth century, the publication of 'street ballads' sold by balladmongers provides a record of the popular song traditions, but the singers and musicians themselves, with occasional exceptions, remain largely anonymous and unidentified until the mid-nineteenth century.

In 1851, Henry Mayhew published his remarkable social document based on interviews, *London Labour and the London Poor*, which threw light on the personalities and lives of a number of street musicians. They could be divided 'into the tolerable and the intolerable performers,' and also 'the skilful and the blind.' Mayhew estimated the musicians in the London streets at a thousand, more numerous than any other class of street performer, and the ballad-singers at a quarter of that number. A blind hurdy-gurdy player had worked the streets for 40 years, while a 'Farm-Yard Player' had performed animal imitations on the violin for half as long. A trio of blind Scotsmen who played violoncello, clarinet and flute had been performing for two or three decades. Another Scotsman, an ex-corporal of the Southern Highlanders, played the bagpipes while his daughter danced the Highland fling and the sword dance. Life on the streets was neither lucrative nor easy: an elderly harp player was persecuted by ruffians, while another performed on drum and pipes and complained of the competition of German performers. Foreign street entertainers were numerous, among them an Italian who played for his dancing dogs and another, from Parma, who had a 'flute harmonicon organ' that played eight tunes. A French hurdy-gurdy player had an Italian violin-playing wife, and a few German street bands also performed, working out of Whitechapel. They undercut the English groups, of which there were some 250, among which wind instrument ensembles were superseding the formerly popular string bands. Also on the streets were some 50 Ethiopian serenaders working in blackface and singing the popular songs of minstrelsy to banjo and bones accompaniment. Many of the common street singers had become 'Ethiopians' as the fashion for glee-singing waned, but the long-song ballad-sheet sellers continued to ply their popular trade and kept the remaining 'chaunters' supplied with new songs.

Street singers and musicians or 'buskers' continued to work the streets of English towns and cities in the twentieth century, even selling song sheets from trays or handheld T-frames. In the 1950s, their numbers declined as Britain approached a period of full employment and legislation was introduced to restrict street entertainment. With the greater economic disparities of the 1980s, street musicians returned, some now playing blues in emulation of African-American street singers, some performing 'oldies' and Beatles hits; and, occasionally, even music students, unable to obtain work, played excerpts from popular violin concertos in resonant doorways. Elsewhere, one new category of street musicians to appear in the 1980s was the Andean panpipe groups in -Peru.

Bibliography

Cohen, David, and Greenwood, Ben. 1981. *The Buskers*. Newton Abbot: David and Charles.

Engel, Carl. 1929 (1864). *The Music of the Most Ancient Nations*. London: William Reeves.

Henderson, W., ed. 1937. *Victorian Street Ballads: A Selection of Popular Ballads Sold in the Street in the Nineteenth Century*. London: Country Life.

Jusserand, J.J. 1909 (1888). *English Wayfaring Life in the Middle Ages*. London: T. Fisher Unwin.

Lee, Edward. 1970. *Music of the People: A Study of Popular Music in Great Britain*. London: Barrie and Jenkins.

Mayhew, Henry. 1969 (1851). *Mayhew's London. Being Selections from London Labour and the London Poor*, ed. Peter Quennell. London: Spring Books.

Pinto, V. de Sola, and Rodway, A.E., eds. 1957. *The Common Muse: An Anthology of Popular British Ballad Poetry, XVth-XXth Century*. London: Chatto and Windus.

Shepard, Leslie. 1973. *A History of Street Literature*. Newton Abbot: David and Charles.

Tanenbaum, Susie J. 1995. *Underground Harmonies: Music and Politics in the Subways of New York*. Ithaca, NY: Cornell University Press.

PAUL OLIVER

String Band

Combinations of stringed instruments are found across the entire spectrum of Western music, from the Amadeus String Quartet to the Big Ben Banjo Band. Students of US music, however, reserve the term 'string band' for groups within the Anglo-American and African-American vernacular traditions loosely gathered under the heading 'old-time music.'

In the rural South in the nineteenth and early twentieth centuries, the music furnished for dances and for entertainment at other community events such as county fairs, store openings and weekend picnics, as well as for smaller-scale functions like the house dance, was generally played by a fiddler or fiddlers, with accompaniment, if any, on banjo or guitar, or both. In accordance with local performance practise, the banjo might take a melodic lead part in unison with or in counterpoint to the fiddle, or a chordal timekeeping role together with the guitar, or some mixture of the two.

In Appalachia and other parts of the southeastern United States, the five-string banjo (which was used almost everywhere in preference to the four-string model) preceded the guitar as a unit of the string band. Many musicians had seldom or never seen guitars until inexpensive models began to be sold after World War I through the catalogs of the mail-order companies Sears, Roebuck and Montgomery Ward. The addition of the guitar to the fiddle–banjo combination may have been responsible for the disappearance of some modal tunes and unusual tunings.

Nevertheless, some students of old-time music are disposed to think of this instrumental trio formation as 'classic,' possibly by analogy with the supposedly archetypal instrumentation of the early jazz band (trumpet, trombone, clarinet, piano, banjo, brass bass, drums). Likewise, bluegrass, a refined form of string band music that developed in the Southeast in the mid-1940s, has an instrumental formation (fiddle, banjo, mandolin, guitar, string bass) that its adherents regard almost as statutory.

Yet, in practise, old-time string bands and, to some extent, bluegrass bands have been heterogeneous. The cello was used extensively in the late nineteenth and early twentieth centuries, evidently as a rhythmic anchor, although by the 1930s it had virtually disappeared, to be replaced, if at all, by the plucked string bass. The mandolin and various instruments in the mandolin, banjo and guitar 'families,' such as the mandola, banjolele, tenor guitar, tiple and ukulele, were also common. The mandolin or the ukulele was a customary first instrument for young players and, in many family string bands, preteen children of both sexes played those instruments. The strummed autoharp and plucked Appalachian dulcimer made occasional appearances. Non-stringed instruments, such as the piano, organ, accordion, harmonica, hammered dulcimer, clarinet, washboard and jug, were also added to essentially string lineups. Bluegrass, although imposing a somewhat stricter immigration policy on 'foreign' instruments, has opened its gates to some of the above, and has warmly welcomed the Dobro resonator guitar.

The rural tradition of string bands as informal groupings of unsettled lineup, the latter depending on the availability of players and instruments, afforded a contrast to the parallel and largely urban tradition of stringed instrument clubs sponsored by manufacturers like Gibson, Martin, Weymann and National. Here, whole bands, sometimes numbering 20 players or more, would be devoted to a single instrument type such as the banjo, range and color being provided by bass banjos, piccolo banjos and so forth. Such ensembles appear to have played chiefly from written music, often including specially scored ragtime compositions.

The rural string bands, on the other hand, were usually composed of players who, whether musically literate or not (and, thanks to music teachers in the rural school system, many were the former), played chiefly from a repertoire of breakdowns (reels), hornpipes, jigs, waltzes, schottisches and other kinds of tunes, which they typically acquired not from scores but through personal tuition from older players, often family members. Although originating as dance music, any of this repertoire might be played, particularly on the fiddle, with other functional or aesthetic objectives – an expansion of purpose that eventually led to the hermetic discipline of 'contest fiddling,' a 'fiddling superstyle,' as it has been called, which values intricate melodic variation and technical virtuosity more than virtues like an irresistible call to the floor or emotional expressiveness.

Some elements of string band practise were implicitly codified by the record industry, which discovered old-time music in the early 1920s and began to promote it briskly in much the same way as it had previously learned to market African-American jazz and blues, or the musics of ethnic communities such as those of Irish Americans and Greek Americans. Most of the popular old-time recording acts of the 1920s were string bands like Charlie Poole's North Carolina Ramblers (which had the 'classic' trio formation), Gid Tanner's Skillet Lickers and Fiddlin' John Carson's Virginia Reelers from Geor-

gia, the Fiddlin' Powers Family and Ernest Stoneman's Dixie Mountaineers from Virginia and the Leake County Revelers from Mississippi. The last-named group's 1927 recording of 'Wednesday Night Waltz' sold almost 200,000 copies, its success demonstrating the national, or at any rate pan-Southern, market potential of this kind of music.

In some of these bands and their scores of contemporaries, what appealed to the record buyer was as likely to have been the singer or song as the instrumental music (for a time, most of the old-time singers recorded for their own qualities were required to have some kind of string band accompaniment, whether it was their accustomed setting or not). At the same time, however, there continued to be a demand for recordings of dance music played on fiddle and guitar, uncluttered by vocal refrains but, in some instances, fitted with dance calls. It was duly supplied by the Kessinger Brothers from West Virginia, the Stripling Brothers from Alabama, Narmour and Smith from Mississippi and innumerable other acts from the eastern seaboard to the Southwest. Many distinct regional fiddling styles were thus documented.

Purely instrumental recordings featuring banjo or guitar, whether as solo or lead instrument, were far less common, but this seems to have reflected the commercial approach of recording scouts and producers rather than the musical culture itself. A similar bias has been crucial in the documentation of the African-American string band music that certainly flourished alongside, and often in a musically and socially intricate relationship with, the white tradition. The instant and overwhelming popularity of the blues appears to have blinded the record industry to other secular African-American idioms such as dance fiddling or string-ensemble ragtime. A scattering of records by the Dallas String Band, Hayes and Prater, and other even more obscure groups, together with a handful of non-blues pieces by the popular fiddle-and-guitar team of the Mississippi Sheiks, hint at a virtually lost world of African-American string band music that predated and briefly coexisted with the earliest blues.

By the end of the 1930s, the fiddle-dominated string band was no longer the primary expressive vehicle of what would come to be called country music. As in other genres, the song had overtaken the tune: personalities like Jimmie Rodgers and the Carter Family, whose songs were set more or less exclusively to guitar accompaniments, pointed the directions in which country music would develop. String band music's last significant flings were the rural quasi-vaudeville of J.E. Mainer's Mountaineers, a versatile show band from North Carolina, and the jazz-influenced and not exclusively string-based music of the Southwest that came to be termed western swing. While fiddle and guitar, particularly pedal steel guitar, have continued to be important signifiers in country music, it is chiefly in bluegrass that the lineage of string polyphony is prolonged.

Bibliography

Wolfe, Charles. 1998. *The Devil's Box: Masters of Southern Fiddling*. Nashville, TN: Vanderbilt University Press/ Country Music Foundation Press.

Discographical Reference

Leake County Revelers, The. 'Wednesday Night Waltz.' *Mississippi String Bands Volume Two*. County CO-CD-3514. 1927; *1998*: USA.

Discography

Dallas String Band, The. 'Dallas Rag.' *Texas: Black Country Dance Music 1927–1935*. Document DOCD-5162. *1993*: Austria.

Mississippi String Bands Volume One. County CO-CD-3513. 1927–30; *1998*: USA.

Mississippi String Bands Volume Two. County CO-CD-3514. 1927–35; *1998*: USA.

Poole, Charlie. *Old-Time Songs*. County CO-CD-3501. 1925–30; *1993*: USA.

Rural String Bands of Tennessee. County CO-CD-3511. 1925–30; *1997*: USA.

Rural String Bands of Virginia. County CO-CD-3502. 1926–30; *1993*: USA.

TONY RUSSELL

Swing Band

The term 'swing band' is used most frequently as a synonym for 'big band,' but it has a slightly wider meaning, encompassing small groups while excluding those big bands that specialize in post-bop styles of jazz. The term 'swing' came into use at the end of the 1920s to describe an emergent style of ensemble jazz, whose main characteristics included an even four-beats-to-the-measure rhythm, carried by piano, bass, drums and guitar, over which riff-based themes were played to begin and end each number. Soloists were featured between these opening and closing themes.

By 1932, when Duke Ellington employed the term in his song title 'It Don't Mean A Thing If It Ain't Got That Swing,' the word 'swing' itself was being used to summarize many of the characteristics of 'playing hot,' coupled with the underlying rhythmic characteristics described above. The word was used in a large number of song titles, ranging stylistically from the blues of Victoria Spivey's 'Black Snake Swing' (1936) to the prototype jump music of Fats Waller's 'Yacht Club Swing' (1938).

Waller's sextet was a typical small swing band, in which the four musicians of the rhythm section were complemented by trumpet and saxophone or clarinet. Some other contemporaneous small groups or 'combos' adopted the words 'Swing Band' into their names, notably Gene Krupa's 1936 interracial studio group that featured Roy Eldridge in the tune 'Swing Is Here.' By this time, however, the term was used more widely to describe large orchestras such as Benny Goodman's, which is said to have launched the 'swing era' at the Palomar Ballroom in Los Angeles on 21 August 1935. This led eventually to Goodman being dubbed the 'King of Swing.'

African-American big bands of the same period, notably those of Duke Ellington, Cab Calloway and Count Basie, broadly defined the style of music played by swing bands, but their playing allowed considerable latitude for individual instrumentalists to play solos and to shape the ensemble sound. Contemporary press and advertising copy referred to these bands less often as 'swing bands' and, in general, it was white big bands, such as Goodman's or those of Charlie Barnet, the Dorsey Brothers, Woody Herman, Harry James, Artie Shaw, Jack Teagarden and Charlie Ventura, to which the term clung. As a general rule, there was more uniformity and thus less opportunity for individuals to shape the sound of these bands than in their African-American counterparts. Goodman's band owed much of its success to arrangements by the African-American band leader Fletcher Henderson, but its sound was equally dependent on charts by Benny Carter, Deane Kincaide, Spud Murphy and Edgar Sampson, interpreted with Goodman's well-disciplined fastidious approach.

The term 'swing band' continued to be used until postwar economics and a change in public taste put an end to most big bands in the late 1940s. One factor in Goodman's success and the widespread appeal of other white swing bands was their effective targeting of the 'youth market.' Erenberg (1998) argues that the 1950s rock 'n' roll youth culture had its origins in the swing era, and that 'girl-next-door' vocalists like Goodman's singer Helen Ward owed their success to how accurately they targeted teenagers with money to spend. Another factor was the greater economic control of the industry afforded to white bands, and many writers, including Mitchell and Pearson (1994), suggest that the modern jazz or bebop movement was inspired among African-American musicians largely in reaction to the economic and stylistic stranglehold exercised by white swing bands over recording and radio broadcasting.

In the 1980s, a swing revival began, spearheaded by young US musicians such as Scott Hamilton, Warren Vaché, Jr., Harry Allen and Ken Peplowski. These players split their time between reviving the art of swing small-group playing and working in repertory bands such as

Loren Schoenberg's New York-based orchestra, which revived arrangements from the 1930s and 1940s.

Bibliography

Collier, James Lincoln. 1989. *Benny Goodman and the Swing Era*. New York: Oxford University Press.

Erenberg, Lewis A. 1998. *Swingin' the Dream: Big Band Jazz and the Rebirth of American Culture*. Chicago: University of Chicago Press.

Firestone, Ross. 1993. *Swing, Swing, Swing: The Life and Times of Benny Goodman*. London: Hodder and Stoughton.

Levet, Jean-Paul. 1992. *Talkin' That Talk: Le Langage du blues et du jazz* [Talkin' That Talk: The Language of Blues and Jazz]. Paris: Hatier.

Mitchell, Jeremy, and Pearson, John. 1994. 'Jazz 1920–45.' In *The United States in the Twentieth Century: Culture*, ed. Jeremy Mitchell and Richard Maidment. Sevenoaks: Hodder and Stoughton/Open University Press.

Schuller, Gunther. 1989 (1968). *The Swing Era: The Development of Jazz 1930–1945*. New York: Oxford University Press.

Stokes, W. Royal. 1994. *Swing Era New York: The Jazz Photographs of Charles Peterson*. Philadelphia: Temple University Press.

Sheet Music

Ellington, Duke, comp., and Mills, Irving, lyr. 1932. 'It Don't Mean A Thing If It Ain't Got That Swing.' New York: Mills Music.

Discographical References

Ellington, Duke. 'It Don't Mean A Thing If It Ain't Got That Swing'/'Rose Room.' Brunswick 6265. 1932: USA.

Krupa, Gene. 'Swing Is Here'/'I Hope Gabriel Likes My Music.' Victor 25276. 1936: USA.

Spivey, Victoria. 'Black Snake Swing'/'I'll Never Fall in Love Again.' Decca 7203. 1936: USA.

Waller, Fats. 'Yacht Club Swing'/'Muskat Ramble.' Bluebird 10035. 1938: USA.

ALYN SHIPTON

Syncopated Band

Syncopated bands were, in the main, large orchestras led or directed by African Americans between 1900 and 1925 that nurtured the development of early forms of syncopated popular music, such as the cakewalk, via ragtime, to large-band jazz. The earliest such band, drawn from members of the New York Clef Club, was led by James Reese Europe (1881–1919) and appeared at Carnegie Hall in 1914. Initially, Europe featured unwieldy instrumentation, including numerous mandolins and banjos, but his 369th Infantry Band (the 'Hell Fighters'), which he led in France during World War I, had a con-ventional brass band lineup. In 1919, this band made numerous recordings, including 'Memphis Blues' and 'Hesitating Blues,' which contain jazzy breaks and syncopated clarinet solos. After Europe's murder in 1919, Will Marion Cook's band, the Southern Syncopated Orchestra, which came to London in 1919 and visited other European cities between then and 1922, became the best-known such ensemble. Although Cook himself preferred a symphonic repertoire, his band featured Sidney Bechet's syncopated clarinet playing, reviews of which have enshrined the band's importance as a proto-jazz group. The children's 'piccaninny' bands of the Jenkins' Orphanage in Charleston, South Carolina shared many characteristics of syncopated bands and, in common with Cook, traveled widely in the United States and Europe in the 1920s. Other syncopated orchestras were led by Tim Brymn, Gene Mikell, Ford Dabney, Eubie Blake and Noble Sissle. Sissle (who had played and sung with Europe) and Blake (who was a ragtime pianist and composer) launched their characteristic form of African-American revue with *Shuffle Along* in 1921, incorporating elements of the syncopated orchestra and ragtime into the black show tradition of song and dance.

Bibliography

Charters, Samuel B., and Kunstadt, Leonard. 1981 (1962). *Jazz: A History of the New York Scene*. New York: Da Capo Press. (First published New York: Doubleday, 1962.)

Chilton, John. 1980. *A Jazz Nursery: The Story of the Jenkins' Orphanage Bands of Charleston, South Carolina*. London: Bloomsbury Book Shop.

Chilton, John. 1987. *Sidney Bechet, The Wizard of Jazz*. London: Macmillan.

McCarthy, Albert. 1974. *Big Band Jazz*. London/New York: Barrie and Jenkins/G.P. Putnam's Sons.

Discographical References

Europe, James Reese. 'Memphis Blues' and 'Hesitating Blues.' *James Reese Europe's 369th U.S. Infantry 'Hell Fighters' Band*. Memphis Archives 7020. 1919; *1996*: USA.

ALYN SHIPTON

Tribute Band

A 'tribute band' is one that markets its live performances as reproducing the sound and repertoire of a single, very well-known group. Frequently, the tribute band will attempt to re-create not only the music but also the total experience of a live show by the famous group it is emulating. This may include costumes, between-song banter, stage lighting and even recruiting singers or musicians who resemble (as well as sound like) the members of the star group. The desire to create a theatrical illusion links the tribute band to forms of musical theater. One of the most successful tribute bands was, in fact, a touring Broadway show that began in the late 1970s, called *Beatlemania*, which sought to reproduce various moments in the sound/image history of the Beatles. While many tribute bands offer a 'live experience' of defunct bands such as the Doors or Led Zeppelin, other tribute bands emulate existing groups such as Metallica or U2. These tribute bands offer a live show in smaller, more intimate venues than the huge arenas that feature still-touring superstar groups, thus providing a closeup (and less expensive) experience of favorite songs and sounds.

Whether re-creating a lost musical past or providing easier access to a virtual version of contemporary stars, the tribute band seeks to reconcile conflicting imperatives around live performance and musical originality within rock culture. Tribute bands are frequently found within musical formations that value live performance but desire familiar repertoire, and so they may prefer tribute bands over unknown groups with original material. The tension between the tribute band's authentic 'liveness' in its performance and its inauthentic 'unoriginality' in its material is evidenced in its somewhat derogatory nickname, 'human jukebox.' This is tied to the development of a 'record aesthetic' within rock culture, in which live performance is frequently evaluated in terms of the faithful reproduction of a recorded 'original.' However, rock culture also celebrates composition, and views songwriting as a key marker of a band's originality and authenticity. The tribute band's explicit theatricality tends to alleviate audience anxieties about authorship and focuses attention instead on the spectacle of live performance.

Nonetheless, the links to musical theater mean that the tribute band may also operate outside rock culture, and thus more pop- or dance-oriented groups such as the Village People or ABBA may be 'tributed' (ABBA, for example, by Australia's Bjorn Again). This also suggests that talent shows such as *Stars in Their Eyes*, impersonations of famous vocalists by drag queens and even forms of lipsynch performance may share the tribute band's paradoxical investment in an illusion of authenticity.

Bibliography

Bennett, Andrew. 1997. '"Going Down the Pub!": The Pub Rock Scene as a Resource for the Consumption of Popular Music.' *Popular Music* 16(1): 97–108 (see pp. 102ff. for a discussion of a Pink Floyd tribute band).

KEIR KEIGHTLEY

Trio

A trio is an instrumental or vocal or mixed musical ensemble containing three performers. Unlike in Western classical music, in which trio formats are determined by the demands of a written score, in popular music most trio formats have evolved in less formal ways.

The most common instrumental trio lineup has been that of piano, bass and drums, sometimes featuring vocals as well. In US popular music, piano-led trios enjoyed considerable popularity in both the R&B and jazz fields from the 1940s onward. The best-known of the trios featuring vocals was the Nat King Cole Trio, while in jazz Oscar Peterson, Ahmad Jamal and Mose Allison led popular trios. Less common jazz trio formats have included saxophonist Jimmy Giuffre's group with guitarist Jim Hall and trombonist Bob Brookmeyer.

Preceded by the three-member Carter Family group, the folk revival of the 1960s included the Kingston Trio, and Peter, Paul and Mary, combining vocals with guitars and the occasional double bass or banjo.

In guitar-led rock 'n' roll and rock music, the rockabilly era produced some important trios. Johnny Cash and the Tennessee Two and Elvis Presley's first group with Scotty Moore and Bill Black used only guitar and string bass, but a more common lineup was guitar, bass and drums as used by Johnny Burnette and the Rock & Roll Trio. In the 1960s, the Big Three from Liverpool was one of the few British beat groups with three rather than four members, but there were a number of famous heavy rock trios, including the Jimi Hendrix Experience, Cream and Mountain. Later, progressive rock spawned such three-piece groups as Emerson, Lake and Palmer (organ, bass and drums) and Genesis in its 1980s and 1990s incarnation. Although most British punk groups adopted the beat group quartet format, the era produced important trios in the Jam and the Slits. The most significant pop trio of the 1990s was the Norwegian group A-Ha.

Three-voice harmony singing has been a feature of mainstream popular music in the United States since Paul Whiteman added the Rhythm Boys (who included Bing Crosby) to his orchestra in 1927. In the following decade, the Andrews Sisters became the forerunners of numerous 'sister' vocal trios like the Boswell Sisters and the British-based Beverley Sisters. But the greatest flowering of such trios was in black pop and soul music through the Ronettes, the Supremes, the Three Degrees and others. Most of these groups had a de facto lead singer and two backing vocalists.

Male trios were less prominent, although the Impressions strongly influenced a Jamaican tradition of harmony singing by the Wailers, Toots and the Maytals, and others. In white pop music, the Bee Gees were a vocal trio for much of their career, and Crosby, Stills and Nash, followed by America, combined three-part harmony singing with soft rock music.

Rap and hip-hop ensembles have been of varying sizes, but have included such trios as the Beastie Boys and De La Soul.

Discography

A-Ha. *Hunting High and Low*. Warner Brothers 25300. *1985*: USA.

America. *History: America's Greatest Hits*. Warner Brothers 2894. *1975*: USA.

Andrews Sisters, The. *The Andrews Sisters: 50th Anniversary Collection*. MCA 42044. *1987*: USA.

Beastie Boys, The. *Paul's Boutique*. Capitol 91743. *1989*: USA.

Bee Gees, The. *Their Greatest Hits: The Record*. Uptown/Universal 589400. *2001*: USA.

Beverley Sisters, The. *Together*. Music for Pleasure MFP 411066-3. *1985*: UK.

Big Three, The. *Cavern Stomp*. Edsel 112. *1982*: UK.

Boswell Sisters, The. *The Boswell Sisters Collection, Vol. 1: 1931–32*. Collector's Classics 21. *1996*: USA.

Burnette, Johnny, and the Rock & Roll Trio. *Rockabilly Boogie*. Bear Family 15474. *1989*: Germany.

Carter Family, The. *Anchored in Love: Their Complete Victor Recordings, 1927–1928*. Rounder 611064. *1994*: USA.

Carter Family, The. *Can the Circle Be Unbroken?: Country Music's First Family*. Columbia/Legacy 65707. *2000*: USA.

Cash, Johnny, and the Tennessee Two. *The Sun Years*. Rhino R2-70950. *1990*: USA.

Cream. *The Very Best of Cream*. Polydor/Chronicles 523752. *1995*: UK.

Crosby, Stills and Nash. *Crosby, Stills & Nash*. Atlantic 19117. *1969*: USA.

De La Soul. *3 Feet High and Rising*. Tommy Boy 1019. *1989*: USA.

Emerson, Lake and Palmer. *The Best of Emerson, Lake & Palmer*. Rhino 72233. *1996*: USA.

Genesis. *And Then There Were Three*. Charisma CDS 4010. *1978*: UK.

Impressions, The. *The Very Best of the Impressions*. Rhino 72583. *1997*: USA.

Jam, The. *In the City*. Polydor 2383 447. *1977*: UK.

Jamal, Ahmad. *Poinciana*. Chess 31266. *1992*: USA.

Jimi Hendrix Experience, The. *Are You Experienced?*. Track 612-001. *1967*: UK.

Jimmy Giuffre 3, The. *Trav'lin' Light*. Atlantic 1282. *1958*: USA.

Kingston Trio, The. *Capitol Collectors Series*. Capitol 92710. *1990*: USA.

Mountain. *The Best of Mountain*. Columbia 32079. *1973*: USA.

Nat King Cole Trio, The. *The Nat King Cole Trio Recordings*, Vols. 1–4. LaserLight 15746-15749. *1991*: USA.

Oscar Peterson Trio, The. *I Got Rhythm*. Giants of Jazz 53340. *1999*: USA.

Peter, Paul and Mary. *Ten Years Together: The Best of Peter, Paul and Mary*. Warner Brothers 3105. *1990*: USA.

Ronettes, The. *The Best of the Ronettes*. ABKCO 7212. *1992*: USA.

Ross, Diana, and the Supremes. *The Ultimate Collection*. Motown 530827. *1997*: USA.

Slits, The. *Cut*. Island ILPS 9573. *1979*: UK. Reissue: Slits, The. *Cut*. Island 8186. *2000*: UK.

Three Degrees, The. *The Best of the Three Degrees: When Will I See You Again*. Epic 64915. *1996*: USA.

Toots and the Maytals. *The Very Best of Toots & the Maytals*. Island 542345. *2000*: UK.

Wailers, The. *The Best of the Wailers*. Jet Set 403. *1998*: USA.

DAVE LAING

Vocal Groups

Informal singing in groups (with or without instruments) has flourished since the Renaissance period, when people would gather at each other's houses to sing madrigals and part songs. Since the eighteenth century, this domestic music-making has largely given way to public concerts and professional ensembles, and most people now experience vocal groups through recordings and concerts rather than by actually participating themselves.

An ideal vocal group consists of between three and eight singers; if the ensemble is much larger than this, it becomes a choir. A vocal group is able to take responsibility for its own artistic output, whereas a choir is usually dependent on its conductor. Until the early twentieth century, the repertoire for vocal groups in the West was generally created by classically trained composers using formal compositional techniques. Renaissance madrigals and *chansons* were composed for group performance, but the idea of a specific group of people gathering together to sing dates from much later (although there is some evidence that the barbershop tradition goes back to the sixteenth century). In nineteenth-century Germany, there was a tradition of convivial meetings for informal music-making among singers. At the same time in England, fixed groups also met regularly to sing madrigals and glees. In the United States, the Hutchinson Family (one of a number of family groups, which included the Rainer Family, émigrés from Switzerland) wrote and arranged their own material (often of a political nature), and can perhaps be considered the first successful professional vocal group. US composers were especially aware of the possibilities of popular compositions involving vocal groups. Stephen Foster's mid-nineteenth-century songs for the Christy Minstrels are a case in point: they contained four-voice choruses which could be sung by amateur or professional groups. From the early twentieth century onward, the corpus of popular standards increased, and more groups began to arrange their own material or to call on the services of arrangers.

There has always been a strong element of European formal harmony in the music of vocal ensembles, and the commercially successful groups have often inspired many amateur groups to take an interest in singing together. Especially successful in the 1920s and 1930s was the German group known as the Comedian Harmonists, whose vocalizations of Strauss and Rossini and arrangements of jazz classics, such as 'Night and Day,' were acclaimed all over Europe and the United States. The Comedian Harmonists were a quintet, and the fifth part may have given them a greater harmonic breadth than some of their contemporaries. North American groups such as the Mills Brothers and the Ink Spots were influenced both by the Comedian Harmonists' 'instrumental' numbers and by their close harmony singing (in which the vocal lines were closely spaced, with generally no more than an interval of a twelfth between top and bottom voices). The Mills Brothers found success in New York in the early 1930s with a radio show and a hit recording of a vocalized 'Tiger Rag.' The Ink Spots, who were all ushers at New York's Paramount Theater until success overtook them in the mid- to late 1930s, followed in the footsteps of the Mills Brothers; by expanding its repertoire and changing its membership, the group continued to perform for most of the rest of the twentieth century.

There were equally successful 'girl groups' during this period. The three Boswell Sisters, who also accompanied themselves on instruments, developed a virtuosic close harmony style with immaculate tuning. Born in New Orleans, the Sisters (who were among the first white female jazz singers) came from a prosperous background, and are said to have learned jazz from their (presumably black) servants. The group folded in 1935, but its place was taken by the Andrews Sisters, who were also a trio with a similarly rhythmic approach. The Andrews Sisters had many hits in the 1940s, and were especially successful in films (in which they usually appeared as themselves).

In the 1950s, the close harmony tradition continued with doo-wop, so called because of the onomatopoeic harmony sounds used in the backing vocals in early rhythm and blues. Black groups such as the Orioles, the Platters, the Coasters and the Drifters had major successes, followed later in the decade by Frankie Lymon and the Teenagers, and by the Chantels, the first of the great girl groups that were to dominate the 1960s. Other girl groups included the more rock 'n' roll-oriented Shir-

elles, the Crystals, the Ronettes and the Shangri-Las, all of which had hits with well-crafted songs from established songwriters, such as Leiber and Stoller, or from emerging writers, such as Carole King. Producers often had a strong musical influence on their protégés, and many of the girl groups benefited from the Phil Spector sound. In the mid-1960s, the Supremes held sway, and their producer Richard Barrett went on to produce the Three Degrees, a group whose visual image was so powerful that the music was only one of several elements contributing to its success.

Many of the girl group members began their singing career in the churches of the black community, which were the cradle of the gospel tradition. This had its origins in the spirituals and nonconformist hymns of the nineteenth century and earlier. Groups such as the Jubilee Singers (who toured Europe in 1875) popularized the more visceral and uninhibited singing that was eventually to be called gospel. During the 1930s, charismatic soloists emerged to lead a very rhythmic, jazz-influenced singing style that was given worldwide impetus by the success of later groups such as the Golden Gate Quartet (which toured the United Kingdom in 1956). The founding of Tamla Motown Records in 1959 helped to ensure the commercial future of gospel (and its related soul music) throughout the 1960s and 1970s with groups such as the Temptations as well as star soloists.

The beginnings of rock music in the 1960s also produced the legendary male groups the Beatles and the Beach Boys, both of which could sing in four-part harmony while playing instruments. Many British groups of the period (the Hollies, the Zombies and many other Liverpool bands) were equally competent vocally and instrumentally.

On the whole, later rock music did not produce much harmony singing. The bands of the period from the 1970s to the 1990s preferred synthesizers (or earlier versions, such as the Mellotron) when they wanted to use vocal color. What did survive into the late twentieth century was a tradition of jazz-influenced close harmony. Toward the end of the century, entrepreneurs in the music industry realized that it was possible to create and market vocal groups according to a formula that would appeal to specifically targeted audiences. Groups were created by audition, an ability to sing being only one of many criteria applied by the producers. Groups such as the Backstreet Boys in the United States, the Spice Girls in England and Westlife in Ireland (known colloquially as boy bands or girl bands, according to gender) began life as creations of the industry, and attempts by the singers to control their own group strategies have had varying success.

In addition to recorded material, two publications have been significant in enabling amateur groups to create their own music based on styles ranging from spirituals and barbershop to doo-wop and even bop. These are *The Yale Song Book* (from which many student groups take their informal starting point), and the series of volumes known as *The Real Book*. *The Yale Song Book* is a volume of college and barbershop songs arranged for four or five voices. The volumes of *The Real Book* consist of piano and/or guitar transcriptions of standards (or of pieces that have become standards as publication proceeds) from which putative arrangers can easily create their own versions.

Major influences on the vocal group movement (for such it is) have been the Manhattan Transfer and Take 6. These two groups owe a certain stylistic debt to doo-wop, and also to the extreme virtuosity of Lambert, Hendricks and Ross. This trio was formed in 1957 by Annie Ross, Dave Lambert and Jon Hendricks to sing Lambert's 'vocalese' versions of a wide variety of music from Count Basie to bop. The possibility of putting words to existing tunes immediately opened up a potentially huge repertoire for vocal groups without any need for them to get involved in the banalities of imitating instruments.

A parallel influence was a group known as the Swingle Singers, formed by American Ward Lamar Swingle in the late 1960s. While working in Paris as a singer and pianist, Swingle began scatting Bach with French session singers. Swingle's arrangements, which later encompassed pop songs as well as classical pieces, have provided material for countless amateur groups to work on. In 1974, Swingle moved to England and formed the group Swingles II with English singers. This group and various subsequent versions (drawn mainly from the Oxbridge choral tradition) have been able to combine light jazz with more serious avant-garde works by composers such as Luciano Berio.

The influence of the Manhattan Transfer, Take 6 and Swingle has been profound, especially in Scandinavia, where many semiprofessional ensembles have flourished in a stylistic world that revolves around arrangements of pieces recorded by each of them. Some groups, such as the Real Group from Sweden, have made highly original contributions to the genre, incorporating post-Bobby McFerrin vocalized instrumental techniques. Finland hosts a biennial ensemble singing competition in Tampere, to which vocal groups come from all over the world.

A further dimension to the tradition of vocal group performance has been added by the King's Singers and the various British a cappella groups that began life in university or cathedral choirs. The King's Singers have been especially influential in bridging the gap (both commercially and musically) between classical and popular music and in collaborating with other musicians in crossover projects. The same has been true of the Hilliard Ensemble, which began collaborating with Norwegian saxophonist Jan Garbarek in the 1990s. Its music was initially predicated on adding improvised saxophone descants to medieval and Renaissance music. However, as the singers learned from the saxophone, the style evolved toward total improvisation, both free and structured. The harmonic meeting point for the two sides was the juxtaposition of modality exploited by Garbarek's folk-influenced European jazz background with a similar modality found in early music. Another British early music vocal group, the Orlando Consort, has collaborated with the jazz trio Perfect Houseplants to produce medieval/jazz crossover pieces that blend medieval modality with North American chromatic harmony. The British dimension also includes the Tallis Scholars' performance with rock singer Sting.

Sting is one of a number of solo singers (Phil Collins, Peter Gabriel and many others, especially those successful in the 1970s progressive rock era) who use vocal harmonies in the manner of a virtual vocal group. This is achieved by multitracking recorded vocals and adding more singers for live performance. Like the tradition of the soloist and his/her backing singers, this kind of 'ensemble' can have the effect of a group musical experience, but control remains in the hands of the soloist.

Although singing in small ensembles has been highly developed in the Western world, vocal groups are by no means confined to the industrialized West. Many cultures have a tradition of improvised polyphony, in which members of a community come together for spontaneous music-making. Notable examples are Corsica and Georgia (and other states of the former Soviet Union), where groups of three or more men form temporary vocal groups for special occasions. In Bulgaria (and the Balkans generally), there is a tradition of female vocal groups. The Trio Bulgarka and other ensembles from the state radio choir have had considerable success in the West with music based on traditional folk tunes. In some Asian cultures, there is a tradition of massed singing, such as the Balinese *kecak* in which a chorus of men imitate monkey cries.

Singing in a vocal group is a convivial activity that is not confined to commercially successful recording stars. It is a symbol of a type of social cohesion (and, indeed, a successful and happy group may in some sense represent a microcosm of an ideal society). There appears to be little logic behind the flourishing of the medium in the twentieth and twenty-first centuries: singers get together to celebrate or mourn, to make money or simply to have fun, and the tradition exists alongside that of solo singing. A minimum amount of vocal technique and an instinctive musicianship are often all that is required in the first instance. The recorded and published models from virtually the whole of the twentieth century should ensure that this flourishing tradition continues well beyond the foreseeable future, as groups diversify into other areas. As cultures move closer together in their appreciation of each other, world music can be expected to have an increasing influence on vocal groups of the twenty-first century.

Bibliography

Greig, Charlotte. 1989. *Will You Still Love Me Tomorrow?: Girl Groups from the 50s On*. London: Virago Press.

Hamm, Charles. 1979. *Yesterdays: Popular Song in America*. New York: Norton.

Potter, John. 1998. *Vocal Authority: Singing Style and Ideology*. Cambridge: Cambridge University Press.

Potter, John, ed. 2000. *The Cambridge Companion to Singing*. Cambridge: Cambridge University Press.

Southern, Eileen. 1983. *The Music of Black Americans: A History*. 2nd ed. New York: Norton.

The Real Book. n.d. Syosset, NY: The RealBook Press.

The Yale Song Book. 1906. New York: G. Schirmer.

Discographical References

Comedian Harmonists, The. 'Night and Day.' *Comedian Harmonists*. Hannibal 1445. 1933; *1999*: USA.

Mills Brothers, The. 'Tiger Rag'/'Nobody's Sweetheart.' Brunswick 6197. 1931: USA. Reissue: Mills Brothers, The. 'Tiger Rag' and 'Nobody's Sweetheart.' *The Mills Brothers, Vol. 1: 1931–1934*. Giants of Jazz 53086. *1998*: USA.

Discography

Andrews Sisters, The. *Greatest Hits: The 60th Anniversary Collection*. MCA 11727. *1998*: USA.

Backstreet Boys, The. *Greatest Hits – Chapter One*. Jive 9222672. *2001*: USA.

Boswell Sisters, The. *The Boswell Sisters Collection, Vol. 1: 1931–1932*. Collector's Classics 21. *1996*: USA.

Chantels, The. *We Are the Chantels/There's Our Song Again*. Westside 564. 1957–61; *1998*: USA.

Coasters, The. *The Very Best of the Coasters*. Rhino 32656. *1995*: USA.

Comedian Harmonists, The. *Comedian Harmonists*. Hannibal 1445. *1999*: USA.

Crystals, The. *The Best of the Crystals*. ABKCO 7214-2. *1992*: USA.

Drifters, The. *The Very Best of the Drifters*. Rhino R2-71211. *1993*: USA.

Garbarek, Jan, and the Hilliard Ensemble. *Mnemosyne*. ECM 21700. *1999*: USA.

Ink Spots, The. *Best of the Ink Spots*. MCA 001. *1997*: USA.

Lambert, Hendricks and Ross. *Twisted: The Best of Lambert, Hendricks & Ross*. Rhino R2-70328. 1957–61; *1992*: USA.

Lymon, Frankie, and the Teenagers. *The Very Best of Frankie Lymon and the Teenagers*. Rhino R2-75507. *1998*: USA.

Orioles, The. *Sing Their Greatest Hits*. Collectables 5408. *1991*: USA.

Orlando Consort, The, and Perfect Houseplants. *Extempore*. Linn Records CKD 076. *1998*: UK.

Platters, The. *Enchanted: The Best of the Platters*. Rhino R2-75326. *1998*: USA.

Real Group, The. *Commonly Unique*. Gazell GAFCD-1032. *2000*: Sweden.

Ronettes, The. *The Best of the Ronettes*. ABKCO 7212-2. *1992*: USA.

Shirelles, The. *Anthology (1959–1964)*. Rhino R2-75897. *1986*: USA.

Spice Girls, The. *Spice*. Virgin 42174. *1996*: UK.

Sting. *Mercury Falling*. A&M 540486-2. *1996*: UK.

Swingle Singers, The. *The Best of the Swingle Singers*. SWINGCD14. *1998*: UK.

Vox Humana: Ancestral Voices for Modern Europe. Nascente NSCD 030. *1999*: UK.

Westlife. *Coast to Coast*. RCA 74321808312. *2000*: UK.

JOHN POTTER

Washboard Band

Washboard bands were so named for the novelty value of the washboard used as an instrument, for the band rarely if ever had more than one washboard player. The groups of washboard bands formed by pianist Clarence Williams, with Floyd Casey 'on the boards,' did much to popularize the instrument (1927–37). The Washboard Rhythm Kings, a large band with Leo Watson or Ghost Howell frequently playing the boards, made nearly a hundred recordings between 1931 and 1933.

Bibliography

Lord, Tom. 1967. *Clarence Williams* (Bio-discography). London: Storyville Publications.

PAUL OLIVER

Wedding Bands

The term 'wedding bands' or 'wedding orchestras' is associated with the revival in the early 1980s of a traditional instrumental music in Bulgaria that was played live for various celebratory purposes, especially village weddings.

The music of these bands is based on Balkan urban folklore traditions that emerged during the mid-nineteenth century. More specifically, it is based on the music of the *chalga*, which, in giving rise to a new level of professionalism in instrumental playing, exemplified one aspect of the transition from rural to urban cultures in the Balkan region.

A *chalga*, also called *chalgija*, is a small folk band that introduced instruments like the clarinet, the fiddle and, later, the accordion – instruments that were new to the Balkans. The word *chalga*, incorporated into Bulgarian and into all Balkan languages, comes from the Turkish language and implies music played for pleasure that meets people's everyday musical needs. Performed predominantly by gifted Gypsies and Jewish musicians at fairs and other communal celebrations, *chalga* played a significant role in the emerging eclectic popular music of the time, freely mixing and interpreting diverse material derived from various local folk traditions and from modern foreign urban popular music sources. However, *chalga* still emphasized the hedonistic aspects of oriental tunes and dance rhythms. During the first decades of the twentieth century, *chalga* was brought to the United States by Jewish immigrants from Eastern Europe and, to some extent, shaped klezmer music.

Another traditional source of wedding band music is associated with the military brass band, widely introduced into Bulgaria following the National Liberation of 1878. These bands often interpreted local folk-song tunes according to European major-minor tonality. However, whereas *chalga* musicians played spontaneously and without any particular musical preconceptions, thereby affording more opportunity for improvisation, the brass bands, for the most part, performed 'written' music. In Bulgaria, both *chalga* and brass bands continued to exist, although, over the years, *chalga* has been marginalized in village culture far from the attention of the national media. Brass bands, on the other hand, looking to aspire to more 'lofty' musical ideals, developed a more formal style, less suited to the everyday musical needs of ordinary people.

The gap created by these two styles of music was filled by wedding bands, which flourished in the early 1980s in response to keen local demand for festive music to be played at celebratory events. Wedding bands updated the traditional sound by keeping the clarinet, accordion and trumpet in leading roles, and introducing electric instruments and amplifiers. The acoustic fiddle was replaced by the electric guitar, and the electric organ, bass and drums were added to the lead instruments. Inheriting the style and, especially, the spirit of the *chalga* musicians and adopting their enthusiasm for improvisation, wedding bands developed a highly virtuosic instrumental style, sometimes termed 'Balkan jazz,' which contributed to the modern Balkan 'non-Western' sound.

Becoming increasingly popular nationally, wedding bands were initially ignored by the national media. When, finally, they gained media attention, it resulted in, among other things, the establishment of a special festival, held annually from the mid-1980s in Stambolovo, Trakija, in southern Bulgaria. The powerful music of wedding bands was soon noticed by foreign producers, who first recorded live performances of the most successful clarinet player, Ivo Papasov, and his orchestra. This opened the door for wedding band musicians to be heard outside Bulgaria and to gain international fame. Among the most influential wedding bands were Horo, Kanarite and Konushevskata Groupa, as well as the orchestras of Ivan Milev and Nicola Iliev. Most of these bands, however, began to include vocal performances in their shows. In emphasizing the vocal rather than the instrumental, these bands gradually gave rise to another indigenous style of music known as 'folk-pop,' 'ethno-pop' or *chalga*. This style flourished as part of Bulgarian popular music during the 1990s.

Bibliography

Bakalov, Todor. 1992. *Svatbarskite orkestri* [The Wedding Bands]. Sofia: Muzika.

Gaitandjiev, Gencho. 1990. *Populjarnata muzika: pro? contra?* [Popular Music: Pros? Cons?]. Sofia: Narodna prosveta.

Kaufman, Dimitrina. 1990. 'Ot vuzrojdenskata chalgija kum suvremennite svatbarski orkestri' [From the Music Bands of the National Revival Period to the Modern Wedding Orchestras]. *Bulgarski Folklore* 3: 23–32.

Rice, Timothy. 1994. *May It Fill Your Soul: Experiencing Bulgarian Music.* (Compact disc included.) Chicago: University of Chicago Press.

Discography

Papasov, Ivo, and His Bulgarian Wedding Band. *Orpheus Ascending.* Hannibal HNCD-1346. *1989*: USA.

Papasov, Ivo, and His Orchestra. *Balkanology.* Hannibal HNCD-1363. *1991*: USA.

CLAIRE LEVY

Western Swing Band

Western swing bands developed during the early 1930s in the United States to provide music for the dance venues of the oil boomtowns of the southwestern states of Oklahoma and Texas, where young couples raised on hillbilly music wanted swing music appropriate for the couple-dance styles of the time.

String bands, like that of Bob Wills, tried to play the new swing music, but it was Milton Brown who, in 1932, found the mix that would become the basis of western swing, a term that only came into use in World War II to describe this music. Brown added a vocalist, a piano and the newly developed electric steel guitar to the established string band lineup, which featured a fiddle complemented by other unamplified stringed instruments, most commonly guitar, string bass, and mandolin or banjo.

Bob Wills followed this lead with his own Texas Playboys in 1933, and over the years he added drums and a full brass section. Whereas Brown always performed in the formal dress attire appropriate for a jazz swing band, Wills and others – including Cliff Bruner's Texas Wanderers, the Cowboy Ramblers, the Prairie Ramblers, Pee Wee King and the Golden West Cowboys, Patsy Montana, Tex Williams and Hank Thompson – began to favor the newly devised western outfit worn by the singing film cowboy. The repertoire of the 1930s western swing bands included covers of current swing-band pop hits, old sentimental songs, hillbilly favorites, risqué blues numbers, novelty songs and, when the situation called for it, inspirational hymns.

Western swing moved to the west coast with the migrants from the southwest, and the final developments of the style took place in the World War II boomtowns of southern California. The leading bands, such as that of Spade Cooley, increased in size to create enough sound to fill the largest California dance halls and, like pop swing bands, depended on ever more complete written scores to deliver a clear polished sound. In calling himself the 'King of Western Swing,' Cooley named the music, and in his hands the genre, with the addition of woodwinds and classical harp, moved yet closer to the middle-of-the-road stylings being developed by Lawrence Welk. The move to ever larger bands terminated, as it did in jazz, in the years right after World War II. Most of the surviving bands, such as those of Tex Williams and Hank Thompson, played with eight or fewer members, and to get the sounds supplied by horns, experimented with the new pedal steel and the revolutionary electric guitars then being developed by Leo Fender.

Bibliography

Boyd, Jean A. 1997. *The Jazz of the Southwest: An Oral History of Western Swing*. Austin, TX: University of Texas Press.

Malone, Bill C. 1985. *Country Music U.S.A.* Austin, TX: University of Texas Press.

Peterson, Richard A. 1997. *Creating Country Music: Fabricating Authenticity*. Chicago: University of Chicago Press, Chapter 10.

Townsend, Charles R. 1976. *San Antonio Rose: The Life and Music of Bob Wills*. Urbana, IL: University of Illinois Press.

Discography

Cooley, Spade. *Spadella: the Essential*. Columbia/Legacy 57392. *1994*: USA.

Heroes of Country Music, Vol. 1: Legends of Western Swing. Rhino 72440. *1996*: USA.

Texas Music, Vol. 2: Western Swing & Honky Tonk. Rhino 71782. *1994*: USA.

Wills, Bob, and His Texas Playboys. *Anthology 1935–1973*. Rhino R2-70744. *1991*: USA.

RICHARD A. PETERSON

Wind Band

Terminology

The term 'wind band' is used to differentiate this type of group from the brass band, and other ensembles such as dance, jug, mummers, rock, steel, string and theater bands. The wind band, also known as circus, college, concert, military, parade or town band, normally consists of conventional woodwind, brass and percussion instruments. The largest ensemble is the symphonic band, which includes a full range of available instruments – English horn, contraalto and contrabass clarinets, contrabassoon, string bass (and, in some traditions, such as the Spanish, cello), harp, gongs and a full range of auxiliary and mallet percussion – and a larger proportion of flutes and clarinets. Because of its size and instrumentation, the symphonic band is sometimes referred to as a wind orchestra, or symphony of winds, in spite of its lack of stringed instruments, which are the foundation of the symphony orchestra. Except for the wind ensemble, a concept discussed below, and big bands, wind bands share a common heritage, traditions and basic repertoire.

Much of the multiplicity is the result of historical traditions and customs, the terms 'band' and 'orchestra' often being used interchangeably, and the specific purpose served by each organization. Until the twentieth century, their differences were mainly functional, with size, instrumentation and selections determined by the occasion and the place, rather than the performers, who were expected to be competent in all genres and proficient on both stringed and wind instruments. In 1745, for example, J.S. Bach testified that one of his musicians had proven competent 'on the various instruments a *Stadtpfeifer* must profess, namely the violin, oboe, traverse flute, trumpet, horn, and other instruments.' By the end of the nineteenth century, as more technical proficiency was demanded by the music, musicians would be expected to concentrate on one stringed instrument and several woodwinds or brasses. A cellist in the orchestra, for example, would be expected to play trombone or euphonium in the band. Bands, associated with the human Marsyas in Greek mythology and descended from the medieval 'high' instruments, were generally mobile, the musicians performing outdoors on the louder brass and percussion instruments. Bands had a vernacular appeal, frequently provided music for ceremonial occasions, were often associated with the military (its members were accordingly uniformed) and generally performed lighter forms of popular music as entertainment for a mass public. Orchestras, on the other hand, associated with the god Apollo and descended from the medieval 'low' instruments and the concept of chamber music, were stationary, the musicians normally performing indoors using predominantly strings and the softer woodwinds. Orchestras were usually associated with the church, nobility or paid public concerts and, with more serious compositions, appealed to a more sophisticated audience. The function determined the ensemble, with the same performers forming a band for outdoor occasions or an orchestra for indoor concerts and entertainments.

Another reason for its multiple terms is the evolution of the band itself. While there are great differences in size and instrumentation between baroque and post-Romantic works, one can still use the term 'orchestra' because of the basic string-family component. A similar historical evolution can be seen in the wind band, but the lack of a basic family core and the variety of instrumental combinations gave each stage its own name and implications. While orchestral music was always 'downwardly compatible,' in that later groups could still play the music of the earlier ensembles, band music was not. The changes in instrumentation forced later groups to neglect and frequently discard earlier repertoires. Before discussing this evolution, it must be made clear that the band is different from the field music in military organizations. The latter, at various times, consisted of the drummers, fifers, buglers and pipers who sounded the camp duties that regulated military life. The trumpeters and drummers of antiquity and the medieval period served primarily as field musicians.

Early Development

The earliest recognized stage of wind band music is that of the *Stadtpfeifer* and civic waits. In the fifteenth century, many towns and cities employed professional musicians to provide music for civic ceremonies, festivals and official social occasions. In smaller towns, the musicians might also be required to serve as watchmen, providing 'tower music.' To earn additional income, the musicians were often permitted to play for private functions, such as weddings, funerals and dances. The common 'loud' band consisted of two to three shawms with one or two slide trumpets or sackbuts, although wealthier cities might have larger groups. A. Holborne (?1584–1602), D. Speer (1636–1707), J.C. Pezel (1639–94), G. Reiche (1667–1734) and J. Clarke (ca. 1674–1707)

are only a few of the composers with major works for these ensembles.

A second stage of wind band music dawned when the oboe, evolving from the shawm, was introduced into French army units in 1663. Louis XIV's *mousquetaires* had three oboes and five drums to each company in 1665, and by 1677 had a fourth oboist and a sixth drummer. Jean-Baptiste Lully (1632–87) and André Danican Philidor (ca. 1647–1730) arranged many military compositions in four-part harmony, standardizing a combination of oboes, curtals (precursor of the bassoon) and bassoons. The term *hautbois*, 'hautboy' or 'hoboy' referred to the instruments, and also to the musicians and the mixed ensemble. The British were quick to follow the French example, and hautboys were soon found in many regiments. The practise extended to the North American colonies as well: hautboys and trumpets led a military parade in New York in 1714.

With the addition of two French horns to the hautboys in the early eighteenth century, a new stage of wind music evolved: the *Harmoniemusik*. At first, the combination consisted of pairs of oboes and horns, with one or two bassoons. As clarinets gained in popularity, they either replaced the oboes or were included, the latter combination becoming standardized as the ideal classical woodwind octet. The Harmonie separated itself from the drummers, who remained with the field music. The musicians were fully professional, and provided music for military ceremonies and social occasions. The Harmonie's size was determined by the ability of the nobleman or regiment to pay and uniform the musicians, with lesser nobles supporting five musicians while wealthier regiments and noblemen had full octets. Its repertoire, composed by Haydn, Mozart, Beethoven, Krommer, Pleyel and others, included partitas, divertimenti, cassations, serenades, nocturnes, marches, *pièces d'harmonie* and transcriptions of popular stage works. No military or civic occasion would be complete without a band providing inspiring music. Pleasure gardens, theaters, coffeehouses and taverns all attracted customers with bands performing medleys, battle pieces, popular selections and patriotic songs. Bands became particularly important during the French Revolution as accompaniment to the ceremonies and festivities of the new Republic.

The second half of the eighteenth century found Europe increasingly captivated by Turkish fashions. Expressed in literature, costume and art, an especially strong influence was that of the military bands of the Janissaries, the formidable Turkish army. Their instruments – the bass drum, cymbals, triangle, tambourine, timpano and Turkish crescent – were added to the Harmonie. Often played by musicians in colorful costumes rather than uniforms, these percussion instruments forced the ensemble to add more woodwinds to restore some musical balance. The more exotic instruments soon fell out of fashion, but the bass drum and cymbals, along with the snare drum from the field music, soon became regular constituents of the band.

Piccolos, flutes, bass clarinets, contrabassoons, trombones, bass horns and serpents were added to bands in the early nineteenth century. In 1810, Joseph Halliday applied keys to the regulation bugle, producing a fully chromatic brass instrument. Virtuosos on the keyed bugle, such as John Distin and others in Europe, and Richard Willis, Frank Johnson and Edward (Ned) Kendall in the United States, popularized the instrument. Ophicleides and keyed bass horns were developed, and bands became increasingly larger with a greater percentage of brass instruments. The Industrial Revolution fostered improvements such as new keys on the woodwinds and the development of valves for the brass instruments. In Paris, the Belgian Adolphe Sax created the saxhorn family of conical-bored, valved chromatic brass instruments ranging from soprano to contrabass. He also added the clarinet single-reed and fingering system to a brass conical tube, forming a new family of instruments, the saxophones.

Beginning in the 1830s, the homogeneous saxhorn family soon supplanted the mixed wind instruments, leading to the formation of all-brass bands, with percussion. Within 20 years, saxhorn, cornet or brass bands became the most common outdoor instrumental ensemble in the United States. Published arrangements were playable by bands of four to 21 musicians, and percussion. Brass bands became very popular in Victorian England, and followed a development which has continued. The brass band movement was popular in the United States through the Civil War, but, except for its continuance in the Salvation Army, gave way to the rise of concert and symphonic bands following the war. Since 1982, however, British-style brass bands have had a revival in the United States and Canada.

The larger professional and military ensembles had always maintained their woodwind complement. Reformers, such as Wilhelm Wieprecht in Prussia, Andreas Leonhardt in Austria and Adolphe Sax in France, reorganized military bands, setting high standards for other organizations to emulate. The publication of band journals, or periodic editions of symphonies, operatic overtures, fantasias, solos, dances and other popular works available by subscription, helped standardize band instrumentation. Many French editions were published during and after the Revolution. New journals, such as *Jullien's Journal for Military Bands*, *Boosey's Military Journal* and Chappell's *Army Journal* began in England during the 1840s and 1850s. Simultaneously, in the United States, G.W.E. Friederich published his *Brass Band Journal* and W.C. Peters his *Sax-Horn Journal*.

The 'Golden Age'

The period following the Civil War in the United States is often called the 'golden age' of bands. Irish-born Patrick S. Gilmore attracted international attention and fame with his Peace Jubilees (1869, 1872). In 1873, he took over the 22nd Regiment Band and soon made it the finest professional band in the United States. With his tours, he was an inspiration to bands all over the United States, and may be considered 'the father of the American symphonic band.' Other fine professional bands included those led by Matthew Arbuckle, Alessandro Liberati, David W. Reeves, Claudio Grafulla, Jean Missud and Carlo Cappa. Next to Gilmore, the towering figure of the US golden age of bands was John Philip Sousa. Touring regularly with his band from 1892 to 1932, he brought music to every corner of the United States. With his world tour and four European tours, he may be said to have brought US music, including jazz, to the world. While a major figure, Sousa was not alone in this golden age. Other successful bandmasters included Victor Herbert, Francesco Fanciulli, Herbert L. Clarke, Bohumir Kryl, Frank Simon, Arthur Pryor, Simone Mantia, Herman Bellstedt, Giuseppe Creatore, Frederick Innes, Patrick Conway, Edwin Franko Goldman and the leader of a ladies brass band, Helen May Butler.

In addition to these professional bands, there were the amateur bands. By the end of the century, it was estimated there were more than 10,000 bands active in the United States. G.F. Patton wrote, in 1875, 'it is a fact not to be denied that the existence of a good brass band in any town or community is at once an indication of enterprise among its people, and an evidence that a certain spirit of taste and refinement pervades the masses.' William Dana expressed a similar opinion: 'a town without its brass band is as much in need of sympathy as a church without a choir. The spirit of a place is recognized in its band.' A French survey noted that no community was so small as not to have a band of some sort. Dedicated 'professors' organized town bands and taught amateurs of all ages, providing music for parades, summer park concerts and civic festivities. Many American states passed 'band laws' that levied special taxes to support a professional municipal band to provide music for 'occasions of public importance.' Industrial bands, some directed by outstanding soloists such as Herbert L. Clarke and Frank Simon, provided recreational activity for the employees and positive community relations for the employer. Circus bands, often performing their music at faster tempos, provided music for the many touring circuses. Some famous circus bandmasters of the past include Henry Fillmore, Karl King, Russell Alexander, Fred Jewell and J.J. Richards. Bands in New Orleans, in improvising on favorite spirituals on the return from grave sites, were significant in the development of jazz. Bands proliferated everywhere, appearing at civic or military ceremonies, parades, celebrations, concerts, amusement parks, seaside resorts, state fairs, and national and international expositions. They played marches, dances, characteristic pieces, operatic selections, fantasias on popular themes and transcriptions of classical orchestral works. In many communities, the only music available was from the local band. At a time when there were orchestras only in the major cities, bands brought music of all kinds, vernacular and cultivated, to the masses.

Recent Developments

The arrival of radio, the phonograph, moving pictures and the automobile prompted a gradual decline in professional band activities and popularity. The golden age basically ended with the outbreak of World War I. Amateur and some professional bands continued after the war, but the greatest activity was now to be found in the schools. There were school and university bands in North America as early as 1827. Many universities offered courses in military training which required bands for their drills and ceremonies. Bands often performed at sporting events. To fill the stadiums with sound, bands increasingly added more brass and percussion, and often approached more than 300 musicians. Marching bands adopted some of the traditions of the old military field music, such as the color guard, precision marching, learning by rote and the emphasis on percussion (referred to as 'corps style').

Albert A. Harding became director of the University of Illinois Band in 1907, and in the next 40 years brought it to a high professional level, setting standards for college bands throughout the country. He enlarged the band to symphonic proportions, adding color winds (alto and bass flutes and clarinets, the full family of saxophones and sarrusophones, contrabassoon and so on) and making his own arrangements of modern orchestral works. He is considered the first to have developed non-military marching formations for football half-time shows. His work was greatly emulated and he was considered the dean of university band directors.

Musical instrument manufacturers encouraged the growth of music in the schools, and in 1923 organized the first national school band contest. Reaction was so positive that state contests were organized, and school groups flourished. Musical organizations were established to support and encourage this new enthusiasm.

Kappa Kappa Psi, a National Honorary Band Fraternity, was founded in 1919, with a National Honorary Band Sorority, Tau Beta Sigma, following in 1946. To honor outstanding achievement and to enhance the cultural standing of bands, Goldman, Sousa and others formed the American Bandmasters Association (ABA) in 1929. Other professional organizations soon followed: the College Band Directors National Association (CBDNA, 1941), the National Association of College Wind and Percussion Instructors (NACWPI, 1951), the American School Band Directors Association (ASBDA, 1953), the National Catholic Bandmasters' Association (NCBA, 1953), the National Band Association (NBA, 1960), the Women Band Directors National Association (WBDNA, 1969) and the Association of Concert Bands (ACB, 1977). Windjammers Unlimited was founded in 1971 to preserve and promote circus music. Some of these organizations have journals and all have newsletters to advance their goals. Similar organizations, such as the Japanese Band Directors Association and the Österreichischen Blasmusikverband, were formed in other countries. Three international organizations were also created: Die Internationale Gesellschaft zur Erforschung und Förderung der Blasmusik (the International Society for the Promotion and Investigation of Band Music) (IGEB, 1974), the International Military Music Society (IMMS, 1977) and the World Association for Symphonic Bands and Ensembles (WASBE, 1983). Each has national chapters and publishes a journal or proceedings. A direct offshoot of WASBE was BASBWE, the British Association of Symphonic Bands and Wind Ensembles.

One of ABA's goals was the establishment of a standardized international instrumentation. For some years, band music was published according to ABA recommendations in two classifications: 'standard band' and 'concert band.' The former had basic woodwinds and brass, including piccolo in D♭, E♭ horns and single double reeds. The 'concert' band included parts for 2nd flute and piccolo in C, 2nd oboe and bassoon, alto and bass clarinets, F horns, string bass and timpani. CBDNA had a similar goal, and in 1958 William Revelli, one of its founders, proposed a new international instrumentation that he had coordinated with the Comité International pour la Musique Instrumentale (CIMI). The plan called for bands of two basic sizes, 60 and 100 players. In addition to the instruments in the ABA recommendation, it included English horn, contrabassoon, contralto and contrabass clarinets, soprano and bass saxophones, flügelhorns and mallet percussion. Some success has been achieved in the standardization of parts, with publishers such as Molenaar in The Netherlands providing sufficient parts for North American and European-style bands.

Partially in reaction to the large symphonic bands, in 1952 Frederick Fennell formed the Eastman Wind Ensemble. Rather than a fixed standard instrumentation, the wind ensemble is fundamentally a concept. Basic tenets include a chamber music philosophy of flexible instrumentation with one player per part, and freedom of programming in that the same concert may include works ranging from small ensembles to works with full symphonic instrumentation. Fennell's work at the Eastman School of Music has been carried on since 1965 by Donald Hunsberger. The results of their work may be seen in the multitude of wind ensembles throughout the world.

Bands at the end of the twentieth century seemed to be in a position similar to that of the end of the previous century. Except for the lack of the old professional bands, an opportunity continued primarily by the military bands, there was a continuing interest in amateur bands throughout the world. As then, hardly any village or town was without its band, whether it was a youth, student, community or senior-citizen ensemble. In North America alone, a 1973 survey reported the existence of some 50,000 secondary-school and 2,000 college/university bands. Recent studies show that community bands are on the rise and, with their primary aim of popular entertainment, they often reach professional levels. The biennial WASBE conferences attract bands from all parts of the globe, and while instrumentations, uniforms and languages may differ, the musicians share the common bond and repertoire of the wind band.

Bibliography

Adkins, H.E. 1958. *Treatise on the Military Band*. London: Boosey. (First published London: Boosey & Co., 1931.)

Anesa, Marino. 1988. *Musica in Piazza: Contributi per una Storia delle Bande Musicali Bergamasche* [Music in the Square: Contributions for a Story of the Musical Band of Bergamo]. Bergamo: Sistema Bibliotecario Urbano di Bergamo.

Anesa, Marino. 1993, 1997. *Dizionario della Musica Italiana per Banda* [Dictionary of Italian Music for Bands]. 2 vols. Bergamo: n.p.

Bainbridge, Cyril. 1980. *Brass Triumphant*. London: Frederick Muller Ltd.

Battisti, Frank. 1997. *The Twentieth Century American Wind Band/Ensemble: History, Development and Literature*. Fort Lauderdale, FL: Meredith Music Publications.

Bierley, Paul. 1986. *John Philip Sousa, American Phenomenon*. Columbus, OH: Integrity Press. (First published Englewood Cliffs, NJ: Prentice-Hall, 1973.)

Binns, LTC P.L. 1959. *A Hundred Years of Military Music Being the Story of the Royal Military School of Music, Kneller Hall*. Gillingham, Dorset: The Blackmore Press.

Birsak, Kurt, and König, Manfred. 1983. *Das Große Salzburger Blasmusikbuch* [The Grand Wind Music Book of Salzburg]. Wien: Christian Brandstätter.

Booth, Gregory D. 1990. 'Brass Bands: Tradition, Change and the Mass Media in Indian Wedding Music.' *Ethnomusicology* 34(2): 245–61.

Brand, Violet, and Brand, Geoffrey. 1986. *The World of Brass Bands*. Baldock, Herts.: Egon.

Brenet, Michel (pseud. for Marie Bobillier). 1917. *La Musique Militaire* [Military Music]. Paris: Henri Laurens.

Brixel, Eugen. 1984. *Das Große Oberösterreichische Blasmusikbuch* [The Grand Wind Music Book of Upper Austria]. Wien: Christian Brandstätter.

Brixel, Eugen, and Suppan, Wolfgang. 1981. *Das Große Steirische Blasmusikbuch* [The Grand Wind Music Book of Styria]. Wien: Fritz Molden.

Brixel, Eugen, Martin, Gunther, and Pils, Gottfried. 1982. *Das ist Österreichs Militärmusik* [That Is Austrian Military Music]. Graz: Edition Kaleidoskop.

Bythell, Duncan. 1991. 'The Brass Band in Australia: The Transplantation of British Popular Culture.' In *Bands: The Brass Band Movement in the 19th and 20th Centuries*, ed. Trevor Herbert. Milton Keynes: Open University Press, 145–64.

Camus, Raoul F. 1989. 'Early American Wind and Ceremonial Music 1636–1836.' *The National Tune Index*, phase 2. New York: University Music Editions.

Camus, Raoul F. 1992. *American Wind and Percussion Music*. Three Centuries of American Music, 12. Boston, MA: G.K. Hall & Co.

Camus, Raoul F. 1993. *Military Music of the American Revolution*. Westerville, OH: Integrity Press. (First published Chapel Hill, NC: University of North Carolina Press, 1976.)

Cipolla, Frank J. 1979, 1980. 'A Bibliography of Dissertations Relative to the Study of Bands and Band Music.' *Journal of Band Research* 15(1): 1–31; 16(1): 29–36.

Cipolla, Frank J., and Hunsberger, Donald. 1994. *The Wind Ensemble and Its Repertoire*. Rochester, NY: University of Rochester Press.

Clappé, Arthur A. 1911. *The Wind-Band and Its Instruments*. New York: Henry Holt.

Dana, William H. 1878. *J.W. Pepper's Practical Guide and Study to the Secret of Arranging Band Music or, the Amateur's Guide*. Philadelphia: J.W. Pepper.

Degele, Ludwig. 1937. *Die Militärmusik, ihr Werden und Wesen, ihre kulturelle und nationale Bedeutung* [Military Music, Its Development and Nature, Its Cultural and National Importance]. Wolfenbüttel: Verlag für Musikalische Kultur und Wissenschaft.

Deutsch, Walter. 1982. *Das Große Niederösterreichische Blasmusikbuch* [The Grand Wind Music Book of Lower Austria]. Wien: Christian Brandstätter.

Dodworth, Allen. 1853. *Dodworth's Brass Band School.* New York: H.B. Dodworth. (Reprinted St. Paul: Paul Mayberry, n.d.)

Dudgeon, Ralph T. 1993. *The Keyed Bugle.* Metuchen and London: Scarecrow Press.

Dvorak, Raymond F. 1937. *The Band on Parade.* New York: Carl Fischer.

Egg, Erich, and Pfaundler, Wolfgang. 1979. *Das Große Tiroler Blasmusikbuch* [The Grand Wind Music Book of Tirol]. Wien: Fritz Molden.

Farmer, Henry G. 1912. *The Rise & Development of Military Music.* London: Wm. Reeves.

Farmer, Henry G. 1950. *Military Music.* New York: Chanticleer Press.

Fasman, Mark J. 1990. *Brass Bibliography: Sources on the History, Literature, Pedagogy, Performance, and Acoustics of Brass Instruments.* Bloomington, IN: Indiana University Press.

Fennell, Frederick. 1954. *Time and the Winds.* Kenosha, WI: G. Leblanc Co.

Garofalo, Robert, and Elrod, Mark. 1985. *A Pictorial History of Civil War Era Musical Instruments & Military Bands.* Charleston, WV: Pictorial Histories Publishing Company.

Gmaz, Sepp, and Hahnenkamp, Hans. 1987. *Das Große Burgenländische Blasmusikbuch* [The Grand Wind Music Book of Burgenland]. Wien: Christian Brandstätter.

Goldman, Richard Franko. 1946. *The Concert Band.* New York: Rinehart & Co.

Goldman, Richard Franko. 1961. *The Wind Band.* Boston, MA: Allyn and Bacon. (Reprinted Westport, CT: Greenwood Press, 1974.)

Griebel, Armin, and Steinmetz, Horst. 1993. *Militärmusik und 'zivile' Musik: Beziehungen und Einflüsse* [Military Music and 'Civil' Music: Connections and Influences]. Uffenheim: Stadt Uffenheim.

Griffiths, Lt. Samuel Charles. (1896). *The Military Band: How to Form, Train, and Arrange for Reed and Brass Bands.* London: Rudall, Carte & Co.

Habla, Bernhard. 1990. *Besetzung und Instrumentation des Blasorchesters seit der Erfindung der Ventile für Blechblaserinstrumente bis zum Zweiten Weltkrieg in Österreich und Deutschland* [The Composition and Instrumentation of Wind Orchestras Since the Invention of Valves for Brass Instruments up to World War II in Austria and Germany]. 2 vols. Alta Musica, 12. Tutzing: Hans Schneider.

Hall, Harry H. 1963. *A Johnny Reb Band from Salem.* Raleigh, NC: The North Carolina Confederate Centennial Commission. (Reprinted New York: Da Capo, 1980.)

Hazen, Margaret Hindle, and Hazen, Robert M. 1987. *The Music Men: An Illustrated History of Brass Bands in America 1800–1920.* Washington, DC: Smithsonian Institution Press.

Herbert, Trevor. 1990. 'The Repertory of a Provincial Brass Band.' *Popular Music* 9(l): 117–32.

Herbert, Trevor, ed. 1991. *Bands: The Brass Band Movement in the 19th and 20th Centuries.* Milton Keynes: Open University Press.

Herbert, Trevor. 1992. 'Victorian Brass Bands: The Establishment of a "Working-Class Musical Tradition."' *Historic Brass Society Journal* 4: 1–11.

Hind, Harold C. 1934. *The Brass Band.* London: Hawkes & Son.

Hofer, Achim. 1988. *Studien zur Geschichte des Militärmarsches* [Studies in the History of Military Marches]. 2 vols. Mainzer Studien zur Musikwissenschaft, 24. Tutzing: Hans Schneider.

Hofer, Achim. 1992. *Blasmusikforschung: Eine kritische Einführung* [Wind Music Research: A Critical Introduction]. Darmstadt: Wissenschaftliche Buchgesellschaft.

Horwood, Wally. 1980. *Adolphe Sax 1814–1894 – His Life and Legacy.* Baldock, Herts: Egon Publishers Ltd.

Huber, Richard. (1991). *Die Blasmusik in Kärnten* [Wind Music in Carinthia]. Klagenfurt: Kärntner Heimatwerkes.

Kalkbrenner, August. 1882. *Wilhelm Wieprecht: sein Leben und Wirken* [Wilhelm Wieprecht: His Life and Works]. Berlin: Emil Prager.

Kalkbrenner, August. 1884. *Die Organisation der Militärmusikchöre aller Länder* [The Organization of Military Music Bands in All Lands]. Hannover: Louis Oertel.

Kallmann, H. 1960. *A History of Music in Canada, 1534–1914.* Toronto: University of Toronto Press.

Kallmann, H., Kopstein, J., McMillan, B., and Wardrop, P. 1992. 'Bands.' In *Encyclopedia of Music in Canada.* 2nd ed. Toronto: University of Toronto Press, 76–85.

Kappey, J.A. 1894. *Short History of Military Music.* London: Boosey & Co.

Kastner, (Jean) Georges. 1848. *Manuel Général de Musique Militaire à l'usage des Armées Françaises* [General Manual of Military Music for the Use of the French Armies]. Paris: Didot Frères.

Kendrick, Ian. 1995. *The Bands and Orchestras of Oman.* Sultanate of Oman: Diwan of Royal Court.

Kreitner, Kenneth. 1990. *Discoursing Sweet Music: Brass Bands and Community Life in Turn-of-the-Century Pennsylvania.* Urbana, IL: University of Illinois Press.

Lawn, G.R. 1995. *Music in State Clothing: The Story of the Kettledrummers, Trumpeters and Band of the Life Guards.* London: Leo Cooper.

Lord, Francis Alfred, and Wise, Arthur. 1966. *Bands and Drummer Boys of the Civil War.* New York: Thomas Yoseloff. (Reprinted New York: Da Capo Press, 1979.)

Maloney, S. Timothy. 1988. 'A History of the Wind Band in Canada.' *Journal of Band Research* XXIII(2): 10–29.

Manfredo, Joseph. 1995. *Influences on the Development of the Instrumentation of the American Collegiate Wind Band and Attempts for Standardization of the Instrumentation from 1905–1941.* Alta Musica, 17. Tutzing: Hans Schneider.

Miller, George. 1912. *The Military Band.* London: Novello & Co., Ltd.

Mortimer, Harry. 1981. *On Brass.* Sherborne: Alphabooks.

Neukomm, Edmond. 1889. *Histoire de la Musique Militaire* [The History of Military Music]. Paris: Librarie Militaire de L. Baudoin.

Newsom, Jon. 1979. 'The American Brass Band Movement.' *The Quarterly Journal of the Library of Congress* 36: 115–39.

Olson, Kenneth E. 1981. *Music and Musket: Bands and Bandsmen of the American Civil War.* Westport, CT: Greenwood Press.

Panov, Peter. 1938. *Militärmusik in Geschichte und Gegenwart* [Military Music in History and the Present]. Berlin: Karl Siegismund.

Patton, G.F. 1875. *A Practical Guide to the Arrangement of Band Music.* Leipzig: John F. Stratton. (Reprinted St. Paul: Paul Mayberry, n.d.)

Railsback, Thomas C., and Longellier, John P. 1987. *The Drums Would Roll: A Pictorial History of US Army Bands on the American Frontier, 1866–1900.* Poole: Arms and Armour Press.

Rameis, Emil. 1976. *Die Österreichische Militärmusik von ihren Anfängen bis zum Jahre 1918* [Austrian Military Music from Its Beginnings to 1918]. Alta Musica, 2. Tutzing: Hans Schneider.

Rehrig, William H. 1991. *The Heritage Encyclopedia of Band Music: Composers and Their Music,* ed. Paul Bierley. 3 vols. Westerville, OH: Integrity Press.

Rose, Algernon S. 1895. *Talks with Bandsmen: A Popular Handbook for Brass Instrumentalists.* London: William Rider & Son, Ltd. (Reprinted London: Tony Bingham, 1995.)

Russell, J.F., and Elliot, J.H. 1936. *The Brass Band Movement.* London: J.M. Dent & Sons Ltd.

Schafer, William J., with Allen, Richard B. 1977. *Brass Bands and New Orleans Jazz.* Baton Rouge, LA: Louisiana State University Press.

Schneider, Erich. 1986. *Blasmusik in Vorarlberg* [Wind Music in Vorarlberg]. Lustenau: Vorarlberger Blasmusikverbandes.

Schwartz, H.W. 1957. *Bands of America.* New York: Doubleday & Co. (Reprinted New York: Da Capo Press, 1975.)

Smith, Norman E. 1986. *March Music Notes.* Lake Charles, LA: Program Note Press.

Soyer, M-A. 1929. 'De l'orchestration militaire et de son histoire' [Of Military Orchestration and Its History]. *Encyclopédie de la musique et dictionnaire du Conservatoire.* 2nd Part, Vol. 4. Paris: Librarie Delagrave, 2135–2214.

Steinmetz, Horst, and Griebel, Armin. 1990. *Das Große Nordbayerische Blasmusikbuch* [The Great Wind Music Book of Northern Bavaria]. Wien: Christian Brandstätter,

Suppan, Wolfgang. 1983. *Blasmusik in Baden: Geschichte und Gegenwart einer traditionsreichen Blasmusiklandschaft* [Wind Music in Baden: The History and Present of a Landscape Rich in the Tradition of Wind Music]. Freiburg: Musikverlag Fritz Schulz.

Suppan, Wolfgang, and Suppan, Armin. 1994. *Das Neue Lexikon des Blasmusikwesens* [The New Encyclopedia of Wind Music]. Freiburg-Tiengen: Blasmusikverlag Schulz.

Taylor, Arthur. 1979. *Brass Bands.* St. Alban's: Granada.

Taylor, Arthur. 1983. *Love and Lore: An Oral History of the Brass Band Movement.* London: Elm Tree Press.

Thompson, Kevin. 1985. *Wind Bands and Brass Bands in School and Music Centre.* Cambridge: Cambridge University Press.

Turner, Gordon, and Turner, Alwyn. 1995. *The History of British Military Bands.* Vol. 1: Cavalry and Corps. Vol. 2: Guards and Scottish Division. Staplehurst: Spellmount.

Turner, Gordon, and Turner, Alwyn. 1996. *The Trumpets Will Sound: The Story of the Royal Military School of Music Kneller Hall.* Tunbridge Wells, Kent: Parapress Ltd.

Wagner, Joseph. 1960. *Band Scoring.* New York: McGraw-Hill Book Co.

White, William C. 1944. *A History of Military Music in America.* New York: Exposition Press.

Whitwell, David. 1972. *A New History of Wind Music.* Evanston, IL: The Instrumentalist Co.

Whitwell, David. 1979. *Band Music of the French Revolution.* Alta Musica, 5. Tutzing: Hans Schneider.

Whitwell, David. 1982. *The History and Literature of the Wind Band and Wind Ensemble.* 11 vols. Northridge, CA: Winds.

Whitwell, David. 1985. *A Concise History of the Wind Band.* Northridge, CA: Winds.

Wright, Al G., and Newcomb, Stanley. 1970. *Bands of the World.* Evanston, IL: The Instrumentalist Co.

Wright, Frank, ed. 1957. *Brass Today.* London: Besson & Co. Ltd.

RAOUL CAMUS

2. Individuals

Cabaret Singer

The term 'cabaret' refers to both an entertainment venue and a type of entertainment provided there. Both senses have two distinct though connected histories, one mainly in France and Germany, and the other mainly in the United States. The types and styles of cabaret singers are varied, with the one element in common being the requirement for the singer to adapt to a small performance environment.

The word 'cabaret' was used in French from the sixteenth century on (and later also in English) to mean a drinking house, often with informal musical entertainment provided by strolling players. In the early 1880s in Paris, the word began to be used to describe a club-type venue, with tables and chairs grouped around a small stage on which was offered provocative entertainment specializing in social satire. Cabaret emerged partly because, although the dominant form of Parisian entertainment, the 'café-concert,' had developed a role for social commentary, particularly in song, it was seen as limited in its ability to comment fully on society, or to encourage new, more challenging styles of performance. The café-concert format, closely related to music hall, was a loosely connected series of acts including songs, monologs and short plays. Cabarets such as Le Chat Noir (which opened in Montmartre in 1881 and is usually cited as the first of this type) and Le Mirliton built on the café-concert format but created a more experimental form. The crucial element of this innovation was the close relationship between performer and audience, 'one at once of intimacy and hostility, the nodal points of participation and provocation' (Appignanesi 1975, 12).

In this early form of cabaret, major figures often assumed a number of roles, including that of singer. The founder of Le Mirliton, Aristide Bruant, wrote and performed his own songs, which were characterized by biting satire and imaginative (some said lewd) use of the life and language of the street. What made Bruant's guitar-accompanied performance style distinctive was that, rather than performing his embryonic protest songs in such a way as to gain the sympathy of his audience (both for his downtrodden characters and his arguments), he specialized in insulting the audience before, after and even during his songs. Even the sign outside said 'for audiences that enjoy being insulted'; inside, Bruant circulated among the customers' tables in his trademark velvet suit, broad-brimmed hat and long red scarf, as one contemporary recalled, 'calling one person by his first name, flicking a ribald epithet at another, hailing women as they enter with a saucy refrain in which everyone joins' (quoted in Frèches-Thory et al. 1991, 285).

Late nineteenth-century French cabaret was male-dominated, but within the neighboring world of the café-concert, at venues such as the Café du Divan Japonais, women singers began to develop a style that bore the influence of cabaret's concerns with challenging expectations. Without imitating Bruant's own style, Yvette Guilbert became known in the 1890s for her performances of his and other cabaret songwriters' material in the style of the diseuse, which would come into its own in the next century (for example, in the singing of Edith Piaf). Guilbert has been described as having a 'hoarse mournful voice with [a] touch of hysteria,' an 'actress in song' with 'sharp angular gestures and bright reddish hair [whose] presence and delivery were a set of contradictions' (Appignanesi 1975, 30). She herself wrote of these contradictions:

I was looking for an impression of extreme simplicity
. . . I wanted above all to appear highly distinguished,

so that I could risk anything, in a repertoire that I had decided would be a ribald one ... To assemble an exhibition of humorous sketches in song, depicting all the indecencies ... of my 'contemporaries,' and to enable them to laugh at themselves ... that was to be my innovation. (Quoted in Frèches-Thory et al. 1991, 311.)

Both Bruant and Guilbert were immortalized in the posters, drawings and paintings of Henri de Toulouse-Lautrec, those of Guilbert being especially interesting for the performance poses that the artist captured.

In the very early years of the twentieth century, cabaret developed in Germany, Austria and Switzerland, and writers who performed their own work became an important feature in these countries too. One of the most important, dramatist-poet Frank Wedekind, a member of the Eleven Executioners cabaret group in Munich, was influenced by Bruant. He performed satirical songs, with his own guitar accompaniment, in a confrontational manner calculated to shock his mainly middle-class audience. Germany's stricter censorship laws led to more frequent brushes with the law than had been the case in France, and Wedekind spent time in jail. He was a powerful influence on another writer who began as a cabaret poet-performer, Bertolt Brecht. When Wedekind died in 1918, Brecht paid homage to his impact: 'There he stood, ugly, brutal, dangerous, with close-cut red hair ... He sang ... in a brittle voice, rather monotonous and entirely untrained. No singer has ever inspired me or shocked me as much' (Brecht 1967, 3; author's translation). Heinrich Mann remembered Wedekind strumming awkwardly and 'as if annoyed ... twisting and writhing under his own ulterior motives' (Mann 1960, 247; author's translation).

In the 1920s, with Berlin as its focal point, German cabaret thrived, and the cabaret as a venue became more important than ever as an intellectual and artistic meeting ground. Greater emphasis was given to short plays, but song continued its important role in the work of writers like Walter Mehring, Kurt Tucholsky and Brecht. Each now often worked in collaboration with composers, among whom were Friedrich Holländer, Hanns Eisler and Kurt Weill. Although many songwriters began as performers, they now preferred to entrust their songs to specialist monolog performers such as Paul Grätz and, increasingly, to women.

Women performers had been central to the development of German cabaret from its earliest days. Marya Delvard, for example, helped put the Eleven Executioners on the Munich map in 1901, with her performance of a Wedekind song. In the more permissive environment of post-World War I Berlin, performers such as Gussy Holl, Rosa Valetti, Blandine Ebinger and Trude Hesterberg came into their own (some also ran cabarets), developing a style of performance that comfortably embraced the political and the erotic, the comic and the tragic, and that appeared improvisatory but was often highly rehearsed. Out of this environment came one of the most famous of all cabaret performances – Marlene Dietrich as Lola-Lola in Josef von Sternberg's film *Der blaue Engel* (1930), singing Friedrich Holländer's song 'Ich bin von Kopf bis Fuss auf Liebe eingestellt' (the English version of which, with lyrics by Sammy Lerner, appeared in the same year, with the title 'Falling in Love Again'). The same kind of setting – and same central role for a female performer – would later (1966) be evoked in the US musical *Cabaret*, John Kander's and Fred Ebb's adaptation of *The Berlin Stories* of Christopher Isherwood. In *Cabaret*, the outside world's fascination with the style is captured in the person of Sally Bowles (played to great acclaim in the 1972 movie version by Liza Minnelli), an expatriate singer in the seedy world of Berlin's Kit Kat Club, for whom – despite the encircling grip of fascism – 'life is a cabaret.'

With the advent of the Third Reich, German cabaret continued in exile but without any significant developments in performance styles. Although the cabaret-tinged theater of Brecht and Weill had an impact in the United States in the 1930s, in many parts of the English-speaking world the influence of cabaret and of French styles was somewhat belated. In Britain itself, for example, when political and cultural satire suddenly came to prominence in the 1960s, a highly topical, satirical style of cabaret singing had a brief but spectacular success, most notably with the performances of Millicent Martin on the Saturday night television show *That Was The Week That Was*.

For the most part, however, to 'do cabaret' in Britain meant one of two things, both of them different from the continental European concept. One was synonymous with performing in the after-dinner floor show at a 'function' (usually private), and typically involved sharing the bill with comedians and strippers (the cabaret singer might double up as the former but rarely as the latter!). The second, related sense was that of providing the musical entertainment at classy city nightspots, such as London's Talk of the Town. Working in this kind of cabaret usually indicated a performing career in its later stages.

In this latter sense, cabaret singing in Britain owed much to developments in the United States. The North American 'beat clubs' of the 1950s, featuring jazz and poetry, were close relatives of European cabaret, but the United States already had a slightly different use for the term 'cabaret,' albeit one with a somewhat confusing array of variants. None of these variants included the directly challenging ethos of cabaret performance in continental Europe, and although they did have in common with Europe the idea of a small club environment, the leading idea was one of a standard of entertainment to distinguish the venue from saloons and dance halls.

In the rapidly expanding urban entertainment world of early twentieth-century North America, the emergence of the cabaret in the century's second decade was closely connected to the rise in popularity of dance and the need for up-market, intimate clubs. Its increase in popularity in the 1920s owed much to the Prohibition legislation of 1919, which 'required that saloons find something effervescent with which to camouflage the sale of alcohol. The solution most often taken was to upgrade the entertainment into a small vaudeville show' (Kenney 1993, 69).

By the early 1920s, the cabaret had acquired a particular place in the growing urban communities of African Americans. Successors of the basement rathskellers of the late nineteenth century, the cabarets were nevertheless clearly distinguishable from more lowdown venues, and the distinction crept into the repertoire of the jazz and blues performers who, with the dancers, were the main providers of entertainment. To his partner 'Coot' Grant's invitation to 'Find Me at the Greasy Spoon,' blues singer 'Kid Sox' Wilson responded, 'That ain't no cabaret/It's only a barrelhouse saloon.' Raising the standard of a particular saloon to something closer to a cabaret was an achievement singer Ethel Waters was proud of. When she first sang at Edmond's Cellar in Harlem, it was 'the last stop on the way down in show business,' but when the proprietor 'saw the different class of people I was drawing into his low-class dump, he realized I was a real attraction. I'd changed the clientele . . .' (Waters 1951, 118, 126).

Although the band was often the main attraction, singers were increasingly hired to add glamor. Performers such as Waters, Edith Wilson and Lucille Hegamin epitomized the different type of singer coming to the fore through the cabaret stage: sleekly stylish and urbane – 'more cosmopolitan, less emotional' (Harrison 1988, 12) – and with a repertoire based in the vaudeville blues but borrowing widely from contemporary popular song. These singers became particularly popular with the white audiences who frequented the 'black and tans' (interracial cabarets) where, as comedian Jimmy Durante put it, white people could go expecting to find 'Negro melody artists bearing down something terrible on the minor notes' (quoted in Lewis 1981, 208). In this context, they 'deserve credit for popularizing and standardizing blues performance so that it became a staple in American song repertoire' (Harrison 1988, 12).

By the late 1920s, not only the black and tans but the previously all-black venues were attracting white customers, who came 'flooding the little cabarets and bars where formerly only colored people laughed and sang and where now the strangers are given the best ring side tables' (Hughes 1940, 225). Perhaps as a result of this, Waters in particular seems to have responded to the joint demands of the cabaret and the theater by working hard at her delivery. 'Her genius was for characterization, and characterization . . . begins with language. Her diction was immaculate and flexible. She colored vowels, diphthongs and consonants to suit both the substance and the style of a song' (Pleasants 1974, 92).

As popular music vocal styles proliferated in the twentieth century, cabaret performance, in its various guises, never again occupied as prominent a place in the opportunities available to singers as it had in urban centers in the early years of the century. But the cabaret itself proved remarkably resilient in a broad sense, as an intimate performance environment featuring a jazz- and show-based repertoire, and by the late twentieth century, virtually all over the world, the North American concept of cabaret singer had all but obliterated the earlier European one. In the United States itself, though cabaret was badly dented by rock and pop in the 1960s, it revived in the 1980s. While the majority of performers were unpublicized, workaday musicians, some, like Julie Wilson, who had built reputations in the 1950s based on cabaret appearances, were able to reestablish themselves in clubs such as the Rainbow and Stars, and the Russian Tea Room in New York, with repertoires ranging from Weill to Sondheim (Winer 1996).

Bibliography

Appignanesi, Lisa. 1975. *The Cabaret*. London: Studio Vista.

Brecht, Bertolt. 1967. 'Frank Wedekind.' In *Gesammelte Werke* [Collected Works], Vol. 15, ed. Werner Hecht. Frankfurt: Suhrkamp, 3–4.

Frèches-Thory, Claire, et al. 1991. *Toulouse-Lautrec*. New Haven, CT: Yale University Press.

Harrison, Daphne Duval. 1988. *Black Pearls: Blues Queens of the 1920s*. New Brunswick, NJ: Rutgers University Press.

Hazzard-Gordon, Katrina. 1990. *Jookin': The Rise of Social Dance Formations in African-American Culture*. Philadelphia: Temple University Press.

Hennessey, Thomas J. 1994. *From Jazz to Swing: African-American Jazz Musicians and Their Music, 1890–1935*. Detroit, MI: Wayne State University Press.

Hughes, Langston. 1940. *The Big Sea*. New York: Knopf.

Isherwood, Christopher. 1945. *The Berlin Stories: The Last of Mr. Norris, Goodbye to Berlin.* New York: James Laughlin.

Kenney, William Howland. 1993. *Chicago Jazz: A Cultural History, 1904–1930.* New York: Oxford University Press.

Lewis, David Levering. 1981. *When Harlem Was in Vogue.* New York: Knopf.

Mann, Heinrich. 1960. 'Erinnerungen an Frank Wedekind' [Recollections of Frank Wedekind]. In *Essays.* Hamburg: Claasen, 243–62.

Pleasants, Henry. 1974. *The Great American Popular Singers.* New York: Simon and Schuster.

Waters, Ethel. 1951. *His Eye Is on the Sparrow: An Autobiography (with Charles Samuels).* London: Allen.

Winer, Deborah Grace. 1996. *The Night and the Music: Rosemary Clooney, Barbara Cook, and Julie Wilson Inside the World of Cabaret.* New York: Schirmer.

Sheet Music

Holländer, Friedrich, comp. and lyr. 1930. 'Ich bin von Kopf bis Fuss auf Liebe eingestellt' [I Am Focused on Love from Head to Foot]. Berlin: Ufaton Verlag.

Hollander, Frederick, comp., and Lerner, Sammy, lyr. 1930. 'Falling in Love Again (Can't Help It).' New York: Famous Music Co.

Kander, John, comp., and Ebb, Fred, lyr. 1966. 'Cabaret.' *Cabaret.* New York: Times Square Music.

Discographical References

Dietrich, Marlene. 'Falling in Love Again.' Victor 22593. 1931: USA. Reissue: Dietrich, Marlene. 'Falling in Love Again.' *Falling in Love Again.* MCA 11849. *1998*: USA.

Dietrich, Marlene. 'Ich bin von Kopf bis Fuss auf Liebe eingestellt.' EL EG-1770. 1930: Germany. Reissue: Dietrich, Marlene. 'Ich bin von Kopf bis Fuss auf Liebe eingestellt.' *The Essential Marlene Dietrich.* EMI CDEMS 13299. *1991*: UK.

Grant, 'Coot,' and Wilson, 'Kid Sox' (Leola Wilson and Wesley Wilson). 'Find Me at the Greasy Spoon (If You Miss Me Here).' Paramount PM 12337. 1925: USA. Reissue: Grant, 'Coot,' and Wilson, 'Kid Sox' (Leola Wilson and Wesley Wilson). 'Find Me at the Greasy Spoon (If You Miss Me Here).' *Complete Recorded Works, Vol. 1 (1925–1928).* Document 5563. *1998*: Austria.

Discography

A Collector's Sondheim (with Millicent Martin). RCA RCD3-5480. *1985*: USA.

Cabaret [Original Broadway Cast]. CBS 03040. *1966*: USA.

Cabaret [Original Soundtrack]. MCA 37125. *1972*: USA.

Dietrich, Marlene. *Falling in Love Again.* MCA 11849. *1998*: USA.

Dietrich, Marlene. *The Essential Marlene Dietrich.* EMI CDEMS 13299. *1991*: UK.

Guilbert, Yvette. *Le fiacre.* Pearl/Flapper 9773. *1991*: UK.

Waters, Ethel. *Ethel Waters 1926–1927.* Charly Classics 688. *1993*: UK.

Wilson, Julie. *Julie Wilson Sings the Kurt Weill Songbook.* DRG CDSL 5207. *1988*: USA.

Wilson, Julie. *Julie Wilson Sings the Stephen Sondheim Songbook.* DRG CDSL 5206. *1987*: USA.

Filmography

Cabaret, dir. Bob Fosse. 1972. USA. 124 mins. Musical Drama. Original music by Fred Ebb, John Kander.

Der blaue Engel [The Blue Angel], dir. Josef von Sternberg. 1930. Germany. 103 mins. Romance. Original music by Friedrich Holländer (composer and songwriter), Franz Waxman (composer).

DAVID HORN

Chansonnier

In French, the word 'chansonnier' has had a number of different, although related, meanings: (a) it is used regularly by contemporary scholars working in the field of medieval and early Renaissance music to designate a manuscript collection of French songs; (b) in a broader sense, the term was also employed during the period of the French Revolution (from around 1750 to 1850) to designate collections of French songs of that period; (c) in France the term is, in addition, used in reference to contemporary collections of songs; (d) the term was also used in France during the fifteenth century to refer to someone who enjoyed singing, from the eighteenth century to designate someone who produced *chansons*, and from the nineteenth century to refer to an artist who would write his/her own lyrics (but not music) and perform songs of a satirical and political character; and (e) the term has been used since World War II in Québec to describe a particular kind of singer-songwriter.

To gain an appreciation of the resonances of the word as it is used in contemporary France and Québec to refer to types of performers, it will be useful to examine the term's provenance.

The Chansonnier as Song Anthology

Manuscript Anthologies

The word 'chansonnier' is employed by contemporary scholars to designate a collection of French songs from the Middle Ages or from the early Renaissance period. The songs in these anthologies are usually short, often anonymous and, in the case of the older ones at least, frequently collected as texts only, without music. Extensive repertoires of sacred and secular songs from the sixteenth century onward have been preserved through manuscripts.

While medieval copyists would often use a single manuscript for the rendition of one lengthy *chanson de geste* (approximately 10,000 lines), they would sometimes make the most of a manuscript by bringing together shorter songs. The short songs of the troubadours (singer-songwriters of the South of France) and those of the *trouvères* (singer-songwriters of northern France), as well as a large number of later secular and religious songs (motets, rondeaux, ballades, *lais* and *virelais*) have survived by means of this kind of handwritten document. Some of these manuscripts are highly decorated, with elaborate illuminations, as they were prepared for kings, princes, rich merchants and other wealthy people. While the songs of the *trouvères* and troubadours focus on themes of love, the chansonniers of the fourteenth and fifteenth centuries are genuine miscellanies (mixing romances with songs and other kinds of texts). The most famous is the Bayeux manuscript, copied around 1514, containing *L'Amour de moy* (a love song), *Dieu merci j'ai bien labouré* (a song about country works), *A la duché de Normandie* (a song about war) and several drinking songs.

Lists of medieval and early Renaissance chansonniers, as well as bibliographical information, can be obtained from Paris (1856), Raynaud (1884), Droz and Piaget (1925), Jeanroy (1918), Lachèvre (1922), Atlas (1975–76), Perkins and Garey (1979) and Fallows (1999).

The Anthologies of the Revolution

While a few anthologies of songs were still copied as manuscripts during the sixteenth, seventeenth and eighteenth centuries, most were printed. From the beginning of the sixteenth century to the end of the eighteenth century, anthologies of *chansons* – texts with music – were brought out primarily by the king's printers: Pierre Attaingnant during the first half of the sixteenth century (Heartz 1969), and the Ballards from the sixteenth to the eighteenth century (Lesure and Thibault 1955). Several anthologies of French songs were also published by printers in the Low Countries.

While Attaingnant and the Ballards were bringing out an extensive collection of *chansons* for the court and the wealthy, a popular form of song entertainment was also emerging. In the sixteenth century, small chansonniers were sold on the streets of cities such as Paris and Lyon. According to Jeffery (1971), they contained drinking and dancing songs, as well as songs of an historical and satirical character. When the texts were published without music, they were probably associated with 'monophonic settings' of what later came to be described as 'popular' or '*volkstümlich*' music (Jeffery 1971, 32).

In the following two centuries, these kinds of songs would become increasingly popular. In the seventeenth century, more than 6,000 *mazzarinades*, political and satirical songs named after Mazzarin (1602–61) and describing Parisian life, were distributed in Paris. In 1620, Maître Guillaume, the 'folle' Mathurine, Maillet and Philippot were singing political, satirical and vulgar songs on the streets of Paris. By the end of the seventeenth century, Étienne (the coachman of Mr. de Verthamond), Michel Minard (whose nickname was 'Le Picard') and several others were singing and selling their *complaintes* (laments) in small blue booklets (hence their name, *bleuettes*). On the banks of the Seine, near the Pont Neuf, street singers of uncertain social status were also performing and selling their *ponts-neufs*. A *pont-neuf* was typically a text without music, but a text that was nonetheless associated with an *air*. The texts of the *ponts-neufs* were probably of a political and satirical nature (on the subjects of French street singers and *ponts-neufs*, see Coirault 1953, 63–137; Isherwood 1986, 3–22; Mason 1996, 20–33).

By the middle of the eighteenth century, anthologies of 'popular' *chansons* began to be printed as periodicals – once every two months in the case, for example, of *Le Chansonnier françois ou Recueil de chansons, Ariettes, Vaudevilles & autres couplets choisis. Avec les Airs notés à la fin de chaque recueil*. This anonymous anthology was published regularly on 16 occasions, probably in Paris (although by an unknown printer) between 1760 and 1762. Typically, an issue would consist of one or two pages announcing the forthcoming Parisian theater plays, followed by a table of contents and then by the songs themselves. During its two years of publication, the *Chansonnier françois* brought out some 2,500 songs.

During the years of the French Revolution, the chansonniers were used as political weapons, by revolutionaries and royalists alike, singing in the streets of Paris. For example, the famous 'Ça ira' was sung by 200,000 people as they built the Champ de Mars; royalists in large groups and in the king's armies would sing 'O Richard, ô mon Roi.' A list of these anthologies appears in Delon's and Levayer's *Chansonnier révolutionnaire*, a twentieth-century selection of songs from the Revolution (1989), and in Mason's book, *Singing the French Revolution* (1996). These anthologies, created in the context of specific social or political events, were often short-lived. Dating from the Napoleonic era, *Le Chansonnier des amis du Roi et des Bourbons* is an example of such a publication. These anti-Napoleonic texts were written shortly after Napoleon returned from the island of Elba in March 1815, the first issue dating from May 1815. The second one was published in August 1815, two months after the Napoleonic armies were defeated at Waterloo. The publication was then stopped. Some songs may never have been sung.

Around 1800, several chansonniers were brought into existence by singing societies, and especially by the members of the Caveau society. Founded in 1730, disbanded 10 years later, reestablished in 1762 and disbanded again in 1777, the Caveau was again reestablished in September 1796 under the name Les Dîners du Vaudeville. Commitments were made to bring out 12 periodical anthologies of *chansons*, containing neither political nor religious texts. Between 1797 and 1801, 52 issues were published, with mostly new and original songs and texts with music. These chansonniers contain many songs by the important members of the society, which was finally disbanded in 1939.

Contemporary Anthologies

By the middle of the nineteenth century, the manner in which *chansons* were disseminated had changed. In 1851, the Société des Auteurs, Compositeurs et Editeurs de Musique (SACEM) was established. The rights of songwriters became important; songwriters were now in a better position to earn a living by publishing their songs. At the end of the nineteenth century, Aristide Bruant made his living by singing and selling his songs in small booklets, each containing one or two songs. Copyright laws limited the distribution of songs; consequently, as collections of contemporary songs, chansonniers became more difficult to produce.

However, chansonniers continued to be produced, but they became oriented toward the past. This trend was further strengthened by the contemporary invention of 'folklore.' In 1852, the Ministre de l'Instruction publique, Fortoul, requested that an official inquiry be conducted into the *chansons folkloriques*. Usually, the focus was on the text and not on the music. One such chansonnier focusing on the past was *Le Chansonnier huguenot du XVIᵉ siècle*, published by Bordier in 1870–71. In similar vein, Delon and Levayer brought out their *Chansonnier révolutionnaire* (a collection of songs from the French Revolution) in 1989. More recently, in 1999, Mironneau assembled, under the title *Chansonnier Henri IV*, 132 songs evoking King Henry IV and his time.

The Chansonnier as Performer

France

According to *Le Petit Robert* (1989), the term 'chansonnier' is employed to designate someone 'who writes, composes songs, mainly satirical songs' (II, 486); Gilles Potvin, in *The New Grove Dictionary of Music and Musicians* (2001), proposes a similar definition: 'a term used in France to describe a writer and performer of satirical songs, monologues and skits' (V, 486). Both definitions assert that the songs of a chansonnier are essentially satirical. This description seems appropriate for a large

number of the songs written by the chansonniers of the nineteenth and early twentieth centuries, especially the songs of the 'chansonniers de Montmartre.' However, the term 'chansonnier' has come to be used in a much broader sense, in which the output of chansonniers seems not to be mainly satirical.

According to Rey (1992), the word 'chansonnier' was used in the fifteenth century as an adjective, and not as a noun, to designate someone who enjoyed singing. However, the term 'chansonnier' is used as a noun in the *Dictionnaire de l'Académie Françoise* (1786): 'someone who produces *chansons*' (I, 190). At the beginning of the nineteenth century, a chansonnier was someone who wrote his/her own lyrics (but not music), who sang songs of a principally satirical and political character, and who often performed in a *goguette* (a popular singing society). Pierre-Jean de Béranger was famous as such a chansonnier, along with Émile Debraux and Hegésippe Moreau.

While Béranger wrote the texts of his *chansons*, he did not compose the music. He composed songs, but as a nineteenth-century chansonnier: for each song he would choose between music already composed and a traditional *air*. For example, 'Le petit homme gris' (1811) would be sung to the music of Édouard Pilloire, a composer. 'Les gueux' (1812), however, would be sung to the *air* 'La première ronde du vaudeville, Le départ pour Saint-Malo.' 'Le Roi d'Yvetot' (1813) would be sung to the *air* 'Quand un tendron vient en ces lieux,' while 'Le sénateur' (1813) would be sung to the music of Radet and Desfontaine.

While Béranger frequently performed for selected members of the Caveau singing society, he was also one of the greatest leaders of the Moulin vert, or Moulin de beurre, a *goguette*. Most probably, the choice of venues for performance was limited: chansonniers were not welcome in the large official theaters of Paris and especially not at the Opera.

In 1830, another generation of chansonniers came into being. Their aim was to promote a utopian socialism and to protect the working class. François Vinçard and Jules Mercier defended the ideas of Saint-Simon in their songs. Philosopher and chansonnier Louis Festeau promoted the ideas of Fourier. Pierre Dupont wrote an important selection of *romance* songs with allusions to vague socialist ideas. Charles Gille founded La Ménagerie, a *goguette* hostile to the Bourbons and to Napoleon III. Gille was also responsible for meetings of the Lice Chansonnière, a *goguette* often closed by the Paris police. Eugène Pottier promoted socialist ideas, writing, among other songs, the famous 'Internationale.' Again, the chansonniers wrote the text of their songs but not the music. Not all of these songs were satirical. During the

Second Empire, the *goguettes* were obliged to remain silent (Brochon 1956). By the end of the war of 1870, the *chanson* had evolved further, and was no longer of a 'social' nature (Brochon 1956, 87).

The chansonniers began to perform in the cabarets of Montmartre, above all in the Club des Hydropathes, the Chat-Noir and the Mirliton. The Club des Hydropathes was established by Émile Goudeau in 1878: Jules Jouy (a specialist in black humor) and Maurice Mac-Nab (who laughed at the popular classes), as well as several other chansonniers, met there. In 1885, Émile Goudeau and Rodolphe Salis opened the Chat-Noir. As the manager of the show, Rodolphe Salis used irony to insult his clientele while introducing the songs of the chansonniers and the poems to be read. When Salis and Goudeau sold their building to increase the size of their cabaret, Bruant bought it to create his own club, the Mirliton.

The success of these cabarets was exceptional. Other cabarets were soon established in Montmartre: the Quat-Z'Arts, the Lune Rousse, the Ane Rouge, the Boite à Fursy, the Coucou and the Perchoir. The Chien Noir, the Carillon, the Pie Qui Chante and a few other cabarets provided entertainment for a clientele outside Montmartre. Lists of the Montmartre cabarets are provided by Valbel (1879), by De Bercy and Ziwès (1951), and by Vernillat and Charpentreau (1971). The lives of some 50 chansonniers (for example, Mac-Nab, d'Erville, Boukay, Héros, Xanrof, Trimouillat, Privas, Quinel, Mouton, Salis, Fragerolle, Montoya, Goudezki, Brun, Blès, Joyeux, Richar, Zamacois) are contained in Valbel (1879), while De Bercy and Ziwès (1951) provide information on more than 100 chansonniers.

The meaning of the term 'chansonnier' has more recently become less precise, and is used in a much broader sense. An example of this is to be found in Léo Ferré's book on Jean Roger Caussimon, in which he employs the word to refer to Caussimon, Jacques Brel and himself (Ferré 1967, 7, 32, 37). Similarly, Serge Dillaz employs the term to refer to Pierre-Jean de Béranger, Georges Brassens and Jean Ferrat (Dillaz 1971, 71). However, all these popular artists had one characteristic in common: from Béranger to Ferré, they sang the words they wrote and, in some cases, the music they composed.

Québec

French-speaking singer-songwriters/composers have practised their art in Québec since the middle of the nineteenth century. However, the related term 'chansonniers' (literally, song craftsmen) has been used in Québec more specifically since World War II to describe a special kind of singer-songwriter. This use of the word differs from that current in France during the heyday of Montmartre, when it referred to singers commenting on current events. In Québec, the chansonnier movement reached its height during the 1960s and 1970s.

Even if they wrote most of their material, performers like La Bolduc (1894–1941), Lionel Daunais (1902–82) and Roland Lebrun (1919–80) were not regarded as chansonniers in their own time. The father of Québec's modern chansonniers is Félix Leclerc. Leclerc was well known as a writer of theater and radio plays, but his singing career owes much to a twist of fate. After French producer Jacques Canetti heard Leclerc in Montréal, he invited him to France for a couple of weeks in 1950. Leclerc stayed for a couple of years. That visit provided the genesis of a new means of expression for decades to come, as much in France as in Québec.

Although the French loved the rustic nobility of Québec's vast wilderness as expressed in Leclerc's poetry, other Québec songwriters found their inspiration on the Parisian *Rive gauche* (Left Bank). Future leaders of the chansonnier movement such as Raymond Lévesque, Claude Léveillée and Jean-Pierre Ferland, who all lived in Paris for a while, represented a move toward modernity. Meanwhile, in Québec, individuals such as Gilles Vigneault, Jean-Paul Filion, Claude Gauthier, Tex Lecor and Laurence Lepage were creating a new *chanson québécoise*, more rooted in local tradition. Many of these individuals were discovered by folk talent scout Jacques Labrecque, a folk singer himself. Although most of the chansonniers were men, women were also present from the beginning, the best known among them being Monique Miville-Deschênes, Jacqueline Lemay, Marie Savard and Clémence Desrochers.

Every chansonnier's stage equipment was minimal: one instrument, usually a guitar or piano, and a microphone. For a brief period, in the early 1960s, cosy *boîtes à chansons* (coffeehouses) provided the setting in which these artists grew up and where their songs were born. The most renowned had names like Chez Bozo, La Poubelle, Le Cro-Magnon, La Piouke, Le Cochon Borgne, Le Patriote and La Butte à Mathieu. Located in nearly every school, sometimes in renovated barns, church basements or cabaret cellars, these *boîtes* had handmade decorations with rustic elements like fishing nets, seashells, antiques, farmyard equipment or any other ancient-looking object that was at hand. However, this archetypal image was short-lived. As time passed, the chansonniers' fame grew and their venues had to adjust accordingly. As their audience spread beyond students and young people, medium-size and major halls became a necessity. Television also helped the movement emerge, with programs like *Jeunesse Oblige*, in which a wide variety of artists could perform.

As the context evolved, so did the content. As the 1960s approached, the chansonniers' poetic, even courtly, preoccupations were making way for a new social and political awareness. The affirmation of Québec's growing national identity was also clearly perceptible by this time. Chansonniers became the artists most suited to represent Québec in great cultural events instead of – or along with – traditional folklore acts, a situation that has continued to persist. Some of the best-known female vocalists (Pauline Julien, Monique Leyrac, Renée Claude, Ginette Ravel and Louise Forestier) premièred songs by Québec chansonniers at many international festivals, such as those held at Spa (Belgium), Sopot (Poland), Rio (Brazil) and Tokyo (Japan), as well as in prestigious venues such as Carnegie Hall (New York) and the Olympia (Paris). Ironically, people in Québec had to wait until the 1970s to hear some of these female singers, like Julien and Forestier, record their own songs.

Musically, basic classic and traditional influences slowly gave way to jazz and, after 1962, to more exotic arrangements such as those using bossa nova styles. With the preeminence of rock music in the second part of the 1960s – mainly folk-rock à la Bob Dylan, and the San Francisco psychedelic movement – many second-generation chansonniers were pleased to rediscover their North American roots. Important among these chansonniers were Robert Charlebois, Claude Dubois and the unparalleled duo Les Alexandrins. Expo '67, held in Montréal from April to October 1967, was the major event of the decade in Québec from many points of view, including that of popular music. Out of more than 2,000 submissions from 35 countries around the world, Stéphane Venne's 'Un jour, un jour'/'Hey Friend, Say Friend' was chosen as the official theme song of the event. His work with both popular singers and well-known artists from the chansonnier movement established solid ties between these hitherto seemingly different worlds, as did the music of Robert Charlebois.

The success enjoyed by Venne and Charlebois laid the foundations for what was to become mainstream Québécois *chanson* a few years later, when a new generation came to the fore. Leaders of the mid-1970s generation were groups such as Octobre, Beau Dommage and Harmonium, and individuals such as Raôul Duguay, Plume Latraverse and Paul Piché.

In parallel with local rock acts, many representatives from this new generation of chansonniers tended toward a pop-rock format that has dominated the airwaves since the 1980s. The music scene has evolved into more of a music industry undertaking, in which individual approach has sometimes been sacrificed in favor of *esthétique du genre* (genre aesthetic).

Meanwhile, a new left-wing back-to-the-roots movement with a more urgent feel sprang from the underground through such songwriters as Stephen Faulkner, Anne-Marie Gélinas and, especially, Richard Desjardins. Desjardins has acted as the spokesperson for the social and ecological concerns of which more and more people are becoming aware. Thus, the passage into the twenty-first century has witnessed a revitalized *chanson* in reaction to the formatted music that has come to dominate mainstream radio.

Bibliography (France)

Atlas, Allan W. 1975–76. *The Cappella Guilia Chansonnier*. New York: Institute of Medieval Music.

Avenel, Henri. 1889. *Chansons et chansonniers* [Songs and Chansonniers]. Paris: Flammarion.

Bailly, René. 1936. *Ange Pitou: Conspirateur et Chansonnier (1767–1846)* [Ange Pitou: Conspirator and Chansonnier (1767–1846)]. Paris: Éditions 'À l'Étoile.'

Ballard, Jean-Baptiste-Christophe. 1717. *La Clef des chansonniers ou Recueil de vaudevilles depuis cent ans & plus notez et recueillis pour la première fois* [The Key Chansonnier, or the Collection of Ballads of the Last Hundred Years and More, Noted and Collected for the First Time] (2 vols.). Paris: Ballard.

Béranger, Pierre-Jean de. 1840. *Oeuvres complètes. Illustrées par Grandville* [Complete Works, Illustrated by Grandville]. Paris: Fournier.

Béranger, Pierre-Jean de. 1876. *Oeuvres* [Works]. Paris: Garnier.

Bordier, Henri-Léonard. 1969 (1870–71). *Le Chansonnier huguenot du XVIᵉ siècle* [The Huguenot Chansonnier of the Sixteenth Century]. Geneva: Slatkine Reprints.

Brochon, Pierre. 1956. *La Chanson française (I). Béranger et son temps* [The French Song (I): Béranger and His Times]. Paris: Éditions sociales.

Brochon, Pierre. 1957. *La Chanson française (II). Le Pamphlet du pauvre. Du socialisme utopique à la révolution de 1848* [The French Song (II): The Pauper's Pamphlet (Satirical Booklet). From Utopian Socialism to the 1848 Revolution]. Paris: Éditions sociales.

Brochon, Pierre. 1961. *La Chanson sociale de Béranger à Brassens* [The Social Song from Béranger to Brassens]. Paris: Éditions ouvrières.

Brown, Howard Mayer, ed. 1983. *A Florentine Chansonnier from the Time of Lorenzo the Magnificent* (Florence, Biblioteca Nazionale Centrale, MS Banco Rari 229). Chicago: University of Chicago Press.

Capelle, Pierre. 1811. *La Clé du Caveau à l'usage de tous les chansonniers français, des amateurs, auteurs, acteurs du vaudeville, et de tous les Amis de la chanson . . . Contenant 2030 airs, rondes, chants . . . Précédée d'une table alphabétique des timbres, et suivie de plusieurs autres tables renfermant l'Ordre des coupes pour chaque genre, par. . .* [The Key to the Caveau, for the Use of All

French Chansonniers, Amateurs, Authors, Vaudeville Actors, and All the Friends of the Song . . . Containing 2,030 Airs, Rounds and Songs . . . Preceded by an Alphabetical Table of Melodies, and Followed by Other Tables Including the Order of Parts for Each Kind, by . . .]. Paris: Janet & Cotelle.

Chailley, Jacques. 1950. *Histoire musicale du Moyen Age* [A History of the Music of the Middle Ages]. Paris: Presses Universitaires de France.

Chansonnier de la Montagne, ou Recueil de Chansons, Vaudevilles, Pots-pourris, et Hymnes patriotiques par différens auteurs [The Chansonnier of the Democratic Party of the National Convention, or the Collection of Patriotic Songs, Ballads, Medleys and Hymns by Different Authors]. 1794. Paris: Favre.

Chansonnier patriote, ou Recueil de chansons, vaudevilles et pots-pourris patriotiques par différens auteurs [The Patriotic Chansonnier, or Collection of Patriotic Songs, Ballads and Medleys by Different Authors]. 1793. Paris: Garnery.

Coirault, Patrice. 1942. *Notre chanson folklorique* [Our Folk Song]. Paris: Picard.

Coirault, Patrice. 1953. *Formation de nos chansons folkloriques* [The Development of Our Folk Songs]. Paris: Éditions du Scarabée.

Condemi, Concetta. 1992. *Les Cafés-concerts. Histoire d'un divertissement* [Coffeehouse Concerts: A History of an Entertainment]. Paris: Quai Voltaire.

De Bercy, Anne, and Ziwès, Armand. 1951. *A Montmartre . . . le soir. Cabarets et Chansonniers d'hier* [To Montmartre . . . in the Evening Cabarets and Chansonniers of Yesteryear]. Paris: Bernard Grasset.

Delon, Michel, and Levayer, Paul-Édouard. 1989. *Chansonnier révolutionnaire* [The Revolutionary Chansonnier]. Paris: Gallimard.

Dictionnaire de l'Académie Françoise. 1786. Nismes: Pierre Beaume.

Dillaz, Serge. 1971. *Béranger*. Paris: Seghers.

Diners du Vaudeville [Vaudeville Dinner Parties]. 1798–1800, and 1802. Paris: Imprimeurs des diners.

Dottin, Georges. 1991. *Les Chansons françaises de la Renaissance* [French Songs of the Renaissance]. Paris: Gallimard.

Droz, Eugénie, and Piaget, Armand. 1968 (1925). *Le Jardin de plaisance et fleur de rhétorique, reproduction en fac-similé de l'édition publiée par Antoine Vérard* [The Pleasure Garden and Flower of Rhetoric, a Facsimile Reproduction of the Edition Published by Antoine Vérard]. New York and London: Johnson Reprint.

Erismann, Guy. 1967. *Histoire de la chanson* [A History of the Song]. Paris: Hermes.

Étrennes des Troubadours, chansonnier lyrique et anacréontique pour l'an VIII [The Troubadours' New Year's Gifts: Convivial Lyric Songs for the Year 800]. 1801. Paris: Gaillot.

Fallows, David. 1999. *A Catalogue of Polyphonic Songs, 1415–1480*. Oxford: Oxford University Press.

Ferré, Léo. 1967. *Jean Roger Caussimon*. Paris: Pierre Seghers.

Feschotte, Jacques. 1965. *Histoire du music-hall* [A History of the Music Hall]. Paris: Presses Universitaires de France.

Heartz, Daniel. 1969. *Pierre Attaingnant: Royal Printer of Music – A Historical Study and Bibliographical Catalogue*. Berkeley, CA: University of California Press.

Herbert, Michel. 1967. *La Chanson à Montmartre* [The Montmartre Song]. Paris: Table ronde.

Hewitt, Helen, ed. 1942. *Harmonice musices odhecaton* [One Hundred Songs of Harmonic Music]. Cambridge, MA: Mediaeval Academy of America.

Imbert, Charles. 1967. *Histoire de la chanson et de l'opérette (Histoire de la musique, vol. 17)* [A History of Song and Operetta (The History of Music, Vol. 17)]. Lausanne: Rencontre.

Isherwood, Robert M. 1986. *Farce and Fantasy: Popular Entertainment in Eighteenth-Century Paris*. New York and Oxford: Oxford University Press.

Janin, Jules. 1846. *Béranger et son temps* [Béranger and His Times]. Paris: René Pincebourde.

Jeanroy, Alfred. 1875–1925. *Le Chansonnier d'Arras. Reproduction en phototypie. Introduction par . . .* [The Chansonnier of Arras: A Reproduction in Phototype. Introduction by . . .]. Paris: Didot.

Jeanroy, Alfred. 1971 (1918). *Bibliographie des chansonniers français du moyen age (manuscrits et éditions)* [A Bibliography of French Chansonniers of the Middle Ages (Manuscripts and Editions)]. New York: Burt Franklin.

Jeffery, Brian. 1971. *Chanson Verse of Early Renaissance*. London: Brian Jeffery.

Lachèvre, Frédéric. 1967 (1922). *Bibliographie des Recueils collectifs de Poésie publiés de 1597 à 1700* [A Bibliography of Collected Selections of Poetry Published from 1597 to 1700]. Geneva: Slatkine Reprints.

Laforte, Conrad. 1977–83. *Le Catalogue de la chanson folklorique française (5 vols.)* [The Catalog of French Folk Song (5 vols.)]. Québec: Presses de l'Université Laval.

Laforte, Conrad. 1993 (1976). *Poétiques de la chanson traditionnelle française. Classification de la chanson folklorique française* [The Poetics of the Traditional French Song: A Classification of French Folk Song]. Sainte-Foy: Les Presses de l'Université Laval.

Lapointe, Savinien. 1857. *Mémoires sur Béranger. Souvenirs, confidences, opinions, anecdotes, lettres* [Memories of Béranger: Recollections, Confidences, Opinions, Anecdotes, Letters]. Paris: Gustave Havard.

Le Chansonnier des amis du Roi et des Bourbons [The Chansonnier of the King's Friends and of the Bourbons]. 1815. Paris: Guyot et Depelasol.

Le Chansonnier françois ou Recueil de chansons, Ariettes, Vaudevilles & autres couplets choisis. Avec les Airs notés à la fin de chaque recueil [The French Chansonnier or Collection of Songs, Ariettas, Ballads and Other Selected Couplets, with Airs Noted at the End of Each Collection]. 1971. Geneva: Slatkine Reprints.

Leclerc, Jean-Baptiste. 1797. *Essai sur la propagation de la musique en France, sa conservation, et ses rapports avec le gouvernement* [An Essay on the Propagation of Music in France, Its Preservation, and Its Connections with the Government]. Paris: Imprimerie Nationale.

Leclerc, Jean-Baptiste. 1800. *Rapport fait par Leclerc (de Maine et Loire) sur l'établissement d'écoles spéciales de musique* [The Report of Leclerc (of Maine and Loire) on the Establishment of Special Music Schools]. Paris: Imprimerie Nationale.

Lesure, François. 1981. *Catalogue de la musique imprimée avant 1800 conservée dans les bibliothèques publiques de Paris* [A Catalog of the Music Printed Before 1800 Kept in the Public Libraries of Paris]. Paris: Bibliothèque nationale.

Lesure, François, and Thibault, Geneviève. 1955. *Bibliographie des éditions d'Adrian Le Roy et Robert Ballard (1551–1598)* [A Bibliography of the Editions of Adrian Le Roy and Robert Ballard (1551–1598)]. Paris: Heugel.

Level, Brigitte. 1988. *À travers deux siècles. Le Caveau. Société bacchique et chantante. 1726–1939.* [Through Two Centuries: Le Caveau – A Drinking and Singing Society]. Paris: Presses de l'Université Paris-Sorbonne.

Mason, Laura. 1996. *Singing the French Revolution: Popular Culture and Politics, 1787–1799.* Ithaca, NY: Cornell University Press.

Meyer, Paul, and Gaston, Raynaud. 1892. *Le Chansonnier français de Saint-Germain-des-Prés (B.N. fr. 20050). Reproduction phototypique avec transcription* [The French Chansonnier of Saint-Germain-des-Prés (Bibliothèque National Français 20050): A Phototype Reproduction with Transcription]. Paris: Didot.

Mironneau, Paul. 1999. *Chansonnier Henri IV* [The Henry IV Chansonnier]. Graulhet: Éditions du Pin à Crochets.

Nisard, Charles. 1879. *Études sur la chanson des rues contemporaines* (2 vols.) [Studies of Contemporary Street Song (2 vols.)]. Paris: Dentu.

Nouveau chansonnier patriote, ou Recueil de chansons, vaudevilles, et pots-pourris patriotiques, par différens auteurs [The New Patriotic Chansonnier, or Collection of Patriotic Songs, Ballads and Medleys by Different Authors]. 1794. Lille and Paris: Deperne and Barba.

Paris, Paulin. 1971 (1856). 'Chansonniers.' In *Histoire littéraire de la France, vol. 23* [A Literary History of France,

Vol. 23]. Nendeln (Liechtenstein): Kraus Reprint, 512–831.

Pénet, Martin. 2001. *Mémoire de la chanson. 1200 chansons du Moyen-Age à 1919* [A Commemoration of the Song: 1,200 Songs from the Middle Ages to 1919]. Paris: Omnibus.

Perkins, Leeman L., and Garey, Howard B., eds. 1979. *The Mellon Chansonnier.* 2 vols. New Haven, CT: Yale University Press.

Potvin, Gilles. 2001. 'Chansonnier (ii).' In *The New Grove Dictionary of Music and Musicians*, Vol. 5, ed. Stanley Sadie. 2nd ed. New York: Grove, 486.

Raunié, Émile. 1879. *Recueil Clairambault-Maurepas. Chansonnier historique du XVIIIᵉ siècle. Publié avec Introduction, Commentaires, Notes et Index par E.R.* [The Clairambault-Maurepas Collection: An Historical Chansonnier of the Eighteenth Century, Published with an Introduction, Notes and Index by E.R.] 10 vols. Paris: Quantin.

Raynaud, Gaston. 1972 (1884). *Bibliographie des chansonniers français des XIIIᵉ et XIVᵉ siècle* [A Bibliography of French Chansonniers of the Thirteenth and Fourteenth Centuries]. New York: Burt Franklin.

Rey, Alain, ed. 1992. *Dictionnaire historique de la langue française* (Historical Dictionary of the French Language). Paris: Dictionnaires Le Robert.

Rieger, Dietmar, ed. 1988. *La Chanson française et son histoire* [The French Song and Its History]. Tübingen: Gunter Narr Verlag.

Robert, Paul. 1989. *Dictionnaire alphabétique et analogique de la langue française (Le Petit Robert).* Paris: Le Robert.

Roncaglia, Aurelio. 1991. 'Rétrospectives et perspectives dans l'étude des chansonniers d'Oc' [Retrospectives and Perspectives in the Study of the Chansonniers from South of the Loire]. In *Lyrique romane médiévale: la tradition des chansonniers* [Lyrical Medieval Romance: The Tradition of the Chansonniers], ed. Madeleine Tyssens. Geneva: Droz.

Sallée, André, and Chauveau, Philippe. 1985. *Music-Hall et Café-concert* [Music Hall and Coffeehouse]. Paris: Bordas.

Tiersot, Julien. 1889. *Histoire de la chanson populaire en France* [A History of the Popular Song in France]. Paris: Plon.

Tyssens, Madeleine, ed. 1991. *Lyrique romane médiévale: la tradition des chansonniers* [Lyrical Medieval Romance: The Tradition of the Chansonniers]. Geneva: Droz.

Valbel, Horace. 1879. *Les Chansonniers et les Cabarets Artistiques de Paris* [The Artistic Chansonniers and Cabarets of Paris]. Paris: Dentu.

Vernillat, Françoise, and Charpentreau, Jacques. 1971.

La Chanson française [The French Song]. Paris: Presses Universitaires de France.

Zumthor, Paul. 1983. *Introduction à la poésie orale* [Introduction to Oral Poetry]. Paris: Seuil.

Bibliography (Québec)

Bertin, Jacques. 1987. *Félix Leclerc: Le Roi Heureux* [Félix Leclerc: The Happy King]. Paris: Les Éditions Arléa.

Chansons d'aujourd'hui [Songs from Today]/*Chansons* [Songs]. 1984–97. Montréal: Office des communications sociales/Ces-éditions-ci.

Kallmann, Helmut, and Potvin, Gilles, eds. 1993 (1983). *Encyclopédie de la musique au Canada/Encyclopedia of Music in Canada*. Montréal: Fides.

L'Herbier, Benoît. 1974. *La chanson québécoise: Des origines à nos jours* [Québec's Singing: From the Start]. Montréal: Les Éditions de l'Homme.

Thérien, Robert, and D'Amours, Isabelle. 1992. *Dictionnaire de la musique populaire au Québec: 1955–1992* [Dictionary of Popular Music in Québec, 1955–1992]. Quebec City: IQRC.

Tremblay-Matte, Cécile. 1990. *La chanson écrite au féminin: 1730–1990, de Madeleine de Verchères à Mitsou* [Songwriting by Women: 1730–1990, from Madeleine de Verchères to Mitsou]. Laval: Éditions Trois.

Sheet Music

Degeyter, Pierre, comp., 1888, and Pottier, Eugène, lyr. 1871. 'Internationale.' In *Chants révolutionnaires*. Paris, 1887.

Discographical Reference

Venne, Stéphane. 'Un jour, un jour'/'Hey Friend, Say Friend.' *Le temps est bon*. Citation CCD-3238. *1998*: Canada.

Discography

Beau Dommage. *L'intégrale*. Capitol CD4L 56358. 1974–77; *1991*: Canada.

Charlebois, Robert. *Robert Charlebois (Collection Québec Love)*. Gamma GCD-501. 1967–71; *1993*: Canada.

Charlebois, Robert, and Forestier, Louise. *Lindberg*. Gamma GS-120. *1968*: Canada.

Claude, Renée. *Renée Claude (Collection Les Refrains d'abord)*. Fonovox VOX 7853-2. *1997*: Canada.

Cousineau, Luc (including songs from Les Alexandrins). *Comme tout le monde*. Mérite 22-1083. 1967–89; *2001*: Canada.

Cousineau, Luc (including songs from Les Alexandrins). *Vivre en amour*. Mérite 22-1082. 1969–89; *2001*: Canada.

Desjardins, Richard. *Au Club Soda*. Fukinic FUK-LV-2. *1993*: Canada.

Dubois, Claude. *Claude Dubois 1958–1970 (L'intégrale, coffret I)*. Pingouin PNC 124. *1999*: Canada.

Duguay, Raoul. *Monter en amour*. Capitol S22C 26606. 1975–78; *1993*: Canada.

Faulkner, Stephen. *Si j'avais un char: anthologie 1975–1992*. DisQuébec QUÉC-2-1101. 1975–94; *1995*: Canada.

Ferland, Jean-Pierre. *Les 20 premiers succès*. Select SQCD 20001. 1961–65; *1974*: Canada.

Forestier, Louise. *Louise Forestier (Collection Québec Love)*. Gamma GCD-503. 1967–78; *1993*: Canada.

Gauthier, Claude. *Claude Gauthier (Collection Québec Love)*. Gamma AGEK-2204. *1993*: Canada.

Gélinas, Anne-Marie. *Le tango de l'amor*. Leïla CPLCDSP-10. *1999*: Canada.

Harmonium. *Harmonium*. Celebration CEL 1893. *1974*: Canada.

Julien, Pauline. *Rétrospective*. Mérite 22-1017. 1971–74; *1999*: Canada.

Labrecque, Jacques. *La parenté est arrivée*. London MLP-10014. *1958*: Canada.

Latraverse, Plume. *Plume Pou digne*. Deram XDEF 101. *1974*: Canada.

Leclerc, Félix. *L'intégrale Félix Leclerc*. Philips 838 459-2. 1950–78; *1989*: Canada.

Leclerc, Félix, et al. *Heureux qui comme Félix: une histoire de Félix Leclerc*. GSI GSIC-10-981. *2000*: Canada.

Lecor, Tex. *Mes premières chansons*. Mérite 22-1084. 1960–63; *2001*: Canada.

Lecor, Tex. *Tex Lecor (Collection Québec Love)*. Gamma GCD-506. 1967–77; *1993*: Canada.

Léveillée, Claude. *Claude Léveillée (Collection Emergence)*. Sony Music C2K 91057. 1961–67; *1997*: Canada.

Lévesque, Raymond. *Quand les hommes vivront d'amour*. Amberola ambp cd 7107. 1954–77; *1999*: Canada.

Piché, Paul. *Intégral*. Audiogram ADCD 2000. *1986*: Canada.

Vigneault, Gilles. *Chemin faisant – Cent et une chansons*. Le Nordet GVNC-1017. 1962–87; *1990*: Canada.

CHARLES DOUTRELEPONT (France) and
RICHARD BAILLARGEON (Québec)

Clog Dancer

A clog dancer performs step dances characterized by boisterous, fast footwork, a rigid torso and an up-and-down knee motion. On his/her feet, the dancer wears either oxford shoes with steel plates or taps on the soles, or traditional clogs. The latter are wooden shoes, or shoes with wooden soles and heels, originally worn by peasants and industrial workers in northern Europe.

Clog dancing in Britain in the nineteenth century was a solo dance in which the dancer kept the rhythm by tapping with heel and toe. There were numerous clog-dancing competitions held in northern England, including the Pitman's Championship of Durham and Northumberland. One of the most famous dancers was George Galvin, who won 'World Championships' in 1880 in Leeds and in 1883 in Oldham. As Dan Leno, he later became a famous music hall comedian and singer.

Clog dancers themselves appeared on music hall variety bills, and Charlie Chaplin and Stan Laurel were at different times members of the Eight Lancashire Lads clog-dancing team. Most teams danced to well-known tunes, such as 'Men of Harlech,' 'Auld Lang Syne' and 'The British Grenadiers.' There was a renewal of interest in the dance form as part of the English folk revival, and clog-dancing workshops and competitions have continued to be held at some folk festivals.

Clog dancing developed differently in North America, where its first center was the Appalachians. The influences included the Irish jig, French *danse*, German *plotl*, Scottish highland dancing and, according to some experts, African steps and Native American dance. The resulting dance was also known as buck dancing or flat footin'.

Clog dancing or 'clogging' became a feature of vaudeville performance from the 1830s and was featured in a musical, *The Black Crook*, in 1866 in New York. John Queen, a celebrated lyricist of the 1900s who wrote 'Just Because She Made Dem Goo-Goo Eyes' and 'I Got Mine,' was a champion clog dancer from New Orleans.

As a spectacle, clogging later lost popularity to a more syncopated step dance – tap. However, as in Britain, interest in clogging was rekindled by its inclusion in such folk revival events as the Mountain Dance and Folk Festival, founded in Asheville, North Carolina in the 1920s. The style as it has subsequently evolved has eight basic steps, such as heel, toe, brush, drag and slide. There are line and partner dances, some resembling square dance formations.

Bibliography

Dobson, Bob. 1979. *Concerning Clogs*. Clapham: Dalesman Books.

Pilling, Julian. 1967. *The Lancashire Clog Dance*. London: English Folk Dance and Song Society.

Ratcliffe, Caroline. 2001. 'The Ladies' Clog Dancing Contest of 1898.' In *Step Change: New Views on Traditional Dance*, ed. Georgina Boyes. London: Francis Boutle, 76–98.

Spalding, Susan Eike, and Woodside, Jane Harris, eds. 1995. *Communities in Motion: Dance, Community, and Tradition in America's Southeast and Beyond*. Westport, CT: Greenwood Press.

Sheet Music

Cannon, Hughey, comp., and Queen, John, lyr. 1900. 'Just Because She Made Dem Goo-Goo Eyes.' New York: Howley, Haviland and Co.

Cartwell, Charlie, comp., and Queen, John, lyr. 1901. 'I Got Mine.' New York: Howley, Haviland and Dresser.

DAVE LAING

Folk Singer

The term 'folk singer' can be used to describe various types of performer of traditional songs or songs inspired by traditional works. These can range from singers of ritual or work songs in tribal or preindustrial societies to professional vocalists whose repertoire consists of newly composed material. The complexity of the folk singer's role in a range of social, geographical and cultural contexts is discussed by Bohlman (1988). The role of performers of such genres as 'newly composed folk music' and *narodna muzika* in Communist Eastern Europe is evaluated by contributors to Slobin (1996), while Cantwell (1996) excavates the origins of the most prevalent present-day version of 'folk singer' to be found in Anglophone music cultures.

Such folk singers occupy an uneasy space within the overall sphere of contemporary North American popular music. Embodying for the folk music audience an aesthetic that rejects music as a commodity and thus many elements of popular music production, promotion and distribution, the folk singer must negotiate an irresolvable tension between audience and industry. More than most popular music performers, the folk singer is constrained by the expectations of the audience, whose conservatism verges at times on dogmatism. Conceived of as the carrier of a tradition, the folk singer's role is more that of custodian than creator or innovator, and, for reasons dating back to Herder, the modern folk singer represents for many the voice of a people resisting the hegemonic pressures of a predominating capitalist/technological society.

At the beginning of the twenty-first century, 'folk singer' normally suggests an ideological stance toward the selection of repertoire and toward the presentation and performance of it, manifest in a preference for traditional musical materials and performance practises, such as the use of acoustic instead of amplified instruments. Moreover, the folk singer generally must conform to audiences' highly developed ideas concerning authenticity and display the sincerity they regard as absent in other modes of popular music performance, while meeting the requirements of the record companies that produce, disseminate and profit by the music.

The contemporary folk singer follows one of two general tendencies toward these ends. The first is the continual revival and preservation of traditional folk song material, sometimes lampooned as the scruffy singer, hand cupped over ear and intoning in an archaic accent. The second tendency is exemplified in the 'singer/songwriter' whose material exhibits sufficiently overt connections to 'roots' and traditional performance practise to mitigate the fact that it is newly composed and not folk music at all.

Therefore, it is in his/her role as representative for the audience's ideologies, drawn from the vague concept of folk music and its oppositional ethos with regard to the hegemonic capitalist culture, that distinguishes the folk singer from simply the singer.

Bibliography

Bohlman, Philip V. 1988. *The Study of Folk Music in the Modern World*. Bloomington, IN: Indiana University Press.

Cantwell, Robert. 1996. *When We Were Good: The Folk Revival*. Cambridge, MA: Harvard University Press.

Slobin, Mark, ed. 1996. *Retuning Culture: Musical Changes in Central and Eastern Europe*. Durham, NC: Duke University Press.

TIM WISE

Jazz Singer

A jazz singer is a singer who, in performance, uses some or all of the elements of jazz: melodic or harmonic improvisation, syncopation and swing, and a style of interpretation comparable to that of a jazz instrumentalist. In practise, a definition such as this is often treated quite fluidly, as in many aspects of repertoire and performance the distinction between a jazz singer and a popular singer is not always clear-cut.

The part played by the jazz singer in a jazz performance has varied historically, from that of a contributor of a vocal line to what is essentially an ensemble concept, to that of being the central focus of attention for whom the other musicians provide accompaniment. In both cases, and in others in between, the jazz singer's role has most often been that of a soloist, although there have been numerous examples of jazz vocal collaborations (for example, Sarah Vaughan and Billy Eckstine) and ensembles (for example, Manhattan Transfer).

The status of the singer in a jazz ensemble has been similarly varied, as have the opportunities for performance. The period in jazz history during which singers had most opportunities was that of the swing era. It coincided with – and was at least partially explained by – the prominence of popular songs in the repertoire of swing bands. Even in this period, however, not all band leaders considered the presence of a singer obligatory. The rise of bebop, with its concentrated focus on small-group instrumental music, curtailed the opportunities for singers, leaving many to continue to seek employment in the surviving big bands (something that some, such as Anita O'Day, did with considerable success) or to turn more explicitly to popular music, as did Frank Sinatra, following his tenure with Tommy Dorsey's swing band.

As jazz idioms that evolved in the late twentieth century continued to allow little scope for singers – with notable exceptions – the persistence of earlier styles, and their eventual coexistence, has sustained opportunities for jazz singers at local, national and international levels. At the same time, a new generation of musicians who both play an instrument and sing (in a variety of styles, from the intimacy of Canadian pianist-singer Diana Krall to brass band-style New Orleans trumpeter-vocalists Kermit Ruffins and James Andrews) has made undiluted pleasure in singing central to what they do.

The term 'jazz singer' first attained prominence through the 1927 movie of the same name, starring Al Jolson. Celebrated historically as the first 'talking picture,' the film's choice of title reflected the contemporary popularity of the idea of jazz, but not its actuality. Al Jolson's performance in the film was a stereotypical blackface vaudeville turn, and had no direct connection with the kind of performance that could then be found in clubs, dance halls and theaters.

The art of jazz singing developed during the 1920s, and the first significant practitioner was Louis Armstrong, whose performances of Fats Waller's song 'Ain't Misbehavin'' from the 1929 revue *Connie's Hot Chocolates* helped him become known to a mass audience as a popular entertainer rather than a jazz instrumentalist. Yet, Armstrong's singing was entirely consistent with his instrumental work. He reshaped melodic lines, altered his timing, occasionally amended lyrics or substituted nonsense 'scat' syllables, but he retained many of the performance techniques of the black musical theater of the day. This latter characteristic was even more marked in the work of Cab Calloway, whose diction, sense of pitch and timing allowed him to transfer effortlessly in later life to musical theater roles in *Hello, Dolly!* and *Porgy and Bess*, but whose frenetic stage persona and 'hi-de-hi' nonsense language remained consistent with the improvisational principles of jazz. Calloway's most typical material involved the Harlem lowlife characters 'Minnie the Moocher' and 'Smoky Joe.' Similar results were achieved by vocalists influenced by him, such as Billy Banks, and by those who followed a different route to attain a comparable effect, such as Fats Waller, whose talent for ironic and humorous comment on his material did not detract from the intrinsic jazziness of his singing. The 1930s saw the birth of such vocal ensembles as the Spirits of Rhythm, and a small number of vocal groups subsequently specialized in jazz singing – notably, in the 1960s, Lambert, Hendricks and Ross, who contrived new lyrics to recordings of improvised solos.

While male singers initiated the art of jazz singing, it has been taken to its greatest artistic heights by female vocalists. The remarkable vocal flexibility of Ella Fitzgerald and Sarah Vaughan, which was combined with improvisational ability, allowed both to improvise in the manner of an instrumentalist, while Billie Holiday's interpretation of lyrics brought the art of improvisation to bear on both words and music. She worked within a limited pitch range and created dramatic effects through subtle manipulation of timing.

The bebop era ushered in singers like Joe Carroll and Johnny Hartman, who transferred the rapid melodic lines and intricate phrasing of bebop to singing. Although Billy Eckstine led a bebop big band from 1944 onward, his own singing was rooted in blues and ballads, and he did not attempt to tackle the harmonic and melodic innovations of modern jazz. In a similar paradox, in the 1950s trumpeter Chet Baker emulated the instrumental innovations of Miles Davis, but his vocals were contrastingly simple, being light, airy and often ballad-based.

In the free jazz era, from the 1960s onward, some singers successfully transferred instrumental techniques to the voice, while still interpreting lyrics in the same way as an instrumentalist might tackle a 'head' arrangement. Abbey Lincoln has been consistently successful in this area, notably in her own compositions and arrangements, such as 'Caged Bird.' Lincoln's idiosyncratic material, with themes that ranged from childhood to universal questions, has been matched by the work of Brazilian singer Flora Purim, who has worked not only with Dizzy Gillespie, but most consistently with percussionist Airto Moreira. Betty Carter made the transition from a bop singer to a radically inventive vocalist who employed free jazz notions of time and pitch within the context of the standard repertoire.

Al Jarreau and Bobby McFerrin both experimented with the concept of singing entirely unaccompanied. McFerrin, in particular, used the resonating chambers of his body and unorthodox vocal techniques to create the impression of an accompanimental line for his vocals, while actually creating the entire effect vocally.

In Britain, singers associated with the band leader and composer Mike Westbrook have explored links between jazz, vaudeville and free improvisation. Phil Minton has employed constriction and distortion techniques more often found in the art music of composers such as Peter Maxwell Davies in his interpretations of Westbrook's William Blake settings, while Kate Westbrook has explored the common ground between these settings and cabaret songs. Both Maggie Nicols and Julie Tippetts have worked in similar areas, most notable examples being Nicols with the European trio Les Diaboliques, playing the music of Irène Schweizer, and Tippetts performing material by Keith Tippett and Swiss-Irish pianist John Wolf Brennan. Norma Winstone has specialized in the use of the voice as an instrument, particularly as an improvising foil to the trumpeter Kenny Wheeler.

Musicians connected with the Association for the Advancement of Creative Musicians (AACM) in Chicago have taken radically different directions with regard to jazz singing. Anthony Braxton has worked with the experimental US singer Lauren Newton (who is also a regular member of the Vienna Art Orchestra), using her classically derived avant-garde techniques to explore trance music, scores dictated by chance events, such as the spinning of a wheel, and minimalist motifs. By contrast, Lester Bowie in his band Brass Fantasy employed singers such as the trombonist Frank Lacy to inject elements of urban funk, rap and hip-hop into the band's work.

Ingredients similar to those developed by the AACM musicians lay behind the M-Base Collective and its experiments of the 1980s involving singer Cassandra Wilson, who successfully broke down barriers between jazz, blues and contemporary African-American music.

At the end of the twentieth century, jazz singers were confronting the whole range of stylistic and improvisational techniques developed since the beginning of jazz, and a convincingly postmodern approach had been developed by the Chicagoan Kurt Elling, who combined scat singing with remarkable speed, and consistently experimented with the form and shape of lyrics.

Bibliography

Crowther, Bruce, and Pinfold, Mike. 1997. *Singing Jazz: The Singers and Their Styles.* London: Blandford.

Feather, Leonard. 1988. 'Singing.' In *The New Grove Dictionary of Jazz*, Vol. 2, ed. Barry Kernfeld. London: Macmillan, 455–62.

Friedwald, Will. 1990. *Jazz Singing: America's Great Voices from Bessie Smith to Bebop and Beyond.* London: Quartet.

Sheet Music

Brooks, Harry, and Waller, Fats, comps., and Razaf, Andy, lyr. 1929. 'Ain't Misbehavin'.' New York: Mills Music.

Discographical References

Armstrong, Louis. 'Ain't Misbehavin'.' OKeh 8714. 1929: USA. Reissue: Armstrong, Louis. 'Ain't Misbehavin'.' *This Is Jazz, Vol. 1.* Sony 64613. *1996*: USA.

Lincoln, Abbey. 'Caged Bird.' *Wholly Earth.* PolyGram 559538. *1999*: USA.

Filmography

The Jazz Singer, dir. Alan Crosland. 1927. USA. 89 mins. Drama. Original music by Louis Silvers.

ALYN SHIPTON

Lead Singer

The term 'lead singer' has two meanings in popular music. In its more common usage, it denotes a singer who is a member of a vocal ensemble and whose role in that ensemble involves being regularly placed in the foreground, against a vocal background provided by the other singers. In some stylistic contexts, lead singers may be members of vocal-instrumental ensembles, and so be instrumentalists as well as vocalists. In this usage, a solo singer performing with a backing group can be considered to be a lead singer only when the unit to which all members belong is a collective one, and, in most instances, when it has its own name.

Although it is unclear when the phrase 'lead singer' first began to be used, the sources of the practise and its route into popular music can be identified with reasonable certainty as emanating principally from a method of organization found in African-American group singing. Descriptions of slave work songs often mentioned that they were structured antiphonally around a leading solo voice (the 'call') and a group reply (the 'response'). The same idea also clearly informed the singing of religious songs. Writing in 1867, the compilers of *Slave Songs of the United States* (a collection consisting predominantly of religious songs) commented: 'There is no singing in *parts*, as we understand it, and yet no two appear to be singing the same thing – the leading singer starts the words of each verse, often improvising, and the others, who "base" him, as it is called, strike in with the refrain, or even join in the solo, when the words are familiar. When the "base" begins, the leader often stops, leaving the rest of the words to be guessed at, or it may be they are taken up by one of the other singers.' The effect is one of 'marvellous complication and variety' (Allen, Ware and Garrison 1867, v). The compilers also noted that in the most common arrangement the leading voice's verse occupies lines one and three, and the refrain lines two and four. Other arrangements include giving the solo voice three lines and the group one, and vice versa (1867, xlvii).

The custom was no doubt influenced to some degree by the increasingly common verse-chorus structure that characterized both secular song and religious hymnody of the time, and by the fact that secular songs in particular were often arranged so that a solo voice delivered the verse, while the refrain was allocated to a chorus. But it differed from these types in that the structure was more fluid, and especially in the fact that the solo voice and the chorus engaged much more obviously in closely timed exchanges and dialogs with each other – as is apparent in the most common arrangement described above. Importantly, the solo voice was not merely an individual charged with delivering certain lines; he/she had connections with the group and responsibilities toward it. That is one reason, no doubt, why Allen, Ware and Garrison did not speak of soloists, but of 'leading voices' and 'leaders.'

While work songs died out, except in special contexts such as penitentiaries, religious music flourished, and it was here that the lead singer format was first developed and modified. In the earliest known recordings by African-American male vocal groups, some of the basic alternatives offered by the principle of lead singer and group can be heard in practise. In the Standard Quartette's 1894 cylinder recording 'Keep Movin',' the leading voice is charged with the verse (into which other members of the group occasionally interject) and the group with the chorus. In the Dinwiddie Colored Quartet's 1902 recording 'Down on the Old Camp Ground,' the verse itself consists of a line sung by the lead singer (tenor Sterling Rex) alternating with a repeated line, 'way down on the old camp ground,' sung by the group. Both lead singer and group then join together for the refrain.

Patterns such as these, and variations on them, can be found regularly in recorded gospel music of the 1920s and 1930s, although the term 'lead singer' itself may not have been in use. Gospel historian Anthony Heilbut uses the term 'lead singer' to refer to singers such as Norman 'Crip' Harris, first tenor in the Norfolk Jubilee Quartet from 1937. Harris's style, according to Heilbut (1985), involved 'high-pitched, staccato phrasing' (42). During the late 1930s, the approach of some quartets became increasingly jazz influenced and sophisticated, while not losing stylistic aspects with clear gospel roots. The Golden Gate Quartet, whose music often edged toward the secular, featured three different lead singers, one of whom, Henry Owens, Heilbut describes as slurring and moaning 'with an understated tact,' while William Langford (aka Landford) 'was more showmanly, switching registers from baritone to falsetto, and using a sly, satisfied tone, oily with vibrato' (1985, 44).

Gospel music continued to use and develop the role of lead singer in groups such as the Dixie Hummingbirds and, later, Sam Cooke and the Soul Stirrers. The first major transfer of this format to secular music appears in the late 1930s/early 1940s performances of groups such as the Mills Brothers and the Ink Spots (who featured both a high tenor and a bass lead), both of which were among the first groups to 'cross over' and have success in the white market. By the late 1940s, male vocal groups, all with a prominent role for lead singers, were a central feature in what had become known as 'rhythm and blues.' Beginning around 1950, and possibly influenced by a conscious use of young, gospel-trained singers, the lead singer's contribution tended to become more emotional and highly charged. Gillett (1983, 155–56) has drawn attention to the gospel influence in the singing of Clyde McPhatter with the Dominoes and the Drifters. At the same time, the arrangement of voices became dominated by a format in which the lead singer was placed more consistently in the foreground, singing against a background (sometimes consisting of wordless singing) provided by the rest of the group. Although attention was focused on the lead singer, the format allowed for what was by now often functioning in effect as a backing group to contribute in various ways. In the Drifters' witty 'Money Honey,' for example, in which lead singer McPhatter narrates cameo episodes (in a style that Gillett describes as one of 'deadpan over-involvement' (1983, 156)), the backing group intervenes to underline the irony of the various ways in which other people's financial requirements impinge upon the lead singer's daily life.

Throughout the 1950s, with doo-wop groups like the Five Royales and the Coasters, the format of lead singer plus backing group continued to be widely used. It became an ingredient in rock 'n' roll (for example, with Frankie Lymon and the Teenagers) and achieved Top 10 success in recordings such as the Platters' 'The Great Pretender' (featuring lead singer Tony Williams). Its persistence can be seen in Phil Spector-produced recordings of girl groups such as the Crystals (with lead singer La La Brooks) and in many Motown records.

The influence of US rhythm and blues recordings may well be a crucial one in the assimilation of the format of lead singer plus backing group into the guitar-based British 'beat' groups of the early 1960s, and in US groups such as the Beach Boys. From these various points – including Motown – it went on to become a standard device in much rock and pop music. In some groups – most famously, the Beatles – the role of lead singer alternated (in this case, principally between two performers), while in others – for example, Herman's Hermits – one lead singer dominated.

A second, less common usage of 'lead singer' occurs in contexts in which the lineup of an instrumental ensemble features alternative solo singers, one of whom is regarded as principal (hence, 'lead') singer. Big bands of the 1930s often employed more than one singer and operated a pecking order (which could be the subject of dispute between the singers and the band leaders).

Bibliography

Allen, William Francis, Ware, Charles Pickard, and Garrison, Lucy McKim, eds. 1867. *Slave Songs of the United States*. New York: Simpson. (Reprinted New York: Peter Smith, 1951.)

Gillett, Charlie. 1983 (1970). *The Sound of the City: The Rise of Rock and Roll*. Rev. ed. London: Souvenir Press.

Heilbut, Anthony. 1985. *The Gospel Sound: Good News and Bad Times*. Rev. ed. New York: Limelight.

Discographical References

Dinwiddie Colored Quartet, The. 'Down on the Old Camp Ground.' Monarch 1714. 1902: USA. Reissue: Dinwiddie Colored Quartet, The. 'Down on the Old Camp Ground.' *The Earliest Negro Vocal Quartets, 1894–1928*. Document DOCD-5061. *1991*: Austria.

Drifters, The. 'Money Honey.' Atlantic 1006. 1953: USA.

Platters, The. 'The Great Pretender.' Mercury 70753. 1955: USA.

Standard Quartette, The. 'Keep Movin'.' Unnumbered cylinder. 1894: USA. Reissue: Standard Quartette, The. 'Keep Movin'.' *The Earliest Negro Vocal Quartets, 1894–1928*. Document DOCD-5061. *1991*: Austria.

DAVID HORN

Session Musician

'Session musician' is a generic term that refers to a range of practises, all of which involve the participation of a musician in a recording session featuring an artist or band with which the session musician does not regularly perform onstage. While this practise goes back to the earliest recordings at the turn of the century, by and large the phenomenon of the session musician is a product of two interrelated factors: professionalism and the cost of recording sessions. Consequently, the first session musicians were centered in London and New York, and typically they were music hall and vaudeville musicians who were hired for recording sessions that featured the vocal talents of British and North American stars of the stage. In the United States, the majority of the earliest jazz, country, blues, gospel and Cajun recordings in the 1920s and early 1930s tended to be made by self-contained bands or individual artists, and consequently they did not require the hiring of session musicians. In the case of country, gospel, blues and Cajun music, most recording sessions were done with portable recording units 'on location' in southern cities away from the heart of the recording industry. A minority of recordings in this period, such as those by classic blues singers like Bessie Smith and 'Ma' Rainey, did routinely involve the hiring of players on a per-session basis. In these cases, the session musicians were typically jazz players who made their living mostly through live performances, the infrequent sessions they were hired for simply serving as an additional, albeit small, source of revenue.

While the big band era (from the early 1930s through the mid-1940s) was dominated by the recordings of self-contained bands, over time a number of spin-off recordings were made by jazz musicians, which involved a leading instrumentalist or vocalist recording with a small group, employing a handful of selected players as session musicians. The blues recording scene in Chicago in the late 1930s and early 1940s also began to involve sessions in which a leader (usually a vocalist/instrumentalist) was paired with various session musicians for a given recording; and, of course, Tin Pan Alley pop recordings, largely centered in New York City during this period, continued to rely primarily on session musicians to provide the accompaniment for star vocalists.

In the postwar era, all major genres of North American popular music, including jazz, country, pop, rock, rhythm and blues, and blues, increasingly utilized session musicians. In Nashville, New York, Los Angeles and eventually Toronto, the session musician scene became highly competitive, with certain players clearly considered the first, second or third choice on their instrument for sessions in a given style. Musicians were paid for three-hour sessions, and terms and conditions were regulated by contracts between musicians' unions and the recording industry. It thus became possible for a select group of players to make a lucrative living playing sessions on a daily basis, enabling them to forgo working the road as performing musicians. A similar situation developed in the late 1950s in London.

In smaller North American recording centers, such as Memphis and New Orleans, the session musician scene tended to be less formally fixed and less lucrative, with no individual musician able to make his/her living entirely by playing sessions.

To be a session musician, one was generally expected to be able to sight-read musical notation quickly and accurately, to be able to transpose a part from one key to another instantly, to be able to play in a wide range of styles and emulate the licks, techniques and stylistic nuances of other notable instrumentalists and, in some genres, to be able to continuously develop appropriate and catchy grooves, riffs and lines for recording after recording. The latter requirement involved what Memphis trumpeter Wayne Jackson has termed 'slate memory': the musician creates a part, plays it for however many takes are necessary to get a satisfactory recording and then 'wipes the slate clean' to begin working on the next tune (Bowman 1997). Historically, the occupation of session musician has been dominated by men, exceptions being the excellent west coast bass player Carol Kaye and the percussionist Bobbie Hall.

One of the major threads in the history of rock music has been the development of self-contained bands that maintain total control over all aspects of their recording career. Since this involves a number of practises/crafts associated with recording – playing one's own instrument, writing one's own songs and producing one's own records – it directly affected the need for and deployment of session musicians. Whereas Roger McGuinn (then Jim McGuinn) was the only member of the Byrds allowed by Columbia Records to play (as opposed to sing) on the group's debut single 'Mr Tambourine Man,' and none of the Beach Boys played (as opposed to sang) on their earliest recordings, by the late 1960s it was an accepted tenet and part of the ideology of rock music that the members of a group under whose name a recording was released would want to, be able to, and be expected by their audience to play their own instruments on their own recordings.

This development, while significant in the overall history of popular music, did not completely spell the end of the session musician. Country music, easy listening and movie soundtracks still relied almost exclusively on session musicians. In the case of blues and, eventually, soul music, a number of small, independent record labels, including Chess, Motown, Stax and Sugar Hill, developed what were termed 'house bands': the same set of session musicians was hired for virtually every session the company recorded, consequently giving all the records issued by a particular label a recognizable sound or identity. In the case of Motown and Stax, these musicians were expected to work for no one else, thereby ensuring that no other company could release products with the same basic sound. Some house bands (such as Booker T. and the MGs from the Stax Studios in Memphis and Area Code 615 from Nashville) and top session players (like saxophonist David Sanborn and drummer Bernard Purdie from New York) had parallel careers as artists in their own right.

Subsequently, a variety of practises developed that fell under the rubric of session musician. While a number of players continued to work in major urban centers, playing session after session in a variety of styles, there were other 'superstar' session musicians, such as guitarist Steve Cropper, who were booked for sessions by different artists in a variety of cities throughout the world. Cropper could spend two weeks in Chicago recording on a blues album and then fly to Tokyo for two weeks of work with a Japanese pop artist. Another development was the practise of hiring for a specific project a particular instrumentalist who did not normally play sessions. When Bob Dylan, for example, made a record, he did not use his road band; neither did he hire the standard session players in whatever city he was recording. Instead, he would handpick players such as Eric Clapton or Mark Knopfler for a given tune or for a whole album. Finally, for all genres, strings and wind instruments tended to be played by session musicians, and background vocals were typically supplied by a provider of a related practise, the session singer.

In the 1980s, changes in music technology had an impact on the employment of session musicians. The invention of synthesizers, MIDI and sequencers resulted in the replacement of keyboard players by programmers and of drummers by drum machines on many pop and rock sessions.

In the late 1990s, session musicians were still ubiquitous on most country and pop sessions, while any combination of the above-cited practises might be used for jazz, blues, rap or rock recordings.

Bibliography

Blaine, Hal, and Goggin, David. 1990. *Hal Blaine and the Wrecking Crew: The Story of the World's Most Recorded Musician*. Emeryville, CA: Mix Books.

Bowman, Rob. 1997. *Soulsville U.S.A.: The Story of Stax Records*. New York: Schirmer Books.

Faulkner, Robert R. 1971. *Hollywood Studio Musicians: Their Work and Career in the Recording Industry*. Chicago: Aldine-Atherton.

Discographical Reference

Byrds, The. 'Mr Tambourine Man.' Columbia 43271. *1965*: USA.

Discography

Area Code 615. *Area Code 615*. Polydor 24-4002. *1969*: USA.

Booker T. and the MGs. *Green Onions*. Stax 701. *1962*: USA.

Purdie, Bernard. *Soul Is . . . Pretty Purdie*. Fly 10154. *1972*: USA.

Sanborn, David. *Taking Off*. Warner Brothers WB 2873. *1975*: USA.

ROB BOWMAN

Shout/Shouter

A shout in customary usage is a loud cry, or vocal expression, projected with considerable exhalation and strain on the vocal cords. Generally used to attract attention, it can be arresting, indignant, vehement, exultant or, indeed, expressive of a range of emotions. A shout may be angry or joyous; it may be directed to one person or many; and, sometimes, its purpose may be merely for the satisfaction of release or of hearing an echo. Because of the effort and breath required to shout, only one or two words may be used: the name of a friend, a welcome to a sportsman or sportswoman, a cry of warning or fear. Certain shouts, such as, in former times, 'Hail!' to a hero,

'Hooray!' to mark an achievement or 'Fore!' on the golf course, have become standardized.

The musical potential of the shout would therefore seem limited, but certain singers in the blues, jazz and swing fields cultivated a shouting technique in order to project their lyrics above the volume of sound produced by the supporting band. Prominent among these were Jimmy Rushing, who first recorded in 1930 with Bennie Moten's Kansas City Orchestra, and bartender Big Joe Turner, also from Kansas City, who came to prominence as a singer with boogie-woogie pianists. Both men were large, with big chest cavities and powerful voices. Willie Mae Thornton, known as 'Big Mama,' was one of the smaller number of women blues shouters who recorded after World War II. All favored blues, even when singing with jazz and swing groups, and it is possible that the 'call(or shout)-and-response' structure allowed them time for the necessary intake of breath. Their lines were often short exclamations of the 'Yeah, yeah!' type, appropriate to the shouting technique.

The origin of the shouting technique may, however, be sacred rather than secular, having been used by African-American preachers since Emancipation, and probably before. Rev. J.C. Burnett and Rev. A.W. Nix were among these exhorting preachers whose partially shouted sermons were recorded in the 1920s. Their half-shouting sermons should not be confused with the ring shout (a sacred, anti-clockwise shuffling dance).

PAUL OLIVER

Singer

The centrality of the singing voice in popular music is inseparable from the centrality of the person or persons doing the singing – the singers. The contribution made by singers is seen most obviously in the context of performance, but it is also important in other areas of activity, especially marketing and promotion, and reception. Within and between these three categories numerous histories interweave themselves, involving matters as varied as vocal technique, performance arenas, genre development, gender roles, technological change and image creation.

The Singer in Performance

Because the singer's instrument – the voice – is the most portable of all instruments, there are no contexts or venues, public or domestic, amateur or professional, in which the singer may not physically perform. In the historical development of popular music, this has been an important element in the central role that the singer has played, but the apparent advantage that it brings has not been a permanent feature, and establishing and retaining prominence has often been dependent on other factors. Before the advent of amplification, for example, in large public venues such as theaters, voices, like instruments, were often grouped into ensembles to create the necessary volume, and only the more powerful individual voices had a chance of success in a solo capacity. With the advent of amplification all this changed; at least, it changed in theory, as it took some time for the different character of the voice that the microphone produced to be generally accepted. Acceptance came through recordings rather than through public live performance. Once the change was established, singers found that those with 'smaller' voices now had opportunities across a range of performance contexts – in recorded performance, and in live performance both in public venues and on radio.

A contextual factor that has regularly influenced both the function of the singer and the style of performance has been that of genre. Sometimes this has mainly involved matters of technique and expression. Much soul and soul-derived singing of the 1960s and after, for example, required the singer to be a master of melisma. Sometimes it has involved both technique and opportunity. In much dance band music of the 1920s and 1930s, the singer's function was to come in partway through a number, typically using a low-key delivery, and in so doing offer a partial contrast to the instrumental sound of the band. Another challenge frequently posed to singers by generic conventions has been that of role-playing. In perhaps the most obvious example of this, the musical theater, singers face the task of choosing and applying the best musical means to bring out the character in the dramatic role being played. The demands made when singers switch from one genre to another are considerable. Pleasants (1974) has suggested that Elvis Presley had an acute sense of the vocal style appropriate to different generic contexts, and so developed what Pleasants refers to as a 'vocal multiplicity . . . a sound for country, a sound for gospel, a sound for ballads, and a sound for rhythm and blues' (276).

Whatever the physical or generic context, one of the most basic functions of the singer is to add vocally produced sounds to a particular sound event. In such events, the singer's voice is one happening among many, all occurring at roughly the same time, and its prominence can vary. In many areas of popular music, conventions dictate that sounds produced by a solo singer have a high level of prominence, while those produced by supporting, or 'backing,' singers have a lower level. These and other concepts were all available to performers before the advent of recording technology, but limitations on the projection of the human voice meant that in many performance contexts – in theatrical productions with orchestral accompaniment, for example – listeners were accustomed to relatively low levels of

prominence. But, with the arrival of the microphone and amplification, it became possible to enhance the prominence of the singer's contribution beyond what was normally achievable by using the voice's natural ability. In live performance, this created a shift in the way in which sonic and visual perception combined and interacted. In recorded performance, where the visual element was absent, technology enabled styles to be created – most notably, that of the crooners in the late 1920s and 1930s – in which the foregrounding of the singer's vocal contribution produced a sense of imagined physical proximity (and hence of intimacy) as a matter of course. All of this also changed the listener's expectations.

Subsequent technological developments, such as sound mixing, created a situation in which subtleties of choice regarding the level of prominence of the singer became matters of style. In some cases, it is apparent that the increase in choices offered by technology can also affect the character of a genre. Burston (1998) has pointed out how, in the 'megamusicals' such as *Les Misérables*, the combination of an in-house mixing desk and radio microphones (taped to singers' bodies and able to pick up all of their contributions equally well, even those uttered sotto voce from the back of the stage) created a sonic environment akin to that of FM radio (207).

The intervention of technology has, of course, impacted on other aspects of the singer's contribution than simply the prominence of the singing voice or the sonic environment in which it is embedded. Lacasse (2000) employs the term 'vocal staging' to refer to 'any deliberate practice whose aim is to enhance a vocal sound, alter its timbre, or present it in a given spatial and/or temporal configuration with the help of mechanical or electrical process' (4). Although in popular music most such processes involve the use of recording technology in some form, not all do, and the practise is in fact an old one. Exploiting the acoustics of a building, for example, can also be considered vocal staging, in Lacasse's formulation. As Lacasse shows, the expressive possibilities achieved by vocal staging are immense and complex, as are those for extramusical connotations (2000, 237ff.).

Alongside the singer's role in introducing vocally produced sounds to the sound event is that of introducing words. All the functions that lyrics perform in a song – whether it is their own addition to the sonic environment, their qualities as performed poetry, or the countless ways in which they refer to and insert the world of lived experience – are made possible by the singer's involvement. In a great deal of popular music, the singer's relationship to lyrics is far from being that of a straightforward 'channel of communication.' Rather, it offers a range of choices about delivery (timbre, dynamics, phrasing and so on) and, perhaps especially, interpretation. (Not all choices are necessarily made by the singer in person; others may exert influence, and technology may be used to alter the singer's sound.)

The singer's presence as the conveyor of lyrics is also one of the principal means through which lyrics are able to explore narrative and dramatic conventions. By themselves, lyrics can and do use such conventions widely, whether in the more or less straightforward telling of a story, or in the (more common) instance of 'dropping' the listener into a particular moment of a story already in progress. What the singer does, through a range of technical and stylistic elements, is personalize – and so dramatize – the situation in a particular way.

The closeness of the relationship between singer and lyrics does not, of course, preclude the possibility of 'wordless' singing. Examples of this are plentiful, and range from the 'scat' singing of performers such as Ella Fitzgerald and Anita O'Day – a technique that offers singers the opportunity to improvise like instrumentalists – to John Lennon's use of evidently meaningless sounds on the Beatles' recording 'You Know My Name (Look Up the Number)' in parody of club singers. Another option that the singer has is to ignore or disrupt the conventional processes of signification and treat words for their sounds alone. Writing of Van Morrison's 1968 album *Astral Weeks*, Hoskyns (1991) remarks that 'what Lester Bangs called Van's "whole set of verbal tics" is really a primal subversion of meaning, an attempt to outstrip language through incantation and repetition' (127–28).

Because words are also very often tied to melody, the singer's role, whether performing solo or in a group, also includes responsibility as the main bearer of melody. As melody and words are often inseparable, the choices that melody offers the singer are much the same as those offered by words, with the addition of factors such as register and pitch. A singer's performance is often marked by its awareness of the interplay between words and melody (or by its lack of awareness, since such disparity is permissible in certain stylistic contexts). But delivery of the melody line also differs in that it offers much greater opportunities than do words for introducing variation in the course of performance, and genres of popular music in which interpretive vocal performance is central have often made use of this. The range is wide, from the subtle inflections of Elizabeth Fraser of the Cocteau Twins (whose singing also employs wordless sounds) to the vocal improvisations of jazz singers as varied as Billie Holiday and Karin Krog.

For many singers, using musical parameters to explore the means of interpretation depends more on elements such as timbre. In this, as Losseff (1999) notes in the case of Kate Bush's 'Wuthering Heights,' particularly interesting things can happen 'when well-defined boundaries are *crossed*.' In this recording, Bush's voice – in the persona of Cathy – 'in effect occupies a timbral space that had not been heard before, not least because she never really exploits the chest register at all ... but sings entirely in the middle and head registers, while manipulating her vibrato/soft palette to produce different vocal effects' (229–30).

In live or filmed contexts, a further function of the singer occurs at the level of the kinetics of the performance. The singer's movements and gestures not only add another dimension to performance, but are also, as the focal point of the visual gaze, the fulcrum around which movement and gesture proceed. In the case of genres in which singers also perform instrumentally, gesture and movement are often constrained – although many guitarists, to give the most obvious example, have made stage movement involving the instrument an element of their acts. In other cases, where the constraints or opportunities offered by instruments do not exist, some singers choose to use movement and gesture very economically (although the effect can still be dramatic), while others prefer athleticism. The signification possibilities are often very rich. The particular combination of singing and dancing has offered a range of opportunities to incorporate the singer into a highly choreographed, often very theatrical, display, from the debonair virility of Gene Kelly in *Singin' in the Rain* to the energetic eroticism of Madonna.

The Singer in Ensembles

Popular music is rich in the alternative ensemble formats in which singers perform. Few, if any, are unique to popular music, but popular music as a whole has explored the possibilities that are offered more thoroughly than any other area of music. Even in a category such as music by unaccompanied singers, which makes up a relatively small component of the whole of popular music, and which draws on practise with a long history, the results can be spectacularly different, as can be seen, for example, in both music by a cappella gospel groups and music by gospel choirs.

The history of popular music ensembles involving singers is dominated by three categories: self-accompanied singers; solo singers with instrumental accompaniment; and singing ensembles. Each of these has its own history and has continued to maintain a separate identity, but it is also the case that each format has both overlapped with and influenced the others.

Self-accompanied solo singing is often associated with folk and traditional music, and its passage into commercial popular music often followed a route from vernacular tradition (as, for example, in the case of the first recorded figures in country music, fiddle players who also sang, such as Fiddlin' John Carson). As is shown in the example of perhaps the most famous and influential genre to follow this path – blues – the self-accompanied solo singer was not necessarily a long-established role in vernacular music, but could also be a quite recent response (late nineteenth-century, in this case) to changed social and cultural circumstances. Blues also offers the reminder that self-accompanied solo performance could be one option among several in these traditions.

In the broad sweep of popular music, self-accompanied solo singing has often involved the performance of music created by the singer. This was already the case with one of the earliest professional examples of the self-accompanied soloist, the pianist-songwriter Henry Russell, in the 1830s and 1840s. It was the case with a large proportion of commercially recorded solo blues, and it became a part of country music following the success of Jimmie Rodgers in the late 1920s and early 1930s. Around 1940 in the United States, a threefold connection began to be made, particularly among a new generation of folk-influenced musicians on the political left, between singers performing self-composed songs, ideas of authenticity, sincerity and integrity, and a belief in the power of song to raise social and political awareness. The connection was embodied especially in the songs of Woody Guthrie (for example, his *Dust Bowl Ballads*).

Notions of authenticity, sincerity and integrity (and with them, an often implied hostility to the commercial motivation of the music industry) became a defining element in the emergence at the very end of the 1950s of the category that became known as the singer-songwriter. Although not all singer-songwriters accompanied themselves, many did. The figure of the singer-songwriter became evident – and often influential – in many different places: Bob Dylan in the United States, Jacques Brel and Georges Brassens in France, Violeta Parra in Chile, Atahualpa Yupanqui in Argentina. It was characteristic of the phenomenon, too, that, although live performances were seen as quintessential, the music of the singer-songwriters began to take on a separate existence as texts in their own right.

In at least partial contrast to the tradition of self-accompanied singers and singer-songwriters lies the practise of a solo singer performing pre-composed music (typically by someone other than the singer), with accompaniment provided by an instrumental ensemble. This clearly has roots in the classical tradition, but its earliest popular manifestation lies most probably in the popular theater of the nineteenth century, especially vaudeville, revue and early cabaret. In due course, and thanks in part to the impact of recordings, the format was able to spread beyond the confines of the theater. During the 1920s, solo vocalists were regarded by dance bands and jazz bands largely as nonessential appendages, but by the 1930s they had secured a place in their own right. The role of specific individual singers was crucial to this process. The achievement of Louis Armstrong and Bing Crosby in particular in gaining popular appeal was significant in 'propell[ing] popular attention towards singers rather than players' (Potter 1998, 105).

The period from the late 1930s to the 1950s saw a blossoming in the role of the spotlighted individual singer with band or small group accompaniment, epitomized by performers such as Frank Sinatra in the United States and (in a very different style) Edith Piaf in France. In the Anglophone world especially, the format and the idiom – and the particular ideology of individualized performance that had grown up around them – were challenged by rock 'n' roll and rock music, which scorned the whole sonic world (and often the age) of the star singers, and by styles of the 'folk revival,' which scorned the whole idea of 'stardom' on which the format had come to depend.

Yet, not only did the format of the spotlighted individual singer with instrumental backing not go away, but it remained, albeit with many stylistic shifts, to become a standard presence in a great deal of pop music of the late twentieth and early twenty-first centuries. Among these stylistic shifts, one of the most prevalent was the introduction of backing singers – a development that came into the mainstream via a different route, one with its roots in vocal ensembles.

Although music centered around a solo voice has been such a dominant format, much music has been created around other ensembles of various sizes and combinations. The format is an international one and can be seen in manifestations as different as the Trio Bulgarka from Bulgaria and the Ladysmith Black Mambazo ensemble from South Africa. As with both of these examples, many vocal ensembles have been exclusively female or male. Big bands often employed groups of female and male singers (such as the Andrews Sisters and the Four Freshmen). The practise was maintained, from the African-American all-girl and all-boy groups of the 1950s and 1960s such as the Ronettes and the Platters to 1990s pop groups such as the Spice Girls and Take That. Gender divides were also frequently present when the vocal ensemble format was adapted in genres that were based on musicians who both played and sang. Country music, for example, regularly featured male duets (such as the Blue Sky Boys), while the typical four-piece rock band – all of whose members often sang together at some time, as did the Beatles and the Beach Boys – was resolutely male.

In a great many different generic contexts, small ensembles of singers structure what they do around the interplay of solo voice and group. The results not only are musically expressive, but also have the potential to suggest social and political relationships. The repertoire of the Chilean *nueva canción* group Inti-illimani, for example, includes songs (such as 'La muerte no va conmigo') in which a succession of individual male voices, establishing identity on an egalitarian basis, alternates with non-hierarchical unison singing.

The example of African-American rhythm and blues (R&B) vocal groups illustrates the types of changes that can be introduced over time while remaining faithful to the subtle expression of self–other relationships. The R&B vocal group of the late 1940s and 1950s had its origins in an earlier style of gospel group (typically a quartet) in which no single voice dominated, but in which collective harmony and unison singing was combined with moments when individual voices were foregrounded, often in a form of dialog (such as call-and-response) with the rest of the ensemble. By the late 1930s, this style was changing, in both sacred and secular contexts. The Ink Spots in particular developed an approach in which a high tenor 'lead' was highlighted throughout against a vocal background divided into a single bass voice and two middle voices singing in harmony. By the time of groups such as the Dominoes and the Drifters, placing a tenor, or sometimes bass, lead out in front of a harmonizing group had become standard. The lead singer's role now offered more possibilities for individual-centered expression than had the earlier gospel style, while the remaining singers represented a kind of support group, underpinning and commenting on (sometimes with ironic humor) the lead singer's contribution.

Once established, the format of lead singer and backing group became an available resource, to be adapted in different stylistic contexts. Its most obvious line of succession can be followed through Motown and soul, but it also became fundamental (most probably under the influence of US R&B) to guitar-based styles such as Merseybeat. In time, it became so widespread as to warrant no comment.

The example of Merseybeat also points to how, in many of the subgenres making up one of the twentieth century's most dominant popular music genres – rock – the role of the singer was formed from a merger of the self-accompanied singer or singers and the small vocal ensemble. One of the things that has often enabled a distinction to be drawn between 'rock' and 'pop' is that the role of singers in the latter is more likely to be formed by a different merger: that between small vocal ensemble and the singer with instrumental accompaniment. A parallel distinction has also often been drawn between self-accompaniment, in both rock and the singer-songwriter tradition, as signifying creativity, and non-self-accompaniment as signifying performance – and interpretation – alone.

Marketing and Promotion

The first signs that commercial music concerns recognized the potential of using the singer's individual identity to help sales of music were seen as early as the beginning of the eighteenth century, when music publishers first began to include singers' names on sheet music. By the mid-nineteenth century, this had extended to making the singer(s) the subject of lithographed illustrations on sheet music covers. By the 1920s, it was common to find small photographs of singers incorporated into the covers. In due course, the ultimate tribute appeared: sheet music covers consisting only of a single large publicity-style photograph. The use of the singer's image on the product continued, and was further developed, on LP album covers. A full range of iconography was employed – from live performance shots to cartoon images to a variety of ways in which images suggested that the singer was prepared to share public or private moments.

Marketing through images on the product itself was always limited, however, and, since a relatively early point in the twentieth century, much more attention has been paid to advertising. Especially after the rise of the music press and the expansion of the popular press, advertising and publicity became the main avenues by which all musicians were marketed and promoted. Singers have always been heavily featured. In the main, it appears that what has often made singers so marketable, whether they are individual performers or members of ensembles, is the basic fact that they are regularly the center of attention in performance, rather than any factors specifically connected to their performance skills or attributes. Once a singer's centrality has been established, the creation of an image may, if desired, be based almost entirely on extramusical factors, involving biographical events, character traits and so on. Yet, at the same time, it is unusual for the processes by which a singer's image is created and disseminated to overlook the fact that in performance singers not only are spotlighted, but also have the principal role in the creation of mood and meaning. Hence, marketing and image creation are also responsive to the idea of the singer as the main site of personality and individuality in performance.

There are also plentiful examples of marketing and promotion that do make reference to specific attributes, either of a performer in general or of a particular performance. The voice of Karen Matheson, singer with the Scottish band Capercaillie, for example, is regularly described as 'pure' and 'ethereal.' In an earlier era, press advertising for blues singer Ida Cox's recording 'Blues Ain't Nothin' Else But!' stressed the realism in her performance by asserting: 'Every verse is a picture. Hear it and discover how many kinds of blues you've got' (Oliver 1990, 286).

Reception

In the reception of singers by listeners, the singer's contribution to the sound event is distinguished from instrumentally produced sounds by the fact that listeners apprehend it as being directly produced by the body. The fact that all listeners have developed expertise in their daily lives in interpreting the physical attributes of the spoken voice at any one moment – whether it is the character and mental state it suggests, or the nature of an event it is describing – means it is a relatively small step to transfer interpretive skills to the more stylized world of the singing voice, and hence to 'read' the character and mood of the singer as belonging to a sentient individual. The singer therefore becomes the key site at which sound is linked to personality and to mood in the listener's understanding.

Listeners' responses are also influenced by the knowledge they have accumulated – very often subconsciously – about the ways in which the sound that is produced in the body also expresses social and cultural meaning. As is shown in work by Frith and McRobbie (1979) and by Shepherd (1991), the singer's sound is particularly rich in meaning for listeners in the area of gender relations. To Frith's and McRobbie's comparison of 'cock rock' and 'soft rock' voices Shepherd adds a distinction between 'woman as nurturer' (for example, Canadian singer Anne Murray) and 'the boy next door' (for example, Paul McCartney singing 'Yesterday'). Whereas in the case of the former 'the physiology of sound production . . . seems to speak to a person more fully aware of her inner experiential being in offering herself as a source of emotional nourishment,' in the case of the latter 'the physiology of sound production . . . reflects an experiential emptiness in avoiding the resonating chambers of the chest cavity' (Shepherd 1991, 167).

These two skills that the listener develops – the ability to recognize in the singer's voice characteristics of that person as an individual human being acting in individual human situations, and the ability to understand how the voice expresses social and cultural relations –

are central to the phenomenon of fandom. The singer's ability to engender responses at both a personal and a sociocultural level is reflected in the ways in which fans may choose to fashion a 'relationship' with the singing star that is highly personal, or one that is group-based (as, for example, in the appeal of certain singers to the gay community), or both.

Audience responses, including those of fans, are, of course, dependent both on the nature of the singer's contribution to performance and on the way that he/she is marketed – in other words, on the singer's role in a complex, interconnected musical communication process. Taken together, the singer's preeminence in each part of this process, across a wide range of popular musics, is a powerful indication of the primary role that the singer is regularly asked to play in that process.

Bibliography

Burston, Jonathan. 1998. 'Theatre Space as Virtual Place: Audio Technology, the Reconfigured Singing Body, and the Megamusical.' *Popular Music* 17(2): 205–18.

Frith, Simon, and McRobbie, Angela. 1979. 'Rock and Sexuality.' *Screen Education* 29: 3–19. (Reprinted in *On Record: Rock, Pop, and the Written Word*, ed. Simon Frith and Andrew Goodwin. London: Routledge, 1990, 371–89.)

Hoskyns, Barney. 1991. *From a Whisper to a Scream: The Great Voices of Popular Music*. London: Fontana.

Lacasse, Serge. 2000. *'Listen to My Voice': The Evocative Power of Vocal Staging in Recorded Rock Music and Other Forms of Vocal Expression*. Ph.D. thesis, University of Liverpool.

Losseff, Nicky. 1999. 'Cathy's Homecoming and the Other World: Kate Bush's "Wuthering Heights."' *Popular Music* 18(2): 227–40.

Oliver, Paul. 1990. *Blues Fell This Morning: Meaning in the Blues*. 2nd ed. Cambridge: Cambridge University Press.

Pleasants, Henry. 1974. *The Great American Popular Singers*. New York: Simon & Schuster.

Potter, John. 1998. *Vocal Authority: Singing Style and Ideology*. Cambridge: Cambridge University Press.

Shepherd, John. 1991. *Music as Social Text*. Cambridge: Polity Press.

Discographical References

Beatles, The. 'Yesterday.' Capitol 5498. *1965*: USA.

Beatles, The. 'You Know My Name (Look Up the Number).' Apple R 5833. *1970*: UK.

Bush, Kate. 'Wuthering Heights.' *The Kick Inside*. EMI EMC 3223. *1978*: UK.

Cox, Ida. 'Blues Ain't Nothin' Else But!' Paramount 12212. 1924: USA.

Guthrie, Woody. *Dust Bowl Ballads*. Folkways F-5212. *1964*: USA.

Inti-illimani. 'La muerte no va conmigo.' *De Canto y Baile*. RCA 2L 34393. *1986*: Italy.

Morrison, Van. *Astral Weeks*. Warner Brothers 1768. *1968*: USA.

Singin' in the Rain (Original soundtrack). Columbia 45394. *1990*: USA.

Filmography

Singin' in the Rain, dir. Stanley Donen and Gene Kelly. 1952. USA. 103 mins. Musical Romance. Original music by Nacio Herb Brown, Lennie Hayton.

DAVID HORN

Soloist

A soloist is a musician who performs alone, either accompanied or unaccompanied. In Western classical music, the term was used to describe singers, those musicians who played the solo parts in concertos, and those principal members of orchestral sections who played any solos required within the symphonic repertoire. In classical music, the majority of soloists play music that has been composed and set down previously, although solo cadenzas (passages of unaccompanied playing that link sections of a concerto) were often improvised during the Classical and Romantic periods in the eighteenth and nineteenth centuries. In jazz, however, solo passages are almost always improvised by the performer. Louis Armstrong is credited with being the first significant soloist in jazz but, since his innovations of the 1920s, almost all jazz musicians improvise solos and play collective improvisation or passages of composed or arranged material.

Soloists appear in many genres of popular music in most cultures. Anglo-American popular songs from the early twentieth century onward included a segment to be filled by a brief solo from a pianist, saxophonist, guitarist or other instrumentalist which generally followed the chordal or melodic structure of the chorus or verse. In such genres as rhythm and blues, rock 'n' roll and others involving groups or bands, soloists took the opportunity to demonstrate their virtuosity with an improvisational stance that resembled the approach (but not the sound) of the jazz soloist.

ALYN SHIPTON

Songster

Since the first decade of the twentieth century, and possibly for much longer, the term 'songster' has been used, in Howard Odum's words, 'to denote any Negro who regularly sings or makes songs' (Odum and Johnson 1925, 156–57). Such a songster was usually expected to accompany himself (few were women) on guitar or, more rarely, banjo. He was compared with the 'musicianer,' who claimed 'to be an expert with the banjo or fiddle.' Also used was the term 'music physicianer,' which probably distinguished a performer on a medicine show from the 'doctor' or 'medical physician.' While the latter term was short-lived, both 'musicianer' and 'songster' were still used in the 1960s.

It is possible that the word 'songster' was used in reference to singers who had as broad a repertoire of songs as was expected by those who purchased the songbooks of the same name. The earliest such singers to have recorded were Johnny 'Daddy Stovepipe' Watson (1867–1963) and Henry Thomas, known as 'Ragtime Texas' (1874–ca. 1958). Both played guitar, and Thomas also played 'quills' or syrinxes (short reed pipes). Although there may have been earlier musicians of similar range and abilities who entertained on the plantations before the American Civil War or worked the 'colored' minstrel shows, Watson and Thomas appear to have been the oldest representatives of a generation of singers born between the era of Reconstruction (1867–77) and the turn of the century.

Folklorists paid little attention to songsters until the years following World War I, so that it was the first to record who gave the best indication of their music. Papa Charlie Jackson, a banjo-playing songster from New Orleans, recorded from the mid-1920s, as did Sam Jones, known as 'Stovepipe No. 1,' who probably came from Cincinnati. Singers from northern Mississippi, like Jim Jackson (guitar) and 'Banjo Joe,' Gus Cannon (who later led Cannon's Jug Stompers), and others such as Frank Stokes or Walter 'Furry' Lewis from Memphis, Tennessee, were typical entertainers who performed in the medicine shows that worked the small southern towns. Other songsters, such as Luke Jordan, Peg Leg Howell and Pink Anderson, performed in the shows of the eastern and southeastern states. Such rural entertainments, like the larger minstrel shows, provided work for both black and white musicians, whose presence in the same companies permitted the exchange of songs. Roy Acuff, Fiddlin' John Carson, Uncle Dave Macon and Jimmie Rodgers were among the white showmen whose repertoires paralleled those of the black songsters.

Apart from the traveling show songsters, there were many who remained in their hometowns, and whose reputations were often considerable but local – like Mississippi John Hurt from Avalon, Mississippi, the New Orleans boatman, Richard 'Rabbit' Brown, or the Virginia barber, William Moore. Most songsters continued performing through the 1930s, although the number who were recorded in the peak period of the popularity of the blues was far less. Even so, it was possible for songsters like Elizabeth Cotton, originally from North Carolina, Mance Lipscomb from Navasota, Texas, the erstwhile companion of Blind Blake (Blind Arthur Blake),

Bill Williams from Florida and the Alabama slide guitarist Johnie Lewis to be discovered and recorded in the 1960s.

The range of songs performed by the songsters almost defies classification, but it includes 'coon' and minstrel songs, ballads and heroic *cante-fables* (part-song, part-narrative epic performances), dance songs and routines, parodies and comic numbers, adapted prison and work songs, spirituals and gospel songs, as well as others as learned, or as required, by their audiences, and sung as the occasion demanded. The audiences comprised both blacks and whites, although frequently in segregated venues: most songsters could recall playing for dances at the 'big house,' as well as in jukes ('juke joints' or bars where 'freshly cooked food, homebrew, and moonshine were sold cheaply . . . there was usually some gambling, talking and flirting on the periphery of the gatherings, but [where] the center of activity was the dancing' (Barlow 1989, 29)) or for country suppers. Many claimed large repertoires, like Mance Lipscomb, who numbered some 300 songs in his, or the best-known of all songsters, Huddie Ledbetter ('Leadbelly'), who claimed to know over 500 songs. These singers were born at the close of the nineteenth century, and few songsters were younger; the last of the genre was John Jackson, who was born in Virginia in 1924. The songsters were overtaken by blues singers, whose music was energetically promoted by the record companies. Some songsters, such as Charley Patton and 'Big' Bill Broonzy, rapidly adapted to the new music and, although the range of their repertoires demonstrated their songster origins, they were soon recognized as principal exponents of the blues.

Bibliography

Alyn, Glen, comp. 1993. *I Say Me for a Parable: The Oral Autobiography of Mance Lipscomb, Texas Bluesman*. New York: W.W. Norton & Company.

Barlow, William. 1989. *'Looking Up at Down': The Emergence of Blues Culture*. Philadelphia: Temple University Press.

Bastin, Bruce. 1986. *Red River Blues: The Blues Tradition in the Southeast*. Urbana, IL: University of Illinois Press.

Lomax, John A., and Lomax, Alan, eds. 1936. *Negro Folk Songs as Sung by Lead Belly*. New York: Macmillan.

Odum, Howard W., and Johnson, Guy B. 1925. *The Negro and His Songs: A Study of Typical Negro Songs in the South*. Chapel Hill, NC: University of North Carolina Press.

Oliver, Paul. 1984. *Songsters and Saints: Vocal Traditions on Race Records*. Cambridge: Cambridge University Press.

Russell, Tony. 1970. *Blacks, Whites and Blues*. London: Studio Vista.

Thomas, Will H. 1912. *Some Current Folk-Songs of the Negro and Their Economic Interpretation*. Austin, TX: Folk-Lore Society of Texas, Pamphlet 1.

Discography

Songsters and Saints: Vocal Traditions on Race Records, Vol. 1 (2 LP set). Matchbox Bluesmaster Series MSEX 2001/2002. *1984*: USA.

Songsters and Saints: Vocal Traditions on Race Records, Vol. 2 (2 LP set). Matchbox Bluesmaster Series MSEX 2003/2004. *1985*: USA.

PAUL OLIVER

Tap-Dancer

The tap-dancer specializes in a form of dance in which the feet execute rhythmic patterns that are often – though not necessarily – complex in nature and in which the sounds made by the feet during the dance are enhanced by the metal 'taps' worn on the toes and heels of the shoes. Most famously associated with movie musicals of the 1930s and 1940s (in which it often featured in couple dancing as an element in a kind of courtship ritual), tap is essentially a theatrical exhibition dance combining a visual display of agility with musical expressivity.

The origins of tap are thought to lie in the coming together of British clog and jig dancing and African-American dance steps. Historians see early evidence of this process in the late eighteenth century in the hornpipe dancing of John Durang from Pennsylvania, whose stage dancing included features such as a 'double shuffle' and a 'grasshopper step'; Durang even incorporated 'beating down' on his toes in a possible predecessor to a tap movement (Stearns and Stearns 1994, 38–39). The development of new theatrical dance styles along these lines took place both in dance houses such as those in the Five Points district of New York, where the African-American dancer William Henry Lane, known as Juba, performed in the 1840s, and in the stage acts of blackface minstrels. Although Juba (who was also one of the first African Americans to perform in minstrel shows) was described as a 'jig dancer,' the meaning of the term was shifting away from that of 'Irish dancing' toward a collective expression for black dance; and, in that dance, the rhythmic use of the feet was a key factor. In reporting on Juba's dancing in London in 1848, a critic referred wonderingly to 'the manner in which he beats time with his feet and the extraordinary command he possesses over them' (quoted in Stearns and Stearns 1994, 46).

One particular minstrel dance, the soft shoe (performed in leather shoes), has been cited as tap's most likely immediate precursor, especially as performed by George Primrose (Norton 1986). Tap-dancing itself first appeared on the public stage in the context of vaudeville, where the tap-dancer was soon featured as a specialty act. One of the earliest shows to follow this pattern was the all-black revue, *Darktown Follies* (1913), in which dancers Eddie Rector and Toots Davis surprised New York audiences with their contrasting tap styles, one graceful and precise, the other more angular and dramatic. With the all-black musical *Shuffle Along* (1921), which featured a stunning array of dancing, including tap routines, dancers began to introduce a greater variety of rhythms; for the most part, however, the outstanding African-American tap-dancers of the time appeared infrequently, if at all, on Broadway, until the success of Bill 'Bojangles' Robinson in *Blackbirds of 1928*.

Trained in the touring vaudeville circuit – and already 50 years old by the time of his Broadway success – Robinson subsequently appeared in several Broadway shows and a total of 14 Hollywood movies, among them *Stormy Weather* (1943). Tap was absolutely central to Robinson's style. Writer Langston Hughes described his dancing as 'human percussion . . . creating little running trills of rippling softness or terrific syncopated rolls of mounting sound' (1957, 49) – although among fellow entertainers Robinson was not always unanimously admired, and his range was limited to several basic steps. His major contribution was that 'he brought tap up on the toes, dancing upright and swinging' (Stearns and Stearns 1994, 187). He also enhanced the sonic elements: in his most famous dance, the 'stair dance,' each step was made to resonate at a different pitch.

The tap-dancing of Robinson's outstanding contemporary, John W. Bubbles, did not bring the latter the same rewards (although his overall skill as an entertainer impressed George Gershwin sufficiently to give him the part of Sportin' Life in *Porgy and Bess*), but he is generally credited with being more rhythmically inventive. Bubbles' dancing in the early to mid-1920s, at the Hoofers Club in Harlem and in revues, shifted the basic rhythm toward a more even four-in-the-bar, allowing greater scope for inventive accenting, in which he used both heel and toe.

With *The Broadway Melody* (1929), tap – mostly in the form of 'precision tapping' and 'toe tapping' – began to be a regular feature of early Hollywood musicals, but few who did it, whether actors or chorus girls, had received much training. That did not prevent the occasional individual, such as James Cagney, from developing a singular approach to dance that incorporated basic tap routines into an overall performing style. Among the first female Hollywood stars to become known for their tap-dancing were Ruby Keeler and Ann Miller, although

both were overshadowed in terms of tap-dancing accomplishment by Eleanor Powell. Powell acknowledged the influence of jazz musicians, especially drummers: 'I used to practise all the time to those records,' she once admitted.

With the dancing of Fred Astaire, first with his sister Adele in Broadway musicals such as George and Ira Gershwin's *Lady, Be Good!* (1924), later with Ginger Rogers in Hollywood musicals such as *Top Hat* (1935) and *Swing Time* (1936) and with Powell in *Broadway Melody of 1940*, tap steps and routines were extensively combined with other dance steps into one integrated whole. In the Astaire-Rogers films in particular, tapping was used as a kind of dialog between the two characters, an exploration and articulation of the chemistry between them. Although Astaire used tap steps a great deal, he never thought of himself – and did not wish to be thought of by others – as a tap-dancer. But, as Marshall and Jean Stearns remark, 'his consistent use of tap reinforced the acute sense of rhythm on which all of his dancing is based' (1994, 224). The practise of integrating tap's particular expressivity and potential for display into wider routines was continued by Gene Kelly in films such as *Singin' in the Rain* (1952). Although trained in tap, Kelly's more athletic approach and his greater interest in incorporating elements of ballet meant tap became one of a set of available styles, for use in appropriate moments, especially to express inner emotions (Delamater 1981, 158).

As the tap-dancer became more of a rarity in popular stage and film entertainment in the latter part of the twentieth century, making appearances only in revivals or in contexts where tap helped to evoke an earlier era, so tap-dancing came to be seen in dance circles more as an art form, and as such was ripe for further technical experimentation. The contemporary tap-dancer, one observer noted, 'can accomplish feats that were impossible even five years ago' (quoted in Emery 1988, 351). At the same time, tap-dancing has become popular as an amateur activity in many parts of the world, used partly as an aid to physical fitness and partly in preparation for amateur performance, but chiefly no doubt for the pleasure of doing it.

Bibliography

Delamater, Jerome. 1981. *Dance in the Hollywood Musical*. Ann Arbor, MI: UMI Research Press.

Emery, Lynne Fauley. 1988. *Black Dance from 1619 to Today*. 2nd rev. ed. London: Dance Books. (First published Palo Alto, CA: National Press Books, 1972.)

Hughes, Langston. 1957. *Famous Negro Music Makers*. New York: Dodd, Mead.

Malone, Jacqui. 1996. *Steppin' on the Blues: The Visible*

Rhythms of African American Dance. Urbana, IL: University of Illinois Press.

Norton, Pauline. 1986. 'Soft Shoe.' In *The New Grove Dictionary of American Music*, Vol. 4, ed. H. Wiley Hitchcock. London: Macmillan, 255.

Stearns, Marshall, and Stearns, Jean. 1994 (1968). *Jazz Dance: The Story of American Vernacular Dance.* New York: Da Capo.

Filmography

Broadway Melody of 1940, dir. Norman Taurog. 1940. USA. 102 mins. Musical. Original music by Roger Edens, Cole Porter, Walter Ruick.

Singin' in the Rain, dir. Stanley Donen and Gene Kelly. 1952. USA. 103 mins. Musical. Original music by Nacio Herb Brown, Arthur Freed, Lennie Hayton.

Stormy Weather, dir. Andrew L. Stone. 1943. USA. 77 mins. Musical. Musical direction by Emil Newman.

Swing Time, dir. George Stevens. 1936. USA. 103 mins. Musical. Original music by Robert Russell Bennett, Hal Borne, Dorothy Fields, Jerome Kern.

The Broadway Melody, dir. Harry Beaumont. 1929. USA. 104 mins. Musical. Original music by Nacio Herb Brown, George M. Cohan, Arthur Freed, Willard Robinson (II).

Top Hat, dir. Mark Sandrich. 1935. USA. 97 mins. Musical. Original music by Irving Berlin.

DAVID HORN

Torch Singer

The term 'torch singer' began to be used in the United States in the mid- to late 1920s to refer to a singer whose repertoire included a large number of love songs performed in an intimate style and typically centering around unreturned devotion. Although 'torch singer' came to be applied to female singers, and although a 'torch song' came to be thought of as a song sung from a female standpoint, a gender distinction was not always present, at least at first. *Vanity Fair* (November 1927), for example, reports singer Tommy Lyman as announcing a song he was about to perform as 'My famous torch song, "Come To Me My Melancholy Baby."'

The same article credits Lyman with inventing the term 'torch song,' but its origins and those of 'torch singer' are more obscure. Wilder (1972, 21) dates the first evidence of the torch song genre (though not necessarily the term) as early as ca. 1915, with songs expressing 'a new, more personal point of view,' such as Spencer Williams's 'I Ain't Got Nobody.' Moore (1989, 31) identifies the 'formula for the torch song' in the French song 'Mon Homme,' which (as 'My Man') was a success for Fanny Brice in the 1921 *Ziegfeld Follies*. There is no evidence, however, that the terms themselves were in wide circulation in this period. If the music business was not the actual source of the terms, it was the first to make wide use of them. Given the subject matter in which the torch singer specialized, the emergence of the terms seems to be connected with the phrase 'to carry a torch for someone,' and the image of the flambeau was often used in discourse around them.

The best known of the female torch singers – performers such as Ruth Etting, Libby Holman and Helen Morgan – were New York-based musicians whose professional life consisted of performing in an interdependent mix of environments: the club (usually gangster-run), the revue stage and network radio; most also made recordings, and both Etting and Morgan made appearances in Hollywood movies. Where the so-called flappers who were popular at much the same time (for example, Helen Kane) projected an energetic, youthful image that reflected a comparatively untroubled view of the post-World War I years, the torch singers presented a more mature, reflective, but basically less optimistic, response. The paradox that the torch singer represented in the midst of the apparently liberating changes to social and sexual behavior that had characterized this period was noted by Walter Winchell, who remarked on 'those female Troubadours with voices of smoke and tears, who moan and keen love's labours lost in the rhythm and boom of the Roaring Twenties' (quoted in Bradshaw 1985, 73). Although unmistakably urban and urbane, and clearly perceived as exotic figures, the torch singers also clung resolutely – and usually in spite of all the evidence – to ideals of constancy, and in doing so they reflected the tensions and ambiguities felt by both women and men as the decade drew to a close.

The advent of the torch singer's more personal style was made possible by the technological changes involving the introduction of the microphone and electrical recording in the mid-1920s. Although some singers, such as Brice and Lee Morse, made the transition from the vaudeville style of public performance to the new environment, the majority of white singers – including the torch singers – who dominated the records and the radio waves in the United States in the late 1920s and early 1930s came to the fore in response to the new stylistic opportunity offered by the technology. Perhaps because they were more used to singing in the private surroundings of the home, female singers were less afraid than male singers of the new technology's ability to reveal the personal idiosyncracies of a voice and to offer an opportunity for the expression of emotion at close quarters.

No torch singer's repertoire consisted solely of torch songs, and no one torch singer's performance idiom conformed to one torch song mold. Even singers most closely identified with the term, such as Ruth Etting (billed by record company, Columbia, as 'The Queen of the Torchsingers'), included numbers of a more humorous, optimistic nature, like 'Button Up Your Overcoat'; and songs that began wistfully as typical torch songs, such as 'If I Could Be With You One Hour Tonight,' could be transformed before the end, with the help of impatient-sounding session musicians, into a more upbeat performance – although, by the 1930s, Etting's performances had tended to part with this particular feature. A singer such as Annette Hanshaw illustrates well the range of performance styles that existed (as well as revealing some of the pitfalls of using the term as a retrospective critical category). She sang many of the songs that became torch song classics, such as 'My Sin' and 'What Wouldn't I Do For That Man?,' each of which was recorded by several other singers, but she employed a more jazz-influenced style and generally quicker tempos, and was frequently accompanied by recognized jazz musicians.

Although the presence of blues inflections and tonality can be seen in some torch songs – for example, in 'Moanin' Low' – these were the same elements that Tin Pan Alley songwriters had been incorporating into their products for some time. As far as performance was concerned, Libby Holman was not Bessie Smith; 'the two traditions,' Moore says, 'remained separate throughout the 1920s' (1989, 32). One writer, familiar with both traditions, wrote scathingly about the torch song as 'a low type song of sentimentality . . . practised by the Nudists of the musical world, in which the whining voice complains of unrequited love.' If torch songs did come from the blues, 'they were in no sense a development or an improvement' (Cuney-Hare 1936, 144).

Nevertheless, the torch singer did exercise an influence on the jazz singer, most notably on Billie Holiday. As torch songs such as 'Body and Soul' and 'Mean to Me' became jazz standards, Holiday's highly intimate style built on the torch singer's mix of sophistication, glamor and defenselessness. At least one major difference, of course, was that, whereas torch singers typically sang their torch songs 'straight,' with occasional mannerisms, Holiday was a pioneer of the idea of musical and emotional interpretation.

The term 'torch singer' had died out in contemporary use by the mid-twentieth century, only to resurface in the 1980s and 1990s, but with a very different gloss. Singers such as k.d. lang and Alison Moyet have been described in the music press as 'torch singers,' but the connotation has shifted away from vulnerability toward a greater manifestation of inner strength.

Bibliography

Bradshaw, J. 1985. *Dreams That Money Can Buy: The Tragic Life of Libby Holman*. New York: W. Morrow.

Cuney-Hare, Maud. 1936. *Negro Musicians and Their Music*. Washington, DC: Associated Publishers.

Maxwell, G. 1974. *Helen Morgan: Her Life and Legend*. New York: Hawthorn Books.

Moore, John. 1989. '"The Hieroglyphics of Love": The Torch Singers and Interpretation.' *Popular Music* 8(1): 31–58.

Rust, Brian, and Debus, Allen G. 1973. *The Complete Entertainment Discography: From the Mid-1890s to 1942*. New Rochelle, NY: Arlington House.

Wilder, Alec. 1972. *American Popular Song: The Great Innovators, 1900–1950*, ed. James T. Maher. New York: Oxford University Press.

Sheet Music

Ahlert, Fred E., comp., and Turk, Roy, lyr. 1929. 'Mean to Me.' New York: DeSylva, Brown and Henderson, Inc.

Gorney, Jay, comp., and Harburg, E.Y., lyr. 1929. 'What Wouldn't I Do For That Man?' New York: Remick Music Corp.

Green, Johnny, comp., and Eyton, Frank, Heyman, Ed & Sauer, Robert, lyrs. 1930. 'Body and Soul.' New York: T.B. Harms, Inc.

Henderson, Ray, comp., and Brown, Lew & DeSylva, Buddy, lyrs. 1928. 'Button Up Your Overcoat.' New York: DeSylva, Brown and Henderson, Inc.

Henderson, Ray, comp., and Brown, Lew & DeSylva, Buddy, lyrs. 1929. 'My Sin.' New York: DeSylva, Brown and Henderson, Inc.

Johnson, James P., comp., and Creamer, Henry, lyr. 1926. 'If I Could Be With You One Hour Tonight.' New York: Remick Music Corp.

Rainger, Ralph, comp., and Dietz, Howard, lyr. 1929. 'Moanin' Low.' New York: T.B. Harms, Inc.

Williams, Spencer, comp., and Graham, Roger & Peyton, Dave, lyrs. 1915. 'I Ain't Got Nobody.' New York: Triangle Music Pub. Co.

Yvain, Maurice, comp., and Willemetz, Albert & Charles, Jacques, lyrs. 1920. 'Mon Homme.' New York: Leo Feist, Inc.

Discographical References

Brice, Fanny. 'My Man.' Victor 45263. 1921: USA.

Etting, Ruth. 'Button Up Your Overcoat.' Columbia 1762-D. 1929: USA.

Etting, Ruth. 'If I Could Be With You One Hour Tonight.' Columbia 2300-D. 1930: USA.

Hanshaw, Annette. 'My Sin.' Harmony 910. 1929: USA.

Hanshaw, Annette. 'What Wouldn't I Do For That Man?' Harmony 1012. 1929: USA.

Holiday, Billie. 'Body and Soul.' Vocalion 5481. 1940: USA.

Holiday, Billie. 'Mean to Me.' Columbia 35926. 1937: USA.

Holman, Libby. 'Body and Soul.' Brunswick 4910. 1930: USA.

Holman, Libby. 'Moanin' Low.' Brunswick 4445. 1929: USA.

Yerkes Orchestra. 'Mon Homme.' Columbia A-3403. 1921: USA.

DAVID HORN

Troubadour

'Troubadour' is a term that has been used extensively in popular music to describe a performer with an attractive manner, often itinerant and self-accompanied, or a small band of accomplished musicians with similar appeal. Troubadours have been assumed to be among the earliest of popular music exponents, and use of the word also has implications of a time-honored role. It is questionable whether the original troubadours were popular musicians or singers in the sense in which the term is customarily applied, although certain of their functions and their accompanying musicians give some justification for the application of the term. Nonetheless, owing to frequent popularization in Hollywood films and cartoons, a stereotype of the 'troubadour' has become entrenched in popular culture over the last century.

Deriving from 'trobar,' a dialect term meaning 'to invent' or 'to compose,' troubadours were first evident in eleventh-century France at the time of the first crusade. Identified with Provence, writing in the *langue d'oc* dialect, and far removed from the northern French *langue d'oïl*, the troubadours emerged at a time when the courts were maintained in the castles of the Provençal counts and dukes. Between conflicts, court life was liable to be boring, and the troubadours, courtly poets and song composers created entertainments of wit and artifice.

The title of 'first troubadour' is often assigned to Duke William IX of Aquitaine, seventh Count of Poitiers (1071–1127), but there is evidence that other troubadours were of less noble birth: Aimeric de Peguilhan was the son of a draper in Toulouse, while Peire Vidal, a celebrated singer in the late twelfth century, was the son of a furrier from the same city. Guilhem Figueira was a tailor and the son of a tailor, and Perdigon was a fisherman's son, while Bernart de Ventadorn was fathered by the furnace-tender at Ventadorn Castle. Bernart took advantage of his upbringing in the castle to acquire the skills of a troubadour, eventually becoming a favorite of Henry II and Queen Eleanor. Several troubadours, such as Peire de Maensac and Sordello of Sirier (Mantua), were poor knights or cavaliers who learned to sing and compose songs, thus ingratiating themselves at court. Among the most famous troubadours were aristocrats from beyond Provence, like the Dauphin of Auvergne, Prince Sancho of Navarre and Alphonso II, King of Aragon. A very famous king, Richard Coeur de Lion, fit the troubadour profile, although he was actually a *trouvère*, rooted in the northern Angevin language and culture. Although some troubadours came from humble origins, they aspired to the sophisticated life at court, where they joined with those of more noble station to practise their art.

Although the *vidas* and *razos*, or introductory notes, on the lives of the troubadours and the explications of their songs are not always reliable, much is known about the poets, as they moved in a highly literate and bilingual society, and many hundreds of their songs have survived. The songs are variously classified according to the development of writing styles, song structures, themes and approaches. Although the troubadours' *épitres*, or letters, were intended to be read, most of their poems were accompanied with music played by the jongleurs or accompanists: the lyric poems were sung to music, while the epic poems were recited with musical interludes. Among the simpler poems were those comprised of couplets, of which there were sometimes seven to a verse, while the *chanson* (*canso*) consisted of five or six stanzas. Many of these were love songs, refined in text, exhibiting the later 'gentil lovyng' of Chaucer, portrayed as the music unfolded. A romantic type of song was the *pastorelle*, which took the form of an exchange between the troubadour and a shepherdess. The songs frequently involved the subtleties of *amour courtois* as the troubadour culture gained favor with women at court. A number of troubadours took mistresses, and the indiscretions of some were notorious. There were also female troubadours, such as the Comtessa de Dia, who likewise composed songs and took aristocratic lovers.

Numerous songs were expressions of pleasure, such as the *alba* or dawn song, which was sometimes of an erotic nature, although often sprinkled with religious sentiments. Riddle songs, which obscured their meaning in teasing verses, tantalized the troubadours' listeners, but the complexities of the *trobar clus*, or abstruse poems, disguised more contentious attitudes, including ridicule of the Church, in enigmatic stanzas. Jealousies in the court extended to the troubadours themselves, whose *sirventes* or *pasquinades* were challenging, satirical and provocative songs that were addressed to other troubadours but also conveyed grievances. Disputes and contrary opinions were acted out in the *tenson* or poetic dialog, in which the combatants took alternate verses, using the same number of rhymed lines in each. An elaborate form of *tenson* was the *tournament*, in which opinions were expressed in verse by several combatants who had to obey the rules of rhyming.

Apart from mastering a large number of song types and verse forms, the troubadours also exercised their talents by devising rhyme schemes. Among the more common were the ABABCDCD, ABABCCD and ABACCDD forms. Others were more demanding – few more so than the *sixtine*, which consisted of six stanzas, each comprising six verses. Only six rhyming words were permitted, which had to appear in each stanza in inverted form, the sixth rhyme-word of the first stanza becoming the first rhyme-word of the second stanza, the remainder following in sequence and with successive inversions. Over 1,500 different metrical schemes have been identified, of which the majority were used only once. Of the music, far less is known, only a handful of examples having been analyzed; these, however, reflect the general melodic character of contemporary secular and sacred song.

As might be expected, a number of troubadours, like the widely traveled Gascon, Cercamon (the successor to William IX), or the master of the *trobar clus* and *sixtine*, Arnaut Daniel, were jongleurs before they were encouraged or protected by their lords in order that they might become troubadours – as Daniel was by Richard I. Troubadours were intent upon writing their own songs, and many, but not all, also sang them. Most had one or two, or even a retinue, of jongleurs – versatile musicians who were often their masters' singers, and who performed acrobatics, juggled and generally entertained. Their accomplishments included the playing of the lute, primitive violin, bagpipe, syrinx, harp, gigue, gittern, psaltery, *organistrum* (a form of hurdy-gurdy), *regal*, tabor and rote, among other instruments. The jongleur might also tell tales, do trained animal acts, juggle with knives and practise acrobatics.

Jongleurs were usually of common birth, but many gained fame for their musical accomplishments, and some, skilled at devising songs, were accepted as troubadours. Others, perhaps not so lucky, traveled as wandering minstrels, performing throughout much of Europe. Without the protection enjoyed and, as a consequence, afforded by the troubadours, jongleurs forfeited their legal rights, but many formed guilds of minstrels to protect themselves and each other. Some women (*jongleuses*) joined the traveling jongleurs, playing instruments, singing to the crowds, even dancing

with dancing bears; a few, like Marie de France, became famous at court.

The activities of the jongleurs long outlasted the troubadour movement in the south. The Provençal troubadours, who had fueled their *pasquinades* with disputes, recklessly wrote new ones concerning the conflicting theologies of the Church of Rome and the Albigenses. When Pope Innocent III authorized a crusade against the Albigensian heretics, numerous Provençal troubadours were massacred with them, although the *trouvères* of northern France continued the troubadour tradition. The jongleurs' activities were more extended. As more people became literate and poetry was increasingly read rather than sung, the jongleurs adapted their talents, becoming street entertainers, acting in mystery plays, performing with companies of minstrels and singing ballads in inns and hostelries. They – more than the troubadours for whom they had sung and performed – were likely the real antecedents of popular musicians in subsequent generations.

Bibliography

Aubrey, Elizabeth. 1996. *The Music of the Troubadours*. Bloomington, IN: Indiana University Press.

Gaunt, Simon, and Kay, Sarah, eds. 1999. *The Troubadours: An Introduction*. Cambridge: Cambridge University Press.

Pound, Ezra. 1954 (1913). 'Troubadours – Their Sorts and Conditions.' In *Literary Essays of Ezra Pound*, ed. T.S. Eliot. London: Faber & Faber, 94–108.

Stevens, John. 1986. *Words and Music in the Middle Ages: Song, Narrative, Dance and Drama, 1050–1350*. Cambridge: Cambridge University Press.

Topsfield, L.T. 1975. *Troubadours and Love*. Cambridge: Cambridge University Press.

Werf, Hendrik van der. 1972. *The Chansons of the Troubadours and Trouvères: A Study of the Melodies and Their Relation to the Poems*. Utrecht: A. Oosthoek's Uitgeversmaatschappij.

Werf, Hendrik van der (collector and transcriber), and Bond, Gerald A. (text editor). 1984. *The Extant Troubadour Melodies: Transcriptions and Essays for Performers and Scholars*. Rochester, NY: H. van der Werf.

Wilhelm, James J. 1972. *Mediaeval Song: An Anthology of Hymns and Lyrics*. London: George Allen & Unwin.

PAUL OLIVER and BRYAN GILLINGHAM

3. Performance Techniques

Air Guitar

'Air guitar' is the term for an imaginary guitar that a person pretends to play, often to recorded music or to live music when excited by a performance. Since the instrument is imaginary, the person is playing 'air.' Air-guitar playing is also seen at presentations or competitions involving 'air bands.' Air bands use real instruments or theater props to pantomime the performance of those who recorded the music. Since air bands do not really play instruments, they are judged on their acting rather than on their musical ability. 'Air' band is rather a misnomer, since the instruments used in such pantomimes may be real.

Air guitar playing is usually associated with popular music styles dominated by the electric guitar, such as rock, blues and heavy metal.

WAYNE EAGLES

Barré

'Barré' is a technique that involves pressing adjacent guitar strings using only one finger. In most cases, it is the forefinger that is used, pressing all six strings; but other forms of barré, using the little finger or the ring finger, and occasionally the middle finger, are found in the fingering of classical or popular pieces. Some chords can be played either with open strings or with a barré. While open-string chords are preferred by amateur guitarists, who may find it difficult to sound all the strings properly when applying the barré, or on occasions when a sustained, fully resonant sound is required, barré chords offer better control for electric guitar sounds since they can be more easily dampened or stopped. A supreme example of barré chords is to be found in the Kinks' 'All Day and All of the Night' (1964). To obtain an open-string sound on higher frets, acoustic guitarists use a capo (an abbreviation of the Italian *capotasto*), a mechanical substitute for the barré.

Discographical Reference

Kinks, The. 'All Day and All of the Night.' Pye 7N 15714. *1964*: UK.

FRANCO FABBRI

Bottleneck Guitar

Commonly associated with rural acoustic blues guitar styles, bottleneck guitar is a variation of the slide guitar technique. It is similar to the Hawaiian guitar technique and was possibly influenced by it, but it probably derived from another source, the diddley-bow, an improvised one-string instrument whose pitch could be varied continuously rather than by stepwise motion. 'Bottleneck' refers specifically to the implement used for fretting the guitar, cut perhaps from a beer or wine bottle, sanded smooth and typically slid over one of the fingers of the player's left hand. However, the actual manner of manipulating the bottleneck, tuning or even holding the guitar can vary from player to player.

As with the metal slide in slide guitar, the use of a bottleneck liberates the guitarist from the limitations of the equally tempered pitches determined by the guitar's frets. In conventional guitar playing, the fingers of the player's left hand press the strings onto the fretboard just behind the frets; the frets then determine the pitch of the string. The use of a glass cylinder on the strings makes it unnecessary for the player to press the strings hard with the fingers against the frets because the glass now determines the speaking length of the strings. A pitch can be produced at any point on the fretboard, not just at the frets. The guitarist is thus freed from the regime of discrete half-step increments established by the frets. With glissando and all shades of vibrato thus possible, the guitar's pitches can be molded with the same flexibility as the human voice. While guitarists commonly bend strings to add tonal interest, as well as to achieve the correct intonation of the blue notes, the use of an implement to slide along the strings offers far greater range and flexibility, including whole-chord glissandi.

As with slide guitar and Hawaiian guitar, for bottleneck guitar the instrument is tuned in such a way that the open strings form chords or consonances. This is because the bottleneck is most easily held either at a right angle or at a slight angle to the line made by the strings; to make chords possible, the strings are therefore tuned in combinations of fifths and thirds.

Among the guitarists noted for the bottleneck technique, Walter 'Furry' Lewis, James 'Kokomo' Arnold and Tampa Red deserve special mention.

Bibliography

Evans, David. 1987 (1982). *Big Road Blues: Tradition and Creativity in the Folk Blues*. New York: Da Capo Press.

Titon, Jeff Todd. 1977. *Early Downhome Blues: A Musical and Cultural Analysis*. Urbana, IL: University of Illinois Press.

Discography

Finger, Peter. *Bottleneck Guitar Solos*. Kicking Mule 116. *1975*: USA.

Lewis, 'Furry.' 'Why Don't You Come Home Blues.' Vocalion 1134. 1927: USA.

Tampa Red. *Bottleneck Guitar (1928–1937)*. Yazoo 1039. *1992*: USA.

Weldon, Casey Bill, and Arnold, 'Kokomo.' *Bottleneck Guitar Trendsetters of the 1930s*. Yazoo 1049. *1992*: USA.

TIM WISE

Brush Playing

An alternative to drumsticks for drumset players are brushes, which generally consist of a fan-shaped arrangement of wire strands attached to a handle. Such brushes were developed around 1912 and were often referred to as 'flyswatters.' Brushes are most often used on the snare drum for timekeeping, but they are sometimes used on cymbals to produce a delicate sound. Brushes can also be used on tom-toms for fills and solos.

The term 'brush' reflects the appearance of the device, as well as the way in which it is typically used. Drummers generally slide the left-hand brush over the snare drum head in a rhythmic, circular motion, producing a sustained 'swish' sound, while using either a sideswiping motion or direct taps to play rhythmic patterns with the right-hand brush. Brushes are especially popular with jazz drummers, who often use them in ballads to produce a very legato style of timekeeping. But brushes can also be used for fast tempos, as demonstrated by Philly Joe Jones on the Miles Davis recording 'Billy Boy,' and drummer Dave Tough was noted for his ability to power a big band with brushes. Other notable jazz brush players include 'Papa' Jo Jones and Ed Thigpen.

When playing the Brazilian bossa nova, drummers often use a brush in one hand and a drumstick in the other, swishing the brush back and forth across the drumhead to simulate the sound of a shaker while using a cross-stick technique with the stick to imitate the sound of claves. Rock, pop and country drummers often use brushes much like drumsticks, playing hand-to-hand rhythms on the snare drums and producing accents by striking the rim of the drum with the handle of the brush. Drummer Russ Kunkel influenced many rock and pop drummers to use brushes for acoustic-based rock when he used brushes on James Taylor's recording 'Fire and Rain.'

Variations of the traditional wire brush include brushes with thick nylon or fiberglass strands, and bundles of thin wooden dowels that produce a sound in between that produced by traditional brushes and that by drumsticks.

Bibliography

Erskine, Peter. 1987. 'Brushes.' In *Drum Concepts and Techniques*. Milwaukee, WI: Hal Leonard, 87–89.

Riley, John. 1994. 'Brushes.' In *The Art of Bop Drumming*. New York: Manhattan Music, 47–54.

Discographical References

Davis, Miles. 'Billy Boy.' *Milestones*. Columbia 9428. 1958; *1959*: USA.

Taylor, James. 'Fire and Rain.' *Sweet Baby James*. Warner Bros. 1843. *1970*: USA.

RICK MATTINGLY

Busk/Busking

'Busking' was originally a cant, or underworld, term used of pirates and others who traversed the seas and cities seeking illicit gains from nefarious practises. Early in the nineteenth century, 'busking' referred to the selling of obscene books and song sheets in public houses and inns, especially in London. By mid-century, it was used to describe vagrants, or street entertainers held in low regard. It was this usage that persisted and was adopted by the street musicians themselves to describe their improvisatory playing. If they were asked to perform a tune or setting for a song, they might 'busk it' or invent an accompaniment if they did not know the theme. Soon, street musicians were commonly termed 'buskers' in England and, by the 1920s, the long lines that formed outside theaters and the 3,000 or so local cinemas constituted ready-made audiences for their playing. 'The buskers were at the bottom of the profession' (Pearsall 1976, 136).

Soon, the term was adopted by jazz musicians, some learning by working the streets. Of the busking jazz groups that played in the gutters of the London streets in the 1950s, none were as well known or as frequently moved on by the police as the Happy Wanderers, a group of middle-aged Londoners playing saxophone, trumpet, banjo and washboard.

Although not widely used in the United States, the English term was sometimes adopted, being indirectly linked with the word 'busk' as used in US circuses. In this context, it denoted performances that earned tips or donations from an audience rather than charging standard entrance fees. 'Busking' has continued to be used to denote jazz improvisation without rehearsal, with an implication of the perfunctory or the unpolished.

Bibliography

Cohen, David, and Greenwood, Ben. 1981. *The Buskers*. Newton Abbot: David and Charles.

Pearsall, Ronald. 1976. *Popular Music of the Twenties*. Newton Abbot: David and Charles.

Tanenbaum, Susie J. 1995. *Underground Harmonies: Music and Politics in the Subways of New York*. Ithaca, NY: Cornell University Press.

PAUL OLIVER

Calls/Calling

A 'call' is a vocal form of address to a distant person or animal, frequently pitched high and without the harshness of a shout. Calls were a vital form of communication before the advent of the telephone and other electronic media. As such, the melodic and rhythmic characteristics of calls have fed into many early forms of popular music, and 'calling' has continued to be important to different kinds of square-dancing.

Typically, calls are made with exhaled air, using the roof of the mouth to project the sound. Often, they are of one or two notes only, but some may be melodically constructed. In pastoral and peasant communities, calling to hogs, cattle and geese at feeding times was, and in some regions has continued to be, common practise. Some calls, such as the Australian bush 'coo-ee,' which was popularized during World War I, are based on bird imitations, while others are enhanced by echoes between hills or amplified across lakes and other stretches of still water. Calls are also used to attract the attention of relatives, friends or work mates, some calls being devised so that they can be distinguished from others, on, for example, a fairground site where booths

are being erected and prizes delivered. A specific type of call was the cry of vendors, pedlars and hawkers.

Where wagons and teams of horses, mules or oxen were driven, the calls of 'whoa,' 'haw' and 'gee' were customary when giving directions to the lead animals. Calls were professionally used in occupations where information had to be passed to another worker, the 'sounding calls' of riverboat pilots, leadsmen and watchmen being among the most celebrated. Samuel Langhorne Clemens, who trained as a riverboat pilot on the *Paul Jones* out of New Orleans in the mid-nineteenth century, noted the calls of the leadsmen: 'Quarter less three! . . . Half twain! . . . M-a-r-k twain!,' from which he took his pseudonym. As described by Mary Wheeler (1944), the lead pipe on the lead line would be dropped plumb and laid on the riverbed, 'Quarter Less Twain' being 10 1/2 feet deep and 'Mark Twain' being 2 fathoms. Joe Shores and Sam Hazel recorded a few Mississippi sounding calls for the Library of Congress in 1936. Reissued with them is a recording made by an unknown 'Old Train Caller from New Orleans,' who called train destinations, also included in 'Railroadin' Some' by the Texas songster Henry Thomas.

The rapid-fire lists of weights, qualities and prices of tobacco and cattle given by auctioneers might also be classified as calls, although they were, in fact, extended descriptions uttered in a monotone. A number of recordings by both black and white songsters incorporated the calls of Appalachian 'set-running' and the square dances of Texas and Arizona. Eventually becoming international in its appeal, square-dancing involves sets and movements that are controlled and directed by a 'caller.' The caller may sometimes be a dancer but more frequently he/she stands before the dancers and intersperses directions with 'patter':

Jaybird lit upon the groun'
Crow hopped up an' knock 'em down
Promenade your partners 'round.'

In the 1930s, callers such as Bob Lapsley of El Paso and, in particular, Jimmy Clossin, formerly of the Texas Panhandle, became famous. 'Calling involves the memorizing of each and every dance routine . . . Chant the Call in a clear voice as you would a nursery rhyme . . . Keep in time with the music and come in on the down beat for the next line of the call,' Jimmy Clossin advised. Although they have not died out, calls have diminished in the workplace, due to changing labor patterns, the decline of peasant farming and the common use of mobile telephones. But on the dance floor, a caller's skills are still greatly in demand, as the popularity of square-dancing has spread worldwide.

Bibliography

Clossin, Jimmy, and Hertzog, Carl. 1951 (1940). *The American Cowboy Square Dance Book*. London: G. Bell and Sons.

Twain, Mark. 1883. *Life on the Mississippi*. Boston, MA: James R. Osgood and Co.

Wheeler, Mary. 1944. *Steamboatin' Days: Folk Songs of the River Packet Era*. Baton Rouge, LA: Louisiana State University Press.

Discographical References

Field Recordings, Vol. 3: Mississippi 1936–1942 (with unknown train caller, Joe Shores, Sam Hazel). Document DOCD-5577. *1997*: Austria.

Thomas, Henry. 'Railroadin' Some.' *Night Train, Vol. 3: Classic Railroad Songs*. Rounder 1144. *1998*: USA.

Discography

Brown, Enoch. 'Complaint Call.' *Music Down Home: An Introduction to Negro Folk Music, U.S.A.* (ed. Charles Edward Smith). Folkways Records FA 2691. *1965*: USA.

Dodson, Annie Grace Horn. 'Children's Call.' *Music Down Home: An Introduction to Negro Folk Music, U.S.A.* (ed. Charles Edward Smith). Folkways Records FA 2691. *1965*: USA.

Dodson, Annie Grace Horn. 'Field Call.' *Music Down Home: An Introduction to Negro Folk Music, U.S.A.* (ed. Charles Edward Smith). Folkways Records FA 2691. *1965*: USA.

PAUL OLIVER

Claw Hammer

'Claw hammer' or 'clawhammer' is a term broadly designating a style of 'old-time' five-string banjo playing, traditional in the southeastern United States and now adopted widely, characterized by a distinctive right-hand technique.

In its simplest form, the player's fingers are held in a fairly fixed position, with thumb and index finger forming a curved (claw hammer) shape, as if the whole hand were gripping an invisible cylinder that is slightly too large to permit the thumb and index finger to touch at their tips. In 2/4 time, a single measure of claw hammer playing consists of a quarter note, struck (or 'stroked,' to use the minstrel-era term) by the player's index fingernail or middle fingernail with a downward movement. This technique has occasionally been called 'down-picking,' but most banjoists reserve the word 'picking' for styles in which the digits opposed to the thumb sound strings with an 'upward' or flexion motion. In claw hammer, the initial quarter-note stroke is always downward. Two eighth notes follow, the first sounded by a repetition of the initial noting movement with index or middle finger, the last invariably being the

high droning 'fifth' or chanter string sounded by the player's thumb.

For many players, the term 'claw hammer' is roughly synonymous with 'frailing.' However, there are subtypes – for example, the 'drop-thumb' style, in which the player's thumb 'drops' down to sound a string on the second eighth note of the measure. The drop-thumb technique in the hands of masterful players like Kyle Creed is especially adaptable to slow and subtle tempos; the rollicking 'sawmill' approach of banjoists like Louis Marshall 'Grandpa' Jones or Ralph Stanley generally works best for 'barn-dance' numbers and banjo songs at moderate to rapid tempos.

Bibliography

Krassen, Miles. 1974. *Clawhammer Banjo: Traditional Appalachian Banjo Tunes Transcribed in Tablature and Based on the Playing of Wade Ward*. New York: Oak Publications.

Rosenbaum, Art. 1968. *Old-Time Mountain Banjo: An Instruction Method for Playing the Old-Time Five-String Mountain Banjo Based on the Styles of Traditional Banjo-Pickers*. New York: Oak Publications.

Rosenbaum, Art. 1981. *The Art of the Mountain Banjo*. Fullerton, CA: Centerstream.

Seeger, Mike, and Cohen, John, eds. 1964. *The New Lost City Ramblers Songbook*. New York: Oak Publications.

Discography

Creed, Kyle. *Liberty*. Heritage 28. *1977*: USA.

Jones, 'Grandpa.' *Everybody's Grandpa*. Bear Family 15788. *1996*: Germany.

Library of Congress Banjo Collection, 1937–1946. Rounder 0237. *1990*: USA.

Macon, Uncle Dave. *Go Long Mule*. County 3505. *1995*: USA.

Old Five String, Vol. 1: Clawhammer Banjo Solos. Heritage 39. *1983*: USA.

Stanley, Ralph. *Songs My Mother Taught Me & More: 'Clawhammer' Style Banjo*. Freeland 655. *1998*: USA.

Steele, Pete. *Banjo Songs and Tunes*. Folkways FS 3828. *1958*: USA.

The Music of Kentucky, Vol. 1: Early American Rural Classics, 1927–37. Yazoo 2013. *1995*: USA.

THOMAS A. ADLER

Close Harmony Singing

Close harmony is an approach to vocal group voice leading that underlies a wide variety of North American genres of vernacular harmony, from bluegrass to doo-wop. The guiding principle in close harmony singing is to preserve close intervallic voicings, usually on proximate chord tones, and for this reason it is most often practised by gender-segregated trios, quartets and quintets.

Many close harmony styles feature a high harmony part (tenor or soprano) above the melody line, allowing the melody part (air) to cross with one or more lower voices to preserve the closely harmonized chords.

North America's fascination with close harmony dates to the late 1830s, when various singing troupes from the Austrian and Swiss border region of the Alps undertook a series of tours. The members of the original Rainer Family (Anton, Franz, Maria, Felix and Joseph) had been touring Europe for a decade when they decided to bring their act, the Tyrolese Minstrels, to North America in 1834, performing German part songs and arrangements of Tyrolese folk songs. They were followed by the German Minstrels (1837), the Alpine Minstrels (1837), the Strasser Family Singers, and a different group of Rainer Family members, again calling themselves the Tyrolese Minstrels (also known as 'the Tribe of Rainer'), who toured the United States between 1839 and 1843. At a New York concert in 1839, the Rainers premièred 'Silent Night/Stille Nacht' for US audiences.

North American audiences thrilled to the (latter) Rainers' precise enunciation and timing, and a harmony so well blended that listeners were unable to determine which singer was singing which part. An English-language publication of their songs by Ditson helped US singers, such as the Euterpian Quartette, the Hughes Family, Ossian's Bards, the Illsleys, the Boston Minstrels, the Alleghenians and the Hutchinson Family Singers, to imitate the Tyrolean close harmony style.

John Hutchinson first heard the Tyrolese Minstrels in Lynn or Boston, Massachusetts around 1840 and taught the rest of his family to sing in the style of the Rainers. In the best-known arrangement of the group, sister Abby sang the high harmony part to Judson's tenor, accompanied by John and Asa as first and second bass. The Hutchinsons, the most popular of many touring close harmony groups after 1840, helped to establish and to define this tradition and its repertoire by virtue of their popularity over decades.

North American music publishers from the 1840s onward produced four-part close harmony arrangements of hymns for Masonic lodges, early college fraternity songs, and military, patriotic, sentimental and comic ballads, often in tandem with S-A-T-B (soprano-alto-tenor-bass) arrangements. The most ardent popularizers of close harmony in the period were the blackface minstrel show quartets, which were performing close harmony choruses 'in the style of the Hutchinsons' as early as 1843–44. The four-part chorus minstrel song became a fixture of minstrelsy (blackface *and* African-American troupes) and went with the shows across North America.

This style of singing passed into recreational practise in African-American communities from Florida to Hampton Roads, Virginia, and could be heard in black barbershops, on street corners, in saloons and in black fraternal organizations all across the South. The recreational black quartets contributed the particularly flexible approach to rhythm, the chromatic voice leading on ragtime chord progressions and the practise of 'snaking' from chord to chord that came to characterize the 'barbershop' style of close harmony singing. However, the publication of close harmony arrangement books in 1876 and 1879 by both W.T. Giffe and Dr. J.B. Herbert showed the extent to which different repertoires, including spirituals, sentimental 'hearth-and-home' parlor ballads, minstrel songs and comic songs, were being performed by both black and white close harmony groups.

Close harmony quartets were widely recorded in the early decades of the recording industry. Two African-American quartets, the Unique Quartette and the Standard Quartette, recorded between 1890 and 1897, and the Manhansett Quartette produced a series of recordings that formed the basis for subsequent white groups (for example, the Haydn, the Peerless and the American quartets). Polk Miller and His Old South Quartette (ca. 1909–10) was a rare mixed group at the time – a white entertainer with a black quartet. However, African-American groups such as Lieutenant Jim Europe's Four Harmony Kings, the Norfolk Jazz Quartet/Norfolk Jubilee Quartet, the Southern Negro Quartette, the Harmony Four (aka the Bessemer Quartet, the Southern Harmony Quartette and the Southern Serenaders), the Mobile Four, the Southernaires and the Mills Brothers all were recording by the late 1920s, mixing sacred and secular repertoires. Even the jubilee gospel quartets of the 1930s, such as the Golden Gate Quartet and the Silver Leaf Quartet, included secular material in their shows and recordings and carved out an important space for close harmony gospel singing at Friday church socials, on stage and on radio. Close harmony gospel quartets persevered through the 1940s and 1950s – the era of groups such as the Dixie Hummingbirds, the Fairfield Four, the Five Blind Boys of Alabama, the Soul Stirrers and the Spirit of Memphis Quartet – and they have remained a fixture in many North American communities.

Close harmony worked its way into many parallel streams of country and western music. Gospel publishing companies such as J.D. Vaughan (Lawrenceburg, Tennessee), the Hartford Publishing Company (Arkansas) and the Trio Music Company (Texas) sponsored close harmony quartet tours through the rural South at the turn of the century. Home- and church-based singing of gospel and country songs in harmony arrangements proliferated throughout the region, found especially in the 'brother' style of close and high harmony. Bill and Charlie Monroe, Ira and Charlie Louvin, Ralph and Carter Stanley, Jim and Jesse McReynolds, and many others carried this 'high lonesome harmony' tradition into what would become known as bluegrass music, following the ensemble model of Bill Monroe's Blue Grass Boys. Most of the Blue Grass Boys' choruses featured a high and reedy lead voice harmonized still higher by the first tenor, and often supported below by a baritone or (more rarely) by a baritone and bass.

Close harmony groups were featured in Hollywood western films of the 1930s to the 1950s. Two Illinois farm girls who sang close harmony, Millie and Dolly Good, were repackaged as the Girls of the Golden West. A radio quartet, the Maple City Four, performed in the 1937 hit western *Git Along Little Dogies*, starring Gene Autry, and the same group appeared with Roy Rogers in the 1938 film *Under Western Stars*. In 1933, Roy Rogers had formed his own close harmony vocal group called the Pioneer Trio, which was renamed the Sons of the Pioneers in 1934. The trio grew into a quartet with the addition of bass singer and fiddler Hugh Farr. 'Cool Water,' 'Tumbling Tumbleweeds' and other Sons of the Pioneers hits demonstrate a smooth close harmony style with obvious jazz influences and a 'western ambiance' accompaniment.

Some mainstream recording quartets of the 1930s, such as the Revelers, became jazz vocal groups. Others, like the Boswell Sisters and Frank Sinatra's early vocal quartet, the Hoboken Four, started in swing music and fronted swing orchestras. The Boswell Sisters (and 'the Boswell sound') inspired later female pop groups like the Andrews Sisters and the Chordettes ('Mr. Sandman'), although the Chordettes also had roots in barbershop revival singing.

African-American harmony swing and rhythm and blues (R&B) groups like the Ink Spots, the Mills Brothers, the Hudsonaires, the Five Red Caps and the Charioteers enhanced the role of close harmony in jazz. In the 1930s, the Mills Brothers, one of the most oft-cited influences by later R&B (and doo-wop) vocal harmony groups, helped to make the imitation of instrument sounds and an active bass part (dubbed the 'talking bass') a part of R&B vocal group style. Directly inspired by some of these groups, a movement took shape in men's harmony in the late 1940s and 1950s (eventually called doo-wop) that reemphasized the romance of the street corner and formed recognizable harmony sounds, and it was based in such major east coast cities as Baltimore (the Orioles, the Cardinals and the Swallows), Washington, DC (the Clovers, the Rainbows) and New York (the Crows, the Chords, the Cadillacs, and Frankie Lymon and the Teenagers).

Close harmony did not disappear from jazz in this era. The Four Freshmen, an Indiana group that started with barbershop harmony, expanded their chord vocabulary to include extended jazz chords, inversions and octave displacements that imitated Stan Kenton's jazz combo arranging. The Four Freshmen influenced such jazz harmony groups as the Hi-Lo's, the Modernaires and Manhattan Transfer, as well as post-doo-wop pop harmonizers such as the Beach Boys, the Lettermen, the Mamas and the Papas, Frankie Valli and the Four Seasons, the Chaperones and the Happenings. It was often the departures from close harmony that helped to mark these arrangements as revolutionary and arresting. Nonetheless, close harmony was the foundation on which many of these innovations were constructed, and it has continued to sustain hip-hop and soul group harmonies.

Bibliography

Allen, Ray. 1991. *Singing in the Spirit: African-American Sacred Quartets in New York City*. Philadelphia: University of Pennsylvania Press.

Averill, Gage. 2002. *Four Parts, No Waiting: A Social History of American Barbershop Harmony*. New York and London: Oxford University Press.

Cockrell, Dale, ed. and comp. 1989. *Excelsior: Journals of the Hutchinson Family Singers, 1842–1846*. Sociology of Music No. 5. Stuyvesant, NY: Pendragon Press.

Dixon, Robert M.W., Godrich, John, and Rye, Howard. 1997. *Blues and Gospel Records 1890–1943*. 4th ed. Oxford: Clarendon Press.

George, Nelson. 1988. *The Death of Rhythm & Blues*. New York: Pantheon Books.

Giffe, W.T. 1876. *Giffe's Male Quartet and Chorus Book, Containing a Choice Variety of New Quartets, Choruses and Part Songs for Male Voices*. Indianapolis, IN: H.L. Benham.

Gracyk, Tim, with Hoffmann, Frank. 2000. *Popular American Recording Pioneers, 1895–1925*. New York: Haworth Press.

Gribin, Anthony J., and Schiff, Matthew M. 1992. *Doo-Wop: The Forgotten Third of Rock 'n' Roll*. Iola, WI: Krause Publications.

Groia, Philip. 1974. *They All Sang on the Corner: New York City's Rhythm and Blues Vocal Groups of the 1950's*. Rev. ed. Setauket, NY: Edmond Publishing Company.

Herbert, J.B. 1879. *Herbert's Male Quartet and Chorus Book*. Cleveland and Chicago: S. Brainard's Sons.

Lornell, Kip. 1995. *Happy in the Service of the Lord: African-American Sacred Vocal Harmony Quartets in Memphis*. 2nd ed. Knoxville, TN: University of Tennessee Press.

Pruter, Robert. 1996. *Doowop: The Chicago Scene*. Urbana, IL: University of Illinois Press.

Sampson, Henry T. 1980. *Blacks in Blackface: A Source Book on Early Black Musical Shows.* Metuchen, NJ: Scarecrow Press.

Sampson, Henry T. 1988. *The Ghost Walks: A Chronological History of Blacks in Show Business, 1865–1910.* Metuchen, NJ: Scarecrow Press.

Warner, Jay. 2000. *The Da Capo Book of American Singing Groups: A History, 1940–1990.* Boulder, CO: Da Capo Press.

Sheet Music

'The Celebrated Melodies of the Rainer Family.' 1841. Boston, MA: Oliver Ditson.

Discographical References

Chordettes, The. 'Mr. Sandman.' Cadence 1247. 1954: USA.

Sons of the Pioneers, The. 'Cool Water.' *Tumbling Tumbleweeds.* MCA 20359. *1987*: USA.

Sons of the Pioneers, The. 'Tumbling Tumbleweeds.' *Tumbling Tumbleweeds.* MCA 20359. *1987*: USA.

Filmography

Git Along Little Dogies, dir. Joseph Kane. 1937. USA. 60 mins. Western. Original music by Fleming Allen, Smiley Burnette, Stuart McGowen, Sidney D. Mitchell, Sam Stept.

Under Western Stars, dir. Joseph Kane. 1938. USA. 67 mins. Western. Original music by Edward Cherkose, Jack Lawrence, Johnny Marvin, Charles Rosoff, Peter Tinturin.

GAGE AVERILL

Crooning

'Crooning' denotes a relaxed style of singing associated with the development of the microphone in the 1920s and 1930s, initially used for radio broadcasts and subsequently for amplified singing in public concerts. The word 'crooning' is found in English literary sources as early as the fifteenth century, meaning 'to sing or speak in a low, murmuring tone.'

Before the invention of the microphone, singers had to project their voices in much the same way as classical singers, that is, by lowering the larynx to gain access to additional frequencies that amplify the sound without having to exert extra effort. The result of this technique is a richer sound than is normally heard in speech. The early blues 'shouters,' for example, often produced a complex sound with vibrato and the sustained vowels associated with projecting the sound as far as possible.

The microphone removed the need to project the sound, and enabled performers to sing as though they were talking to their listeners on a one-to-one basis. The effect on singing technique was dramatic, and meant that popular singing evolved away from the sound of trained singers toward the more 'natural' sound that has characterized it ever since. The earliest crooners (Whispering Jack Smith, Rudy Vallee and Bing Crosby, for example) soon saw the benefits of using the new speech-related technique in amplified concert singing, where the microphone quickly replaced the short-lived and unsatisfactory megaphone.

Common to all crooning is a sense of intimacy with the microphone, and therefore with the listener (whose ears are, in effect, only a very short distance from the singer's mouth). Although the sound may be small, a wide dynamic range is possible, and the shapes of vowels and syllables can be retained from speech, rather than distorted in an effort to project. Nonvocal emotional inflections (such as sighing or particular ways of breathing) become available to the performers as additional rhetorical colors; throwaway lines that would not normally be heard become part of the singer's potential stylistic armory; and small chromatic inflections become possible in a singing style where the vibrato is closely controlled or absent altogether.

Inevitably, these effects tended to facilitate a certain sort of repertoire, and it was a surfeit of this that eventually led to the marginalization of the technique. Bing Crosby was followed by others (including Russ Columbo, Perry Como and Dean Martin), whose distinctive voices responded well to the microphone, but who themselves had few successors as the genre declined in popularity among mainstream audiences. Improved microphones and more risk-taking by later singers, such as Billy Eckstine and, supremely, Frank Sinatra, enabled a more robust singing style to develop without compromising the benefits of close miking.

Bibliography

Dunne, John Gregory. 1990. *Crooning: A Collection.* New York: Simon and Schuster.

Friedwald, Will. 1991. *Jazz Singing: America's Great Voices from Bessie Smith to Bebop and Beyond.* London: Quartet.

Goldstein, Howard. 2001. 'Crooning.' In *The New Grove Dictionary of Music and Musicians*, Vol. 6, ed. Stanley Sadie. 2nd ed. New York: Grove, 720.

McCracken, Allison. 1999. '"God's Gift to Us Girls": Crooning, Gender, and the Re-Creation of American Popular Song, 1928–1933.' *American Music* 17(4): 365–95.

Discography

Como, Perry. *A Portrait of Perry Como.* Gallerie 448. *2000*: UK.

Crosby, Bing. *I Surrender Dear.* All Star Series CD 23106. *1991*: USA.

Eckstine, Billy. *Basie/Eckstine Incorporated.* Roulette RCD 59042. 1986: USA.

Martin, Dean. *The Best of Dean Martin*. Capitol CDP7 90718 2. *1989*: USA.

Sinatra, Frank. *Sinatra-Basie*. Reprise 927023-2. *1963*: USA.

Smith, Whispering Jack. *The Roaring Twenties*. Saydisc CD-SDL 344. *1984*: UK.

The Greatest Crooners. Disky BX 85312/22/32. *1998*: The Netherlands.

JOHN POTTER

Crushing

'Crushing' is a term used metaphorically to describe a particular piano technique in which adjacent notes are played almost simultaneously. The technique appears in blues and, occasionally also, in jazz. According to Oliver (1986), it was developed by blues and boogie-woogie pianists in response to the ability of blues guitarists and harmonica players to 'bend' notes, sliding off the pitch microtonally. Lacking the same options, 'blues pianists achieve illusions of bent and passing notes by "crushing" adjacent keys or sliding the third finger across them' (1986, 171–72). One of the two notes 'crushed' is hit 'a fraction before the other so that the implied passing note hits the ear in a manner similar to a guitarist's slide' (Oliver 1969, 86). The technique occurs in Meade 'Lux' Lewis's recording of 'Honky Tonk Train Blues' (1927).

In jazz, the pianist Thelonious Monk was noted for including 'crushed' notes in his repertoire of techniques.

Bibliography

Oliver, Paul. 1969. *The Story of the Blues*. London: Barrie & Rockliff.

Oliver, Paul. 1986. 'Blues.' In *The New Grove Gospel, Blues and Jazz*, ed. Paul Oliver, Max Harrison and William Bolcom. London: Macmillan, 36–188.

Discographical Reference

Lewis, Meade 'Lux.' 'Honky Tonk Train Blues.' Paramount 12896. 1927: USA.

DAVID HORN

Cueing

The term 'cueing' has a number of different meanings depending on the context. In radio broadcasting, for example, cueing is the technique by which one prepares a tape or disc for playback, ensuring that sound is present immediately upon starting the playback device. Commercials and spot announcements are often recorded onto tape cartridges, which are then loaded into special playback devices that have automatic cueing functions. A more subtle and musically significant variation on basic turntable cueing technique is employed by dance club DJs, allowing them to cut between different songs or instrumental breaks while maintaining a

sense of tempo and flow. Cueing in dance clubs is usually done with the aid of headphones, so that the process of preparing the discs for playback is inaudible to the audience.

In musical performance and in recording, the band leader, producer or engineer usually has the responsibility of cueing the musicians (verbally or with hand signals) to begin playing.

Because of the physical and temporal discontinuities inherent in multitrack recording, a specific approach to cueing has also become part of studio technology. Modern mixing consoles are equipped with a special set of circuits, often referred to as the 'cue section' or 'foldback.' These circuits permit the producer or engineer to speak to the musicians via headphones, and allow the musicians to hear a mix of prerecorded tracks so that they can play in sync with what is already on tape. The 'cue mix' is usually tailored to the needs of the individual musicians or the particular overdubbing session, and bears little resemblance to the final mix destined for the master tape.

Bibliography

Alten, Stanley R. 1994. *Audio in Media*. 4th ed. Belmont, CA: Wadsworth.

PAUL THÉBERGE

Declamation

In general, 'declamation' refers to the way in which words may be delivered in an overtly dramatic or impassioned manner to impart emotional effects greater than those customarily obtained through the patterns of ordinary speech. Declamation tends to be in evidence in the making of speeches and the recitation of poetry, as well as in the dramatic situations of plays and films.

In the context of music, 'declamation' refers to the manner in which – for the purposes of emotional effect – the delivery of words through the sounds of music takes on dimensions additional to those customarily found in ordinary speech. In music, the term covers the way in which the words are stressed, pronounced and enunciated, and includes musical devices such as slurring, accenting and phrasing.

In most Western popular music, amplification reduced the need for the larger vocal gestures that were necessary before the invention of the microphone, and as a consequence forms of declamation more closely related to the patterns of ordinary speech tend to be used. Historically, different styles have produced specific varieties of declamation. The sub-classical style used by many music hall and variety show singers, for example, employed a declamatory style that owed something to the formality of classical music. Jazz widened the declamatory possibilities considerably, and added, among many other rhetorical stances, a cool delivery related to the atmosphere of the nightclub. Rock 'n' roll saw a much more energetic declamatory style, with a wider range of facial gestures supporting the vocal delivery. Rock music has taken almost all declamatory styles on board, with singers adopting whatever feels appropriate for the music they wish to put across. Rap has further widened the boundaries of what is possible by legitimizing street language as performance rhetoric.

Bibliography

Bartminski, Jerzy. 1989. 'On Melic and Declamatory Versions of Folk Songs.' *Slavica* 18: 57–80.

Jander, Owen, and Carter, Tim. 2001. 'Declamation.' In *The New Grove Dictionary of Music and Musicians*, Vol. 7, ed. Stanley Sadie. 2nd ed. New York: Grove, 122.

Mitchell, Tony. 1995. 'Questions of Style: Notes on Italian Hip Hop.' *Popular Music* 14(3): 333–48.

Walser, Robert. 1995. 'Rhythm, Rhyme, and Rhetoric in the Music of Public Enemy.' *Ethnomusicology* 39(2): 193–217.

JOHN POTTER

Deejaying (DJing)

One of the most important strands in reggae, and certainly the most popular with its core audience in Jamaica, the performance technique of deejaying (also known as 'toasting') consists of rhythmically talking or semi-singing ('chanting') over prerecorded music, 'live' in dance halls and sound systems (mobile discothèques) or in the recording studio. A predecessor of US rap, the practise shares a number of its characteristics: deejays' musicality revolves around rhythm and tone rather than discrete pitches, and a high premium is placed on being able to 'ride' the rhythm with agility.

Deejaying is generally presented in Jamaican Creole (patois) or in approximations of it, often with a helping of phrases in the Rastafarian idiom. It is in many ways a collective tradition, and deejays draw and expand on a shared vocabulary of themes and formulaic stock phrases. Topics range from the nonsensical or hedonistic to matters of social, political and religious concern, as well as various aspects of modernity and globalization – which they address good-humoredly or antagonistically, as the case may be. Sexual prowess and social injustice constitute the somewhat unlikely pair of deejaying's most enduring themes.

The practise of deejaying originated in Jamaican sound systems in the early 1950s, where disc jockeys, commonly working with a single turntable, would fill the silent space between records – as well as talking over them – with improvised chatter and lively interjections, promoting their respective sound systems and encouraging crowds to dance. For their inspiration, the progenitors of the practise looked to the jive-talking US R&B radio disc jockeys of the 1940s and 1950s, as well as drawing on the rich oral traditions of Jamaican folk culture. Early dance hall deejays, such as Count Machuki and Sir Lord Comic, recorded only sparingly (and late in their careers). 'Girls Town Ska' by the Baba Brooks Band (1965), featuring an uncredited Count (Cool) Sticky, is one of the earliest studio recordings featuring a Jamaican deejay. No 'live' recordings from the early days exist, although a 1993 album by King Stitt, *Dance Hall '63*, attempts to re-create the atmosphere of an early 1960s session.

Initially performed exclusively in the dance hall, the practise of deejaying gradually evolved into a recorded art form (deejays leaving the spinning of discs to a 'selector'). Following hugely successful recordings by King Stitt and, subsequently, U Roy, the popularity of the practise increased dramatically in the early 1970s. U Roy, widely regarded as deejaying's great popularizer, revolutionized the Jamaican music scene with a number of bestselling records in 1970. For these, the musical background consisted of purposely created 'dub versions' of recent hits, remixed rhythm tracks with the original voice(s) largely absent, leaving room for the deejay's nimble wordplay. With only minor variations, the formula has been adhered to ever since.

Around 1972–73, there appeared a new kind of deejay. While toasting the pleasures of the dance – and commenting on the latest Clint Eastwood movie – did not go out of style, jive-talk and hedonism began to give way to spiritual concerns and social comment. The pan-African and Rasta themes so characteristic of 'roots reggae' in the 1970s were, in fact, largely established by 'cultural' deejays such as Big Youth, Prince Jazzbo and I Roy. Correspondingly, the accompanying dubs grew heavier – bass and drums were brought to the fore and few, if any, vocal fragments remained in the mix.

The musically sparse 'dance hall' era of the early 1980s saw a shift to more secular concerns and a less optimistic outlook in the lyrics, possibly a reflection of the deteriorating social conditions and increased violence within the lower echelons of Jamaican society. Still, the deejays – Lone Ranger, Brigadier Jerry, General Echo, Ranking Joe – ruled the dance, none more popular than Yellowman, who offered social commentary as well as humor and 'slackness,' i.e., sexually explicit lyrics.

The availability of unofficial 'live' cassettes further popularized deejaying in the 1980s and helped to spread the work of deejays whose natural habitat was the dance hall, not the studio. As reggae permutated into 'ragga' in 1985, the trend to toast 'slack' lyrics and to depict ghetto life unadorned continued unabated, evolving into the homophobic and misogynistic – as well as violent 'gun talk' – lyrics of the early 1990s (Buju Banton and Shabba Ranks causing considerable controversy in this respect). By mid-decade, a counter reaction in the form of a return to 'cultural' themes was evident, sometimes involving the same artists who had been performers of the bawdy variety only a few years previously.

With the origins of deejaying in the highly competitive sound system scene, rivalry and self-aggrandizement have long been conspicuous characteristics of the practise. The verbal duels between Prince Jazzbo and I Roy in the mid-1970s are legendary, and the trend has continued. Deejaying is largely a male domain, but important exceptions to the rule included, in the 1980s, Sister Nancy and Lady G, and, in the 1990s, Lady Saw and Tanya Stephens. While deejays frequently engage in a critique of capitalism – explicitly, in their lyrics, and implicitly, in the communal aesthetic that informs their performance (see Gilroy 1993) – the practise of deejaying is utterly commercialized and commodified. The recording of 'specials' – personalized sound system tributes cut onto unique, one-off acetates – is so lucrative that it has become many deejays' most important source of income. Lyrics, too, as often as not extol the material side of life.

In the 1990s, deejaying 'crossed over' on an unprecedented scale, Chaka Demus & Pliers, Mad Cobra (Cobra), Shaggy and Beenie Man enjoying international pop hits on major labels. Closer ties between Jamaican deejays and US rappers began to evolve, the influence of the latter in one sense an instance of cultural 're-exportation.' By the beginning of the twenty-first century, deejaying was covering a wide range of performance techniques, from melodic 'sing-jaying' to gravel-voiced 'ragga' toasting, and subject matter ranging from the whimsical to the uncompromisingly hardcore (as in the late 1990s work of Bounty Killer, Capleton and Sizzla).

Deejaying is the voice of a small, postcolonial nation 'talking back,' a musical practise that, despite humble beginnings, has exerted a tremendous influence on popular music – not least on rap in the United States, where its erstwhile and ongoing impact has yet to be fully acknowledged.

Bibliography

Barrow, Steve, and Dalton, Peter. 1997. *Reggae: The Rough Guide*. London: Rough Guides Ltd.

Bilby, Kenneth. 1995. 'Jamaica.' In Peter Manuel, with Kenneth Bilby and Michael Largey, *Caribbean Currents: Caribbean Music from Rumba to Reggae*. Philadelphia: Temple University Press, 143–82.

Cooper, Carolyn. 1994. 'Lyrical Gun: Metaphor and Role Play in Jamaican Dancehall Culture.' *Massachusetts Review* 35: 429–47.

Gilroy, Paul. 1993. *Small Acts: Thoughts on the Politics of Black Cultures*. London: Serpent's Tail.

Hewitt, Roger. 1986. *White Talk Black Talk: Inter-Racial Friendship and Communication Amongst Adolescents*. Cambridge: Cambridge University Press.

Jones, Simon. 1988. *Black Culture, White Youth: The Reggae Tradition from JA to UK*. Basingstoke: Macmillan Education.

Kaski, Tero, and Vuorinen, Pekka. 1984. *Reggae Inna Dancehall Style*. Helsinki: Black Star.

Rose, Cynthia. 1999. 'Black Punks Re-write History: Raggamuffins Walk on the Dark Side.' In *Trade Secrets: Young British Talents Talk Business*. London: Thames & Hudson, 38–53.

Ross, Andrew. 1998. 'Mr. Reggae DJ, Meet the International Monetary Fund.' In *Real Love: In Pursuit of Cultural Justice*. New York: New York University Press, 35–69.

Stolzoff, Norman C. 2000. *Wake the Town and Tell the People: Dancehall Culture in Jamaica*. Durham, NC: Duke University Press.

Discographical References

Baba Brooks Band, The. 'Girls Town Ska.' Ska Beat 218. *1965*: UK. Reissue: Brooks, Baba, and His Band. 'Girl's Town Ska.' *Trojan Ska Box Set, Volume 2*. TRBCD 014. *2000*: UK.

King Stitt. *Dance Hall '63*. Studio One 03193. *1993*: USA.

Discography

A Dee-Jay Explosion in a Dancehall Style. Heartbeat 04. *1982*: USA.

Alcapone, Dennis. *Forever Version*. Studio One 8025. *1971*: Jamaica.

Banton, Buju. 'Boom By-By.' Shang 4385. *1992*: Jamaica.

Banton, Buju. *'Til Shiloh*. Loose Cannon 314 524 119. *1995*: USA.

Beenie Man. *Maestro*. Greensleeves 234. *1996*: UK.

Beenie Man. 'Who Am I.' Greensleeves 588. *1997*: UK.

Big Youth. *Screaming Target*. Trojan 61. *1973*: UK.

Bounty Killer. *Down in the Ghetto*. Greensleeves 210. *1994*: UK.

Capleton. *More Fire*. VP 1587. *2000*: USA.

Demus, Chaka, & Pliers. 'Murder She Wrote.' Mango 530131. *1992*: USA.

Great British MC's. Fashion 001. *1985*: UK.

I Roy. *Presenting*. Trojan 63. *1973*: UK.

I Roy. 'Straight to Prince Jazzbo Head.' *Step Forward Youth*. Live and Love LALP 03. *1975*: UK.

'Keep On Coming Through the Door': Jamaican Deejay Music 1969–1973. Trojan 255. *1988*: UK.

Lady G. 'Nuff Respect.' *Music Works Showcase 88.* Greensleeves 118. *1988*: UK.

Lady Saw. 'What Is Slackness.' *Give Me the Reason.* VP 1470. *1996*: USA.

Mad Cobra (Cobra). 'Flex.' Columbia 74373. *1992*: USA.

Prince Jazzbo. *Choice of Version.* Studio One 1959. *1991*: USA.

Prince Jazzbo. 'Gal Boy I Roy.' *Straight to Babylon Chest.* Live and Love 06. *1976*: UK.

Shabba Ranks. *Just Reality.* VP 1117. *1990*: USA.

Shaggy. 'Oh Carolina.' Greensleeves 361. *1993*: UK.

Sister Nancy. *One, Two.* Techniques. *1982*: Jamaica.

Sizzla. *Black Woman and Child.* Greensleeves 243. *1997*: UK.

Smiley Culture. 'Cockney Translation.' Fashion 028. *1985*: UK.

Stephens, Tanya. *Ruff Rider.* VP 1521. *1998*: USA.

U Roy. *Your Ace from Space.* Trojan 359. *1995*: UK.

Yellowman. *Mr. Yellowman.* Greensleeves 35. *1992*: UK.

HASSE HUSS

Drumroll

A drumroll consists of a series of strokes played so close together as to simulate a single long tone. Rolls can be 'closed,' meaning that the strokes are extremely close together, or 'open,' meaning that the individual strokes are more apparent.

Double-stroke rolls are associated with the rudimental tradition and are performed by playing two strokes (i.e., a double stroke) with each hand in quick succession, ending the roll with a single tap. Short rolls are often designated according to the number of strokes – five-stroke roll, seven-stroke roll, nine-stroke roll and so on. Double-stroke rolls are especially appropriate for deep field drums that require a more powerful stroke. In rudimental settings, double-stroke rolls are generally played as thirty-second notes.

Multiple-bounce rolls, also called buzz rolls, are played by pressing the drumsticks into the drumhead in quick succession so that each stroke produces a smooth series of bounces. Bounce rolls are most typically used by orchestral percussionists and jazz drummers, as well as by Scottish pipe-band drummers performing on modern, high-tension side drums. Although bounce rolls can be performed on any drum, they are most often performed on the snare drum, where the vibration of the snares helps sustain the sound. A popular guideline among drummers is to make a multiple-bounce roll sound like the tearing of sandpaper. Before the advent of ride cymbals, early jazz drummers (for example, Baby Dodds) kept time on a snare drum with short 'press' rolls, which were played as tight multiple-bounce rolls.

Single-stroke rolls consist of rapidly alternating individual strokes and are best suited to drums that produce sustained tones, such as timpani, bass drums and tom-toms. Rock and pop drumset players typically use single-stroke rolls to go 'around the kit' in fills and solos. The single-stroke roll can also be thought of as a tremolo.

Rolls are often used to create a sense of drama or anticipation in music (as well as in circus acts); frequently, such rolls are combined with crescendos. A roll is often played before the start of a country's national anthem as a way of bringing the listeners to attention, and it is frequently sustained throughout most or all of the piece. A 'roll-off,' consisting of a short, repeated rhythmic figure followed by a long roll, is often used to set the tempo of military music. Drummers in Scottish bagpipe bands use a pair of long rolls to signal the beginning of a tune, as well as to drown out the sound the bagpipes make as they are filling with air prior to being played.

Discography

Dodds, Baby. 'Careless Love Blues.' *Footnotes to Jazz, Vol. 1: Baby Dodds Talking and Drum Solos.* Folkways Records 2290. *1951*: USA.

Dodds, Baby. 'Shimmy Beat and Press Roll Demonstration.' *Footnotes to Jazz, Vol. 1: Baby Dodds Talking and Drum Solos.* Folkways Records 2290. *1951*: USA.

RICK MATTINGLY

Drum Rudiments

Often called the 'building blocks of drumming' and equated with the scales played on melodic instruments, drum rudiments consist of short rhythmic phrases with specific stickings. Rudiments first developed in the military bands of the 1800s, in which instruction was by rote, and as a result many rudiments were given onomatopoeic names; for example, the long roll was called the 'daddy mammy' to reflect its right-right left-left sticking, and the name 'flam' imitated the combined sound of a grace note and a primary note. Popular rudiments include the paradiddle, flam accent, ratamacue and various numbered rolls (for example, five-stroke roll, nine-stroke roll and so on).

The first set of standardized drum rudiments was created by the National Association of Rudimental Drummers (NARD) in 1933 and consisted of 26 rudiments that were considered essential by its members. The Percussive Arts Society (PAS) expanded this set in 1984 by compiling a list of 40 International Drum Rudiments, which included the original 26 NARD rudiments, along with drum corps, European, orchestral and contemporary snare drum rudiments that had become popular, such as 'Swiss Army Triplets' and the 'Pataflafla.'

Rudiments are primarily used in military, marching and drum corps settings, and popular snare drum solos have been written entirely based on rudiments (for example, 'Connecticut Half-Time' and 'Three Camps'). Many drumset players use rudiments for technique development and adapt rudiments to other styles of music. Jazz drummers such as Buddy Rich and Joe Morello often displayed a rudimental influence; rock drummer Spencer Dryden played a rudimental-style snare drum introduction on Jefferson Airplane's 1960s hit 'White Rabbit'; and Steve Gadd's drum part on Paul Simon's 1970s hit '50 Ways to Leave Your Lover' was rudimentally based.

Bibliography

Wanamaker, Jay. 1998. 'PAS International Drum Rudiments.' *Percussive Notes* 26(4): 6–9.

Discographical References

Fennell, Frederick. 'Connecticut Half-Time.' *The Spirit of '76: Ruffles and Flourishes*. Mercury 434386. *1997*: USA.
Fennell, Frederick. 'Three Camps.' *The Spirit of '76: Ruffles and Flourishes*. Mercury 434386. *1997*: USA.
Jefferson Airplane. 'White Rabbit.' RCA 9248. *1967*: USA.
Simon, Paul. '50 Ways to Leave Your Lover.' Columbia 10270. *1976*: USA.

RICK MATTINGLY

Dub Plates/Specials

In reggae, the terms 'dub plates' and 'specials' refer to custom-made 10″ (25 cm) acetates featuring exclusive mixes of songs for use on sound systems. An understudied phenomenon, the practise of 'cutting dubs' is one of the defining characteristics of Jamaican popular music. By most accounts, the practise dates back to the late 1950s. In fact, after an initial run of *mento* recordings (from producers such as Stanley Motta and Ken Khouri) in the early 1950s, some of the first discs made in Jamaica were dub plates, specially recorded and manufactured by the leading sound system entrepreneurs of the day (Duke Reid and Coxsone Dodd, most notably) to provide original, exclusive musical entertainment. Dub plates featuring alternative mixes (and, sometimes, unreleased songs) were a prominent feature of the sound systems' repertoire long before DJs and singers began adding their voices over rhythm tracks in the early 1970s.

Typically, at the height of the dub plates' popularity in the mid-1970s, a sound system operator would go to a recording studio and have the engineer mix two or four cuts 'live' from the multitrack tape onto an acetate disc on the cutting lathe. These were unique, customized mixes for the exclusive use of the commissioning sound system; subsequent visits by other sound system operators would yield different mixes. Cutting two dubs per acetate side has always been the general rule. Dub plates

(in the form of alternative mixes) largely went out of style in the early 1980s. A contributing factor was no doubt the major changes in recording technology of the 1970s and 1980s, most crucially the shift from four- to 16- and 24-track recording. Based on relatively 'simple' recording techniques, cutting and mixing 'dub' did not adapt well to the more complex recording approaches of later eras. Most important, however, was the increasing popularity of a particular kind of dub plate: the 'special.' Specials, too, are individually commissioned 10″ (25 cm) acetates, ideally featuring an exclusive version of a famous song by a famous artist, but with the lyrics altered from the original to name-drop and 'big up' (praise) the purchaser in question – be it a sound system (most commonly), a radio DJ or a store.

Since the 1990s, major sound systems have played hardly anything but specials; with every new hit recording, literally hundreds of sound systems require their special versions. Up-and-coming sound systems (and budding artists) do their best to keep up. In the 1990s and early 2000s, famous DJs (and, occasionally, singers) were virtually able to name their price: US$1,000 for a single special was not unknown. Prices were, and have remained, highly variable, however, determined by a number of factors, not least the relative negotiating powers of artist and customer. Getting a special played on a leading sound system may benefit a DJ just as much as the sound system may gain from being able to 'drop' a special by a famous DJ. In the fierce (and lucrative) competition between sound systems – in the 1990s and early 2000s, an increasingly global affair – specials are the prime currency. Most DJs in Jamaica, whether unknown or famous, arguably make more money from cutting specials than from either recording or performing. To some, the concentration on specials has been detrimental to reggae. But, as Stolzoff (2000) points out, 'the dub plates are often the catalysts to the creation of new musical styles' (130).

Single copies of dub plates and specials, or a handful of copies at the very most, are cut, and thus they rarely, if ever, circulate beyond the closed, informal economy of the sound systems. On the other hand, as cassette recordings of sound systems in action – so-called 'sound tapes' (or 'yard tapes') – are widespread, the musical performances cut onto the dub plates and specials do reach a larger audience. Particularly impressive offerings often acquire cult status, and have, on rare occasions, gained official release – I Roy's 'Coxsone Affair' is a good example. More often than not – such as in the case of the late Tenor Saw's literally show-stopping specials for Killamanjaro – even the best recordings will remain unavailable to the general public. Legitimate (i.e., major company) collections of classic dub plates and specials scarcely exist. A rare exception is the French compilation, *King Jammy's Presents Dub Plates, Volume 1.*

Although test pressings and acetates are nothing new in popular music, the impact of the specials, along with many other practises originating in reggae, has been quite spectacular; not least, the so-called 'white labels,' so prominent in many current dance genres, clearly take their cue from their Jamaican equivalent. In addition, dub plates and specials offer an example of alternative practises of recording and distribution (and an interesting take on Paul Gilroy's (1993a, 1993b) famous discussion of the creative possibilities that arise from various kinds of versioning in black music, as well as of the interaction of production and consumption) – all the more remarkable for their coexistence in the alleged homogeneity of the international popular music marketplace.

Bibliography

Barrow, Steve, and Dalton, Peter. 1997. *Reggae: The Rough Guide.* London: Rough Guides Ltd.

Bradley, Lloyd. 2000. *Bass Culture: When Reggae Was King.* London: Viking.

Gilroy, Paul. 1993a. '"Jewels Brought from Bondage": Black Music and the Politics of Authenticity.' In Paul Gilroy, *The Black Atlantic: Modernity and Double Consciousness.* London: Verso, 72–110.

Gilroy, Paul. 1993b. 'One Nation Under a Groove.' In Paul Gilroy, *Small Acts: Thoughts on the Politics of Black Cultures.* London: Serpent's Tail, 19–48.

Larkin, Colin, ed. 1998. *The Virgin Encyclopedia of Reggae.* London: Virgin.

Stolzoff, Norman C. 2000. *Wake the Town and Tell the People: Dancehall Culture in Jamaica.* Durham, NC: Duke University Press.

Discographical References

I Roy. 'Coxsone Affair.' *Presenting.* Trojan 63. *1973*: UK.

King Jammy's Presents Dub Plates, Volume 1. Celluloïd 79210. *1998*: France.

Discography

Tenor Saw. *Fever.* Blue Mountain BMLP 013. *1986*: UK.

Thomas, Jah, and Levy, Barrington. 'Tribute to Moa Anbessa' [Moa Ambassa]. Nigger Kojak NK 001. *1980*: UK.

HASSE HUSS

Dub Version

Of all Jamaica's contributions to popular music, arguably none has had greater worldwide impact than the dub version. Indeed, the term 'dub' has become a commonplace, its referent many kinds of instrumental music, particularly in the dance genres of the late 1990s – for example, house and techno. While many of the versioning practises characteristic of reggae involve the re-recording of a song or rhythm track, the term 'dub,' 'dub version' or 'version' refers specifically to a recording engineer's remix of an existing recording. Almost without exception, these remixes highlight the bass and drum of the backing track – sometimes with snippets of the original vocals remaining, usually with the added effects of echo or reverb.

The first remixes began to appear in Jamaica in 1967. As with most innovations in Jamaican popular music, they grew out of the needs and practises of sound systems (mobile discothèques), where exclusive sounds were always at a premium. Some of the remixes were pressed in very limited quantities and played in the dance halls only; others were commercially available. Initially, they were mostly straight instrumentals, commonly featuring the organ as the lead instrument. Remixes displaying more of the engineer's input first emerged in 1968. In 1970, Lynford Anderson mixed the first true 'multitrack' dubs at Dynamic Sounds – including 'Phantom,' the dub version of the Clancy Eccles-produced 'Herbsman' by King Stitt. Around the same time, sound system owner 'Ruddy' Redwood played custom-made instrumental versions of producer Duke Reid's rocksteady classics. The impact in the dance hall was phenomenal. One contributing factor to the success of the remixes was their usefulness in providing rhythm tracks for deejays to talk and toast over. Riding the rhythms of Duke Reid, U Roy effectively launched the toasting phenomenon in 1970. Two years later – now bearing the name 'versions' – they were on the B side of virtually every single released in Jamaica.

Around 1972, the first dub versions to feature more radical alterations of sound appeared. These featured the fading (or cutting) in and out of the various channels, as well as added effects such as echoes, phasers and equalizers. Most accounts credit their design to one man, King Tubby (Osbourne Ruddock), an electronics engineer and the owner of a leading sound system, Tubby's Hi Fi. With the support of his friend, producer Bunny Lee, he began to remix not only Lee's rhythms, but also those of other prominent producers of the era, including Lee 'Scratch' Perry, Glen Brown, Augustus Pablo and Carlton Patterson, on a recently acquired four-track mixing board. One of the first discs to credit King Tubby on the label was the 'version' side to Larry Marshall's 'I Admire You,' released as 'Water Gate Rock' in 1974.

Three albums by three different producers vie for the title of the first dub album: Herman Chin-Loy's *Aquarius Dub*, Lee Perry's *Blackboard Jungle Dub* and Clive Chin's *Java Java Java Java*, all released in 1973. A veritable deluge followed, the quantity of dub albums released by the end of the 1970s numbering in the hundreds. While dub albums are often attributed to the producer, the real star is the engineer. In addition to the renowned King Tubby, important innovators include Errol 'E.T.' Thompson, Studio One's Sylvan Morris, Lloyd James ('Prince Jammy,' later 'King Jammy') and Hopeton 'Overton' Brown ('Scientist').

By most accounts, the dub boom had run its course by 1982, although a number of enthusiasts, particularly in the United Kingdom, have kept the scene alive. Reggae singles have continued to come with a dub version, although it is perhaps fair to say that the practise has become somewhat perfunctory. However, the techniques and recording practises of dub live on most conspicuously in many other styles – not least in the multifaceted genre of drum 'n' bass, as so clearly indicated by its name.

Part of dub's original attraction may have been the relatively meager technological arsenal of its engineers. Echo came from tape recorders and reverb was provided by 'spring reverbs' – all analog equipment. Most of the recordings that define the style were recorded and mixed on four-track equipment; only rarely were the additional four or 12 channels of latter-day studios utilized as well. While dub has occasionally inspired accounts that border on the metaphysical, the sensation of hearing a favorite song (or rhythm) stripped to its bass and drum essentials and played at earth-shattering volume in a dark, crowded dance hall is in many ways one of the defining experiences of reggae.

Bibliography

Barrow, Steve, and Dalton, Peter. 1997. *Reggae: The Rough Guide*. London: Rough Guides Ltd.

Hendley, Dave, and Hurford, Ray. 1987. 'King Tubby in Fine Style.' In *More Axe*, ed. Tero Kaski and Ray Hurford. Helsinki and London: Black Star and Muzik Tree, 91–98.

Potash, Chris, ed. 1997. *Reggae, Rasta, Revolution: Jamaican Music from Ska to Dub*. New York: Schirmer Books.

Toop, David. 1996. *Ocean of Sound*. London: Serpent's Tail.

Discographical References

Chin, Clive. *Java Java Java Java*. Impact. *1973*: Jamaica.

Chin-Loy, Herman. *Aquarius Dub*. Aquarius 001. *1973*: Jamaica.

Dynamites, The. 'Phantom.' Dynamite. *1970*: Jamaica.

King Stitt. 'Herbsman.' Clan Disc. *1970*: Jamaica.

King Tubby. 'Water Gate Rock.' Black & White. *1974*: Jamaica. (B side of Marshall, Larry. 'I Admire You.') Reissue: King Tubby. 'Watergate Rock.' *Larry Marshall Meets King Tubbys: I Admire You in Dub*. Motion FASTCD/LP 0004. *2000*: UK.

Marshall, Larry. 'I Admire You.' Black & White. *1974*:

Jamaica. Reissue: Marshall, Larry. 'I Admire You.' *I Admire You*. Heartbeat 57. *1992*: USA.

Perry, Lee. *Blackboard Jungle Dub*. Upsetter. *1973*: Jamaica.

Discography

King Tubby. *Dub Gone Crazy*. Blood and Fire 002. *1994*: UK.

King Tubby. *The Dub Organiser*. Black Solidarity 57. *2000*: UK.

Pablo, Augustus. *King Tubby Meets Rockers Uptown*. Yard. *1976*: Jamaica.

Roots Dub. Studio One. *1979*: Jamaica.

U Roy. *Your Ace from Space*. Trojan 359. *1995*: UK.

Vital Dub. Well Charge. *1977*: Jamaica.

HASSE HUSS

Fade-In

The term 'fade-in' is used to describe the process of gradually increasing the loudness of an audio signal from silence. In music recording, a fade-in at the beginning of a song is rarely used, partly because the technique sounds artificial in strictly musical contexts. The fading-in of individual tracks during the mixdown of a multitrack tape, however, is more common. Fade-ins are routinely used in radio programming to create transitions between speech and music selections, to maintain the pacing of program material and, in the production of radio and television commercials, to bring up music or sound effects at the end of a spot announcement. In narrative film and television, a fade-out followed by a fade-in can be used as a transitional device to signify changes in time, place or dramatic action.

PAUL THÉBERGE

Fade-Out

The term 'fade-out' (or 'fade') is used to describe the process of gradually decreasing the loudness of an audio signal to silence. A fade-out is sometimes used in popular music recording as an alternative to conventional musical endings, where a song comes to a more or less abrupt halt with a harmonic cadence. Typically, a musical phrase, often derived from a part of the song's chorus, is repeated a number of times by the musicians while the engineer slowly lowers the volume of the recording with a console fader. Use of the technique results in a gradual disengagement of the listener from the music, and has sometimes been described as lending an air of nostalgia to the ending of a pop song. 'Open the Door, Richard!' – an early R&B crossover hit recorded by saxophonist Jack McVea and produced by Ralph Bass in 1946 – is reputed to have been the first pop song to end with a fade. Fade-outs became more common in the late 1960s, especially in psychedelic and electronic music.

Fade-outs are also routinely used in radio programming: for example, to cut short prerecorded music, thus increasing the pace of program material. In narrative film and television, a fade-out followed by a fade-in can be used as a transitional device to signify changes in time, place or dramatic action.

Bibliography

Hicks, Michael. 1999. *Sixties Rock: Garage, Psychedelic, and Other Satisfactions*. Urbana, IL: University of Illinois Press.

Discographical Reference

McVea, Jack, and His All Stars. 'Open the Door, Richard!' Black & White 792. 1946: USA. Reissue: McVea, Jack, and His All Stars. 'Open the Door, Richard!' *Open the Door, Richard!* Jukebox Lil JB 607. *1984*: Sweden.

PAUL THÉBERGE

Faking

Faking has two meanings in popular music. The first concerns the performance practise of, mainly, reed and brass instruments in which false or substitute fingerings are employed. The second concerns the practise of 'busking' or improvising an arrangement of a piece that usually benefits from a written arrangement, and embraces the description of nonreading musicians within an ensemble of musically literate players who improvise to give the impression that they, too, are playing the written parts.

Fake fingering is used for two reasons. Firstly, it is used to assist a woodwind or saxophone player in negotiating a fast passage in which it is virtually physically impossible to configure the orthodox fingering of a note or notes. An alternative is used that may slightly affect pitch or tonality, but that does not hinder the rapidity of fingering the surrounding notes. Secondly, it is used as a deliberate ploy to create unusual tones or pitches that contrast with more legitimately produced notes. A saxophonist, for example, may alternate an orthodox and a fake fingering for a single note, thus creating a timbral difference between each repetition of the sound. One of the most celebrated examples of this can be found in the playing of the jazz saxophonist Lester Young, notably in a piece such as 'Lester Leaps In,' which has been thoroughly analyzed by Porter (1985). Brass players can achieve the same effect by alternating valve combinations and adjusting their embouchure accordingly. Trombonists will use their embouchure to 'bend' out-of-tune notes created by 'fake' slide positions: in other words, to avoid excessive manipulation of the slide, the player uses a different tube length from normal and adjusts the pitch of the resultant note from a different harmonic series to approximate the intended note.

Faking or busking tunes involves either playing entirely by ear on any instrument or group of instruments, and attempting in doing so to capture the correct harmonies, rhythms and melody lines of a piece, or playing some elements by ear within formal written arrangements. Famous examples of semiliterate musicians who used the accuracy and speed of their ear to play creditably in bands that performed written arrangements include the trumpeters Bix Beiderbecke (with Paul Whiteman's big band) and Chet Baker (with Gerry Mulligan's quartet). Ensembles that play pieces largely by ear often underpin their work with the use of a 'fake book.' Such a publication is a collection of skeletal arrangements, often published in breach of the original composer's copyright, each of which presents little more than the melody line and guitar chord symbols. Because they are often published illegitimately, fake books have a varying level of accuracy, but the best ones contain playable versions of many hundreds of tunes.

Bibliography

Baudoin, Philippe. 2001. *Oh Play That Thing!*. Paris: n.p.

Kernfeld, Barry. 2002. 'False Fingering.' In *The New Grove Dictionary of Jazz*, Vol. 1, ed. Barry Kernfeld. 2nd ed. London: Macmillan, 738.

Levet, Jean-Paul. 1992. *Talkin' That Talk: Le Langage du blues et du jazz* [Talkin' That Talk: The Language of Blues and Jazz]. Paris: Hatier.

Porter, Lewis. 1985. *Lester Young*. Boston, MA: Twayne Publishers.

Sher, Chuck. 1983. *The World's Greatest Fake Book*. San Francisco: n.p.

The Real Book. ca. 1972. Boston, MA: n.p.

Witmer, Robert. 2002. 'Fake Book.' In *The New Grove Dictionary of Jazz*, Vol. 1, ed. Barry Kernfeld. 2nd ed. London: Macmillan, 735–36.

Wong, Herb. 1988. *The Ultimate Jazz Fakebook*. Milwaukee, WI: Hal Leonard Corporation.

Discographical Reference

Basie, Count. 'Lester Leaps In'/'Dickie's Dream.' Vocalion 5118. 1939: USA.

ALYN SHIPTON

Falsetto

'Falsetto' denotes the higher of the two main 'registers' of the male voice. (Although female voices work in a similar way, the difference in registers is often not noticeable.) The normal, or modal, register used for speech and much singing is known as the chest register. With this disposition, the vocal cords vibrate symmetrically and produce the individual sound that characterizes each voice. In falsetto, the folds (cords) vibrate symmetrically, but are thin, stretched and rarely close the glottis completely. The arytenoid cartilages come together in such a way that the vibrating length of the folds is considerably reduced. This produces the characteristic high-pitched sound associated with the 1960s North American 'surfing' groups (such as the Beach Boys, and Jan and Dean) and the dance music of the 1970s (such as that sung by the Bee Gees). The technique was not new, and can be heard in the blues singing of Tommy Johnson and the rapid register switching of Howlin' Wolf. Many male vocal groups from the 1920s onward used a high falsettist on the top line.

Despite the apparent artificiality of the tone, all singers are capable of singing in falsetto (although many, such as Jason Kay (vocalist with Jamiroquai), are able to sing high passages in 'head voice' without resorting to falsetto). Leo Sayer is a notable example of a singer who has exploited both registers and head voice to the full.

Women singers frequently break into falsetto for emotional effect (the 'breaking' of the voice occurs in speech at moments of especially strong emotion). Nina Simone and Sinéad O'Connor have used this device particularly effectively.

Falsetto is also part of the rhetoric of much African-American soul singing, where the association of high-pitched sounds with women's and children's voices often adds irony or pathos.

Bibliography

Negus, V.E., Jander, Owen, and Giles, Peter. 2001. 'Falsetto.' In *The New Grove Dictionary of Music and Musicians*, Vol. 8, ed. Stanley Sadie. 2nd ed. New York: Grove, 537–38.

Sundberg, Johan. 1987. *The Science of the Singing Voice.* De Kalb, IL: Northern Illinois University Press.

Welch, G.F., Sergeant, D.C., and MacCurtain, F. 1988. 'Some Physical Characteristics of the Male Falsetto Voice.' *Journal of Voice* 2(2): 151–63.

Discography

Beach Boys, The. *Endless Summer.* CDP 746 467-2. *1987*: USA.

Bee Gees, The. *Bee Gees: Their Greatest Hits – The Record.* Polydor 589449-2. *2001*: USA.

Jamiroquai. *Emergency on Planet Earth.* Sony 474069-2. *1993*: UK.

Jan and Dean. *Jan and Dean: Anthology.* United Artists UAS-9961. *1971*: USA.

O'Connor, Sinéad. *So Far . . . The Best of Sinéad O'Connor.* Chrysalis 821581-2. *1997*: UK.

Sayer, Leo. *Silver Bird.* Chrysalis 1050. *1973*: USA.

Simone, Nina. *Nina Simone.* Compact Jazz 838 007-2. *1989*: USA.

JOHN POTTER

Frailing

'Frailing' (sometimes 'flailing,' 'thrashing,' 'sawmill style,' 'rapping,' 'knocking' or 'claw hammer') is a generic term for a range of 'old-time,' five-string banjo-playing styles, all considered traditional in the southeastern United States and now adopted widely. The most commonly heard term, 'frailing,' is undoubtedly a variant of 'flailing,' which refers by analogy to the repetitive circular motion that would have been very familiar to preindustrial farmers accustomed to using wooden flails to thresh various grain crops by hand. The basic technique of frailing likely was derived from the minstrel's so-called 'stroke style' of banjo playing, briefly described in the entry on claw hammer.

Bibliography

Krassen, Miles. 1974. *Clawhammer Banjo: Traditional Appalachian Banjo Tunes Transcribed in Tablature and Based on the Playing of Wade Ward.* New York: Oak Publications.

Rosenbaum, Art. 1968. *Old-Time Mountain Banjo: An Instruction Method for Playing the Old-Time Five-String Mountain Banjo Based on the Styles of Traditional Banjo-Pickers.* New York: Oak Publications.

Rosenbaum, Art. 1981. *The Art of the Mountain Banjo.* Fullerton, CA: Centerstream.

Seeger, Mike, and Cohen, John, eds. 1964. *The New Lost City Ramblers Songbook.* New York: Oak Publications.

Discography

Creed, Kyle. *Liberty.* Heritage 28. *1977*: USA.

Jones, 'Grandpa.' *Everybody's Grandpa.* Bear Family 15788. *1996*: Germany.

Library of Congress Banjo Collection, 1937–1946. Rounder 0237. *1990*: USA.

Macon, Uncle Dave. *Go Long Mule.* County 3505. *1995*: USA.

Old Five String, Vol. 1: Clawhammer Banjo Solos. Heritage 39. *1983*: USA.

Stanley, Ralph. *Songs My Mother Taught Me & More: 'Clawhammer' Style Banjo.* Freeland 655. *1998*: USA.

Steele, Pete. *Banjo Songs and Tunes.* Folkways FS 3828. *1958*: USA.

The Music of Kentucky, Vol. 1: Early American Rural Classics, 1927–37. Yazoo 2013. *1995*: USA.

THOMAS A. ADLER

Fuzz

The word 'fuzz' is applied to an instrument or a sound processor to indicate a distinctive distorted sound: a fuzz guitar or a fuzz bass has a harsh, square-wave sound, usually generated by a fuzz box plugged between the instrument and its amplifier. Although mellower, violin-like distorted sounds can be created on the guitar by means of overdriven tube amplifiers, the fuzz box became a standard accessory for guitarists in the mid-1960s after the success of the Rolling Stones' '(I Can't Get No) Satisfaction' (1965). Fuzz bass sounds can be heard in the Beatles' 'Think for Yourself,' featuring 'Paul on fuzz bass,' on *Rubber Soul* (1965). As feedback and distortion were integrated into the 'sound vocabulary' of all lead guitarists in the late 1960s – and influenced by Jimi Hendrix, Eric Clapton, Jeff Beck and others – amplifier manufacturers began to include preamplification controls in their products. These allowed distortion without the need for either a fuzz box or excessive volume. Since the introduction of digital sound processors, fuzz sound has become just one of the presets in guitar multi-effect pedals.

Discographical References

Beatles, The. 'Think for Yourself.' *Rubber Soul*. Parlophone PMC 1267. *1965*: UK.
Rolling Stones, The. '(I Can't Get No) Satisfaction.' Decca F 12220. *1965*: UK.

FRANCO FABBRI

Hammering-On

'Hammering-on,' a term widely used by players of fretted instruments, is a left-hand technique in which a given note is sounded by bringing a finger down onto the appropriate noting position on the fingerboard quickly and forcefully. The 'hammer-on' is loudest, clearest and most pronounced if the string being played by the left hand has just been sounded by a picking or striking motion of the right hand. Hammering-on is therefore frequently used by players of five-string banjos using the 'frailing' or 'claw hammer' styles in order to vary a repetitious right-hand rhythm; a quarter note followed by two eighth notes (in a measure of 2/4 time) thus is elaborated into a measure of four eighth notes. Hammering-on is often characterized as the opposite of the left-hand 'pulling-off' or pizzicato movement, in which a string is forcefully and rapidly unfretted.

THOMAS A. ADLER

Hawaiian Guitar

'Hawaiian guitar' is a term that usually refers to the technique of playing the guitar flat in the lap while fretting the strings with a steel bar or similar implement. In Hawaii, this style is known as *kīkā kila* (steel guitar), but when it was introduced to the mainland United States and elsewhere it was called 'Hawaiian guitar.'

Hawaii has produced two very distinctive approaches to playing the guitar: slack key (*kī hō'alu*) and steel (*kīkā*

kila); thus, there has been some confusion over the exact denotation of 'Hawaiian guitar.' Logically, the term can refer to either of these approaches and, originally, it designated the older slack key style, in which the guitar is held in the conventional manner. However, with the explosion of enthusiasm for Hawaiian music in the first decades of the twentieth century, the term became attached to the technique of playing the guitar flat in the lap and fretting with a steel bar. Now, with the term 'steel guitar' universally adopted, 'Hawaiian guitar' generally connotes the early twentieth-century styles and instruments.

The guitar's popularity in Hawaii dates from 1832, when Mexican *vaqueros*, invited to the islands to deal with the ever-increasing population of cattle, brought their guitars with them. The Hawaiians devised the so-called slack key tunings, that is, tunings producing consonances or complete chords on the open strings – for example, an open A chord (E, A, e, a, $c\sharp^1$, e^1, from the lowest string to the highest, sounding an octave lower than written). In the 1860s, Portuguese sailors introduced steel strings to the Hawaiians, and the final step was the fretting of the strings with a steel bar, an innovation usually attributed to Joseph Kekuku, who claimed to have developed the technique in 1885.

The Hawaiian guitar technique involved raising the height of the strings on the fretboard, accomplished by increasing the size of the nut, as well as the use of picks on the thumb and fingers of the right hand. The playing mirrored Hawaiian vocal practise in the cultivation of gentle glides into notes from above or below the pitch, subtle use of vibrato, and the employment of string harmonics, which are considered analogous to Hawaiian falsetto singing.

The success of the Hawaiian pavilion at the Panama-Pacific International Exposition of 1915 in San Francisco triggered the vogue for Hawaiian music on the mainland United States. Instrument makers such as Weissenborn and Knutsen responded with guitars expressly designed for lap-style playing, incorporating wide, hollow necks with flat fretboards, high nuts and flush frets. The resonator guitars of John Dopyera and the earliest electric lap steel guitars manufactured by Rickenbacker and others were also a direct response to the interest in Hawaiian guitar music.

Hawaiian musicians transported the technique all over the globe: to India, China, Australia, Europe and Latin America. Important exponents of the Hawaiian guitar include Frank Ferrara, Tau Moe, Mike Hanapi, King Bennie Nawahi and, especially, Sol Ho'opi'i. Non-Hawaiians Alvino Rey and Roy Smeck introduced the style into mainstream North American popular music. Jimmie Rodgers made the first hillbilly recording featuring Hawaiian guitar, 'Dear Old Sunny South by the Sea' (1928), and the instrument's impact on this genre has been particularly profound. Ultimately, the distinction between the Hawaiian steel guitar and the blues slide guitar became blurred, so that the technique of playing the guitar flat in the lap lost its Hawaiian connotations. However, it is difficult to overstate the significance of the Hawaiian style for the world's music.

Bibliography

Gruhn, George, and Carter, Walter. 1993. *Acoustic Guitars and Other Fretted Instruments*. San Francisco: Miller Freeman Books.

Ruymar, Lorene, ed. 1996. *The Hawaiian Steel Guitar and Its Great Hawaiian Musicians*. Anaheim Hills, CA: Centerstream Publishing.

Discographical Reference

Rodgers, Jimmie. 'Dear Old Sunny South by the Sea.' *Jimmie Rodgers: First Sessions (1927–1928)*. Rounder CD-1056. 1928; *1990*: USA.

Discography

Hawaiian Music: Honolulu-Hollywood-Nashville 1927–1944. Frémeaux et Associés FA 035. *1995*: France.

History of Hawaiian Steel Guitar. Hana Ola Records HOCD34000. *1999*: USA.

Sol Ho'opi'i: Master of the Hawaiian Guitar, Volume 1. Rounder CD-1024. 1977; *1991*: USA.

TIM WISE

Hocket

'Hocket,' from the French *hoquet* (Latin *hoquetus*), meaning 'hiccup,' is a contrapuntal performance technique in which individual notes or chords within musical phrases, not the complete phrases, are alternated between different voices, instruments or recorded tracks. Although the term is traditionally used to describe the technique in late medieval French motets (as in 'In seculum,' an instrumental motet in the *Codex Bamberg*, cited in Davison and Apel 1949, 34), hockets are far from uncommon in modern popular music. A well-known example is the African woman shifting to and fro between voice and one-note pan pipe in the introduction to Herbie Hancock's 1973 version of 'Watermelon Man.' Indeed, hockets are a prominent feature of several African music cultures, not only among the Ba-Benzélé featured on the Hancock recording, but also among the Mbuti, the Basarwa (Khoisan) and Gogo (Tanzania) (Nketia 1974, 167). In a more general sense, fast alternation of one or two notes between voices, instruments and timbres not only contributes massively to the dynamic of timbral and rhythmic distinctness that is intrinsic to the polyphonic and polyrhythmic structure of much music in Sub-Saharan Africa (Nketia 1974;

Chernoff 1979), but also gives evidence of 'social partiality for rapid and colourful antiphonal interchange' (Sanders 1980). Such partiality may also help to explain the predilection for hocketing found in funk music, where the technique is intentionally employed for purposes of zestful accentuation and interjection. Typical examples of funk hocketing are the quick, agogic interplay between high and low slap bass notes, or the fast interchange between extremely short vocal utterances, stabs from the horn section and interpunctuations from the rest of the band (for example, Larry Graham, James Brown). These affective qualities of hocketing were certainly recognized by medieval European clerics, who characterized it as *lascivius* ('fun') *propter sui mobilitatem et velocitatem*. In 1325, Pope John XXII issued a papal bull banning its use in church (Sanders 1980).

Another type of hocketing has been developed in response to the restrictions of instrument technology. For example, the Andean practise of sharing the tonal vocabulary of a piece between two or more pan pipes (*zampoñas*) and their players demands skillful hocketing to produce runs of notes that are in no way intended to sound like hiccups (e.g., Ennio Morricone's 'No Escape,' in which the *zampoñas* are played by Raffaele and Felice Clemente). Advanced hocketing is also practised in Balinese gamelan music, in which very short portions of melody are allocated to many different players to produce highly complex sound patterns.

Bibliography

Chernoff, John Miller. 1979. *African Rhythm and Sensibility*. Chicago: University of Chicago Press.

Davison, A.T., and Apel, W. 1949. *Historical Anthology of Music*, Vol. 1. Boston, MA: Harvard University Press.

Nketia, J.H. Kwabena. 1974. *The Music of Africa*. New York: Norton.

Sanders, Ernest H. 1980. 'Hocket.' In *The New Grove Dictionary of Music and Musicians*, Vol. 8, ed. Stanley Sadie. London: Macmillan, 608.

Discographical References

Hancock, Herbie. 'Watermelon Man.' *Head Hunters*. Columbia CK 32731. *1973*: USA.

Morricone, Ennio. 'No Escape.' *Casualties of War*. CBS 466016 2. *1989*: USA.

Discography

Brown, James. 'Get on the Good Foot,' 'Get Up Offa That Thing,' 'Papa's Got a Brand New Bag.' *Cold Sweat*. Hallmark 30580. 1978; *1999*: USA.

Graham Central Station. *Release Yourself*. Warner Brothers 56062. *1974*: USA.

'Ifu.' *Music of the Ba-Benzélé*. Bärenreiter-Musicaphon BML 30L 2303. *1969*: Germany.

Musik från Tanzania (ed. K. Malm). Caprice RIKS LPX 8. *1974*: Sweden.

PHILIP TAGG

Holler/Hollering

Related to the call and the shout, the holler may be distinguished from these forms of hailing by the detachment of the person who transmits the holler from his/her addressee. Whereas the call is normally addressed to a specific person, animal or domesticated fowl, and the shout projected to a distant but identifiable target, the holler is emitted to whomever may be within earshot. As a term, 'holler' is considered to be North American in origin, and to be a dialect form of the earlier 'hallo' or 'halloo,' used since the early eighteenth century to urge hunting dogs in the chase. It was also employed to drive unwanted animals away, and to call in the hounds after the hunt. In the United States, the word may also be derived from the greeting 'hallo,' 'halloah' or, in its current form, 'hello,' when used as a general cry to seek human contact or to establish the location of the hailer in a wilderness area. This latter usage suggests an affinity with Shakespeare's 'Holla your name to the reverberate hills' (*Twelfth Night*, I, v, 239). The term 'holler' also referred to the announcement of food prepared by camp cooks and available at the cowboys' chuck wagon, and to the bellowed instructions to a work gang, such as a railroad track-lining crew.

In Southern white communities, especially in the Appalachians, calls or hollers were the customary means of keeping in contact with neighbors. Sometimes, neighbors would holler jointly, taking separate parts in harmony, though frequently the holler was used as a call for aid. The term was also employed for calling hogs or hunting dogs.

Although 'holler' has a general application to cries for contact, attention or succor, or for assistance directed to an unseen and usually unknown potential listener or respondent, the term became more specifically applied to a form of field call used by African-American agricultural workers. It is believed that the 'field holler' came into more general use when the collective work song declined with the diminution of the plantation system after the American Civil War. At that time, Frederick Law Olmsted noted a field hand raising 'a long, loud, musical shout rising and falling and breaking into falsetto, his voice ringing through the woods in the clear, frosty air, like a bugle call' (1953, 166). He did not refer to it as a holler, but the term was in use in the early twentieth century. Howard W. Odum and Guy B. Johnson gave examples of 'the lonely singer, with his morning yodel or "holler"' (1926, 253), and a couple of 'cornfield' hollers, 'sung mostly in falsetto,' were phonophotograph-

ically recorded by Milton Metfessel in 1925 (Metfessel 1928, 120, 121).

Although it has been generally assumed that hollers were the antecedents of the blues, there is no documentary evidence confirming this. Recordings of hollers were made for the Library of Congress from 1933 onward, when a 'steel-laying holler' was contributed by Rochelle Harris in Tennessee. 'Track-lining hollers' were also made some years later, in 1940, by Henry Truvillion in Texas. Singers such as Enoch Brown and Richard Amerson made a number of 'cornfield hollers' that were not issued, but Thomas J. Marshall's 'Arwhoolie' (cornfield holler), made in 1939, was issued, although as he was a student it was probably mimicry. Of undoubted importance were the hollers recorded by Son House in 1942, in a style that is clearly related to the blues, even though the influence may have been of the blues on the holler, rather than the reverse. In Alabama in 1950, Harold Courlander recorded Enoch Brown and Annie Grace Horn Dodson singing several hollers, which bore out his summary that the holler 'might be filled with exuberance or melancholy. It might consist of a long "hoh-hoo" stretched out with intricate ornamentation of a kind virtually impossible to notate ... Sometimes this elemental music, carried beyond a single line or phrase, would take on the form of an elemental song' (1963, 81).

In the late 1960s, a revival of interest in the white tradition of hollering in North Carolina led to the institution of an annual hollering contest – the National Hollerin' Contest – held in Spivey's Corner, Sampson County. Some of the champions have appeared on Johnny Carson's television show or have been featured on radio programs.

Hollers could certainly be exuberant, but the term 'whooping,' dating from the sixteenth century, was frequently used for exultant calls of a similar kind. Combining both terms was a practise familiar to revelers in the nineteenth century, when George Whyte Melville (1821–78) declared, in his song 'Drink, Puppy, Drink,' that 'merrily we'll whoop and we'll holloa,' anticipating by many decades boogie pianist Montana Taylor's 'Whoop and Holler Stomp.'

Bibliography

Browne, Ray B. 1954. 'Some Notes on the Southern "Holler."' *Journal of American Folklore* 67: 73–77.

Courlander, Harold. 1963. *Negro Folk Music, U.S.A.* New York: Columbia University Press, Ch. IV.

Hudson, S.F., et al. 1995. *Hollerin': The Ceased Music.* Notes to *Hollerin'*. Rounder CD 0071.

Metfessel, Milton. 1928. *Phonophotography in Folk Music.* Chapel Hill, NC: University of North Carolina Press.

Odum, Howard W., and Johnson, Guy B. 1925. *The*

Negro and His Songs: A Study of Typical Negro Songs in the South. Chapel Hill, NC: University of North Carolina Press.

Odum, Howard W., and Johnson, Guy B. 1926. Negro Workaday Songs. Chapel Hill, NC: University of North Carolina Press.

Oliver, Paul. 1998 (1969). The Story of the Blues. Boston, MA: Northeastern University Press.

Olmsted, Frederick Law. 1953 (1856). The Cotton Kingdom: A Traveller's Observations on Cotton and Slavery in the American Slave States, ed. Arthur M. Schlesinger. New York: Knopf.

Sheet Music

Melville, George Whyte. 1879. 'Drink, Puppy, Drink.' London: n.p.

Discographical References

House, Son. The Complete Library of Congress Sessions, 1941–1942. Travelin' Man 2. 1996: USA.

Taylor, Montana. 'Whoop and Holler Stomp.' Vocalion 1275. 1929: USA.

Discography

Field Recordings, Vol. 2: NC & SC, GA, TN, AR (1926–1943). Document Records DOCD-5576. 1998: Austria.

Field Recordings, Vol. 3: Mississippi (1936–1942). Document Records DOCD-5577. 1998: Austria.

Field Recordings, Vol. 13: Texas, Louisiana, Arkansas, Mississippi, Florida, Alabama, Georgia, Tennessee, South Carolina, Delaware (1933–1943). Document Records DOCD-5621. 1998: Austria.

Negro Folk Music of Alabama, Vol. 1: Secular Music. Smithsonian/Folkways 4417. 1951: USA.

PAUL OLIVER

Honking

'Honking' is an onomatopoeic term used to describe a particular sound produced on the saxophone. It is associated especially with certain rhythm and blues (R&B) tenor saxophonists of the 1940s and 1950s, usually known as 'honkers.' The essential feature of honking is repetition of the same note using a blaring tone. Saxophone performances using honking were also likely to include screeching or screaming sounds. Recalling his first exposure to honking in Harlem in the 1940s, writer Arnold Shaw described how 'the [tenor sax] performer kept honking on one note. It had no particular rhythm; it was just repeated at intervals.' The saxophonist responsible then 'switched to a very high note and kept screeching that one note' (1978, 169).

LeRoi Jones (Imamu Amiri Baraka) has noted that honking was part of a culture of competition that incorporated more than just honking itself. Honking contests involved 'men like Eddie "Lockjaw" Davis, Illi-

nois Jacquet, Willis "Gatortail" Jackson, Big Jay McNeeley [sic], Lynn Hope ... [trying] to outshout and outstomp any other saxophonist who would dare to challenge them' (1965, 172). McNeely specialized in making honking part of a 'wild-man stage persona' that he developed for black and white audiences in and around Los Angeles in the early 1950s. 'Trailed by his baritone-playing brother (Robert), Big Jay marched back and forth across the stage or off it, down into the aisles or through the crowd. He would take off his coat, lie down on his back and kick his feet in the air; a band member would hold a microphone over him to catch every decibel' (Millar 1985). For a photo spread in Ebony magazine, McNeely took his saxophone into the street outside the Club Oasis in Los Angeles, honking at passing drivers and pedestrians during the shoot (Millar 1985).

Jones sees three root causes for honking: to 'spend oneself with as much attention as possible'; 'to make the instruments sound as unmusical, or as non-Western as possible'; and to embody reaction against the 'softness and "legitimacy"' that had crept into black instrumental music with the advent of swing' (1965, 172). To this could be added that repeated honking as used in R&B was also a means to engender an excited audience response. As such, it stood in a line of succession stretching from earlier practises using drumming and body percussion (for example, clapping) to the development of other repetitive instrumental techniques used later in rock 'n' roll and rock.

Bibliography

Jones, LeRoi (Imamu Amiri Baraka). 1965. Blues People: Negro Music in White America. London: MacGibbon & Kee.

Millar, Bill. 1985. Liner notes to Road House Boogie. Saxophonograph BP-505.

Shaw, Arnold. 1978. Honkers and Shouters: The Golden Years of Rhythm and Blues. New York: Macmillan.

Discography

Honkers & Bar Walkers. Delmark CD DL438. 1989: USA.

McNeely, Big Jay. The Best of Big Jay McNeely. Saxophonograph BP-1300. 1985: UK.

McNeely, Big Jay. Road House Boogie. Saxophonograph BP-505. 1985: UK.

DAVID HORN

Humming

'Humming' is usually taken to refer to vocalizing with the mouth closed. The lungs provide air pressure, activating the vocal cords, which send the raw sound through the nasal passages instead of allowing it to be modified by the acoustic spaces in the mouth. Provided the epiglottis is lowered, thus directing air through the nose and blocking the airway to the mouth, humming can also be done with the mouth open. In closed-mouth mode, it is possible to change the tone of the sound by altering the shape of the vocal tract (the space between the vocal cords and the lips) and changing the position of the tongue. With the mouth open, a similar effect can be achieved by changing the shape of the mouth, emphasizing particular harmonics resonating in the vocal tract. Humming is part of the repertoire of expressive devices that people use, consciously or unconsciously, to externalize the personal musical thoughts that accompany their daily lives.

Humming is used as an additional tone color for singers when no text is required. Its use in popular music postdates the invention of the microphone, without which the delicate sounds would not be heard (although there are exceptions to this, notably the more robust closed-mouth vocalizing of Bessie Smith). Its instrumental-like effect can give singers and listeners time to reflect on the text between sung phrases and can create yet more layers of meaning. Some African languages have humming sounds that can very easily be transformed into musical material. African choirs (such as Ladysmith Black Mambazo) use humming for both vocal color and rhythmic emphasis.

JOHN POTTER

Improvisation

'Improvisation,' from Latin *improvisus* (meaning 'unforeseen'), is a term used to describe the simultaneous composition and performance of music. As its derivation indicates, the term has often had connotations of spontaneous or unpremeditated creation, and it has been contrasted with formal composition, in which the details of a piece are planned and fixed in advance of its performance.

Nettl (1974), however, argues that this is a false dichotomy, and that the two terms may more usefully stand for the opposite ends of a continuum on which the performer is allowed an increasing degree of autonomy. Firstly, even the performance of a complex musical score allows the players some element of choice, however limited, in matters of execution and interpretation. Secondly, and of great importance, there is much evidence that music in a wide range of cultures which appears to be produced spontaneously is in fact based on an underlying learned 'model' of appropriate performance practises, and that the characteristics of this model may not diverge in significant respects from the stylistic features of composed or traditional pieces.

Improvisation plays an important part in many traditions, and notably in much Indian, Indonesian, Middle Eastern and African music. Yet, it has been a relatively neglected area of music scholarship, almost certainly as a result of its insignificance in Western art music during the twentieth century. It has also been widely held in the West that improvised music, due to its assumed spontaneity, is inherently inferior to composed works, and that only a few exceptional individuals possess the ability to improvise. Recent studies, however, have rendered such views highly questionable: 'improvised' music has been shown to be highly organized, often complex, and pre-planned to a considerable extent; moreover, there is increasing recognition that improvisation must be understood as a collaborative cultural practise which is established in particular musical traditions, rather than as a talent bestowed on particular individuals.

Decline and Rebirth

In fact, even in the West, improvisation has been important in both vernacular and art music traditions. Evidence of the former persists in the performances of, for example, flamenco guitarists, Basque folk singers, Jewish klezmer bands, Hebridean vocal musicians and Irish fiddlers, and well into the nineteenth century the improvising soloist was a recognized (and often celebrated) figure at art music concerts and recitals. Figures regarded by posterity as major composers, such as Bach, Handel, Mozart and Beethoven, were at least as well known to their contemporaries for their keyboard improvisations, and players routinely embellished or improved notated parts, which in any case often left much open to the performers' discretion. From the latter part of the eighteenth century, however, two opposed trends were established: on the one hand, vocal and instrumental virtuosos developed unprecedented improvisational skills; on the other hand, the composers of symphonic music increasingly sought to require performers to remain close to the score as a matter of accepted practise.

While virtuoso recitals, particularly by pianists, persisted, it was the latter tendency that prevailed. With the widespread acceptance of the ideology of 'serious' music in the second half of the century, and the retrospective definition of a canon of 'classical' works, the liberties of the performer were sacrificed to the authority of the 'great composer.' The practise of improvisation was restricted to the cadenza – a solo passage interpolated into an otherwise composed work (often at the end of the first movement of a concerto) – and to certain functional contexts, such as pianists accompanying dance rehearsals or organists extemporizing during religious ceremonies.

Thus, by the beginning of the twentieth century improvisation had all but disappeared from the European tradition of art music, and from the 'light' popular music derived from it – Victorian parlor ballads, music hall songs, brass and military band music, and so on. Already, however, quite different traditions of improvisation had been established in the West as a result of the modern African diaspora (Gilroy 1993). In Latin America and in the Caribbean islands, the mixture of African and European elements led to a variety of new musical styles, but it was above all the gradual emergence of distinctive African-American *genres* in the United States between the Civil War and the turn of the century that restored the improvising performer to a position of prominence, and that was ultimately to have an enormous influence on a variety of popular music styles in the twentieth century and beyond. More specifically, it was the achievement of jazz musicians to restore improvisation to a central position in Western musical culture by creating a tradition that had the improvised solo, rather than the written score, at its heart (Peretti 1992, 113).

Studies of Improvisation

As a result of its peripheral status in European art music, and its association with jazz, blues and, more recently, rock, the practise of improvisation has received little attention from music scholars. The work of Ernst Ferand (1887–1972) stood virtually alone until the gradual development, from the 1960s, of jazz studies and ethnomusicological work in western and southern parts of Asia; these and certain other research areas are reflected in the collection of articles edited by Nettl and Russell (1998), which stands, at the beginning of the twenty-first century, as the most authoritative single work on the subject. The period in question also saw the expansion of popular music studies, which – often for the first time – gave serious analytic attention to styles previously regarded as marginal by musicologists. Yet, while improvisation is a crucial element in many of these styles, the topic itself has rarely been the focus of attention. Even within the jazz literature, and despite Schuller's justified claim that 'improvisation is the heart and soul of jazz' (1968, 58), it is only in recent years that the subject has received sustained analytic attention. The most influential of the pioneering studies were those of Hodeir (1956) and Schuller (1968), while Bailey (1980) sought to put the subject in cross-cultural perspective. To date, Berliner (1994) is the most exhaustive treatment of performance practise in the jazz tradition, focusing on the lengthy process through which players become capable improvisers and are recognized as such within the artistic community. Sudnow (1978) explores ways in

which the practises involved in keyboard improvisation become embodied in the performer, Tirro (1974) identifies the 'constructive elements' that players utilize repeatedly in building up their solos, while Monson (1996) examines the interactional exchanges among groups of improvising jazz players.

With increasing recognition of the achievements of improvisers in the jazz and rock fields, and the growing provision of practical classes and courses in academic contexts, the recordings of master improvisers have acquired canonic status, and their solos have been transcribed and published. Instruction in improvisation is thus becoming formalized and institutionalized in the manner of the European conservatoire, a pattern that contrasts starkly with the informal (though no less rigorous) apprenticeships of the earlier innovators, and that has been viewed as leading to a violation of the fundamentally 'dialogical' nature of the African-American aesthetic (Tomlinson 1992). There are, too, a number of published instruction manuals that treat jazz improvisation as a learnable skill rather than as an innate gift, and that aim to teach players how to create effective melodic and rhythmic patterns appropriate to underlying harmonic sequences. As a result, in the United States and in major cities throughout the world there are substantial numbers of improvising musicians of great technical accomplishment, although some critics have argued that the stylistic hegemony of bebop and its derivatives is unduly restrictive, and that the work of formally trained musicians tends to lack the originality and individuality of earlier players.

Like musicology, other academic disciplines have largely neglected improvisation. Insofar as improvisation has been considered, research has largely reflected conventional assumptions by treating it as an individual accomplishment (as opposed to a socially organized practise), and hence as a topic for the psychology of creativity. Pressing (1988) provides a review of this material. The ethnographically grounded work of Berliner (1994) and Monson (1996), however, has opened up the possibility of a more sociologically satisfactory account by demonstrating that musical improvisation is above all a collaborative, interactional practise based on the performance conventions, or model, upheld by specific artistic communities. In thus emphasizing its communal, as opposed to individual, aspects, this work has moved the study of improvisation closer to the practise of generations of players in the African-American traditions. Moreover, this approach is likely to prove fruitful across the whole spectrum of popular music styles in which improvisation is an ingredient; as Nettl (1998, 15) has emphasized, improvisers in all styles and traditions work on the basis of a set of shared performance conventions – how to proceed, what the music ought to sound like, and so on – which enables them to create music that is simultaneously spontaneous and organized (Martin 2002).

The Effects of the African Diaspora

With the growing influence of African-American styles on popular music generally, improvisation emerged in a variety of contexts. Improvised solos, often by guitarists or saxophonists, were a feature of many rhythm and blues recordings in the postwar period, and of the electrified blues bands of Chicago and Memphis. As a direct consequence, such instrumental passages were also evident in the evolving rock 'n' roll of the 1950s and, most importantly, in the progressive rock of the 1960s, which provided extended opportunities for guitarists to develop improvisations, usually over simple harmonic progressions or riff patterns. British groups such as Cream, Led Zeppelin and Fleetwood Mac, all featuring lengthy blues-derived guitar solos, were particularly influential, and it was blues traditions that were both developed and subverted in the work of the iconic guitarist Jimi Hendrix (1942–70). Such groups and their successors gave the soloist a position of prominence equaled only in modern jazz, and restored improvising instrumentalists to the forefront of popular music, as in the 1930s.

The effects of the African diaspora are also evident in the various musical traditions that emerged in Latin America. Manuel (1988), for example, notes the widespread influence of Afro-Cuban rhythms on twentieth-century styles as they evolved, also pointing out that much of this music derives its vitality from rhythmic improvisations – from slight nuances to 'overtly audible passages' – rather than from the flamboyant solos of instrumentalists (133). The African influence is thus apparent in respect of both the rhythmic foundation and the performance as a collective accomplishment as opposed to an opportunity for individual virtuosity. However, it is also important to recognize the extent to which twentieth-century communications, in this field as in others, accelerated syncretic processes in the development of new styles, notably in South Africa, where African-American forms – from ragtime through swing to rock – demonstrate that the transatlantic influence has been a two-way process (Manuel 1988, 106–11). As these examples suggest, the international influence of US jazz players on the development of popular music styles has been considerable; in recent years, moreover, the tradition of improvisation in jazz has been studied more extensively than any other.

Improvisation in Jazz

Although the details are lost to history, it is clear that the development and codification of particular African-American styles occurred in the last decades of the nineteenth century. These new styles were essentially oral-tradition music that incorporated collective performance conventions. Thus, early players, such as blues singers or itinerant pianists, would be expected to shape their performances to suit the immediate responses of their audiences, and within groups of instrumentalists a degree of spontaneous musical interaction was normal rather than exceptional. The distinctively African elements in all the emergent syntheses – including an emphasis on rhythm, call-and-response patterns, use of the 'blues' scale and other contrasts with diatonic convention – have often been noted; in 1918, the early black band leader James Reese Europe spoke of the tendency of his musicians to 'embroider' their parts so as to produce 'new, peculiar sounds' and to add to their music 'more than I wish them to' (Badger 1995, 195). The ambiguous connotations of the term 'ragtime' convey something of the contrast between the European and the African emphases: the piano rags of Scott Joplin and others, while making extensive use of syncopated rhythms, are precisely notated pieces that allow the player little interpretive freedom, whereas to 'rag' a tune soon came to mean to recast it with the use of syncopation and rhythmic 'swing,' melodic paraphrases, 'blue' notes, embellishments and other elements drawn from black music styles. This latter usage, common in the second decade of the twentieth century, in turn gave way to the term 'jazz,' particularly after the appearance in 1917 of the Original Dixieland Jazz Band at Reisenweber's restaurant in New York.

The ODJB was a white group from New Orleans whose exuberant 'Dixieland' style derived from (and parodied) that of the many brass and parade bands which played a central role in the city's cultural life. Within the black New Orleans bands, however, far more significant musical developments were taking place. Players from rural backgrounds brought with them the oral tradition of the plantations, and they were often self-taught. In contrast, the urban Creoles were musically literate and familiar with the conventions of European art music. Despite friction between these groups, what emerged was an increasingly complex musical culture in which improvisation was an important ingredient. At first, in both parade bands and smaller groups that played for dancers, this seems to have involved the embellishment and reinterpretation of familiar melodies. The leading figures in early New Orleans jazz were all cornet or trumpet players, such as Buddy Bolden (1877–1931), Freddie Keppard (1890–1933) and Joe 'King' Oliver (1885–1938), renowned for their ability to provide a strong lead around which other instruments could weave compatible lines. In the 'classic' New Orleans jazz band, the clarinet would create a counter-melody or ornamentation above the cornet, with the trombone providing both a harmonic and a rhythmic foundation (although the idea of a 'pure' New Orleans style is largely a retrospective creation of 'revivalist' musicians and enthusiasts).

The essence of New Orleans jazz was thus a collective improvised polyphony, which depended on the ability of players to respond instantly to each other's contributions. Before long, however, individual instrumentalists began to distinguish themselves from the ensemble: by 1914, Sidney Bechet (1897–1959) was renowned in New Orleans for his skill as an improvising clarinetist (Chilton 1987, 19); he was soon followed by trumpeter Louis Armstrong (1901–71), generally regarded as the first great jazz soloist. Indeed, Armstrong's recordings in the mid-1920s did much to establish the jazz solo as a passage in which an individual instrumentalist would improvise while being provided with a harmonic and rhythmic framework by the rhythm section (usually some combination of piano, guitar or banjo, bass and drums). Armstrong approached the solo in terms 'not of a pop song more or less embellished, but of a chord progression generating a maximum of creative originality' (Schuller 1968, 103). It was on this basis that what Nettl (1974) calls the 'model' underlying jazz improvisation became elaborated. Its meter and structure were usually determined by that of the piece being performed, often a popular song or a 12-bar blues, although, as Armstrong's early recordings indicate, musicians were already composing pieces primarily as vehicles for improvisation. In time, a repertoire of jazz 'standards' would accumulate – pieces selected for their comfortable or challenging harmonic sequences rather than for their melodic attractions (for example, blues such as George Gershwin's 'I Got Rhythm,' or 'ballads' such as Johnny Green's 'Body and Soul' or Jerome Kern's 'All the Things You Are').

Early improvised solos often consisted of simple syncopated phrases and basic arpeggios. However, more than any other individual, Armstrong revealed the musical and aesthetic possibilities of jazz improvisation. His formidable technique and range were matched by bold melodic imagination and superb rhythmic poise; his urgent, 'hot' solos were unprecedented and, through recordings, enormously influential. Armstrong's work not only acted as a catalyst for the development of other jazz players, notably tenor saxophonist Coleman Hawkins (1904–69), but also placed the improvised solo in the mainstream of mass culture through his own career as an entertainer, and through his direct influence on the instrumental stars of the swing era big bands. Trumpeters Roy Eldridge, Harry James and Bunny Berigan, for example, all based their work on Armstrong. This stylistic legacy was unchallenged until the late 1930s and the emergence of tenor saxophonist Lester Young (1909–59), with his sinuous melodic lines, 'cool' tone and minimal use of vibrato.

Alto saxophonist Charlie 'Bird' Parker (1920–55) has often been compared with Armstrong in the extent of his influence on a new generation of players. The bebop style pioneered in the 1940s by Parker and associates such as trumpeter Dizzy Gillespie (1917–93) eventually supplanted the tradition of Armstrong and his followers, and became accepted as the orthodox approach to improvisation in modern jazz (Owens 1995, 4). Parker's brilliant solos, combining imagination, virtuosity and emotional intensity, have been heard as integrating elements of both Hawkins and Young (DeVeaux 1997, 267–68); with Parker as their inspiration, the bebop players soon pushed conventional improvisation to its limits through the use of sophisticated harmony, intricate melodic patterns, rapid tempos and complex rhythms. Their achievements both ensured that improvised music could once again be accepted as a valid mode of artistic expression and paved the way for the appearance of an avant-garde, since subsequent innovators were increasingly forced to break with the 'model' established since the 1920s. Saxophonist Ornette Coleman (b. 1930) abandoned accepted harmony and formal structures in the late 1950s, and in the final phase of his career saxophonist John Coltrane (1926–67) experimented with collective 'free' improvisation. Since the 1960s, groups of 'free' improvisers have pursued these ideas, notably in Europe and New York City.

Bibliography

Badger, Reid. 1995. *A Life in Ragtime: A Biography of James Reese Europe*. New York: Oxford University Press.

Bailey, Derek. 1980. *Improvisation: Its Nature and Practice in Music*. Ashbourne: Moorland Publishing Company.

Berliner, Paul F. 1994. *Thinking in Jazz: The Infinite Art of Improvisation*. Chicago: University of Chicago Press.

Chilton, John. 1987. *Sidney Bechet: The Wizard of Jazz*. London: Macmillan.

DeVeaux, Scott. 1997. *The Birth of Bebop: A Social and Musical History*. Berkeley, CA: University of California Press.

Gilroy, Paul. 1993. *The Black Atlantic: Modernity and Double Consciousness*. London: Verso.

Hodeir, André. 1956. *Jazz: Its Evolution and Essence*, trans. David Noakes. New York: Grove Press.

Manuel, Peter. 1988. *Popular Musics of the Non-Western World: An Introductory Survey*. New York: Oxford University Press.

Martin, Peter J. 2002. 'Spontaneity and Organization.' In *The Cambridge Companion to Jazz*, ed. David Horn and

Mervyn Cooke. Cambridge and New York: Cambridge University Press, 133–52.

Monson, Ingrid. 1996. *Saying Something: Jazz Improvisation and Interaction*. Chicago: University of Chicago Press.

Nettl, Bruno. 1974. 'Thoughts on Improvisation: A Comparative Approach.' *Musical Quarterly* LX(1): 1–19.

Nettl, Bruno. 1998. 'Introduction: An Art Neglected in Scholarship.' In *In the Course of Performance: Studies in the World of Musical Improvisation*, ed. Bruno Nettl and Melinda Russell. Chicago: University of Chicago Press, 1–26.

Nettl, Bruno, and Russell, Melinda, eds. 1998. *In the Course of Performance: Studies in the World of Musical Improvisation*. Chicago: University of Chicago Press.

Owens, Thomas. 1995. *Bebop: The Music and Its Players*. New York: Oxford University Press.

Peretti, Burton W. 1992. *The Creation of Jazz: Music, Race, and Culture in Urban America*. Urbana, IL: University of Illinois Press.

Pressing, Jeff. 1988. 'Improvisation: Methods and Models.' In *Generative Processes in Music: The Psychology of Performance, Improvisation, and Composition*, ed. John A. Sloboda. Oxford: Clarendon Press, 129–78.

Schuller, Gunther. 1968. *Early Jazz: Its Roots and Musical Development*. New York: Oxford University Press.

Sudnow, David. 1978. *Ways of the Hand: The Organization of Improvised Conduct*. London: Routledge and Kegan Paul.

Tirro, Frank. 1974. 'Constructive Elements in Jazz Improvisation.' *Journal of the American Musicological Society* 27(2): 285–305.

Tomlinson, Gary. 1992. 'Cultural Dialogics and Jazz: A White Historian Signifies.' In *Disciplining Music: Musicology and Its Canons*, ed. Katherine Bergeron and Philip V. Bohlman. Chicago: University of Chicago Press, 64–94.

Sheet Music

Gershwin, George, comp., and Gershwin, Ira, lyr. 1930. 'I Got Rhythm.' New York: New World Music.

Green, Johnny, comp., and Heyman, Ed, Sauer, Robert, & Eyton, Frank, lyrs. 1930. 'Body and Soul.' New York: Harms.

Kern, Jerome, comp., and Hammerstein, Oscar, II, lyr. 1939. 'All the Things You Are.' New York: Harms.

PETER MARTIN

Jamming

'Jamming' is the term used to describe informal collective improvisation, often in a competitive situation (known as a 'jam session'); it has its origins in jazz, although it is now widely used in most areas of popular music. The term (like 'jazz' itself) originates from early twentieth-century US black argot for sexual intercourse.

Although there is some evidence of jamming in the earliest days of New Orleans jazz, that city's complex social structure, racial divides and the intensely competitive environment between bands more often led to public 'cutting contests' in which soloists or entire groups vied for public acclaim. Jamming in the modern sense dates from the earliest attempts by Chicago musicians to emulate the music of such New Orleans bands as Joe 'King' Oliver's or the New Orleans Rhythm Kings in after-hours get-togethers at clubs, speak-easies or hotels. Initially, such sessions almost always took place in private or semiprivate settings, and their primary purpose was to foster camaraderie and competition between musicians. However, the so-called Austin High School Gang of young white Chicagoans adopted such sessions into their musical ethos, and many of these players formed the core of the New York jam sessions presented in public by guitarist Eddie Condon from the 1940s until the early 1970s.

Musicians' clubs or societies hosted jam sessions for black musicians in several US cities, notably New York, where the Clef and Rhythm clubs were the scenes of many after-hours contests between the city's players. The rapid development of clubs in that city's 52nd Street and in Harlem fueled an atmosphere of informal jamming, in which musicians such as trumpeter Roy Eldridge and tenor saxophonist Chu Berry became famous for 'cutting' all-comers in the mid-1930s. The most notable other regional center for after-hours jamming was Kansas City, Missouri, where the 'wide-open' policies of the Pendergast regime encouraged numerous clubs to flourish, thereby attracting an unusually high level of musical competition.

In the early 1940s, the New York clubs Minton's and Monroe's Uptown House presented jam sessions at which the club provided a rhythm section and encouraged soloists to come and compete against one another. In this atmosphere, bebop, or modern jazz, developed rapidly, and the copious opportunities for jamming allowed the musicians to experiment with new harmonic and rhythmic ideas in public. Here, as in the earlier Chicago tradition, there was a strong element of oral transmission of techniques from one generation to another.

Director Gjon Mili's 10-minute film *Jammin' the Blues* (1944), produced by entrepreneur Norman Granz to feature many of the musicians who indulged in public jam sessions during his *Jazz at the Philharmonic* concerts, such as Lester Young, Illinois Jacquet and Harry 'Sweets' Edison, attempts to capture the atmosphere of a jam session from this era. However, owing to the extraordinary visual beauty of Mili's photography, and the way he directed the musicians for visual rather than musical effect, the informality of a genuine jam session is sacrificed to achieve different artistic ends.

In jazz, such an atmosphere did not return until the 'loft jazz' movement of the 1960s to the 1980s, but other styles of popular music adopted the idea of the jam session. Just as in jazz, where the harmonic and rhythmic structure of 'standards' allows a lingua franca between musicians, the most popular areas for jamming are where a similarly universal core repertoire exists, such as 1960s rock music. In this field, the 'supergroups' assembled for festivals and benefit concerts generally jam on well-known tunes, rather than attempting new pieces.

In the late 1990s, a new form of jazz fusion emerged in New York clubs that brought together elements of jazz-rock and funk into a potent mixture popular in dance clubs. So-called jam bands were at the center of this movement, which was triggered by the jazz-rock trio Medeski, Martin & Wood and also involved such groups as Deep Banana Blackout. Another such band, with connections to John Zorn's New York downtown scene and the Knitting Factory club, is Sex Mob, which includes drummer Kenny Wolleson and bassist Tony Scherr.

Bibliography

Barker, Danny. 1988. *A Life in Jazz*, ed. Alyn Shipton. New York: Oxford University Press. (First published London: Macmillan, 1986.)

Condon, Eddie. 1974 (1948). *We Called It Music: A New Generation of Jazz*. London: Hale.

Gitler, Ira. 1985. *Swing to Bop: An Oral History of the Transition in Jazz in the 1940s*. Oxford and New York: Oxford University Press.

Levet, Jean-Paul. 1992. *Talkin' That Talk: Le Langage du blues et du jazz* [Talkin' That Talk: The Language of Blues and Jazz]. Paris: Hatier.

Meeker, David. 1982 (1981). *Jazz in the Movies*. New York: Da Capo Press.

Pearson, Nathan W. 1987. *Goin' to Kansas City*. Urbana, IL/London: University of Illinois Press/Macmillan.

Schuller, Gunther. 1988. 'Jam Session.' In *The New Grove Dictionary of Jazz*, Vol. 1, ed. Barry Kernfeld. London: Macmillan, 577.

ALYN SHIPTON

Karaoke

Karaoke is a performance technique using a piece of equipment that enables a person to sing along to a prerecorded accompaniment. The word 'karaoke' is a combination of two Japanese words: *kara*, meaning 'empty' or 'vacant,' and *oke*, a shortened form of the word for 'orchestra.' Karaoke equipment consists of microphones, a music player, a power amplifier, including a circuit for mixing and a circuit for echo, speakers, and a television monitor or songbooks. The source of the music – music that is minus the main vocals, but has a guiding melody – varies from audiotape, CD, videotape, video disc or wired network to communication satellite.

Karaoke started in Japan at the beginning of the 1970s as entertainment for customers in bars, and won huge popularity among middle-aged men, who sang old-fashioned *enka* songs. It was used as an eclectic style both for raising group consciousness and for intensifying a sense of individualism. Karaoke could reinforce a sense of belonging within a group, and at the same time make it possible for people to express themselves through their choice of songs and performance. But, with the appearance of 'karaoke boxes' (cubicles exclusively for karaoke singing) in the mid-1980s, karaoke quickly became popular among the general public, regardless of people's age, sex or occupation.

Karaoke changed the popular music scene in Japan. First, karaoke created a distinction between songs for singing and songs for listening to. The record industry tried to produce songs that suited karaoke: medleys, duets and songs that could be sung easily. After karaoke boxes became popular, there were more than 10 million 'single' CDs sold each year. These megahits were usually theme songs from television dramas or songs used in television commercials that young people wanted to sing in karaoke boxes. Recording companies added karaoke accompaniment to the original version of songs recorded by a singer. One of the most important attributes of a hit song changed from 'good to listen to' to 'good to sing.'

Secondly, karaoke was responsible for a revival of old popular songs. On the whole, it is the young who are concerned with the current 'flow' of popular music, the latest hit songs. Older generations are more familiar with the songs that were popular in their youth. Karaoke made it possible for people to sing the old popular songs that were part of their society's heritage.

When karaoke first appeared, it was thought to be peculiar to Japanese culture. Outside Japan, it was found only in places frequented mainly by Japanese on overseas business assignments or in their homes. Since the end of the 1980s, that has changed dramatically: karaoke has spread all over the world. In parts of Europe, Scandinavia, Australia, and North and South America, karaoke became quite popular toward the end of the 1980s and had dwindled somewhat in popularity by the mid-1990s. In the United Kingdom and Italy, karaoke was popularized in part through television shows that featured karaoke participants.

More generally, karaoke's popularity has been attributed to longstanding cultural traditions of group or social singing. Karaoke around the world was primarily a source of fun and entertainment, and was often associated with partying. This may be a characteristic of karaoke outside the Japanese tradition, as the latter is more formal. Although karaoke usually took place at a bar or pub, and some bars were designated as karaoke bars, other venues for karaoke were resorts, hotel bars, private parties, banquets and weddings. Often, bars and pubs would feature a karaoke night, where people would get up to sing alone or in groups, for fun and/or as part of a competition. The songs were chosen from traditional, current and 'classic' popular songs in many styles (from the 1930s on) from the country in question and also from the US popular song repertoire.

A further distinguishing feature between Eastern and Western karaoke is that, in Western karaoke, an MC, a KJ (karaoke jockey) or an animator is often hired for the evening. The MC's task is to help maintain a lively and fun atmosphere. This is accomplished in part by pacing the songs to keep an energetic feel to the event. The MC may also sing along, and provide lively banter between songs (Mitsui and Hosokawa 1998, 85–86).

Bibliography

Cusic, Don. 1991. 'Karaoke: High Tech and the Folk Tradition.' *Tennessee Folklore Society Bulletin* 55(2): 51–55.

Finnegan, Ruth. 1989. *The Hidden Musicians: Music-Making in an English Town*. Cambridge: Cambridge University Press.

Hosokawa, Shuhei. 1995. *Sanba no kuni ni enka wa nagareru* [Enka Resounds in the Land of Samba]. Tokyo: Chuo Kouronsha, Chukou Shinsho #1263.

Lum, Casey Man Kong. 1996. *In Search of a Voice: Karaoke and the Construction of Identity in Chinese America*. Mahwar, NJ: Erlbaum.

Mitsui, Tôru, and Hosokawa, Shuhei, eds. 1998. *Karaoke Around the World*. London: Routledge.

Otake, Akiko. 1997. *Karaoke umi o wataru* [Karaoke Crosses the Ocean]. Tokyo: Chikuma Shoten.

Sato, Takeshi, ed. 1993. *Jouhouka to taishuu bunka: Video game to karaoke* [Information-Oriented Society and Popular Culture: Video Games and Karaoke]. Tokyo: Gendai no Esupuri.

Sato, Takumi. 1992. 'Karaoke box no media bunka-shi' [A Media-Cultural History of Karaoke Compartments]. In *Pop communication zensho* [Pop Communication Compendium]. Tokyo: PARCO Shuppan.

Shirahata, Youzaburou. 1996. *Karaoke-anime ga sekai o meguru* [Karaoke Animations Move Around the World]. Tokyo: PHP Kenkyuujo.

HIROSHI OGAWA with MEGAN JEROME

Lay-Back

The term 'lay-back' is one that has been used to describe the performance practise of many jazz drummers who,

in terms of the notion of a strict 4/4 meter drawn from music in the classical tradition, delay the beat or pulse through the manner in which they articulate it by striking the ride cymbal of the drumset. According to Keil (1966), a 'lay-back' drummer 'places a slightly delayed accent on the notes marked plus [in Example 1], letting beats 1 and 3 "lay back" still farther behind the pulse, so that only notes 2 and 4, the off-beats, seem to coincide with the metronome' (342).

Example 1

The term 'lay-back' contrasts with that of 'on top,' which refers to the reverse tendency of other drummers to anticipate the beat. According to Keil, 'this dichotomy by no means exhausts the typology of taps' (1966, 342). Rather, the contrast serves an heuristic purpose in distinguishing 'two common approaches or attacks' (1966, 341). Indeed, 'every drummer has what is known in the jazz argot as a distinctive tap, that is, a manner of applying stick to cymbal.' The primary goal of each drummer's 'characteristic and internally consistent tap is to create as much vital drive as possible, to build a groove or track for the soloist to get into and this is done by pulling against the pulse' (Keil 1966, 341).

The tendency has been for 'lay-back' drummers to combine with 'stringy' bassists, that is, string bass players who pluck 'higher up on the strings, away from the bridge, usually with the full side of the finger, and the tone "emerges"' (Keil 1966, 343). Notable examples of such combinations have been found in the groups of Miles Davis, such as in the 1955–56 pairing of drummer Philly Joe Jones and bassist Paul Chambers on the album *Round About Midnight*.

Bibliography

Keil, Charles M.H. 1966. 'Motion and Feeling Through Music.' *Journal of Aesthetics and Art Criticism* 24(2): 337–49.

Discographical Reference

Miles Davis Quintet, The. *Round About Midnight*. Columbia 949. 1955–56: USA.

JOHN SHEPHERD

Lining-Out

Lining-out is a Protestant vocal practise, in which the minister or leader reads or chants a line of a hymn or psalm, and the congregation follows by singing the same line.

Lining-out dates from the seventeenth century, and was adopted mainly in Britain and the United States. The manner in which the leader lines out the text has varied historically from a slow monotone to a more typically rapid melodic delivery (so as not to break the flow of the congregational singing); whether monotonic or more melodic, the leader's voice does not normally foreshadow the melody to be sung by the congregation (Tallmadge 1975). The style of congregational singing has been consistently slow, often with no detectable rhythm, and in most documented cases has exhibited considerable scope for inflection and elaboration. This singing style (often called 'the Old Way of Singing,' a description already in use in eighteenth-century Britain) has influenced twentieth-century popular music singing styles in the United States.

The first evidence for lining-out occurs in 1644, when the practise was adopted by the Westminster Assembly of Divines for use in English churches 'for the present, where many in the Congregation cannot read.' It spread rapidly to Scotland and to the American colonies, and became inseparably linked with the Old Way of Singing. By the eighteenth century, determined efforts were regularly being made to stamp out both practises in England and New England, by introducing organs and choirs and/or by increasing musical instruction. A number of hostile but detailed descriptions of the Old Way were left by advocates of the newer alternative, 'Regular Singing,' in early eighteenth-century New England. One writer speaks of the twisting and torturing of the melody and deplores the time 'taken up in shaking out these Turns and Quavers'; besides, the writer continues, 'no two Men in the Congregation quaver alike' (Walter 1721).

In Britain, lining-out and the Old Way persisted longest in the Scottish churches – which had initially been antagonistic to lining-out as an English intrusion – and they could still be found in the islands of the Hebrides in the second half of the twentieth century. In the United States, the practises disappeared from New England, but took root in the late eighteenth century in frontier states such as Kentucky and Tennessee (where modernizing European tendencies were less successful), spreading from there to other parts of the South. They became associated in particular with congregational singing using the so-called shape-note hymnals.

Documentary evidence also exists for the practise of lining-out (sometimes called 'deaconing out') among black congregations in the South, where it seems likely that the important part played by call-and-response structures in many services may have created a sympathetic environment for a second, alternative style of antiphony to become established. The two practises were conducted differently, however. Lining-out involved textual repetition, whereas call-and-response typically involved a textual shift, often around a question and answer; lining-out involved two musical statements without an intrinsic connection, while call-and-response involved melodic complementarity.

In time, the original purpose of lining-out lost most of its relevance, but the tradition had become so deeply embedded in the Old Way of Singing that it was inseparable from it. This is apparent in a recording such as that made around 1961 by Lasserre Bradley at Little River Primitive Baptist Church, Sparta, North Carolina, featuring Elder Walter Evans and Congregation singing 'Hosanna! Jesus Reigns.' Both lining-out and the Old Way of Singing can still be found, particularly among Primitive Baptists. As Wicks (1989) has shown, elements of the Old Way of Singing associated with lining-out, such as upward portamentos, vocal shakes and filled-in thirds and fourths, can readily be identified in singers such as Dolly Parton, Emmylou Harris and George Jones.

Bibliography

Chase, Gilbert. 1987. *America's Music: From the Pilgrims to the Present*. Rev. 3rd ed. Urbana, IL: University of Illinois Press.

Pitts, Walter F. 1993. *Old Ship of Zion: Afro-Baptist Ritual*. Oxford: Oxford University Press.

Southern, Eileen. 1997. *The Music of Black Americans: A History*. 3rd rev. ed. New York: Norton.

Tallmadge, William H. 1975. 'Baptist Monophonic and Heterophonic Hymnody in Southern Appalachia.' *Yearbook for Inter-American Research* 11: 106–36.

Temperley, Nicholas. 1981. 'The Old Way of Singing: Its Origins and Development.' *Journal of the American Musicological Society* 34: 511–44.

Walter, Thomas. 1721. *The Grounds and Rules of Musick Explained; or, An Introduction to the Art of Singing by Note*. Boston, MA: J. Franklin for S. Gerrish.

Wicks, Sammie Ann. 1989. 'A Belated Salute to the "Old Way" of "Snaking" the Voice on Its (ca) 345th Birthday.' *Popular Music* 8(1): 59–96.

Discographical Reference

Evans, Elder Walter, and Congregation. 'Hosanna! Jesus Reigns.' Sovereign Grace 6444. *1961?*: USA. Reissue: Evans, Elder Walter, and Congregation. 'Hosanna! Jesus Reigns.' *Folk Music in America, Vol. 1: Religious Music: Congregational and Ceremonial* (ed. Richard K. Spottswood). Library of Congress LBC 1. *1976*: USA.

DAVID HORN

On Top

The term 'on top' is one that has been used to describe the performance practise of many jazz drummers who, in terms of the notion of a strict 4/4 meter drawn from music in the classical tradition, anticipate the beat or pulse through the manner in which they articulate it by striking the ride cymbal of the drumset. According to Keil (1966), an 'on top' drummer 'attacks the cymbal so close to the pulse as to almost be ahead of it or "above" it when dealing with those notes in the tap that fall on 1, 2, 3, and 4 of a 4/4 measure' (342).

The term 'on top' contrasts with that of 'lay-back,' which refers to the reverse tendency of other drummers to hang back behind the beat. According to Keil, 'this dichotomy by no means exhausts the typology of taps' (1966, 342). Rather, the contrast serves an heuristic purpose in distinguishing 'two common approaches or attacks' (1966, 341). Indeed, 'every drummer has what is known in the jazz argot as a distinctive tap, that is, a manner of applying stick to cymbal.' The primary goal of each drummer's 'characteristic and internally consistent tap is to create as much vital drive as possible, to build a groove or track for the soloist to get into and this is done by pulling against the pulse' (Keil 1966, 341).

The tendency has been for 'on top' drummers to combine with 'chunky' bassists, that is, string bass players who pluck 'lower down on the strings, nearer the bridge, usually with the tip of the finger, and the tone "bursts"' (Keil 1966, 343). Notable examples of such combinations have been found in the groups of Thelonious Monk, as in the 1962 pairing of drummer Frankie Dunlop and bassist John Ore on the album *Monk's Dream*.

Bibliography

Keil, Charles M.H. 1966. 'Motion and Feeling Through Music.' *Journal of Aesthetics and Art Criticism* 24(2): 337–49.

Discographical Reference

Thelonious Monk Quartet, The. *Monk's Dream*. Columbia 40786. *1962*: USA.

JOHN SHEPHERD

Picking

'Picking' (sometimes 'plucking') is a generic fretted instrument term designating the right-hand finger movements that actuate and produce individual notes from the strings of a banjo, guitar, mandolin and so on. 'Picking' simultaneously connotes both the selection of a particular string or note and its sounding, either by a flexion movement of any one digit on the right hand (with or without a fingerpick or thumbpick, a shaped plectrum of steel or plastic, worn on the distal end of the digit) or by a flatpick or plectrum held in the right hand. Some players consider picking as the conceptual opposite of 'strumming,' in which a rapid right-hand finger or plectrum movement across several strings pro-

duces a chordal or harmonized effect. Thus, such terms as 'three-finger picking,' 'Scruggs-picking,' 'cross-picking,' 'up-picking' and 'down-picking' designate particular techniques for the production of a sequence of differentiated individual notes. For five-string bluegrass banjo players, Earl Scruggs provided the technical breakthrough into a smooth roll-based picking style that often bears his name. Among bluegrass musicians, too, picking has been semantically extended to mean playing and singing in general; thus, an invitation to join in an impromptu, improvisational small-group jam session or picking party is often extended by one musician – even a fiddler or violinist, whose use of the bow precludes any actual right-hand picking – saying to another, 'Let's pick!'

Discography

Flatt, Lester, and Scruggs, Earl. *Foggy Mountain Banjo*. Columbia CS-8364. *1961*: USA.

Jim and Jesse. *Jim & Jesse: Bluegrass and More*. Bear Family BCD 15716. *1994*: Germany.

Osborne Brothers, The. *Pickin' Grass and Singin' Country*. MCA 468. *1975*: USA.

Watson, Doc and Merle. *Pickin' the Blues*. Flying Fish FF-352. *1985*: USA.

THOMAS A. ADLER

Playing Clean

'Playing clean' might seem to be the opposite of 'playing dirty,' but it has never become such a widely used term in music criticism. 'Playing clean' is generally used to denote the precision with which big band or orchestral musicians render their written parts: a clean player will produce, as precisely as possible, what appears on the page. In other words, the player plays without expressive tone, blue notes, rasps or 'dirty,' coarsened intonation. The term 'clean' has wider applications in jazz, where it is generally used to indicate a musician who is not under the influence of narcotics – although in the case of saxophonist Eddie 'Cleanhead' Vinson, it merely indicated that he sported a shaven pate.

Bibliography

Levet, Jean-Paul. 1992. *Talkin' That Talk: Le Langage du blues et du jazz* [Talkin' That Talk: The Language of Blues and Jazz]. Paris: Hatier.

ALYN SHIPTON

Playing Cool

'Playing cool' is a term that came into use in the late 1940s to describe a style of jazz that was the antithesis of 'playing hot.' Whereas hot jazz was passionate, intense and highly syncopated, using vocal tone and vibrato, cool jazz stressed a legato style, a light, airy tone and a minimum of vibrato. Initially, players following the example of saxophonist Lester Young were described as 'cool,' including alto saxophonist Lee Konitz and tenors Stan Getz, Zoot Sims and Paul Quinichette. However, the term acquired a more specific meaning with the release of Miles Davis's nonet album *Birth of the Cool* (recorded in 1949–50). On this album, not only was Davis's own playing light, vibratoless and clear, but the arrangements by Gil Evans, John Lewis, Johnny Carisi and Gerry Mulligan shared a uniformity of approach that took arranger Claude Thornhill's ideas for large bands and applied them to a small band that included the timbres of French horn and tuba. In the 1950s, this approach continued in the work of the Modern Jazz Quartet, Dave Brubeck's quartets and several groups associated with pianist Lennie Tristano. In addition, the west-coast groups of Shorty Rogers, Jimmy Giuffre and Art Pepper acquired the epithet 'West Coast Cool.' The term 'playing cool' has remained in use, but in the 1990s it acquired a more general usage (beyond jazz) to mean 'good' or 'excellent,' within the bounds of accepted taste or fashion.

Bibliography

Chambers, Jack. 1983. *Milestones I: The Music and Times of Miles Davis to 1960*. Toronto, ON: University of Toronto Press.

Gioia, Ted. 1992. *West Coast Jazz: Modern Jazz in California 1945–1960*. New York: Oxford University Press.

Hellhund, Herbert. 1985. *Cool Jazz: Grundzüge seiner Entstehen und Entwicklung* [Cool Jazz: Basics of Its Emergence and Development]. Mainz: Schott.

Levet, Jean-Paul. 1992. *Talkin' That Talk: Le Langage du blues et du jazz* [Talkin' That Talk: The Language of Blues and Jazz]. Paris: Hatier.

Discographical Reference

Davis, Miles. *Birth of the Cool*. Capitol C21K 92862. 1949–50: USA.

ALYN SHIPTON

Playing Dirty

'Playing dirty' has several meanings in popular music. In blues lyrics, it frequently refers to unethical behavior, as in lyrics like those of Memphis Minnie's 1935 song '[He's a] Dirty Mother for You.' As Jean-Paul Levet points out in his study of blues language (1992), in addition to its derogatory meaning the term is frequently inverted in its sense, in a similar way to 'wicked' meaning 'marvelous' or 'fantastic.' In terms of lyrics, the term is also used to signify lewd behavior, cross-referring to ideas like the 'dirty dozens': a punning reference both to the 12-measure structure of the blues and to the derogatory New Orleans word game known as 'the dozens,' in which increasingly scurrilous implications are made

about the protagonists' mothers. There is a direct correlation between such uses of the term and its application in jazz argot, where it is almost always used to describe vocal or rough instrumental tone. 'Jelly Roll' Morton's 'Dirty, Dirty, Dirty' from 1940 is an example, as was the earlier 'Dirty Guitar Blues' by Bobbie Leecan (1926). Trumpeters produce 'dirty' tone by growling, using a plunger mute, half-closing the valves and singing a multiphonic tone into the mouthpiece. Similar effects can be created by other brass players and saxophonists. In jazz since the 1940s, 'dirty' tone has tended to be a comic effect, used, for example, by trumpeter Clark Terry as part of his 'mumbling' act or by cornetist Rex Stewart in his examination of jazz brass techniques. While many similar sounds are produced by free jazz players, notably those, such as Peter Brötzmann, who explore the boundaries between music and noise, the concept of 'dirty' tone is regarded by them as archaic. The concept is the antithesis of 'playing clean' – in other words, playing with a pure, vibratoless tone, and with perfect execution.

Bibliography

Barker, Danny. 1988. *A Life in Jazz*, ed. Alyn Shipton. New York: Oxford University Press. (First published London: Macmillan, 1986.)

Levet, Jean-Paul. 1992. *Talkin' That Talk: Le Langage du blues et du jazz* [Talkin' That Talk: The Language of Blues and Jazz]. Paris: Hatier.

Discographical References

Leecan, Bobbie. 'Dirty Guitar Blues.' Victor 20251. 1926: USA.

Memphis Minnie. '[He's a] Dirty Mother for You.' Decca 7048. 1935: USA.

Morton, 'Jelly Roll.' 'Dirty, Dirty, Dirty.' General 1711. 1940: USA.

ALYN SHIPTON

Playing Hot

'Playing hot' derives from the various meanings of 'hot' in popular music and jazz. The term was used in tune titles from the ragtime era onward to denote a snappy, syncopated theme. Some female blues singers were known as 'Red-Hot Mamas' on account of their forceful singing style and lyrics that mirrored the sexual come-on of the lead role played by comedienne Gertrude Saunders in Irving C. Miller's 1926 African-American revue *Red Hot Mama*. The Russian-born singer Sophie Tucker (1884–1966) earned the sobriquet 'Last of the Red-Hot Mamas' for an act that began as a blackface vaudeville 'coon-shouting' turn in 1906. She later modified the act by abandoning her burnt cork makeup, but she continued to include a significant proportion of African-

American songs well after the classic blues era of the 1920s–1930s was over.

Also in the 1920s, early jazz musicians were classified as 'hot' players according to the passion and drive of their playing. A 'hot' style involved occasional growls or smears and giving the impression of playing on top of or fractionally ahead of the underlying beat or pulse. The epithet 'hot' was applied directly to some of these individuals, including trumpeter Oran 'Hot Lips' Page, as well as to entire groups, such as Louis Armstrong's Hot Five or Hot Seven or 'Jelly Roll' Morton's Red Hot Peppers. Armstrong epitomized playing hot through his forceful syncopation, occasional use of vocal tone and his relentless rhythmic drive. His style is transcribed in his '50 Hot Choruses for Cornet' (published in 1927).

Eventually, 'hot' jazz came to mean Dixieland or swing, defined by Hugues Panassié in his book *Le Jazz Hot* (1934) as jazz played 'with warmth or heat,' rather than 'played straight.' Panassié was a prime mover in the Hot Club de France, an organization supporting his definition that was subsequently copied in countries from Belgium to Argentina.

Although the term 'playing hot' has barely been used outside revivalist circles since the 1950s, its antonym, 'playing cool,' was applied to an entire movement in modern jazz from the late 1940s onward.

Bibliography

Levet, Jean-Paul. 1992. *Talkin' That Talk: Le Langage du blues et du jazz* [Talkin' That Talk: The Language of Blues and Jazz]. Paris: Hatier.

Panassié, Hugues. 1934. *Le Jazz Hot*. Paris: Editions R.A. Correa. (Published as *Hot Jazz: The Guide to Swing Music*, trans. Lyle and Eleanor Dowling. London: Cassell, 1936.)

Sheet Music

Armstrong, Louis, comp. 1927. '50 Hot Choruses for Cornet.' New York: Melrose.

ALYN SHIPTON

Playing Inside

'Playing inside' is the antonym of the jazz term 'playing outside.' The terminology emerged during the development of free jazz in the 1960s, and a player who 'plays inside' is one who remains within the harmonic, metrical and scalar boundaries of a composition.

ALYN SHIPTON

Playing Outside

The concept of 'playing outside' stems from the jazz of the 1960s, when the emergent ideas of free jazz players coalesced with those developed through other, more conventional, forms of improvisation. Given that, as many free jazz players abandoned traditional notions of meter, pulse, harmony and intonation, their playing went 'outside' or beyond the hitherto commonly accepted boundaries of the popular song form or of a modal harmonic platform, it could be argued that all free jazz is by definition 'outside.' However, the term is seldom applied outright in a free jazz context, but more frequently in a context where, as in the playing of saxophonist Eric Dolphy, for example, elements of free jazz are brought into improvisations over a conventional harmonic or metrical structure. In such circumstances, the 'outside' player provides a startling contrast to the supporting rhythm section. Ornette Coleman has consistently demonstrated the ability to 'play outside,' as have David Murray and two fellow members of the World Saxophone Quartet, Oliver Lake and Hamiet Bluiett. In Europe, saxophonist Peter Brötzmann has used extremes of sound as an 'outside' technique, while Louis Sclavis has extended the ideas of Dolphy, most notably in a trio with bassist Henri Texier and drummer Aldo Romano, which effectively alternates 'inside' and 'outside' elements in its concert programs.

Bibliography

Dean, Roger Thornton. 1992. *New Structures in Jazz and Improvised Music Since 1960*. Buckingham: Open University Press.

Litweiler, John. 1984. *The Freedom Principle: Jazz After 1958*. New York: Da Capo Press.

Such, David G. 1993. *Avant-Garde Jazz Musicians: Performing 'Out There'*. Iowa City, IA: University of Iowa Press.

ALYN SHIPTON

Power Chord

The term 'power chord' refers to a particular guitar voicing commonly heard in rock music. A power chord is not really a chord, since chords contain three or more notes; it is a two-note interval of a perfect fifth, which consists of a root note and the fifth note of the major scale: do and sol in solfège. The root note is often doubled one octave higher in pitch. Generally played on an electric guitar with a distorted amplifier, the perfect fifth is a powerful sound – hence the term 'power chord.'

The power chord involves a movable hand position, playable in many areas of the guitar fretboard, although usually rooted on the lower-pitched strings of the guitar. Generally, the notes of the power chord are played simultaneously; they can also be inverted, with the fifth note of the scale voiced lower than the root (in reality, a perfect fourth). The widespread use of the power chord can be traced to the use of distortion effects; elaborate chord voicings do not necessarily translate well in distorted sound, so power chords allow guitarists to give a sense of the music's harmony, but with less dissonance.

WAYNE EAGLES

Rapping

'Rapping' is a term used to denote a vocal presentation in which a rapper uses spoken or semi-spoken declamations, most usually in the form of rhyming couplets. These declamations, rather than any other, more traditional musical elements, are considered the emotional focal point of the performance.

Rapping's verbal virtuosity has many predecessors in black expressive culture, although direct lines of influence may vary from artist to artist. These include: the dozens and toasting traditions from Jamaica and the United States; children's games like 'Pattin' Juba,' black girls' cheerleading and double-dutch chants; black preaching; jazz vocalese; radio DJs' verbal patter; jive scat; courting rituals; lovers' raps (i.e., Isaac Hayes, Barry White, Millie Jackson); the political storytelling of Gil Scott-Heron and the Last Poets; and the half-spoken vocal delivery of performers such as James Brown and George Clinton, among others.

The practise of rapping emerged during the mid-1970s from the underground 'hip-hop' culture of African-American and Afro-Caribbean youths in the South Bronx and upper Manhattan neighborhoods of New York City. Hip-hop culture comprised graffiti writing, break dancing, a distinctive style of dress and rap music. Most accounts consider the commercial origin of rap performance to be a hit recording, 'Rapper's Delight' by the Sugarhill Gang, which climbed to number 36 in the US charts in 1979.

Within rap practise itself, a musical division of labor appeared which has continued to shape rap developments. In the early days of rap, DJs working in the New York City club scene, in parks and at neighborhood parties supplied music by mixing various 'beats' and snippets of sound from recordings in order both to compel their audiences to dance and to establish their reputations. Some DJs would supply relatively simple 'raps' along with their beats, a practise that ultimately developed into more elaborate rhyming lyrics. Eventually, MCs (a term borrowed from 'Master of Ceremonies') or rappers appeared, and they became the focal point of rap performances as they raised the artistic stakes in rap's lyrical sphere. The role of DJs also attracted keen interest as the technology they used became more electronically sophisticated. DJs began to take recorded 'samples' from a dizzying variety of sources and mix them in inventive ways to create appealing rhythm tracks over which rappers would spin out their dense epic narratives. The historical trajectories of musical developments growing out of the DJ legacy are rich enough to deserve their own attention.

Whether performed 'freestyle' (completely or semi-improvised) or meticulously planned, rap performances are crafted to sound fresh and spontaneous. Equal evaluative weight is given to the poetic invention in the lyrics and to the musical means of delivery, although listeners experience the emotive import of the lyrics, varied timbral intonation and subtle rhythmic delivery as a resolute composite. The poetry itself must convey to listeners – through complex uses of metaphor, simile, irony, parody and double entendre, among many other techniques – both an immediacy of communication and a museful virtuosity. Subtle plays on language use abound in rap practise. Rappers perform their verses primarily in rhyming couplets, but a rich variety of poetic structures exists within the practise. A performance typically encompasses an extraordinary number of intertextual references, including current events, US history, popular culture, black folk culture, other rap performances and up-to-date, geographically specific slang from youth culture. It is impossible to generalize about the subject matter in rap because, as a genre, the lyrics range from the socially responsible to the most outlandish, calculated nihilism designed to generate controversy: acrid social critique, self-help philosophies, notions of racial uplift, misogyny, comedy, phallocentric braggadocio, artistic rivalries with other rappers, inner-city violence, love, racial strife, gender relationships, Islam, sexuality, parties and youthful leisure are among the many topics covered in a typical performance. Although rapping in performance practise has been from its beginning an essentially male endeavor, many female rappers are also recognized as leading figures in its brief history.

While many accounts stress the revolutionary aspects of rap practise, a good number of its aesthetic requirements fit squarely within the traditions of other African-American musical styles. As with the best jazz soloists and virtuoso soul singers, the quality of a rap presentation is judged by a rapper's mastery of several elements of musical performance, including clarity, originality, timbral inflection, emotional focus, culturally coded 'body attitudes,' and rhythmic flexibility and invention. At the same time, the degree to which rapping – an essentially non-sung vocal performance – has become such a widely accepted practise within the popular music sphere indicates that it should certainly be considered a significant development in the history of popular song.

As a set of performance practises that have given rise to a range of successful commodities in the global marketplace, rap music has responded in many strikingly self-conscious ways. Many rappers critique and, in some cases, celebrate, capitalism, their relationships with record labels and conspicuous consumption, among other related topics. Digital sampling itself presents a direct challenge to the traditional legal and ethical issues surrounding ownership of musical gestures and culture. These issues, together with the supply and demand imperative of the music business, continue to shape the narrative, thematic and musical content of rap recordings. If a specific thematic or musical approach is successful in the marketplace, it will most certainly be reproduced by other artists; and it will most certainly be critiqued in practise by others.

That rappers appear frequently as guest artists on non-rap recordings demonstrates the practise's influence in US musical culture. Fashions sported by rap artists have continually influenced trends throughout the United States and the world. The rapping practise itself has attracted an international following and has inspired similar developments in many countries around the world (where rappers perform in their own language rather than in English).

Bibliography

Gaunt, Kyra D. 1995. 'The Veneration of James Brown and George Clinton in Hip-Hop Music: Is It Live? Or Is It Re-memory?' In *Popular Music: Style and Identity*, ed. Will Straw et al. Montréal: The Centre for Research on Canadian Cultural Industries and Institutions, 117–22.

Hager, Steven. 1984. *Hip Hop: The Illustrated History of Break Dancing, Rap Music, and Graffiti*. New York: St. Martin's Press.

Perkins, William Eric. 1996. *Droppin' Science: Critical Essays on Rap Music and Hip Hop Culture*. Philadelphia: Temple University Press.

Rose, Tricia. 1994. *Black Noise: Rap Music and Black Culture in Contemporary America*. Hanover and London: Wesleyan University Press.

Toop, David. 1991 (1984). *Rap Attack 2: African Rap to Global Hip Hop*. London: Serpent's Tail.

Walser, Robert. 1995. 'Rhythm, Rhyme, and Rhetoric in the Music of Public Enemy.' *Ethnomusicology* 39(2): 193–217.

Discographical Reference

Sugarhill Gang, The. 'Rapper's Delight.' Sugar Hill 542. *1979*: USA.

Discography

Arrested Development. *Three Years, Five Months & Two Days in the Life of . . .* Chrysalis F2-21929. *1992*: USA.

A Tribe Called Quest. *People's Instinctive Travels and the Paths of Rhythm*. Jive 1331. *1990*: USA.

De La Soul. *Three Feet High & Rising*. Tommy Boy 1019. *1989*: USA.

Dr. Dre. *The Chronic*. Death Row 57128. *1992*: USA.

Eric B. & Rakim. *Paid in Full*. Island 842 589-2. *1987*: USA.

Grandmaster Flash & the Furious Five. *Greatest Hits*. Sequel NEM622. *1994*: USA.

Guru. *Jazzmatazz: An Experimental Fusion of Hip-Hop and Jazz, Vol. 1*. Chrysalis F2-21988. *1993*: USA.

Heavy D and the Boyz. *Living Large*. Uptown MCAD-5986. *1987*: USA.

Ice Cube. *AmeriKKKa's Most Wanted*. Priority SL-57120. *1990*: USA.

LL Cool J. *Radio*. Def Jam/Columbia CK-40239. *1985*: USA.

MC Lyte. *Lyte as a Rock*. First Priority Music 90905. *1988*: USA.

NWA. *Straight Outta Compton*. Priority SL-57112. *1989*: USA.

Public Enemy. *Fear of a Black Planet*. Def Jam CK-45413. *1990*: USA.

Queen Latifah. *All Hail the Queen*. Tommy Boy 1022. *1989*: USA.

Run-D.M.C. *Together Forever: Greatest Hits, 1983–1991*. Profile 1419. *1991*: USA.

Salt-N-Pepa. *Hot, Cool & Vicious*. Next Plateau PL-1007. *1986*: USA.

2 Live Crew. *Sports Weekend: As Nasty As They Wanna Be, Pt. 1*. Luke Records 91720. *1991*: USA.

Yo-Yo. *Black Pearl*. EastWest America 92120. *1992*: USA.

GUTHRIE P. RAMSEY, JR.

Reading

'Reading' was the term applied to early jazz bands that played from written arrangements rather than from aural memory. In New Orleans at the beginning of the twentieth century, Buddy Bolden's band was not a 'reading' band, whereas the rival group of John Robichaux was. Both played popular songs of the day, but with Robichaux's band using formal arrangements and Bolden's band playing by ear. In syncopated orchestras such as Will Marion Cook's, there was sometimes a mixture of reading and non-reading players. The distinction continued to be an issue in early jazz and in the 'revival' of traditional jazz in the 1940s and 1950s: guitarist Danny Barker classified many illiterate players as 'ratty' or 'ham fat' musicians, who busked an approximation of the correct harmonies and melodies. The harmonic sophistication required of bebop musicians ensures that the majority are fluent 'readers,' but in the swing era many bands managed with poor reading skills. When Count Basie came to New York in 1936–37, he had to replace many of his original Kansas City personnel with more literate players in order to play the floor shows the band was expected to accompany, an experience shared by several other bands of the period.

Bibliography

Barker, Danny. 1988. *A Life in Jazz*, ed. Alyn Shipton. New York: Oxford University Press. (First published London: Macmillan, 1986.)

Barker, Danny. 1998. *Buddy Bolden and the Last Days of Storyville*, ed. Alyn Shipton. London and Washington: Cassell.

Clayton, Buck. 1986. *Buck Clayton's Jazz World*, ed. Nancy Miller Elliott. London: Macmillan.

ALYN SHIPTON

Recording Session

Introduction

A recording session is a unit of time devoted to the production of commercial recordings. In the earlier days of recording, sessions could be held in the field (by 'field units') as well as in recording studios. However, since that time (and with the possible exception occasioned by the advent of home recording studios in the 1990s), the recording session has come to be associated exclusively with the studios of recording companies.

The duration and character of the recording session have been influenced by the technical development of sound recording and the business organizations that control it. Because of agreements that the AFM (American Federation of Musicians – United States) and the MU (Musicians Union – United Kingdom) have had with the recording industry, the standard length of the recording session has been three hours. Generally speaking, producers have reckoned to complete four tracks in a session. Running over the three-hour period results in overtime payments to musicians.

A 'session' is also a coming together of musicians, recording engineers and producers as they create new music. Until the 1990s, when home recording became increasingly common, commercial sound recording had been a collaborative art that drew on the talents of several different professions in synthesizing artistic and technological skills. Most of the popular music recorded since the late 1960s has been the result of this collaboration.

History

The first recording sessions were carried out in laboratories under controlled conditions. In the 1880s, experimenters in Thomas Edison's and Alexander Graham Bell's laboratories perfected the acoustic recording of sound. They created the first recording studios and defined the roles of engineers and musicians.

The acoustic recording horns were sensitive to sound only within a short distance, and little consideration was given to the acoustic properties of the studio, which could be any open room. The equipment was heavy but portable, and this enabled the first recording engineers to take the machine to the artist, often recording in hotel rooms and private homes. The work of recording demanded as many social as technical skills, because performers were often discouraged by the strange sounds of their disembodied voice emerging from the horn of the recording machine. Engineers had to educate musicians on the right way to sing into the horn and console them when the playback sounded nothing like the original. Recordings were carefully timed because of the short duration of the early recording media, but the unit of account was the performance rather than the time it took to record it. Sessions went on as long as required.

The introduction of electronic recording in the mid-1920s drastically changed the studio and the session. Instead of the use of acoustic horns, sound was picked up by microphones and amplified before it was inscribed onto discs. Microphones were very sensitive, and so the musicians were separated from the engineers by baffles and then walls. Musicians performed in the studio while engineers did their work in the control room, which housed the amplification and recording equipment. The distinction between technical and artistic endeavor was reinforced by the growing complexity of the recording machine; only technicians had the knowledge and training to operate it.

The first recording engineers had to carry out all the functions of the session: artistic, technical and managerial. In the electronic era, these functions were divided up and a separate job description established for each. A musical director had the job of hiring musicians and arranging the music. A recording manager supervised the technicians and directed the flow of work in the studio. The recording studio was now part of a large business organization and its output had to be coordinated with the other factors of production.

The transition to electronic recording required heavy investment, and the large companies that accomplished it wanted to maximize the return of their investment in the new technology. Time was now very precisely managed in the studio. The recording session became a fixed unit of time in which a predetermined number of commercial recordings had to be made. Normally, the day's work in the studio was divided into three-hour sessions that were each supposed to produce four commercial recordings. Companies negotiated payments to performers and technicians using the recording session as the unit of account.

Throughout the 1930s and 1940s, most commercial recording was carried out by large, fully integrated companies such as RCA-Victor, which manufactured entertainment for radio, motion pictures and records. The recording session was carried out on the companies' premises and under the strict control of the management; musicians were just another input of production to be incorporated into the business of popular music. The position of 'artist and repertoire' (A&R) person (invariably male) evolved out of the musical director and recording manager positions. The A&R man ran the recording sessions. He picked the songs to be recorded and decided which recordings were to be mass-produced and released. His power was on most occasions absolute and his judgments usually made or broke the careers of performers. One A&R man described the system thus: '[T]he company would pick 12 songs for Peggy Lee and tell her to be at the studio Wednesday at 8, and she'd show up and sing what you told her' (Denisoff 1975, 113).

The corporate control of recording sessions was gradually undermined by technological and economic changes after World War II. The new technology of magnetic recording on tape offered new economy and flexibility in commercial recording. Tape recorders were not as expensive as disc recorders and were much easier to operate, magnetic tape being a more forgiving medium than acetate-covered discs. Much of the mystery of sound recording was dispelled when musicians acquired their own reel-to-reel tape recorders and began to experiment with them.

Magnetic recording lowered the entry costs of commercial recording and enabled smaller companies to compete with the major record companies. During the late 1940s and 1950s, a number of these companies, called 'independents,' recorded new music aimed at new markets. Independents like Sun Records in Memphis or Chess in Chicago have taken the credit for introducing rock 'n' roll.

A recording session in an independent studio in the 1950s was much more relaxed and informal than in the studios of the large corporations. The owner of the independent studio often carried out all the musical, technical and managerial functions, as had been common in the acoustic era. There were no A&R people, and the industry-wide standard of the three-hour session was often disregarded as sessions grew longer and longer. Musicians were allowed to have their say about how a song should be played and recorded. The strict hierarchy of the recording studio was being broken down, and the control room, once out of bounds for musicians, was now open to them.

The recording career of the Beatles illustrates the changes in the recording session in the 1960s. When they first entered EMI's Abbey Road Studios, the Beatles were totally overawed by the experience and did exactly what they were told. Their producer, George Martin, was in control of the proceedings and determined how the songs should be played and what changes had to be made to make them acceptable recordings. The Abbey Road Studios represented not only the most advanced technology of recording, but also the rigid corporate control of the session. This was a factory for recording all kinds of music, with administrative offices, practise rooms and a canteen. The Beatles worked quickly and efficiently within the time frame given to them, recording 14 songs in one memorable day in 1963 for their album *Please Please Me*.

The commercial success of the Beatles and the profits they brought to EMI gave them more influence in their recording sessions. They began to occupy the studios all day, often remaining at Abbey Road well after the facility closed at 10:00 p.m. Their relationship with George Martin changed as they became his equal in the control room. Now they were suggesting changes and employing all the resources of the studio to achieve the sound they wanted in their recordings.

The Beatles' tenure at Abbey Road Studios coincided with a period of rapid technological change in sound recording. Multitrack tape recording and improved methods of noise reduction provided the means to make recordings of recordings – overdubbing meant that a record could be made up of many different recordings rather than just capturing the performance in the studio. When they began working at Abbey Road, the Beatles used two-track tape recorders – one track for vocals and the other for instruments – but within a few years they were utilizing four- and eight-track machines.

The widespread adoption of multitrack recording and overdubbing in recording popular music transformed the recording session. Recording the song onto a tape recorder was now only the beginning of the process, for much of the work in the studio was taken up in editing and mixing the tracks recorded. The strict rules about studio time and the hierarchy of studio work crumbled as recordings were made in a completely different way. The recording session became outmoded as the studio became the place to create rather than to record sound. Musicians were no longer playing their songs directly into the microphones but assembling their music out of many recordings made over long periods of time. Mixing and editing the prerecorded tracks became as important as the original recording. Musicians used the studio to practise and write music and saw it as a workshop where they could use all the technology of sound recording to fabricate new sounds.

The Beatles and their contemporaries played with tape recorders in the studio, inventing such new techniques as 'flanging' – slowing down the turning reels of tape by pressing on the edge of the reel. They brought in exotic instruments to record tracks and pillaged the studio's library of special effects to add unusual noises to their songs. They stayed up all night in the recording studio and filled it with candles and incense. The three-hour recording session was outmoded in many studios as musicians took days and days to record one song. By the late 1960s, a three- or four-minute pop single might represent over 100 hours of studio time.

Two historic recordings emerged from this period that perfectly summed up the innovations and aspirations of popular music in the 1960s. The Beatles' *Sergeant Pepper's Lonely Hearts Club Band* (1967) and the Beach Boys' *Pet Sounds* (1966) showed what could be accomplished with recording technology. They demonstrated that the recording studio was the place where music was created rather than recorded. Both albums took months of studio time to assemble and could not be reproduced live on stage – they were creations of the studio. They set the standards of popular music and the direction that commercial sound recording would follow for the next decade. Making music and recording it had become one indivisible act in the studio. The Beatles and the numerous other groups who attempted to emulate them could say that they made records rather than music.

In the 1970s, studio recording became more complex as the capabilities of multitrack tape recorders increased and more editing techniques were introduced. Recording with 24 tracks was commonplace and some studios used even more inputs. Despite the greater complexity of multitrack tape recorders, their price gradually dropped, which encouraged musicians to buy them and build their own recording studios. The home studio came of age in the 1970s, when many artists equipped a basement or spare room with top-of-the-line recording equipment and made their own master recordings, which could then be mixed and transferred at professional facilities. The recording session had little meaning in the home studio because the equipment was always ready and at hand. The musician operated the machines and managed the process without any help, and could also play a variety of instruments on the recording.

The advent of digital sound recording in the 1980s accelerated this process and brought the home studio within the budgets of many more musicians. Digital recording offers an economical way to achieve the sound quality of the professional studio, and its versatility means that recording can be accomplished in many different formats: tape, minidisc, computer floppy disc and recordable compact disc. The home recording studio of the 1990s was most likely to be built around the computer, which can record, edit, mix and transfer sound. The recording session begins at the flick of a switch.

Bibliography

Denisoff, R. Serge. 1975. *Solid Gold: The Popular Record Industry*. New Brunswick, NJ: Transaction Books.

Escott, Colin, with Hawkins, Martin. 1992. *Good Rockin' Tonight: Sun Records and the Birth of Rock 'n' Roll*. New York: St. Martin's Press.

Gaisberg, Fred W. 1942. *The Music Goes Round*. New York: Macmillan.

Kennedy, Rick. 1994. *Jelly Roll, Bix and Hoagy: Gennett Studios and the Birth of Recorded Jazz*. Bloomington, IN: Indiana University Press.

Lewisohn, Mark. 1988. *The Complete Beatles Recording Sessions*. New York: Harmony Books.

Discographical References

Beach Boys, The. *Pet Sounds*. Capitol T 2458. *1966*: USA.

Beatles, The. *Please Please Me*. Parlophone PMC 1202. *1963*: UK.

Beatles, The. *Sergeant Pepper's Lonely Hearts Club Band*. Parlophone PCS 7027. *1967*: UK.

ANDRE MILLARD

Rehearsal

Introduction

Rehearsal is a form of preparation for performance intended for public presentation. The term 'practise' is sometimes used synonymously with 'rehearsal,' but more often refers to the maintenance and development, in varying proportions, of instrumental skills, with or without specific public presentations in mind.

Several preliminary points need to be made before moving to a discussion of distinctive aspects of rehearsal in various genres of popular music.

Firstly, the differentiations between genres made in the following discussion of the rehearsal are largely notional points of reference, to which no given musical practise will fully correspond. Furthermore, rehearsal protocols that may at first appear to characterize popular music may well be trans-generic, a function of a more generalized politics of social as well as musical production and performance. Gender politics, for example, intrude conspicuously into different styles of popular music rehearsal, partly because they are conducted in relatively informal settings contiguous with everyday life (Cohen 1991; Järviluoma 1997). In her case study of a Finnish *pelimanni* group (a rural group playing folk and traditional dance music), Järviluoma (1997) notes that, when women attended rehearsals, 'at least one of them was always involved in making coffee' (136). Consequences included loss of practising time and therefore the perpetuation of inequities in competence. This situation, however, is more a function of a group's amateur status than of genre, and reproduces the dynamic to be found in amateur art music groups (Finnegan 1989). Similarly, the informal rehearsal venues visualized as peculiar to amateur rock groups have an affinity with classical groups of the same status (Finnegan 1989).

Nonetheless, there are tendencies in popular music that are likely to produce distinctive patterns in rehearsal conditions, such as the emphasis on ear as opposed to score. The category 'popular music rehearsal' embraces a broader range of practises than 'art music rehearsal,' with less distinct boundaries between nonmusical social practise and musical practise.

Secondly, to strengthen the link between popular music practise and its discourses, it is necessary both to uncouple the latter from their traditional associations with, broadly speaking, art music models, and at the same time to refer back to specific instances of popular music practises. The case studies presented here relate to what may be loosely called jazz, rock and folk, because these provide a spectrum of reasonably unexceptionable and representative categories of popular music. Each also supplies sharply focused ethnographically based examples of 'coal-face' studies. With regard to 'folk,' the case study drawn upon here is that of a deeply embedded local tradition, Finnish *pelimanni* music, which is entangled with local cultural life, politics and history. It also has well-established rehearsal protocols which have been the subject of scrupulously researched documentation. While the 'Finnishness' of the choice may surprise some Anglocentric expectations, it is in its eccentric specificity that it becomes an instructive model in the investigation of the global phenomenon known as 'local music tradition.'

Rehearsal Practises in Popular Music

The heterogeneous category of popular music itself embraces wide-ranging variations in rehearsal practises, reflecting, among many other things, different phases in the history of popular music, especially in relation to global mediations and conditions of production and consumption. There is also the very practical question of the function of rehearsal across and within genres. Is the object of a rehearsal to (re)produce a reading of a score, or to prepare for what will, to a large extent, be improvisation? Is the goal a performance or a recording? This diversity can be illustrated by reference to three popular music traditions, which are nonetheless disparate in terms of formal parameters, place and space, and generational appeal: jazz, rock and, more problematically, folk.

Rehearsal Practises in Jazz

Formal rehearsal practises vary enormously within the category 'popular music,' but also within any of its genres. A jazz 'rehearsal' may, on the one hand, consist of several very focused sessions involving scores that set out melodic and harmonic lines against improvised solos. These may be ways of working up original compositions or re-creations of 'classic' recordings for concert performance. Especially in the latter case, the 'score' may be in conventional written notation, chord charts with a running order and written instructions, a recording or a synthesis of collective memory – or any combination or permutation of all of these (Berliner 1994). The role of memory as opposed to a fixed score as the 'storage system' also means that material is likely to be constantly evolving, as in the case of Betty Carter's bands, described in Berliner (1994, 308–309). At one extreme, 'rehearsal' might be as rudimentary as talking through some riffs, themes, breaks and harmonies immediately before a performance, as illustrated, for example, in Eddie Condon's description of a recording session with Fats Waller (Condon 1970, 158–62).

On the other hand, there is also frequent 'rehearsal' of this kind actually on stage – for example, in the briefest rundown before the count-in. If the musicians are immersed in a shared tradition, the leader will frequently announce a song without prior reference to the band, indicate the key with a hand signal and make some comment like 'Do the Ellington ending.' The empathy arising from a shared tradition and repertoire also facilitates continuous 'rehearsal' actually during performance, as in the celebrated Oliver/Armstrong harmonized breaks (Shapiro and Hentoff 1966). This is virtually standard jazz practise, with an extraordinary complexity of spontaneous individual and collective decision-making in jazz rehearsal/performance (Johnson 1996). Perhaps the most minimalist yet continuous form of this rehearsal involves 'eyeballing.' Both a high level of aural alertness and eye contact among members of a jazz group allow continuous 'rehearsal' of the next chorus through signals that call for stop-time choruses, breaks, half-chorus solos, key changes, instrument dropouts and concluding modulations under a cadenza.

Rehearsal Practises in Rock

As in the case of jazz, rehearsal in rock, whether for live or recorded performance, may be much more than the preparation of a preexisting repertoire; rather, it is a major site for the 'composition' of material. Conspicuous exceptions are, of course, concerts that aim to replicate established 'hits' either by their original performers, or by cover or tribute bands. Cohen (1991) documents a range of rock rehearsal formats, many of which overlap with those of jazz groups. Band members may 'workshop' ideas, often using a tape recorder to produce a version of a 'score-in-progress,' which individual members might then work from at home (Cohen 1991, 135). Rehearsal continues in other social practises that are not overtly musical – party and pub conversations or exchange of tapes, for instance (Cohen 1991, 30).

To a greater extent than is the norm in jazz, however, rehearsal in rock is also the compositional phase, with musicians working from fragments as the basis of a collective and largely spontaneous development process (Cohen 1991, 136–38, 151–55). Considerable creative latitude is accorded the 'feel' of each individual, so that the collective dynamic of a rehearsal reflects the broader sociometry of the group (Cohen 1991, 143, 156). In many instances, friends, partners and other musicians attend rehearsals, introducing lines of force that ambiguously traverse the music. Perhaps as a corollary to the play of temperament, musical competence in the traditional sense is regarded ambivalently (Cohen 1991, 138–44, 155–63). The lack of formal musical training that often characterizes rock groups leads to protracted rehearsal phases, although often producing unexpected innovation. An openness to acoustic possibilities that fall outside the institutionalized aesthetics of art music is one reflection of this, producing a very wide field of play in rehearsals.

The Rehearsal Practises of *Pelimannit*

This openness is in strong contrast to the practises employed in Finnish *pelimanni* music, rooted in more traditional, acoustic instrumentation, including accordions, fiddles and mandolins. Sustained by amateur local musicians, the groups include older people playing a predominantly traditional repertoire interspersed with recent local compositions. They play with the music in front of them, although some play only from memory (Järviluoma 2000, 114). Most rehearsal is focused on a forthcoming performance, with considerable discussion of repertoire. While questions of musical form and aesthetics play an important and often primary role in these discussions, close attention is paid to the way in which the group's regional identity will be accentuated by a given item, which may then be chosen even if it is considered 'musically inferior' (Järviluoma 2000, 111). This sense of 'place' might be a function of the title, the style, or even simply knowledge shared by the musicians but not necessarily available to anyone outside the group (Järviluoma 2000, 106–107). The 'place' evoked need not be that of 'self,' but of 'other' (Järviluoma 2000, 108). The 'rehearsal' is thus explicitly a way of preparing a local identity.

This is perhaps the main reason why, notwithstanding similarities with other score-based traditions such as amateur classical groups, the intrusion of local gossip into the rehearsal regime was not regarded as an irritating distraction by the leader/conductor; it also provided a parallel to the larger role played by memory as opposed to reading skills (cf. Finnegan 1989, 242). The *pelimannit* rehearsal was more a process of activating and articulating local lore (including that connected with music) stored in the individual and collective memory than of realizing an inviolable and transcendent design inscribed in a score.

Conclusion

Far from building a comprehensive profile of popular music rehearsal, the foregoing hints at the diversity of practises. Genre as rooted in musical form is no longer a very reliable way of distinguishing musical practises. The frequency, character and location of rehearsal will vary with such factors as the immediate objective, the musicians' level of individual and collective development and their professional status, all of which cut across genre. Because of the high level of improvisation in jazz, for example, it has at least as many resemblances to non-musical improvisatory practises (like theater sports, a form of improvisational theater) as to another form of popular music like that of *pelimannit* musicians (Johnson 1992).

Nonetheless, some broad tendencies in popular music rehearsal can be noted. In popular music *as a whole*, the thrust is likely to be toward a more or less democratic manifestation of individual temperament (within limits imposed by the enveloping social formation), compared with art music rehearsal. Certain broad generalizations may be used to distinguish the rehearsal practises of different musical styles within the category of popular music: in rock, formal rehearsal is likely to play a major role, overlapping with composition, while in jazz formal rehearsal is likely to be rather rare, and in practise to overlap with performance. In the 'folk' form considered here, rehearsal is likely to be implicated explicitly in articulating a sense of place and history.

These samples suggest how variegated the full popular music landscape is. Popular music's practitioners move back and forth along the continuum, linking the local with the global, their rehearsal practises varying accordingly. Perhaps that flexible responsiveness is the common feature by which popular music rehearsals are most likely to be distinguished from rehearsals in the 'classical' music tradition.

Bibliography

The following publications are cited in the foregoing text. The literature on popular music rehearsal is, of course, more extensive. Readers are referred to the reading lists provided in the following publications for a larger sample.

Berliner, Paul F. 1994. *Thinking in Jazz: The Infinite Art of Improvisation*. Chicago and London: University of Chicago Press.

Cohen, Sara. 1991. *Rock Culture in Liverpool: Popular Music in the Making*. Oxford: Oxford University Press.

Condon, Eddie, with Sugrue, Thomas. 1970 (1948). *We Called It Music: A Generation of Jazz*. Westport, CT: Greenwood Press.

Finnegan, Ruth. 1989. *The Hidden Musicians: Music-Making in an English Town*. Cambridge: Cambridge University Press.

Järviluoma, Helmi. 1997. 'Local Construction of Gender in a Rural *Pelimanni*-Musicians Group.' In *Musiikki, Identiteetti ja Ruohonjuuritaso: Amatöörimuusikkoryhmän kategoriatyöskentelyn analyysi* [Music and Identity at a Grass-roots Level: Analyzing the 'Category-Work' of an Amateur Music Group]. Tampere: Acta Universitatis Tamperensis, 129–63. (Reprinted in Moisala, Pirkko, and Diamond, Beverley, eds. 2000. *Music and Gender*. Urbana and Chicago: University of Illinois Press, 51–79.)

Järviluoma, Helmi. 2000. 'From Manchuria to the Tradition Village: On the Construction of Place via *Pelimanni* Music.' *Popular Music* 19(2): 101–24.

Johnson, Bruce. 1992. 'Orality and Jazz Education.' *NMA* (New Music Articles) 10 (October): 39–46.

Johnson, Bruce. 1996. 'Resituating Improvisation.' *The Journal of Improvisational Practice* 2(1)(October): 6–11.

Shapiro, Nat, and Hentoff, Nat, eds. 1966 (1955). *Hear Me Talkin' to Ya: The Story of Jazz by the Men Who Made It*. New York: Dover Publications.

BRUCE JOHNSON

Rhythm (Riddim, Rydim)

To a large degree, reggae revolves around the concept of 'rhythm' ('riddim,' 'rydim' – the orthography varies). Often described as a bass line or a combination of a bass line and a drum pattern, a 'rhythm' may also be conceived in terms of an ostinato. In either case, the term designates a fairly loose musical structure – not quite a song, yet of greater substance than, say, the three chords of the blues or the archetypal I-vi-IV-V 'doo-wop' progression of early 1960s pop.

A 'rhythm' may be said to consist of a recurring musical catch phrase or motif – frequently, but not necessarily (or exclusively), carried by the bass – a chord progression and a recognizable rhythmic pattern. The chord progression is often a two-chord oscillation; common varieties are I-ii (or variations thereof – for example, I^{maj7}-ii^7), I↓VII and i↓VII. Typically, in the studio (or in 'live' performance) a new 'song' (i.e., a set of words and a melody) will be matched with an existing rhythm, rather than being given a unique musical setting.

Of particular significance are the rhythms that were first recorded at Studio One and Treasure Isle in the late 1960s and early 1970s. While these draw on a formidable variety of sources – including German band leader Bert Kaempfert's 'Afrikaan Beat,' the Beatles' 'Norwegian Wood' and the Impressions' 'Minstrel and Queen,' to mention only a few – many of them were, in fact, in-house creations; those from Studio One were more often than not composed by organ player Jackie Mittoo and/or bass player Leroy Sibbles (also lead vocalist with seminal vocal group the Heptones).

Rhythms such as 'Full Up,' 'Joe Frazier' and 'Heavenless' have been recycled countless times since the early 1970s, and in many ways constitute a shared musical repertoire. Indeed, since the 1970s, the number of reggae releases that draw on recycled rhythms has exceeded those that utilize completely original material. Rhythms are far from belonging to the public domain in any legal sense, however, and their reuse has often resulted in fierce battles over copyright and ownership – as in the case of Musical Youth's 'Pass the Dutchie' (1982), an international hit interpretation of the 'Full Up' rhythm. In an extraordinary 1994 recording, 'Original Full Up,' Leroy Sibbles (alongside deejay Beenie Man) explored the fate of a composer of such an 'evergreen,' a poignant reflection on the almost proverbial lack of financial reward in the reggae industry. A handful of rhythms has reached beyond the reggae community – most famously, perhaps, 'Real Rock,' in the shape of Willie Williams's 'Armagideon Time' (1979), covered by UK rock group the Clash in 1980.

In the 1990s, the trend was clearly to 'build' sparser rhythm tracks – sometimes to the point of dispensing with the bass and melody lines altogether in favor of predominantly percussive, 'no-frills' musical backgrounds. Drum patterns, too, became increasingly rudimentary, often consisting of little more than the ubiquitous ♩ ♩ ♩ beat, which, by most accounts, originated with Admiral Bailey's 'Punaany' in 1986. The paradox here, as noted by Bilby (1995), is that while the 'digital' high-tech rhythms so in vogue during the 1990s and early 2000s have been met with scorn by fans of 'authentic' reggae, their percussive character in many ways draws them nearer to an 'African' (or 'Afro-Jamaican') aesthetic than many of the European-derived melodies of so-called 'roots reggae.'

While the rhythms of the 1960s and 1970s have been regularly resurrected, there have been many additions to the canon. Some of them – for example, 'Sleng Teng'

(1985), 'Punaany' (1986) and 'Joy Ride' (1995) – have already become classics. No doubt some of the more recent ones, with colorful names like 'Scarface,' 'Bug' and 'Orgasm,' will eventually join their number.

Tracing the genealogy of rhythms is a favorite pastime of fans and enthusiasts of reggae worldwide. An ambitious first attempt at systematization is the three-volume *Rhythm Wise* series (Hurford and Kaski 1989; Scrivener 1990, 1991). On the Internet, fan-run Web sites offer 'guides' and 'directories' that draw on this work.

All in all, the shared cultural knowledge of rhythms and their origins delineates a translocal community of musicians and fans, as remarkable for its informal character and relative distance from the multinational record companies as for its 'traditional,' yet state-of-the-art, approach to music-making.

Bibliography

Barrow, Steve, and Dalton, Peter. 1997. *Reggae: The Rough Guide*. London: Rough Guides Ltd.

Bilby, Kenneth. 1995. 'Jamaica.' In Peter Manuel, with Kenneth Bilby and Michael Largey, *Caribbean Currents: Caribbean Music from Rumba to Reggae*. Philadelphia: Temple University Press, 143–82.

Hurford, Ray, and Kaski, Tero. 1989. *Rhythm Wise*. London and Helsinki: Muzik Tree and Black Star.

Scrivener, Jean. 1990. *Rhythm Wise Two*. Helsinki: Black Star.

Scrivener, Jean. 1991. *Rhythm Wise Three*. Helsinki: Black Star.

Discographical References

Admiral Bailey. 'Punaany.' Jammys. *1986*: Jamaica.

Beatles, The. 'Norwegian Wood.' *Rubber Soul*. Parlophone PCS 3075. *1965*: UK.

Clash, The. 'Armagideon Time.' *Black Market Clash*. Nu Disk/Epic 4E 36846. *1980*: USA.

Kaempfert, Bert. 'Afrikaan Beat.' *Afrikaan Beat*. Decca DL 74273. *1962*: USA.

Impressions, The. 'Minstrel and Queen.' ABC-Paramount 10357. *1962*: USA.

Musical Youth. 'Pass the Dutchie.' MCA 52149. *1982*: USA.

Sibbles, Leroy, and Beenie Man. 'Original Full Up.' Digital B. *1994*: Jamaica.

Williams, Willie. 'Armagideon Time.' Studio One. *1979*: Jamaica. Reissue: Williams, Willie. 'Armagideon Time.' *Armagideon Time*. Heartbeat 3509. *1992*: USA.

Discography

Burning Spear. 'Joe Frazier.' Studio One. *1971*: Jamaica.

Downbeat the Ruler – Killer Instrumentals: Best of Studio One, Vol. 3. Heartbeat 38. *1988*: USA.

Joy Ride. VP 3103. *1996*: USA.

Minott, Sugar. 'Rydim Matic.' Harry J. *1985*: Jamaica. Reissue: Minott, Sugar. 'Rhythmatic.' *Inna Reggae Dance Hall*. Heartbeat HB 29. *1986*: USA.

Smith, Wayne. 'Under Me Sleng Teng.' Jammys. *1985*: Jamaica.

HASSE HUSS

Rimshot

In drumming, a rimshot is a stroke that involves striking the rim of the drum and the drumhead simultaneously with the same stick. The resulting sound is generally sharper, brighter and more cutting than that made when the drumhead is simply struck. The technique is most often used on the snare drum, and it is frequently employed by rock, pop and blues drummers when they play the loud backbeats (beats 2 and 4 in a 4/4 bar) that characterize that music. Rimshots are frequently employed on tom-toms in Afro-Cuban and reggae music, giving a bright, metallic quality to the notes.

The standard rimshot is played by bringing the stick down so that the shoulder, or shaft, of the stick strikes the rim at the same time as the tip, or bead, of the stick strikes the drumhead. A popular variation of the rimshot technique is one called the cross-stick, in which the tip of the stick rests on the drumhead and the stick is pivoted so that its shoulder strikes the rim, producing a bright 'pop' sound. The cross-stick technique is frequently used to simulate the sound of claves in styles such as the Brazilian bossa nova, and it is also popular among rock, pop and country drummers for ballads.

Another rimshot variation is the stick shot, in which the tip of one stick rests on the drumhead with its shoulder resting on the rim, and is struck by the other stick. Some refer to the technique of striking only the rim as a rimshot, but that is more commonly called a rim click.

RICK MATTINGLY

Ring Shout/Ring Shouting

An anonymous writer in *The Nation* of 30 May 1867 (quoted in Krehbiel 1914) described a plantation 'praise' meeting, which was followed by a gathering of old and young African Americans, some of them 'half-clad field hands' who, 'when the "sperichil" is struck up, begin first walking and by and by shuffling around, one after the other, in a ring. The foot is hardly taken from the floor, and the progression is mainly due to a jerking, hitching motion which agitates the entire shouter and soon brings out streams of perspiration.' The writer's description was of a 'ring shout,' which often 'lasts into the middle of the night, [and] the monotonous thud, thud of the feet prevents sleep within half a mile of the praise-house.' Many similar descriptions exist of the circle of dancers, slowly revolving with shuffling steps in a counterclockwise direction, sometimes to singing or hand-clapping, and with wriggling, hip-shaking and rhythmic heel-tapping (Parrish 1942; Courlander 1963, 194–200; Jones and Hawes 1972).

Ring shouts were ostensibly religious, although some of the words sung to the shout were distinctly profane, and the rhythms made to simulate a railroad train (Carmer 1935). Ring shouts were recorded in the 1950s in the Georgia Sea Islands as part of a project to maintain old traditions, but possibly the three titles recorded by Austin Coleman and a small group in Jennings, Louisiana in July 1934 best convey the intensity and the train-like rhythms of the ring shout.

It is likely that the ring shout is among the most persistent of African survivals, this form of dancing in Africa having been described and recorded on many occasions. The circle formed by the dancers served to define and possess space (Sachs 1937). Dr. Lorenzo Turner traced the word to the Arabic *Saut*, or encircling of the Kaaba, which may account for its use in describing religious ring dances, including those performed at funerals. It may be noted that Colonel Wentworth Higginson recalled the 'rhythmic barbaric chant called a "shout" beside the campfire' during the Civil War, which was sung at nocturnal funerals.

The songwriter and composer George Gershwin became interested in the shout during research in the South Carolina sea islands for *Porgy and Bess* and, if his librettist DuBose Heyward, who accompanied him, is to be believed, participated in a shout on James Island, 'to the delight of the congregation' (Jablonski and Stewart 1973, 221). Dena Epstein has suggested that there is a related style of shouting, in which the singers break into foot-stomping and hand-clapping, and that this may be what Gershwin heard (1977, 286).

In more recent times, the word 'shout' has been applied more loosely to both ecstatic dancing and singing, while in the work of some African-American scholars, notably Sterling Stuckey (1987) and Samuel Floyd (1991, 1995), who applies Stuckey's approach specifically to music, the ring shout has taken on enhanced significance in discussions of survivals and essences, as an activity of 'ancient African provenance' that became 'central to the cultural convergence of African traditions in Afro-America' (Floyd 1991, 266–67).

Bibliography

Carmer, Carl. 1935. *Stars Fell on Alabama*. London: Lovat Dickson and Thompson.

Courlander, Harold. 1963. *Negro Folk Music, U.S.A.* New York: Columbia Press.

Epstein, Dena J. 1977. *Sinful Tunes and Spirituals: Black Folk Music to the Civil War*. Urbana, IL: University of Illinois Press.

Floyd, Samuel A. 1991. 'Ring Shout! Literary Studies, Historical Studies, and Black Music Inquiry.' *Black Music Research Journal* 11(2): 265–87.

Floyd, Samuel A. 1995. *The Power of Black Music: Interpreting Its History from Africa to the United States*. New York: Oxford University Press.

Jablonski, Edward, and Stewart, Lawrence. 1973. *The Gershwin Years*. Garden City, NY: Doubleday.

Jones, Bessie, and Hawes, Bess Lomax. 1972. *Step It Down: Games, Plays, Songs and Stories from the Afro-American Heritage*. New York: Harper and Row.

Kemble, Frances Anne. 1961 (1863). *Journal of a Residence on a Georgian Plantation in 1838–1839*, ed. John A. Scott. London: Jonathan Cape.

Krehbiel, Henry Edward. 1914. *Afro-American Folksongs: A Study in Racial and National Music*. New York and London: G. Schirmer.

Parrish, Lydia. 1942. *Slave Songs of the Georgia Sea Islands*. New York: Farrar, Straus and Company.

Sachs, Curt. 1937. *World History of the Dance*. New York: W.W. Norton and Company.

Stuckey, Sterling. 1987. *Slave Culture: Nationalist Theory and the Foundations of Black America*. New York: Oxford University Press.

Discography

Negro Religious Field Recordings from Louisiana, Mississippi, Tennessee (1934–1942), Vol. 1. Document Records DOCD-5312. *1994*: Austria.

PAUL OLIVER and DAVID HORN

Scat Singing

Scat singing is a style of wordless jazz singing in which meaningless syllables are sung as part of an improvised melodic line, generally over a preexisting harmonic structure. This form of vocalization allows the voice to assume the role of an instrument, that is, to be used as if it were an instrument engaged in improvised solos. Scat singing has been taken by some writers to connect with other aspects of African and African-American musical practises. The scat singing of Louis Armstrong and Cab Calloway, for example, has been described by W.L. James as 'using old folk song principles to supplement the normal means of singing' (quoted in Floyd 1995, 117).

Louis Armstrong's 'Heebie Jeebies' (1926) is considered to be the first recorded example of scat singing, and is reported to have resulted from Armstrong's need to improvise when he dropped his sheet of lyrics while recording. Leading exponents of the genre from the swing era include Cab Calloway (who sang about scat as well as actually scatting) and Ella Fitzgerald. Dizzy Gillespie, with vocalists Joe Carroll and Kenny Hagood, extended the idea into modern jazz in bebop vocals such as 'Oop-pop-a-dah' (1947). This expanded the melodic and syllabic flexibility of scat, and the linguistic possibilities were explored by multi-instrumentalist Slim Gaillard in a nonsense language called 'Vout,' and by the group Lambert, Hendricks and Ross, who created long stream-of-consciousness lyrics to sing to the lines of previously improvised melodies by, for example, Lester Young. Many singers developed the idea, but in the 1990s the technique was extended into other areas of vocal practise, through explorations of constriction or extremes of range and volume, by such performers as Phil Minton and Kurt Elling.

Bibliography

Floyd, Samuel A. 1995. *The Power of Black Music: Interpreting Its History from Africa to the United States*. New York: Oxford University Press.

Friedwald, Will. 1991. *Jazz Singing*. London: Quartet.

Discographical References

Armstrong, Louis. 'Heebie Jeebies.' OKeh 8300. 1926: USA. Reissue: Armstrong, Louis. 'Heebie Jeebies.' *This Is Jazz, Vol. 1*. Sony 64613. *1996*: USA.

Gillespie, Dizzy. 'Oop-pop-a-dah.' Victor LJM 1009. 1947: USA. Reissue: Gillespie, Dizzy. 'Oop-pop-a-dah.' *The Complete RCA Victor Recordings 1937–1949*. Bluebird 66528. *1995*: USA.

ALYN SHIPTON

Screaming (Wailing)

'Screaming' was first used ca. 1940 to describe either passages featuring loud, high notes played on a wind instrument or a single such note. A good example of 'screaming' is the sound of a trumpet player like Roy Eldridge in passages such as those found in his solo from the second bridge to the end on his recording of 'Rockin' Chair' with Gene Krupa.

'Wailing' was used in a similar way as early as the late 1920s, specifically to describe the sound of the brass and clarinet/saxophone sections of bands such as those led by Duke Ellington (e.g., 'The Mooche') or Fletcher Henderson (e.g., 'The Stampede'). Wailing also connotes a more general sense of 'playing well' or 'performing well' with great feeling.

'Screaming' has also been used to describe a specific singing technique, derived largely from African-American gospel and blues styles, in which the voice is extended above the customary register with a corresponding roughness in tone. This technique is much used by soul and soul-influenced singers, and a great deal of skill is required to maintain control of pitch – a skill possessed by the best performers in the style, such as James Brown (e.g., 'Lost Someone' from *Live at the Apollo*), Wilson Pickett and Aretha Franklin.

Bibliography

Brackett, David. 1995. 'James Brown's "Superbad" and the Double-Voiced Utterance.' In *Interpreting Popular Music*. Cambridge: Cambridge University Press, 108–56.

Mabie, Janet. 1993 (1930). 'Ellington's "Mood in Indigo": Harlem's "Duke" Seeks to Express His Race.' In *The Duke Ellington Reader*, ed. Mark Tucker. New York and Oxford: Oxford University Press, 41–44. (First published in *Christian Science Monitor* (13 December 1930).)

Discographical References

Brown, James. 'Lost Someone.' *Live at the Apollo*. King K826. *1963*: USA.

Ellington, Duke. 'The Mooche.' OKeh 8623; mx W.401175-A. 1928: USA.

Henderson, Fletcher, and His Orchestra. 'The Stampede.' Columbia 654-D; mx 142205-3. 1926: USA.

Krupa, Gene, and His Orchestra. 'Rockin' Chair.' OKeh 6352; mx 30830-1. 1941: USA.

DAVID BRACKETT

Sean-nós

Sean-nós, meaning 'old style,' is a style of singing that belongs to the Irish tradition. It is a solo art – the voice is unaccompanied by an instrument, and any accompaniment by other singers is in unison, as Irish traditional music in general does not employ harmonies. *Sean-nós* singing is found primarily in the west of Ireland, in *Gaeltacht* (Irish-speaking) areas, and is performed live at sessions in public houses and at informal social and family gatherings.

Sean-nós songs are sung in Irish, and the language and text are considered to be equally as important as the tune. The melodies are learned aurally – singing is thought to be best learned by imitation rather than from notation or a tutor. The use of ornamentation offers a small degree of variation between singers and between local styles. It takes two forms: melismatic, in which additional notes embellish the main notes; and intervallic, in which changes or additions are made to the intervals between the main notes.

The content of *sean-nós* songs consists of stories and laments. These tales of love, death and mishap may be localized, referring to characters and places known to singers and audience, or they may use symbolism to describe universal subjects, such as sex, nationalism and religion. The respect granted to singers enhances the power of their performance; quiet (*ciuneas*) is often called for and interruption frowned upon. Carson (1996) describes *sean-nós* singers as adrift, alone and isolated when they perform their songs, suggesting that the singers' practise of holding or 'winding' their hands while performing is a form of existential anchor, as is the tendency to speak the last few words of a song as if reentering the real world from some transcendental plane.

'Mouth music' or 'diddling,' in which dance tunes are performed by singers instead of instrumentalists, also derives from *sean-nós*. Like Irish instrumental music, *sean-nós* songs have long been collected and translated by enthusiasts, both in Ireland and abroad, and disseminated through recordings.

The influence of *sean-nós* on popular music is, however, restricted by the emphasis on solo acoustic performance, and, although allied to ballad singing through its narrative form, *sean-nós* is at odds with rock and pop formats through the irregularity and changing nature of its phrasing. It has had some influence, however, perhaps more notably in live performance, and singers such as Sinéad O'Connor and Dolores O'Riordan of the Cranberries reflect this influence in the ornamentation of their vocal melodies. The influence is more pronounced in Irish speakers from traditional music backgrounds, such as Enya, Clannad, and Iarla Ó Lionáird of the Afro Celt Sound System; these musicians have all used synthesizers to great effect in backing their singing, recreating the distance between the voice and ambient background noise.

Bibliography

Carson, Ciaran. 1996. *Last Night's Fun: A Book About Music, Food and Time*. London: Pimlico.

Kopka, Matthew. 1997. *Celtic Mouth Music* (with CD). New York: Ellipsis Arts.

O'Canainn, Tomás. 1978. *Traditional Music in Ireland*. London: Routledge & Kegan Paul.

Discography

Afro Celt Sound System. *Volume 1: Sound Magic*. Realworld CDRW61. *1996*: UK.

Enya. *Enya*. BBC Records REB 605. 1986; *1987*: UK. Reissue: Enya. *Enya: The Celts*. WEA 4509911672. *1992*: UK.

O'Connor, Sinéad. *I Do Not Want What I Haven't Got*. Ensign CHEN 14. *1990*: UK.

Ó Lionáird, Iarla. *The Seven Steps to Mercy*. Realworld CDRW67. *1997*: UK.

ABIGAIL GILMORE

Session

The term 'session' in popular music refers to gatherings of musicians in a particular place over a short but loosely defined period of time. Performance can be for various purposes, as in 'jam session' (collective improvisation, sometimes of a competitive character, and usually for the enjoyment and benefit of the musicians taking part, rather than for those of any audience) or 'recording session' (where non-musicians are also involved), but the term does not denote formality. The comparative lack of formality distinguishes a session from a rehearsal (whose usual aim as a more structured occasion is the preparation of a piece or pieces of music for public consumption – it should be noted that the degree of formality with a rehearsal differs between genres of popular music) and a performance (although 'jamming' may be a part of a performance as, for example, at festivals and benefit concerts).

The term 'session' has, however, taken on a more specific meaning in the world of Celtic music, where it refers, once again, to an informal gathering of musicians, this time usually in a public house (pub). Sessions vary widely, but consist of traditional Celtic music, predominantly Irish and instrumental in content, although variants include Breton, Scottish and English music sessions. Some sessions accommodate singers: *sean-nós* sessions are for singers only, whereas other sessions use songs to contrast with instrumental material. Musicians play traditional tunes in sets of two or more, on acoustic instruments such as fiddles, flutes, *Uilleann* pipes, accordions, banjos and *bodhráns*.

The session represents a very different mode of performance from other forms of musical delivery, and has no direct equivalent in pop, rock or folk music. Musicians may come and go at leisure, switching from audience member to performer in the time it takes to pick up an instrument. No two sessions are identical, since the session's participants, as well as its content, vary. The musical material derives from the repertoires of participants, and its course is dictated by mood, precedence and the dominance of whoever is 'leading the tune.' The traditional music session should not, however, be confused with a 'jam' or improvisational session. Order is maintained through numerous implicit social rules, learned through experience and interaction, which govern both behavior and music. These rules can cover a range of elements, from seating arrangements to the number of times tunes are played, from acceptable instruments to the versions of tunes that are considered correct.

Many factors contribute to the session as an event, from the background and proficiency of musicians, to its location, the time of day and the alcohol consumed. An essential ingredient of a good session is 'crack,' meaning loosely 'fun' or 'play.' This word has become 'gaelicized' as *craic*, lending it more authenticity and authority. However, sessions are also occasions where technical advice and tips on instrument care can be obtained, as well as new tunes and songs. Thus, sessions offer a collective opportunity for refreshing and maintaining musical traditions.

Distinct from the century-old *ceil'*, in which the emphasis is on the dancing rather than the music, the session is a relatively new phenomenon, representing a shift in emphasis in Irish music from solo performance for listening toward group activity. Hosted in pubs or houses, sessions initially presented an opportunity for musicians to gather together in a migratory context, and as such represented disparate and separated communities. Latterly, revivals in traditional music, together with music tourism, and an increase in Irish pubs around the world have popularized the session, which may often be held at the invitation and expense of a pub's landlord and may involve amplification. Sessions now feature participants from different ethnic and musical backgrounds, and have considerable commercial value. The primary function of the session is, however, social rather than remunerative; as a performance, it can be described as introverted, since its purpose is more for the benefit of the participating musicians than for that of the audience.

Bibliography

Carson, Ciaran. 1986. *The Pocket Guide to Irish Traditional Music.* Belfast: The Appletree Press.

Carson, Ciaran. 1996. *Last Night's Fun: About Music, Time and Food.* London: Pimlico.

Fairbairn, Hazel. 1994. 'Changing Contexts for Traditional Dance Music in Ireland: The Rise of Group Performance Practice.' *Folk Music Journal* 6(5): 567–98.

ABIGAIL GILMORE

Shape-Note Singing

'Shape-note' is a system of musical notation, used mainly for religious songs and hymns, that enables choirs and congregations with no formal musical education to sing in tune. The shapes – including rectangles, triangles, pennants and ovoids – represent the solmization syllables (syllables that stand instead of the names of the notes of the scale): do, re, mi and so on. In most of the music that has been used in shape-note singing since its introduction in the early nineteenth century, only four syllables – mi, fa, so, la – and hence only four shapes are used, although seven syllables and shapes were eventually introduced alongside the previous system.

The suggestion that four solmization syllables were enough for the task was found in the English theory books of Thomas Morley (1597) and, especially, John Playford (1674). In Playford's words, 'six notes were thus used for many years past ... but in these latter times, four only are in use, the which are sol, la, mi, fa ... four being found sufficient for expressing the several sounds, and less burthensome for the memory of practitioners' (1–2) (Taddie 1996, 43). The first, and most enduring,

example of the marriage of the four syllables to four distinct shapes occurred in the religious songbooks published in the southern United States, beginning in the first half of the nineteenth century. This music was often collectively named *Sacred Harp* after the songbooks that were published under that name. (In fact, many other publishers of religious songs used similar notation, forming the common basis of the tradition.)

The most influential songbook issued under the title *The Sacred Harp* was first published in 1844, but was far from being the first book of its kind. The honor of introducing the four-shape system goes to *The Easy Instructor*, possibly published in Philadelphia in 1801, and certainly in New York in 1802. In the system presented by compilers William Little and William Smith, fa was shown as a right-angled triangle, sol as a circle, la as a square and mi as a diamond. Many other books of this type were published, among which Ananias Davisson's *Kentucky Harmony*, and *The Southern Harmony*, compiled by William Walker and published in Spartanburg, South Carolina in 1835, were very successful. However, it was *The Sacred Harp* of 1844 (compiled by Walker's brother-in-law Benjamin Franklin White and Elisha J. King, a young and ill-fated fellow Baptist teacher from Georgia) that continued to be the favorite hymnal of the Southern camp meetings from which it emerged, going through many editions and revisions, the most notable of which was Joseph S. James's 'improvement' of 1911.

The four-syllable, four-shape-note system did not flourish unopposed. The brothers Lowell and Timothy Mason published their own *Sacred Harp* in Cincinnati in 1837, in which they attempted to rid congregational singing both of the four notes and of the largely indigenous North American repertoire the songbooks contained, arguing in favor of seven notes and a more contemporary European style of composition. However, their mission was not helped by their publishers, who, nervous of their share of a growing market, issued the book with the four shape-notes still firmly in place.

Although designed to be used by the musically untutored, *The Sacred Harp* assumed an instructional responsibility, with its early editions carrying an introductory section entitled 'The Rudiments of Music,' which drew extensively on the introductions that had been a typical feature of eighteenth-century New England tunebooks. In the form of replies to simple questions, it explained that the natural position for mi was on the line or space represented by b, but that if b and e were flat then mi would be on a, and so on. Likewise, the horizontal book or 'longboy' (8 3/4" (22.2 cm) by 5 3/8" (13.6 cm)) included 'Lessons for Tuning the Voice,' with exercises in 'Common Time, Minor Key' or 'Triple Time, Major Key.' The volume was divided into parts, the first of which included the 'plain and easy tunes' that often had their origins in folk hymnody. These were followed by the 'more lengthy and elegant pieces' that were used by singing or concert societies. Although Part I included titles such as 'A Sicilian Mariner's Hymn' or 'Solitude in the Grove' and Part II 'A Portuguese Hymn' or 'David's Lamentation,' by far the majority of pieces had one-word titles, which frequently had locational associations: 'Stratfield,' 'Tilden,' 'Williamstown,' 'Clare-mont.' The last named was in Part III, which contained anthems and odes 'of the First Eminence.' As in many shape-note songbooks, the music was given in three- and four-part harmony, the melodies carried by the tenor.

Many of the songbook introductions also contained 'general observations' on how the music was to be sung – advice that may often have been honored in the breach, or at least adapted freely to circumstance. Singing master Allen Carden's *The Missouri Harmony* (9th ed., 1846), for example, counseled the book's users that 'each part [should sing] so soft . . . as will permit the other parts to be distinctly heard,' and that 'in applying the words, great care should be taken that they be properly pronounced, and not torn in pieces between the teeth.' He also warned the over-enthusiastic that 'too long singing at one time, injures the lungs' (10).

It seems likely that, as well as being a practical, indeed educational, tool, the combination of solmization syllables and shape-notes in printed and published form played a significant role in enabling a style of group singing to cohere and become stable. But whereas in eighteenth-century New England an orally transmitted singing style, with much ornamentation, had largely withered and fled before the onslaught of 'regular singing' based on note reading from printed volumes, in the South in the nineteenth century, although the printed shape-notes no doubt eliminated many of the varieties inherent in orally transmitted practise, it also helped others to be preserved and to adapt. It did so because it was a reflection of singing practise more than it was an alternative. Also, the shape-notation was regularly regarded by users as the starting point rather than a representation of the ultimate goal. And indeed, as Taddie (1996) notes, when with time the compilers' attempts to underpin shape-note singing with theory 'more and more reflected the shift to a concept of key that was characteristic of the art music of written traditions, the music moved closer and closer to the older oral tradition of folk music, with its pentatonic, hexatonic, and modal scales' (60).

The rural and 'primitive' nature of the shape-notes led to their being termed 'buckwheat notes' by the somewhat more musically sophisticated, who also looked askance at the way in which, in performance, the median note, mi, was placed, after which the singers customarily sang through the rest of the sequence (fa, sol, la) to ensure that they were all in tune before they sang the words of the verse. From this, the style of singing was also called 'fasola.' For many 'fasola singers,' however, adherence to *The Sacred Harp* was a matter of faith. Its appeal lay in the 'fuging' (fuguing) style, gapped scales and modal tunes that dated from before the American Revolution and that knit the voices in a complex, layered polyphony.

Shape-note singing conventions have remained one of the principal contexts in which *Sacred Harp* hymns are to be heard. While some conventions are held in churches (though without services), 'All Day Singing,' in which singers gather from scattered communities to participate in daylong song festivals punctuated by feasts of simple food, has continued to be popular. At many such singing festivals, 'seven shape-note' hymnals are used as well. Called 'dorayme' songbooks, they use the seven-note system advocated by the Mason brothers and introduced by Jesse Aikin in *The Christian Minstrel*, published just two years after Benjamin White's *The Sacred Harp*. Adopted by the Texas-based Stamps-Baxter Music and by the Tennessee publisher James D. Vaughan, the seven-note system became, and has remained, popular with many singing conventions that use both systems freely. Others adhere to the 'old way' of singing – using portamento, fast note clusters, sudden leaps and sharply punctuated short notes, singing from *The Sacred Harp* under the direction of a singing leader. Brooks (1998) has described how, at such conventions, the leader normally sits in the center, with the singers in a square facing inward. 'Anyone may lead, and all the leaders take turns; thus although each song is supervised by a single individual, that individual is simply one among equals' (44–45). When a fine tune like 'Windham' or 'Sardinia' is sung, the volume, complexity and emotional intensity of such singing are profoundly impressive.

In relation to its popularity in seven Southern states, but most markedly in Alabama, Georgia and Kentucky, shape-note singing has been inadequately recorded. *All Day Singing from 'The Sacred Harp'*, recorded by Alan Lomax in 1959, contains remarkable examples of such singing under the direction of a number of leaders, including performances of music by eighteenth-century New England composers Daniel Read and William Billings, and nineteenth-century North American settings of hymn texts by noted English hymn writers Isaac Watts and Charles Wesley. Although *The Sacred Harp* is customarily associated with Southern white communities, shape-note singing has also been popular, though even less recorded, among some black congregations. The

Middle Georgia Singing Convention No. 1, which recorded in Atlanta in 1930, and the Fa Sol La Singers, who recorded there the following year, are evidence of the longevity of the tradition in black communities.

Bibliography

Aikin, Jesse B. 1846. *The Christian Minstrel*. Philadelphia: S.C. Collins.

Brooks, William. 1998. 'Music in America: An Overview (Part 1).' In *The Cambridge History of American Music*, ed. David Nicholls. Cambridge: Cambridge University Press, 30–48.

Carden, Allen D. 1846. *The Missouri Harmony; or, A Collection of Psalm and Hymn Tunes and Anthems*. 9th ed. Cincinnati: Phillips and Reynolds. (Reprint, with a new introduction, Lincoln, NE: University of Nebraska Press, 1994.)

Cobb, Buell E. 1978. *The Sacred Harp: A Tradition and Its Music*. Athens, GA: University of Georgia Press.

Davisson, Ananias. 1826. *Kentucky Harmony; or, A Choice Collection of Psalm Tunes, Hymns and Anthems in Three Parts*. Harrisonburg, VA: Wartman.

Horn, Dorothy D. 1970. *Sing to Me of Heaven: A Study of Folk and Early American Materials in Three Old Harp Books*. Gainesville, FL: University of Florida Press.

Jackson, George Pullen. 1944. *The Story of the Sacred Harp*. Nashville, TN: Vanderbilt University Press.

Jackson, George Pullen. 1964 (1933). *White Spirituals in the Southern Uplands*. Hatboro, PA: Folklore Associates.

James, Joseph S. 1911. *Original Sacred Harp; Containing a Superior Collection of Standard Melodies, of Odes, Anthems, and Church Music, and Hymns of High Repute*. Atlanta: n.p.

Little, William, and Smith, William. 1802. *The Easy Instructor; or, A New Method of Teaching Sacred Harmony*. New York: G. & R. Waite.

Lowens, Irving. 1964. *Music and Musicians in Early America*. New York: Norton.

Mason, Lowell, and Mason, Timothy. 1837. *The Sacred Harp*. Cincinnati: Truman and Smith.

Metcalf, Frank L. 1937. '"The Easy Instructor": A Bibliographical Study.' *Musical Quarterly* 23: 89–97.

Morley, Thomas. 1597. *A Plaine and Easie Introduction to Practicall Musicke*. London: Peter Short. (Reprint, New York: Da Capo Press, 1969.)

Playford, John. 1674. *An Introduction to the Skill of Musick*. London: W. Godbid. (Reprint, Ridgewood, NJ: Gregg Press, 1966.)

Stanley, David H. 1982. 'The Gospel-Singing Convention in South Georgia.' *Journal of American Folklore* 95(375)(January–March): 1–32.

Taddie, Daniel. 1996. 'Solmization, Scale and Key in Nineteenth-Century Tunebooks.' *American Music* 14(1): 42–64.

Walker, William. 1835. *The Southern Harmony, and Musical Companion*. Spartanburg, SC: William Walker.

White, Benjamin Franklin, and King, Elisha J. 1844. *The Sacred Harp*. Philadelphia: T.K. & P.G. Collins.

Wicks, Sammie Ann. 1989. 'A Belated Salute to the "Old Way" of "Snaking" the Voice on Its (ca.) 345th Birthday.' *Popular Music* 8(1): 59–96.

Discographical References

Fa Sol La Singers, The. *Black Vocal Groups, Vol. 4 (1927–1939)*. Document DOCD-5552. 1931; *1997*: Austria.

Middle Georgia Singing Convention No. 1, The. *Atlanta, Ga. Gospel: Complete Recorded Works in Chronological Order, 1923–1931*. Document DOCD-5485. 1930; *1996*: Austria.

Southern Journey, Vol. 9: Harp of a Thousand Strings. All Day Singing from 'The Sacred Harp'. Notes by Alan Lomax. Rounder 1709. 1959; *1998*: USA.

Discography

White Spirituals from 'The Sacred Harp'. Notes by Alan Lomax. Atlantic SD-1349 (Southern Folk Heritage Series). *1960*: USA.

PAUL OLIVER and DAVID HORN

Singing

Singing is a particular form of human utterance that may be defined as a subset of the larger category of vocalization. Within this category, it is often distinguished from speech and para-linguistic types of utterance (howling, whimpering, shrieking and so on) by reference to its qualities of 'musicality,' especially as manifested in features associated with the concept of melody or melodiousness. However, many characteristics of singing – pitch, rhythmic articulation, specific timbres – are common to the whole territory of vocality. Indeed, most singing takes the form of a vocal utterance that carries words. Not surprisingly, therefore, throughout the cultures of the world singing is, for the most part, closely associated with language; in fact, for centuries, this linkage has given rise to speculation concerning the historical relationship and priority of music and language within the development of human society, a debate that has continued among some evolutionary biologists. Ethnographic and historical evidence suggests that the mutual interaction between speech and singing is especially close in the case of vernacular musics. This is what gives the singing in such musics a sound often thought of as 'natural,' as opposed to the more stylized varieties of singing found, for example, in Western classical music. This should, however, not be taken to imply that singing in popular musics cannot take extreme forms (yelling, growling, yodeling, grunting and so on). The term 'natural' in this formulation (which, in any case, may be suspiciously indebted to a historically specific problematic growing out of European Romanticism) is being opposed to 'art' (the cultivated, the trained, the esoteric) rather than to the 'unnatural.'

The Mechanics

The 'vocal set' (the acoustic qualities associated with individual vernacular languages) is an important factor in distinguishing among the different sounds of popular song from country to country. The physical process inherent in the vocal set is often likened to that of playing a wind instrument, but perhaps a better analogy is a sound system. The creation of all vocal sounds involves a three-stage process: there is a power supply (the lungs), a sound generator (the vocal cords – or folds, as they are sometimes called), and a resonator (the vocal tract, which is the acoustic space between the cords and the lips). Air generated by the lungs is forced through the cords under pressure, causing vibrations that create a complex basic sound. The sound is modified and amplified by various resonances in the vocal tract (called formants) and emerges from the lips as specific pitches or vowels. This resultant sound consists of a number of harmonics (sometimes called partials or overtones), which, in combination, make up the color of individual tones or vowel sounds.

It is possible to isolate and emphasize specific harmonics by changing the shape of the vocal tract to access particular formant frequencies in addition to the fundamental pitch being sung, creating a multiphonic texture. This process gives the distinctive sound of overtone singing associated with some Tibetan monks and Tuvan throat singers. Complex multiphonics are also possible on the inhaled breath, but this has limited use in popular music.

There are other resonances that singers sometimes refer to (for example, head voice, chest voice, sinus tone), and these are useful in classifying vocal types. In classical singing (or popular singing that is influenced by the trained variety), an additional resonance called the singer's formant is available if the larynx is lowered, creating extra acoustic space in the vocal tract. This is responsible for the richer sound and greater projection used in classical singing. The technique is generally not used in contemporary popular music, which can achieve projection while still sounding closer to speech thanks to the use of microphones.

Before and After the Microphone

Popular singing is a type of singing that, in principle, is accessible to anyone, and it does not require a schooled technique. As far as it is possible to tell, styles of folk singing have evolved as extensions of, or in association with, practises of speech (whether conversational or rhetorical). Before the invention of the microphone, this generally meant unaccompanied song or the use of a small number of instruments to support the singer. The variety of technique was immense: it ranged, for example, from the nasal tone and restrained narration style of white ballad singers of the US Appalachian region to the highly ornamented, microtonally inflected approach associated with epic singers in the Balkans; and from the open-throated, relaxed production generally used for lyrical songs across most of Northern Europe to the much more intense technique, produced in throat and nose, typical of love song performance in the Middle East.

With the rise of the pleasure gardens in eighteenth-century Europe and North America (later followed by music hall, variety and vaudeville theaters), popular song in these areas became public entertainment on a much larger scale. This meant that singers had to resort to some of the techniques of classical singing in order to project their sound to the back of a hall. The repertoire, too, often consisted of light classics, arrangements of highlights from classical works, or commercially produced songs influenced by these traditions, and many singers would switch easily from classical to popular singing with only minimal changes to their technique.

The advent of the microphone, and electrical recording, in the mid-1920s gave to nonclassically trained singers the means to reach a large or distant audience without modifying a vernacular technique. The most spectacular early beneficiaries of this technological innovation were the crooners – most famously, Bing Crosby – whose on-the-breath intimations of personal feeling not only depended totally on the microphone, but also used the technology to create a new 'theater' for singing: a virtual space where singer and listener could conduct a relationship without ever meeting. The potential of this shift, for vocal technique as well as for the psycho-semiotics of vocal practise, was decisive for the future of popular singing.

Some Techniques

The emergence of jazz as a distinctive popular music began the process by which the partial rapprochement of popular and classical singing in nineteenth- and early twentieth-century Europe and North America was halted, and to a large extent reversed. The success of Louis Armstrong, in particular, had important consequences for popular singing, especially in connection with his concept of swing as applied to sung texts. In Armstrong's trumpet solos (as in jazz generally), swing consisted of subtle manipulations of the rhythm between the main beats. In his singing, Armstrong applied the same principle at the level of the syllable. This allowed him to unite a speech-like way of singing (particularly notable in his case because of his rather throaty timbre) with the rhythms of the new music. This in turn meant that the African-American community had access to a popular song based on speech, at a time when the middle-class white singing style was still based largely on a kind of sub-classical approach.

Louis Armstrong is also credited with the earliest recorded example of scat singing. While recording 'Heebie Jeebies' in 1926, Armstrong dropped his lyric sheet and had to vocalize nonsense syllables until he could retrieve it. He developed the technique further with 'Basin Street Blues' and 'Squeeze Me' as a means of vocal improvisation that could be used in conjunction with his trumpet playing. Although this occasionally involved a direct imitation of instrumental sounds, the use of nonsense syllables offered the possibility of wordless improvising that was specific to itself and not simply a pastiche. The young Bing Crosby picked this up, together with the broader, speech-related dimensions of Armstrong's singing, and his mastery of microphone technique made him and his own disciple, Frank Sinatra, the most influential figures in jazz-influenced popular vocalism.

What was marginalized in this white appropriation of African-American technique was the bundle of more para-linguistic, 'dirty' sounds typical of a good deal of Afro-diasporic singing; indeed, Sinatra's style was very much based on a smooth legato line, which he maintained through the use of a breathing technique similar to that cultivated by classical singers since the nineteenth century, supporting the voice with controlled pressure from the diaphragm (a band of easily controlled muscle surrounding the spinal cord beneath the lungs). The more varied and often emotionally extreme range of sounds to be heard from many early blues singers – Charley Patton, Son House, Robert Johnson and others – continued to be developed, but elsewhere, within rhythm and blues (R&B) (Muddy Waters, Howlin' Wolf, Elmore James and so on), and their commonly felt associations with representations of a domineering masculinity were picked up by white rockers as the central influence in creating the core male rock vocal technique. In the singing of Mick Jagger, Eric Burdon, the young Van Morrison, Robert Plant and Kurt Cobain, the principal characteristics of this technique became clear: a high-pressure wind supply was pushed through a tightened throat across a wide pitch range, generating (especially in the high register) a sound that seemed to encapsulate insistence, frustration and incipient viol-

ence all at once, while the transatlantic diction also established a new Anglo-American vocal norm.

Before this, however, in the mid-1950s, Elvis Presley initiated a new phase in the popularizing of African-American vocal techniques, combining them with influences from country music to create a unique style full of hiccups, between-the-beat accents and striking register shifts, from chest-voice baritone to falsetto. And only a little later, Bob Dylan drew further on country music techniques – particularly the nasal timbre and quasi-talking mode of address – to create a novel blend of poetry and sound; not only in savage message songs like 'Subterranean Homesick Blues,' but also in love songs such as 'She Belongs to Me,' singing (as it is more usually understood) seems to be only half-realized, to be deliberately placed just out of reach. In the 1970s, punk singing such as Johnny Rotten's with the Sex Pistols reached new levels of anti-musical 'naturalism.' At the same time, though, a long line of theatrical 'divas' continued to flourish, influenced (still) by semiclassical techniques, but also by the legacy of the 'Broadway belt' (a female chest voice forced into a higher than normal register); and the female line, from Shirley Bassey to Céline Dion, had male equivalents: Freddie Mercury, Robbie Williams. Cooler but still speech-like voices pervaded 'indie' rock and synthesizer pop (from Morrissey of the Smiths to Neil Tennant of the Pet Shop Boys). Again, by contrast, there was a strong chest-powered, open-throated, wide-range technique, originating in African-American gospel music and pursued through a lengthy line of soul singers, from Ray Charles, Nina Simone and Aretha Franklin on. Toward the end of the twentieth century, the portmanteau of singing techniques widened still further to accommodate rap. Like Greek tragedy, rap 'singing' is a heightened form of speech that fuses speech melody with a highly poetic rhetorical delivery. Rap began as street entertainment for African-American youth but, at the turn of the century, it could be found in almost all industrialized societies.

If this sketch of vocal techniques current in the late twentieth century in the dominant Anglophone popular music markets seems broad enough, the boundaries are pushed even further out when other cultures are added to the picture. What is striking is that, although in virtually all parts of the world the influence of Anglo-American singing has become clear, and often significant, a huge variety of indigenously distinctive approaches has survived and has continued to develop. A few examples might hint at this. The ornate, ecstatic vocalism of *qawwālī*, the devotional Sufi genre, has reached new heights of popularity, especially through the crossovers explored by Nusrat Fateh Ali Khan, while the most famous voice in Bollywood *filmī*, that of Lata

Mangeshkar, retains the nasal quality typical of north Indian singing, even when surrounded by 'Hollywood' strings. The overtone singing of Tibetan monks and Tuvan throat singers has reached the world music market through the recordings of Kaigal-ool Khovalyg, Sainkho Namchylak, Lama Gyurme and others. Characteristic styles of the Middle East have been renovated – for example, by the celebrated Egyptian singer Umm Kulthūm – and blended with rock and funk, in the Algerian genre, *rai*. The South African *iscathamiya* group Ladysmith Black Mambazo combined the wide-range male-group sounds of Zulu traditions – from deep bass to falsetto – with hymn-tune harmonies, while the group's contemporary in the *mbaqanga* genre, Mahlathini, developed the deep, 'groaning' voice also found in his Zulu background in the context of amplified rock-style textures.

Gender, Identification and Meaning

Singing is intrinsically gendered – or so it seems to most listeners. Characteristic pitch ranges and expressive styles appear to define 'male' and 'female' voice types and genres, and, because the subject matter of most popular songs concerns romance, such characteristics map readily enough onto interpretation. Yet, objectively – that is, listening to a recording with no access to contextual information – it is not always easy to identify the gender of a voice with confidence. Nina Simone can sing low enough to sound like a man, the Bee Gees high enough to sound like women. Bessie Smith's voice is sufficiently powerful to be 'manly,' Michael Jackson's sufficiently light to be 'feminine.' And the range of Diamanda Galas – both in pitch and in extremity of technique – is so vast as to make it plausible to hear her gender, judging by sound alone, as indeterminate. To evaluate gender effectively, then, it is often necessary to have the information provided by context, generic convention and song theme. It is this that makes vocality so important to the application of gender theory to music. Singing offers a site where gender boundaries are policed but are also made available for disruption. Van Morrison's 'Gloria' (1964) presents a classic example of rock vocal machismo: the singer waits for Gloria to come to his room to make him 'feel all right,' his scopophilic sense of power embodied in his leering, aggressive, shouted vocal. When Patti Smith remade the song in 1975, she not only took over this typically male role, exaggerating its machismo to the point of parody, but also embedded her conquest within a narrative of religious morality rejected: bells toll in her version, and they do so to mark her scandalous appropriation of patriarchal authority.

Such gender negotiations represent one aspect, albeit the most important, of the general field of identification patterns opened up by singing in its manifold guises. Voice, a prime marker of identity in everyday life as well as in song, is strangely neglected in early psychoanalysis. Its excursions in popular singing offer a rich field for interpretation, although this is under-theorized as yet. In recent years, scholars influenced by Jacques Lacan, Freud's revisionist disciple, have located the 'invocatory drive,' along with the scopophilic 'gaze,' as one of Freud's 'partial objects' – fetishistic objects of desire. Barthes, Kristeva and Zizek all agree that the voice carries language, and hence, on this level, stands for the symbolic law of culture and meaning. More interestingly, however, they identify an underside: here, Barthes' 'geno-song,' Kristeva's 'semiotic,' Zizek's 'object voice' point toward a place where one becomes aware of a voice anterior to meaning – an impossible but nevertheless tantalizing voice outlawed by language but home to desires both profound and disruptive. For popular song, the irony here is acute: singing practises marked by their closeness to speech, by an intense alliance with language, turn out to offer, through their equally intense centering on vocal body (Barthes' 'grain of the voice'), a route to their own deconstruction.

Bibliography

Dolar, Mladen. 1996. 'The Object Voice.' In *Gaze and Voice as Love Objects*, ed. Renata Salecl and Slavoj Zizek. Durham, NC: Duke University Press, 7–31.

Dunn, Leslie C., and Jones, Nancy A., eds. 1994. *Embodied Voices: Representing Female Vocality in Western Culture*. Cambridge: Cambridge University Press.

Frith, Simon. 1988. 'Why Do Songs Have Words?' In *Music for Pleasure: Essays in the Sociology of Pop*. Cambridge: Polity Press, 105–28.

Frith, Simon. 1996. 'The Voice.' In *Performing Rites: On the Value of Popular Music*. Oxford: Oxford University Press, 183–202.

Laing, Dave. 1990. 'Listen to Me.' In *On Record: Rock, Pop and the Written Word*, ed. Simon Frith and Andrew Goodwin. London: Routledge, 326–40.

Middleton, Richard. 1995. 'Authorship, Gender and the Construction of Meaning in the Eurythmics' Hit Recordings.' *Cultural Studies* 9(3): 465–85.

Potter, John. 1998. *Vocal Authority: Singing Style and Ideology*. Cambridge: Cambridge University Press.

Potter, John, ed. 2000. *The Cambridge Companion to Singing*. Cambridge: Cambridge University Press.

Sundberg, Johan. 1987. *The Science of the Singing Voice*. DeKalb, IL: Northern Illinois University Press.

Toop, David. 1994. *Rap Attack 2: African Rap to Global Hip Hop*. London: Serpent's Tail.

3. Performance Techniques

Discographical References

Armstrong, Louis, and His Hot Five. 'Heebie Jeebies'/'Muskrat Ramble.' OKeh 8300. 1926: USA. Reissues: Armstrong, Louis. 'Heebie Jeebies' and 'Muskrat Ramble.' *Louis Armstrong*. Madacy 2383. *1999*: USA.

Armstrong, Louis, and His Hot Five. 'Two Deuces'/'Squeeze Me.' OKeh 8641. 1928: USA. Reissues: Armstrong, Louis. 'Two Deuces' and 'Squeeze Me.' *Hot Fives & Sevens, Vol. 3*. Jsp 314. *1998*: USA.

Armstrong, Louis, and His Orchestra. 'Basin Street Blues.' OKeh 8690. 1928: USA. Reissue: Armstrong, Louis. 'Basin Street Blues.' *Original Jazz Performances*. Nimbus 2124. *1998*: UK.

Dylan, Bob. 'Subterranean Homesick Blues'/'She Belongs to Me.' Columbia 43242. *1965*: USA.

Morrison, Van. 'Gloria.' Decca F 12018. *1964*: UK.

Smith, Patti. 'Gloria.' *Horses*. Arista 4066. *1975*: USA.

RICHARD MIDDLETON

Slapping (Bass)

Slapping is a percussive style of pizzicato jazz bass-playing originally employed on the double bass, but also applicable to the electric bass guitar. The sound is made by the impact of the string on the instrument's fingerboard; this is achieved by pulling the string away and allowing it to 'snap' back on the fingerboard as the note is produced. The technique was originally employed to amplify the volume of the double bass outdoors, in large halls and on record, and was exemplified by such New Orleans players as 'Pops' Foster, Wellman Braud and John Lindsay. Milt Hinton perfected the technique in Cab Calloway's orchestra, recording Roy Eldridge's composition 'Pluckin' the Bass' (1939). The technique was used only selectively in modern jazz, although Charles Mingus employed it. Free improvisers, including Malachi Favors and Barry Guy, have also used the effect to create percussive and dramatic effects. Electric bassists, notably Jaco Pastorius and Stanley Clarke, have added the style to the vocabulary of the bass guitar.

Bibliography

Shipton, Alyn. 1976. 'Styles of New Orleans Bass Playing.' *Footnote* 7(1): 18.

Discographical Reference

Calloway, Cab, and His Orchestra. 'Pluckin' the Bass.' Vocalion 5406. 1939: USA. Reissue: Calloway, Cab. 'Pluckin' the Bass.' *His Best Recordings*. Best of Jazz 4011. *1996*: USA.

ALYN SHIPTON

Slide Guitar

'Slide' is the common term for the technique of fretting a guitar not, or not only, with the fingers but with a hard, smooth implement, to produce glissandi and other effects. The tool may be a steel bar or wedge designed for the purpose, or a found object, such as a broken-off bottleneck (hence the alternative term 'bottleneck guitar,' used chiefly in blues contexts), small glass bottle, polished meat bone, steel knife handle or blade, or any short length of metal bolt or tube. (Bob Dylan has used a girlfriend's lipstick holder.) The device is held in, or between the fingers of, the fretting hand or, if hollow, slipped onto the third or little finger.

Whatever the implement, its straightness and rigidity make it easier to handle when the guitar is tuned to an open chord (the strings often being raised to prevent buzzing on the frets) and the slide used for whole or partial barré chords as well as for single-string lines, although single-string slide playing is also feasible in standard tuning. Open tunings favored by blues and 'old-time' country musicians have been D (D, A, d, $f\sharp$, a, d^1), E (E, B, e, g, b, e^1) and G (D, G, d, g, b, d^1), but musicians using the pedal steel or the acoustic Dobro resonator guitar have employed numerous other tunings. The slide effect is often used as a responsorial second 'voice' or to imitate natural, animal or mechanical sounds, such as wind, wolf howls, bells or train wheels.

The origin of slide guitar in the United States remains obscure. It has often been claimed that it was inspired by the Hawaiian music disseminated by troupes on the vaudeville circuit and at world fairs in the 1890s and 1900s. Hawaiian guitar techniques have incontrovertible links with slide guitar, but the occurrence of related performance practises in other non-North American contexts, such as the vina of Indian music, suggests that the discovery of a slide technique has been both widespread and random.

Abundantly documented in African-American music is the diddley-bow, a monochord made from wire nailed to a board or to the wooden wall of a house, raised with a bottle or tin can as bridge and resonator, and played like a one-string slide guitar. Many blues guitarists who grew up in the South in the early twentieth century have described the diddley-bow as their first, childhood instrument, and a few continued to play it as adults.

Guitarists have developed a remarkable variety of slide styles through a combination of factors, such as tuning, choice of slide device and playing position (conventional or flat on the lap), and techniques such as finger damping behind the slide to produce a less resonant and metallic effect. Influential figures have included the gospel guitarist Blind Willie Johnson and bluesmen Tampa Red, Robert Johnson, Robert Nighthawk and Muddy Waters. Elmore James, playing slide on electric guitar, opened a path of sonic experiment that was followed by many blues and rock guitarists. Similarly, the work of 'old-time' country slide guitarists like Jimmie

Tarlton and Cliff Carlisle, and of Bob Dunn and Leon McAuliffe in western swing, preceded the innovations of pedal steel players like Speedy West. The legacies of these musicians have become significant patches in the quilt of North American popular music.

Discography

(Almost) Everybody Slides. Sky Ranch SR 652301. 1968–89; *1990*: France.

Blues Masters, Vol. 18: More Slide Guitar Classics. Rhino R2 75348. *1998*: USA.

Jones, Eddie 'One-String.' *One String Blues*. Takoma CDTAK 1023. 1960; *1996*: UK.

Slide Guitar: Streamline Special. Columbia/Legacy CK 65518. 1927–94; *1998*: USA.

White Country Blues (1926–1938). Columbia/Legacy CK 47466. 1926–38; *1993*: USA.

TONY RUSSELL

Street Cries

A 'street cry' is a form of call developed for the purpose of attracting customers to purchase commodities from a vendor. Street cries have been sufficiently melodious to be considered a form of popular singing in their own right, and have been incorporated into popular songs.

The caller of street cries is frequently also the salesperson, although the hoarseness that comes with continual street crying often necessitates the employment of another, possibly a young boy, to cry out the names of the wares for sale. Unlike the call used in other circumstances, the street cry has a contour that tends to conclude on a relatively high note. Depending on the length of the call, it may also be more melodious.

As early as 1415 A.D., the rights of Parisian merchants to sell in the street and to attract purchasers with calls were defined and particularized as to the time of day and the days of the week when they could do so. Although no sellers in the city were more fully documented than those in Paris, throughout Europe, and for several centuries, street vendors using their cries to sell their wares and their skills were extensively recorded by artists in numerous series of popular engravings. A series would usually be in a standard format, with the street hawkers sometimes depicted against contemporary urban backgrounds, but often seen in isolation from their context and with no specific setting drawn. Two dozen *marchands ambulants*, many of them women, were commonly heard and noted in a series. In 'Les Nouveaux Cris qui s'observant journellement dans la Ville et Fauxbourg de Paris,' published in the early eighteenth century from Saint-Severin by J. Maillot, some 60 hawkers were depicted, nearly half of them females selling fruit, fish, herbs, flowers and mushrooms: 'Champignons, mes gros champignons . . .' The throng of street sellers at the

Pont-Neuf was famous for centuries and remained a popular subject for engravers.

No less interesting or various were the street vendors and their calls in Cologne, depicted by Franz Hogenberg in 1589, or the 192 different commodities and their sellers in the streets of Rome, drawn by Hogenberg's contemporary there, Ambrosius Brambilla. Other sets were compiled in Venice and Florence, Milan and Naples, their locations reflected in the range, for example, of fish and other seafood on sale. From Göttingen to Danzig, Berlin to Vienna, a remarkable documentation of cries and criers, particularly in the eighteenth century, was provided by popular etchers and engravers. In England, such artists as William Hogarth, Thomas Rowlandson, Gustave Doré and Francis Wheatley left an exceptional record of the hawkers in their surroundings. Hogarth's depiction of 'The Enraged Musician,' driven to despair by the cries of the sellers of milk and mackerel and the noise of rattle, tin drum and barking dogs, was a deft reminder of the cacophony of the streets.

Street cries have a long history, but the earliest indications of their content came from a fifteenth-century ballad poem, noted by an antiquary of the period, John Stowe. 'London Lickpenny,' also listed as 'London Lackpenny,' has been attributed to Dan John Lydgate, Monke of Bery, but this ascription has been dismissed by most authorities, the author remaining unknown.

> In to London I gan me to hy
> of all the lond it bearethe the prise
> hot pescods, one can cry
> strabery, rype, and chery in the ryse
> one bad me come nere and by some spice
> peper and safforne they gan me bede
> but for lack of money I myght not spede

ran the ninth stanza of the ballad, listing several cries, as did the other 15 stanzas. In the ensuing century, many cries were noted and the vendors were often depicted in prints, such as those by Marcellus Laroon, published in a second edition in 1711. Some were familiar over two centuries, as was the musical distich, 'Three Rows a Penny Pins, Short, Whites, and Mid-dl-ings!' Others were enigmatic, like the cry 'Buy a fine mouse trap, or a tormentor for your fleas,' noted as early as 1662. 'Hae ye any rats or mice to sell?,' 'New brooms for old shoes' and 'Any tripe, or neat's foot or calf's foot, or trotters, ho! Hearts, Liver or Lights!' were among the many hundreds of street cries noted. Many were incoherent or obscure, and the essayist Addison was of the opinion that the vendors cried their wares 'so as not to be understood,' attracting notice in so doing.

In the mid-nineteenth century, the assiduous observer Henry Mayhew (1851) noted the 'cries and rounds of Costermongers' in the London streets: 'Real Yarmouth bloaters, 2 a penny,' 'New herrings alive, 16 a groat,' the latter, he commented, being the loudest cry of any. 'All are bawling together – salesmen and hucksters of provisions, capes, hardware, and newspapers – till the place is a perfect Babel of competition.' Although for many years collectors of street lore had regretted the decline of street crying, Mayhew and his contemporaries noted them by the score. Even in the 1940s and 1950s, the cries of chair-menders and knife-grinders, along with those of hawkers, milkmen, paraffin salesmen and rag-and-bone men, were still to be heard in London's suburban streets.

At the same time, the last of the street vendors in the United States could still be heard. In 1925, Emmet Kennedy noted the cries of 'gombo,' French-patois-speaking 'Creole Negroes,' like the potato-cake woman 'in the street below singing: Bel pam pa-tat, Bel pam pa-tat, Madam, ou-lay-ou le bel pam pa-tat, pam pa-tat.' He heard 'a man who used to go around with an old white mule and a rickety spring wagon, and his cry was like this: Mah mule is white, mah chah-coal is black, I sells mah chah-coal two-bits a sack – Chah-coal – Chah-coal.' And there was a blackberry woman, who had picked blackberries in the woods and along the bayou banks before walking into New Orleans: 'Perhaps it is due to her weariness of body that her cry has a suggestion of melancholy: Black ber-ries – fresh an' fine, I got black ber-ries, lady, Fresh from the vine, I got black-berries la-dy, Three glass fo' a dime, I got black-berries, I got black-berries.' That was in 1925; perhaps Dora Bliggen was the same woman, a blackberry seller who was also a priestess in a revival congregation who carried her berries for sale in a basket on her head, and who cried the same words. Frederic Ramsey's recording of her was almost alone in documenting on disc the last cries of a many centuries-old tradition of street vendors. Only in the markets do some latter-day examples survive.

Street cries may well be considered as one of the earliest forms of popular song, the cries having distinct melodic lines. This was sufficient for some of them to be incorporated into longer popular songs, 'Cherry Ripe,' 'Sweet Lavender' and 'Cockles and Mussels' being familiar examples. It has been suggested that blues in the Deep South may have been influenced by street cries, but it may be more appropriate to consider them as a parallel tradition in the formative years of blues.

Bibliography

De Sola Pinto, V., and Rodway, A.E., eds. 1957. *The Common Muse: An Anthology of Popular British Ballad Poetry, XVth-XXth Century*. London: Chatto & Windus.

Hackwood, Frederick W. 1910. *The Good Old Times: The Romance of Humble Life in England*. London: T. Fisher Unwin.

Kennedy, R. Emmet. 1925. *Mellows: A Chronicle of Unknown Singers*. New York: Albert and Charles Boni.

Massin. 1978. *Les Cris de la ville: commerces ambulants et petits métiers de la rue* [Street Cries: Itinerant Trades and Small Street Businesses]. Paris: Gallimard.

Mayhew, Henry. 1969 (1851). *Mayhew's London. Being Selections from London's Labour and the London Poor*, ed. Peter Quennell. London: Spring Books.

Nelson, Raphael. 1941. *Cries and Criers of Old London*. London and Glasgow: Collins.

Ramsey, Frederic. 1960. *Been Here and Gone*. New Brunswick, NJ: Rutgers University Press.

Tuer, Andrew W. 1885. *Old London Street Cries and the Cries of Today: With Heaps of Quaint Cuts*. London: Leadenhall Press.

Sheet Music

Davison, J.W., comp. and lyr. n.d. 'Sweet Lavender.' London: D'Almaine & Co.

Horn, Charles E., comp. and lyr. 1820. 'Cherry Ripe: A Cavatina.' London: I. Willis.

Yorkston, James, comp. and lyr. 1894. 'Cockles and Mussels.' London: Francis Bros. & Day.

Discographical Reference

Bliggen, Dora. 'Blackberries!' *Music from the South, Vol. 10: Been Here and Gone*. Folkways Records FA 02659. *1960*: USA.

PAUL OLIVER

Strumming

To strum generally means to sound the strings of an instrument as one in a single stroke. Stringed instruments – for example, guitars – are conventionally held so that the player's left hand produces the pitches by pressing the strings against the fretboard, while the right hand sets the strings into motion either by plucking the strings individually or by sweeping them collectively. The first of these techniques is called picking, the second strumming. While both may involve the use of a plectrum or pick, strumming is usually conceptualized in contrast to picking, in which individual tones instead of chords are sounded.

Strumming often consists of a pattern of up-and-down strokes freely varied and without any tones of the chord being sounded separately, as exemplified by the guitar in Buddy Holly's 'Peggy Sue' or in the Mamas and the Papas' 'California Dreamin'.' Frequently, however, the instrumentalist will pick (with or without a plectrum) a bass note first and follow it with one or two strums of the remaining strings. This pick-strum-strum pattern is typical of the guitar styles of Jimmie Rodgers and Wilf Carter, for example. Thus, picking and strumming very often operate in combination. Strumming is commonly given a strong rhythmic profile to provide thrust to a song, as in the Beatles' 'All My Loving' or 'This Boy' or at the beginning of the Amboy Dukes' 'Journey to the Center of the Mind.'

The strumming motion of the right hand may be simple up-and-down movements of the wrist or larger arcs of the forearm moving from the elbow, while some more spectacular displays of showmanship involve the entire arm outstretched, pivoting from the shoulder, as practised by Elvis Presley and Pete Townshend.

Strumming also embraces power chords – that is, two- or three-note chords built of fifths and octaves, often played as riffs, as in the Kinks' 'You Really Got Me' and 'All Day and All of the Night.' The staccato 'chops' of the mandolin in bluegrass music can also be classed as strumming.

Although many may associate strumming with the guitar, virtually all stringed instruments may be, and frequently are, strummed. The playing technique of certain of these – for example, the ukulele, the autoharp and the Appalachian dulcimer – involves strumming primarily, if not exclusively.

Discographical References

Amboy Dukes, The. 'Journey to the Center of the Mind.' Mainstream 684. *1968*: USA.

Beatles, The. 'All My Loving.' *With the Beatles*. Parlophone PMC 1206. *1963*: UK.

Beatles, The. 'I Want to Hold Your Hand'/'This Boy.' Parlophone R 5084. *1963*: UK.

Holly, Buddy. 'Peggy Sue.' Coral 61885. *1957*: USA.

Kinks, The. 'All Day and All of the Night.' Pye 7N 15714. *1964*: UK.

Kinks, The. 'You Really Got Me.' Pye 7N 15673. *1964*: UK.

Mamas and the Papas, The. 'California Dreamin'.' Dunhill 4020. *1966*: USA.

TIM WISE

Tailgating

The phrase 'tailgate trombone' most probably originated around 1910 in New Orleans, although elements of the style associated with the term had earlier origins, going back to ragtime and circus bands. The phrase referred to the way in which brass bands and early jazz bands rode the streets in wagons or advertising trucks, with the trombonists positioned by the tailgate so as to be able to use the full length of their slides.

By the 1920s, 'tailgating' had become a generic term to describe the New Orleans style of Dixieland trombone playing. Its best-known exponent, Edward 'Kid' Ory, the 'king of the tailgate trombone,' recorded in Louis Armstrong's Hot Five ensemble. In ensembles like Armstrong's, 'tailgating' sounded akin to riding perilously close to the rear of another vehicle. The trombone accompaniment consisted of 'tailgating' the melodic lead of the trumpet or clarinet by quickly coming up close from behind, overlapping and pushing ahead to the next chordal or harmonic change. Functionally, 'tailgating' involved a mix of leading tones, counter melodies and marching rhythm bass figures, often delivered with glissando slide rips, slurs, falloffs, smears and other vocal effects. Other major exemplars of the tradition were Jim Robinson, who recorded with the bands of Sam Morgan and Bunk Johnson, and Georg Brunis, who recorded with the New Orleans Rhythm Kings and with Bix Beiderbecke.

Both as a term and as a technique, 'tailgating' virtually disappeared in the eras dominated by swing, big band and bebop jazz. It reemerged in the late 1960s when avant-gardists reemployed brass band and Dixieland trombone techniques in free jazz and collective improvisation. For his role in this revitalization, trombonist Roswell Rudd was critically acclaimed as 'playing tailgate on a spaceship.' Other jazz trombonists who have contributed to the presence of 'tailgating' in contemporary ensemble jazz include Ray Anderson and Craig Harris.

Discography

Armstrong, Louis. *The Hot Fives, Volume One*. Columbia 44049. 1925–26; *1988*: USA.

Ory, Edward 'Kid.' *King of the Tailgate Trombone*. American Music AMCD-20. 1948–49; *1990*: USA.

STEVEN FELD

Vamping

'Vamping' was the term used in early jazz to describe an improvised 'oom-pah' ragtime or stride piano accompaniment, played with two hands: the left took the pedal notes on beats 1 and 3 of a measure, and the right played chords on beats 2 and 4. The term derives from the French *avant-pied* (the front part of a shoe) and came into jazz argot from the cobbler's term to 'vamp up' or improvise a boot repair. The usage subsequently narrowed, denoting a short introductory passage repeated ad infinitum until a soloist or singer entered. 'Vamp 'til ready' was the instruction printed on sheet music above such sections. By the 1950s, the term was being used for ostinato introductions (such as the start of Dizzy Gillespie's 'Kush'), and in the 1960s its meaning once more broadened to denote the ostinatos used to accompany entire solos in Latin jazz, jazz-rock and modal jazz.

Bibliography

Root, Deane L. 1988. 'Vamp.' In *The New Grove Dictionary of Jazz*, Vol. 2, ed. Barry Kernfeld. London: Macmillan, 570.

Discographical Reference

Gillespie, Dizzy. 'Kush.' *An Electrifying Evening with the Dizzy Gillespie Quintet.* Verve V6-8401. *1961*: USA. Reissue: Gillespie, Dizzy. 'Kush.' *An Electrifying Evening with the Dizzy Gillespie Quintet.* PolyGram 557544. *1999*: USA.

ALYN SHIPTON

Versioning

The practise of versioning, in one form or another, lies at the heart of reggae. In the Jamaican context, the term does not simply denote the covering of outside material – for example, an international hit record – although this may certainly be one of its referents; it also, and more fundamentally, describes the various kinds of recycling of songs and 'rhythms' (i.e., instrumental backing tracks) that have been typical of reggae since the early 1970s. Thus, 'versioning' may involve not just the re-recording of a song, but also the grafting of a completely new performance (by another vocalist, deejay or musician) onto an existing rhythm track, as well as its remix – a 'dub version' – by a recording engineer. Frequently, elements of both practises are combined, such as when a popular song (or rhythm track) is re-recorded by another producer, voiced by a deejay or singer, and then remixed – often in a great number of only slightly differing permutations.

Partly a product of scant resources in a developing country and partly a response to the increasing pressure on producers to offer alternative cuts of a popular recording, versioning has gradually become a defining characteristic of reggae. The sound system habit of stringing together different cuts of a 'rhythm' into a continuous sequence played an important role in bringing about an ever-increasing number of simultaneously available versions of popular rhythm tracks, particularly in the 1990s.

Covering outside material is nothing new in Jamaican popular music. Acknowledged classics of the ska era include versions of the themes from the James Bond movies, *Guns of Navarone* and *Bonanza*, as well as of international pop hits. The Skatalites' famous 'Independent Anniversary Ska' (1966) is a cover of the Beatles' 'I Should Have Known Better' (1964). During the rocksteady years, appropriations of US sweet soul became legion, with particular attention paid to the songbook of Curtis Mayfield. An important transitional record (as ska turned into rocksteady), Delroy Wilson's 'Dancing Mood' (1966) is a remarkable transformation of an up-tempo original by US soul quintet the Tams (1964). While the 'roots reggae' artists of the late 1970s concentrated on original material, at least one of Bob Marley's most celebrated songs, 'One Love' (1966, 1977), is, in part, a cover – of the Impressions' 'People Get Ready' (1965).

In the mid-1970s, producers such as Bunny Lee, Joe Gibbs and the Hookim brothers began to re-record popular rhythm tracks from the Studio One and Treasure Isle catalogs. Updated, they provided the musical backing for literally thousands of recordings (and 'live' performances), particularly during reggae's 'dance hall' phase in the early 1980s. The 'digital' era (1985 onward) saw the trend continue (and grow) with a number of additions to the repertoire – for example, the endlessly versioned 'Sleng Teng' (1985) and 'Punaany' (1986) rhythms.

One particular instance of versioning is the 'one-rhythm album,' a format initiated in 1974 with the release of producer Rupie Edwards's *Yamaha Skank* (re-released, with extra tracks, in 1990 as *Let There Be Version*). The album *Pepper Seed Jam!* (1995) offers 26 versions of one rhythm track segued together. Many compilation albums are organized around versions of one or two rhythms – for instance, *Good Fellas* (1991), which features five cuts of John Holt's 'A Love I Can Feel' (1970) by artists such as Beres Hammond, Cutty Ranks and Tony Rebel. Holt's version was an interpretation of 'I Want A Love I Can See,' a 1963 non-hit single by the Temptations. The rhythm subsequently served as the blueprint for Inner Circle's international hit, 'Sweat (A La La La La La Long)' in 1993.

Occasionally, a rhythm track will be coupled with a completely different song – for example, Spanner Banner's 'Love Will Save the Day' (1995), a cover of British singer Des'ree's 'You Gotta Be' (1994) over the re-recorded rhythm track of Ernest Wilson's 'Undying Love' (1968), or Mr. Vegas's 'Yu Sure' (1998) over the instrumental backing track of a cover of George Michael's 'Faith' (1987) by local singer Tony Curtis.

While intertextuality to some may be stealing to others (see Harris 2000), versioning in reggae is an important compositional tool as well as an instance of creative musical dialog, albeit between often highly unequal partners. Thus, the arguably most popular record in Jamaica in 1999 was Terry Linen's unassuming cover of Whitney Houston's 'Your Love Is My Love' (1998). The versioning of 'rhythms' – both old and new – has continued unabated. In 2000, no fewer than 28 versions of the 'Scarface' rhythm were released simultaneously in Jamaica, each pressed on a separate vinyl single.

Bibliography

Barrow, Steve. 1990. Liner notes to Rupie Edwards and Friends, *Let There Be Version*. Trojan TRLS 280.

Barrow, Steve, and Dalton, Peter. 1997. *Reggae: The Rough Guide*. London: Rough Guides Ltd.

Bilby, Kenneth. 1995. 'Jamaica.' In Peter Manuel, with Kenneth Bilby and Michael Largey, *Caribbean Currents: Caribbean Music from Rumba to Reggae*. Philadelphia: Temple University Press, 143–82.

Harris, Keith. 2000. '"Roots"?: The Relationship Between the Global and the Local Within the Extreme Metal Scene.' *Popular Music* 19(1): 13–30.

White, Garth. 1983. 'Mento to Ska: The Sound of the City.' In *Reggae International*, ed. Stephen Davis and Peter Simon. London: Thames and Hudson, 37–42.

Discographical References

Beatles, The. 'I Should Have Known Better.' *A Hard Day's Night*. Parlophone PCS 3058. *1964*: UK.

'Bonanza.' *Instrumental Gems of the '60s*. Collector's Choice Music 7765. *1995*: USA.

Curtis, Tony. 'Faith.' 2 Bad. *1998*: Jamaica.

Des'ree. 'You Gotta Be.' Dusted Sound 6601342. *1994*: UK.

Edwards, Rupie. *Yamaha Skank*. Success. *1974*: Jamaica. Re-release: Edwards, Rupie, and Friends. *Let There Be Version*. Trojan TRLS 280. *1990*: UK.

Good Fellas. Penthouse. *1991*: Jamaica.

'Guns of Navarone.' *The Guns of Navarone [Original Soundtrack]*. Columbia CL 1655/CS 8455. *1961*: USA.

Holt, John. 'A Love I Can Feel.' Studio One. *1970*: Jamaica.

Houston, Whitney. 'Your Love Is My Love.' Arista 13730. *1998*: USA.

Impressions, The. 'People Get Ready.' ABC-Paramount 10622. *1965*: USA.

Inner Circle. 'Sweat (A La La La La La Long).' Big Beat 98429. *1993*: USA.

'James Bond Theme.' *Instrumental Gems of the '60s*. Collector's Choice Music 7765. *1995*: USA.

Linen, Terry. 'Your Love Is My Love.' Raggedy Joe. *1999*: Jamaica.

Marley, Bob, and the Wailers. 'One Love'/'People Get Ready.' *Exodus*. Island ILPS 9448. *1977*: UK.

Michael, George. 'Faith.' Sony 07623. *1987*: USA.

Mr. Vegas. 'Yu Sure.' *Heads High*. Greensleeves GRELCD 251. *1998*: UK.

Pepper Seed Jam! Mad House 0003. *1995*: USA.

Skatalites, The. 'Independent Anniversary Ska.' Island 260. *1966*: UK. Reissue: Skatalites, The. 'Independent Anniversary Ska.' *Foundation Ska*. Heartbeat HB 185/196. *1997*: USA.

Spanner Banner. 'Love Will Save the Day.' Digital B. *1995*: Jamaica.

Tams, The. 'Dancing Mood.' *Presenting the Tams*. ABC-Paramount 481. *1964*: USA.

Temptations, The. 'I Want A Love I Can See.' Gordy 7015. *1963*: USA.

Wailers, The. 'One Love.' Coxsone. *1966*: Jamaica. Reissue: Marley, Bob, and the Wailers. 'One Love.' *One Love*. Heartbeat 111. *1991*: USA.

Wilson, Delroy. 'Dancing Mood.' Island 3013. *1966*: UK. Reissue: Wilson, Delroy. 'Dancing Mood.' *Original Club Ska*. Heartbeat 55. *1990*: USA.

Wilson, Ernest. 'Undying Love.' Coxsone. *1968*: Jamaica. Reissue: Wilson, Ernest. 'Undying Love.' *Studio One Showcase, Vol. 1*. Heartbeat 224. *1999*: USA.

Discography

Alphonso, Roland. 'James Bond.' Island 259. *1964*: UK. Reissue: Alphonso, Roland. 'James Bond.' *Intensified! Original Ska 1962–66*. Mango IMCD 51. *1990*: USA.

Banton, Mega. 'Scarface.' Shocking Vibes. *2000*: Jamaica.

Malcolm, Carlos & the Afro Caribs. 'Bonanza Ska.' Island WI 173. *1965*: UK. Reissue: Malcolm, Carlos & the Afro Caribs. 'Bonanza Ska.' *Dance Crasher (Ska to Rock Steady)*. Trojan TRLS 260. *1997*: UK.

Skatalites, The. 'Guns of Navarone.' Island WI 168. *1965*: UK. Reissue: Skatalites, The. 'Guns of Navarone.' *Original Club Ska*. Heartbeat 55. *1990*: USA.

Sleng Teng Extravaganza. Jammys. *1995*: Jamaica.

20 Film and Stage Classics Jamaican Style. Trojan 319. *1992*: UK.

Filmography

The Guns of Navarone, dir. J. Lee Thompson. 1961. UK/USA. 159 mins. War Adventure. Original music by Alfred Perry, Dimitri Tiomkin, Francis Paul Webster.

HASSE HUSS

Vibrato

'Vibrato' (from the Latin *vibrare*, 'to shake') refers to the pulsating of a note. There are two kinds of vibrato: a frequency vibrato, in which the pitch of a note is raised or lowered (usually the former) in a regular rhythm; and an intensity vibrato, in which the strength or amplitude of a note is alternately augmented and diminished while a constant pitch is maintained.

In stringed instruments such as the violin, the player produces vibrato by rocking the finger gently backward and forward to produce a 'wobble,' or pulsing change of pitch. This is normally less than a semitone, so it is perceived as an expressive device applied to a given pitch rather than as a change of note. Guitar vibrato works in a similar way, with electric instruments also having the possibility of a tremolo arm. This device operates on the bridge, stretching the strings and effectively raising the pitch of the entire instrument according to how far the arm is moved by the player. Modern string technology has led to the development of strings that can 'bend' notes up to one-third or more above the note fingered on the instrument.

Players of wind instruments produce vibrato by varying the intensity of the air supply, and in certain circumstances can produce a frequency vibrato by moving the fingers above the finger holes rather than covering them in the conventional way.

Singers use both frequency and intensity vibrato. A pronounced frequency vibrato is characteristic of much classical singing and is a byproduct of a classical technique (involving pulsations in the cricothyroid muscle). Some popular singers (including Frank Sinatra) have also used this technique. More common, however, is an intensity vibrato in which variations in subglottal pressure produce small changes in volume.

Vibrato has tended to have a specific role in particular genres. As a general rule, it is applied less in popular music than in classical music. This is especially true of singing, but less so in the case of some wind instruments. The clarinet, for example, is often played with considerably more vibrato in most forms of popular music. There are specific instances of vocal practises influencing instrumental style and technique, such as Louis Armstrong's tendency to add vibrato toward the end of a long held note. This is almost certainly derived from the vibrato he added to the end of long sung phrases to compensate for the diminishing air pressure below the vocal folds.

Bibliography

Potter, John. 1998. *Vocal Authority: Singing Style and Ideology*. Cambridge: Cambridge University Press.

Sundberg, Johan. 1987. *The Science of the Singing Voice*. De Kalb, IL: Northern Illinois University Press.

JOHN POTTER

Vocalized Tone

'Vocalized tone' is a term used to describe the timbre of sounds produced from non-vocal sources (instrumental, electronic) that are thought to possess characteristics associated with vocal sounds. The particular sort of expressiveness that results is a feature of many popular music styles, particularly African-American styles and those influenced by them.

In many music cultures, the distinction between instrumental and vocal sound is not rigid, 'talking drums' being the most clichéd example. Even in the West, where the 'rise of instrumental music' has been intensively thematized, people have long talked of 'nasal' woodwind, 'keening' bagpipes, 'sighing' strings and so on. But in this culture, the strand of thought that has promoted an ideal of timbral 'purity' for instrumentalists has provoked the need for a term that can mark the opposite of this.

In African-American musics and their derivatives, vocalized tone is actually part of a somewhat broader set of practises within which instruments often try to 'personalize' themselves by imitating the flexibility of pitching, timbre and articulation typically belonging to voices: a singer-guitarist such as B.B. King, who calls his guitar 'Lucille,' clearly thinks of 'her' fills, breaks and solos as 'talking back' to him; slide and 'bottleneck' guitar techniques make possible the equivalent of the expressive intonations of speech. But the most dramatic examples of vocalized tone concern paralinguistic vocal techniques: growls, grunts, howls and so on, and the whole phenomenon of 'dirty' tone, which models the idiosyncrasies, the individual 'grain' of the emoting voice. Brass 'growls' became common in 1920s and 1930s jazz (most famously in the work of the Ellington orchestra); wah-wah pedals facilitated the production of heightened-speech effects on electric instruments; over-driven amplifiers and feedback techniques, most influentially developed by Jimi Hendrix, enabled hard rock and heavy metal guitarists to place dirty vocalized effects at the center of these styles. More recently, in hip-hop and dance music styles, scratched and synthesized 'exclamations' amid the rhythm loops often seem to mimic vocalized interjections.

In a sense, the vocoder engineers the opposite process: vocalized sounds are transformed into an 'instrumentalized' derivative. At the same time, the trace of a voice survives; and this ambivalence may be regarded as confirming the point that in many musics – certainly many popular musics – the boundary between instrumental and vocal sounds is porous.

RICHARD MIDDLETON

Wah-Wah (Wa-Wa)

This onomatopoeic term refers to the vocal-like sound produced by an undulating filtration of high frequencies from a musical note. This was developed in early jazz styles to add a vocal singing quality to brass and woodwind playing. For brass, this effect is created by the opening and closing of the hand over the bell of the instrument, or by using this hand technique in conjunction with a mute. Several types of mutes are employed to attain such an effect; they include hats, plungers, harmons, solotones and wah-wah mutes. A similar effect is produced for woodwind instruments by alternating between false and standard fingerings on the same note. A key exponent of the wah-wah mute was cornetist 'King' Oliver, whose 1923 recording of 'Dippermouth Blues' exemplifies his style. Members of the Duke Ellington Orchestra, such as trumpeters Bubber Miley and Cootie Williams and trombonist Joe 'Tricky Sam' Nanton, were also highly influential in developing wah-

wah techniques. Ellington's recording of 'East St. Louis Toodle-oo' (1926) displays both Miley's and Nanton's virtuosic employment of plunger mute wah-wah effects. The wah-wah was employed less in post-swing styles, such as bebop and hard bop. However, through the efforts of free and avant-garde jazz musicians, such as trumpeter Lester Bowie and trombonists George Lewis, Roswell Rudd and Ray Anderson, a renewed interest in wah-wah mutes and effects has persisted in jazz.

With the advent of electronic instruments and their prominent use in popular music styles, electronic frequency filters were developed to produce the same acoustic effect. Early wah-wah devices, which have continued to be widely used, were pedal-operated tunable filters that gave a player control over an instrument's harmonics. Wah-wah pedals are used mostly by guitarists, although examples exist of keyboards processed through wah-wah pedals (especially before the introduction of more sophisticated controls and signal processors integrated into synthesizers), and these electronic devices have been used by instrumentalists playing acoustic instruments. Trumpeter Miles Davis uses a wah-wah pedal extensively on his 1969 jazz fusion recording *Bitches Brew*.

The wah-wah guitar sound – with its 'spoken' quality – was fashionable in the late 1960s for lead solos, under the influence of Jimi Hendrix (classic examples exist throughout the *Electric Ladyland* album (1968)) and Eric Clapton (on Cream's 'White Room' (1968)); the wah-wah was also adopted as a rhythm guitar technique in soul and disco hits (Isaac Hayes' 'Theme from Shaft' (1971)). Although the wah-wah never completely disappeared (guitarists like Frank Zappa and David Byrne continued to use it throughout the 1980s), it saw a resurgence in popularity with guitar bands in the 1990s and through the influential recordings of Bill Frisell, John Abercrombie and John Scofield.

Discographical References

Cream. 'White Room.' Atco 6617. *1968*: USA.
Davis, Miles. *Bitches Brew*. Columbia 26. 1969; *1970*: USA.
Ellington, Duke. 'East St. Louis Toodle-oo.' Vocalion 1064. 1926: USA.
Hayes, Isaac. 'Theme from Shaft.' *Shaft*. Enterprise 5002. *1971*: USA.
Hendrix, Jimi. *Electric Ladyland*. Reprise 6307. *1968*: USA.
Oliver, Joe 'King.' 'Dippermouth Blues.' Gennett 5132. 1923: USA.

CHRIS WASHBURNE and FRANCO FABBRI

Whistling

Whistling is an oral sound produced by forcing exhaled air through pursed lips, between the tongue and the teeth, or between fingers inserted in the mouth. By the use of the tongue and subtle labial inflections, the sounds in the former method may be emitted melodically. Until the advent of the transistor radio provided independent accompaniment, whistling was used to accompany many types of work, such as labor on building sites. In the West, the delivery of goods and newspapers was enlivened and announced by the whistling of errand boys. Whistling was popular in the nineteenth century, as was reflected in minstrel and ragtime themes – for example, Sam Devere's 'Whistling Coon' and Kerry Mills's 'Whistling Rufus.' The blackface singer Eugene Stratton (1861–1918) entertained as 'The Whistling Coon' at the Oxford Theatre, London, singing and whistling Leslie Stuart's hit tunes 'The Lily of Laguna' and 'Little Dolly Daydream.' In the music halls, performers such as Albert Whelan became famous for whistled interpretations of popular tunes.

In the 1930s, some crooners favored whistled solos, Bing Crosby's 'Where the Blue of the Night (Meets the Gold of the Day)' being a notable example. Whistling by women was still considered vulgar, until the Walt Disney animated cartoon film of *Snow White and the Seven Dwarfs* made the performance by Snow White of 'Whistle While You Work' acceptable. But it was Deborah Kerr, in the Rodgers and Hammerstein film *The King and I* (1956), who broke the stereotype with her declaration 'I Whistle a Happy Tune.' Whistling was seldom heard in jazz, except for the outlining of a theme or sequence, but a few blues singers, such as Whistling Bob Howe and the pianist Whistling Alex Moore, were noted for their whistled blues. Although whistling was encouraged during World War II – to 'keep up the spirits' – and was mythologized in the film *The Bridge on the River Kwai* (1957), the practise largely died out in the mid-1960s. It should be noted that, in many cultures, whistling is unacceptable, being associated with malevolent spirits.

Bibliography

Paskman, Dailey, and Spaeth, Sigmund G. 1928. *'Gentlemen, Be Seated': A Parade of the Old-Time Minstrels*. Garden City, NY: Doubleday, Doran & Co.
Pearsall, Ronald. 1976. *Popular Music of the Twenties*. Newton Abbot: David & Charles.
Spaeth, Sigmund G. 1948. *A History of Popular Music in America*. New York: Random House.

Sheet Music

Ahlert, Fred E., comp., and Crosby, Bing, & Turk, Roy, lyrs. 1931. 'Where the Blue of the Night (Meets the Gold of the Day).' New York: DeSylva, Brown and Henderson, Inc.

Churchill, Frank, comp., and Morey, Larry, lyr. 1937. 'Whistle While You Work.' New York: Bourne.

Devere, Sam, comp. and lyr. 1909 (1888). 'Whistling Coon.' New York: W.A. Pond.

Mills, Kerry, comp. and lyr. 1899. 'Whistling Rufus.' New York: F.A. Mills.

Stuart, Leslie, comp. and lyr. 1897. 'Little Dolly Daydream.' London: Francis, Day and Hunter.

Stuart, Leslie, comp. and lyr. 1898. 'The Lily of Laguna.' London: Francis, Day and Hunter.

Discographical References

Crosby, Bing, and Bennie Krueger and His Orchestra. 'Where the Blue of the Night (Meets the Gold of the Day).' Brunswick 6226. 1931: USA. Reissue: Crosby, Bing. 'Where the Blue of the Night (Meets the Gold of the Day).' *Million Sellers.* Prism 295. *1998*: USA.

Snow White and the Seven Dwarfs (Original soundtrack). Disney 60850. *1993*: USA.

The King and I (Original soundtrack of the motion picture). Capitol 64693. *1993*: USA.

Filmography

Snow White and the Seven Dwarfs, dir. Dorothy Ann Blank, William Cottrell, Richard Creedon, Merrill de Maris, Walt Disney, David Hand, Wilfred Jackson, Larry Morey, Perce Pearce, Dick Richard, Ben Sharpsteen, Webb Smith. 1937. USA. 83 mins. Animated Musical. Original music by Frank Churchill, Leigh Harline, Larry Morey, Paul J. Smith.

The Bridge on the River Kwai, dir. David Lean. 1957. UK/USA. 161 mins. War Drama. Original music by Malcolm Arnold.

The King and I, dir. Walter Lang. 1956. USA. 133 mins. Musical Romance. Original music by Ken Darby, Alfred Newman, Richard Rodgers.

PAUL OLIVER

Yodeling

Yodeling is a singing style that alternates in a controlled way between two distinct registers of the voice. Yodeling has been used in many cultures both for music and for signaling, but its presence in popular music derives from folkloric adaptations of traditional styles from Switzerland and Austria, and from North American country music.

In a yodel, a higher falsetto head voice alternates with the register associated with lower notes – the chest voice – with each style of vocal production using radically different conformations of the vocal folds. Yodelers emphasize the timbral contrast between the registers and the distinctive, abrupt sound-onset envelope of the break while maintaining pitch control. The break is often supported by vowel changes and other changes of the vocal apparatus, typified by the well-known 'yod-el-lay-ee' vocables used.

Yodeling became widely known internationally in the nineteenth century, when singing groups from Alpine Central Europe performing folkloric repertoires – such as the Rainer Family singing group (which flourished between about 1820 and 1840) – became popular on the stage (Nathan 1946). Minstrel show and other theatrical performers continued yodeling on the urban stage throughout the nineteenth century, and the conventional outdoor Alpine connotation was linked with virtuosic display and a theatrical sense of the bizarre. English performer Harry Torrani (born Harry Hopkinson, ca. 1900) had a successful stage and recording career from the 1920s to the late 1940s, and was an inspirational source of style and repertoire for many later performers around the world.

From the late 1920s, hillbilly/country singer Jimmie Rodgers, 'the blue yodeler,' made yodeling an almost indispensable part of country music. Rodgers's stylistic inspiration was probably theatrical performance, reinforced by African-American uses of vocal-register shifts (Coltman 1976). In keeping with his groundbreaking intimacy of delivery, Rodgers's yodeling avoided the athletic exhibitionism of stage yodeling. His yodels were frequently a simple series of parallel sixths, and they founded some of the most characteristic country guitar and slide guitar licks.

Although there is little to link yodeling to cowboy vernacular traditions, by the 1930s 'cowboy' singers such as Gene Autry had coupled yodeling with the mythologized West. In 1935, Patsy Montana became the first female country music million-seller as the yodeling 'cowboy's sweetheart,' and even Harry Torrani was billing himself as 'the Yodeling Cowboy from Chesterfield.' Canadian singers Wilf Carter and Hank Snow were prominent yodeling performers of the 1940s, and other performers, such as Elton Britt and Kenny Roberts, maintained the spectacular effects of the style in their performances.

Yodeling declined in popularity in country music from the 1950s. However, in Australian country music – where, from the 1930s, performers such as Tex Morton made yodeling an indispensable component of the local style – it has remained popular (Smith 1994). At the end of the 1990s, a few North American performers were using yodeling, usually within the 'new traditionalist' historicizing mode of country music that refers back to previous performers.

Many soul, rock 'n' roll, and rock vocalists have used falsetto registers, and singers from Aaron Neville to Michael Jackson and many others have continued this style. A number of popular female singers of the 1990s –

such as Delores O'Riordan of the Cranberries, Alanis Morissette and Tori Amos – employed the breaking voice. Although strictly speaking not yodelers, these performers exploited some of the impact of yodeling's techniques.

Bibliography

Coltman, Robert. 1976. 'Roots of the Country Yodel: Notes Toward a Life History.' *John Edwards Memorial Foundation Quarterly* 42: 91–94.

Nathan, Hans. 1946. 'The Tyrolese Family Rainer, and the Vogue of Singing Mountain-Troupes in Europe and America.' *The Musical Quarterly* 31(1)(January): 63–79.

Smith, Graeme. 1994. 'Australian Country Music and the Hillbilly Yodel.' *Popular Music* 13(3): 297–311.

Discography

Torrani, Harry. *Harry Torrani: Regal Zonophone Collection* (3 CDs). EMI/Regal Zonophone 7243 5 22540. *2000*: Australia.

GRAEME SMITH

Part II
Musical Production and Transmission

4. Personnel

Announcer

An announcer is an individual in broadcasting whose voice is used as the voice of a radio or television station. Depending on the type of station, the announcer might only prerecord voice-over commercials or program trailers, but is more likely to also introduce and link programs live, introduce and play discs, make emergency or public-service announcements and read the news. The all-purpose radio announcer has become almost a creature of the past, except on speech stations, especially national or public-service ones (see Morris 1999).

The importance of the announcer on radio was recognized from the early 1920s. In both the United States and the United Kingdom, station announcers of the 1920s were predominantly male, college-educated and formal in diction. In 1926, the BBC imposed a requirement that its announcers use national 'received' pronunciation and diction and wear formal evening dress (Briggs 1961). Both countries' stations set out to preserve the anonymity of announcers, but in the United States this failed and, by the late 1920s, network announcers were some of the biggest-name radio stars (Douglas 1987; Maltin 1997; Hilmes 1997). These included announcers of programs of popular music, such as George D. Hay (the self-styled 'Solemn Old Judge'), who introduced the *Grand Ole Opry* on station WSM in Nashville, Tennessee, and Ted Husing, who compèred the CBS network broadcasts of the Duke Ellington Orchestra from New York's Cotton Club. Both examples also illustrate the proactive roles that announcers could play at the time. The *Grand Ole Opry* was Hay's idea, and it was Husing who persuaded CBS to put a wire into the Cotton Club for live broadcasting.

In the United States in the late 1940s, many announcers moved across to television, decided to concentrate on news-reading or sports commentary, or, following the pioneering examples of Al Jarvis and Martin Block in the 1930s, became disc jockeys (DJs). The emergence of format radio in the 1950s meant there were fewer stations that required announcers, as DJs became the voices of the station. Ennis (1992, 109–11) argues that the role of the announcer gradually metamorphosed from that of a mere provider of information into that of a salesman for the program sponsor and finally into that of an on-air personality, of which the dominant type was the DJ.

Bibliography

Briggs, Asa. 1961. *The History of Broadcasting in the United Kingdom. Vol. 1: The Birth of Broadcasting*. London and New York: Oxford University Press.

Collier, James Lincoln. 1987. *Duke Ellington*. London: Michael Joseph.

Douglas, George H. 1987. *The Early Days of Radio Broadcasting*. Jefferson, NC: McFarland.

Ennis, Philip H. 1992. *The Seventh Stream: The Emergence of Rocknroll in American Popular Music*. Hanover, NH: Wesleyan University Press/University Press of New England.

Hilmes, Michele. 1997. *Radio Voices: American Broadcasting, 1922– 1952*. Minneapolis, MN: University of Minnesota Press.

Malone, Bill C. 1985. *Country Music, U.S.A.* Rev. ed. Austin, TX: University of Texas Press.

Maltin, Leonard. 1997. *The Great American Broadcast: A Celebration of Radio's Golden Age*. New York: Dutton.

Morris, Nancy. 1999. 'US Voices on UK Radio.' *European Journal of Communication* 14(1): 37–59.

Scannell, Paddy, and Cardiff, David. 1991. *A Social His-*

tory of British Broadcasting. Vol. 1: 1922–1939 – Serving the Nation. Oxford: Blackwell.

KEN GARNER

Arranger

An arranger is a person whose task is to convert a musical text from one form to another. In most instances, this means recasting a piece of music into a version performable by a different instrument or a different kind of ensemble. The activity of arranging can be distinguished from those of transposing, transcribing and orchestrating. Whereas transposing denotes simply moving material into a different key, arranging generally involves other alterations, such as changes to the basic rhythm, to the harmonization and to the ordering of the sections of a piece. Transcribing normally denotes the rewriting of material for another instrument or instruments, but in exactly the same shape as the original, as far as is practicable. Thus, a hit from a Broadway show, for instance, may be transcribed for piano. Transcriptions of ensemble pieces for piano solo are often called reductions. Similarly, orchestrating, or scoring, denotes the assigning of musical lines to particular instruments. Each of these processes is subsumed in the concept of arranging.

Sometimes, the arranger's job involves a single activity, such as creating an easy piano accompaniment to a songwriter's melody. Helmy Kresa, for example, produced such piano arrangements for Irving Berlin and many other noted songwriters. More often, however, the arranger's work, particularly when intended for an ensemble, involves much that is generally understood as composition, including devising harmonies, textures, introductions and codas, and so on. The elaborate choral and instrumental arrangements that Ray Conniff has made of popular songs, for example, demonstrate extensive recomposition. The aim of the arranger, however, is always to ensure that the original material is still recognizable – that the melody will still be identifiable as the original one – although the overall mood of the piece may be drastically altered.

The arranger must have complete familiarity with the instruments' possibilities: their ranges and sonorities, the peculiarities of their notation, conventional instrumental combinations and so forth. The arranger also needs insight into the practicalities of the instruments, such as their fingerings, difficulties of intonation and suchlike, in order to avoid awkward and unidiomatic figures, and must show sensitivity to such requirements as the players' need for rests in which to breathe.

The arranger responds to two particular types of demand: the practical and the commercial. An example of practical motivation would be the arrangement of orchestral music for piano, in the case of a large work for the stage, to facilitate rehearsal. Singers or dancers could thus rehearse their parts with piano accompaniment rather than requiring a full orchestra. Commercial motivation includes the presentation of a piece of music in various forms in order to reach more markets – for example, the many arrangements of popular songs for high-school bands to perform, piano reductions of hit tunes, and the increasingly available 'easy piano' arrangements for pianists of modest ability.

Several specialized types of arranger emerged in the first quarter of the twentieth century, coinciding with the development of new musical genres. The Hollywood method of adding music to film provided employment for arrangers, who expanded the short scores provided by the composers. The development of swing bands, such as Fletcher Henderson's, provided opportunities for talented arrangers like Don Redman, whose innovative arrangements served as a template for the entire genre. The lush 'symphonic' style of arrangers like Ferde Grofé, who created many arrangements for Paul Whiteman's orchestra, including that of Gershwin's 'Rhapsody in Blue,' became a model for radio and television orchestras for almost the remainder of the century.

Of all popular music arrangers, those working in jazz have achieved perhaps the greatest prestige, doubtless owing to the tendency of aficionados to regard jazz as art. Certainly, such ensembles as the Stan Kenton Orchestra provided opportunities for radical experimentation by Pete Rugolo, Bill Russo, Gene Roland and Kenton himself, to mention only a few. But other forms of popular music have fostered equally creative talents. For example, the development of the long-playing phonograph record and of new radio formats, in particular, opened new avenues for arrangers such as Paul Weston, André Kostelanetz and George Melachrino, who created smooth-sounding arrangements of popular songs, as well as well-known classical pieces, and laid the foundations for the string-saturated styles of Percy Faith, Geoff Love and Norrie Paramor, who dominated the 'Beautiful Music' sounds of FM radio in the United States during the 1960s and 1970s. Nelson Riddle also made smooth and soothing arrangements of the mood music type, but his real fame derives from his collaborations with Frank Sinatra on nine Capitol albums, beginning with *Songs for Young Lovers* (1955). Riddle's arrangements for *Songs for Swingin' Lovers!* (1956), with muted brass and easy swinging tempos, are particularly esteemed.

Bibliography

Jasen, David A. 1988. *Tin Pan Alley: The Composers, the Songs, the Performers, and Their Times: The Golden Age of*

American Popular Music from 1886 to 1956. New York: Donald I. Fine.

Lanza, Joseph. 1995. *Elevator Music: A Surreal History of Muzak, Easy-Listening, and Other Moodsong*. New York: Picador.

Petkov, Steven, and Mustazza, Leonard, eds. 1995. *The Frank Sinatra Reader*. New York: Oxford University Press.

Discographical References

Sinatra, Frank. *Songs for Swingin' Lovers!*. Capitol 46570. *1956*: USA.

Sinatra, Frank. *Songs for Young Lovers*. Capitol 48470. 1955: USA.

Whiteman, Paul, and His Orchestra. 'Rhapsody in Blue.' RCA-Victor 35822. 1927: USA.

Discography

Conniff, Ray. *'S Wonderful!*. Columbia 925. *1990*: USA.

TIM WISE

Band Leader

The concept of the band leader emerged in tandem with the US symphonic band, following the arrival in the United States in 1848 of Irishman Patrick S. Gilmore (1829–92). Prior to that, brass and military bands in the United States had been more or less identical. Gilmore introduced reed instruments and, in addition to directing his band, undertook its business management, promotion and musical policy with equal flair and aplomb. After leading an eponymous ensemble, he directed various bands for the state of Massachusetts, before moving to New York in 1873 and taking over the 22nd Regiment Band.

This ensemble set the pattern for military-style symphonic bands for the next 50 years. Gilmore presented important soloists, toured throughout the year with seasons in New York and at Manhattan Beach and, at a time when US symphony orchestras were only barely established, laid the foundations for the band to become the most popular medium for light classics, regimental marches and a newly composed band repertoire. Gilmore set a precedent for the role of band leader in all subsequent forms of ragtime, jazz and popular music, not only through band directing, but also through composing new music – his best-known piece is the song 'When Johnny Comes Marching Home.'

Gilmore's heir as the most significant US band leader was John Philip Sousa (1854–1932). Sousa wrote numerous marches (including 'The Washington Post') that defined the multi-thematic genre of military march; at the same time, he gradually expanded the instrumentation of his band to over 70. His popularity was greatly enhanced by the fact that his career coincided with the emergence of sound recording and, from the late 1890s on cylinders, and then on discs, his music was disseminated as no previous band leader's had been. Many of the musicians who had worked for him, most notably trombonist Arthur Pryor, went on to become band leaders in their own right, continuing the Sousa tradition well up to World War II.

As ragtime and then jazz became established, other leaders began to assume an importance similar to Sousa's, although this was not always recognized at the time. James Reese Europe, Will Marion Cook, Will Vodery and Gene Mikell acquired considerable reputations for leading African-American syncopated orchestras and, like Sousa and Gilmore, all four men directed rather than played in their bands.

In the ragtime and society orchestras of New Orleans, there were playing band leaders such as John Robichaux and Armand J. Piron, and in the wake of cornetist Buddy Bolden, the 'first man of jazz,' other trumpeters and trombonists began to lead prototypical jazz bands, among them Tom Brown, Frankie Dusen, Manuel Perez and 'King' Oliver. Oliver, in particular, continued the traditional role of band leader, although for the first half of his career he was also a formidable soloist. He wrote music, directed and rehearsed his band, hired musicians (showing an astute eye for talent) and undertook much of his band's promotion.

As big bands emerged, first by means of the white band leader Paul Whiteman, and then through African Americans such as Fletcher Henderson, the role of the band leader polarized more sharply into those like Whiteman, who abandoned an instrumental career (as a violinist) to conduct his band and commission music from others (ranging from Grofé to Gershwin), and those like Henderson, who not only played piano but also wrote arrangements. This polarity continued in the 1920s: violinist-leaders such as Erskine Tate and Carroll Dickerson were largely inaudible on their bands' recordings and acted as figureheads, while instrumentalists like Oliver, Duke Ellington and Luis Russell took a full part in the music their bands played. Russell was an unusual case: throughout most of the 1930s, he led the band that backed Louis Armstrong and, although he recorded independently, his band was best known as 'Louis Armstrong and His Orchestra,' even though Armstrong himself had little or nothing to do with leading the band.

There was a further change in the 1930s with the emergence of 'personality band leaders' – men whose job it was to 'front' a band with energy and enthusiasm, but without playing or – for the most part – singing. Examples included Tiny Bradshaw, Baron Lee and Lucius 'Lucky' Millinder. Both Lee and Millinder 'fronted' a big band established by Irving Mills's booking agency. The

Mills Blue Rhythm Orchestra had two functions: to record songs in which Mills had a copyright interest and add to his royalty revenue; and to entice promoters into booking Mills's major acts, such as Duke Ellington, on the principle that they would hire the Mills Blue Rhythm Orchestra first in return for getting Ellington later. Lee and Millinder were used to provide for audiences the focus of an extroverted personality, and thus a selling point, for the band.

The exception was the singer Cab Calloway (also booked by Mills), who took over a band called the Missourians in 1929 and created a convincing persona around a frenetic stage act that involved his vocals, energetic dancing and the use of a 'hi-de-hi' nonsense language. Because Calloway was actually an innovative singer in his own right, and his songs developed a narrative theme about Harlem lowlife characters such as 'Minnie the Moocher,' he became wildly successful, and by 1939 he was the highest-earning black band leader in the United States, although he played no instrument himself.

In the swing era, at the time Calloway was popular, instrumentalist band leaders additional to those already mentioned included clarinetists Benny Goodman and Artie Shaw, saxophonists Jimmy Dorsey, Woody Herman, Charlie Barnet and Charlie Ventura, trumpeters Harry James and Erskine Hawkins, trombonist Tommy Dorsey, pianists Count Basie and Teddy Wilson, and drummers Chick Webb and Gene Krupa. Contemporaneously with the swing orchestras, there were society dance bands led by such men as Sam and Lester Lanin.

The distinction between dance band leaders, instrumentalist jazz band leaders and those who merely 'fronted' a band held true in Europe as well. In Britain, for example, bands like those of Jack Payne, Carroll Gibbons, Geraldo and Ambrose played mostly light dance music, while those of Lew Stone, Jack Hylton and Roy Fox played a significant proportion of jazz pieces. Of the leaders mentioned, only Gibbons (a pianist) and Fox (a trumpeter) were important instrumentalists. Later, during and after World War II, Ted Heath, a trombonist, became the leader of Britain's foremost jazz big band.

In France, leaders like multi-instrumentalist Louis Vola, the clarinetist André Ekyan and trumpeter Philippe Brun led jazz-inflected bands, although the most successful was probably that led by Gregor Kelekian (an Armenian born in Turkey). Gregor et ses Gregoriens was renowned as a group that encouraged talented musicians to flourish, among them violinist Michel Warlop and saxophonist Alix Combelle.

In Belgium, notable band leaders included Charles Remue (who, in 1927, made the first jazz discs by a Belgian band) and Fud Candrix, who led his band during the German occupation in the 1940s. In Switzerland, Teddy Stauffer 'fronted' the 'Original Teddies,' and his sideman Eddie Brunner led bands in Germany and France that included both US and European musicians. Other North Americans traveled to Asia: Teddy Weatherford led a series of bands in India and China, Buck Clayton took a US orchestra to Shanghai, and Canadian-born Jimmy Lequime recorded in Calcutta.

In the postwar period, band leaders have continued to be divided into singers or instrumentalists and those who have confined themselves to conducting and directing. In the jazz field, there has been a gradual move away from the concept of a leader and his/ her orchestra, although some leaders have continued to lead large ensembles. These have included pianist Stan Kenton, trumpeter Maynard Ferguson, pianist Toshiko Akiyoshi and survivors from the swing era, such as vibes player Lionel Hampton and saxophonist Illinois Jacquet. Modern jazz pioneers who also ventured into band leading included Dizzy Gillespie and the drummer Kenny Clarke, who co-led a band in Europe with Francy Boland. One of North America's most innovative band leaders was arranger Gil Evans, whose big band met informally every Monday night in New York, and his son Miles Evans has continued this tradition, as has his protégé Maria Schneider, who has led a similarly sized group in New York into the twenty-first century. In Europe, many of the most influential band leaders have not necessarily lent their names to their ensembles, a good example being the Austrian composer Mathias Rüegg, leader of the Vienna Art Orchestra.

Band leaders who have worked in record studios, radio and television have acquired considerable fame. In the United Kingdom, Victor Sylvester's dance orchestra, along with those of Mantovani and Edmundo Ros, achieved fame on BBC Radio, while the television bands of Jack Parnell, Alyn Ainsworth and Harry Stoneham have had similar success on British television. In the United States, numerous television bands have been important, but particularly notable has been the success of jazz musicians such as Dr. Billy Taylor (on the *David Frost Show*) and Branford Marsalis (on the *Tonight Show*) in combining the elements of directing, organization and promotion with their own first-rate musicianship.

Bibliography

Berendt, Joachim-Ernst. 1982 (1975). *The Jazz Book: From Ragtime to Fusion and Beyond*. Rev. ed. Westport, CT: Lawrence Hill. (First published Frankfurt am Main: Fischer Bücherei, 1953.)

Camus, Raoul. 1986. 'Bands.' In *The New Grove Dictionary of American Music*, Vol. 1, ed. H. Wiley Hitchcock and Stanley Sadie. London: Macmillan, 127–37.

Charters, Samuel B., and Kunstadt, Leonard. 1981. *Jazz: A History of the New York Scene*. New York: Da Capo Press. (First published New York: Doubleday, 1962.)

McCarthy, Albert. 1971. *The Dance Band Era, 1910–1950*. Philadelphia: Chilton Book Co.

McCarthy, Albert. 1974. *Big Band Jazz*. London/New York: Barrie and Jenkins/G.P. Putnam's Sons.

Schuller, Gunther. 1989 (1968). *The Swing Era: The Development of Jazz, 1930–1945*. New York: Oxford University Press.

Sheet Music

Lambert, Louis (aka Patrick S. Gilmore), comp. and lyr. 1863. 'When Johnny Comes Marching Home.' Boston, MA: Henry Tolman & Co.

Sousa, John Philip, comp. 1889. 'The Washington Post.' Philadelphia: Coleman.

ALYN SHIPTON

Composer

Most forms of popular music have been rooted in non-notated traditions. For this reason, the specialized occupation of composer as distinct from that of the performing musician is, in the context of popular music, a rather recent phenomenon, dating back not much further than the middle of the nineteenth century.

Non-notated forms of music are, of course, created by individuals, but through processes of oral transmission this music has remained in a constant state of change and flux. Such music could not therefore be attributed to a single creator or author. In addition, the core of popular music practise has been constituted by performance and the pleasure derived from this. Sharing a common repertoire of songs or dances has been a quite common state of affairs, something that has rendered superfluous the question of who actually created the music.

Even as notation became increasingly common in popular music, authorship was still not an issue. In the early stages of Western popular music's development, handwritten scores were produced by band leaders. These served the need of coordinating musical performances in situations where lineups changed frequently. In the early nineteenth century, music publishers started to target this market. For this reason, authorship became an important question, but it was handled in a rather pragmatic way. It was common for band leaders to publish under their own name regardless of who actually provided the musical ideas. In the mid-nineteenth century, popular and successful leaders, like the father and sons of the Viennese Strauss dynasty or the Komzak family, maintained what were in effect manufacturing studios, where their ideas and proposals for dance tunes were transformed into waltz compositions. The arranger was much more important than the composer in these situations, since the arranger decided how the music was to sound. In this way, the arranger contributed in a much more direct way to the success of a band.

Since this music served clearly defined functions, its structure was prescribed to a high degree. This left little space for compositional imagination. However, commodification and, with this, competition encouraged authorship, and created the need for a single name that could serve to establish ownership of the music. Toward the end of the nineteenth century, the composer was thus more important legally than artistically in serving the requirements of music ownership.

Parallel to these processes, musical forms derived from art music traditions became established in the field of popular music. Typical of such forms were the operetta, music for the bourgeois parlor room, and countless piano compositions intended for musical amateurs. All these required the services of the composer – that is to say, the provision of a notated outline of the music independent of its performance. Thus, musicians emerged who started to write music – in particular, songs – intended primarily for publication as sheet music and not with specific performance situations in mind. With this came the establishment of the conceptual musical artist, the composer, as distinct from the performing musical artist, the musician.

Song composers such as the Austrian Johann Sioly (1843–1911) had an enormous output: to Sioly alone are credited more than 10,000 songs. This kind of productivity occurred because, even at this stage in the history of popular music, popular music works did not last very long. A single composition did not therefore generate much income. This was particularly true in the second half of the nineteenth century, when copyright was handled rather loosely and licensing was still not established. This situation changed with the implementation of musical copyright legislation early in the twentieth century, and the foundation of performing rights organizations such as the American Society of Composers, Authors and Publishers (ASCAP). Copyright legislation and the establishment of performing rights organizations – together with a huge increase in the demand for music brought about by recording technology, and the emergence of the gramophone and, later, the radio – allowed for a stable and more or less calculable income for freelance composers.

Although the first half of the twentieth century was the time when the composer came, in popular as in classical music, to embody the professional activity responsible for the creation of music, most composers nevertheless worked as performing musicians. They did this not least to keep directly in touch with the audience as a condition for writing successful – that is to say, popular –

music. Tin Pan Alley in the United States and equivalent developments in other countries gave rise to the golden age of the composer in popular music. However, composing – the creation and outlining of pieces of music – remained distinct from arranging and, with this, from the actual assignment of sounds to the pieces outlined. In this way, composers normally provided just a sketch or outline of pieces of music, more and more reduced to the bare essentials needed to establish copyright: the eight, 12, 16 or 32 bars that formed the core of the music, together with some indication – frequently in just a symbolic form – as to how this material should be harmonized. The rest was left to the arranger.

Although they were essential to the Tin Pan Alley process, composers were often not widely known by name outside professional music business circles. With a few exceptions, such as the songs of George Gershwin, the music that composers (and lyricists) created was more likely to be associated in the public mind with those who performed it, and especially those who recorded it (even when the public was aware of more than one version). This was to become even more pronounced from the 1950s on.

The artistic and economic growth of the musical theater in the 1920s and 1930s, and the interest of the film industry first in using songs in its films and then in producing complete film musicals, widened the scope for composers, especially in the United States. But, although an entire musical had the potential to give a composer's name more recognition and status than individual songs could ever achieve, this was by no means always the case in practise. While the name of Cole Porter became widely known through shows such as *Anything Goes* (1934), the public profile of Harry Warren, who wrote music for many Hollywood films, including the *Gold Diggers* series (and who received an Oscar for his song 'Lullaby of Broadway'), remained comparatively low.

Some Tin Pan Alley and Broadway composers, such as Irving Berlin and Cole Porter, wrote both music and lyrics, but the majority worked in partnership with lyricists. Some partnerships were longlasting – for example, that between Harry Warren and Al Dubin, or between composer Ray Henderson and lyricists Bud De Sylva and Lew Brown – and often highly productive. In the early days of such partnerships, lyricists generally enjoyed a lower status in the industry than composers, and a lower public profile. By the late 1930s, this had begun to change, and the names of composer-lyricist partnerships became an important selling point in publicity for many musicals (an outstanding example being the two partnerships in which composer Richard Rodg-

ers was involved, with Lorenz Hart and with Oscar Hammerstein II).

In the 1920s, commercial sound recording had become a rival to sheet music as a means of circulating music (it would eventually be its successor). The extension of copyright to include 'mechanical rights' meant that the legal status – and hence the financial reward – of the composer was protected in the new environment, as long as the composer's contribution to a piece being recorded was registered. Records therefore provided an additional means of earning income, without any particular requirement to get directly involved in the record-making process. But in another quarter of the record industry the situation was rather different. Beginning in the 1920s, the record industry opened its doors to non-notated musical traditions, allowing them to enter the wider marketplace for the first time. Although some songwriters in this tradition recognized the need to establish copyright as composers, most were unaware of the system or its advantages, and legal ownership of the material was often claimed by record company personnel or other intermediaries. This situation changed only gradually over the next 20 to 30 years.

The introduction of magnetic tape into music production in the late 1940s brought with it important changes in the situation for the profession of the popular music composer, as it enabled musical parameters that were difficult to notate, such as timbre (the quality of sound itself) and melodic and rhythmic inflection, to be more easily handled on a trial-and-error basis during the recording and mixing process. With this, the function of the composer became integrated into the recording process, which was carried out much more as teamwork. Although for legal reasons there was always someone named as composer, in practise it became more and more difficult to distinguish who exactly contributed what during the recording process. This was particularly the case since the sound of the music was normally finalized after initial recording through the 'mixing down' of a multitrack recording and the editing of this mixdown in a postproduction process. Frequently, in the rock genre, songs were co-credited to the performer and the record producer – for example, Bryan Adams and Robert John 'Mutt' Lange.

While the term 'composer,' having to do with notions of authorship, remained a firm concept in legal contexts, in the actual practise of music the concept became very loosely defined, varying from case to case. The creation and conception of music could result in it being written down by someone in as complete a manner as possible, or the creation and conception could be the result of a more casual process of collective trial and error. In the latter case, either collective or individual authorship could be assigned afterward according to internal agreements.

During the 1960s, it became common to draw a distinction between a songwriter and a composer. The songwriter (who might also be a lyricist) was someone who created the main elements of a song without necessarily being responsible for the way the song sounded or was performed. The difference between the songwriter and the composer was that the songwriter was thought of as expressing himself/herself rather than just 'composing' music. The same period also saw the emergence of the singer-songwriter, whose contribution to the sound and the performance was more central than that of either the songwriter or the composer, and whose image was even more strongly linked to ideas of self-expression.

With the development of deejaying (DJing) during the 1980s, another new type of 'composer' emerged, even if the musicians and performers were rarely termed as such. Programming and networking devices such as the famous Roland TB-303 Bassline Composer or the Roland TR-606 Rhythm Composer became the standard for this type of DJ-composer.

Sheet Music

Warren, Harry, comp., and Dubin, Al, lyr. 1935. 'Lullaby of Broadway.' New York: Witmark.

PETER WICKE and DAVE LAING with DAVID HORN

Disc Jockey

A disc jockey, or DJ, is a person who: (a) presents radio programs or programming consisting mainly of commercially available music, normally played from discs; (b) plays and mixes discs for dancing in a dedicated disco or club, or at any public or private function; or (c) plays, scratches, remixes and samples discs as part of the creation of new live or recorded musical works, either individually or as a member of a group comprising other vocalists and instrumentalists, most commonly in rap or dance music.

The term 'disc jockey' was coined in the United States in the early 1940s to distinguish the new style of presenters of radio shows based on discs from conventional announcers. *Variety*, the US entertainment trade magazine, chose 'disc jockey' to replace 'record jockey' (used by the record company executive Jack Kapp in a magazine feature in 1940), first using it in an article entitled 'Disc Jockey Solves Vacation' on 23 July 1941. It has also been attributed to the gossip columnist and broadcaster Walter Winchell. At first, the word 'jockey' simply referred to how the DJ controlled the loudness of discs, 'riding the gain' on the control panel dial. It also came to suggest how the DJ 'rode the records to success,'

championing and repeating a favored disc until it became a hit.

Who were the first DJs? It is generally agreed that the first notable shows to start the trend toward high-profile programs based entirely on commercial discs were presented by Al Jarvis, who invented *The World's Largest Make-Believe Ballroom* on station KFWB Los Angeles in 1932, and Martin Block, who copied the idea in 1935 for WNEW New York. Each played three or four records in a row by a featured artist, speaking to listeners as if the artist were physically present and playing live. Block's show became a phenomenon, partly because of his talent for coining slogans for advertisers; by the end of its first year, it had over 4 million listeners and was running for 2.5 hours every day. It encouraged national advertisers to sponsor the new chart shows that were based on sheet music sales and records, and the radio networks to introduce more disc jockey shows, especially late at night (Passman 1971; Denisoff 1986; Fong-Torres 1998).

But the act of playing discs on the radio, though still rare, was hardly new in 1932. Discs had featured in many experimental early broadcasts on both sides of the Atlantic. The very first use of radio for broadcasting, by R.A. Fessenden on Christmas Eve 1906 from Brant Rock, Massachusetts, had included a phonograph record of a woman singing Handel's 'Largo.' In Britain, although the BBC devoted less than 1 percent of airtime to discs in 1930, it had introduced *The Week's Concert of New Gramophone Records* in March 1924, and Christopher Stone, generally credited as 'Britain's first disc jockey,' had begun his daily morning show of new discs in 1927 (Briggs 1961, 1965).

The cult of the DJ as heroic, self-appointed expert on the latest sounds can be dated to the late 1940s and very early 1950s, when white DJs like 'Symphony Sid' Torin (the first DJ to champion bebop on his jazz show on New York's WHOM in 1945), Alan Freed – and, a little later, Wolfman Jack – started introducing new R&B records by imitating the new 'jive' talk of the first black DJs on groundbreaking all-black stations like WDIA Memphis. These included Nat D. Williams, B.B. King and Rufus Thomas on WDIA, and Vernon Winslow 'Doctor Daddyo' of New Orleans WJMR and WEZZ (Cantor 1992; Jackson 1991). This perception of the disc jockey survived despite two early assaults on the DJ's integrity as unbiased taste-maker: first, the adoption of Top 40, the first radio format, by hundreds of North American stations between 1953 and 1957, which took the selection of discs out of individual DJs' hands; and then the payola scandals of the late 1950s, in which Freed was the most notable casualty.

But the myth of all DJs being crusading, independent spirits was enhanced by the life style and on- and off-air activities of DJs on the progressive, free-form FM underground stations of late 1960s North America (see Ladd 1991; Keith 1997; Douglas 1999), and by the romance attached in the popular imagination to Britain's offshore pirate stations in the mid-1960s, which, with some exceptions, were in fact tightly programmed and, in some cases, corrupt businesses (Chapman 1992).

It has become rare for any DJ on a commercial, formatted radio station to have any say on the discs he/she plays. At many stations, there are no discs at all in the on-air studio; the music is loaded onto a computer hard drive, and the DJ starts each song by simply touching its title on a computer visual display unit. However, the DJ still has to 'ride the gain' on the volume sliders – 'driving the desk,' as it is called in Britain – preserving one aspect of the DJ's craft. The radio industry has come to prefer terms like 'presenters' and 'on-air talent' to describe its voices. Perhaps the experience of being the public, audio image of a radio station while being excluded from control of the music explains the legendary ego problems of many radio DJs, often documented in hilarious contemporary, behind-the-scenes histories (see, for example, Garfield 1998). The only radio DJs who choose their own discs are those heard on specialist, late-night, public and community radio programs.

The other workplace for a disc jockey – the club – where the DJ publicly plays discs for dancing, has proved a much more creative environment. The first discothèques may have appeared in Paris during the Nazi occupation, but the emergence of the DJ from behind the turntable as a notable person with influence on what discs are played can be dated to the beginnings of the disco scene in New York in the late 1960s and early 1970s. It is possible to argue that a relocation of musical authenticity from live performance to discs took place at this time. From this stemmed the star status of DJs in rap bands, as nightclub performers and as remixers in the 1980s and 1990s. The respect afforded by rappers to 'my DJ,' by clubbers to the world-renowned DJ doing a 'set' in their city, is a sign of the reverence displayed by members of youth culture worldwide for disc culture, discs and those who select and manipulate them for an audience (Thornton 1995; Poschardt 1998; Brewster and Broughton 1999).

Bibliography

Brewster, Bill, and Broughton, Frank. 1999. *Last Night a DJ Saved My Life: The History of the Disc Jockey*. London: Headline.

Briggs, Asa. 1961. *The History of Broadcasting in the United Kingdom. Vol. 1: The Birth of Broadcasting*. London: Oxford University Press.

Briggs, Asa. 1965. *The History of Broadcasting in the United Kingdom. Vol. 2: The Golden Age of Wireless*. London: Oxford University Press.

Cantor, Louis. 1992. *Wheelin' on Beale*. New York: Pharos Books.

Chapman, Rob. 1992. *Selling the Sixties: The Pirates and Pop Music Radio*. London: Routledge.

Denisoff, R. Serge. 1986. *Tarnished Gold: The Record Industry Revisited*. New Brunswick, NJ: Transaction Books.

'Disc Jockey Solves Vacation.' 1941. *Variety* 143(7) (23 July): 34.

Douglas, Susan J. 1999. *Listening In: Radio and the American Imagination*. New York: Times Books/Random House.

Fong-Torres, Ben. 1998. *The Hits Just Keep On Coming: The History of Top 40 Radio*. San Francisco: Miller Freeman Books.

Garfield, Simon. 1998. *The Nation's Favourite: The True Adventures of Radio 1*. London: Faber and Faber.

Jackson, John A. 1991. *Big Beat Heat: Alan Freed and the Early Years of Rock & Roll*. New York: Schirmer Books.

Keith, Michael C. 1997. *Voices in the Purple Haze: Underground Radio and the Sixties*. Westport, CT: Praeger.

Ladd, Jim. 1991. *Radio Waves: Life and Revolution on the FM Dial*. New York: St. Martin's Press.

Passman, Arnold. 1971. *The Deejays*. New York: Macmillan.

Poschardt, Ulf. 1998. *DJ Culture*. London: Quartet.

Thornton, Sarah. 1995. *Club Cultures: Music, Media and Subcultural Capital*. Cambridge: Polity Press.

KEN GARNER

Engineer

Employed to manage the complex task of controlling the movement of sound from a sound source (performer or instrument) to an audience or recording medium, engineers are often considered to be simply technicians. They are, however, responsible for much more than simply technical matters. They are required to achieve particular sounds sought after by musicians and producers, as well as understand the nature and role of those sounds in specific musical genres and audience settings, keep abreast of quickly changing technologies, and maintain technical standards that allow large-scale performances to be mounted and recordings to be mass-produced and distributed.

Prior to the development of rock music, recording engineers generally came from the scientific and technical ranks associated with audio engineering and often held staff positions at recording studios owned and operated by major recording companies. The engineer's role at that time was to ensure a technically good recording, without exceeding the operating limits of existing equipment. In an environment dominated by craft unions and bureaucratic organization, the engineer's job was often governed by the clock: setting up microphones, preparing the recording equipment and getting a series of good takes had to be accomplished quickly and efficiently so that the added cost of musicians' overtime fees was not incurred.

With the advent of R&B, rock 'n' roll and rock music in the 1950s and 1960s, the studio climate began to change: fueled largely by changes in recording technology, independent record labels and the entrepreneurial spirit that guided them, the recording process became more flexible and experimental in character. The engineer's goal was to collaborate with producers and musicians and to experiment with the materials of recording in order to achieve a new kind of sound. To attain such goals, recording engineers worked long hours, and, partly because the musicians associated with the new musical styles often worked outside the confines of the unions, sessions typically started late at night and ended in the early morning hours.

In many instances, recording engineers became part of independent record label production teams and were perhaps as responsible for the sound of some musical styles as the songwriters, producers and artists themselves. Tom Dowd, for example, was sound engineer with Atlantic Records and worked closely with arranger Arif Mardin and producer Jerry Wexler. His experiments with microphone placement, multitrack recording and sound processing helped to produce some of Atlantic's classic R&B and soul hits of the early 1960s. Similarly, while the production team of Holland-Dozier-Holland is well known as the successful songwriting partnership behind many of Motown's early hits, it was engineers Lawrence Horn and Mike McClain who developed an approach to recording and signal processing that put a unique stamp on the sound of Motown's records and made them particularly effective in radio airplay.

By the late 1960s, pop artists began spending increasing amounts of time in the recording studio. For the Beatles, in particular, who eventually quit the concert stage altogether, the studio became the primary site of their creative activities. But, while the members of the Beatles remained the essential songwriting and performing entity on their recordings, it was producer George Martin and engineer Geoff Emerick who were responsible for many of the instrumental arrangements and unique sounds that made the group's late recordings so remarkable. Emerick's work had an impact even on the sound of the group itself, and he is credited with, among other innovations, developing the double-tracking approach to recording John Lennon's vocals.

By the early 1970s, in part because of the rapid changes in recording technology (multitrack recording facilities expanded from eight-, to 16-, to 24-track capability and beyond in the space of only a few years) and in part because of the increasing demands of musicians and producers, most major recording companies had ceased operating their own recording facilities in favor of hiring independent, commercial recording studios. These increased in number during the early 1970s, creating employment for an entire generation of young engineers: 24-track recording had become the norm in most commercial facilities and, because automation was still not widely utilized, there was a great need for experienced recording engineers as well as for assistant engineers, tape operators and maintenance personnel (the latter positions allowing for an informal apprenticeship system in which would-be engineers could gain experience and work their way up to the status of studio engineer).

Over time, some sound engineers were able to develop their own 'signature' sound, which placed them in demand by musicians and record labels. This enabled some to achieve freelance status, setting up their own recording studios or hiring facilities on a per-project basis. Others became producers: for example, Steve Lillywhite's drum sounds won him an opportunity to produce for U2 in the early 1980s, and earned him both critical acclaim and requests from other musical groups and record labels seeking to achieve a similar sound with their music. Still others, such as engineer Bob Clearmountain, used their reputation for creating unique sounds to market original sample libraries, thus opening up new career paths and new sources of freelance revenue for themselves (throughout the 1980s, sampling was a controversial practise, potentially bringing engineers into conflict with musicians, and forcing many engineers to negotiate, and rationalize, a personal stance vis-à-vis sampling activity; see Porcello 1991).

While many engineers are highly skilled and dedicated to their chosen profession, there is some pressure on them to move into other roles, especially that of record producer. Indeed, the boundaries between engineer and producer are extremely fluid, and many successful producers began their career as an engineer: Phil Ramone, for example, undoubtedly one of the best-known independent A&R people and record producers of the past four decades (having produced recordings for artists ranging from Frank Sinatra to Billy Joel to the Rolling Stones), began his career in the music industry as a sound engineer. His interest in the technical side of recording has led him to take a leadership role within the industry in helping to establish technical standards for digital recording and in facilitating early experiments with remote recording and mixing via digital networks.

One of the chief motivations for engineers to shift into record production, however, is financial: producers enjoy legal rights over master recordings while engineers do not, and, aside from the artistic credibility that such rights bestow, rights to a hit recording can be extremely lucrative. Recent changes to copyright law in some countries, known as 'neighboring rights,' have afforded engineers some degree of legal recognition but relatively little financial reward. Nevertheless, the stature of some engineers in the industry has allowed them occasionally to negotiate 'points' (percentages of the profit in recordings) when their records have achieved a certain level of success. The record industry has also recognized the role played by remix engineers in creating unique versions of recordings designed for use in specific industry sectors, such as radio airplay and dance venues, and some have been able to negotiate lucrative long-term contracts with major record companies. Remix engineer Shep Pettibone, for example, established a substantial reputation for work he did in the early 1990s on singles by artists such as Madonna.

At best, however, the status of the recording engineer is still rather tenuous within the record industry. While a few engineers have achieved artistic credibility and independent status, many others labor away in commercial studio settings, typically uninvolved in decisions concerning musical performance, leaving those to a producer or to the musicians themselves. They generally do not offer aesthetic judgments (unless asked to do so), as their job is to take direction and capture as 'authentic' and technically unadulterated a sound as possible. Even this can create some tension regarding their role, however, given the inherently aesthetic nature of judgments of authenticity.

Bibliography

Cunningham, Mark. 1998. *Good Vibrations: A History of Record Production*. 2nd ed. London: Sanctuary Publishing.

Fox, Ted. 1986. *In the Groove: The People Behind the Music*. New York: St. Martin's Press.

Kealy, Edward R. 1979. 'From Craft to Art: The Case of Sound Mixers and Popular Music.' *Sociology of Work and Occupations* 6(1): 3–29.

Porcello, Thomas. 1991. 'The Ethics of Digital Audio-Sampling: Engineers' Discourse.' *Popular Music* 10(1): 69–84.

PAUL THÉBERGE and STEVE JONES

Lyricist

A lyricist is the author of words intended to be sung. The lyricist generally works in collaboration with the composer of the music for a song. The lyrics of a song may also be written by the same person or persons responsible for composing the music, or may consist of a previously created poem or piece of verse.

In European music, many of the first specialist writers of lyrics were librettists, creating words for operas. Thus, Lorenzo da Ponte, a former poet of the Viennese court, created the words for Mozart's *Don Giovanni* and *Cosi fan Tutte*. The majority of operettas and stage musicals also followed this strict division of labor between composer and lyricist in their creation. In England, the humorist W.S. Gilbert provided dialog and lyrics for numerous operettas composed by Sir Arthur Sullivan, while the lyricists of the Broadway musicals of the twentieth-century United States included Oscar Hammerstein II and Moss Hart (both partners of composer Richard Rodgers), Ira Gershwin (with George Gershwin) and Alan Jay Lerner (with Frederick Loewe). Among the smaller number of Broadway composer-lyricists were Irving Berlin, Noel Coward, Cole Porter and Stephen Sondheim. In Europe, the lyricists Tim Rice and Alain Boublil worked with Andrew Lloyd Webber and Claude-Michel Schonberg, respectively.

In the field of popular song composition, many early broadsides were not credited to specific authors, although some, like the seventeenth-century writer Laurence Price, have been identified (Harker 1987). By the eighteenth century, one convention in Britain was for composers to set already published verse to music rather than to commission new lyrics; a similar convention was often used in Western classical music. The exceptions, such as Thomas Moore and Robert Burns, were poets who set their own verses to music that was often drawn from traditional Irish and Scottish sources.

During the nineteenth century, the first great popular songwriter in the United States, Stephen Foster, also wrote both words and music for many of his best-known songs. In the era of vaudeville (United States), music hall (Britain) and *café-concert* (France), lyrics were sometimes written by the singers who performed songs onstage. Examples were George M. Cohan, George Leybourne and Aristide Bruant.

By the time of the formation of Tin Pan Alley, teams of professional lyricists and composers flourished alongside self-contained songwriters (that is, songwriters who wrote both lyrics and music), such as Charles K. Harris, author and composer of 'After the Ball.' Although he soon became a self-contained songwriter, Irving Berlin's first job was as a staff lyricist for a music publisher. Arthur J. Lamb wrote the lyrics to 'A Bird in a Gilded Cage,' a composition by Harry Von Tilzer.

The role of lyricist in vernacular musics such as country and blues was less precise, for two reasons. Firstly, these musics drew from a background of traditional song, whose authors were unknown. Secondly, performers themselves frequently created or embellished songs without committing either lyrics or melody to paper. Nevertheless, early entrepreneurs of country music required a supply of songs that were clearly new so that they could be copyrighted. Thus, the pioneering talent scout Polk Brockman of Atlanta commissioned songs – words and music – from Andrew Jenkins, a blind news vendor and preacher, to be recorded by other artists (Peterson 1997, 24). The position in rural blues was similar, although the hit records by city-based female singers of the 1920s were often composed by a new breed of arrangers, publishers and authors, including Perry Bradford and Clarence Williams.

As the vernacular recording industry grew in the 1940s and 1950s, the need for a constant supply of new songs increased. At some early rhythm and blues record companies, staff arrangers or even producers became songwriters. This was the position at Atlantic, where Jesse Stone and Ahmet Ertegun composed many of the label's early hits by the Clovers, Ruth Brown and others (Gillett 1975). Here, the general trend was for the same writer to create both words and music. There were some exceptions in the rock 'n' roll era. Little Richard's earliest hits, 'Tutti Frutti' and 'Long Tall Sally,' for example, were based on words supplied by nonprofessional female lyricists – Dorothy La Bostrie and Enotris Johnson, respectively (White 1985, 67).

Some jazz-based songs were composed with a division of labor between composer and lyricist. The words for numerous compositions by Fats Waller were supplied by Andy Razaf, while Billy Strayhorn was Duke Ellington's dependable lyricist, even if at times Ellington claimed the credit (and the royalties) for Strayhorn's words, just as manager Irving Mills had done with Ellington.

There are many instances of lyricists migrating to music from written literature. The English comic novelist P.G. Wodehouse provided lyrics for Jerome Kern; the French poet Jacques Prevert wrote 'Les Feuilles mortes' (known in English translation as 'Autumn Leaves'); and the German dramatist Bertolt Brecht provided lyrics for *The Threepenny Opera* with music by Kurt Weill. In the era of Anglo-American rock, cartoonist Shel Silverstein wrote for Dr. Hook and the Medicine Show; poets John Perry Barlow and Robert Hunter wrote for the Grateful Dead; novelist Michael Moorcock wrote for Hawkwind; and Jacques Levy wrote with Bob Dylan. Czech poet Egon Bondy wrote lyrics for the persecuted 1960s avant-garde band Plastic People of the Universe.

Some lyricists have specialized in translation. Since Henry Rowley Bishop made an English version of *Don Giovanni* in 1810, opera librettos have been translated into vernacular languages. In the contemporary musical theater, Herbert Kretzmer made English translations of Boublil's lyrics for *Les Misérables* and *Miss Saigon*. In the late twentieth century, French and Italian hit songs were given English versions, and vice versa. Paul Anka turned 'Comme d'habitude' into 'My Way,' while Bob Dylan's early lyrics were translated into French by Pierre Delanoe and into German by Wolfgang Ambros.

There have been some outstanding examples of 'pure' lyricists in the 1960s and later. These included Bernie Taupin with Elton John, Howard Greenfield with Neil Sedaka and Hal David with Burt Bacharach. Nevertheless, the strict division of labor between members of a songwriting team rapidly dissolved in the 1950s and 1960s. Although such famous partnerships as Leiber and Stoller, Goffin and King, Holland-Dozier-Holland, and Mann and Weil started out with one member primarily responsible for lyrics, no formal distinction was made between composer and lyricist. In the case of John Lennon and Paul McCartney, the most famous songwriters of the 1960s, not only was the role of lyricist shared or passed from one member to the other, but many Beatles' songs were composed by only one of the duo despite being credited to both.

The working methods of lyricists and composers are varied. Since the start of the Taupin-John partnership, Bernie Taupin has provided Elton John with lyrics to set to music. Other composing teams operate in a more dialectical way, with a melodic line or a verbal phrase triggering the process of more or less simultaneous creation of words and music.

Some lyricists have specialized in writing words to set to an existing classical melody or jazz improvisation. Examples of the former are Eric Carmen's 'All By Myself,' using a melody by Rachmaninoff, and the humorist Allan Sherman's lyrics for 'Hello Muddah, Hello Faddah,' which was set to 'Dance of the Hours' by Ponchielli. Jon Hendricks and King Pleasure are each renowned for creating lyrics for recorded jazz solos by James Moody, Charlie Parker and others.

Outside Europe, specialist lyricists have existed in some music cultures. In the Middle East, songs performed by the great Egyptian singer Umm Kulthūm often began as specially written words by recognized poets such as Ahmad Rami, who wrote 70 lyrics for her in the 1930s (Danielson 1997, 73ff.). In Japan, Yaso Saijo was the most successful lyricist of *kayokyoku*, the principal popular music genre of the 1930s. In Brazil, celebrated lyricists such as Haroldo Barbosa, Fernando Brant and Ronaldo Bastos worked with composers Bidu Reis, Milton Nascimento and Celso Fonseca. In contrast, the great *griot* tradition of West Africa involves the production of newly composed works whose words and music are the creation of a single individual usually born into the song-making caste.

The cultural and economic status of lyricists has improved since the eighteenth century, when they were treated as inferior to composers: while opera gives precedence to the composer, the authorship of most stage musicals is credited to both composer and lyricist.

The payment of lyricists was also often inferior to that of the composer; Hamm (1979) states that, in the early days of Tin Pan Alley, a composer in need of a lyric would pay 'an author a sum of perhaps five dollars to write a text for him – the writer having no further claim to his text, financial or otherwise' (290), although the advent of copyright legislation and performing rights organizations such as the American Society of Composers, Authors and Publishers (ASCAP) gave lyricists a legal basis for equality of payment with composers.

Copyright law has also caused legal difficulties for some lyricists when they have been accused of plagiarism or unlawful parody. Although plagiarism cases usually involve musical phrases, the British songwriting team of Guy Chambers and Robbie Williams was found guilty of unlawfully copying lyrics that had appeared in a recording by Loudon Wainwright III in 2002. In the most celebrated parody lawsuit of the late twentieth century, Luther Campbell of the rap band 2 Live Crew was acquitted of copyright infringement in his lewd version of Roy Orbison's lyrics to 'Oh, Pretty Woman.'

Bibliography

Danielson, Virginia. 1997. *The Voice of Egypt: Umm Kulthūm, Arabic Song, and Egyptian Society in the Twentieth Century*. Chicago: University of Chicago Press.

Gillett, Charlie. 1975. *Making Tracks: The Story of Atlantic Records*. London: Panther.

Hamm, Charles. 1979. *Yesterdays: Popular Song in America*. New York: Norton.

Harker, Dave. 1987. 'The Price You Pay: An Introduction to the Life and Songs of Laurence Price.' In *Lost in Music: Culture, Style and the Musical Event*, ed. Avron Levine White. London: Routledge & Kegan Paul, 107–63.

Peterson, Richard A. 1997. *Creating Country Music: Fabricating Authenticity*. Chicago: University of Chicago Press.

White, Charles. 1985. *The Life and Times of Little Richard*. London: Pan.

Sheet Music

Harris, Charles K., comp. and lyr. 1892. 'After the Ball.' Milwaukee, WI: Charles K. Harris & Co.

Von Tilzer, Harry, comp., and Lamb, Arthur J., lyr. 1900. 'A Bird in a Gilded Cage.' New York: Shapiro, Bernstein and Von Tilzer.

Discographical References

Anka, Paul. 'My Way.' *Paul Anka in Vegas*. Delta 12669. *1995*: USA.

Carmen, Eric. 'All By Myself.' Arista 0165. *1976*: USA.

Little Richard. 'Long Tall Sally.' Specialty 572. *1956*: USA.

Little Richard. 'Tutti Frutti.' Specialty 561. *1956*: USA.

Orbison, Roy. 'Oh, Pretty Woman.' Monument 851. *1964*: USA.

Sherman, Allan. 'Hello Muddah, Hello Faddah (A Letter from Camp).' Warner 5378. *1963*: USA.

2 Live Crew. 'Oh, Pretty Woman.' *As Clean As They Wanna Be*. Luke 91652-2. *1989*: USA.

Discography

Piaf, Edith. 'Autumn Leaves (Les Feuilles mortes).' *Edith Piaf: 30ᵉ anniversaire*. Capitol 27097. *1994*: USA.

DAVE LAING

MC

The initials 'MC,' sometimes written as 'emcee,' stand for 'Master of Ceremonies.' More recently, in the genre of rap, the term 'MC' has been used as an abbreviation for 'mic chanter' (Back 1996, 188) or 'mike controller' (Warner 1996, 289) to describe a group member who recites the rhyming couplets of rap verses.

The term 'Master of Ceremonies' has its origins in the designation for a position in the English royal household. It was applied within the sphere of entertainment in eighteenth-century England. In the following century, it was the title given to the person who introduced each act, and sometimes entertained the audience with a comedy routine between acts, at concerts of various types of music as well as at vaudeville shows. The best-known MC of recent times is probably the 'leering, epicene' (Green 1977, 53) fictional Master of Ceremonies created by John Kander and Fred Ebb for their 1966 stage musical *Cabaret*.

In twentieth-century North America, MCs were used in most genres of popular music. In 1926, the *National Barn Dance*, a radio show broadcast by WLS Chicago, was advertised as having 'masters of ceremonies' (Shelton 1966, 43). In the 1940s and 1950s, the MC of a jazz or rock 'n' roll show would often be a well-known local disc jockey such as 'Symphony Sid' Torin of New York jazz station WHOM, who introduced concerts by Dizzy Gillespie in 1945 (DeVeaux 1997, 430), or Alan Freed, champion of black rock 'n' roll artists and promoter of touring 'package' shows featuring up to eight acts. R&B or soul orchestras such as those of James Brown or Ray Charles would employ an MC to whip up the enthusiasm of the audience prior to the entrance of the star.

The word 'MC' has also been used as a verb – by Duke Ellington, for example, who said 'I didn't know the first thing about how to MC . . .' (Collier 1987, 98) when, in 1930, he started to announce to the audience the items in the stage act of his orchestra.

The only occasion when an MC is known to have composed a song lyric during a show was at the Newport Jazz Festival in 1960. The poet Langston Hughes was introducing blues performers and, hearing that this would be the last Newport festival, he wrote a set of blues verses that was spontaneously set to music and sung by Otis Spann, pianist with the show's headline group the Muddy Waters Band (Tooze 1997, 173–74).

Bibliography

Back, Les. 1996. *New Ethnicities and Urban Culture: Racisms and Multiculture in Young Lives*. London: UCL Press.

Collier, James Lincoln. 1987. *Duke Ellington*. London: Michael Joseph.

DeVeaux, Scott. 1997. *The Birth of Bebop: A Social and Musical History*. Berkeley, CA: University of California Press.

Green, Stanley. 1977. *Encyclopaedia of the Musical*. London: Cassell.

Shelton, Robert. 1966. *The Country Music Story*. Indianapolis, IN: Bobbs-Merrill Co.

Tooze, Sandra B. 1997. *Muddy Waters: The Mojo Man*. Toronto: ECW Press.

Warner, Simon. 1996. *Rockspeak!: The Language of Rock and Pop*. London: Blandford.

DAVE LAING

Musician

The term and concept of 'musician' have no more a global currency than does the term 'music.' There are many societies and cultures in which no direct linguistic and epistemological equivalents for these terms exist. Nonetheless, modern Western scholarship has recognized cultural activities across the globe that it has had little difficulty in categorizing as 'musical,' and as being performed by 'musicians.' As Merriam (1964) has observed, 'in all societies individuals exist whose skill at making music is recognized in some way as being superior to that of other individuals so that they are called upon, or simply take their "rightful" place, in musical situations' (124). The character of these places can vary greatly from one society or culture to another. In Sufi culture, for example, musicians perform religious functions, while West African *griots* are important as oral historians and praise-singers.

In Western culture, the term and concept of 'musician' have had a long history. The term is derived from the Latin '*musicus*,' itself owing much to the Greek 'μουσιχός.' The term 'musician' was used in different ways before it came to indicate the performing artist as opposed to the conceptual artist – the composer – in music. In the ancient world, the term '*musicus*' referred to individuals competent in music in the broadest sense of the word. Elsewhere, the term covered a variety of sound-related activities, depending on the culture in which the term – in one of its linguistic equivalents – was used. However, as societies became increasingly stratified, so too did the world of music. With this, the activities of musicians became more specialized: dedicated to dance, entertainment or amusement, with the status of the musician remaining customarily very low in the social hierarchy.

It needed the market forces of developing capitalism in Europe to facilitate the emergence of a type of musician who could offer his/her services directly to a paying audience, and in this way try to make a living. Before this time, popular musicians could be excluded from musicians' guilds because their repertoire, their instruments or their social position lacked the status necessary for admittance. 'Free' or so-called 'traveling musicians' were thus deprived of all rights and had to beg in order to survive.

In Europe, it was not until the end of the eighteenth century that the musicians' guilds, which had regulated professional musical activities since the early Middle Ages, were replaced by specific trade regulations that allowed and, indeed, forced musicians to offer their services to the general public for regular payment. As a consequence, a type of 'all-round musician' emerged, characterized by the ability to cover a broad repertoire, from dance music to folk song, from parlor song to the music of the vaudeville theater. This type of versatile musicianship became a major force in the development of popular music. The vicissitudes and uncertainties of the market and the demands of the consuming audience did not permit a strict division of labor among musicians. Songwriters acted customarily as band leaders, and performing musicians frequently played more than one instrument. Many musicians were forced into an existence that hovered uneasily between that of the professional and that of the semiprofessional. However, with the growth of urbanization and industrialization, an increasing specialization occurred. Toward the end of the nineteenth century, popular musicians had clearly defined areas of work in dance music, in public entertainment and in music halls or musical theaters. These musicians frequently relied on a formal training – graduating from one of the conservatories and then leaving the world of classical music, or taking lessons from one of the many popular musicians who supported themselves by giving lessons in addition to performing.

Technology soon became a major challenge for musicians struggling to survive in popular music. Sound recording was the first step in redefining the role of the musician. Sound recording made it possible for non-notated forms of music to be exploited commercially. With this, well-defined and entrenched standards of professionalism were opened to new forms of musicianship. In the United States, ragtime, tango and early jazz brought into recording studios musicians from non-notated musical traditions. And although the first recordings in these genres were still made by those who conformed to the standards of the musically literate and versatile professional musician, it was not long before the doors of recording studios were opened to musicians – not only blues musicians, but also folk and country musicians – who could not read scores and who could not establish their legitimacy through their professional training.

This development was fostered also by radio. The barn dance format, inaugurated in 1923 by WBAP Fort Worth and taken up by many stations throughout rural North America – the famous *Grand Ole Opry* show, created in 1925 by WSM in Nashville, Tennessee, was one – opened the door for many talented nonprofessionals. However, it was also radio that threatened musicianship in general. From the early 1920s, radio enabled people to hear music at home by way of studio performances and remote broadcasts. This weakened the motivation for people to go out to live performances. Then, in the mid-1930s, radio began using recorded, 'canned' music rather than actual performances in the studio or from remote locations. Radio also militated against the continuing versatility of musicians through its capacity to broadcast any kind of music to any audience. This capacity rendered redundant the ability of musicians to maintain a broad repertoire within their particular genre or musical tradition. The emergence of the film soundtrack at the end of the 1920s had a similar effect by making cinema musicians obsolete.

One of the deepest breaks in the evolving character of the musician was brought about by magnetic tape, which arrived in recording studios in the late 1940s. Its far-reaching consequences have been twofold. First, it rendered established musical competence superfluous. Considerable musical experience had formerly been one of the preconditions for entering the studio, regardless of whether or not this experience had been acquired professionally. Taping provided an easy and cheap way to re-record inexperienced musicians such as the young Elvis Presley as often as necessary and to compensate for imperfections by cutting and splicing. The former line which had distinguished the professional or highly experienced musician from the musical amateur disappeared completely. From this time, literally anybody could become a 'musician' as long as he/she could learn to control the creation of sounds in ways that met the demands of the marketplace. The result was a huge injection of creativity from untapped sources, since all the preconditions that previously had had to obtain if an individual was to be accepted as a 'musician' – education, experience, proven musical competence – ceased to exist. The boundary between 'musicians' and 'non-musicians' became porous in every way: socially, culturally and artistically. The concept of the 'musician' thus became quite unstable.

The second consequence to follow from the advent of magnetic tape was a shift in emphasis from the musician as a performer to the musician as an originator of sounds. To be a musician no longer meant just being involved with the generation of sounds by means of an instrument or the voice; it began to mean being involved with the creation of new sounds, even in the case of music that was already known (as with the making of cover versions). To be a musician increasingly meant to create unique sounds. The line between the performer, the songwriter and the producer became blurred. Although these activities continued to exist as distinct occupations, they increasingly became interchangeable, indistinguishable or united in one person. From the 1960s onward, the term 'musician' began to cover all of these activities.

The final shift in the character of what it meant to be a 'musician' was brought about in the early 1980s by DJs using the turntable as a musical instrument. Making music by means of already existing music through the use of machines such as turntables, sequencers and sampling devices has provided the most far-reaching challenge to traditional notions of what it means to be a 'musician.' Cutting and mixing, sampling and looping have augmented and, to a degree, supplanted the long-established way of being a musician: vocalizing or playing an instrument. With this, the term 'musician' has reverted to what it used to be in previous times: an open category that can subsume any kind of musical competence.

Bibliography

Bayton, Mavis. 1990. 'How Women Become Musicians.' In *On Record: Rock, Pop and the Written Word*, ed. Simon Frith and Andrew Goodwin. New York: Pantheon, 238–57.

Bennett, H. Stith. 1980. *On Becoming a Rock Musician.* Amherst, MA: University of Massachusetts Press.

Coffman, James T. 1971. '"Everybody Knows This Is Nowhere": Role Conflict and the Rock Musician.' *Popular Music and Society* 1: 20–32.

Coffman, James T. 1972. '"So You Want to Be a Rock & Roll Star!": Role Conflict and the Rock Musician.' In

The Sounds of Social Change: Studies in Popular Culture, ed. R. Serge Denisoff and Richard A. Peterson. Chicago: Rand McNally, 261–73.

Faulkner, Robert R. 1971. *Hollywood Studio Musicians: Their Work and Careers in the Recording Industry*. Chicago: Aldine-Atherton.

Finnegan, Ruth. 1989. *The Hidden Musicians: Music-Making in an English Town*. Cambridge: Cambridge University Press.

Hadley, Daniel. 1993. '"Ride the Rhythm": Two Approaches to DJ Practice.' *Journal of Popular Music Studies* 5: 58–67.

Harvith, John, and Harvith, Susan Edwards, eds. 1987. *Edison, Musicians and the Phonograph: A Century in Retrospect*. New York: Greenwood Press.

Julien, Olivier. 1999. 'The Diverting of Musical Technology by Rock Musicians: The Example of Double-tracking.' *Popular Music* 18(3): 357–65.

Kaufmann, Dorothea. 1991. '"Wenn Damen pfeifen, gehen die Gracien flöten": Die Musikerin in der deutschen Tanz- und Unterhaltungsmusik des 19. Jahrhunderts' ['If Ladies Whistle, Refinement Goes for a Burton': The Female Musician in German Dance and Entertainment Music]. *Worldbeat* 1: 81–94.

Köhler, Peter, and Schacht, Konrad. 1983. *Die Jazzmusiker: Zur Soziologie einer kreativen Randgruppe* [The Jazz Musician: Toward a Sociology of a Creative Fringe Group]. Freiburg: Peter Weininger, Roter Punkt Verlag.

Merriam, Alan P. 1964. *The Anthropology of Music*. Evanston, IL: Northwestern University Press.

Ritzel, Fred, and Stroh, Wolfgang Martin. 1985. 'Deutsche Tanzmusiker. Zu einer Sozialgeschichte der populären Musik in Deutschland' [German Dance Musicians: Toward a Social History of Popular Music in Germany]. *Jazzforschung* 17: 69–75.

Salmen, Walter. 1997. *Beruf: Musiker – verachtet – vergöttert – vermarktet. Eine Sozialgeschichte in Bildern* [Occupation: Musician – Despised – Idolized – Marketed. A Social History in Pictures]. Kassel: Bärenreiter.

Seltzer, George. 1989. *Music Matters: The Performer and the American Federation of Musicians*. Metuchen, NJ: Scarecrow Press.

Stebbins, Robert A. 1966. 'Class, Status and Power Among Jazz and Commercial Musicians.' *The Sociological Quarterly* 7(2): 197–213.

Swindell, W.C. 1986. 'Black Musicians' Struggle for Subsistence.' *OneTwoThreeFour: A Rock 'n' Roll Quarterly* 3: 7–38.

PETER WICKE

Orchestrator

An orchestrator is a person who scores a piece of preexisting music for performance by the instruments in an orchestra or ensemble. Working from a variety of possible sources, ranging from a complete original piano score to a collection of miscellaneous notes, or even from a previous orchestration, the orchestrator is responsible for deciding how to assign individual musical lines and notes to specific instruments, for producing the orchestral score itself and for preparing – or supervising the preparation of – the various instrumental parts. Whereas in most art music it is common for the composer also to be the orchestrator, in popular music the orchestrator is frequently an independent professional engaged specifically to orchestrate a particular piece – although some successful bands and orchestras employ their own staff orchestrators. The role of arranger may include that of orchestrator.

Because orchestration is a skill that tends to be formally acquired, many popular music composers who work in an orchestral idiom but whose career route has not included formal musical education do not aspire to be their own orchestrators. Some have worked closely with an orchestrator – as did Paul McCartney with Carl Davis in the scoring of the *Liverpool Oratorio* (Davis was also the first to conduct the piece, in 1991) – but most have preferred to pass the task on. This trend was especially apparent in the musical theater in the first 60 years of the twentieth century. Producers of many of Broadway's most celebrated musicals consistently employed professional orchestrators to produce the orchestral score for the show. It was in the context of the Broadway musical that the status and contribution of the theatrical orchestrator changed – from constituting a routine task with little status to being seen as a significant element in determining the character of the show. This change was largely due to the work of a single man, Robert Russell Bennett. A substantial number of the orchestral scores of major musicals, including *Show Boat* (1927; music by Jerome Kern), *Anything Goes* (1934; music by Cole Porter), *Oklahoma!* (1943; music by Richard Rodgers) and *My Fair Lady* (1956; music by Frederick Loewe), were produced by Bennett, who exploited his background in both classical composition and dance band music to develop a style of symphonic orchestration for the musical that respected, and indeed drew out, the idiomatic nature of the material.

The strong tendency for later composers for the musical who were formally trained, such as Leonard Bernstein and Stephen Sondheim, to continue to employ a separate orchestrator (or orchestrators) was partly a reflection of the established nature of the tradition, but also an acknowledgment that the orchestrator possessed a particular, highly professional expertise. Both Bernstein and Sondheim were keen to act in partnership with their orchestrators. For many of his shows,

Sondheim worked in collaboration with one single orchestrator, Jonathan Tunick, while in Bernstein's case collaboration sometimes shaded into participation, so that for his shows *Candide* (1956) and *West Side Story* (1957) his name appeared among the credits for the orchestration.

The contribution of the orchestrator to the character and reputation of a particular piece of music has sometimes been a subject of dispute, as happened most famously in the case of George Gershwin's 'Rhapsody in Blue,' first performed by Gershwin with Paul Whiteman's band in 1924. Following his first attempt at an extended, 'serious' piece, the one-act 'jazz opera' *Blue Monday* (1922), which had been orchestrated by Will Vodery, Gershwin studied orchestration, but nevertheless 'Rhapsody' was orchestrated by Whiteman's arranger Ferde Grofé from a two-piano score. Sensitive to rumors that Grofé's role had extended beyond that of orchestrator, Gershwin made a point of informing ASCAP in writing that he was the sole composer of 'Rhapsody'; Grofé himself, while inclined to disparage Gershwin's suggestions for the instrumentation of the piece, 'never claimed to have done more than orchestrate it' (Schiff 1997, 11). The fact that Gershwin did not subsequently make his own orchestration suggests that Grofé had had the foresight to negotiate the sole rights to orchestrate the piece (Schiff 1997, 11).

Bibliography

Bennett, Robert Russell. 1975. *Instrumentally Speaking.* Melville, NY: Belwin-Mills.

Holden, S. 1984. 'How the Music Gets That Special Broadway Sound.' *New York Times* (29 January).

Schiff, David. 1997. *Gershwin: Rhapsody in Blue.* Cambridge: Cambridge University Press.

Tucker, Mark. 1996. 'In Search of Will Vodery.' *Black Music Research Journal* 16(1): 123–82.

Sheet Music

Gershwin, George, comp. 1924. 'Rhapsody in Blue.' New York: New World Music Corp.

Discographical Reference

McCartney, Paul, and Davis, Carl. *Liverpool Oratorio.* Angel 54371. *1991*: UK.

DAVID HORN and STAN HAWKINS

Producer

The producer of a recording is generally considered the final arbiter of aesthetic judgments throughout the recording process. Prior to the advent of electrical recording, however, the producer's role did not exist. In large part this was because the recording process itself was relatively straightforward, involving the live performance of a piece of music onto a recording medium.

A recording, once made, could not be changed. Sound engineers played a critical role insofar as they made decisions regarding the placement of musicians and recording devices within a studio, but they made those decisions on the basis of their understanding of the mechanics of recording; they were not involved in aesthetic matters. At that time, an 'A&R' (artist and repertoire) person was analogous to a producer. The former's responsibilities included booking studio time and ensuring that musicians were hired and appeared on time, contracts were drawn up and enforced, the performer's career was progressing (musically and financially) and suitable musical material was on hand.

The advent of tape recording and multitrack recording meant not only that the recording process became more complex, but that there was a need for its supervision. The easy manipulation of sound via equalization, reverberation, layering of tracks and the like, as well as the ability to splice and edit takes, not only opened up new creative avenues and opportunities for experimentation, but also meant that myriad decisions had to be made before, during and after a recording session – decisions that would have a significant impact on the finished recording. A&R people, generally not well versed in recording techniques, were less likely candidates than sound engineers to take on that role, simply because of a lack of understanding of the process. In many cases, therefore, producers have come from the ranks of sound engineers; Phil Ramone, for instance, began his studio career as an engineer, as did Bruce Swedien and Alan Parsons. There were exceptions, however, and some A&R people also made the transition to producer, most notably George Martin, the Beatles' producer. Producers continued to rely routinely on sound engineers, as their new role meant that they were unable to attend to all the details of the recording process.

Producers assumed a role not unlike that of a film director, supervising the step-by-step process of creating a product, organizing and guiding a team (musicians, engineers, guest performers and so on) to bring about its realization, remaining aware of the overall goal (a difficult task for those with specialized roles) and assembling the final product. As the recording process became more complex (industrially as well as technologically) in the late 1950s and early 1960s, the role of a producer evolved to that of overseer of the entire recording process for a given recording project. The seemingly simple matter of bringing musicians together to make a recording, for instance, was forever changed by multitrack recording. Musicians no longer needed to be in the same place at the same time to record together, and it became part of a producer's job to manage and keep track of the fragmented recording process.

At the same time, tape recording and associated technologies reduced the expense of audio recording, allowing independently owned recording studios (such as Sam Phillips' Sun Studios in Memphis) to create professional recordings. The owners of such studios often acted as producers, and over time a producer's role became one not only of a decision-maker and organizer, but of an active participant and collaborator in the recording process, much as George Martin played an active role in the realization of the Beatles' recordings. Producers are, in fact, credited alongside musicians in the notes accompanying almost every commercial recording, according them a status akin to that of the artist (Phil Spector, having achieved great acclaim and notoriety, is the most notable). In some instances, such as that of Alan Parsons or Bill Laswell, producers are musicians in their own right. It is not uncommon for some musicians to act as producers of their own (and others') recordings. For example, the songwriting team of Jerry Leiber and Mike Stoller, responsible for numerous hit rock 'n' roll songs in the 1950s, became involved in production because they sought to make records of their songs as they wished to hear them.

In some cases, a producer will have a long-term relationship with a performer (as George Martin did with the Beatles, or Brian Eno with U2), a record label or a recording studio. Often, producers will be hired for individual projects. But even those who regularly work with the same artists, label or studio find that their role varies from one recording project to another, depending on the performers' desires, the recording studio and/or equipment chosen, or evolving musical styles and tastes. Nevertheless, several of the producer's responsibilities are common to most recording projects. Performers, as well as record labels, rely on a producer to be an objective listener and to assist with making decisions concerning musical arrangements, performances, even songwriting and the choice of music to be recorded. A producer is also relied upon to make decisions about which recording studios and types of equipment are most appropriate for a particular project. The most vital functions, and the ones for which producers are most often chosen and by which they are most often judged, are the ability to motivate performers to produce their best and the competence to determine the appropriate sound of a recording before it is issued. Usually, diplomacy and tact are requisite, since a producer's idea of how a recording should sound can run counter to that of a musician and/or songwriter.

Bibliography

Creekmur, C.K. 1988. 'The Space of Recording: The Production of Popular Music as Spectacle.' *Wide Angle* 10(2): 32–40.

Goodwin, Andrew. 1988. 'Sample and Hold: Pop Music in the Digital Age of Reproduction.' *Critical Quarterly* 30(3): 34–49.

Hennion, Antoine. 1982. 'Popular Music as Social Production.' In *Popular Music Perspectives, 1*, ed. David Horn and Philip Tagg. Göteborg and Exeter: IASPM, 32–40.

Jones, Steve. 1992. *Rock Formation: Music, Technology, and Mass Communication*. Newbury Park, CA: Sage.

Kealy, E.R. 1974. *The Real Rock Revolution: Sound Mixers, Social Inequality, and the Aesthetics of Popular Music Production*. Ann Arbor, MI: University Microfilms International.

Kealy, E.R. 1979. 'From Craft to Art: The Case of Sound Mixers and Popular Music.' *Sociology of Work and Occupation* 6: 3–29.

Kealy, E.R. 1982. 'Conventions and the Production of the Popular Music Aesthetic.' *Journal of Popular Culture* 16(2): 100–15.

Martin, George, with Hornsby, Jeremy. 1979. *All You Need Is Ears*. New York: St. Martin's Press.

Muikku, J. 1990. 'On the Role and Tasks of a Record Producer.' *Popular Music and Society* 14(1): 25–33.

Théberge, Paul. 1989. 'The "Sound" of Music: Technological Rationalization and the Production of Popular Music.' *New Formations* 8: 99–111.

Théberge, Paul. 1997. *Any Sound You Can Imagine: Making Music/Consuming Technology*. Hanover, NH: University Press of New England/Wesleyan University Press.

Tobler, John, and Grundy, Stuart. 1982. *The Record Producers*. New York: St. Martin's Press.

Vignolle, J-P. 1980. 'Mixing Genres and Reaching the Public: The Production of Popular Music.' *Social Science Information* 19(1): 79–105.

STEVE JONES

Sideman

A sideman is a musician (male or female) who is an ordinary member of a band but has no leadership or vocal duties. In the language of the symphony orchestra, a sideman is a rank-and-file member. However, with regard to jazz bands, dance orchestras, big bands, show bands and, by extension, rhythm and blues or soul bands, the term 'sideman' is universally used to describe the constituent musicians. Most musicians' unions in the United States and Europe distinguish leaders and star soloists and vocalists by setting out different rates of pay for them, whereas sidemen are paid the minimum union 'scale' rate.

Bibliography

Levet, Jean-Paul. 1992. *Talkin' That Talk: Le Langage du blues et du jazz* [Talkin' That Talk: The Language of Blues and Jazz]. Paris: Hatier.

Smith, W.O. 1991. *Sideman*. Nashville, TN: Rutledge Hill Press.

ALYN SHIPTON

Singer-Songwriter

Referring to popular music artists who write and perform their own material (often self-accompanied, most frequently on acoustic guitar or piano), the term 'singer-songwriter' is usually (although not exclusively) applied to certain performers in the rock, folk and pop genres. Throughout the nineteenth and twentieth centuries, there were artists who fitted into this category across a number of genres: for example, the US performer of the 1830s Henry Russell, French *chanson réaliste* performer Aristide Bruant, various blues performers of the 1920s and 1930s, the country singer Hank Williams and the rock 'n' roll singer Buddy Holly. However, from the 1960s onward, the term came into popular usage to refer to a specific group of performers following particular stylistic and thematic conventions.

Singer-songwriters have been seen critically and commercially as a 'movement' within popular music, and the term has been privileged as a distinct category contained within an Anglo-American rock perspective. The music of singer-songwriters has tended to adhere to folk, rock and North American pop styles, and to include personal or observational concerns in its lyrics. The term can be viewed as aesthetically loaded, as it connotes particular attributes of a performer – such as emotional honesty, intelligence, authenticity and artistic autonomy. The singer-songwriter has also come to be associated with lyrical introspection, confessional songwriting, gentle musical arrangements and an understated performance style.

The term itself came into common usage in the mid-1960s and had its roots in the folk revival. In a 1965 advertising campaign, the Elektra record company used the slogan 'Singer-songwriters exclusively on Elektra Records' to promote folk and protest singers such as Phil Ochs, Tom Paxton and Fred Neil. The term was originally applied to folk artists (or 'topical songwriters') whose repertoires had moved away from a reliance on traditional material, subject matter and song styles to a more contemporary style generally dealing with more personal issues. Gaar (1993) argues that 'folk artists worked within an established genre steeped in historical tradition whereas the music of the singer-songwriters came from an intensely personal perspective' (184). The emergence of the singer-songwriter has been linked to folk aesthetics and values crossing over to mainstream commercial popular music: '[A]s the folk emphasis on songs and lyrics, on the performers' honesty and insight, were adapted to the commercial needs of rock . . . the rock

songwriter became the poet, the singer/songwriter the archetypal rock artist' (Frith 1978, 186). The advent of the category came in the wake of the huge success and influence of Bob Dylan, who in the early 1960s had begun to move away from traditional folk songs and idioms to a more poetic, less rigidly defined individual style.

Something of an ideological split can be perceived between many in the folk scene who espoused the original concerns of the revival and artists who were veering toward more introspective songwriting. This dichotomy can be characterized as the primacy of the song and tradition on the one hand, and a concentration on the expression of individual views and the craft of songwriting on the other. In 1964, the editor of the US folk journal *Sing Out!* directed criticism at Dylan for diverging from prescribed 'folk' forms and lyrical concerns:

[A]ny songwriter who tries to deal honestly with reality in this world is bound to write 'protest' songs . . . Your new songs seem to be all inner-directed now, inner probing self-conscious – maybe even a little maudlin or a little cruel on occasion . . . you're a different Bob Dylan from the one we knew. The old one never wasted our precious time. (Silber 1964, 22)

At the same time, an emerging dichotomy could be traced between folk aesthetics and the persona of the singer-songwriter. Arguing against elements of 'cabaret' being incorporated into folk performance, the UK folk singer Ewan MacColl wrote, '[T]he entertainer is required to put himself or herself over to the audience; the traditional singer is concerned with putting the songs over' (1964, 18). In contrast, the US singer Phil Ochs eschewed these values in favor of a purely personal explanation of his work: 'I'm not out there to be the spokesman for the Left, for SNCC [the Student Non-Violent Co-ordinating Committee], for my generation, or for anybody but myself. I'm only singing about my feelings, my attitudes, my views' (1965, 11). This new concentration on the personal also had a major effect on the lyrical content of the material. Singer-songwriters can be seen as representative of the widening of the discursive space between the folk and rock traditions. Dylan and Ochs were no longer purely writers of 'protest songs' – their lyrical palette had been enlarged to include almost limitless subject matter. This thematic broadening by figures such as Dylan and Ochs is in contrast to their direct forerunners, such as Woody Guthrie, who, while writing and performing their own material, did so with regard to a set of much more rigidly circumscribed topics. The label 'singer-songwriter,' then, gave later artists a certain amount of freedom of expression. In the 1970s, for instance, the perception of Christian artists such as Larry Norman and Bruce Cockburn as singer-songwriters allowed them to address broader issues than religion and spirituality, such as politics and personal relationships.

From the mid-1960s onward, a number of solo artists came to be represented as part of the singer-songwriter 'movement' by the record industry and in popular criticism. The phrase was used as a marketing vehicle to group together particular artists for new signings by certain US record labels. In the late 1960s, for example, the singer-songwriter became a central element of the identity of the Warner-Reprise label. Artists on the roster included Joni Mitchell, Arlo Guthrie, Van Morrison and James Taylor. While artists such as Mitchell had their roots in the folk movement, the category of 'singer-songwriter' had become associated with a wider group of performers who came from a variety of backgrounds, including those – such as Randy Newman, Neil Young, James Taylor and Carole King – with a rock and pop songwriting pedigree. Newman had been a staff songwriter at the US company Metric Music since 1964, while King had been a successful songwriter working out of New York's Brill Building for almost 10 years, during which time she had written a number of pop hits for artists such as Little Eva, the Chiffons, Herman's Hermits and Dusty Springfield. King's second solo album, *Tapestry* (1971), went on to sell over 15 million copies.

This inclusion of 'professional' industry writers is indicative of ideas of 'craftsmanship' that have come to be associated with the singer-songwriter idiom. The international commercial and critical success of artists such as Mitchell, Taylor and King in the late 1960s and early 1970s helped to establish the conventions through which the singer-songwriter has come to be understood (the aforementioned associations between singer-songwriters and introspective, emotionally expressive performance). These conventions were incorporated into various international traditions, such as the *canzone d'autore* in Italy and other European folk traditions. They also influenced Latin American performers such as the Brazilians Caetano Veloso and Gilberto Gil, the Japanese singer-songwriter movement and such artists as Freddie Aguilar from the Philippines, who was one of the first performers to have major domestic success singing in the Tagalog language and addressing Filipino concerns.

It has been suggested that the self-accompanied performance and thematic conventions in the singer-songwriter idiom have a marked effect on the way in which the music of singer-songwriters is listened to and understood. It has been argued that their music is received differently from other rock styles, provoking a personal rather than a collective reaction from listeners. Street (1986) contends that, '[w]here rock was concerned with public life (even when dealing with personal concerns), the singer-songwriters made music for an audience that either finds itself, or feels itself, alone in the isolation of the nuclear family or the bed-sitting room' (198). The implication is that this connection with the individual listener is made not purely through the lyrical themes of the songs, but through the communication of the persona of the singer-songwriter. This interpretation assumes a strong identification between the performing artist and his/her listeners. As Fabbri (1982) argues, a distinction must be made between a listener's engagement with lyrical sentiment and his/her identification with the song's creator: '[In] the case of the *canzone d'autore* . . . the listener must always remember that the song's protagonist is another person, and, if there is identification, it is directly with the singer, not with the protagonist of each song. The *cantautore* is a poet with whom the listener relates' (68).

The singer-songwriter idiom also has particular conventions in terms of live performance. The very nature of self-accompanied performance serves to construct an apparently direct relationship between the singer and his/her audience. The projection of direct communication is a balance between the sharing of the singer-songwriter's personal material and the inherent theatricality and projection of public performance. To maintain the impression of intimacy, the concert setting may be understood as an act of baring one's soul in which the performer must be seen as somewhat vulnerable or even ill at ease. As Fabbri (1982) points out, 'the *cantautore* must always give the impression of being uncomfortable in front of his audience, because privacy is his "true" dimension' (70). Moreover, this relationship is also reflected in the conventions of the listening audience in the live setting. Middleton (1990) points out that there are many different conventions within popular music performance and that there is a great deal of variation in the listening experience between 'the "distracted" environment of many club settings and the hushed concentration typical of singer-songwriter concerts' (95).

While the concentration on the personal and 'authentic' is certainly a major strain of the singer-songwriter idiom, individual songs are not necessarily presented as a reflection of the writer's feelings or, indeed, as indicative of his/her point of view. Many singer-songwriters have adopted the point of view of a variety of characters in their work. The Randy Newman songs 'Short People' and 'You Can Leave Your Hat On,' for example, cannot be judged purely as reflections of the songwriter's true views. Rather, they can be seen as comments on life through the eyes of a constructed protagonist. The term 'singer-songwriter' has also been applied to performers who have attempted to explore notions of perspective and 'honesty' in songwriting by the deliberate use of artifice and constructed performer personae. In 1990s independent rock, for example, the UK performer Momus presented the persona of an amoral, effete intellectual, while the US performer Will Oldham (who began his career as an actor) has consistently written from the perspective of a Southern backwoods, blue-collar melancholic. Both write songs from the point of view of their respective adopted personae. However, these constructed, often ironic positions are part of the legitimated space of the idiom in that they are concurrent with ideas of the command of the 'art' of songwriting and the singer-songwriters' perceived status as masters of their craft.

The relative complexity of the lyrics of singer-songwriters, along with the prevalence of self-accompanied performance, has meant that song words have been privileged in the way these artists have been understood. This privileging – witnessed in the title of Bob Sarlin's (1992) study of singer-songwriters, *Turn It Up! (I Can't Hear the Words): Singer/Songwriters Then & Now* – is reflected in the forms of analysis that have been applied to their work. For instance, the plethora of studies on Bob Dylan and books such as Gouldstone's (1989) study of Elvis Costello attempt to explain their subjects' work through extensive analysis of their lyrics. These works are perhaps indicative of the way in which singer-songwriters have often been situated critically as singing poets who offer insights into the human condition (Sarlin 1992). For instance, while emphasizing that his subject – Bob Dylan – is a songwriter rather than a poet, Gray (1999) places Dylan within a literary tradition, comparing his work with that of writers from Walt Whitman to William Burroughs. Indeed, the singer-songwriter can be seen as part of the general trend in late-1960s Anglo-American popular music toward a high/low culture demarcation, with the form being a central part of the critical elevation of rock as superior to pop forms.

There are, however, contradictions in the way in which singer- songwriters have been represented as 'craftsmen' [*sic*] on the one hand, and a channel for non-rational, intensely personal emotions on the other. Singer-songwriters have frequently been valued and understood as autonomous artists at a remove from the compromising pressures of the entertainment field. The notion of an independent artist who is visited by a muse is often alluded to in biographies and appraisals. In these instances, artists are often presented as seers through which songs are channeled. In his anthology of interviews with songwriters, for instance, Zollo (1997) describes songwriting as 'much more than a mere craft. It's a conscious attempt to connect with the unconscious; a reaching beyond ordinary perceptions to grasp images that resonate like dreams, and melodies that haunt and spur the heart' (xii). Indeed, any notions of work or craft are often denied in the songwriting process in favor of explanations that emphasize the activity as a metaphysical or even mystical experience. In discussing the process of writing the song 'Eve of Destruction,' P.F. Sloan comments: 'It was a fantastic feeling of being in another place. Pure witnessing. I was allowed to be present at times. The excitement was so great that I wouldn't even bear to witness it . . . Sometimes I'd see a whole chorus that was written' (quoted in Zollo 1997, 183). Thus, musicians may seek to enhance their status by presenting themselves as conduits of emotional insight. Lou Adler, the founder of Dunhill Records (where Sloan was employed at the time), gives a very different, more prosaic account of the writing of the same song. He states that, in an attempt to capitalize on the commercial potential of folk rock, he gave staff writer Sloan the task of writing songs in the same style: 'I gave Phil Sloan a pair of boots and a copy of the Dylan album, and a week later he came back with ten songs . . . he's a great mimic' (quoted in Laing 1975, 57).

The qualities that have become synonymous with the singer-songwriter have affected their working practise in that their perceived autonomy has been seen as influencing every aspect of an artist's business life. Gillett (1984) argues that, in the late 1960s, artists regarded as 'serious' were afforded unprecedented space in which to work: 'The success of Dylan had virtually reversed the balance between the record company and artist to the point where lawyers and managers now dictated many of the terms by which their protégés signed to companies, and the artist subsequently recorded apparently by whim rather than according to release schedules' (407). The perception of an artist as a singer-songwriter also allows for a longer time scale for artistic development in contrast to that for pop or rock performers, who may need to remake or reposition their musical style or public image in order to maintain the momentum of their career. This perceived integrity and concentration on individual talent also allow a performer to cross genres and work with musicians performing other musical styles while maintaining a public persona. Record companies will often give artistic support and financial backing to performers who have been successful over the long term: for example, Joni Mitchell in her use of jazz and fusion players in the mid-1970s, Paul Simon in his introduction of African musics on *Graceland* or Elvis Costello in his forays into classical arrangements with the Brodsky Quartet.

The connotations and tropes of the singer-songwriter have meant that the term has become an effective method of selling and marketing a performer to the extent that journalists and critics have used it as a framing device for a wide variety of artists in order to convey their worth and integrity. In some cases, the artist concerned may not fit the accepted definition of a singer-songwriter (i.e., a self-accompanied solo artist). However, the allusion may still be made with qualification to convey certain modes of authenticity. For example, during the promotion of the album *13* by the British group Blur, the band's vocalist Damon Albarn was referred to in media accounts as a 'singer-songwriter with a band,' and the album, represented as confessional, was considered as Albarn's equivalent of *Blood on the Tracks* (Bob Dylan's 1975 album dealing with his divorce).

The conventions of the singer-songwriter have been viewed as a departure from the macho articulations associated with conventional rock music. Indeed, the introspection of the lyrics has been interpreted by some critics as forging alternative tropes of masculinity within the rock genre. Chambers (1985) points out that the 'personal lyrics and the insecurities of a lone male, a man and a guitar, came to occupy certain positions more usually associated with female singing (self-doubt and self-pity)' (121). This association between the public persona of the singer-songwriter and a less aggressive mode of public display offered an opportunity to female musicians wishing to find acceptance as rock performers. The singer-songwriter idiom became a space in which the participation of women was legitimized. Since the success of Joni Mitchell and Carole King, there have been a number of women performers who have been successfully marketed as singer-songwriters, including Carly Simon, Joan Armatrading and Rickie Lee Jones in the 1970s, Tracy Chapman and Suzanne Vega in the 1980s, and Alanis Morissette, Jewel, Tori Amos and Liz Phair in the 1990s. Laing (1975) sees the success of female singer-songwriters as 'an implicit challenge to the macho stance of the conventional rock band' (80). However, Woodworth and Dodge Hanson (1998) raise the point that the label 'sensitive singer-songwriter' is a potentially constraining one, which ignores, or flattens out, the differences between performers. They comment that it has become a category in which to group female artists without acknowledging their individuality: 'Why should we assume that the experiences of Suzanne Vega, who grew up in East Harlem to the taunts of "you're the whitest girl I've ever seen" and those of Kate Campbell, who was raised as the daughter of a socially progressive Baptist preacher in rural Mississippi, would somehow say the same things?' (x). Although women play a central role within the singer-songwriter idiom, this may be read as a confined space of legitimacy that is not echoed in other rock genres.

The term 'singer-songwriter,' then, has become so entrenched within the discourses of popular music that it is often seen as constricting and narrow. Some performers have remarked that the term is overbearing and unwelcome. For instance, the US solo performer Elliott Smith has stated that he feels uncomfortable with the label, commenting that critics use the term to pigeonhole his work and link it with particular well-worn associations. Nevertheless, it is clear that the term and the artists associated with it have continued to be important in the development of the aesthetics, ideologies and discursive space of popular music.

Bibliography

Chambers, Iain. 1985. *Urban Rhythms: Pop Music and Popular Culture*. London: Macmillan.

Fabbri, Franco. 1982. 'A Theory of Musical Genres: Two Applications.' In *Popular Music Perspectives, 1*, ed. David Horn and Philip Tagg. Göteborg and Exeter: IASPM, 52–81.

Frith, Simon. 1978. *The Sociology of Rock*. London: Constable.

Gaar, Gillian G. 1993. *She's a Rebel: The History of Women in Rock & Roll*. London: Blandford.

Gillett, Charlie. 1984. *The Sound of the City: The Rise of Rock and Roll*. London: Book Club Associates.

Gouldstone, David. 1989. *Elvis Costello: A Man Out of Time*. London: Sidgwick.

Gray, Michael. 1999. *Song & Dance Man III: The Art of Bob Dylan*. New York: Cassell.

Laing, Dave. 1975. 'Troubadours and Stars.' In *The Electric Muse: The Story of Folk into Rock*, ed. Dave Laing et al. London: Methuen, 45–82.

MacColl, Ewan. 1964. 'The Singer and the Audience.' *Sing Out!* 14(4) (September): 16–20.

Middleton, Richard. 1990. *Studying Popular Music*. Milton Keynes: Open University Press.

Ochs, Phil. 1965. 'Topical Song and Folksinging: A Symposium.' *Sing Out!* 15(4)(September): 10–12.

Sarlin, Bob. 1992. *Turn It Up! (I Can't Hear the Words): Singer/Songwriters Then & Now*. New York: Citadel Underground. (First published New York: Simon and Schuster, 1974.)

Silber, Irwin. 1964. 'An Open Letter to Bob Dylan.' *Sing Out!* 14(5)(November): 22–23.

Street, John. 1986. *Rebel Rock: The Politics of Popular Music*. Oxford: Blackwell.

Woodworth, Marc, and Dodge Hanson, Emma, eds. 1998. *Solo: Women Singer-Songwriters in Their Own Words*. New York: Delta.

Zollo, Paul. 1997. *Songwriters on Songwriting*. 2nd ed. New York: Da Capo Press.

4. Personnel

Discographical References

Blur. *13*. Virgin 99129. *1999*: UK.

Dylan, Bob. *Blood on the Tracks*. Columbia PC-33235. *1975*: USA.

King, Carole. *Tapestry*. Ode 34946. *1971*: USA.

McGuire, Barry. 'Eve of Destruction.' Dunhill 4009. *1965*: USA.

Newman, Randy. 'Short People.' Warner 8492. *1977*: USA.

Newman, Randy. 'You Can Leave Your Hat On.' *Sail Away*. Reprise MS-2064. *1972*: USA.

Simon, Paul. *Graceland*. Warner Brothers 2-25447. *1986*: USA.

ROBERT STRACHAN and MARION LEONARD

Songwriter

A songwriter is a person who, alone or in collaboration with others, invents a song and preserves its basic features by writing them down. Although at first glance the definition might seem straightforward, its application depends crucially on an understanding of what constitutes a song and of what counts as writing. These understandings vary. Matters are complicated by the fact that words and music can be produced or used separately, or in different ways. The function of a songwriter may be sharply distinguished from, or alternatively may overlap with, those of other participants in the music-making process. A song can be 'written down' on paper, on a recording or on a computer disc – and sometimes on more than one of these, in which case the different versions can be partial or even in conflict.

In many music cultures, especially those commonly described as 'traditional,' the inventors of songs are often unknown, and songs are preserved in memory and performance. In Western art music, songwriters are almost always identified, and almost always claim compositional primacy through production of a score. Popular music practise is located somewhere between these two extremes, although its exact mode of operation is itself variable.

The Tin Pan Alley System, and Before

In Europe (starting at least as early as the sixteenth century) and, subsequently, in North America, producers of printed broadside material for vocal performance (such as street ballads, *Gassenlieder* and *chansons*) often followed an existing folk practise, putting new words to an existing tune. Little is known about such writers – in most cases, not even their names.

As a more organized commercial leisure apparatus developed in the eighteenth and nineteenth centuries, a new category of writers and composers emerged, producing original sheet music and songbooks for a growing bourgeois domestic market and for performers working in popular theaters, pleasure gardens, music halls and (in the United States) minstrel shows. At first, there was a tendency to draw on the techniques of, and even to adapt the repertoire from, more elite genres on the one hand and folk genres on the other. Indeed, the generic and socioeconomic boundaries were blurred, especially in the case of the various eighteenth-century comic opera traditions (such as ballad opera, *opéra comique* and *singspiel*). The establishment of separate popular song genres in the nineteenth century, however, facilitated the emergence of specialist writers in the United States – for example, Dan Emmett (1815–1904) in minstrelsy, Felix McGlennon (1856–1943) in music hall and Henry Clay Work (1832–84) in domestic balladry. Such men were among the first to benefit from the exploitation of sheet music as a mass-market commodity.

The first music copyright legislation appeared in the nineteenth century, and the first royalty collection agencies were founded (the French *Société des Auteurs, Composeurs et Editeurs de la Musique* in 1850). The laws defined the songwriter as an 'author' comparable to a novelist or poet. However, the legislation was weakly enforced, and piracy was widespread. Financial success for a songwriter depended on individual deals struck with a performer (whose artistic success with the song was therefore vital) or a publisher, and in general, because of oversupply, the songwriter was in a weak negotiating position. Not surprisingly, therefore, the status of popular songwriters was low. Most of the exceptions had a foot in more elite spheres – opera composers such as Michael Balfe (1808–70), Arthur Sullivan (1842–1900) or Jacques Offenbach (1819–80) – or at least worked in a style adjacent to an up-market genre (domestic lied composer Franz Abt (1819–85), for example). Perhaps the low status of songwriters explains why popular songwriting was the only area of nineteenth-century musical composition to allow a role for women, at least in the genre of 'respectable' domestic song (Claribel – real name Charlotte Alington Barnard (1830–69) – is an example). Moreover, despite the growing prominence of specialist genres, the repertoire remained decidedly mixed. Tunes migrated between genres, arrangements and parodies were a mainstay (including arrangements of 'traditional' tunes, such as the *Irish Melodies* of Thomas Moore (1779–1852)), and hymns might appear in almost any vocal program. Perhaps the only songwriter from this period to survive with a reputation of substance built entirely on popular song production is the North American writer of pieces for parlor and minstrel show, Stephen Foster (1826–64).

The 'Tin Pan Alley system' of song production, pioneered in the United States in the 1880s, 1890s and early twentieth century, and copied soon after in Western

European countries, replaced the individualistic basis of previous practise with something more akin to a factory process. Publishing firms, especially those located in New York's 'Tin Pan Alley,' employed writers and composers (and also arrangers and orchestrators), researched markets, plugged their products and ruthlessly exploited successful formulae. Songwriters were simply one component (or more often two – lyricists and composers, generally paid separately) within an efficient division of labor. Copyright protection and royalty collection were tightened, especially in relation to performing rights. The American Society of Composers, Authors and Publishers (ASCAP) and the Performing Right Society (PRS) in Britain were both founded in 1914. The popularity of player pianos, and the swift development of recording, radio and, later, sound film, contributed (at least at first) to an increase in sheet music sales (10 million annually in the United States by 1910), as well as multiplying the revenue streams, increasing the possibilities of media symbiosis and corporate integration, and forcing quicker turnover of songs. There is some justice in the observation that growing corporate control reduced songwriters' freedom to maneuver.

An alternative (and to some, more congenial) source of employment lay in the musical theater (centered on New York's Broadway), and it may be significant that virtually all of the best-remembered US writers of the inter-war period (Jerome Kern (1885–1945), Irving Berlin (1888–1989), Cole Porter (1891–1964), George Gershwin (1898–1937) and Ira Gershwin (1896–1983), Richard Rodgers (1902–79) and Lorenz Hart (1895–1943)) built major reputations there. A theater role could give a greater degree of autonomy (Berlin, for instance, formed his own publishing company); partnerships of composers and lyricists (such as the Gershwins, Rodgers and Hart), while modeled on the typical Tin Pan Alley mode of operation, were often unusually close (and in some cases – Berlin, Porter – the same individual wrote both words and music). Nevertheless, there were close links between Broadway and Tin Pan Alley – most shows contained hit songs – and all writers, from the least 'schooled' (Berlin) to the most (Porter, Rodgers), based their work on standard forms and conventions. Moreover, all songwriters, however well known, were less significant to most of their listeners than the celebrated performers of the time, and their tunes and words (and sometimes their harmonies) were regularly modified and even recomposed by singers, dance bands and commercial arrangers.

However, the worldwide power and influence of the Tin Pan Alley/Broadway song-production system was immense. Just as ASCAP (and similar organizations elsewhere) built a virtual monopoly and hence, arguably, exerted a conservative effect on mainstream song style and technique, so the US model and its leading practitioners came to enjoy a broad international dominance. It is interesting, then, that although this might appear to represent an urban Euro-US hegemony, many of the songwriters came from ethnic minorities (Jewish, African-American) with roots in 'premodern' cultures (those of Russia or the US South), or were influenced by their musics. To the sociologist Max Weber, this might have looked like a significant 'disturbance' within an increasingly rationalized system.

The Rock System

Even within the ASCAP monopoly, songwriters from 'marginal' social spheres – most particularly, blues, jazz and hillbilly performers – could, from the 1920s on, sell their work to publishers or record companies, often via entrepreneurial middlemen. They were usually musically illiterate, and sold their work for an exploitative pittance (a one-off fee, sometimes plus a tiny royalty). Talent scout and record producer Ralph Peer, for instance, set up his own publishing company, linked to Victor Records, to manage such contracts (Sanjek 1988, 64–65, 69–70). From 1939 to 1941, a protracted dispute between ASCAP and the US broadcasting corporations, together with the formation of Broadcast Music Inc. (BMI), a rival royalty collection agency, opened up the system. At the same time, records were taking over from sheet music as the principal dissemination medium.

Before long, new, cheaper technologies (vinyl, recording tape) were transforming the production apparatus, and the focus shifted from piano and paper to microphone and mixing desk. Those working in genres where notation was generally an afterthought to orally/aurally based composition – rhythm and blues (R&B), hillbilly/country music – were ideally placed to exploit the new situation. Their audiences had moved in large numbers to cities in the northern and western United States, creating expanded markets and giving them greater prominence, and a wave of new radio stations spread their appeal. BMI members worked primarily in these repertoires.

The cultures of both R&B and country music, as well as the requirements of the new production processes, militated against a rigid division of labor. The importance of recorded sound, the role of loose 'head' arrangements, and the central aesthetic significance of a sense of identity between performers and the emotional message of a song all made it increasingly likely that performers themselves would be involved in generating material. Many performers invented songs for themselves – in country music, Hank Williams (1923–53), for instance; in R&B, Louis Jordan (1908–75), B.B. King (b.

1925) and many others. Musicians who were or who had been performers often wrote songs for others and, in many cases, such musicians were also involved in arranging, directing and producing; Atlantic Records' musical director Jesse Stone (1901–99) and Chess Records' Willie Dixon (1915–92) are examples. Even nonperforming writers frequently combined composing with other roles; thus, the hugely successful partnership of Jerry Leiber and Mike Stoller (both b. 1933) was built around record production as well as songwriting. Many of the most successful rock 'n' roll singers recorded songs written by such musicians – either material created especially for them or material that existed already in other recorded versions and that they covered. This trend also opened the way for unscrupulous producers and record company bosses to cut themselves into copyright credits on songs to which they had made no contribution whatsoever; Don Robey ('Deadric Malone') of Duke/Peacock comes to mind.

But rock 'n' roll also confirmed the incipient rise to dominance of the new category of songwriter, which can be called that of composer/performer. In particular, Chuck Berry (b. 1926) drew on a range of R&B techniques and materials, but stamped them with a new personality bound up equally with his memorable guitar riffs and solos, and with his unique style of witty, affecting lyric narratives of contemporary teenage life; and Buddy Holly (1936–59), in close collaboration with his group, the Crickets, and record producer Norman Petty, produced perhaps the first fully integrated pop records – that is, the roles of 'composition,' particular singing styles, instrumental arrangements and of the recording of sound can hardly be distinguished as separate aspects of the complete act of 'songwriting' (and the songs are accordingly credited to various combinations of Holly, band members and Petty). The work of Chuck Berry on the one hand and Buddy Holly on the other points toward the two main approaches to songwriting that were to become dominant in the 'rock system': that of the singer-songwriter and that of group composition. (The fact that singer-songwriters had existed in other cultures for centuries, and that their role could flourish relatively independently of the influence of the rock system, as in the 'New Song' movement in Cuba or the *chansonnier* tradition in France, suggests that, in some ways, rock was aligning itself with a more widely existing mode of song production.)

The modalities of the two approaches – that of the singer-songwriter and of group composition – were influentially developed in the 1960s by Bob Dylan (b. 1941) on the one hand and the Beatles on the other. Dylan wrote his songs for himself to sing, and although their published lyrics were treated by many fans and critics as if they were poetry, Dylan stressed that it was in performance (live or recorded) that they lived. For most listeners, then and since, the *sound* of Dylan's voice is an integral part of the composition. While many of Dylan's songs (and those of subsequent singer-songwriters) have been covered by other artists, this aesthetic principle lies at the core of the approach. It is a principle that has spread much more widely to include a large number of the most accomplished songwriters in popular music: Bruce Springsteen, Prince, Björk, Elvis Costello and many others.

For the Beatles, John Lennon (1940–80) and Paul McCartney (b. 1942) agreed early in their careers that all songs they wrote would be jointly credited. Sometimes the initial compositional process was genuinely collaborative, but more often, it seems, their songs were associated principally with one or the other. Nevertheless, accounts of the Beatles' methods make it clear that at later stages of production, in the recording studio, all four band members – not to mention, frequently, additional performers and, crucially, producer George Martin – were involved in 'writing' the songs. This method is documented on the Beatles' *Anthology* albums.

Whether singer-songwriters or members of composing groups, songwriters under the rock system enjoyed a significant rise in status (and, very often, in financial rewards). Moreover, the differences between the two types can be exaggerated: John Lennon's post-Beatles career demonstrates explicitly his singer-songwriter tendencies, and Bob Dylan's *Basement Tapes* document his use of collaborative studio composition, while pop/rock bands in general have drawn on a range of approaches. However, the specialist songwriter survived the advent of rock. In the 1960s, so-called 'Brill Building pop' – involving such writers as Neil Sedaka (b. 1939) and the partnerships of Barry Mann (b. 1939) and Cynthia Weil (b. 1942), Gerry Goffin (b. 1939) and Carole King (b. 1942), and Burt Bacharach (b. 1928) and Hal David (b. 1921) – updated the Tin Pan Alley model of song production. At the same time, the songs for Motown Records' black pop were written by company owner Berry Gordy (b. 1929), and by writing teams such as Holland/Dozier/Holland (Brian Holland (b. 1941), Lamont Dozier (b. 1941) and Eddie Holland (b. 1939)) – an example followed in the 1970s by Philadelphia Records' Kenny Gamble (b. 1943) and Leon Huff (b. 1942). But both Gordy, and Gamble and Huff worked as producers as well as writers (and owned the record and associated publishing companies, too), just as the celebrated producer (and onetime Leiber and Stoller associate) Phil Spector (b. 1940) wrote or co-wrote many of the songs he produced.

Under the rock system, then, it became difficult to offer a simple answer to the question of who the songwriter now was. If a record could, in a sense, be regarded as 'a song,' then its singer might have a claim to be regarded as one of its writers, even if it was a version of a piece originally created by others. Perhaps in recognition of this (or perhaps to increase royalty payments), singers (Elvis Presley, for example) have sometimes been cut into copyright credits, even if they would appear to have played little or no role in the original composition process.

Collaborative studio composition processes have occasionally led to quarrels among band members over royalty distribution. In 1999, three members of the British group Spandau Ballet took their ex-colleague Gary Kemp to court for reneging on a verbal agreement to share songwriting royalties equally. Kemp wrote the songs, but the others argued that he was ignoring what happened subsequently in the studio: 'He's trying to take away our creative input. The great thing about band music is that it is a collaboration' (*The Guardian*, 5 May 1999, 4). Nevertheless, Kemp won the case. At an extreme, the dialogic aspect of much rock song production has sometimes resulted in more wide-ranging legal disputes. One celebrated case concerned the allegedly plagiaristic relationship between Led Zeppelin's 'Whole Lotta Love' of 1969 and Willie Dixon's earlier composition 'You Need Love.' Equally celebrated might be the argument made by Duane Allman's daughter in 1999 that the famous guitar riff in Eric Clapton's 'Layla' (1970) was actually 'written' (and played) by her uncredited father.

Of course, Dixon and other blues musicians themselves often drew on collectively owned or uncopyrighted material when writing songs. Such processes as those described above, together with their implications for song ownership, mimic, in an electronically mediated environment, those that were widely characteristic of song production before the adoption of notation. It is not surprising, therefore, that in cultures where notation has come only recently, or not at all, to songwriting, the emergence of modern popular music industries, coinciding with the global spread of the rock system, has made the latter seem the natural way of bringing tradition into the orbit of commodity production. Throughout the 'world music' peripheries, songwriters are generally performers working through a mixture of oral and studio techniques, either relatively alone (as singer-songwriters) or in bands and more or less complex collaborations.

Since Rock

Much of the rock system has survived. Many late twentieth-century rock bands continued to generate songs collaboratively: records by R.E.M., Nirvana, Radiohead and many others are credited to band members, although often with fulsome thanks to other participating musicians, engineers and producers. Even bands that relied increasingly on digital studio technology, and perhaps hardly performed their work live at all – the Pet Shop Boys, for example – followed basically the same model. Singer-songwriters – PJ Harvey, k.d. lang, Tori Amos and others, not to mention the host of rap performers – continued to write for their own voices, supported by collaborating musicians and producers. Moreover, the more 'industrial' chart pop model survived too – for example, in the work of the Motown-like late-1980s UK songwriting and production team of Mike Stock (b. 1951), Matt Aitken (b. 1956) and Pete Waterman (b. 1947) for such singers as Kylie Minogue, or that of the Spice Girls' various songwriters in the 1990s (Richard Stannard and Matthew Rowe being the best known).

Nevertheless, in many contexts (particularly that of 'dance music'), digital technology has changed the songwriter's role substantially. When materials are generated from interlinked samplers and synthesizers, held in computer memory and worked at on screen, the gap between 'composition' and 'recording' is potentially elided completely, and the 'songwriter' is often arranger, programmer, sound engineer and composer in one. At the same time, the sampling process brings out the extent to which composition involves a *community* of originators, a point confirmed in a different way by club DJs mixing live between complex sequences of records and extracts from records. In this sense, such producers, DJs and remixers as Derrick May, Jeff Mills, Kevin Saunderson, Paul Oakenfold and Arthur Baker could be regarded as songwriters in their own right. Indeed, the degree of control they exert over one-off, finished pieces carries them further toward the role of *auteur*, as it exists in classical music, than popular music has perhaps ever previously reached.

Yet, the new technology did not of itself destroy traditional songwriting roles, as the success in the 1990s of such crossover dance/rock bands as the Prodigy, with their writer Liam Howlett (b. 1971), demonstrates. Other facets of the dance music culture were crucial here: an aversion to rock's typical star system; a declining interest in vocalism; and an emphasis on rhythmic functionality rather than discrete musico-emotional experiences. Given the prevalence of remixing and reuse of materials on the one hand, and of small record companies, each associated with its own sub-style, on the other, it sometimes appeared that, at the extreme, record labels themselves could in a sense now be regarded as songwriters.

By the 1990s, for many popular music fans the term 'song' seemed to refer to any reasonably identifiable musical product, regardless of the extent of vocal content, while for musicians 'writing' denoted any and all parts of the production process. Yet, in a 1999 BBC Radio poll of the 'Top 100 Tunes of the Twentieth Century,' virtually all the songs selected originated between about 1930 and about 1980 – that is, they were produced within either the Tin Pan Alley or the rock system – and no piece of 'dance music' figured at all. Admittedly, the channel was middle-of-the-road (Radio 2), but at the very least the poll seemed to confirm that, within a sizable portion of the popular musical memory, songwriters of familiar type still held sway.

Bibliography

Goodwin, Andrew. 1990. 'Sample and Hold: Pop Music in the Digital Age of Reproduction.' In *On Record: Rock, Pop and the Written Word*, ed. Simon Frith and Andrew Goodwin. London: Routledge, 258–73.

Hamm, Charles. 1979. *Yesterdays: Popular Song in America*. New York: W.W. Norton.

Laing, Dave. 1969. *The Sound of Our Time*. London: Sheed and Ward.

Macdonald, Ian. 1994. *Revolution in the Head: The Beatles' Records and the Sixties*. London: Fourth Estate.

Marcus, Greil. 1997. *Invisible Republic: Bob Dylan's Basement Tapes*. New York: Henry Holt & Co.

Martin, George. 1979. *All You Need Is Ears*. London: Macmillan.

Martin, George, ed. 1983. *Making Music: The Guide to Writing, Performing and Recording*. London: Pan Books.

Moore, Thomas, comp. 1808–34. *Irish Melodies*. 10 vols. London and Dublin: J. Power and W. Power.

Sanjek, Russell. 1988. *American Popular Music and Its Business: The First Four Hundred Years. Vol. 3: From 1900 to 1984*. New York: Oxford University Press.

Discographical References

Beatles, The. *Anthology 1*. Apple CDPCSP 727. *1996*: UK.

Beatles, The. *Anthology 2*. Apple CDPCSP 728. *1996*: UK.

Beatles, The. *Anthology 3*. Apple CDPCSP 729. *1996*: UK.

Derek and the Dominoes. 'Layla.' Atco 6809. *1970*: USA.

Dylan, Bob. *The Basement Tapes*. Columbia 4678502. *1996*: USA.

Led Zeppelin. 'Whole Lotta Love.' Atlantic 2690. *1969*: USA.

Muddy Waters. 'You Need Love.' Chess 1839. *1962*: USA.

RICHARD MIDDLETON

Video Jockey

'Video jockey' (VJ) is the term used to denote a host or compère of television programs devoted to music videoclips. It is a variation of DJ ('disc jockey'), which, since the 1930s, has been used to designate those who play records in the contexts of radio broadcasting or nightclubs. VJ (or 'veejay') became accepted terminology in the 1980s, when such hosts as Martha Quinn (of US-based MTV) and J.D. Roberts (of the Canadian network *MuchMusic*) became well-known media personalities. It should be noted that, unlike most radio disc jockeys, VJs typically prerecord their segments for insertion between videoclips.

Typically, VJs introduce upcoming videoclips, interview artists, and read letters or other forms of communication from listeners. While VJs may be associated with specific styles of music, the choice of videoclips they introduce is usually made by a programming director or committee. (This is one reason why there have been few payola scandals involving VJs.) Since the early 1980s, many music video networks, including MTV, have reduced the amount of 'flow' programming (in which VJs introduce videoclips) in favor of a range of other formats (such as concert documentaries, talk shows, and even drama and comedy programming).

In the original planning of MTV, there was uncertainty as to how presenters should appear. In particular, it was unclear whether VJs should sit behind desks, like the hosts of television news programs and talk shows, or strive for an informality more appropriate to the world of youth-oriented music. The manner of presentation developed at MTV, and copied elsewhere around the world, is one in which VJs dress casually and either sit on stools or chairs or stand, sometimes even strolling around the studio. In all these ways, music video networks have sought to develop an informal rapport between VJs and viewers which resembles that between radio hosts and their listeners. In his study of music television (1992, 139–42), Andrew Goodwin enumerated several functions that VJs perform: an information function (offering information on clips and performers); an anchoring function (providing a stable, consistent presence amid the flow of often-unrelated videoclips); a relaying function (anticipating upcoming videos and introducing them in ways that direct the viewer's attention, potentially distracted as it is, to the screen); and an identificatory function (offering an 'ordinariness' which, set against the celebrity and glamor of music performers, may be comforting to viewers).

Bibliography

Goodwin, Andrew. 1992. *Dancing in the Distraction Factory: Music Television and Popular Culture*. Minneapolis, MN: University of Minnesota Press.

WILL STRAW

5. Processes: Interpretive

Interpretation

In discourse about music, 'interpretation' usually refers either to the verbal act of explaining or elucidating the meaning of a piece, or to the act of planning and executing a performance via the decoding of Western staff notation (which could be understood as making a piece 'meaningful' in the course of performing it). Broad views of 'interpretation' also include dancing, and singing/playing along with a recording or a performance (see Scruton 1993).

Music scholarship has hitherto paid the most attention to interpretation via performance. This focus has resulted from the emphasis in formal music education on the study and performance of Western art (or 'classical') music which relies on Western staff notation for its transmission. Music notation, in addition to providing information on pitches, rhythms, dynamics, articulation and phrasing, gives clues to the performer about musical style. The ability to infer stylistic aspects of a score is developed through oral tradition typically provided by individual instruction. An interpretation is thus judged on the basis of its stylistic appropriateness and, in some instances, on whether the performer has accurately rendered the presumed intentions of the composer (Randel 1986). With the blossoming of the 'performance practise' movement over the last three decades of the twentieth century, the degree to which performers have considered historical evidence may be taken into account in evaluations of their interpretations (see Kenyon 1988).

Popular music scholarship has also used 'interpretation' in this sense when the performer is not identical with the songwriter/composer, in particular with respect to 'standards' written in the Tin Pan Alley style (ca. 1910–50), in which many versions of the same song were typically recorded, some of which diverged considerably in musical style and genre (see Hamm 1995a). Although almost all of these songs were composed using Western staff notation, performers usually worked from a lead sheet that would convey the melody and harmony alone. The performer and/or the arranger would then decide on a realization of this template. Thus, for example, in 1944 several recordings of the song 'I'll Be Seeing You' were released, including those by Bing Crosby, Frank Sinatra and Billie Holiday, all of which diverged in treatment of melody and harmony, tempo, instrumentation, key and overall mood/affect (for a detailed comparison, see Brackett 1995, ch. 2).

An extreme form of this interpretive flexibility may be found in jazz versions of Tin Pan Alley standards. For example, a comparison of three recordings of the Rodgers and Hammerstein chestnut 'The Surrey with the Fringe on Top' – by Miles Davis, Sonny Rollins and Wes Montgomery – reveals significant differences of rhythm, phrasing, timbre and even pitch, and all deviate from the notated sheet music (and the original cast recording of *Oklahoma!*), and yet the tune remains recognizable in all three versions. Another form of interpretation in jazz utilizes improvisation on harmonic changes so that only faint glimmers of the melody as notated remain, as in Charlie Parker's recording of 'Embraceable You' (composed by George and Ira Gershwin) (see Williams 1987). The evaluation of interpretation in popular music and jazz, in which spontaneity and the imprint of the performer's personality are prized, almost neatly inverts that of current classical music performance practise, with its insistence on fidelity to the score (see Taruskin 1995, 281–82).

In music derived from rhythm and blues (R&B), country music and rock 'n' roll, interpretations of previously written material are frequently described as 'cover versions.' (Exceptions to this are songs written in a neo-Tin Pan Alley style, such as Lennon's and McCartney's 'Yesterday,' or rock interpretations of standards, such as Janis Joplin's 'Summertime' (with Big Brother and the Holding Company).) A cover version differs from an interpretation of a Tin Pan Alley tune due to its derivation from a recording closely identified with the style of a particular performer rather than from notated sheet music. In the United States, the cover version gained prominence in the early 1950s, when ('mainstream') pop performers began recording songs categorized as 'R&B' and 'country and western' with greater frequency. What began arguably as an exploitative phenomenon has become, by turns, a way of paying tribute (for example, the Beatles' and the Rolling Stones' early recordings of songs by Chuck Berry and other 1950s rock 'n' roll songs), or a way of reviving a moribund career or fending off creative stagnation (for example, various artists' recordings of Motown songs in the 1980s). Clearly, however, terms such as 'cover,' 'interpretation' and 'improvisation' are unstable: a 'cover' that departs too much from the original will eventually become an 'interpretation,' while an 'interpretation' that loosens its connection to the underlying tune sufficiently will seem improvisatory. The actual usage of these terms by musicians, fans and critics tends to result from the intersection of genres with specific historical and cultural contexts.

An example of how these terms can shift historically may be seen in a later form of performative interpretation, the 'remix,' in which artists release either several different versions of a song simultaneously or a new version of an earlier recording, a practise traceable to 'versioning' and dub in Jamaican music, and to DJ mixing in disco and hip-hop (Hebdige 1987). The 1990s' remix altered the balance between different tracks in a multitrack recording and/or replaced or superimposed additional tracks onto a basic recording. Highly electronic and dance-oriented genres have made the greatest use of the remix, which can produce radically different versions of the 'same' song. For example, the CD by L.A. Style, *James Brown Is Dead*, consists solely of eight different mixes of the title track (plus one track of 'outtakes') in which the texture and groove are slightly altered, and vocal tracks are added or substituted for one another in order to adapt the song to different formats; this is illustrated by some of the titles: 'Original Mix,' 'Rock Radio Mix' and 'Crossover Radio Mix.' Other approaches to the remix may result in a change of genre such that the initial recording of the song is barely recognizable. Some of the songs on Björk's *Telegram* – an album of remixes of her earlier *Post* – are a case in point. The song 'Cover

Me,' for example, is transformed from an atmospheric ballad accompanied primarily by harpsichord with no discernible groove or percussion to a 'drum 'n' bass' song in which bits of the vocal line from the initial recording are submerged in the mix.

Although performer-based interpretation has traditionally dominated music scholarship, the 1980s and 1990s witnessed a growing interest in criticism highlighting the role of listener-based interpretations (see McClary 1991; Kramer 1995; for representative collections, see Solie 1993, and Brett, Wood and Thomas 1994). Interpretation of this sort (which also goes by the name 'hermeneutics') has increasingly played a role in both scholarly criticism and music analysis, and in some ways has represented a resurgence, albeit in a more highly theorized form, of a kind of interpretation popular in nineteenth- and early twentieth-century criticism. Listener-based interpretation involves an articulation of a musical text and the sociocultural circumstances of the listener/critic with (implicitly or explicitly) a set of theoretical concerns. Listener-based interpretation has been prominent in popular music scholarship, and has concerned itself with detailed 'readings' of individual songs (see Brackett 1995; Bradby and Torode 1984; Cubitt 1984; Fiori 1987; Griffiths 1988; Hamm 1995b; Hawkins 1992; Kruse 1990; Negus 1997; Tagg 1991; Walser 1995; Winkler 1987), as well as with surveys of entire genres, styles or oeuvres (see Bradby 1990; Mellers 1973; Middleton 1995; Moore 1993; Walser 1993; Whiteley 1992; for a detailed overview, see Frith 1996).

Bibliography

Brackett, David. 1995. *Interpreting Popular Music*. Cambridge: Cambridge University Press.

Bradby, Barbara. 1990. 'Do-Talk and Don't-Talk: The Division of the Subject in Girl-Group Music.' In *On Record: Rock, Pop and the Written Word*, ed. Simon Frith and Andrew Goodwin. New York: Pantheon Books, 341–68.

Bradby, Barbara, and Torode, Brian. 1984. 'Pity Peggy Sue.' *Popular Music* 4: 183–206.

Brett, Philip, Wood, Elizabeth, and Thomas, Gary C. 1994. *Queering the Pitch: The New Gay and Lesbian Musicology*. New York and London: Routledge.

Cubitt, Sean. 1984. '"Maybelline": Meaning and the Listening Subject.' *Popular Music* 4: 207–24.

Fiori, Umberto. 1987. 'Listening to Peter Gabriel's "I Have the Touch."' *Popular Music* 6(1): 37–43.

Frith, Simon. 1996. *Performing Rites: On the Value of Popular Music*. Cambridge, MA: Harvard University Press.

Griffiths, Dai. 1988. 'Three Tributaries of "The River."' *Popular Music* 7(1): 27–34.

Hamm, Charles. 1995a. 'Genre, Performance, and Ideology in the Early Songs of Irving Berlin.' In Charles Hamm, *Putting Popular Music in Its Place*. Cambridge: Cambridge University Press, 370–80. (First published in *Popular Music* 13(2) (1994): 143–50.)

Hamm, Charles. 1995b. 'Privileging the Moment of Reception: Music and Radio in South Africa.' In Charles Hamm, *Putting Popular Music in Its Place*. Cambridge: Cambridge University Press, 249–69.

Hawkins, Stan. 1992. 'Prince: Harmonic Analysis of "Anna Stesia."' *Popular Music* 11(3): 325–35.

Hebdige, Dick. 1987. *Cut 'n' Mix: Culture, Identity, and Caribbean Music*. London: Methuen.

Kenyon, Nicholas, ed. 1988. *Authenticity and Early Music: A Symposium*. Oxford and New York: Oxford University Press.

Kramer, Lawrence. 1995. *Classical Music and Postmodern Knowledge*. Berkeley and Los Angeles: University of California Press.

Kruse, Holly. 1990. 'In Praise of Kate Bush.' In *On Record: Rock, Pop and the Written Word*, ed. Simon Frith and Andrew Goodwin. New York: Pantheon Books, 450–65.

McClary, Susan. 1991. *Feminine Endings: Music, Gender, and Sexuality*. Minneapolis, MN: University of Minnesota Press.

Mellers, Wilfrid. 1973. *Twilight of the Gods: The Beatles in Retrospect*. London: Faber & Faber.

Middleton, Richard. 1995. 'Authorship, Gender, and the Construction of Meaning in the Eurythmics' Hit Recordings.' *Cultural Studies* 9(3): 465–85.

Moore, Allan. 1993. *Rock, The Primary Text: Developing a Musicology of Rock*. Buckingham and Philadelphia: Open University Press.

Negus, Keith. 1997. 'Sinead O'Connor – Musical Mother.' In *Sexing the Groove: Popular Music and Gender*, ed. Sheila Whiteley. London and New York: Routledge, 178–90.

Randel, Don Michael. 1986. 'Interpretation.' In *The New Harvard Dictionary of Music*, ed. Don Michael Randel. Cambridge, MA: The Belknap Press of Harvard University Press, 399.

Scruton, Roger. 1993. 'Notes on the Meaning of Music.' In *The Interpretation of Music: Philosophical Essays*, ed. Michael Krausz. Oxford and New York: Oxford University Press, 193–202.

Solie, Ruth A., ed. 1993. *Musicology and Difference: Gender and Sexuality in Music Scholarship*. Berkeley and Los Angeles: University of California Press.

Tagg, Philip. 1991. *Fernando the Flute: Analysis of Musical Meaning in an Abba Mega-Hit*. Liverpool: Institute of Popular Music, University of Liverpool.

Taruskin, Richard. 1995. *Text and Act: Essays on Music and Performance*. New York and Oxford: Oxford University Press.

Walser, Robert. 1993. *Running with the Devil: Power, Gender and Madness in Heavy Metal Music*. Hanover and London: Wesleyan University Press.

Walser, Robert. 1995. 'Rhythm, Rhyme, and Rhetoric in the Music of Public Enemy.' *Ethnomusicology* 39(2): 193–217.

Whiteley, Sheila. 1992. *The Space Between the Notes: Rock and the Counter-Culture*. London: Routledge.

Williams, Martin. 1987. *The Smithsonian Collection of Classic Jazz*. Washington, DC: The Smithsonian Collection of Recordings.

Winkler, Peter. 1987. 'Randy Newman's Americana.' *Popular Music* 7(1): 1–26.

Sheet Music

Gershwin, George, comp., and Gershwin, Ira, lyr. 1930. 'Embraceable You.' New York: New World Music Corp.

Rodgers, Richard, comp., and Hammerstein, Oscar, lyr. 1943. 'The Surrey with the Fringe on Top.' New York: Williamson Music.

Discographical References

Beatles, The. 'Yesterday.' *Help!*. Parlophone PCS 3071. *1965*: UK.

Big Brother and the Holding Company. 'Summertime.' *Cheap Thrills*. Columbia KCS 9700. *1968*: USA.

Björk. *Post*. Elektra 61740-2. *1995*: USA.

Björk. *Telegram*. Elektra 61897-2. *1996*: USA.

Crosby, Bing. 'I'll Be Seeing You.' Decca 18595. 1944: USA. Reissue: Crosby, Bing. 'I'll Be Seeing You.' *Million Sellers*. Prism 295. *1998*: USA.

Davis, Miles. 'The Surrey with the Fringe on Top.' *Steamin' with the Miles Davis Quintet*. Prestige 7200. *1956*: USA.

Holiday, Billie. 'I'll Be Seeing You.' Commodore 553. 1944: USA.

L.A. Style. *James Brown Is Dead*. Arista 12387-2. 1991; *1992*: USA.

Montgomery, Wes. 'The Surrey with the Fringe on Top.' *Willow Weep for Me*. Verve 6-8765. 1965; *1969*: USA.

Oklahoma! [Original Cast]. Angel 64691. 1955: USA.

Parker, Charlie. 'Embraceable You.' Dial 1024. 1947: USA. Reissue: Parker, Charlie. 'Embraceable You.' *Masterworks: 1946–1947*. Giants of Jazz 53007. *1998*: USA.

Rollins, Sonny. 'The Surrey with the Fringe on Top.' *Newk's Time*. Blue Note 4001. 1957: USA. Reissue: Rollins, Sonny. 'The Surrey with the Fringe on Top.' *Sonny Rollins*. Blue Note BN-LA401-H2-0798. *1975*: USA.

Sinatra, Frank. 'I'll Be Seeing You.' RCA-Victor 26539. 1944: USA. Reissue: Sinatra, Frank. 'I'll Be Seeing You.' *Popular Frank Sinatra, Vol. 2*. RCA 68712. *1999*: USA.

DAVID BRACKETT

Orchestration

Orchestration is the activity of scoring music for performance by an orchestra. In some areas of popular music, the task of creating an orchestrated version of a preexisting piece is regarded as synonymous with that of making an arrangement, although it is more accurate to say that arrangement generally subsumes orchestration.

The terms 'orchestrating' and 'orchestration' emerged in the European art music tradition in the first half of the nineteenth century to describe the activity of specifying instrumental parts within the documentation of the score and the skill and knowledge involved. It also carried connotations of the expectation of originality.

The practise itself was well established by the early nineteenth century. By the early 1600s, composers such as Michael Praetorius had begun to move away from the accepted convention of providing music that could be performed by a variety of instrumental combinations (as a result of which the sound of a piece was not integral to its conception and would depend on performers' choice and their instrumental resources) toward offering explicit suggestions for instrumentation. By the late seventeenth century, identification of instruments was becoming commonplace. As this happened, overall sonority, together with ideas of cohesion and contrast, became a centrally important component of composition for instrumental ensembles.

The particular importance attached to orchestration during the nineteenth century followed in the wake of developments at several levels: improved instrument technology, such as the development of valves for brass instruments and key mechanisms for woodwind instruments that facilitated a greater degree of agility; the growth of the orchestra into a complex instrumental ensemble (creating, in effect, a compositional tool of unprecedented power and versatility); and the perception that it was in music for the orchestra that the peaks of musical expression were achieved. (One of the composers whose work epitomizes the use of the full symphony orchestra for dramatic effect, Hector Berlioz, wrote a treatise on orchestration in 1843. Another, Nikolay Rimsky-Korsakov, equally renowned for his own orchestrations, followed in Berlioz's footsteps with a book of 'principles' of orchestration, first published in Russian in 1913.)

The importance of orchestration remained in place in art music, through many idiomatic changes, throughout the twentieth century. In popular music, its practise,

though widespread, has never been so central. The orchestra has never enjoyed a position of domination either in the practise or in the ideology of popular music. Its role has more often been one of providing accompaniment than of being itself the focus of attention and, when an orchestral sound is required in an accompanying role, it may well find itself set alongside, combined with or contrasted with sounds not traditionally associated with the orchestra, such as those of a rhythm section, an electric guitar combination or non-Western instruments. Unlike the situation in most art music, therefore, where an orchestral sound cast in an accompanying role in a particular piece will usually be the only such sound, in many individual performances of popular vocal music – especially on record – the orchestral sound becomes one option among many, and orchestrating that sound becomes one tool among many that contribute to the particular outcome. The advent of digitally produced sound in the studio in the latter part of the twentieth century, offering orchestral sounds without the need to pay for an orchestra, increased the possibilities for including and manipulating those sounds in large or small measure.

At least until the rise of digitally produced sound – and to a considerable extent after it – it was and has continued to be common practise for popular music composition and orchestration to be carried out by separate people, thus making orchestrating a necessary – and, eventually, highly respected – skill, but without the connotations of compositional originality. In many such contexts, across a range of genres that make use of orchestral sound in some way, orchestration is carried out as required by the arranger; and indeed, within Anglophone popular music, daily use of the terms 'orchestrating' and 'orchestration' is much less common than that of the umbrella term 'arranging.' Partly, no doubt, this usage grew up simply in order to help create some clarity between the worlds of popular and art music – and the retention of 'orchestrating' and 'orchestration' in stage and screen music perhaps reflects the awareness in those areas of the legacy of nineteenth-century and early twentieth-century art music orchestration. But the distinction also involves a significant shift of emphasis. In both popular and art music, the act of arranging music for a combination of instruments – or, indeed, of arranging ensemble music for a solo instrument, the opposite of orchestration – almost inevitably involves the reworking of an existing piece, whether fully composed or simply sketched out. But whereas in art music an arrangement, orchestrated or not, typically has a much lower status in the aesthetic hierarchy than if the composition in question was original to the person arranging it, in popular music the issue is much less significant. What happens when orchestration is subsumed into arrangement, which occurs frequently, is that attention is drawn to the centrality in popular music of a set of practises based on ongoing processes of remodeling and reinterpreting, of treating 'original' ideas as starting points.

One area where popular music has been very influential and where orchestration has continuously occupied a central place is that of music for the moving image. Film music's often quite ambiguous position in distinctions between popular and art music is reflected in attitudes toward the practise of orchestration. In its use of orchestral sonorities and range of instruments, film music as varied as that of Erich Korngold and Bernard Herrmann owed a debt to art music, from Romantics to modernists. But a number of factors that made composing for films different also affected orchestration. One such factor was technological. The electrical recording process available for early films with synchronized soundtracks tended to make large string sections beloved of the revered art music composers, such as Richard Wagner and Richard Strauss, sound 'too thick and pulpy' (London 1936, 169). The 'microphone orchestra' (said the same commentator) should be 'constituted on a small scale' (London 1936, 184).

A second factor was – and has continued to be – the pressure exerted by tight production schedules. Because the composer is frequently not involved until after the shooting of a film, 'he or she generally has so little time . . . that the producer must also call on an orchestrator or orchestrator-arranger to fill out the score following the composer's more-or-less elaborate notations' (Brown 1994, 63). Although orchestrators were often fellow-composers (Hugo Friedhofer was one of a number of orchestrators working on Korngold's scores, for example), not all film composers were content with the system. As Brown reports, Herrmann for one objected strongly: 'To orchestrate is like a thumbprint. People have a style. I don't understand it, having someone orchestrate. It would be like someone putting color to your paintings' (1994, 292). A further, significant influence was the openness of film studios to popular music styles. In the 1950s and 1960s this led to a variety of scores using jazz band instrumentation (for example, by David Raksin and Elmer Bernstein), while in the 1960s and 1970s Henry Mancini and John Barry (among others) integrated jazz with the sounds of popular orchestral music. (The importance Mancini attached to orchestration is illustrated by the fact that he published a book about it, *Sounds and Scores*, in 1962.)

On top of these various factors influencing film orchestration came one that perhaps surpassed all the others in importance: the particular opportunities for composition and orchestration represented by the link between music and the moving image. While some techniques (for example, to express mood changes) were already present in opera, many had to be developed for the new medium. A good example of this is found in the 'spaghetti western' scores of Ennio Morricone. A key part of Morricone's response to the task of developing sonorities to express and link mood, atmosphere, event (typically, dark) and landscape in films such as *A Fistful of Dollars* (1964) and *The Good, the Bad and the Ugly* (1966) was to involve a huge variety of timbres, including whistling, soprano vocalizing, acoustic and electric guitar, solo trumpet and pan pipes, as well as strings and percussion.

In contrast to music for the moving image, with its close, if ambiguous, relationship to the orchestral art music tradition, the jazz band provides an instructive example of how a popular music genre can use techniques of orchestration derived from elsewhere but explore their usage with a different range of instruments to hand and a different sound concept in mind. In the 1920s and 1930s, for example, 'Jelly Roll' Morton, Don Redman, Duke Ellington, Benny Carter and Fletcher Henderson each developed their own individual styles of band orchestration, around the instrumental resources of the ensemble: brass and wind instruments, keyboard (occasionally), plucked strings (banjo or guitar, double bass) and percussion. The orchestral work of each of these band arrangers was distinctive in its own way (as was that of later arrangers such as Pete Rugolo for Stan Kenton), characterized by its imaginative use of instrumental groups or sections and the way in which solos were embedded in the overall sound. Ellington's orchestration in particular demonstrated two additional factors: his interest in tone color (as exemplified most famously in the voicings for 'Mood Indigo' – the traditional jazz 'front line' instruments of trumpet, clarinet and trombone arranged to give a highly original sound); and his response (and that of Billy Strayhorn, who orchestrated many Ellington compositions from the late 1930s on) to the distinctive instrumental sounds of individual performers in the band and the way in which he integrated them into the scoring. A similar familiarity with the particular sounds of individual players characterized the work of Bill Challis for the Paul Whiteman and Jean Goldkette bands in the 1920s, but here Challis's task was to integrate jazz and dance band sonorities.

Bibliography

Bennett, Robert Russell. 1975. *Instrumentally Speaking*. Melville, NY: Belwin-Mills.

Berlioz, Hector. 1843. *Grand traité d'instrumentation et d'orchestration modernes* [Major Treatise on Modern

Instrumentation and Orchestration]. Paris: P. Schonenberger.

Brown, Royal S. 1994. *Overtones and Undertones: Reading Film Music*. Berkeley, CA: University of California Press.

London, Kurt. 1936. *Film Music: A Summary of the Characteristic Features of Its History, Aesthetics, Technique, and Possible Developments*, trans. Eric S. Bensinger. London: Faber & Faber.

Mancini, Henry. 1962. *Sounds and Scores: A Practical Guide to Professional Orchestration*. Northridge, CA: Northridge Music Co.

Rimsky-Korsakov, Nikolay. 1964 (1913). *Principles of Orchestration, with Musical Examples Drawn from His Own Works*, ed. Maximilian Steinberg, trans. Edward Agate. New York: Dover Publications.

Schuller, Gunther. 1989. *The Swing Era: The Development of Jazz, 1930–1945*. New York: Oxford University Press.

Skinner, Frank. 1950. *Underscore*. New York: Criterion Music Corp.

Tucker, Mark. 1991. *Ellington: The Early Years*. Urbana, IL: University of Illinois Press.

Discographical Reference

Ellington, Duke. 'Mood Indigo'/'When a Black Man's Blue.' Victor 22587. 1930: USA. Reissue: Ellington, Duke. 'Mood Indigo'/'When a Black Man's Blue.' *Centennial Edition: Complete RCA Victor Recordings: 1927–1973* (24-CD box set). RCA 63386. *1999*: USA.

Filmography

A Fistful of Dollars (*Per un Pugno di Dollari*), dir. Sergio Leone. 1964. West Germany/Italy/Spain. 101 mins. Spaghetti Western. Original music by Ennio Morricone.

The Good, the Bad and the Ugly (*Il Buono, il Brutto, il Cattivo*), dir. Sergio Leone. 1966. Italy/Spain. 161 mins. Spaghetti Western. Original music by Ennio Morricone.

DAVID HORN

Parody

According to the *Oxford English Dictionary*, a parody is 'a composition in prose or verse in which the characteristic turns of thought and phrase in an author or class of authors are imitated in such a way as to make them appear ridiculous, especially by applying them to ludicrously inappropriate subjects.' The use of wit and irony closely allies parody with satire, although 'satire' more consistently implies a deprecating effect.

In jazz versions of Tin Pan Alley-derived 'standards,' a performer's interpretation may communicate a parodic stance through exaggerated gestures, an unlikely choice of material or an incongruous combination of stylistic traits, any of which may convey an ironic form of commentary (Monson 1994). Post-Tin Pan Alley Western popular music contains the work both of professional satirists and of those who employ parody occasionally. Among the former are Stan Freberg – whose 'Banana Boat (Day-O)' of 1957 clearly imitates Harry Belafonte's recording from earlier in that year while exaggerating stylistic mannerisms – and 'Weird Al' Yankovic – who has parodied many 1980s and 1990s artists, including Michael Jackson, Madonna and Nirvana. Among those who use parody occasionally are Paul Simon, whose 'A Simple Desultory Philippic' parodies Bob Dylan's style from the period 1965–66 without burlesquing a particular song, and Peter, Paul and Mary, whose 'I Dig Rock and Roll Music' satirizes the Mamas and the Papas' vocal style in particular, and rock 'n' roll hipsters' concession to commercialism in general.

Many artists engage in self-parody, be it consciously, through quotation of earlier works (for example, the Beatles' quotation of 'She Loves You' in 'All You Need Is Love'), or unconsciously, through an exaggerated re-creation of well-known gestures from earlier moments in a career (as in the post-1969 performances of Elvis Presley).

The work of Frank Zappa from the late 1960s and early 1970s represents an apogee of parody and satire in popular music; its vast range of targets includes psychedelic rock, blues rock, hippy/counterculture in general, earlier rock 'n' roll (for example, 'Duke of Prunes'), doo-wop, Motown, protest songs and classically trained singing, to name a few. The collage-like presentation of these disparate styles introduces concepts from the early twentieth-century avant-garde (see Bürger 1984), and verges on pastiche, thus foreshadowing approaches found in post-modernists of the 1990s such as Beck.

The line between parody, imitation and stylistic allusion is not stable: while the Beach Boys' initially uncredited appropriation in 'Surfin' U.S.A.' of Chuck Berry's 'Sweet Little Sixteen' raised issues of plagiarism, it clearly was not parody (a generous interpretation would cite 'unconscious' influence). On the other hand, the Beatles' 'Back in the U.S.S.R.,' in its conflation of stylistic allusions to both Chuck Berry and the Beach Boys' imitation of Chuck Berry, clearly parodies both of its predecessors through its absurd juxtaposition of comic lyrics and exaggerated vocal mannerisms; however, this is 'clear' only if the listener has prior knowledge of the models. This implies the importance of reception, for parody relies on a 'competent' listener who can recognize the difference between the model and the parody (Stefani 1987).

Quotation via sampling may also lead to a sense of parody in genres such as hip-hop, due to the incongruity of the sampled material in the new context. An example of this is the Wu Tang Clan's use of a phrase from Gladys Knight's version of 'The Way We Were' in 'Can It All Be So Simple.'

No discussion of parody in popular music would be complete without a mention of the movie *This Is Spinal Tap* (1984), which spoofs rock music documentaries as well as a variety of popular music styles (see Covach 1995).

Bibliography

Bürger, Peter. 1984. *Theory of the Avant-Garde*. Minneapolis, MN: University of Minnesota Press.

Covach, John. 1995. 'Stylistic Competencies, Musical Satire, and "This Is Spinal Tap."' In *Concert Music, Rock, and Jazz Since 1945: Essays and Analytical Studies*, ed. Elizabeth West Marvin and Richard Hermann. Rochester, NY: University of Rochester Press, 399–421.

Monson, Ingrid. 1994. 'Doubleness and Jazz Improvisation: Irony, Parody, and Ethnomusicology.' *Critical Inquiry* 20: 283–313.

Oxford English Dictionary. 1989. 2nd ed. 20 vols. Oxford: Clarendon Press.

Stefani, Gino. 1987. 'A Theory of Musical Competence.' *Semiotica* 66(1–3): 7–22.

Discographical References

Beach Boys, The. 'Surfin' U.S.A.' Capitol 4932. *1963*: USA.

Beatles, The. 'All You Need Is Love.' Parlophone R 5620. *1967*: UK.

Beatles, The. 'Back in the U.S.S.R.' *The Beatles*. Apple PCS 706718. *1968*: UK.

Beatles, The. 'She Loves You.' Parlophone R 5055. *1963*: UK.

Belafonte, Harry. 'Banana Boat (Day-O).' RCA 6771. *1957*: USA.

Berry, Chuck. 'Sweet Little Sixteen.' Chess 1683. *1958*: USA.

Freberg, Stan. 'Banana Boat (Day-O).' Capitol 3687. *1957*: USA.

Knight, Gladys, and the Pips. 'The Way We Were.' Buddah 463. *1975*: USA.

Peter, Paul and Mary. 'I Dig Rock and Roll Music.' Warner Brothers 7067. *1967*: USA.

Simon and Garfunkel. 'A Simple Desultory Philippic.' *Parsley, Sage, Rosemary and Thyme*. Columbia CS 9363. *1966*: USA.

Wu Tang Clan. 'Can It All Be So Simple.' *Enter the Wu Tang (36 Chambers)*. RCA 66336-4. *1993*: USA.

Zappa, Frank, and the Mothers of Invention. 'Duke of Prunes.' *Absolutely Free*. Verve V-5013. *1967*: USA. Reissue: Zappa, Frank, and the Mothers of Invention.

'Duke of Prunes.' *Absolutely Free*. Rykodisc 10502. *1995*: USA.

Discography

Beck. *Mellow Gold*. Geffen 24706. *1993*: USA.

Beck. *Mutations*. Geffen 25309. *1998*: USA.

Beck. *Odelay*. Geffen 24823. *1996*: USA.

Beck. *One Foot in the Grave*. K 28. *1994*: USA.

Yankovic, 'Weird Al.' *Greatest Hits*. Scotti Bros. Records 5211-4-SB. *1990*: USA.

Filmography

This Is Spinal Tap, dir. Rob Reiner. 1984. USA. 82 mins. Comedy ('Mockumentary'). Original music by Christopher Guest, Michael McKean, Rob Reiner, Harry Shearer.

DAVID BRACKETT

Pastiche

The *Oxford English Dictionary* defines 'pastiche' as 'a medley of various ingredients; a hotch potch, farrago, jumble.' Subsidiary usages include 'an opera, cantata, or other composition, made up of various pieces from different authors or sources, a pot-pourri,' and 'a picture or design made up of fragments pieced together or copied with modification from an original, or in professed imitation of another artist; also, the style of such a picture.' These latter two definitions come closest to contemporary usage in writing about popular music. The current usage, as found in the theoretical discourse around postmodernism, began to appear in the 1970s. Pastiche became associated with postmodernism with the appearance of two closely related articles by Fredric Jameson (1983, 1984). In Jameson's famous formulation,

Pastiche is the imitation of a peculiar or unique style, the wearing of a stylistic mask, speech in a dead language: but it is a neutral practice of such mimicry, without parody's ulterior motive, without the satirical impulse, without laughter, without that still latent feeling that there exists something 'normal' compared to which what is being imitated is rather comic. (1983, 114)

Described thus, the idea of pastiche blends aesthetics and sociology, as it combines aspects of form (stylistic allusion) with some notion of reception (the audience's attitude toward, and understanding of, this allusion). That is, a sense of pastiche can occur only if a member of the audience understands the reference and perceives that it does not refer to a norm. Pastiche is also linked with other oft-mentioned attributes of postmodernism: 'rhizome/surface' as opposed to 'root/depth,' 'signifier' versus 'signified,' '[blank] irony' versus 'metaphysics' (see Hassan 1985). Because it refers to styles that are not

213

perceived as the artist's unique voice, pastiche is often associated with extreme stylistic eclecticism.

Part of what distinguishes pastiche from parody is that the reference is more subtle in pastiche than in parody, and another style may be evoked only partially, whereas parody tends to refer to the parodied style in its totality. When this partial reference refers to a style with strong links to a prior historical period, it evokes the 'retro' phenomenon (also sometimes referred to as 'historicism' – see Jameson 1984). Much early discussion of pastiche in popular music focused on music video due to the striking links between that medium's visual procedures and those found in advertising and avant-garde cinema (see Kaplan 1987, and Goodwin 1987, 1992 for opposing sides of this debate).

One of the earliest examples of material that verged on pastiche due to its extreme eclecticism is Frank Zappa's work of the late 1960s with the Mothers of Invention, although his stylistic allusions were usually exaggerated enough to conjure up a sense of parody. A clearer example of pastiche is the Beatles' eponymous double album (sometimes referred to as the White Album). This album called into question notions about an integrated group style and progress in terms of the values of Western art music (which were embodied in *Sergeant Pepper's Lonely Hearts Club Band* and continued by numerous progressive/art rock groups), while juxtaposing and alluding to a wide range of different styles. Some of these were straightforward parody, such as 'Back in the U.S.S.R.,' but many other tracks lacked such an obvious satirical impulse. Was 'Yer Blues' a parody of blues revivalists or a heartfelt utterance in blues form? Was 'Good Night' a spoof or a nostalgic glimpse back at the 'light' music of the Beatles' childhoods? Was 'Revolution No. 9' a serious avant-garde electronic music experiment or a throwaway designed to deflate pompous pop artists?

As subgenres continued to proliferate in Western rock music in the 1970s and older styles continued to circulate, instances of pastiche began to rise correspondingly. David Bowie and Elvis Costello provide two contrasting examples of pasticheurs whose careers began during this period (Moore 1993, 171–79). Bowie, as one of the initiators of the glam rock style, inhabited a series of self-consciously 'inauthentic' personae, and released albums that alluded to a succession of musical styles, including hard rock (*The Rise and Fall of Ziggy Stardust and the Spiders from Mars, Diamond Dogs*), soul/funk (*Young Americans*) and early techno/new wave (*Heroes*). Costello (aka Declan McManus), while maintaining a fairly consistent persona, adopted a series of pseudonyms ('Elvis Costello,' 'the Imposter,' 'Napoleon Dynamite' and so on) and also explored a wide range of styles, sometimes

from album to album – *Get Happy* (soul music of the 1960s), *Almost Blue* (country music), *Imperial Bedroom* (early art rock). All of his albums until 1984 featured textural consistency due to the use (with one exception) of the same band, the Attractions. With his turn to different groups of studio musicians for most of his projects after 1986, the eclecticism has increased, and stylistic allusions can be found between tracks on the same album; this is especially true of *Spike* and *Mighty Like a Rose* (see Brackett 1995, ch. 5).

During the 1990s, many artists adapted aspects of the approaches used by Zappa, the Beatles, Bowie and Costello. Beck, in a song like 'High 5 (Rockin' the Catskills),' traversed many styles in a single track, with most of the styles drawn from the 1960s and early 1970s. An artist like Björk created a sense of pastiche not by rapid crosscutting à la Beck, but by mixing styles simultaneously within a song, between songs within an album or between albums.

Historicism or 'retro' performance was also widespread in the 1990s, with the music of an artist like Sheryl Crow on, for example, *Tuesday Night Music Club*, relying almost totally on styles that had existed since the early 1970s. These styles have not been updated, but have been used as models for 'new songs.' The retro idea has been taken to an extreme by tribute bands, who base their entire repertoire, and musical and visual style, on a previous band. For example, the band Dread Zeppelin performs nothing but Led Zeppelin songs in note-perfect arrangements based on the latter group's recordings.

A discussion of pastiche in popular music would not be complete without a mention of Hindi film song, which anticipated many developments in Western popular music of the 1990s. Hindi film songs have featured eclectic pastiches of material dating back to the late 1940s, initially combining 'light' Indian classical with traditional folk music and new forms of popular music, while later drawing on an enormous range of material from around the world – in particular, different styles of Western popular music. However, the dependence of pastiche on reception complicates the straightforward attribution of this concept to musical works outside the Western cosmopolitan context, where concepts such as 'blank irony' and 'stylistic originality' may not either exist or have the same importance (Manuel 1988).

Bibliography

Brackett, David. 1995. *Interpreting Popular Music*. Cambridge: Cambridge University Press.

Goodwin, Andrew. 1987. 'Music Video in the (Post) Modern World.' *Screen* 28(3): 36–55.

Goodwin, Andrew. 1992. *Dancing in the Distraction Fact-*

ory: *Music Television and Popular Culture*. Minneapolis, MN: University of Minnesota Press.

Hassan, Ihab. 1985. 'The Culture of Postmodernism.' *Theory, Culture and Society* 2(3): 119–32.

Jameson, Fredric. 1983. 'Postmodernism and Consumer Society.' In *The Anti-Aesthetic: Essays on Postmodern Culture*, ed. Hal Foster. Seattle, WA: Bay Press, 111–25.

Jameson, Fredric. 1984. 'Postmodernism, or, the Cultural Logic of Late Capitalism.' *New Left Review* 146: 53–92. (Reprinted in Jameson, Fredric. 1991. *Postmodernism, or, The Cultural Logic of Late Capitalism*. Durham, NC: Duke University Press, 1–54.)

Kaplan, E. Ann. 1987. *Rocking Around the Clock: Music Television, Postmodernism and Consumer Culture*. London: Methuen.

Manuel, Peter. 1988. *Popular Musics of the Non-Western World*. New York and Oxford: Oxford University Press.

Moore, Allan. 1993. *Rock, The Primary Text: Developing a Musicology of Rock*. Buckingham and Philadelphia: Open University Press.

Oxford English Dictionary. 1989. 2nd ed. 20 vols. Oxford: Clarendon Press.

Discographical References

Beatles, The. 'Back in the U.S.S.R.' *The Beatles*. Apple PCS 706718. *1968*: UK.

Beatles, The. 'Good Night.' *The Beatles*. Apple PCS 706718. *1968*: UK.

Beatles, The. 'Revolution No. 9.' *The Beatles*. Apple PCS 706718. *1968*: UK.

Beatles, The. *Sergeant Pepper's Lonely Hearts Club Band*. Parlophone PCS 7027. *1967*: UK.

Beatles, The. *The Beatles*. Apple PCS 706718. *1968*: UK.

Beatles, The. 'Yer Blues.' *The Beatles*. Apple PCS 706718. *1968*: UK.

Beck. 'High 5 (Rockin' the Catskills).' *Odelay*. Geffen 24823. *1996*: USA.

Bowie, David. *Diamond Dogs*. RCA-Victor APLI 0576. *1974*: USA. Reissue: Bowie, David. *Diamond Dogs*. Rykodisc RCD 10137. *1990*: USA.

Bowie, David. *Heroes*. RCA-Victor AFL1-2522. *1977*: USA.

Bowie, David. *The Rise and Fall of Ziggy Stardust and the Spiders from Mars*. RCA-Victor SF 8287. *1972*: USA. Reissue: Bowie, David. *The Rise and Fall of Ziggy Stardust and the Spiders from Mars*. Rykodisc RCD 10134. *1990*: USA.

Bowie, David. *Young Americans*. RCA-Victor AQL1-0998. *1975*: USA.

Costello, Elvis. *Almost Blue*. Columbia FC 37562. *1981*: USA.

Costello, Elvis. *Get Happy*. Columbia JC 36347. *1980*: USA.

Costello, Elvis. *Imperial Bedroom*. Columbia FC 38157. *1982*: USA.

Costello, Elvis. *Mighty Like a Rose*. Warner Brothers 9-26575-4. *1991*: USA.

Costello, Elvis. *Spike*. Warner Brothers 25848-4. *1989*: USA.

Crow, Sheryl. *Tuesday Night Music Club*. A&M 31454-0126-4. *1993*: USA.

Zappa, Frank, and the Mothers of Invention. *Absolutely Free*. Verve V-5013. *1967*: USA. Reissue: Zappa, Frank, and the Mothers of Invention. *Absolutely Free*. Rykodisc RCD 10502. *1995*: USA.

Zappa, Frank, and the Mothers of Invention. *Freak Out!*. Verve V-5055. *1966*: USA. Reissue: Zappa, Frank, and the Mothers of Invention. *Freak Out!*. Rykodisc 10501. *1995*: USA.

Zappa, Frank, and the Mothers of Invention. *We're Only in It for the Money*. Verve V6-5045. *1968*: USA. Reissue: Zappa, Frank, and the Mothers of Invention. *We're Only in It for the Money*. Rykodisc 10503. *1995*: USA.

Discography

Dread Zeppelin. *Un-Led-Ed*. IRS IRSD-13048. *1990*: USA.

DAVID BRACKETT

Quotation

In the context of music, 'quotation' denotes a short passage or tune taken from one piece of music to another. In popular music, quotation usually functions as an act of humor, parody or homage. The practise is widespread among jazz improvisers, in whose improvisations often-humorous allusions to non-jazz repertoires may arise from a combining of historically discrete and disparate elements of style (Monson 1994), may represent a borrowing of ideas, or may comment covertly on class and racial politics (Gabbard 1991).

In Western popular music from the mid-1950s to the late 1970s, there was little outright quotation, and what did occur frequently referred to other repertoires: the Byrds' respectful quotation of John Coltrane's 'India' (itself a reference to a recording of Ravi Shankar's) in 'Eight Miles High'; the Electric Light Orchestra's humorous quotation of the opening of Beethoven's 5th Symphony in 'Roll Over Beethoven'; the Beatles' quotations of the Glenn Miller Orchestra's 'In the Mood' and the Marseillaise at the end of 'All You Need Is Love.' In addition to this, much popular music from this era contains a great deal of stylistic imitation and allusion.

With the advent of rap in the mid- to late 1970s, quotation became an integral part of popular music in North America and the United Kingdom. Drawing, in part, on Jamaican practises of toasting and dub (Hebdige 1987), rap performances and recordings frequently used previous recordings as the basis (either literally or re-recorded) of the backing tracks (for example, the backing track on the Sugarhill Gang's 'Rapper's Delight' was based on Chic's 'Good Times'). In this context, quotation acts as a way of projecting the performer's view of his/her cultural lineage. The development of inexpensive sampling technology in the mid-1980s facilitated quotation of everything from one- to two-measure drum parts as the basis for a recording's groove to whole sections of a previous recording as the basis for a 'new' track (for example, Puff Daddy's use of the Police's 'Every Breath You Take' for 'I'll Be Missing You'). For alternative perspectives on this phenomenon, see Goodwin (1990) and Rose (1994).

Bibliography

Gabbard, Krin. 1991. 'The Quoter and His Culture.' In *Jazz in Mind: Essays on the History and Meanings of Jazz*, ed. Reginald T. Buckner and Steven Weiland. Detroit, MI: Wayne State University Press, 92–111.

Goodwin, Andrew. 1990. 'Sample and Hold: Pop Music in the Digital Age of Reproduction.' In *On Record: Rock, Pop and the Written Word*, ed. Simon Frith and Andrew Goodwin. New York: Pantheon Books, 258–73.

Hebdige, Dick. 1987. *Cut 'n' Mix: Culture, Identity, and Caribbean Music*. London: Methuen.

Middleton, Richard. 1990. *Studying Popular Music*. Milton Keynes and Philadelphia: Open University Press.

Monson, Ingrid. 1994. 'Doubleness and Jazz Improvisation: Irony, Parody, and Ethnomusicology.' *Critical Inquiry* 20: 283–313.

Rose, Tricia. 1994. *Black Noise: Rap Music and Black Culture in Contemporary America*. Hanover and London: Wesleyan University Press.

Discographical References

Beatles, The. 'All You Need Is Love.' Parlophone R 5620. *1967*: UK.

Byrds, The. 'Eight Miles High.' Columbia 43578. *1966*: USA.

Chic. 'Good Times.' Atlantic 3584. *1979*: USA.

Coltrane, John. 'India.' *Impressions*. Impulse AS-42. *1963*: USA. Reissue: Coltrane, John. 'India.' *Live at the Village Vanguard – The Master Takes*. Impulse IMPD-251. *1997*: USA.

Electric Light Orchestra, The. 'Roll Over Beethoven.' Harvest HAR 5063. *1973*: UK.

Glenn Miller Orchestra, The. 'In the Mood'/'I Want to Be Happy.' Bluebird 10416. 1939: USA.

Police, The. 'Every Breath You Take.' A&M 2542. *1983*: USA.

Puff Daddy, and Evans, Faith. 'I'll Be Missing You.' Bad Boy 79097. *1997*: USA.

Puff Daddy, and Evans, Faith. 'I'll Be Missing You.' *No Way Out*. Bad Boy 73012. *1997*: USA.

Sugarhill Gang, The. 'Rapper's Delight.' Sugar Hill 542. *1979*: USA.

DAVID BRACKETT

Scratching

'Scratching' is a term used to denote the manipulation by hand of one or more phonograph turntables to create a sound not unlike that made by 'scratching' a record with a needle. The technique was invented by DJs who usually worked in tandem with a rapper, and Grandmaster Flash is most commonly associated with the initial development of scratching. Instead of using a turntable to play records, Flash used the turntable itself as an instrument, spinning it with one hand (forward and backward, mostly in short, rapid bursts) and manipulating its volume controls with the other. Flash often used the sound of needle against vinyl, hence 'scratching,' as a form of sound synthesis.

The sound became fashionable in the late 1970s when hip-hop and rap music performers developed it and found it eminently useful as a rhythmic element, as a 'break' to allow movement from one musical passage to another or as a means of joining together repetitions of a single passage. Scratching sounds were later incorporated in digital audio samplers and synthesizers, allowing their easy addition to almost any piece of music. The technique came to be widely used in alternative rock music by performers like Beck, the Beastie Boys and the Dust Brothers, who incorporated it as a stylistic element in music that relied heavily on digital editing and the juxtaposition of multiple sounds and styles.

Discography

Beastie Boys, The. *Paul's Boutique*. Capitol C2-91743. *1989*: USA.

Beck. *Odelay*. DGC 24823. *1996*: USA.

Grandmaster Flash. 'The Adventures of Grandmaster Flash on the Wheels of Steel' (12″ single). Sugar Hill 557. *1981*: USA.

STEVE JONES

6. Processes: Technological

Backing Track

A backing track is a support line or part that occurs within a recording. It can include any part of the backing, such as the backing vocals and backing musicians, that does not belong to the lead part. In rock or pop songs, the backing tracks usually include the drumkit, bass, rhythm guitar and/or keyboard parts, all of which support the soloist or instrumentalist on the lead track. As with instrumental backing, backing vocals may be recorded on one or more of the backing tracks. As a rule, the backing track is recorded before the soloists record their parts, although this is not necessarily always the case.

STAN HAWKINS

Digital Recording

Digital recording is a method by which an audio signal is converted into discrete values, coded in the form of binary numbers (0's and 1's), and then stored on a tape or disc medium. All earlier recording methods were analog in nature: whether in the form of etched grooves on a record or varying patterns of electrical magnetism on tape, recorded signals were continuous waveforms, similar in pattern to the changes in air pressure created by the original sound. In digital recording, the electrical amplitude of an audio signal is 'sampled' at regular intervals (typically 44,100 or 48,000 times, or more, per second) – referred to as the 'sampling frequency' – and then 'quantized' into discrete values, or 'quantization levels.' These levels are coded into binary numbers of a specific length: typically, 16-bit words, or greater, are used (16 0's and 1's can represent 65,536 discrete levels). The binary code is converted into a series of electrical pulses – on/off states – that can be recorded on magnetic tape or any other digital medium. This process, known

as analog-to-digital conversion (ADC), must be reversed at the playback stage so that the original analog audio signal can be reconstructed; this latter stage is called digital-to-analog conversion (DAC). The entire recording and playback process is sometimes referred to as pulse code modulation (PCM).

The scientific theories that formed the basis for digital recording date from the 1920s and 1930s, and a variety of experiments in digital audio took place at the Bell Laboratories, and elsewhere, during the 1950s. However, it was not until the late 1960s that the first prototypes of a practical digital recording system – using PCM conversion methods in conjunction with videotape recorders (VTRs) as a storage medium – were developed, first at the NHK Technical Research Institute in Japan and, later, at Nippon Columbia and Sony.

Digital recording has several advantages over analog tape recording methods: tape hiss, print through, transport instabilities and the buildup of noise inherent in successive tape generations are all but eliminated in the digital domain. By the late 1970s, these and other advantages had led to the widespread adoption of digital recording methods in the recording industry in the stereo mastering of classical and popular music. In 1983, the compact disc – a digital playback-only format for the consumer market – was introduced in Europe and North America; and, by 1986, low-cost digital audio tape (DAT) recorders had also become available.

During the 1980s, various digital multitrack systems were also introduced, including both tape-based systems and computer-based workstations that used hard drives for data storage. Tape-based multitrack recorders, like their analog counterparts, are a linear medium that allows tracks to be layered one after the other but provides very limited facilities for the editing of individual tracks (limited essentially to 'punching' in and out of record mode). Hard disc systems, on the other hand, are a random-access form of technology that stores and plays back each recorded take as a separate audio file; this allows for both the detailed editing of individual recorded events and engagement in the large-scale rearrangement of the recorded material. As a result, computer workstations became an increasingly popular medium for the composition and remixing of popular music. With the falling prices of computer and audio hardware during the 1990s, hard disc recording systems made significant inroads in the amateur and semiprofessional home studio market, thus bringing these powerful new systems and techniques within the reach of consumers.

Bibliography

Alten, Stanley R. 1994. *Audio in Media*. 4th ed. Belmont, CA: Wadsworth.

Huber, David Miles. 1992. *Random Access Audio*. Carmel, IN: Sams Publishing.

McGill, James F. 1985. 'An Introduction to Digital Recording and Reproduction.' In *Digital Audio Engineering: An Anthology*, ed. John Strawn. Los Altos, CA: William Kaufman, Inc., 1–28.

Nakajima, H., et al., eds. 1983. *Digital Audio Technology*. Blue Ridge Summit, PA: Tab Books.

PAUL THÉBERGE

Distortion

'Distortion' denotes a change in the shape of a sound wave. Although distortion can be produced by a specific processor, the term originated from and is commonly used in relation to an unwanted change of wave shape (hence, of timbre), caused by limits or inadequacies in the signal chain. Distortion occurs in analog systems when, for example, a component in the signal chain does not perform linearly on all frequencies, changing the harmonic content of the transmitted sound. The simplest visual representation of distortion is that of a wave whose crests are flattened, so that it resembles a square wave. Digital systems do not allow smooth distortion (which is why some musicians and producers prefer the ringing sound of slightly distorting analog systems), but they are subject to other forms of distortion. Aliasing, which occurs with sounds that have frequencies of more than half the sampling frequency, is a type of digital distortion.

Bibliography

Borwick, John, ed. 1980. *Sound Recording Practice*. Oxford: Oxford University Press.

FRANCO FABBRI

Double-Tracking

Double-tracking is a recording technique in which a vocal or instrumental performance is recorded twice on separate tracks of a multitrack tape recorder. The slight variations in pitch and timing that are a result of the differences between the two performances produce a fuller sound. The technique was used by the Beatles and other artists from the late 1960s onward, but became prevalent only after 16- and 24-track tape recorders became available. The technique can use up a great many tracks, however (for example, when used on background vocal harmonies), and it is sometimes necessary to pre-mix the doubled performances to free up tracks for other parts.

Bibliography

Julien, Olivier. 1999. 'The Diverting of Musical Technology by Rock Musicians: The Example of Double-Tracking.' *Popular Music* 18(3): 357–65.

PAUL THÉBERGE

Dubbing (Overdubbing)

The term 'dubbing' is sometimes used as an abbreviation for 'overdubbing,' a studio practise in which the various vocal and instrumental sounds are recorded in temporal succession on multitrack tape. Unlike live performance, musicians are seldom required to play together at the same time in the multitrack studio: each musician simply adds his/her individual part while listening to previously recorded material, thus allowing recordings to be made over a period of days or months, and in different geographical locations. In general, rhythm tracks (drums and bass) are recorded first, followed by guitars, keyboards and backing vocals and, finally, solo instruments and lead vocals (a rough vocal track, called a 'guide track,' is sometimes recorded earlier in the process to help orient the musicians to the basic structure and dynamic flow of the song). The various layers of sound are then combined (or stripped away) at the time of mixdown.

The technique of overdubbing was first introduced into mainstream pop of the 1950s when a third track was added to the stereo pair of tracks found on professional recorders. The extra track was used as a means of isolating and enhancing the vocal sound of pop singers, such as Frank Sinatra and Nat 'King' Cole, in relation to the backing orchestra. A somewhat earlier, and much more extensive and creative, use of overdubbing, however, can be found in the multiple guitar and voice recordings of Les Paul and Mary Ford during the 1950s: for example, even before multitrack tape was available, Paul used disc and tape copying methods to build multiple layers in hits such as 'Lover' (1948) and 'How High the Moon' (1951). Les Paul is also credited with having created the design for the first eight-track tape recorder. The fusion in timbre created by a single vocalist performing multiple harmony parts, a technique pushed to its limits by artists such as Joni Mitchell during the early 1970s, can be achieved only through overdubbing.

By the time four-track recorders became available during the early 1960s, producers such as Phil Spector were using the technology as an integral component in an overall strategy for the creation of a new pop sound. During the late 1960s and early 1970s, track capacity expanded rapidly from four- to eight- to 16- and 24-track recording, offering greater possibilities for the control and layering of sounds; performers such as Stevie Wonder made use of these enhanced capabilities and released recordings in which they played and sang all the musical parts. In Jamaican popular music, from the late 1960s onward, it was common for engineers to make a specially mixed version of songs recorded on multitrack, called the 'dub' version, which contained only the instrumental tracks, with an exaggerated emphasis placed on the rhythm and bass. Overdubbing must be considered as a central technique of the multitrack studio when used as a compositional tool and has been an essential component in the evolution of the sound of recorded popular music in the post-World War II era.

The term 'dubbing' is also used in the film industry to describe the process of adding sound to a film or video, or to describe the process of copying material from one tape to another.

Bibliography

Eno, Brian. 1983. 'The Studio as Compositional Tool, Part I.' *Down Beat* 50(7) (July): 56–57.
Eno, Brian. 1983. 'The Studio as Compositional Tool, Part II.' *Down Beat* 50(8) (August): 50–53.
Hebdige, Dick. 1987. *Cut 'n' Mix: Culture, Identity, and Caribbean Music*. London and New York: Methuen.
Jones, Steve. 1992. *Rock Formation: Music, Technology, and Mass Communication*. Newbury Park, CA: Sage.
Sievert, Jon. 1978. 'Les Paul.' In *The Guitar Player Book*, ed. Jim Ferguson. New York: Grove, 184–90.
Théberge, Paul. 1989. 'The "Sound" of Music: Technological Rationalization and the Production of Popular Music.' *New Formations* 8 (Summer): 99–111.

Discographical References

Paul, Les, and Ford, Mary. 'How High the Moon.' Capitol 1451. 1951: USA. Reissue: Paul, Les, and Ford, Mary. 'How High the Moon.' *The Best of the Capitol Masters*. Capitol C2-99617. *1992*: USA.
Paul, Les, and Ford, Mary. 'Lover.' Capitol 15037. 1948: USA. Reissue: Paul, Les, and Ford, Mary. 'Lover.' *The Best of the Capitol Masters*. Capitol C2-99617. *1992*: USA.

Discography

Mitchell, Joni. 'Shadows and Light.' *The Hissing of Summer Lawns*. Asylum Records 7E-1051. *1975*: USA.
Paul, Les, and Ford, Mary. *All-Time Greatest Hits*. CEMA 57262. *1992*: USA.
Wonder, Stevie. 'Living for the City,' 'Higher Ground' and 'Jesus Children of America.' *Innervisions*. Motown T-326L. *1973*: USA.

PAUL THÉBERGE

Echo

'Echo,' from Latin *echo* and Greek *êckhô*, is a term used in popular music to designate either an effect of sonic repetition or the electromechanical device producing such an effect. Although 'echo' and 'reverberation' ('reverb') are used interchangeably in many discussions concerning popular music, they refer to phenomena that are both physically and perceptually distinct. Echo occurs when delay time between the original sound and its repetition is (roughly) larger than or equal to 50 milliseconds. For its part, reverberation is a prolongation, or persistence, of the original sound. Physically, both echo and reverberation are constituted of 'echoes,' but reverberation is a succession of echoes with most delays smaller than 50 milliseconds.

Fascination with the echo effect has its roots in ancient mythology (Melville 1987), and probably even earlier – as far back as resonance in prehistoric caves, where sound may have had an important ritualistic role (Reznikoff 1995). In the seventeenth century, Athanasius Kircher (1602–80) systematically studied the natural effect of echo to attempt to control or 'capture' it for further use (Kircher 1994 (1676)). Echo has also been used in other forms of expression, such as poetry (Hollander 1981), and, of course, classical composers from Bach to Mahler have used motivic repetition to achieve an echo effect (Imberty 1993). But the particular effect produced by the exact replication of the original sound was possible only through the reflection of that sound on particular surfaces or, later, through sound recording techniques.

The systematic use of echo in recorded popular music seems to have its origins in 1950s rockabilly recordings produced in Memphis by Sam Phillips. Known as the 'slap-back echo,' the effect was applied not only to voice, but to drums and guitar as well, and sometimes to the whole mix (as in Elvis Presley's 'Blue Moon of Kentucky'). The effect was produced by sending the sound to a recording machine through a tape-loop.

Historically, different kinds of echo effect – long echo, runaway echo, stereophonic echo, for example – have been used in recorded popular music and applied to any sound source, especially guitars and vocals (for example, the famous guitar solo by David Gilmour in Pink Floyd's 'Time'). Following experimentation in the late 1960s and early 1970s, echo can often be found mixed with other sound processing effects, such as flanging, distortion and reverb (for example, in Björk's 'Hunter'). Such a diversity of effects has become possible mainly because of technological improvements, such as the development of digital delay in the 1980s. For the listener, it produces the effect of enlargement (as in Daniel Lanois' 'Death of a Train') and, in some cases, a feeling of nostalgia (for example, in the bridge section of U2's 'Mofo'). Richard Middleton, when writing about the echo effect in Elvis Presley's early recordings, points out that 'the effect is used largely to intensify an *old* pop characteristic – "star presence": Elvis becomes "larger than life"' (Middleton 1990, 89). On another level, echo also influences the rhythmical, melodic and harmonic structure of a song through the interactions of the periodic repeated sounds with the other sounds of the whole musical texture.

Bibliography

Anderton, Craig. 1985. *The Digital Delay Handbook*. New York: Amsco Publications.

Hollander, John. 1981. *The Figure of Echo: A Mode of Allusion in Milton and After*. Berkeley, CA: University of California Press.

Imberty, Michel. 1993. 'L'utopie du comblement: à propos de l'*Adieu* du *Chant de la terre* de Gustav Mahler' [The Utopia of Fulfillment – With Respect to *The Farewell* from Gustav Mahler's *Song of the Earth*]. *Les cahiers de l'IRCAM: Utopies* 4: 53–62.

Kircher, Athanasius. 1994 (1676). 'Phonosophia anacamptica, ou traité de l'écho' [Phonosophia anacamptica, or Treatise on the Echo], trans. Guy Lobrichon. *Les cahiers de l'IRCAM: Espaces* 5: 13–28.

Lacasse, Serge. 1995. *Une analyse des rapports texte-musique dans 'Digging in the Dirt' de Peter Gabriel* [An Analysis of Text–Music Relations in Peter Gabriel's 'Digging in the Dirt']. M.A. thesis, Université Laval, Québec.

Melville, A.D., trans. 1987. *Ovid's Metamorphoses*. Oxford: Oxford University Press.

Middleton, Richard. 1990. *Studying Popular Music*. Milton Keynes: Open University Press.

Morrison, Craig. 1996. *Go Cat Go!: Rockabilly Music and Its Makers*. Urbana, IL: University of Illinois Press.

Reznikoff, Iégor. 1995. 'On the Sound Dimension of Prehistoric Painted Caves and Rocks.' In *Musical Signification: Essays in the Semiotic Theory and Analysis of Music*, ed. Eero Tarasti. Berlin: Mouton de Gruyter, 541–57.

Shea, William F. 1990. *The Role and Function of Technology in American Popular Music: 1945–1964*. Ph.D. thesis, University of Michigan.

Discographical References

Björk. 'Hunter.' *Homogenic*. Elektra CD 62061. *1997*: Iceland.

Lanois, Daniel. 'Death of a Train.' *For the Beauty of Wynona*. Warner CDW 45030. *1993*: USA.

Pink Floyd. 'Time.' *The Dark Side of the Moon*. Harvest SMAS-11163. *1973*: UK.

Presley, Elvis. 'Blue Moon of Kentucky.' Sun 209. 1954: USA.

U2. 'Mofo.' *Pop*. Island 314 524 334-2. *1997*: Ireland.

SERGE LACASSE

Mixing

Denoting the manipulation and balancing of sounds within a musical performance or recording, mixing is the final process in determining the character of sounds to be presented to an audience. The principles of mixing are largely the same, whether the activity takes place in a recording studio or in a live performance setting, even though the end product is clearly of a different nature. In both cases, multiple sound sources (typically from microphones or electronic instruments, numbering anywhere from two to more than a hundred) are routed to a mixing console, where they are combined and output to (usually) two stereo channels.

Prior to the advent of electrical sound amplification and multitrack recording, a mix of sounds emanating from a musical group was achieved in one of two ways: by the placement of the musicians on a soundstage (for example, the loudest instruments, such as percussion, would be placed furthest from the audience, toward the back of the stage; the softest ones would be to the front of the stage); or, in a recording studio, by the positioning of musicians in relation to the recording device, and the alteration of room acoustics through the use of sound-absorbing or sound-reflecting objects. In a recording situation, songs would be recorded and re-recorded until an engineer or other supervisor at the session was satisfied with the balance, the performance and the room acoustics.

Such techniques have persisted in both live performance and recording settings. Particularly in regard to the former, vocalists often use microphone positioning as a means of controlling volume levels. Microphone placement plays a significant role in the recording process too, as it permits performers to alter the relationship between sound emanating directly from a source and ambient, or reflected, sound. Recording studios are designed with room acoustics as a primary consideration, and studios regularly use curtains, baffles and other objects to alter the acoustic characteristics of enclosed studio space.

Multitrack recording fragmented the recording process. It allowed individual sounds to be recorded to the individual channels, or tracks, of a tape synchronously with previously recorded tracks. At a mixdown session for a final mix (as opposed to a rough mix, created as an aural reminder of the state of a work-in-progress, akin to the use of 'rushes' in the film industry), all tracks are combined into a monoaural or stereophonic master tape. The goal is to create an overall balance of sound, an aesthetic blend between each track.

To achieve the highest degree of control during mixdown, in most contemporary recording sessions individual tracks are recorded separately, in isolation from one another. Moreover, they are often recorded in anechoic fashion. That is, techniques of 'close-miking' (placing a microphone as close to an instrument as possible) and 'direct injection' (plugging an electronic signal directly into a mixing console) were developed to allow as little ambient sound as possible onto a recorded track. As well as multitrack tape recorders, sound processing equipment was developed that permitted numerous sonic parameters to be altered during mixing, including ambiance. Consequently, the final mix is the moment in the recording process most affected by technology. Individual tracks, groups of tracks (a submix) or even the overall mix can be treated with various forms of signal processing, such as equalization, reverberation, echo, limiting and the like, to achieve a perfect blend of sounds. Typically, individual tracks are listened to separately, and signal processing applied. Several tracks are then added until an overall mix is achieved. Of course, the greater the number of tracks, the more complicated the mixdown. The sheer variety of possible treatments of individual tracks, their combinations and the ongoing changes that need to be made to tracks during the mix (often requiring specially designed mixing consoles that record the changes to parameter settings of each channel and thus automate mixdown) can mean that the process of achieving a final mix can take longer than the actual recording sessions.

During a mixdown session, several mixes of a piece of music can be created. Usually, some of these are issued, each targeted to a particular medium. For instance, a mix that is created to sound best when broadcast via television will be used as the soundtrack to a video; another will be created to sound best on FM radio; yet another will be made to sound best on a portable cassette player. The popularity of dance music and the development of 12″ (30 cm) dance records with extended mixes is an additional example of the affiliation of mixing and music format. Club DJs came to be renowned as mixers,

further fragmenting roles associated with the process of music-making, since mixing had been the domain of producers and engineers; it was presumed that they had a better sense of what would be popular in the clubs and could tailor mixes to suit popular tastes.

Mixing can also serve artistic purposes. Particularly after the development of inexpensive digital recording technology, remixing music became a widespread activity. In some instances, as in the case of remixes of Everything But The Girl's 'Missing,' the backing track is dropped out, leaving only vocals, which are then supported by an entirely new musical background. Alternatively, individual elements are edited, made to sound different and rearranged, as in Arthur Baker's remixes of New Order's 'Confusion.' In both cases, digital recording technology facilitated the implementation of a 'cut-and-paste' process not unlike that in word processing. This process allows the manipulation of almost every sonic and musical parameter, including even tempo, length and pitch.

Discographical References

Everything But The Girl. 'Missing.' *Amplified Heart*. Atlantic 82605. *1994*: USA. Re-release: *Amplified Heart* (with Todd Terry's Club Mix of 'Missing' as an additional track). Blanco Y Negro/WEA 4509 96482-2. *1995*: UK.

Remixes

The Full Remix EP (12″). Blanco Y Negro/WEA NEG71T 4509-97134-0. *1994*: UK (Chris & James Full On Club Mix; Chris & James Flossie Dub; Little Joey Remix; Ultramarine Remix).

The Remix EP (album version). Blanco Y Negro/WEA NEG71CD 4509-97133-2. *1994*: UK (Little Joey Remix; Chris & James Full On Club Mix; Ultramarine Remix).

12″. Blanco Y Negro/Eternal/WEA NEG84T 0630-12528-0. *1995*: UK (Todd Terry Mixes; Alex Natale Mix; Chris & James 94 Mix; Album Mix).

New Order. 'Confusion.' Factory FAC 93. *1983*: UK.

12″ Remixes

EMI GOOD 501. *1983*: New Zealand.

Factory 08-22687-20. *1983*: The Netherlands.

Factory/Gap FAC 93. *1983*: Australia.

Factory/Gap FACC 93. *1983*: Australia (8:13 Confusion; 5:19 Confusion Beats; 7:33 Confusion Instrumental; 8:04 Confusion Rough Mix).

Factory/Nippon Columbia YW-7419-AX. *1983*: Japan.

Factory/Virgin 600893. *1983*: France.

Nuevos Medios 31 046 M. *1983*: Spain.

PolyGram FACX 13. *1983*: Canada.

Rough Trade LC5661 (yellow label). *1983*: Germany.

Streetwise SWRL 2213. *1983*: USA (8:04 Confusion
Rough Mix; 8:04 Confusion Rough Mix).

Streetwise SWRL 2213 (white label promotion). *1983*:
USA.

Factory/Festival X14827. *1990*: Australia.

Minimal Records QAL-249. *1990*: USA (5:30 Confusion
(alternative mix); 5:10 Confusion (essential mix); 3:40
Confusion (trip 1-ambient confusion); 1:17 Confusion
(a cappella); 7:05 Confusion (con-om-fus-ars-ion);
6:50 Confusion (ooh-wee dub)).

STEVE JONES

Postproduction

The postproduction stage of a recording project includes
a variety of activities that take place after the musical
material has been recorded and mixed. These activities
are usually coordinated by the producer and/or the
A&R department of the record label. Postproduction
tasks may involve a number of aesthetic, technical and
promotional decisions, such as evaluating and ordering
the recorded tracks, overseeing compact disc and tape
mastering, and selecting songs for release as singles, all
of which can have a significant effect on the success of
the recording project.

Once a series of songs or musical works has been
recorded, the order, or 'sequence,' in which the material
will be arranged on disc or tape must be determined,
usually by the producer or A&R coordinator. The
sequence of the individual songs is important because it
can influence how the overall sound, themes and contours of the album will be perceived by the listener;
timing of the silences between individual cuts will also
have an impact on the overall pacing of the final recording.

After a suitable order has been determined, the material is ready for the mastering stage, during which
inconsistencies in volume and tone quality between the
various cuts can be corrected. The creation of a master
tape is, however, more than a technical task – it is one
that involves aesthetic judgment and an ability to bring
out the subtle timbral characteristics that may be
common to the individual recordings in order to create
a distinctive overall sonic impression of the material.
Mastering is usually performed by specialized engineers,
and may include a variety of technical operations that
modify and shape the recording, such as altering
dynamics through compression or emphasizing specific
frequency characteristics through equalization. Dynamic
limiting may also be applied to meet the requirements
of specific formats or broadcast media.

For promotional purposes, one or more songs are usually selected during the postproduction stage for release
as singles and, once selected, songs destined for radio

or dance club use often require the creation of alternate
mixes. In the past, the original producers and engineers
were usually entrusted with such tasks; however, with
specialization within the industry increasing during the
1980s and 1990s, it has become common for dance club
mixes to be created by independent engineers or DJs.

Finally, the postproduction stage also involves a
number of clerical and legal tasks that must be performed before a recording can be released. These include
the collection of information – credits, duration of the
selections, lyrics and so on – for the creation of liner
notes, and the securing of licenses for sound samples or
songs that may have been used in the recording.

PAUL THÉBERGE

Preproduction

Preproduction is the planning stage of a music recording
in which arrangements for the essential artistic and technical resources required to produce the recording are
made. The specific activities associated with the preproduction stage will vary according to the nature and complexity of the recording project.

In the case of a typical rock band recording, where
most of the song material is original and members of the
band are the only musicians to be recorded, the preproduction stage may involve little more than an initial set
of negotiations with a producer or A&R representative of
a record company; fixing of the overall budget for the
project; selection of the songs to be recorded; and hiring
of a recording studio and engineer. Prior to the actual
recording sessions, rehearsals take place, and additional
discussions between the band, producer and engineer
may be required in order to determine the overall
approach to be taken during the sessions, sound requirements, microphone selection, tracking order, and other
technical and aesthetic issues.

In many pop music recordings, however, artists are
often involved in the recording of material originating
elsewhere, or other musicians may be engaged as performers. In such cases, additional preparations are usually required. These may include securing rights to particular songs, hiring an arranger to score the musical
material, booking soloists and rehearsing session musicians, as well as carrying out the various other activities
associated with the preproduction stage outlined above.

To a large degree, multitrack recording practises have
changed the manner in which many musicians
approach the composition and recording of popular
songs. In the past, most of the writing and rehearsing of
songs took place outside and prior to the actual recording session. Since the 1960s, it has become increasingly
common for songs to be written and arranged in the
studio itself, thus integrating recording technology into

the creative process and blurring the distinction between various aspects of the preproduction and production stages of a recording project. By the 1980s, with the advent of digital synthesizers and sequencers, much of the arranging and actual recording of instrumental parts could be done in low-cost home studios; professional recording facilities became necessary only for recording and mixing additional parts and for finishing the recorded work. In this way, production aspects of a project became part of an extended preproduction process.

While demarcations between the various stages of the production process have changed or disappeared, preproduction has remained an important part of any recording project in that many of the decisions taken at this stage of the process will often have a significant impact on the sound of the final recording. Compatibility between the aesthetic orientations of the artist, producer and engineer, suitability of the musical arrangements and recording facilities, and various other factors can influence both the artistic and commercial success of a recording.

PAUL THÉBERGE

Production

The production stage of a recording project includes the principal recording, processing and mixing of musical material in order to produce a master tape. In other media, such as film and television, the production stage is usually understood to encompass only the actual filming process, with visual and audio editing and mixing relegated to an extended postproduction phase of the project. In music recording, however, editing, processing and mixing are considered part of the overall, integrated studio production process leading to the creation of a master tape recording.

Since the late 1960s, it has become commonplace for popular musicians to write, compose and arrange material in the studio. As a result, distinctions between preproduction and production are often blurred. The number of significant technical, musical and aesthetic operations that take place in the studio – operations that can take anywhere from a few days to several months to complete – have made production the single most important phase in the creation of most popular music recordings.

With the exception of the taping of live concerts, a recording's production phase most often begins in a multitrack studio, where individual instrumental tracks are recorded and layered on a multitrack tape recorder or on a computer. Through a process known as overdubbing, individual instrumental performances are recorded. In most cases, the drums, bass and rhythm guitars (individually or together) are recorded first; a rough

vocal track – known as a guide track – and/or a click track may also be recorded to lay out the basic contours of a song and supply a consistent tempo for the musicians. These tracks are usually followed by the recording of keyboards and other backing instrument tracks, solo instruments such as lead guitar or saxophone, background vocals and, finally, the lead vocal track. In many popular music recordings, drum machines or basic synthesizer tracks may be substituted for any of the above performances. These may be created in the studio or elsewhere – for example, in smaller production facilities (such as a home studio) – during the preproduction phase of the project. Considerable attention is given to each individual track as it is recorded: the producer oversees the recording sessions and ensures that the overall quality of the performances meets the requirements of the project; the recording engineer, through judicious use of microphone placement, equalization, compression and other techniques, ensures the technical quality of the recordings.

In most cases, several takes are required before an adequate performance is obtained. Engineers can 'punch in' on a recording, allowing new material to be recorded over old. When additional tracks are available, several takes might be committed to tape (or to a computer's hard disc) and later combined to create a composite 'performance.' Some initial signal processing, such as equalization and compression, may also be applied as the sounds are committed to multitrack tape in order to enhance their sound quality and tame the often wildly fluctuating dynamics of vocal and instrumental performance.

Since the 1970s, 24-track (or greater) recording capability has been the norm in professional studio production. As far as possible, each performer is allotted at least one track on a multitrack tape; in the case of the drums, the signals from as many as eight different microphones (placed in close proximity to each individual drum and cymbal) may be routed to separate tracks. This allows for maximum control and flexibility in the final mixdown stage of a recording. Because each performer is recorded separately, it is not necessary for all members of a band or ensemble to be present in the studio at the same time. Individual performances can be recorded days, weeks or months apart and, because of the relative standardization of recording technology, tracks can be recorded in different cities when necessary, to accommodate the preferences and schedules of star performers. The layering of different performances allows for considerable flexibility in the overall composition and arrangement of the musical material; this accounts, in large part, for the tendency of many popular musicians to use the production stage of a recording as an integral part of the songwriting process.

Once the music has been recorded, the engineer and producer begin the lengthy task of processing the recorded tracks and preparing them for the final mixdown to stereo. Basic balances between the various tracks are established; further equalization might be required in order to balance the overall frequency spectrum of the recording or to help individual tracks stand out within the musical texture. Additional compression might be applied to even out the dynamic contour of a vocal performance or to add extra 'punch' to drums and bass, and special effects such as chorus, delay or reverb may be added. The spatial location of individual sounds in the stereo field is determined. Decisions to edit, eliminate or add new tracks may also be made at this stage of production.

Once the editing and processing stage has been accomplished, the mixdown takes place. The mixdown is essentially a real-time process in which the engineer 'performs' the prerecorded music at the console, balancing, processing and creating the overall dynamic shape of the music as it is played back from the multitrack recorder and mixed to the stereo master tape. Increasing specialization during the 1980s led to the common practise of employing separate recording and mixdown engineers on many music recording projects. Although most engineers prefer to mix in real time, the process has become so complex that many mixing consoles (and most multitrack software programs) are now equipped with computerized controls allowing for various degrees of automation to be introduced into the mixdown process.

Having a distinct 'sound' is both a musical and an aesthetic goal for many musicians, and a commercial imperative within the record industry. The production stage of the recording process is significant because it is through the various technical and musical practises associated with multitrack recording, signal processing and mixing that the basic 'sound' of a recording is defined and shaped.

Bibliography

Alten, Stanley R. 1994. *Audio in Media*. 4th ed. Belmont, CA: Wadsworth.

Eargle, John. 1980. *Sound Recording*. 2nd ed. New York: Van Nostrand Reinhold.

Moylan, William. 1992. *The Art of Recording: The Creative Resources of Music Production and Audio*. New York: Van Nostrand Reinhold.

Nisbett, Alec. 1995. *The Sound Studio*. 6th ed. Oxford: Focal Press.

PAUL THÉBERGE

Quantizing

Quantizing, or quantization, is a process in which a continuous input is transformed into discrete steps.

(a) In the case of digital audio, quantizing is part of the analog-to-digital conversion process in which the continuous electrical amplitude of an audio signal is converted into digital form – for example, into 16-bit digital numbers.

(b) In drum machines and sequencers, quantizing is used to bring notes played at irregular intervals into line with the basic beat or precise subdivisions of the beat. Sometimes referred to as 'auto-correct,' the rhythmic effect of excessive quantization gives a kind of rigid, mechanical feel, valued by many electro-pop musicians but also deplored by critics of electronically generated music.

PAUL THÉBERGE

Recording

Methods of sound recording production vary greatly depending on the recording medium. The phonograph, analog tape recorder and digital media require different recording methods based on their technical and aural qualities. As editing, multitrack recording and other technological developments came about, the relations of production changed along with individual roles and the functions of performers, engineers and producers. As the technology of sound recording grew more complex, the roles played by the producer and engineer in popular music creation became even more important. However, as music technology became more affordable, many amateur and professional musicians were able to acquire recording equipment and learn more about the recording process.

The process of recording essentially relies on the performance of music before technological equipment that 'fixes' sound onto a recording medium. In the late 1800s and early 1900s, recording was, simply, the mechanical opposite of reproduction. A performer would play or sing into the phonograph's horn, and the sound would be etched onto the disc or cylinder. An article in a 1900 issue of *Scientific American* provides a description of the Edison Phonograph Works and the typical recording method of the time:

> One of the upper floors of a large building in the record department is divided into a number of rooms, in which the specialists who are employed by the Edison Phonograph Works are kept steadily at work speaking, playing or singing into the recording machines . . . the violinist stands with his instrument immediately and closely in front of three converging horns, each of which connects with a recording phonograph . . . One of the first things that strikes a visitor to the record room is the rapidity with which the artists sing, the speed being much greater than that to which one is accustomed in a music hall or opera house. Moreover, the songs are sung with the

full power which would be used before a public audience.

Among the most popular records are those of band music, and for making these the company maintains a full instrumental band . . . the musicians are so grouped around the phonographs that the volume of sound from each instrument strikes full upon the horns, the front row of the performers being seated on ordinary chairs and those behind on raised seats. On the occasion of our visit there were no less than sixteen phonographs on the racks in front of the band, each with its horn pointing toward the musicians. In this case, as in the case of solos, the music is performed at full power. (390)

Recording sound has, from its earliest days, been an unnatural method of trying to create natural-sounding performances. Opera singer Maria Jeritza, in an interview in *The Literary Digest* (1924), described her first recording experience in North America and noted the difficulties that have accompanied studio recording ever since recording sessions began at the Edison Phonograph Works:

I already knew one thing . . . that I must try to sing just as naturally as I would on the stage. But when I arrived, I knew that the only way I could do so would be to forget my surroundings completely, for my setting was anything but a stage-setting.

First of all, the records were made in a small room, a room so small that the members of the little orchestra of ten or fourteen men which accompanied me had to sit close together, knee to knee. Then came the actual singing itself. With the orchestra so close to the singer the sound of the instruments is so overpowering that it drowns the voice, and I could not hear myself sing . . . but I found myself able to overcome this difficulty by holding my hands over my ears . . .

Then there is the matter of adjusting your position, as you stand and sing, so that you are at exactly the right distance from the receiver. For deep register tones one comes closer, for high register tones one moves farther away.

The first record made is always an experimental one. It enables the singer to hear herself as she should *not* be . . . [and then come] as many more recordings as may be necessary to secure perfect results. (28)

The unique recording capabilities of the phonograph, together with the consequent sound manipulations that were to alter forever the relationship between studio performance and public live performance, were discovered early on. Speeding up or slowing down the phonograph during recording, cutting two cylinders in half and editing them together, overlaying the sound of a previous recording with a new performance onto a new cylinder,

and other techniques presaged modern multitrack recording methods. It became apparent very early in the phonograph's existence that the recording studio was a place where sound did not have to be recorded and reproduced exactly as it was during a live performance.

Manipulation of sound for phonograph recording became commonplace once electrical recording was invented. The microphone and the amplifier permitted precise control of loudness and tone, and wrought a significant change in studio performance and recording, a change that resulted in a transformation in recorded music by allowing the capture of softer and ambient sounds, and quieter music.

Electrical recording also affected popular music style in performance as well as in recording. Bing Crosby's style of crooning, for example, would have been impossible without the microphone.

Overdubbing (the layering of sound upon sound), a key element of modern popular music recording, was, at best, a difficult matter with phonograph recording. Two or more phonographs were played and their sound combined onto another phonograph. That was also the process by which a long-playing record (LP) was made: multiple performances on several separate discs were combined onto one longer one by playing back each one onto the new one. Problems with timing, speed and so on were numerous. The widespread use of tape recorders coincided with the advent of the LP, and tape also allowed easier overdubbing and editing.

Tape recording proved very useful and economical in the studio, and by the early 1950s tape recordings could be made in stereo. Phonograph recording continued into the 1950s, although tape recording edged it out of most commercial and consumer applications. In the late 1970s, phonograph recording was reintroduced under the name 'direct-to-disc,' and was marketed for audiophiles. Referred to by some as 'superdisc,' the process was essentially the same as electrical phonograph recording in the 1950s and earlier. It was often cited as a return to a more natural, musical form of recording, one that eliminated tape from the recording process and recorded sound directly onto a disc that would be used for pressing records.

Tape recording brought about many changes in sound recording, but most were concentrated in the control room and not the studio. Splicing, editing and tape manipulation have almost always been accomplished by the engineer or producer in the control room. The parameters of musical performance changed little, however, and much of the recording process remained essentially the same as it was for phonograph recording until the mid-1960s. There was typically no overdubbing, and the musicians performed together in the same room.

During the initial period of the use of tape recording, the most noticeable changes in popular music recording were those brought about by the editing capabilities of tape and by the increased recording time easy editing allowed. For the musician, editing meant that a piece did not necessarily have to be performed all the way through. Instead, parts of it could be performed and then spliced together later. Moreover, editing ability meant that the 'perfect' take could be assembled from several imperfect ones. The best parts of each take would be chosen and carefully joined into one seamless piece. The Beatles' 'Strawberry Fields Forever,' for example, joined two separate takes, one sped up and one slowed down until they were in the same key.

In the mid-1960s, multitrack tape recording brought about the most significant change of all. Not only did multitrack recording incorporate previously used tape techniques; it added several more that were crucial to the development of popular music recordings. First, it allowed overdubbing, a technique whose use is first ascribed to guitarist Les Paul. On one of the tape's tracks a piano could be recorded, then later a guitar could be recorded synchronously with the piano but on another track, and so on.

The process had several immediate consequences. First, an artist could now play all instruments without the help of a group. Second, band members did not have to perform their parts at the same time in the same place. The drummer and bass guitarist could record their parts one night in one studio; then the next day, the tape could be taken elsewhere, where the keyboard player and lead guitarist could go to record their parts the next night.

Third, multitrack recording allowed for easy 'punch-ins.' It was no longer difficult to fix short segments of a performance within a piece of recorded music. Since each instrument was on a separate, isolated track, it became possible to return to it at any given time and replace it. Should it be deemed necessary, it was possible to erase and re-record only a small section of it. Fourth, multitrack recording enabled composers to create music by layering sounds, track by track.

Fifth, and most germane to any discussion of recording, multitrack recording technology put the producer and sound engineer firmly in charge of studio recording. Since sounds could be recorded on discrete tracks, they could easily be manipulated after recording. This manipulation and balancing of sound became known as mixing, and it is the foundation of contemporary popular music. After multitrack recording's introduction, songs were recorded until the performance was satisfactory. The balance and tone of sounds, room acoustics,

even song arrangements, were adjusted during mixing sessions.

The development of sound processing equipment, or 'effects,' also established the control room as the center of production. 'Effects' can be divided into roughly three categories: reverberation-related effects, equalizers and compressors/limiters. Reverberation-related effects include those that can add echo or time delay, or simulate room acoustics. They are usually used to add ambiance to a sound. Since it is quite easy to add ambiance after a recording has been made, acoustic isolation is even more important in the studio room, and performers often play in isolation booths, or alone, to avoid 'leakage' of other sounds into their own track. The goal is to have as primal a sound as possible, so that it can be developed later, in the control room, under the supervision of the producer and engineer.

Equalizers vary the amount of a specific frequency band and are used to alter the tone of a sound. Essentially precise tone controls, they are used to change the color of the sound. A mixing board usually has some form of equalization for each channel.

Compressors and limiters restrict the level of a sound. Although engineers strive for a very wide dynamic range, some instruments can exceed a recording device's range. A limiter ensures that a signal does not exceed a certain level, while a compressor narrows the dynamic range. Noise gates are usually part of a compressor or limiter, and essentially shut off sound from a channel unless it reaches a certain threshold. They are most often used to make certain that low-level, stray, unwanted sounds (such as tape hiss or shuffling feet) do not make their way into a recording. They are also used to make rock recordings sound as loud as possible without exceeding broadcasting limits.

During the late 1960s, innovation in professional audio recording centered on the addition of more tracks to multitrack recorders, and by the early 1970s 24-track recorders were the industry standard. The 1980s saw development of techniques with which it was possible to slave together two 24-track decks for a total of 46 tracks, and 32- and 48-track recorders were developed as well.

Another great leap in recording technology came at the Audio Engineering Society's 1977 convention in New York, when digital recording was introduced as a viable studio technology. Although digital recorders had been developed several years earlier, the 32-track digital tape recorder introduced by 3M in 1977 was the first to be purchased by recording studios. In most ways, the 3M deck introduced at the convention physically resembled analog tape machines. It used 1″ (2.5

cm) tape moving at a slightly faster speed than on an analog tape deck.

Concomitant with the introduction of 3M's digital recorder was the introduction of the digital compact disc (CD), and it is no coincidence that its introduction corresponded to 3M's release of their deck. Without suitable home playback equipment, digital recording would have had little opportunity to find a market.

Recording studios did not quickly acquire digital recorders, not simply because their price was high but because of already heavy investments in analog tape equipment. At 1990 and 1991 audio industry trade conventions, smaller versions of professional digital recorders were exhibited by Alesis (the 'ADAT'), Tascam and Akai. These units allowed for eight-track recording, and could be chained together for up to 24-track (or more) recording. These digital recorders quickly made their way into personal, home studios, as well as into larger, commercial facilities. And soon after, advances in computer technology (particularly the decrease in the cost of hard disc storage and the increase in microprocessor speed and capability) meant that digital recording direct to a hard disc became competitive with tape-based forms of digital recording.

As with the introduction of tape recording, the recording process itself initially changed little as studios acquired digital tape and hard disc recorders. However, just as tape's editing capabilities revolutionized recording, the first prominent change brought about by digital recording also involved editing. Digital recording did away with razor blade splicing. Instead, electronic editing is performed with the aid of a microprocessor. The degree of precision that electronic editing offers is far beyond that of analog recording. With a digital recording, splicing by hand is impossible. Instead, one observes the sound waveforms of a specific track on a computer monitor and locates points at which the waveforms match. The points are stored in a microprocessor's memory and, when they come up during playback, the microprocessor switches from one point to the next imperceptibly. Each track can be previewed in that fashion so that edit points do not have to be the same throughout the recording. The best edit points for each track can be selected. Edit points within 10 microseconds of absolute accuracy can be attained. Moreover, digital editing, unlike tape editing, is non-destructive, since one can recall from the tape or hard disc the 'original' track.

If there has been any single bias in the development of recording techniques and technology, it is toward editing. As it has evolved, recording equipment has allowed more precise editing of music. The traditional roles of producers and recording engineers, though remaining intact in

large, professional studios, have fallen away in other spheres of music production. Preproduction can now be accomplished at home or elsewhere, using digital tape recorders or computer-based hard disc recorders. With much preproduction occurring largely outside the studio and, if desired, under the control of the musician, once in the studio the producer is faced with music that is almost completely realized. However, owing to the malleable nature of digital recording, radical alteration of song structure and arrangements becomes possible even in the late stages of production. The producer and musician are thus faced with more decision-making throughout the recording process, thereby lengthening the time it takes to make a recording.

Modern digital recording offers much that was unavailable, even unthought of, in any previous recording medium. But when faced with a stunning array of possibilities, it becomes difficult to determine exactly what decision to make, what choice is the right one. Recording was once fettered by the medium – phonograph recording allowed for short recordings of a certain volume, for example, and performances had to be live, in the studio. Sound, performance and music can now be entirely flexible, and creativity unbound by the physical restrictions of a recording medium.

Bibliography

Chanan, Michael. 1995. *Repeated Takes: A Short History of Recording and Its Effects on Music*. London and New York: Verso.

Denisoff, R. Serge. 1975. *Solid Gold: The Popular Record Industry*. New Brunswick, NJ: Transaction Books.

Hammond, John. 1977. *John Hammond on Record*. New York: Summit Books.

'How It Feels to Sing for the Phonograph.' 1924. *The Literary Digest* (10 May): 28–29.

Jones, Steve. 1992. *Rock Formation: Music, Technology and Mass Communication*. Newbury Park, CA: Sage Publications.

'The Manufacture of Edison Phonograph Records.' 1900. *Scientific American* (22 December): 390.

Martin, George, with Hornsby, Jeremy. 1979. *All You Need Is Ears*. New York: St. Martin's Press.

Tobler, John, and Grundy, Stuart. 1982. *The Record Producers*. New York: St. Martin's Press.

Wexler, Jerry. 1993. *Rhythm and the Blues: A Life in American Music*. New York: Knopf.

Discographical Reference

Beatles, The. 'Penny Lane'/'Strawberry Fields Forever.' Parlophone R5570. *1967*: UK.

STEVE JONES

Reverb

'Reverb' (a colloquial abbreviation for 'reverberation') is a term used in popular music to designate either an effect of sound prolongation or persistence resulting from successive but imperceptible echoes, or the electro-mechanical device producing such an effect. Historically, many techniques, such as echo chambers, spring reverb and digital units, have been used to produce artificial reverb. First used in radio and cinema, artificial reverb was first heard in popular music recordings in the late 1940s (e.g., the Harmonicats' 'Peg o' My Heart'; Patti Page's 'Confess'). More recently, reverb has been mainly used to re-create the sounds of natural environments or to magnify the sounds of voices and instruments, both on recordings and on stage.

Bibliography

Dodge, Charles, and Jerse, Thomas A. 1985. *Computer Music: Synthesis, Composition, and Performance.* New York and London: Macmillan.

Moylan, William. 1992. *The Art of Recording: The Creative Resources of Music Production and Audio.* New York: Van Nostrand Reinhold.

Shea, William F. 1990. *The Role and Function of Technology in American Popular Music: 1945–1964.* Ph.D. thesis, University of Michigan.

Discographical References

Harmonicats, The. 'Peg o' My Heart.' Vitacoustics 1. 1947: USA.

Page, Patti. 'Confess.' Mercury 70878. 1948: USA.

SERGE LACASSE

Sound Editing

During the first half of the twentieth century, most music recordings were made direct to disc: recorded simultaneously with the musical performance, the disc medium offered no direct means for altering or correcting the recorded material. With the widespread introduction of magnetic tape recording during the post-World War II period, however, the possibility of editing and assembling the recording material (in much the same way as film can be edited in cinema) offered sound engineers new corrective and creative opportunities. (Rough editing had been possible with earlier wire and metal-band magnetic recorders, but the techniques were difficult and the results crude.)

Tape editing is accomplished by physically cutting the magnetic tape (preferably during a brief silence) and then splicing it back together by applying a special adhesive tape over the backing material. Sound engineers have become extremely adept at sound editing – such that it is virtually impossible to discern where edits have been made in a recording, even with close listening. Singer Bing Crosby was one of the first popular performers to use tape editing extensively, assembling programs for network radio broadcast. From the late 1940s onward, the Crosby broadcasts used editing to replace imperfect performances (in whole or in part), to tighten up or correct dialog and commercials, and even to add exaggerated laughter ('laugh tracks') to comic routines (Mullin 1976).

With the increasing use of multitrack tape recording in popular music during the 1960s, the physical editing of the tape became impossible: because the tracks on a multitrack tape run parallel to one another, attempting to cut the tape to correct the performance of a single musician would effectively destroy the performances recorded on all the other tracks as well. Sound engineers developed a technique of electronic editing – called 'punching in' – whereby the recording circuit on a given track is engaged, while the tape is playing, in order to replace a segment of previously recorded material. Multi-track tape recorders are designed in such a way as to allow musicians to listen to the recorded material just prior to the punch-in point in order to match the phrasing and dynamics of the passage, to make the engagement and disengagement of the recording circuit as silent as possible and, in many professional recorders, to automate the punch-in and punch-out points with extreme precision so that the accidental erasing of material is avoided. Critics of multitracking cite punch-in techniques as contributing to an obsession with perfection and a dynamic uniformity that is entirely unlike live performance (Hunter 1987).

While cutting and splicing digital recording tape are possible on some systems, they require special care because of the density of the recorded data; furthermore, the system must include dedicated circuitry so that the edit points can be located and the resulting transitions in the recorded material are smoothed out. A more common practise has been to use computer-based systems: once digitized, audio can be recorded into files on hard discs and, through the use of editing programs, represented and manipulated graphically on the computer monitor. Edit points can be located with a precision unheard of using analog methods and, with digital signal processing (DSP), the material can be altered in various ways (in terms of pitch, dynamics, equalization and so on), thus further enhancing the editing process. In addition to cut-and-paste methods – known as 'destructive' editing because, much like tape editing, the audio file is permanently altered in the process – computer editing allows for various forms of 'nondestructive' editing in which the original sound file is not altered by either the editing or the processing. Through use of the hard disc's capacity to randomly access any point in a file with equal speed and precision, portions of a sound file can be designated for cutting, alterations such as fading in or out, and reordering of the material, without actual damage to the file. Such capabilities have been extended to computer-based multitrack recording programs, affording a level of flexibility that goes far beyond simple analog punch-in techniques. During the 1990s, computer-based recording and editing came into increasing use in a wide variety of popular music genres, but were especially useful in creating remixes in dance music.

Bibliography

Alten, Stanley R. 1994. *Audio in Media*. 4th ed. Belmont, CA: Wadsworth.

Huber, David Miles. 1992. *Random Access Audio*. Carmel, IN: Sams Publishing.

Hunter, Mark. 1987. 'The Beat Goes Off.' *Harper's* 274: 53–57.

Mullin, John T. 1976. 'Creating the Craft of Tape Recording.' *High Fidelity Magazine* 26(4) (April): 62–67.

Woram, John. 1976. *The Recording Studio Handbook*. Plainsview, NY: Sagamore.

PAUL THÉBERGE

Sound Engineering

Sound engineering provides a critical, mediating link between the performance of music and its reception by audiences. Sound engineers serve in several capacities, and they are typically responsible for evaluating the conditions under which music is to be performed and/or recorded and for overseeing the technical aspects of the performance or studio session. Both their technical expertise and their musical sensibilities are called upon as they select, position and operate sound reinforcement and/or recording equipment, and as they mix sound. In the case of recording sessions, sound engineers also prepare recordings for mastering and mass production, making alterations in the sound quality of the recordings that will often have an impact on their suitability for different media and their success in the marketplace. Traditionally, sound engineers are not involved in aesthetic and musical decision-making, as that role is generally undertaken by producers. However, it must be recognized that the decisions made by sound engineers, and the practises in which they are engaged, are inherently aesthetic in nature, and, in many instances, the roles of musician, producer and engineer overlap in subtle, yet significant, ways.

The tasks and responsibilities associated with sound engineering have changed radically over the past century. In some cases, these changes can be related to fundamental changes in the technology of sound recording, and in other cases to the changing economic organization of the record industry, the demands of musicians and the evolution of musical styles. In the early, acoustical days of recording, it was the task of the engineer to position the performers carefully in front of the recording horn in such a way as to achieve an acceptable musical balance, to prepare the mechanical devices associated with the recording turntables and to prepare the wax platters (shaving, polishing and heating them) for recording. The engineer's primary responsibility was to capture the performance as well as possible, given the relatively crude tools available, and to ensure the technical quality of the recording – that is, make sure that the recorded grooves did not over-modulate or otherwise exceed acceptable limits.

With the introduction of electrical microphones and amplification in the 1920s, the role of the sound engineer changed in a subtle way. Now that it was no longer necessary for musicians to crowd around a recording horn to create sufficient sound levels for recording purposes, sound engineers (in many cases, drawn from the radio industry) were confronted with a new set of technical possibilities: selecting the right type of microphone and determining how many should be used (experiments with multiple microphones had already begun by the early 1930s), where they should be placed in relation to the ensemble and how they should be balanced were additional responsibilities for the engineer. Also, with the increased sensitivity of the microphone, new problems arose: for the first time, room acoustics (echo and reverberation) became a central concern in sound engineering. That these practises and concerns were more than technical in nature is evidenced by the debates around recording aesthetics that began to take place during this period and by the growing awareness that the sound of the recording itself (and not just the music) could be regarded as an object of aesthetic criticism.

It was during the 1950s, 1960s and 1970s, however, that sound engineering took on its modern form. During this period, magnetic tape recorders were first introduced into studio recording. The possibility of multiple recorded takes, tape editing, tape echo and other effects and, later, the development of multitrack recording practises all contributed to an increasing complexity in the techniques associated with sound engineering and an increased responsibility (both technical and musical) on the part of the recording engineer. Slowly, sound engineering began to be recognized as an 'art' in its own right and as a significant component in the achievement of a unique and marketable sound for popular recording artists. As entrepreneurial modes of production became dominant in emerging genres such as R&B and rock, an engineer's willingness to experiment with the new techniques of sound recording was increasingly valued.

Mixing consoles and external effects devices also became increasingly complex in their design during this period, and they began to have an impact not only in recording studio practise, but in live performance contexts as well. By the 1970s, major touring acts routinely employed sound engineers, and their task was no longer simply that of maintaining a band's amplifiers and public-address system. Rather, they had to position and balance a large array of microphones, process the signals with equalization, compression, reverberation and other special effects to achieve the kind of sound associated with the band's studio recordings, and compensate for club or stadium acoustics.

By the mid-1970s, the practises associated with studio engineering had become so complex that a certain degree of specialization had become inevitable. For example, in many professional studios recording assistants were employed to help in setting up the numerous microphones, cables and other devices that might be required on a session, to maintain and operate the tape recorders, or to keep detailed logs of the various recorded takes, their position on the multitrack tape, console settings and other aspects of the session. The performance of these seemingly menial tasks by recording assistants not only freed the recording engineer to concentrate on the more creative problems associated with recording, but also, in the essentially craft-oriented structure of studio work, provided many individuals with the experience necessary to become an engineer.

The chief recording engineer associated with a project would be responsible for the following: conferring with the artist and producer prior to a recording session in order to gain an understanding of the musical and aesthetic requirements of the recording; supervising the overall session and any assistants participating in it; operating the recording console; setting balances and tonal quality; ensuring the technical quality of the basic recorded tracks; and (together with the producer) ensuring good performances. Once recorded, the tracks require a different set of engineering considerations, and often different engineers would be employed at this stage of the process.

Engineering a mix (which is not unlike sound engineering in live performance contexts) requires the ability to take a large number of instrumental and vocal inputs and put them into a musically and tonally balanced form, a detailed technical knowledge of a vast array of signal processing equipment, and a sensitivity to the aesthetic character and requirements of the music at hand in order that the desired artistic result may be achieved. Once the mix engineer, artist and producer are happy with a recording, it must be subjected to one last set of engineering requirements during the mastering stage: the adjustment of overall recording levels and additional equalization, for example, to optimize the recording for

particular recording formats or media. Here again, specialized mastering technologies and specialized engineers are usually employed.

Modern sound engineering has thus become a multistage process involving a number of discrete tasks. As recording technology has developed and become more specialized, sound engineers are sought after both for their understanding of the overall recording process and for their knowledge of the state-of-the-art developments in new technology. Sound engineering thus plays a critical role in the recording process, acting as a link between technology, the musicians, sound and music.

Certainly, by the 1980s and 1990s, many popular musicians had recognized the importance of sound engineering in the recording process and had developed close relationships and artistic collaborations with sound engineers. Often, as in the case of rap music, they broke with conventional engineering standards and recording aesthetics, and pushed the technical capabilities of recording devices beyond normal expectations in search of a unique sound. Others took it upon themselves to learn the basic principles of recording, signal processing and mixing, and built expensive recording facilities of their own. But, while the acquisition of such knowledge has become an essential part of every musician's experience, the increasing complexity of sound recording and reinforcement technology (the development of MIDI technology and computer-controlled audio, for instance) and the new demands placed on engineers by the industry (such as those of creating special mixes for dance club use and synchronizing music to videoclips) have ensured the professional sound engineer's central role in musical practises.

A testimony to the increasing complexity and specialization within the art of sound engineering can be found in the emergence, in the latter part of the twentieth century, of sound engineering programs in universities, technical colleges and private institutions. While on-the-job experience has continued to be a major prerequisite for a career as a sound engineer, it is clear that the range of technical knowledge and skill required in modern sound engineering is much greater than can be absorbed through informal apprenticeship in the studio. Sound engineering has become a diverse, technical and artistic practise that requires years of both formal and informal training and a constant renewal of knowledge and skills in relation to the changing contexts of technological development, industry structure and musical style.

Bibliography
Alten, Stanley R. 1994. *Audio in Media*. 4th ed. Belmont, CA: Wadsworth.

Kealy, Edward R. 1979. 'From Craft to Art: The Case of Sound Mixers and Popular Music.' *Sociology of Work and Occupations* 6(1): 3–29.

Morris, DeWitt F. 1977. 'The Audio Engineer – Circa 1977: What Does He (or She) Do?.' *Journal of the Audio Engineering Society* 25(10/11): 864–72.

Moylan, William. 1992. *The Art of Recording: The Creative Resources of Music Production and Audio*. New York: Van Nostrand Reinhold.

Read, Oliver, and Welch, Walter L. 1976. *From Tin Foil to Stereo: Evolution of the Phonograph*. 2nd ed. Indianapolis, IN: Howard W. Sams & Co.

PAUL THÉBERGE and STEVE JONES

Synchronization (1)

Synchronization is a process in which the transport mechanisms of two or more audio, video or other devices are made to operate at exactly the same speed. Synchronization also allows the devices to find precise locations in the recorded material and is essential, for example, in adding dialog, sound effects and music to video or film images. In purely audio applications, synchronization has often been used in professional sound studios since the 1970s to lock together two multitrack tape recorders in order to increase the number of available tracks. For example, two 24-track recorders can be synchronized together, effectively doubling the number of recording tracks. In actual practise, however, one track on each machine must be dedicated to recording synchronization data, so a maximum of 46 tracks are available for recording music. It is also common for engineers to leave at least one blank track adjacent to the synchronization tracks so that any possible leakage between tracks does not interfere with the recorded music. This further reduces the number of actual tracks available for recording. In some digital audio applications, a clock signal, operating at the speed of the digital sampling rate (e.g., 44,100 or 48,000 times per second), can be used to ensure that digital tape recorders, computers and other devices maintain synchronization accuracy down to the level of the individual sample, and it does so without using up recording tracks.

The most common synchronization standard used in professional recording studios is known as 'SMPTE time code,' a digital protocol developed by the Society of Motion Picture and Television Engineers (SMPTE). It consists of digital data that designate time in the form of hours, minutes, seconds and frames. It is used extensively in film and video postproduction, but also in synchronizing audio tape recorders to one another and to computers. However, with the increasing use of electronic instruments (synthesizers, drum machines and sequencers) and computers in recording studios during the 1980s, a number of other protocols have also been employed.

A relatively simple method of synchronization was developed for early drum machines and sequencers: it consists of a clock pulse operating at a precise subdivision of the beat (referred to as 'pulses per quarter-note' or 'ppq'); thus, while the clock rate is fixed (usually at 24, 48 or 96 ppq), the actual speed of the clock pulse is tempo-dependent. The clock of one device can be used to drive another, provided that they both operate at the same clock rate (which was often not the case, especially when an attempt was made to synchronize equipment from different manufacturers). Some drum machines and sequencers can also supply an audio signal, operating at the clock rate, which alternates between two pitches (a technique known as frequency shift keying or FSK); the signal can be recorded and used to synchronize the device with multitrack tape recorders.

Because the internal clock rate of electronic instruments can vary so widely, synchronization was often a hit-or-miss affair until the introduction of the MIDI (musical instrument digital interface) specification in 1983. The MIDI specification includes its own timing data, corresponding to a standard reference of 24 ppq, and data for finding specific locations within a song ('song position pointer'). To bridge the gap between the SMPTE standard and MIDI, yet another protocol – MIDI time code (MTC) – was introduced in 1987: MTC converts SMPTE into MIDI messages and allows the tempo of sequenced music to operate independently while maintaining 'real time' synchronization with external devices.

Bibliography
Alten, Stanley R. 1994. *Audio in Media*. 4th ed. Belmont, CA: Wadsworth.

Anderton, Craig. 1986. *MIDI for Musicians*. New York: Amsco.

Huber, David Miles. 1992. *Random Access Audio*. Carmel, IN: Sams Publishing.

PAUL THÉBERGE

Synchronization (2)

'Synchronization,' in terms of the cinema, refers to the process of perfectly coordinating sound with an image for the exhibition of a motion picture. The practise of synchronization is as old as cinema itself: the test film that inventor William Kennedy-Laurie Dickson made for Edison in 1894–95 shows Dickson playing his violin into a sound-recording device as two assistants dance for the camera. Although sound film processes were available at the very beginning of the twentieth century, and were introduced again about a decade later, problems with amplification and synchronization, which depended on mechanical linkages by means of belts or shafts, made the process impractical. Even in the days of live accompaniment, the synchronization of image and sound was well established. Rapee (1925) referred to the miscue of a technician providing a synchronized sound effect.

By the early 1920s, smaller, undercapitalized companies had introduced synchronous sound achieved through newer electronic technologies, but these were commercial failures until major corporations entered the marketplace. In the United States, Fox Movietone and Warner's Vitaphone were soon followed by RCA Photophone. These three technologies were incompatible with each other. Fox Movietone involved variable density sound on film, a process that controlled the amount of light hitting the photoelectric cell by varying the light transmission ability of the optical soundtrack. Warner's Vitaphone used sound on disc, while RCA Photophone involved variable area sound on film, a process that controlled the amount of light hitting the photoelectric cell by varying the area of the optical soundtrack through which light could pass. At this time, the German Tobis system, whose patents had been licensed by Movietone, became the continental European standard. All systems did result, however, in a standardized filming and projection speed of 24 frames per second. A period of unrest in the film industry ensued, ending with the adoption of a single sound on film variable area process, with the key patents held by or licensed to Western Electric.

Initially, sound film technologies were meant to provide the experience of full orchestral accompaniment or live vaudeville prologs, previously available only in the largest theaters, to any movie house equipped with a synchronous sound system. But the post-synchronized music and effects tracks added to films that had been shot silent, such as *Sunrise* (September 1927), or the musical vaudeville routines reproduced in the Vitaphone shorts were integrated with dialog into film narratives by the time of the October 1927 release of *The Jazz Singer*. By 1930 and the release of *Sunny*, musical numbers were commonly prerecorded, with performers lip-syncing their performances to the recording, and the dubbing of professional singing voices for actors of lesser musical talent had become common.

The adoption of synchronous sound involved changes in camera technology. Soundproofed 'blimped' cameras – cameras that had padding or casing fitted over them to isolate the sound recording equipment from the cameras' mechanical noise – had been introduced by 1930, with the Fox, Mitchell and Debrie machines dominating by the end of the decade. The multiple synchronizer, which allowed simultaneous editing of sound and image, was developed, with the Moviola device

becoming the industry standard. The postwar period saw a great leap forward in synchronization technology, particularly with the introduction of magnetic tape recording, which greatly simplified location sound shooting. By 1950, compact quarter-inch tape recorders were synchronized by means of a common AC pulse from the power source. The 1957 Auricon Cine-Voice cameras permitted single-system synchronized sound filming through the use of a magnetic strip on the edge of 16 mm film. Double-system synchronization connected sound and image recorders by means of a cable. By the 1960s, both systems had been superseded by crystal oscillator technology, permitting tape recorder and camera to operate on their own power sources without any physical connection. The Nagra tape recorder dominated film production, and the cheaper Uher became the television standard. The venerable Moviola editors increasingly were replaced by flatbed synchronizing editing machines (based on prewar Zeiss models), with the German Steenbeck dominating the market.

While multitrack synchronized sound was introduced with Disney's Fantasound stereo process in 1940, theatrical systems using as many as six or seven magnetic soundtracks were in use in the mid-1950s, made possible by advances in electronic mixing technology. Dolby stereo optical soundtracks had replaced magnetic media as the industry standard by the mid-1970s, coexisting with the older analog optical systems. At the beginning of the twenty-first century, the marketplace was served by several competing digital sound systems, with most films being released with both analog and digital optical tracks alongside the image.

Bibliography

Rapee, Erno. 1925. *Erno Rapee's Encyclopaedia of Music for Pictures*. New York: Belwin.

Salt, Barry. 1983. *Film Style and Technology: History and Analysis*. London: Starword.

Schoenherr, Steven E. 1999–2000. *Motion Picture Sound, 1930–1989*. http://history.acusd.edu/gen/recording/motionpicture.html

Filmography

Sunny, dir. William A. Seiter. 1930. USA. 67 mins. Musical Romance. Original music by Oscar Hammerstein II, Otto Harbach, Jerome Kern.

Sunrise, dir. F.W. Murnau. 1927. USA. 110 mins. Romance. Original music by Hugo Riesenfeld.

The Jazz Singer, dir. Alan Crosland. 1927. USA. 89 mins. Drama. Original music by Louis Silvers.

MARK LANGER

Take

'Take' is a term used to identify each recorded playthrough of a piece of music, typically in the setting of recording studios. The term only became common in non-English-language settings with the advent of multi-track studios. The term derives from the notion that something is 'taken' and subsequently inscribed, much as in photography one 'takes' a picture with a camera. Several takes are usually recorded. Before the advent of multitrack studios, the best take would be chosen to make the recording. Since the advent of multitrack studios, the best portions of multiple takes have been edited together to make a single 'ideal' recording. In certain genres, such as rock, where notions of authenticity have been important, musicians have sometimes striven for a 'perfect take,' which requires no later editing or manipulation. In other genres, such as jazz, the process of editing together the best portions of multiple takes, made possible by multitrack studios, is often resisted in the name of preserving the integrity of a particular performance. Takes not used for the final recording issued to the public are referred to as 'out-takes.' The term 'alternate take' is used to refer to out-takes that are released as part of the complete recorded documentation of a musician's or group's work.

STEVE JONES

7. Technologies

Click Track

A click track is often used, much like a metronome, to establish a consistent tempo in multitrack recording. Operating essentially as a guide track, a series of clicks – usually quarter notes – is recorded on a separate track of a multitrack tape before the drums or rhythm section of a song is recorded. The use of a click track is sometimes necessary because of the fragmented nature of the multi-track recording process: any fluctuations in tempo in the early stages of the recording will make it more difficult for singers and other instrumentalists to stay in time when recording overdubs. Click tracks are also often used in soundtrack recording as an aid in synchronizing music to a film sequence.

Bibliography

Alten, Stanley R. 1994. *Audio in Media*. 4th ed. Belmont, CA: Wadsworth.

Karlin, Fred, and Wright, Rayburn. 1990. *On the Track: A Guide to Contemporary Film Scoring*. New York: Schirmer.

PAUL THÉBERGE

Compressor

A compressor is a device used to reduce the dynamic range of an audio signal before it is recorded to tape. This prevents distortion due to momentary overload and allows for a higher, more consistent overall recording level to be achieved. The compressor senses the incoming level of the signal and automatically adjusts it according to parameters set by the recording engineer.

Compression usually takes place only after the signal reaches a predetermined level (the threshold); the input level is then reduced by a preset amount called the compression ratio. With a ratio setting of 4:1, for example, an incoming signal four decibels above the threshold will result in an output of only one decibel. Various other controls can be used to determine the speed at which the compressor is activated ('attack' time) and how long it takes for the signal to return to normal ('release' time). Compressors are commonly used in recording vocals, drums or any other sound where dynamic control is required. In addition, compressors can be used to obtain special effects, such as increasing the apparent fullness and sustain of a bass or electric guitar sound. Compression is also routinely used in radio and television commercials and in film trailers to raise overall loudness and thus capture audience attention.

Bibliography

Alten, Stanley R. 1994. *Audio in Media*. 4th ed. Belmont, CA: Wadsworth.

PAUL THÉBERGE

Computers in Music

Introduction

The practise of applying personal computer (PC) and associated technologies to the production of popular music is commonplace. The use of computers in music became widespread in the mid-1980s. The main reasons for this were: the adoption of integrated-circuit (IC) technology in the manufacture of synthesizers; an agreement among electronic instrument manufacturers to establish a communications 'standard' for the exchange of information between synthesizers (MIDI); and an exponential growth in the use of PCs for business and leisure purposes. Computers have been applied to almost all conceivable technologies and processes in music production – for example, microphones, digital tape recorders, hard-disc recording, mixing desks, dynamics/signal processing, sound generation and sampling.

Definition

In popular music, the term 'computer' has a twofold definition. 'PC' refers to a generic desktop computer system, comprising a central processing unit (CPU), a visual display unit (VDU), an alphanumeric keyboard and a 'mouse' pointer; the term can also refer to circuit boards designed to fulfill a specific musical function (as in the synthesizer, sampler, mixing desk, tape controller and signal processor). For PCs to play a role in the production of music, certain hardware and software developments were necessary. The musical instrument digital interface (MIDI) became a computer 'peripheral'; in response, specific music software applications were spawned by third-party developers.

The primary role of the computer is as a 'sequencer,' allowing storage and retrieval of MIDI data. Dedicated MIDI devices were also developed; however, it was the ability to edit, manipulate and transform MIDI data that led to the widespread usage of computers in music. Working practises have changed significantly as a result.

Computer Applications

Computer music applications bridged the gap between compositional practise and production processes in the realization of the pop song. Sequencer software offers more than simple data storage and retrieval: it provides many creative functions and tools for songwriting. Emulation of multitrack tape recorder functions is a key feature, together with functions that could have come into existence only through the application of computer technology. Many of these functions are not exclusive to music processing: concepts such as 'cut,' 'copy' and 'paste' come directly from word-processing and desktop-publishing (DTP) applications. Other possibilities stem from the mathematical capabilities of computers to manipulate data.

The sequencer does not store the actual sound, but a sequence of instructions that tells other computers (located within synthesizers and samplers, for example) when to emit sound, at what pitch and velocity, and for what period of time. The actual sound emitted is dependent on particular instrument settings within the synthesizer or sampler. In the same way that familiarity with the piano keyboard is taken for granted, a knowledge of, and a willingness to embrace, computer technologies in the production of music have become

almost essential. Sequencers readily impart a 'mode of working' to the user. Their structural framework of 'tracks' and 'patterns,' with loop-cycle, cut, copy and paste functions, auto-correction, quantization and transposition, has influenced two decades of pop music production. (The E-mu Emulator sampler, introduced in 1980, became the first widely available sampler; the Spider Sequencer, produced by Electronic Dream Plant in 1980, has been identified as one of the first low-cost sequencers; in 1983, Roland produced the first MIDI-equipped drum machine in the TR909 model; and in 1986, Steinberg released its Pro 16 sequencer software for the Commodore 64 computer (Russ 1996, 63, 277).) Here, the computer, synthesizer and sampler are more than mere assistants; they are the tools that define the music. While the sound elements that constitute a track may vary, the production method is transparent and markedly consistent – so much so, that musical 'development' and transformation are inextricably linked to technological innovation.

The application of MIDI technology now extends far beyond what was originally envisaged. As a communications interface, it has been used to control many other studio technologies, including patch bays, digital reverberation and delay units, mixer fader movements, mute/solo switches and equalization settings.

Computer Hard-Disc Recording

The limitations of both samplers and analog/digital tape recorders have resulted in the development of computer-based hard-disc recording. Advances in the speed of computer processors, the storage capacity of hard-disc drives, and data transfer rates between computer processors and hard discs have brought digital recording and editing not just to the recording studio, but to the home user. Samplers are restricted by the amount of random access memory available for recording and editing, and both analog and digital tape recorders lack integral editing capability. The computer-based hard-disc recorder addresses both of these problems, since recording time is limited only by the amount of disc space; editing and manipulation tools are usually inbuilt.

Developments at the beginning of the twenty-first century indicate an increasing role for the computer in music production. The ability to handle MIDI sequencing/automation, synthesis sound generation, sampling and hard-disc recording on a single integrated platform (the virtual studio) already exists.

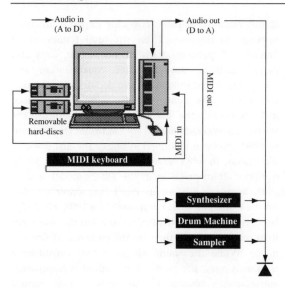

Workstation

The PC forms the core of the workstation. The installation of a MIDI card is required to handle MIDI data input to a software sequencer for recording, and output to MIDI-compatible devices (synthesizers, drum machines, samplers). The installation of an analog-to-digital (A to D), digital-to-analog (D to A) audio card allows direct-to-disc recording of audio source material. Signal processing software provides digital manipulation and 'non-destructive' editing of audio data within the computer. A workstation with these facilities may be used in pre-production writing and arranging, postproduction editing, mixing and remixing, or to realize an entire project from start to finish.

Conclusion

The computer, its allied technologies and associated software are responsible for revolutionizing working practises in the construction and realization of popular music. For those involved with writing and producing such music, there is a preoccupation with technology itself, since the technology gives rise to a musical product that could not have been realized in any other way. While the focus here is on computers in music (music production), computers are playing an ever-increasing role in the delivery of musical products to the consumer. Sales of CDs via the Internet are accelerating. The downloading of music and video as compressed digital data direct to the home may be the next revolution to sweep the industry, leading to the demise of physical media (CDs, videotapes) and the high-street retail outlet.

Bibliography

http://www.obsolete.com/120_years/
Russ, Martin. 1996. *Sound Synthesis and Sampling*. Oxford and Boston: Focal Press.

JONTY STOCKDALE

Cut

The term 'cut' is used to describe the process of making a master recording (usually on a disc) from which other disc or tape copies will be manufactured. The term originated in the early days of phonograph recording when, at the same time as a musical performance, a master was made with a cutting machine directly onto a lacquer or acetate disc. In the vernacular, the expression 'to "cut" a record' has come to be associated, in a more general fashion, with the entire process of recording a song for commercial release. 'Cut' can also refer to a single selection on an LP recording: an album 'cut.'

PAUL THÉBERGE

Drum Machine

Drum machines have made a significant contribution to the sound and style of a wide variety of pop music genres since the late 1970s. Unlike electronic drums, which are usually played in a conventional manner with sticks, a drum machine is most often played (or programmed) by tapping a set of buttons on the instrument's main panel with the fingers – a design that made the instruments accessible to a wide range of musicians, with or without conventional drum skills. A drum machine consists of two distinct subsystems: one provides for the generation of electronically synthesized drum sounds or the reproduction of digital samples of actual percussion instruments, and the other allows for rhythmic patterns to be created, stored and combined in sequence.

The origins of drum machine technology can be found in the automatic accompaniment devices introduced in home organs of the 1950s and 1960s. As early as 1962, Ace-Tone (founded in Japan by Ikutaro Kakehashi, who went on to establish the successful electronic musical instrument company Roland in 1972) began development of what was to be a successful series of portable, stand-alone rhythm boxes, containing a variety of preset rhythm patterns. It was not until the 1980s, however, that drum machines gained favor with professional musicians. Roger Linn's LM-1 (introduced in 1980) and the LinnDrum (1982) are often credited with giving the drum machine professional credibility: the instruments combined sampled drum sounds (giving them a more realistic sound than designs based on synthesis), programmability, quantization (a technique for auto-correcting rhythmic irregularities) and the ability to chain together rhythm patterns into song-like structures.

Perhaps the best-known drum machine, however, is the Roland TR-808 (first introduced in 1980). The TR-808 found favor among dance music producers and, especially, rap artists: the powerful, low-frequency, electronic sound of the 808's bass drum has become closely associated with rap music. The continued popularity of the TR-808 has led Roland to include samples of some of its sounds in later drum machine models and, in 1997, the instrument was re-created in computer software form by Propellerhead, a Swedish software company.

Bibliography

Anderton, Craig. 1988. '20 Great Achievements in 20 Years of Musical Electronics, 1968–1988.' *Electronic Musician* 4(7) (July): 28–97.

Rose, Tricia. 1994. *Black Noise: Rap Music and Black Culture in Contemporary America.* Hanover, NH: Wesleyan University Press.

PAUL THÉBERGE

Equalizer

An equalizer (often referred to by its abbreviated form, 'EQ') is an electronic device used to selectively cut or boost audio frequencies. Originally developed during the 1950s to compensate for deficiencies found in the tape medium, equalizers, which may come in a variety of forms (such as 'parametric' and 'graphic' EQs), were soon put to creative uses by sound engineers. As one of the engineer's primary means of altering the timbral quality of vocal and instrumental sounds, equalizers are an indispensable aesthetic tool, and they have become a standard component found in most mixing consoles. Consumers are familiar with the equalizers – ranging from simple bass and treble controls to more sophisticated graphic EQs – found on domestic hi-fi equipment.

Bibliography

Alten, Stanley R. 1994. *Audio in Media.* 4th ed. Belmont, CA: Wadsworth.

Eargle, John. 1980. *Sound Recording.* 2nd ed. New York: Van Nostrand Reinhold.

PAUL THÉBERGE

Film Music Technology

The sound requirements for music are quite different from those for dialog and sound effects recording in film (or television) production. As a result, music is almost always recorded, mixed, edited and synchronized separately from other elements of the soundtrack. Only at the final dubbing stage of the film postproduction process are all the elements of the soundtrack combined, processed and balanced together.

While at least some dialog and sound effects recording is done during the initial shooting of any film or television program, the acoustics and ambient sound conditions of most sets and outdoor locations are not conducive to good music recording. Furthermore, the recording of musical instruments and voices usually requires close miking techniques and special mixing and processing facilities that are available only under studio conditions.

The practise of recording music separately has been a feature of film soundtrack production since the earliest days of the sound film. For example, in the movie musicals of the 1930s and 1940s it was common to record the speaking voices of star performers, such as Bing Crosby and Fred Astaire, on the film set, while their singing numbers were prerecorded in the studio. To the trained listener, the transition between the speaking and singing voices (at least where obvious instrumental accompaniment is not involved) is evident in subtle changes in vocal quality produced by the relative proximity of the microphone and by differences in ambiance. To the casual listener, however, the transition is virtually imperceptible and is a testament to the technical expertise of the sound mixers and the lip-syncing abilities of the performers.

In conventional background music production, placement of music in a film is usually determined during the postproduction stage. During the 'spotting session,' the composer, director and music editor view a rough cut of the film and discuss elements of style, mood and tempo, as well as the timing of the musical cues. Where music is to be timed to specific events on-screen, the music editor often assists the composer by preparing click tracks. These click tracks, which can be quite complex, link beats to the exact number of film frames, thus ensuring accurate timing and facilitating changes of meter and tempo.

Once composed, the music is usually recorded by an ensemble or orchestra in a special recording studio – known as the 'scoring stage' – equipped with full picture projection facilities and synchronizing equipment. The orchestra is most often positioned with its back to the film screen so that the conductor can view a copy of the film, by now in its final stages of editing, which the music editor has specially prepared with visual markers (such as vertical lines or 'streamers' that warn the conductor of an upcoming musical cue, and light pulses or 'punches' that assist the conductor in setting tempos and in synchronizing the music to the film image); the film is also often supplied with click tracks for each musical cue.

Since the late 1960s, there has been a marked increase in the use of popular music in film soundtracks. Popular songs are most often recorded and mixed in advance (typically in commercial recording studios without special film technology), and the film is then edited to the music, thus reversing the usual priorities of conventional postproduction. Traditional film critics have argued that the process of cutting action to the beat or musical phrase, which is commonplace when popular music is used, is often less fluid than conventional film scoring and has made many films appear mechanical and more like rock videos. Initially, most cinema sound systems were not well suited to the expanded dynamic and frequency ranges of much popular music; by the mid-1970s, the introduction of Dolby stereo and improved playback systems had greatly enhanced the sound of popular music in film theaters.

The use of synthesizers, drum machines and MIDI sequencing has had a profound impact, not only on the sound of much contemporary film music, but on the entire process of composing for film and television. With synthesizers, computers and SMPTE (Society of Motion Picture and Television Engineers) synchronization devices, it has become possible for composers to score (and, in many cases, record) entire soundtracks in their home studios. Using a videotaped copy of the edited film that has been prepared with SMPTE time code, the composer is able to create, perform and synchronize the music with great precision, thus taking over many of the functions of the orchestra, music editor and recording engineer. Furthermore, last-minute changes to the music can be made with greater ease (and at a significantly lower cost) than is possible using conventional methods of scoring and recording.

Both an emphasis on popular music styles and economic factors have led to an increase in the prevalence of electronic music in film scoring. It is estimated that, by the end of the 1980s, over 50 percent of film and television soundtracks were produced either electronically or by using a combination of electronic and acoustic instruments.

Bibliography

Brophy, Philip. 1990. 'The Architecsonic Object: Stereo Sound, Cinema and "Colors."' In *Culture, Technology and Creativity*, ed. Philip Hayward. London: John Libbey & Company, 91–110.

Karlin, Fred, and Wright, Rayburn. 1990. *On the Track: A Guide to Contemporary Film Scoring*. New York: Schirmer.

Williams, Alan. 1981. 'The Musical Film and Recorded Popular Music.' In *Genre: The Musical*, ed. Rick Altman. London: Routledge & Kegan Paul, 147–58.

PAUL THÉBERGE

Guitar Amplifiers

Where there are electric guitars, there are guitar amplifiers, for it is the amplifier that converts the weak electrical signal from the guitar's pickups into audible sound waves. Guitar amplifiers normally consist of two main parts: the amplifier proper and the speaker system. Single-unit boxes containing both parts are known in the industry as 'combo amps,' while separately housed amplifiers are called 'heads,' and the unit containing the speaker or speakers is called the 'cabinet.'

Speakers, which reconvert the intensified electrical signal from the amplifier into sound waves, usually range in diameter from 10″ (25 cm) to 12″ (30 cm), and up to 15″ (38 cm) or even 18″ (45 cm) for bass guitar amplifiers. Cabinets usually contain one to four or even six loudspeakers. Some cabinets for bass guitar amplifiers incorporate folded horn technology to produce very low frequencies. There is also a very large market for extremely small practise amplifiers operating on either batteries or mains electricity, with a single 8″ (20 cm) or 10″ (25 cm) speaker.

Although the original impetus for amplifiers was to make the guitar louder, the development of guitar amplifiers has followed two diverging paths: one is concerned with making the acoustic instrument louder while preserving its tone color; the other is concerned with making an amplifier that in essence creates the tone color. The first is achieved by constructing an amplifier that increases the amplitude of the original signal while remaining 'flat' – that is, affecting the waveform only minimally. This is the same ideal sought by makers of amplifiers for high-fidelity sound recordings. Such amplifiers frequently use transistors, or solid-state technology, which became widely available in the 1960s. The 'flat' or 'clean' sound produced by this type of amplifier is often favored by jazz, dance band and theater orchestra players, as well as by many country guitarists, although there are exceptions to this trend. The second path of development, exemplified by makers such as Fender, has refined the sound of amplifiers using the original technology of vacuum tubes or valves. The crunchy, distorted tone of these amplifiers when they are pushed to their limits, or overdriven, is highly regarded and has been a hallmark of urban blues styles and of blues-based rock and subsequent forms.

Recent trends have included designs that incorporate both tubes and transistors in combination, ranges of amplifiers designed especially for acoustic guitars, and even digital amplifiers that re-create the esteemed sound qualities of vintage tube amplifier designs but without the need for high levels of volume. Thus, in guitar amplifiers one finds the familiar dichotomies of tradition and innovation, of fetishism and iconoclasm, revealing themselves as in so many areas of musical endeavor.

Guitar amplifiers began to be widely available in the mid-1930s. Early examples, such as those manufactured by Epiphone, were designed primarily for use with electric Hawaiian guitars. These were typically built into a single, hard-case (sometimes wooden) cabinet, housing the amplifier and, usually, one speaker with a diameter of 8″ (20 cm), 10″ (25 cm) or 12″ (30 cm) that incorporated a volume control but no tone controls. With the trend toward electrification well established, amplifiers of all shapes and sizes began to appear. Manufacturers such as Danelectro even created small amplifiers built into a guitar's carrying case.

With the rise of guitar-led rock groups in the 1960s, amplifiers assumed an important role in the overall image of rock music. They became bigger, more powerful and more visible. So-called 'stacks' began to appear in the mid-1960s, pioneered by manufacturers such as Marshall; they comprised a head set on top of, usually, two speaker cabinets housing four 12″ (30 cm) loudspeakers. The Marshall stacks represented a new order of power and volume for guitarists and were immediately followed by similar stacked systems from makers such as HiWatt, Sunn and Sound City. Other striking designs began to appear – for instance, the transistor amplifiers made by Kustom, with rolled and pleated covers in unusual sparkle colors, perhaps influenced by the look of hot rod cars.

Tube amplifiers especially have made possible an extraordinarily expanded tone world for guitarists. The ability to sustain tones has increased far beyond the capabilities of the early electric guitarists; feedback, once an annoyance, has become a mainstay of rock guitar technique, and all kinds of effects – from tremolo and reverb to echo, wah-wah, fuzz tone, phasing and beyond – have become commonplace. Amplification created these possibilities.

Guitar amplifiers have probably had their greatest impact on rock music, becoming an important component of that music's imagery as well as its sound. Their distinctive look, their deafening power and their massive stature have symbolized rock's ethos. Familiar images of the Beatles with their Vox amplifiers, or of Jimi Hendrix setting fire to his guitar before a Marshall or of Robert Fripp seated in front of a HiWatt are reminders that the amplifier is the essential element in rock's symbolism of power.

TIM WISE

Harmonizer

A harmonizer is a digital device that can alter the pitch of an audio input without changing its overall duration; the resulting signal can be mixed with the original, thus creating one or more harmonies at predetermined ratios. Harmonizers are sometimes used on vocals in recording studios to create the impression of a chorus of voices; the sonic impression is one of an unusually fused, homogeneous vocal sound. Harmonizers can also be used to create special effects when instrumental parts are recorded.

Bibliography
Alten, Stanley R. 1994. *Audio in Media*. 4th ed. Belmont, CA: Wadsworth.

PAUL THÉBERGE

Lead Sheet

A lead sheet is a sheet of paper displaying the basic information necessary for performance and interpretation of a piece of popular music. Elements usually featured on a lead sheet are: (a) melody, including its mensuration in staff notation; (b) lead sheet chord shorthand, usually placed above the melody; and (c) lyrics (if applicable). Such sheets are used extensively by musicians in the fields of jazz, cabaret, *chanson*, most types of dance music and so on. Lead sheets consisting of lyrics and chord shorthand only are common among musicians in the rock, pop and country music spheres.

Lead sheets originated for reasons of copyright. In the 1920s, the only way to protect authorship of an unpublished song in the United States was to deposit a written copy of it with the Copyright Division of the Library of Congress in Washington, DC. For example, to protect a song recorded by an early blues artist (for example, Beulah 'Sippie' Wallace, Bertha 'Chippie' Hill or Eva Taylor), musicians such as George Thomas, Richard M. Jones and Clarence Williams would provide the Library of Congress with a transcription of the melody's most salient features, along with typewritten lyrics and the basic elements of the song's accompaniment (Leib 1981, 56). Such a document was called a 'lead sheet.' Its function was descriptive rather than prescriptive, not least because: (a) the most profitable popular music distribution commodity of the time was not the recording but three-stave sheet music in arrangement for voice and piano; and (b) most big band musicians read their parts from staff notation provided by the arranger. However, guitarists and bass players of the 1930s usually played from a mensurated sequence of chord names, that is, from 'basic elements of the song's accompaniment' as written on a lead sheet in its original sense.

With the decline of big bands and the rise of smaller combos in the years following World War II, the increasing popularity of the electric guitar as the main chordal instrument in such combos, and the shift from sheet music to records as the primary popular music commodity, lead sheets ousted staff notation as the most important scribal *aide-mémoire* for musicians in the popular sphere. Other reasons for the subsequent ubiquity of lead sheets are that their interpretation demands no more than rudimentary notational skills and that, since they contain no more than the bare essentials of a song, an extensive repertoire can easily be maintained and transported to performance venues.

Bibliography

Circular 50: Copyright Registration for Musical Compositions (Library of Congress). http://lcweb.loc.gov/copyright/circs/circ50.html

Lieb, Sandra R. 1981. *Mother of the Blues: A Study of Ma Rainey*. Amherst, MA: University of Massachusetts Press.

Music Publishing Terminology. http://www.bmi.com/songwriter/resources/pubs/terms.asp

PHILIP TAGG

Lead Sheet Chord Shorthand

Lead sheet chord shorthand is defined as: (a) the symbols used on a lead sheet to represent, descriptively or pre-scriptively, the chords of a song or instrumental number; and (b) the widespread system according to which popular music practitioners most frequently specify chords.

Since there are probably as many variants of lead sheet chord shorthand in circulation as there are musicians, it is impossible to provide a definitive overview of the system. However, although a few of these variants diverge from the codification practises described here (see Flat, Sharp, Plus and Minus, below), most variants follow, by and large, the principles expounded here. Figure 1 provides a selection of tertial chords (that is, chords composed of superimposed thirds) and their lead sheet symbols, all with the note *c* as root. Table 1 shows how the shorthand translates into the terms of spoken English used by musicians (for a song whose lyrics con-

sist entirely of lead sheet names for the chords being played, see 10cc's 'I Bought a Flat Guitar Tutor' (1977)).

Basic Rationale

Lead sheet chord shorthand has a tertial basis. Since the shorthand evolved during the heyday of tertial harmony in jazz-based popular music, its simplest symbols (uppercase letters for note names plus a lowercase m, mi or min to indicate the 'minor') denote common triads built on the designated note (for example, C for a C major triad and Cm for a C minor triad). Moreover, characters placed after the triad name tend merely to qualify that tertial triad, either in terms of notes added to it or by denoting chromatic alteration of any degree within the chord, except for the root and its third. Similarly, the numerals seen most frequently after the triad symbol (7, 9, 11 and 13) represent pitches stacked in thirds above the two thirds already contained within the triad (1-3 and 3-5) on which a more complex chord is based (for example, C^9 containing B$\flat$ and D – flat seventh and major ninth – in addition to C-E-G). The shorthand system also assumes that root and bass notes are the same. Developed in style-specific contexts, lead sheet chord shorthand allows for the concise and efficient representation of chords in many types of popular music – for example, jazz, pop, rock, country music, *chanson*, *schlager* and most styles of dance music. The system is, however, quite cumbersome in its codification of inversions and of non-tertial harmony.

Symbol Components

Lead sheet chord symbols are built from the following components placed in the following order: (1) note

Table 1 Guide to the pronunciation of lead sheet chord shorthand (examples)

Chord Shorthand	Examples in Figure 1	Pronunciation
C^+ or C^{aug}	1c	C plus, C augmented, C aug [o:g]
C^7, C^9, C^{11}, C^{13}	2a, 3a, 4a, 5a	C seven, C nine, C eleven, C thirteen
C^{maj7}, C^{maj9}	2b, 3b	C major seven, C major nine
C^{7-5}, $C^{7\flat 5}$	2c	C seven minus five, C seven flat five
C^{7aug}, C^{7+}	2d	C seven augmented, C seven plus
C^{9+} C^{9aug5}), C^{+9}	3f, 3g	C nine plus (C nine augmented), C plus 9
C^{13+11} (C^{11+13})	5g	C thirteen plus eleven (C eleven plus thirteen)
Cm^7, Cm^9, Cm^{11}	7a, 8a, 8c	C minor seven, C minor 9, C minor eleven
Cm^{maj7}, Cm^{maj9}	7b, 8b	C minor major seven, C minor major nine
Cm^{7-5} or $Cm^{7\flat 5}$ or $C^{ø}$	7c	C minor seven minus five, C minor seven flat five, C 1/2 diminished
$Cdim$ or $Cdim^7$	7d	C diminished, C dim, C diminished seventh
C^6, Cm^6	9a, 9b	C six (C add[ed] sixth), C minor six (C minor add[ed] sixth)
$C^{sus(4)}$, C^{sus9}	10a, 10c	C sus (four), C four suspension, C suspended fourth, C sus nine
C^{add9}, Cm^{add9}	10c, 10d	C add nine, C minor add nine
$C^7_{/3}$, $C^7_{/e}$	11g	C (with) third in bass, C (with) e bass, C first inversion

. = note always omitted from the chord

o (**o**) = note may be omitted from the chord

Stave 1 in each system shows tertial stacking
Staves 2 and 3 together suggest one possible way of
spacing each chord on the piano

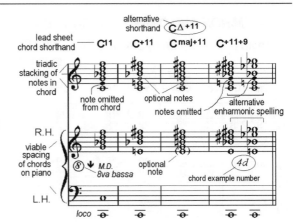

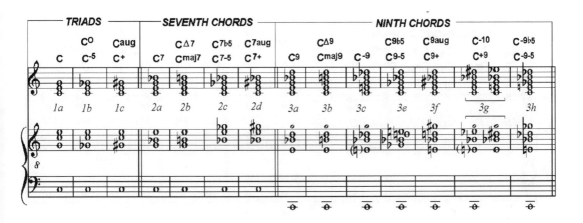

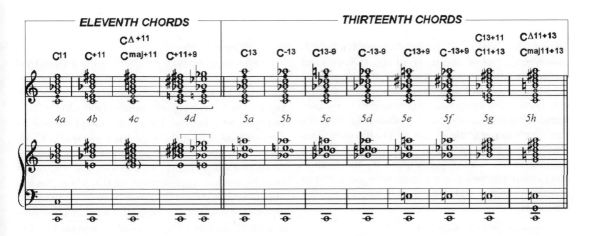

Figure 1 Lead sheet chords (in C).

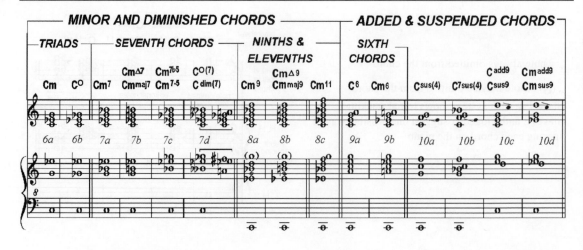

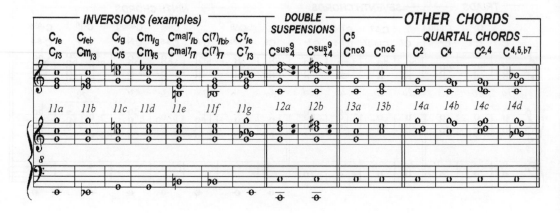

Figure 1 *Continued.*

name of the chord's root, present in every symbol; (2) triad type; (3) type of seventh; (4) ninths, elevenths and thirteenths, with or without alteration; (5) altered fifth; (6) added or omitted notes and suspensions; and (7) inversions. Since components (1) through (7) are only included when necessary, chord symbols range from the very simple (for example, C, Cm, C7) to the quite complex (for example, F♯m^{6add9}, B♭$^{-13+9}$, E omit G♯). Table 2 summarizes the order of presentation for the symbols most commonly used in connection with tertial chords containing neither added notes, nor suspensions nor inversions.

Note Name of a Chord's Root

The note name of a chord's root may be written either in English, as in Table 1 and Figure 1, or according to Germanic- or Latin-language nomenclature. English root-note names are always in uppercase letters.

Types of Tertial Triads

No symbol is necessary for chords using a major triad (for example, C = C major triad), as the qualifier 'major' applies exclusively to sevenths (see Types of Sevenths, below). On the other hand, 'minor' applies to the third and to no other interval. Therefore, chords built as or on a minor triad must include the triad-type qualifier – m, mi or min, always lowercase – immediately after the chord root's note name (for example, Cm = C minor triad; for a different convention, see Flat, Sharp, Plus and Minus, below). Augmented and diminished triads are represented similarly (for example, C+ for an augmented triad on C, see Tab. 1; Fig. 1, chords 1c and 6b; see, also, Types of Sevenths and Inversions, below). To avoid linguistic incongruity, it may be preferable to write the root name and triad type in normal typeface and subsequent symbols in a smaller typeface and/or as superscript – for example, Cm^{maj7} or Cm^{add6} rather than Cmmaj7 or Cmadd6. It should be noted that, while the diminished triad is highly uncommon on its own, the augmented triad (for example, C+) occurs quite frequently in popular music.

Types of Sevenths

Since the minor (flat) seventh (for example, $b\flat$ in relation to c) is more common than the key-specific major seventh (for example, $b\natural$ in relation to c) in the jazz-related styles for which lead sheet symbols were originally developed, and since the qualifier 'minor' is applied exclusively to the third in tertial triads, a major triad with an added minor seventh requires no other qualification than the numeral 7 (Fig. 1, chord 2a); flat seven is, so to speak, the default seventh, in the same way that default triads, or major triads, feature major thirds as the lowest interval in the triad. On the other hand, tertial chords containing a key-specific major seventh need to be flagged by means of 'maj' or 'Δ' (Fig. 1, chord 2b). Since 'maj' and 'Δ' are reserved for use as qualifiers of the seventh and no other degree, the 7 may be omitted in conjunction with these symbols (for example, C^{maj} or CΔ = C^{maj7}). However, the 7 is always present to denote any seventh chord whose 7 has the default value (flat/minor; see Fig. 1, chords 2a, 2c, 2d, 7a and 7c; see, also, Ninths, Elevenths and Thirteenths, below).

Seventh chords containing an augmented fifth indicate such alteration by the notation '7+' or '7aug' (Fig. 1, chord 2d). Diminished fifths in seventh chords containing a major third as the lowest interval appear as '7–5' or '7$\flat$5' (Fig. 1, chords 2c and 7c). Seventh chords containing a minor third as the lowest interval, a diminished fifth and a flat seventh are written as 'm$^{7-5}$' or 'm$^{7\flat5}$,' or sometimes as 'ø' ('half diminished'). The 'dim' chord constitutes a special case, as it contains both diminished seventh and fifth; it is most frequently indic-

ated by 'dim' placed straight after the root-note name, but is sometimes indicated by 'dim7' or, occasionally, by 'o' or 'o7' (Fig. 1, chord 7d).

Ninths, Elevenths and Thirteenths

Chords involving ninths, elevenths and thirteenths are assumed to include, at least theoretically, some kind of tertial triad and some kind of seventh (see Note Name of a Chord's Root, Types of Tertial Triads and Types of Sevenths, above, and Omitted Notes, below). Chords containing elevenths presuppose the presence of a ninth, and thirteenth chords presuppose the presence of an eleventh as well as a ninth, all in addition to a seventh and the major or minor triad of the root note. To save space, shorthand denoting all such chords is usually presented in descending order of intervals requiring qualification – thirteenths, elevenths, ninths, fifths – once the root-note name, the minor-triad marker (if necessary) and the major-seventh symbol (if necessary) have been included (Fig. 1, chords 3a–5h and 8a–c). The only common exception to this practise is the chord containing a major thirteenth and an augmented eleventh, which is usually encoded '13+11,' but is sometimes referred to in reverse order as '11+13' (Fig. 1, chords 5g–h). Shorthand for chords of the thirteenth, eleventh and ninth includes no mention of the eleventh, ninth or seventh below them, unless any of these degrees deviate from their default values (perfect eleventh, major ninth and minor seventh). For example, the '11' in C^{11} assumes the presence of the default ninth and flat seventh (d and $b\flat$), whereas the '9' in C^{+11+9} is included because of its alteration from d to $d\sharp/e\flat$ (Fig. 1, chord 4d).

Altered Fifths

Although simple augmented and diminished triads are encoded '+' or 'aug' and 'dim,' respectively, the symbol for altered fifths (+ and –5 or $\flat$5) in chords of the sev-

Table 2 Basic order of components in lead sheet chord shorthand

1. Root-note name	A, B$\flat$, B, C, C$\sharp$/ D$\flat$, D, D$\sharp$/ E$\flat$, E, F, F$\sharp$/ G$\flat$, G,m G$\sharp$/ A$\flat$				
	Chord/interval type				
	Perfect	*Major*	*Minor*	*Augmented*	*Diminished*
2. Triad Type		[Omit]	m (*or* min/mi)	aug *or* +(5)	[Very unusual]
3. Type of Seventh		maj(7) *or* Δ	7		dim(7) or °(7)
4. (a) Thirteenth		13	–13		
(b) Eleventh	11			+11	
(c) Ninth		9	–9	+9	
5. Fifth	[Omit]			+ *or* aug	–5 *or* $\flat$5

enth, ninth, eleventh and thirteenth is always placed last after all other relevant information (for example, Cm^{7-5} or $C^{7\flat 5}$, Cm^{7-5} or $Cm^{7\flat 5}$, and C^{7+} or C^{7aug}; Fig. 1, chords 2c, 2d, 3e, 3h and 7c).

Omitted Notes

The more notes a chord theoretically contains, the more difficult it becomes to space those notes on the keyboard or guitar in a satisfactory manner. In some cases, the principle of stacking thirds even leads to problems of unacceptable dissonance, usually involving an internal minor ninth, that cannot be resolved by the most ingenious techniques of chord spacing. For example, the major third is always absent from the eleventh chord (Fig. 1, chord 4a), and the unaltered eleventh is always left out of thirteenth chords based on the major triad (Fig. 1, chords 5a–f). Similarly, the perfect fifth is often omitted from thirteenth chords, as well as from certain ninth chords (Fig. 1, chords 5a–h, 3a–e and 3g). These omissions constitute standard practise and need not be indicated. However, one example of a chord that does require indication of an omitted note is the 'bare' fifth, which is often used as the power chord of heavy metal and is usually written (in E) 'E no 3' or 'E omit G ♯' (see Non-tertial Chords, below).

Added Ninths and Sixths

Added chords are those consisting of a simple triad to which another single note has been added without the inclusion of intervening odd-number degrees. For example, 'add9' and 'm^{add9}' chords are triads to which the ninth has been added without an intermediate seventh having been included (Fig. 1, chords 10c–d). Similarly, the two sixth chords shown in Figure 1 (chords 9a and 9b) can be classified as 'added,' because they both consist of a triad to which a major sixth has been added without any intervening sevenths, ninths or elevenths making them into chords of the thirteenth. It should be remembered that the 'm' (for minor) in 'm^6' refers to the minor third, and therefore this notation does not indicate the sixth, which is always major (Fig. 1, chord 9b). Unlike added ninths, added sixth chords are not indicated by the prefix 'add' before the '6.'

Suspended Fourths and Ninths

Suspensions are chords that can be resolved into a subsequent tertial consonance. The most common suspensions in popular music, 'sus4' and 'sus9,' both resolve to common major or minor triads: the fourth of 'sus4' to a third, and the ninth of 'sus9' to the octave (for example, the f in C^{sus4} to the e of C or the $e\flat$ of Cm, and the d in C^{sus9} to the c of C or Cm; see Fig. 1, chords 10a–d). The absence of a numeral after 'sus' assumes that the suspension is held on a fourth. Although 'sus9' and 'add9' may

be identical as individual chords, 'sus9' should typically resolve in the manner just described, while 'add9' need not do so. (For the use of 'sus' in quartal harmony, see Non-tertial Chords, below.)

Inversions

Since inversions tend to occur in popular music mainly in passing-note patterns or anacruses created by the bass player, without reference to notation, no standard lead sheet codification exists for such practises. This lacuna in the system obstructs efficient indication of chord sequences for music in the classical vein. However, one concise way of indicating inversions is to write the relevant bass note, by interval number or note name, following the rest of the chord's symbols and a forward slash – for example, $C^7_{/3}$ or $C^7_{/e}$ for a C seven chord with its third, e, in the bass (see, also, Fig. 1, chords 11a–g). Inversions audible in pop recordings are often absent from published lead sheets and tend to be indicated only if they occur on an important downbeat or its syncopated anticipation.

Anomalies

Flat, Sharp, Plus and Minus

Sharp (♯) and flat (♭) signs are mainly reserved to indicate accidentals qualifying the root-note name. Thus, the '♭' in $E\flat^9$ indicates that the E itself, not the ninth above it, is flat. In this way, it is possible to distinguish between an E flat nine chord ($E\flat^9$) and an E minus nine chord (E^{-9}, i.e., E^7 with a flat ninth). In fact, all altered degrees in any chord, apart from 3 and 7 (see Types of Sevenths, and Ninths, Elevenths and Thirteenths, above), are indicated by '+' (= ♯) or '–' (= ♭). The only exception to this rule is that a flat sign is often used as an alternative for 'minus' before the final 5 of a chord containing a diminished triad (for example, $C^{7\flat 5}$ instead of C^{7-5}; see Fig. 1, chords 2c, 3e, 3h and 7c). It should be noted that conflicting conventions concerning the use of these symbols are in operation. For example, some versions of *The Real Book* use minus signs instead of 'm,' 'mi' or 'min' to denote minor triads, and flat and sharp signs instead of '+' and '–' to signal chromatic alteration.

Enharmonic Spelling

Lead sheet chord shorthand tends to disregard enharmonic orthography. For example, although the ♭II → I cadence at the end of Jobim's 'The Girl from Ipanema' (1963) might appear as $A\flat^{9\flat 5}$ → $Gmaj^7$ on a lead sheet in G, the same ♭II → I cadence would, in E♭, almost certainly be written $E^{9\flat 5}$ → $E\flat^{maj7}$ rather than $F\flat^{9\flat 5}$ → $E\flat^{maj7}$. Similarly, distinction is rarely made between chords containing a falling minor tenth and those that include a rising augmented ninth, the assumption being that, since both '+9' and '−10' refer to the same equal-tone pitch, the difference between them is immaterial. Hence, '+9' is much more commonly used than '−10,' even though the latter may more often be enharmonically correct.

Non-tertial Chords

Since non-tertial chords do not derive from superimposed thirds, they are not easy to express in lead sheet shorthand. Apart from power fifths, already mentioned, there are considerable problems in encoding harmonies used in modal and bitonal jazz, as well as in some types of folk music and avant-garde rock. For example, standard consonances in quartal harmony are frequently indicated by 'sus(4)' (for example, C^{7sus}; see Fig. 1, 10b and 14d), even though harmonic suspension is neither intended nor perceived. Similarly, many musicians often conceptualize chords of the eleventh and thirteenth bitonally rather than in terms of stacked thirds – for example, C^{13+11} as a D major triad on top of C^7, or C^{11} as Gm^7 with C in the bass. No satisfactory consensus yet exists as to how such sonorities might be more adequately encoded. One possible solution to part of the problem may be to refer to some of these chords in the way suggested in Figure 1, chords 13a–14d.

Discographical References

Jobim, Antonio Carlos. 'The Girl from Ipanema.' *The Girl from Ipanema: The Antonio Carlos Jobim Songbook*. Verve 5472. *1996*: USA.
10cc. 'I Bought a Flat Guitar Tutor.' *Deceptive Bends*. Mercury 3702. *1977*: USA.

PHILIP TAGG

Limiter

A limiter is a signal-processing device that prevents an audio signal from exceeding a predetermined dynamic level. While the limiter functions much like a compressor, its compression ratio is usually set at a fixed level between 10:1 and infinity. This device is sometimes used when recording sounds with high-intensity peak levels, such as drum sounds, to prevent overload distortion of a recording device. The limiter is also commonly used in AM radio broadcasting to allow boosting of the overall level of prerecorded music without exceeding regulated spectrum allowances.

Bibliography

Alten, Stanley R. 1994. *Audio in Media*. 4th ed. Belmont, CA: Wadsworth.

PAUL THÉBERGE

Mellotron

The Mellotron is an analog keyboard instrument that uses an ingenious tape loop mechanism to play back recordings of musical instrument sounds. The first prototype (the Mark I) was invented in Britain by Leslie Bradley and his brothers, Frank and Norman, in 1963; but it was the Mark II (introduced into the marketplace in 1964) and the Model 400 (1970) that came to prominence in pop music of the late 1960s and early 1970s, most notably on albums by bands such as the Moody Blues and King Crimson. The sound of its taped string ensembles, brass and wind instruments could also be heard on individual cuts by the Beatles (for example, 'Strawberry Fields Forever'), the Rolling Stones ('2000 Light Years From Home') and many others.

Up to 18 different sets of instrument sounds – solo flutes and strings, as well as choirs, string and brass ensembles, and combo instruments – could be played from the Mellotron's two keyboards. The BBC commissioned a special version of the instrument, loaded with recordings of sound effects, for use in film and television work. Unlike most synthesizers and electronic organs of the day, the Mellotron's exclusive reliance on tape recordings of actual instrument sounds led many to regard the instrument as a precursor of the digital sampler. Its analog tape sound was so distinctive, however, that bands such as the Rolling Stones, on tour during the 1990s, resorted to using samplers and other devices to mimic the sound of the Mellotron in order to reproduce authentic-sounding versions of the hit songs they originally recorded during the 1960s.

Bibliography

Vail, Mark. 1993. 'Mellotron: Pillar of a Musical Genre.' In *Vintage Synthesizers*. San Francisco: Miller Freeman Books, 205–12.

Discographical References

Beatles, The. 'Strawberry Fields Forever.' Capitol 5810. *1967*: UK.
Rolling Stones, The. '2000 Light Years From Home.' *Their Satanic Majesties Request*. London 2. *1967*: UK.

Discography

King Crimson. *In the Court of the Crimson King*. Atlantic 8245. *1969*: UK.
Moody Blues. *In Search of the Lost Chord*. Deram 18017. *1968*: UK.

PAUL THÉBERGE

Microphone

The microphone is the starting point of the audio transmission/reproduction chain and, as such, it plays a significant role in defining the sound of virtually every live performance, broadcast or recording of popular music. Microphones are transducers: they convert acoustic energy into electric energy. They are generally classified according to the type of element that transduces sound and by their directional characteristics. The most common types of microphone used in popular music are 'moving-coil' types (which use a diaphragm and a coil of wire suspended in a magnetic field) and 'capacitor' (or 'condenser') types (which use two electrically charged parallel plates). 'Ribbon' microphones (which utilize a thin metal ribbon instead of a diaphragm) are sometimes used, but are often considered too delicate for the sound pressure levels produced in many forms of pop and rock music; for example, only the most rugged, moving-coil type of microphone is commonly used for 'miking' drums up close, especially bass drums. 'Unidirectional' microphones, exhibiting varying degrees of focused sound pickup (the terms 'cardioid,' 'supercardioid' and 'hypercardioid' are used to describe the increasingly narrow character of a microphone's pickup pattern), are most commonly used in popular music to control feedback in live performance or to isolate vocal and instrumental sounds from one another; 'omnidirectional' microphones (which pick up sound equally from all directions) are used less often.

The first microphones were developed in the United States for use in telephony by Bell and Edison in 1876–77. These early devices employed a carbon-based element and, because their ability to reproduce sound was limited, they have seldom been used outside the telephone industry. Later, in 1916, Edward C. Wente invented the first condenser-type microphone, an improved version of which was introduced in the early 1920s by Western Electric. By the end of the decade, the Wente/Western Electric condenser had become a standard microphone used by professionals throughout the radio, sound recording and sound film industries, and it continued to be popular long after ribbon and moving-coil microphones were introduced (by RCA and Western Electric, respectively) during the 1930s. Initially, during the early 1920s, the record industry had hesitated in adopting electrical methods of recording in favor of protecting the large investments already made in the production and stockpiling of acoustical recordings. However, the microphone, in conjunction with electrical amplification, soon proved to be more powerful than acoustical methods in its ability to render the subtleties of both the human voice and instrumental sounds, and the industry was forced to convert to electrical technologies in order to compete with the new medium of radio.

Beginning in the 1920s, the impact of the microphone on musical style was both subtle and profound. For example, the string bass could be heard clearly, for the first time, in jazz recordings, and the instrument quickly replaced the tuba, which had often been used in earlier recorded jazz. More importantly, a new, intimate style

of singing, known as 'crooning,' evolved in response to the introduction of the microphone. What had become clear to the early crooners, such as Bing Crosby, was that it was necessary not only to sing, but to develop a technique suitable to the microphone. In this sense, contemporary pop performers always sing first and foremost to the microphone, and this is as true when performers sing to a live audience as it is in the studio. In return, the microphone reveals, in intimate detail, every nuance of a performer's vocal style. But it does not do so in a transparent fashion: every model of microphone has its own characteristics and colors the sound in subtle, yet unmistakable, ways. Pop performers have become exceptionally sensitive to the manner in which the microphone can flatter the voice, and they often develop preferences for particular models that appear to lend 'warmth' to a vocal performance. Music listeners' experience of the voice in popular music, as well as their notions of how an acoustic guitar or other traditional instrument 'should' sound, have been subtly influenced by the intercession of the microphone. The sensuous pleasures derived from listening to the sounds produced by pop performers are made all the more powerful by the extraordinary sense of 'presence' afforded by the microphone.

In contemporary live performance and recording, the microphone is never a single technology; it is always plural. Indeed, the evolution of multi-microphone techniques has been central to the development of popular music since the advent of rock 'n' roll during the 1950s. Prior to this time, it was unusual to find more than a handful of microphones used in live performance contexts or in recording studios. But innovative engineers and producers, in search of a new 'sound' for the emerging music, began to experiment with microphones and their placement, 'miking' each instrument individually (Fox 1986, 146). In this way, engineers gradually took over much of the responsibility for achieving musical balance within the overall sound of, first, the recording and, later, live performance. Experiments in multi-microphone technique, which involve the selective placement and isolation of instrumental sounds, were among the first steps taken toward the creation of the modern multitrack studio, and they have continued to be an essential factor in the production of the transparent sound and instrumental separation characteristic of most popular music.

The fundamental importance of the microphone in popular music is underscored, ironically, by the degree to which it has become 'naturalized' and its effects rendered invisible. Whether considering the 1930s notion of 'high fidelity' or the 'unplugged' phenomenon of the 1980s, engineers and critics alike have tended to reinforce the idea that microphones are essentially reproductive technologies, that they are, by design, transparent in their operation. However, such aesthetic discourses only serve to efface the profound impact that microphones have on people's experience of popular music.

Bibliography

Alten, Stanley R. 1994. *Audio in Media*. 4th ed. Belmont, CA: Wadsworth.

Fox, Ted. 1986. *In the Groove: The People Behind the Music*. New York: St. Martin's Press.

Nisbett, Alec. 1989. *The Use of Microphones*. 3rd ed. London: Focal Press.

Woram, John M. 1989. *The Recording Studio Handbook*. Indianapolis, IN: H.W. Sams.

PAUL THÉBERGE

MIDI

MIDI is the acronym for [M]usical [I]nstrument [D]igital [I]nterface, a hardware and software protocol that allows digital information to be transmitted between synthesizers, drum machines, sequencers, computers and other electronic devices. Since its introduction in 1983, it has been adopted by virtually every manufacturer of electronic and digital instruments, thus becoming the de facto standard for electronic musical instrument communication.

During the 1970s and early 1980s, few standards existed in the world of electronic music production: for example, drum machines often operated at different internal clock frequencies, so that, when machines from two different manufacturers (and sometimes even the same manufacturer) were connected, there was no guarantee that they would play at the same tempo. Similar problems existed whenever synthesizers from different manufacturers were used together in live performance or in studio production. However, by the early 1980s, many electronic devices contained microprocessors, and this created the possibility for the development of a digital standard through which hardware manufactured by different companies could be connected. Such a standard was proposed by Dave Smith of Sequential Circuits, a California-based synthesizer manufacturer, as early as 1981; however, it was another two years before, with the help of the Japanese instrument manufacturers, especially the Roland Corporation, MIDI was introduced into the marketplace.

From a hardware perspective, MIDI consists of an inexpensive five-pin DIN (Deutsche Industrie Normen) cable, connected to an optically isolated serial interface (isolating the circuit prevents grounding and other electrical interference when several instruments are connected). Most instruments have three such connectors: for input, output and 'thru' – the latter allowing data to pass through the instrument in such a way that several devices can be chained together in series. By having instruments chained together, sounds from several synthesizers can be played from a single keyboard, allowing musicians to create complex electronic textures in live performance. In the studio, a number of devices can be connected to a central sequencer or computer, where entire musical compositions can be created and reproduced. While the speed and technical characteristics of the interface have been criticized by some, the low cost of implementation permits even the most modest of amateur devices to be connected with sophisticated professional equipment, and this aspect of MIDI has been embraced by many popular musicians.

The software component of the MIDI specification consists of digital data that describe various aspects of a musical performance – for example, what notes are played on a keyboard, when and with what force. MIDI does not carry actual sounds, but only instructions that control how a synthesizer or other device will produce sound. There are two types of MIDI data: channel messages and system messages. Channel messages consist of data describing note duration ('note on' and 'note off' commands), dynamics ('velocity' data), pitch bend, instructions to change the type of sound to be played (program change messages) and other control messages; MIDI can send and receive messages on 16 discrete channels, thus lending itself to multitrack recording techniques. System messages contain data specific to particular devices (system-exclusive messages) and data common to all channels – for example, tuning instructions, and real-time messages that allow clock-based devices, such as drum machines and sequencers, to be synchronized (the standard MIDI timing clock is set at a rate of 24 pulses per quarter note).

By standardizing the transfer of note and timing data, MIDI has become a key technology in the creation of contemporary electronic music, especially various genres of dance music, in which entire musical arrangements can be created and executed by a single individual. The growth of MIDI sequencing software during the 1980s has allowed for the full integration of electronic musical instruments with computers and with the modern recording studio, where MIDI has become central not only in the production of popular music, but also in scoring for film and television.

Bibliography

Anderton, Craig. 1986. *MIDI for Musicians*. New York: Amsco.

Durant, Alan. 1990. 'A New Day for Music?: Digital Technologies in Contemporary Music-Making.' In *Culture, Technology and Creativity in the Late Twentieth Cen-*

tury, ed. Philip Hayward. London: John Libbey & Co., 175–96.

Loy, Gareth. 1985. 'Musicians Make a Standard: The MIDI Phenomenon.' *Computer Music Journal* 9(4): 8–26.

Rothstein, Joseph. 1992. *MIDI: A Comprehensive Introduction*. Madison, WI: A-R Editions.

Théberge, Paul. 1997. *Any Sound You Can Imagine: Making Music/Consuming Technology*. Hanover, NH: University Press of New England/Wesleyan University Press.

PAUL THÉBERGE

Mixing Desk (Mixing Console)

A mixing desk (also referred to as a mixing console or board) is an electronic device used to amplify, combine and modify a variety of inputs – including microphones, musical instruments and prerecorded sounds – and route them to an external device, such as a tape recorder or public-address system. Since the 1950s, mixing desks have become a central component in multitrack recording, broadcasting and live performance, and their design characteristics have become increasingly complex. It is not unusual for a modern, professional recording console to handle as many as 48 simultaneous inputs and 24 outputs, and contain individual subsections devoted to equalization, effects routing (for the addition of reverb and other signal processing) and monitoring.

Bibliography

Alten, Stanley R. 1994. *Audio in Media*. 4th ed. Belmont, CA: Wadsworth.

Eargle, John. 1980. *Sound Recording*. 2nd ed. New York: Van Nostrand Reinhold.

PAUL THÉBERGE

Monitor

The term 'monitor' is used most often to refer to loudspeaker systems used in live performance and in studio recording. In performance, musicians use stage monitors so that they can hear themselves; the loudspeakers, and the mix fed to them, are entirely separate from the speaker systems heard by the audience. In the recording studio, specialized loudspeakers are used to evaluate sound quality and musical balances. A mixing console usually has a monitor section used to isolate sounds, to add effects to them without altering the recording itself, and to feed them back to the performers playing overdubs. 'To monitor' is to listen over speakers or headphones for the purpose of evaluation or overdubbing.

Bibliography

Alten, Stanley R. 1994. *Audio in Media*. 4th ed. Belmont, CA: Wadsworth.

Davis, Gary, and Jones, Ralph. 1989. *The Sound Reinforce-*

ment Handbook. 2nd ed. Milwaukee, WI: Hal Leonard.

Eargle, John. 1980. *Sound Recording*. 2nd ed. New York: Van Nostrand Reinhold.

PAUL THÉBERGE

MP3

The convergence of digital media for music storage and manipulation with the Internet's rise to popularity in the late 1990s created a fertile ground for the digital distribution of music via the Internet. MP3 became the most popular among several competing formats (Real, Liquid Audio and Ogg Vorbis are among the competitors) for the digital storage and delivery of music.

Introduced in 1992, MP3, short for MPEG Layer III (itself an abbreviation for Moving Picture Experts Group I Audio Layer III), is a means of encoding and decoding audio in digital format. It allows for extreme compression of audio files with little or no perceptible loss in audio quality. The development of MP3 meant that songs of three to four minutes' duration could be compressed to data files of 4 megabytes or less and still retain near CD-quality sound. Consequently, with increased bandwidth and transfer rates for Internet connections, the time required to download a song, or even an entire album, became reasonable for many Internet users.

The development of MP3 in conjunction with the Internet's rise in popularity quickly gained the attention of the music industry when it became clear that individuals could easily engage in copying audio CDs in MP3 format and sharing them with friends or strangers online. Many freeware, shareware and commercial MP3 players and 'rippers' (programs that encode CD audio to MP3 format) have become available on the Internet. Although not difficult to use, most require at least some knowledge of computer audio systems. Portable MP3 players began to be marketed in 1998, but were not easy to connect to most computers. In general, MP3, in its earliest incarnation, was a format used mainly by college students, computer enthusiasts and their friends.

Although methods for conducting secure electronic commerce were quickly developed in the late 1990s, the music industry was slow to adopt e-commerce and ceded some turf to e-tailers like cdnow.com and Amazon.com. The industry initially focused instead on piracy of digital music, and under the leadership of the Recording Industry Association of America (RIAA) quickly reacted to the potential threat from unauthorized downloading and uploading of copyrighted music. In 1998, the RIAA formed a committee, the Secure Digital Music Initiative (SDMI), composed of computer hardware and software makers and consumer electronics companies, aimed at creating a means of disabling unauthorized MP3 copying. The difficulty SDMI has continued to face, however, is akin to that faced by the computer software industry in general. Most copy protection schemes are quickly bypassed by hackers and as quickly made publicly available.

By 1999, however, the major record companies had slowly begun to embrace MP3 through such Web sites as Universal Music Group's 'The Farm Club' and Time Warner's 'Entertaindom.' By 2001, music industry-backed initiatives PressPlay and MusicNet had been introduced. However, at the beginning of the twenty-first century, it remained to be seen whether there would be a significant commercial market for downloadable music. 'Peer-to-peer' file-sharing networks continued to proliferate, although the most popular one, Napster, languished after a court-ordered shutdown, and many music fans grew increasingly accustomed to free music downloads. Yet, with apparent disregard for their own market, the major labels persisted in focusing on creating copy protection mechanisms, fighting file-sharing in court and lobbying the US Congress for changes in copyright law. It was clear that the music industry would need to adapt to technology as it had never needed to do before. The industry seemed bent on a slow evolution while the revolution was being downloaded at ever-increasing speed.

Bibliography

Alderman, John. 2001. *Sonic Boom: Napster, MP3 and the New Pioneers of Music*. Cambridge, MA: Perseus Publishing.

Fraunhofer Institut Integrierte Schaltungen. 1998–2001. *MPEG Audio Layer-3*. http://www.iis.fhg.de/amm/techinf/layer3/index.html

Garofalo, Reebee. 1999. 'From Music Publishing to MP3: Music and Industry in the Twentieth Century.' *American Music* 17(3): 318–53.

Haring, Bruce. 2000. *Beyond the Charts: MP3 and the Digital Music Revolution*. Los Angeles: OTC Press.

Hayward, Philip. 1995. 'Enterprise on the New Frontier: Music, Industry and the Internet.' *Convergence* 1(1): 29–44.

Holmes, Tamara E. 2000. *The ABCs of MP3*. http://www.usatoday.com/life/cyber/ccarch/cctam011.htm

Jones, Steve. 2000. 'Music and the Internet.' *Popular Music* 19(2): 217–30.

Laing, Dave. 1997. 'Rock Anxieties and New Music Networks.' In *Back to Reality?: Social Experience and Cultural Studies*, ed. Angela McRobbie. Manchester: Manchester University Press, 116–32.

Lipton, Beth. 1999. *View from the Eye of the Net Music Storm*. http://news.com.com/2009-1082-221683.html?legacy=cnet

Lovering, John. 1998. 'The Global Music Industry: Contradictions in the Commodification of the Sublime.' In *The Place of Music*, ed. Andrew Leyshon, David Matless and George Revill. New York: Guilford Press, 31–56.

MP3 Rocks the Web: A Month-By-Month Wired News Collection. 2002. http://www.wired.com/news/mp3/

Neuenfeldt, Karl. 1997. 'The Sounds of Microsoft: The Cultural Production of Music on CD-ROMs.' *Convergence* 3(4): 54–71.

Ridgley, Mitch. 1999–2000. *The History of MP3 and How Did It All Begin*. http://www.mp3-mac.com/Pages/History_of_MP3.html

Robertson, Michael, and Simpson, Ron. 1999. *The Official MP3.com Guide to MP3*. San Diego, CA: MP3.com.

Taylor, Chris. 2000. 'How to Bring MP3s to the Masses.' *Time* (26 June): 47.

Varanini, Giancarlo. 2000. *MP3: You Can't Stop the Music . . .* http://zdnet.com.com/2100-11-502234.html?legacy=zdnn

STEVE JONES

Multimedia

'Multimedia' is a term associated with computer-based software that integrates audio and visual data to create a semi-virtual world within which a particular theme or subject is explored. The multimedia product emerged in the early 1990s and proliferated from then on as a result of a number of factors: the development of sufficiently fast processors for home computers; the modification and enhancement of CD players to allow fast transfer of data using SCSI (small computer systems interface); the introduction of video and audio 'capture' cards, allowing sound and image to be imported and stored digitally; and the development of multimedia authoring programs, such as Apple's Hypercard and Macromedia's Director software. Multimedia authoring software allows imported audio and visual data to be integrated with text and graphics, with increasing use of 3-D objects and landscape rotation. Media objects (music, video, graphics, text) are nested within an electronic 'storyboard' to create a multimedia program. All possibilities are predetermined within the program, but navigation is usually nonlinear. Users may visit windows (scenes) within the program, and can then browse through or bypass the media objects located there. They may revisit scenes either by retracing their steps through the matrix or by linking through the use of an index or of navigation buttons.

The multimedia product in the form of CD-ROM encompasses a wide range of subject matter, from astronomy to gardening. Specifically music-oriented multimedia account for only a very small proportion of what is available, although audio, whether in the form of music or of sound effects, is usually present. Early contributions to the multimedia music library included Voyager's classical music titles: 'Mozart: The "Dissonant" Quartet,' and 'Beethoven: Symphony No. 9' (both the Voyager Company 1991). More significant, however, was the release of 'Xplora 1 – Peter Gabriel's Secret World' (Peter Gabriel Ltd., Realworld Multimedia 1993). While both Voyager titles and 'Xplora 1' were developed for the Apple computer using Hypercard, the latter set a new standard in CD-ROM multimedia experience by focusing as much on the visual environment as on informational content. The integration of video and sound in 'Xplora 1' resulted from the use of Apple's Quicktime system software extension (subsequently a cross-platform industry-standard multimedia software 'plug-in'), with animated photo-realistic objects implying virtual reality. While the Voyager products were designed as enhanced educational learning tools, 'Xplora 1' was essentially a product aimed at the devoted fan; its significance, therefore, has more to do with the achievements in multimedia presentation than with its content.

Multimedia content is not restricted to CD-ROM software. Internet Web pages now bristle with multimedia content (audio files, videoclips, animated objects, scrolling banners and the like). In addition, games for Sony's playstation, while not labeled as such, are wholly multimedia products. As with CD-ROM packages, music is there largely in support of visual content. SpiceWorld for the Sony playstation is no different in this respect. One of the most successful multimedia products – MYST (Broderbund Software Inc. 1993), subtitled 'The Surrealistic Adventure That Will Become Your World' – is seemingly no more complex than Gabriel's 'Xplora 1.' However, it is the interrelationship between soundscape, digitally rendered photo-realistic landscape, animated object and video that makes this multimedia product so compelling.

JONTY STOCKDALE

Music Software (Professional and Amateur)

Since the introduction of personal computers and, in particular, musical instrument digital interface (MIDI) during the early 1980s, a wide range of music software has been developed and marketed to meet the needs of both professional and amateur popular musicians. Software packages can be classified according to a number of different categories, including music education software (computer aids to ear training, keyboard practise or sight reading); librarian and editing software (applications for organizing large sound and sample collections, creating synthesizer patches or editing samples); sound-generating programs (computer-based samplers and synthesizers); recording software

(including software for hard-disc recording, editing, processing and mixing, as well as MIDI sequencers); music notation packages (software for scoring, arranging and part extraction); and interactive or computer-aided composition programs (applications that can respond to various forms of input and generate musical passages or accompaniments).

The history of music software development dates back to the 1950s, with various experiments, conducted primarily at research centers such as Bell Laboratories, in music composition via computers and in computer-generated sound. Early digital instruments, such as the Synclavier and the Fairlight CMI (Computer Music Instrument), which could be played from a conventional organ keyboard or controlled by a computer, also included unique synthesis, editing and sequencing software, some of which influenced later software innovations. The rise of commercial music software for general-purpose microcomputers, however, essentially began during the early 1980s. The first generation of music software, aimed as much at the computer hobbyist as at the professional musician, addressed issues of musical notation, rudimentary sequencing and sound synthesis. In many cases, these programs exploited the sound-generating capabilities of early personal computers such as the Apple II or the Commodore 64.

The most productive period of music software development occurred during the mid- to late 1980s, following the introduction of MIDI (in 1983) and more powerful personal computer systems. With MIDI, much of the task of generating sound could be shifted to external devices such as synthesizers and drum machines, and more computer power could be devoted to processing musical data. Educational software, synthesizer patch and sample editing applications, and improved notation packages began to appear during this period. However, few of these applications achieved the level of success enjoyed by sequencer software. Adopting the multitrack tape recorder as a metaphor for the user interface, professional and semiprofessional popular musicians began to build powerful production systems in their homes using synthesizers, drum machines, tape recorders and effects devices – all under the central control of the computer and sequencing software. The popularity of software sequencers continued to grow and, by the mid-1990s, a number of developers were marketing different versions of their sequencers – with different options and levels of complexity – to various market segments, including amateurs (so-called 'Lite' versions), semiprofessionals and professionals (the more sophisticated versions, often including elaborate music notation features and digital audio capabilities).

The late 1980s also witnessed the growth of digital

audio recording software. Using the computer's processor (and, in most cases, additional hardware peripherals) for recording, editing and processing of audio, and the hard disc for storage, these applications allowed for a flexibility and precision in editing and processing that far surpassed conventional analog methods. Digidesign, a California-based company, became a leader in this area with Pro Tools, a multitrack hardware/software package for the Apple Macintosh widely used in professional music recording and in postproduction sound for film and video. During the 1990s, many popular MIDI sequencer packages also began to include the type of audio capabilities found in programs such as Pro Tools, eventually growing in complexity to include virtually all elements of studio production, including sequencing, multitrack recording, mixing, editing, equalization and effects.

While computer-aided composition software, especially algorithmic software that generates varying degrees of randomized output, has been accepted among many composers of avant-garde computer music, it has met with relatively little success in the world of popular musicians. Interactive applications that can produce so-called 'intelligent' accompaniment patterns, however, appear to have answered the needs of many amateur and semiprofessional instrumentalists. Not unlike the 'Music Minus One' LP recordings designed for students of jazz, programs like PG Music's 'Band-in-a-Box' allow musicians to play solos over predetermined MIDI arrangements and offer the advantage of greater control over tempo, instrumentation and musical style.

The proliferation of music software, especially multi-track sequencers and digital audio applications, indicates that there is a distinct market for computer programs that meet the specific needs and interests of popular musicians. This development has been closely tied, firstly, to the rise of inexpensive digital synthesizers and MIDI during the 1980s and, secondly, to the increasing power of personal computers and their widespread use in both professional and amateur music-making in the 1990s.

Bibliography

Rothstein, Joseph. 1992. *MIDI: A Comprehensive Introduction*. Madison, WI: A-R Editions.

Yavelow, Christopher. 1992. *Macword Music and Sound Bible*. San Mateo, CA: IDG Books.

PAUL THÉBERGE

Napster

Introduction

Napster is the name of an Internet music company and of a real-time system by which Internet users can locate the MP3 files (a standard technology and format for compressing a sound sequence into a very small file) of other users. Shawn Fanning began developing Napster in early 1999 during his freshman year at Northeastern University in Boston, Massachusetts, where he studied computer science. Motivated by his interest in Windows-based programming and by his roommate's constant frustration in searching for digital music, he set out to create a file-sharing program to solve the reliability problems associated with finding music on-line. He envisioned a system that would combine three integral functions into a single software utility. These functions were:

(a) search engine, dedicated to finding MP3 files only;

(b) file-sharing, with the ability to trade MP3 files directly with other users without having to use a centralized server for storage; and

(c) Internet Relay Chat (IRC), a way to find and chat with other MP3 users while on-line (Tyson 2001).

Fanning left university in early 1999 to devote the majority of his time to developing what would become Napster (also Fanning's nickname). Napster was incorporated in May 1999, and Fanning moved the company to northern California in September 1999. He released an early Beta version of the Napster software during the summer, and news of its existence spread quickly by word of mouth. Download.com featured Napster in its Download Spotlight in early fall 1999, and the Napster user community grew significantly (Fanning 2000).

Napster is estimated to have had over 26 million users (consistently with over 800,000 people using the system simultaneously), while some reports estimate the total number of users to have exceeded 70 million. Despite the employment of filtering technologies that reduced the availability of songs by a number of prominent artists, over 12 million users connected to Napster's file-sharing system in March 2001. According to the analysts Jupiter Media Metrix, Napster's file-sharing system and Web site attracted 17 million users in the United States, or almost 20 percent of those who went on-line that month. Of these users, 15.2 million logged on to the Napster system.

Technology Overview

Napster relied on communication between the personal computers of members of the Napster system rather than providing servers that housed the information. The information was distributed across the Internet, allowing for a depth and scale of information that was virtually limitless.

Napster did not post, host or serve MP3 files from its systems, but used its centralized servers to optimize searching performance. A group of machines at Napster contained members' registrations, shared file lists and music searches. The Napster software allowed users to connect with each other to share MP3 files stored on their individual hard drives. The number of song files available at any given time depended on the number of song files that active users chose to share from their music collections. The transfer was directly from computer to computer or 'peer-to-peer.'

Napster worked in the following way. Using the Napster client, a user logged on to one of Napster's servers, uploading a list of the music files available for sharing on his/her computer. When a search request was issued, the server logged it with the user's Napster username and IP (Internet Protocol) address. Search results arrived immediately, based on the music collections of users logged on to the same server. Napster built a list of the computers containing the song in the 'Results' window. When the user clicked on a search result, a connection was established and the file was downloaded from another Napster user via Napster's proprietary protocol. The client reported back to Napster's server the username, the IP address and the song that had been downloaded. The computer providing the song broke the connection with the computer requesting the song, and the downloaded song was immediately available for other Napster users to download.

Unlike traditional Web-based search engines, the Napster system could not index files based on their content and organize them in a meaningful way for users. During Napster's early development, MP3 and Windows Media Audio (WMA) files were not designed for such content-based indexing. Instead, such files were more easily located and organized on the basis of characteristics such as the file names assigned by users or of personal judgments about the files' contents. Napster provided a directory through which users might find files, by file name, residing on the computers of other Napster users.

One of Napster's goals was to maintain a real-time directory of the music files on the hard drives of all users who were connected at any one time, so that a user could request and get a copy of any file from any other user's hard drive. However, the software showed users only a directory of files for those users connected to the same centralized server. For example, Napster had 100 server computers maintaining the directory of files. When users logged on, they could see only a directory of files for the users connected to that particular server; no information was passed between servers. The users connected to the 99 other servers were invisible to other users (Alsop 2000). The Napster service also provided location information that allowed a computer to connect to another user and transfer the file from its loca-

tion. Napster's functions also included chat rooms, instant messaging and message boards.

Legal Issues

Copyright was at the heart of the Napster debate, which was at its height between 1999 and 2001. Napster provided a service that allowed users to share copyrighted material. The usage policy for the software indicated that Napster was not responsible for the copyright infringement of people who used the service (Alsop 2000). One of Napster's defenses against accusations of copyright infringement was that the downloading of music by its subscribers constituted fair use. Accordingly, Napster attempted to argue that, because the downloading of copyrighted music (by its users) was allowable as fair use, there was no direct infringement upon which to establish Napster's indirect liability as a contributory infringer (Ho 2001).

Many Napster users believed that possessing a digital product conferred the right of unlimited use and distribution. However, enforcement and interpretation of digital rights differed from one geographic region to another. In Europe, at the beginning of the twenty-first century, a directive on Copyright in the Information Society was adopted for the Internet. This directive makes it increasingly difficult for consumers to make copies of content even for private use. In the United States, laws give copyright holders total control over content and allow them to deploy technology to prevent copying, thus making copying a punishable crime (Bassanese 2002). Napster's defense was that MP3 files are personal files that people maintain on their own computers. As a consequence, Napster could not be held responsible for copyright infringement.

In December 1999, the Recording Industry Association of America (RIAA) sued Napster for copyright infringement. The RIAA claimed that Napster was a large, automated system for the unauthorized distribution of copyrighted material. Thousands of people were making thousands of copies of copyrighted songs, and neither the music industry nor the artists were being paid for those copies. Many people embraced Napster because they could get music for free instead of paying for it; however, that was the very reason why the music industry was against it.

As a result of the RIAA's copyright infringement lawsuit, an injunction was issued against Napster in July 2000 that ultimately put its free service out of business. The ruling, which was a major victory for the recording industry, temporarily ordered the on-line music-swapping service to stop permitting the exchange of copyrighted material (Jones 2000).

In February 2001, a US federal appeals court ruled that Napster had to stop trading copyrighted material and might be held liable for 'vicarious copyright infringement' while failing to patrol its system. Napster was alleged to have infringed copyright laws by allowing users to download, copy and distribute digital music for free. Although Napster had already shut down the service of its own volition, in July 2001 a US federal court judge ordered Napster to prevent all music transfers until it could prove that it could effectively block copyrighted songs. The filtering software to block copyrighted material from its file-searching engine was circumvented regularly. Napster kept the free service closed while it continued to work on its membership-based service and to fight its remaining legal battles.

Business Issues

Under a partnership with BMG, Napster was asked at the beginning of the twenty-first century to create a new membership-based service that would pay artists, music publishers and record companies. The service was expected to cost between US$5 and US$10 per month and to begin in late 2002. The release date was to depend on the terms of Napster's licensing agreements with copyright holders. All music that could be copied illegally would be prohibited. It was intended that Napster's servers would record every music file's digital fingerprint (an MD5 hash), which uniquely identifies an MP3 music file. The hashes could be used to track recordings, spot illegal downloads and remove stolen files. Unfortunately, this proved an unviable option, due to differences in recording software and the degree of compression. Different digital recordings of the same song could produce different digital fingerprints. While this would make tracking violators more difficult, the technology would detect most violations (Ante 2000b).

Napster and Loudeye Technologies, Inc. entered into a multi-year strategic agreement in which Loudeye was to provide digital fingerprints and associated descriptive data to Napster for use in its planned membership service. Additionally, Loudeye's service offering was to support Napster's compliance efforts to filter noticed copyrighted content from its free service.

All the music available through Napster's membership service would be legally licensed for sharing by its subscribers. Some music would be shared in MP3 format, and subscribers would have all the freedom with those files that they had with any MP3s. To give artists and copyright holders choices about how their music was shared, Napster created a new secure file format that defined how each file could be used. Subscribers would be unable to play these files – called NAP files – on their portable player at the launch of the new service. The NAP format was introduced because some artists and rights holders would not share their music without a secure format.

Conclusion

Napster and services like it raised the ire of the music industry because they infringed on copyright restrictions. Other peer-to-peer programs gained popularity and began to fill the void left by the closure of Napster.

Bertelsmann and Napster had the task of keeping the focus on the benefits of a viable partnership. Consumers could benefit from greater choice and lower prices; the music industry could benefit from increased sales and a lower cost of doing business (Ante 2000b). The trouble with this scenario was that peer-to-peer programs were distributed quickly, and most forms of commercial digital copy protection were breached quickly and efficiently (Scheschuk 2000). Nevertheless, the pay services believed that the quality of the downloaded files would attract subscribers to their services.

However, the launch of the paid-for Napster was postponed several times, and in May 2002 the Napster board split over the merits of a full takeover by Bertelsmann. Meanwhile, other major record companies introduced competing pay services such as MusicNet and Pressplay.

Part of Napster's legacy was that it taught consumers that the Internet transcends hyperlinked Web pages and e-mail. Napster also ushered in the debate on intellectual property and introduced many businesses to the vast potential of traditional peer-to-peer computing. 'Napster is truly revolutionary – and it will be a precursor of some of the most important Web applications over the next several years,' said James W. Breyer, a managing partner at Accel Partners, a Silicon Valley venture-capital firm (Ante 2000a).

Bibliography

Alsop, Stewart. 2000. 'The Sad Truth About Napster.' *Fortune* (13 November): 83–84.

Ante, Spencer. 2000a. 'Inside Napster.' *Business Week* (14 August).

Ante, Spencer. 2000b. 'Napster: Tune In, Turn On, Pay Up.' *Business Week* (13 November): 52.

Barlow, John Perry. 2000. *The Next Economy of Ideas*. http://www.wired.com/wired/archive/8.10/download _pr.html

Bassanese, Paola. 2002. *File Swapping May Get Your Hands Burnt*. http://www.ovum.com/go/ovumcomments/ 005408.htm

Berg, Al. 2000. 'Tunneling Under.' *Information Security* (November): 14.

Boutin, Paul. 2000. *P2P Pages: Wired's Guide to Global File-Sharing.* http://www.wired.com/wired/archive/8.10/p2p_pages.html

Eliscu, Jenny. 2000. 'Napster Goes Legit.' *Rolling Stone* (14 December): 43–44.

Fanning, Shawn. 2000. *Testimony of Shawn Fanning.* http://www.napster.com/pressroom/001013.html

Ho, Cynthia M. 2001. *What's Unfair About Copying Music from Napster?: Examining 'Fair Use' and Napster.* http://www.luc.edu/schools/law/alumni/copyright.html

Jones, Christopher. 2000. *Napster Copies Move Forward.* http://www.wired.com/news/technology/0,1282,35370,00.html

Kemp, Ted. 2000. 'Napster Means E-Business: Bertelsmann Deal Could Validate Model But Poses Technical Challenge.' *Internetweek* (20 November): 23.

Kuptz, Jerome. 2000. *Napster: Killer Business App.* http://www.wired.com/wired/archive/8.10/architecture_pr.html

Scheschuk, Brice. 2000. 'Napster: The Power of Sharing.' *Maclean's* (13 November): 60.

Tyson, Jeff. 2001. *How Napster Works.* http://www.howstuffworks.com/napster.htm/printable

COREY D. RAMEY

Notation

Introduction

Notation is the visual means of representing music, which can be either graphic or linguistic, or a combination of the two. Examples of notation are provided by scores using five-line staves, and by guitar tablature. One purpose of notation is to convey instructions and directions that relate to a wide range of musical requirements in performance. Notation has also been, and remains, a vital tool in many forms of composition, arranging, orchestration and scoring. In addition, notation can be used for purposes of research and scholarship, when transcriptions of performances are made.

Notation and Popular Music

Many forms of notation are used in popular music. They include guitar tablature, which indicates finger positions on the fret of the guitar's neck for different chords, chordal nomenclature (for example, Co7 Cdim7 – to be explained later in the entry), various signs to indicate the shaping and phrasing of notes in jazz and big band arrangements, and notation to indicate the form of a piece (to be illustrated later in the entry). However, the most common form of notation in popular music – to which most other forms relate – has been that using the five-line stave developed as an integral aspect of the history of Western, classical music. This notation's relationship to popular music differs in some important respects from its relationship to classical music. To understand how this notation and, indeed, other forms related to it function within popular music, it is necessary to understand this difference.

Within the tradition of Western, classical music, this form of notation can prescribe with a high degree of accuracy performance requirements where matters of pitch (which relate to harmony and melody) and rhythm are concerned. Because of its highly prescriptive character, the development of this form of notation has made possible the creation of musical works that are complex in terms of form, and in terms of the use of tightly defined pitches in harmony and melody. Such has been the structural complexity of these works that they could not be created or performed except through the use of this form of notation. Memory alone would not suffice. While many musicians in the Western, classical tradition do perform in concert from memory, it would nonetheless be true to say that Western classical music is not at heart an oral-aural tradition, and that literate mediation through notation is fundamental to its compositional and performance practises.

The practise of popular music on the whole differs in two important ways from that of classical music. Firstly, in most branches of Western popular music, musicians have acquired their skills primarily through processes of aural dissemination. They learn to sing or play an instrument through observation of and interaction with other musicians, and by imitating musical ideas from live performances and recordings. Most forms of popular music are therefore learned and performed in a non-literate, or oral-aural, manner.

Secondly, while deviations from prescribed pitches and rhythms occur in classical music and are, indeed, crucial to good performances, such elements in most forms of popular music are more central to popular music's expressive capacities, and so to its creation and performance. The manner in which the notation of classical music prioritizes certain elements such as pitch and rhythm, and then tightly constrains their variation, means that many of the elements central to popular music's expressive capacities are not represented. These elements might include irregular, polyrhythmic phrases, non-conventional pitch inflections (blue notes, microtonal slurs and slides), the technical features of studio-based effects (reverb, vocoding, flanging, wah-wah) and, very importantly, wide variations in the timbre or tone-color of voices and instruments. It is for this reason that, as early as 1924, Milton Metfessel and Carl Seashore developed the technique of 'phonophotography' in the Department of Psychology at the University of Iowa in order to notate accurately inflections of pitch in performance against time, thus making possible more precise analyses of pitch variation (Oliver 1969, 19; Metfessel 1928).

It is because of popular music's fundamentally oral-aural character, and the extreme difficulty of notating with prescriptive accuracy many of the elements central to its expressive capacities, that the character of the relationship between popular music and various forms of notation (including that derived from classical music) differs from that of the relationship between classical music and its notation.

The role of notation in popular music has thus been significantly different from that found in classical music. Because classically based notation is not ideally suited to most styles of popular music, notation in popular music is often intended as a guide only to performance. For a performance, notation might include anything from a few chords scribbled down beneath the lyrics to more detailed notated arrangements. Performers can use whatever notation is provided as a map to the overall performance of the music. In a piano arrangement, the melody and chords are notated, often in the form of sheet music, on treble and bass staves, while the vocal part and guitar fret positions are included above this in the treble clef. The fundamentally mnemonic character (and role) of this kind of notation is illustrated by the fact that, if played verbatim according to the sheet music, the music often sounds rigid and uninteresting. Within this context, notation does remain generally prescriptive, but only through its role as a literate aide-mémoire in the fundamentally oral-aural relationship between the performer and the performance.

Because of the inadequacies of traditional notation and other forms related to it, the recording has become the principal mode of documentation – the 'score' – in many pop and rock genres. Through software technology developed in the 1980s, such as Cubase, Finale and Notator, the recording can be 'visualized,' thus producing a flexible form of descriptive notation. Yet, even with these programs there is a tendency to stress standard conceptions of pitch as a consequence of the central role played by Western notation in establishing conventional notions of 'music.' However, the scope for analyzing sound shapes, dynamics and spectral ranges through music software has certainly increased the potential for new systems of notation.

Notation as an Aid to Research and Teaching

Functioning in a descriptive as opposed to prescriptive manner, notation can be representative of any performance, and can in this way be an aid to teaching.

An important example of this in popular music has been the 'shape-note' tradition, in which differently shaped notes (rectangles, triangles, pennants and ovoids) represent the solmization syllables (do, re, mi and so on), thus allowing choirs and congregations with no formal musical education to sing together effectively.

In contrast to its function as an instructional aid to the performer, notation can be utilized as a resource for research purposes, and in this respect is normally more complex and detailed than descriptive or, indeed, prescriptive notation. Traditionally, transcribed material is notated as a result of detailed aural perception, which raises the issue of listening competence. However, developments such as that of 'phonophotography' have rendered this issue less important. Oliver reports that, in 1925, Metfessel and Seashore 'made a number of phonophotographic recordings of spirituals, work songs and blues.' As Oliver explains, 'phonophotography combined a "portable sound photography camera," which recorded the music, converted the frequency of vibration, measured the time and filmed the singers. Notations as to text and phonetics were also taken and the "pattern notation" plotted in a graph-curve against an even-tempered scale.' An example of a phonophotographic recording of the 'Cornfield Holler' is reproduced by Oliver (1969, 19).

With advances in digital music technology, it is now possible to access and produce transcribed material more easily. Depending on the sophistication of the technology employed, it is possible to explore a wide range of musical parameters. Technologically transcribed musical data are emerging as an increasingly useful means for exploring compositional and performance processes in music research.

Notation Nomenclature

Standard notation found in jazz and popular music scores and sheet music is derived from Western music notation. There are a number of symbols and nomenclature commonly found in notation.

(a) Chords

In popular music, harmony is commonly represented through a system of chord symbols. Chord symbols provide the performer with the necessary information relating to the specified harmony. Chord nomenclature is not entirely standardized, and there are differences in conventions from one country or culture to another. For example, while chord nomenclature in English-speaking countries is based on the first seven letters of the alphabet (A–G), in non-English-speaking European countries use is often made of the first eight letters, in which the pitch B is replaced with H and B♭ with B.

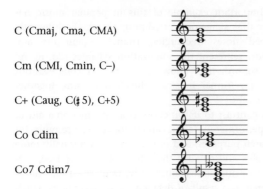

C (Cmaj, Cma, CMA)

Cm (CMI, Cmin, C–)

C+ (Caug, C($\sharp$5), C+5)

Co Cdim

Co7 Cdim7

Example 1 Chord symbols.

Extended chords, which are common in many styles of jazz and popular music, involve diatonic additions to the major, minor, diminished or augmented triads to produce intervals of sevenths, ninths, elevenths and thirteenths. These chords are defined by their uppermost extension, such as Cm^{13}, D^{11} or B^{maj9}. In addition to extensions, altered chords, which involve chromatic changes to components of the chords, are often used in Western popular music. For example, the chord containing the pitches F A C$\sharp$ E G$\flat$ is referred to as $F^{\flat9\sharp5}$. It should be noted that the notation of chord symbols functions only as a general guide and is not intended to indicate the details of harmonic flavoring, such as voicing, inversions and doubling.

(b) Melody

Traditional methods for notating melodies in most popular music have centered on Western diatonic/chromatic and modal music. Generally, little notational innovation has been discernible in the documentation of melodic lines and shapes, although some attempt has been made to represent the microtonal alterations of pitch, such as those found in blues and slide inflections, through a variety of symbols. Pitch fluctuations and nuances, which are so much part of the vocabulary of countless popular styles, are seldom specified in notation. While, for example, symbols for vibrato and trills can be notated or indicated linguistically alongside the relevant note, it is more common to leave such details to the performer's discretion.

(c) Rhythm and Groove

Rhythm is perhaps the most problematic area of notation in jazz and popular music. The nuances and subtleties of the groove are almost impossible to capture within the narrow constraints of Western notation. As so many forms of popular music rely primarily on their 'beat' or groove, it is of concern that transcriptions often fail to represent the intricacies of rhythmic nuance. It is usually simplified representations of a rhythm in notated form, if and when used, that serve as an aid to the character and 'feel' of the music, with the implicit understanding that the performer will fill in the 'gaps.' In some instances, however, the arranger or transcriber is highly meticulous in detailing the representation of a performance through individually devised systems of notation.

(d) Form

Form relates to the shape and structure of a piece of music. A description of the shape and structure is a common type of notation in popular music. Notes on shape relating to the formal characteristics of the music serve to remind the performer of the overall structure and sequence of musical events within that structure.

The majority of popular songs consist of two main sections: the chorus (refrain) and the verse. In addition, the structure can also include passages such as introductions, bridges, middle eights, C sections and codas. Often, the chorus and verse will consist of a total of 16 or 32 bars (constructed of four- or eight-bar phrases). For performance purposes, the structure and form of a song can be notated with or without the inclusion of lyrics. A typical example of this might be represented as follows:

intro – A – A – B – B – A – middle eight – A – B – coda
  4   16 16 16 16 16   8   16 16   4

In another context, the performer might already know the structure of a song, its melodic line, its rhythmic feel, and the nuance and dynamics of its texture and merely requires a chord chart, such as that provided below (Ex. 2).

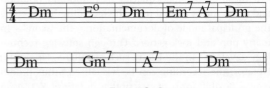

Example 2

Bibliography

Metfessel, Milton. 1928. *Phonophotography in Folk Music: American Negro Songs in New Notation*, with an introduction by Carl Seashore. Chapel Hill, NC: University of North Carolina Press.

Middleton, Richard. 1990. *Studying Popular Music*. Milton Keynes: Open University Press.

Oliver, Paul. 1969. *The Story of the Blues*. London: Barrie and Jenkins.

Read, Gardner. 1978. *Music Notation*. London: Victor Gollancz.

Read, Gardner. 1980. *Modern Rhythmic Notation*. London: Macmillan.

Small, Christopher. 1987. *Music of the Common Tongue*. London: Calder.

Tagg, Philip. 1982. 'Analysing Popular Music: Theory, Method and Practice.' *Popular Music* 2: 37–67.

STAN HAWKINS and JOHN SHEPHERD

Part Writing

Part writing is a compositional technique that involves writing a piece of music for one or more parts. The technique, therefore, is based on the writing of one part or of parts that, when played together, make up a piece of music. The parts have to conform to the criteria for good or acceptable melodic material within any particular style or genre.

If more than one part is involved, the way in which the parts relate to one another has also to conform to the criteria for acceptable harmonic material within any particular style or genre. The balance between emphasis on the melodic and harmonic aspects of part writing may vary between various styles and genres. If the parts contribute to a sequence of block chords, then the part writing may be said to be homophonic in character. Hymns provide good examples of this kind of writing, which is often heard as a melody and accompaniment despite the often significantly melodic character of the parts making up the accompaniment. However, if great stress is placed on the melodic aspects of part writing, with each part possessing striking melodic characteristics and the harmonic aspects of the music arising only as a consequence of the relation of the parts to one another (although still conforming to acceptable harmonic norms), then the part writing may be said to be polyphonic or contrapuntal in character. Procol Harum's 'A Whiter Shade of Pale' and many of the group's other compositions provide good examples of this more linear approach to part writing.

The technique of part writing as a consequence involves placing together various parts of melodic material in a way that determines its overall effect and style.

As a more contemporary illustration of part writing, it can be likened to the process of laying down tracks within a recording, since multitrack recordings invariably consist of tracks working in a somewhat autonomous fashion in relation to one another.

Discographical Reference

Procol Harum. 'A Whiter Shade of Pale.' Deram DM 126. *1967*: UK.

JOHN SHEPHERD and STAN HAWKINS

Pitch Shifter

A pitch shifter is a digital device that can alter the pitch of an audio input without changing its overall duration.

It can be used in recording to correct minor pitch problems – for example, when a singer sings a note slightly sharp or flat – or to create special effects, as when it is used to transpose notes outside a singer's or an instrumentalist's normal range. Some pitch shifters can also be used to change the duration of a recording without changing its pitch; this is called time compression. In radio broadcasting, time compression is sometimes used to change the duration of music and commercials to fit prescribed time limits.

PAUL THÉBERGE

Sampler

A sampler is a hybrid device – both a digital sound recorder and a musical instrument – that was designed to reproduce the sounds of conventional musical instruments, thereby making studio production more economical by eliminating the need for many backing musicians. However, samplers were soon put to more creative uses by hip-hop and rap producers, extending the DJ techniques of isolating break beats and mixing together passages from various recordings. While early digital instruments such as the Synclavier and the Fairlight CMI had sampling capabilities, sampling became widely available to musicians, sound engineers and producers only after the introduction of relatively inexpensive instruments such as the E-mu Emulator (first introduced in 1981) and the Ensoniq Mirage (1984).

Sampling technique is based on the ability to digitally record short fragments of sound (ranging from a few milliseconds to several seconds in duration), digitally loop the sounds to extend their duration, and then make them available to a keyboard, drum pad, sequencer or other input device where they can be played, melodically and rhythmically, like conventional musical sounds. In this regard, the sampler is essentially a computer whose operating system has been optimized for audio and musical purposes. Recorded sounds are stored in RAM (random access memory) where they can be subjected to various forms of digital editing and signal processing, such as cutting, splicing, looping, pitch shifting, time expansion and compression. The sounds can be further shaped using digital simulations of common synthesizer components and techniques: filters, frequency and amplitude envelopes, and modulation. Due to its superior ability to reproduce the sounds of musical instruments, sample playback became the basis of most synthesizer designs, virtually replacing older methods of sound synthesis by the late 1980s.

In many instances, the digital sampler is used specifically for the purposes for which it was intended: as a convenient, flexible and inexpensive replacement for grand piano, drums, string and brass ensembles and, more recently, the sounds of traditional instruments from around the world. In this capacity, and despite the protests of musicians' unions, samplers have become an important part of both contemporary studio recording and live performance. However, in the hands of rap musicians, dance music producers and remix engineers, the sampler has also been used to cut sound fragments and loop together rhythmic grooves from a wide variety of sources – especially commercial recordings of soul, funk and heavy metal music, but also from an increasingly diverse range of sources, including film and television soundtracks. In doing so, sampling artists created a crisis within the music industry with regard to copyright.

While the perceived threat to copyright law was relatively short-lived – the industry essentially bringing would-be samplers into line primarily through intimidation and the threat of litigation – the influence of this chaotic moment in the history of pop should not be underestimated. By the 1990s, sampling had become a tolerated, if not fully accepted, part of pop musical practise: for example, in 1993, the acid jazz group US3 was given extensive access to the back catalog of Blue Note recordings in order to create its particular mix of classic jazz and contemporary rap styles.

Bibliography

Beadle, Jeremy J. 1993. *Will Pop Eat Itself?: Pop Music in the Soundbite Era*. London: Faber and Faber.

Frith, Simon. 1993. *Music and Copyright*. Edinburgh: Edinburgh University Press.

Goodwin, Andrew. 1990. 'Sample and Hold: Pop Music in the Digital Age of Reproduction.' In *On Record: Rock, Pop and the Written Word*, ed. Simon Frith and Andrew Goodwin. London: Routledge, 258–73. (First published in *Critical Quarterly* 30(3)(1988): 34–49.)

Hartley, Ross. 1993. 'Beat in the System.' In *Rock and Popular Music: Politics, Policies, Institutions*, ed. Tony Bennett et al. London: Routledge, 210–30.

Porcello, Thomas. 1991. 'The Ethics of Digital Audio-Sampling: Engineers' Discourse.' *Popular Music* 10(1): 69–84.

Rose, Tricia. 1994. 'Soul Sonic Forces: Technology, Orality, and Black Cultural Practice in Rap Music.' In *Black Noise: Rap Music and Black Culture in Contemporary America*. Hanover, NH: Wesleyan University Press, 62–96.

Discography

US3. *Hand on the Torch*. Blue Note B2 26708. *1993*: USA.

PAUL THÉBERGE

Scoring

Traditionally, a score is the visual representation of the instrumental (and possibly vocal) parts of a piece of music arranged on different staves. 'Scoring' is thus the process of assigning the various parts or elements of a composition to specific instruments and combinations of instruments. By scoring, the arranger or orchestrator considers the musical features (melodies, harmony and rhythm) of a piece of music in terms of the technicalities of the various possibilities for its instrumentation. Scoring is thus fundamental for processes of arranging and orchestration but is not synonymous with them. In this way, scoring may be thought of as necessary but not sufficient for arranging and orchestration.

In traditional terms, 'full scoring' denotes the practise of scoring for a full orchestra or large band. This generally requires considerable skill and expert knowledge of the technical capabilities of the various instruments. A typical full score displays all the parts of the score, which often comprises more than 30 staves. The general layout of a score is in the following sequence, from top to bottom: woodwinds (piccolos, flutes, oboes, English horns, clarinets, bass clarinets, bassoons, double bassoons); brass instruments (French horns, trumpets, trombones, tubas); percussion instruments (for example, tympani, cymbals, side drums, wood blocks); keyboards; voices; and strings (violins, violas, cellos, double basses). Scoring also involves the transposition of certain instruments, so that the actual sound is different in pitch from that represented by the notated notes.

The term 'scoring' or 'to score for' can be used quite flexibly to mean writing or arranging for any group of instruments. In popular music genres, the act of scoring does not necessarily involve the traditional and laborious process of handwriting a score. For example, film scores are often realized electronically through the use of samplers, synthesizers and computer software.

STAN HAWKINS

Sequencer (Sequencer Software)

A sequencer is a device that stores and plays back a series of voltages or performance commands and is used to control synthesizers and drum machines. Hardware sequencers, first in analog and then in digital form, have been a central component in electronic music studios since the rise of the modular synthesizer during the late 1960s. With the advent of musical instrument digital interface (MIDI) during the 1980s, software sequencers became the most common type of computer program used in popular music production.

The manufacture of devices to automate musical performance dates back to at least the invention of the music box in the eighteenth century, and the player piano of the late nineteenth and early twentieth centuries. The player piano, in particular, with its ability to play back musical performances stored on paper rolls, can be considered a mechanical precursor of the modern sequencer. A similar paper-tape mechanism, storing binary data, was used to control playback on the huge RCA Electronic Music Synthesizer, located at the Columbia-Princeton electronic studios, during the 1950s. Much electronic music of this period, however, was created by editing, splicing and looping electronic sounds recorded on magnetic tape.

With the introduction of modular synthesizers during the mid-1960s, it became possible to control the various electronic components through the application of variations in electrical voltage. The analog sequencer was developed to supply to a synthesizer a user-defined series of control voltages (altering the pitch of the oscillators) and gate signals (defining note durations by triggering envelope generators). Sequencers were often designed to repeat a short series of such voltage/gate steps – between eight and 16 steps in early analog devices – and thus, in operation, sounded much like the use of tape loops.

To increase the number of notes that could be produced by the sequencer and to attain greater flexibility in programming, a number of synthesizer designers began to experiment with microprocessor technology during the early 1970s. Among the most popular of the early digital sequencers was Roland's MC-8 Microcomposer, introduced in 1977. Based on design prototypes developed by Ralph Dyck, an independent commercial composer and studio owner working in Vancouver, Canada, the MC-8 had the capability of outputting eight discrete channels of control voltages and had sufficient memory to produce more than 5,000 notes. Following Dyck's innovative design, the device used a numeric keyboard to enter notes and other musical data. Other sequencer innovations of the period included the development of systems for the auto-correction of rhythmic discrepancies and the chaining together of short patterns to create longer sequences, both introduced in Roger Linn's first drum machine, the LM-1, which began development in 1978 and was introduced to the marketplace in 1980.

In 1983, the introduction of MIDI – which allowed digital synthesizers and personal computers to be connected together – created the conditions for the development of the next generation of hardware and software sequencers. These sequencers output MIDI data, rather than control voltages, and can be used to control virtually every aspect of a synthesizer's sound-generating capabilities.

Based on its earlier experiments in designing sequencer-like software for personal computers, Passport Designs introduced the first MIDI sequencer program in 1984. With the increased emphasis placed on the use of simultaneous, multiple channels of MIDI data and the already-established practise of multitrack recording in popular music production, most software programmers adopted the multitrack tape recorder as a metaphor in designing the user interface for sequencer software: the process of inputting MIDI data simulates the practise of recording and overdubbing on a multitrack tape deck (there are even on-screen buttons for record, playback, fast forward and rewind functions), and the data are usually arranged as a series of linear 'tracks.'

The use of sequencers has had a profound impact on a number of popular music genres. During the 1970s and early 1980s, the repetitive patterns and rhythmic precision characteristic of early sequencers became part of the aesthetic of much psychedelic and electro-pop music. Digital synthesizers, drum machines and software sequencers have likewise become essential components in the production of techno and other genres of dance music since the 1980s. Outside these specific genres, the increased use of computers in recording studios during the 1990s has made sequencing software an integral part of recording practise in a wide range of popular and commercial music production.

Bibliography

Holmes, Thomas B. 1985. *Electronic and Experimental Music*. New York: Charles Scribner's Sons.

Théberge, Paul. 1997. *Any Sound You Can Imagine: Making Music/Consuming Technology*. Hanover, NH: Wesleyan University Press/University Press of New England.

Vail, Mark. 1993. *Vintage Synthesizers*. San Francisco: Miller Freeman Books.

PAUL THÉBERGE

Sound Recording Technologies

The technology of sound recording dates back to the late 1800s. The wax and tinfoil cylinders, precursors of the modern phonograph, were among the influential inventions that heralded the end of the nineteenth century and the start of the twentieth century. Communications technology was coming into its own, with initial development of the telephone, telegraph, radio and phonograph occurring during the late 1800s. These inventions were not unrelated. Thomas Edison, who, it is generally agreed, invented the phonograph in 1877, was in some measure involved in the research and development of all of them, as were Alexander Graham Bell and Emile Berliner.

That these inventions were related is not surprising. The driving force behind these communications technologies (and the radio) was the desire to transmit the human voice. One of the earliest uses of the phonograph was for dictation and transcription.

Prior to the phonograph, music notation was the only means, apart from memorization, of preserving a composition. Musical boxes existed, but they could not be said to have 'recorded' music. They relied on a process that involved the repeated striking of small keys or other resonating objects – a process much the same as that used in piano rolls, whereby a piano's keys were guided by a perforated roll of paper, each perforation corresponding to a key. Neither device qualified as an instrument for sound recording simply because they did not fix and store sound.

The first technological method of sound recording dates back to 1857 when Leon Scott, a French scientist, developed the phonautograph. This instrument used a hog's bristle, attached to a diaphragm located at the small end of a conical horn, to cut lateral grooves into a cylinder of heavy paper coated with lamp black. A person could shout into the horn and rotate the cylinder by hand, thereby 'writing' the sound (hence the term 'phonautograph'). Scott, however, had no provision for playing the sound back.

In July 1877, Thomas Edison filed for a patent for a telephonic repeating device with the British patent office. The method was similar to Scott's, although Edison used tinfoil as the medium upon which grooves were cut by a stylus.

The early phonograph was greatly lacking in fidelity. The device would both record and reproduce sound by means of a large acoustic horn (now familiar to many people only from the 'His Master's Voice' logo), thereby necessitating strong sound sources to provide adequate levels of loudness. Yet the sound could not be too loud, since the stylus carved pits into the cylinder and could not be allowed to cut too deeply lest it damage the medium.

The phonograph enjoyed startling popularity from the day of its first public exhibition. Some machines were outfitted with coin slots and sets of hearing tubes with which up to 17 people could listen to a recording.

However, problems lingered. Since the phonograph was initially developed for reproduction of the human voice, with its limited frequency and dynamic range, lack of fidelity limited its popularity – as did the short supply of recordings. The novelty of hearing a recording of the human voice wore off quickly, and technical improvements became necessary if the phonograph was to become an instrument for recording music with any degree of fidelity. Of equal importance, there was no means for mass-producing recordings. Each cylinder could be made only from a unique performance, and to mass-produce cylinders multiple cylinder recording machines had to be arranged in front of the performers. For 100 cylinders to be made, a performer had to play a piece of music 10 times in front of 10 recording machines.

The next step in the phonograph's evolution came from Edison's archrival, Alexander Graham Bell. He developed the graphophone, a device virtually identical to Edison's tinfoil phonograph, except that it used wax-covered paper and not tinfoil. Instead of indenting grooves into tinfoil, the graphophone cut grooves into the wax. The graphophone patent, issued in 1886, included this distinction between indenting and incising, and was the progenitor of the modern phonograph record. Bell also developed a system whereby a jet of compressed air amplified sound reproduction, and a mechanism by which the cylinder could be rotated at a variable speed.

By 1895, with the help of inventor Ezrah Gilliland, Edison had developed an improved, spring motor-driven phonograph. Gilliland had also been working on another invention he called the 'spectacle.' This device allowed for immediate switching between recording and reproduction on the phonograph. The spectacle was important for the phonograph's use as a dictating machine, but the principle of immediate reproduction/ recording remained central to subsequent recording machines like the cassette deck.

During this time, German-born inventor Emile Berliner, inspired by Scott's phonautograph, was working on the gramophone, the direct ancestor of the phonograph, as it became known after the turn of the century. Berliner used a method of photoengraving to etch grooves onto a metal plate. Since he first had to make a metal cylinder for recording, straighten it out for photoengraving, then roll it up again for reproduction, he eventually did away with the cylinder and opted for the convenience of recording on a flat disc instead. Berliner also did away with the photoengraving process, replacing it with a method of plating and duplicating discs similar to the one used in contemporary record pressing plants.

Berliner solved several problems faced by the early phonograph industry. First, he made possible the duplication of records from one master record. The result was the mass production of recordings, which set the scene for the rise of the recording industry. Another result, however, was the separation of recording and reproduction. Second, the recording of discs was no longer a directly acoustical process, but partly a mechanical one. Although the master record's grooves were cut by the stylus, each subsequent record's grooves were not. The grooves were etched by the acid bath, and not cut into the disc by the acoustical energy acting upon the stylus. Third, Berliner's method used grooves that spiraled around the disc and moved laterally, not up and down, increasing fidelity. The result was that louder sounds could be recorded and correspondingly louder volumes reproduced.

Between 1879 and 1885, Bell, while working on the graphophone, attempted magnetic recording and succeeded in recording on tape. Perhaps due to Edison's moderate success with the phonograph, however, Bell abandoned magnetic recording in favor of cylinder recording.

The first practical magnetic recorder was invented by Danish inventor Valdemar Poulsen in 1898, and patented in America in 1900. Its connection to the phonograph is unmistakable, as it employed a cylinder wrapped with magnetic wire. A recording head revolved around the cylinder, magnetizing the wire. Even the name Poulsen chose for the device, the telegraphone, places it alongside the phonograph and telephone.

The general principle of magnetic recording rested on the polarization of metallic particles on a piece of wire (later a length of tape). The orientation of the particles could be altered by passing the wire before a magnetic recording head (itself magnetized by an electrical current resulting from acoustical energy), thereby encoding a signal on the wire. Passage of the wire before a playback head, one sensitive to the particles' orientations, resulted in a reversal of the process. The magnetized particles would set up an electrical current which could be converted into sound.

Several important differences from the phonograph were apparent in magnetic recording. First, the wire could be erased by passing it through a strong magnetic field and could be recorded over without difficulty. By contrast, the wax on a cylinder or disc had to be melted before re-recording could be done.

Second, the recording was of a strictly electrical nature, as opposed to the phonograph's mechanical form of reproduction. The phonograph took sound and converted it into mechanical energy to encode the sound in the form of grooves on a cylinder or disc. The signals encoded onto the magnetic recorder's wire were converted from mechanical energy to electromagnetic energy.

Perhaps most importantly for popular music's development, the magnetic recorder's wire was more suitable for editing and splicing. A phonograph record could be edited only in crude fashion, by starting and stopping it during recording or by attaching different cylinders. Audible pops and clicks would give away the edit points, however. A wire or tape could be cut and reattached with greater ease and better fidelity. And, importantly, minute sections could be cut and reassembled.

Work on magnetic recording proceeded slowly, in part because there was a concentration on improving the

phonograph in the early 1900s, and because the phonograph's acceptance as a device for both recording and reproducing sound meant that there was no concentrated research effort into new methods of recording.

In 1927, J.A. O'Neill received a patent for paper tape coated with a magnetic liquid, and German inventor Fritz Pfleumer developed a metallic oxide formula that adhered to paper. The stage was set for inexpensive magnetic tape. Paper magnetic tape was also extremely easy to edit and splice.

Magnetic tape itself was invented by AEG Telefunken and BASF (who first used it commercially), and presented for the first time at the Broadcast Exhibition held in Berlin in 1935. During World War II, both the Allies and the Nazis showed an interest in magnetic recording. The potential military use foreseen was, in an interesting parallel to initial predictions about the phonograph's usefulness, as a dictation system for pilots. Contrary to the assertion in most audiophile histories, magnetic tape recording was not *invented* in Germany to record Hitler's speeches; it was *perfected* there.

The mass production of tape recordings was made possible in the early 1950s, when the Ampex Corporation developed a high-speed tape copying system that could dub as many as 10 tapes at a time running at 16 times normal speed. The system was purchased immediately by RCA and Capitol Records.

As refinements continued to be made to tape recorders, different recording formats appeared. The first tape recorders could record only monophonic sound in one direction. By the early 1950s, tape heads had been developed that could record on half the width of the tape, so that it could be reversed and the other half recorded on as well. This, in turn, led to the development of two-track stereo tape recording. Stereo eventually became the high-fidelity standard. Because of mechanical difficulties, the stereo disc was not introduced until 1958 – and then it caused some confusion, primarily due to questions of its standardization and compatibility with monophonic equipment. The phonograph had not seen such innovation since the switch from acoustic to electrical phonographs in the 1920s, when the vacuum tube allowed efficient amplifier design.

With the addition of an electrical amplifying circuit as a transducer between the acoustic sound and the mechanical action of the stylus, electrical recording and reproduction made it possible to control loudness.

Recording cartridges were developed in 1930 to make threading wire recorders less difficult, but they were not incorporated in tape recorders until the late 1950s, as a means of ensuring the continued acceptance of tape despite the popularity of the stereo disc. RCA announced in

1958 that it had developed a tape cartridge that played 32 minutes and would retail for about a dollar more than a stereo disc. RCA's cartridge was the precursor of the eight-track cartridge. Although the eight-track cartridge was mass-produced in the 1960s and 1970s, it did not find acceptance among consumers. It was difficult to use for recording and it did not have an efficient means of fast-forwarding and rewinding the tape. A form of the eight-track, referred to colloquially as the 'cart,' became standard equipment in the radio industry for announcements, station identifications and advertisements.

The most widely accepted tape cartridge format to date, the cassette, was introduced by the Philips Company in 1963. To ensure standardization of the cassette format, Philips gave up manufacturing rights to anyone wanting to produce cassettes, provided they used Philips' specifications. By 1965, several companies were making cassette recorders, and reviews were favorable. Cassettes were relatively inexpensive compared with both LPs and reel-to-reel tape recorders and, as shown by the wide variety of people reportedly using them, were easy to operate. Recording was no longer solely in the domain of the technician or hi-fi enthusiast.

The transition from two-track tape decks for stereo recording and reproduction to multitrack recording was relatively quick. In 1958, a four-channel tape recorder was introduced by the Shure Brothers company. It allowed recording and playback of two separate stereo programs, one in each direction.

By 1970, engineers had adapted the four-channel system for playback in one direction, creating four-channel, 'quadrisonic' ('quad') sound. The process was difficult to duplicate with discs (like stereo, it was first available only on tape), and required special encoding and decoding equipment. Quad sound did not catch on with the public and was not well supported by the recording industry.

The four-channel recording system remained, however, and became the backbone of the recording industry. By 1967, the eight-track recorder had become the studio standard, followed by 16-, 24-, 32- and 48-track. Prices had dropped on most multitrack decks by 1980, and companies like Tascam and Fostex were aiming products like the Tascam Portastudio – a small, inexpensive four-track recorder that used cassettes – at amateur and semi-professional musicians. These units usually included a small mixing console for combining the sounds from the four tracks, and their list price was in the $1,000-$1,500 range. In 1985, Fostex introduced an eight-track deck at a list price of $1,600. Studio recording was no longer confined to the studio, and the home recording studio became financially possible.

In the early 1980s, digital audio recording began to become commonplace. Though a seemingly recent phenomenon, digital audio recording's history goes back to the invention of magnetic tape. A common use of magnetic recording was for computer data storage and instrument recording. And, of course, Morse code was the first practical digital code, consisting of dots and dashes (that is, binary ones and zeros, just as digital code for audio and data recording consists of a stream of ones and zeros).

Digital recording was not practical until the microprocessor was invented, primarily because of the enormous amount of data that had to be sorted for conversion from analog to digital and back again. By the late 1970s, microprocessors were abundant and inexpensive enough that the recording industry could begin to use them, and combinations of disc drive and tape recorders made their way into recording studios.

The audio quality of digital recordings is remarkable. Both standard (analog) tape recording and disc recording had an inherent amount of noise in the background – tape hiss for the former, and pops and clicks for the latter. Digital audio, however, is free from such noise. Although professional digital recording machines use tape to store the digital signals, the sound is not bound to the tape's limitations since it is not the signals on the tape that are reproduced (instead, the *information* is processed). By the mid-1990s, much recording was being done directly to computer hard discs, thereby eliminating the need for tape (and potential mechanical problems associated with that medium) and allowing ever-increasing manipulation of recorded music, once it was in the domain of the computer.

Consumer electronics companies initially marketed digital audio with the compact disc (CD) at the 1977 Tokyo Audio Fair. The CD was primarily a playback-only medium, consisting of an optical disc scanned by a laser. Later developments facilitated its use as a recording medium. Other optical-storage media, most notably the minidisc (MD) and the digital versatile disc (DVD – the most likely medium to supplant the CD), soon followed. Optical-storage media are particularly robust as no mechanical contact with the medium is required for recording and playback, thereby increasing longevity.

Tape recording did not disappear, however. Digital audio tape (DAT) became very popular for professional audio production, and found a niche as a data backup medium in computing applications. It did not, however, penetrate the consumer market. In 1991, several semi-professional equipment makers, including Tascam, Akai and Alesis, introduced digital multitrack recorders for the home recording studio. This represented another advance in achieving recording quality at a lower price, and it blurred the distinction between professional and amateur recording equipment.

Digital workstations, machines that record audio directly to a hard disc, have found particular favor in the audio and video postproduction industries, primarily because they are 'all-in-one' systems that embody sound recording, editing and synchronizing all in the digital domain. Although there has been occasional criticism of digital recording as sounding 'harsh' or 'unmusical,' most recordings since the mid-1990s have employed some form of digital recording at some point during the recording process. It is likely that ongoing developments in digital recording technology will continue the trend toward increased storage capacity and microprocessor power, thereby enabling more information to be stored and, presumably, making possible greater fidelity.

Bibliography

Blaukopf, Kurt. 1982. *The Phonogram in Cultural Communication: Report on a Research Project Undertaken by Mediacult.* Wien: Springer-Verlag.

Chanan, Michael. 1995. *Repeated Takes: A Short History of Recording and Its Effects on Music.* London and New York: Verso.

Denisoff, R. Serge. 1975. *Solid Gold: The Popular Record Industry.* New Brunswick, NJ: Transaction Books.

Hammond, John. 1977. *John Hammond on Record.* New York: Summit Books.

Jones, Steve. 1992. *Rock Formation: Music, Technology and Mass Communication.* Newbury Park, CA: Sage Publications.

Martin, George. 1979. *All You Need Is Ears.* New York: St. Martin's Press.

Tobler, John, and Grundy, Stuart. 1982. *The Record Producers.* New York: St. Martin's Press.

Wexler, Jerry. 1993. *Rhythm and the Blues: A Life in American Music.* New York: Knopf.

STEVE JONES

Sound System

At the heart of reggae lies the sound system. In the early days of the phenomenon, during the late 1940s and early 1950s in Jamaica, a sound system was scarcely more than a turntable, an amplifier and a pair of speakers, playing the latest in US rhythm and blues (R&B) (sprinkled with the odd swing and calypso title) before a largely working-class audience. At the beginning of the twenty-first century, the 'sounds' (as they are commonly known) can be large-scale entertainment packages, replete with powerful equipment and crew, touring internationally and attracting a large and enthusiastic following, not unlike supporters of a soccer team. Popular sound systems may consist of more than one 'set' of equipment, enabling simultaneous performances in more than one location. Whether large or small, however, sound systems are the most central institution in reggae, the focal point of audiences and artists alike.

From the start, exclusivity was at a premium. Being able to play obscure US records was one sure way of staying ahead of the fierce competition. As the supply of suitable – i.e., rare – discs began to dwindle in the late 1950s – due in part, paradoxically, to their increased availability (greater numbers of informal importers, larger quantities) and to changing tastes in the United States (rock 'n' roll superseding the beloved 'boogie' of the late 1940s and early 1950s) – creating one's own original material became a necessity. Thus, early sound system entrepreneurs soon found themselves to be the backbone of a fledgling recording industry. Leading operators, such as the legendary Coxsone 'Downbeat' Dodd, Duke 'The Trojan' Reid and Prince Buster, were effectively Jamaica's first record producers. Adaptations of US R&B, mixed with local idioms such as *mento* and calypso, metamorphosed into ska, arguably Jamaica's first modern popular music style (and before long the first indigenous staple of the sound systems).

In the sound systems, a distinction between 'selectors,' who spun the records, and 'DJs,' who talked in between and over them, began to emerge. With the phenomenal success of U Roy (and a host of other DJs in his wake) around 1970, DJing (or 'toasting') on record became reggae's most popular idiom. As virtually anyone, in the permissive environment of the dance hall, could practise being a DJ by chatting over the 'version' sides of the records, young hopefuls were plentiful. Thus, the sound systems became not just the major vehicle for the dissemination of popular music in Jamaica, but also its most important recruiting and testing ground.

In the early 1980s, as the emphasis shifted toward performers rather than the records being played, the sound systems became a showcase for live DJs and (to some extent) singers. Many (but not all) of the performers that were popular in the dance halls went on to become highly successful recording artists as well. In the late 1980s, the 'rhythm' phenomenon took off in earnest; that is, sound system selectors began stringing together different cuts of popular 'rhythms' – the common musical backgrounds that underlie virtually all reggae – into uninterrupted sequences of dance music, a practise known as 'juggling.' In so doing, successful selectors took center stage, becoming stars in their own right. The DJs largely retreated to the recording studio (and to stage shows).

One striking aspect of sound systems' interaction is their intense rivalry, institutionalized in oft-occurring 'clashes,' major ones taking place not just in Jamaica, but in London, New York and Yokohama as well. A clash usually consists of two or more sound systems taking turns playing records, initial rounds lasting perhaps 30 minutes each. As the clash continues, the time allotted to each contestant decreases until, in the final round, the participants play 'one, one' (or 'dub fi dub'), 'drawing' one record at a time. The discs played, at least by the larger sound systems, are invariably 'specials,' one-off recordings of well-known songs by famous artists cut on acetates, with key segments of the lyrics altered to 'big up' (praise) the sound system (and selector) in question. Usually, the clash winner is elected by audience response, measured, quite literally, by the cheers of approval (or jeers of derision, as the case may be) that each participant's choice of music has received. Equally important is the presentation, in particular the selector's spoken introductions. These may range from a refined, almost 'scholarly' approach – as personified by British one-man sound system David Rodigan – to downright verbal abuse (frequently along sexual lines).

For many years a local affair, confined to Jamaica and the Jamaican diaspora – the first British sound system, Duke Vin's, had already begun operating in 1955 – sound system culture had become a truly global phenomenon by the early 1990s. Indeed, two Japanese sound systems, Mighty Crown and Judgement Sound Station, won important international clashes in New York and London, respectively, in the late 1990s. Also noteworthy is the impact of the sound systems on British-Asian music culture in the United Kingdom in the late 1990s and early 2000s.

Sound system nights are invariably recorded; cassettes (and, more recently, CDs and even videotapes) of major events – typically distributed through highly informal channels – will be for sale, at home and abroad, within weeks of their taking place. Since the mid-1970s, a brisk trade has existed in so-called 'yard tapes,' which, although no doubt illicit by major record company standards – and certainly decried by Jamaican producers – serve both as musical newsletters and as career opportunities for a large number of middlemen and small-time entrepreneurs.

A list of important Jamaican sound systems would include: in the 1950s: Tom The Great Sebastian, Count Nick The Champ; in the 1950s and 1960s: Duke Reid The Trojan, Sir Coxsone Downbeat, Prince Buster's Voice of the People; in the 1960s: Sir George The Atomic; in the 1960s and 1970s: King Tubby's Hometown Hi-Fi, Lord Tippertone, El Paso; in the 1970s and 1980s: King Stur Gav, Jack Ruby, Gemini; in the 1980s: Volcano, Virgo, Youth Promotion, Stereophonic; in the 1980s and 1990s: King Jammy's Super Power, Jahlovemusik, Black Scorpio, Metromedia, Stone Love, Killamanjaro; in the 1990s: Bodyguard, Bass Odyssey. Some of the sound systems of the late 1970s – Stone Love and Killamanjaro, most notably – were arguably at the peak of their popularity in the early 2000s, their careers lasting over a quarter of a century.

In reggae, listening to recorded music rather than live performances has been the dominant practise since its inception. In this context, the humble 45 rpm single has remained an important soundcarrier into the twenty-first century. Over the years, live performance by DJs and singers, often in an atmosphere of informal but high-spirited and competitive communality, has commonly taken place over a background of prerecorded music played by a sound system in the archetypal 'dance hall' or 'blues dance' setting, rather than to the accompaniment of 'live' musicians in concert. Although the 1990s saw many big names respond to international success by adopting an 'imported' mode of performance – i.e., appearing with a 'live' band – the sound systems, too, have increasingly become major players in the worldwide spread of reggae, particularly in its latest embodiment, 'dance hall' (or 'ragga'). As outlets for new records, testing grounds for budding talent and the main arenas where the characteristically intimate encounter between audience and performer takes place, the sound systems have been crucial to the development of reggae. In spreading Jamaican popular music, as well as in offering an alternative blueprint for the distribution of recorded dance music more generally, their importance cannot be overestimated.

Bibliography

Back, Les. 1996. '"Inglan, Nice Up!": Black Music, Autonomy and the Cultural Intermezzo.' In Les Back, *New Ethnicities and Urban Culture: Racisms and Multiculture in Young Lives*. London: UCL Press, 183–235.

Barrow, Steve, and Dalton, Peter. 1997. *Reggae: The Rough Guide*. London: Rough Guides Ltd.

Bradley, Lloyd. 2000. *Bass Culture: When Reggae Was King*. London: Viking.

Chude-Sokei, Louis. 1997. 'The Sound of Culture: Dread Discourse and Jamaican Sound Systems.' In *Language, Rhythm, and Sound: Black Popular Cultures into the Twenty-first Century*, ed. Joseph K. Adjaye and Adrianne R. Andrews. Pittsburgh, PA: University of Pittsburgh Press, 185–202.

Hawke, Harry. 1998. Liner notes to *When the Dances Were Changing: Hitbound Selection*. Pressure Sounds PSCD 22.

Kaski, Tero, and Vuorinen, Pekka. 1984. *Reggae Inna Dancehall Style*. Helsinki: Black Star.

Larkin, Colin, ed. 1998. *The Virgin Encyclopedia of Reggae*. London: Virgin.

Stolzoff, Norman C. 2000. *Wake the Town and Tell the People: Dancehall Culture in Jamaica*. Durham, NC: Duke University Press.

Discography

A Dee-Jay Explosion in a Dancehall Style. Heartbeat HBEA 04. *1982*: USA.

Junjo Presents a Live Session with Aces International. Volcano. *1983*: Jamaica. Reissue (with extra tracks): *Junjo Presents a Live Session with Aces International*. Greensleeves GREWCD 48. *2001*: UK.

King Stur-Gav Sounds: Live at Clarendon J.A. Dance Hall Styles Records/Vista Sounds DHS 004. *1983*: UK. [The label has the title *King Stur-gav Sounds Live at Four Paths Clarendon*.]

When the Dances Were Changing: Hitbound Selection. Pressure Sounds PSCD 22. *1999*: UK.

HASSE HUSS

Synthesizer

A synthesizer is a musical instrument that generates sound electronically and usually contains a number of components that can be programmed by the user to control, shape or modify the sound.

Prior to the late 1960s, the use of electronically synthesized sound had been largely the province of avant-garde and, to a lesser extent, film and commercial music composers. As a consequence, most early synthesizers were developed primarily as tools for musical composition in electronic studios, and they sometimes required specialized knowledge in the use of abstract control languages. However, by the 1970s, a number of manufacturers had begun to introduce instruments designed for live performance and, as a result, synthesizers became increasingly used in popular music. Most synthesizers of this period were analog in design, producing and modifying sounds through the application of continuous electronic voltages and waveforms, and were played via conventional organ-like keyboards. During the 1980s, digital principles became dominant in synthesizer design, resulting in greater variety and precision in the production of electronic sounds in live performance, on the one hand, and in the ability to connect synthesizers to personal computers, thus creating elaborate studio production systems, on the other.

Synthesizer History

Among the best-known, and perhaps the most significant, names in the early period of analog synthesizers is that of Robert A. Moog. Working in Traumansburg, New York in the mid-1960s, Moog was a key figure in the development of the modular, voltage-controlled synthesizer. (Other individuals working independently of Moog, and one another, on similar devices during the same period included Donald Buchla in San Francisco and Paolo Ketoff in Rome, Italy.) Moog's early synthesizers integrated the various components used in the creation of electronic sounds – such as oscillators, filters and amplifiers – and applied electrical voltages to control their various characteristics (for example, keyboards and envelope generators produced voltages that could be used to change the pitch and dynamic contour of electronic waveforms). While Moog's large, modular synthesizers were already being used in commercial studios by the late 1960s, it was his introduction of the Minimoog in 1970 that shifted the emphasis of synthesizer design toward the needs of live performance, thus paving the way for the wider acceptance of synthesizer technology within popular music. Most of the early modular systems included a large number of sound-generating and modifying components, and users employed patch cords to configure and connect the various components with one another. In performance systems, the overall number of components was generally reduced, and internal, hard-wired connections were used, thus trading sound-generating power and flexibility for simplicity and ease of use.

During the 1970s, a number of other manufacturers introduced synthesizers designed for live performance. Among the best-known were ARP Instruments, Oberheim Electronics and Sequential Circuits in the United States; EMS (Electronic Music Studios) in Britain; PPG in Germany; and the Roland Corporation and Korg in Japan.

Among the most significant developments in synthesizer design during the 1970s was the introduction of polyphonic keyboards. Keyboard synthesizers of the late 1960s and early 1970s were monophonic (capable of producing only one note at a time) and thus were limited mostly to playing single, solo lines. Polyphonic keyboards, making use of microprocessor technology, increased the number of simultaneous voices that could be played and contributed to the growing popularity of synthesizers among popular musicians.

While many synthesizer manufacturers began using microprocessor technology in a limited fashion to control various aspects of analog synthesizers, the first all-digital synthesizers were also developed during the late 1970s. Digital synthesizers use discrete units of information to describe and modify the characteristics of a waveform; at the output stage, this information must be converted into an analog electrical signal so that it can be fed to an amplifier and loudspeakers. Early digital synthesizers included the Synclavier, based on previous designs developed at Dartmouth College in the United States and made available commercially in 1976, and the Fairlight CMI (Computer Music Instrument), developed in Australia and introduced in 1979. Both could be played via conventional keyboards or programmed with computers and cost US$30,000 or more, and were thus too complex and expensive for the average musician. They nevertheless had an important impact on popular music through their use in commercial studios, in film music production, and by a small number of superstar performers and recording artists (including Stevie Wonder and Peter Gabriel, among others). The popularity of Fairlight CMI's digital sampling capability, in particular, set the stage for later developments in synthesizer design during the 1980s.

A number of significant developments occurred during the early 1980s that changed the nature of the contemporary synthesizer. As microprocessor technology became cheaper and more powerful, manufacturers began increasing the use of digital circuitry in order to make synthesizer technology more stable, economical and easier to use. The manufacturers pursued an aggressive economic and technological strategy that saw the lowering of the cost of synthesizers and samplers, expanded capabilities and an ever-increasing capacity to store and reproduce prefabricated sound programs. The development of this latter capacity coincided with a subtle shift in the way in which musicians were regarded by manufacturers: no longer considered programmers of original sounds, they were increasingly viewed as consumers of prefabricated sounds, and a small cottage industry developed to meet the supposed needs of this new market. Finally, with the introduction of musical instrument digital interface (MIDI) in 1983, the ability to use multiple synthesizers, drum machines and samplers in conjunction with one another and with personal computers was greatly enhanced, thus stabilizing the synthesizer marketplace and offering greater creative possibilities to musicians. More importantly, it allowed electronically generated music to become part of a complete production system, modeled on the multitrack studio, and to become more fully integrated with conventional sound recording than ever before.

The success of these various strategies in expanding the popular market for synthesizer technology can be gauged, in part, by comparing the sales figures of the Minimoog, one of the most popular synthesizers of the 1970s, which sold approximately 12,000 units during the course of the entire decade, and the Yamaha DX7, introduced in 1983, which sold more than 200,000 units in just over three years. In the years that followed, other synthesizers – notably the Roland D series (beginning with the D-50 in 1987) and the Korg M-1 (1988) – would exceed the market success of even the DX7. The Roland and Korg instruments marked a shift in the basic design of the sound-producing capability of contemporary syn-

thesizers: both incorporated prerecorded musical instrument samples, as well as electronic waveforms, as the basis for sound generation. The use of samples enhanced the instruments' ability to imitate conventional instrument sounds and transformed most synthesizers into little more than sample playback instruments well into the 1990s.

At the same time as these developments were taking place in popular music production, large music and consumer electronics corporations, such as Yamaha and Casio, were introducing portable electronic keyboards into the consumer marketplace. While regarded by many as mere toys (and distinguished from synthesizers designed for the professional market by their relative lack of facilities available to the user for programming sounds), portable keyboards increased in popularity throughout the 1980s, almost completely displacing the amateur home organ market. Casio alone is reputed to have sold some 15 million instruments by the end of the decade. The cultural impact of these instruments is immeasurable, and must be counted among the factors contributing to an acceptance of electronic sounds in popular music among amateur musicians and fans alike.

The Role of Synthesizers in Popular Music

Initially, synthesizers were regarded as solo instruments (in part, because of their monophonic limitations) and valued for their ability to create novel sounds and textures. In the early 1970s, rock and jazz keyboardists such as Keith Emerson (of Emerson, Lake and Palmer), Rick Wakeman (of Yes), Stevie Wonder, Chick Corea and Herbie Hancock, among others, made frequent use of analog synthesizers in instrumental solos, and sometimes used the instruments to produce bass lines and other musical parts. In order to increase the musical effectiveness of synthesizers, many players used multiple keyboards in both live performance and studio recording. While such uses of the synthesizer might be considered extensions of conventional instrumental technique, a more experimental approach – which placed greater emphasis on sonic exploration – was adopted by groups such as Pink Floyd and Tangerine Dream.

The use of synthesizers in the production of popular music was not without its opponents, and a campaign against their use in recording was mounted by the musicians' union, which regarded synthesizers as a threat to the livelihood of conventional studio musicians. Such criticism increased as adverse reactions to disco music, which often prominently featured synthesizer sounds, arose during the mid-1970s. Despite such resistance, by the end of the decade analog synthesizers had become a central element in the sound of a variety of experimental rock and electro-pop bands, including Kraftwerk, Devo, Cabaret Voltaire, Yellow Magic Orchestra, Depeche Mode and Human League.

Throughout the early 1980s, synthesizer-based popular music continued to be regarded by many, particularly the rock press, as 'cold' and 'inhuman.' However, with the increasing popularity of digital synthesizers, electronic sounds began to appear in a surprising number of pop genres. For example, the 1980s folk-derived style of Suzanne Vega's music was defined by a combination of acoustic guitar and synthesizers – a combination that would have been unheard-of a decade earlier. An increasing emphasis on the use of synthesizers (and MIDI sequencing) was also evident in a variety of popular dance music styles, such as techno, that emerged during the late 1980s and the 1990s. In these ways, synthesizers have not only achieved a permanent status within popular music, but have also come to play an influential role in the development of new popular music styles.

Bibliography

Anderton, Craig. 1988. '20 Great Achievements in 20 Years of Musical Electronics, 1968–1988.' *Electronic Musician* 4(7)(July): 28–97.

Darter, Tom, and Armbruster, Greg, eds. 1984. *The Art of Electronic Music*. New York: William Morrow.

Holmes, Thomas B. 1985. *Electronic and Experimental Music*. New York: Charles Scribner's Sons.

Théberge, Paul. 1997. *Any Sound You Can Imagine: Making Music/Consuming Technology*. Hanover, NH: Wesleyan University Press/University Press of New England.

Vail, Mark. 1993. *Vintage Synthesizers*. San Francisco: Miller Freeman Books.

PAUL THÉBERGE

Theremin

The theremin was one of the first electronic instruments to achieve a significant level of distinction during the first half of the twentieth century, primarily because of its unique sound and the unusual technique required to play it. Also sometimes known as the 'etherophone,' the theremin was invented in Russia in 1919 by Leon Termen (corrupted to 'Theremin' when he moved to the West) and has continued to be in limited use. Simple in its design, the instrument uses vacuum tube oscillators to create a pure, sweeping electronic tone, the pitch and volume of which can be controlled when the player waves his/her hands in the vicinity of two radio-like antennae.

The theremin has never been widely adopted by professional or amateur musicians. However, its powerful electronic tone, often employing wide vibrato and pro-

nounced glissando effects, and the mysterious method required to play it add an element of bizarre theatricality to performance and may account, in large part, for the interest the instrument has generated as a novelty device. The instrument's novelty status has been all the more reinforced by its occasionally evocative, though primarily anecdotal, use in science fiction, suspense and psychodramatic films of the 1930s and 1940s – *The Day the Earth Stood Still* or Miklos Rózsa's score to Hitchcock's *Spellbound*, for instance – and by its even more rare appearances in popular music, such as in the Beach Boys' 1966 hit, 'Good Vibrations.'

During the 1990s, there was a revival of interest in the theremin due to a retro aesthetic dominant in various genres of popular music, a renewed interest in alternative methods of controlling synthesized sound and, perhaps most important, the continued availability of theremin technology as a result of the manufacturing expertise and long-standing enthusiasm of synthesizer innovator Robert Moog (Hayward 1997). With the recent attention lavished on the instrument, it appears that the theremin is one of the few instruments from the early days of musical electronics that has survived, albeit in a limited capacity, into the twenty-first century.

Bibliography

Darter, Tom, and Armbruster, Greg, eds. 1984. *The Art of Electronic Music*. New York: William Morrow.

Hayward, Philip. 1997. 'Danger! Retro-Affectivity!': The Cultural Career of the Theremin.' *Convergence: The Journal of Research into New Media Technologies* 3(4) (Winter): 28–53.

Mackay, Andy. 1981. *Electronic Music*. London: Harrow House Editions.

Discographical References

Beach Boys, The. 'Good Vibrations.' Capitol 5676. *1966*: USA.

Spellbound (Original soundtrack). DCC 116. *1990*: USA.

Filmography

The Day the Earth Stood Still, dir. Robert Wise. 1951. USA. 92 mins. Science Fiction. Original music by Bernard Herrmann.

Spellbound, dir. Alfred Hitchcock. 1945. USA. 111 mins. Romantic Mystery. Original music by Miklos Rózsa.

Theremin: An Electronic Odyssey (TV documentary), dir. Steven M. Martin. 1993. 90 mins.

PAUL THÉBERGE

Track

In its original sense, the term 'track' refers to a separate strip along the length of a magnetic tape that can contain a discrete audio recording. A stereo tape recording has two 'tracks' – one containing the left channel audio and the other, the right; a conventional audio cassette has four individual tracks – two pairs of stereo tracks – laid out in such a way that only one stereo pair can be accessed from each side of the cassette.

Multitrack tape recorders can have as many as 48 simultaneous tracks available. In the studio, the term 'track' is often used figuratively to refer to the entire process of recording overdubs on multitrack tape – as in 'laying down tracks' – or to an individual performance – 'a great drum track.' The term is also used in MIDI sequencing and in audio recording on computer hard discs, even though neither makes use of a linear medium such as tape.

The term is also used to refer to an individual selection on an album.

PAUL THÉBERGE

Transposer

A transposer allows notes played on a digital piano or synthesizer to be shifted up or down an octave or to an entirely different key. A transposer can be used to extend the playable range of a synthesizer or to transpose an accompaniment to suit the range of a singer or instrumentalist – for example, allowing a performer to play in the key of C while having the pitches sound in the key of A. Many digital pianos, synthesizers and sequencers have transposer functions built into their operating systems; however, a number of manufacturers have also marketed stand-alone hardware devices designed to transpose MIDI note data.

PAUL THÉBERGE

Vocoder

The vocoder is an electronic device that combines the sonic characteristics of a speaking or singing voice with another sound source (most often a synthesized sound), creating an unusual-sounding hybrid between the two. While it has never achieved the status of a mainstream instrument in any particular genre of popular music, the device has nevertheless been used to good effect by a variety of popular musicians, especially those whose musical style depends significantly on the use of electronic musical instruments.

Invented in 1940 at Bell Labs, the vocoder was originally developed as a device to improve voice transmission over telephone wires. When a vocal signal is input to the device through a microphone, it is analyzed by a series of parallel, narrow-band filters. These filters break the signal down into a set of frequency and amplitude components that can then be used to modulate a second, unrelated signal. As a result, the second sound, while retaining much of its original timbre, appears to 'speak' with the characteristic articulation and inflection of a human voice. It was not until almost a decade later that the musical potential of the device began to be recognized, albeit in a limited fashion, by avant-garde composers, first in Germany and then elsewhere.

With the increasing use of analog synthesizers in popular music during the 1970s, a number of electronic instrument suppliers also began manufacturing vocoders. While the devices differed greatly in sound quality (depending on the quality and number of filters employed), capability and ease of use, they nevertheless achieved a limited market success. One such instrument, the Korg VC-10, achieved a measure of popularity because it was simple to use, relatively inexpensive and completely self-contained: the unit included a microphone, filter and synthesizer circuitry, as well as a small, integrated keyboard. During the 1970s, the vocoder found its way into a surprising range of popular music: from the 'robotic,' electro-pop style of Kraftwerk to the more mainstream sound of Stevie Wonder and the Electric Light Orchestra; from the dance music of Giorgio Moroder to the fusion jazz of Herbie Hancock. Often, the device was valued for its ability to 'dehumanize' the voice, giving it a synthetic or machine-like quality.

After its initial introduction in the 1970s, the vocoder found occasional uses in the music of artists such as Laurie Anderson and the Beastie Boys, and even experienced something of a revival in dance music productions of the late 1990s, where the use of electronic instruments was central to the genre. The history of technology is full of curiosities, but perhaps none is so remarkable as the vocoder, a device that never found significant uses in the telephone industry but could, some 60 years later, make notable contributions to dance-inspired hit singles by popular artists such as Cher ('Believe') and Madonna ('Music').

Discographical References

Cher. 'Believe.' *Believe*. Warner Brothers 47121. *1998*: USA.

Madonna. 'Music.' *Music*. Maverick 47598. *2000*: USA.

Discography

Anderson, Laurie. 'O Superman (For Massenet).' *Big Science*. Warner Brothers XBS 3674. *1982*: USA.

Beastie Boys, The. 'Intergalactic.' *Intergalactic [UK]*. Grand Royal 85856. *1998*: UK.

Electric Light Orchestra, The. *Out of the Blue*. United Artists UAR 100. *1977*: UK.

Hancock, Herbie. *Sunlight*. Columbia 34906. *1978*: USA.

Kraftwerk. *Radio Activity*. Capitol SW-11457. *1975*: USA.

Kraftwerk. *The Man-Machine*. Capitol SW-11728. *1979*: USA.

Moroder, Giorgio. *From Here to Eternity*. Casablanca 7065. *1977*: USA.

Wonder, Stevie. 'Ebony Eyes.' *Songs in the Key of Life*. Motown MOT2-340. *1976*: USA.

PAUL THÉBERGE

Workstation

'Workstation' is the term commonly used to describe a keyboard synthesizer/sampler with an integral sequencer and removable storage device. The term is also applied to a desktop computer with added audio/audiovisual production tools. In popular music, the workstation functions as a portable self-contained music production center, integrating all the necessary components into one housing, allowing sound design and modification, and the realization, storage and retrieval of composed ideas. Although workstations are self-contained, a MIDI interface enables both keyboard and sequencer to control external devices (a sampler or drum machine, for example), while allowing an external sequencer to drive the workstation's internal sound module. Although most workstations incorporate a full-size five-octave keyboard, palm-size versions are becoming increasingly popular. The Yamaha QY70 is a good example, providing a miniaturized two-octave keyboard, 24 sequencer tracks, 32-note polyphony, a drum machine, and over 2,000 pre-programmed phrases and patterns (drumbeats, bass lines, keyboard riffs).

JONTY STOCKDALE

Part III
Musical Instruments

8. Found Instruments

Found Instruments

Under this term, derived from Marcel Duchamp's concept of *art trouvé* (found art), may be classed those natural phenomena and manufactured artifacts that have been used for their musical potential. Of these, chest-beating, thigh-slapping, finger-snapping and foot-stamping by the performer are the most accessible, and the most widely employed. But beyond the human body, animal parts have been extensively used – from the conch-shell horn in the Pacific Islands to the Caribbean mule's jawbone with loose teeth – the teeth played as a rattle, or as a scraper with a stick drawn across them. Thighbones have often been used as drumsticks and animal horns as trumpets.

Found objects of diverse kinds have also been employed as musical instruments, with minimal modification or adaptation. Lithophones, or 'musical stones' made of an array of small rocks of different geological type, in shapes and sizes that produce distinctive sounds when struck, are applied to music-making in Togo and other countries, as are hollow logs. Perhaps the most numerous of these natural resources are the leaves and blades of grass that are held vertically between the thumbs and, placed before the mouth, are blown as a mirliton. A similar technique has been observed in Turkey, where a knife blade, or sword blade, has also been employed. In Australia, the gumleaf – the leaf of the eucalyptus tree – is used as a form of reed against the mouth to produce a particularly shrill and penetrating sound, not unlike that of a musical saw or theremin but with more edge, and which a skillful 'player' can control with great subtlety to produce monodic music. It was originally indigenous, but is now played by some Caucasians. An Australian Gumleaf Playing Championship has been held annually since 1980.

It is possible that some utensils have been used as instruments as an outcome of experiments with natural objects. Domestic articles provide a rich source of instruments: a row of glass tumblers partially filled with different quantities of water has been used as a basic 'harmonica,' while cola bottles and other empty vessels have been frequently employed for percussive effects. Empty boxes have provided sharp sounds when beaten with a stick, and West African musicians have displayed considerable ingenuity in using tea-chest tops as frame drums, bicycle pumps as whistles and fish tins as bodies for *sansas*. Such improvisation in the use of available resources as musical instruments is not restricted to rural musicians. For instance, folklorist Tony Schwartz recorded a number of children's bands in New York 19 (southwest of Central Park) in the 1950s. A group of mixed races recorded in a housing-project tenement used 'one bongo drum, several chairs, a long wide bench, metal waste baskets, several sticks and an empty Pepsi-Cola bottle' to produce a rhythmically complex performance.

Household utensils have become instruments played in rural bands and even on the professional stage; as early as the 1830s, the Virginia Minstrels were using fire tongs as castanets. A large saw placed on end can be made to produce a variety of sounds by pressure on the handle, or by drawing a fiddle bow across the non-serrated edge. The playing of fiberboard suitcases with wire brushes became common, while the metal washtub, inverted so as to act as a resonator for a bass, made with a single string running from handle to broomstick, was played by African-American musicians like Dewey Corley of Memphis. It has been argued by Harold Courlander (1963) that this is of African origin; while this may be doubtful, it is undeniable that African-American musicians have been inventive in their use of familiar objects. Some objects, like the jug and the washboard, have been used widely and as a consequence are well known.

Bibliography

Courlander, Harold. 1963. *Negro Folk Music, U.S.A.* New York: Columbia University Press.

Ryan, Robin. 1999. 'Gumleaf Playing Competitions: Aboriginal and Non-Aboriginal Performance Styles and Socio-Cultural Contexts.' *Perfect Beat* 4(3): 66–85.

Schwartz, Tony. 1954. Liner notes to *New York 19*. Folkways FPS8/FD 5558.

PAUL OLIVER

Bones

The bones or, as they were known in the 1840s, the 'bone castanets' were among the simpler 'found' instruments, but ones that have been associated with minstrelsy since the earliest years. An African origin has been posited for them, though with no specific provenance offered. Curt Sachs (1940) referred to a seal from the earliest of urban settlements, Ur, nearly 5,000 years old, on which an animal is depicted playing 'a pair of short *clappers* of the kind that youths call *bones* in our country' (69; emphases in original). Bones were played in Egyptian times and their use appears to have been widespread.

However, it was with the rise of minstrelsy that bones became widely popularized, Frank Brower introducing them when accompanying Dan Emmett at Lynchburg, Virginia in mid-1841. A painting by William Sidney Mount called 'The Bone Player' (1855) depicts a player with two pairs of curved bones, their convex surfaces facing each other. These were held between the first and second, and second and third fingers of each hand, the tips of the forefingers lightly steadying one bone while the other was vibrated or 'clacked' against it. A good player could produce short, sharp sounds or rapid 'rolls' and 'trills.'

The bones were strongly associated with the minstrel show. Credit for standardizing the seating of the minstrel performers in a semicircle is ascribed to E.P. Christy, who placed a 'middleman' in the center and the 'endmen,' 'Mister Tambo' and 'Mister Bones,' at the extremities. The master of ceremonies, 'Mister Interlocutor,' generally engaged in banter with the endmen, who responded with jokes and bursts on the tambourine and bones. The bones players in particular were noted for their accomplished rhythms and expert flourishes, some – like Joe Murphy, who became the champion bones player of the west coast – becoming famous for their performances.

While expert playing might imply complex rhythms and skillful complementing of other instrumentalists, the prime duty of the bones and the tambo players was to put on a show. As explained in Rossiter (1921), 'they must be impressed with the idea that they are to make as *much motion* with as *little noise* as possible' (emphases in original). In other words, they were to make grotesque movements: '[S]haking the bones under the legs, over the head, under the arms, and behind the chair all help to make a good flash, from the front.' Players were advised to use bones that had small metal clappers on the side, which were easier to use with no loss of effect.

The bones were played as a rhythm instrument in British music halls and in US country bands. Although little regarded or recorded, bones players continued to entertain long after the demise of minstrelsy. As late as 1993, Richard Thomas from Washington, DC, a veteran buck-and-wing dancer who had been playing the bones since 1931 when he was nine years old, recorded some spirited accompaniments to the young blues singer, Michael Roach. His playing was indicative of the lively talents of the endmen of a century earlier.

One of the last players of 'dried beef bones,' John Henry 'Bones' Nobles of Beaumont, Texas, performed in the 1970s with zydeco accordionist Clifton Chenier and blues singer-guitarist Clarence 'Gatemouth' Brown. He was filmed playing with pianist Taj Mahal in 1979.

Bibliography

Nathan, Hans. 1962. *Dan Emmett and the Rise of Early Negro Minstrelsy*. Norman, OK: University of Oklahoma Press.

Rossiter, Harold. 1921. *How to Put on a Minstrel Show*. Chicago: Harold Rossiter Co.

Sachs, Curt. 1940. *The History of Musical Instruments*. New York: W.W. Norton & Co.

Wittke, Carl. 1930. *Tambo and Bones: A History of the American Minstrel Stage*. Durham, NC: Duke University Press.

Discography

Roach, Michael (with Richard 'Mr. Bones' Thomas). *Ain't Got Me No Home*. Stella Records STCD.001. *1993*: USA.

Visual Recording

'Bones' (made by Carol Munday Lawrence). 1979. Magic Lantern (MHP). 29 mins. (video).

PAUL OLIVER

Cowbell

A cowbell is a form of clapper bell that is customarily attached to a leather strap and suspended from the neck of herd animals such as cows or sheep. Cowbells are used both on animals in hilly or Alpine areas to indicate their location, and on lead animals to bring in herds for milking or to a sheepfold. Some cowbells, such as the Hungarian *csengo*, take a conventional bell form, which is distinguishable from the quadrilateral shape of the *kolomp* type. This latter type is made of sheet iron or copper, and is welded or has a soldered seam. The larger the piece of sheet metal used, the more mellow and resonant is the sound of the 'instrument.' In some Alpine regions that rely on pastoral economies and have large herds, tuned sets of cowbells mounted on a stand or a portable T-frame are used as musical instruments. Although from mouth to suspension ring they are generally wider than they are high, longer types were used in Slovenia and other regions. These are closer to the African clapperless bell, frequently termed a 'gong,' which is struck with a light hammer. Double gongs, either connected by a single arched handle or mounted one above the other, are common in West and Central Africa. This may account for the clapperless bell being used as a rhythm instrument in African-American folk bands, where the cowbell is usually attached to a washboard or incorporated in the 'traps' of a drumkit.

Bibliography

Ballassa, Ivan, and Ortutay, Gyula. 1984 (1979). *Hungarian Ethnography and Folklore*. Budapest: Corvina Kiado.

Buchner, Alexander. 1971. *Folk Music Instruments*. London: Octopus Books.

PAUL OLIVER

Jug

One of a number of improvised instruments, the jug is a domestic vessel that is employed as a bass instrument. Most effective for this purpose is a jug with a narrow neck of the 'Belamine' type with a capacity of about 2 gallons (7.5 liters). The 'seven-gallon' jug, like the seven-gallon Stetson, is more myth than reality. Blowing across the mouth of the jug produces a booming sound, which is given timbre by forcing the breath through tight lips, sometimes referred to as 'spitting,' although no saliva is emitted. Projecting the breath in this way, to different levels in the jug, alters the column of air disturbed, and a pentatonic scale can be achieved. Although usually termed a 'jug,' other vessels have been used for this purpose. Gus Cannon played a metal kerosene can, with a kazoo mounted on the handle as an alternative mirliton. Sam Jones, known as 'Stovepipe No. 1,' played a length of stove piping. Other domestic articles, from a cola bottle to a length of hose pipe, have been employed to similar effect.

Bibliography

Oliver, Paul. 1990 (1965). *Conversation with the Blues*. Cambridge: Cambridge University Press.

Discography

Cannon, Gus. *Complete Recorded Works, Vols. 1 and 2 (1927–1930)*. Document DOCD-5032, DOCD-5033. *1990*: Austria.

PAUL OLIVER

Kazoo

Technically defined as a mirliton, the kazoo is a quasi-musical instrument that closely resembles a small horn, although simply blowing into it does not produce a musical sound. Kazoos are small in size, some being about 7″ (18 cm) in length and little more than 1″ (2.5 cm) at the widest point. The typical submarine-like form of the kazoo, which is open at both ends, has a broad opening at the mouth or 'stern' end, a 'conning tower' or cup that takes a membrane, and a tapering 'prow.' The membrane may be made of animal gut or flattened reed, and is held in place by a small wire grille and the cup, which, in some types, is screwed into place. Playing the kazoo involves vocalization without the use of the lips, but growls and rasps, as well as throat singing, may be used, the kazoo imparting a buzzing tone to all the sounds. The instrument lends itself to trumpet and trombone imitations, and is often used in folk bands to achieve this effect.

The kazoo may have been a North American device in origin, possibly developed from a canebrake prototype, though made of tinned metal. It was heard at the State Fair in Georgia in 1852, although a patent was not registered until the end of the nineteenth century. Known as a 'bazooka' or 'jazzophone,' among many other terms, it was adopted by folk blues and jug bands, the banjo player and jug band leader Gus Cannon having one affixed to the neck of the kerosene can that he played as a 'jug.' Ben Ramey was a sensitive player who used the kazoo as a blues accompaniment on a number of classic recordings by the Memphis Jug Band; on some of these, including 'Newport News Blues' and 'I'm Looking for the Bully of the Town,' he played extended kazoo solos. The accomplished guitarist Tampa Red also played the kazoo, though to less effect, while many 'one-man bands' included a kazoo in their equipment. The instrument was also used in some contemporary white groups, especially the blues-influenced Allen Brothers, Lee Allen seldom recording without one. For more volume, some performers fixed the kazoo to a toy Kress horn, manufactured for a retail store company, or, like Brownie McGhee, attached it to the bell section of a trombone in order to make a 'jazzhorn.' Jazz bands rarely used kazoos, although the technique of 'blue-blowing' through comb and paper was used in jazz by Red McKenzie, who made over 70 recordings with his Mound City Blue Blowers and other groups. A hair comb wrapped in tissue or copy paper was, in some respects, better than the kazoo, for the lips could be used when blowing through the substitute membrane.

Kazoos or comb and paper were popular with some skiffle groups in the 1950s. But they had a significant precedent in England between the world wars. The kazoo, 'hooter' or 'Tommy Talker' was the lead instrument in the working-class 'Waffen Fuffen' bands of Yorkshire. Otherwise known as 'Tommy Talker bands,' these groups competed at carnivals and popular events, all the instruments being made of tin. Kazoos – often made of plastic – have continued to be made in countries as far apart as Germany and China, but have come to be generally regarded as toys.

Bibliography

Wharton, R., and Clarke, A. 1983. 'The Tommy Talker Bands of the West Riding.' *Musical Traditions* 1: 16–18.

Discographical References

Memphis Jug Band, The. 'I'm Looking for the Bully of the Town.' Victor 20781. 1927: USA. Reissue: Memphis Jug Band, The. 'I'm Looking for the Bully of the Town.' *Complete Recorded Works, Vol. 1 (1927–1928)*. Document Records DOCD-5021. *1990*: Austria.

Memphis Jug Band, The. 'Newport News Blues.' Victor, unissued. 1927: USA. Rerecording: Memphis Jug Band, The. 'Newport News Blues.' *Complete Recorded Works, Vol. 1 (1927–1928)*. Document Records DOCD-5021. *1990*: Austria.

Discography

Allen Brothers, The. *The Chattanooga Boys – Allen Brothers (Austin & Lee Allen): Complete Recorded Works in Chronological Order, Vol. 3 (1932–1934)*. Document Records DOCD-8035. *1998*: Austria.

McKenzie, Red, and the Mound City Blue Blowers. 'Hello Lola'/'One Hour.' Victor 38100. 1929: USA. Rerecording: Mound City Blue Blowers, The. 'Hello Lola'/'One Hour.' *Mound City Blue Blowers 1935–1936*. Jazz Chronological Classics 895. *1997*: USA.

Memphis Jug Band, The. *Complete Recorded Works, Vol. 1 (1927–1928)*. Document Records DOCD-5021. *1990*: Austria.

Tampa Red. *The Bluebird Recordings, 1936–1938*. RCA 66722. *1997*: USA.

PAUL OLIVER

Picking Bow/Mouth Bow

A cave painting, dating back to approximately 15,000 B.C. and discovered at Trois-Frères, France, depicts a masked dancer, probably a huntsman or a shaman, playing a musical bow. Also known as a mouth bow or tune bow, the musical bow was once regarded as a hunting bow used as a plucked musical instrument, but many

musicologists now believe that the instrument is usually made specifically for its musical purpose. In form it is similar to the hunting bow, being made of a tapering wooden wand held in a tension arc by a cord fastened at a notch at each end. The picking bow has served as a musical instrument for literally thousands of years. With one end of the bow held beside the cheek, the string may be plucked to produce a vibrating, harmonic sound, the mouth chamber being used to change or amplify it. The bowstring may be divided by being tied to the arc in unequal division to produce two notes, one division capable of being stopped with the fingers to produce three harmonic chords. The sounds may be modified by the mouth and labial movements.

Reck (1997) indicates the wide geographical spread of the musical bow by mentioning its use in ancient Greece and ancient Japan, in New Guinea (mouth bow/jew's-harp), in India (*mursang*) and among the Maidu Indians of California (although the mouth bow should not be confused with the jew's-harp). A number of musical bows in South Africa have been described by Kirby (1934): they include adapted practical bows, as played by the Angola Bushmen, and others made specifically for music-making, with strings of twisted plant fiber. Among the Swazi and the Thonga, the bowstring was usually divided by a resonator; such resonators, also used elsewhere in Africa, may be made from a calabash, a tin or even a dried-hide milk-sack. Stopping the string with the knuckle or the chin, striking the string with a stick or reed, or holding the bow end between the toes of the foot are among the techniques employed in playing the bow. Archeological evidence (cave drawings) suggests that some multiple-string instruments may be derived from a range of musical bows of different lengths played together.

Few African-American performers in the United States have been noted since the end of slavery, but a mouth bow, also termed a 'homemade jew's harp,' has been described (Evans 1990). A meter-long stick and a length of screen wire or fishing line were used to make the bow, one end of which was placed against the cheek, while the other, with a tin-can resonator attached, was held by the foot. A few white performers have been observed, including Jimmy Driftwood, who was recorded at the Newport Folk Festival playing the 'picking bow,' which he had learned from his father in Arkansas. It is possible that the picking bow relates to the diddley-bow, while the *birimbao* or a version of the 'belly harp' (musical bow with resonator) has been found in African-American communities in Brazil. Mouth bows were noted by several travelers in the nineteenth century in Brazil, where they were termed *benta* or *umcanga*. It has been stated that these were of African origin and were adopted by

Amerindians, although the instrument is no longer played in Brazil.

Bibliography

Balfour, Henry. 1899. *The Natural History of the Musical Bow*. Oxford: Clarendon Press.

Evans, David. 1990. 'African Contributions to America's Musical Heritage.' *The World and I* 5(1) (January).

Fryer, Peter. 2000. *Rhythms of Resistance: The African Musical Heritage in Brazil*. London: Pluto Press.

Kirby, Percival R. 1934. *The Musical Instruments of the Native Races of South Africa*. Johannesburg: Witwatersrand University Press.

Reck, David B. 1997. *Music of the Whole Earth*. New York: Da Capo Press.

Discographical Reference

Newport Folk Festival 1960, Vol. 1. Vanguard 2087. *1961*: USA.

PAUL OLIVER

Rattle

Among the most ubiquitous of all musical instruments, the rattle is an idiophone with loose elements that strike the main body, either internally or externally. Often made of wood or other hard natural materials, the rattle is generally used to produce a rapidly repeated and sharp sound. Among the many types of rattle are the 'vessel' or 'receptacle' type, made from a gourd or other container which may have beans or shells inside that vibrate against the wall of the vessel when it is shaken. The Central and South American maracas are of this type. Also in Central America, some functional ceramic bowls and drinking vessels have hollow feet within which are pebbles that rattle. Other vessels may have a net spread over the outer surface to which seeds or beads are attached; the whole is shaken to similar effect. Woven-basket rattles are found in Central Africa, sometimes consisting of a handle with a basket at each end. Stick rattles share the same principle, the rattle being affixed at one end of a handle; this type is used by the Kwakiutl and other peoples of Canada's Pacific Northwest, especially during rituals. Among the Hopi, a pueblo people of Arizona, animal hoofs, horns and turtle shells, in addition to gourds and pottery vessels, are used for rattles. They may contain pebbles, quartz crystals, seeds or sacred cornmeal, which act as the sound-makers (Simpson 1953, 86).

Suspension rattles are hung and vibrated, often being worn around the neck, on a wristband or at the ankles, in order to amplify the rhythms of the dance while leaving the hands free; these are popular among South Indian peoples, for example, in Kerala. Also classified as a rattle is a form of scraped idiophone, the 'cog rattle,' which consists of a simple wooden cogwheel with a small number of large teeth, set upon an axle that is also the handle. A slender wooden tongue is attached to an encasing frame, which is struck repeatedly by the teeth of the cog when the instrument is revolved rapidly. Used in Central European Orthodox churches, especially during Easter week, the cog rattle is best known as a noisemaker in parades and among soccer crowds. Its musical potential is necessarily limited.

Bibliography

Marcuse, Sibyl. 1964. *Musical Instruments: A Comprehensive Dictionary*. New York: Doubleday and Company.

Sachs, Kurt. 1940. *The History of Musical Instruments*. New York: W.W. Norton.

Simpson, Ruth De Ette. 1953. *The Hopi Indians*. Los Angeles: Southwest Museum, Leaflet 25.

PAUL OLIVER

Spoons

As an alternative to the bones, being louder and more staccato, pairs of spoons were often played as a rhythm instrument by street entertainers, and in rural music in the United States and Britain in the nineteenth and twentieth centuries. At the end of the twentieth century, spoons playing could also be found in Switzerland, Greece, Hungary, Turkey and Central Asia (Reck 1997).

The handles of the spoons were held between the extended fingers, generally of the right hand, so that the bowls were free to make contact when vibrated by wrist action. Several techniques were employed: the bowls of the spoons could be placed so that their backs made contact; alternatively, they could face each other, castanet fashion, a method more suited to wooden spoons. One spoon might be held rigid under thumb pressure, while the other clapped against it, or both might be kept loose, though under control. Different rhythms and qualities of sound could be achieved by using the free hand cupped over the top spoon, or they could be played against the leg or other parts of the body, or between cupped hand and limb.

Playing the spoons was still a 'party trick' in the 1930s, as well as being used in pierrot and amateur shows. Recordings are few, but a couple of titles, including 'Chinese Rag,' were made by the Spooney Five in Atlanta, Georgia in 1927. It probably included the spoons player Herschel Brown, who recorded with guitarist L.K. Sentell in the same city two years later. An otherwise anonymous player known as 'Kid Spoons' played on a few blues recordings at a 1935 session in Jackson, Mississippi with Robert 'Tim' Wilkins, and as one of Minnie Wallace's Nighthawks on 'Field Mouse Stomp.'

Bibliography

Reck, David B. 1997. *Music of the Whole Earth*. New York: Da Capo Press.

Discographical References

Brown, Herschel, and Sentell, L.K. 'Spanish Rag'/'Kohala Rag.' OKeh 45484. 1929: USA.

Spooney Five, The. 'Chinese Rag'/'My Little Girl.' Columbia 15234-D. 1927: USA.

Wallace, Minnie, and Her Nighthawks. 'The Cockeyed World'/'Field Mouse Stomp.' Vocalion 03106. 1935: USA.

PAUL OLIVER

Washboard

Formerly used throughout the Western world for scrubbing clothes, the 'washboard' consists of a corrugated wood or metal platen, usually with legs that stand in a washtub. Concrete washboards molded into concrete tubs have continued to be used for this purpose in Portugal and southern Spain. The antecedents of the washboard were probably the narrow, heavily ridged wooden blocks that were used in Central Europe. In the nineteenth century, African-American women sang 'rubbing songs' to the soft rhythms of scrubbing, which may have provoked young boys seeking a rhythm instrument to adapt it. As a scraped idiophone, the washboard is customarily held vertically, sometimes with another washboard placed back-to-back. It is usually played with forks, or with thimbles on the fingers, and occasionally a board may be suspended flat from a harness around the neck, and played horizontally. Attached to the wooden top of the board (which once held the soap) may be wood blocks, cymbals, cowbells or other improvised instruments. Robert Brown, known as 'Washboard Sam,' used a phonograph turntable attached to his back-to-back boards as a metallophone.

Washboards remained popular with novelty groups such as Spike Jones and his City Slickers, with blues bands and, later, with skiffle groups, especially in Britain in the late 1950s. The instrument gained new life among zydeco musicians in the 1950s, when Cleveland Chenier, brother of the celebrated accordionist Clifton Chenier, made and popularized a 'chest washboard' of corrugated sheet aluminum, worn like a vest and played with the customary thimbles. Known as the 'Louisiana rubboard,' the type has continued to be used in zydeco bands.

Bibliography

Broven, John. 1983. *South to Louisiana: The Music of the Cajun Bayous*. Gretna, LA: Pelican Publishing Company.

PAUL OLIVER

9. Guitars

Guitars

The guitar is a fretted, stringed instrument with a long history of adaptation to a wide variety of styles and sounds. Indeed, the adaptability of the guitar is perhaps its preeminent feature, as the basic six-string design has been reformulated to accommodate a number of fundamental material innovations in the construction of the instrument. That material versatility has paralleled the guitar's tonal evolution, which is most dramatically evident in the shift from acoustic to electric designs in the middle decades of the twentieth century. The combination of flexible design with timbral variability has made the guitar one of the most widely used, and widely heard, instruments in the recent history of popular music.

Basic guitar design consists of a few key features. The neck is a long, thin surface that extends from the much wider body of the instrument. On the neck are the frets, where the player places the fingers in order to sound the desired notes. At the top of the neck is the head, where the strings are attached to a number of tuning pegs (typically six), which are used to vary the tension of the strings so that they play at the necessary pitch. The neck connects to the body at what is called the heel; often, the fretboard will extend several frets beneath the heel onto the body, to allow the player further access to higher-pitched notes. Meanwhile, the body itself is primary to sound production, at least for the acoustic guitar. Body shape tends to be curved in the middle, dividing the guitar into an upper and lower bout. The body itself is hollow, except on certain electric guitar designs, and the round sound hole is typically placed just below the bottom end of the fretboard. Some distance below that is the bridge, where the strings are fixed onto the lower bout of the guitar.

Playing the guitar involves placing the fingers of the left hand onto the desired frets (right-handed players will fret with their left hands), while plucking or strumming the corresponding string with the right hand. Players typically alternate between two basic musical units, single notes and chords, the latter of which are formed by fretting notes on two or more strings and strumming those strings in unison. Historically, the strings are sounded using the bare fingers, although many players use picks – small triangular objects made of metal or plastic. Strumming chords is perhaps the most accessible and widely practised mode of guitar performance, used as it is most regularly for vocal accompaniment; picking melodies comprised of single notes is often seen to be the preserve of the virtuoso. Yet, the guitar is unique in allowing the player to alternate between these two modes of performance with relative ease.

Early History and Construction

Antecedents to the guitar can be traced back to ancient times. The musical cultures of ancient Egypt, Greece and Rome all included stringed instruments that, in the broadest sense, can be said to have given rise to the guitar. However, the guitar as an identifiable object does not seem to have existed before the age of the European Renaissance. Efforts to date the precise origin of the guitar have proven difficult due to scant historical evidence. What is clear is that the guitar emerged from the routes of economic and cultural exchange that existed between Mediterranean Europe and Arabic Asia and North Africa sometime between the fourteenth and sixteenth centuries.

Probably the most important stringed predecessors of the guitar were the lute and the *vihuela*. The lute was the favored stringed instrument of the European aristocracy during the Renaissance and the early modern era, although its origins could be traced back several centuries further. As an instrument of the 'refined' upper classes, it also became subject to increasing complexity of design and technique as the value of contrapuntal music was recognized within the elite circles of Europe. Meanwhile, Spain and Italy saw the emergence of the *vihuela* during the fifteenth and sixteenth centuries, and the instrument found particular favor in Spain, where the lute was held in lower esteem than in the rest of Europe. Whether the *vihuela* was an early version of the modern guitar or a close relative is a matter of some debate among instrument historians. Both the lute and the *vihuela* are distinguished from the modern guitar, however, by the use of double sets of strings or courses rather than the single strings that have become standard. The *vihuela* had six double courses, while the lute could have anywhere from six to 14 such courses.

Fifteenth-century Spain was also home to the four-course *guitarra*, an instrument that seems to have been the most direct predecessor of the modern guitar. The principal distinctions between the *guitarra* and the *vihuela* were the abbreviated number of courses on the former and its smaller body size. By the latter part of the sixteenth century, the smaller guitar began to expand its range with the addition of a fifth course. In line with this innovation, something approximating the modern standard tuning of the guitar also arose, with the five courses assuming the notes of A-D-G-B-E, corresponding to the first five strings of the modern guitar.

The five-course guitar spread widely across Europe during the next century and a half, finding an especially enthusiastic reception in France, Italy and Germany. During the early phases of the guitar's newfound popularity, it was used principally to strum accompaniment to popular songs. By the beginning of the seventeenth century, however, a more melodically complex style began to emerge, predicated upon picking contrapuntal lines that regularly alternated between the lower and upper registers of the guitar. Italy was the locus of these new stylistic developments. The Italian guitarist Francesco Corbetta moved the new style into the French court in the mid-seventeenth century, and from that position also exerted considerable influence on English courtly music; his two publications entitled *La Guitarre Royalle*, published in 1671 and 1674, were dedicated to the English king Charles II and the French monarch Louis XIV, respectively.

It was in these different locations, and amidst these stylistic shifts, that the guitar began to assume its current form as an instrument featuring six single strings (the first six-course guitar may well have been developed in

Spain, but it was an instrument of six double courses). Just who 'invented' the sixth string is difficult to determine, but the idea for a sixth string seems to have taken hold in a range of locations over the latter half of the eighteenth century. The new string was placed a fourth below the lowest string on the five-course instrument, and with it came what is now known as the standard guitar tuning of E-A-D-G-B-E. Other structural modifications accompanied the addition of the sixth string: a more fixed arrangement of frets on the neck of the guitar; a lengthening of the fretboard; an expansion of body size and curvature of the instrument; and a refashioning of the bridge and tuning pegs that allowed for a more secure fastening of the strings. By the turn of the nineteenth century, then, the modern guitar had truly begun to take shape at the design level, and the new instrument was poised to play a significant role in the musical life of Europe and the United States.

The Arrival of the Guitar in North America

The guitar came to the North American continent through the slave trade and the channels of imperial expansion that led to the European colonization of the Americas. Already the product of cultural exchange and collision in Europe, the guitar was to undergo a striking process of creolization within its new setting over the course of the nineteenth and twentieth centuries. Central to this process was the syncretization of African and European musical practises that formed the backbone of so much 'New World' music. When former slaves began to take up the guitar in the years after the American Civil War, and when white musicians influenced by the music of the African-American population approached the instrument during those same years, a new sort of vernacular North American music began to emerge that would dramatically shift the cultural ground on which the guitar stood. Meanwhile, the guitar would also become enmeshed in the North American system of manufacturing during the nineteenth century, and would be produced in larger and larger numbers by the latter decades of the 1800s.

During the early history of the guitar within the United States, the European imprint on the instrument remained strong. For most of the nineteenth century, the guitar featured mainly as a parlor instrument for members of the young nation's growing middle class, used primarily to play versions of European classical music 'lightened' for domestic performance and popular songs – sentimental ballads and hymns, songs from the minstrel stage – distributed by the country's nascent sheet music industry. This was the audience targeted by Christian Frederick Martin, founder of the Martin guitar company and one of the most influential guitar makers of the nineteenth century. Martin came to the United States from Germany in 1833; prior to his arrival, he had worked for some years as an instrument craftsman, and had spent some time as an apprentice and shop foreman with the Viennese guitar maker Johann Georg Stauffer.

Martin set up shop in New York City on his arrival, but relocated in 1839 to Nazareth, Pennsylvania, where the Martin guitar company has remained ever since. The first guitars built by Martin in the United States were largely modeled on the instrumental style he had learned in Europe, but over the course of the next two decades Martin guitars assumed a more distinctive cast. Martin guitars had a body shape marked by a decidedly smaller upper bout than lower bout, and also had a more modest style of ornamentation than was customary on European guitars. The most significant change in design effected by Martin was structural. He introduced a pattern of reinforcing the top of the guitar known as X-bracing, which increased the structural integrity of the instrument and also enhanced its resonating qualities. By the 1850s, the basic design of the Martin acoustic guitar was in place – a design that would have a significant influence on the subsequent development of the acoustic guitar in the United States.

While Martin represented a widely recognized peak in early North American guitar craftsmanship, it was left to the Chicago-based Lyon and Healy company to point the way toward the mass production of the guitar as a commercial object. Founded in 1864, Lyon and Healy was a large-scale manufacturer from the start, and produced more instruments during the nineteenth century than any other single company – possibly as many as 100,000 of its Washburn brand guitars a year by the end of the century. Moreover, the company claimed that its use of mechanized production allowed it to reproduce its guitars with more precision than its competitors, who had to depend 'to a large extent on their workmen, more or less at their mercy, never certain of the result, and often making dismal failures' (Wheeler 1992, citing a Washburn promotional brochure). Through such a corporate philosophy, the guitar became subject to a new degree of standardization; it also became available to a much wider range of consumers than ever before through marketing and distribution in such retail and mail-order outlets as Montgomery Ward.

African Americans and the Guitar

The post-Civil War era was also the time when African Americans first began to take to the guitar in significant numbers. Until then, the banjo rather than the guitar was the stringed instrument most readily identified with black Americans, an association that was reinforced by the prevalence of the banjo among the white performers who took to the nation's stages as blackface minstrels. Indeed, the extent to which the banjo became enmeshed in the increasingly harsh minstrel stereotypes of African Americans during the latter years of the nineteenth century may well have been a key motivation for black musicians to leave the instrument behind in favor of the guitar. Of course, the guitar also offered a significantly different type of sonority from the brighter-toned, percussive banjo – a sound whose relative fluidity fitted the changing styles of black vocalization that gave rise to the blues.

African-American approaches to the guitar offer evidence of the extent to which a musical instrument is by no means limited to the uses envisioned by its designers. As they would also do with European-derived instruments such as the trumpet and the saxophone, African-American musicians who took up the guitar took advantage of the instrument's tonal flexibility in a way that significantly expanded the instrument's range beyond that envisaged by most white players of the day. Although many African-American guitarists played in the standard guitar tuning, fingering standard guitar chords, many others began to detune the guitar into alternate tunings that prepared the way for the droning bass notes and upper-register melodic embellishments which were a prominent feature of much early blues. Black guitarists also employed techniques of string-bending and vibrato that went against the grain of the Euro-American tendency to play in accordance with the tempered musical scale that was outlined by the fret markings of the instrument. Along similar lines was the growing use of slide techniques: running the smooth edge of a bottle, the back edge of a knife or some similar material along the strings in a manner that laid bare the microtonal possibilities of the guitar. By the time of the first recorded blues in the 1920s, these techniques were already well in place among guitarists as diverse as Blind Lemon Jefferson, Charley Patton and Lonnie Johnson.

Spanish Guitars and Flamenco

While the guitar was undergoing some significant transformations on the North American continent, Spain remained a locus of guitar-based activity for much of the nineteenth century. It was in Spain that the modern classical guitar found its shape in mid-century through the work of luthier Antonio de Torres Jurado. More than previous European guitar makers, Torres concentrated on the importance of the guitar's table – the top surface – to the overall construction of the instrument. He introduced a revised pattern of 'fan-bracing' to reinforce that surface, with an increased number of wooden struts fanned out across the bottom half of the table's interior side to achieve what he believed to be the proper amount of string tension and dynamic response. Torres also increased the size of the body and the width of the fretboard to something approximating modern dimensions. The most noted Spanish guitar virtuoso of the late nineteenth century, Francisco Tárrega, was known to have played a Torres guitar, and Torres' example also gave rise to a school of Spanish guitar making that has remained one of the most important in the world.

At the other end of the musical spectrum from the development of the classical guitar was the rise of flamenco, a Spanish song and dance style with a long and complex history. Historically, flamenco is associated with the displaced *gitano* populations of southern Spain, although accounts vary concerning the extent to which *gitano* musical styles intermingled with the surrounding culture of Andalusia. By the 1840s, flamenco music had begun to be featured in local cafés and taverns, and it was in these *cafés cantantes* that flamenco became integrated into the public culture of Spain as a form of music and dance in which folk traditions mingled with entertaining spectacle. The guitar was not initially a central component of the flamenco style, but, as the music developed within the cafés, greater emphasis was placed on the guitar as a melodic and rhythmic accompaniment to the vocals and dance moves, and as a purveyor of melodic improvisation in its own right. Flamenco guitar styles became increasingly driven by a mix of syncopated rhythms and rapidly played *picados* and arpeggios, and the guitar in turn became more and more a symbol of the spirit of flamenco. Paco Lucena is credited as the first significant flamenco guitar soloist, in the days of the *cafés cantantes*, while Ramón Montoya is widely acknowledged to have modernized flamenco guitar styles in the early decades of the twentieth century.

Modern Designs

The construction of US-made guitars moved further away from classically inspired designs as the nineteenth century came to a close. One important innovation was the introduction of guitars that used steel strings rather than the traditional gut. Steel-string guitars took hold gradually, but were clearly in production by the first decade of the twentieth century. Other stringed instruments, such as the mandolin and the banjo, already made use of steel strings, so the idea of a steel-string instrument was not unique to the guitar. Nonetheless, the change in string material created instruments capable of more volume and a brighter tone than gut-string guitars – qualities that would become esteemed in the various string-band traditions that were emerging in the American South and that would become even more valued in the era of sound recording. Among the most important early makers of steel-string instruments were the Larson Brothers, based in Chicago, and the Gibson guitar company of Kalamazoo, Michigan.

Gibson was also responsible for the crafting of the arch-top guitar, one of the more dramatic reconfigurations of the guitar in the modern era. As the name suggests, the arch-top guitar was characterized by an upward curvature of the instrument's top side (the bottom was often correspondingly arched as well), in a manner evocative of the violin. Previous guitar designs had maintained a flat top surface, and the 'flat-top' guitar would remain a significant type of acoustic guitar. But the arch-top assumed a unique presence in popular music, offering the player increased volume and also a smoother, more mid-range-driven tone than its flat-top counterpart.

Orville Gibson, after whom the Gibson company was named, began experimenting with arch-top designs as early as the 1890s, and the earliest existing arch-top from 1900 bears his imprint. The early arch-tops made little impression and, when the Gibson company was established in 1902 by a group of investors who took an interest in Orville Gibson's designs, it was his patented mandolin design that was at the heart of the deal. Arch-top guitars were nonetheless included in Gibson's line of instruments from the beginning, but it was in the 1920s that the arch-top truly came into its own. The change came with the development of the Gibson L-5 arch-top guitar in 1922. Designed primarily by Gibson sound engineer Lloyd Loar, the L-5 departed from both earlier arch-tops and more general guitar styles with the inclusion of f-shaped sound holes carved into the sides of the guitar's top rather than the standard round hole placed in the center. This reorientation of the guitar's sound-producing qualities gave the instrument a unique resonance that became favored among musicians performing the commercial music of the day, especially the burgeoning jazz styles of the decade. While the banjo remained a staple of jazz rhythm sections for most of the 1920s, by the end of the decade the arch-top guitar had begun to supplant the banjo as a key element of contemporary jazz ensembles.

One prominent guitarist from this era, Nick Lucas, connected the transition from banjo to guitar to the new demands created by commercial recording. Cited by James Sallis in *The Guitar Players* (1982), Lucas noted that the banjo 'has a metallic sound, and it penetrates.' In the 1920s, when recordings were made directly onto wax cylinders with a needle imprinting the groove of the music, the sound of the banjo had to be carefully modulated lest it make the needle jump out of the groove. As Lucas recalled, the guitar presented less risk in this regard. When Lucas first used a guitar in a recording session, band leader Sam Lanin responded with relief: 'You know, Nick, it's there and it's not there. But my head-aches are over, and I'm not going to have any more trouble with the wax. From now on play the guitar.' Technology alone did not determine the use of the guitar, however, for the arch-top also allowed a more fluid style of accompaniment to develop, best heard in the mix of chordal comping and rapidly picked arpeg-gios used by Eddie Lang in his duet recordings with viol-inist Joe Venuti and nimble-fingered blues guitarist Lonnie Johnson, respectively.

The late 1920s also saw the further refinement of the flat-top guitar, as the Martin company, having clung rather conservatively to guitars built for use with gut strings, shifted its production almost exclusively to steel-string guitars by 1929. Two years later, Martin intro-duced the first of its 'dreadnought' flat-top guitar models, which would become perhaps the most widely copied acoustic guitar model of the twentieth century. The dreadnought was distinguished from its flat-top pre-decessors by its expanded body size, which in turn gave the guitar a tonal power far removed from earlier Martin designs. Whereas the arch-top became best known as a jazz guitar, the refashioned flat-top quickly became essential to the sounds of country and western, blues and folk music over the decade of the 1930s.

The 12-String Guitar

Another instrument that found favor among rural musicians of the southeastern and southwestern United States was the 12-string guitar. The modern 12-string effectively revived the concept of the double-course guitar, with six pairs of strings tuned to octaves in a manner analogous to the four- and five-string guitars from centuries past. Although the guitar had been trans-formed into a single-course instrument over time, double-course instruments such as the mandolin remained popular, and the move to create a guitar with six doubled courses was likely inspired by such instru-ments. The exact origins of the 12-string are obscure, but the instrument seems to have emerged during the last years of the nineteenth century.

The 12-string's most famous exponent, African-Ameri-can singer and guitarist Huddie Ledbetter (Leadbelly), is said to have purchased his first 12-string in the second decade of the twentieth century, and made his first recordings with the instrument in the 1930s under the auspices of folklorist John Lomax. Leadbelly recorded his best-known songs, 'Irene' and 'Rock Island Line,' in the studio of Moses Asch in the 1940s; both songs feature vigorous strumming and prominent alternating bass notes accentuated by the 12-string's unique powers of projection. Other significant early players of the 12-string were Atlanta bluesman 'Blind' Willie McTell and

Lydia Mendoza, a Mexican-American pioneer of *tejano* music. More recent performers include innovative acoustic stylist Leo Kottke and Roger McGuinn, who used a Rickenbacker electric 12-string guitar on a series of recordings with his band the Byrds in the 1960s that defined a distinctive 'folk-rock' style.

Hawaiian Guitars

Although certain guitar designs are known as 'Hawai-ian,' the term 'Hawaiian guitar' mainly refers to styles of guitar playing that are characteristically Hawaiian. The guitar had entered the musical culture of the Hawaiian islands by the 1830s and 1840s, and had risen to consid-erable popularity by the 1860s. Hawaiian guitarists, like their African-American counterparts, seem to have accommodated the instrument to their indigenous prac-tises, and in turn accommodated their musicianship to the distinctive qualities of the guitar. Two principal styles resulted from this process. The 'slack key' guitar style was predicated on slackening the guitar's strings into a variety of tunings that allowed for harmonically consonant chords to be strummed without fingering the frets. Although other musical traditions (including the blues) have also used such alternate tunings, the Hawai-ian slack key style assumed a unique character by virtue of its origin in the rhythms and melodies of the Hawai-ian chanting tradition. Meanwhile, the 'steel guitar' style involves playing the instrument by sliding a metal bar across the strings to sound the desired notes, typically with the instrument laid flat on its back in the player's lap. The effect of steel guitar playing is one in which the notes slur into one another, creating a very different sense of melody from that produced by fingering and picking clearly articulated single notes.

The techniques of steel guitar playing made unique demands on both the player and the instrument, which entailed certain modifications of the basic guitar design. Hawaiian musicians themselves adapted their instru-ments with special devices designed to raise the strings further off the neck than was typical, to eliminate the unwanted scraping sounds that otherwise resulted from running the steel bar along the fretboard. In later years, commercial guitar makers incorporated this and other features into designs that were meant specifically for Hawaiian steel guitar playing. During the 1920s and 1930s, Herman Weissenborn made some of the most dis-tinctive such guitars, characterized by the use of wood from the koa tree (a species native to Hawaii), a short, square neck, and fret markings that were flat on the sur-face of the fretboard. Weissenborn's innovations met with modest success, but were quickly displaced by a new wave of changes in guitar construction stimulated by the steel guitar concept.

Resonator Guitars

Steel guitar playing was one of the first popular guitar styles to position the guitar as a 'lead' instrument, that is, as an instrument used principally to perform melodies composed of single notes rather than the more typical alternation of strummed chords and melodic embellishments. For that reason, it is perhaps no surprise that the push to enhance the volume of the guitar significantly was largely stimulated by the needs of steel guitarists, who by the 1920s and 1930s were becoming increasingly common not just in Hawaiian performing and recording ensembles but also in the various forms of 'hillbilly' music that were taking shape. Yet, changes in playing style and technique alone do not explain the shifts in guitar design that occurred during these years. During the 1920s, the radio and recording industries both came into their own as major providers of commercial entertainment, and especially of popular music. The combination of new technologies and new techniques prompted a reconsideration of the design and function of the guitar.

The resonator guitar was one product of this historical process at the end of the 1920s. While other types of guitar had been the focus of efforts by designers to enhance the instrument's volume by increasing its size and altering its shape, the resonator guitar marked a more fundamental rethinking of the guitar's basic qualities as a sound-producing mechanism. Resonator guitars were first made under the National guitar brand, and were the result of cooperation between guitar maker John Dopyera and southern California guitar performer George Beauchamp. Beauchamp asked Dopyera for a guitar that had stronger amplifying qualities than anything available on the current market. Accounts vary as to whether the idea for the resonator guitar ultimately originated with Beauchamp or with Dopyera, but Dopyera proceeded to produce a guitar with a unique system of three aluminum cones placed on the underside of the guitar's bridge. The cones faced inward, amplifying the sound into the body of the guitar and then projecting it back out as it resonated against the metal body of the instrument (another innovation). This 'tri-cone' version of the National resonator guitar was first manufactured in 1927 in a square-neck version made for 'Hawaiian' guitarists. This version was most likely patterned after the neck on Herman Weissenborn's Hawaiian guitars, given that Dopyera had worked for a time in Weissenborn's shop.

Dopyera soon broke away from the National company over disagreements with Beauchamp, and in 1928 he founded the competing Dobro company, for which he produced another variation on the resonator guitar. The Dobro resonator guitar was distinct from its National counterpart primarily for including only a single resonator as opposed to National's original three-cone design. Dobro resonators were also shaped differently from those of National – more like a dish than a cone – and the resonating qualities of the Dobro were further reliant on a circular metal plate that supported the bridge and helped to project the guitar's sound outward. Also, unlike the National guitar's body, which was made entirely of metal, that of the Dobro version was made all of plywood, except for its resonating plate; this made the instrument cheaper to produce and also gave it a tone that was different from that of its full-metal counterpart.

Dobro instruments eventually found favor among country and bluegrass steel players such as Josh Graves, who joined the band of Lester Flatt and Earl Scruggs in the 1950s, and, more recently, prominent Nashville session musician Jerry Douglas. Meanwhile, National's own single-resonator models found considerable support among slide-playing bluesmen, with Mississippi guitarist Son House as the most influential early exponent (Chicago-based performer Tampa Red was likely the first African-American performer to record with a National guitar, but he favored the tri-cone model). Together, the National and Dobro resonator guitars gave considerable impetus to the move to make the guitar louder, although in that regard they were soon displaced by another development spurred by the Hawaiian guitar.

The Electric Guitar

The electric guitar was another product of the blending of musical and technological elements that had prompted the creation of the resonator guitar. It was also created within the same southern Californian milieu, although in this instance the first electric instrument was most likely conceived not by John Dopyera but by his associate George Beauchamp, along with two other National employees, Paul Barth and Adolph Rickenbacker. Their creation was an odd-shaped Hawaiian steel guitar, model A-22 in the new instrument line of the Electro String Instrument Corporation established by Rickenbacker, which became better known by its nickname, the 'frying pan.' Like the National resonator guitar, the frying pan was characterized by an aluminum body. However, the shape of the instrument was distinctive, with a long neck and small circular body that was the source of the guitar's nickname. By far the most significant feature of the guitar was a bar-shaped pickup that encircled the strings just above the bridge. The pickup was an electromagnet that converted the vibrations from the guitar's strings into electric currents that could then be transmitted to an external amplifying device. Although pickup designs have varied considerably over the years since the instrument's invention, the inclusion of a pickup is the defining feature of any electric guitar and, with its successful creation, the frying pan became the first significant electric guitar model, available to consumers as early as 1932.

Dobro was almost as quick as Rickenbacker to issue an electric guitar, largely due to the efforts of company instrument maker Victor Smith. (Smith himself, in an interview published in Tom Wheeler's *American Guitars* (1992), claims that the Dobro model was actually developed first.) Smith's first electric instrument was a 'Spanish body' rather than a Hawaiian model, that is, it was more the standard curved guitar shape meant to be played by fingering the frets rather than with a steel bar. By 1935, when National and Dobro had merged to form a single company, electric guitars were becoming an increasingly prominent part of the production line. However, perhaps the most important Spanish-style electric guitar from these early years was the Gibson ES-150, first produced by the Gibson company in 1936. The ES-150 was an electric version of the noted Gibson arch-top line. As Gibson's L-series arch-tops were considered among the highest-quality acoustic guitars in production, especially by professional jazz and popular musicians, the ES-150 conferred a new status on the electric guitar as an instrument of professional quality.

By the end of the 1930s, the ES-150 had been taken up by two accomplished and high-profile jazz musicians, African-American guitarists Eddie Durham and Charlie Christian. Durham, a member of Count Basie's organization, had been experimenting for some years on his own with the idea of amplification, and took to electric instruments readily when they were made available for purchase. Yet, it was Charlie Christian who first brought the electric guitar to public prominence. Having adopted the ES-150 after a meeting with Durham, Christian went on to use it on a series of recordings with Benny Goodman's small groups that established the electric guitar as an instrument suited to single-note solo improvisation. More generally, electric guitars proved to be a valuable resource for swing-era guitarists who needed to be heard amidst the expanding jazz orchestras of the day. The instrument, in its Hawaiian and Spanish versions, also found favor among musicians in the burgeoning style of western swing, a 1930s hybrid of jazz and country sounds that emerged in the southwestern United States. Bob Dunn of Milton Brown and His Musical Brownies and Leon McAuliffe of Bob Wills and His Texas Playboys were two important early exponents of the electric steel guitar, both recording with the instrument by the mid-1930s, while McAuliffe's band mate Eldon Shamblin had brought an electric Spanish model into the Wills organization by the end of the decade.

The Solid-Body Electric Guitar

Early electric guitars tended to be electrified versions of what were essentially acoustic guitar designs. Although often high-quality instruments, in the minds of their designers these earliest electric instruments fulfilled a predominantly pragmatic function, which was to make the guitar louder and thus more audible in the changing circumstances of professional performance. However, in this first era of amplification, some guitarists and designers perceived that an electric guitar need not be so closely tied to the acoustic guitar, that electricity created possibilities for sound production that were unavailable with an acoustic instrument. This recognition gave rise to the solid-body electric guitar, on which the acoustic properties of the instrument were largely displaced from the sound hole, curves and wood of the traditional guitar onto the electronic components.

As the name implies, the solid-body electric guitar is made of a solid block of wood, lacking the hollow interior that was fundamental to existing guitar designs, electric or acoustic. The rationale behind the solid-body is perhaps best explained by musician and inventor Les Paul, one of the main figures in the solid-body's development: 'When you've got the [guitar's] top vibrating and a string vibrating, you've got a conflict. One of them has got to stop, and it can't be the string' (quoted in Sievert 1977). Vibrations from the hollow body of the guitar often interfered with the clarity of the electric signal generated by the strings and pickups in these early stages of electric guitar production. The solid-body electric guitar was designed to minimize resonance from the body of the guitar, which in turn would give the instrument a more thoroughly 'electric' sound and a greater degree of tonal purity. Paul's own efforts toward this end produced 'the Log,' an odd instrument that he assembled in 1941 out of a solid plank of wood, and which is generally recognized as one of the earliest prototypes of a solid-body instrument.

Paul Bigsby, a southern California luthier, made another important solid-body prototype in the mid-1940s in association with noted country guitarist Merle Travis. However, the solid-body electric did not come to public prominence until 1950, when Leo Fender issued the first of his designs for the recently established Fender company. At first called the Broadcaster, the Fender solid-body prepared the way for a new stage in the mass production of the guitar. Fender's ideas for an electric guitar were largely influenced by the thriving country music scene in southern California, and especially by the unique sound achieved by the area's steel guitarists. Yet, his designs were most notable for their relative simplicity, which in turn made them easy to reproduce. Renamed the Telecaster shortly after its initial release,

Fender's solid-body electric soon found success, giving wider impetus to the solid-body concept. Gibson issued its first solid-body, the Les Paul (made in partnership with the guitarist), in 1952, while Fender issued another solid-body guitar, the Stratocaster, in 1954. Together, these three solid-body designs endured throughout the following decades, as the solid-body electric guitar recast the sound and look of popular music.

While the solid-body concept principally involved a change in the body of the guitar, pickup design also underwent revision in the 1950s. During the mid-1950s, Gibson employee Seth Lover created the 'humbucker' pickup, motivated by an impulse similar to that which prompted the invention of the solid-body: to reduce the unwanted noise (or 'hum') generated by early electric guitar models. In this case, the hum in question was the result not of the hollowed instrument, but of the interference that resulted from the intersecting electrical fields of the guitar and amplifier. Standard pickups of the time consisted of a single coil of copper wire wound around six small magnets, one for each string. By adding a second coil and a second set of magnets, Lover found that magnetic hum could be reduced or eliminated, since the humming signal produced by one of the coils would be canceled by the signal of the other. Humbucker pickups were incorporated into Gibson electrics by the late 1950s, although they by no means displaced the earlier single-coil designs. Rather, single- and double-coil pickups became a key mark of distinction between electric guitar models – one that paralleled hollow- and solid-body construction.

New Noises

Not coincidentally, the emergence of the solid-body electric guitar came at a time when popular music in the United States was undergoing some major transformations of its own. The new instruments were to feature prominently in the new music, first at a subcultural level and then at the level of mass culture. Subcultural shifts began to occur during the late 1940s and early 1950s in the nightclubs and recording studios of certain key urban centers, notably Chicago and Memphis. It was in these spaces that African-American musicians once again appropriated the guitar to their own musical ends, as they had done a generation or two earlier. The solid-body electric had been created out of the desire for greater tonal purity, whereas African-American guitarists such as Muddy Waters, Jimmy Rogers, Louis Myers, Hubert Sumlin, Joe Willie Wilkins, Ike Turner and Guitar Slim were often playing at the limits of their equipment, eliciting sounds that sacrificed 'purity' for volume and visceral effect. They did so in part out of necessity, to suit the noisy club environments in which their music

took shape. Yet, they also did so out of a growing recognition that the electric guitar could sound different, that it could cut against the grain of existing popular styles rather than be assimilated into their substance.

This recognition of sonic difference was to lay the groundwork for much of the guitar-based popular music of the next several decades. At this point in the instrument's history, the changes arose less from the way in which the guitar was constructed, and more from the uses to which it was put. The use of distortion or 'fuzz' among guitarists is a case in point. Distortion is what results when the electronic output signal of an amplifier becomes 'clipped' or interrupted in a way that creates an overflow of harmonic resonances. Playing through an amplifier at maximum volume tends to produce such clipped tones – such was the method favored by early electric blues players – but distortion can be achieved through other means. Willie Kizart, guitarist for Ike Turner's Kings of Rhythm, discovered distortion after he dropped his amplifier and tore the speaker cone. The distorted bass notes that he generated with the broken amplifier became a key element of the group's 1951 recording 'Rocket 88' (attributed to Jackie Brenston and His Delta Cats). Just a few years later, Link Wray punctured the speaker of his amplifier with a pencil to get a similar, if more exaggerated, effect on 'Rumble,' his 1958 instrumental.

By the 1960s, what had begun almost as a sonic accident was becoming more readily available. In England, the amplifier designer Jim Marshall and his partner, Ken Bran, began building amplifiers that were dramatically louder than existing models and also designed to produce more 'gain': the amount by which an amplifier multiplies the power of the signal transmitted by the guitar. More gain meant more ready access to distorted tones, and with their unique qualities Marshall amplifiers became coveted among rock guitarists such as Pete Townshend, Jimmy Page, Ritchie Blackmore and Jimi Hendrix. Meanwhile, electronics designer Roger Mayer began producing, for some of London's guitarists, a range of sonic-effect devices, including a distortion-inducing fuzzbox. These devices were small metal boxes containing transistor circuits that, when connected between the line that ran from guitar to amplifier, altered the electronic signal delivered to the amplifier, changing the sound. Through the use of such 'stompboxes,' as they came to be known, guitarists could summon a range of sounds previously available only through the sort of destructive resourcefulness described above or through the manipulation of tape effects in the studio. When stompboxes and more sophisticated amplifiers were popularized during the late 1960s and into the 1970s, electric guitarists in effect became their own audio engineers, as the sound of the instrument could be changed into multiple shades of noise.

For the electric guitar, then, basic guitar design has remained relatively stable since the 1950s, as the electric guitar models of that decade have continued to be the most influential. Acoustic guitar design has remained more or less consistent since the 1920s and 1930s, when the arch-top and flat-top guitars assumed their current forms. However, more and more acoustic guitars are being built with the means of amplification installed, to allow the player to forsake the use of a microphone when playing to a larger audience. In recent years, special piezo pickups have been designed to amplify an acoustic guitar so that it retains some of its 'acoustic' sound qualities rather than simply sounding like an electric guitar. Electric guitars, meanwhile, have been gradually blending with the available 'electronic' sound technologies that have come to prominence in the past three decades, although efforts to create a guitar synthesizer in the 1980s and 1990s did not lead to the production of instruments that were widely used. Rather, the sound of the electric guitar has become increasingly abstracted from its source, with distorted power chords entering into the sampling vocabularies of adventurous techno producers like the Chemical Brothers.

The Guitar in Latin America

While technological developments have moved the guitar into new sonic territories, the instrument has also continued to expand its global reach. Given the significant influence of Spanish colonialism upon Latin America, it should not be surprising that the guitar has figured prominently in many of the musical cultures of the region. As with the development of the guitar in the United States, the instrument has undergone significant indigenization in its transplantation to Latin America, which can be understood by observing the importance of the guitar in two South American countries: Argentina and Chile.

The guitar became the most representative Argentinian national instrument at the end of the nineteenth century. Influenced by other guitar traditions, local makers and aesthetics, it has come to be used in four basic musical genres: folk music, tango, jazz and rock.

In contemporary folk music, Atahualpa Yupanqui, playing guitar as a solo instrument and in accompaniment to his seminal songs, displayed a trademark vibrato along with the use of parallel thirds, closed arpeggios and a specific style of strumming. He produced an exceptional synthesis of traditional styles, mainly from the provinces of Buenos Aires and the northwest of the country. Eduardo Falú played folk music with techniques associated with classical virtuosity, while Juan Falú developed complex harmonic styles. Apart from these individual performers, a range of folk groups from the 1950s and singers of *nueva canción* (new song) in the 1960s made the guitar central to their music, as have musicians of *rock nacional*.

At the beginning of the twentieth century, the guitar formed part of the first tango ensembles. Guitar duets and trios were the instrumental base for the music of Carlos Gardel, the principal singer of tango, and this tradition continued with Edmundo Rivero. Playing with different musicians and orchestras, Roberto Grela was one of the most important tango guitarists. In 1955, avant-garde 'new tango' composer Astor Piazzolla was the first to include the electric guitar in a tango orchestra.

Argentinian jazz guitarist Oscar Alemán gained international recognition in the 1930s as guitarist with the Joséphine Baker troupe in Paris. Beginning in the late 1960s, the powerful, distorted electric guitar sounds of Pappo, and then the sophisticated techniques of Luis Alberto Spinetta, became the most influential styles among Argentinian rock guitarists. Since the late 1980s, Gustavo Cerati has been one of the most outstanding pop guitarists in Argentina.

In Chile, the guitar is played in the countryside and in the cities as an accompaniment to folk and popular songs. Two main groups of interpreters in the use of the guitar can be distinguished, one of Chilean origin and the other of international origin, according to the provenance of the repertoire.

The repertoire of Chilean origin is based on the folk performance techniques of strumming, trilling, picking, arpeggiating and tapping, and on a variety of forms of tuning. The use of the plectrum is less frequent and is exclusive to men. Soloists and folk duos maintain the various tunings and the delicacy of the peasant guitar (Violeta Parra, Margot Loyola, Víctor Jara); groups of folk song and dance use the strumming guitar (Cuncumén); quartets of *huasos* (Chilean cowboys) use the picking and strumming guitar, picking in a contrapuntal fashion with the singing, not in unison or in thirds as the peasants do (Los Cuatro Huasos, Los Huasos Quincheros); Andean groups composed of a varying number of musicians use the strumming and picking guitar to accompany the voice and indigenous Andean instruments (Inti-illimani, Illapu); and instrumental soloists perform folk root and popular music using folk and classical techniques (Sergio Sauvalle, Ricardo Acevedo).

The repertoire of international origin is played by male trios that perform mainly boleros using the *requinto* (Mexican small guitar) and two picking and arpeggiated guitars, which are played using a combination of fingers and plectrum; by male groups based on the Spanish tunas (*estudiantinas*), which use the guitar as an accompaniment to the voice and to other stringed instruments; by masculine duos of Mexican *ranchera* music, which use the strumming guitar as an accompaniment to the voice and to the accordion; by restaurant musicians of Latin American music who use the strumming, arpeggiated and picking guitar; by street singers who perform current repertoire in streets and on urban buses using the strumming guitar; and by singer-songwriters who use the strumming and arpeggiated guitar (Alberto Plaza, Eduardo Peralta, Eduardo Gatti).

The Guitar in Africa

In Africa, as in Latin America, the guitar has become integral to a number of national and regional musical styles. Perhaps the earliest distinct style to emerge on the continent was the 'palm-wine' guitar style, so named for its association with drinking and entertainment at the seaport taverns where it emerged. Palm-wine guitar was developed between the 1920s and the 1950s, largely by Kru musicians – the Kru being an African indigenous group from coastal Liberia whose work as mariners and migrant laborers brought them into contact with a wide range of musical contexts and influences. The palm-wine style was a 'two-finger' style, with the thumb and index finger of the right hand used to pick rhythmic lines and chordal patterns on the bass and treble strings of the guitar.

Palm-wine guitar had a significant influence on the formation of *jújù*, a Nigerian guitar-based music that developed in the 1930s and that has remained a major popular style. *Jújù* took shape in the cosmopolitan location of Lagos, the commercial center of Nigeria and former seat of British colonialism, and is associated with the Yoruba people of Nigeria. Although the name '*jújù*' most likely derives from the use of a tambourine in the music ('*jújù*' is the Yoruban term for the sort of tambourine used in the music, an instrument associated with European influences on local culture), the guitar was a featured instrument from the inception of the style. 'Baba' Tunde King is generally considered the most important early *jújù* performer, if not its founder, and his ensemble during the 1930s included acoustic guitar, tambourine, gourd rattle and cymbals.

The late 1940s saw the beginning of a major stylistic shift in *jújù* with the introduction of amplification, particularly the electric guitar. Ayinde Bakare was the first known *jújù* musician to attach a pickup to his guitar, and many others followed suit. Although the move to amplification modernized the sound of *jújù*, it also opened the way toward a more intensive indigenization of the music, as the new levels of sound allowed for the incorporation of a range of traditional percussion instruments that had previously been excluded from *jújù*, most notably the talking drum (Waterman 1985). These changes laid the basis for the subsequent development of *jújù* in ensuing decades, when it grew both as a symbol of Yoruban identity and as a musical style with global reach. 'Chief Commander' Ebenezer Obey and 'King' Sunny Ade achieved unprecedented levels of popularity with *jújù* during the 1970s and 1980s. By the 1980s, Ade's band, the African Beats, formed in 1966, featured 19 members, including four electric guitarists who played interlocking melody lines, as well as steel guitarist Demola Adepoju.

Guitars entered Zimbabwean music somewhat later than they had Nigerian *jújù*. By the 1950s, the acoustic guitar had become a fairly common presence in urban Zimbabwe, and it was also moving into rural villages. At first, playing styles were largely shaped by the adaptation of US and, especially, South African popular music: US country and South African jive were especially prominent influences. Eventually, such influences began to blend with the practises of the local Shona people, resulting in the indigenous style known as *jit*.

Perhaps the most important merging of tradition and modernity in Zimbabwean music came with the rise of *chimurenga* music during the mid- to late 1970s. Led by Thomas Mapfumo and his accompanying guitarists – Joshua Hlomayi, Jonah Sithole and Leonard Chiyangwa – performers in professional electric bands began drawing on longstanding traditions of Shona mbira music to re-create contemporary popular styles. The mbira is a thumb piano, the Shona version of which has 22 keys and covers three octaves. In *chimurenga*, the rhythmic and melodic functions of the mbira are redistributed among a bassist and two electric guitarists, the latter of whom commonly use the technique of string damping (subtly muting the notes by applying pressure on the strings with the palm of the right hand) to approximate the staccato attack of the mbira. Although guitarists had been playing versions of mbira music since the 1950s, the practise assumed new meaning during the late 1970s, a time of political struggle when popular music became a mode of nationalist expression for black Zimbabweans. As with *jújù*, then, the use of the electric guitar in Zimbabwe led not only to modernization of traditional forms, but also to the indigenization of popular styles of music-making.

In recent decades, Mali has become a major location of African guitar activity. Many of the guitar styles that have developed in Mali are heavily influenced by the traditional practises of the *jelis*, or *griots*, of the Mande people. The *ngoni*, a four- or five-string lute, has historically been the main instrument of Malian *jelis*, and it has continued to be prominent in contemporary Malian groups featuring the acoustic guitar. Djelimady Tounkara, long-time guitarist for the Super Rail Band, is the foremost Malian guitarist in the Mande style – a style based around the use of 'a full diatonic scale with a number of characteristic chromatic passing notes' (Eyre 1997).

Other guitarists in Mali employ scales and melodies more pentatonic in nature, leading to widespread, if sometimes exaggerated, speculation about the connection between Malian music and African-American blues. Bambara and Wassoulou music of Mali make particular use of pentatonic forms – Wassoulou singer Oumou Sangare has recently gained international prominence, although the most noted Malian performer in this connection is Ali Farka Touré, a member of the Songhai people in the northern region of the country. Touré's guitar playing is marked by the use of droning bass patterns combined with almost circular melodies played on the instrument's higher strings. In these melodies can be found the pentatonic content, although there are also passing tones that convey traces of Arabic influence on the music of Mali's northern parts. Touré has gained considerable acclaim outside Africa for his collaborations with Western musicians such as Ry Cooder, although within Mali he remains but one figure in a rich contemporary field of guitarists.

Conclusion

For most of the twentieth century, the guitar was certainly one of the definitive instruments of popular music, finding a place in a vast range of popular styles and attracting an enormous number of amateur players in addition to its professional practitioners. Even at the beginning of the twenty-first century, the acoustic guitar connotes a sort of tradition-based musicianship that has remained vital to those drawing on the wealth of various US and European folk traditions, and confers an almost automatic 'authenticity' on those popular musicians who foreground its use. The electric guitar has become enmeshed in its own traditions as electric blues and rock music continue to place the instrument in a prominent lead position. Electric guitar virtuosity was, for a time, at the peak of rock 'n' roll achievement, although it has lost some of its luster with the rise of non-guitar musics such as disco, rap and techno. Nonetheless, the guitar in both its acoustic and electric forms remains a powerful and pervasive presence in contemporary popular music, and continues to expand its reach by entering the musical styles of Africa and Latin America as well as those of Europe and the United States.

Bibliography

AA.VV. 1996. *Enciclopedia Rock Nacional 30 años de la A a la Z* [Encyclopedia of Rock Nacional: 30 Years from A to Z]. Buenos Aires: Ediciones Mordisco.

Brown, Ernest. 1994. 'The Guitar and the *mbira*: Resilience, Assimilation, and Pan-Africanism in Zimbabwean Music.' *The World of Music* 36(2): 73–117.

Carter, Walter. 1994. *Gibson Guitars: 100 Years of an American Icon*. Los Angeles: General Publishing Group.

Charry, Eric. 1994. 'The Grand Mande Guitar Tradition of the Western Sahel and Savannah.' *The World of Music* 36(2): 21–61.

Corbetta, Francesco. 1671. *La Guitarre Royalle* [The Royal Guitar]. Paris: H. Bonneüil.

Corbetta, Francesco. 1674. *La Guitarre Royalle* [The Royal Guitar]. Paris: H. Bonneüil.

Duchossoir, A.R. 1994. *Gibson Electrics: The Classic Years*. Milwaukee, WI: Hal Leonard Corporation.

Eyre, Banning. 1988. 'Soukous, Chimurenga, Mbaqanga, and More: New Sounds from Africa.' *Guitar Player* 22(10)(October): 80–88.

Eyre, Banning. 1997. 'Mali Hatchets: In Search of West Africa's Master Axmen.' *Guitar Player* 31(7)(August): 35–39.

Faucher, François. 1998–2002. *Classical Guitar Illustrated History*. http://www.info-internet.net/~ffaucher/ffaucher2/guitar_history.html

Ferré, Horacio. 1971. *El libro del tango. Historia e imágenes* [The Book of Tango: History and Pictures]. Buenos Aires: Ossorio.

Gruhn, George. 1981a. 'The Evolution of the Arch-Top Guitar.' *Guitar Player* 15(8)(August): 100.

Gruhn, George. 1981b. 'The Evolution of the Arch-Top Guitar, Conclusion.' *Guitar Player* 15(9)(September): 114.

Gruhn, George. 1981c. 'The Evolution of the Flat-Top Steel-String Guitar.' *Guitar Player* 15(7)(July): 150.

Gruhn, George, and Carter, Walter. 1993. *Acoustic Guitars and Other Fretted Instruments: A Photographic History*. San Francisco: GPI Books.

Grunfeld, Frederic V. 1969. *The Art and Times of the Guitar: An Illustrated History of Guitars and Guitarists*. New York: Macmillan.

Handa, Al. 1998a. *The National Steel Guitar, Part One: An Introduction*. http://www.nationalguitars.com/part1.html

Handa, Al. 1998b. *The National Steel Guitar, Part Three: Tampa Red and Son House*. http://www.nationalguitars.com/part3.html

Jones, LeRoi (Imamu Amiri Baraka). 1963. *Blues People: Negro Music in White America*. New York: William Morrow & Co.

Kaiser, Henry. 1984. 'King Sunny Ade: Nigeria's Juju Superstar.' *Guitar Player* 18(2)(February): 32–42.

Kanahele, George S., ed. 1979. *Hawaiian Music and Musicians: An Illustrated History*. Honolulu: University Press of Hawaii.

Kaye, Lenny, and Kuronen, Darcy. 2000. *Dangerous Curves: The Art of the Guitar*. Boston, MA: Museum of Fine Arts.

Kozinn, Allan, et al. 1984. *The Guitar: The History, the Music, the Players*. New York: William Morrow and Co.

Kubik, Gerhard. 1999. *Africa and the Blues*. Jackson, MS: University Press of Mississippi.

Lafuente, Raúl, Pesce, Rubén, and Visconti, Eduardo. 1977. 'Los guitarristas de Gardel' [The Guitarists of Gardel]. In *La historia del tango* [The History of Tango], Vol. 9. Buenos Aires: Corregidor, 1459–1545.

Longworth, Mike. 1980. *Martin Guitars: A History*. Rev. ed. Nazareth, PA: Mike Longworth.

Luna, Félix. 1974. *Atahualpa Yupanqui*. Madrid: Ed. Jucar.

Palmer, Robert. 1982. *Deep Blues*. New York: Penguin.

Palmer, Robert. 1992. 'The Church of the Sonic Guitar.' In *Present Tense: Rock & Roll and Culture*, ed. Anthony DeCurtis. Durham, NC: Duke University Press, 13–37.

Pujol, Sergio. 1992. *Jazz al sur. La música negra en Argentina* [Jazz to the South: Black Music in Argentina]. Buenos Aires: Emecé.

Rissetti, Ricardo. 1994. *Memorias del jazz argentino* [Memories of Argentinian Jazz]. Buenos Aires: Corregidor.

Sallis, James. 1982. *The Guitar Players: One Instrument and Its Masters in American Music*. New York: W. Morrow.

Schmidt, Cynthia. 1994. 'The Guitar in Africa: Issues and Research.' *The World of Music* 36(2): 3–20.

Sevilla, Paco. 1985a. 'Flamenco: The Early Years.' *Jaleo* 8(1): 17–20.

Sevilla, Paco. 1985b. 'Flamenco, Part II: The Modern Era.' *Jaleo* 8(2): 8–13.

Sievert, Jon. 1977. 'Les Paul.' *Guitar Player* 11(12) (December): 34–64.

Simmons, Michael. 1997. *The Origins of Twelve String Power*. http://www.frets.com/FRETSPages/History/12string/12stOrigins.html

Thanas, Françoise. 1983. *Atahualpa Yupanqui*. Paris: Le livre à venir.

Trynka, Paul, ed. 1995. *The Electric Guitar: An Illustrated History*. San Francisco: Chronicle Books.

Turino, Thomas. 2000. *Nationalists, Cosmopolitans, and Popular Music in Zimbabwe*. Chicago: University of Chicago Press.

Turnbull, Harvey, et al. 2001. 'Guitar.' In *The New Grove Dictionary of Music and Musicians*, Vol. 10, ed. Stanley Sadie. New York: Grove, 551–78.

Waksman, Steve. 1999. *Instruments of Desire: The Electric Guitar and the Shaping of Musical Experience*. Cambridge, MA: Harvard University Press.

Washabaugh, William. 1996. *Flamenco: Passion, Politics, and Popular Culture*. Oxford: Berg.

Waterman, Christopher. 1985. Liner notes to *Juju Roots: 1930s–1950s*. Rounder 5017.

Wheeler, Tom. 1992. *American Guitars: An Illustrated History*. Rev. ed. New York: HarperPerennial.

White, Forrest. 1994. *Fender: The Inside Story*. San Francisco: GPI Books.

'Yupanqui y Viglietti.' 1986. *La del Taller* 7: 3–4.

Discographical References

Brenston, Jackie, and His Delta Cats. 'Rocket 88.' Chess 1458. 1951: USA.

Ledbetter, Huddie (Leadbelly). 'Irene'/'Ain't You Glad.' Asch 343-2. 1943: USA.

Ledbetter, Huddie (Leadbelly). 'Rock Island Line'/'Ol' Riley.' Asch 102. 1942: USA.

Wray, Link, and His Ray Men. 'Rumble.' Cadence 1347. *1958*: USA.

STEVE WAKSMAN with OMAR CORRADO (Argentina)
and SERGIO SAUVALLE (Chile)

Electric Bass Guitar

The sound production of the electric bass guitar, like that of the solid-bodied electric guitar, relies on the vibration of its metal strings in an electromagnetic field, supplied by pickups, with that signal then increased by an electronic amplifier. The fingerboard of the electric bass is fretted in half steps, and the player, either seated or standing, holds the instrument in a horizontal position with the aid of a guitar strap. The standard four-string electric bass guitar is slightly larger than the electric guitar (a total length of 45" (1.15 m)), with each string stretching an octave and a sixth. The strings are tuned to *E A D G*, the same as the acoustic bass and one octave below the lowest four strings of the guitar. The electric bass is ordinarily the lowest-pitched stringed instrument in most popular music ensembles.

The history of the electrically amplified bass guitar is one that reflects technological, economic and musical factors. The instrument was conceived as an answer to popular musicians' growing complaints about the traditional acoustic bass, which was physically cumbersome, difficult to hear and to play in tune, and inconvenient to maintain. During the 1930s, Rickenbacker, Regal, Vega, Gibson and other instrument manufacturers tried to develop acoustic basses with electric amplification to cope with the increasing volume levels of dance bands, in which the guitar was commonly included. As early as 1933, Paul H. Tutmarc of Seattle developed several prototype models in an attempt to create an electric bass guitar, and the following year James Thompson built a solid-bodied electric bass guitar to use for his home recordings. All these early experiments were overshadowed by the enormous success of Leo Fender's solid-bodied Precision Bass, which along with its Bassman amplifier counterpart was marketed in the United States in 1951. As an option to the Precision Bass, the Fender

Jazz Bass was produced in 1960, featuring a thinner neck, two pickups and a modernistic 'offset body' design. Although competitors had produced other electric basses by the mid-1950s, Fender is commonly recognized as the inventor of the instrument owing to the enormous impact of his models, which dominated the marketplace through the 1970s.

In Germany, the electric Violin Bass (model 500/1) was made by the Hofner Musical Instruments Company in 1956. Constructed much like a violin, its hollow body was formed from maple and spruce and its string length was a comfortable 30″ (76 cm). Since the imported Fender bass was much more expensive, young European musicians quickly embraced the Hofner model because of its modest price. The Beatles' Paul McCartney bought a Hofner model 500/1 in 1961 for £30 and performed and recorded with a similar model well into the 1960s.

Techniques for using the electric bass as a melodic instrument were developed in the 1970s by virtuoso players such as Stanley Clarke and Jaco Pastorius, who explored solo playing styles and experimented with the use of electronic special effects and fretless models. But the primitive percussive and rhythmic aspects of the instrument were also exploited in the 1970s by players such as Bootsy Collins, who popularized thumping and popping techniques essential to the funk style. In the 1980s, five- and six-string models were manufactured (adding a low $B1$ string and high c string, respectively), and new designs were fashioned from moldable plastics. In 1981, in an attempt to add sustain and definition to notes, the Steinberger Company manufactured solid-bodied basses using a combination of graphite and glass fiber. Steinberger's revolutionary design eliminated the headstock by moving the tuning keys to the opposite end of the streamlined body.

Nearly all popular music ensembles were affected to some degree by the development of the electric bass guitar. In jazz, for example, Vernon Alley used an electric bass guitar as early as 1940, and Monk Montgomery used one with Lionel Hampton's band in the early 1950s. Montgomery is credited with being the first jazz musician to record using the electric bass guitar, doing so in 1953. In rockabilly and early white rock, sidemen quickly discarded the acoustic bass in favor of the logistically advantageous electric bass. Bill Mack, of Gene Vincent's Blue Caps, was one of the earliest converts in 1956; Elvis Presley's bass player, Bill Black, switched to the electric bass in 1957, as did Buddy Holly's bassist, Don Guess, in 1959. The electric bass quickly found a home in rhythm and blues (R&B) as well: Dave Myers switched from guitar to the Fender Precision Bass in 1958 for his recordings for Chicago blues artists, and in Detroit James Jamerson played electric bass for most of his recordings for the Motown label from 1959 to 1972. In Memphis, the electric bass lines played by Donald 'Duck' Dunn in the early 1960s made a significant contribution to the unique sound of soul recordings made at the Stax studio. B.B. King, Little Walter and 'Big Mama' Thornton all adopted the instrument for their groups to overcome the noise levels found in nightclubs and roadhouses. As rock styles began to influence pop and jazz, notable session musicians such as Ron Carter and Steve Swallow were compelled to learn the electric bass guitar. Country music was one of the last genres to accept the electric bass, but by the early 1960s the punching sound of the electric bass guitar had become a defining element of hard-edged honky-tonk recordings by singers such as Buck Owens. Except for a few instances, the electric bass guitar was deliberately shunned by bluegrass players in an attempt to maintain what they considered to be 'traditional' instrumentation.

The displacement of the acoustic bass by the electric bass guitar was accelerated elsewhere in the world by the performance tours of US rockabilly and pop acts. In England, many young musicians were influenced by the inclusion of the electric bass in instrumentations during the 1959 concert tours featuring Gene Vincent and Eddie Cochran. In Japan, too, Gene Vincent's band and other touring US pop acts used the electric bass during the highly successful and culturally influential Nichigeki Theatre Western Carnival concerts, which began in 1958 in Tokyo and continued seasonally until 1977. The endorsement of the electric bass by these pioneers was trendsetting and caused the acoustic bass to be discarded in Japanese rock until the rockabilly revival period of the 1970s.

Because of the electric bass's similarity to the guitar, many of the first electric bass players were converted guitarists who were familiar with fretted fingerboards and the technique associated with using a pick. Indeed, Leo Fender had solicited the advice of professional guitarists from country, western swing and jazz while developing his prototype Precision Bass. By the early 1960s, there were so many converts that few electric bass players in blues, rock, R&B and gospel had any experience with the acoustic bass.

The effects of the electric bass guitar on popular music have generally been obscured owing to the instrument's role in the ensemble. Most marketing of popular music has tended to place emphasis on either songs, vocalists or solo instruments. So, whereas the electric guitar quickly developed its 'rock image,' driven by first-generation performers like Bill Haley, Chuck Berry and Buddy Holly, the electric bass and its players remained somewhat anonymous. But, toward the beginning of the

1960s, the electric bass began to take on unprecedented levels of importance in pop music. The new role of the bass in the pop ensemble is apparent in the Ventures' 'Walk – Don't Run' (1960), in which the electric bass shares equal importance with the electric guitars rather than remaining hidden in a traditional supporting role. Because of the electric bass's new sonic presence, session players and record producers were obliged to pay more attention to the bass lines chosen for pop recordings. Electric bass lines have gone through several stages and styles: in country, blues and R&B of the 1960s, traditional four- and eight-note walking patterns from the boogie-woogie tradition remained common; the bass lines of 1960s rock were often associated with the recording's electric guitar motifs; and, in the 1970s and 1980s, the bass often played the same rhythmic patterns as the bass drum. The ability of the electric bass to produce fast, clear, repeated notes at a competitive volume played a role in the popularity of early 1960s recordings, such as 'The Twist,' which featured straight eighth-note rhythmic subdivisions rather than 1950s swing patterns.

Bibliography

Bacon, Tony. 1995. *The Bass Book: A Complete Illustrated History of Bass Guitars*. San Francisco: Miller Freeman.

Clevinger, Martin. 1987/99. *Evolution of the Electric Double Bass*. http://www.clevinger.com/Evolution.htm

Goldsby, John. 2000. '100 and Counting: The Players Who Shaped 20th Century Bass.' *Bass Player* 11(1): 28–41.

Jasson, Mikael, and Malandrone, Scott. 1997. 'Jurassic Basses: Was There Electric Bass Before Leo?' *Bass Player* 8(7): 20–22.

Johnson, Alphonso. 1990. 'Bass Guitar.' In *The Guitar: A Guide for Students and Teachers*, ed. Michael Stimpson. Oxford: Oxford University Press, 177–90.

Shimizu, Terumasa. 1998. 'A Musicological Analysis of Melodies and Singing in Japanese Neo-Rockabilly.' In *Popular Music: Intercultural Interpretations*, ed. Tôru Mitsui. Kanazawa, Japan: Kanazawa University Press, 357–65.

Teagle, John, and Sprung, John. 1995. *Fender Amps: The First Fifty Years*. Milwaukee, WI: Hal Leonard.

Discographical References

Ballard, Hank, and the Midnighters. 'The Twist.' King 5171. *1960*: USA.

Checker, Chubby. 'The Twist.' Parkway 811. *1960*: USA.

Ventures, The. 'Walk – Don't Run.' Dolton 25. *1960*: USA.

ROY C. BREWER

Flamenco Guitar

The appearance of the flamenco guitar was contemporaneous with the birth of flamenco as a form of public and professional artistic expression around the 1840s in western Andalusia. In response to the demands of the audiences in the recently established musical cafés, the repertoire of the former gypsy *tonás* (traditional gypsy songs, unmeasured and sung a cappella, probably preceding *cante jondo*) evolved and was enriched by singing accompanied by the guitar. Originally exclusively used for accompaniment, the flamenco guitar quickly found its role as a solo instrument. Ramón Montoya, master guitarist in the first half of the twentieth century, borrowed from the classical tradition complex arpeggio and tremolo techniques, and in this way enriched the primitive and elementary style which was based on the alternation of *rasgueos* (strumming) and simple melodies played with the thumb or in *picados* (rapidly executed scales, plucked with the middle and index fingers alternately). This development led all the great guitarists of the twentieth century to augment or replace their professional activity as accompanists with that of the concert soloist.

Both the instrument and musicians have to be able to adapt to the great contrasts between the extreme speed and sonorous power of a dance *por Bulería* (in the Bulerían style – an extremely rhythmic dance originating in the region of Jerez de la Frontera) and the most delicate melismas of a song *por Granaína* (in the Granaínian style – a free-rhythm, fandango-type song originating in the province of Granada). The contribution of the classical guitar combined with the demands of the art of flamenco has created specific techniques. The use of *rasgueos* and of *golpes* (taps struck on the body of the guitar) makes the flamenco guitar into a genuine percussion instrument, with harmony added. The important role of the thumb, combined with great speed, has led to an increase in the use of notes associated with the left hand. The scales executed in *picados* achieve surprising speeds, exceeding 200 quarter notes per minute broken into sixteenth notes. The regular arpeggios of the classical guitar are often transformed into plucked chords, spread gradually like the coils of a spring, with each strike of the thumb preceded by a melodic phrase played on the bass strings. The thumb itself, caught up in this frenzy of power and virtuosity, becomes a plectrum, playing in one movement a bass string followed by two chords, achieved in an alternate downward and upward motion known as *alzapúa*.

The Almerían guitar-maker Antonio de Torres Jurado (1817–92) resolved the differences between the flamenco guitar and its classical cousin, which had become incompatible with such techniques. The shallower case was mounted in cypress rather than rosewood, thus favoring the sharp sounds (more audible in a popular public environment). The bridge and the less thick soundboard were designed, according to the secrets of each craftsman, with the aim of obtaining an immediate and sudden response suited to the clear audibility of the *rasgueos*. The strings were brought nearer to the frets to facilitate rapid playing with the left hand, particularly for the playing of a series of tied notes. According to an earlier tradition, certain guitars kept wooden pegs, but were replaced in the majority of cases by the current mechanical system. *Golpeadores* (white or transparent tap plates) protect the soundboard from the *golpes*. The systematic use of the *cejilla* (capo) permits the tonality to be adjusted to the range of the singer. The contemporary flamenco guitar, larger and more sonorous, adheres, however, to the same basic principles established by Manuel Torré.

Bibliography

Batista, Andrés. 1979. *Método de guitarra flamenca* [Flamenco Guitar Method]. Madrid: Union Musical Española.

Bellow, Alexander. 1970. *The Illustrated History of the Guitar*. New York: Colombo Publications.

Cano, Manuel. 1986. *La guitarra: historia, estudios y aportaciónes al arte flamenco* [The Guitar: History, Studies and Contributions to the Art of Flamenco]. Granada: Ediciones Aniel, S.A.

Donnier, Philippe. 1985. *Flamenco: Méthode de guitare* [Flamenco: Guitar Method]. Paris: Gérard Billaudot, Éditeur.

George, David. 1969. *The Flamenco Guitar: From Its Birth in the Hands of the Guitarrero to Its Ultimate Celebration in the Hands of the Flamenco Guitarist*. Madrid: Society of Spanish Studies.

Herrero, Oscar, and Worms, Claude. 1996. *Traité de guitare flamenca* [A Study of the Flamenco Guitar]. Paris: Édition Combre.

Martín, Juan. 1978. *Juan Martín's Guitar Method: 'El Arte Flamenco de la Guitarra'*. London: United Music Publisher Ltd.

Peña, Paco. 1976. *Toques flamencos* [Flamenco Pieces]. London: Musical New Services.

Ricardo, Niño, Habichuela, Pepe, and Sabicas. 1987. *Flamenco*. Tokyo: The Gendai Guitar Co.

Discography

Blas Vega, José. *Magna Antología del Cante Flamenco* (20 LPs and book). Hispavox, S.A. S/C 66.201. *1982*: Spain.

Lucía, Paco de. *Fuente y caudal*. Philips 63 28 109. *1975*: Spain.

Marchena, Melchor de. *Guitarra gitana*. Hispavox 530 40 32581. *1987*: Spain.

Montoya, Ramón. *Grandes figuras del Flamenco, Vol. 5*. Le Chant du Monde LDX 74979. *1988*: France.

Ricardo, Niño. *Toques flamencos de guitarra*. Hispavox 530 40 3257 1. *1987*: Spain.

Sabicas. *Adios a la guitarra*. Hispavox 056 744 631. *1990*: Spain.

Sanlucar, Manolo. *Mundo y formas de la guitarra flamenca, Vol. 1*. CBS S 64 660. *1971*: Spain.

Serranito, Victor Monge. *Virtuosismo flamenco*. Hispavox S20.047. *1978*: Spain.

PHILIPPE DONNIER

Tiple

The *tiple*, together with the *cavaquinho* (Brazil), the *cuatro* (Puerto Rico, Venezuela), the *charango* (Argentina, Bolivia, Chile, Peru), the *tres* (Cuba) and others, is part of a group of high-pitched stringed instruments that has had, and has continued to have, an important role in the traditional and popular urban music of Latin America. It is one of the stringed instruments that emerged in the Americas, developed from the Spanish instrumental legacy (*vihuela*, *guitarra*) introduced by the conquistadors five centuries ago. The manufacture and use of the *tiple* have spread to several countries in the Americas, including the United States, and to some countries in Europe, where the instrument has been introduced by popular musicians. In the last 30 years or so in particular, it has been related to musical expressions that have become emblematic of Latin American popular music throughout the continent and in other parts of the world.

The *tiple* also exists in the Dominican Republic (the *tiplecito* or the *guitarrito*) as a melodic instrument, and in Venezuela as an accompanying instrument with 10 strings distributed into four courses (2-3-3-2). But it is in Colombia where the *tiple* has been most relevant, attaining the status of national instrument.

The *tiple* is the size of a small guitar (approximately 35″ (90 cm) in length). Different types of wood are used in the construction of each of its parts: pine, spruce or walnut for the harmonic cover; rosewood or cedar for the lateral hoops and the back cover; cedar or *guayacán* for the neck; and ebony or walnut for the fingerboard.

The *tiple* has 12 strings distributed into four courses of three strings each. The highest course has three thin steel strings, and the lower three courses have two lateral steel strings and one bass string in the middle, tuned an octave lower. The most common tuning used is the same as that of the four upper strings of the guitar: *d*, *g*, *b* and *e*[1], respectively.

The playing techniques used for the *tiple* are strumming and plucking. The first is the more traditional and is used as accompaniment for traditional genres like the *bambuco*, the *pasillo*, the *guabina* and the *torbellino*, the strokes being executed to match their respective rhythmic patterns. The *tiple* has also developed gradually as a versatile solo instrument. By combining the techniques of strumming and plucking, through the execution of a variety of movements with fingertips, nails and the use of the plectrum, the performers have expanded the *tiple*'s musical function.

History

The *tiple* emerged as a Creole variant of the four-course Spanish guitar, a popular instrument during the reign of the Catholic kings (Puerta 1988). Its development was shaped by the process of the political emancipation of what became Colombia from the Viceroyalty of Nueva Granada. Within a context favorable to the emergence of new local musical expression, the instrument became known as the *tiple*. By the second half of the nineteenth century, the *tiple* had become one of the most widely used popular instruments in Colombia, acquiring the basic features – size, number of strings, musical roles – that it has continued to possess.

This evolutionary process culminated in the early part of the twentieth century with two developments that gave the *tiple* its distinct character: the tripling of each of its four courses of strings, a process that was completed about 1915 and that overcame the problem of the heterogeneity or variability of timbre in those courses with a bass string in the middle; and the use of metallic pegs to solve difficulties in tuning in relation to other traditional stringed instruments. Consequently, and from this time (1915), the *tiple* played a prominent role in the composition of tone color in the typical Andean music ensembles in Colombia (duets of guitar and *tiple*; trios of guitar, mandolin and *tiple*; quartets and the so-called *estudiantinas* ensembles).

In the period 1920–30, and with the emergence and establishment of the recording industry and the mass circulation of music through radio, the first solo players of the *tiple* appeared. The legendary Tartarín Moreira, Pacho Benavides and many others contributed to the consolidation of the *tiple*'s local and international musical presence.

By 1970, the instrument had been introduced in Chile by the group Inti-illimani and the songwriter-performer Víctor Jara. In this new context, and together with other folkloric instruments, the *tiple* was firmly integrated into an innovative instrumental fusion whose roots lay in the *nueva canción Chilena* (Chilean new song) movement, a kind of 'new Latin American orchestra' which was spread in the 1970s and 1980s to the continent and throughout the world by Chilean groups like Inti-illimani, Quilapayún and Illapu.

At the beginning of the twenty-first century, experiments are being undertaken in the construction and tuning of the *tiple*. They are designed to diminish its excessively brilliant tones and enhance the sound of the bass strings to achieve a deeper resonance, a more opaque timbre and greater tonal precision that will improve its interaction with the *guitarra*. In the last decade, the *tiple* has acquired new acoustic, rhythmic, timbral and melodic dimensions by means of electronic amplification, especially used for its integration into orchestras of salsa and Caribbean music, or by means of the technically demanding works of Colombian composers, open to innovations and experimentation, as in the work of the Cuatro Palos quartet, the Palo Santo trio and other Colombian groups.

Bibliography

Abadía Morales, Guillermo. 1991. *Instrumentos musicales del folklore colombiano* [Musical Instruments of Colombian Folklore]. Bogotá: Banco Popular.

Davison, Harry C. 1970. *Diccionario folklórico de Colombia: música, instrumentos y danza* [Dictionary of Folklore in Colombia: Music, Instruments and Dance]. Bogotá: Banco de la República.

Puerta, David. 1988. *Los caminos del tiple* [The Evolution of the *Tiple*]. Bogotá: Ediciones AMP.

RODRIGO TORRES

10. Keyboard Instruments

Accordion

The accordion is used in popular music genres in all areas of the world. The musical styles of Brazilian *forró*, Nigerian *jújù*, Cajun, zydeco, Tex-Mex *conjunto*, Dominican merengue, Colombian *vallenato*, Euro-American polka, Finnish tango, French musette and Austrian *Schrammelmusik*, as well as numerous European rural vernacular folk styles, folkloristic, *volkstümlich*, folk-pop and folk-rock genres from Ireland to Bulgaria, all depend on the timbres, playing techniques and socio-musical associations of the accordion. Many dance musics have exploited its penetrating tone and rhythmic bite, and its melodic facility, portability and capacity for self-accompaniment have made the accordion popular with minor professional players everywhere.

The instrument was invented in the early nineteenth century; mass production of tens of thousands per year in factories and workshops, especially in Germany and Italy, ensued from the 1840s onward. Relatively cheap, loud, reliable and easy to play, the accordion was adapted by musicians to local needs and styles through the late nineteenth and the twentieth centuries.

All accordions have a rectangular bellows with tuned metal reeds. These sound when air is forced through them by the bellows, and each wind path, controlled by a button or key, contains a 'bellows compression' and a 'bellows extension' reed. Reeds are typically linked in ranks tuned in octaves or a slightly detuned unison, the latter producing a constant tremolo effect.

The tuning systems of diatonic button accordions, the style which first rose to popularity, derive from the accordion instrument patented by Cyrill Demian in 1829. This 'single-action' system, with different 'press' and 'draw' notes produced from each button, is familiar as that adopted by the harmonica, which produces a diatonic scale with its blow–suck alternation. Thus, the instrument is usually limited to specific keys. A melodic line will require changes in bellows articulation, and these are often exploited by musicians for distinctive phrasing and rhythmic effects. Basses and chords from the left-hand end of the instrument are often limited to tonic and dominant chords. Multiple rows in different keys can expand the scope of the instrument, while maintaining elements of the characteristic sound.

Double-action instruments, where the press and draw reeds for each button are identically tuned, became popular in the twentieth century. These produce a full chromatic scale. Piano accordions have a standard keyboard, while the chromatic button accordion has an array of from three to six rows of buttons spelling out a chromatic scale. Most of these double-action instruments (and a few diatonic accordions) have the left-hand ends in the 'stradella' format, with rows of buttons producing basses and preset chords – major, minor, diminished and so on, arranged in a cycle of fifths. Sometimes, a 'free-bass' left-hand end provides individual pitches in the arrangement of a chromatic button accordion's right-hand end.

All of these systems utilize simplified conceptions of a conventional Western European musical language: a separation of melody and chordal harmonic accompaniment, and a diatonic or tempered pitch gamut, with cycle of fifths harmonic resolutions. In developing popular musical styles that drew on other musical conventions, users adapted these scales and chords to their needs. From the 1920s onward, players of Irish dance music translated the pitch and ornamental effects of fiddle playing to the instrument. Cajun and Creole players make much use of 'cross keying' – playing melodies in the key of the fifth of the row – to exploit the flat seventh this provides. Tex-Mex players have tended to use three-row diatonic instruments, and by moving between the rows, they minimize changes in bellows articulations, and produce fast legato runs of parallel thirds and sixths. Many African musicians aim at a different balance between melodic continuity and rhythmic structure. Jùjú innovator I.K. Dairo, for example, used the single-row diatonic accordion for ostinatos in a multilayered ensemble.

10. Keyboard Instruments

Piano accordions and double-action chromatic button accordions became increasingly popular through the first 30 years of the twentieth century, often replacing diatonic instruments. They became widely used in popular music styles when greater harmonic resources were called for, and the widely understood piano keyboard was an advantage. From the 1950s, keyboards with the intermediate quarter tones of the Arabic modes were used by some players in the Middle East. North American polka music, particularly the postwar Slovenian style, tended to the smoother, controlled sound of the piano accordion. The piano accordion has become the central instrument of reception or wedding bands the world over. In China, it is ubiquitous in entertainment and state-sponsored performances. Models such as the Farfisa Cordovox added electronic rhythm machines to the instrument from the early 1960s, and in the 1980s MIDI-controller accordions were developed that enable the accordionist to drive any timbre.

The chromatic double-action button accordion gives the player access to a range of up to seven octaves, and the right hand can span two-and-a-half octaves without moving. It is favored in Russia and Finland, and is the central instrument of Finnish tango. The characteristic melodic style and timbre of the musette music of Parisian dance halls and recording is based on the chromatic button accordion.

The accordion has been taken up by many subordinate groups, particularly those in transition from rural to urban locations, and those in transition from peasant society to the industrial working class. The genres associated with the instrument have reflected these social transitions (Peña 1985; Giannattasio 1979). Almost universally, the accordion has been subjected to the disdain of bourgeois commentators. Frequently, this rejection has focused on its capacity to evade gatekeepers of taste and style. Thus, the facility with which the instrument could produce the emotive signs of vibrato and crescendo induces European commentators to label it as kitsch, whereas folkloristic commentators in many cultures have seen its involvement in the development of popular music forms from rural vernacular musics as corrupt and deracinating. Meanwhile, its association with pre-rock musical genres assured its rejection by rock musicians, who could also draw on puristic 'folkist' ideologies to reject the instrument. Thus, the accordion is one of a group of instruments whose members are the focus of many pejorative and stereotypic jokes.

Through the 1980s, several aesthetic reassessments and shifts in popular music production and consumption favored the reemergence of the accordion within mass mainstream popular music. Euro-American folk-rock styles and other revivalist groups have included accordions as versatile instruments that could be accommodated to the small band format. This, and the reemergence of a self-historicizing nostalgic mode in North American mainstream rock in the early 1980s, aided the accordion's repopularization. The powerful social connotations of the accordion were also exploited by rock satirist 'Weird Al' Yankovic from 1980 onward. Sectional or regional genres, identified as 'roots' musics, are now effectively marketed to globally dispersed fan bases, and often use the accordion. By the mid-1990s, the presence of a piano accordion in a rock band was no longer surprising.

Bibliography

Giannattasio, Francesco. 1979. *L'organetto: uno strumento musicale contadino dell'era industriale* [The Accordion: A Rural Musical Instrument in the Industrial Age]. Rome: Bulzoni.

Peña, Manuel. 1985. *The Texas-Mexican Conjunto: History of a Working-Class Music*. Austin, TX: University of Texas Press.

Shapiro, Michael, ed. 1995. Track notes to *Planet Squeezebox: Accordion Music from Around the World* (3-CD set). New York: Ellipsis Arts.

Smith, Graeme. 1997. 'Modern Irish-Style Accordion Playing: History, Biography and Class.' *Ethnomusicology* 41(3): 433–63.

Discography

Squeeze Play: A World Accordion Anthology. Rounder ROUN1090. *1997*: USA.

GRAEME SMITH

Bandoneón

The *bandoneón*, the key instrument and sound of tango, is a special large version of the square-built button accordion or concertina, a portable wind instrument made of two harmonic wooden cases joined together by folded cardboard bellows. The bellows cause the loose reeds inside the end cases to vibrate when activated by the small cylindrical nacre-coated buttons. It may have a double or single action.

There are two main types of *bandoneón*: the so-called chromatic *bandoneón*, which has a chromatically arranged keyboard with keys that produce the same sound when pulled in and out; and the diatonic *bandoneón*, most common in the River Plate region of South America, which has a keyboard that is not chromatically arranged and produces two different sounds on the 'pull' and the 'push,' i.e., when opening and closing.

The diatonic *bandoneón* has 38 buttons for the high and medium register of the right-hand keyboard and 33 for the lower register of the left-hand keyboard. The whole register was originally tuned between G^1 and b^6, lacking some notes in the low register. The instruments that are now normally used are tuned between C^2 and b^6, lacking $a^{\#6}$.

The invention of the *bandoneón* in the 1840s is attributed to Heinrich Band, a German accordion manufacturer from Krefeld, although recent studies have suggested that the inventor may have been C. Zimmermann of Carlsfeld. The *bandoneón* was brought to South America by German sailors in the late nineteenth century.

In Buenos Aires, the *bandoneón* definitely became a key part of tango orchestras from 1905, playing as a solo instrument. This playing exploited the expressive qualities of bellows-driven dynamic swells, as well as the full chromatic range of the instrument. As well as producing the iconic sound of the tango, the instrument has been played by folk groups from the coastal provinces of the Paraná River and the northwest regions of Argentina.

Isaco Abitbol and Tránsito Cocomarola were two of the most important *bandoneón* players of *chamamé* (Argentina's most popular roots music). Distinguished *bandoneón* players in tango history include Ciríaco Ortíz, Eduardo Arolas, Pedro Maffia, Pedro Láurenz, Aníbal Troilo, Leopoldo Federico, Juan-José Mosalini, Néstor Marconi, Rodolfo Mederos, Daniel Binelli and Astor Piazzolla. Piazzolla, the avant-garde composer of 'new tango' who revolutionized the genre, bringing it into the world of international jazz and contemporary music, revealed through his own *bandoneón* playing the full, challenging potential of the instrument. Recently, Dino Saluzzi has become one of the most important players of multicultural fusion trends.

Bibliography

Azzi, M.S., and Collier, S. 2000. *Le Grand Tango: The Life and Music of Astor Piazzolla*. Oxford: Oxford University Press.

Dunkel, María. 1987. *Bandonion und Konzertina: Ein Beitrag zur Darstellung des Instrumententyps* [*Bandoneón* and Concertina: A Contribution to the Portrayal of a Type of Instrument]. Berliner Musikwissenschaftliche Arbeiten, Band 30. München/Salzburg: Emil Katzbichler Musikverlag.

Ernie, Héctor, Sierra, Luis Adolfo, and Zucchi, Oscar D. 1977. *La Historia del Tango. Vol. 5: El bandoneón* [The History of the Tango. Vol. 5: The *Bandoneón*]. Buenos Aires: Corregidor.

Manoury, Olivier. 1996. 'Le bandonéon chromatique nouveau est là!' [The New Chromatic *Bandoneón* Is Here!]. *Accordéon Magazine* 15: 48–49.

Monette, Pierre. 1996. 'L'arrivée du premier bandonéon en Argentine' [The Introduction of the First *Bandoneón* in Argentina]. *Accordéon Magazine* 15: 50–53.

Penón, Arturo, and García Méndez, Javier. 1986. *El bandoneón desde el tango/Le bandonéon depuis le tango* [The *Bandoneón* After Tango]. Montréal: Ed. Coatl.

Penón, Arturo, and García Méndez, Javier. 1987. *Petite histoire du bandonéon et du tango* [A Brief History of the *Bandoneón* and the Tango]. Montréal: Diffusion La Librairie du Québec.

Saltón, Ricardo. 1981. 'El bandoneón' [The *Bandoneón*]. *Revista del Instituto de Investigación Musicológica 'Carlos Vega'* 4: 91–105.

Saltón, Ricardo. 1999. '*Bandoneón*.' In *Diccionario de la Música Española e Hispanoamericana* [Dictionary of Spanish and Spanish-American Music], Vol. 2. Madrid: SGAE, 167–71.

Zucchi, Oscar. 1998–. *El tango, el bandoneón y sus intérpretes* [The Tango, the *Bandoneón* and Their Interpreters]. 11 vols. Buenos Aires: Ed. Corregidor.

Discography

Abitbol, Isaco. *Caraí del chamamé*. Music Hall 2243. n.d.: Argentina.

Arolas, Eduardo. *Homenaje a la Guardia Vieja, 1913–1918*. El bandoneon EBCD 125. n.d.: Spain.

Binelli, Daniel. *El bandoneón*. Random Records RR734. 2001: Argentina.

Cocomarola, Tránsito. *Chamamé*. Philips 6347409. n.d.: Argentina.

Federico, Leopoldo. *Sentimiento criollo*. Music Hall CD 236516. 1994: Argentina.

Láurenz, Pedro, and Maffia, Pedro. *Mala junta*. El bandoneon EBCD 98. 1998: Spain.

Los chalchaleros con Dino Saluzzi. *Quiero nombrar a mi pago*. RCA APMS-4129. 1972: Argentina.

Mederos, Rodolfo, and Cuarteto de Cuerdas. *El tanguero*. Teldec Classics International 3984-20641-2. 1998: Germany.

Mosalini, Juan-José. *Bordoneo y 900*. Harmonia Mundi 83/Label Bleu 2507. 1994: France.

Néstor Marconi Trio (with Leonardo Marconi and Oscar Giunta). Melopea CDMSE 5092. 1996: Argentina.

Ortíz, Ciríaco. *Conversando con el fueye*. El bandoneon EBCD 57. 1994: Spain.

Piazzolla, Astor. *Introducción al angel*, Vol. 1. Melopea CDMSE 5041. 1963; 1993: Argentina.

Piazzolla, Astor. *Música popular contemporánea de la*

ciudad de Buenos Aires, Vol. 1. RCA-Victor AVS 4069. *1972*: Argentina.

Piazzolla, Astor. *Suite troileana*. Trova CD 408. *1991*: Argentina.

Piazzolla, Astor, and Pugliese, Osvaldo. *Finally Together*. Lucho 7704–2. *1992*: Benelux.

Saluzzi, Dino. *Kultrum*. ECM Records 1251. *1983*: Germany.

Troilo, Aníbal. *Obra completa en RCA*. 16 vols. *1997–2000*: Argentina.

OMAR CORRADO

Concertina

A concertina is a small bellows instrument supported by the playing hands. The sound is produced by metal reeds, controlled by buttons. Concertinas are used in the British and Irish folk movement, in North American polka, in Argentinian tango and Brazilian *lambada*, and in Sotho and Zulu popular styles, as well as by instrument enthusiasts in the English-speaking world playing a variety of music.

On single-action systems, the 'Anglo-German' types, and the somewhat larger, rectangular-ended Chemnitzer concertinas and *bandoneóns*, each button produces different pitches on extension and compression of the bellows; on double-action systems, such as the 'English' and 'duet' concertinas, the same pitch is produced.

English inventor and scientist Charles Wheatstone patented a concertina-style instrument in 1829, which he had developed into the fully chromatic, English system by about 1840. These instruments were relatively expensive, with reliable intonation and clear and penetrating tone, and suited to composed art music. They were popular with bourgeois amateurs, particularly in England, where the instrument was popularized by theatrical virtuosos (Wayne 1991). Double-action 'duet' systems developed from around the 1880s, which allocated bass and treble notes separately to the left and right hands, thus facilitating solo performance and self-accompaniment. They were often used by music hall artists such as Percy Honri and Alexander Prince (Honri 1974).

Parallel to the development of these chromatic double-action concertinas, single-action concertinas based on diatonic accordions were built by German instrument maker Uhlig from 1834. Expanding to multiple rows, and with extra accidental notes, these evolved into the Chemnitzer concertinas and *bandoneóns*. The hexagonal English body shape was adopted in the 1850s to produce the ubiquitous Anglo-German concertinas. These were manufactured mainly in England and Germany, the English manufacturers tending to produce more expensive and durable instruments, while many of the German concertinas were mass-produced and inexpensive.

Single-action concertinas were widely used by street musicians, and amateur and domestic players of vernacular dance music, who exploited the rhythmic phrasing of the bellows articulation, and the instruments had relatively low socio-musical status (Mayhew 1967, 182–85). Hexagonal concertinas were mainly marketed and used in the British Empire and the Anglophone world. Concertinas of all types were prominent in minstrel show and music hall performances during the nineteenth century and into the twentieth century, and players exploited the theatrical possibilities of the instrument, with dazzling cadenzas and variations, phasing-like effects produced by swinging the bellows, humorous use of miniature and giant instruments, and so on. South African Zulu and Sotho players took up cheap concertinas in the late nineteenth century, and they have continued to use them in local popular dance-music styles that have developed in the past 50 years. Concertinas were adopted from the beginning by Salvation Army street preachers. From the end of the nineteenth century until the mid-twentieth century, concertina bands musically and socially modeled on brass bands were formed in northern England, with annual competitions held to coincide with the annual brass band competitions in Manchester (Pickels 1984, 9).

Concertina accompaniment was used by performers of the British folk revival from the 1950s onward. The well-developed playing styles of Irish rural players have made the instrument important in the Irish traditional music movement. In the British revival, the concertina attained high symbolic status among 'traditional'-style puristic performers, as a contrast to the 'contemporary' reference of the guitar (Eydmann 1995). Many current enthusiasts for the instrument have emerged from this use in the British folk movement, some virtuosos – like Simon Thoumire – developing jazz and genre-fusing styles.

The larger rectangular-ended concertinas were adopted in Germany and Poland and spread throughout the world by German immigrants. These often have a number of linked reed ranks, and are similar in sound to diatonic accordions. The Chemnitzer concertinas, designed to play in a number of keys, were popularly used during the development of ensemble-based polka music in the United States, particularly in the period before 1930. Postwar Chicago players such as Eddie Zima and Li'l Wally Jagiello continued to use concertinas, and the instrument's folksier sound has since been exploited in Chicago-style polka (Keil et al. 1992, 46, passim).

Bibliography

Clapp, Malcolm. 1984. 'Concertinas on 78s.' *Concertina Magazine* 8: 14–15.

Eydmann, Stuart. 1995. 'The Concertina as an Emblem of the Folk Music Revival in the British Isles.' *British Journal of Ethnomusicology* 4: 41–49.

Honri, Peter. 1974. *Peter Honri Presents – Working the Halls: The Honris in One Hundred Years of British Music Hall.* London: Futura Publications.

Keil, Charles, et al. 1992. *Polka Happiness.* Philadelphia: Temple University Press.

Mayhew, Henry. 1967 (1860–61). *London Labour and the London Poor.* London: Frank Cass.

Pickels, Nigel. 1984. 'The History of the Concertina Band.' *Concertina Magazine* 7: 9–10.

Shapiro, Michael, ed. 1995. Track notes to *Planet Squeezebox: Accordion Music from Around the World* (3-CD set). New York: Ellipsis Arts.

Wayne, Neil. 1991. 'The Wheatstone English Concertina.' *The Galpin Society Journal* 44: 113–49.

Discography

Thoumire, Simon. *March, Strathspey and Surreal.* Green Linnet GLCD 1171. *1996:* UK.

GRAEME SMITH

Concert Organ

Although church organs had been used for playing secular music and for performing in public concerts since at least the early seventeenth century, organs were rarely found in secular locations before the eighteenth century. Indeed, secular venues for public concerts were rare until the late seventeenth century and, in England at least, began humbly in taverns where space was set aside for amateur musicians to gather for singing and playing together. By 1700, some taverns had expanded this space and were known as 'music houses'; one such, the Mitre, located near London's St. Paul's Cathedral, is recorded as having had an organ by this date.

At the outset, concert organs were a phenomenon of English-speaking countries. By the middle of the eighteenth century, music rooms larger than those provided in taverns could be found not only in London but also in provincial towns and, by the latter part of the century, in Boston, New York and other colonial centers. These rooms were sometimes called concert rooms, concert halls or even theaters. Concert rooms with any pretensions usually housed a small organ. These were probably used for improvised *entr'acte* music during plays and operas before the time of George Frederick Handel, but it was Handel who first composed major works for this purpose and, from 1735 onward, 'With a Concerto on the Organ' appears frequently in advertisements for performances of Handel's oratorios in venues such as London's Covent Garden. According to the historian Sir John Hawkins, Handel often prefaced a concerto with an improvisation 'concatenated with stupendous art' (1875, Vol. 2, 912). The concertos themselves were composed for chamber orchestra with organ and, during the second half of the eighteenth century and the early years of the nineteenth century, organ concertos continued to be written by composers such as Thomas Arne, John Stanley, William Felton, Thomas Sanders Dupuis, Charles and Samuel Wesley, and by James Hook, the organist of the Vauxhall Gardens theater.

The organs used in these concertos were hardly more than glorified chamber organs, and rarely had more than one keyboard. Solo organ music, beyond the occasional improvisation, was rarely played. By the early nineteenth century, however, the situation was changing rapidly. Concert audiences were growing – a growth fueled partly by an increasing interest in choral music, which had its origins in Handel's popular oratorios. In the early 1830s, a large concert hall was built in Birmingham, England and, in 1834, it was provided with a large four-manual organ made by the William Hill firm; later enlarged, it was still in regular use at the end of the twentieth century. The intended purpose of the organ was the accompaniment of choral festivals but, by 1844, a municipal organist had been appointed, and public organ recitals were instituted.

Other public halls followed suit. In 1840, London's Exeter Hall installed a three-manual instrument built by Walker. Although, like the Birmingham organ, it was largely utilized for accompanying choral music, it too began to be used for solo recitals. By the second half of the nineteenth century, other municipal concert halls had been built in England, most of them containing organs of some distinction. Many of these were still in use at the end of the twentieth century, including the four-manual Henry Willis organs in St. George's Hall in Liverpool (1854) and the Royal Albert Hall in London (1871).

Other countries soon followed England's example. In the United States in the 1850s, Boston constructed its Music Hall, which, in 1863, was provided with a four-manual organ built by the German firm E.F. Walcker. Although this too was intended to accompany oratorios, recitals were by then regarded as an equally important use for the secular organ, and several of the city's leading organists instituted a series of weekly organ recitals. This organ, although ousted a few decades later by the then-new symphony orchestra, was later rebuilt and installed in the Memorial Music Hall in the nearby town of Methuen, where, at the end of the twentieth century, it continued to be used for weekly summer recitals. Other US cities followed Boston's lead, although their organs were all of domestic manufacture. One of the largest, the four-manual 1877 Hook & Hastings organ in Cincinnati's Music Hall, no longer exists, but a large Hook organ built in 1864 and restored in the late twentieth century was still, at the end of the twentieth century, in use in Mechanics Hall in Worcester, Massachusetts.

Paris, already noted for the recitals given on its large church organs, was somewhat of a latecomer to the concert-organ scene, although one of its major builders, Aristide Cavaillé-Coll, had already constructed organs for the Albert Hall in Sheffield, England (1873) and the Palace of Industry in Amsterdam (1875). But it was not until 1877, when Cavaillé-Coll signed another English contract (for Manchester Town Hall), that a campaign was begun for a concert organ in Paris, culminating, in 1878, in the building of the 5,000-seat Trocadéro concert hall, with its large Cavaillé-Coll organ. A series of organ recitals was immediately inaugurated, played by such notables as Alexandre Guilmant, Eugène Gigout, Charles-Marie Widor, Théodore Dubois, César Franck and Camille Saint-Saëns. But perhaps the real zenith of the nineteenth-century concert organ was reached half a world away, with the construction, in 1890, of a Hill & Sons five-manual organ with over 100 stops for the Town Hall of Sydney, Australia, an instrument that has continued to be played by major recitalists from all over the world.

Although organ recitals originated in the church, it was the large concert organs of the latter half of the nineteenth century that spurred popular interest in them. With their transcriptions of orchestral and operatic works, these recitals served to popularize classical music among sections of the population – particularly the working classes – who would not previously have been easily exposed to it. The recitals also encouraged virtuosity among organists and, perhaps most importantly, inspired the composition of large-scale organ works designed to fully utilize the richly varied resources of large instruments. These organs were becoming much more 'orchestral' in their sound, thanks to more string-toned stops and imitative reed colors, as well as improved means of expression and stop manipulation. Because the recitals given on them were attended by people from all walks of life, programs were usually a potpourri, in which a J.S. Bach toccata or a Mendelssohn or Guilmant organ sonata would keep company with a transcription of an operatic overture or oratorio chorus and an improvisation on a popular air such as 'God Save the Queen.' Some of these latter offerings were eventually written down and published by composer–recitalists such as William Thomas Best and Dudley Buck. During the early twentieth century, as organs grew more 'symphonic' in their tonal makeup, Edwin H. Lemare and

other recitalists contrived ever more spectacular and complex transcriptions from Wagner operas or Tchaikovsky symphonies, while other players produced sentimental character pieces depicting sunsets, pastoral scenes, lullabies and the folkways of 'traditional' peoples.

The first half of the twentieth century continued to be a heyday for concert organists, especially in North America, with municipalities such as San Francisco, Minneapolis, Chicago, Chattanooga (Tennessee), Hartford (Connecticut), Springfield (Massachusetts), Toronto and Portland (Maine) constructing large multipurpose halls with sizable organs. In Australia, cities such as Melbourne and Adelaide followed Sydney's example. In addition to municipal halls, halls designed primarily for concert use, such as Boston's Symphony Hall and Pittsburgh's Carnegie Hall, installed organs and promoted both solo recitals and concerts that included music for organ and orchestra. Other, more exotic venues for public organ concerts emerged, some seemingly ephemeral. In 1904, a large organ was built in Los Angeles for the 1904 World's Fair in St. Louis; in 1909, it was purchased by the Wanamaker department store in Philadelphia, enlarged and installed in the Grand Court in 1911. With six manuals and over 400 stops, it remains one of the world's largest organs, and over the years has been played by such noted virtuosos as Alexandre Guilmant, Charles Courboin, Marcel Dupré, Virgil Fox and E. Power Biggs. Although most other 'exposition' organs have long since been dispersed, another notable survivor has been the four-manual Austin 'outdoor' organ built for the 1915 Panama-Pacific Exposition in San Diego, which has remained the musical centerpiece of Balboa Park and has been regularly heard in public concerts.

Organ building worldwide was disrupted by World War II, which also caused the inevitable destruction of many European churches and halls with their organs, but rebuilding eventually occurred. In London, the Royal Festival Hall, with its four-manual Harrison & Harrison organ, was built in a bombed-out sector in 1954; a year later, Vienna's new Stadtsaal opened, housing a four-manual Walcker organ. Leipzig's Gewandhaus was bombed in 1944 and not replaced until 1977, but the new hall boasted an impressive Schuke organ.

In the United States, a lack of funding, along with 'urban renewal' projects, sometimes led to the destruction of older municipal halls, with the dispersal or destruction of their organs, and full-time municipal organists became largely a thing of the past. Yet there was new construction too, as in Boston, where a new Aeolian-Skinner organ was built for the old Symphony Hall in 1949. More recently, older concert organs in Hartford (Connecticut), Portland (Maine) and elsewhere have been restored and, in 1992, I.M. Pei's stunning Meyerson Hall in Dallas, Texas was opened, prominently featuring a four-manual C.B. Fisk Inc. concert organ.

The second half of the twentieth century also saw the spread of concert organs to countries where they had previously not existed, notably Japan and South Korea. Tokyo's NHK (Japanese Broadcasting Company) Hall, centerpiece of a vast broadcasting complex, boasts a large German-made Klais organ of the early 1970s. In 1992, the English firm Mander built an organ for Bungei Hall in Azuchi; in 1998, the US firm Fisk completed an organ for the 2,000-seat Minato Mirai Hall in Yokohama; and more concert organs were, at the end of the twentieth century, planned for other Asian cities.

Bibliography

Biswanger, Ray. 1999. *Music in the Marketplace: The Story of Philadelphia's Historic Wanamaker Organ*. Philadelphia: Friends of the Wanamaker Organ Press.

Hawkins, John. 1875 (1776). *A General History of the Science and Practice of Music*. 3 vols. London: Novello.

Lemare, Edwin H. 1956. *Organs I Have Met*. Los Angeles: Schoolcraft Co.

Lieberwirth, Steffen. 1986. *Die Gewandhaus Orgeln* [The Organs of the Gewandhaus]. Leipzig: Edition Peters.

Ochse, Orpha. 1975. *The History of the Organ in the United States*. Bloomington, IN: Indiana University Press.

Ochse, Orpha. 1994. *Organists and Organ Playing in 19th-Century France and Belgium*. Bloomington, IN: Indiana University Press.

Owen, Barbara. 1987. *E. Power Biggs, Concert Organist*. Bloomington, IN: Indiana University Press.

Thistlethwaite, Nicholas. 1984. *Birmingham Town Hall Organ*. Birmingham: Birmingham City Council.

Wolf, Edward C. 1976. 'The Secular Pipe Organ in American Culture.' In *The Bicentennial Tracker*, ed. A.F. Robinson. Richmond, VA: Organ Historical Society, 142–62.

Discography

Ampt, Robert. *Centenary Plus* (Robert Ampt plays Bach, Handel, Koehne, Dubois and Ampt on the 1890 William Hill organ in the Town Hall of Sydney, Australia). Move MD-3148. *1993*: Australia.

Armstrong-Ouellette, Susan. *A Methuen Mosaic* (Susan Armstrong-Ouellette plays romantic music for organ, brass and violin on the 1863 Walcker/1947 Aeolian-Skinner organ of Methuen Memorial Music Hall, Methuen, Massachusetts). AFKA SK-531. *1994*: USA.

Craighead, David. *The Last Rose of Summer and Other Things They Played* (David Craighead plays music of Paine, Buck, Parker, Ryder and Foote on the 1864 Hook organ of Mechanics Hall, Worcester, Massachusetts). Gothic G-49021. *1986*: USA.

Heywood, Thomas. *Melbourne Sounds Grand* (Thomas Heywood plays a varied program including music of Bach, Mozart, Grainger, Best and Lemare on the 1929 Hill, Norman and Beard organ in the Town Hall of Melbourne, Australia). Move MD-3120. *1992*: Australia.

Krigbaum, Charles. *An Evening at Woolsey Hall* (Charles Krigbaum plays music of Elgar, Mendelssohn, Widor and Duruflé on the 1928 Skinner organ of Woolsey Hall, New Haven, Connecticut. Organ Historical Society OHS-100. *1991*: USA.

Liddle, David. *The Organ Music of Alfred Hollins* (David Liddle plays Hollins's music on the 1911 Forster & Andrews organ in City Hall, Hull, England). Priory PRCD-398. *1991*: UK.

Preston, Mary. *At the Meyerson* (Mary Preston plays music of Reger, Sifler, Greiter, Rinck and Doppelbauer on the 1992 C.B. Fisk organ at Meyerson Symphony Center, Dallas, Texas). Gothic 49094. *1996*: USA.

Stewart, Gordon. *Voluntaries and Interludes* (Gordon Stewart plays music of Whitlock, Elgar, Mozart, Bach, Hollins, Dvořák, Handel, Schubert etc. on the ca. 1860 Willis/1981 Harrison & Harrison organ in the Town Hall of Huddersfield, England). Oryx 72. *1994*: UK.

BARBARA OWEN

Electric Piano

The first electric pianos were created in the 1930s by removing the soundboard of a conventional piano and placing electromagnetic pickups on each string (a principle revived in 1978 in the Yamaha CP80 Stage Piano).

However, what subsequently came to be considered an electric or electromechanical piano was slightly different. The weighted action and mechanism of the keys imitated those of an acoustic piano. The hammer struck a tuned metal tine or bar. In close proximity to this was a coil wound around a soft iron bar – a pickup – which translated the frequency of the tine or bar into an electric signal capable of amplification.

The principal manufacturers of electric pianos were Rhodes, Wurlitzer and Hohner, each of which had slightly different methods of tone creation.

Harold Rhodes (1910–2000) marketed a 32-note Fender Rhodes Piano Bass model in the early 1960s. It was popularized by Ray Manzarek, the keyboard player of the Doors; it complemented the electronic organ and was used instead of a bass player. The Suitcase Piano (1965) used metal bars struck by hammers and had a full-size keyboard with 73 keys; the bottom part of the keyboard contained the speakers and amplifiers, which created the unmistakable Rhodes piano sound. It also had controls for treble and bass, and some versions also had a tremolo circuit. An 88-note model was not released until 1970, the same year as the introduction of the more portable Stage Piano model. Other models followed, but without similar success. Many artists used Rhodes keyboards – for example, Herbie Hancock, Stevie Wonder, Chick Corea and the Carpenters. Adding chorus effect (a smooth and slowly oscillating tonal variation) became a trademark for many performers.

Wurlitzer, the US jukebox and organ company, first manufactured the EP200 electric piano in the very early 1960s. It adapted to a considerable extent a concept used in an early electronic organ: a metal reed struck with a felt hammer, using a genuine piano action. Aimed at the home user, the Wurlitzer model was soon used onstage, as it was smaller and more portable than the Fender Rhodes. Although it had a distinct sound and arguably a better key action, the reeds were prone to break, and it was very difficult to tune and maintain. It was the electric piano used by Supertramp in the 1970s.

Hohner, a company from Trossingen, Germany, built Pianet electric pianos in the early 1960s. Developed from an earlier Cembalet (1958), the compact Pianet had a slightly weighted spring-loaded key action and used metal tines, developed from Hohner's accordions, 'plucked' by a system of adhesive pads. It had few controls and was only slightly touch-sensitive. Its distinct tone can be heard on many recordings of the 1960s, including some by Ray Charles, the Zombies, and on early Small Faces records. Hohner reworked the concept to produce the distinctive Clavinet (1964), which employed plectrums and strings. It has been used extensively in funk music, Stevie Wonder's 'Superstition' being a classic example.

The electromechanical piano was replaced in the late 1970s by the electronic analog piano, which was followed in the 1980s by the digital piano. Ironically, what is perceived to be an electric piano on many recordings is more often than not a digital re-creation with its own distinct timbre, a typical example being a 'ballad' song such as 'Beauty and the Beast' (Céline Dion).

Sometimes, the distinctive sound of electric pianos can be very successfully emulated by software routines used within computer-based audio recording programs.

Bibliography
Forrest, Peter. 1998. *The A-Z of Analogue Synthesizers.* Crediton: Susurreal.
Rhodes Super Site. http://www.badrat.com/
Wurlitzer Electric Piano. http://users.aol.com/KeyMuseum /wurli.html

Discographical References
Dion, Céline. 'Beauty and the Beast.' *Beauty and the Beast: Soundtrack.* Disney B000001M13. *2001*: USA.

Wonder, Stevie. 'Superstition.' Tamla Motown WD 72585/B. *1972*: UK.

Discography
Carpenters, The. *Singles 1969–73.* A & M CDA63601. *1992*: UK.
Charles, Ray. *The Collection.* Collection COL005. *1995*: UK.
Doors, The. *Best of the Doors.* WEA K9603452. *1995*: UK.
Hancock, Herbie. *Head Hunters.* Sony Jazz CK65123. *1992*: UK.
Small Faces, The. *Best of the Small Faces.* Summit SUMCD4001. *1993*: UK.
Supertramp. *Breakfast in America.* A & M CDA3937082. *1994*: UK.
Zombies, The. *Best of the Zombies.* Music Club MCCD002. *1992*: UK.

JON BATES

Electronic Organ

The electronic organ has existed almost since the beginning of the twentieth century. Its purpose has been that of imitation, in a quest to replace the sound of the pipe organ and, subsequently, other instruments of the orchestra and popular music ensembles. Unlike a synthesizer, it is not a creator of new timbres.

The history of the electronic organ mirrors developments in electronic technology. The circuitry for signal generators (oscillators) dates back to 1917. Significant developments in the early 1920s in the production of electron tubes, which had been invented in 1906, as well as amplifiers and loudspeakers, provided the basis for the manufacture of electronic organs for the next 50 years.

Commercial production of electronic organs began in the 1930s. The French inventors Coupleux and Givelet produced and advertised a 'pipeless' organ in 1930 that used punched paper rolls to control four oscillators. The electromechanical Compton (1932) used rotating electrostatic generators. The Hammond (1935) was also electromechanical and used a form of additive synthesis – the adding together of multiple sine waves. It was briefly used at this time by George Gershwin and Fats Waller. The Hammond was also adopted by many churches and has continued to be used by gospel choirs in the United States. Many electronic organs created timbres using subtractive synthesis – wave forms rich in sound partials (sawtooth and square waves, for example) were combined and then shaped by filter circuits that simulated the resonant frequency (the acoustical components) of traditional organ stops. With the addition of sine wave generation circuits, a typical electronic organ of this type would have between 60 and 100 tunable free-phase oscillators.

Various manufacturers favored different methods of producing sound. Experiments using the transformation of light into sound were tried in 1931 by Welte and Rangertone, while both Wurlitzer and Everett (1935) favored an electrostatic reed system keyed by an electromagnetic pallet. Baldwin used frequency division of oscillator-generated frequencies. The advantage of using frequency-dividing systems was that far fewer oscillators were required to create the tones, and tuning the instrument was considerably easier. Eventually, this was to lead to the manufacture of instruments with a single oscillator and powerful division networks.

In the early 1950s, the transistor was introduced as a replacement for the electron tube. Unlike tubes, transistors were small, strong, reliable and easy to work with. Organs became smaller and more attractive for home use, and manufacturers were able to develop and include more features and sounds within a single instrument. Hammond, for example, pioneered the use of the integral reverb unit, which simulated the ambiance of a performance space – a hall or a stage. The market for home organs increased in the postwar years, and companies such as Lowrey, Gulbransen, Conn and Thomas all came into being around the early 1950s. At the same time, jazz artists such as Jimmy Smith were starting to use Hammond organs, creating a new, harder-edged sound.

In the 1960s, the integrated circuit first appeared. This incorporated hundreds (and eventually thousands) of transistors on one piece of silicon. This led to a significant offshoot of electronic organ manufacture: the portable organ. Manufacturers such as Farfisa and Vox made instruments designed for use within small instrumental groups. Portable organs quickly gained in popularity and represented the first use of the electronic organ in rock music. Bands like the Animals, Pink Floyd and the Doors made use of these instruments. At about the same time, the Hammond electronic organ, usually coupled with the rotary 'Leslie' speaker, began to find favor among rock and jazz artists. Emerson, Lake and Palmer and Jon Lord (Deep Purple) explored the use of the Hammond in rock, while the James Taylor Quartet and Joey DeFrancesco have continued to explore its use in the acid jazz genre. Although a successful imitative digital sound synthesis has come to be used for the manufacture of these organs, many artists have continued to prefer the original Hammond models, the production of which ceased in the mid-1960s.

With the advent of cheap silicon components in the early 1970s, the electronic organ gained in popularity. Coupled with this development was that of the rhythm unit. At first it was a separate item, but it quickly became integrated into the instrument, where it was linked to a harmony analyzer and thus became the backbone of the

self-accompaniment unit. A drum pattern plus a chord played on the lower manual were sufficient to derive a bass line and rhythmic chord pattern. The electronic organ became a popular item to have in the home, and many regional organ societies were formed to hear and appreciate concert performances by visiting artists. Mainstream solo artists such as Klaus Wunderlich were very successful commercially, although pop and rock music made little use of the self-accompanying instrument.

There was a shift in technological development from the United States to Japan, where companies like Yamaha and National Panasonic (later Technics) were pushing the limits of electronics in the service of the electronic organ. Yamaha, in particular, had been manufacturing electronic organs since the 1950s.

In the early 1980s, two major technological developments resulted in significant advances. The first was the commercial use of frequency modulation (FM) synthesis. The principle of FM had been known for many years, but it had not been viable because of its complexity and its need for many components. Yamaha funded research and developed the technology; this resulted in the production of its DX series of synthesizers, which used digital means to create sound. This technology was also used in Yamaha organs of the time.

The second major technological development was the use of digitally recorded samples of a real sound either to replace the electronic synthesized sound or, in conjunction with digital synthesis methods, to create authentic tone reproduction. The tone-generating circuit of a modern electronic organ is basically the same as that found in many modern synthesizers. Some organs incorporate digitally recorded sounds from specific theater and church organs for greater realism; others make use of physical modeling, a synthesis technique that allows the interaction of the various elements of the physical sound creation process to be calculated and digitally imitated.

The advent of digital technology has also resulted in advances in self-accompanying instruments. It is possible to have factory-programmed introductions, endings, stylistic variations and several layers of accompanying instruments, plus multitrack recording, on board the organ. Many electronic organs can be pre-programmed by the user; in some cases, the sounds can be reshaped and altered. Most organs are equipped with a computer disc drive to load and store preset sounds, songs, rhythms and performances either created by the user or purchased commercially. The instruments are MIDI-compatible, and some have options for SCSI hard drives. Solo performers such as Max Takano and Glyn Madden have made use of these features both in the studio and live onstage.

Since the boom years of the 1970s and early 1980s, the electronic organ market has fragmented and dissipated somewhat. However, a significant core of electronic organ enthusiasts, who generally want a 'hands-on' instrument that requires little pre-programming, has continued to exist. Conversely, the market for single keyboards – self-accompanying single manual portable instruments with preset sounds – has remained very buoyant. Manufacturers such as Rodgers, Johannus and Viscount, which specialize in electronic church organs that imitate pipe organs, have also continued to produce models.

Bibliography

Bates, Jon. 1989. *The Synthesizer*. Oxford: Oxford University Press.

Crombie, David. 1984. *The Synthesizer and Electronic Keyboard Handbook*. London: Dorling Kindersley.

Towers, T.D. 1976. *Electronics in Music*. London: Newnes Technical.

Vail, Mark. 1997. *The Hammond Organ: Beauty in the B*. San Francisco: Miller Freeman.

Discography

Animals, The. *Best of the Animals*. Laserlight CD16137. *1993*: UK.

Deep Purple. *The Very Best of Deep Purple*. Warner Bros./Rhino 0 8122 797928. *2000*: USA.

DeFrancesco, Joey. *Singin' and Swingin'*. Concord CCD-4861-2. *2001*: USA.

Doors, The. *Best of the Doors*. WEA K9603452. *1995*: UK.

Emerson, Lake and Palmer. *Best of Emerson, Lake and Palmer*. Essential ESSCD296. *1993*: UK.

James Taylor Quartet, The. *Blow Up*. Music Club MCCD333. *1996*: UK.

Madden, Glyn. *Zwei Nacht in Einer Grosser Stadt*. Grosvenor CDGRS1250. *1996*: UK.

Pink Floyd. *Piper at the Gates of Dawn*. EMI CDEMD1073. *1990*: UK.

Smith, Jimmy. *Dot Com Blues*. Blue Thumb 5439782. *2001*: USA.

Takano, Max. *New York, New York*. Grosvenor CDGRS1205. *1996*: UK.

Wunderlich, Klaus. *Golden Sounds of Klaus Wunderlich*. Disky GS864362. *1992*: UK.

JON BATES

Hammond Organ

The Hammond organ, invented by Laurens Hammond at the Hammond company's plant in Chicago in 1933, patented in 1934 and put on the market in 1935, was the first widely known electric organ. Based on the same technical principles as the gigantic (and failed) Telharmonium by Thaddeus Cahill (patented in 1897), it was made possible by various concurring circumstances, such as the availability of valve amplifiers, and Hammond's need to find new applications for his synchronous motor (previously used to power electric clocks) during the Depression years.

Each note on the Hammond organ is generated by an individual electrical alternator, formed by a toothed 'tone wheel' or disc, a permanent magnet and a coil. The rotating wheel modifies the flux supplied by the magnet, and so induces an alternating voltage in the coil, which, when a key is pressed, can be amplified to generate a sound. The number of teeth and the shape of the tone wheel determine the frequency and timbre of the sound. The latter is controlled by a number of stops, similar to those available in traditional mechanical organs that allow the organist to blend various harmonic components. A useful accessory is the Leslie loudspeaker set, with rotating horns that create a distinctive sound as a result of combined Doppler effects.

An expensive instrument for an individual during the Depression years (the initial cost was $1,250), the Hammond organ was nonetheless much cheaper than a pipe organ (whose price was in the $70,000 range), so Hammond organs were sold to churches, theaters, radio stations, hotels and nightclubs. Popular performers at that time and subsequently included Milt Herth ('Stompin' at the Savoy' (1936)) and Ethel Smith (her version of 'Tico Tico' (1944) sold more than 2 million copies). Fats Waller, already known for his pipe organ solos recorded for Victor in a disused church (1926–29) and for his unrivaled ability 'to make the pipe organ swing,' also adopted the instrument.

In the late 1930s, the Federal Trade Commission (FTC) challenged the Hammond company's advertising and decided to appoint an impartial panel to determine whether the Hammond instrument was in fact an 'organ.' Members of the panel, unaware of the actual sound source, listened to a pipe organ and a Hammond instrument; in over 30 percent of their responses they could not tell the difference between them. However, although the FTC subsequently ruled that the Hammond company could call its instrument an organ, and although George Gershwin was said to be the first owner of a Hammond organ, the instrument was inevitably characterized by connotations of 'easy listening,' and its sound subsequently used to evoke (or satirize) typical performance environments, like nightclubs, hotel cocktail lounges and bars. After World War II, cheaper models and an improved economy opened up a thriving home market for Hammond organs in the United States. This was accompanied by the formation of Hammond organ societies. With the added ability to help beginners without any knowledge of chords to play the instrument, the Hammond organ and similar electric organs succeeded in becoming the focal point of musical entertainment in households during the 1950s – at least in North America and some European countries.

Adopted largely in popular music, the electric organ had its greatest success in the 1960s and early 1970s, becoming the lead instrument in hits like the Animals' 'The House of the Rising Sun' (1964), featuring a famous solo by Alan Price, Procol Harum's 'A Whiter Shade of Pale' (1967) and the Band's 'Chest Fever' (1968) (although Garth Hudson was using a Lowrey organ). It brought fame to instrumentalists like Al Kooper, Brian Auger and Keith Emerson, all of whom were indebted to jazz virtuoso Jimmy Smith. Other notable organ sounds from the 1960s, like that of the Doors, were actually electronic organ sounds, that is, they were generated by purely electronic circuits and not by electromechanical devices.

Discographical References

Animals, The. 'The House of the Rising Sun.' Columbia DB 7301. *1964*: UK.

Band, The. 'Chest Fever.' *Music from Big Pink*. Capitol 2955. *1968*: USA.

Herth, Milt. 'Stompin' at the Savoy'/'The Madam Swings It.' Decca 911. 1936: USA.

Procol Harum. 'A Whiter Shade of Pale.' Deram DM 126. *1967*: UK.

Smith, Ethel. 'Tico Tico'/'Lero Lero.' Decca 23353. 1944: USA.

FRANCO FABBRI

Harmonium

The principle of the free reed (as opposed to the beating reed, as in pipe organ reed pipes) can be found in early wind instruments such as the Asian *sheng*, but its application in keyboard instruments dates only from the late eighteenth century, when makers of organs began experimenting with the use of brass free reeds as a substitute for traditional pipes in small domestic and self-playing instruments. Although such instruments eventually became known generically as reed organs, during the nineteenth century they went by a variety of other names. In continental Europe, 'harmonium' was and is the preferred term, but early reed organs were also called 'seraphines' in England and 'melodeons' in North America, and in France the term *'orgue expressif'* was frequently used. The harmonium was patented in 1840 in Paris by Alexandre F. Debain.

Like the organ, the harmonium is a wind-activated instrument, but free reeds can be sounded by either pressure or suction. In Europe, the pressure system was used from the outset, but in North America reed organs using the suction system evolved during the early decades of the nineteenth century, and instruments of this type are commonly referred to in Europe as 'American organs.' The pressure/suction is generated by the action of the player's feet on pedals connected to a bellows, although in the twentieth century reed organs were often made with a small internal motor, and older instruments were frequently retrofitted with one (sometimes contrived from an old vacuum cleaner). Because of the action of the pedals, one often hears harmoniums colloquially referred to as 'pump organs.'

As a domestic instrument, the harmonium quickly became popular. It was cheaper to make than the small domestic pipe organs that it eventually replaced, and it stayed in tune better than the more costly piano. The earliest versions (and many later ones) were also compact and portable, and made a pleasing piece of parlor furniture – hence another of the harmonium's many colloquial names: 'parlor organ.'

By the second half of the nineteenth century, the making of reed organs had become a major industry in the United States, France, Germany and, to a somewhat lesser extent, England, The Netherlands and Scandinavia, although by this time every European country had some harmonium makers and, by the turn of the century, harmoniums were being made in Japan and India. The leading US manufacturers (who counted their output in the thousands) were Estey, Mason & Hamlin, and Kimball. In France, Alexandre and Mustel were the two leading makers, and in Germany the Scheidmeyer firm operated a large harmonium factory.

Just as the mode of reed-organ construction differed somewhat between North America and Europe, so did the instrument's use. While reed organs enjoyed wide domestic and religious use on both continents, European musicians took them more seriously, perhaps because the pressure system allowed more dynamic-expressive variation. Harmoniums were found in salons and smaller concert rooms; harmonium playing was taught at the Paris Conservatory; and such noteworthy French and German composers as Franck, Vierne and Reger wrote serious and substantial works for the instrument. In Germany, full-fledged solo recitals were given on larger instruments, called *Kunstharmoniums*. The harmonium also figured in ensemble music for chamber or string orchestras, and even appeared in opera scores by Rossini and others; as late as the twentieth century, it was specified by Kurt Weill in his score for *The Threepenny Opera*.

While some large instruments, often with elaborate cabinetwork and more than one keyboard, were produced in late nineteenth-century North America – Mason & Hamlin's 'Liszt' model was a notable example – the bulk of reed-organ production consisted of smaller models with two to four sets of reeds, which for a time were the most ubiquitous domestic instruments of the middle class. Hardly a farmhouse or cottage was without one. In the expanding Midwest, ambitious salesmen peddled them from horse-drawn carts in the rural areas, and they eventually appeared in the Sears & Roebuck catalog. Reed organs were also used in smaller churches and in Sunday school rooms, and were part of the equipage of traveling evangelists such as Moody and Sankey. While these instruments were frequently of the basic domestic type, larger church models were also made, often with fake 'pipe tops' to make them resemble a pipe organ. The most impressive of these church models was the Vocalion, which, because it was built on the pressure principle, was louder than the average suction-type instrument; large Vocalions had two manuals and pedals, and with their pipe tops could be mistaken for small pipe organs.

While serious composers wrote for the European harmonium, the musical reed-organ fare in the United States, although produced in considerable volume, was of a more homely variety. The typical reed-organ book, usually prefaced by some basic lessons and instructions for the beginner, was a mélange of popular songs, waltzes and galops, easy transcriptions of operatic melodies, and perhaps a few religious pieces. Any original material was simple and was the work of obscure composers (usually including the collection's compiler), and many books were published by reed-organ manufacturers as a means of promoting their product. But the well-worn condition of surviving examples testifies to the fact that they were frequently used, bringing pleasure and a small degree of musical education to various households.

The harmonium has also been featured in performances by well-known US popular musicians. For example, in discussing the performance styles of women classic blues singers of the 1920s and 1930s, Oliver (1997) notes that 'whereas Ma Rainey liked a rough jazz band to accompany her . . . Bessie Smith preferred the legitimately trained Fletcher Henderson or the organist Fred Longshaw as her accompanist' (70). On some recordings, such as 'St. Louis Blues,' Bessie Smith is accompanied by Louis Armstrong on the cornet and Fred Longshaw playing the harmonium.

By the turn of the century, the factory-produced piano was rapidly usurping the place of the reed organ as a domestic instrument, and by the early decades of the twentieth century many manufacturers had gone out of business, while others, including Kimball and Estey, were downsizing reed-organ production in favor of producing pianos or pipe organs. Kimball eventually phased

out reed organs entirely, leaving the dwindling market to Estey, which by the 1930s and 1940s was producing a small number of two-manual-and-pedal reed organs for use as organists' practise instruments, an idea possibly borrowed from British makers such as Holt. By the time of World War II, Estey's reed-organ output consisted almost entirely of small folding 'chaplain's field organs,' examples of which still occasionally appear in Sunday schools and summer camps.

By the postwar period, reed-organ manufacture was virtually extinct in Europe and the United States, although Yamaha of Japan continued to produce a small number. The final blow to the industry was administered by the growing popularity of domestic electronic instruments, beginning in the 1930s with the Hammond organ; indeed, in the second half of the twentieth century, such instruments occupied virtually the same niche in popular culture as reed organs had a century earlier.

Although many old harmoniums have long been cherished (if not always played) as family heirlooms, the late twentieth-century wave of nostalgia focused new interest on reed organs as collectibles and, while no new ones were being made in the United States or Europe, antique dealers were finding them profitable, and businesses existed for the sole purpose of restoring them.

In 1981, the Reed Organ Society was founded. It publishes an informative journal and, although it is based in the United States, its membership of collectors, hobbyists, restorers and musicians is drawn from many countries. New interest in the serious literature of the European harmonium has resulted in several CD recordings by performers such as England's Anne Page, and even some of the more ephemeral music of the North American continent has been recorded. But while other, older musical instruments have seen revivals within the musical mainstream, the harmonium may be the only instrument to have made the transition from popularity as a musical medium to popularity as an antique in less than two centuries.

Bibliography

Bradley, Van Allen. 1957. *Music for the Millions: The Kimball Piano and Organ Story*. Chicago: Henry Regnery Co.

Fluke, Phil, and Fluke, Pam. 1985. *Victorian Reed Organs and Harmoniums*. Bradford: P. & P. Fluke.

Gellerman, Robert F. 1985. *Gellerman's International Reed Organ Atlas*. New York: Vestal Press.

Gellerman, Robert F. 1996. *The American Reed Organ and the Harmonium*. New York: Vestal Press.

Milne, F.F. 1930. *The Reed Organ: Its Design and Construction*. London: Musical Opinion.

Oliver, Paul. 1997. *The Story of the Blues: The Making of a*

Black Music. London: Pimlico. (First published London: Barrie & Rockliff, 1969.)

Ord-Hume, Arthur W.J.G. 1986. *Harmonium: The History of the Reed Organ and Its Makers*. Newton Abbot: David & Charles.

Whiting, Robert B. 1981. *Estey Reed Organs on Parade*. New York: Vestal Press.

Discographical Reference

Smith, Bessie. 'St. Louis Blues.' Columbia G 30818. 1925: USA. Reissue: Smith, Bessie. 'St. Louis Blues.' *Smithsonian Collection of Classic Jazz, Vol. 1*. Smithsonian 0331. *1991*: USA.

Discography

Barfield, Naomi. *The Old Pump Organ* (Naomi Barfield plays her own compositions on an unidentified US reed organ). Forum 7GS-2510. http://www.bsnpubs .com/forum.html

Desbonnet, Germain. *Music for Harmonium* (Germain Desbonnet plays music of Franck, Boëllmann and Berlioz on an Alexandre). Musical Heritage Society MHS-4192. http://www.musicalheritage.com/

Hasselböck, Franz. *Das Romantisches Harmonium* (Franz Hasselböck plays works of Kienzel, Reger, Bruckner, Bizet, Franck, Liszt, Berlioz, Smetana and von Weber). DaCamera Magna SM-93001. http://www.bayer musicgroup.de

Lueders, Kurt. *L'harmonium au salon* (Kurt Lueders plays music of Widor, Franck, Guilmant and Massenet). Euromusic EURM-2022. http://www.ohscatalog.org/ frenhar.html

Michel, Johannes Matthias. *Sigfrid Karg-Elert: Harmonium Works Vol. 1*. Classic Produktion Osnabrück CPO 999 522-2. *1997*: Germany.

Michel, Johannes Matthias. *Sigfrid Karg-Elert: Harmonium Works Vol. 2*. Classic Produktion Osnabrück CPO 999 523-2. *1998*: Germany.

Michel, Johannes Matthias. *Sigfrid Karg-Elert: Harmonium Works Vol. 3*. Classic Produktion Osnabrück CPO 999 611-2. *1998*: Germany.

Michel, Johannes Matthias. *Sigfrid Karg-Elert: Harmonium Works Vol. 4*. Classic Produktion Osnabrück CPO 999 631-2. *1998*: Germany.

Page, Anne. *French Music for Harmonium II* (Anne Page plays music of Louis and René Vierne, Tournemire, Hakim, Litaize and Langlais on an 1897 Mustel). Voix Celeste CEL 002. *1990*: France.

Verdin, Joris. *César Franck: Oeuvres pour harmonium* (Joris Verdin plays an 1865 Alexandre). Ricercar RIC-75057. *1990*: France.

Verdin, Joris. *Guilmant & Lemmens: Pièces pour harmonium* (Joris Verdin plays an 1891 Mustel). Ricercar RIC-206252. *1997*: France.

BARBARA OWEN

Harmonium (India)

The harmonium was introduced into India in the mid-nineteenth century. It was the small portable version of the harmonium originally used by missionaries that became common in both popular and classical forms of Indian music. The harmonium has hand-operated bellows, which the player (usually a singer) works with the left hand while playing the keyboard with the right hand. Its range is variable, but normally spans two or three octaves.

The Role of the Harmonium in Indian Music

Since its introduction into India, the harmonium has played a controversial role in the history and development of both Indian classical and popular music. Purists have consistently objected to its use, as its tempered scale is viewed as inimical to the subtle pitch inflections of Indian music and its keyboard suggests the possibility of harmonic accompaniment. In 1910, a *śruti* harmonium was developed and manufactured by Henry Keatley Moore, based on the acoustical research of A.J. Ellis, H. Helmholtz and others (Moore had worked as Ellis's assistant). It had 22 intervals to the octave, in keeping with the ancient Indian division of the scale, and was therefore considered more authentic – and hence suitable for Indian music. However, the *śruti* harmonium appeared to be of interest only to musicologists and theoreticians. It quickly became little more than a curiosity, generally ignored by performing musicians.

The harmonium continued to stimulate much heated debate. Among its fiercest critics were the famous Bengali poet, musician and educationalist Rabindranath Tagore and the early twentieth-century Indian musicologist Ananda K. Coomaraswamy. It was finally banned on All India Radio (AIR) from the 1950s until the 1970s. (Interestingly, it appears that this ban was initiated by the English composer John Foulds, who was at that time head of the Delhi station (Neuman 1990).) Nevertheless, in Indian classical music the harmonium has now largely supplanted the *sārangī* as the main accompanying instrument.

The Harmonium in Indian Popular Music

The harmonium has assumed a central role as an accompanying instrument for all forms of popular vocal music. It is ubiquitous in light popular forms, such as *ghazal*, and in forms of religious popular music, such as *bhajans* and *qawwālī*; they in turn have formed the basis for numerous *filmī* songs. The late Nusrat Fateh Ali Khan, the *qawwāl* who had a significant impact on Western popular music in the 1980s and 1990s, used the harmonium as a central element of his ensemble. The harmonium is essentially a support for the voice, and its performance as a solo instrument is less common.

Bibliography

Dick, Alistair, and Owen, Barbara. 1984. 'Harmonium.' In *The New Grove Dictionary of Musical Instruments*, Vol. 2, ed. Stanley Sadie. London: Macmillan, 131.

Neuman, Daniel M. 1990. *The Life of Music in North India*. Chicago: University of Chicago Press.

GERRY FARRELL

Melodeon

A melodeon is a small diatonic button accordion, usually a one-row, one-key version (although English folk revivalists use the term to describe the smaller two-row instrument they tend to play). The sound is produced by drawing air through metal reeds by means of bellows. The instrument has 10 right-hand buttons, and plays two-and-a-half octaves of a single diatonic scale, often with three to four draw stops to select the voices of the right-hand end. The bass keys, sometimes spoon-shaped, select the tonic/dominant chords. The melodeon is used in Brazilian *forró*, Nigerian *jújù*, Cajun, French-Canadian traditional, and English/Irish traditional folk dance music styles, as well as in other minor regional genres.

Discography

Beausoleil. *Cajunization*. Rhino 75633. *1999*: USA.

Brazil Forró: Music for Maids and Taxi Drivers. Rounder 5044. *1989*: USA.

Dairo, I.K., and His Blue Spots. *Definitive Dairo*. Xenophile 4045. *1996*: USA.

La Bottine Souriante. *Xième*. Mille-Pattes MPCD 2040. *1998*: Canada.

Stradling, Rod. *Rhythms of the World*. Rogue FMSD 5021. *1991*: UK.

GRAEME SMITH

Organ

Until the mid-nineteenth century, the term 'organ' (German *Orgel*, French *orgue*, Italian *organo*, Spanish *organo*) referred solely to a keyboard instrument producing its sound by means of wind-blown pipes. The popular term, 'pipe organ,' came into use in the late nineteenth century to distinguish the traditional organ from the reed organ (harmonium) and, more recently, the electronic organ.

The precursor of the organ was a small, loud instrument called a 'hydraulis,' invented in the third century B.C., used outdoors for games and on ceremonial occasions, and popular throughout the ancient Greco-Roman world. By the tenth century, the organ had begun to assume some of its present characteristics, and was appearing in large cathedrals and abbeys in Western Europe, where at first it was used, like bells, to add exciting musical noises to festal occasions or to announce processions. Only later did it begin to have any function in the church's liturgy.

By the end of the fifteenth century, organs of various sizes possessing most of the characteristics of modern organs (multiple keyboards, stops of varying colors and pitches, compasses up to four octaves, pedals) were found in churches, while smaller organs, sometimes with only a single set of pipes, were used in homes and for accompanying songs in outdoor miracle plays. The earliest examples of written organ music appear in the fifteenth and early sixteenth centuries, exhibiting an interesting mixture of sacred and secular. Dances and compositions based on popular songs share the pages with church pieces based on plainsong.

Although the organ was identified with church music during the Renaissance and the Baroque period, it never lost its secular appeal. Its use was banned in the Reformed Dutch Church during the seventeenth century due to the Calvinist belief that instrumental music of any kind was improper in a church service, but composer Jan Pieterszoon Sweelinck used the large instrument in his Amsterdam church to entertain the merchants with lively toccatas and variations on popular songs on market days. During the eighteenth century, J.S. Bach and others gave recitals, and French organists entertained the people with variations on popular folk carols before the Christmas midnight Mass. Theaters often possessed small organs, and Handel's delightful organ concertos were composed to entertain the audience between the acts of his operas.

In the nineteenth century, the secular use of the organ became more widespread. From the 1830s onward, large organs began to appear in concert halls in England, on the continent and in the United States. During the second half of the nineteenth century, recitals played in these venues, as well as in larger churches, attracted substantial audiences and programs were designed for maximum popular appeal. Tourists to Freiburg, Germany and Zurich, Switzerland wrote of hearing the cathedral organists in these cities improvise 'thunderstorm' pieces so realistically that it made them reach for their umbrellas. In Paris, the flamboyant L.-J.-A. Lefébure-Wély wrote rousing marches and character pieces such as the 'Bolero de Concert,' making him the first choice to draw large audiences to organ dedications. At Liverpool's St. George's Hall, William T. Best was cheered by local Welshmen when he played his 'Concert Fantasia' on 'Men of Harlech,' and in the United States Dudley Buck, Eugene Thayer and John Knowles Paine offered audiences variations on popular songs and hymns such as "Tis the Last Rose of Summer,' 'Home, Sweet Home' and 'The Star-Spangled Banner,' a tradition Charles Ives perpetuated with his rollicking 'Variations on "America."'

During the late nineteenth century, recital programs invariably included transcriptions from orchestral and operatic works, and the tonal design of organs gradually became more 'orchestral' in character by the early twentieth century, with increasing numbers of imitative reed stops and massed string-toned effects. While the overture to Herold's opera *Zampa* was a standard crowd pleaser in the late nineteenth century, by the early decades of the twentieth century performers such as Clarence Eddy and Edwin H. Lemare were using these expanded tonal resources and improved registration aids in sophisticated transcriptions of such works as Wagner's 'Ride of the Valkyries' and Saint-Saëns's 'Danse Macabre.' Yet other notable performers, such as Lynnwood Farnam and Joseph Bonnet, also drew good audiences with more traditional fare.

By the close of the 'roaring twenties,' large cinema organs had been installed in places such as New York's Radio City Music Hall, where Jesse Crawford was the featured organist. Radio also made use of the organ, and a cinema-style instrument designed by Reginald Foort was installed in London's BBC studios in 1936.

Radio and phonograph records began to utilize the organ in the period preceding World War II, and while a certain amount of the music broadcast and recorded was classical, much of it was popular. Classical organists such as the United States' E. Power Biggs, England's G.D. Cunningham and France's Charles Courboin made many recordings, as did popular performers such as Crawford, and even jazz great Fats Waller recorded a few organ performances, initially rare collectors' items that have now been reissued on CDs. Biggs also had a nationally syndicated radio program from 1937 to 1958.

In the postwar period, a more eclectic style of organ became current, and classical performers such as Biggs and France's Marcel Dupré did much to popularize organ works of the Baroque and Romantic periods. Others, such as Virgil Fox, took a more radical approach to the classical repertoire; one of Fox's last performances was of souped-up Bach played on an electronic organ with a psychedelic light show at New York's Fillmore East.

Beginning in this period, a trend among some more traditional organ composers toward 'crossover' music employing jazz, blues and other popular idioms derived from big band, piano and cinema organ styles becomes noticeable. Robert Elmore's 'Rhumba' (1954) was an early example; more recently, these idioms have been employed by composers such as Calvin Hampton ('Five Dances'), William Albright ('Sweet Sixteenths: Concert Rag') and William Bolcom, who employs black gospel techniques in his 'Gospel Preludes.' During the 1990s, presenters of organ concerts, such as Canada's Calgary International Organ Festival, increasingly offered a melange of program options ranging from severe classical to transcriptions and theater/pop, successfully drawing audiences with a wide range of musical tastes.

The Organ Historical Society (P.O. Box 26811, Richmond, VA 23261) and The Organ Literature Foundation (45 Norfolk Road, Braintree, MA 02184-5915) both have extensive catalogs of organ-related books and recordings.

Bibliography

Arnold, Corliss R. 1995. *Organ Literature: A Comprehensive Survey.* 2 vols. 3rd ed. Metuchen, NJ: Scarecrow Press.

Bicknell, Stephen. 1996. *The History of the English Organ.* Cambridge: Cambridge University Press.

Lukas, Viktor. 1989. *A Guide to Organ Music.* Portland, OR: Amadeus Press.

Ochse, Orpha. 1975. *The History of the Organ in the United States.* Bloomington, IN: Indiana University Press.

Sumner, William Leslie. 1978. *The Organ: Its Evolution, Principles of Construction and Use.* 4th ed. London: MacDonald & Jane's.

Williams, Peter, and Owen, Barbara. 1988. *The Organ.* London: Macmillan.

Sheet Music

Albright, William, comp. 1976. 'Sweet Sixteenths: Concert Rag.' New York: E.B. Marks.

Bolcom, William, comp. 1984–90. 'Gospel Preludes.' 4 books. New York: E.B. Marks.

Buck, Dudley, comp. 1975. 'The Star-Spangled Banner: Concert Variations.' New York: McAfee Music.

Buck, Dudley, comp. 1977. 'The Last Rose of Summer' (Variations). New York: McAfee Music.

Elmore, Robert, comp. 1954. 'Rhumba' (in *Rhythmic Suite*). New York: St. Mary's Press.

Hampton, Calvin, comp. 1981. 'Five Dances.' Boston, MA: E.C. Schirmer.

Ives, Charles, comp. 1949. 'Variations on "America."' Bryn Mawr, PA: Mercury Music Corp.

BARBARA OWEN

Piano

Introduction

One of the largest musical instruments, the piano is also one of the most versatile. It can perform the roles of soloist, accompanist and participant in a band or orchestra, and it can itself suggest both a single individual sound or voice, and the many sounds or voices of a large ensemble. Its versatility extends to performance contexts – the piano is found at events as diverse as theatrical rehearsals and apartment rent parties, in all kinds of venues, from concert halls to clubs to churches, and it has a long history of association with the home. In the process, it has not only contributed to a large number of different genres and styles of music, but has also been an essential presence in many of them. It has been used in sharply contrasting dramatic contexts, where it has played roles as various as commentator on romantic tragedy and participant in slapstick. An advanced technological product, the piano has also had a central involvement in the growth of music trade and commerce, and has played a major role in social and cultural history. It has been valued, too, in diverse ways: as the epitome of aesthetic sensibility, as a gendered sign of grace and stability, as a tool of cultural hegemony, as the most essential of all practical tools for the working musician, and as an accomplice in barroom carousing. All of these functions and characteristics have separate but interlocking histories and these are reflected in the role that the piano has played in popular music.

Early Design, Manufacture and Marketing

The piano is a keyboard instrument that has its strings struck by rebounding hammers. In this, it is to be distinguished from keyboard instruments of the harpsichord family, whose strings are plucked, and from the clavichord, whose strings are struck by tangents (brass blades) that do not rebound. In its modern form, it has a range of slightly over seven octaves. The piano's invention is usually credited to Bartolomeo Cristofori, who worked for the Medici court in Florence in the late seventeenth and early eighteenth centuries. Shortly after its first appearance around 1700, it was described in a journal of the day as 'gravicembalo col piano e forte' (harpsichord with soft and loud). Not only was this account the source of the piano's name, but it hinted clearly at a key characteristic – the control of volume and dynamics within a phrase – that would lead to the piano's domination as a keyboard instrument.

The piano was first designed and developed in the wing shape that came to be known as 'grand.' These early instruments were intended for the European aristocracy. The first steps toward producing an instrument that incorporated Cristofori's leather-covered hammers and rebounding mechanism in a simpler design and shape, with the intention of reaching a larger – if still largely upper-class – market, were made by the builders of the square piano in the second half of the eighteenth century. London in particular was a site where the square piano – which in shape was close to a clavichord – became the fashionable center of a nascent music business, in which the pianos made by German immigrant

Johannes Zumpe and his successors were promoted via subscription concerts featuring leading musicians of the day, and supported by printed music for the amateur. Such music often came with instructions on how to get the most out of the new purchase. The square piano was intended principally as a domestic instrument, but its marketing linked the public and private worlds in a way echoed by later generations of music entrepreneurs (Parakilas et al. 2002, 21–23). As the idea grew of using the piano as a foundation on which to promote music, a particularly significant part was played by Italian-born composer and pianist Muzio Clementi. Based in London from the mid-1770s, Clementi involved himself in what became an integrated network of activities, touring internationally as a virtuoso performer on the grand piano while having profitable interests in composing, publishing (his own and others' music), piano design (all shapes), writing tuition manuals and collaborating with editors of newly founded music journals. In this, 'he showed a particular genius for understanding how apparently different systems of production and marketing could be coordinated so that each promoted and expanded the others' (Parakilas et al. 2002, 75).

The Rise of the Upright

The first upright pianos were produced in the late 1730s, but in their eighteenth- and early nineteenth-century form tended to be mainly upright grands, and as such were as far out of the reach of middle- and working-class households as grands themselves. Three particular developments that took place in design and manufacture between the 1820s and the 1860s helped the upright piano come eventually to a position of market domination. The first was cross-stringing, or over-stringing. This system, first developed by Henri Pape in Paris in the late 1820s, ran the longer bass strings diagonally across the frame, to be crossed by the shorter treble strings. The second development was the iron frame, patented in Boston in 1825 (originally for a square piano design) and adopted by the Boston firm of Chickering. By the late 1850s, Chickering's chief US rivals, the recently established New York firm of Steinway & Sons, had brought together cross-stringing (in a less crowded, fan-like layout), iron frames and other devices to make the first modern concert grand. Steinway's use of cross-stringing was a recognition of the system's potential to make better use of the soundboard rather than of the instrument's greater compactness. But, in 1863, Steinway applied its cross-stringing design to an iron-frame upright. With its heavier hammers, improved action, an iron frame allowing greater string tension and a system of cross-stringing that combined compactness with enhancement of tone, the instrument, in the words of

Ehrlich (1976), 'marks a watershed . . . [it was] the first really adequate upright, on which virtually all later instruments of quality were based' (50). Like other US manufacturers, Steinway also moved into steam-powered machinery – the third development – greatly increasing the production capacity of all its pianos.

Steinway was also responsible for developing a highly effective approach to marketing the firm's pianos as quality, indeed luxury, items. Like most other manufacturers, however, the company was by no means convinced of – or even interested in – the existence of a more populist market. Changes in design and technology were not sufficient in themselves to place the upright in a dominant market position. It needed the emergence of a new generation of music entrepreneurs, who saw the commercial potential of using modern factory production methods to mass-produce an instrument that could be sold as a feature in homes of all sizes and social levels. In the 1870s, former crockery salesman Joseph Hale set up a factory in New York in which pianos were assembled from parts constructed elsewhere. Soon, he was charging about one-third of the price of the major manufacturers. Hale sidestepped the prevailing agency system and 'sold to anybody – private individual, dealer or jobber anywhere – who paid him' (Loesser 1954, 526). Recognizing that, whether the piano was priced cheaply or not, its social status was such that it sold better if it had some kind of individualization, Hale initiated a stencil system – which operated for many years in the United States and elsewhere – under which dealers could have their own names stenciled on the instruments. Other companies followed in Hale's wake, introducing further initiatives. In one of the most significant, dealers such as W.W. Kimball of Chicago and D.H. Baldwin of Cincinnati offered pianos for sale on a credit system and, by the 1890s, mail-order companies such as Sears Roebuck were offering a range of uprights under their own installment agreements (Hoover 2002, 53–55; Roell 1989, 100).

In this way, the piano was placed at the center of a rapidly expanding capitalist consumer culture, befitting its achievements as, in Robert Winter's description, an 'all-conquering machine' (quoted in Leppert 2002, 216). Yet, this same object had before this time also acquired a different identity, which it still retained. Via a different, albeit related, route, the piano had been allocated a role across a wide range of society that linked it with the essence of femininity. Sometimes, the association was seen as basically trivial, a prelude to – and admittedly useful equipment for – a more responsible role in life (Loesser 1954, 267ff.). But often, as pianos appeared in more and more middle-class homes, the link solidified to make the piano the very symbol of female-centered

familial solidarity. Its establishment in the home – typically in the center of the home – had coincided with, and been encouraged by, the emergence of an ideal of domesticity predicated upon a particular conception of the role of the woman/mother, and the activities that fell into her sphere.

The irony of the coexistence of these dual roles – as instigator of debt and as bastion of family life – is inescapable. Equally striking, however, is that they also make clear how hard it has always been to articulate the piano to one single set of meanings, and how it has often thrived on ambiguity. The piano's place in both domestic stability and consumer culture made it appropriate that it should play a significant role in tensions being played out in popular culture at the turn of the century between the private and public spheres of life.

The rapid expansion of the market for upright pianos, especially in the United States, was a major factor in the growth of popular music publishing in the late nineteenth century. When a new breed of music publishers emerged in the 1890s to revolutionize the market for sheet music, they did so in the confident expectation that an increased demand for music would follow the expanded market for instruments. Already a veteran of promotional schemes, the piano now became an integral part of a new angle on marketing, developed by music publishers: song plugging. Whether plugging took place on publishers' own premises or in major retail chain stores – where it became part of new sonic accompaniment to shopping – it relied on the presence of pianos. The source of much of this music was commercial public entertainment, the nature of which did not always meet with the approval of those whose ideas of the moral value of music had been crystallized around the domestic piano, but which appealed to a younger generation precisely because that image was so restrictive. From the late nineteenth century on, while the piano would retain its role as a provider of domestic popular music, it was increasingly its contribution to forms of musically focused public leisure activities that would mark it out.

Mass Production, International Expansion and Cultural Penetration

In the 1790s, the London firm of Broadwood, England's leading piano maker, was manufacturing an average of 500 grand and square pianos a year. By 1870, the total number of instruments manufactured in Britain, the United States, France and Germany was 85,000. By 1890, the figure had exceeded 200,000 and by 1910 it had reached 600,000, of which 370,000 were manufactured in the United States alone (Ehrlich 1990, 222). The popularity of the piano in this period, often thought of as the instrument's commercial heyday, was further enhanced by the development of the mechanical player piano or pianola, which permitted performance without the obligation to acquire pianistic skills. More importantly, perhaps, in the form of the piano rolls made by professional musicians (often famous ones) and reproduced by a system of punched cards, the player piano brought something close to the actual sound of professional performance into the ordinary home for the first time.

For the four Western countries mentioned above, 1910 marked a peak of production. North American production, which declined steeply in the 1930s and 1940s, was alone in staging a partial recovery. Output gradually grew to reach a fairly regular 200,000 a year in the period from 1970 to 1985, but by that time production in Japan had surpassed it (392,000 in 1980), and Russian production was not far behind (166,000 in the same year) (Ehrlich 1990, 222).

Pianos had arrived in many different parts of the globe before the instrument became a part of capitalist industrial production, but the second half of the nineteenth century saw a significant growth in its international reach. In most cases, the first stage of 'piano imperialism' (Parakilas et al. 2002, 241) was provided by the desire of representatives of Western imperial expansion to have pianos to accompany their lives (and, no doubt, to symbolize their culture). The second stage involved the influence of this arrival on existing musical culture and practise.

In the important example of Japan, the imperial influence worked in a slightly different way. In the 1870s, when the piano first began to acquire a reputation in Japan as a symbol of the modern industrial culture toward which the Meiji government sought to direct the country, it did so following a government mission to the West to discover how this culture operated. The subsequent growth of piano ownership, and with it the circulation of Western piano music, was limited until around 1900. At this time, however, the first evidence was appearing of what would become a remarkable industrial response within the country. Torakichi Nishikawa and Torakusu Yamaha's first ventures into instrument building had both been with reed organs in the 1880s and 1890s. Nishikawa built his first upright piano in 1887, Yamaha his first in 1900. As Western music gained greater acceptance in Japan, manufacture increased and more companies were created, laying the initial basis for the major role that Japanese piano manufacture would later play in the wider world. By 1991, 250 companies were registered, and the Yamaha Corporation was making 14,000 instruments a month (Herd 1994, 189).

In Western countries themselves, the deep social penetration of the piano did not mean it reached everyone. In the judgment of Loesser (1954), in the United States 'there were . . . vast segments of the population – subsistence farmers, agricultural laborers, Southern Negroes, hillbillies, factory workers, mariners', fishermans' and loggers' families, and hordes of city workers in service occupations – to whom the piano and its use were foreign' (540). No doubt, also, many whom it reached, in diverse parts of the world, were put off by the reputation, status and, in some cases, culture that accompanied it. But there is no doubt that the piano did penetrate some ethnic and racial groups, whose contribution to popular music was to be very considerable.

It was often assumed that the spread of the piano would automatically be accompanied by the dissemination of Western music and, indeed, by the adoption of a certain set of established values, most often those associated with the white middle classes. In the case of African-American culture, the response was much more complex. African Americans first began to have access to the piano in significant numbers at a time when, with disillusion widespread following the failure of Reconstruction, there was considerable uncertainty in the African-American community as a whole about its relationship with the dominant culture. In the context of the social and economic marginalization of large swathes of that community, often left substantially to its own devices, cultural forms such as music and dance had the opportunity to develop independent directions. Yet, they did not – could not – do so without some form of acknowledgment of the dominant culture's musical traditions, with which they had become familiar.

African-American musical forms that emerged at this time were creative responses, variously conceived, to the tensions that existed between assimilation and independence; and in the role of the piano these responses can be clearly seen. The 'rag' in ragtime, for example, was derived from African-American performance practise, quite possibly worked out in forms of dancing that were accompanied by 'patting juba,' in which hands were clapped, feet stamped and thighs slapped to provide syncopated rhythms against the main beat. When transferred to the piano, as in Ben Harney's song, 'You've Been a Good Old Wagon, But You've Done Broke Down' (1895), offbeat accents in the right hand set against steady accented bass notes on the first and second beats in the left hand with chords on the offbeats clearly echo earlier vernacular practise. On top of that, the piano's potential as a percussive instrument lends itself well to the syncopations. At the same time, however, the very fact that a piano was played with two hands and that it could sound all the notes in simple or complex chords had produced a stylized transformation of the original idea. Once this stylization was established, other pianistic features and devices followed. The published rags of Scott Joplin, for example, reveal great use of virtuosic running patterns for the right hand while retaining the main syncopated gestures. The left hand, too, has its oom-pah pattern broken up by passages of chromatic octaves and some runs.

An alternative approach to the same underlying tension can be seen in blues piano playing, in which there is simultaneous use of a major and minor third within a chord. These and other juxtapositions in combining the pentatonic and diatonic scales have been explained by Blumenfeld (1992) as 'a deliberate attempt on the part of the early Afro-American blues artist to place the musical scale of his African heritage into conscious and unresolved dissonant relationship with the diatonic mode used by the European settlers' (41).

The Piano in Musical Life and Musical Performance

In the daily life of popular music-making, the piano has performed a centrally important function, providing the supply of music needed for all manner of activities. Much of this centrality has been due to the resources that the piano placed in the hands (and feet) of a single performer. This instrument, equipped with devices such as a sustaining pedal and a pedal to reduce volume, could be played by one person using both hands on the keyboard and operating the pedals with the feet. A player could play a melodic line or several lines, provide harmonic filler, create a strong rhythmic feel with the instrument's percussive possibilities – and at the same time the player could sing. All of these possibilities, together with the piano's potential for volume of sound, made the instrument a one-person substitute in situations that had previously required a group of instrumentalists.

In both amateur and professional spheres, in many different kinds of venues and in diverse types of rehearsal space, the piano has been regarded as a kind of factotum, taken for granted but indispensable. Even though, in recent times, the piano's own progeny, the electronic keyboard – a much more portable instrument – has increasingly taken over the piano's functions, the piano continues to be used in many different daily contexts. It has also been the site at which many musicians and songwriters (including, for example, musical theater composers such as George Gershwin and – with a specially adapted instrument – Irving Berlin) have worked out their ideas. Historically, the piano's only major rival in this role has been the guitar, whose emergence as a multipurpose instrument postdated that of the piano. There are significant differences between them. The guitar's versatility is not as extensive – it lacks the equivalent ability to stand for a large ensemble, for example. It is also apparent that, when used in songwriting, the guitar and piano could produce different results. In a Lennon and McCartney song such as 'I Am the Walrus,' the parallel chordal movements seem likely to be a consequence of the song being worked out on the guitar. In contrast, Brian Wilson of the Beach Boys frequently used the piano to work out his songs. As Nicholson (2000) has pointed out, the piano 'encourages harmonic characteristics of its own,' one of which is the comparative ease with which chords can be played in inversions other than the root. In a song such as 'God Only Knows,' 'the effect of this, combined with the use of extended chords . . . is often somehow to deprive the music of a strict tonal centre' (23).

In the forms in which popular music is performed, the piano's contribution has been equally wide-ranging. The range of styles that have been developed for the piano in popular music is remarkable, as is the scale of the instrument's contribution to a diversity of genres. If, by the late twentieth century, in the wake of various technological changes, there was evidence of few further innovations involving the piano, that does not obscure the fact that its contribution has been made over a length of time greater than that of any other instrument with the exception of the voice (with which it has very often been in partnership).

The piano has been a basic ingredient in the development of genres as diverse as parlor song and tango, bebop and salsa, Brill Building pop and gospel, and its influence has been international. In all of this activity, four principal roles may be identified: solo instrument; the only, or main, accompaniment to a singing voice or voices; participant in an ensemble; and lead instrument in a small ensemble. Several of these roles show a clear line of inheritance from earlier musical practise within the classical tradition, but the results are often markedly different: from Beethoven sonatas to ragtime and boogie-woogie; from Schubert lieder to rock 'n' roll in the style of Little Richard and Jerry Lee Lewis; from piano trios to jazz trios. A crucial reason for such contrasts lies in the fact that approaches to using the piano in all of these roles were transformed by the percussive and rhythmic ideas that were the hallmark of African-American performance practise on the instrument. A significant number of the innovative uses of the piano have been in those genres – either African-American in origin or strongly influenced by African-American music – where performance techniques have been passed on and developed by physical observation, where performance procedures have operated on the basis of working out ideas and approaches in practise rather than from a score, and where performance aspects other than those most easily recordable by notation, such as percussive quality, timbre and attack, have been dominant. (Because the piano lacks the microtonal and note-bending ability of the guitar, it is one of the most 'notat-able' instruments, and notation for the piano can, of course, be found within these genres, but it is often either rudimentary, as in the case of head arrangements for a big band, or 'after the event,' as in the case of transcriptions.)

Not everything in popular music's approach to these roles has simply been the result of contrast and differ-ence, however. There was a continuity between piano music of the Romantic era, for example, and some uses of the piano in accompaniment to silent films. Within the broad historical sweep of popular music itself, as fun-damental practises are adapted by new styles, there are also continuities. It could also be argued, for example, that elements in the style of a performer such as Tori Amos owe much to the persistence of a dramatically conceived approach to song accompaniment evident as far back as Henry Russell in the 1830s and 1840s.

Solo Piano

Solo piano music contains intriguing examples of both continuity and contrast. Nineteenth-century sheet music included many pieces for solo piano in which the object was to capitalize on the piano's ability to 'stand for' a larger ensemble. These published reductions, generally of popular contemporary marches and dances, were intended to be used when the full ensemble would be too expensive to hire. Such sheet music was not gen-erally technically demanding, often including a tuneful melody for the right hand and a rhythmic pattern in the left – such as the common oom-pah pattern (oom-pah-pah in the case of the waltz), alternating pedal notes with chords – in imitation of patterns used by bands.

There seems little doubt that the left-hand figures described here were an important influence on ragtime. But, despite the involvement of sheet music publishers, and the desire of musicians such as Joplin to see their music in print, like classical sonatas, ragtime was also – was perhaps first and foremost – a music of the oral tradi-tion, in which techniques were constantly tested and developed in performance. By the time the next African-American piano style, stride piano, developed just before and during the 1920s, there was still a residue of the earl-ier, march-like oom-pah left hand, but it was part of a very different pianistic conception.

In the person of a musician such as James P. Johnson, one of the leading Harlem-based stride pianists, stride took the rhythms of ragtime and, in the words of

Schuller (1968), 'recast (them) into a more swinging, steadier jazz beat.' The 'reliable rhythmic substructure' contributed by the left hand also provided a 'flow and forward movement' that had not been present before (216–17). Stride pianists often also created a contra-puntal melody in the bass notes by stretching the har-mony and changing the chords every two beats instead of every four or eight. Although a main melody was pre-sent – and its syncopated nature was retained with fre-quent accents and occasional rests – the main interest was often rhythmic. In the case of Johnson and, perhaps especially, his 'disciple' Fats Waller, there was also a pas-sionate desire to create a very full, powerful sound.

At the same time as stride was developing in Harlem, the term 'novelty piano' began to be applied to a virtu-osic tradition that also emerged out of ragtime, but in this case out of a refined, white suburban extension. Pieces such as 'Canadian Capers' and 'Kitten on the Keys,' and pianists, both male and female (such as Zez Confrey, Billy Mayerl, Roy Bargy, Frank Banta, Raie da Costa, Patricia Rossborough and Renara in England, Vera Guilaroff in Canada, Ramona, Edna Fisher and Pauline Alpert in the United States), brought this entertaining new style to the forefront. Based on classical piano-playing traditions from Liszt and on salon repertoire, but using many elements of syncopated music, these pian-ists provided a highly arranged, rhythmically intriguing and often quite melodic piano genre. Great speed and a 'secondary rag' syncopation, grouping the regular quad-ruple subdivisions of the basic pulse into threes, were its hallmarks. The style involved using an orchestral left hand to simulate the rhythm of a dance band, and a right hand that could interpolate filigree with virtuosic figurations. This approach was to have a strong influence on the 'romantic' piano genre that has continued ever since, to some degree, in 'cocktail'-style presentation.

Stride piano is generally considered to have reached its apogee in the style of Art Tatum. But, while Tatum did indeed base his approach on the stride idiom with, in Dick Hyman's words, 'an underpinning of steady dance tempo and jazz/blues tonality' (quoted in Doer-schuk 1995, 59), he brought to it a prodigious technique. The result was an advanced, highly complex style that has sometimes been described as orchestral. A typical Tatum performance would see him take a tune of the day and, by a series of rhythmic and harmonic trans-formations, and with the aid of all manner of orna-mentation (a feature of his play that later often earned him the scorn of jazz critics) and many changes of pace, provide what Priestley (1998) aptly calls 'a completely new experience' (218).

Tatum was unusual in many respects (he was, for example, almost completely blind), one of which was that his virtuoso technique began to blur the division between right and left hand. In jazz in general, however, this distinction had little future, as the pianists moved increasingly in the direction established by Earl Hines. Hines's 'trumpet'-style right hand offered the pianist the chance to create lines and figures like a single-note instrument, supported by the left hand, often in a highly percussive way. Another factor making Tatum unusual was his marked preference for solo performance in an age when small groups were increasingly becoming the main context for jazz pianists to show their prowess. The solo pianist did continue to have a place in jazz – for example, in the work of Tatum's most obvious successor, Oscar Peterson – but did not play the role of innovator until the emergence of Keith Jarrett as a soloist in the early 1970s. In his lengthy solo improvisations, often over 30 minutes long, Jarrett ranged widely over piano styles, popular and classical, incorporating also folk and ethnic musics, and setting up rich and intricate dialogs between them. Jarrett also insisted on playing an acoustic piano, at a time when many musicians were moving to electronic keyboards.

The Piano as Accompanist

If the solo pianist can be seen as a sign of independence, the pianist as accompanist might appear to present a very different image, but two factors resist that interpretation. First, in much popular vocal music accompanied by piano, the singer and the accompanist are one and the same; and second, the conception of the piano's role is in any case often more that of collaborator than simple accompanist.

Playing while singing (or singing while playing) is widespread across popular music genres. No doubt much nineteenth-century sheet music was purchased with the idea that the singer could accompany himself or herself if desired, but in that particular case the printed music generally cast the piano in advance as playing a supporting role. Much more common is an approach that frees up the piano and gives it more options – to be active rhythmically and/or harmonically, percussively and/or melodically, to improvise or not, to be featured as a front-line participant or as backing, as a commentator or as showperson, according to choices that the musician makes. Something of the range can be seen in singer-pianists in rock 'n' roll, pop and rock. Elton John often uses the piano to double the melodic line, while employing three-note chords in the medium to high register to provide an interlude between textual phrases. Little Richard became known for his percussive 'pounding' on the piano, particularly in the high register of repeated chords. These hammered home the harmony and provided additional rhythmic pulse. Jerry Lee Lewis

favored a variety of pianistic devices, ranging from a bass line with boogie patterns to repeated chords in the high register, with glissando flourishes interspersed. Both Richard and Lewis used the piano as an essential partner (almost as a co-conspirator) in an ostentatious, theatrically conceived performance. By contrast, Carole King, on her album *Tapestry*, employed a wide range of techniques much more reflectively.

Many singer-pianists have used the convention (of playing and singing) to engineer a performance in which the piano was presented as an equal partner. In the stride-influenced style of Cleo Brown, for example, as illustrated by her 1935 recording of 'The Stuff Is Here and It's Mellow,' piano and voice alternate as the focus of attention, the piano having a 16-bar introduction of the melody and two further 16-bar choruses following each vocal. Although the piano's contribution to this recording is rhythmically (and somewhat playfully) conceived, it does not need to perform a timekeeping function as such. In this, as in many similar recordings, the singer-pianist is accompanied by a rhythm section of guitar, bass and drums, freeing the piano up for a more front-line role.

Blues piano is particularly notable for the variety of percussive-rhythmic contributions that the piano regularly makes before, underneath, alongside and after a vocal line. Some pianists employed particular piano phrases and figures as a kind of signature; some relied on a basic technique that Priestley (1998) calls a 'hypnotic ostinato much more rudimentary than anything in ragtime' (215). Others were more versatile. As examples, Oliver (1986) singles out Roosevelt Sykes and Leroy Carr, who used a range of devices including walking basses, 'steady 4/4 time with a solid stomping accompaniment ... light and economical left-hand support to filigree right-hand passages ... drone accompaniments on a single chord ... fast and exhilarating boogie basses' (172–73). In Little Brother Montgomery's 1930 recording of 'Vicksburg Blues,' the way the 'rumbling, even threatening character' of the left hand contrasts with the 'taut, braying vocal' is seen by Oliver as an example of close integration of the piano and the vocal (1986, 175).

Blues as a genre also includes in the music of many of the women singers of the 1920s and 1930s, usually known as 'classic blues,' plentiful examples of the separation of the roles of singer and pianist, as, for example, in recordings made by Bessie Smith with various pianists (Fred Longshaw, Porter Grainger, Fletcher Henderson). Whenever this separation is found in popular music, a high degree of importance is attached to the level of understanding between the two performers. Such understanding – regularly aimed for, if not always achieved –

operates on a combination of technical and interpretive elements.

The Piano in the Ensemble

Many pianists developed a style that they could adapt effectively in different situations, including ensemble performance. Roosevelt Sykes, for example, often played with combos in the 1940s, where, as Cohn et al. (1993) point out, his habit of playing a 'deep rumbling bass to hold down the beat while darting all over the keyboard with his right hand, using the latter in the manner of horn players and later electric guitarists' gave him a style 'that worked well on a solo basis and with larger ensembles' (69). Often, the style in which such ensembles performed was relatively short-lived, and as a consequence the piano's role could disappear; but, in other cases, the piano was a regular presence through changes in style and in size of ensemble. In the case of tango, for example, although the piano was not part of the original nineteenth-century instrumentation, it soon became one (often in a trio with violin and *bandoneón*), and remained to become an integral part of the *orquesta típica* ensemble, as it grew in size during the 1920s.

Beginning in the 1950s, Cuban dance music (a mixture of rumba and *son*) evolved in a way that gave the piano a crucial role in the ensemble (Manuel 1988, 34). In part, this role was influenced by that played by the piano in jazz ensembles from the big-band period onward, with an emphasis on chordal accompaniment to soloists, but there were significant differences. For one thing, there was a 'greater stress on volume and percussive intensity' (1988, 35). For another, a key role for the piano was to contribute the *montuno*, a steady, rhythmic/choral, riff-like pattern (in salsa, it is also called *guajeo*) that the pianist repeats, usually with only the slightest variations, throughout the solos by other instruments. In this way the piano inscribes a highly distinctive, audible and persistent rhythmic figure against which other instruments set their own rhythmic lines.

The role of the piano as an integral, but not necessarily spotlighted, member of an ensemble is different from its other roles in one intriguing way. Some areas of popular music appear to have revived – or more likely, discovered for themselves – a practise that the classical tradition had largely abandoned. When a big-band leader such as Count Basie or Duke Ellington directed an ensemble from the piano, making his own diverse pianistic contributions while doing so, there was an echo of the custom often used in the eighteenth century whereby the role of conductor was taken by the keyboard continuo player. According to McVeigh (1993), the habit of including keyboard participation in choral and orchestral music continued in London 'well past 1800,' and conductor Sir

George Smart was wielding his baton from the piano as late as 1834 (218–19). But then, as the role of conductor became more prominent and more celebrated, the practise largely died. Its reappearance in popular big-band music – whether setting a tone, suggesting a tempo, 'comping' behind a soloist or making passing interjections – was a reflection of the sheer practical usefulness of the idea. It also enabled the band leader to be seen both as one of the team and – because the placing of the piano was sure to attract the gaze – as the team leader, and at the same time avoid the stuffy image of 'conductor.'

Small instrumental ensembles in which the piano plays a leading role range from 'lounge music' to accompany food, drink and relaxation, to challenging forms of jazz. The modern version of the first of these appears in a clear line of inheritance from light music of previous eras, while the latter's history and character are more complicated. Within the jazz ensemble, the piano's versatility – whether to use its percussive potential to contribute to the rhythm, its distinctive sound to contribute ornamental extras or its stand-alone capacity to contribute solos – has been consistently recognized. In the history of jazz band development, specific roles have waxed and waned in importance. Particularly significant was the shift that occurred in the small bebop groups in the 1940s, when the rhythmic role that the piano could still be called upon to play was taken over by the drums and bass, and the pianist was free to become one of the front-line soloists, on an equal footing for the first time with saxophones and trumpets. Two of the most celebrated bebop pianists, Bud Powell and Thelonious Monk, developed highly individual styles. Powell was particularly noted for his 'linear' right hand, which fashioned single-note lines and phrases in the manner of saxophonists such as Charlie Parker. Monk, one of jazz's most idiosyncratic figures, played the instrument with his fingers very flat, as if to emphasize percussive qualities, and introduced all manner of rhythmic disjunctures and harmonic dissonances to his music.

Fame and Image

Although they were much admired, bebop pianists tended to be overshadowed in the celebrity stakes by other instrumentalists, and with few exceptions it has generally been the case in popular music history that pianists have not had the same share of the limelight that other performers have had; at least, when pianists have competed at the top in terms of fame, it has not necessarily been because of their piano playing. Partly, this is because the piano has not perhaps lent itself as well as smaller, more portable instruments to image-construction. The particular posture required of pianists (except when they stand up, like Little Richard) has also militated against striking silhouettes and similar images. Yet, in earlier periods, pianists were among the greatest musical celebrities of their day. In describing how enthusiastic fans would steal objects belonging to Franz Liszt, and how his body became 'an object of almost fetishized fascination,' Leppert (2002) refers to him as a 'psychological projection created by his audience . . . a consumer product in the early history of consumption' (210).

The instrument itself has also been overshadowed and has seen its roles taken on by others. Its habit of going out of tune is just one factor in the preeminence of the electronic keyboard. Yet, when extent is combined with variety and versatility, it remains the case that the piano's contribution to popular music is unsurpassed. Whether it will take on new roles in new contexts remains to be seen.

Bibliography

Berlin, Edward A. 1980. *Ragtime: A Musical and Cultural History*. Berkeley, CA: University of California Press.

Blumenfeld, Aaron. 1992. *The Blues, Boogie and Barrelhouse Piano Workbook*. Katonah, NY: Ekay Music.

Cohn, Lawrence, et al. 1993. *Nothing But the Blues: The Music and the Musicians*. New York: Abbeville Press.

Doerschuk, R.L. 1995. 'Dick Hyman: Past 10ths and Other Musical Highlights.' *Keyboard Magazine* 21: 56–63.

Ehrlich, Cyril. 1976. *The Piano: A History*. London: Dent.

Ehrlich, Cyril. 1990. *The Piano: A History*. 2nd ed. Oxford: Clarendon Press.

Hasse, John Edward, ed. 1985. *Ragtime: Its History, Composers, and Music*. New York: Schirmer Books.

Herd, Judith. 1994. 'Japan, Piano Industry in.' In *Encyclopedia of Keyboard Instruments*, ed. Robert Palmieri. New York: Garland, 186–90.

Hoover, Cynthia. 2002. 'Promoting the Piano.' In James Parakilas et al., *Piano Roles: A New History of the Piano*. New Haven, CT: Yale University Press, 53–57.

Leppert, Richard. 2002. 'Cultural Contradiction, Idolatry, and the Piano Virtuoso: Franz Liszt.' In James Parakilas et al., *Piano Roles: A New History of the Piano*. New Haven, CT: Yale University Press, 200–23.

Loesser, Arthur. 1954. *Men, Women, and Pianos: A Social History*. New York: Simon and Schuster.

Manuel, Peter. 1988. *Popular Musics of the Non-Western World: An Introductory Survey*. New York: Oxford University Press.

McVeigh, Simon. 1993. *Concert Life in London from Mozart to Haydn*. Cambridge: Cambridge University Press.

Nicholson, Stuart. 2000. *A Study of the Characteristics of Brian Wilson's Music (with the Beach Boys) During the 1960s*. Unpublished undergraduate thesis, University of Liverpool.

Oliver, Paul. 1986. 'Blues.' In *The New Grove Gospel, Blues and Jazz*, ed. Paul Oliver, Max Harrison and William Bolcom. London: Macmillan, 36–188.

Parakilas, James, et al. 2002. *Piano Roles: A New History of the Piano*. New Haven, CT: Yale University Press.

Priestley, Brian. 1998. 'Ragtime, Blues, Jazz and Popular Music.' In *The Cambridge Companion to the Piano*, ed. David Rowland. Cambridge: Cambridge University Press, 209–25.

Roell, Craig H. 1989. *The Piano in America, 1890–1940*. Chapel Hill, NC: University of North Carolina Press.

Schuller, Gunther. 1968. *Early Jazz: Its Roots and Musical Development*. New York: Oxford University Press.

Sheet Music

Chandler, Gus, White, Bert, and Cohen, Henry, comps., and Burtnett, Earl, lyr. 1915. 'Canadian Capers.' New York: Warner Brothers.

Confrey, Zez, comp. 1921. 'Kitten on the Keys.' In *Modern Novelty Piano Solos*. New York: Mills.

Harney, Ben, comp. and lyr. 1895. 'You've Been a Good Old Wagon, But You've Done Broke Down.' Louisville, KY: Greening Music Company.

Lennon, John, and McCartney, Paul, comps. 1967. 'I Am the Walrus.' London: Northern Songs.

Wilson, Brian, comp. and lyr., and Love, Mike, lyr. 1966. 'Good Vibrations.' Hollywood: Irving.

Discographical References

Beach Boys, The. 'God Only Knows.' Capitol 5706. *1966*: USA.

Brown, Cleo. 'The Stuff Is Here and It's Mellow.' Decca 410. 1935: USA.

King, Carole. *Tapestry*. Epic EK-34946. *1971*: USA.

Montgomery, Little Brother. 'Vicksburg Blues.' Paramount 13006. 1930: USA.

DAVID HORN with ELAINE KEILLOR

Residence Organ

Records show that organs were being used for domestic music-making in homes throughout Europe prior to the sixteenth century. These early house organs, or chamber organs, were small and easily portable, usually with from three to five sets of gently voiced wood and/or metal pipes, and were used to accompany singing or stringed instruments. King Henry VIII of England owned more than a dozen such organs, and they also appear in the inventories of other members of the nobility. Musicians, too, often owned these small organs, and a chamber organ with four stops, said to have once belonged to the sixteenth-century composer Claudio Merulo, has been preserved at the Conservatory of Music in Parma, Italy.

These domestic instruments became more popular during the seventeenth century, and many households used them as ensemble instruments with the equally popular consort of viols. The practise was particularly common in England, where a considerable amount of music for this purpose was written by composers such as Lawes, Jenkins, Ferrabosco and Coperario.

During the eighteenth century, larger domestic organs began to be built, particularly in England, Holland and France. Marie Antoinette of France owned a rather elaborate specimen, since preserved at Versailles, and a number of English instruments from this period have survived. Most of these had a single keyboard, although many had between five and 10 stops; a few possessed two keyboards and, occasionally, a pedalboard. In general, these organs were built by instrument makers who also produced larger church organs, although in the Toggenburg region of Switzerland the domestic organ approached the status of folk instrument, and many were made by amateurs or local instrument makers.

Little documentation exists on the music played on chamber organs in the eighteenth century, but what there is suggests that these instruments were used just as keyboard instruments have continued to be used in the home – for practising lessons, playing pieces that were often 'generic,' in this case for either the organ or the harpsichord, and accompanying singing. This is borne out by accounts from the early and middle nineteenth century, including a charming vignette of a visit by the composer Mendelssohn to Queen Victoria and Prince Albert, who owned a fairly large chamber organ. Prince Albert is said to have played a voluntary, after which Mendelssohn accompanied Queen Victoria in one of his own songs.

While smaller house organs continued to be made for both professional and amateur musicians, by the end of the nineteenth century organs of a substantial size began to appear in the mansions of the wealthy. In 1891, the Willis company built a four-manual organ of near concert-hall proportions for Blenheim Palace, home of England's Churchill family. Salon organs became popular in France, where they were sometimes used with other instruments in private concerts of chamber music. Unlike the musically skilled gentry of earlier days, the owners of these instruments rarely performed themselves, and therefore usually hired professional organists to entertain them.

By the beginning of the twentieth century, opulent residence organs had become established as a status symbol and, indeed, as an almost essential accouterment of the increasingly large and ostentatious mansions of newly rich capitalists, especially in the United States. Accounts of music-making in Whitehall, the Palm Beach residence of the Flagler family, where a fairly modest two-manual Odell organ was installed in 1901, give a glimpse of how these organs were used. At least two local organists were reported as having played there for private concerts or to entertain luncheon guests, as well as to accompany Mrs. Flagler, who was said to have possessed a fine singing voice. Edward Searles of Massachusetts, who married into a railroad fortune, had an organ at both his primary residence in Methuen and a summer estate in Great Barrington. Organist Henry M. Dunham, in his memoirs (Dunham 1931), describes a Christmas party at the latter house in the 1890s. Following a banquet, at around 11:00 p.m., he and Everett Truette 'began playing the organ, the other guests listening from various parts of the house. There was a little balcony . . . where Mrs. Searles sat, a most appreciative listener' (118).

From the early twentieth century onward, however, technology rendered organists unnecessary, except perhaps on special occasions. The recently invented paper-roll playing mechanism used in player pianos was soon adapted and expanded to operate organs made by the US companies Aeolian, Skinner, Moller, Estey and Austin, as well as the German firm Welte, which established branches in England and the United States. Early versions required a person to operate the stops and expression pedals (following directions printed on the paper roll) but, by the second decade of the twentieth century, the mechanism had been perfected to take over all these functions. All that was needed to provide a little dinner music was to have someone put on a roll and start the player.

Advertisements, extant roll collections and Aeolian's handsomely bound books describing the music on their rolls all provide a good idea of the musical tastes of the owners of self-playing residence organs. One advertisement states that 'you have merely to touch a button' to enjoy a Victor Herbert waltz, an overture, a Schubert song or 'a swift new fox trot' – people danced to music from these organs as well. Aeolian's books show a repertoire heavy on transcriptions from symphonic works, operas and oratorios, as well as songs and piano pieces. Legitimate organ works are decidedly a minority, and are largely by romantic and contemporary composers; even Bach is represented more by transcriptions than by actual organ pieces. Companies such as Aeolian, Austin and Welte often hired such well-known organists as Clarence Eddy, Joseph Bonnet, Charles Courboin, Edwin H. Lemare, Sigfrid Karg-Elert and Lynnwood Farnam to cut rolls, but many rolls were also made by anonymous staff organists. Some of the more complex symphonic rolls were cut by hand to produce effects that would have been impossible for a single player to achieve.

The stock-market crash and the Great Depression effectively put an end to the market for residence organs of this type. In his book on the Aeolian firm, Rollin Smith states that, of the 761 organs built between 1894 and 1932, only 65 were known to still exist at the end of the twentieth century, less than half of which were still playable (Smith 1998). Of these, perhaps the most notable was one of Aeolian's largest organs, which was built for Longwood Gardens, the DuPont estate in Delaware, and was still used for concerts and recordings.

During the second half of the twentieth century, electronic instruments firmly captured the home market, yet pipe organs were still being built for home use. At the beginning of the twenty-first century, however, these were generally small in size, found mostly in the homes of musicians, and used primarily for practise, teaching and informal musical gatherings. Exceptions have been the occasional transplanted church or theater organ and, rarely, new installations such as the large French-style organ made by Fisk and used in a private concert hall in California.

Bibliography

Dunham, Henry M. 1931. *The Life of a Musician*. New York: Richmond Borough Printing Company.

Fox, Joseph. 1984. 'Mechanical Music in the American Home.' *Music and Automata* 1(3).

Jakob, Friedrich. 1980. 'Der Hausorgelbau in der Schweiz' [Chamber-Organ Building in Switzerland]. In *Visitatio Organorum* [Looking at Organs], ed. A. Dunning. Buren: Frits Knuf, 363–78.

Murray, Robert G. 1983. 'The Organs at Whitehall.' *The Tracker* 27(2): 16–21.

Smith, Rollin. 1974. 'The Organ of the Frick Collection.' *Music, the A.G.O. and R.C.C.O. Magazine* 8(1): 29–31.

Smith, Rollin. 1997. *The Reynolda House Aeolian Organ*. Winston-Salem, NC: Reynolda House.

Smith, Rollin. 1998. *The Aeolian Pipe Organ and Its Music*. Richmond, VA: Organ Historical Society.

Wilson, Michael. 1968. *The English Chamber Organ*. London: Bruno Cassirer.

Wolf, Edward C. 1976. 'The Secular Pipe Organ in American Culture.' In *The Bicentennial Tracker*, ed. A.F. Robinson. Richmond, VA: Organ Historical Society, 142–62.

Discography

Bate, Jennifer. *From Stanley to Wesley, Vol. 1* (Jennifer Bate plays eighteenth-century English music on five English chamber organs and two church organs). Unicorn-Kanchana DKP-9096. *1990*: UK.

Jones, Brian, and Gordon, Andrew. *Organ and Piano Duets at Longwood Gardens*. AFKA SK-506. *1990*: USA.

Stairs, Michael. *A Longwood Gardens Christmas* (Michael Stairs plays Christmas organ works and popular songs on the 1930 Aeolian organ at Longwood Gardens). Organ Historical Society DTR9102. *1996*: USA.

BARBARA OWEN

Theater/Cinema Organ

The term 'theater/cinema organ' refers to a pipe organ placed in a motion picture theater for accompanying silent films and for other entertainment uses.

The theater or cinema organ represents a unique step in the evolution of the traditional pipe organ of church and concert hall. It was the result of the achievements and inventions of many people, the most important of whom was Robert Hope-Jones. Hope-Jones was a church organ builder in England. He did not set out to invent a theater pipe organ for the accompaniment of silent films; rather, his intention was to make changes to and improve upon church pipe organs. His goal was to produce an organ that would sound like an orchestra.

In the earliest days, the console (keyboards) of a pipe organ was directly connected to the valves beneath each pipe to open the valve, admit the air and sound the note. Hope-Jones developed one of the first and most reliable 'electric actions' with electromagnets beneath the pipes. When an organ key was pressed, the electromagnet opened the valve, admitting the air and sounding the note. This meant that the organ console could be placed anywhere, connected to the pipes by an electric cable.

Hope-Jones demonstrated this new organ design at St. John's Anglican Church, Birkenhead, England in 1886, placing the console out in the churchyard among the gravestones and playing for the congregation seated within the church. His audience was astounded.

In the early 1900s, Hope-Jones emigrated to the United States, where he worked briefly for a number of church organ builders before joining forces with the Rudolph Wurlitzer Company of North Tonawanda, New York. Most of Hope-Jones's inventions predate 1907, several years before organs were placed in theaters in significant numbers. He was responsible for introducing the horseshoe-shaped console, which made the stop controls easier to reach; the tilt-tab stop control; and the electric lighting of the stop rail, which made the stops easier to see in a darkened environment. He also used increased wind pressures in his pipe organs to produce the desired orchestral tones and to operate the various drums, cymbals and percussion instruments that were attached.

The Wurlitzer Company marketed an organ known as a 'unit orchestra,' designed to imitate orchestral sounds. It included, in various forms, additional sound effects useful in accompanying silent pictures, such as doorbells, steamboat whistles, railroad bells, sirens, birdcalls, automobile horns, wood blocks, drums and cymbals. In addition, percussion instruments – pianos, marimbas, xylophones, glockenspiels and various sorts of bells and chimes – were included, depending on the size of the organ.

Although the larger theaters had orchestras to accompany silent pictures (some of them boasting 50 to 60 musicians or more), a single organist with a specially designed theater organ could do some things that an orchestra could not. He/she could time his/her playing to fit the action on the screen; could use the organ's special effects at just the right moment; and could play from memory, improvise and weave together a tapestry of music that would be difficult, if not impossible, for an orchestra to produce. Best of all from the standpoint of the theater management, it was cost-effective to use a single organist rather than 50 or 60 musicians.

The first organs placed in theaters were usually built by church organ builders. They were called 'straight' organs because they were designed to play sacred and classical music and they did not adapt well to cinema entertainment. The earliest motion picture theaters were in small, storefront buildings, sometimes using a bedsheet for a screen. Any musical accompaniment was normally provided by a piano. As motion picture theaters evolved into 'movie palaces' and 'cathedrals of the film' (one US theater/cinema chain advertised its buildings as 'an acre of seats in a palace of splendor'), ever larger and more elaborate organs were installed.

One of the very first theaters to feature an organ was Thomas L. Talley's theater in Los Angeles, which opened in 1905. A Murray M. Harris pipe organ was installed and the result was a huge success.

The earliest account that exists of organ music being used to accompany a film comes from London, England. French inventors Louis and Auguste Lumière staged a showing of their 'cinématographie' (which they had introduced in Paris a few months earlier), and for the London showing a reed organ (harmonium) was played, it is believed, to mask the noise of the projector and – quite incidentally – to provide some background music. The organ was equipped with a compressed-air cylinder, and puffs of air were released from it to accompany pictures of a train pulling into the station. The audience was thrilled by such realistic sound effects. This event occurred on 12 February 1896.

By 1912, the Wurlitzer Company and other organ builders were installing theater organs across the United States, Canada, Great Britain and, to a lesser degree, Europe, Australia and New Zealand. Organ pipes were installed in one or two rooms (chambers) located at either side of the proscenium (sometimes stacked, one on top of the other, especially in British theaters). The console was often placed on a lift or elevator to allow it to be raised into view when needed. It could be lowered out of sight for accompanying silent films.

The National Geographic Society estimated that at least 6,000 theaters in the United States were so equipped. However, this is a very conservative estimate, since the output of the two largest organ builders (Wurlitzer and Robert Morton) would have exceeded this total. Other important US producers included Kimball, Marr and Colton, Kilgen, Barton, Moller and Page. In England, the two best-known organ builders were Compton (the largest, which installed its first instrument in 1908) and 'Christie' (built by Hill, Norman and Beard) beginning in 1926. Other British organ builders included Rutt, Jardine, Ingram, Conacher, Hilsdon, Fitton and Hayley, and Blackett and Howden.

In addition to using an organ to accompany silent pictures, most theaters featured a 'spotlight' organ solo, in which the organist raised the instrument on the lift and, in the spotlight, as one of the many featured attractions, played a special organ solo or 'intermission.' Theater organs were also used regularly to accompany 'community singing,' using song slides with the words projected onto the screen, and often to accompany live vaudeville acts that might be appearing on the same bill with the film.

With the coming of sound pictures, theater organs continued to be used in this fashion even when they no longer provided picture accompaniment. However, in the United States, the Great Depression in the 1930s spelled the end of the theater organ. Theater staffs and budgets were trimmed, organists were let go, and many organs were junked, sold to churches or left to slumber in silence. In England, cinema organs continued to be widely used until after World War II, while in the United States only the largest and most important theaters retained and used their instruments.

Bibliography

Anderson, Gillian B. 1988. *Music for Silent Films, 1894–1929: A Guide*. Washington, DC: Library of Congress.

Barnes, William H., and Gammons, Edward B. 1970. *Two Centuries of American Organ Building*. Glen Rock, NJ: J. Fischer and Bro.

Berg, Charles Merrell. 1976. *An Investigation of the Motives for the Realization of Music to Accompany the American Silent Film, 1896–1927*. New York: Arno Press.

Bowers, Q. David. 1966. *Put Another Nickel In*. Vestal, NY: Vestal Press.

Carter, C. Roy, comp. n.d. *Theatre Organists Secrets*. Los Angeles, CA: C. Roy Carter.

Courtnay, Jack. 1946. *Theatre Organ World*. London: Theatre Organ World Publications.

Foort, Reginald. 1970. *The Cinema Organ*. 2nd rev. ed. Vestal, NY: Vestal Press.

Hall, Ben M. 1961. *The Best Remaining Seats*. New York: Clarkson Nott Potter, Inc.

Hampton, Benjamin B. 1970. *History of the American Film Industry*. New York: Dover Publications, Inc.

Junchen, David L. 1985. *Encyclopedia of the American Theatre Organ*. Pasadena, CA: Showcase Publications.

Landon, John W. 1974. *Jesse Crawford, Poet of the Organ; Wizard of the Mighty Wurlitzer*. Vestal, NY: Vestal Press.

Landon, John W. 1983. *Behold the Mighty Wurlitzer: The History of the Theatre Pipe Organ*. Westport, CT: Greenwood Press.

Lang, Edith, and West, George. 1920. *Musical Accompaniment of Moving Pictures*. Boston, MA: The Boston Music Company.

Ochse, Orpha. 1975. *The History of the Organ in the United States*. Bloomington, IN: Indiana University Press.

Rapee, Erno. 1970 (1925). *Encyclopedia of Music for Pictures*. New York: Arno Press. (First published New York: Belwin, 1925.)

Rudolph Wurlitzer Company. 1926. Reprint. Vestal, NY: Vestal Press.

Tootell, George. n.d. *How to Play the Cinema Organ – A Practical Book by a Practical Player*. London: W. Paxton and Co., Ltd.

Whitworth, Reginald. 1932. *The Cinema and Theatre Organ*. Reprint. London: Musical Opinion.

JOHN W. LANDON

Wurlitzer Organ

The Wurlitzer Company was the best-known producer of theater organs. Its heavy use of advertising brought it a degree of recognition unmatched by other companies. In the United States during the 1920s, advertising led people to call every refrigerator a Frigidaire, every camera a Kodak and every phonograph a Victrola. In the same way, most theater organs were known as 'mighty Wurlitzers.' A popular advertisement for the company shows a young boy at the movie theater with his father, pointing to the organ and saying, 'Gee, Dad, it's a Wurlitzer!'

True to its advertising claim, Wurlitzer did produce an excellent instrument, as shown by the number that have survived and have continued to be played, recorded and enjoyed. Wurlitzer became the industry leader, with most other companies making some attempt to imitate the instrument's appearance and sound.

The Wurlitzer family traces its origins back to Saxony, Germany in the late 1500s. Rudolph Wurlitzer, father of the US branch of the family, was born in Saxony in 1831, emigrating to the United States in 1853 and settling in Cincinnati. He became a naturalized citizen in 1859 and began importing musical instruments such as trumpets and drums, which were needed in large numbers by the Union Army in the American Civil War.

The first keyboard instrument manufactured in the United States under the Wurlitzer name was a piano, produced in 1880. Automatic and coin-operated instruments were added later. Farney Wurlitzer, the youngest son of Rudolph, joined the firm in 1904 and was the first to recognize the importance of building theater organs to accompany silent pictures. The first theater organ left the factory on 3 February 1907. In 1909, Robert Hope-Jones, an organ builder who had immigrated from England, went bankrupt and his assets and patents were purchased by Wurlitzer. Many believe that the first Wurlitzer theater pipe organ incorporating many of Hope-Jones's ideas was the Style 'L,' which the company began producing in 1912. It included a roll-playing mechanism. One of the earliest Wurlitzer horseshoe console instruments was the three-manual (keyboard), 17-rank (sets of pipes) organ installed in the Liberty Theater in Seattle, Washington in 1914.

At its peak in 1926, the company was shipping one complete organ each day. After the stock-market crash in 1929 and the advent of sound films, the theater organ business in the United States declined drastically. However, the 1930s brought the building of super-cinemas in Great Britain, where Wurlitzer did the bulk of its business until the beginning of World War II in 1939.

Some of the most outstanding instruments built by the Wurlitzer Company would include those installed in Radio City Music Hall, New York; the Paramount Theater and ninth-floor Paramount studio, Times Square, New York; the Fox theaters in Detroit, St. Louis and San Francisco; the Empire Theatre, Leicester Square, London; the Paramount theaters in Manchester, Leeds and Newcastle, England; the Trocadero, Elephant and Castle, London; the Granada, Tooting; and the Tower Ballroom, Blackpool, England.

The Wurlitzer Company became one of the major producers of pianos in the United States and, after the heyday of the theater organ, a major producer of jukeboxes.

Bibliography

Anderson, Gillian B. 1988. *Music for Silent Films, 1894–1929: A Guide*. Washington, DC: Library of Congress.

Barnes, William H., and Gammons, Edward B. 1970. *Two Centuries of American Organ Building*. Glen Rock, NJ: J. Fischer and Bro.

Berg, Charles Merrell. 1976. *An Investigation of the Motives for the Realization of Music to Accompany the American Silent Film, 1896–1927*. New York: Arno Press.

Bowers, Q. David. 1966. *Put Another Nickel In*. Vestal, NY: Vestal Press.

Carter, C. Roy, comp. n.d. *Theatre Organists Secrets*. Los Angeles, CA: C. Roy Carter.

Courtnay, Jack. 1946. *Theatre Organ World*. London: Theatre Organ World Publications.

Foort, Reginald. 1970. *The Cinema Organ*. 2nd rev. ed. Vestal, NY: Vestal Press.

Hall, Ben M. 1961. *The Best Remaining Seats*. New York: Clarkson Nott Potter, Inc.

Hampton, Benjamin B. 1970. *History of the American Film Industry*. New York: Dover Publications, Inc.

Junchen, David L. 1985. *Encyclopedia of the American Theatre Organ*. Pasadena, CA: Showcase Publications.

Landon, John W. 1974. *Jesse Crawford, Poet of the Organ; Wizard of the Mighty Wurlitzer*. Vestal, NY: Vestal Press.

Landon, John W. 1983. *Behold the Mighty Wurlitzer: The History of the Theatre Pipe Organ*. Westport, CT: Greenwood Press.

Lang, Edith, and West, George. 1920. *Musical Accompaniment of Moving Pictures*. Boston, MA: The Boston Music Company.

Ochse, Orpha. 1975. *The History of the Organ in the United States*. Bloomington, IN: Indiana University Press.

Rapee, Erno. 1970 (1925). *Encyclopedia of Music for Pictures*. New York: Arno Press. (First published New York: Belwin, 1925.)

Rudolph Wurlitzer Company. 1926. Reprint. Vestal, NY: Vestal Press.

Tootell, George. n.d. *How to Play the Cinema Organ – A Practical Book by a Practical Player*. London: W. Paxton and Co., Ltd.

Whitworth, Reginald. 1932. *The Cinema and Theatre Organ*. Reprint. London: Musical Opinion.

Discography

The Mighty Wurlitzer: Music for Movie-Palace Organs. New World Records NW 227. *1977*: USA.

JOHN W. LANDON

11. Mechanical Instruments

Mechanical Instruments

Introduction

Mechanical instruments are those instruments that produce their sounds automatically from a pre-programmed mechanical source and are operated either without human participation (by clockwork, water, wind or electricity) or with musically unskilled human aid (such as by turning a handle or pumping bellows to provide air for pressure, or exhausters for suction). Because the prime feature of such an instrument is that its mechanism can produce predetermined musical sounds each time it is operated, and since its music is provided from a precise and repeatable mechanical program, each playing is an original performance. By definition, then, this category excludes machines such as gramophones, phonographs and aeolian harps.

History

Mechanical instruments have their origin in the remote past. The first self-playing instruments, based on the flute, are thought to predate the Christian era. Apollonius of Perga (third century B.C.) is credited with having devised automata, including singing birds, worked by a water wheel that also pumped air into a whistle.

It is reliably recorded that the ancient peoples of Asia and Egypt had 'automatic statues' which moved or spoke, and this inspired Hero of Alexandria (first century A.D.) to devise automaton temple doors and a mechanically played instrument. However, self-playing devices of this period seem to have been of the random form that, like the aeolian harp, could not replicate any given theme. They lacked the vital component that distinguishes the automatophon from such instruments – the repeatable element that comes from using a mechanical program to render exact repetition possible.

Just when this was introduced is uncertain, but the first written description of a mechanical instrument with such a program source was provided between 813 and 833 by three of the leading recorders of Arab science in Baghdad, the so-called Banū Mūsa (Brothers Mūsa – Muhammad, Ahamad and Hasan). The mechanism described was a flute played by means of a rotating cylinder made of closely spaced discs, from the surface of which pegs projected to lift levers that uncovered the apertures in the body of the flute.

As both music and technology progressed, the evolution of proper self-playing instruments began. In Europe during the fifteenth to seventeenth centuries, mechanical music was principally provided by the mechanical organ and the self-playing carillon, although stringed instruments such as the automatic spinet had made their appearance by the end of the sixteenth century. This period in European history was one of rich patronage from the noble and ruling classes, and the ancient religious and cultural center of Augsburg became the focus of art and craft. Not surprisingly, automata and mechanical music were part of this scene. The work of craftsmen such as the Bidermanns, father and son, who made mechanical organs and spinets, Achilles and Viet Langenbucher, also making clockwork spinets, Matthias Runggells, Hans Schlottheim and others marked a noble transition from the Middle Ages to the great era of self-playing musical instruments that was to follow.

Much of this immensely fruitful development was halted by the onset of the Thirty Years' War (1618–48). It was not until the start of the eighteenth century that mechanical music once more began to flourish, ushering in its richest period. Indeed, the years from 1720 through to 1820 may rightly be called the 'Golden Century,' as mechanical instruments became true musical interpreters. Because the program-barrels of these instruments preserve the exact style of ornamentation and performance that was expected of them when newly built, they are of importance to the musicologist, providing real clues to such thorny problems as the correct speed of the minuet, the precise difference between allegro and adagio, and the culture of seventeenth- to eighteenth-century musical ornamentation.

During the two thousand and more years of mechanical instruments (with the principal developments having taken place since the end of the seventeenth century), almost every instrument of music has been automated. From the church organ to the harmonica or mouth organ, from the flute to the violin and banjo, all have received the attention of resourceful inventors.

Purpose and Social Implications of Mechanical Instruments

By the time of Augsburg's rise to supremacy in the production of mechanical instruments, there had been a subtle shift in the purpose of these artifacts. Whereas the earliest examples had been created as novelty items, later instruments were designed to provide entertainment. However, because the music they played was in general in the contemporary idiom, they were not specifically revered for musical interpretation, although it must have been essential that they perform technically as well as, if not actually better than, a human performer.

As novelty items they were accessible only to the wealthy, and were considered suitable gifts between monarchs, noblemen and diplomats. When Elizabeth I decided to give a present to the Sultan of Turkey in 1599, she chose a musical clock containing a carillon, barrel organ and automaton birds. In Central Europe, gifts exchanged between rulers were often richly ornamented mechanical instruments, frequently with clocks and automata.

The aristocracy took an almost naive pleasure in incorporating music into the most unlikely objects to surprise and delight their guests. This created an environment for makers to be at their most innovative. At the time of Haydn, for example, small organs built into decorative urns, even a musical settee, were not exceptional. In the Royal Palace in Madrid, there is a chandelier with two separate miniature clockwork organs concealed in its lusters.

This rich sponsorship excluded the ordinary public, for whom the only source of any mechanical music they might hear was a carillon or, later, a barrel organ in church. In Vienna, center of the musical-clock industry during the 'Golden Century,' all fashionable public places, such as cafés and restaurants, had musical clocks that played the best of popular music to their clientele.

While this still fell short of offering music for the masses, by 1834 it was possible to calculate that four-sevenths of the music heard by people in the majority of towns and cities actually came from mechanical instruments played in the streets by itinerant musicians. As the nineteenth century drew to a close, new statistics suggested that street barrel organs and pianos accounted for more than 85 percent of the music heard by the average town dweller.

The increasing availability of the musical box during the second half of the nineteenth century at last brought music into the ordinary home. It was music that united families in life and worship, and for this reason many musical boxes were provided with at least one hymn tune to which the family could sing on Sundays.

If the musical box brought the first music into the nonmusical home, the arrival of the self-playing piano or player piano brought a revolution in domestic entertainment. As formal piano teaching declined in the aftermath of World War I, the player piano brought music of an acceptable quality into homes everywhere. In 1920, 70 percent of the 364,000 pianos manufactured in the United States were player pianos; by the beginning of the Depression in 1929, player pianos still accounted for more than one-third of the 120,000 pianos produced. The player piano was also responsible for educating the general public about the corpus of music available to them. For many who could not master the keyboard, it allowed access to the enjoyment of music through actual 'performance,' and brought within the grasp of those with an inquiring and adventurous nature the works of composers that they might never otherwise have thought to hear. One composer at least attributed his fame solely to the availability of his music on a piano roll – Edward Macdowell (1861–1908).

Principles of Operation

Mechanical instruments comprise four parts: the musical element (pipes, strings, bells, tuned steel teeth); the musical program (barrel or cylinder, tune disc or perforated card, metal or paper); a mechanical interface between the first and second parts; and the source of energy to set the instrument into play.

The musical element is normally familiar and, with the possible exception of the tuned steel tooth (for example, the musical-box comb), recognizable as similar to features of nonmechanical instruments.

The musical program, in its most common form, is a cylinder, the surface of which is provided with projections representing the particular note sequence of the music to be played. The oldest and most common form is a wooden barrel, the outer surface of which is made of a close-grained timber (traditionally poplar) and into which are driven pins (short notes) and staple-like bridges of various lengths (longer notes). Metal cylinders were used for the large church carillons and smaller musical clocks and musical boxes. In general, punched discs with projections were used in disc-playing musical boxes, and pierced metal, card or paper for *organettes*. Perforated paper is used for pneumatic actions found in player pianos and many other early twentieth-century instruments.

The interface comprises a method of linking the program source to the musical element. This is typically a keyframe (a row of mechanical levers) or tracker bar (used in pneumatic actions controlled by a paper roll).

Energy to drive the sequence of performance is provided by a clockwork motor (which may be spring- or weight-driven); by a hand-turned crank; by foot-operated pedals to a pneumatic mechanism (as in a player piano); or by electricity (as in some piano orchestrions, violin players and coin-operated instruments).

Music for Mechanical Instruments

While the essence of the mechanical instrument was that it could play any existing music, a number of composers were inspired to write especially for the mechanical medium. For example, C.P.E. Bach and Handel were among the many who composed for the musical clock, Cherubini for the barrel organ, and Handel, Haydn, Mozart and Beethoven for the clockwork organ.

A number of composers wrote for the player piano, encouraged by the opportunity it provided to exploit the freedom from the human player's limitations. This freedom allowed extended and even simultaneous use of every keyboard register, as well as the playing of chords in excess of 10 notes, while repetition and 'stretch' could be almost limitless. Although Camille Saint-Saëns wrote for the Aeolian Company's 116-note pipe organ ('Fantasie pour Orgue Aeolian'), neither he nor Cecille Chaminade (who composed for the same instrument) truly took advantage of the possibilities open to them. Stravinsky, on the other hand, used the player piano for an early version of 'Les Noces,' while others, including Casella (1883–1947), Goossens (1893–1962), Hindemith (1895–1963), Howells (1892–1983), Malipiero (1882–1973) and Nancarrow (1912–97), experimented with its abilities.

Conclusion

In spite of a revival of interest in mechanical music in the 1960s that saw the restoration of considerable numbers of 'classic' player pianos and the production of several new so-called spinet models, by the end of the twentieth century mechanical instruments performed only a minor role in public entertainment. Other than for the performance of modern compositions for player piano

(which, like some of the eighteenth- to nineteenth-century mechanical organ compositions, cannot be played convincingly by hand), their sole purpose was to entertain and amuse by adding an extra dimension to an existing experience.

At the end of the twentieth century, a whole new generation of player pianos arose thanks to computer technology, which has made possible digitally recorded information that can be used to play a pneumatic or electric player. The MIDI recording/playback system lies at the heart of these new instruments and represents a technique now readily available to produce self-playing pianos, electronic organs and synthesizers. While a feature of all traditional mechanical instruments was that they were visually interesting to watch, new-age electronic instruments that play automatically have replaced that feature with electronic reliability and portability: the electronic organ is far smaller and lighter than a pipe organ with the same tonal responses.

Bibliography

Adlung, Jacob. 1768. *Musica mechanica organoedi* [Mechanical Music of the Organ Player]. Berlin.

Bowers, Q. David. 1972. *Encyclopedia of Automatic Musical Instruments*. New York: Vestal.

Brauers, Jan. 1984. *Von der Äolsharfe zum Digitalspieler: 2000 Jahre mechanische Musik, 100 Jahre Schallplatte* [From the Aeolian Harp to the Digital Memory: 2000 Years of Mechanical Music, 100 Years of the Gramophone Disc]. München: Klinkhardt & Biermann.

Buchner, Alexander. 1959. *Hudební automaty* [Mechanical Musical Instruments]. Prague: Státní nakl. krásné literatury, hudby a umení.

Buchner, Alexander. 1992. *Les instruments de musique mécanique* [Mechanical Musical Instruments], trans. Philippe Rouillé. Paris: Grund.

Caus, Salomon de. 1624 (1615). *Les raisons des forces mouvantes* [The Logic of Moving Forces]. Rev. ed. Frankfurt: I. Norton.

Chapuis, Alfred. 1928. *Automates, machines automatiques et machinisme* [Automatons, Automatic Machines and Mechanisms]. Geneva: Editions Techniques.

Chapuis, Alfred. 1980. *History of the Musical Box and of Mechanical Music*, trans. Joseph E. Roesch. Summit, NJ: Musical Box Society International. (Originally published as *Histoire de la boîte à musique et de la musique mécanique*. Lausanne: Scriptar, 1955.)

Chapuis, Alfred, and Droz, Edmond. 1949. *Les automates, figures artificielles d'hommes et d'animaux: histoire et technique* [The History and Workings of Automatons and Artificial Figures of Men and Animals]. Neuchâtel: Éditions du Griffon.

Chapuis, Alfred, and Gélis, Édouard. 1928. *Le monde des*

automates: étude historique et technique [The World of Automatons: An Historical and Technical Study]. Paris: É. Gélis.

Engramelle, M.D.J. 1971 (1775). *La tonotechnie ou l'art de noter les cylindres* [The 'Tonotechnical,' or the Art of Inscribing Cylinders]. Geneva: Minkoff.

Fludd, Robert. 1618. *Tractatus secundus de naturae simia seu technica macrocosmi historia* [Second Treatise on the Imitation of Nature or the Technical History of the Macrocosm]. Oppenheim: De Bry.

Haspels, Jan Jaap. 1987. *Automatic Musical Instruments, Their Mechanics and Their Music, 1580–1820*. Utrecht: J.J. Haspels.

Haspels, Jan Jaap. 1994. *Musical Automata*. Utrecht: Nationaal Museum van Speelklok tot Pierement.

Hoffmann, E.T.A. 1819. *Die Automate* [The Automaton]. Berlin.

Jüttemann, Herbert. 1987. *Mechanische Musikinstrumente: Einführung in Technik und Geschichte* [Mechanical Musical Instruments: Introduction to Their Techniques and History]. Frankfurt: E. Bochinsky.

Jüttemann, Herbert. 1991. *Schwarzwälder Flötenuhren* [Black Forest Flute Clocks]. Waldkirch: Waldkircher Verlag.

Kircher, Athanasius. 1650. *Musurgia Universalis* [Universal Musical Work]. Rome.

Langwill, Lyndesay G., and Boston, Noel. 1970 (1967). *Church and Chamber Barrel-Organs*. Rev. ed. Edinburgh: L.G. Langwill.

McTammany, John. 1971 (1915). *The Technical History of the Player*. New York: Vestal.

Ord-Hume, Arthur W.J.G. 1973a. *Clockwork Music: An Illustrated History*. London: Allen and Unwin.

Ord-Hume, Arthur W.J.G. 1973b. *The Mechanics of Mechanical Music: The Arrangement of Music for Automatic Instruments*. London: The author.

Ord-Hume, Arthur W.J.G. 1978. *Barrel Organ: The Story of the Mechanical Organ and Its Repair*. London: Allen and Unwin.

Ord-Hume, Arthur W.J.G. 1980. *Musical Box: A History and Collector's Guide*. London: Allen and Unwin.

Ord-Hume, Arthur W.J.G. 1982. *Joseph Haydn and the Mechanical Organ*. Cardiff: University College Press.

Ord-Hume, Arthur W.J.G. 1984. *Pianola: The History of the Self-Playing Piano*. London: Allen and Unwin.

Ord-Hume, Arthur W.J.G. 1986. *Harmonium: The History of the Reed Organ and Its Makers*. Newton Abbot: David & Charles.

Ord-Hume, Arthur W.J.G. 1995a. *The Musical Box: A Guide for Collectors, Including a Guide to Values*. Atglen, PA: Schiffer Pub.

Ord-Hume, Arthur W.J.G. 1995b. *The Musical Clock: Musical and Automaton Clocks and Watches*. Ashbourne: Mayfield Books.

Palmieri, Robert, ed. 1994. *Encyclopedia of Keyboard Instruments. Vol. 1: The Piano*. New York: Garland.

Protz, Albert. 1939. *Mechanische Musikinstrumente* [Mechanical Musical Instruments]. Kassel: Bärenreiter-Verlag.

Roell, Craig H. 1989. *The Piano in America, 1890–1940*. Chapel Hill, NC: University of North Carolina Press.

Schott, Caspar. 1664. *Technica curiosa* [Interesting Technical Devices]. Nuremberg: E.A. and W. Endter.

Schott, Caspar. 1674. *Magia universalis naturae et artis* [Wonders of Universal Nature and Art]. Bamberg: Schönwetteri.

Simon, Ernst. 1980 (1960). *Mechanische Musikinstrumente früherer Zeiten und ihre Musik* [Mechanical Musical Instruments of Earlier Times and Their Music]. Wiesbaden: Breitkopf & Härtel.

Tushinsky, Joseph S. 1978. *The Pianocorder Story*. Chatsworth, CA: Superscope.

Vaucanson, Jacques de. 1738. *Le mécanisme du fluteur automate* [The Mechanism of the Automaton Flute Player]. Paris: Chez J. Guerin.

Vaucanson, Jacques de. 1742. *An Account of the Mechanism of an Automaton*. London: Printed by T. Parker.

Witteloostuijn, Jaco van, and Maas, Ruud. 1984. *Muziek uit Stekels en Gaten* [Music of Pin-studded Cylinders]. Buren: F. Knuf.

Discography

Christmas Bells. Nationaal Museum van Speelklok tot Pierement CD STP 004. *1995*: The Netherlands. (Contains 27 tracks comprising Christmas music played on cylinder and disc musical boxes, automatic violin, musical organ clock, chamber barrel organ, church barrel-and-finger organ, orchestrions, and fairground and dance hall organs.)

The Cuckoo and the Nightingale – Cylinder Organs from 1750 to 1830. Nationaal Museum van Speelklok tot Pierement CD STP 002. *1991*: The Netherlands. (Contains 32 tracks, including music by Handel, Haydn, Mozart and Eberl, played on organ-playing musical clocks made by Pyke, Engeringh, Jaquet-Droz, Per Strand and Davrainville (father and son).)

Fair Organ Follies. Marion Roehl Recordings MRR 1033. *1998*: USA. (Contains 22 tracks of music played on a 57-key Gavioli made in Paris in 1905. Some of the pieces played are from the hands of Europe's top arranger, Tom Meijer.)

Festival of Strings. Nationaal Museum van Speelklok tot Pierement CD STP 003. *1993*: The Netherlands. (Contains 32 tracks of music played on stringed instruments comprising dulcimer musical clocks, compound musical clocks, automatic zither, piano-melodico automatic piano (mechanical), disc-playing piano, clockwork café piano, piano-orchestrion, self-playing violin, Phonoliszt-Violina, reproducing pianos and modern Yamaha Disklavier.)

Grand Piano. Nimbus Records NI 8801-NI 8819. *1995–2000*: UK. (Comprises major pianists performing via Duo-Art reproducing piano roll on a Steinway concert grand using a modern, carefully constructed cabinet push-up piano player created by technicians expressly for Duo-Art performance. Includes performances by Harold Bauer, Percy Grainger, Josef Hofmann, Ignaz Friedman, Ignace Jan Paderewski, Ferruccio Busoni, Frederic Lamond and Nikolay Medtner.)

Klavierleeuwen: Grootmeesters op de pianorol. Nationaal Museum van Speelklok tot Pierement CD STP 006. *1998*: The Netherlands. (Contains 16 tracks of music played on the best reproducing pianos, including Steinway-Welte, Marshall & Wendell Ampico, Hupfeld Triphonola, Steinway Duo-Art.)

The Magic of the Barrel Organ. Erato 4509-92133-2. *1993*: France. (Comprises instruments from the collection of Paul Bocuse, and contains 18 tracks of light music played on three different fairground organs.)

Musical Memories. Nationaal Museum van Speelklok tot Pierement CD STP 001. *1989*: The Netherlands. (Contains 26 tracks played on cylinder and disc musical boxes, automatic violin, musical organ clock, orchestrions, and fairground and dance hall organs.)

Serenade. Nationaal Museum van Speelklok tot Pierement CD STP 005. *1997*: The Netherlands. (Contains 30 tracks of music played on street organs and dance hall organs.)

Two Fairground Organs. Nationaal Museum van Speelklok tot Pierement CLAR 53355. *1996*: The Netherlands. (Contains 18 tracks of music played on a Wilhelm Brüder Söhne organ and the famous Dubbele Ruth concert organs. Music by Waldteufel, Nicolai, Strauss and Lehar, among others.)

ARTHUR W.J.G. ORD-HUME

Automatic Violin

During the two thousand and more years of mechanical instruments (with the principal developments having taken place since the end of the seventeenth century), almost every instrument of music has been automated, but of them all the violin has perhaps presented the greatest challenge, both technical and musical.

Numerous attempts were made to overcome these hurdles, but in the end only two instruments were sufficiently successful to enter production. One was Hupfeld's Phonoliszt-Violina, made in Leipzig, which, although powered by an electric motor, was entirely a pneumatic instrument; the other was the Mills Violano-Virtuoso, made in Chicago, which was an entirely electric instrument.

Hupfeld's instrument was introduced in about 1907–08 and comprised an upright expression piano on top of which was an extension case containing, in the most common models, three violins, only one string of each being fingered. The Mills instrument, on the other hand, entered production around 1910 and comprised a special cabinet housing a symmetrically arranged 44-note piano (lowest notes being in the center) and a violin, all four strings of which could be individually fingered and bowed simultaneously.

Bibliography

Bowers, Q. David. 1972. *Encyclopedia of Automatic Musical Instruments*. New York: Vestal.

Kitner, Mike, and Reblitz, Art. 1984. *The Mills Violano-Virtuoso*. New York: Vestal.

Ord-Hume, Arthur W.J.G. 1984. 'The Violano-Virtuoso and Its Swedish Origins.' *Music & Automata* 1(3): 134–42.

Discography

Christmas Bells. Nationaal Museum van Speelklok tot Pierement CD STP 004. *1995*: The Netherlands. (Contains 27 tracks comprising Christmas music played on cylinder and disc musical boxes, automatic violin, musical organ clock, chamber barrel organ, church barrel-and-finger organ, orchestrions, and fairground and dance hall organs.)

Festival of Strings. Nationaal Museum van Speelklok tot Pierement CD STP 003. *1993*: The Netherlands. (Contains 32 tracks of music played on stringed instruments comprising dulcimer musical clocks, compound musical clocks, automatic zither, piano-melodico automatic piano (mechanical), disc-playing piano, clockwork café piano, piano-orchestrion, self-playing violin, Phonoliszt-Violina, reproducing pianos and modern Yamaha Disklavier.)

Musical Memories. Nationaal Museum van Speelklok tot Pierement CD STP 001. *1989*: The Netherlands. (Contains 26 tracks played on cylinder and disc musical boxes, automatic violin, musical organ clock, orchestrions, and fairground and dance hall organs.)

ARTHUR W.J.G. ORD-HUME

Barrel Organ

'Barrel organ' describes a mechanical instrument of the pipe-organ family in which the musical program is represented by projecting pins and staple-like bridges onto the surface of a slowly rotating barrel or cylinder. Commonly, there is confusion that associates the term 'barrel organ' with the book-playing street organ or, frequently, the barrel piano. While the barrel organ was also used on the streets, the link with the street piano is spurious.

Commonly, the instrument comprises upward of 14 notes in a non-chromatic scale. From one to four stops or registers may be provided, selection being by drawstops. Tunes were frequently pinned in only a few keys, G and D being the most common. The pinned wooden barrel is rotated by a crank that also pumps wind into the organ chest. As the barrel turns, its circumference passes beneath a keyframe of small levers or 'keys.' These engage with the barrel pins, lifting them to allow wind from bellows to enter a particular organ pipe and produce a sound. In all respects, other than the replacement of a manual keyboard by the mechanical keyframe and the barrel, the mechanism is merely a simplification of the conventional pipe organ.

Instruments were made for both secular and church use, frequently with the same style of case. Exchangeable barrels meant that the organ could be 'flexible' in use. Normally, each barrel might contain eight or 10 tunes, so with four barrels the repertoire could be quite large. Because the style was outwardly similar, these are referred to as 'church and chamber' barrel organs. While English and French instruments of this type are invariably hand-turned, fully automatic instruments were made, in particular in Austria, where clockwork organs powered, in the main, by descending weights were common. The smallest barrel organ was the *serinette* or bird organ, typically measuring some 13" (34 cm) wide by 8" (20 cm) deep and standing 7" (18 cm) high. The average church and chamber instrument might be 27" (70 cm) wide and stand 70" (1.8 m) high.

Barrel organs also saw service on the street. Very popular in the late eighteenth and nineteenth centuries, these portable instruments were largely replaced by the more durable street piano.

Also during this period, many clockwork organs were made in Vienna. These attained high musical quality, and such composers as Handel, Haydn, Mozart and Beethoven, among others, wrote music expressly for the instrument. By the early part of the nineteenth century, however, the instrument had lost favor.

The barrel organ enjoyed a particularly rich history in England. Many outlying parish churches had poor music, and for them the mechanical church organ was a boon. The peak period of the church barrel organ was ca. 1760–1840; during this time, hundreds of them were made by over 130 makers, principally in London. Virtually every organ builder also made mechanical instruments. Such was the skill of these makers and their barrel pinners that Dr. Charles Burney, commenting in his *A General History of Music* (1776) on the very general use of barrel organs, added, 'the recent improvements of some English Artists have rendered the barrel capable of an effect equal to the fingers of the first-rate performers.'

By the end of the eighteenth century, barrel mechanisms attached to or built into organs were so common that instruments were described as 'finger organs' or 'barrel-and-finger organs.' The largest barrel-and-finger organ in the world was the Apollonicon, built in London by Flight & Robson and exhibited by them between 1817 and 1845. This gigantic automatic recital automaton, which took five years to build, could produce note-perfect orchestral music: each work in its repertoire was represented as a set of three very large wooden barrels.

The barrel organ, in particular the small street variety, also experienced a strong revival, in particular during the last two decades of the twentieth century. The barrel, however, gave way to alternative technologies. First, perforated-paper rolls were used, allowing much longer pieces of music to be provided. Second, solid-state music memory was applied, to produce a composite instrument that, while still possessing a fully mechanical organ action with bellows and pipes, played from an electronic memory bank that offered up to 100 tunes on one changeable plug-in EPROM (electrically programmable read-only memory) module.

Bibliography

Adlung, Jacob. 1768. *Musica mechanica organoedi* [Mechanical Music of the Organ Player]. Berlin.

Bedos de Celles, François. 1935–36 (1766–78). *L'art du facteur d'orgues* [The Art of Manufacturing Organs]. Paris: L.F. Delatour.

Bormann, Karl. 1968. *Orgel- und Spieluhrenbau* [Organ and Musical Clock Manufacturing]. Zürich: Sanssouci-Verlag.

Buchner, Alexander. 1992. *Les instruments de musique mécanique* [Mechanical Musical Instruments], trans. Philippe Rouillé. Paris: Grund.

Burney, Charles. 1776. *A General History of Music*. London: Printed for the author.

Caus, Salomon de. 1624 (1615). *Les raisons des forces mouvantes* [The Logic of Moving Forces]. Rev. ed. Frankfurt: I. Norton.

Elvin, Laurence. 1968. *Forster and Andrews, Organ Builders, 1843–1956*. Lincoln: L. Elvin.

Elvin, Laurence. 1976. *Forster and Andrews: Their Barrel, Chamber and Small Church Organs*. Lincoln: L. Elvin.

Engramelle, M.D.J. 1971 (1775). *La tonotechnie ou l'art de noter les cylindres* [The 'Tonotechnical,' or the Art of Inscribing Cylinders]. Geneva: Minkoff.

Farmer, Henry G. 1931. *The Organ of the Ancients, from Eastern Sources (Hebrew, Syriac and Arabic)*. London: W. Reeves.

Farmer, Henry G. 1940. *The Sources of Arabian Music.* Bearsden: The author.

Fludd, Robert. 1617–24. *Utriusque cosmi maioris* [History of the Macrocosm]. Oppenheim: Hieronymi Galleri.

Haspels, Jan Jaap. 1987. *Automatic Musical Instruments, Their Mechanics and Their Music, 1580–1820.* Utrecht: J.J. Haspels.

Haspels, Jan Jaap. 1994. *Musical Automata.* Utrecht: Nationaal Museum van Speelklok tot Pierement.

Jüttemann, Herbert. 1991. *Schwarzwälder Flötenuhren* [Black Forest Flute Clocks]. Waldkirch: Waldkircher Verlag.

Kircher, Athanasius. 1650. *Musurgia Universalis* [Universal Musical Work]. Rome.

Langwill, Lyndesay G., and Boston, Noel. 1970 (1967). *Church and Chamber Barrel-Organs.* Rev. ed. Edinburgh: L.G. Langwill.

Malloch, William. 1983. 'The Earl of Bute's Machine Organ: A Touchstone of Taste.' *Early Music* XI: 172.

Mayes, Stanley. 1956. *An Organ for the Sultan.* London: Putnam.

Mendel, Hermann. 1878. *Musikalisches Conversations-Lexicon* [Musical Encyclopedia]. Berlin.

Ord-Hume, Arthur W.J.G. 1973a. *Clockwork Music: An Illustrated History.* London: Allen and Unwin.

Ord-Hume, Arthur W.J.G. 1973b. *The Mechanics of Mechanical Music: The Arrangement of Music for Automatic Instruments.* London: The author.

Ord-Hume, Arthur W.J.G. 1978. *Barrel Organ: The Story of the Mechanical Organ and Its Repair.* London: Allen and Unwin.

Ord-Hume, Arthur W.J.G. 1982. *Joseph Haydn and the Mechanical Organ.* Cardiff: University College Press.

Protz, Albert. 1939. *Mechanische Musikinstrumente* [Mechanical Musical Instruments]. Kassel: Bärenreiter-Verlag.

Quoika, Rudolf. 1959. *Altösterreichische Hornwerke* [Old-Austrian Horn Manufacturers]. Berlin: Merseburger.

Rambach, Hermann, and Wernet, Otto. 1984. *Waldkircher Orgelbauer* [Waldkirch Organ Manufacturers]. Waldkirch: Waldkircher Verlagsgesellschaft.

Schott, Caspar. 1664. *Technica curiosa* [Interesting Technical Devices]. Nuremberg: E.A. and W. Endter.

Simon, Ernst. 1980 (1960). *Mechanische Musikinstrumente früherer Zeiten und ihre Musik* [Mechanical Musical Instruments of Earlier Times and Their Music]. Wiesbaden: Breitkopf & Härtel.

Trichter, Valentin. 1742. *Curiöses Reit-, Jagd-, Fecht-, Tantz- oder Ritter-Exercitien-Lexikon* [A Compendium of Knightly Exercises – Riding, Hunting, Fencing, Dancing]. Leipzig.

Wilson, Michael. 1968. *The English Chamber Organ: History and Development 1650–1850.* Oxford: Cassirer.

Zeraschi, Helmut. 1971. *Das Buch von der Drehorgel* [The Book of the Barrel Organ]. Zürich: Sanssouci-Verlag.

Zeraschi, Helmut. 1973. *Die Drehorgel in der Kirche* [The Barrel Organ in the Church]. Zürich: Sanssouci-Verlag.

Discography

Christmas Bells. Nationaal Museum van Speelklok tot Pierement CD STP 004. *1995*: The Netherlands. (Contains 27 tracks comprising Christmas music played on cylinder and disc musical boxes, automatic violin, musical organ clock, chamber barrel organ, church barrel-and-finger organ, orchestrions, and fairground and dance hall organs.)

The Magic of the Barrel Organ. Erato 4509-92133-2. *1993*: France. (Comprises instruments from the collection of Paul Bocuse, and contains 18 tracks of light music played on three different fairground organs.)

Musical Memories. Nationaal Museum van Speelklok tot Pierement CD STP 001. *1989*: The Netherlands. (Contains 26 tracks played on cylinder and disc musical boxes, automatic violin, musical organ clock, orchestrions, and fairground and dance hall organs.)

ARTHUR W.J.G. ORD-HUME

Barrel Piano/Street Barrel Piano

The barrel piano, which closely followed the barrel organ into the world of automatic music, is a piano played automatically by a pinned barrel or cylinder. The earliest instruments combined a barrel-played repertoire with the capacity to be played manually via a keyboard. In contrast to the barrel organ, clockwork, both weight- and spring-powered, was a common feature of these instruments.

Among the earliest makers of these barrel-and-finger instruments were William Rolfe & Sons ('Makers of Patent Self-Acting Pianofortes,' patented by Thomas Hall Rolfe in 1829) and Clementi Collard & Co. In the form made in London by William Rolfe (1830) and others, the barrel piano was a normal domestic instrument augmented by a pinned wooden cylinder placed inside the case under the keyboard. This barrel was provided with a mechanical keyframe and a series of linkages or stickers that extended behind the soundboard to the top of the pianoforte and operated an additional set of hammers that struck the strings through a gap in the soundboard. The musical barrel was turned by a clockwork motor driven by a heavy weight that was wound up to the top of the case. Their performance prompted Thomas Busby (*Concert Room and Orchestra Anecdotes* (1825)) to write of the instruments produced by Clementi Collard & Co. that 'the *piano* and *forte* passages are given with correctness and effect, the *forzandi* and *diminuendi* are produced by the slightest motion of the hand applied to a sliding ball at the side of the instrument.'

A drawing-room barrel piano with no keyboard that was weight-driven and included a number of effects such as drum, triangle, sordino and buff-stop was introduced by John Longman (ca. 1804). Around 1860, the Black Forest makers Imhof & Mukle made spring-driven clockwork barrel pianos with no manual keyboard that were also for drawing-room use. The mechanical operation of other types of barrel piano was achieved by hand-turning a crank.

While the drawing-room barrel piano sired the less-respected street barrel piano, it was soon replaced in the drawing room by the first of several generations of automatic piano players. The cumbersome barrel was replaced in favor of the studded wooden strip of Debain's Antiphonel, which in turn was replaced by the perforated roll of the piano player and later of the player piano. Further developments produced the expression piano and, eventually, the reproducing piano. Meanwhile, on the streets of every major town in Europe and North America, the keyboardless hand-turned barrel piano, thought to have emanated from Italy around 1800, rapidly took over from the street barrel organ as the public's music disseminator, and enjoyed a century and a half of popularity as a street instrument.

The early portable pianos were an English invention, John Hicks of Bristol being the first maker. By 1805, the Hicks family was making small portable instruments that could be carried by itinerant musicians. The Hicks style of piano was made by various members of the same family: Joseph Hicks, who excelled in making these instruments, which were sometimes, but incorrectly, called 'portable dulcimers,' and George Hicks, who worked for a time in London and then took the craft to New York. Henry Distin was another maker.

The large street piano mounted on a handcart also came from Italy, and was made everywhere in Europe and North America by migrant craftsmen. These open-air instruments, sometimes called 'cylinder pianos,' 'piano organs' or, often (incorrectly), 'barrel organs' or 'hurdy-gurdies,' underwent a variety of improvements. Some models were made with mechanically driven repeating actions and were known as 'mandoline' pianos, while others included percussion in the shape of drum, triangle, and xylophone or wood block. Some were further augmented by mechanical means to show advertisements, and others featured a picture display built into the vertical fall.

Early in the twentieth century, a new style of instrument that had coin-freed spring-driven clockwork motors was introduced and became widely used in public places, particularly in public bars. In France and Belgium, these instruments were developed into large and spectacular barrel-playing café pianos, often with decorative carved cases and embellished with mirrors. In 1950, both Portugal and Spain produced a large number of small novelty barrel pianos on miniature handcarts that performed popular dance music and variety songs.

An unusual form of the barrel piano was the Swedish Pianoharpa or table piano, which was invented in 1889 by I.F. Nilsson of Oster Korsberga, Lemnhult, patented and developed by the brothers Anders Gustaf and Jones Wilhelm Andersson of Näshult, Vetlanda. This was in the form of a shallow living-room table and was intended for the country house that wanted simple music.

Bibliography

Bowers, Q. David. 1972. *Encyclopedia of Automatic Musical Instruments*. New York: Vestal.

Busby, Thomas. 1825. *Concert Room and Orchestra Anecdotes of Music and Musicians, Ancient and Modern*. London: Printed for Clementi Collard & Co.

Harding, Rosamond E.M. 1933. *The Piano-Forte: Its History Traced to the Great Exhibition of 1851*. Cambridge: Cambridge University Press.

Lindwall, B. 1978. 'The Andersson Pianoharpa.' *The Music Box* 8: 330–34.

Ord-Hume, Arthur W.J.G. 1970. *Player Piano: The History of the Mechanical Piano and How to Repair It*. London: Allen and Unwin.

Ord-Hume, Arthur W.J.G. 1973. *The Mechanics of Mechanical Music: The Arrangement of Music for Automatic Instruments*. London: The author.

Ord-Hume, Arthur W.J.G. 1984. *Pianola: The History of the Self-Playing Piano*. London: Allen and Unwin.

Discography

Christmas Bells. Nationaal Museum van Speelklok tot Pierement CD STP 004. *1995*: The Netherlands. (Contains 27 tracks comprising Christmas music played on cylinder and disc musical boxes, automatic violin, musical organ clock, chamber barrel organ, church barrel-and-finger organ, orchestrions, and fairground and dance hall organs.)

Festival of Strings. Nationaal Museum van Speelklok tot Pierement CD STP 003. *1993*: The Netherlands. (Contains 32 tracks of music played on stringed instruments comprising dulcimer musical clocks, compound musical clocks, automatic zither, piano-melodico automatic piano (mechanical), disc-playing piano, clockwork café piano, piano-orchestrion, self-playing violin, Phonoliszt-Violina, reproducing pianos and modern Yamaha Disklavier.)

Musical Memories. Nationaal Museum van Speelklok tot Pierement CD STP 001. *1989*: The Netherlands. (Contains 26 tracks played on cylinder and disc musical boxes, automatic violin, musical organ clock, orchestrions, and fairground and dance hall organs.)

ARTHUR W.J.G. ORD-HUME

Calliope

A calliope is a type of organ that is steam-activated rather than wind-generated by bellows. It is, in principle, a logical extension of the steam whistle that was used on North American locomotives in the nineteenth and early twentieth centuries; some of these whistles had two or more pipes tuned to produce a distinctive coupling of notes. On US riverboats, such whistles, which were blown both to announce arrival or departure and to challenge other riverboats, might have three or four pipes.

In the mid-1850s, A.S. Denny introduced his multiple-piped 'calliope,' named somewhat incongruously after the Muse of Greek epic poetry. Its appearance had a dramatic effect in circuses and fairs, being audible, in suitable conditions, over a distance of approximately 20 kilometers. Although the calliope was used in these large-scale public entertainments, it was on the riverboats that it was most commonly installed. It consisted of one or two rows of short and graduated vertical pipes mounted on substantial pipework directly connected to the steam boiler. The calliope player stood, or sat, at one end before a narrow organ keyboard, the depressed keys operating valves that released steam pressure, which caused the tuned pipes to emit a blast of sound.

Probably the first boat to advertise with the new instrument was the *Floating Palace*, which had a circus and minstrel show aboard, and was operated by Gilbert R. Spaulding and Charles J. Rogers in 1858. Floating theaters, menageries and 'museum concerts' were presented on board specially built showboats, in particular those managed between 1878 and 1907 by Captain French and his wife 'Aunt Callie.' As showboats at this time were towed rather than powered under their own steam, the calliope was mounted on the exposed top deck of the towing riverboat.

In the 1930s, the calliope for the riverboat that towed the original *Cotton Blossom* was played by Eva La Reane. Best known of the calliope players, at least among jazz enthusiasts, was Fate Marable, who played for the Streckfus line, in particular aboard the *Capitol*, where he also led his Jazz E. Saz Band for several years. In the 1980s, the *Natchez* excursion boat from New Orleans still announced its imminent departure by playing 'Waiting for the Robert E. Lee' on the steam calliope.

Bibliography

Graham, Philip. 1951. *Showboats: The History of an American Institution*. Austin, TX: University of Texas Press.

Rosenthal, George S., and Zachary, Frank, eds. 1946. *Jazzways*. New York: Greenberg.

Samuel, Ray, Huber, Leonard V., and Ogden, Warren C. 1955. *Tales of the Mississippi*. New York: Hastings House.

Sheet Music

Muir, Lewis F., comp., and Gilbert, L. Wolfe, lyr. 1912. 'Waiting for the Robert E. Lee.' New York: F.A. Mills.

PAUL OLIVER

Carillon

Carillons first appeared in Europe in the fourteenth century. They consist of a set of bells (each producing one tone of the musical scale) which, unlike those that are 'rung' by swinging, remain stationary and are sounded by hammers that move and strike the bells. They can be played manually, or automatically using a large drum or barrel (initially made of iron, later of bronze) into the surface of which are secured specially shaped iron pegs. As the drum revolves, these pegs engage a series of levers that operate the hammers, which then strike the bells. The carillon seldom has a fully chromatic compass; generally, the lower octaves are abbreviated and delete accidentals.

In The Netherlands and Belgium at the end of the twentieth century, there remained a large number of such carillons that were still playable, despite the attrition caused by two world wars and the normal wear and tear on their mechanisms. While the Low Countries possess the majority of the world's surviving carillons, fine examples exist in the United States, Australia, Canada, Great Britain and South Africa, and new instruments are also occasionally made.

Attempts to replace the cumbersome carillon barrel began in the 1850s. The first of these involved perforated-card playing mechanisms (as installed in an instrument at Bourneville (UK), but no longer used). By the late twentieth century, carillons were being built that operated using solid-state electronics, with EPROM (electrically programmable read-only memory)-based tune libraries and electromagnetic solenoid-driven bell hammers (for example, the one in London's Leicester Square, built in 1988).

Bibliography

Bowers, Q. David. 1972. *Encyclopedia of Automatic Musical Instruments*. New York: Vestal.

Lehr, André. 1971. *Van Paardebel tot Speelklok* [From Horsebell to Musical Clock]. Zaltbommel: Europese Bibliotheek.

Price, Percival. 1983. *Bells and Man*. Oxford: Oxford University Press.

Discography

Christmas Bells. Nationaal Museum van Speelklok tot Pierement CD STP 004. *1995*: The Netherlands. (Contains 27 tracks comprising Christmas music played on cylinder and disc musical boxes, automatic violin, musical organ clock, chamber barrel organ, church barrel-and-finger organ, orchestrions, and fairground and dance hall organs.)

Musical Memories. Nationaal Museum van Speelklok tot Pierement CD STP 001. *1989*: The Netherlands. (Contains 26 tracks played on cylinder and disc musical boxes, automatic violin, musical organ clock, orchestrions, and fairground and dance hall organs.)

ARTHUR W.J.G. ORD-HUME

Electrically Operated Piano

A large number of piano makers produced electrically operated instruments for use in bars and public places. While retaining the principle of pneumatic playing using air suction or, occasionally, pressure, the pumping was undertaken by electric motor. A less-refined development of the piano orchestrion, these instruments incorporated percussion effects, *mandoline* attachments (producing a sound from the piano action by interspersing a metal or leather device between hammer and spring), xylophone and, in many cases, wooden organ pipes. Some were made for automatic playing only, while others could also be played by hand. From this was developed the semi-automatic theater orchestra or 'photoplayer,' intended for the silent cinema. This very large and complex instrument could be played by hand or from one, sometimes two, special piano rolls, and included a variety of sound effects, such as sleigh bells, locomotive whistles, pistol shots and horses' hooves, in addition to full piano and pipe organ. In gambling or arcade machines, mechanical music was also combined with a moving display, one popular device being the horse-race piano.

Bibliography

Bowers, Q. David. 1972. *Encyclopedia of Automatic Musical Instruments*. New York: Vestal.

Ord-Hume, Arthur W.J.G. 1984. *Pianola: The History of the Self-Playing Piano*. London: Allen and Unwin.

Discography

Festival of Strings. Nationaal Museum van Speelklok tot Pierement CD STP 003. *1993*: The Netherlands. (Contains 32 tracks of music played on stringed instruments comprising dulcimer musical clocks, compound musical clocks, automatic zither, piano-melodico automatic piano (mechanical), disc-playing piano, clockwork café piano, piano-orchestrion, self-playing

violin, Phonoliszt-Violina, reproducing pianos and modern Yamaha Disklavier.)

Grand Piano. Nimbus Records NI 8801-NI 8819. *1995–2000*: UK. (Comprises major pianists performing via Duo-Art reproducing piano roll on a Steinway concert grand using a modern, carefully constructed cabinet push-up piano player created by technicians expressly for Duo-Art performance. Includes performances by Harold Bauer, Percy Grainger, Josef Hofmann, Ignaz Friedman, Ignace Jan Paderewski, Ferruccio Busoni, Frederic Lamond and Nikolay Medtner.)

Klavierleeuwen: Grootmeesters op de pianorol. Nationaal Museum van Speelklok tot Pierement CD STP 006. *1998*: The Netherlands. (Contains 16 tracks of music played on the best reproducing pianos, including Steinway-Welte, Marshall & Wendell Ampico, Hupfeld Triphonola, Steinway Duo-Art.)

ARTHUR W.J.G. ORD-HUME

Mechanical Banjo

The mechanical banjo, one of the more unusual mechanical instruments, was introduced in the United States. The Encore Automatic Banjo was made in the mid-1890s and played from a perforated-paper roll, but its particular cleverness concerned the lifelike manner in which it plucked the strings. Also, it was electrically powered, thus making it one of the earliest North American electric instruments.

Bibliography

Bowers, Q. David. 1972. *Encyclopedia of Automatic Musical Instruments*. New York: Vestal.

ARTHUR W.J.G. ORD-HUME

Mechanical Harp

An electrically driven roll-playing mechanical harp was invented by Whitlock of Indiana in 1899. Manufactured by Wurlitzer, it enjoyed only short-lived popularity, because, although it was a highly attractive and musically satisfying instrument, it was too quiet for use in public places.

Bibliography

Bowers, Q. David. 1972. *Encyclopedia of Automatic Musical Instruments*. New York: Vestal.

ARTHUR W.J.G. ORD-HUME

Musical Box

A musical box is a mechanical instrument, usually driven by clockwork, that plays a program of music on a set of tuned steel springs or teeth, as in a comb. The musical box began as no more than a curious novelty adjunct to a utilitarian object. Seals, scent bottles, snuffboxes and watches were produced that played simple melodies on a compass of notes ranging from as few as five to as many as, but seldom exceeding, 14. The mechanism typically consisted of a rotating metal cylinder with projections that 'played' a comb of tuned steel teeth. By the second decade of the nineteenth century, however, the mechanism had been improved and enlarged to the point where the cylinder musical box could be launched as a stand-alone musical interpreter.

At the time of London's Great Exhibition of 1851, the predominantly Swiss makers were able to produce musical boxes that exhibited the greatest possible musical quality. However, the high cost of manufacture and the limited repertoire of its cylinder meant that the musical box had only narrow appeal. When the disc-playing musical box (utilizing punched discs with projections) was invented in Germany in 1886, it offered cheap music from a very large inventory of titles. The effect on the Swiss industry was both to remove its virtual monopoly of the musical-box market and to hasten mass production. However, the overall result was a significant reduction in quality and price.

The arrival of the gramophone encouraged makers to capitalize on the new appliance, and the disc musical box became the *phonopectine* with the incorporation of a device that played both musical-box and record discs.

After World War II, there was a considerable effort to revive the Swiss musical-box industry, with a number of makers concentrating on small mass-produced items for the novelty and tourist markets. The repertoire consisted merely of popular and traditional melodies. The majority of these small firms either went out of business or amalgamated. The surviving business of Reuge embraced modern technology and manufacturing processes, while at the same time producing some very high-quality limited-edition musical boxes for the collectors' and investors' markets.

Beginning in the 1950s, Japan created a musical-box industry. At the beginning of the twenty-first century, the largest maker, Sankyo Seiki, operates a fully automated factory at Suwa, Nagano that is capable of turning out 100 million pieces a year, ranging from simple 12-note mechanisms to those having combs of 50 teeth. There is also a number of small firms in Britain, Japan and the United States that are making both new musical boxes and high-quality arrangements of music for playing on traditional disc machines. At the same time, newly manufactured examples of some of the largest disc-playing musical boxes of the early twentieth century are in limited production by a few specialist firms.

In Britain and North America as well, both new discs and replicas of old discs for musical boxes are available from several businesses. One British firm has an inventory of equipment that can make 100 different brands and sizes of disc.

Bibliography

Chapuis, Alfred. 1980. *History of the Musical Box and of Mechanical Music*, trans. Joseph E. Roesch. Summit, NJ: Musical Box Society International. (Originally published as *Histoire de la boîte à musique et de la musique mécanique*. Lausanne: Scriptar, 1955.)

Ord-Hume, Arthur W.J.G. 1980. *Musical Box: A History and Collector's Guide*. London: Allen and Unwin.

Ord-Hume, Arthur W.J.G. 1995. *The Musical Box: A Guide for Collectors, Including a Guide to Values*. Atglen, PA: Schiffer Pub.

Witteloostuijn, Jaco van, and Maas, Ruud. 1984. *Muziek uit Stekels en Gaten* [Music of Pin-studded Cylinders]. Buren: F. Knuf.

Discography

Christmas Bells. Nationaal Museum van Speelklok tot Pierement CD STP 004. *1995*: The Netherlands. (Contains 27 tracks comprising Christmas music played on cylinder and disc musical boxes, automatic violin, musical organ clock, chamber barrel organ, church barrel-and-finger organ, orchestrions, and fairground and dance hall organs.)

Musical Memories. Nationaal Museum van Speelklok tot Pierement CD STP 001. *1989*: The Netherlands. (Contains 26 tracks played on cylinder and disc musical boxes, automatic violin, musical organ clock, orchestrions, and fairground and dance hall organs.)

ARTHUR W.J.G. ORD-HUME

Musical Clock

A musical clock is a clock that incorporates a mechanical music program played automatically at intervals regulated by the clock mechanism. Notable early examples of musical clocks include the great musical and automaton clock of Strasbourg (1574), the smaller indoor clocks of Isaac Habrecht (1544–1620) and the domestic table musical clock of Nicholas Vallin (dated 1598). However, these early clocks were comparatively crude compared with those produced during the richest era of musical clocks, the period from 1720 through to 1820. The center of the musical-clock industry during this 'Golden Century,' in which the development of all mechanical instruments flourished, was Vienna. It was here that a whole industry sprang up to vie in making the finest instruments that would perform, on a small carillon of bells, an equally small pipe organ or a stringed instrument like a dulcimer, all the popular music. Indeed, in Vienna during this period, all fashionable public places, such as cafés and restaurants, had musical clocks that played the best of popular music to their clientele.

Small comb-playing musical-box movements were incorporated into Viennese mantel clocks, many of the early ones featuring high-quality movements by the best local makers. By the end of the nineteenth century, disc-playing musical mechanisms were built into clocks, including 'long-case' musical hall clocks.

Bibliography

Haspels, Jan Jaap. 1987. *Automatic Musical Instruments, Their Mechanics and Their Music, 1580–1820*. Utrecht: J.J. Haspels.

Haspels, Jan Jaap. 1994. *Musical Automata*. Utrecht: Nationaal Museum van Speelklok tot Pierement.

Ord-Hume, Arthur W.J.G. 1973. *Clockwork Music: An Illustrated History*. London: Allen and Unwin.

Ord-Hume, Arthur W.J.G. 1995. *The Musical Clock: Musical and Automaton Clocks and Watches*. Ashbourne: Mayfield Books.

Discography

Christmas Bells. Nationaal Museum van Speelklok tot Pierement CD STP 004. *1995*: The Netherlands. (Contains 27 tracks comprising Christmas music played on cylinder and disc musical boxes, automatic violin, musical organ clock, chamber barrel organ, church barrel-and-finger organ, orchestrions, and fairground and dance hall organs.)

The Cuckoo and the Nightingale – Cylinder Organs from 1750 to 1830. Nationaal Museum van Speelklok tot Pierement CD STP 002. *1991*: The Netherlands. (Contains 32 tracks, including music by Handel, Haydn, Mozart and Eberl, played on organ-playing musical clocks made by Pyke, Engeringh, Jaquet-Droz, Per Strand and Davrainville (father and son).)

Festival of Strings. Nationaal Museum van Speelklok tot Pierement CD STP 003. *1993*: The Netherlands. (Contains 32 tracks of music played on stringed instruments comprising dulcimer musical clocks, compound musical clocks, automatic zither, piano-melodico automatic piano (mechanical), disc-playing piano, clockwork café piano, piano-orchestrion, self-playing violin, Phonoliszt-Violina, reproducing pianos and modern Yamaha Disklavier.)

Musical Memories. Nationaal Museum van Speelklok tot Pierement CD STP 001. *1989*: The Netherlands. (Contains 26 tracks played on cylinder and disc musical boxes, automatic violin, musical organ clock, orchestrions, and fairground and dance hall organs.)

ARTHUR W.J.G. ORD-HUME

Orchestrion

Creating a mechanical orchestra was a recurring goal through the latter half of the eighteenth century and the nineteenth century. Developed from the barrel organ, one of the earliest instruments of this genre was created by the Black Forest émigré Johann Georg Strasser, who sold it in St. Petersburg for 10,000 roubles in 1801. It is believed that this was the instrument owned by Tchaikovsky's father, which inspired the young Peter Ilich's interest in music.

The name 'orchestrion' was coined by the Abbé Georg Joseph Vogler (1749–1849) for a large organ with which he toured England and the Continent in 1789. During the nineteenth and early twentieth centuries, the term 'orchestrion' was applied to any complex mechanical instrument played by pinned barrels, perforated cards or paper rolls.

Orchestrions were capable of performing the popular classical repertoire to perfection, and makers such as Welte and Imhof & Mukle were renowned for their instruments. Although the instrument originated as a development of the organ, its evolution centered around the mechanical piano, resulting in the production of so-called 'piano orchestrions,' in which percussion effects and, frequently, a pipe organ were included.

Piano orchestrions began as barrel-operated instruments, and there were many makers of these instruments in Bohemia, Prussia, France and the Low Countries. The barrel was soon replaced by perforated-paper music rolls, allowing more compact and musically variable instruments to be made. From this were evolved the fairground or carousel organ and the dance hall organ, varieties that reached their peak of perfection in the first quarter of the twentieth century.

Bibliography

Bender, Gerd. 1975–78. *Die Uhrenmacher des hohen Schwarzwaldes und ihre Werke* [The Clock Manufacturers of the High Black Forest]. 2 vols. Villingen/Schwarzwald: Verlag Müller.

Haspels, Jan Jaap. 1987. *Automatic Musical Instruments, Their Mechanics and Their Music, 1580–1820*. Utrecht: J.J. Haspels.

Jüttemann, Herbert. 1987. *Mechanische Musikinstrumente: Einführung in Technik und Geschichte* [Mechanical Musical Instruments: Introduction to Their Techniques and History]. Frankfurt: E. Bochinsky.

Ord-Hume, Arthur W.J.G. 1978. *Barrel Organ: The Story of the Mechanical Organ and Its Repair*. London: Allen and Unwin.

Discography

Christmas Bells. Nationaal Museum van Speelklok tot Pierement CD STP 004. *1995*: The Netherlands. (Contains 27 tracks comprising Christmas music played on cylinder and disc musical boxes, automatic violin, musical organ clock, chamber barrel organ, church barrel-and-finger organ, orchestrions, and fairground and dance hall organs.)

Festival of Strings. Nationaal Museum van Speelklok tot Pierement CD STP 003. *1993*: The Netherlands.

(Contains 32 tracks of music played on stringed instruments comprising dulcimer musical clocks, compound musical clocks, automatic zither, piano-melodico automatic piano (mechanical), disc-playing piano, clockwork café piano, piano-orchestrion, self-playing violin, Phonoliszt-Violina, reproducing pianos and modern Yamaha Disklavier.)

Musical Memories. Nationaal Museum van Speelklok tot Pierement CD STP 001. *1989*: The Netherlands. (Contains 26 tracks played on cylinder and disc musical boxes, automatic violin, musical organ clock, orchestrions, and fairground and dance hall organs.)

ARTHUR W.J.G. ORD-HUME

Player Piano

A player piano is a pianoforte that has a self-playing mechanism capable of playing from perforated-paper music rolls or piano rolls.

Automatic methods of playing the piano – mechanical devices – became available in the early nineteenth century. These early barrel-programmed automatic pianos were purely mechanical in operation. Alternative actions, but still mechanical in principle, included instruments such as Debain's Antiphonel. Instead of a barrel, this system employed short lengths of wooden board called *planchettes*, one surface of which was provided with metal projections representing the program pattern of the tune to be played; these *planchettes* were drawn across a mechanical keyframe using a rack-and-pinion drive system operated by the turning of a crank handle.

The system of punched cards used by Jacquard in programming cloth-weaving looms in 1801 inspired Claude-Félix Seytre to apply the perforated card to the playing of a musical instrument in 1842. Not until the 1880s, however, was punched card successfully used in production piano players. Still, however, these were mechanical players.

By 1890, the first pneumatically controlled piano players were being manufactured. Suction operated, the piano player, also called a cabinet or push-up player, was the forerunner of the player piano and was generally a self-contained device containing a pneumatic mechanism. It was set in front of an ordinary piano, which it then played with a row of felt-covered wooden fingers (at the back) that rested on the keyboard. From this device, it was a logical step to the player piano, where an 'interior-player' action (the player mechanism wholly contained within the body of the piano itself) was used to play the piano rather than requiring a large and separate cabinet. This system instantly made all earlier mechanical systems obsolete.

Piano players were still being produced as late as 1905, even though the first player pianos had appeared as early as 1892. By 1901, the player piano as a complete unit had taken command of the automatic-piano market. Whereas the early mechanical piano players were operated by a hand-turned crank, the pneumatic actions were operated by foot treadles. These acted on exhaust bellows to provide suction, which controlled the suction-operated mechanism.

In the beginning, these mechanisms did not play on the full compass of the piano, some early examples merely playing on 58 of the keyboard's notes. Other models were produced that worked on 46, 61, 65, 70, 73, 82 and 88 notes. This lack of standardization was a major problem to the manufacturers of music rolls. In 1910, player-piano manufacturers agreed to standardize on 65 and 88 notes for all pianos.

Various pneumatic functions could be incorporated between the music roll and the piano hammer to regulate or vary the force applied to the hammer. Such automatic-expression devices first appeared as early as 1901, but these were rudimentary systems. By 1906, however, player pianos were available that incorporated seven degrees of expression; these paved the way for the development of, first, the expression piano and, subsequently, the reproducing piano.

The Expression Piano and the Reproducing Piano

As early as 1895, both mechanical and pneumatic piano players were provided with a rudimentary means by which the treble notes could be played louder than those in the bass and vice versa. It was this crude system that marked the quest not so much for the automation of the piano and its music as for replication of the real performer's playing.

The first significant development came when the Aeolian Company invented the Themodist expression system, whereby individual notes could be made to sound out over or within an accompaniment. Next, it was found that, by varying the vacuum tension between the separate halves of the valve chest and combining this with a Themodist-type accenter, and applying the same technique to both halves of the keyboard, a much more realistic performance could be produced. Instruments with this type of artificially enhanced music-roll performance were called 'expression pianos' and were produced mainly in Germany and the United States for use in public places.

By 1904, Edwin Welte of Freiburg, followed the next year by Hupfeld of Leipzig, had invented a means of pneumatically controlling expression in several stages between bass and treble. This was a significant step toward introducing an automatic degree of pianistic interpretation or expression, and was achieved using specially made music rolls that could control the operating vacuum pressure within selected parts of the player mechanism, as well as operating the sustaining and soft pedals of the piano.

The reproducing piano was a form of player piano that, when using special reproducing music rolls, could reenact the original touch and expression of the recording pianist. It developed from the expression piano.

The first real reproducing piano was the Welte Mignon, invented by Karl Bockisch and Edwin Welte in 1905. The Welte reproducing system, which produced the various shades of piano playing by the careful adjustment of the suction levels in the piano's expression mechanism, was patented, and formed the basis of all subsequent reproducing pianos.

Many makers built reproducing pianos, but the most successful models following the Welte were the DEA (introduced in 1905) and the Triphonola (1918), both made by Hupfeld of Leipzig, and the Ducanola, produced by Philipps in Frankfurt in 1909. However, by far the most successful was the Aeolian Company's Duo-Art, introduced in the United States in mid-1913, followed by the American Piano Corporation's Ampico, first marketed in the same year.

These instruments depended for their success on obtaining leading pianists and composers to make reproducing piano rolls of their performances. Among the artists who made recordings were Teresa Carreño, Rachmaninoff and Artur Rubinstein, for Ampico; Victor Herbert, for Ampico and Duo-Art; Gershwin and Harold Bauer, for Duo-Art; Paderewski, for Duo-Art and Welte; and Wanda Landowska, Debussy, Mahler and Richard Strauss, for Welte.

The Player-Piano Industry

The manufacture of player pianos became one of the major industries of the nineteenth and twentieth centuries in Europe and North America. The number of manufacturers throughout the world, and in the United States in particular, is almost impossible to assess accurately; many companies were short-lived or insignificant in their contribution to the 2.5 million instruments sold in the United States between 1900 and 1930. In London alone, a 1922 trade directory listed no fewer than 52 makers. In 1900, 171,000 'ordinary' and 6,000 self-acting pianos were made. By 1925, the total of 136,000 ordinary pianos produced had been exceeded by the 169,000 self-acting player pianos produced.

The mid-1920s saw the peak of the player piano's vogue. Every piano retailer sold player pianos and their rolls. Many lending libraries were established where, for a small sum, a number of rolls could be borrowed.

The arrival of the gramophone and, shortly afterward, the radio encouraged some makers to try to increase their market share by incorporating the new appliances into their instruments. As a result, player pianos were produced with gramophones and radios built into the upper part of the case.

During the early years of the Depression, the market collapsed and player-piano sales dwindled virtually to nothing. Despite a concerted attempt to revive the player-piano market in London in the early 1930s, the industry was finished long before the outbreak of World War II in September 1939.

The demise of the player piano was the result of changes in social life. First, cheap automobiles became available, which allowed people greater mobility. With less time spent in the home, music for the masses became less important. The advances of radio and the gramophone tended to some extent to replace what had been lost through diminishing musical participation. It was war, though, particularly World War II, that forever changed the social dependence on mechanical music that had dominated the previous 400 years.

A revival of interest in mechanical music that began in the 1960s also saw an attempt to revive the player piano, and US makers launched small so-called 'spinet' models for the modern home that played ordinary 88-note music rolls. Several styles of key-top player designed to be mounted on an ordinary piano were also produced, but these were not successful, largely because, owing to their ultra-compact size, they could not produce enough suction to provide acceptable playing power.

As owners of classic player pianos increased in number, and instruments were restored rather than scrapped or converted to 'ordinary' pianos, the demand for perforated-paper music rolls expanded. One major supplier in North America, QRS, makes new rolls of both traditional and new popular music. There is also a large manufacturer in Australia, as well as a significant number of small businesses in Britain and North America, that make specialized high-quality rolls, both newly arranged music and recuts of old music rolls.

Digital control of pianos, initially from specially encoded cassette tapes, gave the instrument a new lease on life. The Superscope Marantz Pianocorder, launched in North America in 1978, was the first of these digitally controlled instruments and offered live recording (melographic recording) and playback. At least one Pianocorder was successfully installed in a late twentieth-century harpsichord.

Solid-state electronics and advanced computer technology helped to create a new market in hotels and restaurants for the self-playing piano. Several Japanese companies have introduced instruments that play a pre-recorded program from a floppy disc, and one installation in particular, the Yamaha Disklavier, a concert grand with a computer disc drive, performs to the very best of reproducing-piano capability. Developments in this area have been very rapid, and instruments with extensive repertoires on tiny EPROM (electrically programmable read-only memory) modules have created a new generation of reproducing pianos that are totally automatic in operation. Such instruments cannot, however, be classified as either 'mechanical' or 'pneumatic,' being wholly electronic or 'solid-state.'

Bibliography

Bowers, Q. David. 1972. *Encyclopedia of Automatic Musical Instruments*. New York: Vestal.

Dolge, Alfred. 1980. *Men Who Have Made Piano History*. Rev. ed. New York: Vestal. (First published as *Pianos and Their Makers*, Vol. 2. Covina, CA: Covina Publishing Company, 1913.)

Ehrlich, Cyril. 1976. *The Piano: A History*. London: Dent.

Givens, Larry. 1970. *Re-enacting the Artist: A Story of the Ampico Reproducing Piano*. New York: Vestal.

Howe, Richard J., ed. 1987. *The Ampico Reproducing Piano*. St. Paul, MN: Musical Box Society International.

McTammany, John. 1971 (1915). *The Technical History of the Player*. New York: Vestal.

Ord-Hume, Arthur W.J.G. 1984. *Pianola: The History of the Self-Playing Piano*. London: Allen and Unwin.

Palmieri, Robert, ed. 1994. *Encyclopedia of Keyboard Instruments. Vol. 1: The Piano*. New York: Garland.

Roehl, Harvey N. 1973 (1961). *Player Piano Treasury: The Scrapbook History of the Mechanical Piano in America as Told in Story, Pictures, Trade Journal Articles and Advertising*. 2nd ed. New York: Vestal.

Roell, Craig H. 1989. *The Piano in America, 1890–1940*. Chapel Hill, NC: University of North Carolina Press.

Tushinsky, Joseph S. 1978. *The Pianocorder Story*. Chatsworth, CA: Superscope.

Discography

Festival of Strings. Nationaal Museum van Speelklok tot Pierement CD STP 003. *1993*: The Netherlands. (Contains 32 tracks of music played on stringed instruments comprising dulcimer musical clocks, compound musical clocks, automatic zither, piano-melodico automatic piano (mechanical), disc-playing piano, clockwork café piano, piano-orchestrion, self-playing violin, Phonoliszt-Violina, reproducing pianos and modern Yamaha Disklavier.)

Grand Piano. Nimbus Records NI 8801-NI 8819. *1995–2000*: UK. (Comprises major pianists performing via Duo-Art reproducing piano roll on a Steinway concert grand using a modern, carefully constructed cabinet push-up piano player created by technicians expressly for Duo-Art performance. Includes performances by Harold Bauer, Percy Grainger, Josef Hofmann, Ignaz Friedman, Ignace Jan Paderewski, Ferruccio Busoni, Frederic Lamond and Nikolay Medtner.)

Klavierleeuwen: Grootmeesters op de pianorol. Nationaal Museum van Speelklok tot Pierement CD STP 006. *1998*: The Netherlands. (Contains 16 tracks of music played on the best reproducing pianos, including Steinway-Welte, Marshall & Wendell Ampico, Hupfeld Triphonola, Steinway Duo-Art.)

ARTHUR W.J.G. ORD-HUME

12. Percussion Instruments

Percussion Instruments

Instruments of percussion are among the earliest known musical instruments, with many existing from antiquity. Simply defined, they include any instrument that produces a sound when struck. The striking motion may be expanded to include rubbing, scraping, shaking (sometimes the instrument is attached to the wrist or ankle) or plucking. The striking implement can be a stick, mallet, hand, clapper or the instrument itself; the striking action can also be accomplished via mechanical or electronic means of eliciting a sound from the instrument.

Classification

Percussion instruments can be acoustically classified as membranophones (those having a vibrating membrane) and/or idiophones (those whose entire body vibrates). Idiophones can be further classified according to the material from which they are constructed, resulting in xylophones (made of wood) and metallophones (made of metal). Percussion instruments are sometimes categorized into those having definite pitch (such as a xylophone) or indefinite pitch (such as a snare drum). Chordophones that are struck with a beater or mechanical device (such as the dulcimer or piano) are sometimes included under the classification of percussion, as is the celesta (keyboard glockenspiel).

A more detailed method of classifying percussion instruments takes into account instrument construction, design and performance application. These categories include: various drums (on the basis of shell shape, type of head, and material used for construction), often arranged in pairs or sets; keyboard or mallet instruments (usually a pitched series of bars arranged either diatonically or in the shape of a piano keyboard); hand per-

cussion instruments (which are held in, or played with, the hands); 'traps' or instruments, traditionally played by a drummer/percussionist, that imitate a wide variety of sounds; and electronic percussion instruments (which produce sounds electronically, but actuate them by the striking of a trigger).

Early Percussion Instruments

Percussion instruments appear in the earliest recorded and depicted annals of humankind, and were at first probably used to accompany dance and ritual music. Sachs (1940) systematically identifies the percussion instruments used in ritual for each continent, as well as indicating early references in literature and archeological discoveries. There is documentary evidence of percussion instruments in art, drawings and other surviving artifacts from the Sumerian, Egyptian, Greek and early Asian cultures. The earliest percussion instruments included shaken gourds (rattles) and clappers, and could also include the sounds of foot stomping and of warriors pounding on shields. Notched bones or branches were also used to produce scraping sounds in various rituals.

Early drums consisted of hollowed logs, sometimes constructed with an open slit; as the instrument evolved, the slit widened into an opening covered by a membrane of animal hide or skin. As manufacturing methods developed, the drum became a highly constructed, variously shaped acoustic shell, covered at one or both ends by a membrane that could be tuned by numerous methods.

Since early percussion instruments were manufactured from indigenous materials, specific instruments are often associated with the music of a particular culture. Instruments made of wood are the most widespread, while gongs (tam-tams) and metallophones constructed of bronze developed as an integral part of the music of Malaysia and other East Asian cultures. Areas that lack old-growth trees developed clay or ceramic drum shells, and the advanced metallurgical techniques of the Near and Middle East integrated the use of cymbals and bells into the cultures of those regions. Conversely, the wide availability of substances such as hard stone resulted in instruments like the lithophone contributing to popular music worldwide.

As the primary traditional function of percussion instruments has been to provide rhythm, early uses of the instruments reflect this practise. Popular dance of all cultures can be defined by and associated with indigenous instruments and rhythms for the song and dance of that culture. Early songs and dances were first accompanied by frame drums, some of which may have had jingles or snares attached and which are often depicted as being performed by women. Early percussion instruments that are linked culturally to regional music include: the gamelan in Malaysia; the *tablā* in India; castanets in Spain; finger cymbals in the Middle East and North Africa; the *bodhrán* in Ireland; *tsuzumi* and *taiko* drums in Japan; the xylophone in Africa; the marimba in Guatemala; claves in the Caribbean islands; the 'talking drum' and mbira in Africa; *nakers* and timpani in the Middle East; cymbals, triangles and the jingling johnny in Turkey (in the janizary bands); and the zither in Eastern Europe.

In Western popular music, early use of percussion included the frame drum (with and without jingles) and the pipe and tabor (performed by one player). Following the Crusades, Eastern percussion instruments began to influence the music of Europe. These included *nakers*, kettledrums, bass drums, cymbals, triangles and the jingling johnny, collectively known as Turkish or 'Mehter' instruments. The kettledrum assumed a preeminent role in music of the military, and pairs of them placed on horseback were often used as a signaling device for commands; ultimately, the kettledrum was accepted as a standard orchestral instrument during the Classical era. Large snare or field drums were later used as accompaniment for marching or for the movement of troops in battle, as well as for ceremonial functions.

Percussion Instruments in Western Cultures During the Nineteenth and Twentieth Centuries

During the nineteenth century, percussion instruments played a prominent role onstage as the accompaniment for all types of theatrical or minstrel performances, especially those including dance. Instruments that were prominent early in the century included bones and tambourines for minstrel shows, and snare or field drums of various sizes to accompany dances or other performances.

In the European ballet and operetta traditions, popular songs and dances were often set in 'ethnic' or exotic locations, and were accompanied by percussion instruments that evoked these locations. This involved the traditional use of timpani, snare drum, bass drum and cymbals to accompany waltzes or quadrilles; gongs (tam-tams) and Chinese tom-toms to accompany 'Oriental' numbers; the xylophone or marimba to imitate clog dancing or polkas; and the zither or cymbalom for traditional Eastern European pieces. Early North American theatrical songs and medley overtures, such as those of David Braham (written for Edward Harrigan's productions), continued to use the xylophone to imitate clogging, establishing a foundation for the orchestrations of later US and European musicals. Popular orchestrations of Tchaikovsky, Suppé, Johann Strauss, Victor Herbert, George Gershwin, Percy Grainger, Ferde Grofé, Erich Korngold, Leonard Bernstein, Morton Gould, Robert Russell Bennett, Rodgers and Hammerstein, and Andrew Lloyd Webber all make use of a wide variety of percussion instruments, including the cymbalom, glockenspiel, xylophone, vibraphone, various drums, metallophones, timpani, chimes, gongs, cymbals and other small traps.

As brass or military bands (like those of Patrick S. Gilmore and John Philip Sousa) came to be drawn on for entertainment at social functions during the late nineteenth century, the percussion section adopted a standard contingent of three players (one each on snare drum, bass drum and cymbal), and often featured one of the players as a soloist on bells (glockenspiel) or xylophone. The practise of having one person playing the bass drum with an attached cymbal allowed timpani to be included too. This practise, which was derived from the traditional accompaniment of marches, quadrilles, polkas and waltzes, evolved into the standard two-person arrangement that was used in early theater orchestras and jazz bands. The development and perfection of the bass drum pedal at the turn of the twentieth century reduced the percussion section of the standard popular band or orchestra to one percussion player who performed on the bass drum, snare drum and traps – instruments that produced an assortment of sound effects. This 'trap drummer' became the mainstay of most small Western popular musical ensembles during the early twentieth century, functioning as the foundation of the rhythm section and as the 'color' person for sound effects.

With the introduction of silent motion pictures, the role of the trap drummer was expanded to include all the sound effects considered necessary for a realistic representation of the action on the screen. Depending on the type of ensemble, the trap drummer's basic 'kit' included a snare drum, pedal-operated bass drum and cymbal, crash cymbal, Chinese tom-tom and a set of Chinese wood blocks. The kit could then be expanded to include any or all of the following traps: triangle, timpani, glockenspiel, xylophone, tambourine, ratchet, castanets, sandpaper blocks, slapstick (whip), various bird whistles, slide (Frisco) whistle, train whistle, boat whistle, bell plate (anvil), klaxon horn, siren, fire engine or locomotive bell, chimes, locomotive imitation, gunshot imitation, horse hoof imitation (coconut shells), dog bark imitation, bear growl imitation, baby's cry imitation, police whistle, sleigh bells, gongs (tam-tams), marching men imitation, car or train crash machine, wind machine, thunder sheet and rain imitation.

The advent of sound for motion pictures greatly reduced employment opportunities for musicians in local theaters. This resulted in a rise in the number of musicians pursuing careers in society orchestras (for hotels or private clubs) and in the newly developed medium of radio. Radio allowed percussionists to contribute their talents in much the same way as they had for silent movies, but significantly fewer positions were available.

In live theater, the trap drummer, when performing in a pit orchestra, was expected to support the dancing and action onstage with appropriate cymbal crashes, rimshots or other punctuative sounds. During the first half of the twentieth century, live theater entertainment (including vaudeville) provided many percussionists with the opportunity to abandon their supporting role and pursue a career as a main-stage performer. Three types of headlined solo percussion performers were typical of the vaudeville era: the child drummer; the solo marimbist (xylophonist); and the novelty drummer. Significant representatives of such types of performers included the young Buddy Rich as 'Traps Drum Wonder,' Jess Libonati, Professor Lamberti, El Cota, Teddy Brown, George Hackford and Jack Powell.

During the late nineteenth and early twentieth centuries, additional performance opportunities for percussionists both as members of popular ensembles and as solo performing artists were provided by the Chautauqua circuit, traveling circus bands, cowboy bands, local bands or community orchestras, and the recording industry. Chautauquas had a high demand for solo artists on the xylophone or marimba, and were especially keen to hire female performers for the traveling shows as inspiration for families and for female attendees interested in the performing arts.

Owing to its acoustic properties, the xylophone was one of the most successful instruments during the acous-

tic recording era. The many well-known solo xylophone artists included Charles P. Lowe, George Hamilton Green, Jr., Joseph Green, Charles Daab and Lou 'Chiha' Frisco. Also popular for both recordings and touring-circuit performances during the early twentieth century were marimba ensembles performing Mexican, Central American, Hawaiian folk and other popular tunes. Drums are often absent from early recordings because of their poor acoustic quality, which tended to overpower the recording mechanism. This has resulted in a somewhat inaccurate assessment of their use in popular ensembles during the early recording era.

As silent movies gave way to motion pictures with recorded soundtracks, the percussionist became invaluable as a studio musician who not only kept time for the other musicians, but also continued to provide sound effects as needed to support the action in feature films. Sound effects, often on 'found' instruments, were also quite prominent in early animated films (such as Walt Disney's Mickey Mouse features), which firmly established the studio percussionist's role as a provider of creative sound effects for popular film soundtracks.

As popular music evolved throughout the twentieth century, so did the function and role of the percussionist. With the rise of jazz came the prominent use of the vibraphone (vibraharp) by such noted players as Lionel Hampton, Milt Jackson, Red Norvo, Gary Burton and Adrian Rollini, which proved its viability as a solo instrument. The swing era ushered in larger ensembles that often featured extensive setups for the drummer, who was usually on a raised platform centered behind the orchestra. Pictures of Chick Webb, Cozy Cole (with Cab Calloway), George Marsh (with Isham Jones and Paul Whiteman) and Sonny Greer (with Duke Ellington) show elaborate setups that include timpani, chimes, gongs (tam-tams), a vibraphone, several tom-toms, and numerous cymbals and traps, in addition to the basic bass drum, snare drum and hi-hat. Often having a colorful painting on the front bass drumhead, these large setups were intended more for show than for actual performance, although all the instruments were played occasionally during an evening performance. Gene Krupa brought the drummer to the forefront as a soloist during the swing era, opening the door for later drummers as soloists in all types of popular music ensembles.

The dissemination of popular Latin dances, such as the rumba, tango and bossa nova, during the 1930s brought more Latin American percussion instruments to popular attention. Especially prominent were the bongos, claves, maracas, *güiros*, cowbells and congas utilized by performers such as George Marsh (with Paul Whiteman). While these instruments were added to the standard percussion kit during the 1930s and 1940s, it was the success of prominent Latin percussion artists, such as Tito Puente, during the 1950s that established a more authentic integration of both the instruments (such as timbales) and the traditional styles associated with the music of other cultures.

The big band era saw a reduction in the number of instruments in a standard drumset to four or five drums with cymbals and a hi-hat, with the set functioning primarily in a timekeeping role. Notable exceptions to this trend were Buddy Rich, Gene Krupa, Louie Bellson and Lionel Hampton, who maintained prominence as solo artists and band leaders. As rock music became prominent during the 1960s and 1970s, the set grew larger again, incorporating as many as eight (or more) tom-toms, cymbals and gongs, but it still functioned primarily as a timekeeper. However, in larger stadium concerts, it became standard practise to feature the drummer in extended solos during the performance. Notable drummers who made use of gongs during this period were John Bonham (Led Zeppelin) and Carl Palmer (Emerson, Lake and Palmer).

Percussion Instruments in Non-Western Cultures

In non-Western cultures, the use of percussion instruments in popular music can be roughly categorized by region. Most of these cultures also make a distinction between the use of percussion instruments for religious purposes and their use in popular entertainment.

Africa

In Africa, percussion instruments used in ritual ceremonies include drums (*dundun* or 'talking drum,' frame drums of various sizes, or *tar*, *naqqara*, *riqq*, *dumbak*, *batá* and barrel drums), shakers (*chekeré* or other indigenous rattles), rattle belts, the double and single bell, percussion sticks, hand cymbals (*kas*) and finger cymbals. These may be commonly used, along with clapping and foot stomping, for ceremonial rites in Islamic prayer, as well as in the ritual rites of passage of other religions to accompany singing and dancing. Typically in African popular culture, percussion instruments are used in ceremonies to mark birth, death, circumcision and marriage, at seasonal feasts and ceremonial hair cutting, and in praise of leaders. In Sudan, kettledrums, often mounted on camels, are used in formal ceremonies for tribal leaders.

The non-ritual use of percussion instruments in African popular culture is to be found in various genres, including *jújù*, highlife and Afrobeat, as well as in other regional folk or popular styles. *Jújù* and highlife make prominent use of the *dundun* and *batá* drums, as well as the characteristic tambourine and cylindrical drums of various sizes and shapes. Typical stylistic drumming patterns include the use of a mother (or master) drum that

improvises over interlocking ostinato patterns played by supporting drums. The *dundun* is of special significance because of its ability to mimic speech and song patterns of the Yoruba language. The evolution of Afrobeat is an example of the Westernization of African popular music; it includes the use of a drumset, featuring an interlocking bass pattern with a snare drum backbeat, along with percussion sticks and *chekeré*. Of regional significance are the use of xylophone bands, accompanied by drums and/or wooden slit-drums, in Central Africa (Uganda), the use of the *djembe* in West Africa, and the use of the cord and peg barrel drum on the Guinea coast. The jazz and big band styles that appeared in South Africa featured the use of the drumset. Pennywhistle bands make use of crude hand drums.

Asia, the Middle East and the Pacific Islands

Within most Eastern cultures, the use of percussion in popular music, excluding imported Western genres, has remained quite traditional: it generally has a ceremonial function or is used as an accompaniment to dance, theatrical productions and, especially, song. The various types of percussion instruments, and the regions and ensembles in which they figure prominently, include: (a) the metallophone and xylophone in Thai *pi-phat* ensembles and Indonesian gamelan; (b) barrel drums in Japanese *taiko* and *noh* ensembles, Tibetan religious ceremonial music, Chinese opera and Afghan song; (c) bells (metal, wooden and ceramic) and gongs (pitched and non-pitched) in Tibet, Indonesia, China and the Philippines; (d) *tablā* and the mridangam in Indian classical music; (e) cymbals in China, Thailand, Indonesia, India, Korea and other Southeast Asian cultures; (f) tambourine, *dumbak* and small kettledrums in the Middle East and in central and southern Asia; (g) ceremonial bamboo instruments, such as the Hawaiian *puili* and the Indonesian *angklung*; and (h) wooden log or slit-drums in China, Australia, Japan, Korea and numerous Pacific Island cultures.

Central America and the Caribbean Islands

In Central America and the Caribbean Islands, percussion instruments constitute a core element of popular music as a result of the African slave trade. Prominent in the evolution of Cuban music has been the use of *batá* (always in sets of three) and *chekeré*, which were originally used in music of the Yoruba people, and *yuka* (also in sets of three), initially used in music of the Bantu people. These instruments, whose role was primarily ceremonial, were gradually integrated into various popular music styles. Bongos, congas, claves, maracas, cowbells and *güiros* were added, eventually becoming the standard instruments for various dances and musical styles, such as the rumba, cha-cha and mambo in Cuba, and the merengue as developed by Johnny Ventura in the Dominican Republic. Tito Puente popularized the use of multiple sets of timbales along with mounted cowbells and cymbals. The invention and popularization of the steel drum or pan proved noteworthy for Trinidad, as has the use of the marimba for Mexico and Guatemala. In the traditional music of Mexican cultures the use of a drum (either a membrane-covered or wooden slit-drum) and various rattles (constructed from gourds or from animal parts, such as hoofs or jawbones) forms the basis of popular ceremonial accompaniment of song and dance.

South America

Percussion instruments used in South American popular music are derived from the cultures of Native South American peoples, as well as of African and European immigrants. Apart from the drumset, an imported element in the Westernization of South American popular music, traditional percussion instruments abound throughout the various cultures as accompaniments to song and dance. Among the most common is the tabor, combined with pipe or pan pipe in the Andean region. This tabor is sometimes a small snare drum (*caja*) and sometimes a larger *bombo* (with or without snare). Samba, in which large groups of percussion instruments – such as *caxixi, tamborim, pandeiro, surdo, berimbau* and *cuíca*, various shakers and scrapers, and *agogô* bells – are featured as an accompaniment to dance and carnival or fiesta celebrations, is widely associated with Brazilian culture. Military drums (snare and bass) are integral parts of both marching and concert bands in Bolivia and Peru. Other percussion instruments associated with particular regional popular musical styles include the *quijada*, the marimba with bamboo resonators, the mbira and the *marimbula*.

Globalization and Cultural Hybridity

Popular music of the non-Western tradition, in addition to continuing traditional styles of drumming for 'authentic' performances, has been highly influenced by the widespread dissemination of jazz, rock 'n' roll, Latin and fusion music of the 1980s and 1990s. As a result of this, and of a reverse influence of non-Western drumming on Western music, it has become common to encounter the Western drumkit in all parts of the world and to hear a wide variety of non-Western music melded into traditional Western song and dance styles. Especially prominent is the use of the *tablā* to evoke the music of India and the gamelan orchestra to reflect the song traditions of Indonesia, the use of African mbira and drum rhythms, the utilization of the steel drum from the Caribbean and the *bodhrán* from Ireland, and

the influence of the Central American marimba tradition.

The widespread influence of both Latin American and Afro-Cuban music has resulted in a fusion of styles throughout the world of popular music, manifest not only in the use of indigenous percussion instruments, but also through the dance rhythms, language and subject matter of the lyrics. This instrumental and rhythmic fusion has resulted in recognizable stylistic influences on performers as diverse as Liberace, Dizzy Gillespie, Stan Kenton, Carlos Santana and Chick Corea, as well as on numerous film and television composers.

A common practise has been to use additional percussionists to support the drummer for live and recorded performances. This 'multi-percussion' setup usually includes several small, handheld drums, shakers and cowbells distributed around congas, bongos, cymbals and timbales. Tambourines, maracas, *chekeré* rattles, *caxixi*, wind chimes, samba whistles, claves and *güiros* have also been used. Among the most prominent artists who have featured a 'world' approach to the use of percussion instruments, often having numerous drummers of different cultural traditions assembled for performance or recording, are Paul Winter and Mickey Hart. In addition, significant use of an African drumming influence can be heard in the television series *Daktari*, scored by Shelly Manne.

Electronic Percussion Instruments

Electronic percussion instruments (the electronic drum pad and the drum machine) had a significant influence on popular music during the last two decades of the twentieth century. The drum pad, actuated by a drumstick, is easily incorporated into the modern drummer's setup, while the drum machine has contributed most significantly as background rhythm for studio recordings of popular dance albums. Peter Erskine and Danny Gottlieb are among the many popular performers who have successfully incorporated electronic percussion instruments into their setups and recordings, and such devices have also been widely used in film and television soundtracks.

Bibliography

Anderson, William M., and Campbell, Patricia Shehan, eds. 1996. *Multicultural Perspectives in Music Education.* 2nd ed. Reston, VA: Music Educators National Conference.

Beck, John H., ed. 1995. *Encyclopedia of Percussion.* New York and London: Garland Publishing.

Blades, James. 1992. *Percussion Instruments and Their History.* Rev. ed. Westport, CT: Bold Strummer.

Diagram Group, The. 1976. *Musical Instruments of the*

World: *An Illustrated Encyclopedia*. New York: Paddington Press.

Meza, Fernando A. 1990. *Percussion Discography: An International Compilation of Solo and Chamber Percussion Music (Discographies, No. 36)*. Westport, CT: Greenwood Press.

Percussive Arts Society Research Publications, 1963–1987 (CD-ROM). 2001. Lawton, OK: Percussive Arts Society.

Peters, Gordon B. 1975. *The Drummer, Man: A Treatise on Percussion*. Rev. ed. Wilmette, IL: Kemper-Peters Publications.

Richards, Emil. 1972. *World of Percussion: A Catalog of 300 Standard, Ethnic, and Special Musical Instruments and Effects*. Sherman Oaks, CA: Gwyn Publishing Company.

Sachs, Curt. 1940. *The History of Musical Instruments*. New York: W.W. Norton.

Tabourot. 1994. *Historic Percussion: A Survey*. Austin, TX: Tactus Press.

The Garland Encyclopedia of World Music. 1998–2002. New York: Garland Publishing.

Discography

African Rhythms and Instruments, Vol. 1. Lyrichord 7328. *1990*: USA.

African Rhythms and Instruments, Vol. 2. Lyrichord 7338. *1990*: USA.

African Rhythms and Instruments, Vol. 3. Lyrichord 7339. *1990*: USA.

Bali: The Celebrated Gamelans. Musical Heritage Society 3505. *1976*: USA.

Java: Music of Mystical Enchantment. Lyrichord 7301. *1976*: USA.

Max Weinberg Presents: Let There Be Drums!. Rhino R2 71547. *1994*: USA.

Percussions d'Afrique. Playasound 65004. *1983*: France.

Percussions d'Asie. Playasound 65026. *1988*: France.

Peru: Music from the Land of Macchu Picchu. Lyrichord 7294. *1976*: USA.

Red Norvo. *Red Norvo*. Time-Life STL-J14. *1980*: USA.

Rhythm-Time: World Percussion. World Music Network 1033. *1999*: UK.

The Engine Room: A History of Jazz Drumming from Storyville to 52nd Street. Proper Records PROPERBOX 2. *1999*: UK.

The Rough Guide to Africa. World Music Network 1. *2001*: UK.

The Rough Guide to Latin America. World Music Network 2. *2001*: UK.

The Rough Guide to World Music. Vol. 1: Africa, Europe and the Middle East. World Music Network 1032. *1999*: UK.

The Rough Guide to World Music. Vol. 2: Latin and North America, Caribbean, India, Asia and Pacific. World Music Network 1044. *2000*: UK.

JAMES A. STRAIN

Batá Drums

The *batá* drum began to find a place as an instrument of popular music only toward the end of the twentieth century. With increasing interest in world music and specifically in Afro-Caribbean music, *batá* drums started to be used in folkloric ensembles and even in certain jazz settings. They can be heard in recordings by such artists as the Conjunto Folklorico Nacional de Cuba, the Machete Ensemble and Mongo Santamaría.

The *batá* drum is distantly related to the conga and bongo drums. Like a conga drum, it has a long, narrow, cylindrical shape; however, the *batá* drum has a head on both ends. The player, holding the drum transversely across his/her lap, strikes one head with each hand. Each head is of a different size and produces a different pitch. The larger of the two heads is called the *enú* (mouth) and the smaller one is called the *chachá* (butt).

A *batá* ensemble consists of three drums of graduated sizes. The *Iyá* is the largest and produces the lowest pitches; the mid-size drum is the *Itótele*; and the smallest drum, the *Okónkolo*, produces the highest pitches.

Batá drums originated as part of the religious ritual of the Yoruba people of West Africa. An intrinsic element of this ritual involved the performance of specific rhythms on the *batá* drums to represent the different deities. These rhythms have been identified and transcribed in early texts by Fernando Ortíz (1974) and in more recent work by John Amira and Steven Cornelius (1992).

In the mid-eighteenth century, many of the Yoruba people arrived in Cuba as slaves. When the Spanish plantation owners tried to suppress their religious beliefs and practises, the slaves applied the names of Christian saints to their own deities and the hybrid religion known as Santería was established. Santería became very popular in Cuba during the twentieth century and, from the 1950s onward, acquired many followers in southern Florida and New York City.

As interest in Santería has grown, exposure to the *batá* ensemble has increased, and gradually, like the congas and bongos, *batá* drums have been incorporated into various popular music styles. Recordings by such groups as Santana and Irakere provide the listener with the opportunity to hear how the *batá* drums may be utilized in popular music and jazz settings. Commercial *batá* drums are available from several manufacturers in the United States and Europe.

Bibliography

Amira, John, and Cornelius, Steven. 1992. *The Music of Santería: Traditional Rhythms of the Batá Drums*. Crown Point, IN: White Cliffs Media Co.

Malabe, Frank, and Weiner, Bob. 1990. *Afro-Cuban Rhythms for the Drumset*. Miami, FL: Warner Brothers Music.

Mauleón, Rebeca. 1993. *Salsa Guidebook for Piano and Ensemble*. Petaluma, CA: Sher Music Co.

Ortíz, Fernando. 1974. *La música afrocubana* [Afro-Cuban Music]. Madrid: Ediciones Júcar.

Uribe, Ed. 1996. *Essence of Afro-Cuban Percussion and Drum Set*. Miami, FL: Warner Brothers Music.

Discography

Cardona, Milton, and the Eya Aranla Ensemble. *Bembé*. American Clave/Pangaea 1004. *1985*: USA.

Cult Music of Cuba. Folkways Records FE 4410. *1977*: USA.

Santamaría, Mongo. *Afro Roots*. Prestige 24018. *1992*: USA.

Santamaría, Mongo. *Our Man in Havana*. Fantasy 24729. *1993*: USA.

Santero, Vol. 1. T.H. Rodven 4060. *1994*: Venezuela.

Santero, Vol. 2. T.H. Rodven 159. *1993*: Venezuela.

JONATHAN WACKER

Bells

Bells, in a variety of shapes, are percussion instruments that date from antiquity. Acoustically classified as idiophones, bells are sounded by striking either with a mallet or by means of an internal clapper. They can be constructed from a variety of materials, although the most common is a resonant, hard metal such as bronze. Bells can be either definite pitched or indefinite (relative to size) pitched instruments. They should not be confused with the modern instruments known as the glockenspiel or chimes, which imitate the sound of bells for concert performances.

Used primarily as ceremonial instruments for worship, bells had little or no function in the popular music of ancient cultures. Since the eighth century, large tower bells in churches and civic centers have been used as a method of calling worshipers or of marking the time of day. Often, small clusters or rows of bells are worn as jingles to accompany folk or ceremonial music used for dancing (for example, anklets of bells used to accompany Native American dancing).

Tuned bells, when suspended in a bell tower and played by means of a keyboard mechanism, are known as a carillon. Carillons have been used in religious and popular music performances since the thirteenth century. Twentieth-century developments of the carillon included the use of tower chimes (tubular bells) to produce the sound, and the use of electronic amplification of tuned rods to imitate the sound of tower chimes or bells. During the mid-twentieth century, electronic carillon concerts of popular music were quite common in the

United States, with the most prominent ones perhaps being the annual Christmas season concerts at the Chicago Tribune Building.

Types of indefinite pitched bells that are known to have been used to accompany popular singing and dancing include the African double bell and the Latin American *agogô* bell. Popular Latin American music is characterized by a wide variety of non-pitched cowbells, which often provide the underlying dance rhythm known as the clave. During the rise of the standard drumset (trap set or 'kit') in the early twentieth century, the cowbell was a prominent fixture, often found in a mounted pair as one of many small 'traps' that attached to the rim of the bass drum. This non-pitched cowbell became a semi-permanent fixture on the drumset. It was then used independently of the drumset, first in Latin American-based dances, and then as a timekeeper for rock-based music of the 1970s and 1980s, whether Latin-influenced or not.

During the late nineteenth century, novelty acts involving tuned handbells became popular throughout Europe and the United States. These bells, sometimes referred to as Swiss handbells, are accurately tuned sets played by several individuals (collectively called a choir), each of whom rings his/her assigned pitches in order, in order to produce popular melodies accompanied by harmony. Several performers gained renown for performing novelty acts on Swiss handbells for vaudeville or radio broadcasts during the first half of the twentieth century. One prominent artist was Clarence Messick, who performed novelty acts using handbells, rows of tuned sleigh bells and a variety of other ringing instruments. He and his brother Arthur, billed as the Messick Brothers Grand Concert Company, appeared for a brief period in the early twentieth century, performing on bells manufactured in all parts of the world. Handbell choirs have continued to be a popular form of entertainment for many civic, church and educational institutions.

The largest manufacturer of tuned bells, chimes, electronic carillon, tower chimes and novelty-type bell instruments during the years 1890 to 1970 was the J.C. Deagan Company of Chicago, Illinois.

Bibliography

Beck, John H., ed. 1995. *Encyclopedia of Percussion*. New York and London: Garland Publishing.

Diagram Group, The. 1976. *Musical Instruments of the World: An Illustrated Encyclopedia*. New York: Paddington Press.

François, Jean-Charles, ed. 1986. 'Deagan Catalogs B, D, E, G, H.' *Percussive Notes Research Edition* 24: 3, 6.

Mack, George. 1977. 'Clarence Messick's Musical Bells.'

In *A Century of Music*, ed. John W. Ripley and Robert W. Richmond. Topeka, KS: Shawnee County Historical Society, 7–11.

JAMES A. STRAIN

Berimbau

The Brazilian *berimbau de barriga*, or simply *berimbau*, is a gourd-resonated, braced musical bow of African origin. The instrument consists of a 4'–5' (1.2 m–1.5 m) branch of *biriba*, bamboo, oak or other wood bent into an arc. The bow is strung with a single metal string, usually recycled from an industrial use.

Attached to the convex back of the bow with a small loop of string is a gourd resonator, although coconut, calabash or a tin can is occasionally substituted for a gourd. The string loop also serves as a bridge, dividing the metal string into two sections. The little finger of the musician's left hand (assuming a right-handed player) passes underneath the string loop to hold the *berimbau*.

The string is struck with a thin stick called a *vaquita* or *vareta*, which is held in the player's right hand along with a small basket rattle called *caxixi*. A small coin (*dobrão*) or stone (*pedra*) held between the musician's left thumb and index finger is pressed to the string, resulting in a pitch change of about a minor or major second above the *berimbau*'s fundamental tone.

The *berimbau* originated in an early nineteenth-century Brazilian slave culture. Several historical notices and depictions from this period demonstrate the continued presence of a variety of central African musical bows (Koster 1816, 122; Graham 1824, 199; Walsh 1830, 175–76; Debret 1834, 39; Wetherell 1860, 106–107). Popular among African-Brazilian vendors and street musicians, these musical bows were known by African names such as *urucungu*, *madimba lungungo*, *mbulumbumba* and *hungu* (Shaffer 1976, 14; Kubik 1979, 30). As a result of pan-African technology-sharing, organological traits of these various musical bows were fused to create a single African-Brazilian instrument (Graham 1991, 6).

Sometime in the late nineteenth century, this new musical bow received a Lusophone name – *berimbau de barriga*, or 'jaw harp of the stomach' – and entered a new cultural context, the African-Brazilian martial art form known as *capoeira* (Kubik 1979, 30–33). Beginning at least as early as the eighteenth century, *capoeira* was fought to the music of an African-derived hand drum or to simple handclapping. *Capoeira* is now fought to the *toques* (rhythms) of the *berimbau*, which accompany the songs known in Brazil as *cantigas de capoeira*.

The musical ensemble employed in contemporary *capoeira* features one to three *berimbaus*, an *atabaque* (conical hand drum), a *pandeiro* (tambourine) and an *agogô* (double bell). Where multiple *berimbaus* are employed in an ensemble, they are often tuned to separate pitches. In Salvador de Bahia, the cultural epicenter of *capoeira*, different names are used for *berimbaus* of various sizes, including *viola* (small), *medio* (medium) and *gunga* (large) (Lewis 1992, 137). From the 1940s, a number of *capoeira* schools in Bahia began to paint their *berimbaus* with colorful stripes and other decorations, reflecting their pride in their individual *academias* (traditional *capoeira* schools) (Shaffer 1976, 26).

The *Berimbau* in Popular Music

Besides its close association with *capoeira*, the *berimbau* has long been used in a variety of Brazilian folk and popular music forms, such as *samba de roda*, *carimbo*, bossa nova, *afro-samba* and *tropicalismo*. Art music composers such as Mario Tavares (*Gan Guzama*), Luiz Augusto Rescala (*Musica para Berimbau e Fita Magnetica*) and Gaudencio Thiago de Mello (*Chants for the Chief*) have also written music for the instrument.

The *berimbau* experienced a creative renaissance in 1960s Brazilian popular music, followed by its spread to areas outside Brazil and its use in 1970s international jazz. Although the international diffusion of *capoeira* was a phenomenon that contributed to the spread of the *berimbau*, this occurred only after the instrument had already spread through popular musics. As a result of Brazilian popular musical movements in the 1960s, the *berimbau* began to be heard internationally independently of *capoeira*. Baden Powell and others brought the *berimbau* to the attention of musicians outside Brazil in *afro-samba* songs that mimicked the sound and rhythm of the *berimbau* on the guitar. In 1965, Astrud Gilberto recorded a jazz-bossa nova version of Powell's 'Berimbau' that featured Dom um Romão on the instrument. Gilberto Gil recorded an important *tropicalismo* album in 1968, which featured the *berimbau* with electric guitars. By the end of the 1960s, the *berimbau* had entered rock and jazz in both Brazil and the United States.

Several expatriate Brazilian percussionists began the process of reinterpreting the *berimbau*, using it outside of *capoeira* in 1970s jazz, and this resulted in innovative technical and organological developments. Airto Moreira, Dom um Romão, Guilherme Franco and Naná Vasconcelos had explored the possibilities of using the *berimbau* in jazz, and they were followed by Paulinho Da Costa and Djalma Corrêa (and Papete in Brazilian pop). Airto Moreira, who left Brazil in 1968, played the *berimbau* on recordings by Miles Davis in 1969, made a solo recording in 1970 and played with the group Weather Report in 1971. Dom um Romão replaced Moreira in Weather Report and continued to use the *berimbau* during a Japanese tour in 1972. Subsequently, Romão developed an electric *berimbau*, which greatly increased the volume of the instrument and allowed for subtle changes in its timbre through the use of signal processors. Guilherme Franco had been using the *berimbau* in an experimental percussion trio in Brazil in 1972. After moving to New York, he played the *berimbau* on jazz recordings by Archie Shepp and McCoy Tyner. Naná Vasconcelos played the *berimbau* with Argentinian Gato Barbieri in 1971 and made three successive recordings between 1971 and 1973, in Argentina, France and Brazil, all featuring extended improvisatory solos. Subsequently, non-Brazilian percussionists extended the process of reinterpretation, incorporating the *berimbau* into jazz. Among them were Luis Agudo and Onias Carmadelli from Argentina, Okay Temiz from Turkey and African-American Bill Summers, among others.

The use of the *berimbau* in jazz provided a nontraditional context for contact, in which percussionists with little or no experience with *capoeira* could freely exchange ideas about *berimbau* techniques. Luis Agudo moved to France in 1970, where he built his own *berimbau* with a double *caxixi* and experimented with African, Brazilian and Argentinian rhythms. While touring Europe, Agudo met Okay Temiz in Sweden in 1974 and instructed him in how to build a *berimbau*. By 1975, Temiz had developed a completely new technical approach to the *berimbau*, involving numerous effects – pedals, microphones and a free-hand grip similar to that used for the violin, where the instrument is held between the chin and the shoulder, so that both hands were free for playing. A similar cultural exchange occurred through contact between Naná Vasconcelos and percussionists in Italy and Japan. In the 1990s, Vasconcelos performed a series of solo concerts and held workshops in Japan and Italy. As a result of personal contact with Vasconcelos, percussionists Seichi Yamamura of Japan and Peppe Consolmagno of Italy began to play the *berimbau* in a style heretofore peculiar to Vasconcelos, effectively contributing to a kind of *berimbau* performance lineage.

New *Berimbau* Techniques

By the 1990s, a number of organological developments and new techniques were evident in the way that the *berimbau* was played in popular musics. Tuning became an issue when the *berimbau* was played in new musical contexts where pitch was a consideration. Some musicians, such as Vasconcelos and Temiz, actually tied the gourd resonator to the wooden bow in a new manner, so that it was fixed in place, keeping the pitch accurate. Brazilian Dinho Nascimento built a large bass *berimbau*, called a *berimbum*, which used the string and tuning hardware of an acoustic bass.

Another organological development consisted of doubling the number of strings, which required new performance techniques. Double-string *berimbaus* were used by Vasconcelos, Temiz and Franco (who also developed a double-*berimbau* – literally two instruments joined as one). Romão, Temiz and Franco developed electric *berimbaus*. Temiz also developed an electric double-string *berimbau* that featured the addition of separate microphones and signal processors for the string, gourd and *caxixi*. His technique involved using as many as nine signal processors simultaneously in conjunction with a free-hand grip, which allowed the left hand to slide the coin farther up and down the string, producing many more than the traditional two pitches. By amplifying each part of the *berimbau*, Temiz could exploit other possibilities, such as tapping on the gourd with the coin, fingers and stick, successfully producing traditional Turkish rhythms.

Vasconcelos expanded many technical aspects of the *berimbau*. Such technical developments included plucking the string with the fingers, striking the wood of the bow with the stone, muting the string, scraping and striking the gourd and other parts of the instrument with the stick, increasing the number of pitches from two to three with a special angled stone stroke, and playing inside the bow with the stick by alternating between the wood and string, thereby achieving many kinds of harmonics and percussive effects. He also redefined the role of the *caxixi*. Keeping one rhythm with the *caxixi* as an ostinato, the fingers of the same hand played different accents on the string with the stick. Similar techniques, and others, appear in Luiz Almeida Da Anunciação's *berimbau* method book of 1990. Argentinian Luis Agudo and Brazilian Dom um Romão both employed an unusual technique for string bending by bracing the gourd against the body while pulling back on the bow. In the 1990s, Dinho Nascimento developed a blues-like slide-*berimbau* technique: it involved holding the bow against the body in a free-hand fashion so that a glass slide could be used to bend the tones of the string. Also in the 1990s, Italian Rosario Jermano developed another slide-*berimbau* technique that called for a new left-hand grip and the use of a metal guitar slide in place of the stone or coin. Through both a methods book and teaching, Jermano's technique spread to other musicians in Italy, including percussionist Paolo Sanna.

Both inside and outside Brazil, the *berimbau* continues to be used in new ways in popular musics. Brazilian artists who have recently used the *berimbau* in heavy metal, rap and rock include Sepultura, General Frank and Mônica Feijó, among others. Artists outside Brazil who have also recently used the *berimbau* in new genres include Alex Pertout (Australia, orchestral), François

Malet (France, jazz), Nuno Rebelo (Portugal, experimental film/dance/theater) and Rich Goodhart (United States, progressive world-rock). The *berimbau* has also been used in New Age and music therapy genres, with recordings by anthropologist Michael Harmer of the Foundation for Shamanic Studies, among others.

Conclusion

The *berimbau* has become somewhat emblematic of Brazilian popular culture, its image appearing frequently in murals, sculpture, jewelry, tattoos and the electronic media. The diffusion of the *berimbau* into popular musics outside of *capoeira* and beyond Brazil has led to its increased sophistication and technical diversity as a musical instrument. Because of the various styles of music in which the *berimbau* was increasingly used, new techniques were developed to better meet the challenges of *berimbau* performance outside of *capoeira*. These new attributes of contemporary *berimbau* performance include an increased tendency toward improvisation, the use of electronics, additional strings, combinations with new instruments, new rhythmic styles and solo performances. Following the innovations of Brazilian percussionists, many non-Brazilian musicians who creatively adopted the *berimbau* did so without a prior knowledge of *capoeira* and approached the instrument solely in the context of jazz and rock. Through the process of reinterpretation, the increased range of diverse performance techniques came to better fit the needs of musicians who used the *berimbau* in new contexts, and this facilitated the use of the instrument outside of *capoeira* and beyond Brazil.

Bibliography

'A História do Berimbau' [The History of the *Berimbau*]. 1999. *Revista Capoeira* 2(7).

Almeida, Bira [Mestre Acordeon]. 1986. *Capoeira: A Brazilian Art Form (History, Philosophy, and Practice)*. Berkeley, CA: North Atlantic Books.

Balfour, Henry. 1899. *The Natural History of the Musical Bow*. Oxford: Clarendon Press.

Coelho, Raquel. 1993. *Berimbau*. São Paulo: Editora Atica.

Consolmagno, Peppe [Giuseppe Consolmagno]. 1998. 'Il Berimbau' [The *Berimbau*]. *World Music* 8(33) (August): 44–52.

Cunha, Tustão. 2000. 'Como Montar e Cuidar do seu Berimbau' [The Care and Assembly of a *Berimbau*]. *Batera & Percussão* 4(36) (August): 44–45.

Da Anunciação, Luiz Almeida. 1990. *A percassão dos ritmos brasileiros suo técnica esua escrita. Caderno 1: O berimbau* [The Percussion Instruments of the Brazilian Typical Rhythms: Its Techniques and Its Musical Writing. Book 1: The *Berimbau*]. Rio de Janeiro: Europa Empresa Gráfica e Editora.

Debret, Jean-Baptiste. 1834. *Voyage pittoresque et historique au Bresil* [A Picturesque and Historical Voyage to Brazil]. Paris: Firmin Didot Frères.

'Dinho Nascimento: Fábrica de Sons' [Dinho Nascimento: Maker of Sounds]. 1999. *Mundo Capoeira* 1(1) (May): 10–11.

Faleiros, Gustavo. 2000. 'Papete: Música e Pesquisa' [Papete: Music and Research]. *Batera & Percussão* 4(32) (April): 16–20.

Germinario, Fabio. 2001. 'Luis Agudo.' *Jazzit* 3(6) (September/October): 48–50, 52–53.

Gomes, Sergio. 2000. 'O berimbau' [The *Berimbau*]. *Batera & Percussão* 4(36) (August): 40–42.

Graham, Maria. 1824. *Journal of a Voyage to Brazil*. London: Longman.

Graham, Richard. 1991. 'Technology and Culture Change: The Development of the *Berimbau* in Colonial Brazil.' *Latin American Music Review* 12(1) (Spring/Summer): 1–20.

Graham, Richard, and Robinson, N. Scott. 1988. 'Historical and Musical Introduction to the *Berimbau*.' LP *Highlights in Percussion* 3(1): 14, 16.

Herskovits, Melville J. 1958. *The Myth of the Negro Past*. Boston, MA: Beacon Press.

Jermano, Rosario. 1999. '*Slide Berimbau' – Nuova Technica per suonare il Berimbau* ['Slide *Berimbau*' – New Technique for Playing the *Berimbau*]. Rome: Rosario Jermano.

Koster, Henry. 1816. *Travels in Brazil*. London: Longman.

Kubik, Gerhard. 1979. *Angolan Traits in Black Music, Games and Dances of Brazil: A Study of African Cultural Extensions Overseas*. Lisbon: Junta de Investigações Científicas do Ultramar.

Lewis, J. Lowell. 1992. *Ring of Liberation: Deceptive Discourse in Brazilian Capoeira*. Chicago: University of Chicago Press.

Moreira, Airto. 1985. *Airto: The Spirit of Percussion*. Wayne, NJ: 21st Century Music Productions.

Nazário, Zé Eduardo. 2000. 'Entre Amigos: Zé Eduardo Nazário entrevista Guilherme Franco' [Between Friends: Zé Eduardo Nazário Interviews Guilherme Franco]. *Batera & Percussão* 4(38) (October): 54–56.

Pellegrini, Cecília. 2000. 'Dinho Nascimento: *Gongolô*.' *Revista Capoeira* 2(9): 28–29.

Pinto, Tiago de Oliveira, ed. 1986. *Brasilien: Einführung in Musiktraditionen Brasiliens* [Brazil: An Introduction to the Music Tradition of Brazilians]. Mainz and New York: Schott.

Rego, Waldeloir. 1968. *Capoeira Angola: ensaio sócio-etnográfico* [*Capoeira* Angola: Socio-Ethnographic Essay]. Rio de Janeiro: Gráffica Lux.

Robinson, N. Scott. 2000a. 'Naná Vasconcelos: The

Nature of Naná.' *Modern Drummer* 24(7) (July): 98–102, 104, 106, 108.

Robinson, N. Scott. 2000b. 'Rhythm Legend Airto: Then & Now.' *Modern Drummer* 24(6) (June): 68–72, 74, 76, 78, 80, 82.

Robinson, N. Scott. 2002. *The New Percussionist in Jazz: Organological and Technical Expansion*. M.A. thesis, Kent State University.

Roisman, Eli. 2000. 'Dinho Nascimento: O mago do Berimbau' [Dinho Nascimento: The Magician of the *Berimbau*]. *Batera & Percussão* 4(38) (October): 32–34, 36.

Shaffer, Kay. 1976. *O berimbau-de-barriga e seus toques* [The *Berimbau* and Its Rhythms]. Rio de Janeiro: Ministerio da Educação e Cultura.

Walsh, Robert. 1830. *Notices of Brazil in 1828 & 1829*. London: F. Westey & A.H. Davis.

Wetherell, James. 1860. *Brazil – Stray Notes from Bahia: Being Extracts from Letters, &c., During a Residence of Fifteen Years*. Liverpool: Webb and Hunt.

Discographical References

Baden Powell. 'Berimbau.' *Os Afro-Sambas*. Forma FM-16. *1965*: Brazil.

Gilberto, Astrud. 'Berimbau.' *Look to the Rainbow*. Verve 821556-2. *1965*: USA.

Discography

Agudo, Luis. *Afrosamba & Afrorera*. Red RR123185. *1984/85*: Italy.

Agudo, Luis, and Vieire, Afonso. *Jazz a Confronto 33*. Horo HLL 101-33. *1975*: Italy.

Anderson, Marc. *Time Fish*. East Side Digital ESD 80842. *1993*: USA.

Australian Art Orchestra and Sruthi Laya Ensemble. *Into the Fire*. ABC Classics ABC 465 705-2. *2000*: Australia.

Baker, Ginger. *Horses & Trees*. Terrascape TRS 4123-2. *1986*: USA.

Berimbau e Capoeira – BA. Documentario Sonoro do Folclore Brasileiro INF 46. *1988*: Brazil.

Brock, Jim. *Pasajes*. Mbira MRLP-1001. *1988*: USA.

Codona. *Codona 2*. ECM 1177 78118-21177-2. *1981*: USA.

Consolmagno, Peppe [Giuseppe Consolmagno]. *Timbri Dal Mondo*. Cajù 4158-2. *1999*: Italy.

Corrêa, Djalma. *Djalma Corrêa e Banda Cauim*. Barclay 821 375-1. *1984*: France.

Da Costa, Paulinho. *Agora*. Pablo OJCCD-630-2 (2310–785). *1976*: USA.

Daniele, Pino. *Pino Daniele*. EMI 3C 064-18391. *1979*: Italy.

Davis, Miles. *Big Fun*. Sony SRCS 5713. 1969–72: USA.

Davis, Miles. *The Complete Bitches Brew Sessions*. Columbia C4K 65570. *1969*: USA.

De André, Fabrizo. *In Concerto (live)*. Ricordi 74321656992. *1999*: Italy.

Deguchi, Khorey. *Blowin' Green Breeze*. MAHORA Japan MFS-5801. *2000*: Japan.

Favata, Enzo. *Il cielo è sempre piu' blu*. San Isidro SND 1001-2. *1996*: Italy.

Feijó, Mônica. *Aurora 5365*. Sonopress MRO178. *2000*: Brazil.

Folklore e Bossa Nova do Brasil (Jazz Meets the World 1: Jazz Meets Brazil). MPS 533 133-2. *1966*: Germany.

Franco, Guilherme. *Capoeira: Legendary Music of Brazil*. Lyrichord 7441. *1997*: USA.

Gil, Gilberto. *Gilberto Gil*. PolyGram 1029. *1968*: Brazil.

Goodhart, Rich. *The Gathering Sun*. Beginner's Mind Productions BMP 0404. *1999*: USA.

Guzman, Viviana. *Planet Flute*. Well-Tempered 5187. *1997*: USA.

Harmer, Michael. *Shamanic Journey Tapes: Musical Bow for the Shamanic Journey*. The Foundation for Shamanic Studies No. 6. *1991*: USA.

Headhunters, The. *Survival of the Fittest*. BMG France 74321409522. *1975*: USA.

Jobim, Antonio Carlos. *Urubu*. Warner Archives BS-2928. *1976*: USA.

Jones, Elvin. *Mr. Thunder*. East West EWR7501. *1974*: Sweden.

Jones, Marti. *Used Guitars*. A&M 5208. *1988*: USA.

Klug, Slats, and Friends. *A Brown County Christmas, Volume Two*. Rebo Music 1231. *2001*: USA.

Kokelaere, François. *Berimbau: The Art of Berimbau (Brazilian Musical Bow)*. Musique du Monde 92678-2. *1993*: France.

Liotta, Saro. *L'attesa*. RCA TPL1-1209. *1976*: Italy.

Lunar Bear Ensemble. *Lunar Bear Ensemble*. Muworks CD 1006. *1988*: USA.

Maeda, Yuki. *Jazz Age: Gershwin Song Book I*. Ewe EWCD002. *1997/98*: Japan.

Metheny, Pat, and Mays, Lyle. *As Falls Wichita, So Falls Wichita Falls*. ECM 78118-21190-2. *1981*: USA.

Moraz, Patrick. *Patrick Moraz*. Charisma 0798. *1978*: UK.

Moreira, Airto. *Natural Feelings*. Buddah BDS-21-SK. *1970*: USA.

Nascimento, Dinho. *Berimbau Blues*. Velas V 20166. *1996*: Brazil.

Nascimento, Dinho. *Gongolô*. Genteboa GB 002. *2000*: Brazil.

Nascimento, Milton. *Miltons*. Columbia CK 45239. *1989*: USA.

New Dave Pike Set with Baiafro, The. *Salomão*. MPS MB-21541. *1972*: Germany.

OM. *OM with Dom um Romão*. ECM 19003. *1977*: USA.

Oriental Wind. *Life Road*. JA & RO 08-4113. *1983*: Sweden.

Papete [José de Ribamar Vianna]. *Berimbau e Percussão: Music and Rhythms of Brasil.* Universal Sound US CD7. *1975*: Brazil.

Papete [José de Ribamar Vianna]. *Planador.* Continental 1.01.404.244. *1981*: Brazil.

Passport. *Iguaçu.* Wounded Bird WOU 149. *1977*: USA.

Rebelo, Nuno. *Azul Esmeralda.* Ananana AN-LLL0001-CD. *1998*: Portugal.

Redmond, Layne, and Brunjes, Tommy. *Trance Union.* Golden Seal CD 0100. *2000*: USA.

Red Red Meat. *There's a Star Above the Manger Tonight.* Sub Pop 387. *1997*: USA.

Robinson, N. Scott. *Things That Happen Fast.* New World View Music NWVM CD-02. *2001*: USA.

Robinson, N. Scott. *World View.* New World View Music NWVM CD-01. *1994*: USA.

Rudolph, Adam. *Adam Rudolph's Moving Pictures.* Flying Fish FF 70612. *1992*: USA.

Sepultura. *Roots.* Roadrunner 8900. *1996*: USA.

Shepp, Archie. *The Cry of My People.* MCA 23082. *1972*: USA.

Temiz, Okay. *Drummer of Two Worlds.* Finnadar SR 9032. *1975/80*: Turkey.

Temiz, Okay. *Oriental Wind.* Sonet SNTF 737. *1977*: Sweden.

The Discoteca Collection: Missão de Pesquisas Folclóricas. Rykodisc RCD 10403. 1938: Brazil.

Tibbetts, Steve. *Exploded View.* ECM 1335 831 109-2. *1986*: USA.

Vasconcelos, Naná. *Africadeus.* Saravah SHL 38. *1972*: France.

Vasconcelos, Naná. *Amazonas.* Phonogram 6349.079. *1973*: Brazil.

Vasconcelos, Naná. *Nanatronics: Rekebra/Nanatroniko.* Bagaria BAG-X 0190784. *1984*: Italy.

Vasconcelos, Naná. *Saudades.* ECM 1147 78118-21147-2. *1979*: USA.

Vasconcelos, Naná, and Lucena, Agustin Pereyra. *El Increible Naná con Agustin Pereyra Lucena.* Tonodisc TON-1020. *1971*: Argentina.

Voicequn. *Peace Birthday.* Funny Time Label & Records SB-202. *2002*: Japan.

Watson, David. *Skirl.* Avant 77. *1999*: USA.

Weather Report. *Live in Tokyo.* Sony International 489208-2. *1972*: Japan.

Weather Report. *Weather Report.* Columbia/Legacy CK-48824. *1971*: USA.

Yamamura, Seichi. *Voice of TEN.* Funny Time Label & Records HOC-356. *1997*: Japan.

Visual Recordings

Almeida, Bira [Mestre Acordeon]. 1983. 'Capoeira Bahia.' World Capoeira Association (video).

'Bahia de Todos os Sambas.' 1983. Sagres (video).

'Batouka: First International Festival of Percussion.' 1989. Rhapsody Films (video).

Moreira, Airto, and Purim, Flora. 1985. 'The Latin Jazz All-Stars Live at the Queen Mary Jazz Festival.' View NTSC1311 (video).

'Pernambuco em concerto.' 2000. África Produçoes (video).

'The JVC Video Anthology of World Music and Dance. Vol. 28: The Americas 2.' 1988. JVC, Victor Company of Japan (video).

'The Spirit of Samba: Black Music of Brazil.' 1982. Shanachie (video).

Vasconcelos, Naná. 1971. 'Berimbau.' New Yorker Films (documentary film).

Vasconcelos, Naná. 1990. 'Goree, On the Other Side of the Water.' UNESCO (documentary film).

'Woodstock Jazz Festival.' 1981. Pioneer Artists PA-98-596-D (DVD).

RICHARD GRAHAM and N. SCOTT ROBINSON

Bodhrán

A *bodhrán* is the Irish version of the frame drum that has appeared in cultures from the North American continent to the Far East. The word '*bodhrán*' means 'skin tray' in Gaelic; '*bodhor*' also means 'soft' or 'dull-sounding.' It is believed that the instrument was developed in Ireland from the skin trays made for carrying peat. The rim of the *bodhrán* is usually made from ash, and the skins used are sheep, goat, calf or deer. The *bodhrán* measures 16"–20" (40 cm–50 cm) in diameter. The player holds the instrument in the left hand by a crosspiece of wood inserted into the frame, damping the skin with the left hand while the right hand either beats directly or with a stick on the skin to produce the rhythms of Irish jigs, reels, slip jigs and so on. The stick (or 'tipper') was originally a double-ended knuckle bone, but now single or double-ended tippers are usually made from ash, holly or hickory.

The instrument has always been revered in Ireland. It is played together with whistle, pipes, fiddles and, latterly, guitars, mandolins and *mandolas*. The *bodhrán* has also enjoyed increasing popularity and interest outside Ireland. For example, an oversize synthetic *bodhrán* has been made by the North American drum company Remo. These instruments are typically 20" (50 cm) in diameter, with plastic frames and skins, and are marketed in the United States for hand drumming. Hand techniques involve the application of several drumming methods derived from southern India, Persia, Egypt and southern Italy, as well as newly invented techniques, such as using a drumset brush in the left hand while playing with the bare right hand. The noted US frame drum virtuoso Glen Velez has developed innovative hand techniques specifically for this instrument. Innovative techniques for playing the *bodhrán* have also been developed in Ireland. In the 1990s, Rónán Ó Snodaigh perfected a pitch-bending technique by pressing a metal pipe against the skin from the inside of the *bodhrán*. This technique has been adopted by other *bodhrán* players in Ireland, including Brian Fleming.

Despite its worldwide, multicultural lineage, during the late twentieth century the *bodhrán* resonated a sense of fashionable 'Irishness' to many across the world. The growth of 'Irish theme pubs' in many major cities is not disconnected from this phenomenon. *Bodhráns* are much in evidence at traditional Irish sessions, where as many as 10 are sometimes played simultaneously, each instrument carrying advertisements on their skins for Irish stout.

Bibliography

Blank-Edelman, David N. 1994. 'Glen Velez: A Unified Approach to the Frame Drum.' *Rhythm Music* 3(8): 38–43.

Brooks, Iris. 1995. 'Glen Velez: Hands Dancing.' *Jazziz* 8: 60, 61, 63, 65, 67.

Hannigan, Steáfán. 1991. *The Bodhrán Book*. Cork: Ossian.

Keane, John B. 1992. *The Bodhrán Makers*. New York: Four Walls Eight Windows.

Marrin, Pat. 1996. 'The Irish *Bodhrán*.' *Reach into the Pulse* 2(3): 7, 14.

Mulvaney, Paul. 1988. 'Tommy Hayes – On a Wing and a *Bodhrán* Player.' *Drums & Drumming* 4(4): 12–13.

Murphy, Martin. 1997. *The International Bodhrán Book*. Cork: Ossian.

Ó Súilleabháin, Mícheál. 1984. *The Bodhrán: An Easy to Learn Method for the Complete Beginner, Showing the Different Regional Styles and Techniques*. Dublin: Waltons Musical Instrument Galleries Ltd.

Discography

Byrne, David, and Eno, Brian. *My Life in the Bush of Ghosts*. Sire SRK 6093-2. *1981*: USA.

Chieftains, The. *Tears of Stone*. BMG 09026-68968-2. *1999*: USA.

Chieftains, The. *The Chieftains 1*. Claddagh Records CC2. *1964*: Ireland.

Dalglish, Malcolm. *Hymnody of Earth*. Musical Heritage Society 512926M. *1991*: USA.

Dalglish, Malcolm, and the Ooolites. *Hymnody of Earth (revised)*. Ooolitic Music OM 1111. *1997*: USA.

Dalglish, Malcolm, and the Ooolites. *Pleasure*. Ooolitic Music OM 1112. *1997*: USA.

De Jimbe. *De Jimbe*. Malgamu MALGCD115. *2001*: Ireland.

Gallen, Ray. *Masterclass – Celtic Beat: Traditional Music from Ireland*. Outlet CHCD 1010. *1997*: Ireland.

Kíla. *Tóg é Go Bog é.* Key KRCD005. *1997*: Ireland.

Ní Riain, Nóirín. *Celtic Soul*. Living Music 0031. *1996*: USA.

Satake, Akira. *Cooler Heads Prevail*. Alula ALU-1003. *1997*: USA.

Velez, Glen. *Handance*. Nomad NMD 50301. *1984*: USA.

Velez, Glen. *Internal Combustion*. CMP CD 23. *1985*: Germany.

Velez, Glen. *Pan Eros*. CMP CD 63. *1993*: Germany.

Velez, Glen. *Ramana*. Music of the World CDH-307. *1991*: USA.

Velez, Glen. *Rhythmcolor Exotica*. Ellipsis Arts CD 4140. *1996*: USA.

Velez, Glen. *Rhythms of the Chakras*. Sounds True M006D. *1998*: USA.

Velez, Glen. *Seven Heaven*. CMP CD 30. *1987*: Germany.

Velez, Glen, with Levy, Howard. *Border States*. Interworld Music CD-21907. *1993*: USA.

Visual Recordings

Anders, Robin Adnan, and Menton, Todd. 1991. 'Percussion of the World.' Mid-East Mfg. (video).

Chieftains, The. 1984. 'The Chieftains in China.' Shanachie SH204 (video).

Gallen, Ray. 1997. 'Masterclass – Celtic Beat: Traditional Music from Ireland.' Outlet VHIRL 808 (video).

Hannigan, Steáfán. 1991. 'The *Bodhrán* Video: A Complete Audio-Visual Course for the Traditional *Bodhrán*.' Ossian (video).

Hayes, Tommy. 1994. '*Bodhrán*, Bones and Spoons.' C.W. Productions (video).

Mercier, Mel. 1993. '*Bodhrán* & Bones.' Interworld Music (video).

Smith, Robin M. 1993. 'Power *Bodhrán* Techniques: The New Approach to the Celtic Drum.' Mid-East Mfg. (video).

Velez, Glen. 1990. 'The Fantastic World of Frame Drums.' Interworld Music (video).

MIKE BROCKEN with N. SCOTT ROBINSON

Bombo Legüero

A drum with a wooden frame approximately 24" (60 cm) high and 16" (40 cm) in diameter, a *bombo legüero* has leather or skin drumheads at both ends. The drumheads are usually fastened with wooden hoops to which thin strips of leather are introduced for the adjustment of tension. The instrument is played with two sticks – one of plain wood, the other with one end covered in leather. Both sticks beat on different parts of one of the drumheads and on the corresponding hoop edge. The drum was called 'legüero' because it was said that its sound could be heard several leagues (about 5 kilometers) away. Played by Argentinian folk groups widely promoted by the media since the 1950s, and in Bolivia during the same period, the instrument played a key part in the Argentinian folk revival of the 1960s and the parallel seminal *nueva canción* (new song) movement in neighboring Chile. Later, the *bombo legüero* was used by folkloric groups as an instrument in the percussion section.

Bibliography

Pérez Bugallo, Rubén. 1993. *Catálogo ilustrado de instrumentos musicales argentinos* [Illustrated Catalog of Argentinian Musical Instruments]. Buenos Aires: Ediciones del Sol.

Vega, Carlos. 1943. *Los instrumentos musicales aborígenes y criollos de la Argentina* [Indigenous and Creole Musical Instruments of Argentina]. Buenos Aires: Centurión.

OMAR CORRADO

Bongo Drums

Like their larger relations the conga drums, the bongo drums derive from the mixing of cultures that occurred after settlers from Spain brought African slaves to the islands of the Caribbean to work on their plantations. These slaves brought with them the handmade drums that were part of their traditional music. At first, the Spanish plantation owners did not use these instruments in their aristocratic music but, over time, it began to incorporate aspects of the African music, the mixture of both Spanish and African characteristics combining to form Cuban popular music. The bongo drums, developed in the Oriente region of Cuba by the descendants of African slaves, were part of that evolution.

Bongo drums consist of a pair of small wooden drums that are joined together by a small block of wood. The drums are generally about 8″ (20 cm) high, with head diameters of approximately 8″ (20 cm) and 10″ (25 cm). Like the congas, the bongos usually have calfskin heads that the player strikes with his/her hands. Early versions of these drums had the heads attached to the shell of the drum with metal tacks. The drums were then tuned by holding them over a fire so that the heat would dry out the head and raise the pitch. Modern versions of the bongo drums have steel hardware holding the head to the drum so that it may be tuned with a wrench. Many contemporary bongo players use plastic heads so that they can play the drums with sticks and not break the heads.

The earliest known use of the bongo drums was in the music of the peasant class, which was known as *son*. *Son* was strongly influenced by the African rural class, and incorporated maracas, claves, bongos and the *marimbula*. Gradually, *son* evolved into *septeto* and eventually into *conjunto*, which became quite popular in the early and mid-twentieth century.

Bongo drums were the principal percussion instrument in the *conjunto* bands that performed during *carnaval* celebrations in the middle- to lower-class regions in Cuba. These bands consisted usually of guitar, *tres* (a Cuban version of the guitar, with three sets of double strings), contrabass, bongos, trumpets and vocalists. Gradually, congas and piano were added as the popularity of this ensemble grew.

In the *conjunto* band, the bongo player performs on the bongos and the *campana* or cowbell, depending on the music. During sections of relatively low volume or intensity, he/she might play a repetitive rhythmic pattern, known as the *martillo*, with his/her hands on the heads of the bongos. In louder, more active sections, the performer would switch to playing a simple pattern on the cowbell with a stick.

The mambo and salsa bands of the mid-twentieth century would often employ five or more percussion players to handle all the instruments that were necessary for an authentic-sounding Afro-Cuban rhythm section. As this music spread to the United States and Europe, the number of percussionists performing in such an ensemble gradually diminished. In modern usage, ensembles often use one percussionist to play all the Latin percussion instruments in one large setup.

Leading bongo players who have contributed to the increase in popularity of the bongo drums in contemporary Afro-Caribbean music include Chano Pozo, Armando Peraza, Orestes Vilató, Poncho Sánchez and Ray Romero.

Bibliography

Blades, James. 1984. *Percussion Instruments and Their History*. Rev. ed. Boston, MA: Faber and Faber.

Malabe, Frank, and Weiner, Bob. 1990. *Afro-Cuban Rhythms for the Drumset*. Miami, FL: Warner Brothers Music.

Mauleón, Rebeca. 1993. *Salsa Guidebook for Piano and Ensemble*. Petaluma, CA: Sher Music Co.

Quintana, José Luis, and Silverman, Chuck. 1998. *Changuito: A Master's Approach to Timbales*. Miami, FL: Warner Brothers Music.

Uribe, Ed. 1996. *Essence of Afro-Cuban Percussion and Drum Set*. Miami, FL: Warner Brothers Music.

Discography

Los Van Van. *Aquí el que Baila Gana*. Alex 3202. *1993*: USA.

Machito. *Machito and His Afro-Cubans – 1941*. Palladium 116. 1941: Canada.

Pacheco, Johnny. *Early Rhythms*. Musical Productions 3162. *1991*: USA.

Palmieri, Charlie. *A Giant Step*. Tropical Budda TBLP-003. *1984*: USA.

Palmieri, Eddie. *Azucar Pa'ti*. Tico 1122. *1995*: USA.

Sánchez, Poncho. *El Conguero*. Concord Picante 4286. *1985*: USA.

JONATHAN WACKER

Castanets

Castanets date from the ancient civilizations of the Orient as well as of Egypt. It is assumed that the Moors who invaded the Iberian Peninsula brought the instruments to Spain. It is probable that the metal shells of the Egyptian instruments were replaced by chestnut (*castaña* in Spanish) hulls in the Spanish castanets. Since the Renaissance, castanets have been associated with the music and dance of Spain. However, while they are most commonly used to evoke the image of Spain or Spanish-flavored music, in the twentieth century the instrument could be found in a variety of settings that had no connection with Spanish music or locales.

Castanets are comprised of two shells of hard wood (ebony or rosewood), which are strung together so that their concave sides face one another. As the shells strike each other, a sharp, crisp, high-pitched sound is produced. Traditionally, castanets are played by passing the thumb through the string loop, which creates enough tension to force the castanets apart. The player's four fingers then strike one castanet against the other. Mastering this technique requires considerable practise. The nontraditional percussionist generally uses either paddle or machine castanets.

There are two types of paddle (or handle) castanets. The first consists of a handle on which the two castanets are mounted and a thin board that passes between the wooden shells. This instrument is rather awkward for use in reproducing intricate rhythms, but it is very successful in producing loud, raucous rolls. The other type of paddle castanets is similar in construction to the first except that there is no board between the two shells. This greatly facilitates the execution of intricate rhythms while still allowing the instrument to retain its capacity to produce louder sounds.

Machine (mounted) castanets are capable of playing intricate rhythms and can produce them in very soft dynamic ranges. However, these castanets are somewhat at a disadvantage when trying to produce louder sounds. The mounting system makes it possible for the percussionist to play the castanets with the fingers or with a pair of soft mallets. One technique that produces a tremendously loud roll is to strike the machine castanets with a pair of paddle castanets.

In general, the use of castanets in popular music is associated with Spanish or Latin American music, with the former being more common. The most widely recognized use of castanets is in conjunction with flamenco dancing. Flamenco dancers often hold the castanets in their hands and perform intricate rhythms with them as they produce equally aggressive rhythmic patterns with their feet. Other uses for castanets have been found in orchestral music, and in popular music not associated with Spain. However, these settings often lack the intricate rhythmic complexity found in the traditional use of the instrument.

Bibliography

Blades, James. 1975. *Percussion Instruments and Their History*. Rev. ed. London: Faber and Faber.

Peinkofer, Karl, and Tannigel, Fritz. 1976. *Handbook of Percussion Instruments: Their Characteristics and Playing Techniques, with Illustrations and Musical Examples from the Literature*. London and New York: Schott.

Peters, Gordon B. 1975. *The Drummer, Man: A Treatise on Percussion*. Rev. ed. Wilmette, IL: Kemper-Peters Publications.

Tabourot. 1992. *Castañuelas, Olé!: A Book About Castanets*. Austin, TX: Tactus Press.

Discography

Traditional

Montoya, Carlos. *The Art of Flamenco*. LaserLight 12177. *1993*: USA.

Montoya, Enrique, de Alicante, El Nino, and Flamenco Ensemble. *Flamenco Fire*. Tradition/Rykodisc 1073. *1998*: USA.

Jazz

DiMeola, Al. *This Is Jazz, Vol. 31*. Legacy 65047. *1997*: USA.

Mingus, Charlie. *Tijuana Moods [Expanded]*. RCA 63840 *2001*: USA.

Classical

Albéniz, Isaac, and de Falla, Manuel. *Albéniz: Iberia Suite; Falla: The Three-Cornered Hat*. Chandos CHAN 8904. *1990*: UK.

Prokofiev, Sergei. *Rachmaninov, Prokofiev: Piano Concertos*. BBC Legends 4092. *2002*: UK.

ANDREW SPENCER

Claves

In Cuba, the word 'clave' is used to refer to a key rhythmic pattern that underlies much Cuban music, notably *son*. In the plural, the word 'claves' is the name for a Cuban percussion instrument that consists of a pair of short, round hardwood sticks which are played by being struck together. The instrument is found throughout Latin America and is used for ritual rural and urban popular musics. In some writings, the pair of claves is referred to as 'a clave,' but this does not tally with popular or oral historical usage. The sound made by claves is chunky and richly hollow. The sticks may be of the same length, or one may be slightly longer and fatter than the other. In some places, classic gender categories are assigned to the sticks: the shorter stick is designated female and the longer stick male.

The origins of the claves are unclear, but probably date back to the beginnings of time when people struck together resonant natural objects, such as stones and sticks, to beat out rhythms. In Cuba, the *soneros* of the east (Santiago de Cuba) used two river stones beaten together to produce the rhythmical basis for the songs of the troubadours known as '*trova*' (*clave de trova* (Ex. 1) (Segundo 1999)). There is also evidence that, in Brazil, Afro-Brazilians would improvise instruments: they would attend dances carrying two stones, which they would beat together to produce rhythms.

While the origin of the instrument continues to be the object of investigation, some scholars believe that the tendency to assign a gender to the sticks may come from Africa. It is more common in African ideologies to endow natural phenomena – trees, plants, rivers and stones – with a sexual identity in the same way as deities and animals. However, as the Amerindians of South America also ascribe gender properties to musical instruments, such theories, while valid, are largely hypothetical. Similar instruments are found in many parts of the Spanish-speaking world, and therefore investigation into origin, while fascinating, is inconclusive.

However, the name of the instrument is probably Spanish, derived from the resemblance of its two hardwood pieces to *clavijas* or *claves* – the small, cylindrical pegs used in naval architecture. It is also a term that can be used to refer to a nail and to hammering in a nail. Interestingly, '*clave*' is the Spanish name of the precursor of the piano in the seventeenth and eighteenth centuries; it is also a Spanish noun meaning 'key' and, in many instances, the two meanings are related in Cuban music. Hence, 'clave' in the singular is used to refer to each individual stick that constitutes the instrument (and, in some situations, to the instrument itself, made up of the pair of sticks), as well as to the unique sound produced by the instrument – *la clave*. In Cuba, it is on occasion called the *clave xilofónica*.

According to Cuban ethnologist Fernando Ortíz, claves were originally made of *ácana* wood, which comes from a group of woods known as 'heart woods' or 'core woods' (*maderas de corazón*). The word '*ácana*' derives from '*acane*,' a word of Bantu origin meaning 'good' (Ortíz 1991); many forcibly enslaved people brought from West Africa were of Bantu origin. However, claves can also be made from other kinds of wood, such as *yaití*, *yaba* and *jabí*, also called *quiebra hacha* because it is hard to cut. If made of *yaití*, each of the two cylindrical sticks has a white and a dark side, as the sticks are made from a vein in the heart of the tree. There are also claves made of pieces of *jiquí* (a compact and granite-like wood), and of *guayacán negro* (also called *palo santo* or *guayaco*), the wood used to make castanets ('*palo santo*' may link claves to the Afro-Cuban religion known as *Palo*). Modern claves have been made of *granadillo*, a glassy material that produces a fine timbre. Claves made out of ebony by furniture workers called *ebanistas* are rare. Claves can also be made of bone, shells, metal, plastic, bamboo, stone, iron, bronze and ivory. They can also be improvised out of a simple stick and bottle, box or other hard surface for a different sound aesthetic.

Many examples of clave-like instruments can be found around the world. The onomatopoeically named *quitipla* belongs to the clave family and comes from Venezuela. It consists of two pieces of wood or bamboo, which are beaten alternately against the ground and each other to produce three different sounds and an even rhythm (Ex. 2). In Spain, an instrument similar to claves is called *tejoletas*. It is played simply by holding one stick between the left-hand index finger and thumb and beating it with another stick held with the right hand. In the Canary Islands, a type of claves called *palitos sonoros* is used exclusively to accompany a dance called *saltona*.

Example 1 The Santiago of Cuba clave of Compay Segundo.

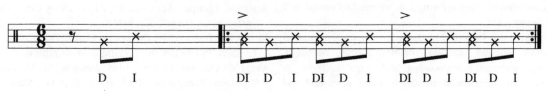

D I   DI D   I DI D   I   DI D   I DI D   I

Example 2 Venezuelan *quitipla* beat.

Some researchers also include the castanets used in Spanish music in the clave family.

In Michoacán (Mexico), a dance called *paloteos* is performed during Holy Week, in which the musicians (*paloteadores*) use a type of claves called the 'sonorous sticks of *tepehuate*' (*palitos sonoros de tepehuate*). This instrument is made of almost petrified wood, and when the sticks are struck together they produce a sound similar to that of the xylophone. A type of claves called *crótalos*, made of pieces of wood and ivory and dating back to some 5,000 years before Christ, has been found in Egypt. There is also information about instruments found in India made of two loose boards that are struck together. In Tripoli and Tangier, the *skachek* is used. It originated in the Sudan and is a type of double *crótalos* made of iron with a rod serving as a handle. Among Arab populations, these double *crótalos*, made of bronze, are called *kerkabú*, and are similar to the *znodj* of Morocco and Algeria. Comparable instruments, according to available data, can be found in Asia.

To play the claves, the player (who may be known as a *clavista*) holds one stick in the left hand and hits it rhythmically in the middle with the other, held in the right hand. Usually, but not always, the left hand may be cupped to function as a resonance chamber, a hollowing of the palm of the hand over which the stick, steadied by the fingertips, rests firmly but gently so that no air can enter from either side. This left-hand cavity, or resonance chamber, gives the sticks a sharp, clear sound when they are struck together. Tuning can be altered by increasing or decreasing the size of the chamber: a sharper sound is produced when it is closed and a deeper one when it is open. In Cuba, rumba claves (which may be known as *clave africana*) may be made hollow with a smooth curved indentation in the middle, thus not necessitating the creation of a chamber by the left hand; this makes for easier playing over a prolonged period. Claves generally produce a high-pitched and dry sound that carries effectively in the open air without amplification and that resonates strongly and can be heard clearly beneath layers of other instruments. In Cuba, some claves are 'cured' by a notch in the left stick to produce a deeper sound. In Puerto Rico and Cuba, the sticks may be thicker, sometimes double the width of conventional ones, creating a more muffled sound and a 'lower voice.'

Claves can be found in the following Cuban musical styles: *son*, *son montuno*, mambo, *danzón*, *pachanga*, *songo*, *guaguancó*, *mozambique* and *conga habanera*. In Brazil, the instrument appears in bossa nova and *Axê* music.

Bibliography

Arnold, Denis, ed. 1983. *The New Oxford Companion to Music*. Oxford and New York: Oxford University Press.

Basso, Alberto. 1983. *Dizionario Enciclopedico Univerzale Della Musica e Dei Musicisti* [World Dictionary Encyclopedia of Music and Musicians]. Torino: UTET (Unione Tipográfico Editrice Torinece).

Blades, James. 1984. 'Claves.' In *The New Grove Dictionary of Musical Instruments*, Vol. 1, ed. Stanley Sadie. London: Macmillan, 415.

Casanova Oliva, Ana Victoria. 1988. *Problemática Organológica Cubana* [Cuban Organological Problematic]. Havana: Ediciones Casa de las Américas.

Garay, Narciso. 1982. *Tradiciones y Cantares de Panamá* [Traditions and Songs from Panama]. 2nd ed. Panama: Litho Impresora Panamá S.A.

Lapique Becali, Zoila. 1963. *Catalogación y clasificación de la música cubana* [Cataloging and Classification of Cuban Music]. Havana: Departamento de Publicaciones de la Biblioteca José Martí.

Marcuse, Sibyl. 1975. *A Survey of Musical Instruments*. New York: Harper & Row.

Mauleón, Rebeca. 1993. *Salsa Guidebook for Piano and Ensemble*. Petaluma, CA: Sher Music Co.

Orovio, Helio. 1981. *Diccionario de la música cubana. Biográfico y técnico* [Dictionary of Cuban Music: Biographical and Technical]. Havana: Editorial Letras Cubanas.

Ortíz, Fernando. 1952. *Los instrumentos de la música afrocubana* [The Instruments of Afro-Cuban Music]. Havana: Dirección de Cultura, Ministerio de Educación.

Ortíz, Fernando. 1984. *La Clave xilofónica de la música cubana* [The Xylophonic Clave of Cuban Music]. Havana: Editorial Letras Cubanas.

Ortíz, Fernando. 1991 (1924). *Glosario de afronegrismos* [Glossary of Black African Words]. 2nd ed. Havana: Editorial de Ciencias Sociales.

Perdomo Escobar, José Ignacio. 1980. *Historia de la Música en Colombia* [History of the Music of Colombia]. 5th ed. Bogotá: Plaza & Janes, Editores Colombia Ltda.

Roberts, John Storm. 1982. *El Toque Latino* [The Latin Beat], trans. Aurora Merino. México, D.F.: Editores Asociados M., S.A. EDAMEX.

Segundo, Compay (Francisco Repilado). 1999. Interview with author, 9 April. São Paulo.

Sinzig, Frei Pedro. 1959. *Diccionario Musical* [Musical Dictionary]. Rio de Janeiro: Livraria Kosmos Editora.

Veiga de Oliveira, Ernesto. 1966. *Instrumentos Musicais Populares Portugueses* [Portuguese Popular Musical Instruments]. Lisbon: Fundação Calouste Gulbenkian.

Zarate, Manuel F. 1962. *Tambor y Socavón* [Drum and Hollow]. Panama: Imprenta Nacional.

EDWIN RICARDO PITRE VÁSQUEZ (trans. ZUZANA PICK) and JAN FAIRLEY

Conga Drums

The hand drums commonly referred to as 'conga drums' or, simply, 'congas' made their way into popular music by way of a long history that began with the folkloric and ritual musics of the peoples of Africa. Beginning in the fifteenth century, these people were brought, as slaves, to the newly discovered islands of the Caribbean and South America. They brought with them their religious practises, their music and their instruments, including the predecessors of the modern conga drum.

Modern conga drums are barrel-shaped and usually appear in three standard sizes, although a wide range of actual sizes may be found. The smallest of these is called the *quinto*, the mid-size drum is called the conga and the largest is referred to as the *tumbadora*, a term often used to describe the entire family of conga drums. Each of the drums has a playing head at one end and the other end is open. The length of the barrel is approximately three to four times the width of the playing head.

The earliest versions of these drums were constructed from hollowed sections of tree trunks, which were open at both ends. An animal hide was stretched across one opening. When the animal hide was struck, it created a resonant sound. Modern congas are often made of slats of wood held together with glue or, frequently, from a molded fiberglass shell.

The playing heads of conga drums are almost exclusively made of animal skins, usually cattle or mule. In early versions, the heads were attached to the drum with strips of animal hide. Later, the heads were attached to the drums using tacks nailed into the body of the drum. Contemporary manufacturers use steel hardware to mount the heads in such a way that the player can tune the drum by tightening or loosening the head to raise or lower the pitch. Modern heads are being produced of fibrous plastic material that attempts to imitate the sound of natural animal skin and is impervious to changes in weather.

Music, and drumming in particular, was central to the social life of Caribbean plantation slaves. This emphasis on music and rhythm has been passed down through generations of post-slavery Afro-Caribbean people. For centuries, rural Cubans have participated in improvisational performances that involve only percussion instruments, singing and dancing, and are traditionally called rumbas or rhumbas. Conga drums were central to the rumba performance.

As the music of rumba spread to the cities, it gradually became infused with characteristics of the music of the aristocracy, members of which were primarily of Spanish origin. One of the leading genres that merged the African and Spanish musical styles in Cuba was *son*. *Son* is the root of many Afro-Caribbean popular music genres, and it included instruments and musical characteristics of the rumba. Conga drums gradually became a central instrument in these musical styles.

Similar musical developments can be found in other Caribbean countries, including the *bomba* in Puerto Rico and the merengue in the Dominican Republic. Congas, however, are not always used in performances of these styles of music.

In the early twentieth century, the popularity of Afro-Cuban music in the United States grew at a rapid pace due to the proximity of the island of Cuba. North Americans vacationing in Cuba brought back an appreciation for the Cuban style of music. This appreciation has steadily grown, largely through the efforts of composers and band leaders such as Don Apiazu, Paul Whiteman, Xavier Cugat and Stan Kenton. The 'Latin style' was also adopted by popular jazz musicians, including Dizzy Gillespie, Stan Getz, Machito, Charlie Parker and Cal Tjader.

The conga drums are at the center of the Latin percussion player's setup of instruments. They are heard in pop, rock and jazz performances and on recordings (including soundtracks), and are fast being incorporated into the curriculum of most major music schools.

Bibliography

Blades, James. 1984. *Percussion Instruments and Their History*. Rev. ed. Boston, MA: Faber and Faber.

Malabe, Frank, and Weiner, Bob. 1990. *Afro-Cuban Rhythms for the Drumset*. Miami, FL: Warner Brothers Music.

Mauleón, Rebeca. 1993. *Salsa Guidebook for Piano and Ensemble*. Petaluma, CA: Sher Music Co.

Quintana, José Luis, and Silverman, Chuck. 1998. *Changuito: A Master's Approach to Timbales*. Miami, FL: Warner Brothers Music.

Uribe, Ed. 1996. *Essence of Afro-Cuban Percussion and Drum Set*. Miami, FL: Warner Brothers Music.

Discography

Blades, Ruben. *Antecedente*. Elektra 60795. *1988*: USA.

El Gran Combo. *25th Anniversary, Vols. 1 & 2*. Combo 1114/1116. *1987*: USA.

Gillespie, Dizzy, with Machito. *Afro-Cuban Jazz Moods*. Pablo/Fantasy 1348. *1975*: USA.

Irakere. *Bailando Así*. Babacan 2408. *1995*: USA.

Machito. *Machito at the Crescendo*. GNP 100216. *1961*: USA.

Santamaría, Mongo. *Afro Roots*. Prestige 24018. *1992*: USA.

Santamaría, Mongo. *Live at Yankee Stadium*. Vaya 26. *1992*: USA.

Santamaría, Mongo. *... Y Sus Ritmos Afro-Cubanos-Yambú*. Fantasy 10058. *1958*: USA.

JONATHAN WACKER

Cymbal

Introduction

One of the most ancient of instruments, dating back some 5,000 years, the cymbal is a round 'plate' made of bronze that can be used in pairs, which are crashed together, or mounted individually on a stand and struck with drumsticks or mallets. In most styles of popular music, including rock, jazz, blues and country music, a drumset player will typically use a variety of cymbals for different purposes, including timekeeping, coloration, marking of musical sections and accenting. For example, a jazz drummer will generally keep time by defining the pulse of the music on a ride cymbal, and marking the second and fourth beats in a measure of 4/4 with the hi-hat cymbals, while often using a crash cymbal to mark the beginning of a new chorus, to accent the climax of an ensemble figure, or for ornamentation.

Most modern cymbals are based on the design of cymbals that were originally made in Turkey. These are sometimes referred to as Turkish cymbals, whether they are made in Istanbul or in the United States, Canada, Switzerland, Germany or Italy, which is where the majority of high-quality cymbals are manufactured.

Most cymbals have a bell or cup, which is a raised section in the center of the cymbal. The bell has a small hole in the center through which straps can be attached for playing cymbals in pairs; it can also be used to mount the cymbal on a stand. Generally, the bell produces a much clearer, brighter sound than the body of the cymbal, and drummers sometimes ride on the bell of a ride or crash cymbal to produce a more cutting, articulate sound or to imitate the sound of a cowbell.

In the Dixieland era, some drummers would hammer nails or insert several rivets into holes drilled through the cymbal, usually near its edge. Rivets add shimmer to the vibration of a cymbal, making a ride cymbal more legato or smooth and prolonging the 'sustain' of a crash cymbal (the length of time the sound persists). Some bebop drummers of the 1950s also used riveted cymbals, which became standard products in cymbal catalogs. Drummers sometimes achieved a similar effect by attaching a beaded chain to the top of a cymbal stand and letting it hang over the bow of the cymbal.

Types of Cymbal

The ride cymbal is typically 18"–22" (45 cm–55 cm) in diameter (20'' (50 cm) being the most common) and is used in jazz, rock, pop, blues, country and some Brazilian styles to provide a rhythmic continuum that defines the underlying subdivisions of the main pulse (i.e., straight eighth or sixteenth notes, 'swung' eighth notes, shuffle and so on).

The crash cymbal is typically 15"–19" (38 cm–48 cm) in diameter (16" (40 cm) and 18'' (45 cm) being the most common) and is used for explosive accents and punctuations. A variation of the crash cymbal is the splash cymbal, which can be from 8" to 12" (20 cm to 30 cm) in diameter and which produces a short, high-pitched sound with little sustain.

The hi-hat consists of a pair of cymbals, typically 13" or 14" (33 cm or 35 cm) in diameter, mounted on a pedal-operated stand. When played with the foot pedal, the cymbals come together to produce a 'chick' sound, which is often used to maintain backbeats (beats 2 and 4 in a 4/4 bar). The hi-hat can also be played in a closed or semi-closed position with a drumstick, and is often used instead of a ride cymbal in rock music to maintain a rhythmic continuum.

China cymbals and swish cymbals are based on Oriental rather than Turkish cymbals, and have flanged edges. Depending on their diameter, they can be used as ride cymbals or as crash cymbals, but in either case they are generally regarded as special-effects cymbals due to their extremely loud, overtone-rich sound.

History

Bronze is an alloy that was used in Asia around 3000 B.C., and China, India and Turkey have all been suggested for the origin of the cymbal. Cymbals were associated with the worship of gods, and are mentioned in the Bible in connection with David. They were also used in the military, not only to accompany marching music but also to frighten enemies. In the 1800s, classical composers such as Haydn used cymbals to imitate Turkish janizary music, but it was not until well into the nineteenth century, through composers such as Berlioz and Wagner, that cymbals became a regular part of symphonic percussion sections. At first, cymbals were used primarily in symphonic music when a military sound was desired, but gradually composers began using cymbals to reinforce climactic moments in a composition, and also used various cymbals for ornamentation and color. Debussy's composition 'La Mer' is notable for its effective use of cymbal colors.

In military and marching music, cymbals were generally played in pairs by a single player, usually duplicating the bass drum part. In some cases, a cymbal was mounted on the top of the bass drum shell so that a single player could play the bass drum with a mallet while crashing a handheld cymbal against the mounted one.

As the drumset developed in the early 1900s, drummers used individual cymbals of the type employed by orchestral and military bands, mounting them on stands. These cymbals were generally 10″–15″ (25 cm–38 cm) in diameter and were used for short crashes and accents.

In the early 1920s, a device called the 'snow-shoe' or the 'Charleston pedal' appeared: it consisted of two cymbals mounted on hinged boards that could be clapped together with the foot. Around 1925, a drummer named Vic Berton developed the low-boy or 'sock cymbals,' which resembled the later hi-hat except that the cymbals were only about 15″ (38 cm) above the floor. These devices were generally played with the left foot to reinforce the backbeat. Soon afterward, the tube that held the cymbals was extended so that the cymbals could be played with sticks, and the low-boy became the hi-hat. Drummers could then play the standard jazz ride-cymbal pattern on the hi-hat to obtain a different effect.

As jazz drummers of the 1940s began using larger cymbals to maintain a continuous timekeeping pattern, cymbals began to be classified as rides or crashes, and different weights were developed, ranging from 'paper thin' to heavy, to accommodate an increasing demand for a variety of cymbal sounds. The modern drumset often features more cymbals than drums, and cymbals have evolved from merely providing sound effects to being crucial elements in a drummer's performance, with the ride cymbal and hi-hat considered equal in importance to the snare drum and bass drum for basic timekeeping.

Bibliography

Blades, James. 1984. *Percussion Instruments and Their History*. Rev. ed. London and Boston: Faber and Faber.

Jones, Larry C. 1979. 'Cymbal Acoustics, Selection, and Care.' In *Percussion Anthology: A Compendium of Articles from 'The Instrumentalist' on Percussion Instruments*. Evanston, IL: Instrumentalist Co., 560–63.

Pinksterboer, Hugo. 1992. *The Cymbal Book*. Milwaukee, WI: Hal Leonard Corporation.

Schofield, Colin. 1989. 'Cymbal Rivets.' *Modern Drummer* 13(9): 90–91.

Discography

Davis, Miles (with Jimmy Cobb). *Kind of Blue*. Columbia 8163. *1959*: USA.

Franklin, Aretha (with Bernard 'Pretty' Purdie). *Live at the Fillmore West*. Atlantic 7205. *1971*: USA.

Hancock, Herbie (with Tony Williams). *Maiden Voyage*. Blue Note 40020. *1966*: USA.

Jarrett, Keith (with Jack DeJohnette). *Tokyo '96*. ECM 21666. *1998*: Germany.

Metheny, Pat (with Danny Gottlieb). *The Pat Metheny Group*. ECM 1114. *1978*: Germany.

Roach, Max. 'Pies of Quincy.' *Max Roach: Award Winning Drummer*. Bainbridge 1042. 1959: USA.

RICK MATTINGLY

Cymbalom

The largest of Europe's plethora of hammered zithers, the cymbalom or cimbalom is closely identified with Hungary, with both its Magyars and its mostly settled Roms (also called Gypsies), but in slightly modified forms it has also spread to Romania, Ukraine, Belarus, the Czech and Slovak Republics, Poland and Russia. Although the cymbalom is related to a great variety of smaller but similar hammered zithers (sometimes called dulcimers) that derived from East, South and Southeast Asia and spread through Western Asia to Europe and North America, the Hungarian form is distinguished by its great size and the presence of pedal-operated dampers.

Most innovations that make the cymbalom distinctive are attributed to the Budapest musical instrument manufacturer Jozef V. Schunda, who was active around 1870. The modern cymbalom, based on Schunda's model, has multi-stringed courses over chessmen-type bridges covering a range of four octaves ($E - e^3$) plus the lower D, including chromatic pitches. Players use two wooden beaters whose tips are covered with cotton, providing a slightly muffled tone that contrasts, for example, with that of the Persian santur, which has a more metallic sound.

Before Schunda standardized the instrument, the cymbalom was just one of many 'folk' dulcimers, with local variations, found throughout Central Europe. Schunda's model was more closely identified with city life, and indeed this instrument attained status both as Hungary's 'national' instrument and as a legitimate orchestral instrument. Franz Liszt (1811–86), a German-speaking composer who was born in what would become Hungary and who later asserted his Hungarian identity through some of his compositions, sought to elevate the cymbalom's status by imitating it in certain works and actually scoring for it in others. The cymbalom was also required in certain works by several later composers, including Hungarians Zoltán Kodály and Béla Bartók, Russian Igor Stravinsky and German Carl Orff.

The cymbalom's association with popular music would be relatively insignificant were it not for the fact that the instrument is an integral part of the Gypsy ensembles that have long entertained diners and drinkers in Hungary's restaurants and cafés. Even

Johannes Brahms seems to have absorbed Gypsy music as he ate and drank in Vienna's cafés, for Brahms's 'Hungarian Dances' include passages inspired by cymbalom masters. In the Gypsy ensembles, the cymbalom plays a secondary role most of the time, accompanying the violin by playing arpeggiated harmonies and other figurations. A minimal ensemble also includes a string bass, but some groups add a viola to emphasize the harmonies.

Gypsy bands like those that perform in Hungary's cafés and restaurants are occasionally found elsewhere in Europe and even in the United States. Cleveland, Ohio, considered to have the largest Hungarian population outside Hungary, at one time had at least two restaurants where Gypsy groups entertained regularly. Senior cymbalom player John Udvary dominated the scene for many years until his retirement and death around 1990. His son, Alex Udvary, professionally trained in both cymbalom and piano, has regularly appeared with major orchestras, playing the cymbalom part for works by Kodály and Stravinsky.

The cymbalom remains little noticed by popular musicians generally, apart from members of Gypsy groups. However, the cymbalom does make occasional appearances in the context of 'world music.' These can take the form of the simple addition of the instrument to a non-Hungarian mixed ensemble, where it is played by someone with no knowledge of the instrument's tradition or its repertoire, or it can involve cross-cultural collaborations between musicians representing vastly different traditions. At the close of the twentieth century, perhaps the most active such player was Alexander Fedoriouk, a Ukrainian cymbalom player based in Cleveland, Ohio, who had also collaborated with a number of non-Ukrainian musicians playing non-traditional music.

The cymbalom is unlikely to attain widely popular status because the instrument is acoustic, demands the talents of a highly skilled musician/specialist and is fairly expensive. For these reasons, the cymbalom's popularity will likely remain largely confined within the context of Gypsy bands.

Bibliography

Hartman, Arthur. 1916. 'The Czimbalom, Hungary's National Instrument.' *Musical Quarterly* 2: 590–600.

Leach, John. 1972. 'The Cimbalom.' *Music and Letters* 53: 134–42.

Ling, Jan. 1997. *A History of European Folk Music*. Rochester, NY: University of Rochester Press.

Sárosi, Bálint. 1978. *Cigányzene* [Gypsy Music], trans. Fred Macnicol. Budapest: Corvina Press.

Discography

Café Noir. 'Window to the Sea.' *Window to the Sea*. Carpe Diem Records 31007. *1993*: USA.

Celtic Zen. *Celtic Zen*. Yin Yang Records YY11116-2. *1997*: USA.

Hungary and Romania: Descendents of the Itinerant Gypsies – Melodies of Sorrow and Joy. Music of the Earth series. Multicultural Media MCM 3010. *1997*: USA.

Unblocked: Music of Eastern Europe. Ellipsis Arts CD 3570. *1997*: USA.

The World in Our Backyard: Ethnic Music of Our Neighborhoods (comp. Ray Alden). Chubby Dragon Productions CD 1005. *1997*: USA.

TERRY E. MILLER

Drums

Construction

Drums, perhaps the most ubiquitous of instruments, are percussion instruments with a vibrating membrane that is sounded by striking or rubbing. Most drums consist of a rounded or oblong hollow body (shell) with a vibrating membrane (drumhead) stretched across the open end. The striking or rubbing implement can be a stick, mallet, brush or hand. Early drums consisted of hollowed logs, sometimes carved with vibrating tongues or slits, that resonated when struck. Notable exceptions to the definition (that is, drums without a vibrating membrane) include the log drum, slit-drum, steel drum (pan) and wood drum.

The shell of a drum can have any number of possible shapes, with an opening at one or both ends. Either end may be covered with a head made of animal hide or plastic. Drum shells have been constructed from most known materials, evolving from wood through clay, bronze, brass, copper, steel, aluminum, fiberglass and plastics to modern composite materials.

Although most shells are made with a circular opening, the openings can be square, rectangular or oval, or can have any number of sides (such as an octagonal construction). Most vertical shapes for the drum shell are tubular and, based on their specific construction, can be described as cylindrical, conical, barrel, waisted, goblet or footed. Other possible constructions include vessel and frame-shaped shells. The various shapes result in a wide variety of tonal characteristics, some of which are easily recognized as indigenous to specific cultures or regions of origin. Shells are sometimes elaborately decorated, especially when the drums have some type of ceremonial function.

Narrow-shelled drums (frame drums) often have a single head, and sometimes have jingles attached (tambourines). Early methods of attaching the drumhead and tuning its tension used gut or rope bindings laced through the head. These bindings wrapped round the entire drum or were pegged into the side. Later developments for tensioning the head have included gluing, tacking and mounting with tuning mechanisms that lap the head onto wood or metal hoops attached to the drum via screw mechanisms and a counter-hoop made of metal. Before the advent of Mylar (plastic) drumheads in 1957, all heads were made from animal skin or hide. Drumheads are sometimes decorated with ceremonial paintings, popular paintings, manufacturers' logos, advertisements, or the name of a performer or group.

During the Middle Ages, a cord of gut called a snare was attached to the drum (first to the top head), which resulted in a buzzing sound. This snare evolved into a multiple-strand device, also manufactured from a wide variety of materials, and is the definitive element distinguishing the snare drum from various types of tom-toms. Most small drums without snares are generically referred to as tom-toms, while larger drums without snares are referred to as bass drums. Snares have for some time been manufactured from both natural and synthetic materials and have as many as 20 strands, and they are attached to the bottom head. Some types of drums might have snares attached to both the bottom and the inside of the top head. Friction drums, such as the *cuíca* and the lion's roar, have a stick or cord attached to the center of the head. Players produce the sound by rubbing or pulling the stick or cord, thereby vibrating the head. They can change the pitch by varying the pressure on the head with their free hand.

Playing Techniques

When playing drums, players can hold them in their hands, place them in their lap, hold them between their knees, hold them under their arm, attach them to their body with a neck strap, hang them from their waist or shoulder, place them on the ground, mount them on a stand or rack, or mount them on the back of a horse or other animal. The drums may be positioned or held vertically, horizontally or at any angle necessary or convenient for performance.

Some types of drums are traditionally used in pairs or sets, played by a single player. Examples of this configuration include the kettledrums (timpani), *tablā*, bongos, timbales, congas, roto-toms and the drumkit. Other types consist of a group of similar drums used as an ensemble for performances. Examples of this configuration include the steel pan ensembles of the Caribbean, *taiko* drum ensembles of Japan and various drumming ensembles of Sub-Saharan Africa. A third configuration includes a wide variety of types of drum played by several performers simultaneously, each with an established function in the ensemble. These ensembles include the Brazilian samba band, Latin or Afro-Cuban ensembles, European and North American drum corps (often accompanying fifes or bugles) and the Western percussion ensemble found in public secondary schools and universities.

Roles and Functions

Drums have played, and continue to play, an integral role in popular music in most cultures of the world. Although sometimes ceremonial in function, drums are traditionally used to establish tempo and to maintain rhythmic unity. Traditional popular music of many Aboriginal cultures (such as Native American and African) utilized the drum as the primary, and sometimes exclusive, instrument to accompany song. Throughout the twentieth century, the drumkit or drumset (consisting primarily of a bass drum, snare drum, one or more tom-toms, cymbals and hi-hat) functioned in rhythm sections as the primary vehicle for maintaining time in Western popular song and dance music.

Drums play an integral part in the accompaniment of traditional song in Native music of North, Central and South America, especially in the ceremonial music of Indian cultures of the central and northern continent, and in the pipe and tabor tradition of the Andes Mountains regions. Drums of African origin are used both in ceremonial music and in a variety of popular musical styles not only in Africa, but in regions of the world, such as the Caribbean, where African cultures were transplanted as a result of the slave trade. Afro-Cuban, Afro-Brazilian, Afro-American (blues and jazz), Afro-pop and Latin American musical styles have all integrated traditional African drumming styles into mainstream popular music in one form or another, often as a definitive component of the style of music.

Drums are found in larger musical ensembles in most Asian cultures, such as the gamelan orchestras of Bali, and in the theatrical and ceremonial musics of Japan, China, Korea and Tibet. Frame drums are used to accompany song and dance, and are also members of larger musical ensembles, in the Middle East, North Africa, Russia and Europe. The kettledrum and various types of snare and bass drums can be found in types of popular concert and marching music with European origins.

A significant influence in popular music of the last century has been the development of the drumset and its role in various styles of Western popular music. From its first appearance in early theater and jazz music, to its contribution to the role of drummers (such as Chick Webb, Gene Krupa and Buddy Rich) as band leaders, the drumset has consistently influenced and defined styles of Western popular music. Jo Jones's and Dave Tough's use of the cymbal ride pattern helped to define the jazz and bebop genres, establishing the foundation from which drummers such as Kenny 'Klook' Clarke, Max Roach, 'Big' Sid Catlett, Shelly Manne and Jack DeJohnette could expand the drummer's role as soloist in these styles. Rock, funk and fusion music are clearly defined by the drumming styles of such artists as Tony Williams, John Bonham, Billy Cobham, Bill Bruford, Steve Gadd, Peter Erskine and Steve Smith.

Bibliography

Anderson, William M., and Campbell, Patricia Shehan, eds. 1996. *Multicultural Perspectives in Music Education.* 2nd ed. Reston, VA: Music Educators National Conference.

Beck, John H., ed. 1995. *Encyclopedia of Percussion.* New York and London: Garland Publishing.

Diagram Group, The. 1976. *Musical Instruments of the World: An Illustrated Encyclopedia.* New York: Paddington Press.

The Garland Encyclopedia of World Music. 1998–2002. New York: Garland Publishing.

Discography

Max Weinberg Presents: Let There Be Drums!. Rhino R2 71547. *1994*: USA.

The Big Bang (4 CDs). Ellipsis Arts 3400-3403. *1994*: USA.

The Engine Room: A History of Jazz Drumming from Storyville to 52nd Street. Proper Records PROPERBOX 2. *1999*: UK.

Visual Recordings

Holender, Jacques. 1989. 'The Buddy Rich Memorial Scholarship Concert.' DCI Music Video (video).

Holender, Jacques. 1991. 'Kodo, Heartbeat Drummers of Japan.' Rhapsody Films, Inc. (video).

Holender, Jacques. 1997. 'Live at the Modern Drummer 10th Anniversary Festival Weekend 1997: Steve Gadd & Giovanni Hidalgo.' DCI Music Video (video).

JAMES A. STRAIN

Drumset

Introduction

The term 'drumset' or 'drumkit' refers to a collection of drums and cymbals played by a single performer, generally using all four limbs. A modern drumset typically consists of a bass drum (played with the drummer's foot via a pedal); a snare drum; two or more tom-toms; and various cymbals, including a ride, one or more crash cymbals and a hi-hat. Drumsets are used in most styles of popular music, including rock 'n' roll, jazz, country and blues.

History

The modern drumset traces its origins to the invention of the bass drum pedal, which first appeared in the 1890s. However, the bass drum pedal did not achieve widespread popularity until perfected by the Ludwig Drum Company (located in Chicago) in 1909. The pedal allowed a single performer sitting on a stool to play both snare drum and bass drum. This manner of playing was sometimes referred to as 'double drumming.' Gradually, other drums, cymbals and percussion instruments were added. The individual components were borrowed from a variety of cultures. The snare drum and bass drum were of the type used by European military and concert bands. The original tom-toms used with drumsets were Chinese drums with tacked-on heads. The cymbals were of Turkish and Chinese origin and were of the type used in concert bands and orchestras. Combining these instruments into a single drumset is considered a US innovation.

Early drumsets were often called 'trap' sets or 'traps.' The term originated around the 1920s as a result of the various wood blocks, cowbells, ratchets, temple blocks and sound-effects devices that adorned the drumkits used by vaudeville, theater and dance band drummers (for example, Sonny Greer with the Duke Ellington Orchestra), and that were often referred to as 'trappings.' (One alternative explanation for the term is that the drumset was considered a conTRAPtion. Another explanation is that the various foot pedals resembled bear traps.) Theater drummers in the early part of the twentieth century also used drumsets along with timpani, xylophones and other percussion instruments, functioning as one-person percussion sections.

The Dixieland and early jazz-band drummers developed a performance style from which modern drumset playing evolved. At first, jazz drumset players such as Baby Dodds and Chick Webb did most of their accompanimental playing on the snare drum and bass drum, much in the style of military drummers, using a lot of rolls and rudimental figures. By the time of the swing era, drummers such as Jo Jones, Gene Krupa and Buddy Rich were playing 'time' on a ride cymbal or hi-hat (which was invented around 1927), maintaining a steady pulse on the bass drum and using the snare drum to reinforce accents in ensemble riffs or in a comping style. Tom-toms were used primarily in conjunction with the snare drum for fills and solos, but sometimes drummers would perform primarily on tom-toms to produce a 'jungle' sound. The swing drummers also pioneered the use of wire brushes on the snare drum, which provided a very soft, legato sound that was especially useful in ballads. By this time, few drummers were using the small percussion instruments and sound effects that had previously been included as part of the drumset, and most drumsets consisted entirely of drums and cymbals. A typical drumset of the period had a 26" (66 cm) bass drum, a snare drum, one tom-tom mounted over the bass drum, one tom-tom standing on legs (commonly called a floor tom), a pair of hi-hat cymbals, a ride cymbal and two or three crash cymbals.

The bebop drummers of the 1940s, such as Kenny Clarke, Max Roach, Art Blakey, Philly Joe Jones and Elvin Jones, put more emphasis on the ride cymbal as the primary timekeeper, maintained hi-hat (with pedal) on the second and fourth beats of the bar (backbeats) and de-emphasized the bass drum, using it for occasional loud accents ('dropping bombs') rather than to maintain a constant pulse. Because bebop was typically played by groups with three to seven players, it was not necessary for the drummer to hold the band together with a loud bass-drum pulse, as was the case with the big band drummers of the swing era. Also, because bebop was not considered dance music, drummers were freer to use the bass drum for syncopated accents rather than for maintaining a dance beat. Some bebop drummers did, however, often maintain a soft quarter-note pulse on the bass drum, a technique often referred to as 'feathering' the drum. The typical bebop drumset had the same configuration as the drumsets used by big band drummers, but the sizes of the drums tended to be smaller, especially the bass drums, with 18″ (45 cm) and 20″ (50 cm) bass drums becoming common.

In the early 1950s, with the advent of rhythm and blues (R&B), which combined bebop and blues with a steady dance beat, the shuffle became the dominant rhythmic pattern, often played simultaneously on the snare drum and ride cymbal, or on the snare drum alone with brushes.

When rock 'n' roll developed in the 1950s, drummers started putting emphasis on the snare drum and bass drum again, using them to play repetitive patterns (beats) that emphasized the backbeats on the snare drum. Because of the volume of rock 'n' roll, drummers preferred larger drums than those used by bebop drummers, and 22″ (55 cm) bass drums became standard. As late as the mid-1960s, such rock drummers as Ringo Starr (with the Beatles) and Charlie Watts (with the Rolling Stones) were still using the same basic configuration of drums and cymbals that had been standardized by bebop drummers (bass drum, snare drum, two tom-toms, ride cymbal, hi-hat and one or two crash cymbals). But in the mid-1960s, many drummers added another tom-tom mounted on their bass drums, and from the late 1960s some rock 'n' roll drummers, such as Ginger Baker (of Cream), Keith Moon (of the Who) and Neil Peart (of Rush), used two bass drums (pioneered by jazz drummer Louis Bellson in 1938), as many as eight tom-toms and a wide variety of cymbals. Some drummers added other percussion instruments, such as Carl Palmer's use of large gongs with Emerson, Lake and Palmer, John Bonham's use of timpani with Led Zeppelin, and Peart's use of tubular chimes with Rush. Such instruments were used only as special effects, however. The rock influence also affected the setups of jazz drummers such as Tony Williams and Billy Cobham, whose drumsets resembled the larger kits used by rock drummers.

Construction

Drums were originally made with wooden shells and were mounted with calfskin heads. Most drumset players switched to plastic heads when they were perfected by companies such as Remo and Evans in the 1950s. In the 1970s, drum manufacturers experimented with other shell materials such as plastic, fiberglass and stainless steel. But by the 1980s most drum shells were again being made from wood.

Electronic drumkits first appeared in the 1980s, manufactured by companies such as Simmons, ddrum and Yamaha. The kits featured various types of pads that were played with the same technique as acoustic drums, but sent an electronic signal to a separate tone generator that produced a synthetic or sampled sound. Despite the versatility of electronic kits and the advantages in terms of amplifying the volume easily, only a small percentage of drummers (notably Bill Bruford with King Crimson) abandoned their acoustic drums for electronic pads. Most of the drummers who did use electronic pads continued to use acoustic cymbals.

The early 1980s also saw the perfection of the drum machine, which was a sequencer with sampled drum sounds. Because of the quality of the sounds, drum machines were sometimes used on recordings. Drummers could also use electronic pads or triggers attached to acoustic drums to access the sounds from drum machines, allowing them to quickly change the timbre of their individual drums and cymbals, or combine various drum and percussion sounds. As a result, many drummers who did not utilize electronic technology began adding special-effects cymbals (for example, splash cymbals and china cymbals), extra snare drums (for instance, piccolo snare drums and soprano snare drums) and various percussion devices in order to supply more color to the music.

Performance

When playing 'time' in the context of a band, a drumset player will generally maintain a rhythmic continuum on the ride cymbal or hi-hat, defining the underlying rhythmic feel of the music. Jazz drummers typically play a triplet-based swing pattern on the ride cymbal, sometimes referred to as 'spang-a-lang.' Rock drummers typically play ride patterns based on straight eighth-note subdivisions, and often play their ride patterns on the hi-hat cymbals rather than on the ride cymbal.

The drumset player will often use the bass drum to play a rhythm that is identical or complementary to the part played by the acoustic or electric bass. In most popular styles of music, the snare drum supplies the backbeat, which consists of beats 2 and 4 in a 4/4 measure. Rock-based music is said to be played on the drums 'from the bottom up,' meaning that the bass drum and snare drum are the most prominent, with the ride cymbal or hi-hat more in the background. Jazz is said to be played 'from the top down,' with the ride cymbal pattern being the focus, the pedal-operated hi-hat cymbals supplying the backbeats, and the snare drum and bass drum providing accents and punctuation rather than repetitive patterns. Tom-toms are used primarily for fills and solos, although they are sometimes incorporated into timekeeping patterns along with, or instead of, the snare drum.

Although the drumset is not typically used in 'authentic' Brazilian and Afro-Cuban music, US and European drumset players often use the different sounds of the drumset to imitate the sounds produced by Latin percussionists. Tom-toms are often used to imitate bongos and congas, the snare drum can be made to sound much like timbales when the snares are released, the bell of a cymbal can be used to imitate a cowbell sound and a cross-stick technique on the snare drum can be used to reproduce the sound of claves. Jazz players in particular use such techniques to give a Latin flavor to the music.

Bibliography

Cangany, Harry. 1996. *The Great American Drums and the Companies That Made Them, 1920–1969*. Cedar Grove, NJ: Modern Drummer Publications.

Cohen, Jon. 1995. *Star Sets: Drum Kits of the Great Drummers*. Milwaukee, WI: Hal Leonard Corporation.

Nicholls, Geoff. 1997. *The Drum Book*. London: Balafon Books.

Read, Danny L. 1981. 'The Evolution of the Drum Set, Part 1.' *Modern Drummer* 5(8): 18–21.

Read, Danny L. 1982. 'The Evolution of the Drum Set, Part 2.' *Modern Drummer* 6(1): 26–29.

Discography

Beatles, The (with Ringo Starr). *Abbey Road*. Apple S0383. *1969*: UK.

Cream (with Ginger Baker). *Wheels of Fire*. Atco 2700. *1968*: USA.

Dodds, Baby. *Footnotes to Jazz, Vol. 1: Baby Dodds Talking and Drum Solos*. Folkways Records 2290. *1951*: USA.

Goodman, Benny (with Gene Krupa). *Carnegie Hall Concert (1938)*. Columbia 40244. 1938: USA.

Gretsch Drum Night at Birdland (with Art Blakey, Elvin Jones, Philly Joe Jones and Charlie Persip). Roulette 52049. *1960*: USA. Reissue: *Gretsch Drum Night at Birdland*. Blue Note 28641. *1994*: USA.

King Crimson (with Bill Bruford). *Three of a Perfect Pair: Live in Japan*. Warner Bros. 25071. *1984*: USA.

Led Zeppelin (with John Bonham). *Led Zeppelin IV*. Atlantic 7208. *1971*: USA.

Mahavishnu Orchestra (with Billy Cobham). *Birds of Fire*. Columbia 468224. *1972*: USA.

Rich, Buddy. *Swingin' New Big Band*. Pacific Jazz 20113. *1966*: USA. Reissue: Rich, Buddy. *Swingin' New Big Band*. Blue Note 35232. *1996*: USA.

Roach, Max. *Drums Unlimited*. Atlantic 1043. 1965–66: USA.

Rolling Stones, The (with Charlie Watts). *Sticky Fingers*. Rolling Stones Records 59100. *1971*: USA.

Rush (with Neil Peart). *Moving Pictures*. Mercury 4013. *1981*: USA.

Who, The (with Keith Moon). *Who's Next*. Decca 79182. *1971*: UK.

Williams, Tony. *Believe It*. Columbia 33836. *1976*: USA.

RICK MATTINGLY

Frame Drums and Tambourines

Introduction

Technically, a frame drum is a drum that has a shell depth smaller than the diameter of the skin, which can be from 6" to 20" (15 cm to 50 cm) or more; in simple terms, it is a hoop with a skin stretched across it. Although the frame is most commonly round, it can be square or hexagonal; it is made from various woods, metals or clay, and has a single or double head. The head of a frame drum is made either from an animal skin – cow (calf), goat, fish, lizard, deer, whale, seal or snake – or from an animal's internal organs. The skin is attached to the frame with glue, tacks or a counter-hoop system with tuning hardware (devices such as screws to tune the skin to a particular note or pitch by tightening or slackening its tension over the frame). Construction styles for most frame drums often vary from region to region. North American drum companies such as Cooperman have successfully made synthetic plastic skins, removable jingles and tunable frames.

There are two major types of frame drum: those without jingles, which can be played with the hands or with sticks; and those with jingles, which are played with the hands (tambourines). Tambourine jingles are usually round metal discs set into the frame, but they can also be pellet bells or brass rings attached to the inside of the frame.

Frame drums are found in many cultures and have a long history. Examples of different types are depicted in pottery, reliefs, paintings and folk art. The earliest depictions of frame drums appear in Mesopotamian art from the third millennium B.C. These frame drums are much larger than those used in popular music of the late twentieth century. Depictions of smaller frame drums similar to some still used can be found in the artwork of Greece, Egypt, Persia and India. They mainly show women playing frame drums in ritual, but men often appear in Arabic examples when a frame drum is employed for martial purposes. The first appearance of a frame drum with jingles attached to the frame is found on a second-century Roman stone coffin.

Grips and Technique

A consistent feature of the depictions of frame drums throughout their history has been the use of two main grips for holding the instrument. From the iconographical evidence, the most common was what can be called the Oriental grip. The player is always shown with the left hand holding the instrument at the bottom with the skin facing away from him/her and the fingers of both hands playing. This grip allows the player to produce numerous sounds from the skin: for example, a low-pitched natural ringing sound produced by striking the drum off-center; a high-pitched sound produced by striking the edge; a stopped stroke produced by slapping the instrument in the center; various jingle sounds; brushing sounds produced by grazing the skin with the fingernails or fingertips; a drone produced by the friction of a moistened finger rubbed on the skin; and the sound produced by knocking the frame with the knuckles. In Arabic drumming, the first three sounds mentioned above are onomatopoeically known as *doum*, *tak* and *kah*. Persian drumming does not use the *kah* stroke, but employs snapping techniques for the high-pitched rim sounds. Indian drumming has similar names for drum strokes, as well as rhythmic solfège systems known as *bols* and *solkattu*. The Indian technique has developed in such a way as to allow fast and clear repetitions of specific sounds, usually stopped sounds.

The other main grip can be called the European grip and first appears in Dutch artwork from the seventeenth century. This grip seems to be reserved largely for specific tambourine playing, such as that used in African-American minstrelsy, gospel, rock, European orchestral playing, and folk musics of Spain and Brazil. The player holds the instrument in the left hand so that the drumhead faces up toward the sky, with the thumb touching the skin; most of the playing is done with the right hand. Compared with the multiple skin sounds (and jingle sounds, if the instrument is equipped with jingles) that the Oriental grip permits, the European grip allows for a more jingle-based sound.

The sitting position facilitates another playing grip. The seated player holds the instrument on the left knee with the left hand resting on top; this allows for similar manipulations of the skin as with the Oriental grip. This 'sitting' grip becomes a necessity when the frame drum is too large for handheld playing.

Numerous methods of gripping are used for frame drums played with sticks, as for Native North American frame drums, the Irish *bodhrán*, the *tapou* of Martinique, Ukrainian tambourines, frame drums in Chinese opera (*jing xi*) called *bangu* and in the silk and bamboo music (*jiangnan sizhu*) of Shanghai called *biqi gu*, and frame drums with handles attached, such as *uchiwa daiko* (*daimoku daiko*) from Japan and the North American *kilaut* (*cauyuq*) played by the Inuit. These grips constitute exceptions to the three already discussed. The hand-beaten frame drum of Brazil's *Bumba Meu Boi* rituals, the *pandeirão*, is also an exception.

Lastly, a grip called a free-hand position was developed by John Bergamo. The player holds a frame drum between the legs so that the skin slants away from him/her; this allows both hands to be used for playing. This style was actually first used in New York in the early 1980s by electric tambourinist Peter Wharton, who damped the jingles and amplified the tambourine while playing.

Nomenclature

The nomenclature for frame drums is problematic, as similar instruments have different spellings and names in different cultures, reflecting differences in regional preferences. In addition, drum companies such as Remo have continued to market newly invented versions of frame drums simply as 'frame drum.' Other inventions have included a one-piece all-wooden frame drum used by Glen Velez, a one-piece all-clay frame drum made by the Wright Hand Drum Company, and Carlo Rizzo's 'polytimbral tambourine,' with which he can control the tension of the skin, damping of the jingles and application of snares to the skin while playing.

Frame Drums (Without Jingles)

Following are brief descriptions of the most common frame drums (without jingles) found in popular music.

The *adufe* (*pandeiro quadrado*, *pandero cuadrado*) is a double-headed square frame drum, 12"-16" (30 cm–40 cm) in diameter, played mainly in Portugal and Spain, but also found in Egypt, Guatemala and Brazil. It can have pellet bells attached to the inside frame, and is held in the Oriental grip. The Egyptian version is quite old, dating back as far as 1400 B.C. The Brazilian version was stick-beaten and may have been a precursor of the *tamborim* (see below). The European versions are hand-beaten, and triangular-shaped drums may also be found.

There is also a Spanish version for which the seated player's right hand uses a stick to strike the frame and skin while the left hand plays the skin as well.

The *bendir* (*bendyr*, *bendire*) of Morocco and Tunisia is similar to the *tar* (see below), with the addition of snares stretched across the inside of the skin so that the instrument produces a buzzing sound. This drum can range from 10'' (25 cm) to 16'' (40 cm) in diameter, and is held in the Oriental grip. Large versions that include jingles are sometimes found.

Traditionally used in Irish pub music, the *bodhrán* is 16"–20" (40 cm–50 cm) in diameter and is played with a double-ended stick known as a 'tipper.' Both traditional and innovative hand techniques also exist. New techniques in Ireland involve the use of a metal pipe pressed against the inside head to change the pitch. Although the *bodhrán* can have jingles, it is a frame drum that usually has no jingles.

The *gombe* (*gome*) is a large square frame drum played by the Ashanti and Ga people of Ghana. Its dimensions are usually 18" (45 cm) by 15" (38 cm). This drum is set on the ground, and the player, reaching down between his/her legs, strikes the goatskin to achieve open tones, slaps and bass tones. It is played in much the same way as an Afro-Cuban conga drum, except that the *gombe* player presses the heels of the feet into the skin to change the pitch. This drum may be used in highlife music in place of a bass. (Similar drums are played by the Maroon people of Jamaica.)

The Puerto Rican *pandereta* is usually available in three sizes – diameters of 10" (25 cm), 12" (30 cm) and 14" (35 cm) – has tuning hardware and a thick skin, and is used in traditional *bomba* and *plena* music. The playing technique is similar to that for playing the congas, and the instrument is held in the Oriental grip.

The *pandero* is a large frame drum from Spain and Portugal, 16"–20" (40 cm–50 cm) in diameter. It can be played in the sitting position, or held in the Oriental grip if the frame depth is shallow enough. ('*Pandero*' is also a term sometimes used for tambourines in Portugal.)

The *rammana* is a frame drum, 10" (25 cm) in diameter, used in the classical music of Thailand. It is often played simultaneously, either by the same player or by another, with a clay or wooden goblet drum called a *thon*. The instruments are known collectively as *thon-rammana*. When they are played by the same player, the *thon* lies on the player's lap and is played with the right hand, while the player holds the *rammana* in the sitting position and plays it with the left hand. The playing technique involves low-pitched, rim and stopped sounds similar to those used in Arabic drumming, and snapping techniques similar to those of Persian drumming are used on the *rammana*.

The *samba* drum is a rectangular frame drum from Nigeria, usually 14" (35 cm) in diameter. It was used, along with tambourines, in early forms of *jújù* music. The Christian church introduced tambourines; Nigerian-made versions (*jújù* drums) may be square, octagonal or hexagonal, but they are often referred to as tambourines. Both types of drum were also used by street musicians and small ensembles of Yoruban palm-wine and *asìkó* musicians. (Round, clay, stick-beaten frame drums without jingles, called *sakara*, usually 12" (30 cm) or more in diameter, are also played in Nigeria and Liberia.)

The *tamalin* is a large rectangular frame drum played in parts of Ghana. It is found in three sizes: 17" (43 cm) by 14" (35 cm); 19" (48 cm) by 16" (40 cm); and 24" (60 cm) by 19" (48 cm). These drums are used by the Ashanti and Ga people in traditional ensembles, as well as to play highlife music. Each drum has a crosspiece at the back (as in the Irish *bodhrán*), and the player's hand achieves open and closed sounds.

The Brazilian *tamborim* (*tambourim*) is a frame drum used for samba. It is 6"–8" (15 cm–20 cm) in diameter, and has a wooden or metal frame, with a plastic or skin head. The stick used to play the *tamborim* has a frayed tip that produces a thicker sound than a regular stick. Using the European grip, the player employs a technique that involves turning the hand holding the drum so that rhythms are produced on the skin as the drum rotates around the stick. The hand holding the instrument also damps the skin from underneath.

The Egyptian *tar* – not to be confused with the *tar* used in Persian music, which is a lute – is a circular frame drum found in Arabic music traditions throughout North Africa. It ranges from 12" (30 cm) to 16" (40 cm) in diameter, and is held in the Oriental grip. *Tar* and *bendir* are often used interchangeably in Arabic culture.

Tambourines

Tambourines vary in size, shell, skin and jingle type, as well as in playing technique, and are usually circular (the Chinese octagonal snakeskin tambourine *bafang gu* being an exception). The generic tambourine, used in popular and orchestral music of the West, is held in the European grip. The playing technique involves shaking the frame to activate the jingles and striking the skin for accents. This approach seems to be focused on producing a jingle sound, with no exploration of the expressive possibilities of the skin. The playing techniques of African-American tambourinists are an exception: in gospel music and in vaudeville, the players, using the European grip, rock the instrument from side to side while striking it with the thumb for low sounds and slapping it with the palm in the center for stopped sounds; the famous African-American vaudeville tambourinist,

Master Juba (William Henry Lane), performed in this style between 1840 and 1850. Another exception is African-American tambourinist Joe Habad Texidor, who performs on several recordings by jazz virtuoso Rahsaan Roland Kirk (*Volunteered Slavery* in 1969) in a style untypical of African-American musics featuring tambourine.

What is most commonly called a tambourine in the context of popular music often does not have a skin and is technically neither a tambourine nor a frame drum. Its proper name is 'jingle ring.' The distinction between a tambourine and a jingle ring is rarely made, and usually only by knowledgeable percussionists. Similar instruments are also common in India.

Following are brief descriptions of tambourines found in popular music.

The *bassé* (*bas*, *tanbourin*) is a Haitian frame drum, 12″–16″ (30 cm–40 cm) in diameter, that can be with or without jingles. Used traditionally in some *rara* and voodoo music, it is also sometimes played in Haitian popular music along with other traditional drums. Held by a cross-brace or rope-tension system at the back, the instrument is slapped for stopped and low sounds.

The *doira* or *gaval* is a tambourine played in Afghanistan, Xinjiang (China), Turkey, Iran, Israel and in parts of the former Soviet Union. The preferred skin is fish, and the jingles are brass rings and/or pellet bells attached to the inside of the frame. The instrument is held in the Oriental grip, and the playing technique involves snapping the fingers against the rim for accented high-pitched sounds, as well as stroking the fingers toward the center to produce low ringing sounds. The frame can also be struck or shaken to activate the jingles.

Although frame drums in India are numerous, there is one that has been incorporated into Western popular music. The *kanjira*, used in the *Karnatik* classical tradition in southern India, is a tambourine with a 6″ (15 cm) lizard-skin head and one pair of coin jingles. The skin, held in the Oriental grip, is moistened so that it is loose enough for the player to bend the low sound by pressing into it with the holding hand. The playing technique involves rotating the right hand so that two different parts of the palm alternate as playing surfaces. This technique allows fast, clear repetitions of the stopped sound along with a low sound produced by strokes of the index finger.

The Egyptian *mazhar* looks like a large *riq* (see below). It is about 12″–14″ (30 cm–35 cm) in diameter, has huge brass jingles and is very loud. The playing technique involves shaking the instrument and striking the skin for low and stopped sounds.

The *pandeiro* is a tambourine used in traditional Brazilian music, such as samba, *choro* and *capoeira*, and in Brazilian pop music. It is 10″–12″ (25 cm–30 cm) in diameter, with a plastic head or a skin head of calf or boa constrictor. The frame can be made of plastic, wood or metal. The jingles are arranged in a single row in the frame, sometimes with three per slot; the third jingle restricts jingle movement, which allows the skin articulations to be heard clearly. The European grip is used, and several playing techniques exist that involve the player damping and turning the drum from right to left with the holding hand while striking it with different parts of the playing hand, moving the instrument up and down to get jingle articulations while striking, and playing on the edge of the skin with the fingers.

The Basque tambourine from Spain, the *pandereta*, is usually 10″–12″ (25 cm–30 cm) in diameter, with a staggered row of jingles, and is held in the European grip. The player rocks the instrument back and forth while playing various rhythms with the knuckles of the right hand, using the thumb to create jingle sounds by rubbing the skin. In Galicia in Spain, the Italian technique is used (see *tamburello*, below). The terms '*pandeiro*' and '*pandeireta*' are used generically in both Spain and Portugal to indicate a tambourine.

The *riq* or *deff* (*riqq*, *duff*), a tambourine played in many parts of the Arabic Middle East and Israel, is 10″ (25 cm) in diameter, with five double pairs of jingles set into a wooden or metal frame. The preferred skin is fish or plastic, but it can also be goat or calf. The instrument is used in both popular belly-dance music and the Arabic classical traditions. The Oriental grip is used, and the playing technique involves three basic skin sounds (*doum*, *tak*, *kah*): playing on the jingles with the fingers (the resultant sound is called *tik*); shaking the frame; and striking the frame itself. The instrument can be played dramatically with a great deal of jingle strokes and shaking, or in a softer style in which no jingle strokes are used and the index fingers of both hands damp the skin while the middle and ring fingers of both hands alternate skin sounds.

The *tambour di bass* is a large tambourine – 20″ (50 cm) in diameter – played in Martinique. It is played in an ensemble, along with two barrel drums, a bamboo flute, a shaker and a stick-beaten bamboo tube.

The *tamburello*, a southern Italian tambourine, is usually 10″–14″ (25 cm–35 cm) in diameter, with tin-can jingles. It is held in the Oriental grip. The playing technique, which involves only right-hand strokes, is demanding and is based on producing a triple stroke by means of a pivotal motion in the center of the skin that moves from the thumb to the side of the hand to a full-hand slap. A large version of the instrument, with a deep frame and loose skin, is called a *tammorra*. This tambourine is typically 14″–18″ (35 cm–45 cm) in diameter, is held in the Oriental grip, and requires a different technique, which involves bouncing the playing hand across the skin to produce duple rhythms.

The *terbang* is an Indonesian tambourine, usually 10"–12" (25 cm–30 cm) in diameter, with four to five pairs of jingles. Held in the Oriental grip, the drum is played with the fingers utilizing the *doum-* and *tak*-style sounds. The frame of the tambourine is made from wood and has a characteristic convex shape like that of the Thai *rammana*, Malaysian frame drums (*rebana*) and Mongolian frame drums. Coming to Indonesia by means of Islam, the *terbang* was used in older central Javanese Islamic ritual music called *terbangan* and was occasionally used in some central Javanese gamelan ensembles and in other parts of Indonesia.

Frame Drums in Popular Music

In the late 1700s, the tambourine was briefly popular in the salon music of England. Some composers, such as Joseph Dale, Franz Steinglaw and Frank Stybelt, even created pieces that called for up to 30 different tambourine strokes (many for show) involving different types of rubbing, twirling and striking. Tambourines in England at this time often had a thumb hole that allowed the drum to spin freely around the thumb of the holding hand, an effect called for in the notation.

North American vaudeville/minstrelsy performers developed new tambourine techniques, and the tambourine experienced a rise in popularity as the primary minstrel rhythm instrument. According to Charles Dickens, by the 1840s Master Juba was astounding audiences with a highly stylized manner of tambourine playing that included the ability to mimic the sounds of trains and other mechanical devices. Breaking the color barrier by performing for white audiences, he toured the United States with a group called the Ethiopian Serenaders in 1843, going with them to London in 1848. By 1929, recordings featuring this African-American tambourine style had been made by Paramount Records, featuring tambourinist Uaroy Graves of the Mississippi Jook Band playing a variety of gospel and blues songs.

The innovative African-American technique, however, remained exclusive to gospel music. During the post-World War II era, the Salvation Army adopted the tambourine in its bands, preferring the biblical term 'timbrel.' The Salvation Army's use of the tambourine did not involve an innovative playing technique; rather, it was a symbolic and militaristic use in the style of a marching band. Routines for large ensembles of timbrel players were choreographed for visual appeal. Two editions of a manual for timbrel playing were published between 1955 and 1960, which detailed routines involving formation marching with ensemble movement of timbrels to various positions. Such routines were part of the Salvation Army's efforts through the 1960s.

From the free-jazz movement of the late 1950s through the sonic inventions of jazz fusion of the 1970s, non-Western influences on Western popular music increased, culminating in the 1980s and 1990s with the popularization and commercial packaging of 'world music.' The term is often used generically for indigenous musics from various parts of the world, rock/pop music with non-Western influences, creative new-age offerings, and an offshoot of jazz fusion involving multicultural influences with a jazz aesthetic. It was within this jazz context that an innovation in the playing of frame drums and a subsequent rise in their popularity occurred, prompting Western percussionists to learn non-Western instruments. The first recording of a jazz-inspired world music fusion involving frame drums – *Jazz Sahara* – was made in 1958 by Ahmed Abdul-Malik. As well as US jazz saxophonist Johnny Griffin, this recording includes jazz musicians playing with North African Arabic musicians and features the *riq* played throughout in a typically traditional style. On George Gruntz's *Noon in Tunisia: Jazz Meets Arabia* (1967), featuring several other European and US jazz musicians, as well as traditional Bedouin musicians from Tunisia, the *bendir* is prominent. An hour-long performance film with the same title was also released in Germany in 1969, but with the added feature of trumpeter Don Cherry. The *bendir* players on these recordings perform in a traditional manner within a nontraditional setting: jazz.

The use of Native frame drums and players on jazz recordings was uncommon, but there are several recordings that provide an historical continuum up to the major innovations of the 1980s. For example, in 1971 Native American jazz saxophonist Jim Pepper, along with his father Gilbert Pepper, featured Native American frame drums on several tracks of his debut recording, *Pepper's Pow Wow*. Moreover, the addition of Brazilian percussionist Airto Moreira on recordings by high-profile jazz artists like Miles Davis (in 1969–70), Weather Report (in 1971) and Return to Forever (in 1972) instigated the inclusion of traditional Brazilian percussion instruments within this new jazz context. Brazilians Dom um Romão and Paulinho da Costa, along with Airto Moreira (who became known for wild *pandeiro* solos), began to feature the Brazilian frame drums, *pandeiro* and *tamborim*, on their jazz-inspired solo recordings through the 1970s. Again, with regard to technique and rhythm patterns these frame drums were played very much as they would be in traditional settings. Another example of the use of frame drums within the jazz context was *Natural Elements* (1977) by the group Shakti, on which Indian master percussionist T.H. 'Vikku' Vinayakram performed on *kanjira* alongside jazz guitarist John McLaughlin. Jazz-inspired recordings throughout the 1970s that featured frame drums did so mainly with Native players of the respective traditions performing in much the same way as they would within traditional contexts. This meant that frame drums were used only where Native rhythmic patterns were compatible with the jazz context. There were two notable exceptions. Collin Walcott, performing on the Paul Winter Consort's *Road* (1970), was most likely the first Western percussionist to use a foreign frame drum technique on a jazz recording (Ukrainian-style stick-beaten tambourine), while *Diga* (1976), by the multicultural percussion group Diga Rhythm Band, featured Zakir Hussain of India on the Egyptian *tar*.

The use of frame drums in popular music during the 1980s blossomed into an innovative renaissance largely as a result of the work of frame drum virtuoso Glen Velez. The innovation in the work of Velez, a type of new percussionist, centered around detailed studies of unrelated frame drum techniques, such as Egyptian *riq* and *tar*, Persian *gaval*, Moroccan *bendir*, Indian *kanjira*, Brazilian *pandeiro* and Italian *tamburello*, with their subsequent application as a composite performance technique to drums such as Irish *bodhrán* (played with bare hands and/or drumset brush and hand), Thai *thon-rammana*, Native American frame drums and Spanish *adufe*. This approach was successful because nearly all frame drums have a similar basic physical construction that allows for the transposition of techniques and ideas, resulting in a unified sonic possibility (such as the three onomatopoeic sounds from Arabic drumming – *doum*, *tak* and *kah*). The only criterion for this unified approach to frame drumming is that the drum's skin be thin enough to respond to the various hand techniques (stick-beaten frame drums usually have thicker skins and are not always the best choice for the application of hand-drumming techniques). The early work of Velez on recordings by Horizontal Vertical Band in 1980 and 1981, Manzanita in 1981 and 1985, and the Paul Winter Consort in 1983 and 1985 demonstrates this approach. Velez's first solo recording, *Handance* (1984), reveals a refinement of his unified technique, which continued to develop in both breadth and depth throughout his recorded work in the 1990s.

Velez's approach to frame drumming had an impact on Western popular music in two ways. First, his stylized approach created interest among many other percussionists, causing the Velez approach to playing to spread among his students; this resulted in more performers of this style in the New York area (Mark Nauseef, Layne Redmond, N. Scott Robinson, Jan Hagiwara, Eva Atsalis,

Randy Crafton, Rich Goodhart and Glen Fittin are all proficient frame drum specialists with recording careers). Second, the Velez unified and improvisational approach freed the frame drum in Western popular music from a reliance on the compatibility of traditional rhythmic patterns, which subsequently expanded the kinds of musics they could be used in beyond jazz (see recordings by Rabih Abou-Khalil, Kimberly Bass, Malcolm Dalglish, Horizontal Vertical Band, Patty Larkin, Manzanita, Mokave, New York's Ensemble for Early Music, Pilgrimage, Steve Reich, Akira Satake, Richard Stoltzman, Trio Globo, Suzanne Vega and Paul Winter).

Another innovator during the late 1980s was multi-percussionist John Bergamo. Located on the US west coast at the California Institute of the Arts (a music school with diverse world music opportunities), Bergamo began applying North Indian tabla and South Indian *kanjira* techniques, as well as conga, *dumbeck* and other drumming techniques, to generic tambourines, frame drums and the *bodhrán*, developing his own unified approach to frame drumming. Differing widely from the Velez school, Bergamo developed a grip in which large frame drums were held between the legs so that both of the player's hands were free for playing. His approach also explored the sonic possibilities of frame drums in new ways – for example, obtaining harmonic pitch blends by sweeping the hands upward across the skin, and rubbing superball mallets on the skin for increased sustain and harmonics. Bergamo did not limit his unified approach to drumming to frame drums, but explored possibilities with African and Indonesian hand drums as well as suspended Indonesian nipple gongs and found objects, such as metal pots and jars of water, all played with the hands. As a leading instructor at a prestigious music school, Bergamo was successful in creating his own pool of students who went on to professional careers (Mark Nauseef and Rich Goodhart (both of whom had studied briefly with Velez before moving west to study with Bergamo), Randy Gloss, Austin Wrinkle, Andrew Grueschow, Peter Fagiola). His impact on popular music as a recording artist with frame drums has been more restricted to highly creative styles of music (see recordings by Bracha, Mokave and Repercussion Unit).

By the late 1980s, in Europe, the Italian virtuoso Carlo Rizzo had developed a unique and highly individual unified approach to tambourine playing with a synthesis of Italian, Persian and Indian drumming techniques. By constructing his own 'polytimbral tambourine,' Rizzo could control the tension of the skin, application of snares and damping of the jingles, making his instrumental solos sound distinctly like a *tamburello*, *tammorra*, *kanjira*, *bendir*, *dumbeck* or snare drum within a single performance. Residing in France, he recorded with a host of diverse European artists (Luc Ferrari, Michael Riessler, André Velter, Justin Vali Trio, Valentin Clastrier, Antonio Placer and Rita Marcotulli) throughout the 1990s before his first solo recording, *Schérzo 'Orientale'*, was released in 1997.

Also in the late 1980s, in Brazil, the *pandeiro* underwent a liberating innovation as a result of the work of percussionist Marcos Suzano, who unified Brazilian, Indian and drumset techniques/rhythms in such a way as to sound like *pandeiro*, *kanjira* and funk drumset during performance. Residing in Brazil, he recorded with many Brazilian and US artists (Hendrik Meurkens, Maria Bethania, Joan Baez, Ana Gabriel, Ashley Cleveland, Gilberto Gil, Marisa Monte, Boca Livre, Joyce, Carlinhos Brown and Carlos Malta). In 1996, his solo recording, *Sambatown*, was released.

As the result of a new type of Western percussionist approaching frame drums as a single family of instruments, it has become common to mix the playing techniques, grips and concepts associated with each instrument to create a composite vocabulary that can be used on almost any frame drum as its playing technique. Since this approach operates mostly outside each instrument's respective cultural tradition, the innovative use of frame drums in Western popular music has continued alongside traditional frame drum use in various regional world musics.

Bibliography

Belloni, Alessandra. 1997. 'Sud e Magia – South and Magic: A Living Tradition of Southern Italian Frame Drums and Tambourine Festivals.' *Percussive Notes* 35(5): 37–41.

Bergamo, John, with Bergamo, Janet. 1990. 'Exploring Tambourine Techniques.' *Percussive Notes* 28(3): 12–14.

Braund, Simon. 1989. 'Tambourine Man: Airto Moreira.' *Rhythm: Total Percussion Magazine* 2(4): 23–24, 27–28.

Brooks, Iris. 1987. 'Meet the Composer: Glen Velez.' *Ear: Magazine of New Music* 12(6): 16–19.

Brooks, Iris. 1996. 'Alessandra Belloni.' *Percussion Source* 1(2): 26–29.

Brooks, Iris. 1997. 'Colors & Scents: Glen Velez Draws Inspiration from the World Around Him.' *Drum!* 6(1): 75–78.

Cally, Sully. 1990. *Musiques et danses afro-caraïbes: Martinique* [Afro-Caribbean Music and Dance: Martinique]. Gros-Morne, Martinique: Sully-Cally/Lezin.

Consolmagno, Peppe (Giuseppe). 1999. 'Alessandra Belloni.' *Percussioni* 10(94): 56–63.

Courlander, Harold. 1960. *The Drum and the Hoe: Life and Lore of the Haitian People*. Berkeley, CA: University of California Press.

Courlander, Harold. 1973 (1939). *Haiti Singing*. New York: Cooper Square Publishers.

Da Anunciação, Luiz Almeida. 1990. *The Percussion Instruments of the Brazilian Typical Rhythms: Their Technique and Their Music Writing. Percussion Manual – Volume 1, Book 2: The 'Pandeiro' Brazilian Style*. Rio de Janeiro: Europa Gráfica e Editora Ltda.

Deal, Scott. 1998. 'The Eskimo Drums of Alaska.' *Percussive Notes* 36(1): 54, 56–59.

Deane, Christopher. 1992. 'Improving Your Tambourine Skills.' *Percussive Notes* 31(1): 29–30.

Desroches, Monique. 1996. *Tambours des dieux: Musique et sacrifice d'origine tamoule en Martinique* [Drums of the Gods: Music and Sacrifice of Tamil Origin in Martinique]. Montréal: Harmattan.

Diagram Group, The. 1976. *Musical Instruments of the World: An Illustrated Encyclopedia*. New York: Paddington Press.

Doerschuk, Andy. 1996. 'Layne Redmond: Following in the Footsteps of the Drumming Goddesses.' *Drum!* 5(2): 38–40, 42, 45.

Doerschuk, Andy. 1998. 'Layne Redmond: Chasing the Frame Drum Through History.' *Drum!* 7(1): 78–79, 81–82, 84.

Donald, Mary Ellen. 1985. *Arabic Tambourine: A Comprehensive Course in Techniques and Performance for the Tambourine, Tar, and Mazhar*. San Francisco: Mary Ellen Books.

Dorsey, Ed. 1987. 'An Interview with Glen Velez.' *Percussive Notes* 25(4): 56–60.

Doubleday, Veronica. 1999. 'The Frame Drum in the Middle East: Women, Musical Instruments and Power.' *Ethnomusicology* 43(1): 101–34.

Emsheimer, Ernst. 1977. 'On the Symbolism of the Lapp Magic Drum.' *The World of Music* 19(3/4): 45–61.

Fagiola, Peter. 1997. 'A Discussion of Frame Drums.' *Percussive Notes* 35(6): 30–33.

Fagiola, Peter. 1999. *Frame Drumming: Free Hand Style – The Basics*. Milwaukee, WI: Hal Leonard Publishing Corporation.

Falvo, Robert. 1997. 'Beginning with the *Tar*.' *Sticks & Mallets* 1(1): 54–55, 64.

Fonseca, Duduka da, and Weiner, Bob. 1991. *Brazilian Rhythms for Drumset*. Miami, FL: Manhattan Music, Inc.

Gershuny, Diane. 1990. 'Steve Amadee: Sometimes Less Is More.' *Drums & Drumming* 2(5): 10, 12.

Goldberg, Norbert. 1984. 'Brazilian Percussion.' *Percussive Notes* 22(5): 51–52.

Goltheim, Vivien I. 1988. '*Bumba-meu-boi*: A Musical Play from Maranhão.' *The World of Music* 30(2): 40–68.

Gottlieb, Gordon. 1984/85. 'The Percussion of *Carnaval*.' *Modern Percussionist* 1(1): 12–17, 46–47.

Gould, Michael. 1998. '*Taiko* Classification and Manufacturing.' *Percussive Notes* 36(3): 12–14, 16–20.

Graham, Richard. 1985/86. 'Glen Velez's Tambourines.' *Modern Percussionist* 2(1): 48–50.

Graham, Richard. 1992. 'Trans-Atlantic African Organology: The Tradition of Renewal.' *Experimental Musical Instruments* 8(1): 29–35.

Graham, Richard, and Robinson, N. Scott. 1989. 'The *Tamborim*: Little Drum with a Big Sound.' *Highlights in Percussion* 4(1): 11, 14.

Grover, Neil, and Whaley, Garwood. 1997. *The Art of Tambourine and Triangle Playing*. Fort Lauderdale, FL: Meredith Music Publications.

Guizzi, Febo. 1988. 'The Continuity of the Pictorial Representation of a Folk Instrument's Playing Technique: The Iconography of the *Tamburello* in Italy.' *The World of Music* 30(3): 28–58.

Guizzi, Febo, and Staiti, Nico. 1989. *Le forme dei suoni: l'iconografia del tamburello in Italia* [Shaping the Sound: The Iconography of the *Tamburello* in Italy]. Sicily: Arte e Musica.

Hannigan, Steáfán. 1991. *The Bodhrán Book*. Cork: Ossian.

Houston, Bob. 1987. 'The Development of the Orchestral Percussion Section (c. 1675–1890).' *Percussioner International* 1(4): 44–48.

Johnson, Tom. 1981. 'The Real Tambourine Man: Glen Velez.' *The Village Voice* 26 (11 March): 70.

Kampmann, Wolf. 1996. 'Mister Tambourine Man: Der Perkussionist Carlo Rizzo' [Mr. Tambourine Man: The Percussionist Carlo Rizzo]. *Neue Zeitschrift für Musik* 6: 34–36.

Kujahn, Lars Bo. 1990. *Oriental Percussion*. Frederiksberg, Denmark: Percussion Center Publications.

Lang, Morris. 1986. 'The Tambourine.' *Percussioner International* 1(2): 60–61.

Levine, David. 1977. 'Playing Rock Tambourine.' *Modern Drummer* 4(1): 14.

Liang, Mingyue (David Ming-Yüeh Liang). 1985. *Music of the Billion: An Introduction to Chinese Musical Culture*. New York: Heinrichshofen Edition.

Li Castro, Emiliano, and Dado, Fabrizio. 1991. 'I tamburi a cornice di Glen Velez' [The Frame Drums of Glen Velez]. *Percussioni* 2(6): 36–39.

Loney, Glenn, ed. 1984. *Musical Theatre in America: Papers and Proceedings of the Conference on the Musical Theatre in America*. Westport, CT: Greenwood Press.

Marcuse, Sibyl. 1975. *A Survey of Musical Instruments*. New York: Harper & Row.

Mason, Bernard S. 1938. *Drums, Tomtoms and Rattles: Primitive Percussion Instruments for Modern Use*. New York: A.S. Barnes.

Moreira, Airto. 1985. *Airto: The Spirit of Percussion*. Wayne, NJ: 21st Century Music Productions.

Mulvaney, Paul. 1988. 'Tommy Hayes – On a Wing and a *Bodhrán* Player.' *Drums & Drumming* 4(4): 12–13.

Murphy, Martin. 1997. *The International Bodhrán Book*. Cork: Ossian.

Napolitano, Giuliana. 1999a. 'Carnaval: a história das baterias de samba' [*Carnaval*: The History of the Samba Schools' Percussion Orchestras]. *Batera* 3(21): 24–26.

Napolitano, Giuliana. 1999b. 'Marcos Suzano: A força do pandeiro' [Marcos Suzano: The Power of *Pandeiro*]. *Batera* 3(22): 70–73.

Nathan, Hans. 1952. 'The First Negro Minstrel Band and Its Origins.' *Southern Folklore Quarterly* 16: 132–44.

O'Mahoney, Terry. 1999. 'The Irish *Bodhrán*.' *Percussive Notes* 37(2): 34–40.

Ó Súilleabháin, Mícheál. 1984. *The Bodhrán: An Easy to Learn Method for the Complete Beginner, Showing the Different Regional Styles and Techniques*. Dublin: Waltons Musical Instrument Galleries Ltd.

Paulinho (Paulo Fernando Magalhaes). 1965. *Rhythms and Instruments of Brazil*. Reseda, CA: Swing House, Inc.

Payson, Al. 1971. *Techniques of Playing Bass Drum, Cymbals, and Accessories*. Park Ridge, IL: Payson Percussion Products.

Pinto, Tiago de Oliveira. 1991. *Capoeira, Samba, Candomblé: Afro-brasilianische Musik im Recôncavo, Bahia* [*Capoeira*, Samba, *Candomblé*: Afro-Brazilian Music in the Recôncavo, Bahia]. Berlin: Dietrich Reimer Verlag.

Powell, Stephen. 1996. 'Drums of the Southwest.' *Percussion Source* 1(3): 26–29.

Pryor, Andrea. 1997. 'Samba Schools of Rio de Janeiro.' *Percussive Notes* 35(1): 68–72.

Redmond, Layne. 1990. 'Rhythm and the Frame Drum: Attributes of the Goddess.' *Ear: Magazine of New Music* 15(4): 18–19, 21.

Redmond, Layne. 1996. 'A Short History of the Frame Drum.' *Percussive Notes* 34(5): 69–70, 72.

Redmond, Layne. 1997a. '*Bumba Meu Boi*: Frame Drum Festival in São Luis, Maranhão.' *Percussive Notes* 35(3): 39–42.

Redmond, Layne. 1997b. *When the Drummers Were Women: A Spiritual History of Rhythm*. New York: Three Rivers Press.

Redmond, Layne. 1998. 'Rhythms of the Goddess, When Women Were Ecstatic Drummers.' *Shaman's Drum* 48: 40–53.

Reimer, Terry. 1998. 'Layne Redmond.' *Chicago Percussion and Rhythm* 1(3): 12–13.

Renaud, Philippe. 1998. 'Carlo Rizzo: le tambourin dans

tous ses états' [Carlo Rizzo: The Tambourine in All Its Forms]. *Improjazz* 46: 6–10.

Robinson, N. Scott. 2000. 'Glen Velez: A World of Sound in His Hands.' *Modern Drummer* 24(4): 72–76, 78–80, 82, 84, 86.

Robinson, N. Scott. 2001. 'John Bergamo: Percussion World View.' *Percussive Notes* 39(1): 8–17.

Sabanovich, Daniel. 1994. *Brazilian Percussion Manual: Rhythms and Techniques with Application for the Drum Set*. 2nd ed. Van Nuys, CA: Alfred Publishing Company.

Salvation Army, The. 1955. *Timbrel Manual*. San Francisco: The Music Bureau, Western Territorial Headquarters.

Sankaran, Trichy. 1986. 'Talavadya Kacceri: The Percussion Ensemble of South India.' *Percussioner International* 1(2): 16–19.

Santos, John. 1987. 'The Brazilian *Tamborim*.' *Modern Percussionist* 3(3): 44, 46–47.

Schuyler, Philip D. 1978. 'Moroccan Andalusian Music.' *The World of Music* 20(1): 33–46.

Sofia, Sal. 1987. 'John Bergamo: Rhyme, Rhythm, and Raga.' *Percussioner International* 1(4): 50–55.

Sulsbrück, Birger. 1986. *Latin American Percussion: Rhythms and Rhythm Instruments from Cuba and Brazil*. Copenhagen: Den Rytmiske Aftenscoles Forlag/Edition Wilhelm Hansen.

Sumarsam. 1995. *Gamelan: Cultural Interaction and Musical Development in Central Java*. Chicago: University of Chicago Press.

Taylor, Eric. 1989. *Musical Instruments of South-East Asia*. New York: Oxford University Press.

Thomas, T. Ajayi. 1992. *History of Juju Music: A History of an African Popular Music from Nigeria*. New York: Thomas Organization.

Uribe, Ed. 1993. *The Essence of Brazilian Percussion and Drum Set*. Miami, FL: Warner Bros. Publications.

Velez, Glen. 1980. 'The Tambourine in Ancient Western Asia.' *Ear Magazine East* 5(5): 3.

Velez, Glen. 1982. 'A Monograph on the Frame Drum, Ancestor of Our Modern Tambourine.' *Ear Magazine East* 7(3–4): 8–9.

Velez, Glen. 1999. *Handance Method: An Introduction to Frame Drumming*. New York: Frame Drum Music.

Velez, Glen. 2000. *The Cueing and Performance Guide*. New York: Frame Drum Music.

Vincent, David. 1987. 'Basic Tambourine Technique.' *Percussive Notes* 25(5): 23–24.

Waterman, Christopher A. 1990. *Jùjú: A Social History and Ethnography of an African Popular Music*. Chicago: University of Chicago Press.

Wentz, Brooke. 1984. 'An Interview with Glen Velez.' *Op Magazine* V: 42–43.

Discographical References

Abdul-Malik, Ahmed. *Jazz Sahara*. Riverside OJCCD-1820-2. *1958*: USA.

Diga Rhythm Band. *Diga*. Rykodisc RCD 10101. *1976*: USA.

Gruntz, George. *Noon in Tunisia: Jazz Meets Arabia*. MPS 15.132. *1967*: Germany.

Horizontal Vertical Band. *Direct to Disc*. Other Media 5681. *1981*: USA.

Horizontal Vertical Band. *Spontaneous Music*. Other Media 80-7-1. *1980*: USA.

Kirk, Rahsaan Roland. *Volunteered Slavery*. Rhino R2 71407. 1969; *1993*: USA.

Manzanita. *La Quiero a Morir*. CBS S 26716. *1985*: Spain.

Manzanita. *Talco y Bronce*. CBS S 85313. *1981*: Spain.

Paul Winter Consort, The. *Canyon*. Living Music LD0006. *1985*: USA.

Paul Winter Consort, The. *Road*. A&M CD 0826. *1970*: USA.

Paul Winter Consort, The. *Sun Singer*. Living Music LMR-CD 003. *1983*: USA.

Pepper, Jim. *Pepper's Pow Wow*. Embryo SD-7312. *1971*: USA.

Rizzo, Carlo. *Schérzo 'Orientale'*. Al Sur ALCD 214. *1997*: France.

Shakti. *Natural Elements*. Columbia 48122. *1977*: USA.

Suzano, Marcos. *Sambatown*. MPB 063016719-2. *1996*: Brazil.

Velez, Glen. *Handance*. Nomad NMD 50301. *1984*: USA.

Discography

Abou-Khalil, Rabih. *Between Dusk and Dawn*. Enja MMP-170886 2. *1987*: Germany.

Abou-Khalil, Rabih. *The Sultan's Picnic*. Enja ENJ-8078-2. *1994*: Germany.

Bergamo, John. *On the Edge*. CMP CD 27. *1986*: Germany.

Bergamo, John, and Dorsey, Ed. *Cloud Hands (Tambo)*. Interworld Music C-903. *1990*: USA.

Bracha. *Bracha*. CMP CD 34. *1988*: Germany.

Clastrier, Valentin, Riessler, Michael, and Rizzo, Carlo. *Paludes*. Wergo 8010-2. *1995*: Germany.

Crafton, Randy. *Duologue*. Lyrichord LYRCD 7430. *1997*: USA.

Dalglish, Malcolm, and the Ooolites. *Pleasure*. Ooolitic Music OM 1112. *1997*: USA.

De Jimbe. *De Jimbe*. Malgamu MALGCD115. *2001*: Ireland.

Friesen, Eugene. *The Song of Rivers*. New England Town Media NECD-3102. *1997*: USA.

Goodhart, Rich. *Affirmative Reply*. Beginner's Mind Productions BMP 1002. *1991*: USA.

Goodhart, Rich. *Divining Signs*. Beginner's Mind Productions BMP 1001. *1988*: USA.

Goodhart, Rich. *Never Give a Sword to a Man Who Can't Dance*. Beginner's Mind Productions BMP 0403. *1995*: USA.

Goodhart, Rich. *The Gathering Sun*. Beginner's Mind Productions BMP 0404. *1999*: USA.

Good Time Blues: Harmonicas, Kazoos, Washboards, and Cow-bells. Columbia Legacy CK 46780. *1991*: USA.

Hands On'Semble. *Hands On'Semble*. Tala Mala TM 1414. *1998*: USA.

Hellborg, Jonas, Lane, Shawn, and Selvaganesh, V. *Good People in Times of Evil*. Bardo 040. *2000*: Italy.

I Giullardi di Piazza. *Earth, Sun & Moon*. Lyrichord LYRCD 7427. *1996*: USA.

Jazz Meets the World No. 4: Jazz Meets Africa. MPS 531 720-2. *1997*: Germany.

Kíla. *Tóg é Go Bog é*. Key KRCD005. *1997*: Ireland.

Larkin, Patty. *Strangers World*. High Street 72902 10335-2. *1995*: USA.

Lockwood, Annea. *Thousand Year Dreaming*. What Next? WN 0010. *1993*: USA.

Mississippi Jook Band, The. 'Hittin' the Bottle Stomp.' Melotone 6-11-65. 1936: USA.

Mokave. *Mokave Volume 1*. Audioquest AQ-CD 1006. *1991*: USA.

Musical Traditions of Portugal. Smithsonian Folkways CD SF 40435. *1994*: USA.

Oskorri. *Ura*. Elkarlanean KD-556. *2000*: Spain.

Pilgrimage. *9 Songs of Ecstasy*. Point Music 314536 201-2. *1997*: USA.

Redmond, Layne, and Brunjes, Tommy. *Being in Rhythm: A Guided Meditation*. Interworld CD 927. *1997*: USA.

Redmond, Layne, and Brunjes, Tommy. *Lotus of Light: Chanting the Chakras*. Interworld CD 930. *1999*: USA.

Redmond, Layne, and the Mob of Angels. *Since the Beginning*. Redmond Recordings RRCD11. *1992*: USA.

Reich, Steve. *Tehillim*. ECM 1215 78118-21215-2. *1982*: USA.

Repercussion Unit. *In Need Again*. CMP CD 31. *1987*: Germany.

Robinson, N. Scott. *Things That Happen Fast*. New World View Music NWVM CD-02. *2001*: USA.

Satake, Akira. *Cooler Heads Prevail*. Alula ALU-1003. *1997*: USA.

Songs & Rhythms of Morocco. Lyrichord LYRCD 7336. *1979*: USA.

Stoltzman, Richard. *New York Counterpoint*. RCA 5944-2-RC. *1987*: USA.

Trio Globo. *Trio Globo*. Silverwave SD 806. *1994*: USA.

Vega, Suzanne. *Days of Open Hand*. A&M 7502-15293-2. *1990*: USA.

Velez, Glen. *Assyrian Rose*. CMP CD 42. *1989*: Germany.

Velez, Glen. *Internal Combustion*. CMP CD 23. *1985*: Germany.

Velez, Glen. *Seven Heaven*. CMP CD 30. *1987*: Germany.

Visual Recordings

Bergamo, John. 1990. 'The Art & Joy of Hand Drumming.' Interworld Music (video).

Bergamo, John. 1991. 'Finding Your Way with Hand Drums.' Interworld Music (video).

Bergamo, John. 1997. 'Hand Drumming with John Bergamo.' Tala Mala (video).

Dalglish, Malcolm. 1993. 'Hymnody of Earth (revised).' KET (video).

Dalglish, Malcolm. 1997. 'The Selchie and the Fisherman.' Live Multimedia, Inc. (video).

Gil, Gilberto. 1994. 'Unplugged.' Warner Music Vision (video).

Gruntz, George, with Cherry, Don, and Bedouin Musicians from Tunisia. 1969. 'Noon in Tunisia: Jazz Meets Arabia.' Des Arts Populaires Tunisiennes (film).

Hannigan, Steáfán. 1991. 'The *Bodhrán* Video: A Complete Audio-Visual Course for the Traditional *Bodhrán*.' Ossian (video).

Harms, Ben. 1997. 'Basic Technique for Hand Drum and Tambourine.' Harms Historical Percussion (video).

Hayes, Tommy. 1994. '*Bodhrán*, Bones and Spoons.' C.W. Productions (video).

'Konkombe: The Nigerian Pop Music Scene.' 1980. Shanachie Record Corp. (video).

'Modern Drummer Festival Weekend 1998 (Sunday).' 1999. Warner Bros. (video).

Moreira, Airto. 1985. 'Harvest Jazz.' Sony (video).

Moreira, Airto. 1993. 'Brazilian Percussion.' DCI Music Video VH0182 (video).

Paul Winter Consort, The. 1985. 'Canyon Consort.' A&M/Windham Hill (video).

Redmond, Layne. 1992. 'Ritual Drumming (A Sense of Time: Explorations of the Tambourine and *Riq*).' Interworld Music/Warner Bros. (video).

Redmond, Layne. 1999. 'Rhythmic Wisdom.' Interworld Music (video).

Robinson, N. Scott. 1996. 'Hand Drumming: Exercises for Unifying Technique.' Wright Hand Drum Company WHD-01 (video).

Sankaran, Trichy. 1994. '*Mrdangam* and *Kanjira* Clinic.' Percussive Arts Society PAS9401 (video).

'The JVC/Smithsonian Folkways Video Anthology of Music and Dance of Africa. Vol. 1: Egypt/Uganda/Senegal.' 1996. JVC, Victor Company of Japan (video).

'The JVC Video Anthology of World Music and Dance, Vols. 1–30.' 1988. JVC, Victor Company of Japan (video).

Velez, Glen. 1989. 'Drumbeats.' Remo HD-7514-DB (video).

Velez, Glen. 1990. 'The Fantastic World of Frame Drums.' Interworld Music (video).

Velez, Glen. 1996a. 'Handance Method for Personal Rhythmic Development and Hand Drumming 1.' Interworld Music/Warner Bros. VH0284 (video).

Velez, Glen. 1996b. 'Handance Method for Personal Rhythmic Development and Hand Drumming 2.' Interworld Music/Warner Bros. VH0285 (video).

N. SCOTT ROBINSON

Glockenspiel

The glockenspiel (orchestra bells; Fr.: *(jeux de) timbres*; It.: *campanelli*) is a metallophone comprised of graduated tuned bars of steel, bronze or aluminum alloys, arranged in two rows as a piano keyboard, and struck with knobbed mallets or sticks. The normal range of the glockenspiel is 2 1/2 octaves, sounding g^2 to c^5.

From the eighth to the eighteenth centuries, the glockenspiel was a set of European small bells or a miniature carillon. Mechanical glockenspiels were developed in the thirteenth century as practise instruments for carillons. Bar glockenspiels were introduced in Holland in the seventeenth century, likely influenced by the Dutch explorers' acquaintance with Native bar metallophones (*gendèr, saron*) of the Malaysian archipelago. Late eighteenth-century bar glockenspiels were also played from a mechanical piano-like keyboard. In the nineteenth century, the bell lyre, a portable bar glockenspiel on a lyre-shaped frame, was introduced by marching military bands.

In military bands, the glockenspiel normally played the melody, thereby enhancing the high register. By the early twentieth century, the glockenspiel was a featured solo instrument in band concerts and on acoustic recordings such as those made by Charles P. Lowe ('Blue Bells of Scotland,' 'Chiming Bells') for the Columbia Graphophone Company in 1898. Typically, due to its long-ringing sound, the glockenspiel played the melody only, with minimal elaboration.

Throughout the twentieth century, the glockenspiel was used for its tone color in film scores (*Raiders of the Lost Ark*), musicals (*Camelot*) and symphonic pops concerts (*An American in Paris*). The glockenspiel is virtually absent in rock music.

Bibliography

Apel, Willi. 1969. *Harvard Dictionary of Music*. 2nd ed. Cambridge, MA: Harvard University Press.

Blades, James. 1970. *Percussion Instruments and Their History*. New York: Praeger.

Cahn, William. 1996. *The Xylophone in Acoustic Recordings (1877–1929)*. Rev. ed. Bloomfield, NY: William L. Cahn Publishing. (First published Holcomb, NY: Cahn, 1979.)

Marcuse, Sibyl. 1975a. *A Survey of Musical Instruments*. New York: Harper & Row.

Marcuse, Sibyl. 1975b. *Musical Instruments*. New York: Norton.

Peinkofer, Karl. 1969. *Handbook of Percussion Instruments*. London: Schott.

Discographical References

'Blue Bells of Scotland.' Orchestra bells, prob. played by Charles P. Lowe. Cylinder. Columbia Graphophone 12502. ca. 1898: Bridgeport, CT.

'Chiming Bells.' Orchestra bells, prob. played by Charles P. Lowe. Cylinder. Columbia Graphophone 12516. ca. 1898: Bridgeport, CT.

Discography

An American in Paris [O.S.T.]. Rhino 71961. *1996*: USA.

Camelot. Jay 1295. *1996*: USA.

Raiders of the Lost Ark. DCC 90. *1995*: USA.

Filmography

An American in Paris, dir. Vincente Minnelli. 1951. USA. 113 mins. Musical Romance. Original music by George Gershwin, Ira Gershwin.

Camelot, dir. Joshua Logan. 1967. USA. 150 mins. Musical. Original music by Ken Darby, Frederick Loewe.

Raiders of the Lost Ark, dir. Steven Spielberg. 1981. USA. 115 mins. Adventure. Original music by John Williams.

WILLIAM L. CAHN

Güiro

The *güiro* is a percussive scraper found in the Caribbean, Panama and South America and now used in many bands and orchestras throughout the world, particularly in Latin orchestras and big bands. It has an attractive curvy textured sound which, when the instrument is played rhythmically, allows the rhythms to be broken down into many components and timbres. The *güiro* is usually a size that can be easily and lightly held in the hand. Formally categorized as an idiophone, the instrument is commonly made from a gourd, either oblong or spherical in shape (like those used by the *Cunas* Indians (*Kantules*)), but it is most often made out of wood, metal and bamboo. There are examples made from industrial spare parts, armadillo shells, sea shells, turtle shells, coconuts, bone – indeed, anything to hand with a grooved surface that can be scraped. In some areas of Africa and the Americas, Fanta orange drink bottles are popular!

The front of the instrument is scored with parallel grooves, which mark the surface (but without cutting through it) and offer a rough edge that can easily be scraped and that makes a good sound. The instrument is known by a host of names: *guacharaca* in Colombia; *guira* (made of metal and played with a fork) in the Dominican Republic; *reco-reco* in Brazil; *guayo* or *ralladera* in Cuba; and *guayo*, *güiro*, *candungo*, *carracho* or *guícharo* in Puerto Rico. The most common name, however, is *güiro*. It is an essential instrument in Cuban *son* and *trova* groups and in salsa orchestras, where it keeps a regular rhythm in the time line and is often played by one of the singers, lead or second. In Panama, the *churuca* or *guáchara* has a key role in an ensemble known as the *Gallino* (with the *rabel* (lute), *mejoranera* (guitar) and drum). It is made from a strong cane with an uneven surface or a deer shinbone with holes that is scraped with sticks.

The musician who plays the *güiro*, sometimes called a *güirero*, normally holds the instrument in the left hand and scrapes the playing stick across the grooves with the right hand. Players have been known to play the *güiro* with a fork, in which case the instrument's percussive capacity is duplicated.

For those for whom origin is important, opinion is divided as to whether the *güiro* was first created in Africa or in the Americas. Some authors support a Bantu (Congolese) origin for it. Indeed, there is no evidence to suggest that indigenous people in the Americas did not have their own equivalent of the *güiro*. The important thing is that the instrument has always played a key role in many different cultural groups, and that these cultures have found the *güiro* aesthetic an integral part of music-making. In Cuba, the *güiro* is found in an enormous number of different popular ensembles, and indeed many top orchestras have a musician whose sole purpose is to play the *güiro*. In other groups, the *güiro* player may also sing (and vice versa – i.e., one of the singers may play the *güiro*). As a percussion instrument, the *güiro* plays a key role and may be used to start pieces off.

In the former Belgian Congo, the indigenous Ikoko people use an instrument made of a long bamboo cane with numerous transverse grooves that are scraped with a very thin, hard stick. In Angola, there is a four-foot instrument made from the bark of a type of palm tree, which has a hollow core and an exterior carved into grooves that are forcefully scraped with a stick. In Nigeria, an instrument called *kirana* is used, which is made from the dried stem of the euphorbia cactus and which has irregular notches that are scraped with a small stick. *Guayos* typical of the Antilles have been found belonging to the Zuni, Hopi and Maya cultures.

In Cuba, where on occasion the *güiro* is known as *guayo* from its indigenous name *guyey* or *guajey*, the instrument may be made from the *guira* tree, from which

a branch is taken, hollowed out and notched horizontally so that it can be scraped with a small stick. In some groups that play *son*, the instrument is scraped from the bottom to the top, ending with two short top turns, as the different curve of sound is integral to the timbre of the music. There are and have been many famous Cuban *güiro* performers, including Gustavo Tamayo, Osvaldo 'Chihuahua' Martinez, Francisco 'Panchito' Arbolaez and Rolando Valdes. Musicians sometimes play the *guayo* by beating a stick on its back ('*el virao de guayo*'), hitting the smooth surface as if it were a clave. There is a certain tendency in Afro-Cuban music to use it to produce top-quality texture for huge bands and orchestras and more elementary percussive effects in other groups, even to the point of improvising with the instrument in unexpected ways – depending on the instrumental lineup of the group.

In Cuban popular music, the *güiro* is found in an enormous number of instrumental groupings, including the *Charanguita* (*guateques*) with accordion, *timbales* (drums) and *güiro*; the *orquesta típica*, which performs a repertoire of local *contradanza* with two clarinets, one trumpet, two horns, two violins, one double bass, one timpano (small drum) (*pailas* or *timbales*) and one *güiro*; and *Charanga Francesa* with two violins, piano, double bass, *timbales* and *güiro*.

In Cuban music, the term '*güiro*' may also denote a type of music used in popular Santería religious ceremonies and other Afro-Cuban cults that may use a 6/8 or 12/8 measure and is played with three *chekerés*, a *cencerro* (cowbell) and *tumbadoras* (conga drums). (A *chekeré*, also found in Brazil, is a large gourd filled with seeds, with a fret of string around the outside involving woven beads which moves against the body of the gourd when shaken to produce a double scratchy shake against the shaken seeds.)

In the music of the Dominican Republic, the *güiro* is part of the merengue trio together with the accordion and *tambora* (drum). In Puerto Rico, it is found with the accordion and tambourine in *plena* groups. In Colombia, the *cumbia* and *vallenato* use the accordion, *tumbadoras* and *güiros* (*guacharacas*).

In Brazil, the *güiro* is most often called *reco-reco*. It is found in different regions and is used in folkloric celebrations and dances, as well as in much contemporary popular music. The instruments are made of various materials and in different shapes, often improvised from what the musician can find to hand. The most representative types include: *Reco-reco da Aldeia de Carapicuíba*, São Paulo, which may be of indigenous origin; *Casaco do Espírito Santo*, used in *Jongo*; *Reco-reco de mola em Góias*, found in Congolese groups; *Reco-reco de mola para samba*, found in the samba schools of São Paulo; and *Reco-reco do luthier Nadir Rovari*. There are different types of *reco-reco* in the states of Pernambuco, Sergipe, Mato Grosso, Goiás, Minas Gerais, São Paulo, Rio de Janeiro and Espírito Santo.

The *güiro* is an essential part of Cuban *son* and Latin American salsa orchestras in both North and South America, Africa and indeed the rest of the world. Musicians from various periods who have promoted the *güiro* are: Johnny Pacheco, Ismael Rivera, Guillermo Amores, Enrique Lazaga, Juliol Noroña and Ismael Quintana. The musical styles that use the *güiro* include: *danzón*, *Afro*, *chachachá*, *pachanga*, *songo* (*chekeré*), *bomba*, *plena*, merengue (*guira*), Haitian *méringue*, *compas*, salsa and *guajira*. Cuban musician Arsenio Rodríguez's song 'Dile a Catalina' or 'El guayo de Catalina' describes the usefulness of the *guayo* in the kitchen for scraping off the skin of the yucca, although the lyrics are full of double-entendres based on the rhythmic playing/stroking of the instrument and its shape. The chorus says:

Tell Catalina to buy herself a *guayo* because . . .

the yucca is getting spoiled.

Bibliography

Arnold, Denis, ed. 1983. *The New Oxford Companion to Music*. Oxford and New York: Oxford University Press.

Austerlitz, Paul. 1993. 'Local and International Trends in Dominican Merengue.' *The World of Music* 35(2): 70–89.

Basso, Alberto. 1983. *Dizionario Enciclopedico Univerzale Della Musica e Dei Musicisti* [World Dictionary Encyclopedia of Music and Musicians]. Torino: Unione Tipográfico Editrice Torinece (UTET).

Casanova Oliva, Ana Victoria. 1988. *Problemática Organológica Cubana* [Cuban Organological Problematic]. Havana: Ediciones Casa de las Américas.

Garay, Narciso. 1982. *Tradiciones y Cantares de Panamá* [Traditions and Songs from Panama]. 2nd ed. Panama: Litho Impresora Panamá S.A.

Lapique Becali, Zoila. 1963. *Catalogación y clasificación de la música cubana* [Cataloging and Classification of Cuban Music]. Havana: Departamento de Publicaciones de la Biblioteca José Martí.

Marcuse, Sibyl. 1975. *A Survey of Musical Instruments*. New York: Harper & Row.

Mauleón, Rebeca. 1993. *Salsa Guidebook for Piano and Ensemble*. Petaluma, CA: Sher Music Co.

Orovio, Helio. 1981. *Diccionario de la música cubana. Biográfico y técnico* [Dictionary of Cuban Music: Biographical and Technical]. Havana: Editorial Letras Cubanas.

Ortiz, Fernando. 1952. *Los instrumentos de la música afro-cubana* [The Instruments of Afro-Cuban Music].
Havana: Dirección de Cultura, Ministerio de Educación.

Perdomo Escobar, José Ignacio. 1980. *Historia de la Música en Colombia* [History of the Music of Colombia]. 5th ed. Bogotá: Plaza & Janes, Editores Colombia Ltda.

Roberts, John Storm. 1982. *El Toque Latino* [The Latin Beat], trans. Aurora Merino. México, D.F.: Editores Asociados M., S.A. EDAMEX.

Schechter, John M., and Blades, James. 1984. 'Güiro.' In *The New Grove Dictionary of Musical Instruments*, Vol. 2, ed. Stanley Sadie. London: Macmillan, 86–87.

Sinzig, Frei Pedro. 1959. *Diccionario Musical* [Musical Dictionary]. Rio de Janeiro: Livraria Kosmos Editora.

Stasi, Carlos Eduardo di. 1993. *Instrumentos de Raspar no Brasil: Documentação* [Scraping Instruments in Brazil: Documentation]. São Paulo: ArteUnesp, Vol. 9.

Stasi, Carlos Eduardo di. 1998. *Representations of Musical Scrapers: The Disjuncture Between Simple and Complex in the Study of a Percussion Instrument*. Ph.D. thesis, University of Natal, Durban.

Veiga de Oliveira, Ernesto. 1966. *Instrumentos Musicais Populares Portugueses* [Portuguese Popular Musical Instruments]. Lisbon: Fundação Calouste Gulbenkian.

Zarate, Manuel F. 1962. *Tambor y Socavón* [Drum and Hollow]. Panama: Imprenta Nacional.

Discographical Reference

Rodríguez, Arsenio. 'Dile a Catalina.' *Arsenio Rodríguez*. DiscMedi 206. *1995*: Spain.

EDWIN RICARDO PITRE VÁSQUEZ (trans. ZUZANA PICK)

Jew's-Harp (Jew's Harp)

The jew's-harp, or jaw harp, is a small instrument consisting of a bamboo, bone or, most often, metal frame on which is mounted a flexible tongue or key, usually made of the same material. The end of the frame on which the tongue is mounted is closed. The instrument is held in the mouth, against the teeth, and the tongue is plucked by the player's finger. The type of sound produced can be changed by altering the shape and size of the mouth cavity.

The instrument is found in many parts of the world and has a particularly long history in Asia and Europe. It was introduced by Europeans to Africa and the Americas. It is known by many different names (for example, *Maultrommel* ('mouth drum') in Germany, *zamburak* in Iran and *genggong* in Bali). In England, it was originally known as 'trump,' a name that has persisted in Scotland and Ireland. The source of the later English name 'Jew's harp' is obscure, although almost certainly it has nothing to do with Jews. Another English name for the instrument is 'gewgaw.'

The jew's-harp was introduced to the concert stage in Europe in the eighteenth century, and numerous virtuoso performers emerged, some of whom performed on two instruments at once, one pitched lower than the other, in order to obtain a complete scale. For the most part, however, in the West the instrument often came to be associated with novelty songs or with children. Indeed, numerous musicians born in the late nineteenth or early twentieth century are known to have played a jew's-harp as children, among them blues musician Robert Johnson, and country musicians Vernon Dalhart and Roy Acuff.

In the 1950s and 1960s, in the wake of the revival of interest in folk and traditional music in both the United States and Europe, the jew's-harp was played on a number of recordings. Generally in the hands of multi-instrumentalists such as Mike Seeger, rather than in those of specialist performers, it was rarely featured with any prominence, although Folkways Records did make an entire album of blues musician Sonny Terry performing on the instrument. It was also featured in the eclectic music of the Incredible String Band (*The Hangman's Beautiful Daughter*, 1968) and in singer-songwriter Leonard Cohen's 'Bird on a Wire' (from the album *Songs from a Room*, 1969). One of its more unusual appearances was when it was played by British disc jockey John Peel on the Third Ear Band album *Alchemy* (1969).

Considerably greater interest in the jew's-harp began to develop in the 1990s, especially in Scandinavia, The Netherlands and the United States, with a regular festival in Norway entirely devoted to the instrument, an annual North American Jew's Harp Festival, and an international congress in Yakutsk, eastern Siberia in 1991 and in Molln, Austria in 1998. One result of this revival of interest and of the accompanying emergence of a new generation of specialist performers was an alteration in the common perception of the instrument as having a poor and restricted sound and as being at best an instrumental curiosity. In the late twentieth century, Dutch jew's-harp authorities Phons Bakx and Henk Postma could write that the jew's-harp was appearing in electronic pop, avant-garde jazz and world music; indeed, they say, 'the overtones of the tiny instrument even shimmer in techno beat dance halls' (1998).

Bibliography

Bakx, Phons, and Postma, Henk. 1998. *The Jew's Harp Column*. http://www.folkworld.de/7/jewsharp.html

Fox, Leonard, ed. 1988. *The Jew's Harp: A Comprehensive Anthology*. Lewisburg, PA: Bucknell University Press.

Pertout, Adrian. 1999–2000. *The Jew's Harp*. http://www.users.bigpond.com/apertout/Jew'sHarp.htm

Wright, Michael. 2000. 'The Jew's Harp, the Fool of Instruments: A Personal View.' *The Living Tradition* 37.

Discographical References

Cohen, Leonard. 'Bird on a Wire.' *Songs from a Room*. Columbia 09767. *1969*: USA.

Incredible String Band, The. *The Hangman's Beautiful Daughter*. Elektra EVKS7 258. *1968*: UK.

Terry, Sonny. *Sonny Terry's New Sound: The Jawharp in Blues and Folk Music*. Folkways FT 3821. *1961*: USA.

Third Ear Band. *Alchemy*. Harvest 756. *1969*: UK.

Discography

Genggong: Balinese Jew's Harp Orchestra. World Music Library 5228. *1997*: Japan.

Trân Quang Hai. *Guimbardes du Monde: Jew's Harps of the World*. Playasound 66009. *1998*: France.

DAVID HORN

Kulintang (also *Kolintang, Kulintangan, Gulintangan, Kakolintang, Engkremong*)

'*Kulintang*' is the name for a set of bossed, pitched bronze gongs used as a traditional instrument in the southern Philippines (Mindanao, Palawan and the Sulu Archipelago), the East Malaysian provinces of Sarawak and Sabah, portions of Kalimantan (Indonesian Borneo) and Brunei. The gongs of the *kulintang* (generally eight in the Philippines but ranging from six to 11 elsewhere) are laid horizontally on two parallel lengths of rope stretched across a wooden frame. The instrument is played by a single player who, either standing or seated on the floor, strikes the gongs both on their bosses and on their rims with a pair of thick, light wooden beaters. The *kulintang* is usually played with an ensemble of drums and other gongs. In the Philippines, the *kulintang* has a central role in and is the main melodic instrument of an ensemble referred to as 'the *kulintang* ensemble' or as simply '*kulintang*.' This ensemble generally consists of one or two large bossed gongs called *agong* (or *agung*), a goblet-shaped drum played with sticks, called *debakan* (or *dadabuan*), a medium-size bossed gong called *babandil* (or *babandir*), and sometimes other gongs or percussion instruments. Smaller versions of the *kulintang*, with wood, bamboo or metal keys rather than gongs (such as the *saronay*, a metallophone with bossed metal keys), are used by children or for practise.

The *Kulintang* in the Philippines

Although gongs of various types were used throughout the Philippine Islands before contact with Europe, more than 400 years of Westernization and colonization have relegated them to more isolated and less Westernized parts of the country. In the Philippines, the *kulintang* is used primarily in the southern islands, where it is played by Muslim and other non-Christian (animist) ethnic groups, each of which has its own repertoires and playing styles. The largest of these groups are the Maranao (from the central part of Mindanao), the Maguindanao (or Magindanao, from the Cotabato area of Mindanao, near Lake Lanao) and the Tausug (from the Sulu Archipelago). Of the three, the Maguindanao playing style is the most virtuosic, although all styles require great skill in both technique and improvisation. Traditionally, the *kulintang* was played by unmarried women (and sometimes young men), although this restriction has gradually eased.

In the 1950s, an awakening interest in indigenous music and dance led to a diffusion of the *kulintang* throughout the Philippines. In the late 1950s and early 1960s, composers such as Lucrecia Kasilag and José Maceda began experimenting with the use of the *kulintang* in combination with various other Western and Filipino instruments; they were joined in the 1970s by Ramón Pagayon Santos and Edru Abraham. Also in the 1950s came the formation of folkloric dance troupes such as the famous Bayanihan Philippine Dance Company. These groups, which presented dances from all parts of the country, used *kulintang* music to accompany their performances of Muslim dances from the southern Philippines. Most of the *kulintang* players in these groups, however, were Christian and were rarely members of the ethnolinguistic groups in which the music is traditionally performed. As a result of the widespread performances of such groups, *kulintang* music, although indigenous only to the southern Philippines, emerged as one of the most visible forms of Filipino traditional music both in the Philippines and around the world.

By the 1960s, a few of the *kulintang* performers in these dance troupes had begun to experiment with popular music, trying out rock 'n' roll or Latin rhythms on the *kulintang*. However, it was not until the mid-1970s that a small number of Filipino folk-rock groups began using the *kulintang* (and other indigenous instruments) alongside acoustic guitars and other Western instruments, creating a distinct, 'neo-ethnic' subgenre of Filipino popular music. For these groups, whose Tagalog-language lyrics centered on environmental and social issues as well as protests against the government of Ferdinand Marcos, the *kulintang* not only served as an aural representation of indigenous, pre-colonial identity, but also showed solidarity with the Muslim and other non-Christian groups of the southern Philippines (some of which were engaging in armed resistance against the central government at that time). Although the 'neo-ethnic' style came to be described by its players and listeners as *katutubo* (literally, 'of our own' or 'indigenous'), most of the *kulintang* players in these groups (as in the dance troupes) were Christian rather than Muslim.

The first Filipino group to achieve fame for using the *kulintang* in a folk-rock context was Asin (literally, 'Salt'),

in which the instrument was played by the late Cesar 'Saro' Bañares, Jr. The group's classic song, 'Ang Bayan Kong Sinilangan' (recorded in 1978 but written a year earlier), is generally considered to be the first recorded popular song to feature the *kulintang*. Although the patriotic song 'Ako ay Pilipino' (commissioned by Imelda Marcos, wife of the president, and composed by songwriter George Canseco in 1979) featured a brief excerpt of *kulintang* music in its introduction, the *kulintang* music was likely taken from an ethnographic recording. Another important early recording featuring the *kulintang* was Apo Hiking Society's 1982 hit 'American Junk,' with humorous lyrics critical of the United States' cultural dominance of the Philippines.

In the 1980s and 1990s, an increasing (but comparatively small) number of like-minded folk-rock groups began to use the *kulintang* as an integral part of their sound. Among these were Ang Grupong Pendong (the *kulintang* played by Chat Coloma-Aban), Waling-Waling, studio-only pop music 'supergroup' Lokal Brown (the *kulintang* played by Saro Bañares), Popong Landero and Grace Nono. Many of these artists found common ground in the record label operated by the nongovernmental organization DEMS (Development Education Media Services Foundation), based in Davao, Mindanao. By the early 1990s, Joey Ayala and his group Bagong Lumad ('New Native') (with the *kulintang* played by Ayala's sister Cynthia Alexander, and later by Bayang Barrios) had achieved widespread fame with their brand of socially conscious 'neo-ethnic' pop music, bringing the style to new audiences. At the beginning of the twenty-first century, Ayala's *kulintang* player was the young virtuoso Malou Matute, the first graduate of the University of the Philippines' traditional music program.

The trend of using the *kulintang* in popular music has led to a greater number of more mainstream Filipino artists and groups sporadically employing the *kulintang* (or, occasionally, an electronically sampled *kulintang*) in their music, usually for 'exotic' effect. Since the late 1980s, the instrument has been featured in the contexts of hard rock (in the work of the band Pen-Pen), jazz (in the work of saxophonist Tots Tolentino), reggae (in the work of the group Tropical Depression) and industrial music (in the work of the group Identity Crisis). Additionally, composer Ryan Cayabyáb has featured the *kulintang* in his successful theatrical productions, and pop singer Gary Valenciano often plays the instrument in his live shows.

Groups utilizing the *kulintang* in more experimental contexts include KONTRA-GAPI (a contraction of 'Ang *Kont*emporaryong *Ga*melan *Pi*lipino,' or 'The Contemporary Filipino Gamelan'), a pan-indigenous 'total theater' ensemble formed by University of the Philippines professor Edru Abraham in 1989; the improvisational percussion ensemble Pinikpikan; 'neo-ethnic' multi-instrumentalist Arthur 'Ato' Mariano and his project Earth Music; and the world fusion group Makiling Ensemble. Abraham selected the Indonesian term 'gamelan' for his group's name to reinforce the historical connections between the Malay cultures of island Southeast Asia and their shared gong-chime musical tradition, a heritage that he feels has largely been obscured in the Westernized Philippines.

The lack of a single standard *kulintang* tuning presents a challenge to those wishing to integrate the instrument into popular music ensembles. Typically, slight alterations in the tuning of individual gongs are made so that they will match the tuning of guitars and other Western instruments. Nevertheless, one or more gongs will often retain their idiosyncratic tunings. This, combined with the instrument's complex acoustics, can cause it to sound slightly out of pitch with the equally tempered scale, but players acknowledge that this is part of the charm of using a traditional instrument. Some players combine two sets of *kulintang* in order to obtain a greater number of pitches.

The Filipino *Kulintang* in North America

Within the United States, where (according to the 2000 census) those of Filipino ancestry form the second-largest Asian group, the *kulintang* has had a presence since the late 1960s, through the instruction of transplanted *kulintang* masters Usopay Hamdag Cadar and, later, Danongan Kalanduyan. Through study with Filipino teachers both in the United States and abroad, a number of North American musicians (of both Filipino and non-Filipino descent) have gained proficiency in playing the instrument. By the 1980s, a few of these musicians had begun mixing *kulintang* music with popular musics and jazz. At the forefront of this trend has been the California-based ensemble Kulintang Arts (founded in 1985), which has used the *kulintang* in jazz and in Afro-Cuban and other nontraditional contexts. Other North American musicians who have used the *kulintang* in new contexts include former Kulintang Arts member Frank Holder; world percussionist and ethnomusicologist Royal Hartigan; Asian-American jazz composer Fred Ho; Filipino-American free jazz drummer/percussionist Susie Ibarra; Asian-American multi-instrumentalist Forrest Fang; Filipino-American singer-songwriter Eleanor Academia; San Francisco-based pan-Asian ensemble Asian Crisis; multiethnic ensemble Mahal (also from San Francisco); Ohio-based ensemble Pointless Orchestra; and Vancouver multi-instrumentalist Randy Raine-Reusch. Since the late 1990s, an electronically sampled *kulintang* has featured promin-

ently in the electronic drum-and-bass music of Filipino-American artist e:trinity (Elson Trinidad).

The *Kulintangan* and Other Bossed Gong Rows in Borneo

For centuries, Borneo's close proximity to the Philippines has resulted in the intermingling of the various cultures found throughout these regions. Gong rows are found throughout Borneo, especially in the northernmost parts of the island: in Sabah and Sarawak, in Brunei and in parts of Kalimantan. Sabah is located on the northeast coast of Borneo, the closest to the Philippines, and its gong row is called a *kulintangan*. The *kulintangan* is usually played in a small ensemble with a drum called *gendang* and two sizes of hanging bossed gongs called *tawak* and *bandil*. Although the *kulintangan* is still used mostly in traditional music, some of the musicians of the Sabah Museum are experimenting with its use in more contemporary music.

The greatest use of the Bornean *kulintang* is found in Sarawak, where young musicians have an active interest in integrating traditional instruments into pop and world music. Although the Melanau of the central north coast of Sarawak have a six-gong *kulintang*, the instrument of choice for contemporary musicians seems to be the Iban *engkremong*, with a series of either six or eight bossed gongs. Traditionally, the *engkremong* was accompanied by the *gendang*, the *tawak* and a smaller suspended bossed gong called *babendai*. These accompanying instruments are occasionally used in contemporary music as well.

There are a number of groups located in Kuching, the capital of Sarawak, that regularly use the *engkremong* in contemporary music, mostly for its percussive possibilities. The most active is the group Tuku Kame, made up of the musicians employed by the Sarawak Cultural Village and led by composer and arranger Narawi Rashidi. The group regularly performs internationally and released its first, eponymous CD in 1999. Another fairly active group that regularly uses the *engkremong* is Mitra, comprising the musicians of the Ministry of Social Development. This group has also made a CD and regularly performs at state functions and festivals in Sarawak. A third group worthy of mention is the newly formed Sayu Ateng, supported by the Ibraco company. Sayu Ateng, which recorded its debut CD in 2000, has performed only a few times in Sarawak (at the Rainforest World Music Festival), but has also performed in Singapore. These three groups have helped to stimulate an even greater interest in traditional instruments, both in Sarawak and in the surrounding regions of Singapore and Peninsular Malaysia.

Bibliography

Baes, Jonas, and Baes, Amapola. 1998. 'East-West Synthesis or Cultural Hegemony?: Questions on the Use of Indigenous Elements in Philippine Popular Music.' *Perfect Beat: The Pacific Journal of Research into Contemporary Music and Popular Culture* 4(1): 47–55.

Butocan, Aga Mayo. 1987. *Palabunibunyan: A Repertoire of Musical Pieces for the Maguindanaon Kulintangan*. Manila: Philippine Women's University.

Cadar, Usopay Hamdag. 1996. 'The Maranao Kolintang Music and Its Journey in America.' *Asian Music* 27(2): 131–48.

Familara, Len. *The Politics of Pop Music*. http://www.upd.edu.ph/~updinfo/sep_oct99/popmusic.htm

Kontemporaryong Gamelan Pilipino (KONTRA-GAPI). http://www.univie.ac.at/Voelkerkunde/Asian-Pacific/aufi/music/ kgapi.htm

Kularts (Kulintang Arts Incorporated). http://www.kul-arts.org/

Lockard, Craig A. 1996. 'Popular Musics and Politics in Modern Southeast Asia: A Comparative Analysis.' *Asian Music* 27(2): 149–99.

Maceda, José Montserrat. 1963. *The Music of the Magindanao in the Philippines*. Ph.D. thesis, University of California, Los Angeles.

Otto, Steven Walter. 1985. 'The Muranao Kakolintang: An Approach to the Repertoire.' *The Technician* 3(1) (Special issue).

Roche, David. 1996. 'Brave New Worlds: Mindanaoan Kulintang Music and Cambodian Classical Dance in America.' In *The Changing Faces of Tradition: A Report on the Folk and Traditional Arts in the United States*, ed. Elizabeth Peterson. Washington, DC: National Endowment for the Arts, 34–41.

Santos, Ramón Pagayon. 1991. 'The Philippines.' In *New Music in the Orient: Essays on Composition in Asia Since World War II*, ed. Harrison Ryker. Buren, The Netherlands: Frits Knuf Publishers, 157–76.

Discographical References

Apo Hiking Society. 'American Junk.' *The Best of Apo Hiking Society*. Bell Films Inc./Universal CD-P-94,075. *1982*: Philippines.

Asin. 'Ang Bayan Kong Sinilangan.' *Masdan Mo Ang Kapaligiran*. Vicor VCD-K-073. *1994*: Philippines.

Ledesma, Kuh. 'Ako ay Pilipino.' *Ako ay Pilipino*, Vol. 2. Vicor BCD-K-053. *1994*: Philippines.

Sayu Ateng. *Sayu Ateng*. Ibraco. *2000*: Malaysia.

Tuku Kame. *Tuku Kame*. Sarawak Cultural Village. *1999*: Malaysia.

Discography

Abraham, Edru, and Ang Kontemporaryong Gamelan Pilipino. *Edru Abraham at ang Kontemporaryong Gamelan Pilipino*. Produksyong Itawit-Ibanag. *1992*: Philippines.

Abraham, Edru, and Ang Kontemporaryong Gamelan Pilipino. *Gong at Ritmo, Lunggating Pilipino*. Produksyong Itawit-Ibanag. *1995*: Philippines.

Abraham, Edru, and Ang Kontemporaryong Gamelan Pilipino. *World Beat—World Music: Filipino*. Produksyong Itawit-Ibanag. *1995*: Philippines.

Academia, Eleanor. *Oracle of the Black Swan*. Black Swan Records. *1998*: USA.

Ang Grupong Pendong. *Dito sa Lupa*. Neo (Viva) VCD-94-87. *1994*: Philippines.

Ang Grupong Pendong. *Panahon*. National Council of Churches. *1991*: Philippines.

Asin. *Masdan Mo Ang Kapaligiran*. Vicor VCD-K-073. *1994*: Philippines.

Asin. *Pag-ibig, Pagbabago, Pagpapatuloy*. Vicor SCD-070. *2001*: Philippines.

Asin. *Sa Atubiling Panahon*. Ivory IRC-L-A215. *1985*: Philippines.

Ayala, Joey. 'Tayo ang Lupa.' *Lupa't Langit*. Star. *1997*: Philippines.

Ayala, Joey, and Bagong Lumad. 'Sariwang Hangin.' *Mga awit ng Tanod-lupa*. WEA Philippines (now Universal). *1990*: Philippines.

Bayanihan Philippine Dance Company, The. *Bayanihan Philippine Dance Company as Presented by S. Hurok*. Monitor MFS 322. *ca. 1959*: USA.

e:trinity. *e:trinity*. Pacific City PACD 0001. *1999*: USA.

Fang, Forrest. *The Blind Messenger*. Cuneiform Rune 98. *1997*: USA.

Hanopol, Mike. *Tribu Kemistri*. Yikes Y7771-2. *1997*: USA.

Hartigan, Royal. *Blood Drum Spirit* (2 CDs). Transparent. *1998*: USA.

Ho, Fred Wei-han. *A Song for Manong: The Soundtrack to Part 3 of Bamboo That Snaps Back*. Asian Improv AIR 0003. *1988*: USA.

Ibarra, Susie, and Charles, Denis. *Drum Talk*. Wobbly Rail WOB005. *1998*: USA.

Ibarra, Susie, and Tsahar, Assif. 'Dream Song #3.' *Home Cookin'*. Hopscotch HOP 1. *1999*: USA.

Kulintang Arts. *Ancient Rhythms/Urban Sounds*. Kulintang Arts Inc. *1989*: USA.

Kulintang Arts. *Cycles: Timeless Rituals to Ancient Icons*. Kulintang Arts Inc. *1992*: USA.

Ledesma, Kuh. 'Narito ang Eden.' *Ako ay Pilipino*, Vol. 1. Vicor BCD-K-052. *1994*: Philippines.

Lokal Brown. *This Is Lokal Brown*. Ivory IRC-L-B047. *1988*: Philippines.

Makiling Ensemble. *Medyo Modern*. N/A. *2000*: Philippines.

Nono, Grace. 'Ani.' *Isang Buhay*. BMG Pilipinas Asia CD 65. *1997*: Philippines.

Ori Kaplan Percussion Ensemble, The. 'Sky Drops' and 'Dark Sun.' *Gongol*. Knitting Factory KFW 284. *2001*: USA.

Pinikpikan. *Atas*. Tao Music 008. *1999*: Philippines.

Pinikpikan. *Metronomad*. Tao Music 003. *1996*: Philippines.

Pointless Orchestra. 'Yet Another Abstract Piece.' *Lives: A Pointless Night Out*. Without Fear WFR 0001. *1997*: USA.

Razon, Bo. 'Maracatu Ti Saronay.' *Biyahero*. BMG Pilipinas Asia CD 120. *1998*: Philippines.

Tolentino, Tots. 'Etnik Daw.' *Color Real*. Dyna DYP 90/35. *1993*: Philippines.

Tropical Depression. *Kapayapaan*. Neo (Viva) VIVA94092. *1995*: Philippines.

Waling-Waling. *Earth Flight*. Star Records. *1997*: Philippines.

Visual Recording

Geffrey, William. 1997. 'Jewels of the Islands: Filipino Music.' Centre Pacific Productions (video).

DAVID BADAGNANI, PEDRO R. ABRAHAM, JR.

and RANDY RAINE-REUSCH

Lagerphone

In its modern form the lagerphone is of Australian origin and is a percussive instrument that produces a rhythmic effect similar to that of the tambourine. The instrument is so named because it is generally made from an old broom handle with beer-bottle tops loosely nailed onto part of the shaft and the broom head; small bells and miniature cymbals are also often added. Other names attributed to the instrument include the 'boozaphone' (coined in the 1950s by the Gay Charmers Old Time Band of Lake Charm, in the Australian state of Victoria) and the Murrumbidgee Rattler (Atherton 1990).

To play the instrument, the player strikes it with a serrated stick to the beat of the tune it is accompanying, and thumps the pole on the floor on the offbeat. Drawing the serrated edge of the stick across the broom handle at intervals creates interesting sound and rhythmic effects, while shaking the instrument makes the bottle tops rattle even more. More sophisticated models have a cowbell or car-light reflector added, which produces 'glock' sounds when struck – a style of lagerphone featured in an article in the *Australasian Post* in the mid-1950s (Meredith 2000). Colored bottle tops are often used to spell out a band's logo on the broom head or on a separate signboard.

Forerunners of the lagerphone include the Napoleonic Jingling Johnny, a marching stick covered in bells and used like a baton or staff to beat time and to keep marchers in step, and rhythm sticks covered in shells and used for ceremonies by the Torres Strait Islanders and the Cape York Aboriginals (Edwards 1979). Similar instruments may have been used by British skiffle bands. In 1988, the Victorian Folk Music Club publication *Collector's Choice* (Vol. 3, p. 84) published a photograph of a miners' highland band in Costerfield, Victoria, taken in 1925, showing a kettle containing stones, attached to a pole, that was used for keeping time; and Campbell Holmes, trombonist with the Wedderburn Oldtimers Band, recalls seeing a lagerphone-style instrument used by a makeshift band near Darwin in 1943 (Holmes 1999).

The first known record of the lagerphone in its modern form dates back to a 1950s country talent quest and concert that took place in the town of Holbrook, New South Wales. A rabbit poisoner won first prize with the instrument, which is now held by the Woolpack Inn Museum in Holbrook. A local man, Claud Meredith, was so impressed that he constructed his own model, using beer-bottle tops, and presented it to his brother, John Meredith. He in turn, as founder of the Bushwhackers Band of Sydney in 1952, introduced the instrument to the band, dubbing it the 'lagerphone' (J. Meredith 1999).

The Bushwhackers were active in collecting and performing 'bush songs' from rural Australia, using the button accordion, lagerphone and 'bush bass' as accompaniment. The band raised the profile of the lagerphone through its recording of some of this material on 78 rpm records for the Wattle label, which were in turn broadcast widely over the radio, and through its appearance in 1954 in a popular play entitled *Reedy River*. The instrument's profile was raised further by articles on how to construct a lagerphone that appeared in such popular magazines as the *Australian Magazine* and the *Australasian Post*. This national publicity inspired the formation of a number of 'bush bands' across Australia over the following decades (for example, the Cobbers, the Melbourne-based Bushwackers and Mulga Bill's Bicycle Band). However, John Manifold, writing in the *Australian Tradition* in 1973, points out that their instruments had never been typically used in the bush, but were reminiscent of the 'foo foo' or skiffle groups that played on ships.

The lagerphone can be an extremely interesting and effective rhythm instrument in the hands of a master player such as Brian Loughlin, a character actor and the original lagerphone player with the Bushwhackers (his performances can be heard on the Bushwhackers' Wattle label recordings of the early to mid-1950s). Other excellent lagerphone players were Barry Golding and Liz Eager of Mulga Bill's Bicycle Band, which recorded in the

1970s. More contemporary recordings include those of the Cobbers and the Melbourne-based Bushwackers.

Bibliography

Atherton, Michael. 1990. *Australian Made – Australian Played: Handcrafted Musical Instruments from Didjeridu to Synthesiser.* Kensington: New South Wales University Press.

'Bottle Tops in D♭.' 1954. *Australian Magazine* (16 February): 42.

Edwards, Ron. 1979. *Skills of the Australian Bushman.* Adelaide: Rigby.

Ellis, Peter. 1993. 'Musical Instruments: Lagerphone.' In *The Oxford Companion to Australian Folklore,* ed. Gwenda Beed Davey and Graham Seal. Melbourne and New York: Oxford University Press, 289.

Holmes, Campbell. 1999. Personal communication with author.

Manifold, John. 1973. 'The Bush Band.' *Australian Tradition* 32 (September): 21.

Meredith, John. 1999. Personal communication with author.

Meredith, John. 2000. Personal communication with author.

Discography

Australian Bush Songs by Bushwhackers Band (Sydney) (EP). Wattle B1. *1957*: Australia.

Bullamakanka. *Bullas Live.* EMI TCEMX 430029/TCFA 157145. *1985*: Australia.

Cobbers, The. *All for Me Grog.* WEA 600039. *1978*: Australia. Reissue: Cobbers, The. *All for Me Grog.* Festival C37484. *1980*: Australia.

Colonials, The. *Waltzing Matilda.* Harbour Records MLF 264. *ca. 1971*: Australia.

Mulga Bill's Bicycle Band. *In Concert Recording.* Basket BBBS-002. *1973*: Australia.

The Bushwackers Dance Album. Image LP 815. *1980*: Australia.

The Bushwackers (Melbourne) (EP). Image IEP-5. *1976*: Australia.

Wild Colonials, The. *Euabalong Ball.* EMI SOEX 9738. *1971*: Australia.

PETER ELLIS

Maracas

A maraca is a rattle used as a percussion instrument, most commonly played in pairs for popular music, but played singly as a healing instrument in numerous rituals throughout South America and the Caribbean. Often made of the dried-out gourd of the *guira* (squash), or of stretched and stitched leather, maracas can also be made from wood, straw, coconut, metal or plastic. The common factor is that they will be filled with seeds or material that resonates inside the gourd to create a good shaking, rattling sound. The type of material used, the number of seeds and so on depend on the aesthetic of the maker or player. Belonging to the family of musical instruments called idiophones or autophones, maracas are a key part of Cuban *son*, salsa, rumba, *charanga* and *trova* ensembles, and they are found all over the world in big bands and orchestras that play any form of 'Latin'-influenced music. Maracas, which may be played by a lead or second singer, have a key role in maintaining the complex rhythms of ensembles and are often used to start a piece off.

Attached to each rattle or gourd is a cylindrical wooden stick, by which the instrument is held. When a maraca is held by the stick and shaken, the seeds or other material within the container hit the inside wall of the rattle or gourd and produce the instrument's characteristic rhythmic sound. Maracas have a sharp sound, which in some cultures is said to imitate the sound of rain or of rattlesnakes. Sometimes, one of the rattles has a deeper tone than the other, and traditionally the deeper-toned rattle is held in the left hand.

Maracas range in size from small egg-shaped forms to large apple and more elongated shapes. Those used in Venezuelan *joropo* tend to be small; those used to accompany South American bolero singing are often medium; those used in pan-Latin salsa tend to be medium-large; and those used for open-air carnival processions tend to be large. Difference in size may depend upon usage and, again, the aesthetic of the player. Different maracas also have different timbres, which may correspond to the type of music to be performed.

Played in a variety of ways, maracas are shaken rhythmically in time with many of the movements made by dancing feet, and most players dance as they shake them. Occasionally, only one maraca is played, held in one hand and shaken from up to down to produce a constant rhythm. As part of Afro-Cuban ritual, notably Santería healing ceremonies, one maraca is used and shaken both regularly and irregularly. A solo maraca made from a gourd and often covered with woven material is also used by Chilean Araucanian/Mapuche female shamans in healing ceremonies. For popular music, two maracas, held in two hands, are usually played. The shaking pattern is the same, from up to down, but the maracas may also be used alternately to produce a constant rhythm and a great deal of timbral texture. The difference in tone between the two rattles of the maracas is particularly noticeable in African-Caribbean music: the maraca played with the left hand may be tuned deeper and is used to mark the weaker tempo (in contra-tempo), while the maraca played with the right hand may be sharper and marks the strong tempo as well as the ornamentations (appoggiatura, syncopations and so on). As an instrument, maracas are limited, and require the player (generally called a *maraquero*) to develop sophisticated rhythmical and gestural techniques. In most musics that are improvised, maraca players can display virtuoso qualities. Maraca players have a key role in much popular music, and this role should never be underestimated. For the Venezuelan *joropo* (played in 3/4 or 6/8 time), it is said that virtuosos of the instrument, such as Maximo B. Teppa, have apparently created original polyrhythms.

Maracas have long been used throughout the Americas. The origin of those used in tropical regions may have coincided with the use of the *totumo*, a squash fruit still used to make maracas. The instrument played a prominent role in the ancient religious rituals of pre-Columbian Indians, who often richly decorated maracas with feathers, incisions, varied coloring, and even gold coverings. The maraca has long been associated with religious ceremony and ritual.

In Brazil, the *maracá* or *maracaxá* is derived from the Tupi *mbara'ká*, a root percussion instrument used by Brazilian Indians in religious and war ceremonies. It is analogous to the ancient Egyptian sistrum, the Hebrew *salterio* and the Christian organ. Made from a squash containing little stones, with an inserted wooden handle, it was decorated on top with feathers of the *guará* (a Brazilian bird) and sometimes with human hair. The sound of a *maracá* made of palm leaves tied with fibrous strings closely imitated that of the rattlesnake, while another made of *cipós* (aerial tree-climbing plants) had small stones inside. The *maracá* exercised a powerful influence over the vision and imagination of Amerindians, and was used as a war staff by the Tupis. Other Brazilian instruments included in the same family are the *pau de chuva*, the *caxixi*, the *ganzá* and the *cabaza*.

In Brazil, the maraca was held in such deep respect that, after receiving a blessing from the *Pajé* (shaman) of a tribe, it was kept in a special ritual tabernacle, to be taken out only by the *Pajé*; it was thus made his personal instrument. Called *chocalho*, it is still played by the *Pajé*; the seeds inside are called '*contas de nossa senhora*' (the counters of Our Lady). The *chocalho* is also used as a toy by children in indigenous Brazilian villages. Among the indigenous people of the Amazon, a *maracá* representing a type of idol made of a hollow human skull has been found; others are in the form of *jabutís*, made from cooked mud and containing balls of the same material.

Different kinds of maracas are used throughout Latin America for many types of rural and urban popular music. In Colombia, they are used in *cumbia* and *gaitas* groups; smaller maracas called *gapachos* are played in the *chirimía* ensembles of the Andean regions. In the Col-

ombian plains, maracas (called *clavellinas*) are used, as in Venezuela, to accompany the music of the plains (*pasajes*, *joropos* and so on). In Paraguay, maracas made of a fruit called *porrongo* are used for certain rituals in which they are played only by men.

In Panama, an instrument called *zambumbia* (a closed hollow cylinder with dried seeds inside) on occasion replaces the maracas when *cumbia* is played. The *Cunas* Indians (*Kantules*) use a maraca called a *nasisi* (*sonajero*) for a religious ceremony: the player shakes it with the right hand while playing a melody on the *kamu* (pan flute) with the left hand. Since pre-Columbian times, maracas called *sonajas* or *ajacaxtli* have been played in Mexico. In Haiti, maracas are called *asson*, and in some places in Chile they are known as *huada*.

At carnival time in countries such as Panama, Martinique, Cartagena and Brazil, a variation on the traditional maraca may be found: it is made of wood or metal with balls at both ends, filled inside with little metal balls or seeds and attached by a wooden or metal cylinder. Such maracas are capable of great volume and allow the performance of acrobatic movements. They are often painted with different motifs and colors.

Ritual instruments similar to maracas include the Cuban *erikundi*, which is covered in leather and is the sole instrument used for the *carabalí-efik* in the Afro-Cuban *Abakuá* cult. In pairs, such maracas are also used in popular music groups, particularly *vieja trova* and old *son* groups in Havana, and may indicate the player's allegiance to the *Abakuá* cult. In Haiti, there is a similar instrument called *chachá*. The *chekeré*, also known as *agué* or *aggbé*, originally a Yoruba ritual instrument found in Brazil, Cuba and other countries, is a large shaker gourd covered on the outside with crossed and knotted string net, with beads woven into the knots. The instruments vary in diameter, but are often large, and they are filled with dry seeds to provide rhythm. The player shakes the net while beating the sides of the gourd with the palm of the hand. The beads of the net and the seeds inside the instrument vibrate at a different rate to give rise to a 'double shake.' This produces rocketing levels of rattling, which seem to increase in power as the instrument is used. The *chekeré* is used in various Afro-Cuban rituals.

Maracas are an integral part of the rhythm sections of Latin American ensembles. The traditional trio of the Cuban *son* uses *tres* (a small guitar with three sets of double strings), guitar and maracas; the traditional trio of the Venezuelan *joropo* uses *cuatro* (a small guitar with four strings), harp and maracas; the traditional trio of Mexican boleros uses *requinto* (a small guitar like the *cuatro*), guitar and maracas; and the traditional trio of Paraguayan music uses harp, guitar and maracas. There

Example 1 The Cuban *son* maracas beat.

Example 2 The Puerto Rican *bomba* maracas beat.

are various ways of playing the maracas, depending on the musical style (mambo, bolero, *son*, *guaracha* and so on) and the musician. Often, the playing of the maracas is assigned to the lead singer of the group (the *sonero*).

Cuban musical groups incorporate both European and traditional instruments into groups and orchestras without any distinction. These will include percussion instruments (such as maracas or bongos). These instruments are found in fixed numbers in ensembles like trios, quartets, sextets, French *charanga* orchestras and *orquestas típicas* (incorporating some variations), and also in band-type groups that include saxophones, clarinets and other instruments like those used in jazz. Several examples of the use of traditional instruments like maracas are found in the repertoire of Cuban chamber music. One such example is the Afro-Cuban capriccio for six mixed voices and percussion, entitled *Maracas y Bongó*, by the Cuban composer Emilio Grenet.

Modern composers have used maracas in their works, including Edgard Varèse ('Ionisation, for 13 Percussion Instruments'), Sergei Prokofiev (*Romeo and Juliet*) and Malcolm Arnold (*Symphony No. 4*). Occasionally, the maracas are used as batons for drums; this effect was used by Leonard Bernstein in his *Symphony No. 1* ('Jeremiah'), Harold Farberman in his *Concerto for Jazz Drummer and Orchestra*, and Marius Constant in the ballet *Le Paradis Perdu*. Pierre Boulez uses three pairs of maracas, of different sizes, and with tunings from the sharpest to the deepest in *Rituel*. Maracas are also found in *Saudades do Brasil* by Darius Milhaud, and in *Cuban Overture* by George Gershwin.

Makers of maracas and luthiers include the Venezuelan known as 'Pan con queso' and the Colombian known as 'El Piernas.' Such brand names of percussion instruments as Latin Percussion (LP), Afro Percussion and Meinl have promoted the instrument worldwide. Instrumentalists and singers of Caribbean music have also promoted maracas in various periods – for example, Machito (Frank Grillo), Beny Moré, Rubén Blades, Pete 'El Conde' Rodriguez, Issac Delgado, Pérez Prado, Hector Lavoie, Ismael Quintana and Adalberto Santiago.

Among the musical styles that use the maracas are *son* (Ex. 1), *son montuno*, mambo, *danzón*, *pachanga*, *songo*, *chachachá* and *bomba* (Ex. 2).

Bibliography

Arnold, Denis, ed. 1983. *The New Oxford Companion to Music*. Oxford and New York: Oxford University Press.

Basso, Alberto. 1983. *Dizionario Enciclopedico Univerzale Della Musica e Dei Musicisti* [World Dictionary Encyclopedia of Music and Musicians]. Torino: UTET (Unione Tipográfico Editrice Torinece).

Blades, James, and Schechter, John M. 1984. 'Maracas.' In *The New Grove Dictionary of Musical Instruments*, Vol. 2, ed. Stanley Sadie. London: Macmillan, 611–12.

Casanova Oliva, Ana Victoria. 1988. *Problemática Organológica Cubana* [Cuban Organological Problematic]. Havana: Ediciones Casa de las Américas.

Garay, Narciso. 1982. *Tradiciones y Cantares de Panamá* [Traditions and Songs from Panama]. 2nd ed. Panama: Litho Impresora Panamá S.A.

Lapique Becali, Zoila. 1963. *Catalogación y clasificación de la música cubana* [Cataloging and Classification of Cuban Music]. Havana: Departamento de Publicaciones de la Biblioteca José Martí.

Marcuse, Sibyl. 1975. *A Survey of Musical Instruments*. New York: Harper & Row.

Mauleón, Rebeca. 1993. *Salsa Guidebook for Piano and Ensemble*. Petaluma, CA: Sher Music Co.

Orovio, Helio. 1981. *Diccionario de la música cubana. Biográfico y técnico* [Dictionary of Cuban Music: Biographical and Technical]. Havana: Editorial Letras Cubanas.

Ortíz, Fernando. 1952. *Los instrumentos de la música afrocubana* [The Instruments of Afro-Cuban Music]. Havana: Dirección de Cultura, Ministerio de Educación.

Perdomo Escobar, José Ignacio. 1980. *Historia de la Música en Colombia* [History of the Music of Colombia]. 5th ed. Bogotá: Plaza & Janes, Editores Colombia Ltda.

Roberts, John Storm. 1982. *El Toque Latino* [The Latin

Beat], trans. Aurora Merino. México, D.F.: Editores Asociados M., S.A. EDAMEX.

Sinzig, Frei Pedro. 1959. *Diccionario Musical* [Musical Dictionary]. Rio de Janeiro: Livraria Kosmos Editora.

Veiga de Oliveira, Ernesto. 1966. *Instrumentos Musicais Populares Portugueses* [Portuguese Popular Musical Instruments]. Lisbon: Fundação Calouste Gulbenkian.

Zarate, Manuel F. 1962. *Tambor y Socavón* [Drum and Hollow]. Panama: Imprenta Nacional.

Discographical References

Arnold, Malcolm. *Symphonies Nos. 3 and 4*. Naxos 553739. *1998*: UK.

Bernstein, Leonard. *Jeremiah/The Age of Anxiety*. Chandos 9889. *2001*: UK.

Boulez, Pierre. *Boulez: Rituel/Éclat/Multiples*. Sony 45839. *1990*: France.

Farberman, Harold. *Farberman: Concerto for Jazz Drummer and Orchestra; Shchedrin: Carmen Suite*. Bis 382. *1986*: Sweden.

Gershwin, George. *Rhapsody in Blue/Cuban Overture/Porgy and Bess Suite/An American in Paris*. Deutsche Grammophon 431625. *1990*: Germany.

Milhaud, Darius. *La Création du monde/Le Boeuf sur le toit/ Saudades do Brasil*. EMI 47845. *1987*: France.

Prokofiev, Sergei. *Romeo and Juliet Suites*. ASV 885. *1994*: UK.

Varèse, Edgard. 'Ionisation, for 13 Percussion Instruments.' *Varèse: The Complete Works*. London 460208. *1998*: UK.

EDWIN RICARDO PITRE VÁSQUEZ (trans. ZUZANA PICK)
and JAN FAIRLEY

Marimba

Introduction

The marimba is considered to be a type of xylophone, the origins of which date back many centuries. More specifically, marimbas may be classified as struck idiophones. Some of the earliest of these instruments are thought to have originated in Indonesia or Africa. Wherever their origins lie, at the close of the twentieth century many of the world's cultures had some type of xylophone-like instrument(s), some of which could be classified as marimbas.

In Europe, North America, Asia and other regions, the marimba has a limited role as a solo concert instrument, and is also heard occasionally in contemporary chamber music as well as in jazz, New Age music and other popular genres. In other parts of the world, namely Africa and Latin America, it is often heard and performed in the context of traditional and folk music. In Mesoamerica, the instruments have an extended range, and groups of players often perform simultaneously on the same instruments, as opposed to the concert-hall approach of a single player performing on a single instrument. It is in Latin America, most especially in Mexico and the nations of Central America, that the marimba enjoys its greatest popularity.

In Mesoamerica, the term '*marimba orquesta*' indicates that other instruments will accompany the marimba (usually trumpets, saxophones, drumset, bass and auxiliary percussion). The term '*marimba*' or '*marimba pura*' denotes an ensemble that includes several players on one marimba or two (ranging from four to seven players) but no other instruments. In Guatemala, however, *marimba pura* (ironically) also means a trio consisting of a *marimba doble* (also called *grande*), *marimba cuache* and trap drumset.

Forms of Marimba

The Chiapan (Mexican) and Guatemalan marimbas used in popular music have two basic forms: the diatonic instrument, sometimes called the *marimba sencilla* (single keyboard); and the chromatic instrument, the *marimba doble* (double keyboard), the latter being similar in configuration to a piano. The part of the instrument that is struck is a set of graduated wooden bars (15″ (38 cm) to 4″ (10 cm) in length, with graduated widths), commonly referred to as *teclas* or keys.

In North America, Europe, Japan, Mexico and Guatemala, the wooden bars are suspended by means of holes drilled through each bar at two (non-vibrating) nodal points. Each bar is then connected consecutively with a long cord that is threaded through each hole and then strung through suspension pegs, thus permitting maximum freedom of vibration. Not all *marimba sencillas* are constructed in this way. Nicaraguan marimbas and some Honduran ones have two vertical holes drilled in each key and a cord threaded through that wraps directly onto rubber or other material already fixed onto the frame. The keys are graduated in size and suspended on their cords over rectangular resonating chambers that are open at the top and closed at the bottom. The length of each resonator (along with its air volume) is measured precisely so that it will acoustically amplify and resonate with the fundamental pitch of its own key, thus producing the optimum enhancement of tone. Just above the closed bottom of each resonator is a protruding piece of wax fastened over an aperture. Over this opening is stretched a thin sheath of pig intestine that vibrates sympathetically when the bars are struck, creating a buzzing effect. This is called *tela* (often referred to as *telilla* in Nicaragua, Honduras and Guatemala).

The Guatemalan keyboard is distinct in that the chromatic notes are aligned in a different manner from that of other marimbas. The accidental pitches are moved to the left and are placed directly above their corresponding pitches (i.e., C♯ above C and so on). This presents particular challenges to performers unfamiliar with Guatemalan marimba performance practise. The difference in the keyboard is indeed a distinctive feature of instrument construction as well as another source of nationalistic pride in the marimba, identifying these instruments as unmistakably Guatemalan.

The range of each particular instrument determines the number of keys (and corresponding resonators). The sizes and ranges of instruments vary from maker to maker, but the full-size chromatic instrument is usually 6 1/2 octaves (C^1 to f^4). Smaller chromatic instruments (called *requintas*) are usually less than five octaves, but do not go below the second 'C' on the full-size instrument. A large instrument would have upward of 78 keys, and a smaller one fewer than 60.

To play the marimba, players stand behind the instrument and use rubber-headed mallets to strike the wooden bars. The rubber heads of the mallets are mounted on wooden shafts that are approximately 15" (38 cm) in length. Players hold at least two mallets and as many as four (two in each hand); the mallets are graduated in weight and hardness – large soft-headed mallets for the bottom (or bass) notes, and very small and hard sticks for the upper keys.

Marimba Ensembles

Much of the marimba activity in Mexico is focused in the state of Chiapas and in Mexico City, although the marimba may also be heard in the states of Oaxaca, Tabasco and Veracruz. The Mexican recording industry actively releases recordings of current groups, as well as re-releases of older LP recordings on CDs and cassettes. In the state of Chiapas, the municipal governments of the largest cities (such as the capital Tuxtla Gutiérrez and Tapachula) sponsor daily live open-air marimba performances. In Tuxtla, these performances take place every evening from 7:00 to 9:00 p.m. in *El Jardin de la Marimba* (the Marimba Park), which was designed and built especially to host these performances. The park was dedicated in 1995, and in 1998 the performances were well attended, with many of the patrons dancing to the music of *las maderas que cantan* ('the wood that sings'). In 1997, there were four full-time marimba ensembles sponsored by various governmental agencies in Tuxtla Gutiérrez.

To procure the services of a marimba group in Mexico City, one simply needs to walk down Calle Francisco Gonzalez Bocanegra (the street named after the composer of Mexico's national anthem) in the city's marimba district. Also located on this street is *La Escuela de la Música Mexicana*, founded in 1990 as an institution to teach popular Mexican musical styles, including marimba. Mexico City is also home to several international touring marimba ensembles, which make recordings that are widely distributed. The best known of these are Marimba Nandayapa (led by the dynamic and innovative performer/arranger Zeferino Nandayapa), Los Mecateros (the Moreno Brothers) and Marimba Aquino. Through recordings, radio broadcasts and television appearances, these ensembles have a considerable following.

In Guatemala, the marimba is widely regarded as the national instrument – a fact confirmed by listening to the radio at any hour of the day. Over the years, federal law has mandated a daily minimum number of hours of marimba music. This met with some early resistance from listeners but eventually had the desired effect. The largest station, TGW, often airs live broadcasts of marimba music from its studios in Guatemala City. The laws may be moot, as any radio station would experience a severe drop in the number of listeners if it did not broadcast marimba music. Marimba groups are highly sought after in both urban and rural areas to celebrate almost any occasion.

In both Mexico and Guatemala, there is also an active market for CDs and cassettes of marimba music, which spans all genres – marimba players showing no hesitation in acquiring any type of repertoire, be it classical transcriptions, folkloric and traditional musics, or the many songs that comprise dance music in these nations. In the late 1990s, CDs and cassettes were routinely sold by roving vendors while people listened to the music in the Marimba Park in Tuxtla Gutiérrez. While CD recordings of marimba music are quite popular in the urban areas of Chiapas and Guatemala, cassettes are sold in greater numbers – especially in the countryside.

Large *marimba doble* ensembles were extremely popular up to and throughout the 1950s in El Salvador, Honduras, western Nicaragua and Costa Rica. In these republics, marimbas were first imported and later re-created in imitation of Guatemalan *marimba dobles*. However, the arrangement of the keys corresponded to that of a standard piano keyboard, as in the marimbas from Chiapas. The surge in popularity of this form of the instrument derived from its acceptance by the middle classes and much of the upper classes. The large chromatic marimbas allowed for the performance of a repertoire formerly restricted to the more limited world of parlor piano, a domain reserved to a great extent for young female performers. The *marimba doble* ensembles performed waltzes, schottisches, polkas, fox trots and other forms linked to European dance repertoires that had been thoroughly creolized in the Americas. The ability of the chromatic marimbas, patterned after pianos, to produce these musical styles on an instrument identifiably indigenous to the region and nation coincided with an awakening of national consciousness among the middle classes that was an important factor in the popularity of marimba ensembles.

The Marimba in Popular Music

After the 1940s, the importance of the marimba within popular music throughout the greater Mesoamerican region suffered a decline. The availability of inexpensive radios and record players meant that they gradually supplanted live marimba performances. This change was hastened in the 1950s by the advent of rock 'n' roll, a musical style that does not translate well to the marimba. The decline in the marimba's importance was most marked outside southern Mexico and Guatemala. In El Salvador and Honduras, large *marimba dobles* have now become restricted to tourist venues and special government-sponsored programs; in Nicaragua, they had completely disappeared by the 1980s. Several full *marimba doble* ensembles have continued to perform in Costa Rica, particularly in the northwest province of Guanacaste.

Diatonic *marimba sencillas* and small, usually single-player chromatic marimbas of various types and diverse instrumentations have continued to hold an important position as providers of popular music in parts of Honduras, Nicaragua and Costa Rica, particularly among the lower classes. In Nicaragua, the premier instrument is called the *marimba de arco*, a 22-key diatonic instrument named for the arc or hoop attached to the frame within which the player sits while performing. Especially in urban areas, this instrument is often modified by the replacement of the arc with folding legs that allow for easy transport and performance in a standing position. These movable marimbas are used in restaurants in the cities and provide music for parties in smaller towns. Both the traditional *marimba de arco* and modified marimbas with legs are always accompanied by a guitar with six metal strings and the small *guitarilla*, which has four metal strings. This trio provides the accompaniment for the main folk dance (generically termed 'Dance of the Marimba'). It is augmented with scrapers and other small percussion instruments for a host of other commercial musical styles of dance, including *cumbias* and merengues, and *palo de mayo* (an Afro-Creole dance form from eastern Nicaragua). Marimba ensembles were virtually absent from the *Volcanto/Nueva canción* ('New Song') movement, with the notable exceptions of Carlos Mejía Godoy in Nicaragua, Yolacamba-Ita from El Salvador (whose exile status forced them to use a Nicaraguan instrument) and the Guatemalan group Kin Lalot. *Marimba sencillas* of various sizes have remained an

important part of the popular musical landscape in Costa Rica. While the greatest concentration has always been in Guanacaste, in the 1990s there was a certain resurgence of marimbas in the capital, San José. It should be kept in mind that the marimba has remained a key instrument within several vital folk traditions throughout Central America. While the marimba is often viewed as an outdated instrument by some youth culture members, its use in popular music evokes its special role as an instrument identified exclusively with this part of the world and further blurs an already tenuous distinction between folk and popular contexts.

In Colombia and Ecuador, the marimba is an important instrument among the African-American communities on the western Pacific littoral. The large diatonic Colombian marimba is played in an ensemble with various drums and small percussion instruments and is used much more as a percussion instrument than it is in Central American styles. The marimba was once somewhat restricted to folk contexts but it has begun to be used in ensembles oriented toward popular audiences. Similarly, the various types of small to medium-size Ecuadorean marimbas have begun to achieve a nominal acceptance as part of popular music ensembles, both within the Afro-Ecuadorean Esmeraldas region and among the general population.

In Mexico, one of the foremost representatives of the connection between popular music and the marimba is the composer/marimbist Alberto Domínguez. He began his career in his family marimba ensemble, the legendary Los Hermanos Domínguez, in San Cristóbal de las Casas, Chiapas. He went on to compose such well-known standards as 'Perfidia' and 'Frenesi,' which were first heard on the marimba. The movie industry in Hollywood often incorporated the marimba into motion pictures. Ironically, while Mexican marimbas were sometimes seen, the soundtracks were occasionally dubbed with traditional North American instruments. The Domínguez Brothers made appearances in several popular films, most notably *Tropic Holiday*.

Through wide distribution of numerous original recordings on the very successful A&M label, an ensemble led by Julius Wechter, called the Baja Marimba Band, achieved a degree of national visibility in the United States in the 1960s. Like the Mesoamerican marimba orchestras, Wechter's ensemble included brass instruments and a rhythm section in addition to marimbas. In terms of musical material, many of the first albums the Baja Marimba Band released had the sound and flavor of Mexican folkloric and traditional musical genres. As time progressed, Wechter attempted to reach a broader audience by incorporating tracks that were steeped in North American pop, Dixieland and other musical styles of the day. The ensemble's concert appearances took on the air of a variety show, with comic skits and showmanship that played alongside the musical genius of the group's leader.

Some called Herb Alpert's Tijuana Brass 'Ameriachi' because of its Americanization of this distinguished Mexican musical genre. A Mexican mariachi band typically has: two trumpets; three or four violins; a *vihuela* (a type of guitar); and a *guitarron* (a large lute-type instrument that functions as the bass of the ensemble). Herb Alpert's Tijuana Brass had: two trumpets; a trombone; a keyboard; a guitar; a bass; drums; and a marimba/auxiliary percussion.

The Baja Marimba Band shared some similarities with the Mexican marimba orchestra, which is often heard throughout southern Mexico (most prominently in the state of Chiapas) as well as in Mexico City. A Mexican marimba orchestra has: brass and reeds (the wind complement varies widely); seven marimbists on two instruments; a bass; drums; and auxiliary percussion. Julius Wechter's Baja Marimba Band had: two marimbists on two instruments; a trumpet; a trombone; reeds; a guitar; a piano; a bass; and drums.

It should also be noted that, throughout the twentieth century (as late as the 1990s), marimba groups from Mexico, Honduras and Guatemala toured the United States, South America, Asia and Europe. Guatemalan family-based ensembles (Bethancourt, Hurtado and others) made many US recordings in the 1920s and 1930s, while Marimba Nandayapa and Los Mecateros were making CD recordings of Mexican popular music during their tours of Japan as late as 1997.

Bibliography

Acevedo Vargas, Jorge L. 1986. *La Música en Guanacaste* [Music in Guanacaste]. 2nd ed. San José: Editorial de la Universidad de Costa Rica.

Anderson, Lois A. 1967–68. 'The African Xylophone.' *African Arts* 1(1): 46–49, 66, 68–69.

Anderson, Lois A., et al. 1984. 'Xylophone.' In *The New Grove Dictionary of Musical Instruments*, Vol. 3, ed. Stanley Sadie. London: Macmillan, 869–79.

Chamorro, Arturo. 1984. *Los instrumentos de percusión en México* [Percussion Instruments in Mexico]. Zamora: El Colegio de Michoacán.

Chenoweth, Vida. 1964. *The Marimbas of Guatemala*. Lexington, KY: University of Kentucky Press.

Garfias, Robert. 1983. 'The Marimba of Mexico and Central America.' *Latin American Music Review* 4(2): 203–12.

Julius Wechter and the Baja Marimba Band. http://www.amcorner.com/bmb/index.php3

Kaptain, Laurence D. 1989a. 'Chiapas and Its Unusual Marimba Tradition.' *Percussive Notes* 26(5): 28–31.

Kaptain, Laurence D. 1989b. 'Heart of Wood Song.' *Mexico Journal* 2(25): 25–26.

Kaptain, Laurence D. 1990. 'Focus on Performance: Interview with Zeferino Nandayapa.' *Percussive Notes* 28(2): 48–50.

Kaptain, Laurence D. 1991. *Maderas que cantan* [The Wood That Sings]. Tuxtla Gutiérrez, Chiapas: Instituto Chiapaneco de Cultura.

Kaptain, Laurence D. 1992. *The Wood That Sings: The Marimba in Chiapas, Mexico*. Everett, PA: HoneyRock Publications.

Kaptain, Laurence D. 1995. 'The Marimba in Mexico and Related Areas.' In *Encyclopedia of Percussion*, ed. John H. Beck. New York and London: Garland Publishing, 239–56.

Kaptain, Laurence D. 2001. 'Julius Wechter.' *Percussive Notes* 39(1): 53–62.

Knopper, Steve, ed. 1998. *Music Hound Lounge: The Essential Album Guide to Martini Music and Easy Listening*. Detroit, MI: Visible Ink Press.

Monsanto Dardón, Carlos Hugo. 1982. 'Guatemala a través de su marimba' [Guatemala Through Its Marimba]. *Latin American Music Review* 3(1): 60–72.

Montiel, Gustavo. 1985. *Investigando el origen de la marimba* [Investigating the Origin of the Marimba]. México, DF: Gustavo Montiel.

Muñoz Tábora, Jesús. 1988. *Organología del Folklore Hondureño* [Organology of Honduran Folklore]. Tegucigalpa: Secretaría del Turismo y Cultura.

O'Brien, Linda L. 1982. 'Marimbas of Guatemala: The African Connection.' *The World of Music* 24(2): 99–103.

O'Brien, Linda L. 1998. 'Guatemala.' In *The Garland Encyclopedia of World Music. Vol. 2: South America, Mexico, Central America, and the Caribbean*, ed. Dale A. Olsen and Daniel E. Sheehy. New York and London: Garland Publishing, 721–38.

Pineda del Valle, César. 1990. *Fogarada: Antología de la marimba* [Fogarada: Anthology of the Marimba]. Tuxtla Gutiérrez, Chiapas: Instituto Chiapaneco de Cultura.

Ritter, Jonathan Larry. 1998. *La marimba esmeraldeña: Music and Ethnicity on Ecuador's Northern Coast* [The Marimba of Esmeraldas: Music and Ethnicity on Ecuador's Northern Coast]. M.A. thesis, University of California at Los Angeles.

Rudish, Neil. *Julius Wechter, 1935–1999*. http://www.amcorner.com/gallery/julius.php3

Salazar Salvatierra, Rodrigo. 1988. *La marimba: empleo, diseño y construcción* [The Marimba: Its Use, Design and Construction]. San José: Editorial de la Universidad de Costa Rica.

Scruggs, T.M. 1991. 'Review of *Nicaragua . . . ¡Presente! –*

Music from Nicaragua Libre.' *Latin American Music Review* 12(1): 84–96.

Scruggs, T.M. 1994. *The Nicaraguan baile de la marimba and the Empowerment of Identity.* Ann Arbor, MI: University Microfilms.

Scruggs, T.M. 1998a. 'Cultural Capital, Appropriate Transformations and Transfer by Appropriation in Western Nicaragua: El baile de la marimba.' *Latin American Music Review* 19(1): 1–30.

Scruggs, T.M. 1998b. 'Honduras.' In *The Garland Encyclopedia of World Music. Vol. 2: South America, Mexico, Central America, and the Caribbean,* ed. Dale A. Olsen and Daniel E. Sheehy. New York and London: Garland Publishing, 738–46.

Scruggs, T.M. 1998c. 'Nicaragua.' In *The Garland Encyclopedia of World Music. Vol. 2: South America, Mexico, Central America, and the Caribbean,* ed. Dale A. Olsen and Daniel E. Sheehy. New York and London: Garland Publishing, 747–69.

Scruggs, T.M. 1999a. 'Central America: Marimba and Other Musics of Central America.' In *Music in Latin American Culture: Regional Traditions,* ed. John M. Schechter. New York: Schirmer Books, 80–125. (Field recordings on accompanying CD.)

Scruggs, T.M. 1999b. 'Nicaraguan State Cultural Initiative and "the Unseen Made Manifest."' *Yearbook for Traditional Music* 30: 53–73.

Shaw, Steve. 1997. 'I'll Marimba You: The Julius Wechter Story.' *Cool and Strange Music! Magazine* 4 (February-April): 37–39, 45.

Solís, Theodore. 1980. 'Muñecas de chiapaneco [Supple Wrists]: The Economic Importance of Self-Image in the World of the Mexican Marimba.' *Latin American Music Review* 1(1): 34–46.

Solís, Theodore. 1983. *The Marimba in Mexico City: Contemporary Contexts of a Traditional Regional Ensemble.* Ph.D. thesis, University of Illinois.

Taracena Arriola, Jorge Arturo. 1980. 'La marimba: ¿un instrumento nacional?' [The Marimba: A National Instrument?]. *Tradiciones de Guatemala* 13: 1–26.

Vela, David. 1958. *Information on the Marimba,* trans. and ed. Vida Chenoweth. Auckland, New Zealand: Institute Press.

Vela, David. 1962. *La marimba: estudio sobre el instrumento nacional* [The Marimba: A Study of a National Instrument]. Guatemala: Ministerio de Educación Pública.

Discography

Baja Marimba Band, The. *The Baja Marimba Band.* A&M SP-104. *1964*: USA.

Baja Marimba Band, The. *The Baja Marimba Band's Back.* Bell 1124. *1973*: USA.

Baja Marimba Band, The. *Naturally.* Applause APLP-1008. *1982*: USA.

Ecuador & Colombia: Marimba Masters Sacred Songs. Multicultural Media ASIN B000005BMR. *1998*: USA.

15 Exitos Nicaraguenses en marimba. Discos Fenix, Mántica-Waid & Co. *1999*: Nicaragua.

Garlaza, Faustino. *Marimba de Guatemala.* A World of Music 12531. *1997*: Guatemala.

Los Alegres Hermanos de Ticuantepe. Discos Fenix, Mántica-Waid & Co. 1988; *1999*: Nicaragua.

Maracas, Marimbas, and Mambos: Latin Classics at MGM. Rhino Records R272722. *1997*: USA.

Marimba Claro de Luna. *Romanticismo Tropical.* Sonox M.R. CDSC-3101. *1995*: Mexico.

Marimba Diriá. *Viva Guanacaste.* CBS-Indica S.A., 20.054, n.d.: Costa Rica.

Marimba: Los Mecateros de Oscar Moreno. Producciones Fonográficas S.A. de C.V. PFCD-2014. n.d.: Mexico.

Marimba Music of Tehuantepec. University of Washington Press UWP-1002. *1972*: USA.

Marimba Nandayapa. *Colección Musical Danzón con Marimba.* KCT, S.A. de C.V. PHCD2016. *1995*: Mexico.

Marimba Nandayapa. *La Magica de Chiapas, México.* Discos y Cassettes Master-Stereo, S.A. de C.V. CDNW-7005. *1995*: Mexico.

Marimba Nandayapa. *Los Grandes Temas de La Pantalla.* Compañia Fonográfica Internacional, S.A. de C.V. CD-IMI-1047. *1992*: Mexico.

Marimba Nandayapa. *Los Grandes Valses.* Compañia Fonográfica Internacional, S.A. de C.V. CD-IMI-1102. *1994*: Mexico.

Marimba Nandayapa. *Marimba Nandayapa.* EMI CDPE 003. n.d.: Mexico.

Marimba Orquesta Maribel. *Presente.* Onda Nueva. n.d.: Guatemala.

Marimbas de Chiapas. Mexican Landscapes, Vol. 4. Playasound 65904. *1994*: Mexico.

Marimbas de Guatemala, Vol. 1. Hemisphono 2101. *1995*: Guatemala.

Marimbas Hermanos Paniagua y Corona. *Rincón de México en Maderas.* Fábrica de Discos Peerless, S.A. de C.V. PCD-013-1. *1988*: Mexico.

Marimba Yajalón. *Echoes of Chiapas.* Mark Records 2552-MCD. *1997*: USA.

Música Mexicana. *La Internacional Marimba.* Producciones RCS CD-05. *1994*: Mexico.

Música Mexicana. *Música Mexicana para el mundo con el sonido en marimba de Zeferino Nandayapa.* Alfa Records, S.A. de C.V. CDAMI-4. *1992*: Mexico.

Nicaragua: música y canto (7-CD set). Radio Güegüense/ Alcaldía de Managua. *1992*: Nicaragua.

Nicaragua ... ¡Presente! – Music from Nicaragua Libre. Rounder Records 4020/4021. *1989*: USA.

Nicaraguan Folk Music from Masaya (comp. T.M. Scruggs). Flying Fish Records 474. *1988*: USA.

20 Exitos: Voces, guitarras y marimba. Discos Fenix, Mántica-Waid & Co. *1999*: Nicaragua.

Wechter, Julius, and the Baja Marimba Band. *I'll Marimba You*. Rondor Music International, Selection BMBPJ087. *1998*: USA.

Visual Recordings

Scruggs, T.M. 1995. 'Los Chinegros: El Baile de las Negras.' JVC/Smithsonian Folkways Video Anthology of World Music and Dance of the Americas, Vol. 6 (VTMV-230) (video).

Filmography

Holiday in Mexico, dir. George Sidney. 1946. USA. 127 mins. Musical. Original music by George Stoll.

Tropic Holiday, dir. Theodore Reed. 1938. USA. 78 mins. Musical. Original music by Boris Morros.

LAURENCE D. KAPTAIN with T.M. SCRUGGS

Mbira (Thumb Piano)

The mbira or thumb piano is a percussion instrument of African origin. It consists of a wooden board or box with strips of metal or wood attached in such a way that the player's thumbs or fingers can pluck the metal strips to produce a rhythmic melody. Mbira are made from an assortment of materials, such as wood, metal gas and insecticide cans, gourds and coconut shells, and in a great variety of sizes, shapes and types, and they exist as acoustic or electric instruments. The number of traditional African types alone would take an entire book to detail, and a diverse assortment of these instruments can be found in the Western world as well.

Nomenclature

The terms 'thumb piano' and 'finger piano' are the most popular names for the instrument and yet, at the same time, they are the most inappropriate from an African perspective (also incorrect are African piano, African nail violin, hand piano and Kaffir piano). Ethnomusicologists use another term that places all these instruments in a single generic category: 'lamellaphone' (also lamellophone) designates any instrument with plucked keys (or lamella) attached to a soundboard, with the possible addition of a resonator. What is called a 'thumb piano' or 'finger piano' is often a specific instrument from an African culture. Such instruments may be used, in an African traditional setting, in ritual ceremonies, such as those performed by the Shona people of Zimbabwe. Renaming the instrument for Western purposes is akin to calling a concert violin a 'fiddle.' Nevertheless, 'thumb piano' and 'finger piano' are names found on many recordings and in many publications. To complicate matters further, on Western recordings a generic name like mbira, kalimba or *sanza* may appear, but it is more often used as an exotic name than as an identifier of a specific African instrument. Although the term 'mbira' is a Shona term meaning an instrument specific to the Shona culture, the term is used here generically, as is often the case in non-African popular musics.

Following is a list of mbira-type instruments (with their usual number of keys) and the country where they are found. All of the instruments listed are used in musics native to Africa or the African diaspora. The list demonstrates the number of instruments of similar appearance and construction that are found in different places and often with only slightly different names.

Africa

Mboton, timbrh – Cameroon; *sanza* (9–12), *sanzi* (9–12) – Cameroon and the Central African Republic; kalimba, *lukembe* – Congo; *fang* (6), *likembe, kisansi, lukembe* (10 wooden keys), *luba* (4), *mbanja* (8), *yombe* (10), *zande* (7) – Democratic Republic of Congo (formerly Zaire); *tom* – Ethiopia; *aprempensuah* – Ghana; *bonduma, gbelee, kongoma* – Liberia; kalimba, *malimba* – Malawi; *danda, malimba* (26), *tomboji, utee* – Mozambique; *jidiga* – Niger; *agidigbo* (5), *akpata, sologun, ubo* – Nigeria; *mbila dza madeza* (27), *mbila tshipai* (11–18) – Republic of South Africa; *kondi, kongoma, kututeng* – Sierra Leone; *afosangu* – Sudan; *chilimbe* (15), *ilimba* (66–72), *malimba* – Tanzania; *lukeme* – Uganda; kalimba (14), *luvale* (13) – Zambia; *hera* (26), *karimba* (15), *matepe* (29), *mbira dzavadzimu* (22, 24, 25), *mbira dzaVandau* (29–30), *munyonga* (50), *ndimba* (17), *njari* (29–35), *nyonga nyonga* (15), *nyunga nyunga* (15) – Zimbabwe.

African Diaspora

Laongo bania, madimba de Btsche, marimba (16), *sanza* – Brazil; *marímbula* (7) – Colombia; *marímbula* (4–7) – Cuba; marimba, *marímbola* (5–6) – Dominican Republic; *malimba* (4–7) – Haiti; rhumba box (5–7) – Jamaica; *marímbula* (3–5) – Martinique; *marímbula* (6) – Puerto Rico; *banja* (5), box bass (5–6), *marímbula* (5–6) – Trinidad and Tobago; *marimba brett* – United States; *quisanche* – Uruguay; *marímbola* (5–6) – Venezuela.

In addition to the traditional instruments found in Africa and the African diaspora, more generic versions, based on those of traditional African design, have been made by Western instrument makers. Makers in North America often give the instrument the generic name of thumb piano, mbira or kalimba. A Western innovation is the purely electric mbira, made by Lucinda Ellison, which is constructed in a similar fashion to the solid-body electric guitar, with internal pickups under the bridge and a jack to plug into an amplifier. One difference between African and Western lamellaphones is that the former most often have shells, metal rings or bottle caps attached which make a buzzing sound when the keys are plucked – a desired African aesthetic. Western-made lamellaphones often do not have buzzers attached, which gives the instruments a plainer sound but makes recording in popular music less problematic.

Tuning and Technique

Tuning represents another important difference between African and Western instruments. African instruments use mainly two types of scales for lamellaphones – a five-pitch scale and a seven-pitch scale – although other types may be found as well. Tuning in Africa is regional, which means that a tuning from one particular area might not match exactly with a tuning from another area if the scale intervals were compared. This is part of an African aesthetic in music – tuning varies across the continent and the variations add to the beauty of an area's music. In contrast, tuning in the West has become standardized, and variations are considered 'out of tune.' A few different heptatonic scales are played on lamellaphones, such as on the *mbira dzavadzimu* of the Shona people in Zimbabwe. These scales may appear to be major, natural minor or Phrygian, with some interval differences from Western scales. An African version of a major scale is close to a Western major scale, but with the fourth scale degree possibly a little sharper and the seventh scale degree lowered to a flat seventh, albeit somewhat more flat than a Western minor seventh interval.

Another difference between African and Western instruments is in how the keys are arranged. A Western keyboard (as on the piano) is arranged from lowest pitches to highest from the left to the right. Most lamellaphones are arranged with the lowest key in the center, and the player alternately plucks right and left or vice versa (depending on how the keyboard has been set up) to ascend the scale. The Shona mbira are an exception – they make use of three keyboards on a single instrument. The left side of the instrument is played with the left and right thumbs and has two rows of seven keys in octaves arranged from the center to the left for ascending, while the right side, which is played with the right thumb and forefinger, is arranged from the center to the right for ascending. The basic technique for playing the mbira involves plucking the keys, or lamellae, with the fingertips and fingernails. Some techniques involve playing with the index, middle and ring fingers of each hand, as on the Nigerian *agidigbo*. Other techniques involve the use of the thumbs plucking down on the keys while the index fingers pluck up from beneath them, as on the *mbira dzavadzimu* from Zimbabwe. The thumbs are used to pluck the keys of the *sanza* in the Central African Republic. The material used for the keys varies: some are made from a heavier, stiffer metal that requires the player to have a longer thumbnail to play comfortably, while others may be of a softer, more flexible metal that makes plucking with the fingertip comfortable. The mbira can be played melodically by plucking out a melody on the keys, or in a rhythmic fashion by plucking a pattern on one side of the keyboard while a pattern that fills in between the first is plucked on the other side.

The Use of Mbira in Popular Music

In a very broad sense, two types of popular music make use of mbira: popular musics of Africa and parts of the African diaspora, and Western popular musics (non-African).

Africa and the African Diaspora

In Africa, popular music can be considered an urban phenomenon. That is to say, urban situations make possible a detribalized zone of cultural interaction in which strict adherence to specific cultural traditions may not operate. Urban musics in Africa are the result of the combining of local traditional elements with Western influences, such as the radio, the microphone and music business, and instruments like the electric guitar, saxophone, trumpet, electric bass, keyboards and drumset. The urban music of the Shona people of Zimbabwe, known as *chimurenga* (uprising), involves a mixing of mbira music with rock, Christian hymns, jazz and various types of traditional songs. This music came about as a result of the uprising of indigenous black Africans against white European colonialism. The uprising began in the 1890s and, by the 1970s, fully Western influences (in terms of the use of electric instrumentation) in *chimurenga* songs had become evident.

Formed in 1977, Thomas Mapfumo and the Blacks Unlimited often incorporated traditional *mbira dzavadzimu* patterns played on multiple electric guitars; they also included up to three mbira players, including Chartwell Dutiro. Another important Zimbabwean artist is Ephat Mujuru with the Spirit of the People, whose music involves the use of electric Shona mbira. Hukwe Ubi Zawose of Tanzania may be viewed as a neo-traditionalist who has rebuilt his instrument, the *ilimba*, to include between 66 and 72 keys tuned in just intonation, many of which are used for 'sympathetic' resonance. Another African musician, Francis Bebey, has studied various musical traditions in Africa and mixes them together on his recordings, often including lamellaphones. The music of the Orchestre Bana Luya (children of the Baluba people) in the Democratic Republic of Congo (formerly Zaire) also features an electric lamellaphone. An important figure in early Zairian-Congolese urban music was Antoine Moundanda, who formed the band Likembé Géant in the early 1950s. The band used three giant *likembe* and played Congolese rumba, polkas and traditional music, and it recorded many LPs for the Ngoma label. All of these examples of recorded African uses of lamellaphones in urban music are from the past 50 years, but one of the earliest examples of the use of these instruments in recorded popular music is from the African diaspora.

Giant-size, box-shaped instruments with between five and seven keys attached appeared all over the Caribbean and parts of South America as a result of the slave trade. These instruments were used to provide a bass sound in various musics. Although they have mostly been replaced by the acoustic bass, some can still be found in Jamaica (for example, in the *mento* music of the Jolly Boys), Trinidad, Puerto Rico and, occasionally, Cuba. The earliest surviving recordings were made in Cuba in 1925 by the bands Terceto Yoyo and Sexteto Habenero, with Gerardo Martinez and Chucho Aristola, respectively, on the *marímbula*.

The West

Even though they are not traditional Western instruments, mbira appear on many kinds of popular music recordings in Europe and the United States, from neo-traditional African music, blues, jazz and movie/television/radio soundtracks to Broadway shows and creative 'world music.' One of the earliest US recordings to include the instrument was the neo-traditional *Drums of Passion*, recorded by Babatunde Olatunji in 1959. Olatunji had come from Nigeria to study in the United States and, with the growing trend among African Americans to promote African awareness, his music became popular. Olatunji plays a kalimba on this recording, which features a host of jazz musicians, including Yusef Lateef. An earlier recording, *Kind of Blue* by Miles Davis (1959), is an example of a melodic/harmonic concept in jazz (modal jazz) inspired by the mbira. In his autobiography (1989), Davis states that, having been inspired by African lamellaphone music, he was trying to limit the scales and chords of his compositions on this recording in an effort to work in a restricted melodic/harmonic framework as a lamellaphone does. Another jazz recording, *The African Beat* (1962) by Art Blakey and the Afro-Drum Ensemble (an ensemble of African drummers and African-American jazz musicians), features Yusef Lateef on the kalimba. In 1966, the Broadway play *Wait a Minim!* featured folk music from southern Africa, with Paul Tracey playing the mbira (Tracey also appeared on Johnny Carson's *The Tonight Show*, demonstrating the mbira and several other African instruments). A recording that features a blend of electronic music and world instruments by composer Jon Appleton and world jazz-

man Don Cherry (on kalimba) is *Human Music* (1970). Bluesman Taj Mahal started playing solos on a Hugh Tracey kalimba in his concerts after first hearing the instrument in a movie. His recording *Recycling the Blues and Other Related Stuff* (1972) features a live solo.

As a novelty device, the instrument made an unusual appearance in a comedy act by Robert Klein, an example of which is included on his 1973 recording *A Child of the Fifties*. Even composer George Crumb scored for a Hugh Tracey kalimba in his *Music for a Summer Evening (Makrokosmos III)* (1974). Perhaps the most mainstream use of the instrument occurs in recordings by the group Earth, Wind & Fire, featuring Maurice White as one of three percussionists. White also used a Hugh Tracey kalimba (the earliest example is on *Spirit* (1976)), and he was able to successfully perform fast solos on the instrument and incorporate it into the body of his ensemble's music.

One of the most creative lamellaphone players in the United States was the inimitable percussionist/sitarist Collin Walcott. Walcott played a *sanza*-type instrument made from an insecticide can, which had nine keys and was tuned to a scale with no third or sixth and a flat seventh in Western tuning (E-F♯-A-B-D-E-F♯-A-B from the center, alternating right to left). His technique was unusual in that he flipped the instrument over so that the keys faced away from him, and he plucked with the index, middle and ring fingers of both hands. He used this instrument first on a recording of composer Irwin Bazelon's 'Propulsions: Concerto for Percussion' (composed/recorded in 1974), then on the group Oregon's recording *Out of the Woods* (1978) and later on Barry Wedgle's *Kake* (1982); it also featured prominently in many of his compositions recorded between 1979 and 1983 with the trio Codona (with Don Cherry and Naná Vasconcelos). Since Walcott's death in 1984, one of his students, Rich Goodhart, has perpetuated the technique and style on his own recordings.

During the 1980s and 1990s, percussionists such as Adam Rudolph, Glen Velez, Paolo Vinaccia, Layne Redmond, John Bergamo, Okay Temiz, Rich Goodhart, N. Scott Robinson, Nexus, Chocolate (Julio Algendones), Jack DeJohnette and Bob Moses used mbira creatively in their music, as did jazz musicians Ishmael Wadada Leo Smith, Steve Tibbetts, Egberto Gismonti, Jean-Jacques Avenel and the Canadian multi-ethnic pop band Ashkaru (with Chip Yarwood on mbira). Composers for Hollywood movies and for radio recordings have used the lamellaphone creatively on soundtracks as well. One example is the film *Lethal Weapon 2* (1989), with music by Michael Kamen, which has mbira in the background music to several scenes. Television viewers may be misled by hearing a similar-sounding instrument on an occasional soundtrack to *The X-Files* (1990s), with music by Mark Snow, but this is an example of sampling technology on contemporary keyboards and is not a real mbira (keyboards such as the Korg M-1 featured a kalimba sample as early as 1988).

Conclusion

Organological, technical and timbral diversification by Western percussionists in popular music was fairly common after 1960. Lamellaphones were adopted by some musicians after they had been exposed to African sources either directly or indirectly through films and recordings. Western companies have continued to construct various types of lamellaphones and distribute them. However, although such instruments are abundant in the West, their use is largely limited to creative percussionists and jazz musicians on occasional recordings.

Bibliography

App, Lawrence J. 1998. 'Afro-Colombian Traditions.' In *The Garland Encyclopedia of World Music. Vol. 2: South America, Mexico, Central America, and the Caribbean*, ed. Dale A. Olsen and Daniel E. Sheehy. New York and London: Garland Publishing, 400–12.

Averill, Gage, and Wilcken, Lois. 1998. 'Haiti.' In *The Garland Encyclopedia of World Music. Vol. 2: South America, Mexico, Central America, and the Caribbean*, ed. Dale A. Olsen and Daniel E. Sheehy. New York and London: Garland Publishing, 881–95.

Berliner, Paul F. 1981. *The Soul of Mbira: Music and Traditions of the Shona People of Zimbabwe*. Berkeley, CA: University of California Press.

Brandt, Max H. 1998. 'Venezuela.' In *The Garland Encyclopedia of World Music. Vol. 2: South America, Mexico, Central America, and the Caribbean*, ed. Dale A. Olsen and Daniel E. Sheehy. New York and London: Garland Publishing, 523–45.

Brown, Ernest D. 1994. 'The Guitar and the Mbira: Resilience, Assimilation, and Pan-Africanism in Zimbabwean Music.' *The World of Music* 36(2): 73–117.

Burt-Beck, Carol. 1979. *Playing the African Mbira*. New York: Ludlow Music, Inc.

Cally, Sully. 1990. *Musiques et danses afro-caraïbes: Martinique* [Afro-Caribbean Music and Dance: Martinique]. Gros-Morne, Martinique: Sully-Cally/Lezin.

Chawasarira, Chaka. 1992. *Muridziro weKarimba naChawasarira* [How to Play the Karimba, by Chawasarira]. Harare: Kunzwana Trust.

Chernoff, John Miller. 1996. 'The Soul of Mbira Twenty Years On: A Retrospect, Part 2.' *African Music* 7(3): 91–95.

Dandemutande: Zimbabwean Music & Culture Worldwide. http://www.dandemutande.com

Davis, Miles, with Troupe, Quincy. 1989. *Miles: The Autobiography*. New York: Simon and Schuster.

Drouet, Héctor Vega. 1998. 'Puerto Rico.' In *The Garland Encyclopedia of World Music. Vol. 2: South America, Mexico, Central America, and the Caribbean*, ed. Dale A. Olsen and Daniel E. Sheehy. New York and London: Garland Publishing, 932–41.

Goddard, Keith. 1996. 'The Soul of Mbira Twenty Years On: A Retrospect, Part 1.' *African Music* 7(3): 76–90.

Graham, Richard. 1993. 'The Giant Lamellaphones: A Global Perspective.' *Experimental Musical Instruments* 9(12): 10–12.

Guilbault, Jocelyne. 1998. 'Dominica.' In *The Garland Encyclopedia of World Music. Vol. 2: South America, Mexico, Central America, and the Caribbean*, ed. Dale A. Olsen and Daniel E. Sheehy. New York and London: Garland Publishing, 840–44.

Howland, Harold. 1981. 'Master Percussionist: Oregon's Collin Walcott.' *Modern Drummer* 5 (April): 24–26, 39, 64–65, 70.

Kaemmer, John E. 1998. 'Music of the Shona of Zimbabwe.' In *The Garland Encyclopedia of World Music. Vol. 1: Africa*, ed. Ruth M. Stone. New York and London: Garland Publishing, 744–58.

Kubik, Gerhard. 1998. *Kalimba, Nsansi, Mbire: Lamellophone in Afrika*. Berlin: Museums für Völkerkunde.

Kubik, Gerhard, and Cooke, Peter. 2001. 'Lamellophone.' In *The New Grove Dictionary of Music and Musicians*, Vol. 14, ed. Stanley Sadie. London: Macmillan, 171–81.

Lewin, Olive. 1998. 'Jamaica.' In *The Garland Encyclopedia of World Music. Vol. 2: South America, Mexico, Central America, and the Caribbean*, ed. Dale A. Olsen and Daniel E. Sheehy. New York and London: Garland Publishing, 896–913.

McDaniel, Lorna. 1998. 'Trinidad and Tobago.' In *The Garland Encyclopedia of World Music. Vol. 2: South America, Mexico, Central America, and the Caribbean*, ed. Dale A. Olsen and Daniel E. Sheehy. New York and London: Garland Publishing, 952–67.

Nembire, Katonje Judah ('Mr. Kanga-Fry'). 1993. *How to Play Zimbabwe's Mbira Huru, Using a Very Simple Number Method, Staff Notation, and Tonic Solfa. Distance Education: Step One*. Mount Darwin, Zimbabwe: Nembire School.

Novitski, Paul. 1996. 'Percussion Discussion: Embracing Mbira.' *Rhythm Music* 5(8): 18–22.

Ortiz, Fernando. 1995. *La marímbula*. La Habana, Cuba: Editorial Letras Cubanas.

Rodríguez, Olavo Alén. 1998. 'Cuba.' In *The Garland Encyclopedia of World Music. Vol. 2: South America, Mexico, Central America, and the Caribbean*, ed. Dale A.

Olsen and Daniel E. Sheehy. New York and London: Garland Publishing, 822–39.

Theirmann, David. 1971. 'The Mbira in Brazil.' *African Music Society Journal* 5(1): 90–94.

Tracey, Andrew T.N. 1970. *How to Play the Mbira (dzavadzimu)*. Roodepoort, Transvaal: International Library of African Music.

Turino, Thomas. 1998. 'The Mbira, Worldbeat, and the International Imagination.' *The World of Music* 40(2): 85–106.

Udow, Michael W. 1972. 'African Percussion Music.' *Percussionist* 9(4): 19–28.

Williams, B. Michael. 1997. 'Getting Started with *Mbira dzaVadzimu*.' *Percussive Notes* 35(4): 38–49.

Discographical References

Appleton, Jon, and Cherry, Don. *Human Music*. Flying Dutchman FDS 121. *1970*: USA.

Bazelon, Irwin. 'Propulsions: Concerto for Percussion.' *Music of Irwin Bazelon*. CRI American Masters CD 623. *1974*: USA.

Blakey, Art, and the Afro-Drum Ensemble. *The African Beat*. Blue Note BST-84097. *1962*: USA.

Codona. *Codona*. ECM 1132 78118-21132-2. *1979*: USA.

Codona. *Codona 2*. ECM 1177 78118-21177-2. *1981*: USA.

Codona. *Codona 3*. ECM 1243 78118-21243-2. *1983*: USA.

Crumb, George. *Music for a Summer Evening (Makrokosmos III)*. Nonesuch H-71311. *1974*: USA.

Davis, Miles. *Kind of Blue*. Columbia Legacy CK 64935. *1959*: USA.

Earth, Wind & Fire. *Spirit*. Columbia CBS CK 34241. *1976*: USA.

Klein, Robert. *A Child of the Fifties*. Rhino R4 70769. *1973*: USA.

Olatunji, Babatunde. *Drums of Passion*. Columbia CK 8210. *1959*: USA.

Oregon. *Out of the Woods*. Discovery 71004. *1978*: USA.

Taj Mahal. *Recycling the Blues and Other Related Stuff*. Mobil Fidelity Sound Lab MFCD764. *1972*: USA.

Tracey, Andrew, and Tracey, Paul, with Pegram, Nigel. *Wait a Minim!*. London AM 58002. *1966*: USA.

Wedgle, Barry. *Kake*. Wonderful World Records 1201. *1982*: USA.

Discography

African

Africa: Shona Mbira Music. Nonesuch H-72077. *1977*: USA.

Azim, Erica Kundidzora. *Mbira Dreams: Trance Music of Zimbabwe*. The Relaxation Company CD3261. *1996*: USA.

Bebey, Francis. *Africa Sanza*. Makossa ADSC-11-86015. *1982*: USA.

Bebey, Francis. *Didiye*. Pee Wee Music PW 017. *1997*: France.

Central Africa: Sanza Music in the Land of the Gbaya. VDE CD-755. *1993*: Switzerland.

Chiweshe, Stella Rambisai. *Kumusha*. Piranha Pir 42-2. *1990*: Germany.

Mapfumo, Thomas, and the Blacks Unlimited. *Chimurenga '98*. Anonym 0001. *1999*: USA.

Mapfumo, Thomas, and the Blacks Unlimited. *Shumba: Vital Hits of Zimbabwe*. Virgin 3-1022-1. *1990*: USA.

Maraire, Dumisani, and Mujuru, Ephat. *Shona Spirit*. Music of the World CDT-136. *1996*: USA.

Moundanda, Antoine, and Likembé Géant. *Kessé Kessé*. Indigo/Label Bleu LBLC 2541/HM 83. *1997*: France.

Samite of Uganda. *Dance My Children Dance*. Shanachie 65003. *1988*: USA.

The Soul of Mbira: Traditions of the Shona People of Rhodesia. Nonesuch H-72054. *1973*: USA.

Suso, Foday Musa. *The Dreamtime*. CMP CD 3001. *1990*: Germany.

Tracey, Hugh. *Reeds (Mbira) 1: The Music of Africa, Series v. 28: Musical Instruments 2*. Gallatone GALP 1323. *1960*: South Africa.

Zaire: Musiques Urbaines à Kinshasa. Ocora C559007HM65. *1987*: France.

Zawose, Hukwe Ubi. *The Art of Hukwe Ubi Zawose: Songs Accompanied by Ilimba and Izeze*. JVC VIGC-5011. *1990*: USA.

Zengea Karimba Ensemble, The. *Vadzimuwe*. ABF Skane ABFSK001. *1992*: Sweden.

African Diaspora

Chocolate (Julio Algendones). *Chocolate: Peru's Master Percussionist*. Lyrichord LYRCD 7417. *1990*: USA.

Hot Music from Cuba: 1907–1936. Harlequin HQCD-23. *1993*: UK.

Jolly Boys, The. *Sunshine 'n' Water*. Rykodisc RCD 10187. *1991*: USA.

Lititz Mento Band, The. *Dance Music and Working Songs from Jamaica*. Haus Der Kulturen Der Welt SM 1512-2. *1992*: Germany.

Musik från Västindien: Små Antillerna. Caprice CAP 2004. *1977*: Sweden.

Sexteto Habenero. *Loma De Belen*. Victor 594. 1925: Cuba.

Terceto Yoyo. *El Congrejito*. Victor 578. 1925: Cuba.

Western/Non-African

Adam Rudolph's Moving Pictures. *Skyway*. Soulnote 121269. *1994*: USA.

Alfano, Jorge. *One Heart*. Lyrichord 7431. *1997*: USA.

Ancient Future. *Dreamchaser*. Narada 62754. *1988*: USA.

Andersen, Arild. *Arv.* Kirkelig Kulturverksted FXCD 133. *1994*: Norway.

Ashkaru. *Mother Tongue.* Triloka 7214. *1995*: Canada.

Asza. *Asza.* PacificLine Music PM0410CD. *1995*: Canada.

Bandt, Ros. *Stargazer.* Vox Australis VAST 004-2. *1989*: Australia.

Bloque. *Bloque.* Warner Bros. 9-47060-2. *1998*: USA.

Bridges. *Bridges.* Interworld 921. *1996*: USA.

Crafton, Randy. *Duologue.* Lyrichord LYRCD 7430. *1997*: USA.

Dalglish, Malcolm, and the Ooolites. *Pleasure.* Ooolitic Music OM 1112. *1997*: USA.

Dietrichson, Tor. *Global Village.* Global Pacific R2-79302. *1987*: USA.

Do'a World Music Ensemble. *Companions of the Crimson Coloured Ark.* Philo CD-PH-9009. *1986*: USA.

Earth, Wind & Fire. *Faces.* ARC/Columbia CK2 36595. *1980*: USA.

Earth, Wind & Fire. *I Am.* Columbia CK 35730. *1979*: USA.

Earth, Wind & Fire. *Powerlight.* CBS CK 38367. *1983*: USA.

Eliovson, Steve, and Walcott, Collin. *Dawn Dance.* ECM 1198 829 375-2. *1981*: USA.

Gismonti, Egberto. *Sol do meio dia.* ECM 1116 78118-21116-2. *1978*: USA.

Goodhart, Rich. *Affirmative Reply.* Beginner's Mind Productions BMP 1002. *1991*: USA.

Goodhart, Rich. *Divining Signs.* Beginner's Mind Productions BMP 1001. *1988*: USA.

Goodhart, Rich. *Never Give a Sword to a Man Who Can't Dance.* Beginner's Mind Productions BMP 0403. *1995*: USA.

Hancock, Herbie. *Head Hunters.* Columbia/Legacy 471239 2. *1973*: USA.

Harrison, Lou. *The Music of Lou Harrison.* Phoenix PHCD 118. *1971*: USA.

Headhunters, The. *Survival of the Fittest.* BMG France 74321409522. *1975*: USA.

Hooker, John Lee. *Free Beer and Chicken.* Beat Goes On BGO CD123. *1974*: USA.

Kaiser, Henry, and Lindley, David. *Sweet Sunny North: Henry Kaiser and David Lindley in Norway, V. 1.* Shanachie 640-57. *1994*: USA.

King Crimson. *Larks' Tongues in Aspic.* EG EGCD-7. *1973*: USA.

Live at the Knitting Factory, Volume 2. Knitting Factory Works KFWCD-98. *1989*: USA.

Moses, Bob. *Time Stood Still.* Gramavision R2 79493. *1994*: USA.

Moye, Famoudou Don. *Sun Percussion, Volume One.* Aeco 001. *1975*: USA.

Nakai, R. Carlos, with Wind Travelin' Band, and Ohkura,

Shonosuke & Kano, Oki. *Island of Bows.* Canyon CR-7018. *1994*: USA.

Nauseef, Mark. *Personal Note.* CMP 16. *1981*: Germany.

Nauseef, Mark. *Wun-Wun.* CMP CD 25. *1992*: Germany.

Oregon. *Oregon in Performance.* Elektra 9E 304. *1980*: USA.

Oregon. *Roots in the Sky.* Discovery 71005. *1979*: USA.

Ottopasuuna. *Ottopasuuna.* Green Linnet GLCD 4005. *1992*: Finland.

Redmond, Layne, and the Mob of Angels. *Since the Beginning.* Redmond Recordings RRCD11. *1992*: USA.

Reid, Sandra. *Hal-An-Tow: Songs of Six Nations.* Lyrichord 7425. *1995*: USA.

Reijseger, Ernst, and Moore, Michael. *Cellotape & Scotchtape.* Data 822. *1982*: The Netherlands.

Robinson, N. Scott. *Things That Happen Fast.* New World View Music NWVM CD-02. *2001*: USA.

Robinson, N. Scott. *World View.* New World View Music NWVM CD-01. *1994*: USA.

Sanders, Pharaoh. *Save Our Children.* Verve 557 297-2. *1998*: USA.

Santana. *Welcome.* Columbia 16142. *1973*: USA.

Shadowfax. *The Odd Get Even.* Atlantic 20652P. *1990*: USA.

Shadowfax. *Too Far to Whisper.* Windham Hill WD-1051. *1977*: USA.

Simon, Ralph. *As.* Postcards POST 1004. *1981*: USA.

Smith, Ishmael Wadada Leo. *Kulture Jazz.* ECM 1507. *1993*: USA.

Mustaphas 3. *Heart of Uncle.* Rykodisc RCD 20156. *1989*: USA.

Tibbetts, Steve. *Exploded View.* ECM 1335 831 109-2. *1986*: USA.

ToKenKi. *Dance Latitude.* TKM 2001. *1991*: USA.

Velez, Glen. *Handance.* Nomad NMD 50301. *1984*: USA.

Velez, Glen. *Rhythmcolor Exotica.* Ellipsis Arts CD 4140. *1996*: USA.

Velez, Glen. *Seven Heaven.* CMP CD 30. *1987*: Germany.

Velez, Glen, with Levy, Howard. *Border States.* Interworld Music CD-21907. *1993*: USA.

Volans, Kevin. *White Man Sleeps.* Cala 88034-2. *1982*: USA.

Weather Report. *Weather Report.* Columbia/Legacy CK-48824. *1971*: USA.

Whelan, John. *Flirting with the Edge.* Narada 45444. *1998*: USA.

Visual Recordings

Dzamwarira, Thomas. 1975. 'Mbira Matepe dza Mhondoro: A Healing Party.' Pennsylvania State University (video).

Earth, Wind & Fire. 1990. 'Earth, Wind & Fire Live in Japan '90.' Pioneer Artists PA-98-582D (DVD).

Earth, Wind & Fire. 1994. 'Earth, Wind & Fire Live.' PolyGram Video 800 635 727-3 (video).

Gates, Henry Louis, Jr. 1999. 'Wonders of the African World: 3 – The Slave Kingdoms.' PBS B8103 (video).

Gwenzi, Gwanzura. 1975. 'Mbira dza Vadzimu: Religion at the Family Level with Gwanzura Gwenzi.' Pennsylvania State University (video).

'Konkombe: The Nigerian Pop Music Scene.' 1980. Shanachie Record Corp. (video).

Mashoko, Simon. 1975. 'Mbira: Njari-Karanga Songs in Christian Ceremonies with Simon Mashoko.' Pennsylvania State University (video).

'Mbira Music: The Spirit of the People (The Spirit of Zimbabwe).' 1990. Films for the Humanities & Sciences (video).

Mude, Hakurotwi. 1978. 'Mbira dzaVadzimu: Urban and Rural Ceremonies.' Pennsylvania State University (video).

Mujuru, Ephat. 1975. 'Mbira: The Technique of the Mbira dzaVadzimu.' Pennsylvania State University (video).

Mujuru, Muchatera, and Mujuru, Ephat. 1975. 'Mbira dza Vadzimu: Dambatsoko – An Old Cult Center with Muchatera and Ephat Mujuru.' Pennsylvania State University (video).

Robinson, N. Scott. 1996. 'Hand Drumming: Exercises for Unifying Technique.' Wright Hand Drum Company WHD-01 (video).

Sandler, Patricia. 1994. 'The Mbira and the Music of the Shona People of Zimbabwe.' Percussive Arts Society PAS9422 (video).

'The JVC/Smithsonian Folkways Video Anthology of Music and Dance of Africa. Vol. 2: The Gambia/ Liberia/Ghana/Nigeria.' 1996. JVC, Victor Company of Japan (video).

'The JVC Video Anthology of World Music and Dance. Vol. 17: Middle East & Africa II: Egypt/Tunisia/ Morocco/Mali/Cameroon/Zaire/ Tanzania.' 1988. JVC, Victor Company of Japan (video).

'The JVC Video Anthology of World Music and Dance. Vol. 19: Middle East & Africa IV: Ivory Coast/Botswana/Republic of South Africa.' 1988. JVC, Victor Company of Japan (video).

Wemba, Papa. 1987. 'La vie est belle' [Life Is Rosy]. Lamy Films (video).

Filmography

Lethal Weapon 2, dir. Richard Donner. 1989. USA. 114 mins. Action Thriller. Original music by Eric Clapton, Michael Kamen, David Sanborn.

N. SCOTT ROBINSON

Rhythm Section

The rhythm section of a musical group is defined as that section which provides the harmonic and rhythmic foundation, and is primarily concerned with accompanying the solo instruments and/or voices. The modern-day rhythm section usually includes a chord-playing instrument, such as the piano and/or guitar, an acoustic or electric bass and drums. However, the exact composition of the rhythm section is determined to a large degree by the style of music. While many styles of popular music involve a rhythm section, the term is mostly associated with jazz and rock. In the early stages of jazz, the bass part was most commonly played on the tuba; later, the acoustic string bass replaced the tuba as the dominant bass instrument. By the 1960s, the electric bass had become very prominent in jazz, rock, soul, and rhythm and blues (R&B). The banjo, which was commonly found in early jazz rhythm sections, was almost completely replaced by the guitar by the mid-1930s. It is important to note that both the acoustic bass and the guitar were also found in some of the earliest jazz rhythm sections.

The Function of the Instruments

The foundational instrument of the rhythm section is the bass. The bass provides a harmonic basis for the music, generally playing a line that emphasizes the roots of the chords. In addition, the bass provides a rhythmic component by playing a walking bass line in jazz, or a repetitive rhythmic pattern in rock. The bass part, when combined with a melody instrument, creates a complete musical sound, with melody, harmony and rhythm.

The drums, typically a drumset, provide both rhythmic drive and timbre. In jazz, the most important component of the drumset is the ride cymbal, which melds with the walking bass to create a unified time pulse. In rock-oriented music, the snare drum backbeat and the bass drum lock in with the bass part, again producing a composite groove.

The keyboard and the guitar each provide chordal harmony along with rhythmic 'comping,' a jazz term that comes from the words 'complementing' and 'accompanying' and refers to the playing of chords in a rhythmic fashion to support the soloist. Keyboard players and guitarists typically eliminate the roots of chords and leave that function to the bass player. If both a guitar and a keyboard are present in the rhythm section, each must leave space for the other so as to create an uncluttered sound.

Rhythm sections are usually set up at the back of the band in a formation that allows for eye contact among the players. The players must also be close enough to hear each other easily so that a balanced and synthesized sound can be achieved. The rhythm section is the most difficult section in which to create a blended, unified sound, because, unlike a trumpet or saxophone section, each rhythm section instrument is quite different. Great rhythm sections are able to create a composite effect in which each instrument contributes to the whole without obscuring the other instruments. Probably the most complete treatment of the rhythm section can be found in the CPP Media instructional video series, 'The Contemporary Rhythm Section,' which contains a master video on the rhythm section as a whole, along with individual videos on each of the rhythm section instruments.

Important Rhythm Sections

The original Count Basie rhythm section, with Count Basie on piano, Walter Page on bass, Jo Jones on drums and Freddie Green on guitar, was one of the most important such sections in jazz. Freddie Green's guitar style has become a standard approach for jazz rhythm guitar, especially in a big-band setting. Many of the most important innovations in jazz combo rhythm sections occurred in the Miles Davis groups: 1955–58 (Red Garland, piano; Paul Chambers, bass; Philly Joe Jones, drums); 1959–63 (Wynton Kelly, piano; Paul Chambers, bass; Jimmy Cobb, drums); and 1963–68 (Herbie Hancock, piano; Ron Carter, bass; Tony Williams, drums). The more rock-oriented groups that Davis led in the 1970s and later in the 1980s also made important contributions. Another influential jazz rhythm section was John Coltrane's, with McCoy Tyner on piano, Jimmy Garrison on bass and Elvin Jones on drums. In jazz, there has been a general movement toward more interaction between the rhythm section and the soloist. Musicians such as John Coltrane and Ornette Coleman, who were working in the free-jazz idiom, also formed rhythm sections containing no piano or guitar, which allowed more harmonic freedom for the soloist.

It could be argued that most rock bands are nothing more than rhythm sections accompanying vocalists. The rhythm section has become the focus in rock, and the electric guitar has moved into a solo position. Classic rock rhythm sections would include bands such as the Beatles, the Rolling Stones, the Grateful Dead, the Jimi Hendrix Experience and Cream, among many others. Funk and R&B bands also focus heavily on the rhythm section, and James Brown's rhythm sections have been particularly influential despite frequent personnel changes. Important members include Sam Thomas, David 'Hooks' Williams, Bernard Odum, bass; Melvin Parker, John 'Jabo' Starks, Clyde Stubblefield, drums; and Jimmy Nolen, Alphonso 'Country' Kellum, guitar. Also noteworthy is the Stax Studio rhythm section, consisting of Booker T. Jones, keyboard; Lewis Steinberg and Donald 'Duck' Dunn, bass; Al Jackson, Jr., drums; and Steve Cropper, guitar. This rhythm section accompanied Wilson Pickett, Aretha Franklin, Otis Redding and many others.

Brazilian and Afro-Cuban rhythm sections typically use more percussion instruments along with the keyboard and bass. These instruments include bongos, congas, timbales, maracas, claves, cowbells and many others. The drumset is often used in conjunction with these instruments and can even be played in such a way as to replace the other percussion instruments if they are unavailable.

Bibliography

Campbell, Michael. 1996. *And the Beat Goes On: An Introduction to Popular Music in America 1840 to Today*. New York: Schirmer Books.

Gridley, Mark C. 1997. *Jazz Styles – History and Analysis*. 6th ed. Upper Saddle River, NJ: Prentice-Hall.

Slutsky, Allan, and Silverman, Chuck. 1996. *The Great James Brown Rhythm Section – 1960–1973*. Miami, FL: Warner Bros. Publications Inc.

Szatmary, David P. 1996. *Rockin' in Time: A Social History of Rock-and-Roll*. 3rd ed. Upper Saddle River, NJ: Prentice-Hall.

Uribe, Ed. 1993. *The Essence of Brazilian Percussion and Drum Set*. Miami, FL: CPP/Belwin Inc.

Discography

Jazz

Armstrong, Louis, and His Hot Five. *The Louis Armstrong Story*, Vol. 1. Columbia CL 851. 1925: USA.

Basie, Count. *Basie*. Roulette SR-52003. *1958*: USA.

Basie, Count. *Basie Straight Ahead*. Chessmates GRP-822. *1998*: USA.

Coleman, Ornette. *Change of the Century*. Atlantic 81341-2. 1959; *1992*: USA.

Coleman, Ornette. *The Shape of Jazz to Come*. Atlantic 1317-2. *1959*: USA.

Coltrane, John. *A Love Supreme*. Impulse! 155. *1995*: USA.

Coltrane, John. *Coltrane Live at Birdland*. Impulse! 198. 1963; *1996*: USA.

Coltrane, John. *Coltrane Live at the Village Vanguard*. Impulse! 251. 1961; *1998*: USA.

Davis, Miles. *A Tribute to Jack Johnson*. Columbia 30455. *1971*: USA.

Davis, Miles. *The Complete Concert 1964: My Funny Valentine + Four and More*. Columbia/Legacy C2K-48821. 1964; *1992*: USA.

Davis, Miles. *In a Silent Way*. Columbia 9857. *1969*: USA.

Davis, Miles. *Milestones*. Columbia CK-40837. 1958; *1991*: USA.

Davis, Miles. *Tutu*. Warner Bros. 25490-2. *1986*: USA.

Davis, Miles. *Workin' with the Miles Davis Quintet*. Prestige 7166. *1956*: USA.

The Smithsonian Collection of Classic Jazz, Vols. 1–5. Smithsonian 0331-0335. *1991*: USA.

Rock
Beatles, The. *Meet the Beatles!*. Capitol 2047. *1964*: USA.
Cream. *Best of Cream*. Polydor 583 060. *1969*: UK.
Jimi Hendrix Experience, The. *Are You Experienced?*. MCA 11602. *1997*: USA.
Rolling Stones, The. *Exile on Main Street*. Rolling Stones COC 69100. *1972*: UK.

Motown
The Motown Story, Vols. 1–5. Motown MS-727 to MS-731. *1971*: USA.

Funk/R&B
Brown, James. *20 All-Time Greatest Hits*. PolyGram 314 511 326-2. *1991*: USA.
Pickett, Wilson. *Greatest Hits*. Atlantic 81737. *1976*: USA.
Redding, Otis. *Remember Me*. Stax SCD-8572-2. *1992*: USA.

Afro-Cuban
D'Rivera, Paquito. *Why Not!*. Columbia FCT-39584. *1984*: USA.
Puente, Tito. *Goza Mi Timbal*. Concord Picante CCD-4399-2. *1990*: USA.
Sanchez, Poncho. *Bien Sabroso!*. Concord Picante CCD-4239. *1992*: USA.

Brazilian
Bertrami, José Roberto. *Blue Wave/Dreams Are Real*. Milestone 47082. *1999*: USA.
Canta Brasil: The Great Brazilian Songbook. Verve 843115-2. *1990*: USA.
Donato, João. *Amazonas*. Elephant Records ER-203. *2000*: USA.
Elias, Eliane. *Eliane Elias Sings Jobim*. Blue Note 95050. *1998*: USA.
Mendes, Sergio. *Brasileiro*. Elektra 61315-2. *1992*: USA.

Visual Recordings
Houghton, Steve. 1994. 'The Contemporary Rhythm Section – Drums.' CPP Media (video).
Houghton, Steve, et al. 1994. 'The Contemporary Rhythm Section – Master.' CPP Media (video).
Ranier, Tom. 1994. 'The Contemporary Rhythm Section – Piano.' CPP Media (video).
Viapiano, Paul. 1994. 'The Contemporary Rhythm Section – Guitar.' CPP Media (video).
Warrington, Tom. 1994. 'The Contemporary Rhythm Section – Bass.' CPP Media (video).

TOM MORGAN

Slit-Drum

The slit-drum, also known as a wooden gong and a log drum, belongs to the category of musical instruments in which sound is produced by the vibration of solid material. As such, it is organologically classified as an idiophone. Sachs (1940) places the origin of the slit-drum in the 'middle stratum,' among prehistorical idiophones that appeared during the Neolithic period together with aerophones (such as the trumpet) and chordophones (such as the ground zither, ground harp and musical bow). While agreeing with Sachs that, in its earliest form, the slit-drum was a hollowed-out tree trunk, placed over a pit in the ground and stamped on, Marcuse (1975) places the origin of this instrument at the beginning of the Paleolithic period. However, despite the slit-drum's obscure origins, it is found in various cultures around the world – in Africa, the Americas, New Zealand and the Pacific Islands, where it is known by a variety of names ('Slit-drum' 1984).

Although the construction of slit-drums throughout the world is based on the same principle – cutting or gouging a slit in a piece of hollowed-out wood, carving the two sides (lips) of the slit to different thicknesses to produce two pitches (high and low) – they vary in size and shape, depending on the availability of raw materials and on the primary function that the instrument will fulfill in the community. Accordingly, the length of a slit-drum measures between 12" (30 cm) (with a diameter of 8" (20 cm)) and 8' 2" (2.5 m) (with a diameter of 36" (90 cm)). Whereas the larger slit-drums are usually kept in a central location in a village for communal use, the smaller ones are part of the array of tools used by healers in the making of invocations or the casting of spirits. These smaller drums are handheld and are played with one wooden mallet. Although the most common shape of the slit-drum is cylindrical, in one region of central Africa a diversity of shapes is found, with such morphological structures as trapeze, croissant, rectangle and half-moon (Laurenty 1968).

The decoration of the slit-drum according to cultural aesthetic norms, and/or to reflect features of a ceremony with which it is associated, reveals further cultural idiosyncracies associated with the instrument. Human and reptile (crocodile) motifs are common forms that provide the contour of the slit-drum. Other figures and geometric designs are also used, where appropriate, on the wall of the instrument. Examination of the variety of slit-drums and their functions in diverse cultures reveals aspects of the instrument that are often ignored in the discourse about the slit-drum. Although one of the most common functions fulfilled by the slit-drum is communication over long distances, especially in cultures where tonal languages contain only two tones (high and low), the instrument does not faithfully reproduce the tonal sequence of the language, but derives its musical phrases from the essence of the message contained in the traditional proverb (Mukuna 1987). In an atonal language, slit-drums do not communicate codes or signals, but musical phrases, which are recognized by the receiver as a given proverb, then interpreted as a message; those slit-drums utilized in these contexts are often cylindrical and unadorned.

Often ignored is the fact that not all slit-drums are made to be used as a surrogate language. Some are constructed for musical purposes and are played with rubber-tipped mallets. This characteristic is often not considered in the classification of the instrument. Although the technique of sound production on the slit-drum is percussive – a technique that qualifies the instrument to be classified as percussion – it is pertinent to point out that, just as the concept of percussion is not universal, so the conceptualization of the slit-drum is not uniform across all cultures. What may be valid for one culture may cause offense if applied cross-culturally. The conceptualization of the slit-drum is culturally defined, and the roles that are attributed to it are peculiar to each culture where it is found.

In Africa, for example, an instrument capable of producing only one tone is considered a percussion instrument. However, any percussion instrument on which two or more tones can be produced introduces the possibility of melody (Nzewi 1998). An illustration of this can be found among the Tetela and the Luba in the Democratic Republic of Congo (DRC), for example, where the trapeze-shaped slit-drum is primarily a musical instrument, carried on a strap around the neck and shoulder, and is used in a musical context to produce melody. Therefore, to classify the slit-drum of the Tetela (*engungu*) as a percussion idiophone along with similar instruments with which it shares morphology is totally erroneous and misleading; it is a melorhythmic instrument.

As both a percussion and a melorhythmic idiophone, the slit-drum has broadened its zone of cultural interaction (a geographic space in which the slit-drum has been accepted as part of the catalog of musical instruments). It has continued to be added to catalogs of musical instruments throughout the world. Its structural concept has continued to be emulated in mass production (utilizing different materials) in industrial countries. As the process of globalization has developed, the slit-drum has acquired new musical and percussive roles, in both traditional and popular musical expressions, if only for the unique timbre of its tones.

The Slit-Drum in Popular Music

The incorporation of the slit-drum into popular music is primarily possible where the instrument is used traditionally, although the instrument is also to be found occasionally in more contemporary forms of popular music. In most urban societies of Africa, where popular music fulfills functions equivalent to those fulfilled by traditional music in rural areas, the slit-drum is incorporated into popular music to provide special effects. In folk or traditional songs interpreted on imported musical instruments – known in Kinshasa (DRC), for example, as 'Folklore' – or in songs composed in that style with a strong traditional character, the slit-drum is often assigned to providing rhythmic patterns. This is the case, for example, in the use of the slit-drum (*lokole*) by the OK Jazz ensemble, one of the most prolific bands in Kinshasa between 1956 and 1994, in its 1984 series of compositions. In 'Maya Ozali Coupable ya Misere na Ngai' (Maya, You Are Responsible for My Miseries), composed by Simarro Massiya and released in 1984, the slit-drum suggests to the dancers a walking motion with its two tones (high and low) in a quasi-duplex meter. Between 1984 and 1989, OK Jazz used the slit-drum in most of its compositions for special effect. Since the slit-drum is not a melodic instrument, its use in popular music – in the Democratic Republic of Congo, for example – is to achieve a special effect aimed at inserting a traditional element into a composition.

Bibliography

Carrington, John F. 1949. *Talking Drums of Africa*. London: Carey Kingsgate Press.

Laurenty, Jean-Sebastien. 1968. *Les Tambours à fente de l'Afrique Centrale* [Slit-Drums of Central Africa]. Tervuren: Musée Royale de l'Afrique Centrale.

Marcuse, Sibyl. 1975. *A Survey of Musical Instruments*. New York: Harper & Row.

Mukuna, Kazadi wa. 1987. 'Function of Musical Instruments in Surrogate Languages in Africa.' *Africa: Revista de Centro de Estudos Africanos de Universidade de Sao Paulo* 10: 3–8.

Nketia, J.H. Kwabena. 1971. 'Surrogate Languages of Africa.' *Current Trends in Linguistics* 7: 699–732.

Nzewi, Meki. 1998. *African Music: Theoretical Content and Creative Continuum – The Cultural Exponent's Definitions*. Oldershausen: Institut für Didaktik Populärer Musik.

Sachs, Curt. 1940. *The History of Musical Instruments*. New York: W.W. Norton.

'Slit-drum.' 1984. *The New Grove Dictionary of Musical Instruments*, Vol. 3, ed. Stanley Sadie. New York: Macmillan, 405–406.

Discographical Reference

'Maya Ozali Coupable ya Misere na Ngai.' *Le Poete Simarro Massiya dans Maya*. L'Industrie Africaine du Disque PF-77012. *1984*: Congo.

Discography

Allen, Michael Graham. *In Medicine River*. Coyote Oldman Music CO-5-CD. *1992*: USA.

Cherry, Don. *Organic Music Society*. Caprice CAP 2001 (1-2). *1972*: Sweden.

Crumb, George. *Music for a Summer Evening (Makrokosmos III)*. Nonesuch H-71311. *1975*: USA.

Goodhart, Rich. *Never Give a Sword to a Man Who Can't Dance*. Beginner's Mind Productions BMP 0403. *1995*: USA.

Goodhart, Rich. *The Gathering Sun*. Beginner's Mind Productions BMP 0404. *1999*: USA.

Gurtu, Trilok. *Kathak*. Times Music TDIFU 004P. *1999*: UK.

Hancock, Herbie. *Head Hunters*. Columbia/Legacy 471239 2. *1973*: USA.

King Crimson. *Discipline*. Virgin EGCD 49. *1981*: USA.

Moreira, Airto. *I'm Fine. How Are You?*. Warner Music Japan WPCR2154. *1979*: Japan.

Moye, Famoudou Don. *Sun Percussion Volume One*. Aeco 001. *1975*: USA.

Music of the Abelam, Papua Niugini. Musicaphon BM 30 SL 2704. *1966*: Germany.

Music of the World's Peoples, Vol. 5. Folkways FE 4508. *1961*: USA.

Oregon. *Oregon*. ECM 1258 811 711-2. *1983*: USA.

Oregon. *Oregon in Performance*. Elektra 9E 304. *1980*: USA.

Oregon. *Roots in the Sky*. Discovery 71005. *1979*: USA.

Papua Niugini: The Middle Sepik. Musicaphon BM 30 SL 2700. *1962*: Germany.

Poole, Elissa. *Strange Companions*. Artifact Music ART 003-CD. *1991*: Canada.

Temiz, Okay. *Drummer of Two Worlds*. Finnadar SR 9032. *1980*: USA.

Traditional Music of Tonga. Hibiscus HLS 65. *1973*: New Zealand.

Wedgle, Barry. *Kake*. Wonderful World Records 1201. *1982*: USA.

Winter, Paul. *Earth: Voices of a Planet*. Living Music LD 0019. *1990*: USA.

Visual Recordings

'Musique Are'are: Part 2, Slit Drum Music.' 1979. C.N.R.S. VC#1870 (video).

'The JVC Video Anthology of World Music and Dance. Vol. 19: Middle East & Africa IV: Ivory Coast/Botswana/Republic of South Africa.' 1988. JVC, Victor Company of Japan (video).

'The JVC Video Anthology of World Music and Dance. Vol. 29: Oceania I: Micronesia/Melanesia/Australia.' 1988. JVC, Victor Company of Japan (video).

KAZADI WA MUKUNA

Snare Drum

The snare drum can be traced back 250 years to the tabor and the side drum. These earlier instruments were generally very large and were used exclusively for military purposes. In the eighteenth and nineteenth centuries, the side drum was incorporated into opera orchestras for use in military scenes. During the middle and latter parts of the nineteenth century, the instrument gradually made its way from the opera pit to the concert stage.

The principal difference between the modern instrument and the earlier ones is the use of tension rods for the drumheads as opposed to that of rope tensioning or simple tacked-on heads. This change was first introduced in 1837 by Cornelius Ward. His drum used screw tensioning instead of rope, had a brass shell, and was considerably smaller than earlier drums. The size of the drum was reduced to accommodate its use in nonmilitary events.

The snare drum can be found in any part of the world, having been influenced by European colonization. It appears in various forms for use in popular marching or military bands in North, Central and South America. Drum corps, in which performers use highly stylized sticking patterns called drum rudiments and in which they are often accompanied by fifes, bugles or bagpipes, are especially popular in the United States, Canada, Britain and Switzerland.

Also found in the military and concert bands of Bolivia and Peru, the snare drum appears throughout South America in various other contexts. These include its use in the pipe and tabor tradition in Peru, as well as in Ecuador, where a larger *bombo* with snare is used. The snare drum is found as a predominant instrument in the musical ensembles of Chile (as the *caja chayero*) and Brazil (as the *caixa*) for carnival celebrations and samba performances. Snare drums are often played simultaneously by dozens of performers.

The most significant role played by the snare drum in modern music is as a vital part of the drumset. In the drumset, the snare drum is the soprano voice and is frequently used to define the backbeat (beats 2 and 4 in a 4/4 measure). While the size of drumsets can range from two to 15 drums (or more), there is always a snare drum in the kit, and it always plays a prominent role in the rhythmic patterns. As a member of the drumset, the snare drum has contributed to the evolution of many styles of dance and popular music, including jazz, swing, rock, bebop, country, country and western, disco, Latin-rock, Afro-rock, reggae, Afrobeat and numerous other fusion styles.

The modern snare-drum shell is made from metal (steel, aluminum, brass), wood (maple, rosewood) or a synthetic material. A diameter that ranges from 13" (33 cm) to 15" (38 cm) and a depth that ranges from 4" (10 cm) to 8" (20 cm) are the most common dimensions. The heads are made from either synthetic material or calfskin. In addition, the bottom head has a number of snares stretched across it that rattle against the membrane when the drum is struck. The snares are generally made of wire, cable or catgut.

Snare drums are generally struck with a pair of wooden sticks, which have been turned in such a fashion as to produce a tip at the end of the stick that strikes the head. Other items used to strike the drum include wire brushes and, on occasion, a timpani mallet.

Of all the percussion instruments, the snare drum requires a playing technique that is one of the most demanding and exact. For that reason, it is often the first instrument studied by young percussionists. The fine degree of muscle control needed for playing the snare drum, especially for performances involving extremely soft dynamics, requires many years of practise. The player must be able to control a variety of strokes and sticking patterns which are used to achieve various effects and musical shadings.

The snare drum has a distinctive high-pitched, dry and crisp sound when the snares are engaged across the bottom head. When the snares are not in contact with the bottom head, the drum has a hollow sound much like that of a high-pitched tom-tom. It is possible to create other effects with the snare drum, which can produce sounds very similar to those of gunshots, wood blocks and claves.

In the context of marching, the role performed by the snare drum is much different from its function on the concert stage or in the jazz club: it serves as the soprano voice in the percussion section and, as such, often provides the most prominent rhythmic voice in the marching ensemble.

Bibliography

Tamlyn, Garry. 1998. *The Big Beat: Origins and Development of Snare Drum Backbeat and Other Accompanimental Rhythms in Rock 'n' Roll.* Unpublished Ph.D. thesis, University of Liverpool, UK.

ANDREW SPENCER

Steel Pans (Steel Drums)

A steel drum or pan is an instrument generally fabricated from an oil or chemical barrel with a capacity of about 55 US gallons (208 liters). The end of the barrel is sunk inward to form a concave shape; individual sections are then grooved on this surface and manipulated to produce tones. Pitch is determined by the size of the section and the amount of tension in the metal. A lead or tenor pan often consists of 28 notes tuned on one barrel. For other types of pans, notes are distributed between two or more barrels to create a set played by one musician. Multiple pans, with different registers, are typically combined to form a steel band, although pans are also used in ensembles that include other types of instruments.

Steel bands and ensembles with pans can be found throughout the world; however, it is not long ago that this unique form of making music existed only in the context of local festivity in Trinidad.

The Development of Steel Pans

Steel pans emerged in Trinidad around 1940 as a replacement for bamboo percussion instruments used during pre-Lenten carnival street processions. Through beating on the bottoms of assorted metal containers, percussionists discovered that containers could be shaped to produce one or more tones. By the early 1940s, there were three common types of pans: a kittle, a three-note lead instrument often made from a zinc or paint can; a cuff boom or slap bass, a large biscuit container that produced one low sound of indefinite pitch; and a bass kittle or dud-up, a caustic soda container divided into two notes that provided counter-rhythms. In the course of the 1940s, more notes were added to pans by grooving additional sections on the bottoms of containers and, by the end of the decade, the full-size oil barrel had become the most popular source of instruments. Meanwhile, the tonal quality of pans improved, and the wrapping of playing sticks with strips of rubber helped to create a mellower sound. By the early 1950s, steel band instrumentation included a lead ping pong, a second pan, a tenor boom (consisting of two barrels) and a bass (consisting of three barrels). All pans now contained sufficient notes to make conventional Western harmony possible. While steel bands played only simple melodies during the World War II period, by the early 1950s they were performing local calypsos, popular music of the Americas and European classical selections.

Experimentation with the tuning (fabricating) of pans has continued, both in Trinidad and in other countries. Among the leading tuners at the end of the twentieth century were Ellie Mannette, Bertie Marshall, Lincoln Noel, Leo Coker, Bertram Kellman and Roland Harrigin. Central areas of innovation have included the selection of optimum types of metal for pans, tuning techniques, and the standardization of the ranges and layouts of notes on different pans. Although pans are not yet standardized, there are several common types of instruments. One version of the tenor pan has 28 notes, ranging from d to f^2. A nine bass, consisting of nine barrels, has 30 notes, ranging from G^2 to c. Among the instruments with registers between those of the tenor and the nine bass are the double tenor (two barrels), the double second (two barrels), the quadraphonic (four barrels), the guitar (two or three barrels), the cello (three or four barrels), the tenor bass (four barrels) and the six bass (six barrels). While the six bass and the nine bass consist of complete barrels, the sides of the barrels used for the other instruments are cut to various lengths to form 'skirts.'

For performances, basses rest on blocks on the floor, while the other instruments are suspended from stands. When steel bands play in street processions, all pans are mounted on large metal frames with wheels. In a steel band, different sections of pans are assigned specific melodic and harmonic roles in musical arrangements. In addition to pans, a steel band typically includes a trap set and various Caribbean percussion instruments.

Steel Pans as Global Instruments

Although the making and playing of pans have continued to have their most vibrant manifestation in Trinidad, the instruments also exist in many other countries. The use of pans first spread to other parts of the Anglophone Caribbean during the 1940s, through migration to and from Trinidad. By the 1950s, there were steel bands in immigrant communities in New York and London. Gradually, steel bands were established in other cities with substantial West Indian populations. Meanwhile, the presence of many West Indian panists abroad and the distribution of steel band recordings inspired non-West Indians to form steel bands. In the United States, for example, there are numerous bands associated with colleges, high schools and elementary schools. Steel bands can also be found in such countries as Venezuela, Switzerland, Nigeria and Japan.

Since the 1950s, pans have been closely associated with Caribbean tourism. Visitors to the Anglophone West Indies, in particular, expect to hear steel bands in hotels and other tourist-oriented venues. Pans are also common in the cruise ship industry, and in tourist and private party settings in Florida. Touristic performances typically feature small steel bands (fewer than 10 musicians) or one or two panists in ensembles that also include an electric guitar, bass and/or keyboard. In addition, panists have increasingly been using electronic sequencers or minidiscs to provide prerecorded rhythm, bass and/or keyboard tracks. Pans also feature as soundtracks for fantasies of tropical leisure in movies, television shows and commercials.

While touristic engagements are sometimes viewed as musically limiting by panists, jazz has provided a particularly fruitful avenue of expression. For example, three of Trinidad's best-known pan soloists, Othello Molineaux, Rudy Smith and Robert Greenidge, have lived overseas for many years and have played with numerous jazz musicians. Molineaux, based in Miami, plays at jazz clubs and festivals throughout the world and has worked with such artists as Jaco Pastorius, Ahmad Jamal, McCoy Tyner and Monty Alexander. Smith, based in Denmark, leads an ensemble that has

been instrumental in introducing the pan to the European jazz scene. Greenidge, based in Los Angeles, has recorded with many popular musicians, including Grover Washington, Jr., Ralph MacDonald, Jimmy Buffett, and Earth, Wind and Fire. Recordings by Andy Narell, a US panist, have also helped to popularize the instrument.

The attraction of the steel pan for musicians and audiences throughout the world springs from the uniqueness of the instrument's construction and sound. While the pan is sometimes treated as a novelty instrument, musicians in many countries have demonstrated its capacity to provide original interpretations of a wide range of musical forms and styles. Panists continue to seek ways of developing the instrument's potential in educational, concert and mass-media contexts.

Bibliography

Goddard, George 'Sonny.' 1991. *Forty Years in the Steelbands: 1939–1979*, ed. Roy D. Thomas. London: Karia Press.

Stuempfle, Stephen. 1995. *The Steelband Movement: The Forging of a National Art in Trinidad and Tobago*. Philadelphia: University of Pennsylvania Press.

Thomas, Jeffrey. 1992. *Forty Years of Steel: An Annotated Discography of Steel Band and Pan Recordings, 1951–1991*. Westport, CT: Greenwood Press.

Thomas, Jeffrey. 1995. 'Steel Band/Pan.' In *Encyclopedia of Percussion*, ed. John H. Beck. New York: Garland Publishing, 297–331.

Discography

Greenidge/Utley. *Club Trini*. Margaritaville Records 162-531 041-2. *1996*: USA.

Molineaux, Othello. *It's About Time*. Big World BW2010. *1993*: USA.

Narell, Andy. *The Long Time Band*. Windham Hill 01934 11172-2. *1995*: USA.

Pan Is Beautiful V: World Steelband Festival, Vols. I & II (Classics in Steel). Trini-T Records PBV 01/88 & PBV 02/88. *1989*: Trinidad and Tobago.

Pan Odyssey: Steelbands of Trinidad and Tobago. Sanch CD 9504. *1995*: Trinidad and Tobago.

Panyard Sketches: Steel Orchestras of Trinidad and Tobago. Sanch CD 9801. *1998*: Trinidad and Tobago.

Patasar, Mungal and Pantar. *Nirvana*. Rituals Records CO2597. *1997*: Trinidad and Tobago.

STEPHEN STUEMPFLE

Tablā

Tablā (from Persian-Arabic *tabl*) constitute a set of hand drums, originating in North India. Each set consists of two tuned drums – *daya* (right) and *baya* (left), higher- and lower-pitched, respectively. The *daya* is made from one piece of hollowed-out wood; the *baya* is made of either metal or clay. The drumheads, usually of goatskin, have three different layers, the distinct sounds of which are manipulated by the player. A system of mnemonics, known as *bols* (from the Hindi *bolnā*, 'to speak'), has developed as a form of notation, as a memory aid and as an aspect of performance. Sounds such as *dha*, *dhin*, *ta* and *tete* represent combinations of single- or double-handed strokes and can be combined in various permutations to make striking and complex rhythmic compositions.

Performance Contexts

The *tablā* perform both a solo and an accompanying role in a number of musical contexts. In North Indian classical music, their function is to keep the *tāl* (time cycle) and also to interact in an improvisatory manner with the vocalist or solo instrumentalist. There is also a tradition of solo *tablā* performance in which a number of compositional models, such as *qāidā*, *relā* and *tukrā*, are used as the basis for extensive extemporization. In such performances, the *tablā* are often accompanied by a melodic instrument, usually the *sārangā* or harmonium, which delineates a repeated melody, *lahra*, for time-keeping.

The *Tablā* in Popular Music

The widespread use of the *tablā* in South Asian folk, religious and classical musics has meant that they have also become one of the central instruments in Indian popular music that draws on a variety of musical sources to create its unique sound. The driving eight-beat rhythm, *keharvā* (divided 4 + 4), played on the *tablā*, underpins musics as different as *bhangra* and *qawwālī* and defines their rhythmic identities. The percussion sections in *filmī* songs invariably feature the *tablā* beside other Indian and Western instruments. Indian musical identity in *filmī* songs owes much to the presence of the *tablā*, which are usually employed to keep the *tāl*, firmly anchoring the songs in the world of Indian rhythm.

The *tablā* have also had significant success in Western popular music. They were first heard with the *sitār* during the 'great sitar explosion' of the 1960s, but their flexibility and distinctive tone color have meant that they have now become a standard part of the pop, rock and jazz percussionist's array of musical resources. *Tablā* players such as Zakir Hussain, Trilok Gurtu and Talvin Singh have become prominent figures in Western popular music.

Bibliography

Dick, Alistair, and Sen, Devdan. 1984. 'Tablā.' In *The New Grove Dictionary of Musical Instruments*, Vol. 3, ed. Stanley Sadie. London: Macmillan, 492–97.

Gottlieb, Robert S. 1977. *The Major Traditions of North Indian Tabla Drumming*. Munich: Emil Katzbichler.

GERRY FARRELL

Timbales

Timbales, also known as *pailitas cubanas*, *pailes*, *timbaletas* and *bongó*, have a rich history that is closely tied to the settling of the island of Cuba by the Spanish. Like many other Afro-Caribbean percussion instruments, these drums developed out of the cultural fusion that occurred when Europeans settling in the Caribbean and South America brought slaves from Africa to work on their plantations. As a result of the gradual commingling of the cultures of these peoples, aspects of their music mixed and developed into a new style with new instruments. The timbales were a product of this social and musical fusion.

The timbales evolved from early orchestral timpani that the Spaniards brought with them to Cuba – in fact, the word 'timbale' is the Spanish translation of the English word 'timpani.' Early timbales closely resembled the timpani used in baroque and classical orchestras. These consisted of two metal bowls approximately 18"–20" (45–50 cm) in diameter, with calfskin heads stretched across the top. These heads were tucked into wooden hoops, which were tightened or loosened with metal screws, thus increasing or decreasing the tension of the heads.

Modern timbales usually consist of two drums of brass or steel, approximately 13" and 14" (33 cm and 35 cm) in diameter, with a head on the top of each drum and an open bottom. The heads are mounted on a steel rim, which is fastened to the shell with steel bolts that are tightened with a wrench. In early versions of the timbales, an animal hide (usually calf or mule) was used for the playing head; modern timbales often have plastic heads, allowing the performer to play more loudly with less risk of breaking the head. The drums are commonly mounted on a stand, and the player usually stands while playing.

The early timbale setup consisted of two drums, placed on the floor or on a stand; the performer played on the shells and the heads with sticks. In modern usage, the setup commonly consists of two to four drums, with cowbells, wood blocks and cymbals mounted on the stand along with the timbales. Thus, modern timbale players can provide a much wider range of sounds than their predecessors.

Timbales were central instruments in the *charanga francesca*, a type of ensemble that originated in the European tradition brought to Cuba by the Spanish and that often performed at elegant aristocratic functions. As the music of the Spanish elite evolved through various genres, including the *contradanza*, the *charanga francesca* and the *conjunto*, it was gradually influenced by the rhythms and instruments of the African slaves.

The *conjunto* orchestras played the music of rural Cubans primarily at the *carnaval* celebrations. The instrumentation for this type of orchestra included various percussion instruments. These instruments were often made by the performers from implements used on the plantations, and included the claves, bongos, congas and cowbells. These *conjunto* orchestras gradually evolved into mambo bands and modern salsa bands, where the traditional *conjunto* percussion instruments are augmented with the timbales. Among the leading mambo/salsa timbale players are José Luis 'Changuito' Quintana, Tito Puente, Walfredo de los Reyes Sr., Willie Bobo and Humberto Morales.

The strong interest in Afro-Caribbean music that has arisen since the early 1980s has resulted in the incorporation of many instruments of traditional Afro-Cuban bands, including the timbales, into US and European pop and rock music. Leading this movement are bands such as the Miami Sound Machine and Santana and popular singers such as José Feliciano and Tania Maria.

Bibliography

Blades, James. 1984. *Percussion Instruments and Their History*. Rev. ed. Boston, MA: Faber and Faber.

Malabe, Frank, and Weiner, Bob. 1990. *Afro-Cuban Rhythms for the Drumset*. Miami, FL: Warner Brothers Music.

Mauleón, Rebeca. 1993. *Salsa Guidebook for Piano and Ensemble*. Petaluma, CA: Sher Music Co.

Quintana, José Luis, and Silverman, Chuck. 1998. *Changuito: A Master's Approach to Timbales*. Miami, FL: Warner Brothers Music.

Uribe, Ed. 1996. *Essence of Afro-Cuban Percussion and Drum Set*. Miami, FL: Warner Brothers Music.

Discography

Barretto, Ray. *Indestructible*. Fania 456. *1993*: USA.

Barretto, Ray. *Ritmo de la Vida*. Fania JM605. *1982*: USA.

Batacumbele. *Afro Caribbean Jazz*. Montuno MLP 525. *1993*: USA.

Batacumbele. *Con Un Poco De Songo*. Disco Hit DHT 008. *1981*: USA.

Fania All Stars, The. *Lo Que Pide La Gente*. Fania 629. *1989*: USA.

Machito. *Live at North Sea '82*. Timeless 168. *1982*: USA.

Puente, Tito. *Cuban Carnival*. RCA 2349-2-RL. *1956*: USA.

Puente, Tito. *The Mambo King: His 100th Album*. Sony Discos 80680. *1991*: USA.

Puente, Tito. *Un Poco Loco*. Picante CJP-329. *1987*: USA.

JONATHAN WACKER

Vibraphone

The vibraphone ('vibraharp' or 'vibes') is a tuned percussion instrument that was invented in the United States in the early twentieth century. It was developed from a 'steel marimba,' a novelty instrument in which a marimba's traditional wooden bars were replaced with metal ones. Beneath each bar was a tubular resonator, closed at one end. Resonators focus the sound of bar percussion instruments to make them louder. In 1916, Hermann Winterhoff of the Leedy Drum Company developed a motor-driven mechanism to raise and lower the banks of resonators, producing a fluctuation in volume. In 1921, this awkward arrangement was replaced by a system in which a rotating disc was positioned at the top (open) end of each resonator. The resultant pulsation of sound inspired the name 'vibraphone' (Blades 1992). Competing manufacturer J.C. Deagan, Inc. created a version of the instrument that had tempered aluminum bars in place of steel and named the instrument a 'vibraharp' (Peters 1975).

Little has changed in the basic design of the instrument since then. The bars are made of an aluminum alloy and vary in length and sometimes in width. Smaller bars are higher in pitch. An arch trimmed lengthwise from the bottom center half of the bar reduces the number of overtones, resulting in the clear, mellow tone associated with the instrument.

The standard range of the vibraphone is three octaves, F to f^2, with the notes arranged in the same configuration as a piano keyboard. Because the bars ring for 10 to 15 seconds after being struck, a foot-operated damper bar stretches the length of the instrument below the inner ends of the bars.

Vibists use mallets to strike the bars. The mallets are approximately 15" to 16" (38 cm to 42 cm) long, and players may hold one or two mallets in each hand. The handles are most commonly made of rattan, which flexes to absorb the shock of contact. The head of the mallet consists of yarn wrapped around a rubber core.

The vibraphone found its first widespread popularity during the swing era. In the 1930s, it was championed by Lionel Hampton, playing with the Benny Goodman Quartet. In the early 1940s, jazz xylophonist Red Norvo switched to the newer instrument. Vibists at this time typically eschewed the harmonic possibilities of four mallets, favoring the melodic potential inherent in the use of two.

The late 1940s witnessed Milt Jackson exhibiting the speed and musical agility needed to become the first bebop vibist. In the 1950s, as a founding member of the Modern Jazz Quartet, Jackson used the vibraphone's mellow sound and new variable-speed motor to help establish the cool-jazz era. Vibraphones became a part of the George Shearing quintet sound, with a succession of players including Margie Hyams and Cal Tjader. Tjader later led his own groups, which emphasized popular Latin rhythms within the context of jazz.

In the late 1960s, Gary Burton developed a manner of playing that moved the vibraphone into the rhythm section, emulating the function of a piano. He changed the grip used to hold two mallets in each hand, and developed a system of mallet-dampening that gave him the option of silencing individual notes while the sustain pedal allowed others to ring. Through this adroit use of four mallets, melody and harmony could overlap, allowing Burton to play entire solo concerts by himself. Burton also popularized the idea of not using the motor, the very innovation in the 1920s that gave the instrument its name!

The lure of electronics periodically influences vibists. Burton, a pioneer in jazz-rock fusion, briefly experimented with a rock guitar-like system of amplifying and distorting his sound. In the 1970s, manufacturers vainly tried to market an electronically amplified version of the vibraphone in which resonators were replaced by transducers.

The 1970s found Mike Mainieri pioneering efforts to marry a synthesizer to a mallet keyboard. By the late 1980s, manufacturers had produced MIDI (musical instrument digital interface) triggers that were either attached to the bars or, with the vibraphone eliminated entirely, mounted within rubber pads laid out in a mallet keyboard configuration.

Although it is most strongly associated with the jazz tradition, the vibraphone appears sporadically throughout rock history, most often as background to soft rock or Motown recordings: examples include the Fortunes, the Supremes and Tim Weisberg. Frank Zappa's groups included percussionist/vibist Ruth Underwood, who was later replaced by Ed Mann.

Because of the vibraphone's relative youth and its beginnings as a novelty instrument, orchestral composers have rarely written for it. It owes its development almost entirely to the realm of popular music, especially jazz. A visually dynamic instrument in performance, the vibraphone has appeared throughout most styles of popular music in the United States, but it has never been indispensable to any.

Bibliography

Blades, James. 1992. *Percussion Instruments and Their History*. Rev. ed. Westport, CT: The Bold Strummer, Ltd. (First published London: Faber and Faber, 1970.)

Peters, Gordon. 1975. *The Drummer, Man: A Treatise on Percussion*. Rev. ed. Wilmette, IL: Kemper-Peters Publications. (Previous ed. published as *Treatise on Percussion*. Rochester, NY: Eastman School of Music, 1962.)

Discography

Burton, Gary. *Alone At Last*. Atlantic SD 1598. *1971*: USA.

Burton, Gary. *Artist's Choice*. Bluebird 6280-2-RB. 1963–68; *1987*: USA.

Burton, Gary. *Good Vibes*. Atlantic SD 1560. *1970*: USA.

Burton, Gary. *The Time Machine*. RCA-Victor LSP-3642. *1966*: USA.

Burton, Gary, and Corea, Chick. *In Concert, Zürich, October 28, 1979*. ECM 821 415-2. *1980*: USA.

Burton, Gary, and Piazzolla, Astor. *The New Tango*. Atlantic 81823-2. *1987*: USA.

Fortunes, The. *Here Comes That Rainy Day Feeling Again*. Capitol 809. *1973*: USA.

Gillespie, Dizzy. *'Diz'*. Camden QJ-25071. 1947–49; *1978*: USA.

Goodman, Benny. *Trio and Quartet Live 1937–1938*. CBS 62853. *1973*: USA.

Jazz-Club Vibraphone. Verve 840034-2. *1991*: USA.

Modern Jazz Quartet, The. *The Art of the M.J.Q. – The Atlantic Years*. Atlantic SD 2-301 0698. *1973*: USA.

Motown Story. Motown MS-5-726. *1971*: USA.

Shearing, George. *George Shearing – Verve Jazz Masters 57*. PGD/Verve 31451 29900 2. 1949–54; *1996*: USA.

TERENCE GUNDERSON

Xylophone

The xylophone (Ger.: *xylophon*; It.: *silofono*; Sp.: *xilofóno*) consists of a series of wooden bars of graduated lengths which are sounded by being struck with mallets or sticks. All wooden-bar instruments (marimbas, xylorimbas and so on) may be classified as xylophones, but the word usually refers specifically to the European/North American/Japanese two-row, chromatically tuned instrument that has rosewood bars, metal tube resonators and a range of three to five octaves, with the highest pitched bar tuned to c^5. Xylophones of North American or Japanese origin are 'quint' tuned, with a predominance of the second upper partial of each bar (a 12th above the fundamental pitch), while xylophones of European origin are tuned with a predominance of the third upper partial (two octaves above the fundamental pitch) or the first upper partial (one octave above the fundamental pitch).

Scholars believe (Marcuse 1975; Jones 1971) that the xylophone originated in Asia and migrated to Africa, possibly through Madagascar, before the arrival of the Portuguese in the fourteenth century. It may have been introduced into Europe by the Portuguese, or it may have been brought by Europeans returning from the

Crusades. In the seventeenth century, the marimba (the xylophone of Central and South America) was introduced into the New World by African slaves; its use became widespread among the Native Indians, and it was played on social and religious occasions.

In early nineteenth-century Europe, the instrument was popularized by Michael Josef Gusikov, a Pole whose concertizing throughout Europe led to recognition for the instrument. In late nineteenth-century North America, several factors increased the popularity of the xylophone: (a) the immigration of skilled European xylophonists; (b) the invention of the phonograph, which closely reproduced the xylophone's sound; and (c) the manufacture of high-quality xylophones by the J.C. Deagan Company of Chicago.

Early twentieth-century concert bands featured xylophone soloists performing arrangements of popular music, including marches, waltzes, patriotic and popular songs, and transcriptions of classical music. The xylophone provided rhythmic clarity in the dance music of the 1920s, in which two styles of xylophone performance, both refined by George Hamilton Green, were dominant: (a) the obbligato (optional embellishment) style, also called 'noodling'; and (b) the 'Novelty Ragtime' style, an elaborate, highly technical, syncopated embellishment, often improvised.

In vaudeville, xylophonists William Coates ('El Cota') and Teddy Brown attained wide public recognition. Performances were highly visual, with added tricks or gags to entertain the audience. Another vaudeville phenomenon was the popularity of Central American marimba bands, which introduced their music and instruments to new audiences.

From 1890 to 1929, thousands of phonograph recordings were made that featured xylophonists playing popular music. Beginning in the 1930s, electric-process recordings introduced 'swing' music featuring xylophonists Red Norvo (United States), Harry Robbins (England) and Kurt Engel (Germany). Xylophonist Sammy Herman hosted an NBC radio network program in the mid-1930s, reaching many listeners through live broadcasts. Around 1936, the vibraphone replaced the xylophone, which thereafter disappeared from the mainstream of popular music.

Since then, the xylophone has been featured in cartoons (*Betty Boop*), in musicals (*West Side Story*), on television (*The Lawrence Welk Hour*) and in symphonic pops concerts (*Hong Kong Fireworks* by Henry Mancini). In the 1970s, interest in Novelty Ragtime xylophone music was revived by Bob Becker through recordings and performances with the percussion group, NEXUS. The xylophone is virtually absent in rock music genres, except for rare use of the marimba.

Bibliography

Blades, James. 1970. *Percussion Instruments and Their History*. New York: Praeger.

Cahn, William. 1995. 'The Xylophone.' In *Encyclopedia of Percussion*, ed. John H. Beck. New York: Garland, 347–61.

Cahn, William. 1996. *The Xylophone in Acoustic Recordings (1877–1929)*. Rev. ed. Bloomfield, NY: William L. Cahn Publishing. (First published Holcomb, NY: Cahn, 1979.)

Jones, A.M. 1971. *Africa and Indonesia: The Evidence of the Xylophone and Other Musical and Cultural Factors*. Leiden: E.J. Brill.

Marcuse, Sibyl. 1975. *A Survey of Musical Instruments*. New York: Harper & Row.

Sadie, Stanley, ed. 1984. *The New Grove Dictionary of Musical Instruments*. 3 vols. London: Macmillan.

Discography

All Star Trio. 'Fluffy Ruffles.' Victor 18641. 1919: USA.

Becker, Bob. 'The Ragtime Robin.' *NEXUS Ragtime Concert*. NEXUS 10284. *1991*: USA.

Green, George Hamilton. 'Triplets.' *Masters of the Xylophone*. Xylophonia Music Company XMC 001. *1993*: USA.

Red Norvo and His All Stars. 'Knockin' on Wood.' *Red Norvo and His All Stars*. Epic LN-3128. 1933–38: USA.

Valley Tonga (recorded by Hugh Tracey). 'Ulumbundu-bundu.' *Music of Africa Series: Musical Instruments 5. Xylophones*. Kaleidophone KMA 5. *1972*: USA.

West Side Story [Original Cast]. Double Play 113. *1995*: USA.

Filmography

West Side Story, dir. Jerome Robbins and Robert Wise. 1961. USA. 151 mins. Musical Drama. Original music by Leonard Bernstein, Saul Chaplin, Irwin Kostal, Sid Ramin, Stephen Sondheim.

WILLIAM L. CAHN

13. Stringed Instruments

Appalachian Dulcimer

The Appalachian dulcimer, sometimes also called the 'mountain' or 'plucked' dulcimer, is a type of 'box-zither' found in the upland south of the United States, hence the term 'Appalachian' dulcimer. It evolved from the German *scheitholt* brought to this region by Pennsylvania German settlers, probably during the late seventeenth century and after. Similar instruments also developed in Sweden, Norway and other European countries. The narrow fingerboard, the arrangement of frets and resulting tunings, predominantly Ionian, came from the *scheitholt*. In the twentieth century, various local forms eventually culminated in the Appalachian dulcimer as it is known today.

The Appalachian dulcimer has either an hourglass-shaped or a teardrop-shaped wooden resonator with sound holes, which can be up to three feet long. The fingerboard sits lengthwise on top of this resonator and usually has full-width frets. There are three, four or six strings, and tunings vary to accommodate different styles of playing. These include melody playing on one string only, using the others as 'drones,' chord accompaniment and more elaborate counter-melody playing. The right, or rhythm, hand mostly uses a flatpick, but sometimes even fingerpicking techniques are applied.

To play the Appalachian dulcimer, the player must be in a sitting position, holding the instrument on his/her lap. This enforced immobility and the instrument's small volume may have been among the reasons why it was not much used other than to accompany ballad singing in Appalachian folk music. The instrument was popularized in the early folk music revival by performers like Jean Ritchie, Paul Clayton and Howard W. Mitchell. In addition, books and articles promoted it as a surviving symbol of an alleged 'Elizabethan' culture of the southern mountains. Subsequently, as with other instruments, the folkloric image of the instrument has been far more popular than its actual usage, even within folk music itself. Attempts to increase the Appalachian dulcimer's volume and thus its general appeal to musicians by enlargement of the instrument's body and amplification with pickups have not changed this situation.

Thus, while the dulcimer has never achieved the popularity of instruments such as the guitar or piano, it has nonetheless maintained a steady presence in popular music since the folk revival of the late 1950s. In the 1960s, Richard Fariña, Roger Nicholson and others followed Ritchie, Clayton and Mitchell, and were in turn followed by subsequent dulcimer players like Leo Kretzner, Robert Force, Albert d'Ossché and Lorraine 'Lee' Hammond.

Pioneering the use of the dulcimer within the context of rock music and thus bringing the instrument to the attention of wider audiences was US singer-songwriter and author Richard Fariña (1936–66). First introduced to the dulcimer in the early 1950s by Ritchie, by the mid-1960s Fariña was performing and recording with his wife Mimi, accompanied by a rock band made up of New York studio musicians; the group gained notoriety after performing at the 1965 Newport Folk Festival. Fariña's intense strumming style and dramatic use of sliding represented a dulcimer style far removed from earlier, traditional idioms. In the years following Fariña's death (in a motorcycle accident), increasing numbers of musicians, largely due to his example, began to use the dulcimer in popular music contexts; many of these groups have continued to perform Fariña's compositions.

The dulcimer was also used in a rock context by Brian Jones (1942–69), a founding member of the Rolling Stones; it can be heard in the group's Elizabethan-tinged

'Lady Jane' (1966). (Jones's 1965 Bill Kindy dulcimer now resides in the Rock and Roll Hall of Fame and Museum in Cleveland, Ohio.) In the early 1970s, Canadian-born folk luminary Joni Mitchell began to employ the instrument in her music, featuring it prominently on her 1971 recording *Blue*. US singer-songwriter Wendy Waldman also began using the instrument in the early 1970s. Again in the early 1970s, the dulcimer, in both amplified acoustic and solid-body electric forms, was adopted by several UK folk-rock groups, including Fairport Convention (in which it was played by Richard Thompson and Simon Nicol), the Strawbs (played by Dave Cousins) and Steeleye Span (played by Tim Hart). In the early 1980s, the dulcimer also featured in the John Renbourn Group, played by John Molineux. More recently, dulcimers have been employed by traditional/rock hybrid bands such as the Minnesota-based Boiled in Lead (played by Drew Miller), the North Carolina group the Offramps (played by Michael Futreal) and the Southern California group Common Ground (played by Mark Cloud).

Within more mainstream rock groups, the dulcimer has been less frequently used, but has been featured in the work of R.E.M., Aerosmith, Cyndi Lauper, Jimmy Page and Tori Amos. The Nashville-based rock band Bare Jr. is among the very few mainstream rock bands to include a full-time dulcimer player (Tracy Hackney).

The dulcimer has also been used periodically in country and bluegrass music, notably by the group the Textones (in which it is played by George Callins). As yet, the only dulcimer player to enjoy success as a full-time studio musician is the eminent Nashville-based performer David Schnaufer, who has recorded with numerous artists, including Johnny Cash, Emmylou Harris, the Judds and Hank Williams, Jr. Within the genre of Christian contemporary music, US performer Rich Mullins (1955–97) often used the dulcimer.

Among the first to use the dulcimer in a jazz context was the versatile US musician Collin Walcott (1945–84), who played it on a track from the group Oregon's 1974 release *Winter Light*. Jazz piano great McCoy Tyner, perhaps sensing an affinity between his own modal jazz and the modal character of the dulcimer, included the instrument in his composition 'Mode for Dulcimer,' which appeared on his 1976 album *Focal Point*. Since the 1980s, Maine-based dulcimer soloist Barbara Truex has been at the forefront of experimentation with the electric dulcimer in the contexts of jazz and improvised music.

Among numerous other dulcimer soloists who have recorded in popular styles are: Sam Sistler, Ron Ewing, Jerry Rockwell, Bonnie Carol, Neal Hellman, Lois Hornbostel, Dallas Cline, Randy Raine-Reusch, Thomas-ina, Susan Carpenter, Heidi Muller, Gail Rundlett and Larkin Bryant.

Bibliography

Hickerson, Joe. 1973. *A Bibliography of Hammered and Plucked (Appalachian or Mountain) Dulcimers and Related Instruments*. Washington, DC: Archive of Folk Music, Library of Congress.

Jeffreys, A.W., Jr. 1958. *Tuning and Playing the Appalachian Dulcimer*. Staunton, VA: The author.

Murphy, Michael. 1976. *The Appalachian Dulcimer Book*. St. Clairsville, OH: Folksay Press.

Ritchie, Jean. 1963. *The Dulcimer Book*. New York: Oak Publications.

Seeger, Charles. 1958. 'The Appalachian Dulcimer.' *Journal of American Folklore* (January-March): 40–51.

Smith, L. Allen. 1980. 'Toward a Reconstruction of the Development of the Appalachian Dulcimer: What the Instrument Suggests.' *Journal of American Folklore* (October-December): 385–96.

Smith, Ralph Lee. 1994. 'Mountain Dulcimer Tales and Traditions: Is This How the Dulcimer Began? A Scheitholt Mounted on a Soundbox.' *Dulcimer Player's News* (January-March): 30–31.

Smith, Ralph Lee. 1997. *Appalachian Dulcimer Traditions*. Lanham, MD: Scarecrow Press.

Discographical References

Mitchell, Joni. *Blue*. Reprise 2038. *1971*: USA.

Oregon. *Winter Light*. Vanguard VSD-79350. *1974*: USA.

Rolling Stones, The. 'Lady Jane.' *Aftermath*. Decca LK 4786. *1966*: UK.

Tyner, McCoy. 'Mode for Dulcimer.' *Focal Point*. Milestone M-9072. *1976*: USA.

Discography

Clayton, Paul. *Dulcimer Songs and Solos*. Folkways Records FG 3571. *1962*: USA.

Fariña, Richard, and Fariña, Mimi. *The Best of Mimi and Richard Fariña*. Vanguard VSD-22B. *1971*: USA.

Leibovitz, Jay, and Kretzner, Leo. *Pigtown Fling*. Green Linnet 1019. *1979*: USA.

Mitchell, Howard W. *The Mountain Dulcimer*. Folk-Legacy FSI 29. *1965*: USA.

Ritchie, Jean. *The Appalachian Dulcimer: An Instructional Record*. Folkways Records FI 8352. *1963*: USA.

Ritchie, Jean. *Sweet Rivers*. June Appal JA 037. *1981*: USA.

Ritchie, Jean, and Watson, Doc. *Jean Ritchie and Doc Watson at Folk City*. Folkways Records FA 2426. *1963*: USA.

Roth, Kevin. *Kevin Roth Sings and Plays Dulcimer*. Folkways Records FA 2367. *1975*: USA.

ARMIN HADAMER and DAVID BADAGNANI

Autoharp

The autoharp is a 'box-zither' invented by Karl August Gütter (1823–1900) of Markneukirchen, Germany, around 1880. Production in the United States was started in 1885 by the German American Charles F. Zimmermann (1817–98), who created the term 'autoharp' and popularized the instrument on a very large scale.

The autoharp has a small zither-like wooden body, a varying number of steel strings, and crossing bars which, when pushed, mute certain strings and leave others open to produce a chord. Note and chord options depend on the model used. Playing styles include long arpeggiating strokes, rhythmic finger–thumb snapping, and picking of individual strings; players sometimes hold the instrument in a horizontal lap-style fashion or vertically against the chest.

The autoharp started as a school and parlor instrument, often to accompany hymn singing. It gained special popularity in Appalachian folk music after the 1920s through the recordings of Ernest 'Pop' Stoneman, and as a rhythm instrument in the music of the Carter Family. After World War II, it was Maybelle Carter who featured the autoharp as a solo instrument, holding it vertically for greater mobility on stage. More recently, this tradition was carried on by players such as Mike Seeger and Bryan Bowers. Electric autoharps were made from the late 1960s and successfully used by, among others, John Sebastian and Lindsay Haisley in popular styles such as folk-rock and contemporary folk.

Bibliography

Blackley, Becky. 1983. *The Autoharp Book*. Brisbane, CA: i.a.d. Publications.

Moore, A. Doyle. 1963. 'The Autoharp: Its Origin and Development from a Popular to a Folk Instrument.' *New York Folklore Quarterly* (December): 261–74.

Sachs, Curt. 1940. *The History of Musical Instruments*. New York: W.W. Norton & Co.

Stiles, Ivan. 1994. 'The True Story of the Autoharp.' *Bluegrass Unlimited* (August): 26–28.

Taussig, Harry A. 1966. 'Teach-In: Autoharp.' *Sing Out!* (February-March): 38–39.

Discography

Bowers, Bryan. *By Heart*. Flying Fish FF 313. *1984*: USA.

Carter, Maybelle. *Mother Maybelle Carter*. Columbia KG 32436. *1973*: USA.

Haisley, Lindsay. *Christmas on the Autoharp*. Armadillo Records ARL 82-1. *1982*: USA.

Jones, Clayton. *Traditional Autoharp*. Sunny Mountain Records EB 1006. *197?*: USA.

Nitty Gritty Dirt Band, The. *Will the Circle Be Unbroken*. United Artists Records UAS 9801. *1971*: USA.

Sebastian, John. *Lovin' Spoonful, the Very Best*. Buddah BDM 5706. *1967*: USA.

Seeger, Mike. *Old-Time Country Music*. Folkways Records FA 2325. *1962*: USA.

Snow, Kilby. *Country Songs and Tunes with Autoharp*. Folkways Records FA 3902. *1970*: USA.

Snow, Kilby, Stoneman, Ernest, and Benfield, Neriah and Kenneth. *Mountain Music Played on the Autoharp*. Folkways Records FA 2365. *1962*: USA.

Stoneman, Ernest. *Tribute to Pop Stoneman*. MGM Records SE 4588. *1969*: USA.

ARMIN HADAMER

Balalaika

The balalaika is a Russian plucked chordophone with a triangular body, a relatively short neck and three strings. It is related to a large family of long-necked lutes used in many parts of Asia, such as the *domra*, *dombra* and *tanbur*.

The origin of the balalaika is unclear. First mentioned in 1688, it seems to have become popular among the lower classes of central Russia during the eighteenth century. The oldest instruments had a round or triangular body, two gut strings tuned at a fourth or a fifth, and a long neck with four to six movable gut frets. Later, the neck was shortened and a third string was added. Two types of tunings were common: unison-fourth and *razlad*, a broken major or minor chord (i.e., d-f♯-a).

The balalaika was used as both a solo and an ensemble instrument. In ensembles, it was played with a *gudok* (fiddle), *volynka* (bagpipe), *buben* (drum) and *dudka* (flute) to accompany dancing and singing, especially *chastushki*, short rhymed ditties that became popular throughout Russia in the nineteenth century. From around the mid-nineteenth century, the popularity of the balalaika diminished. This was due to the growing national market for industrially made accordions, which soon took the place of the balalaika as the most popular instrument among ordinary people.

The modern balalaika was created in the late 1880s by Vassilij Vassilevich Andreev, a young nobleman from Tver. From violin-makers V.V. Ivanov and F. Paserbskij in St. Petersburg, he ordered a new type of instrument, made from the finest woods, with a larger triangular body, a shorter neck, three strings tuned e-e-a and metal frets, in order to obtain an almost two-octave chromatic scale. A few years later, in addition to the first *balalaika prim*, he ordered a whole family of instruments: descant, second, alto, bass and contrabass. With these instruments, Andreev formed the first balalaika orchestra in 1887. It was an immediate success among the nationally oriented nobility. Within a decade, the new instruments had been disseminated, and orchestras were formed all over the Russian Empire, even in regions where Russian instruments had never before been played. By the turn of the century, Andreev's orchestra, known as the 'Veliko-russkij orkestr' and consisting of balalaikas in six sizes and *domras* in three to five sizes, had become a model for all other orchestras.

Few musicians of the old balalaika are known. Among the great soloists on Andreev's balalaika are B. Trojanovskij, N.P. Osipov and B. Feoktistov.

With the introduction of the balalaika among the musically educated nobility, its repertoire changed from rather short and simple dance tunes and song accompaniments to larger compositions, based either on folk songs and dances or on transcriptions of well-known classical pieces. To meet the needs of the broadened repertoire, other instruments were also included in the orchestras: a *gusli* (psalterium), *bajan* (accordion), *brolka* (shawm), *rozhok* (wooden trumpet), *dudka* and a variety of percussion instruments.

During the Soviet years, the balalaika was cultivated as both a solo and an orchestral instrument. It was promoted in schools at all levels, factories, trade unions and so on. It was promulgated as a symbol of both Old Russian folk tradition and the modernity and progress instigated by Soviet rule. After the fall of the Soviet Union, many of the orchestras were disbanded and the popularity of the instrument declined.

Bibliography

Peresada, Anatolij I. 1977. *Spravotjnik balalaetjnika* [The Balalaika Player's Reference Book]. Moskva: Sovjetskij kompositor.

Ronström, Owe. 1976. *Balalajkan C en instrumentstudie* [The Balalaika: An Instrument Study]. Stockholms Universitët: Institutionen för musikvetenskap.

Sokolov, F.B. 1962. *Russkaja narodnaja balalajka* [The Russian Folk Balalaika]. Moskva: Sovjetskij kompositor.

Vertkov, Konstantin A. 1975. *Russkie narodnye muzykalnyje instrumenty* [Russian Folk Instruments]. Leningrad: Muzyka.

OWE RONSTRÖM

Banjo

A banjo is a stringed instrument characterized by the invariable presence of a tightly stretched drum-like membrane or 'head' (typically made of thin leather, calfskin or plastic) which comprises its principal resonating surface. The head, which is usually but not invariably circular, is supported by a body, which may be completely closed, as in the prototypical gourd construction, or which may be an open-backed wooden or metal hoop. The head supports the instrument's single bridge, over which strings (between three and 12, but most often four or five in number) pass from their attachment at the 'tailpiece' to their respective tuning pegs or tensioning devices at the opposite end of a narrow neck.

The banjo's typical structure and form have varied considerably over the instrument's history, providing evidence of its ongoing reinvention at the hands of its builders and players. Early African, West Indian, North American and European examples prior to the mid-nineteenth century were individually built; surviving instruments and documented observations indicate a wide range of sizes, number of strings, and methods of attaching and tensioning the head. The African precursors of all modern types of banjo may have been called by a variety of names, depending on the language and cultural roots of the builders: *halam, bania, banja, banjar*.

The concept of the instrument was carried everywhere that the West African slave trade took its victims: South America, Europe, the Caribbean and North America. Banjos were built and played by slaves and were documented, albeit briefly, by early Caribbean and North American travelers in particular. Before the end of the eighteenth century, the supremely observant Thomas Jefferson included in his *Notes on the State of Virginia* an acknowledgment that 'the instrument proper to them [the slaves] is the Banjar, which they brought hither from Africa' (see Peden 1954, 288).

The nineteenth century witnessed the North American embrace and first great physical transformation of the typical banjo and, more importantly, its complex cultural redefinition at the hands of several new constituencies of players. At the beginning of the nineteenth century, the instrument already seemed to be familiar to many, and therefore barely worthy of detailed description, but it was familiar in the Jeffersonian sense as the instrument 'proper' to African and African-American slaves. Yet, by the 1830s, white Americans had taken up the instrument, always acknowledging its solid association with Southern and Caribbean black slaves, and had planted the seeds that would become blackface minstrelsy by the 1840s. In the minstrel era, the banjo, played by 'blacked-up' white minstrels in the 'stroke style,' was completely subsumed as a stereotypical symbol of the black race itself, even as more and more of its players were, inevitably, white aficionados and presenters of the style. Among the most famous early banjo-playing minstrels was Joel Walker ('Joe') Sweeney of Virginia, sometimes erroneously acclaimed as the inventor of the banjo's fifth string, and Daniel Decatur Emmett (Emmit), composer of 'Old Dan Tucker,' 'De Blue Tail Fly' and other banjo melodies. Such compositions were played on the minstrel stage and were also sold as sheet music, often adorned with outrageous images of slaves dancing, cavorting and always playing the banjo.

During this period, too, banjos began to be commercially manufactured in significant numbers. Although four-string banjos continued to be used, especially in Europe, in the United States the instrument was physically standardized as a frame-built five-string, with 'brackets' to tension the head, and with four long strings and one asymmetrically positioned drone ('chanter') or 'fifth string.'

Minstrelsy and the post-Emancipation black North American diaspora carried knowledge of the banjo and its new minstrelized form a long way. At the beginning of the twentieth century, the banjo continued its minstrel role and imagery; but it was also adopted in the southeastern United States by rural white string-band musicians and folk singers, even as its popularity declined among African Americans in favor of the guitar. The 'stroke style' of minstrel banjo performance may have inspired a group of folk 'down-picking' methods of sounding the banjo's strings, including the types now known as 'frailing' and 'claw hammer.' Yet, undeniably, the playing styles of African-American banjoists were repeatedly transmitted to white Southern banjoists by direct example, as well as through the filter of minstrelsy.

At this time, the banjo was still riding the rising crest of its popularity as a classicized parlor instrument. While it retained its connotative connections to blackface minstrelsy, it had also acquired a much more standardized physical form: the distinctive five-string type, with a high-pitched 'thumb string' whose sound was most often realized by placing that string's tuning peg or mechanism partway down the neck, not on the peghead with the rest of the tuning pegs.

The status of the banjo was systematically 'elevated' as it was Americanized by manufacturers, promoters and some players. Many banjo instruction manuals were published from the 1860s onward. These self-tutoring guides brought some knowledge of the instrument – its 'authentic history,' as George Dobson (1880, 4) termed it while asserting its 'uniquely American' identity – and its varied styles and tunings to a new generation of players. With the advent of the instruction books, tunings became more systematized, and evolved from the minstrel-era 'standard A' tuning (e, A^1, E, $G\sharp$, B) to 'standard C' (g, C, G, B, d) and eventually to 'standard G' (g, D, G, B, d). But banjoists, perhaps as a legacy of the era before frets, have always invented tunings freely: more than 135 documented tunings exist for the five-string banjo.

Those who learned from the instruction manuals of the 1880s and after brought the instrument into appropriately formal musical contexts, where it could be played from written music in 'finger style' or with a plectrum or pick. Above all, in these new contexts the banjo's voice and (to a lesser extent) its associated repertoire were perceived as 'real music' by the North American and British urban middle and upper classes. These were profound changes. Nevertheless, the banjo continued throughout the nineteenth century with its strong connotations of comedy, minstrelsy and rural unsophistication: one has only to look at nineteenth- and early twentieth-century sheet music and popular poetry to find titles like 'Rastus' Banjo' and 'De Banjo Am de Instrument for Me.'

In the first quarter of the twentieth century, the banjo developed several physical sub-types, each said to be more suited to the rhythmic needs of the jazz groups and popular ensembles of the day. These developments produced the British zither-banjo and the four-string 'tenor' and 'plectrum' varieties, with both open backs and enclosed 'resonator' backs – all typically played with a single flatpick held in the right hand. In Britain, the tenor banjo began to be enthusiastically adopted by Irish musicians during this period, and virtuoso North American players of these instruments, such as 'Vess' Ossman, who began recording in the era of cylinders, became well known even before World War I.

After the war, the availability of radio receivers and phonograph recordings of banjo music changed everything, and the banjo found new listeners and some memorable players. In the 1920s and 1930s, *Grand Ole Opry* pioneer Uncle Dave Macon seemed to embody directly the historic link between minstrelsy, vaudeville and the new era of recorded and broadcast music. After the advent of the jazz age, Eddie Peabody and Harry Reser became well known through widely sold 78 rpm recordings featuring their exuberant banjo solos. Kentucky-born Buell Kazee influenced generations of later banjoists (like Pete Seeger), who found in Kazee's 1920s banjo-accompanied recordings of traditional balladry an important example of the instrument's deep reach and complex role in southern Anglo- and African-American cultures. The string-band music released in the late 1920s by Charlie Poole and the North Carolina Ramblers also kept the banjo visible and popular, and Poole's unique and complex picking style clearly prefigured the 'three-finger' style associated with bluegrass music.

Despite such successes, the five-string banjo fell almost completely out of favor in North American popular music by World War II. The tenor and plectrum instruments (manufactured in their largest numbers in the 1920s and early 1930s for the jazz band craze) began to be heard less and less after the Depression. While the older five-string instrument continued to be played, it was used, as before, to evoke images of minstrelsy, nostalgia and (invariably) comic associations in the deliberate playing of such 'old-time' or radio and recording artists as Louis Marshall 'Grandpa' Jones and David 'Stringbean' Akeman. In the 1930s and 1940s, such five-string banjo players helped to consolidate the foundations of the country music industry in the United States.

Yet another banjo revolution began in 1945, when the 21-year-old banjo virtuoso Earl Scruggs joined *Grand Ole Opry* star Bill Monroe and his Blue Grass Boys. Scruggs's many technical breakthroughs on the instrument, all built on his brilliant extension of a 'three-finger' picking style learned in his native western North Carolina, were catapulted into the forefront of media exposure. Over the next 15 years, the small ensemble style pioneered by Monroe's Blue Grass Boys became known generically as 'bluegrass music,' and its sonic center was, and has remained, the hard, 'driving,' fast Scruggs-style picking sound of the banjo. During the remainder of the twentieth century, hundreds of thousands of would-be bluegrass banjoists revitalized the instrument in the United States and ensured its continued spread to other cultural scenes in Europe, Japan and other parts of Asia.

Just as bluegrass began to make an impact in the early 1950s, Pete Seeger published a modest book of banjo instruction, presenting (like its nineteenth-century predecessors) the instrument's history and also offering useful instruction in the wide range of playing techniques that Seeger had used to advantage in his recordings with the Weavers. Beginning in 1957, the Kingston Trio's highly visible use of Dave Guard's banjo playing in their smooth redactions of folk and folk-like songs helped to lay the cornerstone of the 'folk music revival.' Part of that popular revival in North America was the arrival of the Clancy Brothers (with Tommy Makem playing an extended-neck five-string), which helped to bring the Irish banjo into renewed popular prominence. A host of talented modern banjoists, including Don Reno, Bill Keith and Béla Fleck, have adapted and extended the three-finger technique to give the instrument a flexible leading voice in many musical contexts. While older modes of playing have by no means been supplanted, the adaptable three-finger technique has extended the voice of the banjo into novel settings and uses. The distinctive sound of the banjo has come to be heard in a variety of popular musical styles and contexts: bluegrass, 'old-time' string-band, Irish revival, even modern jazz and bebop. In all the places in which it is heard, the banjo's distinctive voice carries forward the connotations of its complex historic development and all its many cultural associations.

Bibliography

Conway, Cecelia. 1995. *African Banjo Echoes in Appalachia: A Study of Folk Traditions*. Knoxville, TN: University of Tennessee Press.

Dobson, George C. 1880. *Complete Instructor for the Banjo, with an Authentic History of the Instrument*. Boston, MA: White, Smith & Company.

Heier, Uli, and Lotz, Rainer E., eds. 1993. *The Banjo on Record: A Bio-Discography*. Westport, CT: Greenwood Press.

Kubik, Gerhard. 1989. 'The Southern African Periphery: Banjo Traditions in Zambia and Malawi.' *The World of Music* 31(3): 3–29.

Linn, Karen. 1991. *That Half-Barbaric Twang: The Banjo in American Popular Culture*. Urbana, IL: University of Illinois Press.

Lornell, Kip. 1990. 'Banjos and Blues.' In *Arts in Earnest: North Carolina Folklife*, ed. Daniel W. Patterson and Charles G. Zug III. Durham, NC: Duke University Press, 216–31.

Peden, William, ed. 1954. *Thomas Jefferson, Notes on the State of Virginia*. Chapel Hill, NC: University of North Carolina Press.

Seeger, Peggy. 1960. *The Five-String Banjo: American Folk Styles*. New York: Hargail Music Press.

Seeger, Pete. 1962 (1948). *How to Play the Five-String Banjo*. 3rd ed. New York: Oak Publications.

Shrubsall, Wayne. 1987. 'Banjo as Icon.' *Journal of Popular Culture* 20(4): 31–60.

Toll, Robert C. 1974. *Blacking Up: The Minstrel Show in Nineteenth-Century America*. New York: Oxford University Press.

Trischka, Tony, and Wernick, Pete. 1988. *Masters of the 5-String Banjo: In Their Own Words and Music*. New York: Oak Publications.

Tsumura, Akira. 1984. *Banjos, the Tsumura Collection*. Tokyo and New York: Kodansha International.

Tsumura, Akira. 1994. *1001 Banjos*. Tokyo: Kodansha International.

Webb, Robert Lloyd. 1984. *Ring the Banjar!: The Banjo in America from Folklore to Factory*. Cambridge, MA: MIT Museum.

Winans, Robert B., and Kaufman, Elias J. 1994. 'Minstrel and Classic Banjo: American and English Connections.' *American Music* 12(1): 1–30.

Sheet Music

Emmett (Emmit), Daniel Decatur, comp. and lyr. 1843. 'Old Dan Tucker.' Boston, MA: C.H. Keith.

Emmett (Emmit), Daniel Decatur, comp. and lyr. 1846. 'De Blue Tail Fly.' Boston, MA: Keith's Music House.

Rutledge, John T., comp. and lyr. 1877. 'De Banjo Am de Instrument for Me.' Bath, ME: Thos. P.I. Magoun.

Discography

American Banjo Tunes and Songs in the 'Scruggs' Style. Folkways FA 2314. *1956*: USA.

Black Banjo Songsters of North Carolina and Virginia. Smithsonian/Folkways SF 40079. *1998*: USA.

Flatt, Lester, and Scruggs, Earl. *Foggy Mountain Banjo.* Columbia CS-8364. *1961*: USA.

Flatt, Lester, and Scruggs, Earl. *Foggy Mountain Jamboree.* Columbia C-1019. *1957*: USA.

Fleck, Béla. *Tales from the Acoustic Planet.* Warner Brothers 45854. *1995*: USA.

Folk Banjo Styles. Elektra 7217. *1962*: USA.

Kazee, Buell. *Buell Kazee.* June Appal 009. *1978*: USA.

Kingston Trio, The. *The Kingston Trio.* Capitol DT-996. *1958*: USA.

Masters of the Banjo. Arhoolie CD-421. *1994*: USA.

Minstrel Banjo Style. Rounder 321. *1994*: USA.

Peabody, Eddie. *Man with the Banjo.* Dot 110. *1955*: USA.

Reser, Harry. *Banjo Crackerjax, 1922–1930.* Yazoo L 1048. *1975*: USA.

Seeger, Pete. *Goofing-Off Suite.* Folkways FA 2045. 1954: USA.

Seeger, Pete. *How to Play the Five-String Banjo.* Folkways FI 8303. 1954: USA.

Van Eps, Fred, and Ossman, Vess L. *Kings of the Banjo: Ragtime.* Yazoo L 1044. *1974*: USA.

Weavers, The. *Best of the Weavers.* Decca DL 8893. 1953: USA.

Weissberg, Eric, and Brickman, Marshall. *New Dimensions in Banjo and Bluegrass.* Elektra 7238. *1963*: USA.

THOMAS A. ADLER

Bouzoúki

The *bouzoúki*, a lute-shaped, tempered, plucked stringed instrument, is the most important melodic instrument of modern Greek popular music. It has a soundbox similar to but larger than that of the mandolin, a long neck and immovable frets. In its traditional form, the *bouzoúki* has three double strings, but a more recent version that emerged during the 1950s has four double strings. The *bouzoúki* belongs to a large family of similar melodic stringed instruments, known by various names in different parts of the Near and Middle East, along with the Turkish *saz*, the Persian *tar* and the Moroccan *buzuk*. Instruments similar to the *bouzoúki* can be found in ancient Greek sculptures and in Byzantine icons, indicating the long historical presence of the instrument in the eastern Mediterranean. The name varied in different periods: *pandouris* in ancient Greece, *tambouras* in the Byzantine period and later. However, these instruments were different from the *bouzoúki* in that they had movable frets and could, therefore, produce modal scales.

There are two smaller versions of the *bouzoúki*: the *tzouras* and the *baglamas*, both of which have three double strings. The *tzouras* is the size of a mandolin or even smaller, and has a long neck; the *baglamas*, still smaller, has a very high pitch and is used mostly for playing chords as an accompaniment to *bouzoúki* music.

The first pair of strings of the traditional *bouzoúki* is for playing the melodic part of the music, while the two lower double strings are for adding a simple accompaniment. The four-stringed *bouzoúki* is also played as a melodic instrument, but the two lower double strings and new tuning are used to produce a harmonically richer music. The addition of a fourth string has drastically changed the texture of the music performed by the instrument: the monophonic, melodic style of the past has gradually given way to a polyphonic, harmonic one. This reflects the general trend of modern Greek music after the 1940s to emulate Western standards.

The *bouzoúki* was the most important instrument for *rebetika* songs, which flourished in the port of Piraeus between the 1930s and the 1950s. The most famous player of the traditional *bouzoúki* was Markos Vamvakaris, while the four-stringed *bouzoúki* was introduced by Manolis Chiotis. The old three-stringed *bouzoúki* has been replaced by the newer four-stringed version in most popular music orchestras. However, older versions of the instrument, like the *tambouras* and the *saz*, were reintroduced by music groups formed in the last decade or so of the twentieth century, influenced by a revitalized interest in Greek traditional music.

The *bouzoúki* found worldwide fame through the music that Mikis Theodorakis composed for Michalis Kakogiannis' film *Zorba the Greek*, based on the novel by Nikos Kazantzakis. In the 1960s and 1970s, it became a principal symbol of the Greek tourist industry. It was also introduced into other countries and music cultures around the world, its influence on Irish music in the late 1960s probably being the most interesting instance of its dissemination.

Bibliography

Anogeianakis, Foivos. 1976. *Ellinika Laika Mousika Organa* [Greek Traditional Music Instruments]. Athens: Ekdosi ethnikis trapezas.

Holst, Gail. 1977. *Road to Rembetika: Music from a Greek Subculture. Songs of Love, Sorrow and Hashish.* Athens: Anglo-Hellenic Publishing.

Pennanen, Risto Pekka. 1999. *Westernisation and Modernisation in Greek Popular Music.* Tampere: University of Tampere.

Discography

Zorba the Greek (Soundtrack). 20th Century 826245-1. *1964*: USA.

Filmography

Zorba the Greek, dir. Michael Cacoyannis. 1964. UK/ Greece. 142 mins. Drama. Original music by Mikis Theodorakis.

PANAYOTIS PANOPOULOS

Bullroarer

Archeologists have uncovered evidence in Paleolithic tombs that suggests that the bullroarer is among the earliest – if not *the* earliest – and longest-surviving of artifacts that can be termed musical instruments. The bullroarer customarily consists of a thin, flat piece of bone, or a slat of wood, which is elliptical in shape and pierced at one end. A length of string, cord or thong is threaded through the hole and tied; the user holds the string in one hand, and whirls the slat over his/her head. As the slat spins on its axis, the whirling movement produces a wailing or even a roaring sound. Found in Australia, New Guinea, India, West Africa, Europe and the Americas, the bullroarer is not only one of the oldest but also one of the most widely distributed of instruments.

Although the bullroarer is musically limited, for more than a century its social role and its symbolic significance have been the subject of intense study and innumerable scholarly papers (Lang 1884). Although it seems little more than a toy, it has been employed for ritual purposes, and initiation ceremonies in particular, in cultures the world over. In classical Greece, as in tribal societies, the bullroarer was whirled by men daubed in paint or feces. Women were prohibited from using, seeing or touching it, and it has been widely argued that the fish-shaped bone or slat is a phallic symbol (van Baal 1966). But the bullroarer makes 'wind,' as well as 'thunder,' and is, in Ernest Jones's words, symbolic of 'flatus, particularly paternal flatus, [as] is well known to all psychoanalysts' (1964, 287). In an exhaustive study of the phenomenon and the literature, folklorist Alan Dundes argues that the pervasive use of the bullroarer is 'based upon notions of male pregnancy envy, anal eroticism, and ritual homosexuality' (1976, 236).

The Maori version of the bullroarer, the *purererhua*, has been used extensively in New Zealand popular music by, for example, the Upper Hutt Posse, and Hirini Melbourne and Richard Nunns, as well as in the soundtrack to *Once Were Warriors*. In contrast, the bullroarer has been little used in Australian popular music, there being considerable taboos surrounding its use in Aboriginal culture. A controversial example of its use is, however, to be found in 'Bullima' by Kooriwadjula (Dunbar-Hall 1994, 106–108).

Bibliography

Dunbar-Hall, Peter. 1994. *Style and Meaning: Signification in Contemporary Australian Popular Music, 1963–1993.*

Ph.D. thesis, School of Music and Music Education, University of New South Wales, Sydney.

Dundes, Alan. 1976. 'A Psychoanalytic Study of the Bullroarer.' *Man* 11: 220–38.

Jones, Ernest. 1964 (1951). *Essays in Applied Psycho-Analysis. Vol. 2: Folklore, Anthropology and Religion.* New York: International Universities Press.

Lang, Andrew. 1884. 'The Bull-Roarer: A Study of the Mysteries.' In *Custom and Myth.* London: Longmans, Green and Company, 29–44.

Mitchell, Tony. 1995. 'New Urban Polynesians: *Once Were Warriors*, the *Proud* Project and the South Auckland Music Scene.' *Perfect Beat* 2(3) (July): 1–20.

van Baal, J. 1966. *Dema: Description and Analysis of Marind-Anim Culture (South New Guinea).* The Hague: Martinus Nijhof.

Discographical Reference

Kooriwadjula. 'Bullima.' *Kooriwadjula.* Enrec EN 149CD. *1992*: Australia.

Discography

Melbourne, Hirini, and Nunns, Richard. 'Purerehua.' *Te Ku Te Whe.* Rattle Records RAT 10004. *1994*: New Zealand.

Upper Hutt Posse, The. 'Whakakotahi.' *Movement in Demand.* BMG/Tangata TANG CD619. *1995*: New Zealand.

Filmography

Once Were Warriors, dir. Lee Tamahori. 1994. New Zealand. 99 mins. Drama. Original music by Murray Grindlay, Murray McNabb.

PAUL OLIVER with BRUCE JOHNSON

Cello

Known for its deep resonant tone, the violoncello or cello is a larger version of the violin. Like the latter, the cello has four strings, is constructed of wood and has a fretless neck. The body has opposing 'f' holes. It is played with a bow, but can also be plucked (pizzicato) or strummed by the right-hand fingers for special effect. The left-hand fingers stop the strings along the neck to achieve the desired pitch, and the smooth neck allows for portamenti (or sliding up or down the string while bowing).

To play this bulky instrument (which is approximately 48.5″ (1.2 m) in length, depending on the maker), the musician sits and places the cello between his/her legs, the neck in a vertical position and resting on the shoulder. A tail pin at the base of the instrument allows it to rest off the ground, facilitating easier left-hand fingering.

As an ensemble instrument, the cello is extremely versatile. In a string quartet, it provides the bass line, but it can also handle fleeting contrapuntal or slow melodic passages. These qualities also make it an ideal solo instrument. Composers such as Dmitri Shostakovich (1906–75) and Antonín Dvořák (1841–1904) wrote concertos for cello and orchestra. The repertoire of solo cello compositions is extensive and boasts a number of masterpieces, including J.S. Bach's six cello suites. Lauded nineteenth- and twentieth-century cellists include Bernhard Romberg (1767–1841), David Popper (1843–1913), Pablo Casals (1876–1973), Jacqueline du Pré (1945–87) and Mstislav Rostropovich (b. 1927).

In popular music and jazz, cellos or their simulation through synthesizers occur in many songs as part of string arrangements. In their simulation through synthesizers, violins, violas and cellos are often distinguishable only through the range in which they are played. A 'cello sound,' for instance, can often be simulated if a keyboardist plays a violin patch well below the violin range. Depending on the sampled rate of the sound and the processing, simulations of the cello can vary.

Simulated or acoustic string arrangements in popular music and jazz are used to create background atmosphere and foreground interest. As part of the background, the cello can be heard as part of an ensemble in songs ranging from early to the most recent popular music recordings. Producers of jazz and popular singers such as Sarah Vaughan ('Lush Life') and Whitney Houston ('I Will Always Love You') have all employed strings.

Strings are often featured in film music. While it is a standard musical cliché that they color emotive moments in films, strings can also be scored to create drama and excitement. In these instances, the cello or cello sound usually provides support for the higher-pitched violins and violas, as in John Williams's score for *Star Wars* or Bernard Herrmann's score for *Psycho*.

During the early years of rock 'n' roll, stringed instruments were of little importance in arrangements except occasionally in ballads. Later, the Beatles' use of strings on recordings such as 'I Am the Walrus' (scored by George Martin) helped to legitimize and reclaim the use of musical practises generally considered to be part of the Western art music tradition. This trend of musical integration continued with Roy Wood's use of cellos on the Move's recording 'Night of Fear' (1968). Later, as a member of the Electric Light Orchestra, Wood declared in 1971 that he intended to carry on where 'I Am the Walrus' had left off.

The use of strings and, indeed, other classical orchestral instruments during the late 1960s and the 1970s became a means of buying into Western art music practises. Deep Purple and Procol Harum both featured symphonic orchestral arrangements – including as many as 10 cellos – on their 1969 and 1972 albums, respectively.

Drawing inspiration from Western art music, popular musicians created hybrids between classical and popular music. This led to the establishment of the 'classical rock' movement. 'Classical rock' was a term that gained currency during the 1970s. The Electric Light Orchestra encapsulated this tradition, and its '10538 Overture' stands as an implicit homage to the Western art music tradition. The cello plays an important role in this song.

During the late 1970s, producers of disco used strings extensively. However, by the late 1970s disco's musical clichés, its incessant quarter-note bass drum thump and octave bass lines, combined with 'swishy' orchestral arrangements, were undermining whatever musical innovations had been made in assimilating the aesthetics and status of the Western art music tradition to popular music.

During the 1980s, the cello continued to feature in a variety of popular music genres, either through sampling or in occasional live performances. However, by this time disco had exhausted the sound, pushing it into the world of Aquarian 'new ageness' and meditation tapes.

Rap, soul and R&B group Soul II Soul's 1989 album *Club Classics, Vol. 1* features the cello. Massive Attack and Sweetbox also use cellos on their recordings. The Irish group the Divine Comedy (Neil Hannon) infuses many of its recordings with strings, particularly cellos, and the lineup of British group My Life Story included a permanent cello player.

Unlike its uncertain history in popular music, the cello has enjoyed a gradual, if not slow, rise in interest as a jazz instrument. However, renowned artists who play jazz cello are few in number. Significant exceptions include Ray Brown and Oscar Pettiford, bass players who, during the 1950s, occasionally traded their stand-up basses for the cello. They sometimes retuned the instrument from its usual series of fifths (C, G, D, A) to a series of fourths (E, A, D, G, like a bass guitar) and played it pizzicato. During the 1960s, Fred Katz and Ron Carter were among the first to bow the cello in a jazz ensemble. String groups that feature the cello and undertake jazz improvisations include Turtle Island String Quartet and Black Swan Quartet.

The cello has continued to signify virtuosity, while its multiple uses in all aspects of music testify to the instrument's great versatility.

Bibliography

Harry, Bill. 1992. *The Ultimate Beatles Encyclopedia*. London: Virgin.

Discographical References

Beatles, The. 'I Am the Walrus.' *Magical Mystery Tour*. Capitol SMAL 2835. *1967*: USA.

Deep Purple and the Royal Philharmonic Orchestra. *Concerto for Group and Orchestra*. Tetragrammaton 131. *1969*: UK.

Electric Light Orchestra, The. '10538 Overture.' *No Answer*. United Artists UAS-5573. *1972*: UK.

Houston, Whitney. 'I Will Always Love You.' Arista 12490. *1992*: USA.

London Symphony Orchestra, The. *Star Wars* (Original soundtrack). PolyGram 13588. *1977*: USA.

McNeely, Joel, and the Royal Scottish National Orchestra. *Psycho* (Original soundtrack). Varèse Sarabande 5765. *1997*: USA.

Move, The. 'Night of Fear.' *Move*. Regal-Zonophone 1002. *1968*: UK.

Procol Harum. *Procol Harum Live: In Concert with the Edmonton Symphony Orchestra and the Da Camera Singers*. A&M 4335. *1972*: USA.

Soul II Soul. *Club Classics, Vol. 1*. 10 Dix 82. *1989*: UK.

Vaughan, Sarah. 'Lush Life.' *The Complete Sarah Vaughan on Mercury, Vol. 1*. Mercury 826320. 1954–56: USA.

Discography

Beatles, The. 'Eleanor Rigby.' *Revolver*. Capitol C1-90452. *1966*: USA.

Black Swan Quartet. *Black Swan Quartet*. Minor Music 009. *1986*: Germany.

Divine Comedy, The. *Casanova*. Tristar 36863. *1997*: USA.

Electric Light Orchestra, The. *The Electric Light Orchestra*. Harvest SHVL 797. *1971*: UK.

Massive Attack. *Blue Lines*. Atlantic 91685. *1991*: USA.

Massive Attack. *Mezzanine*. Virgin 45599. *1998*: UK.

Massive Attack. *Protection*. Virgin 39883. *1995*: UK.

My Life Story. *The Golden Mile*. Parlophone 7386. *1997*: UK.

Sweetbox. *Sweetbox*. RCA 67699. *1998*: USA.

Turtle Island String Quartet. *Windham Hill Essential Series*. Windham Hill 11226. *1997*: USA.

Filmography

Hilary and Jackie, dir. Anand Tucker. 1998. UK. 125 mins. Drama. Original music by Barrington Pheloung.

Psycho, dir. Alfred Hitchcock. 1960. USA. 109 mins. Thriller. Original music by Bernard Herrmann.

Star Wars, dir. George Lucas. 1977. USA. 121 mins. Science Fiction. Original music by John Williams.

BHESHAM SHARMA with MIKE BROCKEN

Charango

The *charango* is a 10-string, plucked chordophone. This hybrid instrument was created with considerable ingenuity by Native American people from the different types of stringed instruments brought from Europe by Spanish colonizers during the conquest of South America. The *charango* is believed to be in large part an indigenous reworking of the Spanish *vihuela de mano*. It became the only stringed instrument to be found in the central Andean region of Bolivia, central and southern Peru, northern Chile, northern Argentina and parts of Ecuador. A comparison of *charangos* shows that some are more like mandolins and others more like lutes. The majority are small in size, and their unique high-pitched sound quality – produced by a thin soundbox and short strings – reveals that, when the Andean people made their own versions of the *vihuela*, they transferred to it their preference and passion for the high musical sounds of the pre-Columbian period. There is no definite information about the instrument's name. However, it is possible that the name derived from an aesthetic, onomatopoeic approximation of how Amerindians heard Spanish musicians playing: '*sumaj cha'ajranku*' ('rich scratch'). Amerindians continue to say 'cha'ajranka' rather than '*charango*.'

The body of the *charango* was originally made from the shell of a *quirquincho* (armadillo). And while *charangos* have been made of a round gourd, the most favored material is wood. The pear-shaped soundbox has a round vaulted back made of a single piece of carved wood. The flat wooden back can be made of cedar or walnut. The neck has between five and 18 wooden, bone or metal frets. The face, which has a round sound hole, is usually made of pine, spruce, cedar or walnut, with a bridge that is usually made of cedar or walnut. The instrument can vary in length between 18″ (45 cm) and 26″ (65 cm). Its strings, made of metal, nylon or gut, are arranged usually in five pairs, but they can also be found in four or five single, double or triple courses fastened by means of rear wooden or metal pegs inserted at the sides to the peg-disc or head, which is slightly bent back.

Although there are different tunings that match the aesthetic predispositions of individual players, the most common and extended one is A minor, in five double courses of metallic strings. Accounts of *charango* tunings and stringing can be idiosyncratic and confusing, in that some players talk of the *charango*'s first, second, third (and so on) strings as being numbered from bottom to top, while other players refer to the order of tuning – that is, the first string as the bottom one; the second as the fourth (second to top); the third as the second from the bottom; the fourth as the fifth string; and the fifth as the third string, that is, the middle one. Some players have the same thickness and quality for each pair of strings. Others have strings of different thicknesses, using different guitar and mandolin strings. Again, the strings do not go in straight order from fine to thick. Both the middle and top strings are thicker than the others to handle the tuning adequately.

Playing styles vary among performers. One of the foremost *charango* musicians has been Jaime Torres, a Bolivian by birth but based in Argentina for most of his life. Torres plays the *charango* with his first and fourth fingers picking at the same time, the lower finger tucked under the string, plucking it from below. The various techniques he uses to play are called *rasgueo* (strumming), *punteo* (picking) and *tremelo* (in which one finger does a fast repetitive flick up and down the strings). It is thought that playing techniques using the thumb and index finger are similar to the Baroque playing styles of Southern Europe, which also used the terms '*punteado*' and '*rasgueado*.' In the playing of Scotland-based self-taught Chilean musician Carlos Arredondo, thumb and index finger (with elongated thickened nails) dominate. Arredondo uses his second and third fingers to create an accompaniment for the melody, which is played on the first string. The melody is played on this string because space for hand movement is restricted on the other strings. Arredondo also at times uses all his fingers, particularly for strumming arpeggios.

There are also different ways of holding the *charango*. While some players cradle it across their mid-chest, others hold it high to the shoulder. Arredondo has a classic guitar position, with the *charango* lying across his right knee, his right foot raised on a footrest.

According to Turino (1993), there are two distinct contemporary *charango* traditions. First, there is the tradition of the Quechua- and Aymara-speaking rural *campesinos* of Peru and Bolivia, who favor a small, wooden flat-backed instrument with five double or triple courses of thin metal strings, producing a thick treble sound that carries well in the open air. Second, there is the tradition of the *campesinos* in northern Argentina and the Lake Titicaca region of Peru and Bolivia, who play a metal-stringed armadillo *charango*. Players strum a single melodic line rapidly, with the remaining open strings producing a dense texture.

In the Lake Titicaca region of Peru and in the province of Canas, the *charango* is used by men to woo and court the woman of their choice. One of the most romantic traditions has been that observed by Turino (1993) in Canas. The prime activity takes place on the day of San Andrés, 3 December, and the day of Santa Cruz, 3 May, both established times when young people pair off with an all-night dance party. In the weeks leading up to these two days, young men arrive by foot or on horseback at the weekly market to lurk as suitors around the girl of their choice, saying nothing, but strumming the same tune over and over until the girl responds with a positive (or negative) glance. Many young men in this area therefore play some *charango*. Many have a mermaid (*sirena*) carved into the *charango* head, as it is believed that *sirenas* give supernatural aid when it comes to seduction. By leaving a *charango* overnight by a spring or a place where a *sirena* is known to live, it is thought that the instrument will be endowed with perfect tuning and a pure voice. After the *sirena* has woven her magic, not only will the instrument's power to conquer women be much greater, but the strings will only have to be struck for beautiful music to emerge. Once a man has a partner, he usually puts away his *charango* and seldom plays; if he does, he is thought of as a womanizer.

The *charango* was regarded in both Peru and Bolivia as a rural, lower-class, 'Indian' instrument until the 1950s and 1960s, following the Bolivian Revolution which reevaluated indigenous traditions. It was at this time that use of the *charango* as played by rural migrants was brought by them to urban areas, where it was taken up by Spanish-speaking city-based musicians, most notably the group Los Jairas whose pioneering styles have influenced musicians over the whole Latin American continent.

In the late 1960s and early 1970s, the key Chilean 'new song' group Inti-illimani was responsible for making Andean sounds key to the *nueva canción* (new song) movement. The musicians of Inti-illimani were among a whole generation of Latin Americans who, in the 1960s and 1970s, embraced the sound of the indigenous communities of the Americas as their own, bringing the *charango* to the concert platform. The group was influenced by one of Latin America's most significant folklorists, Chilean singer-composer Violeta Parra, who worked with members of Bolivia's Los Jairas and went on to play the instrument as accompaniment to her own songs. Inti-illimani and members of the *nueva canción* movement, including the group Quilapayún, brought the musical sounds of the Andes to urban audiences not only in Chile but all over Latin America. Following a visit by Quilapayún to Cuba, for example, a group of Cuban musicians went to live in Chile to work with all the 'new song' musicians for a number of months. When both groups were exiled in Europe following the 1973 Chilean coup, they took the Andean sound with them and it became enormously popular, particularly in Italy and France where Inti-illimani and Quilapayún were based – Inti-illimani was exiled in Italy for 17 years. When General Pinochet seized power in Chile in 1973, the music of 'new song' and the Andean instruments emblematic of its sound were severely discouraged – effectively banned. However, the *charango* and pipes began a discreet comeback when a group called Baroco Andino used them to play Baroque music in Santiago churches only months after the death of 'new song' singer-songwriter Víctor Jara in 1973.

If the *charango* is familiar to people worldwide, from Sweden to Japan, France to Australia, it is also due to the many groups of young musicians from Bolivia, Peru, Chile and Ecuador who have busked all over the world, playing Andean music on bamboo pan pipes, *quena* flutes and *bombo* drums. These groups usually include the small mandolin-like instrument in their lineups. The high-pitched sound of the strings, picked and strummed quickly like a trilling bird, is at the heart of the infectious dances and songs of these popular musicians.

Bibliography

Turino, Thomas. 1993. *Moving Away from Silence: Music of the Peruvian Altiplano and the Experience of Urban Migration.* Chicago: University of Chicago Press.

Discography

Inti-illimani. *Imagination.* Redwood 8505. *1984*: USA.
Torres, Jaime. *Charango.* Messidor 15949. *1986*: USA.

JAN FAIRLEY with CÉSAR QUEZADA

Diddley-Bow

An improvised one-stringed instrument, the 'diddley-bow,' also known as a 'doodle-bow' or, more frequently, a 'jitterbug,' was often the first instrument taken up by blues guitarists in Mississippi and adjacent states. Although variants exist, the diddley-bow was usually made by stapling a length of cotton-baling wire, broom wire (used to bind broom hair or fibers), hay-baling wire or a similar thin metal strand to a wall or a wooden fence. The wire could be affixed vertically or horizontally, and two bridges might be made with a fork, a snuff bottle or a metal bolt at each end. The instrument would be played with a nail, a bottleneck, a pocketknife or even a leather strap, these implements generally held in the left hand and stroking the string, while the string was picked with the fingers of the right hand. Most diddley-bow players were children between six and 12 years old, but older children would experiment with a lard can or other container adapted to make a resonator, and some endeavored to make multi-stringed instruments, although the latter were rarely successful. It has been suggested that guitar playing with open tuning and a slider, such as a bottleneck or Hawaiian bar, may have derived from the use of the diddley-bow (Evans 1971).

Although the use of the instrument may simply have arisen from instances of children mimicking adult musicians, there are many types of African one-stringed instruments that may have been precursors of the diddley-bow. While some of these are one-stringed fiddles, such as the *riti* of the Wolof, or the Songhay *goge*, many are one-stringed lutes, such as the *kuntigi*, played in Niger and Nigeria, or the Senegalese *molo*, both of which bear comparison with the diddley-bow.

A number of blues guitarists, including Big Joe Williams and Elmore James, have recalled playing the diddley-bow, but few have been recorded doing so. Two titles were made by One-String Sam for the Detroit JVB label in 1956, and four years later Eddie 'One-String' Jones recorded five songs with one-string accompaniment in Los Angeles. But the diddley-bow's most indelible impression on popular music was made by the R&B guitarist Ellas McDaniel, who performed under the name of Bo Diddley; his playing technique and childhood lyrics on his first titles adequately qualify his pseudonym.

Bibliography

Evans, David. 1971. 'Afro-American One-Stringed Instruments.' *Western Folklore* 29(4): 229–45.

Discography

Jones, Eddie 'One-String.' *Rolling and Tumbling Blues/The Dozens.* Takoma LP 1023. *1960*: USA.
One-String Sam. *My Baby Ooo/I Need a Hundred Dollars.* JVB 40; Blues Classics BC-12. *1956*: USA.

PAUL OLIVER

Double Bass

The double bass, also known as a contrabass, string bass or acoustic bass, is the largest member of the orchestral string section. Although it is generally regarded as the bass of the violin family, it has as much in common with the viol family as it does with the violin. In particular, this is because it is tuned in intervals of a fourth (E-G-D-A, unlike the rest of the violin family which use fifths), and the body of the instrument generally retains the sloping shoulders of the viola da gamba. The double bass has further affinities with the viol, as it is the only instrument of the modern violin family to have a five-string variant in regular use, although a bottom C can be obtained on the more usual four-string instrument by means of a mechanical extension to the lowest E string.

In Western popular music, the double bass has retained its orchestral role as the foundation of the ensemble, and it was frequently used from the start of the twentieth century in early ragtime and jazz ensembles, even though in the earliest years of recording it became fashionable to employ a tuba instead. This was partly also due to the fact that the bass does not project its sound easily in large spaces, and until means could be found to amplify it, the tuba offered a more audible alternative. Bassists sought to overcome the acoustic limitations of the instrument by several methods: firstly, by bowing each note, rather than using a plucking or pizzicato technique; secondly, by adding a percussive slap to the production of each pizzicato note; and, thirdly, by altering the physical characteristics of the instrument. Such alterations included raising the action (the height of the strings from the fingerboard), using different materials, such as aluminum, for constructing the body of the instrument, and adopting various types of string, of which the most commonly used were gut and steel, although nylon strings (from the mid-twentieth century) offered a robust and loud alternative.

Examples of all these various strategies abound in early jazz. Steve Brown (one of the earliest virtuoso players) used arco and pizzicato techniques in his recordings with Jean Goldkette and Paul Whiteman, as did Wellman Braud with Duke Ellington. Braud was part of a notable tradition of bassists from New Orleans that also included 'Pops' Foster, Bill Johnson, John Lindsay, Al Morgan and Robert Ysaguirre, and between them these men did much to cement the use of the double bass in jazz groups from the late 1920s onward.

In the 1930s, bass-playing was advanced by Walter Page, who popularized the 4/4 'walking bass' in his recordings for Count Basie, by Israel Crosby who initiated ostinato patterns of the kind favored by later bebop players, and by Milt Hinton whose virtuoso recordings for Cab Calloway contain both pizzicato solos (as in 'Pluckin' the Bass') and arco features ('Ebony Silhouette'). Their work was consolidated by that of Jimmy Blanton in Duke Ellington's orchestra from 1939 to 1941. His mobile bass lines in the ensemble freed the instrument from the kind of tonic-based figures that dated back to ragtime, and opened up the way for the bass to become both the principal timekeeper and the agent of harmonic change in the modern jazz groups of the 1940s.

From the late 1940s onward, effective amplification became possible, therefore further freeing bassists and allowing them to apply more technique rather than merely making the instrument audible. Oscar Pettiford, with Duke Ellington and a succession of bebop groups, demonstrated what was possible, and other players, including Ray Brown, Red Callender and Charles Mingus, developed his ideas. By the 1950s, players were exploiting the tonal opportunities offered by steel strings and ever more effective amplification, and were afforded greater speed and facility in solo playing by a slightly lower action. Significant soloists of the 1950s and 1960s included Ron Carter, Scott La Faro, Charlie Haden, Eddie Gomez and Jimmy Garrison.

As jazz itself reached a crossroads in the late 1960s, so too did the development of bass-playing. Avant-garde players, such as Malachi Favors of the Art Ensemble of Chicago, added percussive and drone techniques to the repertoire, and in Europe players such as Barry Guy and the US expatriate Barre Phillips experimented with using the body of the instrument and the harmonics of the strings below the bridge to create new sounds. Others, such as Eberhard Weber, experimented with the instrument itself, using amplification to allow the construction of more compact solid-bodied instruments, adding extra strings, and combining the bass with such effects as echo delay and phasing units. The avant-garde tradition has been continued by players such as William Parker, Jr., Joëlle Léandre and Paul Rogers.

Equally, there has been a simultaneous development of more orthodox playing techniques. Niels-Henning Ørsted Pedersen has shown how, by plucking with three or more fingers of the right hand, he can articulate melody lines as subtle and as rapid as those of a saxophone or trumpet, and this approach has been adopted by such players as Neil Swainson and John Clayton, Jr. Other outstanding exponents of the late twentieth century included Christian McBride, Ray Drummond and James Genus. In the early twenty-first century, players like Avishai Cohen and Omer Avital have been exploring ways of integrating other traditions, including Middle Eastern music, into jazz bass-playing.

Styles of music outside jazz have not developed the same degree of virtuoso bass-playing, but the bass has had a fundamental role in blues or rhythm and blues ensembles. It was used as the bass instrument in early rock 'n' roll groups such as Bill Haley's Comets, although for much of the period from the mid-1950s until the late 1990s, when there was something of a revival in slapping bass techniques, it was supplanted by the bass guitar. The bass has also been used in a variety of other Western popular music styles, from polka to the music of Scottish dance groups.

Bibliography

Berendt, Joachim-Ernst. 1982. *The Jazz Book: From Ragtime to Fusion and Beyond*. Rev. ed. Westport, CT: Lawrence Hill. (First published Frankfurt am Main: Fischer Bücherei, 1953.)

Feather, Leonard. 1957. *The Book of Jazz: A Guide to the Entire Field*. London: Arthur Baker.

Shipton, Alyn. 1988. 'Double Bass.' In *The New Grove Dictionary of Jazz*, Vol. 1, ed. Barry Kernfeld. London: Macmillan, 301–303.

Discographical References

Calloway, Cab, and His Orchestra. 'Ebony Silhouette.' Vocalion 6192. 1941: USA. Reissue: Calloway, Cab, and His Orchestra. 'Ebony Silhouette.' *1940–1941*. Classics 629. *1996*: France.

Calloway, Cab, and His Orchestra. 'Pluckin' the Bass.' Vocalion 5406. 1939: USA. Reissue: Calloway, Cab, and His Orchestra. 'Pluckin' the Bass.' *His Best Recordings*. Best of Jazz 4011. *1996*: USA.

ALYN SHIPTON

Fiddle (Europe/World)

Europe

Emerging in its modern form in sixteenth-century northern Italy, the violin spread rapidly to all strata of society wherever there was an indigenous tradition of bowed string playing. Where that instrument was used for folk and vernacular musics, it is referred to as a 'fiddle.' In Finland and western Norway (early seventeenth century), Scandinavia, the Baltic States and the British Isles (early eighteenth century), and France and the Low Countries, it was played using open strings as drones. Until the mid-twentieth century, the fiddle was held either on the chest or under the chin but not gripped by it, with the neck of the fiddle resting on the palm of the fingering hand, and with the bow held about one-third of the way along its length. Shetland fiddler Aly Bain recalls that the fiddlers he heard as a boy held the instrument under the top of the ribs and, instead of moving the bow, moved the fiddle (Bain 1980).

The United Kingdom and Ireland

The fiddle entered the popular music arena in the United Kingdom through the 1960s–70s folk revival, which went on to develop into 'folk-rock,' 'roots' and then 'world music' scenes. Drawing to varying degrees on rural fiddle styles of the late nineteenth and early twentieth centuries, when the instrument was played at harvest homes and 'tune-ups' to accompany morris dancing in England and at *ceilidhs* in Ireland and Scotland, neo-traditional fiddlers attempted to broaden the appeal of the music by introducing and developing fusion styles. To understand the way in which contemporary fiddlers are situated in the United Kingdom, it is necessary to understand the traditions on which they draw.

English fiddle styles are perhaps the least known within the UK spectrum. A broad distinction can be made between styles from the north and from the south of England. Until World War II, the fiddle, the melodeon and the mouth organ were used to accompany dancing in leisure time and at harvest suppers in the scattered hillside farms of the border counties of Northumberland, Cumberland and parts of Yorkshire. The repertoire differed in rural and urban areas, but mostly consisted of rants (lively, short country dances) and reels. After the war, for instance, the Cheviot Ranters played melodies such as 'The Morpeth Rant' or 'The Eightsome Reel.' In the early twenty-first century, northern fiddle music

demonstrates a greater Scottish influence, with strathspeys and Scottish tune variants predominating.

Southern English traditional fiddlers play a mixture of morris and step-dance tunes, mostly hornpipes, and tunes for social dancing including polkas and marches. Morris fiddlers, such as William 'Jinky' Wells (1918–53), who played for the Bampton morris team, and Stephen Baldwin (1873–1955), who played for the Gloucestershire and Worcestershire teams, inspired early folk music revival musicians. So too did East Anglian fiddlers such as Harcourt 'Harkie' Nesling (1890–1978), Fred 'Eely' Whent (1901–76) and Fred 'Pip' Whiting (1904–86) from East Suffolk, and Harry Cox (1885–1971) from Norfolk.

Southern English fiddlers use a vibratoless tone, with notes punched out by choppy bow strokes. Integral to this type of sound are drones, together with slides and turns used as rhythmical devices to produce pulsating 'drops and raises' (Kennedy 1951; Pegg 1985). Sometimes, musicians sing or hum as they play. The rough-sounding southern style of fiddling was introduced into the British folk-rock movement in the early 1970s through the playing of Carole Pegg, fiddler with the band Mr. Fox, and the sweeter and more dexterous northern style through the playing of Dave Swarbrick, who performed first with the Ian Campbell Folk Group, then with Fairport Convention and later with Steeleye Span and Martin Carthy. Eliza Carthy, daughter of Martin Carthy and Norma Waterson, represents the younger fiddlers now drawing on the tradition to produce a pan-British sound, while Emma Hancock, fiddler with the Borders band Tarras, brings a classical touch to the fusion of traditional music and rock.

In contemporary Wales, the fiddle is played by folk bands such as Pigyn Clust, but no single fiddler stands out although there is a fiddle tradition there: the *ffidil* superseded the *crwth* during the eighteenth century as the principal bowed folk instrument and replaced the harp as accompaniment for popular dance.

The outstanding Sligo fiddler Michael Coleman (1891–1945), with his elaborate fingering, faultless rhythm and vibratoless style, prefigured the cross-fertilizations of 'world musics' when he moved to New York during the 1920s. He came to represent a pan-Irish style later developed by bands such as the Chieftains. Michael Gorman (1895–1970), who had the same teacher as Coleman (James Gammon), moved to England, where he gained renown for accompanying the colossal voice and sparse banjo playing of the Irish street singer, Margaret Barry. Within Ireland, regional traditions in style and repertoire have continued to predominate – for instance, the Donegal repertoire inclines toward reels, flings and Scots-influenced melodies, while the Kerry repertoire has more polkas, jigs and slides. The young sisters Liz and

Yvonne Kane, from the west of Ireland, are currently breathing life into the tradition, and the all-Ireland fiddle champion Máiréad Nesbitt, brought to the fore by Michael Flatley's show *Lord of the Dance*, has also accompanied country and rock musicians such as Emmylou Harris and Van Morrison.

In Scotland, Hector MacAndrew of Aberdeen is the most celebrated contemporary player in the Gow traditional style. The Gow family dominated fiddle playing from the mid-eighteenth to the mid-nineteenth century. 'Famous Niel' Gow (1727–97), who composed many tunes, is thought to have developed the 'Scottish snap,' a characteristic up-bow stroke used in the strathspey. A listening repertoire developed, including the slow air, the 'slow strathspey' and song tunes followed by instrumental variations. James Scott-Skinner (1843–1927) is the most famous in a line of fiddle composers: his air 'The Bonny Lass of Bon-Accord,' strathspey 'Laird of Drumblair' and schottische 'Miller o'Hirn' have become part of the national Scottish repertoire. Much of the fiddle music of the Scottish mainland is influenced by the bagpipe. Aly Bain, albeit from the Shetlands, continues to dominate the Scottish music scene.

The Shetland Isles are nearer to Norway than to Scotland both geographically and culturally, and their relationship with both is expressed in fiddle music. On the one hand, some of the six Scottish tunings identified by James Oswald in *The Caledonian Pocket Companion* have remained in use in the Shetlands. On the other hand, both Shetland and Norwegian fiddlers use microtonal intervals (Cooke 1987) and Shetland fiddlers raise their G strings to A, which is very close to the tuning of the Norwegian *hardingfele* or *hardanger* fiddle.

Scandinavia

The *hardingfele*, which uses double stops and drones and is played to accompany dancing, is typical of western Norway. It usually has four melody strings above the fingerboard and four or five 'sympathetic' or drone strings below it. Popularized by Trond Isaksen Flateboe (1713–72), the son of Isak Nielsen (Skaar) Botnen (1663–1759), it is traditionally narrower than the ordinary fiddle and often has deeper ribs and a more pronounced arching of the belly and back. During the nineteenth century, the instrument's shape became closer to that of the violin. The ordinary fiddle, or *flatfele*, is found in the northern and eastern parts of the country. In the late twentieth and early twenty-first centuries, both the *flatfele* and the *hardingfele* have flourished in the Norwegian folk revival that centers on competitions for players of regional instruments, tunes and styles. The most famous *hardingfele* fiddler is Torgeir Augundson or 'Myllarguten'

(Miller's Boy), who died over a century ago. The Björgum and Buen families dominate the contemporary scene.

Fiddle music is also widespread in the rest of northern Europe. In Finland, where waltzes and polkas are popular, the fiddle is often joined by the harmonium. Many compositions of the Kaustinen fiddler Konsta Jylhä are part of the standard repertoire of Finnish folk musicians. One of the most important fiddle groups, JPP (Järvellan Pikkupelimannit), contains from four to nine fiddlers backed by an acoustic bass and harmonium.

Sweden has rich regional fiddle traditions, including those identified with Lapp-Nils or Nils Jonsson (1804–70) from Jämtland, Lejsme Per Larsson (1822–1907) from Malung and Pekkos Per (d. 1877) from Bingsjö. Hjort Anders Olsson (1865–1952) continued the Bingsjö tradition, followed by his grandson Nils Agenmark (1915–94). Päkkos Gustaf (b. 1916), who continues to play in Bingsjö, is highly influential among contemporary Swedish fiddlers. Also notable is fiddler and singer Lena Willemark, who draws on the Dalarna tradition in different contexts, including the fusion band Enteli and the jazz piano-led Elise Einarsdottir Ensemble. Fiddles adapted to take 'sympathetic' drone strings, such as the *stakefiol* and *lat fiol*, are being used increasingly, as is the keyed fiddle or *nyckelharpa*.

Central and Eastern Europe

Despite the sanitization of traditions under Communism, many Central and Eastern European fiddle traditions have managed to survive. In Poland, for instance, the angular melodies of the Tatra Mountain string bands, particularly from the Podhale region, have burst onto the 'world music' stage. Comprising two to four fiddles and a three-string bass, they collectively improvise with both the melodic line and the harmonic accompaniment, often using the 'Lydian mode' with its sharpened fourth.

In Romania, the *taraf* instrumental ensemble appeared in village musical life during the second half of the nineteenth century. Professional musicians (*lăutari*) introduced a number of instruments from the Persian-Arab-Turkish and Greek urban cultures and from Western Europe. In the early twenty-first century, much attention is focused on the rich traditions of contemporary Transylvania. *Lăutari* there have continued to form bands, in which the fiddle takes the lead over the *tambal* (cymbalom) and double bass, to play for weddings and other celebrations. Hungarian fiddlers in Transylvania play in a highly ornamented style, using double stopping and irregular rhythms.

The *smuikas* of Lithuania is found in a great variety of sizes and forms and may have three, four or more strings, usually tuned in fifths. Similar traditions of fiddle playing are also found in neighboring countries such as Estonia (*viiul*), and Belorussia, Moldavia and Ukraine (*skripka*). In southwest Moldavia, the fiddle usually has seven 'sympathetic' strings.

In the late twentieth century, klezmer bands – in which the fiddle plays an important symbolical role – emerged from Eastern Europe: for instance, the Budapest-based bands Odessa Klezmer Band and Di Naye Kapelye.

Gypsy and Traveler Musicians

In Western, Central and Southeastern Europe, the fiddle is the favored instrument of Gypsies and Travelers. In the United Kingdom, they play mostly in their own camps, occasionally participating in the music-making of local communities. In Wales, the fiddle was played only by Gypsies and Travelers until World War I because of the condemnation of dance by Nonconformist religion. In southern England, Gypsies and Travelers use the instrument to accompany step-dancing.

Two fiddles, a string bass and a plucked instrument are typical of Gypsy ensembles in Central Europe and the Balkans, although in Romania and Moldavia the fiddle repertoire also includes virtuoso instrumental versions of the song form *hora lunga* or *doina*. The two main fiddlers with the Gypsy band Taraf de Haïdouks, which may consist of a dozen or so members, epitomize two kinds of fiddle playing: the plaintive style of 77-year-old Nicolae Neacşu, who accompanies ballads, and the virtuosity of the boy fiddler Caliu illustrate the traditional and modern ends of the fiddle spectrum. The progression from the status of local wedding band to international supergroup is charted by the band's CDs, the first of which was made in 1986 for Ocora and was followed by four more on the Crammed Discs label.

Africa, South Asia, Southeast Asia and the Middle East

The fiddle traveled with colonizers, such as the Portuguese, Dutch and British, and also infiltrated areas where there was European influence. During the 'Discoveries' period of the sixteenth and seventeenth centuries, the Portuguese took the instrument with them to their trading posts and colonies. It was used to entertain them on the long voyages, and was initially used in slave orchestras that comprised harp, fiddle and bassoon. The fiddle thus reached Africa (Mozambique, São Tomé, Principe, Cape Verde), South Asia (Goa and along the Malabar Coast in India, Sri Lanka), Southeast Asia (Malacca, Sumatra, East Timor) – where it became known as the *biola* (from the Portuguese *viola*) – and parts of Latin America (Brazil), where it was incorporated into indigenous musics in different ways (see Môças's *A viagem dos sons/ The Journey of Sounds* (1998)). Around the Strait of Mal-

acca, for instance, the fiddle is played along with the harmonium and frame drum (*rapai*), its music combining implied harmonic musical textures with gong or drum parts that are cyclical (Sarkissian 1998); in Sumatra, the fiddle may sound sweet, as when accompanying a vibrato-laden Javanese vocal style, or wonderfully hard as in *kapri* music (fiddle, vocalist, frame drums), in which it provides a counter-melody to the similarly hard but highly melismatic vocal line (Kartomi 1998); and in Sri Lanka, rich fiddle drones combine with African-inspired syncopated percussive accompaniment provided by triangle, tambourine, guitar, English mandolin, ukulele and accordion (Jackson 1998). Tamils in Sri Lanka also use the fiddle in Karnatic music and to accompany string-puppet plays (*rukada*).

Similarly, in Middle Eastern areas, each society has adapted the instrument's name, sound ideal, playing techniques and holding position to its own requirements. In North Africa and Turkey, the fiddle is usually called *keman* (from the generic term 'kemençe' or 'kamānche,' the latter used to refer to indigenous bowed spiked chordophones) and is played in an upright position, resting on the seated player's thigh. The instrument was often introduced first in popular music contexts, such as the urban café environment. A typical orchestra accompanying Judeo-Spanish songs for Jewish events in Ottoman and Moroccan areas was often comprised of non-Jewish and Gypsy musicians playing the fiddle, *'ūd* (plucked lute), *qanun* (plucked box-zither) and frame drum. In Morocco, one or more fiddles take a leading role in the vocal–instrumental *nawbā* suites played by traditional orchestras. In Iran, the instrument is used to play the whole of the four-string *kamānche* spike fiddle repertoire and, at the beginning of the twentieth century, it temporarily threatened the existence of the *kamānche*. The fiddle features in Gypsy jazz groups in contemporary Turkey, such as the Istanbul Oriental Ensemble.

The fiddle was introduced into India almost two centuries ago. It became a popular element in nineteenth-century urban theater music. It has become prominent in southern Indian classical music, being particularly compatible as accompaniment to the tense, bright timbre of the southern Indian vocal style. It is also an important solo instrument in India. The player usually sits cross-legged, resting the scroll on the right foot and the tail of the fiddle against the left shoulder.

Latin America

Under the Spanish colonial system, where the fiddle was taught and disseminated by missionaries, Indian peasants in Latin America incorporated the instrument into their own cultural and aesthetic frameworks, using it in local musical ensembles during the numerous public festivals and for dance-dramas (Béhague 1979). Jesuits, Franciscans and Dominicans considered the instrument fit to be played by Indians (unlike the guitar) and an effective means of spreading Catholicism. Although preserving the basic characteristics of the European model, the fiddle soon became regarded as an 'Indian' instrument. Fiddles were used in musical groups (*conjuntos*), forerunners of the contemporary *orquesta típicas* (Romero 2001). At the end of the nineteenth century, small ensembles based on the Andean harp and the fiddle began to add instruments such as the mandolin and *charango* (small Andean guitar) and, in the mid-twentieth century, clarinets and saxophones. In contemporary Latin America, most *orquesta típicas*, although dominated by saxophones, continue to include the fiddle, which plays a supportive role overall, but which leads and improvises during the compulsory introduction as well as in interludes between different tunes.

The Ethnomusicological 'Fiddle'

Ethnomusicologists use 'fiddle' as a generic term for any chordophone of the lute type that is sounded by a bow. One of numerous examples is the short-necked South Asian fiddle, *sarangi*, found in Hindustani classical *rāga* music of north India and Pakistan, related forms of which are used in folk musics in Rajasthan and the northwest. There are also similar 'fiddles' in Kashmir and Afghanistan. The Chinese two-string *erhu* is frequently referred to as a 'fiddle' by Westerners, as is the Mongolian two-string 'horse-head fiddle' or *morin huur*. Such instruments are finding a place in popular musics because of the late twentieth-century and early twenty-first-century engagement with 'world music.'

Bibliography

Alburger, Mary Anne. 1996. *Scottish Fiddlers and Their Music*. Edinburgh: Hardie Press.

Bain, Aly. 1980. 'Focus on Fiddlers.' *Acoustic Music* 27: 8–10.

Béhague, Gerard. 1979. *Music in Latin America: An Introduction*. Englewood Cliffs, NJ: Prentice-Hall.

Broughton, Simon, Ellingham, Mark, and Trillo, Richard, eds. 1999. *World Music: The Rough Guide. Vol. 1: Africa, Europe and the Middle East*. London: Rough Guides Ltd.

Cooke, Peter. 1987. *The Fiddle Tradition of the Shetland Isles*. Cambridge: Cambridge University Press.

Cooke, Peter, et al. 1984. 'Violin, §IV: Extra-European and Folk Usage.' In *The New Grove Dictionary of Musical Instruments*, Vol. 3, ed. Stanley Sadie. London: Macmillan, 801–804.

Goertzen, Chris. 1997. *Fiddling for Norway: Revival and Identity*. Chicago: University of Chicago Press.

Hall, Reg. 1999. Notes to *The Voice of the People*, Vol. 9: *Rig-a-Jig-Jig: Dance Music of the South of England*. Topic TSCD659.

Hall, Reg. 1999. Notes to *The Voice of the People*, Vol. 19: *Ranting & Reeling: Dance Music of the North of England*. Topic TSCD669.

Jackson, Kenneth D. 1998. Notes to *Sri Lanka. Baila Ceilão Cafrinhai!/Dance Ceylon Kafrinha!*. Tradisom VS03.

Kartomi, Margaret. 1998. Notes to *Sumatra. Kroncong Moritsko/Kroncong Moritsko*. Tradisom VS06.

Kennedy, Peter, ed. 1951. 'Introduction.' In *The Fiddler's Tune-Book*. London: Oxford University Press.

Oswald, James. 1743–60. *The Caledonian Pocket Companion*. London: The author.

Pegg, Carole A. 1985. *Music and Society in East Suffolk*. Ph.D. thesis, Cambridge University.

Romero, Raúl R. 2001. *Debating the Past: Music, Memory, and Identity in the Andes*. New York: Oxford University Press.

Sarkissian, Margaret. 1998. Notes to *Kantiga di padri sa chang, Malaca/Songs of the Priest's Land, Malacca*. Tradisom VS05.

Discography

A viagem dos sons/The Journey of Sounds (12 CDs) (ed. José Môças). Tradisom VS0-112. *1998*: Portugal.

Baldwin, Stephen. *Stephen Baldwin – English Village Fiddler*. Leader LED 2068. 1954: UK.

Carthy, Eliza. *Red Rice*. Topic Records TSCD493 and TSCD494. *1998*: UK.

Coleman, Michael. *Classic Recordings of Michael Coleman*. Shanachie 33006. *1979*: USA.

Finlande: Musique traditionnelle. Ocora 600004. *1996*: France.

Gienek Wilczek's Bukowina Band. *Music of the Tatra Mountains: Poland*. Nimbus Records NI 5464. *1996*: UK.

Gorman, Michael. *The Sligo Champion*. Topic Records TSCD525. *2001*: UK.

Hall, Reg, et al. *English Country Music*. Topic Records TSCD607. *2001*: UK.

Hungarian Music from Transylvania: Traditions of Gyimes and the Great Plain. Inédit W260098. *2001*: France.

Istanbul Oriental Ensemble. *Caravanserai*. Network 36990. *2001*: UK.

Mr. Fox. *Mr. Fox/The Gypsy*. Castle Communications ECM CD 433. *1997*: UK.

Odessa Klezmer Band. *Isaac's Dry Tree*. Etnofon ER-CD022. *2002*: Hungary.

Roumanie: Musiques de Villages: Oltenia – Moldavia – Transylvania. Constantin Brailoiu Collection (1933–43). AIMP IX, X, XI; Vide-Gallo CD 537, 538, 539. *1988*: Switzerland.

Shetland Fiddlers. Leader LED 2052. *1973*: UK.

Tarras. *Walking Down Main Street*. Topic Records TSCD524. *2002*: UK.

Trebunia Family Band, The. *Music of the Tatra Mountains: Poland*. Nimbus Records NI 5437. *1996*: UK.

Whent, Fred 'Eely,' et al. *Sing, Say and Play: Traditional Songs and Music from Suffolk*. Topic Records 12TS375. *1978*: UK.

Whiting, Fred, et al. *The Earl Soham Slog: Step Dance and Country Music from East Suffolk*. Topic Records 12TS374. *1978*: UK.

CAROLE PEGG

Fiddle (US)

'Fiddle' is the colloquial name for the violin, in reference particularly to its use as a vernacular dance instrument and generally to its use in folk and popular music. During the Middle Ages, the term 'fiddle' came to refer to one particular type of bowed instrument, known today as the medieval fiddle (Remnant 1984); variant forms of the term have been used over time to designate many different bowed stringed instruments. When the modern violin emerged in the mid-sixteenth century, it replaced its predecessors as a popular dance instrument throughout Europe and, seemingly, usurped the older name as well. Fiddling is extremely widespread, and fiddle traditions exist throughout much of Europe and areas colonized by Europeans.

Although fiddling is usually viewed as a form of folk music, the fiddle has often served as a link between commercially produced and distributed popular music genres and local, community-based, orally transmitted folk traditions. The fiddling of the British Isles, Ireland and North America, especially the United States, has had a particularly strong impact on world popular music. Fiddling traditions in these regions have common roots in the body of popular dance music and tune types that crystallized throughout the British/Irish diaspora in the mid- to late eighteenth century, but the subsequent history of fiddling in these areas is quite complex. Numerous local repertoires and performance styles have developed on top of this core, and so, although there are certain tunes common to fiddlers in such far-flung locations as Texas and the Shetland Isles, the differences between fiddling in various regions generally outweigh the commonalities. Even a relatively small geographic area such as Ireland has supported distinctive regional styles and repertoires.

Whether or not discrete local traditions will endure in the current era of mass communications is a subject of concern and debate among scholars, players and fans. Irish fiddling, for example, has been greatly influenced by the playing of a trio of virtuoso fiddlers – Michael

Coleman, James Morrison and Paddy Killoran – who emigrated from County Sligo to New York City and who began making commercial phonograph records in the 1920s. Their records were sought after both in Ireland and in Irish-American communities in the United States, and their repertoire and styles served as models for many young musicians who might otherwise have chosen to emulate players in their own locales (Moloney 1982). However, the many later recordings of fiddlers who represent other Irish regional traditions indicate that variety continued to thrive throughout the rest of the century. The recent surge in popularity of Irish music has created a new group of star performers, and concerns about the continued viability of older, local styles have likewise begun to surface again.

In North America, there has been a considerable amount of cross-cultural musical interchange centered around the fiddle. Native peoples are reported to have learned to play the fiddle as early as 1663 and some Native traditions have continued to flourish (Wells 1978; Mishler 1993). The fiddling traditions of non-English-speaking immigrants from mainland Europe have exerted varying degrees of influence on mainstream North American fiddling styles. There has been significant impact from French traditions in parts of Canada (primarily Québec) and Louisiana, but the fiddling of other ethnic or national groups, such as Hispanic in the US Southwest and Scandinavian in the upper Midwest, respectively, has generally remained more discrete. Even certain Irish and Scottish traditions that have been transplanted to North America have by and large remained unassimilated. The music of the Irish immigrants who flowed to urban centers in North America throughout much of the nineteenth century, for example, has remained largely separate from the Irish-influenced mainstream of North American fiddling. A similar situation obtains in Cape Breton, Nova Scotia, where a strong fiddling tradition was brought by Scottish highlanders in the late eighteenth century, and which has retained much of its original identity.

African slaves are known to have been playing the fiddle by the end of the seventeenth century, and did so both for dances in the homes of their owners and at their own gatherings (Epstein 1977). Free blacks in the North played for white dances into the early twentieth century (Wells 1978). The fiddle has provided an important but little-recognized avenue for interchange between African- and European-American musical traditions. It has been argued that the fiddle and the dance music played on it provided one of the earliest and most deeply influential points of intersection between European and African musical cultures in the New World (Wells 1991). This interchange has been especially important in terms of the development of popular music genres. The European fiddle, often played in conjunction with the African-derived banjo, was one of the primary dance instruments among plantation slaves, and the fiddle/banjo combination was adopted and adapted by black-face minstrels (Winans 1984). Minstrelsy, in turn, was enormously popular throughout much of the nineteenth century, internationally as well as in North America, and is often regarded as one of the earliest distinct genres of popular music.

As African-American dance music evolved in the years following Emancipation, pianos and brass instruments began to displace the fiddle and banjo combination as the favored instruments for providing dance music. It has been suggested that, as ragtime emerged from the older forms of dance music, the percussive and chordal accompaniment that had been provided by the banjo was transferred to the left hand of the piano player, and the melody played on the fiddle to the right (Southern 1983). Fiddlers played small, but significant, roles in ragtime orchestras and early jazz and pre-jazz dance bands. Many of the society and concert bands in New Orleans carried a violinist, as did some of the territory bands that worked the North American heartland in the 1920s and 1930s. Claude Williams emerged from the Kansas City/territory band scene as an important jazz violin soloist; he also played guitar with the Count Basie band. Other influential early jazz violinists were Stuff Smith, Eddie South, and white musicians Joe Venuti and Stéphane Grappelli. Blues fiddlers were similarly few in number. Eddie Anthony recorded numerous pieces with Peg Leg Howell in the 1920s. Lonnie Johnson, better known and more influential as a guitarist, also showed his skills as a blues fiddler on a few recordings.

Fiddlers continued to figure in African-American string bands of the rural South, although relatively little of their music was documented by the record companies that were involved in marketing 'race' (blues and gospel) or 'hillbilly' (white country) music. This oversight was likely due to preconceived notions on the part of record executives regarding the types of music that were salable to particular audiences: African-American musicians playing a type of music that was thought to appeal only to whites were probably regarded as unmarketable anomalies. Yet the existence of a healthy tradition of black fiddlers can be inferred from interviews with many white fiddlers and other musicians who grew up in the second decade of the century, and who either learned directly from black fiddlers in their communities or were greatly influenced by them. A very few recordings of integrated string bands were made, notably those by Taylor's Kentucky Boys, featuring the fiddling of Jim Booker, a black man, and the banjo playing of Marion Underwood, a white man. Cousins Joe and Odell Thompson, from Orange County, North Carolina, were brought to public attention in the 1980s and 1990s and gave contemporary audiences a glimpse of a once-flourishing tradition.

There has been considerable African-American influence on white Southern fiddle traditions, and this influence extends to the various subgenres of country music that feature the fiddle. The fiddle and banjo combination that is at the heart of Southern string band music derives from African-American tradition. It was absorbed into white folk tradition in the Southeast, probably through the combined influence of the professional minstrel stage and direct contact with black folk musicians. The presence of the banjo and the effect that the traditional playing style has had on fiddle repertoire and style in the South have given the fiddling and string band music of this region a unique character. The insistent eighth-sixteenth-sixteenth-note rhythmic pattern that comes from the 'downstroking' or 'frailing' technique of playing the banjo provides the pulse that underlies the region's fiddle tunes.

Fiddle music originated as dance music, and fiddling has been linked with dancing throughout much of its history. In the eighteenth and early nineteenth centuries, dancers in all levels of society moved to the strains of fiddlers in settings ranging from manor houses to taverns. Changes in society and concomitant changes in dance fashions throughout the nineteenth century gradually relegated fiddling to dances in rural areas, or to ethnic neighborhoods in some cities. Industrialist Henry Ford developed an interest in fiddling and 'old-fashioned dancing' in the mid-1920s. This brought national attention to several fiddlers and at least a temporary revival of dancing to fiddle music. Boston, with a mix of emigrants from Ireland and from French and Scottish Canada, was home to a lively fiddle and dance scene in the 1930s, 1940s and 1950s. The fiddle-based western swing bands of the Southwest and West played to large crowds in dance halls from the mid-1930s through much of the 1950s. The counterculture movement of the 1960s and 1970s, with an interest in getting 'back to the land,' helped spur the contradance revival that spread from New England to most other parts of the United States.

Fiddling contests have also played an important role in sustaining and nurturing traditional fiddling. There is evidence of some contests in Colonial America, but a comprehensive history of the fiddle contest tradition has yet to be written. Texas has been home to a long tradition of fiddle contests, and Atlanta, Georgia was the site of a big annual contest from ca. 1913 to 1935 (Daniel 1990, 15–44). Henry Ford's interest in fiddling also spawned a national movement of fiddling contests. In 1926, many communities throughout the United States held fiddle contests that to at least some degree owed their existence to the Ford-inspired fiddling mania.

It was not uncommon for the winners in many of the contests in the first half of the twentieth century to be decided by popular acclaim, and for showmanship to triumph over musicianship. Beginning in the 1950s, contests in the West and Southwest began to use new standards of judging and to impose not only a time limit on the contestants, but also rules concerning the number and types of tunes that could be played. Contests experienced a new surge of popularity in the mid-1960s, in part spurred by the interest in all forms of folk music generated by the folk music revival. In 1963, a contest in Weiser, Idaho, which was first a local and then a regional event, was renamed the 'National Oldtime Fiddlers' Contest' and began to draw competitors from throughout much of the United States and Canada (*History of Fiddling* 1996–99). The success in the Weiser contest of fiddlers from Texas and Oklahoma who played a style featuring elaborate and carefully worked-out variations on two-strain fiddle tunes led to the widespread adoption of this style by players at contests in other areas of the country. Sometimes termed 'contest-style fiddling,' this has become a matter of much controversy, and has generated fear that its popularity will lead to the elimination of older regional styles of traditional fiddling.

In addition to dances and contests, there is a long history of fiddling as professional entertainment. Stage dancers such as Charles Durang danced to the music of fiddlers in the late eighteenth century, and the role of the fiddle in the early blackface minstrel troupes of the nineteenth century has already been noted.

In the modern era, country music is the popular music genre in which the fiddle figures most strongly, as the instrument lies at the heart of most subgenres within the broad spectrum of country music. The recordings of fiddlers A.C. 'Eck' Robertson (1922) and Fiddlin' John Carson (1923) were seminal in the growth of the country music business. Other Southern fiddlers such as Clark Kessinger from West Virginia, Clayton McMichen from Georgia, Charlie Bowman and Fiddlin' Arthur Smith from Tennessee, and Doc Roberts from Kentucky recorded extensively during the 1920s and 1930s. Their work serves as a bridge between older, community-based folk traditions and the new world of mass dissemination of music via recordings and broadcasting.

In the Southwest in the 1930s, Bob Wills and Milton Brown developed a new style that combined elements of jazz and country music and that came to be called 'western swing.' Fiddles were prominent in many western swing bands. Jazz violinists such as Joe Venuti, Stuff Smith and Stéphane Grappelli found many more disciples among the young fiddlers in Texas and Oklahoma than they did among mainstream jazz players. Cecil Brower, J.R. Chatwell, Hugh Farr, Cliff Bruner, Joe Holley, Johnny Gimble and others brought a new swing to their playing of traditional fiddle tunes, and improvised 'takeoff' solos on the jazz/pop standards and new original songs that comprised the repertoires of the western swing bands.

The jazz approach of featuring solos or 'breaks' by individual instrumentalists is also a key aspect of bluegrass performance style as developed by Kentuckian Bill Monroe, beginning with the formation of his band, the Blue Grass Boys, in 1939. Fiddle music was one of many threads of Southern vernacular music upon which Monroe drew in synthesizing bluegrass music. Monroe was greatly influenced by the music of his uncle, Pendleton Vandiver, who was a master Kentucky old-time fiddler. Monroe recorded many tunes that he learned from his Uncle Pen, and also wrote many new pieces in the fiddle tune mold. African-American influence can clearly be seen in bluegrass fiddling in the sliding into and out of notes that is one of the hallmarks of the style, and in the extensive use of the lowered thirds and sevenths employed by many bluegrass fiddlers. These stylistic traits can be heard in the pre-bluegrass fiddling of Tennessee musician Fiddlin' Arthur Smith, and were brought to bluegrass music by such early stylists as Chubby Wise and Vassar Clements. Other important bluegrass fiddlers have included Benny Martin, Kenny Baker, Tommy Magness, Bobby Hicks, Scott Stoneman, Richard Greene, Byron Berline, Stuart Duncan, Paul Warren and Clarence 'Tater' Tate.

Fiddlers have been strongly featured in the touring bands and recordings of such mainstream country artists as Hank Williams, Roy Acuff, Hank Snow, Ray Price, Buck Owens, Porter Wagoner, Merle Haggard, Emmylou Harris and Ricky Skaggs. Fiddlers in these bands often shared solo work with conventional and steel guitarists. Musicians such as Jerry Rivers, Dale Potter, Tommy Jackson, Tommy Vaden, Howdy Forrester, Buddy Spicher and Tommy Williams played on the road and in recording sessions with a variety of country singers. Mark O'Connor, an extraordinarily talented multi-instrumentalist who is best known as a fiddler, made extensive contributions as a Nashville session musician in the 1980s and early 1990s. He has since pursued a path as a classical composer; his 'Fiddle Concerto for Violin and Orchestra' has been recorded and has been performed by numerous symphony orchestras.

Although no particular style of rock fiddling has developed, fiddles have found their way into rock bands, often when a musician with grounding in some other genre has gravitated to rock. Richard Greene, a Los Angeles violinist who mastered bluegrass fiddle style and who had a short, but influential, tenure as a member of Bill Monroe's Blue Grass Boys in the late 1960s, brought a fusion of rock and bluegrass to the group Seatrain in the early 1970s. Another Angeleno, Don 'Sugarcane' Harris, performed in an R&B duo ('Don and Dewey') with Dewey Terry, but is better known for his blues/rock violin work with a variety of artists, including Frank Zappa and John Mayall. Violinist David LaFlamme led the 1960s group It's a Beautiful Day, which enjoyed modest success. LaFlamme had been the first violinist with Dan Hicks and His Hot Licks, a somewhat quirky, pseudo-nostalgic, jazz-influenced group, also from San Francisco, in the late 1960s, that later featured the swingy fiddling of Sid Page. In the late 1990s, the Dave Matthews Band included the violin playing of Boyd Tinsley.

The late 1990s also saw a tremendous growth of interest in Irish and Scottish music, and the emergence of 'Celtic' music as a new genre of popular music. Fiddlers played key roles in bands such as the Chieftains (Seán Keane and Martin Fay), Altan (Mairéad Ní Mhaonaigh and Ciaran Tourish), Solas (Winifred Horan) and Skyedance (Alasdair Fraser). Young musicians such as Irish-American fiddler Eileen Ivers, and Cape Breton fiddlers Ashley MacIsaac and Natalie MacMaster garnered considerable attention with music that was strongly rooted in tradition but that incorporated elements of rock, jazz and other genres. It is perhaps worth noting that it is within the world of modern Celtic music that women fiddlers have, for almost the first time, emerged as prominent players.

Bibliography

Alburger, Mary Anne. 1983. *Scottish Fiddlers and Their Music*. London: Victor Gollancz.

Boyden, David D. 1989. 'The Violin.' In *The New Grove Violin Family*, ed. David D. Boyden et al. New York and London: W.W. Norton, 5–35.

Bronner, Simon J. 1987. *Old-Time Music Makers of New York State*. Syracuse, NY: Syracuse University Press.

Cauthen, Joyce H. 1989. *With Fiddle and Well-Rosined Bow: Old-Time Fiddling in Alabama*. Tuscaloosa and London: University of Alabama Press.

Daniel, Wayne W. 1990. *Pickin' on Peachtree: A History of Country Music in Atlanta, Georgia*. Urbana and Chicago: University of Illinois Press.

Emmerson, George S. 1971. *Rantin' Pipe and Tremblin' String: A History of Scottish Dance Music*. Montréal: McGill-Queen's University Press.

Epstein, Dena J. 1977. *Sinful Tunes and Spirituals: Black Folk Music to the Civil War*. Urbana, Chicago and London: University of Illinois Press.

History of Fiddling, Contests, and the National Oldtime Fiddlers' Contest & Festival. 1996–99. http://www.fiddlecontest.com/History.htm

Jabbour, Alan. 1996. 'Fiddle Music.' In *American Folklore: An Encyclopedia*, ed. Jan Harold Brunvand. New York and London: Garland Publishing, 253–56.

Jabbour, Alan. 2000. *American Fiddle Tunes* (Annotated sound recording). Cambridge, MA: Rounder Records.

Johnson, David. 1984. *Scottish Fiddle Music in the 18th Century: A Music Collection and Historical Study*. Edinburgh: John Donald Publishers.

Mishler, Craig. 1993. *The Crooked Stovepipe: Athapaskan Fiddle Music and Square Dancing in Northeast Alaska and Northwest Canada*. Urbana and Chicago: University of Illinois Press.

Moloney, Mick. 1982. 'Irish Ethnic Recordings and the Irish-American Imagination.' In *Ethnic Recordings in America: A Neglected Heritage*. Washington, DC: Library of Congress, 85–101.

Remnant, Mary. 1984. 'Fiddle.' In *The New Grove Dictionary of Musical Instruments*, Vol. 1, ed. Stanley Sadie. London: Macmillan, 733–40.

Southern, Eileen. 1983. *The Music of Black Americans: A History*. 2nd ed. New York and London: W.W. Norton.

Wells, Paul F. 1978. *New England Traditional Fiddling, 1926–1975*. Annotated sound recording. Los Angeles: John Edwards Memorial Foundation.

Wells, Paul F. 1991. 'Fiddling: A Little-Known Avenue of Black-White Musical Interchange.' Paper Read at the Annual Meeting of the Sonneck Society for American Music, Hampton, Virginia. April.

Winans, Robert B. 1984. 'Early Minstrel Show Music, 1843–1852.' In *Musical Theatre in America: Papers and Proceedings of the Conference on the Musical Theatre in America*, ed. Glenn Loney. Contributions in Drama and Theatre Studies, No. 8. Westport and London: Greenwood Press, 71–97.

Wolfe, Charles. 1997. *The Devil's Box: Masters of Southern Fiddling*. Nashville and London: Country Music Foundation Press and Vanderbilt University Press.

Discographical Reference

O'Connor, Mark. 'Fiddle Concerto for Violin and Orchestra.' *The Fiddle Concerto*. Warner Brothers 45846. *1995*: USA.

Discography

American Fiddle Tunes. Rounder Records 18964-1518-2. *2000*: USA.

Baker, Kenny. *Kenny Baker Plays Bill Monroe*. County Records CO-2708-CD. *1994*: USA.

Black Fiddlers 1929–c. 1970. Document Records DOCD-5631. *1999*: Austria.

Carson, Fiddlin' John. *Complete Recorded Works in Chronological Order*, Vols. 1–7. Document Records DOCD-8014/8015/8016/8017/8018/ 8019/8020. *1997*: Austria.

Cormier, Joseph, and Friends. *Old Time Wedding Reels and Other Favorite Scottish Fiddle Tunes*. Rounder Records 7013. *1992*: USA.

Humeniuk, Pawlo. *King of the Ukrainian Fiddlers, New York, 1925–1927*. Arhoolie Folklyric 7025. *1993*: USA.

Milestone at the Garden: Irish Fiddle Masters from the 78 rpm Era. Rounder Records 1123. *1996*: USA.

New England Traditional Fiddling. John Edwards Memorial Foundation JEMF-105. *1978*: USA.

Now That's a Good Tune: Masters of Missouri Traditional Fiddling (2-LP set). Grey Eagle Records 101. *1989*: USA.

Polish Village Music: Historic Polish-American Recordings, Chicago and New York, 1927–1933. Arhoolie Folklyric 7031. *1995*: USA.

Possum Up a Gum Stump: Home, Field and Commercial Recordings of Alabama Fiddlers. Alabama Traditions AT-103-CD. n.d.: USA.

Prince Edward Island Fiddling, Vols. 1–2. Rounder Records 7014/7015. *1997*: USA.

Robertson, Eck. *Old-Time Texas Fiddler, 1922–1929*. County Records 3515. *1999*: USA.

Robichaud Brothers, The. *The Slippery Stick: Traditional Fiddling from New Brunswick*. Rounder Records 7016. *1996*: USA.

String Bands 1926–1929 [African-American]. Document Records DOCD-5167. n.d.: Austria.

Thomasson, Benny. *Say Old Man, Can You Play the Fiddle*. Voyager Records VOY-345-CD. *1999*: USA.

Traditional Fiddle Music of Kentucky, Vol. 1: Up the Ohio and Licking Rivers. Rounder Records 376. *1997*: USA.

Traditional Fiddle Music of Kentucky, Vol. 2: Along the Kentucky River. Rounder Records 377. *1997*: USA.

Traditional Fiddle Music of the Ozarks, Vol. 1: Along the Eastern Crescent. Rounder Records 435. *1999*: USA.

Traditional Fiddle Music of the Ozarks, Vol. 2: On the Springfield Plain. Rounder Records 436. *2000*: USA.

Traditional Fiddle Music of the Ozarks, Vol. 3: Down in the Border Country. Rounder Records 437. *2000*: USA.

Wood That Sings: Indian Fiddle Music of the Americas. Smithsonian/ Folkways SF-40472. *1997*: USA.

PAUL F. WELLS

Guitarrón

The *guitarrón* is a guitar-like acoustic bass used primarily in the Mexican mariachi ensemble. Its construction is virtually identical to that of the Mexican *vihuela*, except that the *guitarrón* is much larger, has six wound strings and is fretless. The higher-pitched three strings are made of nylon, the lower three of metal. Tuning, listed from sixth to first string, is A^2, D^1, G^1, C, E, A^1 (in a playing position, the first would be closest to the floor, the sixth closest to the ceiling). The intervallic relationship between the strings is the same as that of the guitar, except that the first string is displaced an octave lower than would be expected. The vibrating length of the strings – about 26" (66 cm) – is unusually short for the low pitches these produce. String elevation is normally quite high off the fingerboard.

Since at least the nineteenth century, the *guitarrón* has been associated with the mariachi tradition of the Cocula region of western Mexican, in what is now the state of Jalisco. At that time, it had five strings and was tuned like the modern instrument, but without the lower A string. This prototype produced insufficient volume for the urban mariachi and, by the 1930s, it had been superseded by the contemporary six-string version that allows the player to pluck two strings at a time and thus render the bass line in parallel octaves. This technique creates a full, well-defined sound with surprising volume relative to the size of the instrument. Dexterity is the price paid for this sonority, however, and rapid, complex passages are difficult to play on the *guitarrón*. Nonetheless, its tone, volume, versatility and portability make the *guitarrón* the ideal bass instrument for the mariachi, and it is a central component of the traditional mariachi sound.

'*Guitarrón*' literally means 'large guitar' in Spanish. Other lesser-known types of low-pitched guitars of the same name, but unrelated to the instrument described above, exist in other Latin American musical cultures, most notably those of Argentina and Chile.

Bibliography

de Santiago González, Natividad. 1982. *Método Práctico de Guitarrón* [Practical Method for the *Guitarrón*]. México, D.F.: Cuicatl Ediciones.

Eremo, Judie, with Pillich, Simeon. 1988. 'Nati Santiago: Linda Ronstadt's Guitarrón Master.' *Bass Player* (November/December): 9, 11.

Kaihatsu, Tim. 1981. 'Guitarrón: The Saga of Mexico's Bass Guitar.' *Frets* 3(2) (February): 32, 34.

Turner, Rick. 1995. 'Bass Tech: The Guitarrón.' *Bass Player* 6(1) (January/February): 72.

Vela, John A. 1990. *The Guitarrón Book*. San Antonio, TX: Southern Music Company.

JONATHAN CLARK

Hammered Dulcimer

The hammered dulcimer is a 'box-zither' of uncertain origin. However, its appearance and development in Europe have been well documented since the late Middle

Ages. As a result of technical improvements and standardizations, it temporarily enjoyed popularity in the eighteenth century, although it had already been part of various regional folk traditions in continental Europe and Britain before that. While the dulcimer itself became relatively uniform, the names for it varied. The term 'dulcimer' came to North America with English colonists who, along with other European groups, had brought the instrument over, probably in the seventeenth century. The name changed to 'hammered dulcimer' in the United States in more recent times to distinguish it from the 'Appalachian dulcimer.'

The dulcimer is trapezoidal and case-like in shape, with a two- to four-feet length at the front end. It has an average of 60 strings, arranged horizontally in groups of two to six. A vertical and central bridge divides each string group to produce different pitches. The instrument is positioned on a flat surface and the strings are struck with two hammers, usually wooden. Playing styles range from simple melody and accompaniment to more elaborate forms, such as arpeggiated chord movements and harmonized solos.

In the nineteenth century, the dulcimer gained its greatest popularity as a string band instrument. According to Groce (1983), some dulcimer recordings were made by Thomas Edison very early in the twentieth century. However, because of changing musical tastes and the competition of other instruments such as the piano, the hammered dulcimer went out of fashion, despite its promotion by John Ford, industrialist and old-time music supporter, and radio appearances by solo performers such as Cora Cline in the 1920s. During the folk revival of the 1960s, players like Howard W. Mitchell and Chet Parker staged a late, but impressive, comeback of the instrument. In subsequent years, it eventually became an instrument of high artistic expression in the hands of players like John McCutcheon and Walt Michael, and it has been used for the many styles of new acoustic music.

Bibliography

Baines, Anthony. 1966. *European and American Musical Instruments*. New York: Viking Press.

Groce, Nancy. 1983. *The Hammered Dulcimer in America*. Washington, DC: Smithsonian Institution Press.

Hickerson, Joe. 1973. *A Bibliography of Hammered and Plucked (Appalachian or Mountain) Dulcimers and Related Instruments*. Washington, DC: Archive of Folk Music, Library of Congress.

Holmes, Michael I., ed. 1977. *The Hammered Dulcimer Compendium*. Silver Spring, MD: MIH Publications.

Kettlewell, David. 1984. 'Dulcimer.' In *The New Grove Dictionary of Musical Instruments*, Vol. 1, ed. Stanley Sadie. New York: Macmillan, 620–32.

Pickow, Peter. 1979. *Hammered Dulcimer*. New York: Oak Publications.

Sachs, Curt. 1940. *The History of Musical Instruments*. New York: W.W. Norton & Co.

Sackett, S.J. 1962. 'The Hammered Dulcimer in Ellis County, Kansas.' *Journal of the International Folk Music Council* 14: 61–64.

Discography

Dalglish, Malcolm. *Hymnody of Earth: A Ceremony of Songs for Choir, Hammer Dulcimer and Percussion*. Amerco 7058-2-C. *1990*: USA.

McCutcheon, John. *Hammer Dulcimer and Old Time Fiddle Music: Fine Times at Our House*. Flying Fish GR 710. *1982*: USA.

McCutcheon, John. *The Wind That Shakes the Barley*. June Appal JA 014. *1977*: USA.

Michael, Walt, and McCreesh, Tom. *Dance, Like a Wave on the Sea*. Front Hall Records FHR 023. *1978*: USA.

Mitchell, Howard W. *The Hammered Dulcimer: How to Make It and Play It*. Folk-Legacy FSI 43. *1972*: USA.

Parker, Chet. *The Hammered Dulcimer*. Folkways Records FA 2381. *1966*: USA.

Trapezoid. *Now and Then*. Flying Fish Records 239. *1980*: USA.

ARMIN HADAMER

Harp

Introduction

The harp is broadly defined as a chordophone whose strings are positioned on a plane perpendicular to its soundboard. Harps are found in a wide variety of forms in Africa, Europe, North and South America, and localized parts of Asia. All harps have a neck, a resonator and strings. Some harps, called 'frame harps,' also have a forepillar extending from the lower end of the resonator to the neck, providing structural support and helping to counter the strain of the tightened strings. Harps that lack this forepillar are termed 'open harps.' European or European-derived harps are all frame harps and most non-European harps are open harps.

The resonator is topped with a membrane soundtable or wood soundboard, as well as a string holder to which the strings are usually affixed. At the other end, strings are normally tied in such a way as to be tunable through special knots or tuning pegs. African harps are normally fitted with mechanisms whose effect is to produce a buzzing sound when a string is plucked. Harps have between one and 90 strings, which may be tuned pentatonically, tetratonically or heptatonically, or chromatically. Chromatic alteration is achieved through a wide variety of mechanisms ranging from manually operated hooks to complex pedal-activated systems. The musician may pluck, strike or strum the strings with fingers or a plectrum while damping unwanted strings. The soundboard may also be struck for percussive effect (Griffiths, Rimmer and de Vale 1984).

The harp's history goes back thousands of years. Harps were used in ancient Egypt, Persia, Mesopotamia and China and are mentioned numerous times in the Old Testament. With the passage of the centuries and the harp's geographical dissemination, it diversified into a multitude of constructions, styles and timbres. Harps exist on all continents and in a variety of cultures. They are played by women or men in solo and ensemble settings in a variety of situations, such as religious rituals and court music, and as accompaniment for the singing of ballads and the reading of epic poetry and historical narratives. Harps are also used for entertainment purposes and appear in many forms of popular music.

Harp players benefit from national and international conferences, where they can meet, perform and engage in competition with other players, and gain exposure to other harp traditions. The highest-profile international event is the non-profit, triennial World Harp Congress.

The Harp in Western Popular Music

The harp may have migrated to Europe from Egypt. In Europe, harpists worked for kings and chieftains in the Middle Ages and, later, as wandering troubadours. From the middle of the fourteenth century until the sixteenth century, the large Gothic harp was used; this was an ancestor of the modern Celtic and pedal-operated concert harps, which appeared in the eighteenth century, and the folk harps of Latin America. Members of the former Gaelic nations brought the harp to the colonies of various European countries, most notably Spain and Britain.

Although the harp remains important as a concert instrument, with the advent of the piano and, later, the electric guitar it decreased in popularity as an instrument for the masses. Nevertheless, in contemporary times the harp is frequently used in a wide variety of types of music as diverse as New Age, easy listening, jazz, pop, world music and Celtic-derived music, as well as in film and television music. Most harpists working in these genres are classically trained. While some remain classical harpists and become involved in folk or popular music as a secondary interest, others explore these genres as a priority. Most use the standard concert harp or Celtic harp, while others have amplified their instruments or otherwise adapted them to respond to personal or contemporary needs. Since these artists often draw from a variety of musical genres, they tend to move between various music charts, including world music, New Age, classical and jazz.

The person who made the harp most visible in North American popular culture in the twentieth century was undoubtedly Arthur 'Harpo' Marx, whose filmed performances and comedic persona between the 1920s and the 1950s earned him international status as an entertainer and US icon. Marx played entirely by ear, in an unorthodox manner based on playing techniques and style of his own invention. Known as the 'silent' Marx Brother, he expressed himself through pantomime, whistles and horn honks and by interjecting harp music into the story line under the most remote of pretenses. Another high-profile harpist in the 1950s was Robert Maxwell, who appeared in numerous radio shows, films and television programs, playing the popular music of the day.

The harp is regularly used in film and television soundtracks, and many harpists incorporate this type of work into their activities. Notwithstanding the work of Harpo Marx, the harp's longstanding stereotypical associations with female beauty and delicacy, dreams, angels, and the magical or ethereal are strongly reinforced in television and film soundtracks. For example, the harp underscores Ann Darrow's innocence and helplessness in *King Kong* (1933), as well as Queen Nefertiti's beauty in *The Ten Commandments* (1956). In *The Golden Voyage of Sinbad* (1973), the harp is one of the instruments used during Sinbad's visions. A contemporary example is the use of the harp to introduce the theme song for the popular television program *The Simpsons*, initiating the viewer's passage from reality into the Simpsons' fictional world.

Because of its soft timbre and stereotypical associations, the harp lends itself well to what the music industry has broadly termed 'New Age music.' This music, often instrumental, is designed to relax the listener through its gentle, serene approach, minimization of musical tension, and frequent associations with spiritual or physical health. It features simple harmonies and arrangements, a lack of percussiveness, duple meter, repetition and crystal-clear recording quality. A great many Western harpists work in this idiom, appearing alone or as part of small ensembles together with acoustic and/or electronic instrumentalists. New Age music borrows heavily from folk and classical repertoire as well as from ethnic sources, and there is much crossover with 'world music,' another broad industry term. Switzerland's Andreas Vollenweider, playing an electro-acoustic harp, was one of the first artists to reap the benefits of the New Age marketing category in the mid-1980s.

New Age music, such as that of Joel Andrews and Georgia Kelly, is often played in such environments as birthing rooms, therapy sessions and massage parlors. Kelly was seminal in defining the genre as it was coming into its own in the 1970s. The harp's healing qualities are now so well recognized in the field of music therapy that the quarterly *Harp Therapy Journal* was launched in 1996 and the annual International Harp Therapy Conference was established in 1999.

Because of its marginal portability and quiet sound, the harp's use as a jazz instrument was limited until recent decades, when it was successfully amplified. Jazz harpists tend to be female, typically starting out as piano players and later moving to the harp. To increase the harp's volume, jazz and popular music harpists either amplify the acoustic harp, a common choice, or use an electric harp with pickups for each string. The biannual Lyon & Healy International Pop and Jazz Harpfest provides jazz and popular music harpists with a prestigious competition and important networking opportunities.

The first jazz harpists emerged during the swing era. Classically trained Casper Reardon, who was the first, and only significant, male jazz harpist, was active in the 1920s, appearing regularly on George Gershwin's radio program and guesting with major swing orchestras such as those of Benny Goodman, Duke Ellington and Paul Whiteman. Adele Girard Marsala played and recorded with the band of clarinetist Joe Marsala, her husband, until the late 1940s.

Specializing in hard bop and jazz-funk, Dorothy Ashby was notable not only because she was successful in adapting the harp to bebop, but also because she led her own trio. Alice (McLeod) Coltrane played the harp with her husband, saxophonist John Coltrane. After his death in 1967, she saw to the posthumous release of some of his sessions, controversially overdubbing some of them with her own harp and string arrangements.

Deborah Henson-Conant has had a major impact on the harp's image with her black leather miniskirts, hair extensions and small blue electric harp strapped to her body. Although she has many contemporaries, in 1989 she became the only jazz harpist signed to a major label (GRP).

The harp is occasionally used as the lead instrument in contemporary Western pop music. Dee Carstensen leads her band with her harp, which she uses like a guitar in her folk/pop compositions, and Monica Ramos features the harp in her dance music and electronica. More commonly, though, the harp is used as a supporting instrument in individual pieces. Among the many examples are the Beatles' 'She's Leaving Home' (1967), Stevie Wonder's 'If It's Magic' (1976) and Björk's 'Like Someone in Love' (1993).

There are a number of jazz harpists of Latin American origin who became harpists before immigrating to Western countries. Generally, these harpists work within the light Latin-jazz idiom and their playing is informed by the folk harp traditions of their home countries. Such artists include Carlos Guedes and Roberto Perera, trained in the Venezuelan *arpa llanera* and the Paraguayan harp, respectively.

The Harp in Celtic Music and in the British Isles

The harp was widely used in what were previously known as the Celtic nations (Ireland, Scotland, Wales, Brittany, Cornwall, Isle of Man) for over a thousand years. It continues to act as an important cultural emblem in the area, strongly associated in the popular imagination with Celtic culture and with magic, legend and fantasy. Irish coins, for example, are graced by an image of the fourteenth-century Trinity College wire-strung harp. The same harp inspired the logo for Guinness, the popular Irish brewery.

There are several types of harp in use in the British Isles and in areas populated by people of British origin, such as Canada and the United States. These are the wire-strung Gaelic harp, the Celtic harp, the Welsh triple harp and the concert harp.

The massive Gaelic harp, known as *cláirseach* in Ireland, *clàrsach* in the Scottish highlands, *telyn* in Wales and Cornwall, and *telenn* in Brittany, was used from around 1100. The Gaelic harp is characterized by its metal strings. These strings, plucked with the fingernails and damped with the fingerpads, lend the instrument a loud, bell-like timbre with a prolonged sustain rich in harmonics. Gaelic harpists were employed by royalty and clan chiefs until the subjugation of the Gaelic people by England and France in the fourteenth and fifteenth centuries, after which they became wandering minstrels catering to the gentry. Although the Gaelic wire-strung harp had disappeared completely by the early nineteenth century, it was revived in the late twentieth century based on the historical research of harpists such as Ann Heymann (United States), Alison Kinnaird (Scotland) and Keith Sanger (Scotland).

In the early nineteenth century, a large gut-strung pedal harp based on a smaller parent from continental Europe appeared in the British Isles. It was adopted by the Irish, Scottish and English aristocracy for use in chamber music and orchestras, and was fitted with a pedal mechanism to enable the use of chromaticisms. It continues to serve as a concert harp.

Smaller versions of the concert harp, featuring a lever system instead of pedals, were produced in Ireland starting around 1820. Although this new lever harp was substantially different from the ancient Gaelic harp in construction, playing techniques and repertoire, it became the main focus of attention during a nineteenth-century renewal of interest in Gaelic culture and language. Nevertheless, by the first half of the twentieth century, it had declined, surviving primarily in *ceilidh* bands (Irish or Scottish dance bands) until its revival starting in the 1950s. It is now known as the folk or Celtic harp (also 'neo-Celtic,' 'neo-Irish') and is considered a traditional Irish and Scottish instrument.

The Welsh triple harp is regarded as the national instrument of Wales. This harp, used for both folk and concert purposes, has two diatonic rows of strings tuned in unison and a third row in between allowing for chromaticisms. The triple harp originated in the seventeenth century and was widely played in Europe until the mid-nineteenth century, when it was supplanted everywhere – with the exception of Wales – by the concert harp. Through meticulous research and numerous recordings and tours, contemporary triple harpist Robin Huw Bowen has been instrumental in helping to maintain the triple harp as a living tradition and in introducing it to an international audience.

In the 1950s, a renewal of interest in traditional Gaelic music took root and, after reaching a peak in the early 1970s, has continued. This movement includes the revival of both the Gaelic harp and the Celtic harp, the latter being the more widespread of the two. Both are frequently used in contemporary popular music.

In Ireland, Seán Ó Riada set the Gaelic revival in motion when he formed Ceoltóirí Cualann in 1961. Ceoltóirí Cualann's repertoire included a considerable amount of music originally meant to be played on the harp, but instead executed on the harpsichord to simulate the wire-strung Gaelic harp. Ceoltóirí Cualann mutated into the highly influential group known as the Chieftains, who were joined by harpist Derek Bell in 1973. Clannad, another group featuring the harp, was formed in the early 1970s.

By the mid-1970s, the Gaelic renaissance was well under way and had caught the attention of numerous harpists. The harp revival blossomed in Brittany under the impetus of multi-instrumentalist Alan Stivell. Stivell almost single-handedly brought traditional Breton and other Gaelic music to the attention of French and international audiences and, indeed, of his own Breton compatriots, hundreds of whom took up the harp after his example. Stivell used wire- and nylon-strung harps and other Gaelic instruments alongside the electric guitar, drums and bass in the genres of folk-rock, progressive rock, New Age and even techno, drawing frequently from traditional Gaelic repertoire.

Interest in the Celtic harp was not limited to Europe. The instrument was also enthusiastically adopted in Canada and the United States, particularly in the Maritimes and in New England, respectively, where large numbers of Scottish and Irish descendants have lived for over 200 years and maintain a vibrant musical tradition.

Canadian singer and harpist Loreena McKennitt, whose modern arrangements of traditional melodies have enjoyed international crossover chart success, is probably the most commercially successful Celtic harpist in North America. The Gaelic harp has also received attention in North America, with both the Maritimes and New England attracting harpists from elsewhere wishing to explore Gaelic roots music.

The Celtic and Gaelic harp movement continues to be fed by an infrastructure of associations, festivals, competitions, conferences and journals. For example, the Hent Telenn Breizh association was founded in 1995 to promote the development of the wire-strung Gaelic harp in Brittany. The Gaelic Mods, cultural festivals organized annually in the British Isles and in Canada, provide harpists with important opportunities to develop their craft. Two important sources of material and information for folk harpists are *Sounding Strings* magazine, published in Scotland, and the *Folk Harp Journal*, published in the United States.

Because Gaelic music is a major source of inspiration for both New Age and world music, many Celtic harpists are involved in these genres. For example, the Gaelic-inspired, harp-accompanied mood music of Irish singer Enya catapulted her to the top of the New Age charts. The wire-strung harp played by Brittany's Myrdhin may be heard in the music of Afro-Celt Sound System which, in the late 1990s, dominated world and dance music charts with its blending of Celtic and West African sounds with contemporary electronica and jungle rhythms. Spain's Milladoiro, combining traditional Gaelic and Galician music, also has a permanent harp player.

The Harp in Other European Countries

A folk harp tradition exists in the southwest German region of Bavaria and the adjoining Tyrol region straddling Austria and Italy. The harp is played as a solo instrument or with other instruments, such as the accordion, recorder or zither, to interpret genres such as polka, ländler and yodel. On the one hand, there has been a renewed interest in traditional music such as that played by the Bavarian *stubenmusik* ensembles, composed entirely of strings (harp, zither, guitar, hammered dulcimer), of which hundreds are in operation, many with established recording careers, such as Munich's Fraunhofer Saitenmusik. On the other hand, there are those who inject the traditional music with other influences. BavaRio, for example, which includes the harp, combines the music of descendants of early twentieth-century Bavarian immigrants to Brazil with contemporary samba rhythms.

The metal-strung Norwegian harp has also been the subject of a modest revival led by singer and harpist Tone Hulbækmo.

A remnant folk harp tradition exists among German-speaking villages in the Lake Balaton region of northwest Hungary, but this has not transferred into popular music.

The Harp in Latin America

Latin American harps are descendants of the harp used in Spain in the sixteenth century, now lost, itself derived from a harp brought by the Arabs during their 700-year occupation of Spain. Before the arrival of Europeans, there were no chordophones present in the Americas, with the possible exception of the musical bow in a few isolated areas. The harp and other chordophones such as the guitar and the violin were brought to the Americas by Spanish conquistadors and settlers establishing their territories in Central and South America and the Caribbean between the sixteenth and the eighteenth century and, in particular, by members of religious orders who came to establish schools to Christianize the indigenous peoples and educate them in the European way. These missionaries used music as an essential tool in their Christianizing work and, if the harp survives in many parts of Latin America, albeit as a folk instrument, it is largely a testament to their legacy.

Over the centuries, racial and cultural mixing and integration occurred between people of Spanish, African and indigenous descent. As this mixing took place, distinct but related harp traditions developed in various parts of Latin America based on Spanish repertoire, style and performance contexts fused, to varying degrees, with local characteristics. Major Latin American harp traditions continue to be found in Mexico, Venezuela/Colombia, Paraguay and the Andes region of Peru/Ecuador, with secondary traditions in Chile and Argentina. Contexts in which the harp is used include liturgy, evangelism, entertainment, processions, weddings and wakes (Schechter 1992, 87). Latin American playing styles and techniques, which are orally transmitted, tend to be vibrant and dynamic. The harp is played almost exclusively by men.

Latin American harps, lighter than their Spanish parent and tuned diatonically, tend to consist of a resonator with a ribbed back, a flat soundboard, a straight forepillar in low-headed form and a single rank of strings without pedals (Griffiths, Rimmer and de Vale 1984). Nylon strings are generally employed, although metallic strings are used in some cases. Halftones are produced in various ways, such as by applying the thumb or a small object to the string, or through tuning the harp before performance according to the requirements of the piece.

Mexico

There are two general types of harp in Mexico, that of the tropical eastern state of Veracruz and that of western Mexico, the latter shared by the mariachi ensemble, and the *arpa grande* tradition of the *tierra caliente* (hot lands) region of the state of Michoacán. Folk harp traditions also exist among certain indigenous groups and rural populations located in various parts of the country.

In Veracruz, where a large proportion of the people are of African descent, the harp known as *arpa jarocha* or *arpa veracruzana* thrives as a component of the *conjunto jarocho*, blending Spanish musical instruments and forms with African-derived rhythms and meter. Mainly through arpeggiated melodies, the 5′ (1.5 m) *arpa jarocha* leads an ensemble that also includes the eight-string *jarana* guitar and the four-string *requinto* melody guitar. In the *arpa jarocha*, the top of the soundbox arches slightly outward, stretched by the tension of the strings, making it, technically, a zither.

The popularity of the *jarocho* tradition in the latter half of the twentieth century was due, in large part, to the success of certain individuals and groups in the popular media in the 1940s and 1950s. The recordings and film appearances of Andrés Huesca, seen in his unusual standing position, set a new precedent for the Veracruz harp. His recordings were highly influential in establishing a more standardized style of harp playing and in securing the instrument's place within Mexican popular music. With Huesca, Lino Chávez and his Conjunto Medellín were also major promoters of *jarocho* music in the twentieth century through their numerous recordings of longstanding traditional and original *sones*, the principal musical form of the Veracruz region. The instrumentation, style and *son* renditions of those recordings set the standard for most professional *jarocho* musicians, including harpists, for decades to come.

In the *tierra caliente* area of the western state of Michoacán, the regional musical ensemble known as the *conjunto de arpa grande* (large harp ensemble) experienced a revival during the 1990s. The group's instrumentation typically consists of *arpa grande*, two violins playing in parallel thirds, and one or both of two regional guitars, the five-string *vihuela* and the *jarana* or *guitarra de golpe* (struck guitar). The *arpa grande* differs from the *arpa jarocha* in that it has three or four sound holes located on the top of the soundbox, which is slightly wider; the string tension is lower, producing a shorter note duration; the melodic style is characterized mainly by homophonic, chorded melodies; and the region's fast-tempo *sones* are distinct and may include a loud rhythmic accompaniment beaten on the harp's soundbox.

Mariachi ensembles perform Mexico's most popular folk-rooted music. Historically, the harp played a leading role in mariachi. Now, it is only included by a few of the larger, most prosperous groups, such as Mariachi Vargas de Tecalitlán, for its elegant appearance, its identification with tradition, and its ability to provide occasional flourishes and melodic foregrounding.

Venezuela

In Venezuela, the harp is second only to the *cuatro* (a four-string lute) as a musical symbol of national pride. The harp is prominent in two folkloric musical traditions in Venezuela, that of the Venezuelan central *llanos* ('plains'), spilling over into Colombia, and that of the regions of Aragua and Miranda surrounding Caracas, the capital of Venezuela, near the Caribbean Sea. In the plains area, the harp is most commonly known as *arpa llanera* or *arpa criolla*. In the coastal area, it is usually known as *arpa aragüeña*, although sometimes as *arpa mirandina* or *arpa tuyera*, appellations deriving from local place names. The harp itself, with 33 or 34 strings, is essentially the same instrument in both areas, but with minor regional variations: in the plains area, the harp has a slightly narrower soundboard; and in the coastal region, the nylon or gut strings in the upper register have been substituted with metallic ones, resulting in a bright, bell-like tone. The difference between the *arpa llanera* and the *arpa aragüeña* lies mainly in performance style.

Llanera music, also known as *música criolla* ('Creole music'), has rural origins in the traditional ranching culture of the plains region and dominates the area's musical life. *Llanera* music includes both music for listening (*coplas*, *romances* and *tonadas*) and music for dancing (*joropo*). The *arpa llanera*, which had spread through the plains by the end of the nineteenth century, is the lead instrument in the standard *llanera* ensemble, appearing alongside the *cuatro*, maracas (container shakers) and sometimes voice. An electric or acoustic bass is generally employed to enhance the bass traditionally provided by the lower strings of the harp. The music associated with the *arpa llanera* is characterized by sesquialteral meter (the superimposition of triple and duple time), melodic counterpoint, percussive articulation and delivery, brisk speeds, flamboyant execution, and melodies with Andalusian roots, a legacy of the high proportion of descendants of colonists from that part of Spain.

In Venezuela's coastal area, the *arpa aragüeña* is usually accompanied only by a singer who also plays maracas. The *joropo* music of this region is less flamboyant than that in the plains area and features shorter phrases, complex melodic patterns, and more repetition and improvisation. These characteristics attest to the stronger Afro-Caribbean influence in this region.

During the 1980s and 1990s, when the economy faltered due to changes in the oil industry, many rural people migrated to cities and towns. The result was a marked increase in the number of folkloric musical groups in urban areas and in new influences on the folkloric tradition. What was once seen as an inferior cultural form by the urban upper classes has become a source of pride for Venezuelans of all classes and walks of life. Miniature models of harps are even sold in the country's tourist areas.

Many agree that the leading exponent of the *arpa llanera* is Juan Vicente Torrealba, who grew up in the Venezuelan plains. His compositions, many of which are *tonadas* (a genre reflecting the activities of daily life in the rural ranching areas), have achieved such status that symphony orchestras have performed them. Rural-born *arpa llanera* player Ignacio 'Indio' Figueredo is credited as having been one of the first to bring the *joropo* to Caracas, and *joropo* now enjoys immense popularity and frequent radio play. Many other contemporary *arpa llanera* exponents, such as Hugo Blanco, Rafael Ángel Aparicio and Mario Guacarán, have followed in their footsteps.

Llanera music has inspired the development of a harp-based form of urban popular music in Venezuela, which enjoys great popularity and a status similar to that of country music in North America. This music, while sentimentally and stylistically rooted in the rural folkloric idiom that spawned it, is influenced to varying degrees by Latin- and Anglo-pop. Lyrical subjects, no longer centered around the ranching life style, also include love and relationships, social issues and patriotism. The genre is led by singer Simón Díaz. Singer Reynaldo Armas added an electric bass to the traditional instrumentation and successfully toned down the *joropo*'s flashiness and complexity for the commercial market. In the case of singer Luis Silva, the harp accompanies Anglo-style romantic ballads, although *llanera* influence is still discernible.

An interesting phenomenon – but one with limited success – arose when top Venezuelan salsa group La Dimensión Latina attempted to integrate the *joropo* instrumentation into its salsa sound, the idea being to create a truly Venezuelan form of salsa.

Paraguay

In Paraguay, about 95 percent of the population are of mixed Spanish and indigenous Guaraní descent, a situation that has contributed to Paraguay's relative cultural homogeneity. A strong sense of national pride is exhibited in the country's folkloric music in general (Watkins 1998, 452) and in the harp in particular, to the extent that it has been named Paraguay's official instrument, and references to it appear in elements of popular culture such as sayings and jokes (Schechter 1992, 205). There are a number of annual harp festivals in the capital, Asunción.

In practise, Paraguayan music, including harp music, is primarily of European inspiration. Within the dominant popular idioms, little has survived of the Guaraní heritage besides the use of texts in Guaraní or in the Guaraní-Spanish colloquial hybrid known as *jopará*.

The two most important instruments in Paraguayan folkloric music are the guitar and the *arpa paraguaya* ('Paraguayan harp'), sometimes known as the *arpa india* ('Indian harp'). The current design of the Paraguayan harp, in place since the mid-twentieth century, includes a divided neck with strings running vertically through its middle and holding the instrument together without glue, an exaggerated inverted arch, low string tension, structural strength, light weight, and tight spacing of its 36 nylon strings.

The typical folkloric ensemble is comprised of a harpist (who plays standing), two or three guitarists and sometimes a musician playing a *requinto* (smaller guitar). The musicians may also sing. The harp commonly serves as the lead instrument and the harpist as the ensemble leader. In Asunción, such ensembles, along with dancers, appear in numerous *parrilladas* ('steakhouses') primarily catering to tourists. The harp is equally important as a solo instrument.

The Paraguayan playing style includes a wide variety of special effects and techniques, such as tremolo, muffling, glissandi, and playing the melody in octaves, thirds or sixths, although in general there is a lack of standardization (Watkins 1998, 456). Sesquialteral meter is common in Paraguayan musical styles such as the nostalgic *guaranía* songs and the patriotic *polca* tunes, with harpists playing the bass in triple meter and the melody in duple meter.

Félix Pérez Cardozo (1908–53), Paraguay's most influential composer, was one of the first harpists to popularize the Paraguayan harp outside the country when he took it to Buenos Aires. The Paraguayan harp has achieved greater international recognition than any other Latin American harp, in part because of numerous tours abroad, beginning in the 1970s, by Paraguayan folkloric groups such as Los Paraguayos, Luís Bordón and Enrique Samaniego. Non-Paraguayan harpists all over South America and in North America, Europe and Japan, such as Cuban folkloric and concert harpist Alfredo Rolando Ortiz, have enthusiastically adopted the Paraguayan harp and folkloric repertoire. In fact, Europeans have recorded the Paraguayan harp more often than the Paraguayans have done (Schechter 1992, 204). A Paraguayan melody, the anonymous *polca* 'Pájaro Campana' (Bell Bird), has become an international solo harp classic

and has been recorded innumerable times by harpists worldwide.

The Andes

The harp is used in many parts of the indigenous and mestizo Andes in a variety of settings, such as festivals and religious rituals, and in the home. Harp music in the Andes has deeper indigenous roots than any other harp tradition in South America and has largely resisted replacement by the guitar. Although tuning is diatonic, as it is with other Latin American harps, the Andean music that is played on it is quite often pentatonic, which can be plainly heard in much of the harp music. The harp may provide bass, harmonic support or melody.

In Ecuador, the two centers of harp usage are the provinces of Imbabura and Tungurahua (Schechter 1992, 65). In Imbabura, the harp, characterized by a huge soundbox and short forepillar, is played solo with *golpeador* (a second person beating the soundbox in rhythm) by the indigenous Quichua people at festive occasions such as weddings and at children's wakes. Repertoire is dominated by the duple-meter *sanjuán* genre. The larger harps used in Tungurahua, some of which resemble the Paraguayan harp in structure, are generally used by mestizos for entertainment purposes. Harpists interpret various national Ecuadorean folk forms such as the *pasillo*, the *yaraví* and the *albazo*, often in conjunction with a wind instrument like the *rondador* pan pipes (Schechter 1992, 85–86). Harps are included in numerous Ecuadorean groups, such as Inkhay, promoting a pan-Andean repertoire which enjoys great popularity in Ecuador and has been successfully exported to northern countries.

The harp is found in most of Peru's states (Schechter 1992, 220). Peruvian harps are often made of plywood and usually have 30 to 35 metal, nylon or gut strings and a large soundbox to maximize the instrument's projection. Olsen (1986–87) identifies five main types of musical and physical manifestations of the harp in Peru, the main one being the long, triangular-shaped *arpa indígena* ('indigenous harp').

In Peru, the harp is often used during processions, at which times it is carried on the shoulder via a system of straps, and played upside down (Schechter 1992, 44). Traditional ensembles often feature the harp and violin together. In the large orchestras typical of the Cuzco and Huancayo regions, two harps may appear together, supplying the bass for a variety of wind, brass, stringed, and Western and Latin percussion instruments, as well as for singers.

The harp is used in interpretations of typical Peruvian genres, most notably the *huayno*, a duple-meter pair dance of probable pre-Incan origin enjoying continued widespread popularity in the Peruvian Andes and among Andean migrants in the coastal capital city of Lima (Schechter 1992, 215). Played in homes at birthdays, baptisms and weddings and in the streets during festivals, *huaynos* have also been commercially recorded by numerous indigenous Andean artists. Harpists interpret the *huayno* as solo performers or as part of an ensemble (for example, with a violin), sometimes with a singer as accompaniment. Better-known exponents include Raúl García Zarate, Florencio Coronado, Luciano Quispe and Antonio Sulca. Several examples can be found on *From the Mountains to the Sea: Music of Peru – The 1960s*, a 1996 compilation of music from the now-defunct Peruvian record label Discos Smith.

In the Andes, it is not uncommon for visually impaired men, unable to engage in agricultural pursuits, to become street musicians, with the solo harp being a common instrument of choice. Many have made recordings that are available in Western countries.

In Chile, the harp, traditionally played by women, accompanies the *cueca* national dance, either alone or in an ensemble with a guitar and perhaps a singer, a piano, a *pandero* (frame drum), an accordion and handclapping. Rhythmic accompaniment may be provided by striking the harp's soundboard.

The Harp in Africa

In Africa, harps are found in a belt stretching from Uganda to Mauritania. Unlike in Latin America, where all the harps are descendants of a European ancestor, in Africa harps are indigenous. All African harps, while occurring in many forms, are open harps; that is to say, they have a resonator, a neck and a string holder, but no forepillar. The resonator (through which the neck passes, protruding at the lower end) is made of a halved calabash (gourd) in the savanna region of West Africa and of wood in the forest regions farther south; it is covered with animal skin and has a bridge. Many African harps also have a buzzing mechanism built into them that is activated by playing the strings or striking the resonator. With the exception of Mauritania's *ardin*, which is a true harp, the West African calabash harps are actually harp-lutes because of their two rows of strings, which are parallel to each other but at right angles with the soundboard.

While most harps in Africa are used primarily in a traditional fashion, several have migrated into the realms of contemporary African popular music or world music. The most important of these is the *kora*, a 21-string harp-lute with a large gourd resonator. The *kora* is the preferred instrument of the Mande (or Manding) people of West Africa, in particular the Mandinka of Senegal and Gambia. Mande musicians, called *jelis* in Mali and *griots* in other parts of West Africa, are members of an ancient hereditary class who play the role of historians, praise-singers, entertainers and mediators. The *jelis* work under the auspices of patrons, previously noble families and, in modern times, politicians and businesspeople. In the traditional ensemble, the *kora* appears with the *balafon* (a wooden xylophone) and the *ngoni* (an oblong three-to five-string wooden lute), accompanied by a singer. The *kora* may also appear with the *bolon*, a related three-to four-string harp-lute used to provide bass.

The *kora* came to the attention of a wide international audience with Guinean *kora* player Mory Kanté's 1988 dance hit, 'Yéké Yéké,' which reached the Top 10 in Europe. The emigration of *kora* players to North America and Europe, in particular Paris, helped to promote an awareness of the *kora* that has resulted in numerous *kora* masters touring Europe, North America and Japan and collaborating successfully with Western musicians. *Kora* players who have participated in such collaborations include Toumani Diabaté, who worked with Spanish flamenco group Ketama and who also pioneered the *kora* as a solo instrument; Ballaké Sissoko, who collaborated with North American blues musician Taj Mahal; and Foday Musa Suso, who worked with Philip Glass, Bill Laswell and Pharoah Sanders. The *kora* has also been adopted by Western musicians, such as David Gilden (United States) with his group Cora Connection. Ravi (United Kingdom) uses an electric *kora*.

Related to the *kora* is the long-necked, six-string harp-lute known as the *kamele n'goni*. The *kamele n'goni* is the fundamental instrument of contemporary *wassoulou* music, named after the region in Mali (south of Bamako) from which it comes. *Wassoulou* is an urban phenomenon created by Wassoulou migrants to Bamako in the mid-1970s as a response to the strict conventions of the *griot* tradition and Mande society. It surged in popularity in the late 1980s. A powerful dance music appreciated by the young, *wassoulou* is often used as a vehicle for social criticism.

The pentatonically tuned *kamele n'goni*, or 'youth's harp,' was created by Wassoulou youth as an adaptation of the larger *donso n'goni*, used traditionally as a hunter's harp and for festivals. As a result, melodies of traditional hunters' songs have filtered into modern *wassoulou*. The *kamele n'goni* provides low staccato lines, drives the rhythm and defines the harmony. Other instruments appearing in a typical *wassoulou* ensemble include the *djembé* drum, the electric guitar, and sometimes the *donso n'goni* and the *bolon*.

Oumou Sangaré is the singer who brought *wassoulou* to Western audiences in the 1990s. She features traditional instruments in her arrangements, using the *kamele n'goni* as the lead instrument and the electric guitar and bass as part of the backdrop. Another *kamele n'goni* player and singer from the Wassoulou region is Issa Bagayogo, who overlays his *kamele n'goni* work with *balafon*, horns and guitar and with loops and electronic beats in a genre known locally as 'Afro-electro.'

The *ardin*, a large gourd harp in use in the Western Saharan country of Mauritania, is closely related to the West African harp-lutes. This 10- to 16-string harp is played by female members of the *iggawin* musicians' class, whose role is similar to that of the West African *griots*. Besides the *ardin*, the traditional *iggawin* ensemble also includes the four-string *tidinit* lute (played by men), the *tbal* kettledrums, the *daghumma* gourd shaker and sometimes a tambourine. The *ardin* player also sings. In modern times, the *ardin* and the *tidinit* seem to be increasingly supplemented or replaced by the electric guitar.

Singer and *ardin* player Dimi Mint Abba, a traditionalist, was embraced by the Muslim world after she won the Umm Kulthūm song contest in Tunis in 1977. She went on to become the first Mauritanian to tour the English-speaking world, and recorded an album for international release that has been received with interest by Western audiences. Another contemporary Mauritanian female singer and *ardin* player is Tahra, who merges her Moorish singing and playing style with synthesized electronic music, drawing on contemporary styles of African pop and Western styles such as rap.

Occasionally, other African harps appear in world music. An example is the *ngombi*, a small arched harp used by some Pygmy groups in central Africa, as well as by Martin Cradick in his Celtic-African fusion group Baka Beyond.

The Harp in Asia

While harps were once found in many regions of Asia, for the most part they became obsolete many centuries ago, giving way to zithers, which continue to be used throughout the continent. The harps that did survive in Asia include the *saung-gauk* in Myanmar, the *kafir* or *waji* in Nuristan, the *changi* in the Svaneti region of Georgia and the *bin-baja* of the Pardhan people in India. In a few cases, ancient harps have been revived for use in traditional ensembles, generally interpreting ancient court music. These include the *konghou* in China and the *kugo* in Japan. The Western concert harp is used in Asian classical orchestras. With the exception of the *saung-gauk*, Asian harps are seldom, if ever, used in popular music.

The oval-shaped Myanma (Burmese) arched harp, known as the *saung-gauk*, is the only Asian harp with a classical repertoire that has been used continuously to this day. The *saung-gauk* features a hollow boat-shaped wood body covered with a piece of deer hide. The long arch curves over to rest on the player's left shoulder. The 16 nylon strings, traditionally made of spun silk, are attached to the instrument's neck by a cotton cord with hanging tassels. The *saung-gauk* is placed on a stand or held in the lap.

The harp was introduced in Myanmar by Buddhist missionaries at least 2,000 years ago, and for centuries was the most important instrument in Myanma royal court music. The last court harpist died in 1933, but the music continues to be widely played as Myanma chamber music. The current *saung-gauk* playing style, featuring rapid runs, complex ornamentation and showmanship, spread to other instruments and is now dominant in all Myanma traditional music. The piano version of *saung-gauk* arose in Myanmar shortly before World War II.

The *saung-gauk* continues to enjoy great popularity and prestige in Myanmar, as demonstrated in private dwellings where it is used symbolically to adorn the 'top room.' Traditionally, it is paired with the *patala* bamboo xylophone, and these two instruments are now sometimes joined by the Hawaiian-style slide guitar and the Western piano. The *saung-gauk* is a mainstay in modern popular and film musics in Myanmar, which are founded on the traditional Myanma playing style and structure and infused with Western characteristics.

Bibliography

Afropop Worldwide: Celebrating the Musical Cultures of Africa and the African Diaspora. 2002. http://www.afropop.org

Bens, Jax, and Bens, Toby. 2001. *Remote Harpists & Tropical Harps.* http://members.ozemail.com.au/~jaxbens/index.html/

Cardozo Ocampo, Mauricio. 1988. 'El arpa paraguaya: instrumento trasculturado' [The Paraguayan Harp: A Transcultural Instrument]. In *Mundo Folklórico Paraguayo* [The World of Paraguayan Folklore]. Asunción: Editorial Cuadernos Republicanos. http://www.musicaparaguaya.org.py/arpa.html

Charry, Eric. 2002. 'West African Harps.' In *West African Music.* http://echarry.web.wesleyan.edu/Afmus.html

Clairseoiri na hEireann (The Harp Foundation). 2001. http://www.mayo-ireland.ie/harp/BHO/Fndation.htm

Clarsach.net: A Gateway to the Gaelic Harp of Ireland and Scotland. 2001. http://www.clarsach.net/

Duran, Lucy. 1999. 'Mali/Guinea.' In *World Music – The Rough Guide. Vol. 1: Africa, Europe and the Middle East*, ed. Simon Broughton, Mark Ellingham and Richard Trillo. London: Rough Guides Ltd., 553–54.

Ferrier, Claude. 2002. *Arpa Peruana: Generalidades* [The Peruvian Harp: Generalities]. http://www.musicaperuana.com/arpa/general.htm

Garfias, Robert. 1995. *Tonal Structure in Burmese Music as Exemplified in the Piano Music of U Ko Ko*. http://aris.ss.uci.edu/anthro/courses/rgarfias/burma/burma1.html

Garfias, Robert. 1997. *Recordings: Recordando a Venezuela, Rafael Angel Aparicio y los Hermanos Aparicios: Introduction* [Recordings: Recorded in Venezuela, Rafael Angel Aparicio and Los Hermanos Aparicios: Introduction]. http://www.nwfolklife.org/P_REC/RAA_Intro.html

González Aborno, Carlos Raúl. 1987. 'The Paraguayan Harp.' *Folk Harp Journal* 59: 27.

Griffiths, Ann, Rimmer, Joan, and de Vale, Sue Carole. 1984. 'Harp.' In *The New Grove Dictionary of Musical Instruments*, ed. Stanley Sadie. London: Macmillan, 131–61.

Kinnaird, Alison, and Sanger, Keith. 1992. *Tree of Strings (Crann nan teud): A History of the Harp in Scotland*. Temple: Kinmor Music.

Muddyman, David, and Trillo, Richard. 1999. 'Mauritania and Western Sahara.' In *World Music – The Rough Guide. Vol. 1: Africa, Europe and the Middle East*, ed. Simon Broughton, Mark Ellingham and Richard Trillo. London: Rough Guides Ltd., 563–66.

Olsen, Dale A. 1986–87. 'The Peruvian Folk Harp Tradition: Determinants of Style.' *Folk Harp Journal* 53–59.

O'Sullivan, Donal. 1958. *Carolan: The Life, Times, and Music of an Irish Harper*. London: Routledge & Kegan Paul.

Romero, Raúl R. 1998. 'Peru.' In *The Garland Encyclopedia of World Music. Vol. 2: South America, Mexico, Central America, and the Caribbean*, ed. Dale A. Olsen and Daniel E. Sheehy. New York: Garland Publishing, 466–90.

Ruadh of the Isles, Robert. 2001. *Gaelic Harps & Harpers in Ireland & Scotland*. http://www.tullochgorm.com/harps.html

Schechter, John M. 1992. *The Indispensable Harp: Historical Development, Modern Roles, Configurations, and Performance Practices in Ecuador and Latin America*. Kent, OH: Kent State University Press.

Sheehy, Daniel. 1999. 'Popular Mexican Musical Traditions: The Mariachi of West Mexico and the Conjunto Jarocho of Veracruz.' In *Music in Latin American Culture: Regional Traditions*, ed. John M. Schechter. New York: Schirmer Books, 34–79.

Taylor, Bill. 2000. *Traditional and Historical Scottish Harps*. http://www.clarsach.net/Bill_Taylor/traditional.htm

Watkins, Timothy D. 1998. 'Paraguay.' In *The Garland Encyclopedia of World Music. Vol. 2: South America, Mexico, Central America, and the Caribbean*, ed. Dale A. Olsen and Daniel E. Sheehy. New York: Garland Publishing, 452–65.

Weiser, Glenn. 1996. 'Turlough O'Carolan.' *Acoustic Musician*. http://www.celticguitarmusic.com/carolan.htm

Windling, Terri. 1997. 'The Enchanted Harp.' *Realms of Fantasy*. http://www.endicott-studio.com/forharp.html

Yeats, Gráinne. 2002. 'The Rediscovery of Carolan.' *Harp Spectrum: Exploring the World of the Harp*. http://www.harpspectrum.org/folk/yeats_long.shtml

Discographical References

Beatles, The. 'She's Leaving Home.' *Sergeant Pepper's Lonely Hearts Club Band*. Parlophone PMC 7027. *1967*: UK.

Björk. 'Like Someone in Love.' *Debut*. Elektra 61468. *1993*: USA.

From the Mountains to the Sea: Music of Peru – The 1960s. Arhoolie Productions 400. *1996*: USA.

Kanté, Mory. 'Yéké Yéké.' London LON 171. *1988*: UK.

King Kong (Original soundtrack). Southern Cross 5006. *1993*: USA.

Los Fabulosos. 'Pájaro Campana.' *Tres Paraguayos*. Kubaney 146. *1990*: Cuba.

The Golden Voyage of Sinbad (Original soundtrack). Prometheus PCD 148. *1998*: USA.

'The Simpsons Main Title Theme.' *Songs in the Key of Springfield*. Rhino 72723. *1997*: USA.

The Ten Commandments (Original soundtrack). MCA MCAD-42320. *1989*: USA.

Wonder, Stevie. 'If It's Magic.' *Songs in the Key of Life*. Motown 157357. *1976*: USA.

Discography

Abba, Dimi Mint, and Eide, Khalifa Ould. *Moorish Music from Mauritania*. World Circuit WCD 019. *1990*: UK.

Afro-Celt Sound System. *Sound Magic, Vol. 1*. Real World 62359. *1996*: UK.

Andrews, Joel. *Seven Wheels of Light*. The Relaxation Company 3187. *1996*: USA.

Aparicio, Rafael Ángel. *Recordando a Venezuela*. Northwest Folklife 102. *2000*: USA.

Armas, Reynaldo. *Carta de sus Éxitos*. Vedisco 5193. *1997*: Venezuela.

Ashby, Dorothy. *In a Minor Groove*. Prestige PCD-24120-2. *1958*: USA.

Bagayogo, Issa. *Timbuktu*. Six Degrees 1062. *2002*: USA.

Baka Beyond. 'Ndaweh's Dream.' *The Meeting Pool*. Hannibal 1388. *1995*: UK.

Ball, Patrick. *Finnegans Wake*. Celestial Harmonies 14113. *1997*: USA.

Barra MacNeils, The. *The Question*. Mercury/Polydor/PolyGram 314 529 077-2. *1995*: USA.

BavaRio. *Hoi*. Meilton 2097. *1995*: Germany.

Blanco, Hugo. *Festival Tropical.* Kubaney 410. *1995*: Cuba.

Blind Street Musicians of Cusco, The. *Peruvian Harp & Mandolin.* Music of the World 105. *1995*: USA.

Bowen, Robin Huw. *Telyn Berseiniol Fy Ngwlad (The Sweet Harp of My Land).* Flying Fish FF-70610. *1991*: USA.

Burmese Folk and Traditional Music. Folkways Records FE4436. 1953: USA.

Carstensen, Dee. *Regarding the Soul.* New York City 9001. *1995*: USA.

Ceoltóirí Cualann. *Ó Riada sa Gaiety.* Gael Linn CEF 027. *1970*: UK.

Chieftains, The. *The Chieftains 5.* Shanachie 79025. *1975*: USA.

Chieftains, The. *The Wide World Over: A 40-Year Celebration.* RCA 63917. *2002*: USA.

Clannad. *Clannad.* Philips 6392013. *1973*: UK.

Coltrane, John. *Infinity.* Impulse! 9225. *1965*: USA.

Conjunto Alma Jarocha. *Sones Jarochos. Music of Mexico, Vol. 1: Veracruz.* Arhoolie 354. *1994*: USA.

Conjunto Medellín de Lino Chávez. *Veracruz y Sus Sones.* Orfeon Videovox, S.A. CDN-13619. *1998*: Mexico.

Diabaté, Toumani, and Sissoko, Ballaké. *New Ancient Strings.* Hannibal HNCD 1428. *1999*: UK.

Diabaté, Toumani, Ketama, and Thompson, Danny. *Songhai.* Hannibal HNCD 1323. *1988*: UK.

Díaz, Simón. *Luna de Margarita.* Palacio 66591. n.d.: Venezuela.

Enya. 'Orinoco Flow.' *Watermark.* Atlantic 9242332. *1988*: USA.

Fatala. *Gongoma Times.* Real World RWMCD4. *1993*: UK.

Fraunhofer Saitenmusik. *Excursionen.* Briton Musikverlag 2084. *1993*: Germany.

Gordon Quartet, Bobby, with Marsala, Adele Girard. *Don't Let It End.* Arbors 19112. *1992*: USA.

Guacarán, Mario. *Arpa Llanera.* Playasound 65163. *1996*: France.

Guedes, Carlos. *Churún Merú.* Heads Up 3006. *1990*: USA.

Harpestry. PolyGram 536142. *1997*: UK.

Henson-Conant, Deborah. *Alter Ego.* Golden Cage 96-004. *1996*: USA.

Huayno Music of Peru, Vol. 1: 1949–1989. Arhoolie 320. *1989*: USA.

Hulbækmo, Tone. *Konkylie.* Grappa GRCD 4095. *1995*: Finland.

Inkhay. *Soul of the Andes: String Flutes from Ecuador.* Music of the World 50615. *1998*: USA.

Jali Kunda: Griots of West Africa & Beyond. Ellipsis Arts 3511. *1997*: USA.

Kelly, Georgia. *Seapeace.* Seventh Wave 7021. *1978*: USA.

Los Paraguayos. *Los Paraguayos.* Latin Sounds 62005. *1999*: USA.

Los Pregoneros del Puerto. *Music of Veracruz: The Sones Jarochos of Los Pregoneros del Puerto.* Rounder 5048. *1990*: USA.

Mariachi Vargas de Tecalitlán. *Mexico's Pioneer Mariachis, Vol. 3. Mariachi Vargas de Tecalitlán, First Recordings: 1937–1947.* Arhoolie 7015. 1937–47: USA.

Marx, Harpo. *Harpo in Hi Fi/Harpo at Work.* Collectors' Choice Music 151. *2000*: USA.

Maxwell, Robert. *The Harp in Hi-Fi.* Mercury MG 20138. *1972*: USA.

McKennitt, Loreena. *The Mask and the Mirror.* Warner Brothers 945420-2. *1994*: USA.

Mexico: A Magical Tour – Veracruz & the Jarocho Sones. RCA International 55549. *1998*: USA.

Milladoiro. *Auga de Maio.* Green Linnet 3134. *2000*: USA.

Musa Suso, Foday, et al. *Jali Kunda.* Ellipsis Arts 3510. *1996*: USA.

Ortiz, Alfredo Rolando. *The South American Harp of Alfredo Rolando Ortiz, Vol. 2.* Alfredo Rolando Ortiz 1023. *1992*: Paraguay.

Perera, Roberto. *Harp and Soul.* Heads Up 3036. *1996*: USA.

Ramos, Monica. *Behind That Light.* Climate Records 3005. *2001*: USA.

Ravi. *The African Kora: Journeys of the Sunwalker.* Arc 1502. *1999*: USA.

Reardon, Casper. *Jack Teagarden and His Orchestra, 1934–1939.* Classics 729. 1934: USA.

Sangaré, Oumou. *Moussolou.* World Circuit WCD 021. *1989*: UK.

Sìleas. *Harpbreakers.* Lap Wing 127. *1990*: UK.

Silva, Luis. *20 Grandes Éxitos.* Musart 1424. *1996*: Spain.

Stivell, Alan. *Renaissance of the Celtic Harp.* Rounder 3067. *1987*: USA.

Tahra. *Yamen Yamen.* EMI 790914-2. *1989*: USA.

Torrealba, Juan Vicente. *Música Venezolana de Gala*, Vols. 1 and 2. Vedisco 5084 and 5085. *1995*: Venezuela.

Vollenweider, Andreas. *Caverna Magica.* Columbia MK-37827. *1983*: USA.

Filmography

King Kong, dir. Merian C. Cooper and Ernest B. Schoedsack. 1933. USA. 105 mins. Fantasy. Original music by Max Steiner.

The Golden Voyage of Sinbad, dir. Gordon Hessler. 1973. UK. 105 mins. Adventure. Original music by Miklos Rózsa.

The Ten Commandments, dir. Cecil B. De Mille. 1956. USA. 219 mins. Epic. Original music by Elmer Bernstein.

MONA-LYNN COURTEAU with DANIEL SHEEHY

Hurdy-Gurdy

A hurdy-gurdy (Lat. *organistrum, symphonia*; Fr. *vielle*; It. *lira tedesca*; Sp. *zanfonía*; Ger. *Drehleier*; Hun. *tekerö*; Rus.

relja) is a guitar-, viola- or lute-shaped keyed stringed instrument, played by turning a handle-moved wheel or 'never-ending bow.' The earliest representation of an *organistrum* dates back to ca. 1150 and was found in Spain. The size of this instrument meant that it required two players, one of whom turned the wheel while the other played the melody with both hands. Smaller instruments, called *symphoniae* and requiring only one player, were documented from the twelfth century onward.

The traditional musical sound of medieval Europe, before the establishment of polyphonic music, was characterized by a 'linear' structure. This structure generally consisted of three parts, similar to those of the still-surviving old styles of Eastern European folk music: the melody, which was played by one or more instruments; a continuously rumbling bass sound, which closely accompanied the melody; and perhaps a rhythmic accompaniment. The requisite sound was achieved by the use of various combinations of instruments, such as pipe-drums, bagpipes, stringed instruments, zither and jew's-harp.

The only instrument that in itself combines all the elements required to produce such a sound is the hurdy-gurdy. To produce the melody, the pitch of the notes is changed by the insertion of wooden keys; this differs from the violin, where the player presses the melody string to the soundboard. The sound of the freely vibrating string, touched by small wooden keys from the side, is reminiscent of that produced by brass instruments.

The strings providing the bourdon sound or bass accompaniment have no keys attached to them, so the pitch of the notes cannot be changed; the strings can only be switched on or off.

The buzzing sound of the rhythmic accompaniment is regulated by a small piece of wood pressed down by the *trompette* string. One edge of the wood is supported by the soundboard, while the other is suspended by a small bridge. The rhythmical movement of the handle creates an impulse through the string that causes a brief, intermittent lifting of the wood from the soundboard. The quality of the buzzing sound can be controlled by the peg that regulates the tightness of the string.

During its history, the hurdy-gurdy has traversed the whole social spectrum: after being played in churches, royal courts, noble houses and then middle-class parlors, it gradually fell from favor as new musical trends came into fashion. Moving from west to east, it increasingly became the instrument of peasants, traveling musicians and, later, beggars, who used it for popular and folk music and dances. Toward the end of the twentieth century, its rural use, which previously could have been traced up to Ukraine, could be continuously docu-

mented only in Brittany and Hungary. However, interest in the hurdy-gurdy has begun to increase again as a result of historical music movements and folklore revivals.

The Hurdy-Gurdy in Popular Music

In the twentieth century, the use of the hurdy-gurdy in popular music was a result of the folk music revival of the 1960s, the folk-roots movement in the 1980s and the more recent Celtic–world fusion. Beyond its role in traditional folk music, the hurdy-gurdy was used increasingly in rock, folk-based rock and pop, and jazz within the last 30 years of the twentieth century. Garth Brooks even introduced the hurdy-gurdy to 'new country' music on his CD *Fresh Horses*. Donovan's 'Hurdy Gurdy Man' (1968) might seem to be the most obvious example of the hurdy-gurdy in popular music, but the hurdy-gurdy is not actually featured on the recording.

Typically, bands in North America and Europe that have used the hurdy-gurdy either have been interested in exploring the music of other regions of the world, or have looked to their own roots and experimented with traditional folk music to give it a more modern context.

Musicians such as Pierre Imbert have explored not only French, but also French-Canadian, culture, taking an avant-garde approach to playing an electric hurdy-gurdy, as on *Menage à Quatre*, for example. While their individual styles are unique, Loreena McKennitt (on *The Book of Secrets*), Laurel MacDonald (on *Kiss Closed My Eyes*), and the groups the Tea Party (*The Edges of Twilight*) and Spirit of the West (*Weights and Measures*) have experimented with styles and instruments from various cultures, and have incorporated the hurdy-gurdy into folk-pop and alternative rock contexts. Jimmy Page and Robert Plant of Led Zeppelin included the internationally known hurdy-gurdy player Nigel Eaton on three tracks of *No Quarter*. Eaton then joined Page and Plant on their 1995 world tour, on which he played as his concert solo 'Laridé,' which would become the first track on *Ancient Beatbox*. Jimmy Page also appears briefly in a Led Zeppelin concert film, *The Song Remains the Same* (1976), sitting by a pond and playing the hurdy-gurdy. The sound of the hurdy-gurdy was used by these bands to explore the psychedelic possibilities of the music with a view to producing an 'altered state' in the listener.

Particularly in the United Kingdom, the roots movement saw folk music, and the hurdy-gurdy, being modernized by bands such as the Pogues (on *Waiting for Herb*), the Levellers (on their eponymous CD), Blowzabella (on *Pingha Frenzy*) and Shave the Monkey (on *Mad Arthur*). The foremost hurdy-gurdy player in popular music in North America and Europe was Nigel Eaton, who played and recorded with most of the bands mentioned above.

Toward the end of the twentieth century, the hurdy-gurdy was being used in popular music in other countries as well, including France, Spain (particularly in Asturias and Galicia), Germany, Italy and Sweden. Musicians who used the hurdy-gurdy in popular music at this time were described as iconoclastic, adventurous and open to multicultural influences, yet also rooted in tradition.

In France, the hurdy-gurdy was used in jazz settings by such groups as Aquartet (on their modal jazz CD *Roue Libre*) and the Pascal Lefeuvre Quartet (on *Alicante*), and by hurdy-gurdy players Gilles Chabenat (on *Bleu Nuit*) and Valentin Clastrier (on *Hurdy-Gurdy from the Land of Cathars*). Groups such as Le Gop and Malicorne (on their eponymous CDs) have explored the use of the hurdy-gurdy in folk-rock. Funky jazz and Spanish music met the hurdy-gurdy on La Musgaña's recording *Lubican*. The German group Adaro used the hurdy-gurdy along with wind instruments, electric guitars and drums to play medieval rock on *Words Never Spoken*. Hölderlin Express, a German electric/hip-hop/folk group, featured progressive and nationally recognized hurdy-gurdy player Elke Rogge on *Electric Flies*. In Italy, Lou Dalfin fronted a rock band, singing and playing hurdy-gurdy on *Radio Occitania Libra*. Garmarna (on *God's Musicians/Guds Spelemän*) used the hurdy-gurdy to blend Nordic folk music and rock. In Sweden, Folk och Rackare (on a compilation CD *1976–1985*) and Hedningarna (on *Fire*) incorporated the hurdy-gurdy in their music.

Every year, the hurdy-gurdy can be heard, danced to and celebrated at two major festivals: the St. Chartier music festival in France; and the Over the Water Hurdy-Gurdy Festival in the US state of Washington. Extensive hurdy-gurdy discographies can be found at http://www.hurdygurdy.com and http://chpc06.ch.unito.ib/~ravera/hg/hg-disco.html.

Bibliography

Allmo, Per-Ulf, and Winter, Jan. 1985. *Lirans hemligheter* [Secrets of the Hurdy-Gurdy]. Stockholm: Ordfront.

Bröcker, Marianne. 1977. *Die Drehleier, Ihr Bau und ihre Geschichte* [The Hurdy-Gurdy: Its Construction and Its History]. Rev. ed. Bonn-Bad Godesberg: Verlag für systematische Musikwissenschaft GmbH. (First published Düsseldorf, 1973.)

Broughton, Simon, et al., eds. 1994. *World Music: The Rough Guide*. London: Rough Guides Ltd.

Sárosi, Bálint. 1967. *Die Volksmusikinstrumente Ungarns: Handbuch der europäischen Volksmusikinstrumente Serie I Band I* [Folk Music Instruments of Hungary: Handbook of European Folk Music Instruments, Series I, Vol. I]. Leipzig: VEB Deutscher Verlag für Musik.

Sebö, Ferenc. 1998. *Népzenei Olvasókönyv* [Folk Music Reader]. Rev. ed. Budapest: Planétás. (First published Budapest, 1994.) http://www.hurdygurdy.com (esp. Alden and Cali Hackmann's Hurdy-Gurdy Web site)

Discographical References

Adaro. *Words Never Spoken*. Akku Disk ADCD 3030. *1999*: Germany.

Ad Vielle Que Pourra (Pierre Imbert). *Menage à Quatre*. Xenophile 4048. *1997*: USA.

Aquartet. *Roue Libre*. Mustradem DPCD 96014. *1996*: France.

Blowzabella. *Pingha Frenzy*. Some Bizarre Product BIGH 01. *1988*: UK.

Brooks, Garth. *Fresh Horses*. Capitol 32080. *1995*: USA.

Chabenat, Gilles. *Bleu Nuit: Musiques Pour Vielle à Roue*. Ocora 559046. *1988*: France.

Clastrier, Valentin. *Hurdy-Gurdy from the Land of Cathars*. Silex 225070. *1997*: France.

Dalfin, Lou, and Sustraia. *Radio Occitania Libra*. Baracca & Burattini 487849-2. *1997*: Italy.

Donovan. 'Hurdy Gurdy Man.' Pye 7N 17537. *1968*: UK.

Eaton, Nigel. 'Laridé.' *Ancient Beatbox*. Cooking Vinyl 21. *1996*: UK.

Folk och Rackare. *1976–1985*. Resource RESCD 515. *1996*: Sweden.

Garmarna. *God's Musicians/Guds Spelemän*. Omnium 2014. *1996*: USA.

Hedningarna. *Fire*. Tristar 36756. *1996*: USA.

Hölderlin Express. *Electric Flies*. Akku Disk ADCD 3028. *1996*: Germany.

La Musgaña. *Lubican*. Green Linnet GLCD-4010. *1994*: USA.

Le Gop. *Le Gop*. Le Gop 2. *2000*: France.

Levellers, The. *Levellers*. Elektra/Asylum 61532. *1994*: USA.

MacDonald, Laurel. *Kiss Closed My Eyes*. Improbable Music IMACD-01. *1994*: Canada.

Malicorne. *Malicorne*. Acousteack 9301. *1997*: France.

McKennitt, Loreena. *The Book of Secrets*. Warner Brothers 46719. *1997*: USA.

Page, Jimmy, and Plant, Robert. *No Quarter: Jimmy Page & Robert Plant Unledded*. Atlantic 82706. *1994*: USA.

Pascal Lefeuvre Quartet, The. *Alicante*. Scalen Disc PLQ0190. *1990*: France.

Pogues, The. *Waiting for Herb*. Elektra 61598. *1993*: UK.

Shave the Monkey. *Mad Arthur*. Percheron Musique APE 3003. *1996*: UK.

Spirit of the West. *Weights and Measures*. Warner Music CD19716. *1997*: Canada.

Tea Party, The. *The Edges of Twilight*. Capitol 32350. *1995*: USA.

Filmography

The Song Remains the Same, dir. Peter Clifton and Joe Massot. 1976. USA/UK. 135 mins. Documentary. Original music by John Bonham, John Paul Jones, Jimmy Page, Robert Plant.

FERENC SEBÖ and MEGAN JEROME

Kantele

A chordophone, whose age is reckoned at between 1,000 and 3,000 years, the *kantele* is related to other zither-style instruments in the category of Baltic psaltery. It is traditionally a five-stringed, hollowed soundbox, played on the lap; the player uses picking techniques. Recent design developments have included soundboxes made of separate boards, the addition of more strings (up to 36 and, occasionally, more) and a chromatic lever mechanism. These developments have been accompanied by changes in playing technique and a repertoire that extends beyond the instrument's traditional gamut.

The *kantele* has been regarded as Finland's national instrument since the rise of Finnish nationalism in the nineteenth century, with the development of the folklore collection assembled by Elias Lönnrot as *The Kalevala*, in which the *kantele* is a significant presence. Its popularity declined during the period of cultural internationalist modernism that submerged 'folk' regionalism, but enjoyed a major renaissance with the folk music resurgence from the late 1960s onward, centered in Kaustinen. Kaustinen hosts an annual music festival and is the home of the Folk Music Institute, which initiated the introduction of the instrument to Finnish school curricula in 1982. The *kantele* was also taught at the Sibelius Academy after the appointment of Martti Pokela in 1975. The Kantele Association, established in 1977, publishes the journal *Kantele*. These developments marked the *kantele*'s transition from a 'museum' folk instrument to its dynamic engagement with contemporary music, ranging from concert artwork to integrations with jazz/rock/pop forms, in which both acoustic and recently developed electronic versions of the instrument have come to constitute a distinctive Finnish contribution to the sound of contemporary popular music.

Bibliography

Asplund, Anneli. 1997a. 'Folk Music.' In *Finland: A Cultural Encyclopedia*, ed. Olli Alho et al. Helsinki: Finnish Literature Society, 110–12.

Asplund, Anneli. 1997b. 'Kantele.' In *Finland: A Cultural Encyclopedia*, ed. Olli Alho et al. Helsinki: Finnish Literature Society, 169–70.

Cornell, Diane. 1990. *Musical Instruments as Symbols of Culture: The Impact of the Finnish Folk Music Institute's 'Kantele to the Schools' Project Upon the Role of the Kantele in Finnish Society*. Unpublished M.A. thesis, University of Washington.

Cronshaw, Andrew. 1998. 'The Kantele Conquering New Areas.' *Finnish Music Quarterly* 2(98): 26–31.

Hakala, Joyce. 1997. *Memento of Finland: A Musical Legacy*. St. Paul, MN: Pikebone Music.

Lönnrot, Elias. 1989. *The Kalevala*, trans. Keith Bosley. Oxford and New York: Oxford University Press.

Rahkonnen, C.J. 1989. *The Kantele Traditions of Finland*. Unpublished Ph.D. thesis, Indiana University.

Saha, Hannu. 1988. 'Kantele: New Life for Finland's National Instrument.' *Finnish Music Quarterly* 1(88): 20–29.

Saha, Hannu. 1996. 'Style and the Process of Variation in Folk Music.' Five-page summary in, and of, Kansanmusiikin tyyli ja muuntelu. Kaustinen: Folk Music Institute, Publ. 39. (Includes a CD.)

Saha, Hannu. 1998. 'The Kantele – From Epic to Eclecticism.' *Finnish Music Quarterly* 2(98): 16–25.

The Kantele Shop. http://www.kantele.com/

Discography (with assistance from Helmi Järviluoma)

Karelia. *The Sounds of Birchbark Flute*. Bluebird BBCD 1013. *1980*: Finland.

Pokela, Martti, Pokela-Sariola, Eeva-Leena, and Kontio, Matti. *Kantaleet: Finnish Kantele Music*. LJLP/LJMK 1027. *1983*: Finland.

Primo (Primitiivisen Musiikin Orkesteri). *Haltian Opissa*. Olarin Musiikki Oy OMLP8. *1984*: Finland.

Salamakannel. *Salamakannel*. OMCD 25. *1989*: Finland.

Värttinä. *Musta Lindu*. Olarin Musiikki Oy OMLP22. *1989*: Finland.

Newer improvisatory kantele ethnoperformers/groups include:

Kastinen, Arja. *Kantele Meditation* (60-minute improvisation, with English notes). Finlandia 0630-18064-2. n.d.: Finland.

Loituma. *Things of Beauty*. NSD 6010. *1995*: Finland.

Sirmakka. *Tsihi tsihi* (with English notes). Finlandia 0630-18066-2. n.d.: Finland.

'Classical':

Koistinen, Ritva. *Tradition of Kantele Vol. 3: The New Era 1993* (Works by Pärt, Nordgren, Bashmakov and others). 3984-22113-2. *1993*: Finland.

BRUCE JOHNSON

Khalam

The *khalam* is a form of lute used by professional musicians and *griots* (or *jelli*, *jewel* or *gewel*) – professional entertainers and storytellers – in the savanna regions of West Africa. Variants with four or fewer strings are found among the Soninke, Manding, Tukolor and Fulani

(Fulbe, Peul). Specifically, the *khalam* (or *halam* or *xalam*) is associated with Wolof (or Ouolof) musicians in Senegal, among whom the five-stringed instrument is widely used.

With a body that is as long as, or longer than, the exposed part of the rod-like neck (*banti*), the *khalam* is approximately 2' 5" (0.75 m) overall. Four types are identified by the Wolof, the principal difference between them being the depth of carving of the wood from which the hollow body or resonator of the instrument is made. An elongated ovoid (*kook*), over which a hide (*pawd*) is stretched and fixed with pegs or sewn with a thong along the back, the instrument has a sound hole at the end of the body that permits the strings of horsehair or nylon to be fastened and to be laid along the instrument to the tuning rings (*kachiri*), which are made of thongs bound about the neck. The *khalam* is usually plucked with the fingernails of the thumb, index and middle fingers, although only the two long strings are stopped, the remaining three being played as open strings. Two tunings, 'high' and 'low,' are used.

As a four- or five-stringed instrument, the *khalam* of the Senegambia is believed to have been a forerunner of the North American banjo, which is known to have originated in Africa. Certainly, the short notes and mode of playing are comparable with the more archaic styles of banjo playing, and a number of other parallels have been noted.

Bibliography

Bebey, Francis. 1975 (1969). *African Music: A People's Art*. London: Harrap.

Coolen, Michael T. 1984. 'Senegambian Archetypes for the American Folk Banjo.' *Western Folklore* 43(2): 117–32.

Oliver, Paul. 1970. *Savannah Syncopators: African Retentions in the Blues*. London: Studio Vista.

Discography

Ames, David. *Wolof Music of Senegal and Gambia* (notes and recordings). Ethnic Folkways FE 4462. *1955*: USA.

Nikiprowetzky, Tolia. *La Musique des Griots: Senegal* (notes and recordings). Collection Radio-Diffusion Outre-Mer (Disques Ocora) OCR 15. *ca. 1965*: France.

Oliver, Paul. *Savannah Syncopators: African Retentions in the Blues* (notes and recordings). CBS 52799. *1970*: USA.

PAUL OLIVER

Kora

The *kora* is one of the most popular instruments to have come out of Africa. Its presence in some of the best-known African pop bands of the 1980s and 1990s, such

as that of Baaba Maal, is all the more remarkable given its limited geographical and social origins.

The *kora* was originally exclusive to the Manding people of West Africa, in particular to the Mandinka of Gambia and Senegal, and the Maninka of Mali and Guinea. Less than 300 years old in its modern form, it was first mentioned in the late eighteenth-century writings of explorer Mungo Park (Park 1799).

The *kora* belongs to the unusual family of the harp-lute. It is made from a calabash gourd cut in half and covered with cowhide, through which is fixed a wooden stick. Between 21 and 25 nylon strings are attached to this stick with the help of tuning rings; they are stretched across the soundboard via a bridge, which splits them into two parallel rows at right angles to the calabash. The musician holds the instrument vertically and plays it by plucking and occasionally strumming the strings with the thumbs and forefingers.

Traditionally, the *kora* is played by male musicians belonging to the caste of the *jalis* (sometimes better known as *griots*), whose important and multifaceted hereditary role in Manding society is one of historian, praise-singer, entertainer and mediator. Historically, *jalis* were attached to the courts of the kings who ruled the Manding empire between the thirteenth and late nineteenth centuries. While their role has remained essentially the same since then, the source of their patronage has shifted from kings to businesspeople, politicians and members of other wealthy classes. Their repertoire consists in the main of praise-songs dedicated to their patrons and to great historical figures, as well as songs containing advice, moral judgments and comments on contemporary society. The function of the *kora* is essentially to provide accompaniment to these songs, although solo instrumental parts are not uncommon. In traditional ensembles, the *kora* is most often joined by the *balafon* (a wooden xylophone), but it remains the main instrument accompanying the singer, who can be of either gender. In urban pop bands of the late twentieth and early twenty-first centuries, however, the *kora* has usually been one of many acoustic and non-acoustic instruments.

The *kora* made its debut on the international music scene in the 1970s, with a first appearance by Gambian virtuoso player Alhaji Bai Konteh (Konte) at the Woodstock festival, and an early collaboration between another Gambian master, Foday Musa Suso, and US jazz musician Don Cherry. Since then, many *kora* musicians have visited North America, Europe and Japan, and have sometimes settled in cities there (particularly in Paris), giving the instrument a higher profile abroad. The 1980s saw acclaimed tours and releases by a number of small acoustic ensembles, such as the one led by Jali Musa

Jawara from Guinea or the famed duo, Dembo Konteh and Kausu Kouyaté, from Senegambia. However, the real turning point for *kora*, and possibly Manding, music abroad occurred in 1988 with Guinean musician Mory Kanté's hit 'Yeke Yeke,' which reached the Top 10 charts in Europe and took the club scene by storm with numerous, successive acid-house dance-floor remixes. Another important occurrence for *kora* music, also in the late 1980s, was the successful collaboration between Malian musician Toumani Diabaté and the Spanish flamenco group Ketama, which confirmed the instrument's clear potential for crossover.

While collaborations of this kind multiplied over the years, involving especially jazz musicians, but also rock musicians (for example, Herbie Hancock, Pharoah Sanders and Bill Laswell), a handful of non-Manding professional musicians ventured into forming their own *kora* groups: Ravi of Kora Colours in Britain, who designed his own aluminum electric version of the instrument; South African multi-instrumentalist Pops Mohammed; and David Gilden of the US trio Cora Connection. Rather than drawing directly on the intricate Manding repertoire and playing styles, these musicians usually chose to develop their own, creating an extra dimension to *kora* music – a dimension more in tune with late twentieth-century 'world music' trends.

The increased popularity of Manding music has meant that, since the 1990s, more artists have been touring and recording in the West, while numerous new talents have flooded the West African market. Women in particular (for instance, Kandia Kouyaté and Oumou Dioubaté), who had been confined to a more local African scene, have begun to achieve fame abroad. This intensified activity has resulted in increased visibility and dissemination of the *kora* worldwide. As a consequence, the *kora* has become much more than a Manding instrument. It has become a powerful symbol of African music in the modern world.

Bibliography

Anderson, Ian. 1987. 'Red Dust and Wild Koras.' *Folk Roots* 46: 28–30.

Anderson, Ian. 1996. 'Hard Kora.' *Folk Roots* 157: 19.

Broughton, Simon, et al., eds. 1994. *World Music: The Rough Guide*. London: Rough Guides Ltd.

Cathcart, Jenny. 1996. 'Pops Goes the Kora.' *Folk Roots* 161: 14–15.

Durán, Lucy. 1989. 'Djely Mousso.' *Folk Roots* 75: 34–39.

Durán, Lucy. 1998. 'Techno-Griot.' *Folk Roots* 175/176: 40–46.

Durán, Lucy, and King, Anthony. 1984. 'Kora.' In *The New Grove Dictionary of Musical Instruments*, ed. Stanley Sadie. London: Macmillan, 461–63.

King, Anthony. 1972. 'The Construction and Tuning of the Kora.' *African Language Studies* 13: 113–36.

Park, Mungo. 1799. *Travels in the Interior Districts of Africa: Performed Under the Direction and Patronage of the African Association, in the Years 1795, 1796 and 1797, with an Appendix Containing Geographical Illustrations of Africa by Major Rennell*. London: G. and W. Nicol.

Prince, Rob. 1989. 'The Kora Prince.' *Folk Roots* 69: 15–16.

Stapleton, Chris. 1988. 'Golden Guinea.' *Folk Roots* 61: 27–29.

Discographical Reference

Kanté, Mory. 'Yeke Yeke.' *Akwaba Beach*. Barclay 8331191. *1987*: UK.

Discography

Diabaté, Toumani, Ketama, and Thompson, Danny. *Songhai*. Hannibal HNCD 1323. *1988*: UK.

Dioubaté, Oumou. *Wambara*. Stern's Africa STCD 1086. *1999*: UK.

Gilden, David. *Ancestral Voices*. Kora Productions KPCD01. *1991*: USA.

Hancock, Herbie (with Foday Musa Suso and Bill Laswell). *Sound-System*. CBS CDCBS 26062. *1984*: USA.

Jawara, Jali Musa. *Direct from West Africa*. Go!Global GGXCD 1. *1988*: UK.

Konteh (Konte), Alhaji Bai. *Alhaji Bai Konte*. Rounder 5001. *1972*: USA.

Konteh, Dembo, and Kouyaté, Kausu. *Simbomba*. Rogue FMSL 2011. *1987*: UK.

Kora Colours. *Ravi*. New Earth CD 77111. *1997*: UK.

Kouyaté, Kandia. *Kita Kan*. Stern's Africa STCD 1088. *1999*: UK.

Maal, Baaba. *N'der Fouta Tooro #1*. Stern's Africa STCD 1061. *1994*: UK.

Mandingo Griot Society (with Foday Musa Suso and special guest Don Cherry). *Mandingo Griot Society*. Flying Fish FF 076. *1978*: USA.

Sanders, Pharoah (with Foday Musa Suso). *Message from Home*. Verve 529578-2. *1995*: USA.

MARIE-LAURE MANIGAND

Koto

This 13-stringed, plucked zither first arrived in Japan from China before the ninth century, as part of the orchestra of *gagaku*, an upper-class art music that was assimilated from continental Asia between the fifth and ninth centuries. In the Edo period (1603–1867), it came to be used among the upper and upper-middle classes as a solo and small ensemble instrument. Since that time, the leading masters of koto music have generally been men, while most of the practitioners have been women. Along with flower arrangement and tea ceremonies, koto performance became established in the Meiji era (1868–1912) as one of the traditional accomplishments of young women. In modern popular music, the koto has been used occasionally to represent indigenousness, although much less frequently than the shamisen.

Bibliography

Kubota, Toshiko. 1984. 'Koto.' In *Hôgaku Hyakkajiten* [The Encyclopedia of Japanese Music], ed. Eishi Kikkawa. Tokyo: Ongakunotomo, 395–97.

TÔRU MITSUI

Lira

The *lira* of modern Greece is a bowed stringed instrument, part of a large family of similar instruments found in the geographical area extending from Europe to the Far East. Other important instruments in this group, which has its origins in ancient India, are the Bulgarian *gudulka*, the Persian *kemence*, the Middle Eastern and North African *rabab*, the Indian *sarangi* and the medieval troubadours' *vielle*. The violin is the classical European exponent of this type of instrument. An instrument called the 'lira' also existed in ancient Greece. It was a plucked stringed instrument, similar to the *kithara* and very different from the modern Greek *lira*.

The *lira* has three single strings that are played with a bow, which sometimes has small bells attached to it to produce a simple rhythmic accompaniment. The pitch of the strings is changed not by pressing the string with the finger on the fingerboard (as is the case with the violin), but by touching the string from the side with the fingernail. The *lira* is held upright, with its base placed on the knee of the player and its head on the player's chest. Thus, the player is able to rotate the instrument like a spike fiddle (a fiddle that rests – and can thus be turned – on a spike, in much the same manner as a cello) in order to accommodate the bowing of each string.

Two types of *lira* exist; they differ according to the shape of the soundbox. The most common type is the pear-shaped *lira*, found in parts of Macedonia, Thrace, Crete and the islands, especially the Dodecanese (mostly Kárpathos and Kásos). Cretan *lires* are of the same shape but are usually larger. The second type is the bottle-shaped *lira*, which is played by refugees from Pontus (a region in northern Turkey). In Crete and most of the islands, the *lira* is usually played with the lute as accompaniment, while in Kárpathos it is played accompanied by the bagpipe (*tsambouna*). The *lira* player in Crete is called 'liraris,' while in the Dodecanese he/she is called 'liristis.'

The *lira* was the main melodic instrument of folk music in many parts of Greece, but in the 1960s and 1970s it was replaced by the violin. This change has pro-foundly influenced the music traditionally performed on the *lira*. Even in places where the *lira* has survived, it has assumed many of the characteristics of the violin: its shape, methods of tuning, techniques of playing (such as legato), acoustics (an expanded melodic range and a larger soundbox) and repertoire. Since World War II, the only place where the *lira* has increased in popularity – albeit with major changes – is Crete, where it has become an important symbol of local identity. The *lira* also has a strong presence in certain ritual contexts in Greece, such as the Kárpathian *glendi* (Kavouras 1992) and the spirit-possession ritual of the Anastenaria in northern Greece (Danforth 1989).

As a result of a revitalized interest in traditional music that took place toward the end of the twentieth century, recordings of the famous Cretan *lirarides* and Dodecanesian *liristes* can easily be found in most record stores throughout Greece. However, despite the fact that many different Greek folk instruments have come to be used in new contexts by new groups and musicians in their songs and musical compositions, the *lira* has not been among the most popular of them, probably because it has retained strong local (mostly Cretan) connotations.

Bibliography

Anogeianakis, Foivos. 1976. *Ellinika Laika Mousika Organa* [Greek Traditional Musical Instruments]. Athens: Ekdosi ethnikis trapezas.

Danforth, Loring M. 1989. *Firewalking and Religious Healing: The Anastenaria of Greece and the American Firewalking Movement*. Princeton, NJ: Princeton University Press.

Kavouras, Pavlos. 1992. 'O Choros stin Olympo Kárpathou: Politistiki allagi kai politikes antiparatheseis' [Dance in Olympus, Kárpathos: Cultural Change and Political Controversies]. *Ethnografika* 8: 47–70.

Liavas, Lambros. 1983–85. 'I kataskevi tis achladoschimis liras stin Kriti kai sta Dodekanisa' [The Construction of the Pear-Shaped Lira in Crete and the Dodecanese]. *Ethnografika* 4–5: 117–42.

Malm, William P. 1977. *Music Cultures of the Pacific, the Near East, and Asia*. Englewood Cliffs, NJ: Prentice-Hall.

PANAYOTIS PANOPOULOS

Mandolin

The modern mandolin is descended from the form standardized by the Vinaccia family of Naples, Italy (ca. 1770), which consisted of four pairs of steel strings tuned to g, d, a and e. These original Neapolitan instruments were initially used for classical music written by Italian virtuosos such as Fouchetti, Bortolazzi and Pietro Denis in the Baroque period.

The mandolin fell out of fashion during the first half of the nineteenth century, but mandolin circles (*circolos*) – a mix of amateur and professional players – began to develop in Italy around 1850. The concept spread to Spain and was adopted by *bandurria* players, and on 1 January 1880 a touring *bandurria* group, the 'Spanish Students,' began a visit to the United States. Their concerts and performances inspired Carlo Curti to form his own 'Spanish Students' mandolin orchestra, thus starting a grass-roots mandolin orchestra craze throughout the country.

In 1894, instrument builder Orville Gibson of Kalamazoo, Michigan started building carved-top mandolins and guitars. This led to the creation of the Gibson Mandolin and Guitar Company. Through teacher-agents, students were sold mandolin-family instruments and were taught in groups how to play them. By the turn of the century, the mandolin had become one of the most popular instruments in the United States. After a 20-year run, the craze started to diminish with the onset of World War I and, by the end of the war, interest in the mandolin had waned.

Within African-American culture, the impact of the mandolin was never as great as that of the guitar or the banjo, but several blues musicians, born in the early years of the twentieth century, learned the instrument in their youth, and for a small number it became their main instrument. One of the best known was James 'Yank' Rachell, who as a teenager formed a duo with a fellow-Tennessee musician, guitarist Sleepy John Estes, to play on the streets and at house parties. Rachell made numerous recordings, with Estes and others, between 1929 and 1941, teaming up with Estes again in the 1960s. Another musician, Charlie McCoy, played on a hybrid banjo-mandolin in recordings under his own name and as an accompanist to others, such as his sister-in-law, Memphis Minnie, during the mid-1930s (Dixon, Godrich and Rye 1997, 559). Johnny Young appears to have been unique in using the instrument successfully in the later, electric form of Chicago blues.

Ironically, the most lasting improvements to the instrument came at the end of the mandolin orchestra's heyday. Acoustic engineer Lloyd Loar, working for the Gibson Company, applied what he called the 'principles of Stradivarius arching' to the designs of the existing models of the time, and developed a new line of instruments called the Artist Model F-series. All mandolins, *mandolas*, *mandocellos* and guitars were included in this line and featured carved tops and backs which were tuned and had violin-style f-holes.

During the 1920s, the more raucous-sounding tenor banjo was by far the more popular instrument. The 1930s, however, saw Loar's concepts put to great use by Russian-born mandolinist Dave Apollon. He appeared in Hollywood film shorts and vaudeville, and his F-5 mandolin would easily fill the halls with the sound that Loar had envisioned. Also, around 1936, Bill Monroe was performing in a duo with his brother Charlie, featuring mandolin and guitar. Country musicians had previously never heard the mandolin played with such speed and power. Monroe started recording his 'bluegrass' style of music in September 1946, and this sound proceeded to inspire the next two generations of mandolinists. Among them were Frank Wakefield, Bobby Osborne, Jesse McReynolds, David Grisman (who created the instrumental genre 'Dawg Music') and Andy Statman (who performed modern jazz mandolin).

The mandolin also forged an ongoing relationship with pop music. Homer and Jethro, a mandolin–guitar duo, did comic parodies of everything from Tin Pan Alley tunes to country music of the 1950s and 1960s. In the 1970s, Rod Stewart's hit song 'Maggie May' featured mandolin and fiddle throughout. Rock groups such as Led Zeppelin, the Grateful Dead and Fairport Convention also used mandolin from time to time.

With Bill Monroe probably the greatest influence on most mandolinists in the United States, the instrument has developed an ongoing presence in all styles of music through his followers. In the 1990s, active groups like the Nashville Mandolin Ensemble recorded and performed repertoire from Bach to the Beatles to twentieth-century music and orchestrations of Monroe's 'bluegrass music.' Soloist Paul Glasse delved further into the modern jazz format, while the Modern Mandolin Quartet explored classical, Latin and modern works. North American soloist Evan Marshall took the techniques of violin and early mandolin soloists to breathtaking new levels with his stage and recorded performances, while soloist Neil Gladd, based in Washington, DC, served as the North American standard for 'the classical mandolin' repertoire exclusively.

The mandolin appears to have found its way into almost every musical genre and idiom, and has become particularly popular in the United Kingdom and Australia. From European classical to the most avant-garde forms of jazz and twentieth-century performances, and with constant collaborations between classical, bluegrass, jazz, world music and other folk traditions, the mandolin's future and place in music, both live and recorded, are assured.

Bibliography

Carter, Walter. 1994. *Gibson Guitars*. Los Angeles: General Publishing Group.

Dixon, Robert M.W., Godrich, John, and Rye, Howard. 1997. *Blues & Gospel Records 1890–1943*. 4th ed. Oxford: Clarendon Press.

Morey, Stephen. 1993. *Mandolins of the 18th Century*. Cremona: Editrice Turris.

Tyler, James, and Sparks, Paul. 1989. *The Early Mandolin*. Oxford: Clarendon Press.

Discographical Reference

Stewart, Rod. 'Maggie May.' Mercury 73224. *1971*: USA.

Discography

McCoy, Charlie. *Complete Recorded Works (1928–1932)*. Document 6018. *1992*: Austria.

Rachell, Yank, and the Tennessee Jug Busters. *Mandolin Blues*. Delmark 606. *1998*: USA.

Young, Johnny. *Chicago Blues*. Arhoolie 325. *1965*: USA.

JEROME 'BUTCH' BALDASSARI

Sarod

A *sarod* is a short-necked, fretless plucked lute from North India, related to the *rabāb* of Afghanistan. The *sarod* developed from the *rabāb* in the courts of North India during the eighteenth and nineteenth centuries and became a central solo instrument in North Indian classical music in the twentieth century.

The *sarod* has a wooden body, usually made of teak, with a parchment sound table, and a small secondary resonator at the top of the neck. An unusual feature of the *sarod* is that the neck is covered with a sheet of smooth, polished metal. As there are no frets on the *sarod*, the subtle pitch inflections central to Indian music are achieved by sliding the finger on the string as it is pressed down on the metal surface. Typically, the *sarod* has four or five main playing strings, three to five drone and *chikari* strings and up to 16 sympathetic strings. The strings are plucked with a plectrum, which is usually made of coconut shell. Two of the twentieth century's greatest exponents of the *sarod* were Ali Akbar Khan (b. 1922) and Amjad Ali Khan (b. 1945).

In popular music, the use of the *sarod* has been limited. Like other Indian classical instruments, it is occasionally used in *filmī* song, but not as frequently as the *sitār*. Similarly, it has not found a home in Western popular music, as the *sitār* and *tablā* have. One example of the *sarod*'s use in Western popular music was on recordings by the band Kula Shaker in the mid-1990s.

Bibliography

Miner, Allyn. 1993. *Sitar and Sarod in the 18th and 19th Centuries*. Wilhelmshaven: Florian Noetzel.

Discography

Kula Shaker. *K*. Columbia 67822. *1996*: UK.

GERRY FARRELL

Sāz

The Persian and Turkish word '*sāz*' is a very broad term meaning 'musical instrument.' As such, it has been used historically for many types of instruments. In Iran, Central Asia, Turkey and other Muslim cultures of southeastern Europe, '*sāz*' (or other related terms) has come to refer to a family of plucked or strummed long-necked lutes with rounded, pear-shaped resonators made of wood, and between eight and 10 metal strings in double, or sometimes triple, courses. The *sāz*, in turn, is part of the *tanbūr* family, another generic term for long-necked lutes, thought to have derived from Baghdad and the Khorāsān regions of Iran and Afghanistan.

The *sāz* has different names in different places: in Iran it is generally referred to as the *dotār*, while in central Asia it is called the *dutar*, *tampur* or *dambura*. In Turkey, a very widespread type of *sāz*, used in much entertainment and dance music, is the *bağlama*, which has a shorter neck than the parent instrument.

The *sāz* is the most common lute in Turkey, where it is central to most forms of popular music. Soloists (*aşiklar*) use the *sāz* as accompaniment in performing epic folk poetry and tales in a popular tradition called *ozan*. Aşik Veysel, who died in 1974, was one of the foremost exponents of *ozan*, and his recordings have continued to flood the market. More frequently, however, singers are accompanied by ensembles that include several *sāz*, plus other melody and rhythm instruments. *Amanédhes*, café music popular in the first half of the twentieth century in Izmir, Istanbul and then in centers in Greece, used violin, *kanonáki* (Ar. *qanūn* (zither)), *sandoúri* (Ar. *santūr* (hammer dulcimer)), *oúti* (Ar. '*Ūd* (short-necked lute)) and *sāz*. Rosa Eskenazi was one of the most famous *Amanédhes* singers. The *Türkü*, which fuses *ozan* with other styles of urban music, is played on a mixture of Turkish, Arabic and Western instruments. Performers like Belkis Akkale and Besir Kaya feature most often in the charts. *Arabesk* is derived from Arabic entertainment music that became popular in Turkey due to state bans on the broadcast of local music. Orhan Gencebay and Küçük Emrah were among the most popular *Arabesk* performers in the late 1990s.

In live and recording contexts, where instruments are heavily amplified, a new instrument, the *elektrosaz* (a *sāz* with an electric pickup), is used. One of the main differences between the *sāz* and the *elektrosaz* is that, while the former has strings in double or triple courses, the latter has single strings – the emphasis being on more complex fretwork and simpler strumming. These techniques bring the performance style closer to monophonic urban art music styles and *Arabesk*. Ensembles using the *elektrosaz* in popular urban music often comprise only one *elektro*, a *darbuka* (goblet drum) and either a *kaval* (end-blown flute), an accordion or a violin as additional melody instruments.

Bibliography

Broughton, Simon, et al. 1994. *World Music: The Rough Guide*. London: Rough Guides Ltd.

Spector, Johanna, et al. 1984. 'Sāz.' In *The New Grove Dictionary of Musical Instruments*, Vol. 3, ed. Stanley Sadie. London: Macmillan, 319–20.

Stokes, Martin. 1992. 'The Media and Reform: The Sāz and Elektrosaz in Urban Turkish Folk Music.' *British Journal of Ethnomusicology* 1: 89–102.

Discography

Asya iclerinden balkanlara saz. Kalan 00195. *1998*: Turkey.

Traditional Music of the World, Vol. 6: Song Creators in Eastern Turkey. Smithsonian/Folkways 40432. *1993*: USA.

Turquie: L'art vivant de Talip Özkan. Ocora C 580047. *1993*: France.

JANET TOPP FARGION

Shamisen

The *shamisen* is a plucked, unfretted, three-stringed instrument developed from a prototype that was brought to the main islands of Japan in the mid-sixteenth century from the Ryûkyû island of Okinawa. This prototype was adapted by players of the *biwa* (a type of lute with notably raised frets), among others, to create a unique Japanese instrument. The new instrument, with silk strings and a body covered with cat or dog skin, was first used to accompany popular and folk songs before being introduced into art music and widely utilized as an accompanying instrument in various vocal genres. In popular music since the emergence of the recording industry, the sound of the *shamisen* has often been used to represent indigenousness. It has also been featured most notably in Takio Itô's contemporary min'yo band, Takio Band, played by Shinichi Kinoshita.

Bibliography

Kamisangô, Yûkô. 1984. 'Shamisen.' In *Hôgaku Hyakka-jiten* [The Encyclopedia of Japanese Music], ed. Eishi Kikkawa. Tokyo: Ongakunotomo, 495–500.

Discography

Itô, Takio. *Takio*. CBS/Sony 32DH5123. *1988*: Japan.

Itô, Takio. *Takio Spirit*. FXD-7033. *1991*: Japan.

TÔRU MITSUI

Sitār

A *sitār* (from the Persian *setār* (meaning 'three strings')) is a long-necked plucked lute that originated in North India. The *sitār* represents a synthesis of Indo-Islamic cultures and is related to a number of Middle Eastern lutes, as well as to South Asian instruments such as the *bīn* and *vīnā*. It dates from the thirteenth century, but its structure and playing techniques underwent radical and rapid change in the nineteenth and twentieth centuries. The present-day *sitār* has a gourd soundbox with a wooden table and neck; there are up to seven main playing strings and 13 sympathetic strings running over two bridges. Notes are stopped on 21 movable, raised, curved metal frets. The strings are plucked with a wire plectrum, a *mizrab*, worn on the first finger of the right hand. An important feature of the *sitār* is a technique called *mīnd* – the manner in which notes can be raised and lowered with the fingers of the left hand by the lateral deflection of the string to produce subtle tonal nuances.

Styles and Forms

The *sitār* is associated primarily with North Indian or Hindustani classical music that is based on the structuring principles of *rāg* and *tāl*, systems of modal and metrical organization. All instrumental music in India is closely connected to vocal music. Several distinct styles of *sitār* playing have emerged in the last 100 years. Vilayat Khan (1924–) is the leading exponent of the *gāykī* or 'vocal' style. He has taken this style to new levels of sophistication and complexity and is considered one of the greatest *sitār* players of the twentieth century. He has developed new tunings for the *sitār*, and his performances emphasize the subtle manipulation of *mīnd*. The formal and expressive aspects of the *gāykī* style are influenced by vocal forms such as *khyāl* and *thumrī*. Ravi Shankar (1920–) represents a different stylistic lineage. Although still drawing on vocal forms for performance structure, Shankar's playing is characterized by the complexity of *bols* (right-hand stroke patterns) and the performance of compositions in many different *tāls*. The oldest style of *sitār* playing that has continued to be performed is that of the *Seniā gharānā*. The major twentieth-century exponent of this style was Mustaq Ali Khan (1911–89), whose senior disciple is Professor Debu Chaudhuri (1935–). The *seniā* style emphasizes clarity in the delineation of the *rāg*, particularly in the *alap* sections, and is austere and serious in its delivery, eschewing musical pyrotechnics in favor of detailed musical development. Players in the *seniā* style use an older form of *sitār* that has 17 frets.

The Sitār in Popular Music

Since the beginnings of the Indian popular music industry in the second and third decades of the twentieth century, the *sitār* has featured as an ensemble instrument. The most widespread form of popular music in South Asia to emerge during this period is *filmī gīt* (film song). The *sitār* is often prominent in *filmī* song, although in this context its musical function is redefined. Rather than performing as a solo instrument, the *sitār* is used as another texture within larger orchestral groups alongside other Indian and Western instruments. This often requires adjustments to the usual tuning of the instrument, and *sitārs* are often played in registers not normal in classical music. Electric *sitārs* have been developed, but are not commonly used.

The *sitār* is one of the few Indian instruments to have had a significant influence on Western popular music. This is due mainly to Ravi Shankar's popularity in the West from the late 1950s onward. In 1961, he recorded an album, *Improvisations*, with the jazz flautist Bud Shank. The *sitār* was used by the Beatles and featured in some of their most famous songs. In 1965, George Harrison, the Beatles' lead guitarist, who later became Shankar's student, introduced a *sitār* in the song 'Norwegian Wood,' and this started a fad among pop bands. The Rolling Stones, Traffic, the Byrds and others incorporated Indian elements into their music (see Reck 1985; Farrell 1997). The guitar had been the ubiquitous instrument of pop and rock since the mid-1950s and in the *sitār* guitarists recognized an exotic, albeit remote, version of their own instrument. Several aspects of the *sitār*'s sound and construction helped it to cross over into Western pop: superficially, it resembled the guitar, as it was plucked and fretted; its ability to bend tones linked its sound to that of the electric guitar and enabled it to function like a lead guitar; and, although it was not a chordal instrument, its modal possibilities fitted well with pop music, in which blues-based forms were still a significant influence. Shankar would later call this period the 'great sitar explosion' (Shankar 1968). In fact, the fad was short-lived and reached its zenith in 1966. However, the sound of the *sitār*, and other aspects of Indian culture, such as joss sticks, Indian clothing and mystical philosophies, have come to be essential cultural referents to the hippie era and this phase in the history of Western popular music.

The *sitār* and Indian musical concepts have continued to appear in popular music and jazz. Sampled *sitār* may be heard in many forms of contemporary popular music. Recent manifestations of Indian influence can be found in the music of Kula Shaker and others. Such influences refer retrospectively to the 1960s, but also relate to the upsurge in popularity of South Asian musical forms throughout the South Asian diaspora in recent decades.

Bibliography

Dick, Alistair. 1984. 'Sitār.' In *The New Grove Dictionary of Musical Instruments*, Vol. 3, ed. Stanley Sadie. London: Macmillan, 392–400.

Farrell, Gerry. 1997. *Indian Music and the West*. Oxford: Oxford University Press.

Miner, Allyn. 1993. *Sitar and Sarod in the 18th and 19th Centuries*. Wilhelmshaven: Florian Noetzel.

Reck, David. 1985. 'Beatles Orientalis: Influences from Asia in a Popular Song Form.' *Asian Music* XV(1): 83–150.

Shankar, Ravi. 1968. *My Music, My Life*. New York: Simon & Schuster.

Discographical References

Beatles, The. 'Norwegian Wood.' *Rubber Soul*. Parlophone PMC 1267. *1965*: UK.

Shankar, Ravi. *Improvisations*. Ravi Shankar Music Circle RSD-6. *1961*: USA. Reissue: Shankar, Ravi. *Improvisations*. Angel 67049. *1999*: USA.

GERRY FARRELL

Tea-Chest Bass ('Bush Bass')

The tea-chest bass is a rhythm instrument made from a thin plywood tea chest measuring approximately 27 cubic inches (70 cm³). In the center of the base of the chest, a strong cord, fine rope or hay-band is knotted through a hole and strung to the top of a pole, which is often a broom handle or a tent pole measuring approximately 72" (182 cm) (Atherton 1990). The pole has a nail at the bottom end to anchor it through a hole into the corner of the tea chest. (In an early model, volume was increased and sound improved by using a hollow roller blind for the pole, and tennis-racket gut, doubled over and braided anticlockwise, for the string or cord.) Sound holes similar to those of a violin are sometimes cut into the walls of the box. To play the instrument, the player generally places the chest on the ground with its open top face down or, sometimes, with its side out and partly reinforced with a board. The player keeps the box steady by placing one foot on it, and plucks the cord in time to a tune. Straining the pole sideways pulls the cord taut and makes possible a range of bass notes covering at least an octave.

Modifications have included cutting the tea chest down to about 20" (50 cm) in height to suit the average player (although some players have reverted to the full-size tea chest), and bracing the open end. In some instances, legs (approximately 1" × 1" (2.5 cm × 2.5 cm)) are fixed inside the corners, protruding about 2" (5 cm) at the front and 1" (2.5 cm) at the rear, to raise the box off the ground and let the sound out. Another variation is the use of a metal ring that slides up and down the pole to alter the length of the string.

Although its origins in Australia are unknown, the tea-chest bass, along with the cigar-box fiddle, is part of a tradition of improvised bush instruments (Edwards 1979). An equivalent instrument, made from a washtub and used by 'jug bands,' exists in North America (Cline 1977), and indigenous peoples in New Guinea are known to have played a similar instrument made from oil drums. Like the lagerphone, the tea-chest bass is linked to makeshift bands, skiffle groups, the occasional minstrel troupe and the Australian 'bush band.'

The tea-chest bass was played as early as the 1930s. Stuart Robinson, a former member of the Wedderburn Oldtimers Band, remembers that the Black & White Minstrel Troupe (St. Arnaud), which played in the 1930s, used a tea-chest bass; when Robinson joined the revived band in 1945, he was shown by an older member how to make the instrument (Robinson 1999). For the opening of the Redbank Hall in 1946–47, Robinson was in a band that consisted of piano accordion, tea-chest bass and electric steel guitar, amplified by wiring into a radio.

However, it was not until the early 1950s that the Bushwhackers Band of Sydney, founded by John Meredith in 1952 and featuring Jack Barrie as the first tea-chest bass player, introduced the instrument in a form that was quickly taken up by similar groups nationwide (Pitt 1965) and that has remained popular. It was Meredith who introduced the 'bush bass' to the Bushwhackers Band after a friend made a drawing from an instrument he had seen played on the Sydney wharf (Meredith 1999). The Bushwhackers were active in collecting and performing 'bush songs' from rural Australia, using the button accordion, lagerphone and 'bush bass' as accompaniment. The band raised the profile of the tea-chest bass through its recording of some of this material on 78 rpm records for the Wattle label, which were in turn broadcast widely over the radio, and through its appearance in 1954 in a popular play entitled *Reedy River*. The instrument's profile was raised further by articles on how to construct a tea-chest bass that appeared in popular magazines and the *Australian Tradition* (Pitt 1965). This national publicity prompted many old-time bands of the day to use the tea-chest bass for a brief period, while 'bush bands' like the Bushwhackers sprang up across Australia over the following decades. However, John Manifold, writing in the *Australian Tradition* in 1973, points out that their instruments had never been typically used in the bush, but were reminiscent of the 'foo foo' or skiffle groups that played on ships.

Talented tea-chest bass players can convincingly produce the rhythm of a double bass (bull fiddle) over a range of at least one octave. The tea-chest bass has been well represented on recordings by the original (Sydney) Bushwhackers, as well as by groups from the 1970s, such as the Melbourne-based Bushwackers, the Cobbers and Mulga Bill's Bicycle Band.

Bibliography

Atherton, Michael. 1990. *Australian Made – Australian Played: Handcrafted Musical Instruments from Didjeridu to Synthesiser*. Kensington: New South Wales University Press.

Cline, Dallas, comp. and ed. 1977. *How to Play Nearly Everything from Bones and Spoons to the Washtub Bass*. New York: Oak Publications.

Edwards, Ron. 1979. *Skills of the Australian Bushman*. Adelaide: Rigby.

Ellis, Peter. 1993. 'Musical Instruments: Tea-Chest Bass.' In *The Oxford Companion to Australian Folklore*, ed. Gwenda Beed Davey and Graham Seal. Melbourne and New York: Oxford University Press, 288.

Manifold, John. 1973. 'The Bush Band.' *Australian Tradition* 32 (September): 21.

Meredith, John. 1999. Personal communication with author.

Pitt, Frank. 1965. 'How to Make a Bush Bass.' *Australian Tradition* 2(3) (November): 27.

Robinson, Stuart. June 1999. Personal communication with author.

Discography

Australian Bush Songs by Bushwhackers Band (Sydney) (EP). Wattle B1. *1957*: Australia.

Cobbers, The. 'All for Me Grog.' WEA 600039. *1978*: Australia. Reissue: Cobbers, The. 'All for Me Grog.' Festival C37484. *1980*: Australia.

Jindi Plays Joe (*Collected Tunes from Joe Yates' Book*). Self-published CD by Jindi 0001. *1999*: Australia.

Mulga Bill's Bicycle Band. *In Concert Recording*. Basket BBBS-002. *1973*: Australia.

The Bushwackers Dance Album. Image LP 815. *1980*: Australia.

The Bushwackers (Melbourne) (EP). Image IEP-5. *1976*: Australia.

PETER ELLIS

'*Ūd*

The '*ūd* is a short-necked plucked lute. Since the earliest times, it has been the most important instrument in the Arab world. Its use extends down the east coast of Africa, where it is a principal instrument in Somalia, Sudan, Kenya and Tanzania. The '*ūd* is also commonly used in Turkey, Iran, Iraq, Armenia, Azerbaijan and Greece. It is thought to be the direct ancestor of the European lute.

The term ''*ūd*' derives from the Arabic *al 'ūd*, which has been described as either 'the stick, branch,' referring to the wooden neck of the instrument, or 'the lute,' a generic term for plucked stringed instruments in which the strings lie parallel to the neck and soundboard. Its introduction has been variously attributed to Lamech of Genesis 4, the Greeks Pythagoras, Plato and Euclid, and Ptolemy. Initially, the instrument was made from a single piece of wood with a skin stretched over a rounded soundbox. As such, it was called the *mizhar*. The wooden face was introduced in the sixth century. The '*ūd* with a separate neck fixed onto the soundbox was introduced in Spain in the eighth century. The early instrument had four strings, then five (reported in the ninth century), then seven double strings (reported in the nineteenth century). It is usually played with a plectrum.

Two types of *'ūd* are now commonly used. The *'ūd mashriqi* (eastern *'ūd*) is the more common, being played all over the Arab world. It usually has five double strings. The *'ūd maghribi* (western *'ūd*) is found in North Africa, where it is variously called *'ūd 'arabi*, *quwaytarah* and *kwitra*. It is smaller than the eastern *'ūd*, although with a slightly longer neck.

The *'ūd* was used primarily to accompany secular song, either as a solo instrument or in ensembles with bowed instruments and percussion. In Egypt during the nineteenth century, the *'ūd* was the principal instrument in the music of the *takht* ensemble. By the early twentieth century, the *takht* ensemble had become standardized to include violin (replacing the *kamancha* at the end of the century), *qanūn* (zither), *riqq* (tambourine) and *darabukka* (y-shaped, handheld drum). The ensemble accompanied a solo singer and chorus in popular songs called *taqtūqah*, and the love songs of more 'learned' singers such as Umm Kulthūm. The *takht* was expanded during the 1940s to include several more violins, cellos, double bass and accordions, and in the 1960s to include electric guitars and electronic keyboards. This expanded ensemble was called the *firqah*. This same tradition, with only minor regional variations, forms the backbone of popular music throughout the countries of the former Ottoman Empire and those under its influence, from Zanzibar to Greece. In Zanzibar, the orchestra (sometimes in reduced form) accompanies popular *taarab* songs; in Sudan, the *'ūd* constitutes an essential instrument in both urban and rural music styles; in Morocco and the rest of the Maghreb, the *'ūd* is incorporated into such Arab-Andalusian traditions as *milhûn* and *ghanati*.

The *'ūd* may also be used as a solo instrument, although in this case it is usually within a classical or 'learned' tradition. One of its most popular exponents is the Iraqi performer Munir Bashir.

Bibliography

al-Faruqi, Lois Ibsen. 1981. *An Annotated Glossary of Arabic Musical Terms*. Westport, CT and London: Greenwood Press.

Broughton, Simon, et al. 1994. *World Music: The Rough Guide*. London: Rough Guides Ltd.

Poché, Christian. 1984. "Ūd.' In *The New Grove Dictionary of Musical Instruments*, Vol. 3, ed. Stanley Sadie. London: Macmillan, 687–93.

Discography

Bashir, Munir. *Art of the Ud*. Ocora 580068. *1998*: France.

JANET TOPP FARGION

Ukulele (Ukelele)

As a multi-stringed, fretted instrument, the ukulele is capable of playing complex melodies, rhythms and chords. Due to its relatively small size, it is sonically a 'soft' instrument. Its timbre and tone vary depending on the kind of wood used, the number of strings and the size of the instrument.

There are four main ukulele sizes: baritone, tenor, concert and soprano. The usual four (but up to eight) strings are commonly tuned (from fourth to first string) at guitar concert pitch (d, g, b, e^1) for baritone, and a fourth above (g, c^1, e^1, a^1) for tenor, concert and soprano. Occasionally, ukuleles are tuned a fifth above (a, d^1, $f\!\!\sharp^1$, b^1). The ukulele is often used to accompany singing and, in some contexts, dance. In popular culture, it has linkages to Hawaii and Polynesia, and therefore visual clichés such as hula shirts, leis and tropical decorations are commonplace in its iconography. The ukulele has evolved into a popular instrument that can be played by musicians of any age, ethnic heritage or gender.

The Hawaiian name 'ukulele' has several possible derivations. A common explanation is that the rapid movements of a player's fingers reminded Hawaiians of 'jumping fleas.' Other possible derivations are Queen Lili'uokalani's description of the instrument as 'the gift to come' (*uku* meaning 'gift,' *lele* meaning 'to come'); and a description associated with Edward Purvis, an early popularizer of the instrument in the court of King David Kalakaua. In Hawaiian, the proper pronunciation of the word 'ukulele' is 'oo-koo-le-le,' not the more commonly used 'you-koo-le-le.'

The instrument is derived from the *braguinha* (*machete*), a Portuguese instrument. It arrived in Hawaii in 1879 with Portuguese migrants from the islands of Madeira. Within a decade of their arrival in Hawaii in 1879, Portuguese instrument makers and musicians such as Augusto Dias, Manuel Nunes and Jose do Espirito Santo established ukulele workshops and began popularizing the instrument. Importantly, it received royal patronage. Music was an important part of Hawaiian performing arts, and members of the royal family were skilled instrumentalists, composers and dancers. They helped champion the incorporation of the ukulele into hula dances, instrumental ensembles and modern compositions.

In its original form in Madeira, the *braguinha* used four metal strings tuned in fifths, but the ukulele evolved into an instrument that was easy to chord (becoming similar in tuning to the guitar) and used gut strings. It was relatively easy to play at a basic level and very portable. It also became associated with touristic images of Hawaii circulating on mainland North America around the turn of the twentieth century.

The evolution of the ukulele as a transnational instrument began in earnest in 1915 when it was featured in the Hawaiian music and dance presentations at the Panama-Pacific International Exposition in San Francisco. It was integral to songs such as Henry Kailimai's 'On the Beach at Waikiki,' which is an early example of what became known as *hapa-haole* ('half-white') songs. The lyrics of *hapa-haole* songs are usually in English, with a smattering of Hawaiian words or place names and iconic images such as palm trees, soft winds, moonlight and 'dark-eyed maidens.' Along with songs by Hawaiian-based tunesmiths and performers such as Albert 'Sonny' Cunha, there inevitably followed over several decades many imitative songs by mainland composers. Songs such as 'Lovely Hula Hands,' 'My Little Grass Shack in Kealakekua' and 'Sweet Leilani' are typical of *hapa-haole* songs, and the ukulele is integral to their sound and ambiance. The ukulele remained very popular during the 1920s, but this popularity began to wane in the 1930s, only to revive in the immediate post-World War II era and into the early 1950s. In the mid-1990s, the instrument experienced another revival.

In its Hawaiian homeland, the ukulele had a unique musical niche, along with the lap-style steel guitar, and many fine performers. However, only a few of these performers gained widespread exposure outside Hawaii or the tourist industry. Noted early Hawaiian ukulele players included Ernest Kaai, Jesse Kalima and Eddie Kamae, who established a vibrant tradition continued by musicians such as Eddie Bush, John Kameaaloha Almeida, King Bennie Nawahi and Nelson Waikiki. Outside Hawaii, there were influential performers who contributed to the popularity of the ukulele. Among them were Cliff 'Ukulele Ike' Edwards, a fine musician and singer; Roy Smeck, a multi-instrumentalist, teacher and arranger; George Formby, the quintessential British dance hall performer and master of the double-entendre; May Singhi Breen, an active teacher and composer; and Arthur Godfrey, a US television performer who helped to popularize ukuleles in the 1950s, especially the baritone ukulele. Tiny Tim was an influential and media-conscious performer in the 1970s, and his repertoire and performances drew substantially on those of earlier performers. The styles of all the aforementioned musicians varied considerably, but collectively they made the ukulele seem an accessible and, most importantly, an enjoyable and entertaining instrument.

George Formby, in particular, became internationally famous for his monolog-style songs, laden with double-entendres (for example, 'When I'm Cleaning Windows,' 'Chinese Blues,' subsequently renamed 'Chinese Laundry Blues,' and 'Leaning on a Lampost'). Formby played the banjolele or ukulele–banjo, an instrument that was developed as a hybrid of the ukulele: it was strung like the 'uke,' but shaped like the banjo. It was a louder instrument than the ukulele (the skin on the banjolele amplified the sound) and was more suitable for performance in larger venues. Formby developed a unique sound by playing complex solos and frailing at breakneck speed.

In the latest transnational revival of interest in the ukulele, there are influential performers who either revisit popular historical styles or take the ukulele into musically 'sophisticated' genres such as jazz and Western classical music. Among the former, Bob Brozman, Janet Klein, Estelle Reiner, Ralph Shaw and Ian Whitcomb specialize in roots, vaudeville, dance hall or novelty styles. Among the latter, Lyle Ritz, Herb Ohta and Iwao are versatile and well-trained musicians performing complex and interesting music on the ukulele. There are also larger performance ensembles that make extensive use of the ukulele as a musical component or a visual icon. Examples are the Ukulele Orchestra of Great Britain, Mic Conway's National Junk Band and the Old Spice Boys (featuring Azo Bell) from Australia, the Serious Ukulele Ensemble from New Zealand, Shorty Long from Austin, Texas, the Ukulogical Museum from Belgium (Luc Tegenbos and Peter Van Eyck) and various 'Hawaiianesque' ensembles from Japan. Other unique uses of the ukulele are provided by the Ukulele Trance Project, which intriguingly links the ukulele to flying saucers and space aliens, and the Ukulele Summit recording projects, produced by Mark Cass, featuring the music of Bob Marley and Brian Wilson of the Beach Boys in ukulele-based versions of well-known songs. A key figure in the latest revival is musician, tunesmith and writer Jim Beloff, who has also set up a marketing and informational Web site to cater to enthusiasts (http://www.fleamarketmusic.com). In the ukulele's Hawaiian homeland, performers such as Rick Cunha, Daniel Ho, the Ka'au Crater Boys, Keoki Kahumoku, Israel Kamakawiwo'ole, Alden Levi and Jake Shimabukuro have followed a long tradition of innovation and continuity in ukulele music. Of special note in the recent revival are a burgeoning collector's market for unique or antique instruments and an increase in skilled ukulele makers and designers.

The ukulele, its image and transnational popularity are interesting phenomena. The ukulele can be argued to be an egalitarian instrument because of its playability and relative simplicity of construction. Even young children can play it with ease because of its size and nylon strings, and basic chords for vocal accompaniment can be taught quickly. In the United States, Japan and elsewhere, the ukulele is again being used as an ideal instrument for instructing large groups of children. It is especially effective at camps or in school programs, where ensemble playing is encouraged over virtuosity. The same playability and social attributes of the instrument make it appropriate for adult players too. In regions such as Melanesia and Polynesia, the instrument can be made from locally available materials such as coconut shells and fishing line, and it is therefore affordable and fixable. Overall, the ukulele requires neither a high level of musical talent nor expensive construction materials.

The ukulele is also assumed by many to be an exotic instrument because of its long association with tropical places such as Hawaii and Polynesia and the accompanying stereotyped images of indolence and ease. For consumers living in nontropical climates, the ukulele sonically and visually encapsulates a life style and an ambiance that they can usually experience only vicariously or through mass tourism. A ukulele or a ukulele recording can be either a projection or a memento of an idealized way of living in a distant place where there are no social problems and where music creates social solidarity and animates romance. Even though such idealized notions rarely survive scrutiny, mass tourism and, to some extent, entertainment are predicated on initiating and maintaining such myths. By intention or accident, the association of the ukulele with exotic people and places is recurrent.

The ukulele is also thought to be an enjoyable and entertaining instrument partly because it is egalitarian and exotic, but also because its popularizers positioned, and have continued to position, it as an instrument of fun. Although it is musically possible to play minor-key, somber music on it, the ukulele's early repertoire and its association with mass tourism projected either tropicality or lightheartedness, and sometimes both. Arguably, non-Hawaiian popularizers of the instrument such as Cliff 'Ukulele Ike' Edwards, George Formby, Arthur Godfrey and Tiny Tim were known as entertainers who played the ukulele rather than as ukulele players per se. The egalitarianism of the instrument meant that merely competent musicianship could suffice to provide accompaniment for the main objective: verbal cleverness in the form of wordplay, nonsensical vocables or quirky song themes. This focus of entertainment over musicianship has continued in the work of performers such as Boo Takagi in Japan, Ralph Shaw in Canada, Stefan Raab in Germany, and Jim Beloff and others in the United States. That is not to say they are unmusical; rather, they are entertaining in part because the ukulele is a musical means to an end – entertainment – and not the end itself. It is only when the ukulele is associated with

'sophisticated' genres such as jazz or Western classical music that the focus switches clearly from fun to finesse. In general, the ukulele provides the perfect sonic and visual prop to announce that 'this music is fun and entertaining.'

Ukuleles have remained in general use throughout the world. In Portugal and Brazil, for example, ukulele-style instruments have continued to be played. In Madeira, an instrument known as the *cavaquinho* has remained popular and has been commercially manufactured. In the United Kingdom and the United States, ukulele devotees have held gatherings and festivals to publicize the instrument.

As its history shows, the instrument lends itself to use in different musical genres. Stylistically, contemporary ukulele music encompasses many genres, such as jazz, vaudeville, reggae, exotica and trance. In parts of Polynesia, Melanesia and Southeast Asia, it is integral to daily music culture, and in North America, Japan and Europe there are active recording and performance scenes. Over its history, it has been associated with heritage, novelty and popular culture. Although ukulele music is a mixture of egalitarianism, exotica and entertainment, one constant is that the ukulele is associated with fun and therefore will probably remain attractive to performers, consumers and enthusiasts.

Bibliography

Beloff, Jim. 1997. *The Ukulele: A Visual History*. San Francisco: Miller Freeman Books.

Simmons, Michael. 1996. 'The Real Ukulele.' *Acoustic Guitar* 7(5): 51–57.

Sheet Music

Anderson, R. Alex, comp. and lyr. 1940. 'Lovely Hula Hands.' New York: Miller Music Corp.

Cogswell, Bill, Harrison, Tommy, and Noble, Johnny, comps. and lyrs. 1933. 'My Little Grass Shack in Kealakekua.' San Francisco: Sherman, Clay and Co.

Kailimai, Henry, comp., and Stover, G.H., lyr. 1915. 'On the Beach at Waikiki.' Honolulu, Hawaii: Bergstrom Music Co.

Discographical References

Crosby, Bing. 'Sweet Leilani.' Decca 1175. 1937: USA.

Formby, George. 'Chinese Blues.' Decca F-3079. 1932: UK.

Formby, George. 'Chinese Laundry Blues.' *I'm the Ukulele Man*. Empress RAJCD 801. *1998*: USA.

Formby, George. 'Leaning on a Lampost.' Regal Zonophone MR-2490. 1937: UK; Decca F-9444. 1950: UK. Reissue: Formby, George. 'Leaning on a Lampost.' *I'm the Ukulele Man*. Empress RAJCD 801. *1998*: USA.

Formby, George. 'When I'm Cleaning Windows.' Regal

Zonophone MR-2199. 1936: UK; Decca F-9444. 1950: UK. Reissue: Formby, George. 'When I'm Cleaning Windows.' *When I'm Cleaning Windows.* President PLCD 538. *1995*: UK.

Discography

Beloff, Jim. *For the Love of Uke.* Flea Market Music FMM 1002. *1998*: USA.

Formby, George. *I'm the Ukulele Man.* Empress RAJCD 801. *1998*: USA.

Formby, George. *When I'm Cleaning Windows.* President PLCD 538. *1995*: UK.

Legends of Ukulele. Rhino Records R2 75278. *1998*: USA.

Ohta, Herb. *Duo: I'll Keep Remembering.* M&H Hawaii MHCD-1421. *1999*: USA.

Ritz, Lyle. *Time.* Roy Sakuma Productions RSCD 5583. *1998*: USA.

Ukulele Summit 2/V.A. Meldac Records MECI 25152. *2000*: Japan.

Vintage Hawaiian Treasures, Vol. 1: Hapa-Haole Hawaiian Hula Classics. Hana Ola Records HOCD 17000. *1993*: USA.

KARL NEUENFELDT with MIKE BROCKEN

Vihuela

The *vihuela* is a small, guitar-like instrument used primarily in the Mexican mariachi ensemble. Its five strings, usually made of monofilament nylon, are strummed with the player's fingernails, or by plastic fingerpicks worn backward over the nails. Tuning is similar to that of a guitar with the lowest string missing. The displaced octaves of its reentrant tuning – *A, d, g, B, E* – discourage the *vihuela*'s use as a melodic instrument. Average vibrating length of the strings is about 20" (50 cm).

The body of the *vihuela* has a distinctive convex, vaulted back, reminiscent of a V-shaped boat hull. Although machine gears have replaced wooden tuning pegs on the modern *vihuela*, the tied frets and saddleless bridge of its Renaissance predecessor have been retained. The top of the instrument is traditionally made of a soft wood called *tacote*, which contributes to the *vihuela*'s characteristic sound; the remaining parts are usually constructed of cedar or other hardwood. The *vihuela*'s sharp attack decays rapidly, making it the most percussive element of the contemporary mariachi, in which its inclusion is essential.

The Spanish *vihuela* – similar in construction to the Renaissance guitar – was a favorite of the Spanish elite during the fifteenth and sixteenth centuries. It was first brought to the Americas by Ortiz, a musician on Cortés's initial expedition to Mexico, in 1519. The indigenous peoples quickly adopted the instrument, and eventually modified its construction and function. By the seventeenth century, the *vihuela* had virtually disappeared in Spain, but in western central Mexico it was transformed into a folk instrument that kept the name of its precursor. While the Spanish *vihuela* is occasionally revived by early music specialists, the Mexican *vihuela* has remained a popular instrument.

Bibliography

García López, Abel. 1997. . . . *Y las manos que hacen de la madera el canto* [. . . And the Hands That Make Wood Sing], Vol. 1. Morelia, Mexico: Fondo Estatal para la Cultura y las Artes de Michoacán.

Sheehy, Daniel. 1999. 'Popular Mexican Musical Traditions: The Mariachi of West Mexico and the Conjunto Jarocho of Veracruz.' In *Music in Latin American Culture: Regional Traditions*, ed. John M. Schechter. New York: Schirmer Books, 34–79.

JONATHAN CLARK

Violin

A descendant of ancient Asian instruments such as the *rebab* (Arabia), *sarinda* (India) and the *erhu* (China), the violin is a small, usually wooden stringed instrument played with a bow. Its structure has remained relatively constant since the sixteenth century, when it emerged in northern Italy, chiefly in the Milanese area around Brescia and Cremona, and Venice. The belly (front), the back and the middle section (or ribs) are constructed as separate pieces from a soft wood such as spruce. The bottom, top and corners of the rib section are reinforced with blocks. The belly is pierced by two sound holes shaped like an 'f,' and a bass bar, which runs parallel to the lower strings, is attached to the underside; its position is determined by one foot of the bridge which supports the strings. Underneath the opposite foot of the bridge is the sound post, which runs vertically toward the back of the instrument. At one end of the neck, which is made separately of a harder wood, is the scroll containing the tuning pegs. The strings run from the tuning pegs over the bridge to the tailpiece, which is looped around the end button.

Most violins tune to G, d, a, e^1, but the pitch is now higher than it was, say, in the time of violin maker Antonio Stradivari (1644–1737). This has resulted in greater tension on the strings, necessitating the strengthening of certain parts of the instrument. In addition, the compass of the music has generally increased since Stradivari's day, and so the fingerboard has been extended.

To play the violin, the player bows the strings around the 'f' holes with one hand, while altering the pitch by 'stopping' the strings with the fingers of the other hand. The bow is about 30" (76 cm) long. In the classical tradition, the violin is placed under the player's chin and above the collarbone for playing. Violinists sometimes use a chin rest to help avoid having the left hand support the instrument while playing at the same time.

The violin's eminence in classical music, as a solo, featured, chamber and orchestral instrument is due to the range of emotions the instrument can evoke. Few instruments have the violin's large emotional palette or its general facility for virtuosity. In the hands of a fine player, the violin can conjure delicate, ethereal glassy tones or brash gnarly skitters.

Although virtuosic passages can be accomplished on the violin, its unfretted and relatively small neck makes it an unforgiving musical partner. The violin is especially unforgiving of amateur and even professional performers in live performances, those whose ears cannot discern pitches quickly or those whose sense of touch is uncertain. Despite its challenges, however, there have been many excellent violinists. They include Jascha Heifetz (1901–87), arguably the greatest violinist of the twentieth century, and Yehudi Menuhin (1916–99).

The violin is also renowned as a 'folk' instrument, and for hundreds of years the 'fiddle' has remained a premier instrument in the folk musics of many Western and non-Western communities. Despite describing instruments that are effectively the same or quite similar, the words 'violin' and 'fiddle' connote different musical traditions, the former generally associated with the Western art music tradition. They also denote a different archetypal sound, that of the violin being resonant, rich and glossy, and that of the fiddle being more raw, earthy and nasal.

The violin, as opposed to the fiddle, has featured in a range of popular music and jazz. Stéphane Grappelli and Jean-Luc Ponty stand out as the most visible jazz violinists. The violin has also featured in dance bands when the need has been felt to signal a more 'cultured' ambiance – as, for example, in the recordings of Europe's Society Orchestra (led by James Reese Europe), the orchestra that provided the music for the renowned ballroom dance team of Irene and Vernon Castle. In addition, the violin is on occasion featured as a solo instrument in the arrangements of popular songs. A particularly notable example is to be found in the extended, classically oriented violin solo on Céline Dion's recording of 'It's All Coming Back to Me Now,' the song written by Meat Loaf's classically trained pianist and composer, Jim Steinman.

Violins have also been used frequently in more orchestral settings in popular music as part of string arrangements, as in Sarah Vaughan's 'Lush Life' and Whitney Houston's 'I Will Always Love You.' The violin has also played an important role in the string arrangements of rock groups, as in the Beatles' 'Eleanor Rigby,' 'I Am the Walrus' and 'Yesterday' (which uses a string quartet), the 1969 and 1972 albums of Deep Purple and Procol Harum,

respectively, and the Electric Light Orchestra's '10538 Overture.' Violins have also been used in a very special way to add a lushness to music. The best-known example of this is to be found in the recordings of Mantovani and his orchestra. And in film music, the violin can be heard in all its manifestations, exploiting the wide range of emotions that it can evoke, as in John Williams's score for *Star Wars* or Bernard Herrmann's score for *Psycho*.

Electronic amplification has also affected the role of the violin in both traditional and contemporary musical genres. In the work of, for example, Jerry Goodman (rock) and Ashley MacIsaac (folk-rock), the magnetic pickup and amplifier have both been used to amplify and, in some cases, alter the sound through the use of distortion and reverberation.

The violin's overall versatility has resulted in its adaptation by a host of Western and non-Western communities. To those familiar with Asian musical traditions, for example, the instrument may sound similar to the instruments from which it evolved. And despite the many electronic and technological innovations that have influenced music, the violin and its sound have remained popular. The violin has provided a means of expression in radically different musical settings and contexts.

Discographical References

Beatles, The. 'Eleanor Rigby.' *Revolver*. Capitol C1-90452. *1966*: USA.

Beatles, The. 'I Am the Walrus.' *Magical Mystery Tour*. Capitol SMAL 2835. *1967*: USA.

Beatles, The. 'Yesterday.' Capitol 5498. *1965*: USA.

Deep Purple and the Royal Philharmonic Orchestra. *Concerto for Group and Orchestra*. Tetragrammaton 131. *1969*: UK.

Dion, Céline. 'It's All Coming Back to Me Now.' *Falling into You*. 550 Music/Epic 67541. *1996*: USA.

Electric Light Orchestra, The. '10538 Overture.' *No Answer*. United Artists UAS-5573. *1972*: UK.

Houston, Whitney. 'I Will Always Love You.' Arista 12490. *1992*: USA.

London Symphony Orchestra, The. *Star Wars* (Original soundtrack). PolyGram 13588. *1977*: USA.

McNeely, Joel, and the Royal Scottish National Orchestra. *Psycho* (Original soundtrack). Varèse Sarabande 5765. *1997*: USA.

Procol Harum. *Procol Harum Live: In Concert with the Edmonton Symphony Orchestra and the Da Camera Singers*. A&M 4335. *1972*: USA.

Vaughan, Sarah. 'Lush Life.' *The Complete Sarah Vaughan on Mercury, Vol. 1*. Mercury 826320. *1954–56*: USA.

Discography

Europe's Society Orchestra. 'Castle House Rag.' Victor 35372. 1914: USA.

Goodman, Jerry. *On the Future of Aviation*. One Way 35147. *2000*: USA.

Grappelli, Stéphane. *1935–1940*. Classics 708. 1935–40; *1996*: USA.

Grappelli, Stéphane. *1941–1943*. Classics 779. 1941–43; *1998*: USA.

MacIsaac, Ashley. *Hi How Are You Today?*. A&M 540522. *1995*: USA.

Mantovani and His Orchestra. *The Collection*. Castle CCS130. *1992*: UK.

Ponty, Jean-Luc. *Le Voyage: The Jean-Luc Ponty Anthology*. Rhino 72155. 1975–93; *1996*: USA.

Ponty, Jean-Luc. *The Very Best of Jean-Luc Ponty*. Rhino 79862. *2000*: USA.

Filmography

Psycho, dir. Alfred Hitchcock. 1960. USA. 109 mins. Thriller. Original music by Bernard Herrmann.

Star Wars, dir. George Lucas. 1977. USA. 121 mins. Science Fiction. Original music by John Williams.

BHESHAM SHARMA and MIKE BROCKEN

Zither (Alpine Zither)

The Alpine zither is a 'box-zither' that evolved from the German *scheitholt* in regions of the areas that subsequently became south Germany and Austria. The German term '*Zither*' was applied to this instrument in the eighteenth century and was later used as the generic term for this family of instruments.

Originally a folk instrument of the mountains, the Alpine zither was introduced to Austrian and German concert halls in the 1800s. Virtuosos like the Austrian Johann Petzmayer (1803–84) and the German Adam Darr (1811–66) also included classical music in their repertoires. This demand for greater musical flexibility led to the development of various forms, among which the 'Salzburg zither' has been the most prominent. This type eventually became the modern 'concert zither.' It has a flat wooden body, with five melody strings above a chromatically fretted fingerboard at the front end, and 35 to 38 open strings running parallel over the resonator. Characteristic is the S-shaped back end, which has a scroll at the left and a semicircle with a sound hole at the right. From 1869, zithers were also made and improved in the United States by the Austrian American Franz Schwarzer (1828–1904), who created prize-winning instruments and new models.

Zither playing essentially consists of three parts: melody, chords and bass. The left hand positions the melody notes on the fretboard, while the thumb and fingers of the right hand pick the individual strings – the five closest for melody, the open strings for mid-range and bass accompaniment.

A growing body of original compositions featured the zither as an artistic solo instrument from the middle of the nineteenth century. In the early twentieth century, especially in the 1920s, it was also used in various fields of popular music entertainment, such as salons, beer halls, cafés and vaudeville theaters. The leading player of this era was Georg Freundorfer (1881–1940) from Munich. He teamed up with a piano player to meet the new demand for a jazzier sound. However, his repertoire remained traditional. Zither music had its first and last international success with the soundtrack for the movie *The Third Man* (1949), which was set in postwar Vienna. The theme tune was an adaptation by the Viennese Anton Karas (1906–85) from a zither instruction book. As a single, it became a Top 40 hit in the United States and one of the first movie soundtracks in its own right. Since then, despite this success, the zither's traditional Alpine and Viennese identity has limited its appeal to those looking for this particular regional flavor. The increasing number of zither clubs throughout the world, however, documents a limited revival in very recent years.

Bibliography

Brandlmeier, Josef. 1963. *Handbuch der Zither* [Handbook of the Zither]. Munich: Süddeutscher Verlag.

Nikl, August V. 1927. *Die Zither, ihre historische Entwicklung bis zur Gegenwart* [The Zither: Its Historical Development to the Present]. Wien: Arion-Verlag.

Sachs, Curt. 1940. *The History of Musical Instruments*. New York: W.W. Norton & Co.

Stessl, Janet, ed. 1987–. *Zither Newsletter of the USA*. Chicago: Janet Stessl.

Discographical References

Karas, Anton. 'The Third Man Theme.' London 536. 1950: UK. Reissue: Karas, Anton. 'The Third Man Theme.' *Cinema 100: The Official Cinema 100 Album*. EMI Premier PRDFCD1. *1996*: UK.

The Third Man (Original soundtrack). Soundtrack Factory 33538. 1949; *2000*: USA.

Discography

Karas, Anton. *Anton Karas at His Best*. Request Records SRLP 10088. *1973*: USA.

Karas, Anton. *Anton Karas at the Café Mozart*. Columbia CS 9376. *1966*: USA.

Welcome, Ruth. *Christmas in Zitherland*. Capitol ST 1782. *1962*: USA.

Welcome, Ruth. *The Third Man Theme and Other Zither Hits*. Capitol DT 942. *196?*: USA.

Filmography

The Third Man, dir. Carol Reed. 1949. UK. 104 mins. Mystery. Original music by Anton Karas.

ARMIN HADAMER

14. Voice

Voice (as Instrument)

Voice is the faculty whereby human beings (and some other creatures) produce sound (speech, music and other sounds) through use of the lungs, throat and mouth as an acoustic system. Considered as a musical instrument, the voice is structurally comparable to other instruments. At the same time, it may well be the earliest instrument, with developmental priority, both onto- and phylogenetic. Musically, its most characteristic product is song. It is not surprising, therefore, that, just as singing is a universal in human culture, vocal production, especially in the form of songs, remains at the core of popular music, and singers are among its most esteemed performers.

Sound Production

Putting it crudely, the lungs supply wind, which passes over the vocal cords, creating vibrations of variable frequency (and hence pitch), and these are then given added power and particular timbral characteristics through the use as resonators of the various cavities in the chest, throat and head. Both the physiology and its manipulation for vocalization are complex, and can be studied in the scientific literature. (For an introduction, see Sundberg 1987, 2000.) While vocalization can be said to 'come naturally' (it does not require conscious thought), its techniques, especially in musical contexts, are far from innate; rather, they are produced for particular purposes and are intensely variable, along lines of difference created by culture, social function, ideology and aesthetic.

Types of Singing

Since rock 'n' roll, much popular singing in the West has been thought of as being ruled by a 'naturalistic' technique: timbres, intonations and articulations seem to be close to (or at most, heightened versions of) those in everyday speech. Commonly, a contrast is drawn with classical singing, where highly cultivated technique (controlled breathing, low larynx position, carefully deployed resonance cavities and so on) in the service of pure, consistent tone and rationally organized phrasing draws upon an ideal in which singing does not so much imitate instrumental technique as join with it in the faithful delivery of an almost abstract 'text.' The dichotomy, though it has historical and empirical weight, is too crude. To listen to early recordings by opera stars is to realize just how much they could indulge in spontaneities of ornament, timbre and expression. Conversely, while it is true that after rock 'n' roll the focus of pop singing shifted away from the pseudo-classical styles that had dominated popular vocal genres in the nineteenth and first half of the twentieth centuries, this tradition has continued to resonate: from Caruso through Al Jolson, Dean Martin and Elvis Presley the balladeer to Meat Loaf is an unbroken trajectory (though fed from several sources, for example the Neapolitan *canzona*). When Freddie Mercury and Montserrat Caballe duet on 'Barcelona' (1987), one hears not only the rock/classical dichotomy but also the extent to which each singer can draw on elements in his/her own tradition to approach the other.

Rock 'naturalism' is indebted to both the narrativistic and the conversational modes of country music and folk singing, and to the speech-like approach and effects of much African-American vocalism; but it can also draw on not dissimilar techniques, in cabaret and music hall, from the mainstream popular repertoires. Even more significant, perhaps, is the approach to character portrayal, to stylization, in those repertoires and in musical theater, and its influence on such rock performers as David Bowie and Kate Bush. This reveals both classical 'purity' and rock 'naturalism' as constructs. It is now clear, for instance, that the aggressively anti-technique demotic of punk-rock singing was the product of careful contrivance. When Sid Vicious and the Sex Pistols cover 'My Way' (1979), both the elevated tone of the sub-classical legacy and punk's own naturalism are unmasked through exaggeration to the point of grotesquerie.

It is this ideologically organized triangulation – classical, natural, stylized – that has governed the development and tensions of the popular song field since, probably, the late eighteenth century.

Voice as Instrument

When 'his master's voice' began to emerge from the gramophone horn rather than directly from the master's body, the voice's status as instrument was dramatically underlined. But long before this, it was clear, to musicians anyway, that in many respects the voice's constraints and potentials – in terms of range, timbre, pitching and articulation – could, in principle, be considered in similar ways to those of other instruments, except that it is hard to disguise the individuality of the particular voice, and its physiological and emotional correlatives seem to be that much more directly experienced (compare, for example, the sound, technique and effect of, say, the 1965 Bob Dylan and the 1967 Aretha Franklin). Nevertheless, it *can* be treated with relative anonymity, as in some backing singer accompaniments and the 'heavenly choirs' decorating some ballad perorations and movie soundtracks. Microphone technique – developing from the 1920s – can be used to enhance and project intimate particularities (as in crooning and torch song), but also to blur and amplify vocal nuance for large auditoria. African-American inputs are important to these developments: 'From work song grunts through 1930s jazz styles (Louis Armstrong singing "like a trumpet"; Billie Holiday "like a sax") to the short, mobile vocal phrases of funk and scratch textures, one hears vocal "personality" receding as the voice is integrated into the processes of the articulating body' (Middleton 1990, 264). In the melody- and heterophony-oriented traditions of the Middle East and South Asia, solo voice and instrument are also regarded as two sides of a coin, and this attitude has continued to influence popular styles there. In Western pop – especially where African-American influence is strong – solo instruments are often played, as it were, 'like voices': hence the effects of vocalized tone.

The Vocal Body

Even though instruments can attempt to imitate vocal grunts, whoops and sighs, their inability to succeed completely marks the voice as not just another instrument but as unique – the bearer of a human personality; not a technological extension of the body, more an emanation from its intensional core. Thus, voices are always heard as gendered (and popular styles treat the various voice types, from low-pitched female to falsetto male, in a variety of ways and with a variety of associations), as bearers of a message (usually verbal as well as musical), as markers of an identity (even if sometimes this identity is in some respects a collective one, as in gospel quartets, doo-wop, South African *iscathamiya*, 1990s pop 'boy bands'). The sensuality of a voice, then, seems to be inextricable from its source in a particular body, and for Roland Barthes (1990), this quality (its 'grain' or lack of 'grain') is intimately connected to its erotic effects.

The Popular Voice

The use of the voice in popular music moves the discussion beyond the sphere of the voice as instrument into that more properly considered under the subject of performance. What should be stressed again is the centrality of this instrument: typically it dominates popular music textures, fronts the mix, takes 'the lead.' Vocalization is both vernacular and universal: all listeners can engage and identify with, hence participate in, the activity of singing. Popular music is 'singable music' (Stefani 1987) – even if there are genres and historical periods in which this aspect temporarily retreats somewhat from view, as in the swing-band music of the 1930s, and perhaps the dance pop of the 1980s and 1990s – and indeed perhaps this factor may be thought to help characterize Bourdieu's 'popular aesthetic' (1984), embedded as this is in the 'physicality' of 'real life.'

Bibliography

Barthes, Roland. 1990. 'The Grain of the Voice.' In *On Record: Rock, Pop and the Written Word*, ed. Simon Frith and Andrew Goodwin. London: Routledge, 293–300.

Bourdieu, Pierre. 1984. *Distinction: A Social Critique of the Judgement of Taste*. London: Routledge.

Frith, Simon. 1996. 'The Voice.' In *Performing Rites: On the Value of Popular Music*. Oxford: Oxford University Press, 183–202.

Middleton, Richard. 1990. *Studying Popular Music*. Buckingham: Open University Press.

Potter, John. 1998. *Vocal Authority: Singing Style and Ideology*. Cambridge: Cambridge University Press.

Potter, John, ed. 2000. *The Cambridge Companion to Singing*. Cambridge: Cambridge University Press.

Stefani, Gino. 1987. 'Melody: A Popular Perspective.' *Popular Music* 6(1): 21–35.

Sundberg, Johan. 1987. *The Science of the Singing Voice*. DeKalb, IL: Northern Illinois University Press.

Sundberg, Johan. 2000. 'Where Does the Sound Come From?' In *The Cambridge Companion to Singing*, ed. John Potter. Cambridge: Cambridge University Press, 231–47.

Discographical References

Mercury, Freddie, and Caballe, Montserrat. 'Barcelona.' *Barcelona*. Polydor POSP 887. *1987*: UK.

Sex Pistols, The. 'My Way.' *The Great Rock 'n' Roll Swindle*. Virgin CDVD 2410. *1979*: UK.

RICHARD MIDDLETON

15. Wind Instruments

a. Brass and Horns

Bugle

The term 'bugle' comes from the Latin *buculus*, meaning 'bullock' or 'steer.' From simple bovine origins as a hunting instrument, it quickly became a signaling device of tower watchmen, shepherds and soldiers. In the Renaissance, the bugle was fashioned in copper, brass or silver and designed as a short, wide-bored curved horn. By the eighteenth century, it was formed in a *Halbmond* (half-moon) and used by Hanoverian Jäger companies. The English adopted this form at the beginning of the nineteenth century and termed it the 'bugle horn' and soon condensed it with a single loop. It was this instrument that spread to the rest of Europe after the Allied victory at Waterloo. Primarily a signal instrument, it was admitted to early military bands to spell the first six harmonics (*c* to *g*^{1}) of the key it was built in, usually B♭ or C. There are a considerable number of bugle horn parts in early British band repertoire. The French called the single-wound conical bugle the 'clarion' and the Germans called it the 'Signalhorn.'

In 1810, the Irish bandmaster Joseph Haliday added woodwind-style keys to the British military bugle and formed the keyed bugle. Completely chromatic, the keyed bugle was able to play all the old signals of the military – hunt, post and coach – and negotiate obligatos to vocal pieces, airs and variations on operatic and popular tunes. It became a new voice in the nineteenth-century brass band. A decade after the invention of the keyed bugle, valves were applied to soprano bugles and the valved post horn emerged. Adolph Sax changed the instrument's bore and christened the valved bugle the 'saxhorn.' 'Bugle' (*à pistons*) in modern French denotes the saxhorn or its modern offspring, the flügelhorn.

Natural, keyed and valved bugles coexisted in the nineteenth century and many of the traditional forms retained some usage in their native areas until the beginning of the twenty-first century. US bugle traditions are a mixture of English and French military heritages. North Americans used the bugle and the military signal trumpet and confusingly called them both bugles. In the United States, the English-style bugle is called the 'cavalry bugle' and the signal trumpet pitched in G is thought of as the ordinary bugle. The latter instrument has been adapted with valves for use in drum and bugle corps. Valved bugles were made famous by the Bersaglieri corps of the Italian army in 1861 who played them in a homogeneous grouping of soprano through basso. The soprano bugle has three valves and the lower instruments have one valve that lowers each partial by a fourth, making a diatonic scale possible from the fourth partial upward. In the United States, drum and bugle corps of the late twentieth century developed their own musical cultures, with specific repertoires, field competitions and unique marching styles. These styles have been reflected in the pageantry of corps-style half-time shows presented at high school and college football games by US bands.

Certain bugle players are known by inscriptions to them made on 'presentation' instruments that were given in appreciation of services to a troop or corps. Special compact bugles were created to be played on high-wheel bicycles in the nineteenth century. In the twentieth century, military reenactors created a demand for copies of historic bugles.

While some bugle calls can be traced from the Crusades, the majority of today's calls are documented from the eighteenth century by examination of method books and military records. John Hyde (1799) summarized

English military calls; continental calls were documented by Georges Kastner (1848); and German hunting calls have been preserved in a variety of publications. In the United States, military calls were standardized after 1867 and many of these have remained in use. Bugle calls have been directly quoted and parodied by composers in opera, symphony, military band music, film scores and popular song. Buglin' Sam DeKemel, a New Orleans street vendor and vaudevillian, recorded popular and jazz tunes using a standard G bugle in the 1950s. Soldiers have invented texts to the calls for centuries and a few of the most popular (and printable) versions were published in the *Army Song Book* (1918). Texts to accompany *Jagdsignale*, in the German repertoire, also have a long tradition.

The telegraph and radio eliminated the need for bugle signaling in the military. Today's military bases use recorded calls and buglers appear for ceremonial occasions. Boy Scouts retained bugle traditions patterned after the military. Generations of Scouts have memorized calls to obtain a bugling merit badge.

Bibliography

Army Song Book. 1918. Washington, DC: US Government Printing Office.

Benzinger, Karl. 1967. *Schule für Fürst-Pless-Horn* [Instruction for Hunting Horn Playing]. München: Musikverlag Max Hieber.

Dudgeon, Ralph T. 1993. *The Keyed Bugle*. Metuchen, NJ and London: Scarecrow Press.

Hyde, John. 1799. *A New and Complete Preceptor for the Trumpet and Bugle Horn . . .* London: Button & Whitaker.

Jacob, Heinrich. 1980. *Anleitung zum Jagdhornblasen* [A Guide to Playing the Bugle]. Hamburg and Berlin: Verlag Paul Parey.

Kastner, Georges. 1973 (1848). *Manuel général de musique militaire à usage des armées françaises* [General Handbook of Military Music for the Use of the French Armies]. Geneva: Minkoff Reprint.

Music and Bugling. 1984. Irving, TX: Boy Scouts of America.

Rach, Randy. 1997. *The Music Imprints Bibliography of Field Bugle and Field Trumpet Calls, Signals and Quicksteps for the United States Army, Navy and Marine Corps: 1812–1991*. Hartford, MI: Field Music Books.

Discography

DeKemel, Sam (aka Buglesam or Buglin' Sam). 'Bugle Call Rag'/'Has Anybody Seen My Kitty?' Capitol 238. ca. 1948: USA.

DeKemel, Sam, and Almerico, Tony. *Clambake on Bourbon St.* Cook 1085. ca. 1950: USA.

DeKemel, Sam, and Miles, Lizzie. *Queen Mother of the Rue Royale*. Cook 1181. ca. 1950: USA.

DeKemel, Sam, with Almarico, Tony. *Native New Orleans*. Dot DPL 309. ca. 1955: USA.

DeKemel, Sam, with Almarico, Tony, and His Dixieland All Stars. *Tony Almarico and His Dixieland All Stars*. Vik LX 1057. 1956: USA.

DeKemel, Sam, with Almarico, Tony, and His Parisian Room All Stars. *New Orleans Dixieland Express*. GHB (George H. Buck) 133. 1955; *1970*: USA.

Dudgeon, Ralph. *Music for Keyed Bugle: The Miss Lucy Long Social Orchestra and Quick Step Society*. Spring Tree STE 101. *1983*: USA.

James, Harry. 'Bugle Call Rag.' *The Metronome All-Star Bands*. RCA Camden CAL-426. 1949; *1958*: USA.

Krupa, Gene, and His Orchestra. 'Boogie Woogie Bugle Boy.' OKeh Records 6046. 1941: USA.

RALPH T. DUDGEON

Horn (French Horn)

The horn (French horn), like most brass instruments, has its heritage in Western art music. Descended from animal horns, conches and other lip-blown signaling devices, its circular shape and predominantly conical tubing eventually separated it from the trumpet family. Its signaling role, however, was most often associated with hunting parties, as a means of keeping participants informed and safe from each other. Its early role in art music resembles that of the natural trumpet in terms of musical content, although its hunting heritage did cause composers to rely on it for appropriate scenes or effects (for example, compared with the trumpet's military associations). This role continued to evolve through the eighteenth and nineteenth centuries, with its inclusion in European and North American orchestral and chamber music and the development of a varied solo repertoire. The fact that its flared bell points backward is due, in part, to the early practise of manipulating the hand (normally the right) in the bell to effect pitch changes outside the natural harmonic series. With the invention of the valve around 1815, this particular need for the hand in the bell disappeared, but the hand remained there, participating in the shaping of the instrument's characteristic sound. Later, these same manipulations came to be used for different purposes – to produce brassy, hand-muted or 'stopped' notes, and other timbral effects.

The use of the horn in popular music began with its inclusion in bands in the late eighteenth century. As a featured instrument, it did not enjoy the same image as the trumpet or trombone, perhaps because of its inherent acoustical problems (for example, the bell pointing backward, mellow timbre, mid-range tessitura), and did not transfer to idiomatic forms of popular music very readily. Eventually, however, thanks to the perseverance of enthusiastic performers and interested composers/arrangers, the horn finally made inroads in jazz big bands in the early 1940s, being added especially in larger formats that also included strings and other 'orchestral' colors. The inclusion of the horn on Miles Davis's *Birth of the Cool*, featuring noted player and future jazz scholar Gunther Schuller, among others, did much to improve the image of the horn and encourage its inclusion in smaller settings. Player/composer/arranger John Graas was the first to spotlight the horn as an improvising instrument, but it was not until Julius Watkins arrived in New York in the early 1950s that the horn achieved equal footing as a solo/combo instrument. By the end of the twentieth century, it was less visible than other instruments, but maintained an active presence in jazz as a solo and ensemble instrument.

The horn did not remain as present in mainstream North American popular music after the latter's divergence from jazz, although the instrument continued to be heard frequently in orchestral settings, especially in soundtracks. The horn has frequently been utilized to augment scenes featuring heroic actions or characters, often using leaping musical gestures, reminiscent of its 'outdoor' heritage. Various pop/rock styles that included orchestral colors encouraged composers and arrangers to use horns in the mix, but, while the instrument was given occasional solo passages, it was rarely featured. Unlike some other Western brass instruments, the modern horn is rarely heard outside Western art and US pop/jazz musical contexts. Its mellow and at times majestic sound is found, however, in many isolated, yet surprising circumstances and styles, its use being dependent on the interests of the performer, composer and/or arranger.

Bibliography

Agrell, Jeffrey. 1982. 'Jazz and the Horn.' *Brass Bulletin* 40: 41–45.

Blake, Curtiss. 1982. 'Jazz Discography by Player.' *The Horn Call* XIII(1) (October): 83–88.

The Horn Call Annual, No. 7. 1995. Durant, OK: International Horn Society.

Kernfeld, Barry. 1988. 'Watkins, Julius.' In *The New Grove Dictionary of Jazz*, Vol. II, ed. Barry Kernfeld. London: Macmillan, 600–601.

Ormsby, Verle Alvin, Jr. 1988. *John Jacob Graas, Jr.: Jazz Horn Performer, Jazz Composer, and Arranger*. D.A. thesis, Ball State University.

Schaughency, Steven. 1994. *The Original Compositions of Julius Watkins*. D.A. thesis, University of Northern Colorado.

Schuller, Gunther. 1989 (1968). *The Swing Era: The Development of Jazz, 1930–1945*. New York: Oxford University Press.

Strunk, Steven. 1988. 'Graas, John (J.).' In *The New Grove Dictionary of Jazz*, Vol. I, ed. Barry Kernfeld. London: Macmillan, 445.

Varner, Tom. 1988. 'Julius Watkins, Jazz Pioneer.' *The Horn Call* XIX(1) (October): 21–25.

Varner, Tom. 1989. 'Jazz Horn – Post-Julius Watkins.' *The Horn Call* XIX(2) (April): 43–45.

Discographical Reference

Davis, Miles. *Birth of the Cool*. Capitol Jazz CDP 7-92862-2. *1989*: USA.

Discography

Jazz: Big Bands/Jazz Orchestras

Amram, David. *Havana/New York*. Flying Fish FF 70057. *1978*: USA.

Best of the Big Bands: Claude Thornhill. Columbia CK 46152. *1990*: USA.

Carla Bley Band, The. *Musique Mécanique*. ECM Records 78118-23109-2. *1979*: USA.

Davis, Miles. *Porgy and Bess*. Columbia CK 40647. 1958; *1991*: USA.

Evans, Gil, and the Monday Night Orchestra. *Live at Sweet Basil. Farewell*. Evidence ECD 22031-2. *1992*: USA.

Ferguson, Maynard. *New Vintage*. Columbia 34971. *1977*: USA.

Johnson, J.J. *The Brass Orchestra*. Verve 314-537-321-2. *1997*: USA.

Jones, Quincy. *The Quincy Jones Big Band: Lausanne 1960*. Swiss Radio Days Jazz Series Vol. 1. TCB 02012. *1995*: Switzerland.

Kenton, Stan. *Cuban Fire*. Capitol Jazz CDP 7-96260-2. *1991*: USA.

Kenton, Stan. *Kenton/Wagner*. Creative World ST-1024. *1964*: USA.

Lester Bowie's Brass Fantasy. *Serious Fun*. DIW Records 834. *1989*: Japan.

Mancini, Henry. *The Blues and the Beat*. RCA-Victor LSP-2147. *1960*: USA.

Mangione, Chuck. *Chase the Clouds Away*. A&M Records SP-4518. *1975*: USA.

Robb McConnell and the Boss Brass: Volumes 1 and 2. Pausa Records PR 7140/7141. *1978*

Jazz: Combos led by or featuring horn players

Chancey, Vincent. *Next Mode*. DIW Records 914. *1996*: Japan.

Clark, John. *I Will*. Postcards POST 1016. *1997*: USA.

Four French Horns Plus Rhythm. Savoy Jazz SV-0214. *1993*: USA.

Graas, John. *Coup de Graas*. Mercury MG 36117. *1959*: USA.

Heath, Jimmy. *The Quota*. Riverside OJCCD-1871-2 (formerly RLP-9372). *1995*: USA.

Les Jazz Modes: The Rare Dawn Sessions. Biograph BCD 134-135. *1995*: USA.

Snedeker, Jeffrey. *First Times*. JS2. *1998*: USA.

Taylor, Mark. *QuietLand*. Mapleshade 05232. *1997*: USA.

Todd, Richard. *Rickter Scale*. GunMar GM3015CD. *1990*: USA.

Varner, Tom. *Martian Headache*. Soul Note 121286-2. *1997*: USA.

Varner, Tom. *The Window Up Above: American Songs 1770–1998*. New World Records 80552-2. *1998*: USA.

Watkins, Julius. *French Horns for My Lady*. Philips PHS 600-001. *1961*: USA.

Miscellaneous: Selected recordings in various styles led by or featuring horn players (*), or those that include prominent horn parts

Alan Parsons Project, The. *Tales of Mystery and Imagination: Edgar Allan Poe*. 20th Century Records T-508. *1976*: USA.

*Amram, David. *No More Walls*. Flying Fish CD FF 752. *1997*: USA.

*Amram, David, and Friends. *At Home/Around the World*. Flying Fish CD FF 094. *1996*: USA.

Beatles, The. *Yellow Submarine*. Apple SW 153. *1969*: USA. Reissue: Beatles, The. *Yellow Submarine*. Parlophone CDP 46445 2. *1987*: USA.

Emerson, Lake and Palmer. *Works: Volume 1*. Atlantic Records SD 2-7000. *1977*: USA.

George Shearing and *Barry Tuckwell Play the Music of Cole Porter. Concord Concerto CCD-42010. *1986*: USA.

Holmes, Rupert. *Partners in Crime*. Holmes Line Records INF 9020. *1979*: USA.

Jesus Christ Superstar: Original Soundtrack. MCA Records MCA2-10000. *1970*: USA.

Moody Blues, The. *Days of Future Passed*. Threshold 820006-2. *1967*: USA. Reissue: Moody Blues, The. *Days of Future Passed*. Polydor PGD/A&M 844767. *1997*: USA.

Moscow Art Trio, The. *Prayer*. JARO 4193-2. *1994*: Russia.

Paul Winter Consort, The. *Canyon*. Living Music Records LD 0006. *1985*: USA.

*Shilkloper, Arkady. *Hornology*. CD-RDM 608144. *1997*: Russia.

Wakeman, Rick. *Journey to the Center of the Earth*. A&M Records SP 3621. *1974*: USA.

*Watson, Joan. *Songs My Mother Taught Me*. Peros Music Studios PM 0211–2. n.d.: Canada.

Who, The. *Tommy: Original Soundtrack Recording*. Polydor PD 2-9502. *1975*: USA.

*Wiley, Ken. *Highbridge Park*. Natural Elements Records NE 2006. *1996*: USA.

JEFFREY L. SNEDEKER

Horn Section

A horn section, within the context of rock and pop music, denotes a backing group of brass and reed instruments added to the standard rhythm instruments of a band. The term derives from jazz argot and, specifically, the use of the word 'horn' to mean any wind instrument (and, in some instances, any instrument at all). As early as the 1920s, jazz musicians described playing together as 'blowing,' and instrumentalists were described as those who 'blew their horns,' the most able being said to 'get around on their horns.' Levet (1992) points out the sexual pun in this usage, since 'horn' is also jazz and blues slang for a male erection.

With the beginning of big band instrumentation and, in particular, the founding of large African-American orchestras in the early 1920s, the groups of brass and wind instruments were referred to by musicians and arrangers alike as 'sections,' so that most bands had trumpet, trombone and saxophone (or reed) sections. In the Western classical tradition, symphony orchestras included a section of French horns, but in popular music this instrumentation is relatively rare, and so the term 'horn section' began to be applied, from the 1930s onward, to denote the collective big band wind instruments, distinguishing these from the piano, guitar, bass, drums and percussion of the 'rhythm section.'

With the advent of rhythm and blues (R&B) in the 1940s, the term 'horn section' was applied to the smaller numbers of brass and reed instruments included in the lineups of bands like those of Louis Jordan, Earl Bostic, Bullmoose Jackson and 'Big' Joe Turner. In Jordan's Tympany Five, the principle is clearly exemplified: his own alto saxophone plus trumpet and tenor saxophone constituted the horn section, and the instruments were generally deployed to play unison riffs, either in the opening and closing ensembles of a piece, or to back up Jordan's vocals (to which end, by the mid-1950s, he often added an additional saxophone).

In soul music, the use of a horn section became *de rigueur* in bands such as those of James Brown. Brown's sections were well drilled, and the art of providing 'horn' backings was perfected by musicians like altoist Maceo Parker, who led Brown's horn section. Another significant section leader was trumpeter Pee Wee Moore, who moved on from Brown to work with a variety of soul and rock artists, including Van Morrison.

Although the singer and pianist Ray Charles generally led a big band, he and his arrangers tended to use the brass and reed sections in the manner of an R&B horn section, with a much greater emphasis on unison or close harmony riff ensembles than was heard in the more open writing of jazz arrangers of the time.

In rock music, horn sections have tended to follow the pattern established by R&B and soul artists. British rock bands such as the Kinks and the Rolling Stones have added horn sections for international touring, whereas various US bands, notably Blood, Sweat and Tears, and the Chicago Transit Authority (known as Chicago from 1970), made the horns an integral part of their group's sound.

Bibliography

Berendt, Joachim-Ernst. 1982 (1975). *The Jazz Book: From Ragtime to Fusion and Beyond*. Rev. ed. Westport, CT: Lawrence Hill. (First published Frankfurt am Main: Fischer Bücherei, 1953.)

Levet, Jean-Paul. 1992. *Talkin' That Talk: Le Langage du blues et du jazz* [Talkin' That Talk: The Language of Blues and Jazz]. Paris: Hatier.

ALYN SHIPTON

Mutes

Mutes are devices used to change the timbre or to lessen the volume of an instrument. Although mutes are made for many instruments, their primary use in popular music has been with trumpets and trombones. Wooden mutes for the trumpet date from the seventeenth century, but those used with modern instruments are typically made of aluminum, cardboard, plastic or rubber. They are usually wedged into the bell of the instrument or held in front of it. Early mutes raised the trumpet's pitch by half a step, but modern mutes are designed to be non-transposing.

Dozens of different types of mutes are commercially produced, each with its characteristic timbre. Straight mutes, which are infrequently used in popular music, are simple cones that give the instrument a softer, 'buzzy' sound. Cup mutes, often used by brass sections in jazz big bands, are essentially straight mutes with an attached cup that smooths the sound. Other variants include the bucket, the hat and the solotone. The Harmon, or 'wa-wa,' mute produces a soft and very buzzy sound; its adjustable stem, usually removed by jazz musicians, can be covered and uncovered by one hand to create a 'wa-wa' sound. The Harmon mute has long been associated with Miles Davis, who used it extensively and increased its popularity. The plunger mute – normally an actual bathroom plunger with the handle detached – has been deployed by many brass players; despite the Harmon mute's nickname, it is the plunger that has most often been used to create 'wa-wa' and other vocal sounds. Joe 'King' Oliver's solos with the plunger mute in the early 1920s were much admired and copied; this mute is also associated with the 'growlers' of Duke Ellington's bands, especially trumpeters Bubber Miley and Cootie Williams, and trombonist Joe 'Tricky Sam' Nanton. An assortment of mutes is an essential tool of the trade for brass players who work in jazz bands, pops orchestras, musical theater, film music and other recording contexts. When in need, musicians have been known to improvise mutes with bar glasses or other objects.

Discography

Davis, Miles. 'Flamenco Sketches.' *Kind of Blue*. Columbia CL 1355. *1959*: USA.

Ellington, Duke. 'Concerto for Cootie.' Victor 26598. 1940: USA.

Ellington, Duke. 'East St. Louis Toodle-o.' Vocalion 1064. 1926: USA.

King Oliver's Creole Jazz Band. 'Dipper Mouth Blues.' Gennett 5132. 1923: USA.

ROBERT WALSER

Sousaphone

A sousaphone is a variant of the tuba, pitched at Bb^3 or Eb and designed in the 1890s for marching bands by John Philip Sousa (1854–1932). The circular brass instrument is worn over the player's left shoulder. Its three (occasionally four) valves fall beneath the player's right hand. A detachable bell faces forward above the player's head. Since the 1960s, sousaphones have sometimes been made of fiberglass to reduce their weight. The instrument is strongly directional, and replaced the tuba in some 1920s jazz bands, since it projected toward the audience. It is used in military and civic marching bands, especially when popular music and parades coincide, such as during Mardi Gras in New Orleans.

Since the 1970s, the sousaphone has provided an essential basis for the revival and refashioning of street music, especially as practised by a new generation of New Orleans bands such as the Dirty Dozen Brass Band and the Rebirth Brass Band. The Dirty Dozen Brass Band distinguished itself from traditional New Orleans street bands by mixing the music of John Coltrane and Thelonious Monk, as well as influences from contemporary funk and soul music, into the street hymns and marches that made up the repertoires of traditional bands. The band has worked with artists such as Miles Davis, Elvis Costello and Branford Marsalis. Traditional bands have not always appreciated such innovations. 'We got a lot of static from . . . oldtimers . . . who said we weren't playing traditional music,' said Roger Lewis, a founding member of the Dirty Dozen Brass Band in a recent interview. However, 'the people loved it, because we were picking up the beat' (Rogovoy 2001). Players such as the Dirty Dozen Brass Band's Kirk Joseph have amplified the sousaphone to emulate many characteristics of the electric bass guitar.

Bibliography

Bevan, Clifford. 1978. *The Tuba Family*. London: Faber and Faber.

Rogovoy, Seth. 2001. 'Dirty Dozen Updates New Orleans Street-Band Music.' *Berkshire Eagle* (30 November). http://www.rogovoy.com/150.shtml

Schafer, William J. 1977. *Brass Bands and New Orleans Jazz*. Baton Rouge, LA: Louisiana State University Press.

Discography

Dirty Dozen Brass Band, The. *My Feet Can't Fail Me Now*. Concord Jazz 43005. *1984*: USA.

ALYN SHIPTON

Trombone

The European trombone (German *posaune*, Old French *sacqueboute*, Old English *sackbut*) has existed in similar form since 1551. Over the course of its existence, the instrument has evolved into five types marked by bore and bell sizes: the alto, tenor, symphonic tenor, bass and contrabass trombone. With the later development of mechanized brass, the trombone also developed a valve variant, consisting of a tenor trombone bell section and a section with three piston or rotary valves replacing the slide. All forms of the instrument except the valve version have been widely used in European art music ensembles. Popular music uses are dominated by the tenor slide and valve trombone, although the bass trombone has also developed distinctively in European brass bands and in big band jazz ensembles.

The worldwide spread of brass instruments and brass band music was a direct result of the diffusion and consolidation of European colonialism, particularly in the eighteenth and nineteenth centuries. This led to the presence of the trombone in military, church and other popular ensembles in various parts of Africa, Latin America and Asia-Pacific. In the years since, numerous fusion, hybrid and Creole forms of indigenized brass, percussion and brass, or bamboo and brass music have emerged in these regions. The trombone is part of many of these musical forms, although, as in the brass bands of Eastern and Western Europe, valve instruments (bass trumpet, baritone horn, euphonium) appear more often than the slide or valve trombone.

In the New World, the continuous and increasingly popular presence of the trombone in instrumental music is largely due to its role in jazz from the beginning of the twentieth century. Jazz has produced distinctive trombonists in every era and genre – performers who have cumulatively expanded the possibilities for trombone range, sound quality capabilities and performance speed in ways completely unanticipated and unimaginable in European art music. It is here, in the popular sphere, that the trombone has made its most expressive impact as an instrument with unique vocal and emotional qualities.

The 'tailgate' trombone style, critical to the sound of Dixieland collective improvisation, was developed substantially in the second and third decades of the twentieth century by Edward 'Kid' Ory and Jim Robinson. Jack Teagarden, Jimmy Harrison, Vic Dickenson, Benny Morton and Dicky Wells extended the melodic and rhythmic capabilities of the trombone in the 1920s and 1930s in the transition to swing. Band leader trombonists like Glenn Miller and Tommy Dorsey developed the trombone's role as a lyrical lead instrument with the big bands.

The timbral range and sound qualities of the trombone developed substantially in the vocal and muting techniques of Lawrence Brown, Quentin 'Butter' Jackson, Britt Woodman, Juan Tizol and Joe 'Tricky Sam' Nanton, all longstanding members of Duke Ellington's band and important interpreters of his music. As a soloist in the Count Basie band and other ensembles, Al Grey developed the art of the plunger mute to virtuoso standards on the trombone. The whisper and soft-tongue trombone solo work of Bill Harris while a member of the Woody Herman Herd further developed the instrument's vocal capabilities.

The bebop era in jazz produced players with remarkable tonguing speed, dexterity and ability to play the slide using alternate positions, thus overcoming limitations set by the natural overtone series of the instrument. Bop trombonists, with J.J. Johnson, Curtis Fuller, Slide Hampton, Kai Winding and Jimmy Knepper among the most recorded and admired, were able to keep up with stylistic developments largely associated with players of the trumpet and saxophone. The bop era also produced big band soloists like Carl Fontana, Frank Rosolino, Urbie Green and Phil Wilson, all of whom played in Stan Kenton's groups, and all of whom took the speed and register capabilities of the instrument to new heights.

In important avant-garde ensembles, like those of Archie Shepp or the Jazz Composer's Orchestra, as well as in groups of their own, trombonists Roswell Rudd and Grachan Moncur III restored and expanded many Dixieland and swing techniques in the new free jazz trombone vocabulary of the 1960s and 1970s. Albert Mangelsdorff developed the trombone's capability as a multiphonic instrument during the same period, mastering the technique of singing and playing notes simultaneously. These approaches were developed and extended by George Lewis and Ray Anderson in the ensembles of Anthony Braxton and in other groups. Other often-recorded consolidators of this avant-garde jazz trombone legacy include Craig Harris and Frank Lacy.

In addition to the trombone's success in every style and variety of jazz, the distinctiveness of a vernacular trombone voice developed in other African-American instrumental genres. Harlem's McCullough Sons of Thunder, an ensemble consisting of 10 trombones plus sousaphone and percussion, provides an example of the instrument's use in contemporary gospel music. Another example of the distinctiveness of a vernacular trombone voice is provided through the role of the trombone in the New Orleans brass band tradition. This role has developed continuously and is well represented in contemporary performance and recording by the Rebirth Brass Band, the Dirty Dozen Brass Band and DeJeans Olympia Brass Band. The most recent innovation in the New Orleans trombone tradition is the band Coolbone and its style, known as brass-hop, a fusion of hip-hop and vocal rap backed by a trombone-led horn section playing funk and New Orleans brass band riffs.

Distinctive creolized styles of New World African-Latin trombone playing also developed in dialog with jazz, rhythm and blues, and indigenous genres in the Caribbean. Among the most popular examples is Jamaican ska, whose best-known trombonists, Don Drummond and Rico Rodriguez, both performed with the prolific Skatalites. Distinctive styles of playing also developed in Cuba, especially with Generoso 'Tojo' Jiménez and Juan Pablo Torres, and in Brazil, with Raúl de Souza.

Although Latin trombone influence was introduced by Juan Tizol in Duke Ellington's band, trombones contributed most distinctively to the Afro-Latin jazz fusion sound that developed in New York City in the 1940s and 1950s, particularly under the guidance of big band arranger-leaders like Dizzy Gillespie, Chico O'Farrell, Tito Puente, Tito Rodriguez and Beny (sometimes spelled 'Benny') Moré. Trombonist Barry Rogers played a prominent role in the emergence of Eddie Palmieri's New York brass and percussion small group salsa sound in the 1960s, a role developed further in the 1990s by Conrad Herwig. In the 1970s, New York Puerto Rican trombonist and band leader Willie Colón developed the three-trombone sound in the fusion of Puerto Rican and Cuban salsa. That sound also developed in the Fania All Stars and Tito Puente's bands, with trombonists Reynaldo Jorge and Lewis Kahn. Trombonists Steve Turre and Angel 'Papo' Vasquez also played an important role in

the 1980s New York Latin jazz during the same time, in bands like Manny Oquendo's Conjunto Libre and Jerry Gonzalez's Fort Apache Band. Turre went on to develop a style fusing Afro-Cuban, Brazilian and bebop jazz forms featuring a combination ensemble of trombones and conch shells. The legacy of this trombone-rich New York Puerto Rican-Cuban salsa sound crossed over into mainstream pop in the late 1980s when it was incorporated into projects by David Byrne and Talking Heads.

Trombones were rarely heard in rock music during its formative years. By the late 1960s, some rock and electric blues bands regularly or occasionally augmented the core band with a horn section consisting of trumpet, trombone and saxophone. Well-known examples, where the trombone contributed distinctively, include Chicago, the Paul Butterfield Blues Band, Blood, Sweat and Tears, the Buddy Miles Express, Dreams, the Average White Band and Roomful of Blues.

In soul and funk, the trombone had a major presence in the horn section of James Brown's classic bands. By the early 1970s, trombonist Fred Wesley was featured both as a key soloist and as the arranger and leader of Brown's instrumental backup ensemble, the JBs. Wesley later played with other members of the JBs (Maceo Parker and Pee Wee Ellis), and with Bootsy Collins and George Clinton, in Parliament and Funkadelic. The trombone was also represented in forms of avant-garde and jazz-influenced rock by Bruce Fowler's work in some of Frank Zappa's 1970s and 1980s ensembles.

Discography

Anderson, Ray. *Big Band Record*. Gramavision R2 79497. *1994*: USA.

Brown, James. *Doing it to Death: The JB Story 1970–73*. Polydor 422-821232-2. *1984*: UK.

Byrne, David. *Rei Momo*. Luaka Bop/Sire 25990-2. *1989*: USA.

Colón, Willie. *Salsa's Bad Boy*. Caliente CD Charly 238. *1990*: UK.

Coolbone. *Brass-Hop*. Hollywood HR 62066-2. *1997*: USA.

Drummond, Don. *Don Drummond, Greatest Hits*. Treasure Isle TICD 004. *1989*: USA.

Frozen Brass: Africa and Latin America. PAN 2026CD. *1993*: The Netherlands.

Frozen Brass: Asia. PAN 2020CD. *1993*: The Netherlands.

Herwig, Conrad. *The Latin Side of John Coltrane*. Astor Place TCD 4003. *1996*: USA.

Ifi Palasa: Tongan Brass. PAN 2044CD. *1994*: The Netherlands.

Jazz-Club: Trombone. Verve CD840 040-2. *1989*: USA.

Johnson, J.J. *J.J. Johnson, The Trombone Master*. Columbia CK 44443. *1989*: USA.

New Orleans Brass Bands, Down Yonder. Rounder CD 2062. *1989*: USA.

Shepp, Archie. *Four for Trane.* Impulse IMPD 218. *1997*: USA.

Talking Heads. *Naked.* Fly/Sire 25654-2. *1988*: USA.

Turre, Steve. *Sanctified Shells.* Antilles 314 514 186-2. *1993*: USA.

STEVEN FELD

Trumpets and Cornets

Trumpets and cornets are the highest-pitched modern brass instruments, all of which are lip-vibrated aerophones – that is, instruments in which a vibration is produced within the air column by means of air blown between the player's lips, which are pressed against a mouthpiece. Trumpets in the broadest sense of the term – a length of (usually) metal tubing with a flared bell and a mouthpiece that is more or less cup-shaped – have existed for millennia. Upon the invention and application of valves early in the nineteenth century, brass instruments became fully chromatic, no longer limited to the notes of the overtone series. Most modern trumpets and cornets are pitched in B♭, with three piston valves and a tubing length of about 51" (130 cm). Orchestral players generally prefer to play C trumpets most of the time, with occasional use of instruments in B♮, D, E♮, F, G, and high A and B♮ (piccolo trumpets). However, in popular music, the standard B♮ trumpet has been almost universally used since the late 1920s.

Cornets are distinguished from trumpets by their more compact shape (tubing of the same length is differently folded), a more conical bore and a softer, mellower sound. Cornets were generally favored over trumpets in the nineteenth and early twentieth centuries; in certain respects more agile than trumpets, cornets are, however, capable of less brilliance, power and upper range. Louis Armstrong also remembered the difference as one of cultural prestige, at least in the second decade of the twentieth century:

> Of course in those early days we did not know very much about trumpets. We all played cornets. Only the big orchestras in the theaters had trumpet players in their brass sections. It is a funny thing, but at that time we all thought you had to be a music conservatory man or some kind of a big muckity-muck to play the trumpet. For years I would not even try to play the instrument. (Armstrong 1986, 213–14)

Armstrong and most other jazz players switched from cornet to trumpet in the following decade, but the brilliant and powerful style of much jazz trumpeting can sometimes make it difficult to discern by ear whether a trumpet or cornet is being played on a given recording. The flügelhorn, a similar instrument with a larger bell, deeper mouthpiece and correspondingly darker sound, was used in jazz from the 1930s, and especially after Miles Davis popularized it in the 1950s. Noted players of the flügelhorn include Clark Terry and Art Farmer. Most jazz trumpeters now double on it at least occasionally.

There have arguably been four great styles of trumpet virtuosity: the valveless, high-range 'clarino' playing of eighteenth-century Europe; the cornet soloists of the late nineteenth and early twentieth centuries; modern orchestral and concert trumpeting; and twentieth-century jazz and jazz-influenced popular genres. The second category includes virtuosos such as Herbert L. Clarke, who was for a time featured with John Philip Sousa's immensely popular band. This was the peak of a tradition of trumpet use by military and civic bands that continued throughout the nineteenth and twentieth centuries. However, it is the last of these categories that is of primary importance to popular music, since twentieth-century players of jazz and other popular music reinvented the trumpet, extending its power, lyricism, agility and expressive potential. The sheer volume produced by the trumpet facilitated its leadership role within a host of modern musical styles, and trumpet mutes allowed a great range of timbres.

Early jazz cornet players of note include band leader Joe 'King' Oliver, whose bluesy solos and use of mutes were widely imitated, as well as the legendary Buddy Bolden (who never recorded) and Freddie Keppard. The most influential cornet and trumpet player of this era, and arguably of the entire century, was Louis Armstrong. He set new standards for the instrument in terms of range, endurance, brilliance and power. His sense of rhetoric, swing and timing, together with his thrilling imagination and technical precision, brought him fame as the first great jazz soloist and affected virtually all jazz musicians who followed him. Armstrong's white contemporary, Bix Beiderbecke, was an imaginative soloist in a restrained, cooler style; appropriately, he continued to use the cornet throughout his career.

The swing era was marked by saxophonists' challenges to the trumpet's dominance, but trumpeters continued to be central to popular music both as soloists and as members of sections of up to five players. The 'growlers' of Duke Ellington's band – trumpeters Bubber Miley and Cootie Williams, as well as trombonist Joe 'Tricky Sam' Nanton – developed a rough, expressive manner of playing that Ellington used for what he called 'jungle' music. Roy Eldridge continued to develop the brilliant approach of Armstrong, and the trumpet's technical possibilities began to rival those of the saxophone. These were glory days for the trumpet: players such as Armstrong and Harry James were stars of mainstream popular culture – a phenomenon that would not really occur again, except for such anomalous successes as Eddie Calvert or Herb Alpert and the Tijuana Brass in the 1960s, or flügelhorn player Chuck Mangione in the late 1970s.

With the birth of bebop in the 1940s, trumpeters were among the musicians who strove to set new speed records for instrumental virtuosity and musical imagination. Foremost among them was Dizzy Gillespie, whose fantastic agility and inventiveness gained him recognition as the co-founder (with alto saxophonist Charlie Parker) of bebop. After Gillespie came many bebop trumpet virtuosos, including Kenny Dorham, Fats Navarro, Clifford Brown and Art Farmer. Some players of the 1940s and 1950s, notably Cat Anderson and Maynard Ferguson, continued to stretch the upper range of the trumpet until they had surpassed even the extraordinary demands of late eighteenth-century practises.

The most artistically restless musician in jazz, Miles Davis, started as a bebop trumpeter but went on to pioneer cool jazz, hard bop and jazz fusion; his last album even mixed jazz with hip-hop. Davis made use of a variety of risky techniques – pressing the valves down only halfway, bending notes, using a great range of timbres and articulations and, later, electronic effects such as echo units and wah-wah pedals – in order to articulate musical sensibilities and models of virtuosity that were quite distant from the beboppers' fiery technique (Walser 1993). Free jazz trumpeters pushed even further in this direction. Don Cherry used a 'pocket trumpet' (of normal length but tightly coiled), which contributed to his strained sound, flexible sense of intonation and seemingly unstable technique. Don Ellis developed a four-valved trumpet that could play quarter tones, reflecting Eastern European influences that also fueled odd-meter improvisations; he also distorted his tone electronically. Players such as Freddie Hubbard went in the opposite direction, cultivating the technical perfection of Gillespie and his followers, but with a warmer, fuller sound than Gillespie used.

Wynton Marsalis, the most popular and acclaimed jazz musician of his generation, came to fame as a trumpeter and band leader during the 1980s. Marsalis's impressive technique and improvisational facility helped him become a respected spokesperson for jazz, and he created new institutional berths for the music. Other influential players of the late twentieth century included Tom Harrell and Cuban trumpeter Arturo Sandoval, both of whom often used the flügelhorn.

The trumpet's virtuosic potential was most effectively exploited and extended in the twentieth century by jazz musicians. Thus, nearly all the innovative, influential players mentioned above were American; most were African American. But their influence has been global, as the trumpet has been an important element not only of non-US jazz, but also of a great variety of popular styles worldwide. From *banda* and other Mexican genres, with their brilliant trumpet duets, to Chinese political pop songs featuring former orchestral trumpeter Cui Jian, from jazz-influenced Cuban popular music to the traditional music of Afghanistan, from Polish-American polka bands to jazz ensembles in schools and pops orchestras in parks, from jazz-rock fusions to ska and swing revivals – in all these, the trumpet has maintained a significant presence in a musical landscape dominated by electronic sounds.

Bibliography

Armstrong, Louis. 1986 (1954). *Satchmo: My Life in New Orleans*. New York: Da Capo.

Bate, Philip. 1978. *The Trumpet and Trombone*. 2nd ed. New York: W.W. Norton.

Davis, Miles, with Quincey Troupe. 1989. *Miles: The Autobiography*. New York: Simon and Schuster.

Feather, Leonard. 1957. 'The Trumpet.' In Leonard Feather, *The Book of Jazz: A Guide to the Entire Field*. New York: Horizon Press, 72–78.

McCarthy, Albert J. 1945. *The Trumpet in Jazz*. London: The Citizen Press.

Tarr, Edward. 1988. *The Trumpet*. Portland, OR: Amadeus Press. (Translation, by S.E. Plank and Edward Tarr, of Edward Tarr, *Die Trompete* (Bern: Hallwag AG, 1977).)

Walser, Robert. 1993. 'Out of Notes: Signification, Interpretation, and the Problem of Miles Davis.' *Musical Quarterly* 77(2) (Summer): 343–65.

Discography

Armstrong, Louis. *Portrait of the Artist as a Young Man, 1923–1934*. Columbia Legacy 57176. *1994*: USA.

Clarke, Herbert L. *Cornet Soloist of the Sousa Band: Complete Collection*. Crystal 450. *1996*: USA.

Davis, Miles. *Kind of Blue*. Columbia CL 1355. *1959*: USA.

King Oliver's Creole Jazz Band. 'Dipper Mouth Blues.' Gennett 5132. 1923: USA.

Retka, Gene, and the Cousins. *High Steppin' Polkas*. Aleatoric A-3101. *1979*: USA.

Ustad Nangialai. 'Trumpet.' Sitara Melodies SM-110. n.d.: India.

ROBERT WALSER

Tuba

The tuba is basically a valved bugle, a brass instrument used as a bass or contrabass in orchestras, jazz bands, brass bands, military bands and marching bands. Held on the player's lap, it is a wide-bored instrument, with a flared bell pointing upward. The first instrument was a five-valve bass tuba, introduced in the German states in 1835. Adopted by bands and orchestras in the German states in the mid-nineteenth century, tubas were accepted more slowly in other countries. While English bands accepted the tuba around the middle of the nineteenth century, for example, English and French symphony orchestras replaced the tuba's predecessor, the ophicleide, with the tuba only toward the end of the century.

The term 'tuba' has been applied to instruments of various shapes and sizes. Other members of the tuba family are the euphonium, the bombardon, the sousaphone and the helicon. This group of instruments together is known generally as 'brass bass.' The sousaphone has been an important military instrument, is found most often in marching bands, and has played an important role since the 1970s in the revival of New Orleans street music. The standard brass band format established for contests in Britain during the late nineteenth century contained two euphoniums and four basses of two different sizes.

The symphony orchestra tuba is pitched at C^2, the brass or jazz instrument generally at $B\flat^3$. In 1920s jazz, the tuba was interchangeable with the double bass, but it later took on a more independent role, following Bill Barber's work in Miles Davis's *Birth of the Cool* nonet (1949–50). Jazz musicians such as Don Butterfield, Ray Draper and Howard Johnson extended the instrument's solo possibilities in jazz; Johnson also experimented with tuba ensembles. In the 1990s, Marc Steckar's French ensemble Tubapack continued this development. At the same time, jazz soloists such as the British player Orin Marshall introduced electronic effects into the tuba's solo vocabulary.

The tuba has occasionally taken on a novelty role in popular music, as in George Kleinsinger's and Paul Tripp's children's song, 'Tubby the Tuba.'

Bibliography

Berendt, Joachim E. 1983. *The Jazz Book: From New Orleans to Jazz Rock and Beyond.* 5th ed. London: Granada Publishing.

Bevan, Clifford. 1978. *The Tuba Family.* London: Faber and Faber.

Laplace, Michel. 1986. 'Les tubas dans le jazz et les musiques populaires' [Tubas in Jazz and Popular Musics]. *Brass Bulletin* 56: 18.

Laplace, Michel. 1987. 'Les tubas dans le jazz et les musiques populaires' [Tubas in Jazz and Popular Musics]. *Brass Bulletin* 57: 84.

Richard, Marc. 1988. 'Tuba' (incl. discography of tuba in jazz). In *Dictionnaire du Jazz* [Dictionary of Jazz], ed. Philippe Carles, Andre Clergeat and Jean-Louis Comolli. Paris: Robert Laffont.

Discographical References

Davis, Miles. *Birth of the Cool*. Capitol C21K 92862. 1949–50: USA.

Kaye, Danny. 'Tubby the Tuba.' *Entertainer Extraordinary 1941–1947*. ASV/Living Era 5270. *1998*: USA.

ALYN SHIPTON

b. Reeds and Woodwinds

Bagpipes (British Isles)

Introduction

The bagpipes of the British Isles take several forms, and are used to perform a range of distinctive music. The predominant instrument is the *Piòb Mhór*, or Great Highland Bagpipe, which had become established in the Gaelic-speaking part of Scotland by the late sixteenth century, and was later adopted as the principal instrument of the Scottish regiments in the British Army. By the time of the Crimean War (1853–56), regimental pipe bands were being formed, and the combination of bagpipes with snare, bass and tenor drums has proved the model for a worldwide pipe band movement spanning several continents and involving many thousands of participants.

The Highland Bagpipe

The Highland bagpipe is a mouth-blown instrument. Air is fed by way of a non-return valve into a bag (traditionally made from sheepskin or cowhide, but increasingly from synthetic materials such as Gore-Tex), and from there to a set of three drones and a chanter. The chanter is similar to the medieval shawm, conically bored, with a double reed of Spanish cane (*Arundo donax*) and a fixed scale of nine notes. The tone is characteristically strident, and is well suited to the instrument's early function on the dance floor, parade ground and battlefield. The drones use single reeds, with two tenors sounding an octave below the keynote of $b\flat^1$, and a bass two octaves below the keynote.

Through almost four centuries of unbroken tradition, Highland pipers have evolved an intricate system of embellishment on the chanter, using complex sequences of grace notes to add rhythm and texture to the melodies. This is at its most advanced in the 'classical' tradition of *Ceòl Mór* (great music), in which melodies are built from a ground (*ùrlar*), through movements of increasing complexity to a final 'crowning' movement in the *crunludh*, a rippling sequence of eight grace notes built on each melody note. Over 400 pieces exist in this early repertoire, which peaked in the years leading up to the Jacobite risings of 1715 and 1745, and flourished in the hands of noted exponents such as the MacCrimmons and MacArthurs in Skye, and the Macgregors and Cummyngs in the Central Highlands.

The Piobaireachd Society (established in 1903) has ensured continued interest in *Ceòl Mór*, but of much more enduring popular appeal has been the light music or *Ceòl Beag* repertoire comprising traditional dance melodies (jigs, strathspeys and reels) and more recent formats such as marches and hornpipes.

Marches evolved with the introduction of properly paved roads in the early nineteenth century, and were initially closely associated with the army and the rapid movement of marching troops (hence the term 'quickstep,' and titles such as 'The 72nd Highlanders' Farewell to Aberdeen'). From the 1820s, piping competitions encouraged the development of a distinctive repertoire, and a 'march, strathspey and reel' format evolved that placed heavy emphasis on precision of technique and less on the free-flowing styles traditionally associated with dance music. Competitions have remained a core element of the tradition, and most of the famous exponents of the Highland bagpipe (such as John Ban Mackenzie, Donald Cameron, George S. MacLennan and Donald Macleod) have been successful competitors.

In 1930, the Scottish Pipe Band Association was established to help regulate the rapidly growing pipe band movement, and to run a series of major pipe band competitions that culminated in the World Pipe Band Championships held each August in Scotland. Typically, a band comprises a pipe corps of 10–15 pipers, normally playing in unison, with a drum corps featuring bass and tenor drums, and up to eight snare drummers. The use of elaborate uniforms and the encouragement of military deportment bear witness to the origins of pipe bands in the British Army, and were established features by the end of World War I, when a large number of army pipers returned to civilian life, bringing with them an ingrained sense of military decorum.

At the end of the twentieth century, the Scottish Pipe Band Association had over 400 member bands in the United Kingdom, with countless others affiliated worldwide through 15 independent associations; world champions had emerged from Australia, Canada and Ireland, as well as from Scotland. Aside from the evident social aspects of the pipe band movement, the bands have been a focus for genuine musical innovation, encouraging the playing of new and borrowed tune types such as hornpipes and mazurkas, and allowing a degree of experimentation with harmonies, albeit within the restrictions imposed by the nine-note scale.

Since the 1980s, Highland bagpipes have been increasingly incorporated into Scottish folk groups, usually in combination with fiddles, flutes, guitars, harps, bouzoukis and keyboards. Scottish fiddlers frequently tune their instruments up a semitone in order to play comfortably with the pipes, and discrepancies in volume are ironed out through judicious use of public-address systems. Among the pioneering groups in this respect have been the Tannahill Weavers, Ossian, and the Battlefield Band, and their efforts have done much to popularize pipe tunes among the wider traditional music community. A new generation of musicians has taken the pipes into ever more experimental fields, the work of Martyn Bennett best epitomizing the happy congress of traditional piping with modern electronic forms.

The 'Cauld Wind' Tradition

Scotland's lesser-known piping tradition involves much smaller and quieter instruments, which are usually cylindrically bored and are inflated not by mouth but by the use of bellows strapped under the arm. This is a dry-air system (hence the term 'cauld wind'), which means that reeds are less affected by moisture and therefore last longer.

Although bellows pipes were used throughout the country, they were particularly associated with the towns and burghs of Lowland Scotland and the border region with England. 'Town pipers' were a colorful and characteristic feature of border life, playing reveille and curfew for the townsfolk and featuring prominently on fair and feast days. Pipers such as Habbie Simpson in Kilbarchan and John Anderson in Kelso became the stuff of local legend, but, sadly, by the 1800s the tradition was in decline, and few performers or instruments survived into the twentieth century.

A major revival in Scottish bellows pipes started in the early 1980s, built initially on the activities of the Lowland and Border Pipers' Society. Pipe makers have developed a number of new and sweet-sounding instruments, which play in different keys, and are particularly attractive to those Highland pipers who have a taste for a different sound but are unwilling to adapt to the radically different fingering techniques of Northumbrian and *Uilleann* piping.

Initial efforts focused on the resuscitation of the distinctive border pipe repertoire, but as the instrument became more commonplace, pipers proved ever more adaptable and eclectic in taste. Previous sharp divides between 'folk musicians' and 'pipers' became blurred, and it has become common to hear tunes borrowed and adapted from the Irish, Breton, Asturian and Galician traditions, as well as those reimported from vibrant outposts of the Scottish musical community such as Cape Breton in Canada.

Northumbrian Smallpipes

Whereas the Scottish smallpipe tradition withered in the nineteenth century, across the border in Northumberland the indigenous piping tradition flourished. Both Northumbrian and Scottish smallpipes share common ancestry in a small bellows-blown instrument, with drones fitted into the bag by way of a single stock (known as a 'common' stock), and an open-ended, cylindrically bored chanter, usually pitched in f.

Where the Northumbrian pipe evolved differently from its Scottish cousin was in the implementation of a system of 'closed' fingering (a single finger raised from the chanter produces the desired note), and in the blocking of the end of the chanter. Both differences resulted in a staccato style of playing, and permitted the addition of a number of keys to extend the melodic range. Early pioneers in this regard were John Peacock and John Dunn in Newcastle (ca. 1805), and the father-and-son team of Robert and James Reid in North Shields, who eventually devised a 17-key chanter that produced a full chromatic scale from b to b^2.

The drones also evolved, and many modern sets have four drones, allowing the piper to play in either f or g (the latter being more common for group work); a typical tuning arrangement is g, d^1 and g^1 against the g chanter.

In practise, most pipers favor a simple four- or seven-key chanter system, which allows them to tackle a broad repertoire of dance tunes, many of them fiddle compositions, as well as melodies composed specifically for the pipes. Noted figures in the Northumbrian tradition, such as Jack Armstrong, Tom Clough, Billy Pigg and Joe Hutton, were prolific composers as well as master pipers, and carried on their craft against a backdrop of hard manual work in the collieries and on the upland farms.

The early part of the twentieth century saw a decline in the fortunes of Northumbrian piping, but this trend has been reversed as a result of the efforts of the Northumbrian Pipers Society (established in 1928) and a huge increase in the availability of well-made instruments, produced by specialist Northumbrian pipe makers. The Dukes of Northumberland have employed a personal piper since the 1750s, and the sweet-toned smallpipe has become widely admired, attracting a coterie of high-profile, virtuoso performers, of whom Kathryn Tickell and Pauline Cato are among the best known.

English Revival

Since the 1980s, a number of English instrument makers have turned their attention to early medieval English bagpipes, widely depicted in psalters and wood carvings from the fourteenth to the seventeenth centuries. These instruments represent a pan-European bagpipe type of mouth-blown, single-drone instrument with conically bored chanters and belled drone tops. The tradition of playing these instruments in England had been entirely eradicated, and their revival has involved a great deal of research and ingenuity. Results, however, have been excellent, and the movement has gone hand in hand with renewed interest in the medieval hurdy-gurdy or *vielle*.

Among the leading makers have been Jonathan Swayne (who has played his own instruments in the groups Blowzabella and Moebius), and Julian Goodacre, whose range of bagpipes includes a double-chanter Cornish pipe (based on a sixteenth-century model), and a Leicestershire smallpipe. Performers initially looked to central France for musical inspiration, but they have turned their attention increasingly to composing new material and to researching an authentic English repertoire. Key players in this regard have been brothers John and Peter Goodacre, and members of the Bagpipe Society.

The Irish *Uilleann* Pipe

Although often considered the quintessential Irish instrument, the *Uilleann* pipe was in fact a relative latecomer to Ireland, and in its early years was most commonly associated with the drawing rooms and concert stages of the Anglo-Irish Establishment.

This is the most sophisticated of bagpipes. It appears to have evolved in the mid- to late 1700s through experimentation with preexisting forms of bellows-blown instruments, and by way of a hybrid form, found in both Scotland and Ireland, known as the Pastoral pipe (now defunct). The name '*Uilleann*' (or elbow) pipe has come to widely replace the original term 'Union' pipe.

The chanter is cylindrically bored, the modern instrument being capable of a two-octave range from d to d^2 through overblowing into the top octave. (The piper does this by building up air pressure by means of briefly stopping the foot of the chanter on the knee, or on a 'popping pad' attached to the leg.) The bag is inflated by a bellows, and three drones tuned in octaves are tied into the bag by way of a common stock.

An additional feature found in the more deluxe *Uilleann* pipes is a set of 'regulators' – three or four additional drones, stopped at the end and fitted with keys. These are tied into the bag at an angle to sit comfortably over the knees of the seated player. The piper plays the keys, arranged in groups, with the wrist, while *at the same time* fingering the chanter. The effect is one of sustained chords or vamping over the melody line, but it is extremely difficult to achieve, and is now rarely heard.

As in Scotland, there is a degree of 'performance art' in the Irish pipe repertoire, with sustained pieces such as 'The Fox Chase' making full use of the many voices of the chanter and regulators, and providing a fitting vehicle for past masters such as Leo Rowsome from Ballintore, Willie Clancy from Miltown Malbay and Séamus

Ennis from Finglas. There has also been a fine tradition of traveling pipers, epitomized by Johnny and Felix Doran and, more recently, by Finbar Furey. Fingering styles are less rigidly defined than in the Scottish and Northumbrian traditions and, while modern sets are commonly pitched in d, which is loud, bright and well suited to group work, many soloists have continued to prefer the older, softer-toned chanters pitched in c, b or b♭.

Na Píobairí Uilleann was formed in 1968 under the chairmanship of Breandán Breathnach to foster the art of Irish piping, and it has proved highly influential. The *Uilleann* pipe has come to occupy a prized place in groundbreaking Irish groups such as Planxty, the Bothy Band and Moving Hearts, and the pipers involved (Liam O'Flynn, Paddy Keenan and Davy Spillane) have gone on to work in prestigious projects ranging from Michael O'Sullivan's *Brendan Voyage* to *Riverdance*. The plangent, keening tones of the *Uilleann* pipe played in the upper register have made it a great favorite with Hollywood film directors, and, from the outset, the sheer adaptability of the instrument has suited it to a wide variety of uses, from the concert stage to the pub session.

Bibliography

Cannon, Roderick. 1980. *A Bibliography of Bagpipe Music.* Edinburgh: John Donald.

Cheape, Hugh. 1999. *The Book of the Bagpipe.* Belfast: Appletree Press.

Donaldson, William. 2000. *The Highland Pipe and Scottish Society, 1750–1950.* East Lothian: Tuckwell Press.

Gibson, John. 1998. *Traditional Gaelic Bagpiping, 1745–1945.* Montréal: McGill-Queen's University Press.

MacKenzie, Bridget. 1998. *Piping Traditions of the North of Scotland.* Edinburgh: John Donald.

Vallely, Fintan, ed. 1999. *The Companion to Irish Traditional Music.* Cork: Cork University Press.

Young, Wilson, and Chatto, Allan. 1999. *One Hundred Years of Pipe Band Drumming.* Glasgow: W. Young and A. Chatto.

Discographical References

Dysart and Dundonald Pipe Band, The. 'The 72nd Highlanders' Farewell to Aberdeen.' *Supreme Champions/Dysart and Dundonald Pipe Band.* Lismor LILP 5019. *1975*: UK.

Ennis, Seamús. 'The Fox Chase.' *The Best of Irish Piping: The Pure Drop and The Fox Chase* (2-CD set). Tara TaraCD 10029. *1978*: Ireland.

Discography

Scottish

Grand Concert of Scottish Piping. Greentrax CDTRAX 110. *1996*: UK.

MacDonald, Angus. *A'Sireadh Spòrs.* Temple COMD 2043. *1990*: UK.

McCallum, William. *The World's Greatest Pipers, Vol. 14.* Lismor LCOM 5284. *2000*: UK.

Morrison, Fred. *The Sound of the Sun.* KRL CDLDL 1284. *1999*: UK.

Simon Fraser University Pipe Band, The. *Live at Carnegie Hall.* Lismor LCOM 8019. *1999*: UK.

World Pipe Band Championships 2000. Monarch CDMON 841. *2000*: UK.

Irish

Ennis, Seamús. *The Return from Fingal.* RTE RTECD 199. *1997*: Ireland.

O'Brien, Mick. *May Morning Dew.* ACM ACMCD 101. *1999*: Ireland.

O'Flynn, Liam. *The Piper's Call.* Tara TARACD 3037. *1998*: Ireland.

Spillane, Davy. *Atlantic Bridge.* Tara TARACD 3019. n.d.: Ireland.

Northumbrian

Cato, Pauline, and McConville, Tom. *The Surprise.* Tomcat TCCD 02. 1999: UK.

Northumberland Rant. Smithsonian Folkways SFWCD 40473. *1999*: USA.

Tickell, Kathryn. *Debateable Lands.* Park PRKCD 50. *1999*: UK.

English

Goodacre Brothers, The. *Bag Up Yer Troubles.* White House WHCD02. *1997*: UK.

Moebius. *August.* Rocke ROCCD1. *1993*: UK.

IAIN MACINNES

Clarinet

The clarinet is a single-reed woodwind instrument descended from the chalumeau (an instrument that equates in range and tone to the lowest register of the clarinet) which gained its modern form in stages, from the instrument invented in or around 1700 by Johann Christian Denner. Various models emerged during the late eighteenth and the nineteenth centuries, the most widespread being the instrument designed by Hyacinthe Klosé around 1839. This instrument was based on Theobald Boehm's modifications to the flute, which had given that instrument a better tonal quality. Despite the defining work of Klosé, these instruments have always been referred to as 'Boehm' clarinets. Another design emerged shortly after Klosé's model, during the 1840s, created by the Belgian instrument maker Eugène Albert. Albert clarinets have also been in wide circulation and have been particularly favored by players from Eastern Europe and New Orleans. Albert and Boehm clarinets differ in the degree to which their key systems are articulated and on substantial points of tone hole and bore scaling; their sound can be very different, Albert clarinets having a reedier and harsher sound.

Early instruments were made from boxwood, but most clarinets in the twenty-first century are made from granadilla wood, with metal rings at the joints and nickel-plated silver keys. Other materials occasionally used for the instrument's main cylinder include ebonite (hardened rubber), black or colored plastic, glass and metal.

Clarinets are made in a number of voices (and therefore sizes), from contrabass (almost 10 feet of coiled metal) to sopranino (a straight 18″ (45 cm)), and are pitched in different keys. The most common instrument is the soprano in B♭ (its closest relation, in A, being confined exclusively to classical orchestral and chamber music), but bass clarinets, also in B♭, and the sopranino in E♭ are regularly encountered in jazz. A compass of almost four complete octaves in all voices and a dynamic range from almost inaudible pianissimo to trumpet-like fortissimo, along with a tonal palette from velvet-soft to steel-hard, makes the clarinet one of the most expressive instruments. It is able to blend with an ensemble as well as stand out as a solo voice. Moreover, the relatively straightforward layout of the keys is conducive to fast playing, and this makes the clarinet an ideal vehicle for instrumental virtuosity, enabling a player to switch rapidly between octaves, slide between notes (glissando) and negotiate complex phrases built on arpeggios, scales and grace notes. The character of any particular instrument may be varied by the use of different reed strengths, different ligatures (a ligature being the band that holds the reed in place, which may be made from metal, plastic, fabric or other materials) and mouthpiece calibration (the gap between reed and mouthpiece). Vibrato, particularly if applied at the mouthpiece, can be extreme, and a wide range of effects can also be obtained by varying the embouchure and employing alternative fingerings. Early white jazz clarinet players used these tricks to imitate farm animal sounds (barnyard hokum being a popular ingredient in recordings around 1917–23), while klezmer musicians were able to match the slides and inflections of fiddles, with which they were usually paired. In the second half of the twentieth century, various players extended these unorthodox capabilities by experimenting with multiphonics (the ability to play more than one note simultaneously). While there are many examples of multiphonics in post-1950 classical music, jazz and improvised music, none can be discerned in any form of popular music, where other instruments, such as the electric guitar, are better equipped to deliver the kinds of amplified distortions that musicians and audiences have demanded.

Taking all the clarinet's musical qualities into account, it is not surprising that no two players of the instrument have ever sounded the same. To appreciate this individuality one needs only to listen to the clarinet player at various stages of the career of the Duke Ellington Orchestra: for instance, the New Orleans-born Barney Bigard, who specialized in long glissandi and sweeping runs, compared with Jimmy Hamilton, whose smooth, almost vibratoless tone typified mid-twentieth-century taste. Or one can compare Pee Wee Russell's recordings, replete with unorthodox timbres (growls, slow vibrato, unpredictable rhythmic attack and flow), with the recordings of a swing player such as Artie Shaw, with their uniform artistry based on regular quaver patterns. All these qualities and characters were in circulation during the clarinet's brief tenure at the top of the popular music pyramid – a potent legacy that was promptly passed on to jazz alto and tenor saxophone playing. (The similarities between clarinets and saxophones allow many instrumentalists to double on clarinet and saxophone without difficulty.)

It would be wrong to believe, as some do, that, because the Albert clarinet was favored by New Orleans players, it is the authentic voice of early jazz. The Albert clarinet system is also known as the 'simple' system, but many exponents have claimed that the instrument is harder to play. Paul Barnes, interviewed for *Melody Maker* in 1973 by Max Jones, explained that the main reason for the predominance of Albert clarinets among New Orleans musicians was that these clarinets were French and New Orleans was a French town; Boehm clarinets were German. Some musicians remained faithful to their Albert instruments; others switched later to Boehm. Albert players included Sidney Bechet, Larry Shields, Barney Bigard, Omer Simeon and Edmond Hall, while early (i.e., pre-World War II) jazz players who favored Boehm clarinets included Albert Nicholas, Pee Wee Russell, Frank Teschemacher, Benny Goodman, Artie Shaw and Woody Herman. Almost all post-1945 players play Boehm instruments, although some deliberately favor unorthodox models: the British jazz musician Tony Coe and the klezmer specialist Merlin Shepherd, for example, regularly perform on the brighter- and reedier-sounding soprano clarinet in C – a relic of the nineteenth-century symphony and opera orchestra, and also, significantly, the instrument on which Sidney Bechet learned to play. (Very young beginners are able to play a modern version of the C clarinet made of plastic.)

Early geographical determinants apart, the main point to understand is that in an expressive music like jazz, where distinctive tone and timbre are quintessential, the player may choose from a wide variety of configurations, each with its own strengths and weaknesses. Such refinements are academic when it comes to the amplified wall of sound that typifies Western popular music after the 1950s. The need to generate more sound and punch in popular music (and modern jazz) was certainly one of the factors that led musicians to switch to saxophone or that led groups and arrangers to jettison reed instruments altogether.

The landmarks that chart the clarinet's evolution in popular music can be seen to result from a timely combination of personal musical development (along with the availability of inspirational teachers), arranging skills (usually by people other than the clarinet player) and shifts in popular taste, although some popular traditions, such as New Orleans or Dixieland jazz and klezmer, have remained untouched by fashion.

In late eighteenth-century urban Europe, wind band consorts of the type known as *Harmonie* in Germany and Austria were very popular. The repertoire of these ensembles consisted of transcriptions from operas, operettas, lieder, military music, popular dances and songs. The North American equivalent was the civic concert band, in which a massed section of clarinets replaced the first and second violins of the symphony orchestra. Clarinets became an integral part of the marching band ensembles in parades and sporting events. By the later nineteenth century, the clarinet had joined the violin and guitar as a favorite instrument in domestic or parlor music, a major outlet for popular music until World War II. In the professional and semiprofessional orchestras of the European countryside, the clarinet gradually came to replace, or supplement, the role fulfilled by other wind instruments, such as the bagpipe, the *tarogato*, the *zournás* and the pan flute. In this way, the sound of the clarinet became a characteristic element of Eastern European Gypsy and folk ensembles providing accompaniment at social occasions such as weddings, most notably in klezmer music. The front line of these groups came to consist of at least one violin and one clarinet, sharing melody and counterpoint.

Clarinets were present in the early ragtime, novelty and dance orchestra performances and recordings of the first two decades of the twentieth century, but they were only featured as solo instruments on record (classical orchestral recordings apart) toward the end of World War I. A typical instrumental ragtime performance consisted of syncopated melodies exchanged between violin and clarinet, the rhythmic impetus being provided by a banjo. There are no improvised solos on these pre-jazz recordings. An idea of how the clarinet may have sounded in popular music at that time can be obtained by listening to the recordings of Ted Lewis from 1919 onward, which consist mostly of novelty and show tunes. Not regarded as the most accomplished of clarinet players, Ted Lewis was nevertheless an early influence on the young Benny Goodman and was, during the 1920s, one of Columbia's bestselling artists.

The first recorded jazz clarinet solo break was made in February 1917 by Larry Shields on 'Livery Stable Blues' with the Original Dixieland Jazz Band (ODJB). This is an example of barnyard hokum, as described earlier. A better idea of his musicianship (and also of how far the style of improvised solos had already been developed away from the recording studio) can be heard in the ODJB's recording of 'St. Louis Blues,' made on 25 May 1921, in which Shields improvises two 12-bar choruses. The ODJB was only briefly popular, its most representative recordings being released between 1917 and 1921, but it had many imitators.

Meanwhile, the North American Jewish community had two competing stars on clarinet, Naftule Brandwein and Dave Tarras. Both were recorded regularly from the early 1920s. Brandwein typified the klezmer tradition in that he never learned to read music, but his fiery and rugged solos are underpinned by an awesome technical ability. The playing of Tarras is more refined, a product of his training in a Tsarist military band before he emigrated. Tarras bequeathed his style (and his instruments) to Andy Statman, who was largely responsible for the late 1970s revival of klezmer. One of the reasons why clarinets rather than violins became more associated with recorded klezmer was that the pre-electric (or acoustic) method of recording was able to pick up the sound of the clarinet much better than that of the solo violin. The clarinet, in the hands of a master such as Tarras, was also able to emulate the range and inflections (extravagant slurs) of the violin.

For three full decades, from 1917 until around 1946, clarinets were ubiquitous and a principal voice in popular music that was dominated by instrumental dance music, with or without a jazz ingredient. One person in particular may have been responsible for this: the Victor Talking Machine Company's young musical director during the 1920s, Nat Shilkret. Shilkret was a capable clarinet player, although his recordings mostly feature him as conductor or arranger.

As with klezmer, the voice of the clarinet in popular music takes on two main qualities: schooled and unschooled. These developed respectively from the music of the Creole and black communities in New Orleans, although the importance of German émigré teachers in the Chicago area, such as Franz Schoepp (who taught Goodman and Buster Bailey), and klezmorim must also be considered. Teachers in the Creole community included Lorenzo Tio and Alphonse Picou, who were part of the French classical music scene in New Orleans. Pupils such as Sidney Bechet (who then went on to teach Jimmie Noone), Barney Bigard and Albert Nicholas were therefore given a thorough technical grounding in the established tradition derived from Europe. The musical basis for players in the black community, such as George Lewis and Johnny Dodds, drew much less on this tradition and instead looked to black folk traditions and the blues, prefiguring the major change that was to occur in popular music after World War II.

From these two communities a style of solo and ensemble playing emerged that was consolidated by George Lewis himself (he was not to be recorded until the 1940s) and by Edmond Hall and others in the Louis Armstrong All-Star groups of the 1950s; this style remains prevalent in white revivalist and Dixieland jazz bands half a century later. This style established the clarinet as a front-line partner with the cornet (or trumpet) and trombone, its musical role being to add an embellished counterpoint, usually as the top line to the ensemble. A typical counterpoint is based on arpeggiations of the underlying harmony, while solos are designed to take advantage of the instrument's mobility and tonal variety, ranging from 'hot' and 'dirty' (variations on vocalized tone) to the cooler and softer sounds that come naturally to the instrument.

The New Orleans jazz style is epitomized by the work of what is generally considered the great triumvirate of early New Orleans-born clarinet players: Johnny Dodds, Jimmie Noone and Sidney Bechet.

Dodds, a key figure in the recordings made by Joe 'King' Oliver and Louis Armstrong's Hot Fives and Hot Sevens, was a master at interacting with the other front-line instruments, and his distinctive, declamatory solo style, making use of a wide lip vibrato, has been widely imitated. He was one of the first virtuosos on jazz clarinet, able to scale the higher register of the instrument with ease and in tune.

Noone worked mostly in Chicago. His influence was considerable during his lifetime, although he has become a relatively neglected figure. His style was more controlled and less flamboyant than that of either Dodds or Bechet and can even be described as bland by comparison. The Apex Club Band that he led in Chicago was also unorthodox in that the clarinet shared the front line with only an alto saxophone, played in a sweet manner by Joe Poston – a combination that tends to make the band's recordings sound sentimental and dated. But careful listening to what Noone does with rhythm (aiming just behind the beat) and how he builds his solos reveals the formation of more modern styles of solo playing, such as were about to be consolidated by such players as Benny Goodman and Lester Young. (Several jazz musicians have cited Young as their favorite jazz clarinet player, even though he is always associated with the tenor saxophone.)

Bechet was much more of an individualist. He dominated ensembles with his surprisingly loud projection and a generous vibrato that was difficult to match. Significantly, the player most influenced at the time by Bechet was the alto saxophonist Johnny Hodges. Bechet's influence as a clarinet player was slight because he spent most of his career away from the United States and also because he came to prefer the soprano saxophone, which enabled him to dominate ensembles even more. His lasting legacy is a passionate voice that helped to establish the popularity of the new jazz music beyond New Orleans and beyond North America.

A secondary outlet for the clarinet in jazz was also established during the 1920s in the form of arrangements for sections or choirs of clarinets. One of the earliest examples is Don Redman's arrangement of 'Copenhagen' in 1924 for Fletcher Henderson's orchestra. This calls for a cool clarinet trio, one that was later imitated by 'Jelly Roll' Morton in 'Dead Man Blues' and by Bennie Moten in 'Dear Heart' – the closest the clarinet ever got, incidentally, to being a part of Kansas City jazz, from which it is almost completely absent.

The next and most important phase for the clarinet in popular music was swing. Several dance bands featuring clarinets bridged the gap between the role that had been created in the 1920s and the clarinet's starring role in swing band music. The ground was already being prepared in the work and recordings of earlier dance bands in which leading figures, such as Benny Goodman, Jimmy Dorsey and others, had started their careers. Two such bands were the immensely popular 1920s Isham Jones Orchestra, whose main clarinet player was Al Mauling, and the group of New York-based studio players that recorded prolifically (from 1921 to 1936) under the name California Ramblers. With their deft arrangements of popular dance hits of the 1920s, the Ramblers were clear forerunners of the 1930s swing and big bands and featured one of their main stars in the making, Jimmy Dorsey – yet another player who had been influenced by Jimmie Noone. A little later came the often hot Glen Gray's Casa Loma Orchestra, which was very popular with young white college audiences in the mid-1930s. On clarinet, the Casa Loma Orchestra featured Clarence Hutchenrider, a player whose style simultaneously looked back to the 1920s and forward to later 1930s solo styles. A comparison between his work and that of, for instance, Goodman in 1935 shows how vital it was for a player to have his 'chops' (embouchure) in top condition to negotiate the scope and fluency of the later style. Later recordings show Hutchenrider more on top of the technical demands.

The most discussed landmark of popular clarinet playing is surely the National Biscuit Company's *Let's Dance* radio program, which went out live, nationwide, from Los Angeles on 21 August 1935 to launch what has become known as the swing era. It is certain that listeners that day were not interested in debating the relative merits and ancestry of New Orleans clarinetists, but they were sure that they had discovered a new star, and Benny Goodman was proclaimed 'King of Swing.' As is usual at such times, the listeners would also have been unaware of the preparations for this moment, particularly the subtle networking skills of impresario John Hammond, in the previous year, in bringing about the musical marriage between Benny Goodman, virtuoso clarinet soloist and would-be band leader, and the brothers Fletcher and Horace Henderson, two of the best bigband arrangers at that time. The Hendersons' specialty was to spice up familiar commercial, popular material with a Harlem-oriented musical seasoning. But Hammond's role extended further than that of musical matchmaker: he considered it his job to sell essentially black music played by a white band for a white, commercial audience. The Fletcher Henderson Orchestra had been playing these same arrangements for years, making good records that were heard by very few. Under Goodman's name, they became world hits, and jazz orchestras led by clarinet players, playing similar repertoire, remained fashionable until the mid-1940s.

The swing era of the mid-1930s and early 1940s was initially dominated by Goodman, and of all the clarinetists working at the time he remained the most influential and popular. This can be attributed to his status as one of the all-time great clarinet players, but a more significant ingredient of his popularity, especially in view of his jazz credentials, was his manner of improvising, usually remaining true to the outlines of the melody so that even a lay listener was able to understand what he was doing. Allied to subtle and transparent arrangements, for large band and small ensemble alike, that proved irresistible to dancers, Goodman's work of this period can be considered a peak in the history of popular music.

Goodman had a serious rival in Artie Shaw, whose orchestra toppled Goodman's from pole position in 1938 with the hits 'Begin the Beguine' and 'Nightmare.' The latter became the band's theme song. Although its mildly menacing jungle sounds were characteristic of the music of the swing era, 'Nightmare' avoids a descent into aimless 'noodling' over tom-toms, one of several swing clarinet formulae that caused this kind of music to grow stale. Recordings of coast-to-coast radio broadcasts by Shaw at this time give a better indication of the band's excellence than do the commercial recordings.

Like Goodman, Shaw was classically trained, but whereas Goodman was equally comfortable playing Mozart and Weber, Shaw's crossover ambitions did not lead very far, except for the 'Concerto for Clarinet' which was very popular in 1940.

Other swing bands featured excellent clarinet soloists – for example, Sam Musiker with Gene Krupa (Musiker was also an accomplished klezmer player), Johnny Mince with the Tommy Dorsey Orchestra, and Matty Matlock and Irving Fazola with the Bob Crosby band. Even when the clarinet was not taking the starring role, its sound was prominent, notably as an ensemble voice in the commercial dance music of the Glenn Miller Orchestra. Glenn Miller, along with Claude Thornhill, was an arranger in the short-lived band led by the British musician Ray Noble that featured a choir of saxophones in close harmony topped by sweet-toned clarinet. This became the hallmark of Miller hits, 'Moonlight Serenade' in particular. A similar ensemble voicing also occurred frequently in arrangements for the Duke Ellington Orchestra.

Woody Herman emerged from the Isham Jones Orchestra of the 1930s to become the third most famous name associated with the clarinet at that time. At the end of World War II, Woody Herman's orchestras (which included the famous First Herd of 1945) took over the number one position with a string of hits, including 'Caldonia,' 'Happiness Is Just a Thing Called Joe,' 'Apple Honey' and 'Northwest Passage.' Herman's playing incorporated a stronger blues feel than that of either Shaw or Goodman, and his musical policy in the 1940s successfully embraced modern elements, such as bop harmonies and techniques.

Taken together, these players' mastery of the full range of the clarinet produced some of the most brilliant and well-crafted solos and ensemble writing for clarinet heard until that time: never before had the clarinet been such a popular musical sound.

Suddenly, at the end of 1946, almost all the major swing bands folded. Several later re-formed, but they never regained the status they had enjoyed in the 1930s. The economics of running a large professional ensemble was one factor that led to their demise, but more significant was the change in taste (and the change of generation) that, by the end of World War II, had adjusted its frame of reference to include the newer and fresher African-American models, such as blues and R&B, at the expense of well-drilled, German-Jewish models that were associated with the nineteenth century. That included the clarinet.

It is customary to identify bop, with its new technical and dynamic demands, as one of the other main reasons for the clarinet's decline in popular jazz. However, a more potent challenge emerged in the late 1930s in the form of the popular demand for vocalists, and for music at much slower tempos and with romantic, escapist lyrics. Vocalists, whose contributions during the 1920s and 1930s had consisted typically of a verse and one or two choruses, began to carry the entire performance, to the extent that instruments were relegated to the role of a backing ensemble, adding short solos, not necessarily improvised, in whatever way the arranger deemed suitable. Thus, for instance, Frank Sinatra's 'The Night We Called It a Day' required four clarinets and bass clarinet in an ensemble drawn from the Tommy Dorsey Orchestra, directed and arranged, but as backing, by Axel Stordahl. (The bass clarinet player was probably Fred Stulce, who became a regular performer on Sinatra's recordings up to 1965.)

The popular success of the recordings made by Sinatra and the Pied Pipers with the Tommy Dorsey Orchestra gradually drew Dorsey's musical policy away from instrumentals to vocals with instrumental backing. The drift to vocal popular music was given further impetus by the American Federation of Musicians' recording ban (1942–44): instrumentalists were forbidden to record, but vocalists were not; by the end of the ban (and the war), the singers had taken over the popular music scene almost entirely.

This is not to deny that bop played a part in the decline of clarinet playing. Players were enthralled by Charlie Parker's alto saxophone playing, and avid young clarinet players, such as John Dankworth in England, switched irrevocably after live exposure to bop and Parker on 52nd Street. Clarinets therefore gave way to saxophones in jazz – a trend that was already beginning in the 1930s, so that, by the end of the 1940s, the clarinet began to be regarded, in general, as a training instrument. Nevertheless, several players persevered with the instrument in small-group jazz, adapting the advances of bop and extending technical demands, notably Buddy DeFranco, Tony Scott and the Scandinavians Ake 'Stan' Hasselgård and Putte Wickman. A new generation of musicians arriving in the 1960s revived interest in the expressive possibilities of the clarinet family, Eric Dolphy (a pupil of Joseph Allard) specializing in bass clarinet, Anthony Braxton mastering the entire family, and John Carter proving that there was still plenty of potential in new music for the common soprano instrument. A good representative album of modern clarinet players and writing is *The Clarinet Family* by World Saxophone Quartet member Hamiet Bluiett.

Dixieland clarinetists such as Pete Fountain, Sammy Rimington, Pud Brown and Henry Cuesta have retained a popular following, albeit localized, as is the case with hundreds of capable players who play regularly in clubs and pubs worldwide. But the most prominent popular landmark for the clarinet after 1950 was established by the English 'trad' player Mr. Acker Bilk. Bilk had a hit on both sides of the Atlantic with his own composition (produced by Dennis Preston) 'Stranger on the Shore,' which remained a bestseller for 55 weeks in 1961–62. Although it may have been seen at the time as part of the British trad boom (contemporary UK successes included the feature film and album *It's Trad, Dad*, the number one album *The Best of Ball, Barber and Bilk*, and hits by Terry Lightfoot's band and the Temperance Seven), tuneful instrumentals were again very popular (for example, the Shadows' 'Wonderful Land').

'Stranger on the Shore,' as experienced in the United Kingdom, can also be seen as the culmination of a series of instrumentals featuring British jazz clarinetists, beginning with Monty Sunshine's 'Petite Fleur' (a hit with Chris Barber's Jazz Band in 1959) and Bilk's own 'Summer Set,' 'White Cliffs of Dover' and 'Buona Sera' (all 1960). Later Bilk hits included a cover of 'A Taste of Honey' (1963) and 'Aria' (1976). One outcome of the popularity of 'Stranger on the Shore' was that hundreds of school children in the United Kingdom took up the clarinet in 1962 and years later amateur clarinetists would still pick out this tune as one of their first attempts at playing from memory. Other notable and influential British clarinet players of the 1950s included Wally Fawkes and Sandy Brown.

Elsewhere in popular music destined for the charts, instances of the clarinet are infrequent and musically very limited. The instrument is brought in when subtle warmth, arresting contrasts or nostalgia are required. Appropriately, therefore, the clarinet choir of the 1920s was revived for the Beatles' 'When I'm Sixty-Four.' Among this particular clarinet trio was Henry McKenzie, who led his own jazz groups and played with George Chisholm during the 1960s. Henry Diltz became famous as a photographer and designer of more than 200 album sleeves from the 1960s, but he also played clarinet. His modest contributions can be heard on the Monkees' 'Shake 'Em Up' (duly announced by Mickey Dolenz) and in the backing ensemble to various tracks by the Lovin' Spoonful. Multi-instrumentalist David Tofani's clarinet substitutes for Marc Almond on the B side of the Soft Cell single 'Say Hello, Wave Goodbye' and on various versions of their *Non-Stop Erotic Cabaret*. Joni Mitchell included Paul Horn, better known as a flautist and later as a New Age specialist, on 'For Free,' a song about a clarinet busker.

At the beginning of the twenty-first century, the increased popularity of crossover and world music has brought the clarinet renewed prominence. The eclecticism and variety of world music are creating new roles for the instrument, such as were prefigured by Jimmy Giuffre from the 1950s with his adoption of folk song, gospel and old-time elements into small-group jazz improvisations. Bulgarian wedding music (*svatbarska muzika*) gained wide national popularity among Bulgaria's youth from the mid-1970s, despite official disapproval due to the absence of national folk purity. Its most famous and popular exponent has been Ivo Papasov, who made several recordings, produced by Joe Boyd, that have sold internationally. Like other contemporary wedding music performers, he combined elements of folk dance (very fast, irregular meters; East European scale patterns) with elements of Western popular styles (amplification; bass and drums), while frequently embarking on jazz-style improvisations and borrowings from film music.

Klezmer has also been intermittently popular. It was revived in 1976 by US-based ensembles such as Klezmorim (Ben Goldberg) and the New Orleans Klezmer All-Stars, and later in Australia by KaOz Klezmer, led by clarinetist Pietro Fine, whose repertoire embraces the work of Rimsky-Korsakov, Ellington and Hendrix as well as traditional klezmer music.

At the beginning of the twenty-first century, the future of the clarinet in popular music appears to lie in the hands of performers trained and skilled in more than one idiom, such as Eddie Daniels (jazz, classical) and Don Byron (classical, jazz, Latin, klezmer, avant-garde), both of whom were pupils of Joseph Allard. Byron is considered one of the most influential musicians and composers of his generation, a bestselling jazz artist who has given new voice to the clarinet through a synthesis of styles and genres informed by an engagement with political issues. A selective list of his albums proves the point: *Tuskegee Experiments* (1992), dedicated to Allard, addresses the destructive effects of racism; *Don Byron Plays the Music of Mickey Katz* (1993) is a tribute to Spike Jones's musical director and Yiddish North American music; *Bug Music* (1996) includes versions of John Kirby's classical music takeoffs alongside the quirky melodies of Raymond Scott; *Romance with the Unseen* (1999) includes jazz standards ('Tizol's Perdido') alongside Lennon and McCartney's 'I'll Follow the Sun'; and *A Fine Line* (subtitled *Arias and Lieder*) (2000) blurs stylistic borders still further and in a manner that is more respectful and expressive than most crossover music, expanding the notion of art song to embrace Schumann, Chopin, Puccini, Roy Orbison, Steven Sondheim and Stevie Wonder.

Bibliography

Boatfield, Graham. 1958. 'Things Ain't What They Used to Be: Classic Jazz Clarinet.' In *The Decca Book of Jazz*, ed. Peter Gammond. London: Frederick Muller.

Brymer, Jack. 1976. *Clarinet*. London: Macdonald and Jane's.

Clark, Chris. 1993. 'Byron's [Don Byron] Epiphany.' *Jazz: The Magazine* 18: 22–23.

Collier, James Lincoln. 1989. *Benny Goodman and the Swing Era*. New York: Oxford University Press.

Connor, D. Russell, and Hicks, Warren W. 1969. *BG on the Record: A Bio-Discography of Benny Goodman*. New Rochelle, NY: Arlington House.

Feather, Leonard. 1959. *The Book of Jazz: A Guide to the Entire Field*. London: Arthur Barker, esp. 86–91.

Gracyk, Tim, with Hoffmann, Frank. 2000. *Popular American Recording Pioneers, 1895–1925*. New York: Haworth Press.

Harvey, Paul. 1986. *The Complete Clarinet Player*. 4 vols. London: Wise Publications.

Jones, Max. 1987. *Talking Jazz*. London: Macmillan. (Reprints of interviews with jazz musicians originally published in *Melody Maker*.)

Laplace, Michel. 1996. 'La clarinette à New Orleans' [The Clarinet in New Orleans]. *Jazz Hot Special '97*.

Lawson, Colin, ed. 1995. *The Cambridge Companion to the Clarinet*. Cambridge: Cambridge University Press.

Morrill, Dexter. 1990. *Woody Herman: A Guide to the Big Band Recordings, 1936–1987*. New York: Greenwood Press.

Pino, David. 1980. *The Clarinet and Clarinet Playing*. New York: C. Scribner's Sons.

Porter, Lewis. 2002. 'Clarinet.' In *The New Grove Dictionary of Jazz*, Vol. 1, ed. Barry Kernfeld. 2nd ed. London: Macmillan, 444–47.

Rehfeldt, Phillip. 1994. *New Directions for Clarinet*. Rev. ed. Berkeley, CA: University of California Press.

Richards, E. Michael. 1992. *The Clarinet of the Twenty-First Century* (Book and cassette). Fairport, NY: E&K Publishers.

Schuller, Gunther. 1968. *Early Jazz: Its Roots and Musical Development*. New York: Oxford University Press.

Schuller, Gunther. 1989. *The Swing Era: The Development of Jazz, 1930–1945*. New York: Oxford University Press.

Smith, Bill. 1993. *Jazz Clarinet*. Seattle, WA: Parkside Publications.

Stein, Keith. 1994. *The Art of Clarinet Playing*. Evanston, IL: Warner Brothers/Summy-Birchard Publications.

Discographical References

Barber, Chris, and His Jazz Band. 'Petite Fleur.' Pye Nixa NJ 2026. *1959*: UK.

Beatles, The. 'When I'm Sixty-Four.' *Sergeant Pepper's Lonely Hearts Club Band*. Parlophone PCS 7027. *1967*: UK.

The Best of Ball, Barber and Bilk. Pye Golden Guinea GGL 0131. *1962*: UK.

Bilk, Acker, His Clarinet and Strings. 'Aria.' Pye 7N 45607. *1976*: UK.

Bilk, Mr. Acker. 'Stranger on the Shore.' Atco 6217. *1962*: USA.

Bilk, Mr. Acker, and His Paramount Jazz Band. 'Buona Sera.' Columbia DB 4544. *1960*: UK.

Bilk, Mr. Acker, and His Paramount Jazz Band. 'Summer Set.' Columbia DB 4382. *1960*: UK.

Bilk, Mr. Acker, and His Paramount Jazz Band. 'White Cliffs of Dover.' Columbia DB 4492. *1960*: UK.

Bilk, Mr. Acker, with the Leon Young String Chorale. 'A Taste of Honey.' Columbia DB 4949. *1963*: UK.

Bilk, Mr. Acker, with the Leon Young String Chorale. 'Stranger on the Shore.' Columbia DB 4750. *1961*: UK.

Bluiett, Hamiet. *The Clarinet Family*. Black Saint BSR 0097. *1987*: Italy.

Byron, Don. *A Fine Line: Arias and Lieder*. Blue Note 5268012. *2000*: USA.

Byron, Don. *Bug Music*. Nonesuch 79438. *1996*: USA.

Byron, Don. *Don Byron Plays the Music of Mickey Katz*. Elektra/Nonesuch 79313. *1993*: USA.

Byron, Don. *Romance with the Unseen*. Blue Note 99545. *1999*: USA.

Byron, Don. *Tuskegee Experiments*. Elektra/Nonesuch 79280. *1992*: USA.

Henderson, Fletcher, and His Orchestra. 'Copenhagen.' *Fletcher Henderson and His Orchestra, 1924, Vol. 3*. Classics 647. 1924; *1996*: USA.

Herman, Woody. 'Apple Honey.' Columbia 36803. 1945: USA.

Herman, Woody. 'Caldonia'/'Happiness Is Just a Thing Called Joe.' Columbia 36789. 1945: USA.

Herman, Woody. 'Northwest Passage.' Columbia 36835. 1945: USA.

It's Trad, Dad. Columbia 33SX 1412. *1962*: UK.

Miller, Glenn. 'Moonlight Serenade'/'Sunrise Serenade.' Bluebird 10214. 1939: USA.

Mitchell, Joni. 'For Free.' *Ladies of the Canyon*. Reprise 6376. *1970*: USA.

Monkees, The. 'Shake 'Em Up.' *Missing Links, Vol. 3*. Rhino 72153. *1996*: USA.

Morton, 'Jelly Roll.' 'Sidewalk Blues'/'Dead Man Blues.' Victor 20252. 1926: USA.

Moten, Bennie. 'Sugar'/'Dear Heart.' Victor 20855. 1927: USA.

Original Dixieland Jazz Band, The. 'Dixieland Jass Band One-Step'/'Livery Stable Blues.' Victor 18253. 1917: USA.

Original Dixieland Jazz Band, The. 'Jazz Me Blues'/'St. Louis Blues.' Victor 18772. 1921: USA.

Shadows, The. 'Wonderful Land.' Columbia DB 4790. *1962*: UK.

Shaw, Artie. 'Begin the Beguine'/'Indian Love Call.' Bluebird 7746. 1938: USA.

Shaw, Artie. 'Concerto for Clarinet (1 & 2).' Victor 36383. 1940: USA.

Shaw, Artie. 'Nightmare'/'Non-Stop Flight.' Bluebird 7875. 1938: USA.

Sinatra, Frank. 'Night and Day'/'The Night We Called It a Day.' Bluebird 11463. 1942: USA.

Soft Cell. *Non-Stop Erotic Cabaret*. Sire 3647. *1981*: UK.

Soft Cell. 'Say Hello, Wave Goodbye.' Some Bizarre BZS 7. *1982*: UK.

Discography

Basie, Count (with Lester Young). 'Blue and Sentimental.' Decca 1965. 1935: USA.

Bechet, Sidney. *The Complete Blue Note Recordings*. Mosaic 110. 1939–53; *1986*: USA.

Bigard, Barney. *1928–1948*. Best of Jazz 4028. *1996*: USA.

Brandwein, Naftule. *King of the Klezmer Clarinet*. Rounder CD 1127. *1997*: USA.

Braxton, Anthony. *Five Pieces (1975)*. Arista AL 4064. *1975*: USA.

Carter, John. *Dauwhe*. Black Saint BSR 0057. *1982*: USA.

Clarinet Marmalade: 25 Great Jazz Clarinettists. ASV/Living Era 5132. *1994*: UK.

Coe, Tony. *Canterbury Song*. Hot House CD 1005. *1989*: UK.

Cuesta, Henry. *Lawrence Welk Presents the Clarinet of Henry Cuesta*. Ranwood 8166. *1976*: USA.

Daniels, Eddie. *Breakthrough*. GRP GRD-9533. 1986; *1992*: USA.

Daniels, Eddie. *Swing Low Sweet Clarinet*. Shanachie SH 5073. *1999*: USA.

DeFranco, Buddy. *Complete Verve Recordings of Buddy DeFranco with Sonny Clark*. Mosaic 117. 1954–55: USA.

Dodds, Johnny. *Johnny Dodds*. Jolly Roger 5012. 1954: USA.

Dolphy, Eric. *The Complete Prestige Recordings*. Prestige 4418. 1960–61; *1996*: USA.

Dorsey, Jimmy. *The Fabulous Dorseys Play Dixieland Jazz* (reissues of 1934–35 recordings). Coral CP 27. *1970*: UK.

Fountain, Pete. *Standing Room Only*. Coral 57474. *1965*: USA.

Giuffre, Jimmy. *The Complete Capitol & Atlantic Recordings of Jimmy Giuffre*. Mosaic 6-176. 1954–58: USA.

Goodman, Benny. *After You've Gone, Vol. 1*. RCA/Bluebird 5631-2 R. 1935–37: USA.

Goodman, Benny. *After You've Gone, Vol. 2*. RCA/Bluebird 2273-2-RB. 1937–39: USA.

Hasselgård, Ake 'Stan' (with Benny Goodman). *At Click (1948)*. Dragon DRCD 183. 1948: Sweden.

Herman, Woody. *Blowin' up a Storm* (reissues of mid-1940s hits). Columbia Legacy 5032802. *2001*: USA.

Hutchenrider, Clarence. *Glen Gray and the Casa Loma Orchestra 1940*. Circle CCD 61. *1983*: USA.

Hutchenrider, Clarence. *Glen Gray and the Casa Loma Orchestra on the Air 1934*. Extreme Rarities LP 1005. n.d.: USA.

Klezmorim. *First Recordings 1976–1978*. Arhoolie CD 309. *1989*: USA.

Lewis, George. *The Complete Blue Note Recordings of George Lewis (1943–1955)*. Mosaic MD3-132-3. 1943–55: USA.

Lil's Hot Shots (with Johnny Dodds). 'Georgia Bo-Bo.' Vocalion 1037. 1926: USA.

Mbatsis, Vasilios. *Songs of Epirus*. Society for National Music SDNM 111. *1975*: Greece.

Mince, Johnny (with Tommy Dorsey's Clambake Seven). 'Chinatown, My Chinatown.' Victor 26023. 1938: USA. Reissue: Mince, Johnny (with Tommy Dorsey's Clambake Seven). 'Chinatown, My Chinatown.' *The Music Goes 'Round and Around*. ABM ABMMCD 1208. *1999*: USA.

Noone, Jimmie. 'Apex Blues.' Vocalion 1207. 1928: USA.

Papasov, Ivo. *Balkanology*. Hannibal HNCD 1363. *1991*: UK/USA.

Rêve et Passion: The Soul of Klezmer. Network 30.853. *1998*: Germany.

Shaw, Artie. *Artie Shaw in the Blue Room/In the Café Rouge* (Broadcast performances 1938–39). RCA-Victor LPT 6000. *1972*: USA.

Filmography

It's Trad, Dad, dir. Richard Lester. 1962. UK. 73 mins. Musical Comedy. Original music by Maude Churchill, Ken Thorne.

CHRIS CLARK

Didjeridu

Introduction

The history of the didjeridu in the northern tropical regions of Australia dates back at least 1,500 years. However, the name 'didjeridu' is of relatively recent origin. There are many local Aboriginal names for the instrument in its homeland areas, where it was, and has continued to be, used both on sacred and secret occasions and in secular contexts.

Although often dismissed at one time in Australia as a simplistic and esoteric ethnographic artifact, since the 1980s the didjeridu has become the main aural and visual musical symbol of pan-Aboriginality and 'Australianness.' As a pan-Aboriginal instrument, its use has become commonplace at public and private secular ceremonies. As an Australian instrument, it is extensively used in tourist activities and promotional cultural tours. It has also become an export commodity. Many thousands of instruments made by Aboriginal and non-Aboriginal artisans are sold yearly to tourists or are exported, primarily to North America and Europe. During the 1990s, enthusiasts' discussion groups and retailers' Web sites were set up on the Internet. The emergence and evolution of the didjeridu provide an interesting and instructive example of a musical instrument and musical practises that have moved from local to national and transnational contexts in a relatively short time. As a transnational instrument, it can be heard alone and in ensembles in many contemporary musical genres, such as ambient, Celtic, folk, techno and world musics.

Construction

The didjeridu is a hollow tube without any holes in the sidewalls. A mouthpiece made of beeswax or a similarly pliable material is fashioned to adjust the embouchure. The length of didjeridus varies but is generally around 5' (1.5 m). The combination of the instrument's length, the diameter of the bore and the irregularities of the inside surface determines the fundamental note produced. Historically, didjeridus were most commonly constructed from termite-bored eucalyptus woods and sometimes reamed-out bamboo. Contemporary construction materials include glass, brass, Pyrex and plastic pipe, especially outside Australia where suitable eucalyptuses (and the necessary termites) are rare. Innovations in construction materials have been accompanied by innovations in instrument design. These have included inserting a sliding plastic tube inside another one so that pitch can be changed, and devising ways to add holes and woodwind-like 'keys' for playing more notes and overtones.

Performance

Sound in a didjeridu is produced by 'buzzing' the lips in a way broadly analogous to playing Western brass instruments. A common technique is 'circular breathing' in which players hold air in their cheeks and then expel it while simultaneously inhaling air quickly through their nose. As well as producing a fundamental drone note, the didjeridu is capable of producing rich overtones. A skilled player can produce complex sounds and rhythms by combining the drone and overtones with vocalizations and guttural noises.

In traditional Aboriginal practise, a single didjeridu was generally combined with a songman and a clapstick player. In contemporary non-Aboriginal practise, however, sometimes many instruments are played simultaneously. One hundred and fifty-three didjeriduists played together at Didgfest 1997 in Melbourne, Australia, an achievement registered with the Guinness Book of Records. Unofficial tallies of over 200 players have been noted in Britain and the United States.

Beginning with its novelty use by Rolf Harris in the 1960s and progressing to the inventive recordings of Charlie McMahon with the group Gondwanaland in the 1980s, the didjeridu had by the 1990s become a common part of the soundscape of Australian national culture, heard in commercials, film soundtracks, and radio and television documentaries. Importantly, it also became an integral element in popular Aboriginal bands such as Blekbala Mujik, the Warumpi Band and Yothu Yindi, and in the concert performances, recordings and workshops of Aboriginal didjeriduists such as Mark Atkins, David Blanasi, Alan Dargin, Matthew Doyle, David Hudson and Richard Walley.

A Transnational Instrument

The transnational popularity of the didjeridu and its use in new musical practises have had unforeseen consequences. An environmental consequence has been the overharvesting of suitable eucalyptus wood stocks in some areas of Australia, with concomitant stress on the habitats of particular endangered bird species. Sociocultural consequences have included debates over issues of indigenous intellectual and cultural copyright and cultural appropriation. These debates have arisen from concerns on the part of some Aboriginal people about the didjeridu being played by women, as well as from discomfort over quasi-spiritual activities such as 'healing circles' and sonic massage therapy, and over the use of Aboriginal decorative designs without permission from their traditional owners. There have also been concerns voiced by Aboriginal people over what constitutes an 'authentic' didjeridu, and how artisans and retailers can receive a fair return while respecting the potentially contentious cultural politics that underlie a sizable and profitable, but largely unregulated and undocumented, industry.

The global dissemination of the didjeridu has resulted in its use in many contemporary genres outside Australia, either as a substitute for other drone or percussion instruments or as an instrument in totally new solo or ensemble contexts. Recording artists such as Cyrung, Shaun Farrenden, Ianto Thornber and Graham Wiggins in Great Britain and David Blonski, Jamie Cunningham, Stuart Dempster and Brian Pertl in the United States are some of the didjeriduists responsible for innovations in performance, arranging, pedagogy and marketing. Many of these artists consciously do not draw directly on Aboriginal styles or repertoire. However, there have been didjeridu recordings in which Aboriginal songs or motifs have been imitated or sampled without authorization or acknowledgment. As a consequence, Aboriginal people in Australia asked a didjeridu-oriented Internet site to remove restricted cultural information.

As a transnational phenomenon, the didjeridu has the potential to develop further musically and economically, especially with the global focus on Australia and Aboriginal culture that accompanied the Sydney 2000 Olympic Games. Perhaps because of the didjeridu's deceptive simplicity, it provides a focus for the expression of a myriad of complex musical and extramusical developments.

Bibliography

Dreamtime: A Didjeridu Resource. http://www.mills.edu/LIFE/CCM/DIDJERIDU/index.html

Jones, Trevor. 1967. 'The Didjeridu: Some Comparisons of Its Typology and Musical Functions with Similar Instruments Throughout the World.' *Studies in Music* 1: 23–55.

Moyle, Alice. 1981. 'The Australian Didjeridu: A Late Musical Intrusion.' *World Archaeology* 12(3): 321–31.

Neuenfeldt, Karl. 1993. 'The Didjeridu and the Overdub: Technologising and Transposing Aural Images of Aboriginality.' *Perfect Beat* 1(2): 60–77.

Neuenfeldt, Karl. 1994. 'The Essentialistic, the Exotic, the Equivocal and the Absurd: The Cultural Production and Use of the Didjeridu in World Music.' *Perfect Beat* 2(1): 88–104.

Neuenfeldt, Karl, ed. 1997. *The Didjeridu: From Arnhem Land to Internet*. Sydney: John Libbey/Perfect Beat Publications.

The Didgeridoo University. http://aboriginalart.com.au/didgeridoo/index.html

Discography

Blonski, David. *On Wings of Eagles*. Timeless Productions DAB 102 CD. *1997*: USA.

Dargin, Alan. *Bloodwood: The Art of the Didjeridu*. Natural Symphonies NS 331. *1993*: Australia.

Didgeri Dudes. *Didgeri Dudes*. Didgeri Dudes DD001. *1995*: USA.

Didgeri Dudes (with Stuart Dempster). *Under the Earth Tones: Ambient Didgeridoo Meditations*. Northwest Folklife Recordings NWFL CD003. *1997*: USA.

Gondwanaland. *Let the Dog Out*. WEA 255412-2. *1985*: Australia.

Gondwanaland. *Terra Incognita*. WEA 255411-2. *1983*: Australia.

Gondwanaland. *Wildlife*. WEA 256415-2. *1990*: Australia.

Hudson, David. *Woolunda: Ten Solos for Didgeridoo*. Celestial Harmonies 13071-2. *1993*: USA.

Reconciliation. *Two Stories in One*. Natural Symphonies NS 1131. *1993*: Australia.

Walley, Richard. *Bilya*. Sunset Music SMACD06. *1996*: Australia.

KARL NEUENFELDT

Fife

The fife is a precursor of the piccolo. It is usually made out of wood, is cylindrical and has six holes. The instrument is held in a horizontal or near-horizontal position, with the top (the end of the tube that is closed) placed just under the lips and the bottom (the end of the tube that is open) to the right of the player's body. To create a sound, the player creates an embouchure with his/her lips and blows across the largest hole at the top of the instrument. The flow of air emitted from the player's lips is split on hitting the edge of the hole furthest from the player. The air deflected into the tube vibrates, causing a pitch to be created. Different notes are created by the player covering the remaining holes with his/her fingers, or leaving them open, as the case may be. The sound that is created is high-pitched and tends to be shrill.

The fife has a long history of involvement with military activity, especially when paired with the drum. In the Middle Ages and the Renaissance, fife and drum bands marched with armies throughout Europe from what are now Britain, France and Germany. Fife and drum bands helped in maintaining the speed at which armies marched by using 'fife calls' (small phrases of music). Fife calls were also used to give signals, such as whether members of an army should attack, retreat or run for their lives. Although the piccolo replaced the fife in the British army in approximately 1870, the fife continued to be a part of the US military tradition, particularly in fife and drum combinations. It has remained a staple instrument in Orangemen parades throughout Northern Ireland. Many of the tunes played in these parades have decidedly political connotations. Examples include 'The Battle of Garvagh,' in which the Protestants fight off the Catholics.

The fife has, in various historical periods, been used in dance music. In England, the fife was a popular instrument in the wake of the Napoleonic wars, and it replaced the earlier flageolet in certain types of dance music of the seventeenth century. During the late nineteenth century, US fiddlers, such as Henry Reed (1884–1968), claimed to have learned military and dance tunes from fife players who had served in the American Civil War. The piccolo, the fife's descendant, has remained popular in military bands.

Bibliography

Baines, Anthony. 1967. *Woodwind Instruments and Their History*. 3rd ed. London: Faber.

Camus, Raoul F. 1976. *Military Music of the American Revolution*. Chapel Hill, NC: University of North Carolina Press.

Keller, Kate Van Winkle, and Shimer, Genevieve. 1990. *The Playford Ball: 103 Early Country Dances, 1651–1820: As Interpreted by Cecil Sharp and His Followers*. Northampton, MA: Country Dance and Song Society.

Discographical Reference

Wilson, Sam, and the Loyalists. 'The Battle of Garvagh.' *No Surrender*. Ace of Clubs ACL 1148. *1963*: UK.

BHESHAM SHARMA with MIKE BROCKEN

Flute

The term 'flute' covers a wide range of wind instruments across the majority of the world's cultures where the sound is produced through what is known as an 'edge tone.' The only two locations in which this family of instruments appears not to be indigenous are Australia and Greenland.

An edge tone is created when a column of air is split, with one part going into thin air and the other being driven into a tube or vessel in which it vibrates and produces a tone. Flutes can be divided into those in which the column of air is confined in a channel or duct before it is split, and those in which it is not. Examples of the former are to be found in various kinds of whistles (including pennywhistles) and in the recorder family. Those in which the column of air is not confined are known as 'transverse flutes.' Here, the column of air is shaped and directed by the player's lips across a hole set in the side or at the end of a tube or vessel. The manner in which the player forms his/her lips is referred to as an 'embouchure,' while the hole across which the column of air is directed is known as the 'embouchure hole.' Members of the transverse flute family include modern orchestral flutes as well as fifes and pan pipes.

Before the eighteenth century, the term 'flute' in many European languages referred to the various members of the recorder family, so that the term 'transverse' had to be applied to refer to what is now commonly known in the English language as the 'flute.' The flute in its modern Western manifestation (the concert flute) is based on Theobald Boehm's design of 1841 as modified by nineteenth-century French makers. It is 26" (67 cm) in length with a bore of 0.75" (1.9 cm). The instrument is held in a horizontal or near-horizontal position, with the top (the end of the tube that is closed) placed just under the lips and the bottom (the end of the tube that is open) to the right of the player's body. To create a sound, the player creates an embouchure with his/her lips and blows across the embouchure hole near the top of the instrument. Different notes are created by the player covering the instrument's remaining holes with his/her fingers, or leaving them open, as the case may be.

Unlike reed instruments such as the oboe, the clarinet, the bassoon and the saxophone, whose sound is produced by the pressure of air channeled through the reed, the sound of the flute is produced by the volume and speed of the column of air passed over the embouchure hole. Virtually no resistance is offered to the column of air and, in this sense, the physiology of tone production is closer to that of singing than to that of other woodwind instruments. A good flute tone in the Western art music tradition depends as much on it being properly supported by the diaphragm as does a good vocal tone.

The concert flute has three sections. The top section, which is closed at one end, contains only the embouchure hole. The second, longest section contains six principal holes along the top of the instrument. When all these holes are covered by the player's fingers, the note d is sounded. In this sense, the basic scale of the instrument can be regarded as that of d. One hole on the back of the instrument is covered by the thumb, with alternative positions allowing for the production of b and $b\flat$, respectively. An additional hole on the side of the instrument operated through a lever by the little finger of the left hand allows for the production of $g\sharp$. The bottom and shortest section of the instrument allows for the production of $d\sharp$, $c\sharp$ and c, and, in some versions of this section, B.

The flute has a compass of at least three octaves from c to c^3. The fingerings for the second octave (c^1 to b^1) are almost exactly the same as for the bottom octave (c to b), while alternative, cross-fingerings are used for the top octave (c^2 to b^2); c^3 is regarded as being in the normal range of the instrument, and is also achieved by cross-fingering. Most players can achieve a few notes higher than c^3. Differences in pitch between the bottom and middle octaves are achieved by overblowing, in which, by changing his/her embouchure, the player alters the angle of the air column emitted from his/her lips to nearer the horizontal. The same principle applies to producing the notes of the top octave, the cross-fingerings being necessary to achieve accurate pitches and, within the tradition of Western art music, purity of tone. The flute is regarded as being in C and is not a transposing instrument.

Flutes are made out of nickel-silver, sterling silver, gold, platinum and wood. Wood has become the least common material, as it is more susceptible than metal to climatic change. Also, while the tone produced by a wooden flute is richer than the tones produced by various metal flutes, the sound does not carry as well. Metal flutes allow for a more flexible tone than wooden ones. The sound from a silver flute is more brilliant, while that from a gold flute is more mellow.

Additional members of the concert flute family are the piccolo, which is pitched exactly one octave higher than the concert flute, the bass flute in C, which is pitched one octave lower, the alto flute in G (pitched a fourth lower than the concert flute) and the treble flute in g (pitched a fifth higher than the concert flute). The alto flute is a transposing instrument, with the music being written a fourth higher than it sounds. This makes the transition from the concert to the alto flute easy for the player.

In the Western art music tradition, the flute has an extensive repertoire, extending at least as far back as the Baroque period and coming right through to contemporary avant-garde traditions. With the exception of some avant-garde music for the flute, considerable emphasis is put on producing a pure tone, which can in general be described as liquid, ethereal, hollow and haunting. The tone toward the bottom of the instrument's compass can be described as 'woody,' while that in the top octave, in the hands of a good player, can be described as 'sweet.' Avant-garde music on occasion calls for unconventional tones, including tones that are split (Howell 1974).

The flute has been an important instrument in many forms of popular music around the world. It was, for example, the essential instrument in the Cuban *charanga* orchestra, which was responsible for the development of the *danzón* in the opening years of the twentieth century. The *charanga* orchestra emerged under the influence of French culture, the *charanga francèse* being a French chamber music ensemble consisting of flute and strings that was brought to the Caribbean in the eighteenth century. The *charanga* orchestra was made up of flute, violin, piano, double bass, timbral drum and *güiro*. This format, later expanded to include two violins and three singers, was the basis of the modern Cuban sound, as performed by Los Van Van and NG La Banda. José Luís Cortés, leader of NG La Banda, is one of Cuba's major composers and a leading flute player. Like all modern Cuban musicians, he was schooled in the classical tradition, notably the Russian school, as well as in Cuban popular music.

The flute has been a popular instrument in the West, featuring, for example, in most forms of wind bands, sometimes carrying or doubling the melodic line, but mostly offering an ornamental counterpoint to melodies carried predominantly by clarinets and trumpets. However, because the sound of the flute is weak in comparison to that of other instruments like the trumpet, the trombone, the clarinet and the saxophone, it has not on the whole been prominent in popular music or jazz. The flute's tone is not as well suited to ensemble work in small groups with such instruments or to the noisy ambiance that frequently accompanies performances of popular music. This is not to say, however, that the flute has not had a significant presence in popular music and jazz.

The flute was little used in jazz before the late 1920s, and before the 1950s was a novelty. However, during the 1950s, its use became more frequent. The vast majority of jazz flute players have been either saxophone players who have 'doubled' on the flute, or much more occasionally – as in the case of Herbie Mann – flute players who have doubled on the saxophone. Indeed, the ability of saxophonists to double on the flute is expected in most bands. The one notable exception to this trend was Don Cherry, the cornetist who played a range of non-Western flutes, as in 'Baby's Breath' (1968), when he played a bamboo flute and a Bengal flute simultaneously.

Because the majority of jazz flute players are also saxophonists, the tone they produce on the flute tends to be different to that produced by classical flute players. This is in large part because the embouchure required for the saxophone is muscularly tense and thus quite different to that customary for classical flute players, which is, by comparison, quite relaxed. The result is that flute players in jazz and popular music tend to produce a breathier and less focused tone, which can then be compensated for through amplification. This difference in tone is consistent with the tendency for popular and jazz musicians as a whole to produce vocal and instrumental tones that are more personal, more varied and less pure than those customary in classical music.

One of the first major flute players in jazz was Frank Wess, a member of Count Basie's band. He was followed quickly by Bud Shank and Canadian Moe Koffman, who in 1957 made a name for himself with a catchy flute rendition of 'Swinging Shepherd Blues.' However, Herbie Mann was the first jazz musician to base a career on playing the flute and, in so doing, he became particularly popular during the 1960s. During the 1970s, Mann ceded this position to Hubert Laws, who was rare in having an outstanding classical technique that he adapted to bop and modal jazz.

Jazz flute players have performed on flutes other than the concert c instrument. As well as Don Cherry, who used non-Western flutes, Yusef Lateef has recorded on many wood and bamboo flutes. Arranger Gil Evans's collaboration with Miles Davis on *Porgy and Bess* (1958) is notable for the lyrical alto flute solos of Danny Bank, particularly in 'Fishermen, Strawberry and Devil Crab.' The alto flute has also been played by Herbie Mann ('Tutti Fluttie,' 1957) and Bud Shank ('Lotus Bud,' 1954).

Jazz flute players have also engaged in novel techniques. Because of the similarity in the physiology of sound production between playing the flute and singing, individuals learning the flute frequently vocalize 'in sympathy' while playing. This is something that is routinely discouraged in the Western art music tradition. However, jazz flute players Sam Most and Sahib Shihab have both exploited this similarity in the physiology of sound production in singing or humming, frequently in parallel octaves, while playing. Yusef Lateef has taken this technique further by speaking syllables into the flute, and in this way producing a range of new and unusual sounds.

In popular music, the flute has been present in a wide range of orchestral settings. It is also used from time to time in rock bands to add tone color. Two examples are to be found on Van Morrison's recordings of 'Moondance' and 'Warm Love' (1990). One of the most extraordinary uses of the flute in rock music, however, has been at the hands of Ian Anderson, the leader of Jethro Tull, a group that competed for popularity with Yes during the 1970s, but did not have the latter group's longevity. Anderson's playing is notable for the range of impure tones that he is able to elicit from the instrument, as well as for his ability to bend pitches far beyond what is acceptable in the Western art music tradition.

Bibliography

Bate, Philip. 1969. *The Flute: A Study of Its History, Development and Construction*. New York: W.W. Norton.

Dick, Robert. 1975. *The Other Flute: A Performance Manual of Contemporary Techniques*. London: Oxford University Press.

Howell, Thomas. 1974. *The Avant-Garde Flute: A Handbook for Composers and Flutists*. Berkeley, CA: University of California Press.

Porter, Lewis. 2002. 'The Flute.' In *The New Grove Dictionary of Jazz*, ed. Barry Kernfeld. London: Macmillan, 814–16.

Porter, Maurice. 1967. *The Embouchure*. London: Boosey and Hawkes.

Discographical References

Cherry, Don. 'Baby's Breath.' *Eternal Rhythm*. Saba 15204. *1968*: Germany.

Davis, Miles, and Evans, Gil. *Porgy and Bess*. Columbia CS 8085. *1958*: USA.

Koffman, Moe. 'Swinging Shepherd Blues.' *The Best of Moe Koffman, Volumes 1 and 2*. Anthem 1057. *1989*: Australia.

Mann, Herbie. 'Tutti Fluttie.' *Flute Flight*. Prestige 7124. *1957*: USA.

Morrison, Van. 'Moondance.' *The Best of Van Morrison*. Mercury 841970. *1990*: USA.

Morrison, Van. 'Warm Love.' *The Best of Van Morrison*. Mercury 841970. *1990*: USA.

Shank, Bud, and Levy, Lou. 'Lotus Bud.' *Jazz in Hollywood*. Original Jazz Classics 1890. 1954; *1997*: Germany.

Discography

Jethro Tull. *Stand Up*. Reprise 6360. *1969*: USA.

Lateef, Yusef. *Every Village Has a Song: The Yusef Lateef Anthology*. Rhino 71551. *1994*: USA.

Laws, Hubert. *The Best of Hubert Laws*. Columbia· ZK 45479. *1990*: USA.

Los Van Van. *The Legendary Los Van Van: 30 Years of Cuba's Greatest Dance Band*. Ashe 2007. *1999*: USA.

Mann, Herbie. *The Evolution of Mann: The Herbie Mann Anthology*. Rhino 8122-71634-2. *1995*: USA.

Most, Sam. *Mostly Flute*. Xanadu 1237. 1976; *1995*: USA.

NG La Banda. *The Best of NG La Banda*. Blue Note 21391. *2000*: USA.

Shank, Bud. *The Compositions of Shorty Rogers*. Nocturne NLP 2. 1954: USA.

Shihab Sahib. *All Star Sextets*. Savoy SJL 2245. *1957*: UK.

Wess, Frank. *The Long Road*. Prestige 24247. *2000*: USA.

JOHN SHEPHERD

Harmonica (Mouth Organ, Harp)

Introduction

Less than 200 years after its debut, the harmonica, a small wind instrument played with the mouth, has become ubiquitous. It has been to both poles, down the Amazon and to the summit of Mount Everest. On its most spectacular field trip, it became the first instrument to be played from outer space, when US astronaut Wally Schirra offered a rendition of 'Jingle Bells' on a tiny harmonica during the 1965 Gemini VI spaceflight.

The Free Reed

The harmonica is based on the principle of the free reed, an Asian invention in which a tongue made of metal or wood is attached at one end over a closefitting opening through which the free end vibrates when air passes over it. The pitch of the note is determined by the length and thickness of the reed.

The earliest relic of a demonstrable ancestor of the harmonica is a mouth organ called a *yu*, which was unearthed in China in 1973 during the excavation of a 2,000-year-old tomb from the Han dynasty. The home of the free reed was most likely the region now called Laos, where the greatest variety of Asian free-reed instruments can be found.

From Asia, the free reed was introduced into the Middle East and, by the seventeenth century, free-reed instruments had reached Europe. Contemporary accounts note the unusual speed with which the free reed spread throughout that continent. It was first used in keyboard instruments such as the orchestrion, *terpodion* and harmonium. This experimentation led to a European version of the free reed that consisted of a strip of metal, attached to a metal frame over a slightly larger aperture, which would vibrate when air was moved across it. Fashioning the reed from metal allowed it to be tuned within a semitone. Given the precise pitch requirements of Western music, this was a crucial development.

History

The first European mouth organ to resemble the modern instrument seems to have been the creation of a German instrument maker named Christian Friedrich Buschmann, who in 1821 registered the first European patents for a mouth organ he called the *aura*. This was a horizontal arrangement of 15 steel reeds placed in small channels arranged side by side.

Although some have claimed that the use of two reed plates – one for blow notes and the other for draw notes – was taken from the accordion, which was patented in 1829, it may have been an instrument maker from Bohemia named Richter who introduced this concept in 1825 or 1826. Richter's mouth organ was a 10-hole, 20-reed instrument, with reed plates mounted on either side of a cedar comb whose segments formed separate channels for each pair of reeds. Designed to play simple melodies, the notes of Richter's harmonica were roughly the same as those of the white keys on the piano. Richter placed a full diatonic scale in the center of his instrument, with gapped scales on either side. The blow reeds produced the major tonic chord and the draw reeds sounded the dominant seventh. Richter's variation on Buschmann's theme became the standard configuration.

Germany's Württemberg province, a region on the edge of the Black Forest, was the home of several of the earliest harmonica manufacturers, including Matthias Hohner of Trossingen. In 1857, Hohner turned out 650 instruments with the help of his family and one hired workman. He soon began introducing techniques of mass production, and also showed a flair for marketing, placing his instruments between distinctive, ornate cover plates – prominently featuring their maker's name – that helped to distinguish them from the competition.

It was Hohner's decision in 1862 to become the first harmonica manufacturer to export instruments to North America that made his company a global giant. The demand from this new market became so great that for nearly a decade the Hohner Company sold its products exclusively to North Americans. By 1907, Hohner's annual output exceeded 7 million instruments.

The diatonic harmonica had become one of the most popular instruments in the world, but it had not been able to compete in musical genres that demanded a complete chromatic range. In 1924, Hohner introduced a 12-hole, three-octave chromatic mouth organ that avoided gapped scales by repeating the tonic note at the beginning of each octave. It had two reed plates tuned a semitone apart – for example, C and C♯ – fitted onto a wooden comb. Players could achieve all the notes of the chromatic scale by pushing a spring-loaded button fixed to a slide to alternate between these reed plates. Now armed with a fully chromatic instrument, players began applying it to the classical repertoire and to the new music of jazz.

Nowhere was the mouth organ more popular than in the United States. Several regions settled largely by German immigrants – notably Texas, Illinois and the Carolinas – became known for the high caliber of their harmonica players. By the middle of the nineteenth century, mouth organs were commonly displayed on the shelves of general stores throughout the United States. They usually sold for $0.10, but models for half that price were available until the turn of the century. Harmonica holders, either attached to another instrument or worn around the player's neck, were developed to enable musicians to accompany themselves on the mouth organ while playing other instruments – the guitar in particular.

North American players were quick to put their own stamp on the European instrument. The harmonica's uncanny capacity for impersonation became a fetish among rural players, who perfected a genre of 'talking' harmonica pieces. Players came to be judged by how realistically they could duplicate the feral chaos of fox-and-hounds chases and the aural magnificence of the steam locomotive – themes that had long been staples in fiddlers' repertoires. One of the finest recorded examples of a harmonica train piece is Palmer McAbee's 1928 recording of 'McAbee's Railroad Piece,' in which all the various sounds of the steam locomotive – the hissing of the boilers, the haunting whistle, the clamorous rhythm of the wheels against the tracks, the sudden muting of the machine's roar as it enters a tunnel – are beautifully depicted. DeFord Bailey's 'Pan American Blues' and Freeman Stowers's 'Railroad Blues,' both of which also date from the 1920s, are two other outstanding examples of this motif.

The highlight of the harmonica train pieces, an eerie approximation of the lonesome whine of the steam whistle, was usually achieved by inhaling clusters of notes. The train song may have led to the 'cross-harp' style. Before the advent of this approach, a player who wanted to play a tune in the key of C would use a C harmonica. Because a C harmonica is so designated because its blow notes make up the C major chord, the player would end up playing mostly blow notes. As US harmonica players perfected their train whistles, they came to realize that draw notes not only offered a wider range of tonal effects than blow notes, but also could be 'bent' – that is, players could flatten them to sound a lower note by making slight changes in the shape of the mouth and the direction of the airstream. Many came to prefer the draw scale, an approach they dubbed 'cross harp' or 'second position.' (The traditional method became known as 'straight harp' or 'first position.') Because the draw notes on a C harmonica make up the G7 chord, cross-harp players use a C instead of a G harmonica to play in the key of G.

The 1920s saw the arrival of Borrah Minevitch and His Harmonica Rascals, a much-imitated professional harmonica group that mixed pathos, comedy and music and that for 25 years was one of North American vaudeville's most popular acts. The musical demands resulting from the concept of the harmonica band led to the development of new mouth organ models, including the bass harmonica, the chord harmonica (on which a player could perform an accompanimental role similar to that of a rhythm guitarist) and the polyphonia (which allowed the player to achieve glissandi and other special effects).

A remarkable harmonica soloist named Larry Adler was the next phenomenon to emerge. Both Minevitch and Adler were exponents of the new chromatic harmonica, but while the Harmonica Rascals focused on slapstick and popular songs, Adler performed in formal attire and came to adopt a repertoire more suited to the concert hall.

World War II brought the flow of Hohner harmonicas to the United States and the other Allied nations to a halt, depriving the firm of its largest market. After the war ended, Hohner moved quickly and successfully to recover its worldwide market. The large harmonica groups gave way to smaller, more economic combos – most often trios consisting of a lead chromatic, a chord and a bass harmonica. This approach was applied most successfully by the Harmonicats, whose echo-laden recording of 'Peg O' My Heart' was the surprise number one hit in the United States in 1947.

The harmonica was entering the electronic age. In a 1951 recording session, blues performer Little Walter (Marion Walter Jacobs) blew his harmonica into a cheap public-address microphone plugged into a guitar amplifier and unleashed a raw, intense and exciting torrent of swooping bent notes and slashing phrases. Bluesmen like Little Walter were a primary source of inspiration for Elvis Presley and the small army of performers who followed his lead, but the harmonica was absent from the heyday of rock 'n' roll.

By the end of the 1950s, harmonica sales were sagging. As Hohner celebrated its centennial, the company found itself having to expand its product line to include keyboard instruments. However, the harmonica's decline was suddenly reversed in 1963, when 'Love Me Do,' an engaging pop song driven by a harmonica hook, led to a remarkable cultural reshuffling in which the Beatles became a dominant force in rock 'n' roll. Most of the British bands that followed up on the Beatles' success in the United States were revealed to be disciples of US blues. White North American teenagers began to seek out the black blues artists who were only a subculture away. In the early 1960s, a University of Chicago student named Paul Butterfield began singing and playing the harmonica in the blues bars on the South Side, eventually forming a mixed-race rock/blues group whose 1965 debut album helped – in a fashion that would have been impossible a decade earlier – to bridge the gap between the white rockers and the blues players. It was Butterfield's band that Bob Dylan – who had already entranced folk music aficionados with his combination of a dense lyricism and an utterly basic sound punctuated by bursts of untamed harmonica playing – asked to accompany him when he began to remake himself as a rock star in the mid-1960s.

Harmonica sales in the United States surged, increasing by 66 percent in the single year between 1965 and 1966. The chromatic harmonica still had occasional flashes of glory – Henry Mancini's recording of 'Moon River,' one of the major pop hits of the decade, was framed around a George Fields solo – but the post-Butterfield hipsters were discovering blues players like James Cotton and Junior Wells, while country music fans were becoming reacquainted with the harmonica thanks to the hundreds of recordings featuring the diatonic virtuosity of Nashville session legend Charlie McCoy.

Diatonic harmonica players have subsequently extended that instrument's melodic boundaries. Howard Levy, best known for his work with Béla Fleck and the Flecktones, has pioneered a radical and unique style based on the overblow, the ability to achieve on the blow reed a note that is higher in pitch than the standard blow note. Levy has proved that the diatonic instrument has a role in jazz, which had previously been the province of chromatic harmonica players like Belgian Toots Thielemans.

Bibliography

Baker, Steve. 1990. *The Harp Handbook*. Hamburg: G&F Media.

Field, Kim. 1999. *Harmonicas, Harps, and Heavy Breathers*. New York: Cooper Square Press.

Haffner, Martin. 1991. *Harmonikas: Die Geschichte der Branche in Bildern und Texten* [Harmonicas: Their History in Words and Pictures]. Trossingen: Hohner-Verlag.

Licht, Michael S. 1980. 'Harmonica Magic: Virtuoso Display in American Folk Music.' *Ethnomusicology* 24(2): 211–21.

Raisner, Albert. 1961. *Le Livre de l'harmonica* [The Harmonica Book]. Paris: Presses du Temps Present.

Discographical References

Bailey, DeFord. 'Pan American Blues.' Brunswick 146. 1927: USA.

Beatles, The. 'Love Me Do.' Parlophone R 4949. *1962*: UK.

Harmonicats, The. 'Peg O' My Heart.' Vitacoustic 1. 1947: USA.

Mancini, Henry. 'Moon River.' RCA 7916. *1961*: USA.

McAbee, Palmer. 'McAbee's Railroad Piece.' Victor 21352. 1928: USA.

Paul Butterfield Blues Band, The. *Paul Butterfield Blues Band*. Elektra 7294. *1965*: USA. Reissue: Paul Butterfield Blues Band, The. *Paul Butterfield Blues Band*. Elektra 7559-60547-2. *1995*: USA.

Stowers, Freeman. 'Railroad Blues.' Gennett 6814. 1929: USA.

Discography

Adler, Larry. *Golden Era, Vol. 1*. Prestige 119. *1998*: UK.

Adler, Larry. *Golden Era, Vol. 2*. Prestige 120. *1998*: UK.

Cotton, James. *The Best of the Verve Years*. PolyGram 527371. *1995*: USA.

Fleck, Béla, and the Flecktones (with Howard Levy). *Flight of the Cosmic Hippo*. Warner Bros. 2-26562. *1991*: USA.

Little Walter. *The Essential*. MCA 9342. *1993*: USA.

McCoy, Charlie. *Charlie McCoy's Greatest Hits*. Monument MG7622. *1978*: USA.

Murad, Jerry, and His Harmonicats. *Greatest Hits*. Columbia 9511. *1990*: USA.

Reilly, Tommy. *Serenade*. Chandos CHAN 8486. *1986*: UK.

Reilly, Tommy. *Serenade, Vol. 2*. Chandos CHAN 6568. *1991*: UK.

Terry, Sonny. *Sonny Terry – The Folkways Years, 1944–1963*. Smithsonian Folkways ROSF 40033. *1991*: USA.

Thielemans, Toots. *Harmonica Jazz*. Tristar 80921. *1994*: USA.

Wells, Junior. *Best of the Vanguard Years*. Vanguard 79508. *1998*: USA.

Wells, Junior. *Keep on Steppin': The Best of Junior Wells*. Telarc 83444. *1998*: USA.

KIM FIELD

Khaen (also spelled *Khene, Kaen, Khen, Kehn*)

The *khaen* is a vertically held free-reed mouth organ indigenous to the Lao culture of lowland Laos and the neighboring Isan (Isaan) region of northeastern Thailand. Although *khaen* are made in various sizes and registers, the most commonly used form (called *khaen paet*) is approximately 39" (1 m) in length, and is constructed of 16 slender bamboo tubes of graduated length which pass through and are sealed into a hardwood wind chest (which also serves as the instrument's mouthpiece). The tubes are bound together in raft form, in two flat rows of eight, with a finger hole burned into each tube just above the wind chest. In the wall of each tube, within the wind chest, is mounted a small metal free reed (usually made of an alloy of copper and silver), which responds to both the blowing out and the drawing in of air when the finger hole in the pipe is covered. The instrument's seven-tone tuning system approximates the Western natural minor scale over a compass of two octaves (often ranging from G to g^1, or A to a^1). The *khaen*'s traditional idiom involves the stopping of specific pipes (according to the pentatonic *lai*, or mode, being performed), to produce one or two high drones under which the performer improvises modally, using traditional formulae. The use of drones, combined with melodic playing (often in octaves, fifths or fourths), as well as the use of tone clusters, makes the *khaen* a polyphonic instrument.

The quintessential traditional instrument of the Lao, the *khaen* is indispensable in accompanying the repartee singing known as *mawlam* (also spelled *mor lam*). It is also an integral component of the *bong lang* instrumental ensemble, and is used as a solo instrument (a *khaen* specialist being known as a *maw khaen*). In addition to these traditional uses, the *khaen* is also featured in various Thai and Laotian hybrid popular music forms, including *lam sing* and *luk thung*. In these and other popular genres, however, the sound of the *khaen* is often simulated by Western instruments of similar timbre, including the accordion and, more recently, the electronic keyboard.

In Thai popular music, the *khaen* is featured most prominently in the northeastern genre known as *lam sing* ('*sing*' is derived from the English word 'racing'). *Lam sing*, a highly amplified, danceable hybrid of *mawlam* (particularly *lam klawn*) and various forms of Thai and Western popular music, was developed in the Isan region of Thailand in the mid-1980s, and was popularized in 1989 by *mawlam* singer and impresario Ratri

Srivilai and her brother. This genre supplements the traditional contingent of singers and *khaen* with a band of amplified instruments, including electric *phin* (a northeastern Thai lute), electric guitar, electric bass guitar (often carved in the shape of a *phin*), electronic keyboard and drumset. Additionally, the *khaen* is often employed in the folk-based popular song genre of *luk thung*, although its role is primarily that of evoking the flavor of Lao tradition. It may be heard only during a short solo at the beginning of a selection. One *khaen* performer who achieved widespread fame in Thailand was the late *luk thung* singer Samai Onwong, who played *khaen* in his recordings from the 1970s onward. More experimentally, Fong Nam featured blind *khaen* virtuoso Sombat Simla in a musical dialog with US jazz musicians on its 1994 album *Bang-cock: Bang-kok*.

In Laos, the *khaen* is also used to accompany modernized forms of *mawlam* influenced by the aforementioned Isan styles; recordings of this music, known collectively as *lam lao*, are distributed in the United States by companies based in southern California, and are widely available in Lao markets throughout North America.

Since the 1980s, a number of non-indigenous performers have acquired facility on the *khaen*, often through study with Thai musicians. Rather than playing exclusively in traditional styles, they have frequently developed personal approaches to the instrument for use within the contexts of pop, rock, new age, world fusion and jazz musics. Some of these musicians use the *khaen* to produce Western harmonies rather than the traditional drone (or drones) plus melody. English musician Clive Bell has used *khaen* extensively in the context of free improvisation, as well as with numerous pop and ambient groups, notably the UK-based Japanese pop band Frank Chickens and the UK dub experimenter Jah Wobble. Composer and multi-instrumentalist Randy Raine-Reusch, from Vancouver, uses *khaen* with his intercultural ensemble ASZA, and has played the instrument as a guest with the rock groups Aerosmith, the Cranberries and Yes. Composer-performer Kenneth Newby, also from Vancouver, has used *khaen* with his eclectic ensemble Trance Mission, as well as in various solo projects. In the United States, virtual reality pioneer and multi-instrumentalist Jaron Lanier has explored the improvisational possibilities of *khaen* in collaboration with a number of jazz and rock musicians, including Ornette Coleman, Stanley Jordan, Cyro Baptista, Duncan Sheik and Vernon Reid. Virtuoso *khaen* player (and University of San Diego music professor) Christopher Adler has composed a number of works for solo *khaen*, as well as *khaen* with Western instruments, since 1996.

Australian musicians Collin Offord and Ron Reeves have both used *khaen*: Offord in their duo Australis, and Reeves in the groups Okuta Percussion (based in Germany), Earth Music and Warogus (both based in Indonesia). Other musicians who have used *khaen* in their work include California-based musicians Randy Graves and Larry Cammarata (both of whom have used it in their world fusion ensemble Didginus); Asian-American composer-performer Forrest Fang; US percussionist Charles K. Noyes; San Francisco improvisational ensemble Aono Jikken; Japanese saxophonist Kazutoki Umezu; German cellist Hans Christian; Italian wind player Maurizio Serafini of the group Ogam; Swedish keyboardist Lars Hollmer; Brazilian jazz guitarist Egberto Gismonti; and Russian accordionist Alexei Levin. Jah Wobble's 2000 release *Molam Dub* is an unusual, but successful, collaboration between Wobble's own reggae-inflected band and the Paris-based Laotian ensemble Molam Lao (*khaen* played by M. Khampha Inthisane).

Although the *khaen* has remained popular in both traditional and popular contexts within Thailand and Laos, its integration in popular music ensembles has created problems of balance; in *lam sing*, for example, the *khaen* may often be almost inaudible – either being unamplified or drowned out by the sound of the electronic keyboard. However, the *khaen*'s wide register and its fortuitous compatibility with the Western tuning system have made it the most popular Asian mouth organ utilized by creative Western performers searching for an increased palette of sounds.

Bibliography

Clewley, John. 1994a. 'Old Style Indochina: The Sounds of Laos.' In *World Music: The Rough Guide*, ed. Simon Broughton et al. London: Rough Guides Ltd., 448–49.

Clewley, John. 1994b. 'The Many Sounds of Siam: Thai Music Ranges from Classical to Bikers' Rock.' In *World Music: The Rough Guide*, ed. Simon Broughton et al. London: Rough Guides Ltd., 440–48.

Fetzer, Casey A., and Cottingham, James P. *Acoustics of the Khaen: The Laotian Free-Reed Mouth Organ*. http:// trfn.pgh.pa.us/free-reed/essays/khaen.html

Lilly, Joseph. *An Introduction to the Khaen of Laos*. http:// trfn.pgh.pa.us/free-reed/essays/khaenlaos.html

Miller, Terry E. 1980. *An Introduction to Playing the Kaen*. Kent, OH: Privately published.

Miller, Terry E. 1984. 'Khaen.' In *The New Grove Dictionary of Musical Instruments*, Vol. 2, ed. Stanley Sadie. London: Macmillan, 420–21.

Miller, Terry E. 1985. *Traditional Music of the Lao: Kaen Playing and Mawlum Singing in Northeast Thailand*. Contributions in Intercultural and Comparative Studies, No. 13. Westport, CT: Greenwood Press.

Miller, Terry E., and Williams, Sean, eds. 1998. *The Garland Encyclopedia of World Music. Vol. 4: Southeast Asia*. New York and London: Garland Publishing, Inc.

Molam Dub. http://www.molamdub.com/

Discographical References

Fong Nam. *Bang-cock: Bang-kok*. B&M/Bellezza. *1994*: Thailand.

Wobble, Jah, and the Invaders of the Heart. *Molam Dub*. 30 Hertz 30HZCD 12. *2000*: UK.

Discography

Accordions Go Crazy. *The Art of Paperfolding*. Trikont US-0177. *1991*: Germany.

Accordions Go Crazy. *Overboard*. Trikont CD 00151-26. *1988*: Germany.

Accordions Go Crazy. *Zombie Dancer*. Trikont US-0160. *1989*: Germany.

Aerosmith. 'Hoodoo.' *Pump*. Geffen 9 24254-2. *1989*: USA.

Aono Jikken. *A Page of Madness*. Gold Mountain Supply Company GMSC-01. *1999*: USA.

ASZA. 'Toei Khong.' *ASZA*. Pacificline Music PM1410CD. *1995*: Canada.

Bell, Clive. 'Aventure Birmane.' *Bandes Originales du Journal du Spirou*. Nato NATO 1715/1774. *1989*: France.

Bell, Clive. *Eating*. Sound & Language SLCD 0005. *1997*: UK.

Bell, Clive. *The West Has Won*. MegaRec 97:01. *1997*: Italy.

Bell, Clive, and Cusack, Peter. *Bird Jumps into Wood*. Bead BEAD 22. *1984*: UK.

Beresford, Steve. *Fish of the Week*. Scatter SB-05-CD. *1996*: Scotland.

British Summer Time Ends. *Pop Out Eyes*. Nato NATO 707. *1986*: France.

British Summer Time Ends. *Spy Among the Roses*. Nato NATO DK 53006-2. *1992*: France.

Christian, Hans. *Surrender*. Allemande 9601. *1996*: USA.

Cranberries, The. 'Free to Decide.' *To the Faithful Departed*. Island 314 524 234-2. *1996*: USA.

Didginus. 'Feel This Love.' *Into the Soul*. Ginger Root GRRD-001. *1997*: USA.

Didginus. 'Feel This Love.' *More Than Alive*. Ginger Root GRRD-003. *1998*: USA.

Dolphin Brothers. *Catch the Fall*. Virgin CDV 2434. *1987*: UK.

Everything Play. *Posh*. Crown. *1991*: Japan.

Fang, Forrest. 'The Dragon King's Advice.' *Folklore*. Cuneiform Rune 68. *1995*: USA.

Fong Nam. 'Toi Kai Baw Khio.' *Bang-cock: Bang-kok*. B&M/Bellezza. *1994*: Thailand.

Frank Chickens. 'Annabella.' *Yukasita/Underfloor World*. Toy's Factory 009/TFCK-88715. *1994*: Japan. Reissue:

Frank Chickens. 'Annabella.' *Yukasita/Underfloor World*. Creativeman Discs M38736. *1997*: UK.

Frank Chickens. *Club Monkey*. Flying Records STIR 2 x. *1989*: UK. Reissue: Frank Chickens. *Club Monkey*. Resurgence RES137. *1998*: UK.

Gismonti, Egberto. *Dança Das Cabeças*. ECM 1089 78118-21089-2. *1977*: USA.

Gismonti, Egberto. *Egberto Gismonti*. EMI 31C 064 422940. *1984*: Brazil.

Graves, Randy. *Beginnings, Vol. 2*. Ginger Root RG02. *1996*: USA.

Hollmer, Lars. 'Endlich ein Zamba.' *Planet Squeezebox*. Ellipsis Arts CD3470 (CD3471-3473). *1995*: USA.

Kahondo Style. *Green Tea and Crocodiles*. Nato NATO 1279. *1987*: France.

Kahondo Style. *My Heart's in Motion*. Nato NATO 469. *1985*: France.

Kent, Stephen. *Family Tree*. City of Tribes COTCD-016. *1997*: USA.

Lanier, Jaron. *Instruments of Change*. Point Music 442-132-2. *1994*: USA.

Laswell, Bill, and Sacred System. 'Driftwork.' *Nagual Site*. Wicklow 09026-63263-2. *1998*: USA.

Malakham, Chelimpon, and Ponsri, Pimpa. *Khu Khwan Mawlam #2*. RT 70-4599. *ca. 1994*: Thailand.

Newby, Kenneth. 'Fathom.' *Sirens*. City of Tribes COTCD-015. *1997*: USA.

Newby, Kenneth. 'For a Pavilion of Wind & Cloud ~ Eileithyia.' *The Event Horizon: Psi*. City of Tribes COTCD-009. *1995*: USA.

Phouvieng and Malavanh. *Lam Lao Yawt Hit Chut Phiset*. J.K.B. Productions. *1996*: USA.

Polygenes. *Nine Stones*. Polymuse PM77771. *1996*: UK.

Raine-Reusch, Randy, and Oliveros, Pauline. *In the Shadow of the Phoenix*. Big Cat ABB 1000/3 (third CD of *Driftworks* [4-CD set], Big Cat ABB 1000CD). *1997*: UK.

Schütze, Paul. *Second Site*. Virgin AMBT 23. *1997*: UK.

Srivilai, Ratri. 'Thai Lam Sing Repartee Song.' *The Garland Encyclopedia of World Music. Vol. 4: Southeast Asia – Selected Audio Examples*. Garland Publishing, Inc. *1998*: USA/UK.

Thepsiri, Duangpon. *Pawn Pawn Nai Duangjai*. Sure Audio Co., Ltd. *ca. 1994*: Thailand.

Third Person. *Trick Moon*. Tsuki No Uso TU-001. *1991*: Japan.

Trance Mission. 'Every Stone's Dream.' *Meanwhile*. City of Tribes COTCD-005. *1994*: USA.

Trance Mission. 'Kif.' *Trance Mission*. City of Tribes COTCD-002. *1993*: USA.

Umezu, Kazutoki. *First Deserter*. Off Note ON-7. *1995*: Japan. Reissue: Umezu, Kazutoki. *First Deserter*. Knitting Factory Works KFW 214. *1997*: USA.

Vershki da Koreshki. 'Chimtchak Salghin.' *Vershki da Koreshki*. Al Sur ALCD 204. *1996*: France.

Warogus. 'Lai Kha.' *Celebration*. WML (World Music Library)/Gema Nada Pertiwi CMNW-003. *1997*: Indonesia.

Wobble, Jah. *The Inspiration of William Blake*. All Saints AS29. *1996*: UK.

Wobble, Jah. *The Light Programme*. 30 Hertz 30HZCD 3. *1998*: UK.

Wobble, Jah. *Umbra Sumus*. 30 Hertz 30HZCD 5. *1998*: UK.

Wobble, Jah, and the Invaders of the Heart. *The Celtic Poets*. 30 Hertz 30HZCD 1. *1997*: UK.

Wobble, Jah, and Zi Lan Liao. *The Five Tone Dragon*. 30 Hertz 30HZCD 8. *1998*: UK.

Yes. *The Ladder*. Beyond Music 63985-78046-2. *1999*: USA.

Zorn, John. 'Pool.' *The Parachute Years, 1977–1980*. Tzadik TZ 7316. *1997*: USA.

DAVID BADAGNANI

Klarino

'*Klarino*' is a Greek word for clarinet. In Greek, the word '*klarineto*' is also used, but it refers to the clarinet as part of a symphony orchestra or a jazz band, while the word '*klarino*' is reserved for the same wind instrument as part of a folk ensemble. Because the *klarino* has continued to play such an important role in Greek folk music, it is assumed that it has existed since time immemorial.

The *klarino* was the second classical music instrument of European origin to enter Greece in the middle of the nineteenth century and become part of Greek folk music ensembles, along with the *violi* (the violin). Interestingly, although it was used in wind bands and other orchestras in Corfu and the other islands of the Italian-occupied Eptanese, the *klarino* did not come to the mainland via this route. It was, in fact, introduced in Epirus and western Macedonia by gypsies from the Ottoman Empire, and was soon incorporated into local music groups. Gypsies were renowned and innovative musicians, and some of the best contemporary *klarino* players are gypsies. Eventually, over a period of more than a century, the *klarino* became the most important melodic instrument in the folk music of the mainland. The only parts of Greece where the instrument never became popular were the islands, partly because another melodic instrument, the *lira*, was a strong presence in these areas.

Before the introduction of the *klarino*, the most popular wind instruments of Greek folk music were the *flogera*, a type of recorder made of wood, reed or bone, and the *zournas* (*zurna*), a type of primitive oboe (cone-shaped, with a double reed for the production of sound). The *zournas* was usually played with the accompaniment of the *daouli* (large drum), mostly outdoors. The introduction of the *klarino* facilitated the formation and gradual establishment of a more complex and elaborate music group, the *kompania*, which included the *klarino*, the violin, the *la(g)outo* (lute), the *defi* (drum) and, sometimes, the *santouri* (santur).

Wherever they were introduced, the *klarino* and the violin gradually replaced the local instruments, which were more primitive in construction, harsher in sound, and less demanding in skill and specialized technique. The new instruments profoundly influenced folk music, because they allowed for an increase in the melodic range, a refinement in sound and the adoption of new musical traits. They were also more suitable for playing indoors, in large halls and houses, rather than outdoors, at village feasts, where the older instruments were still prominent.

The playing of the *klarino* was, in turn, also influenced by the playing techniques and sound of older wind instruments, like the *flogera*. Greek *klarino* players do not use the instrument in the typical classical way, as a tempered instrument; rather, they make every effort to imitate the modal scales of Greek music and singing, producing micro-intervals and endless expressive glissandi, using techniques of the *flogera* as well as inventing others of their own.

More than a century after their introduction into Greek music, the *klarino* and the violin, as well as the music traditions associated with them, have continued to flourish, although they have certainly been affected by the introduction of electronic keyboards into Greek folk music in the 1950s and 1960s.

Bibliography

Anogeianakis, Foivos. 1976. *Ellinika Laika Mousika Organa* [Greek Traditional Musical Instruments]. Athens: Ekdosi ethnikis trapezas.

Mazaraki, Despoina. 1984 (1959). *To Laiko Klarino stin Ellada* [Folk Klarino in Greece]. Athens: Kedros.

PANAYOTIS PANOPOULOS

Pan Pipes

Pan pipes, consisting of tubes sealed at the lower end and blown across the open end to create a sound, have developed independently in many parts of the world. The most prevalent forms were traditionally made from natural cane, reeds or bamboo, in which a natural node seals the closed end. While a wide range of different forms of pan pipes and performance techniques are found in, for example, Oceania (Zemp 1978, 1981), Africa (Tracey 1971; Jones 1992, 53–59; Turino 2000, 69) and Amazonia (Taylor 1972; Izikowitz 1970), the most prominent forms of mass-mediated music featuring pan pipes are those of Romania and the Andes.

The tubes of Romanian-style pan pipes (*nai*) are glued together into a wooden curved casing at the lower end of the tubes, and organized in sequence according to size to create a diatonic scale. The most common standardized instrument consists of 20 tubes (b^1-g^4 with F♯s), although other sizes, with variable numbers of tubes, are common. The open ends of the tubes are slightly beveled, which also enables players to achieve chromatic notes by tilting the instrument. It was in the hands of Gheorghe Zamfir, in the early 1970s, that the Romanian pan pipes began to become well known internationally. A virtuoso capable of making this instrument extremely lyrical, Zamfir made many recordings, accompanied on the organ by Marcel Cellier. However, despite Zamfir's many recordings of Romanian music, most of the available CDs of his music are of the 'easy listening' variety, where he has achieved enormous international success.

The Andes are home to an immense range of pan pipes, commonly made from cane, bamboo or plastic tubing. There is ample evidence of the existence of developed pan pipe making and performance traditions in pre-Hispanic times. In the countryside, pan pipes are usually played in consort and often with drums, but not with other wind or stringed instruments. The pipes are sometimes organized sequentially, a single raft including all the notes of the scale (for example, the 17-tube Bolivian *sikuri*). However, it is more common for the notes of the scale to be divided between paired rafts. In the case of a standardized (urban) *zampoña* in G, one of these rafts consists of six tubes and produces the odd tones of the diatonic scale (e, g, b, d^1, f♯^{1}, a^1), while the other consists of seven tubes and produces the even tones (d, f♯, a, c^1, e^1, g^1, b^1). In rural contexts, these paired rafts have traditionally taken the form of separate instruments played by two players, who 'interlock' their complementary pitches to create a melody. These paired sets of pan pipes in rural ensembles (for example, the *Kantu* ensembles of Charazani, Bolivia) often consist of a range of sizes that play in parallel octaves and fifths.

With the rise of Andean urban folk groups – especially since the 1970s and the Chilean *nueva canción* (new song) movement – it has become common to combine pan pipes with other instruments. Los de Ramón were among the earliest Chilean groups to incorporate the *zampoña* (ca. 1967), while from 1969 Los Calchakis were also making recordings in Paris. While the internationally known Chilean groups Inti-illimani and Quilapayún also exploited the pan pipes from the 1970s onward, it was Bolivian ensembles such as Grupo Aymara that developed the musical role of the pan pipes. For example, in the group's first recording, *Concierto en los andes de Bolivia* (1973), Clarken Orosco introduced vibrato into his style, which was quickly imitated by other players, and used pan pipes of different sizes, including the very large *toyos*, to create a range of musical effects (Wara-Cespedes 1984, 229). Andean pan pipes reached a mass market in the United Kingdom in the 1980s with the chart success of the album *Cacharpaya* by the group Incantation, while in the early 2000s Colombian singer Shakira has used pan pipes – ironically of the Romanian variety – on certain recordings.

The typical lineup for urban folk groups from the 1970s was to become pan pipes (*zampoña*), *quena*, *charango*, Spanish guitar and *bombo* (drum). Pan pipes have been used in a range of ways, providing harmonic or polyphonic lines and lyrical melodies, as well as breathy rhythmic textures. In this context, it has become common for a single pan pipe player to play both rafts (of smaller instruments) at once; accordingly, urban *zampoñas* are typically sold with the two rafts tied together. The raft furthest from the player is usually placed slightly higher to facilitate movement between rows.

A number of chromatic pan pipes have been developed in order to extend the tonal capabilities of the instrument, including that of the Chilean group Ortiga (ca. 1978) and the three-row instrument of artists based at (the former) Peña Naira, La Paz, Bolivia between 1973 and 1985. The Bolivian musician Ernesto Cavour developed a two-row instrument, which he describes in detail in his book *Instrumentos musicales de Bolivia* (1994).

Recently, pan pipes have become increasingly associated with background easy listening and mood music. Often in a sampled form, they are used in ambient music to accompany meditation, massage and a range of New Age practises. In particular, these sounds are often used to evoke and create a connection with imagined notions of Andean spirituality.

Bibliography

Cavour, Ernesto. 1994. *Instrumentos musicales de Bolivia* [Musical Instruments of Bolivia]. La Paz, Bolivia: Edición CIMA.

Izikowitz, Karl G. 1970. *Musical and Other Sound Instruments of the South American Indians*. East Ardsley, UK: S.R. Publishers.

Jones, Claire. 1992. *Making Music: Musical Instruments in Zimbabwe Past and Present*. Harare: Academic Books.

Taylor, Donald. 1972. *The Music of Some Indian Tribes of Colombia*. London: British Institute of Recorded Sound.

Tracey, Andrew. 1971. 'The Nyanga Panpipe Dance.' *African Music* 5(1): 73–89.

Turino, Thomas. 2000. *Nationalists, Cosmopolitans, and Popular Music in Zimbabwe*. Chicago: University of Chicago Press.

Wara-Cespedes, Gilka. 1984. 'New Currents in Música Folklórica in La Paz, Bolivia.' *Latin American Music Review* 5(2): 217–42.

Zemp, Hugo. 1978. ''Are'are Classification of Musical Types and Instruments.' *Ethnomusicology* 22(1): 37–67.

Zemp, Hugo. 1981. 'Melanesian Solo Polyphonic Panpipe Music.' *Ethnomusicology* 25(3): 383–418.

Discographical References

Grupo Aymara. *Concierto en los andes de Bolivia*. Lauro LCD-0004. *1973*: Bolivia.

Incantation. *Cacharpaya (Panpipes of the Andes)*. Beggars Banquet BEGA 39. *1982*: UK.

Discography

'Are'are Panpipe Ensemble. *Chants of the Solomon Islands*. Le Chant du Monde 274961. *1994*: France.

Incantation. *Remembrance*. Recall 155. *1998*: France.

Inti-illimani. *The Best of Inti-Illimani*. Xenophile 4055. *2000*: USA.

K'Jarkas. *El Amor y la Libertad*. Tumi 013. *1989*: UK.

Los Calchakis. *El Dorado*. Arion ARN-64204. *1992*: USA.

Ortiga. *Ortiga*. Warner Brothers 1667. *2000*: Germany.

Polyphonies of the Solomon Islands. Le Chant du Monde CNR 274663. *1996*: France.

Quilapayún. *Umbral*. Dom 4282025. *1998*: USA.

Rumillajta. *Takiririllasu*. Rumillajta Recordings 951. *1994*: UK.

Shakira. *Laundry Service*. Sony 63900. *2001*: USA.

Zamfir, Gheorghe. *Gypsy Passion*. Special Music 5153. *1995*: Switzerland.

Zamfir, Gheorghe. *King of the Pan Flute and Other Favorites*. Bescol 315. *2000*: USA.

THE EDITORS with CÉSAR QUEZADA

Pennywhistle (Africa)

Played by urban black South Africans from the early 1900s, pennywhistles were first used extensively in the 1930s and 1940s by the 'Scottishes' – bands of youths who, playing pennywhistles and drums, imitated the dress and marching formations of Scottish pipe bands. The pennywhistle came into its own in the early 1950s with the widespread commercial success of *kwela*, a fusion of North American swing with 'traditional' South African musics and urban black South African styles like *marabi*.

The pennywhistles used were imported mainly from Britain and Germany and cost five to nine shillings each. They consisted of a six-hole cylindrical metal tube (initially brass, later nickel-plated), molded at one end into a fipple mouthpiece. Although the instruments were designed to play two octaves in one major key (B♭

and G instruments being the most popular), *kwela* musicians devised various fingering techniques to produce chromatic and 'bent' notes. By partially covering the fipple opening with their lips, South African pennywhistlers developed a distinctive embouchure which produced a loud, 'buzzy' timbre, and lowered the pitch approximately a semitone.

Kwela was initially played on pennywhistles and guitars, but a drumset and string bass were added to the basic *kwela* lineup when the style was first recorded. By the late 1950s, saxophones increasingly replaced pennywhistles, and guitars were electrified. *Kwela* had mutated into sax jive (Allen 1998).

At the same time, however, pennywhistle *kwela* was being disseminated throughout southern Africa through extensive radio airplay, the export of records and the movement of migrant labor. Particularly popular in Zimbabwe, Zambia and Malawi, pennywhistle *kwela* developed further in Malawi in the 1960s and 1970s, when musicians such as Daniel and Donald Kachamba incorporated local stylistic elements (Kubik 1974).

Bibliography

Allen, Lara. 1998. '*Kwela*: The Structure and Sound of Pennywhistle Music.' In *Composing the Music of Africa: Composition, Interpretation and Realisation*, ed. Malcolm Floyd. Aldershot: Ashgate, 227–63.

Kubik, Gerhard. 1971–72. 'Die Verarbeitung von Kwela, Jazz und Pop in der modernen Musik von Malawi' [The Processing of *Kwela*, Jazz and Pop in the Modern Music of Malawi]. *Jazzforschung* 3/4: 51–115.

Kubik, Gerhard. 1974. *The Kachamba Brothers' Band: A Study of Neo-Traditional Music in Malawi*. Lusaka: Manchester University Press on behalf of the Institute for African Studies, University of Zambia.

Discography

Kachamba, Donald. *Malawi: Concert Kwela*. Le Chant du Monde LDX 274972. *1994*: France.

Mashiyane, Spokes. *King Kwela*. Gallo Music Productions, African Classics CDZAC 50. *1991*: South Africa.

LARA ALLEN

Piccolo

The piccolo (the term 'piccolo' is a shortened version of the instrument's full name, the piccolo flute) is the highest-pitched member of the flute family, with a range that is an octave higher than that of the concert flute. The playing technique for the piccolo is the same as for the larger instrument, and its players are invariably 'doublers' (that is, they play both flute and piccolo). The piccolo's position at the extreme of the tonal range makes it difficult for the instrument to blend in smaller ensembles and to sustain primary melodies. Thus, the piccolo's typical role is that of reinforcing a melodic line in the higher octave during dramatic large-ensemble tutti passages. The piccolo has been prominent in performance situations where its piercing acoustic properties are idiomatic and functional, such as in large venues, at outdoor concerts, in marching ensembles or even in battle. In these contexts, the piccolo can make itself heard over competing sounds.

The piccolo's use in popular music has largely been confined to atmospheric effects, such as the imitation of bird calls or shrieking whistles, orchestral countermelodies (such as the famous passage in John Philip Sousa's 'Stars and Stripes Forever') or special textures, such as Gil Evans's pairing of piccolo and baritone saxophone several octaves apart for his arrangement of 'Blues in Orbit.' Popular jazz flautist Hubert Laws has recorded solos on the piccolo. Prominent in large studio orchestras, the instrument has also made occasional appearances in jazz, salsa and other forms of Latin dance music and, more rarely, in other forms of popular music. The piccolo was used in most New Orleans marching brass bands.

Sheet Music

Sousa, John Philip, comp. and lyr. 1898. 'Stars and Stripes Forever.' Cincinnati: John Church Company.

Discographical Reference

Evans, Gil. 'Blues in Orbit.' *Gil Evans Orch, Kenny Burrell & Phil Woods*. Verve 8838. *1964*: USA.

Discography

Laws, Hubert. *Afro Classic*. Columbia ZK-44172. *1970*: USA.

Laws, Hubert. *Storm Then the Calm*. Music Masters 65118. *1994*: USA.

MICHAEL MORSE

Quena (also spelled *Kena*, *Qina*)

The word '*quena*' is probably derived from the Aymara *quena-quena* (meaning literally 'full of holes'), a type of notched flute still played on the Bolivian altiplano. It is used generically to refer to many types of Andean notched flute, including such rural variants as *lichiwayu*, *mullu*, *phusi pia* and *choquela*. Archeological evidence of Andean notched flutes dates back to at least the Chavín era (900–200 B.C.), with pre-Hispanic examples found along the length of the Andes.

Quena are open-ended, vertically held flutes with a small section cut from the upper end, incorporating a sharp edge. The player's embouchure directs air against this edge to create the sound. Construction materials include cane, bone and plastic or brass tubing; the number of finger holes ranges from four to six, and there is sometimes a rear thumb hole. Rural notched flutes are typically played in a consort with drums, and are designed to play in unison, parallel fourths, fifths or octaves. The playing of *quena* is generally restricted to the Andean dry season (April–October), although in many villages and rural towns mestizo players often associate the *quena* with *Carnaval* (carnival).

The modern urban *quena* is a more standardized instrument, typically constructed from cane or wood, with six finger holes and a rear thumb hole. It is usually pitched in G, with a range of just over three octaves, and, with the use of many awkward half-holes, it can be played fully chromatically. Together with *charango*, pan pipes, Spanish guitar and percussion, the *quena* is an important member of the Andean urban folk ensemble, in which it is played solo or in pairs, typically at the interval of a third. It is noted for its sweet tone and its lyrical capacity.

The association of the *quena* with rural peasant culture hindered its acceptance by urban Creole and mestizo classes, while ironically contributing to its popularity outside the Andes, especially in France. A rise in its status occurred when it was adopted by intellectuals of the Peruvian *indigenismo* movement in the 1920s as an emblem of indigenous culture, and was played alongside mestizo instruments, such as guitars, mandolins and violins. However, the development of an urban *quena* technique has often been associated with Argentina, where important exponents have included Uña Ramos and Facio Santillan. Tito Yupanqui, a Bolivian exponent of the *quena*, also toured internationally during the 1950s. Another key figure was Swiss-born Gilbert Favre. After learning the *quena* in Argentina and conducting a liaison with Violeta Parra (1917–67) – the so-called 'mother' of Chilean *nueva canción* – Favre joined the highly influential group Los Jairas, based at the Peña Naira in La Paz, Bolivia. His idiosyncratic style, with vibrato and many glissandi, has found echoes in such Bolivian virtuosos as Rolando Encinas, Lucho Cavour and Adrian Villanueva.

The adoption of the *quena* by Chilean *nueva canción* groups, such as Quilapayún (1966) and Inti-illimani (1967), greatly increased the instrument's exposure in Europe and North America, especially during those musicians' exile following the military coup of 1973. The *quena* has since become a familiar instrument in the hands of Andean buskers and concert artists in many parts of the world. However, despite the instrument's remarkable expressivity, and a number of excellent exponents from outside the Andes, the *quena* has remained closely identified with Andean music and has only rarely been exploited in other genres.

Bibliography

Carrasco Pirard, Eduardo. 1982. 'The *nueva canción* in Latin America.' *The International Social Science Journal* 34: 599–623.

Cavour, Ernesto. 1971. *Aprenda a tocar quena: método audiovisual* [Learn to Play the *Quena*: An Audiovisual Method]. La Paz, Bolivia: Campo LPC-010.

Cavour, Ernesto. 1994. *Instrumentos musicales de Bolivia* [Musical Instruments of Bolivia]. La Paz, Bolivia: Edición CIMA.

Turino, Thomas. 1993. *Moving Away from Silence: Music of the Peruvian Altiplano and the Experience of Urban Migration*. Chicago: University of Chicago Press.

Wara-Cespedes, Gilka. 1984. 'New Currents in Música Folklórica in La Paz, Bolivia.' *Latin American Music Review* 5(2): 217–42.

Discography

Ramos, Uña. *El Arte de la Quena, Vol. 1*. ALFA (AFCD 9). *1990*: Switzerland.

HENRY STOBART

Recorder

The recorder is an instrument whose ancestors date back to ancient Greek instruments, including the *aulos*, itself a descendant of even older Egyptian instruments. The recorder is a one-, two- or three-piece, flute-like instrument with a conical bore and a 'whistle-like' mouthpiece. All recorders have eight holes, one of which is on the underside of the instrument. To create the recorder's distinct soft, reedy tones, the player blows through the mouthpiece and places his/her fingers on and off select open nodal points or finger holes; the thumb is used to block the hole on the underside. In larger recorders, there is sometimes a padded mechanical lever to help facilitate the opening and closing of the furthest hole down the bore. Initially, the recorder was made of wood, but hard plastic is now often used. There are, in the English tradition, four common sizes of recorder: descant, treble, tenor and bass. The type of recorder heard mostly in schools is the descant, or what is commonly referred to as the soprano, recorder.

The instrument's popularity rose and declined throughout the centuries in different countries. During the Renaissance, it was quite popular and is even mentioned in Shakespeare's *Hamlet*. Describing the technique of playing the recorder, and its effect, Hamlet states, 'It is as easy as lying. Govern these ventages [holes] with your fingers and thumb, give it breath with your mouth, and it will discourse most eloquent music' (3.2.356–67). Composers such as Bach and Handel also wrote for the instrument. However, by the nineteenth century the recorder's popularity was in overall decline among renowned artists and composers. Until a revival of the instrument in European and North American schools in the 1950s, interest in the recorder survived mostly in local communities, and among such folk specialists as Torbjørg Fykerud (1828–1920) and Knut Juveli (1865–1956) in Norway.

Since the 1950s, the recorder has been regarded principally as an instrument for schoolchildren learning to read and play music, although some folk and medieval groups have continued to use the instrument. A large amount of literature for the recorder exists in the form of method books and books of solos, but there are fewer recorded works. The instrument is used in the Orff system of teaching children music through the use of 'folk' tunes, and it has been used by some folk instrumentalists such as Ken Wollitz (United States) and Steinar Ofsdal (Norway).

The sound of the recorder tends to conjure a feeling of nature – of woodlands – and of a distant musical past. Although the recorder's use has been sparse in popular music, some notable exceptions exist. The Beatles' Paul McCartney plays the recorder in 'Fool on the Hill,' John Paul Jones of Led Zeppelin uses the instrument to great effect in 'Stairway to Heaven,' and Keith Jarrett plays the recorder on various tracks of his *Spirits* albums. The recorder has been used more commonly in folk and traditional music and can be heard on recordings by artists such as Scotland's Capercaillie (Scotland) and Fairport Convention.

Bibliography

The Recorder Education Journal. http://www.mwemm.com/arta/service/rej_contents.htm

Discographical References

Beatles, The. 'Fool on the Hill.' *Magical Mystery Tour.* Capitol SMAL 2835. *1968*: USA.

Jarrett, Keith. *Spirits* (2 CDs). ECM 1333/34. *1985*: Germany.

Led Zeppelin. 'Stairway to Heaven.' *Led Zeppelin [Fourth Album].* Atlantic 7208. *1971*: USA.

Discography

Capercaillie. *To the Moon.* Survival SURCD 019. *1996*: Scotland.

Fairport Convention. *The Cropredy Box* (3 CDs). Woodworm WR3CD026. *1998*: UK.

BHESHAM SHARMA and MIKE BROCKEN

Reed Section

A reed section is the part of a jazz orchestra or big band that is constituted of woodwind instruments – generally saxophones, clarinets and flutes. The term was not used to describe the woodwinds of the symphony orchestra, but came into use early in the jazz age. In his arrangements for Paul Whiteman, beginning in 1921, Ferde Grofé wrote for three reed players, with the idea that each musician would double on different instruments. Hence, in Whiteman's 1921–23 reed section, Don Clarke

always played alto saxophone, but Ross Gorman doubled on alto and clarinet, while Hale Byers doubled on soprano and tenor saxophone. This gave the arranger a considerable variety of available tone colors against which to offset the brass sections of trumpets and trombones, and the tradition continued thereafter.

In Fletcher Henderson's band, from 1923 onward, Don Redman continued this approach, writing arrangements in which the three musicians in the reed section (himself, Buster Bailey and Coleman Hawkins) were called on to double variously on goofus (a novelty free-reed instrument), oboe and clarinet, as well as on soprano, alto, tenor, baritone, bass and C-melody saxophones. Other African-American band leaders added the tone colors of less familiar reeds: in Sam Wooding's band, Garvin Bushell played jazz bassoon, and in Chick Webb's band, Wayman Carver repeated his pioneering use of flute from a recording band led by British bassist Spike Hughes.

In the 1930s, reed sections grew to four and then five players. Benny Goodman's orchestra, for example, used two alto saxophones and two tenors (in addition to Goodman's solo clarinet) for much of the 1930s, but in 1940 added an extra alto, and the following year replaced that with a baritone saxophone. Duke Ellington's band, which perhaps made more expressive use of its saxophone section than any other band of the period, had made a similar expansion to five reeds by 1940.

In his writing for Claude Thornhill's orchestra from 1941 onward, Gil Evans began to explore a new tonal palette for the saxophone section, in particular including the bass clarinet, which, although it had already been used by some leaders, took on a more prominent role. By the end of the decade, the most adventurous reed section in jazz was that of Stan Kenton's 'Innovations in Modern Music' orchestra, which, in 1950, called on its players to double on flute, oboe, cor anglais, bassoon, clarinet and bass clarinet, as well as on all the saxophones.

This kind of tonal variety was continued in the experimental big bands of Don Ellis, between the 1950s and 1970s. At the same time, in efforts to explore common ground between Western art music and jazz, the 'third stream' writing of Gunther Schuller and William Russo brought together elements of the symphonic woodwind section and the jazz reed section.

From the 1950s until the 1980s, the orchestras of Sun Ra employed a bewildering variety of reed instruments, but Ra's concept of musical orchestration broke down the more usual ideas of sections, so that he more often wrote for reeds in combination with brass or rhythm instruments than for reeds as a discrete section.

In the 1980s, as an offshoot of his work with the World Saxophone Quartet and other purely woodwind ensembles, such as his own saxophone sextet and octet, Julius Hemphill wrote for large groups in which a freely improvising woodwind ensemble could be accommodated within a conventional big band structure – notably on his double CD, *The Julius Hemphill Big Band*. This showed a radical approach to the treatment of a reed section (and indeed the whole orchestral palette), and comparable experiments continued in the work of Hemphill's former colleague David Murray.

Bibliography

Berendt, Joachim-Ernst. 1982 (1975). *The Jazz Book: From Ragtime to Fusion and Beyond*. Rev. ed. Westport, CT: Lawrence Hill. (First published Frankfurt am Main: Fischer Bücherei, 1953.)

Discographical Reference

Julius Hemphill Big Band, The. *The Julius Hemphill Big Band*. Elektra 60831-2. *1988*: USA.

Discography

Kenton, Stan. *Innovations in Modern Music*. Capitol P-189. 1950: USA.

ALYN SHIPTON

Shakuhachi

The shakuhachi is a vertical bamboo flute of Chinese origin, characterized by microtonal pitch movements and by a wide range of tonal colors. In its short form (*hitoyogiri*), it was used to accompany popular songs. A longer version (*Fuke-shakuhachi*) appeared in the sixteenth century and was used by mendicant Zen priests of the Fuke sect. Its religious associations, as well as its almost exclusive use by male players, have persisted, particularly through the stereotyped image of the samurai priest/shakuhachi player in television period dramas. The conventionalized singing of folk songs by professional 'folk singers' is invariably accompanied by a combination of shamisen and shakuhachi. The shakuhachi has also featured in more recent popular music, most notably in Takio Itô's contemporary min'yo band, Takio Band, and in the Malaysian fusion group Asiabeat, played by North American John Kaizan Neptune.

Bibliography

Tsukitani, Tsuneko. 1984. 'Shakuhachi.' In *Hôgaku Hyakkajiten* [The Encyclopedia of Japanese Music], ed. Eishi Kikkawa. Tokyo: Ongakunotomo, 491–93.

Discography

Asiabeat. *Drumusique*. Domo 71016. *1997*: USA.
Asiabeat. *Monsoon*. Domo 71012. *1996*: USA.
Itô, Takio. *Takio*. CBS/Sony 32DH5123. *1988*: Japan.
Itô, Takio. *Takio Spirit*. FXD-7033. *1991*: Japan.

Neptune, John Kaizan. *Bamboo*. Inner City IC-6077. *1981*: USA.
Neptune, John Kaizan. *Kite*. Kosei Publishing Company KJKN-9200. *1992*: Japan.
Neptune, John Kaizan. *River Rhythm*. Kosei Publishing Company KJKN-9300. *1993*. Japan.

TÔRU MITSUI

Shawm

'Shawm' is a generic term for a type of double-reed woodwind instrument found in many cultures across a wide geographical belt stretching from North Africa and Spain through Central and Southern Europe, the Middle East, India, China and Southeast Asia. The term also covers a family of instruments prevalent in both popular and art music in Europe from the thirteenth to the seventeenth centuries. The various regional names used appear etymologically related. In Turkey, Iraq, Syria and parts of the Caucasus, the instrument is known as the *zurna*. In Greece, it is the *zournas*, while it appears in Iran, Tajikistan, Uzbekistan and Afghanistan as *sorna*, *sornai* or *surnai*. Further east, it is known as the *sahnai* in India, the *sur-na* in Bhutan, and the *sona* or *suona* in China.

The instruments are not identical, but they share many characteristics, both physical and contextual. They have five main parts: the double reed, usually made of cane; a staple, to hold the reed; a pirouette – a small, circular piece of wood or metal through which the reed passes on its way into the instrument and which appears to aid circular breathing, a common technique among shawmists; a forked insert, shaped like a clothespin, which changes the largely cylindrical main bore of the instrument into a stepped conical bore; and the main body, normally made from one piece of wood, and usually with seven roughly equidistant finger holes and a thumb hole. Several smaller holes, sometimes known as 'the devil's finger holes,' are also drilled into the bell; these determine the effective acoustical length of the instrument, and supposedly moderate its often penetrating sound by reducing the number of upper harmonics.

The instruments are primarily heard in folk and traditional music and are often played by Gypsies or other nomads. They are, however, gradually being usurped, particularly in urban areas, by instruments such as the clarinet.

Bibliography

Anoyanakis, Fivos. 1979. *Greek Popular Musical Instruments*. Athens: National Bank of Greece.
Baines, Anthony. 1952. 'Shawms of the Sardana Coblas.' *The Galpin Society Journal* 5: 9–16.
Picken, Laurence. 1975. *Folk Musical Instruments of Turkey*. London: Oxford University Press.

Rice, Timothy. 1982. 'The Surla and Tapan Tradition in Yugoslav Macedonia.' *The Galpin Society Journal* 35: 122–37.

STEPHEN COTTRELL

c. Saxophone

General Description

The saxophone (Ger. *saxophon*, Fr. *saxophone*, It. *sassofone*) is a thin-walled brass instrument with a conical bore that widens to a slightly flared bell. Along its body is a series of holes, sized proportionally to the bore, each covered with a padded key. A single reed mouthpiece, originally made of wood and then of ebonite or metal, connects to the neck. The saxophone is similar to the clarinet and flute for fingering, and somewhat similar to the clarinet for sound production. The saxophone is considered a woodwind instrument.

History

In 1840–41, Adolphe Sax invented the lower-toned members of the saxophone family. The original family of saxophones, completed in 1845, comprised 14 in total: seven orchestral (tuned in the keys of F and C alternately with size) and seven for military bands (tuned in E♭ and B♭). The horns ranged from the smallest and highest-sounding sopranino through soprano, alto, tenor, baritone and bass, to the largest and lowest-sounding, contrabass. The two smallest sizes were usually straight, while the larger sizes were curved at a 90° angle near the neck and U-shaped by the last few holes. Saxophones tuned in E♭ and B♭ were used almost exclusively in all musical contexts by the end of the twentieth century.

The saxophone was designed to bridge the gap between the sounds of brass and woodwind instruments, and to compensate for missing stringed instruments like the cello in a large ensemble. French and Belgian bands were the first to adopt the saxophone, in 1847, followed by bands across Europe and North America. Most bands used at least a quartet (soprano, alto, tenor and baritone). Around the world, saxophones became a part of popular bands in the early 1900s.

The saxophone was not commonly used in classical music, although a few composers, such as Ravel, Berlioz and Debussy, included it in some works. While still not considered a permanent member of the orchestra, the saxophone was more widely used in orchestral and chamber music by the end of the twentieth century, including its use in Cantonese opera. There were many saxophone quartets worldwide that played specially arranged or commissioned classical music, new music, ragtime and popular tunes.

Throughout the twentieth century, the saxophone was used increasingly in numerous genres of popular music worldwide, although it became most commonly associated with jazz.

Range, Tone and Performance Techniques

Each saxophone has a range of approximately 2 1/2 octaves. Using a technique of overblowing to achieve harmonics, players can play in the altissimo register, several octaves above the regular range. Alternate fingerings help with the agility and tuning precision of these high notes.

The tone of the saxophone has been variously described as soulful, sexy, open, raspy, growly, aggressive and like the human voice. In addition to its unique tone colors, it has a wide dynamic range. Part of the appeal of the saxophone is its capacity for individual sounds.

Many factors contribute to an individual's saxophone sound. The player's embouchure is a combination of the position of the lips on the reed, lip pressure, lip control, air pressure, the position of the jaw, the angle of the mouthpiece and the position of the tongue. A player may choose from a myriad of techniques to enhance his/her individual tone: tonguing, vibrato, harmonics, tuning in quarter tones and microtones and circular breathing. As well, a player may explore the multiphonics of the saxophone, as it has the capacity to produce more than one tone at a time throughout its entire range. By using alternate fingerings for one note, a player can attain different timbres. As well, many different makes and models of mouthpiece, reed and saxophone are available, and saxophonists often find a preferred combination. The shape and dimension of the mouthpiece, the hardness and thickness of the reed and the size of facing (the space between the mouthpiece and the reed) all contribute to a player's tone.

In addition to the technical aspects that can combine to produce unique sounds, each genre in which the saxophone is used represents a different musical context, thus allowing, or even necessitating, individual saxophone sounds. The characteristic classical saxophone tone is 'purer' or 'cleaner' than the characteristic jazz tone. The facing of the mouthpiece is smaller in classical saxophone configuration than in jazz, and the reed is harder. By contrast, jazz saxophonists tend to prefer a technique that is achieved by putting less lip pressure on the reed and by relaxing/opening/dropping the jaw, which enlarges the mouth chamber. This technique is more difficult to control than that of the classical saxophone, but lends itself to a wider range of tone colors and to a larger sound.

Tonguing and articulation are important techniques that help to distinguish styles and eras of players. Bop-schooled players like John Coltrane and Sonny Rollins often used very hard tonguing to articulate. Players such as Lester Young produced their characteristic sound in part by not tonguing or by tonguing very softly or lightly. In small jazz ensembles, where amplification was minimal, saxophonists were able to play with a soft, 'woofy' tone and avoid being drowned out by the other instruments.

A specific 'studio' saxophone sound can be heard on soundtrack recordings, in Muzak and in some pop saxophone work. This sound is neither as rough as the jazz sound nor as focused as the classical sound, although it contains elements of both.

In blues, soul and rock, saxophones appeared in horn sections, playing occasional short, high-energy solos. These bands were often amplified and, in order to cut through the volume and texture of the other instruments, saxophonists developed a characteristic tone that was piercing, powerful or edgy. Some players sang from their throats into the mouthpiece and/or used flutter tonguing while playing to achieve a raunchy sound.

The early saxophone sound in Eastern European and Latin American music was characterized by ornamentation and wide vibrato.

Renowned Saxophonists and Their Techniques

The saxophone played a part in the very earliest forms of jazz, as is evident from the celebrated photograph (ca. 1900) of the Buddy Bolden Band from New Orleans. Generally speaking, however, the clarinet was more popular than the saxophone up to the late 1920s, although many reed players played both instruments. Two developments in jazz were especially significant in establishing the saxophone's centrality to jazz. Firstly, as the size of the jazz ensemble grew (in order, in part, to provide music at larger venues), the bigger sound of the saxophone become virtually indispensable. Secondly, the rising importance of the soloist, in both small groups and large ensembles, provided a platform for its emergence as a premier solo instrument.

The first renowned jazz saxophonist and soloist was Sidney Bechet, who played the soprano with a powerful, warm tone and wide vibrato. Soloists did not commonly use the baritone, bass and C-melody saxophones, with the notable exceptions of, respectively, Harry Carney, Adrian Rollini and Frank Trumbauer.

During the 1930s, saxophone or reed sections of up to five musicians were standard in both the 'hot jazz' big bands and the popular 'sweet' bands. Several future soloists began in swing bands, Coleman 'Hawk' Hawkins, the first major tenor saxophone star, being a prime example. Johnny Hodges was representative of big band alto playing/soloing with his swinging style, using quick punchy lines and a swooning, romantic, glissando-like smooth-

ness. Ben Webster, Duke Ellington's tenor player in the early 1940s, also stood out as a ballad player.

Lester Young became well known through his work both with Count Basie's big band and with jazz vocalist Billie Holiday. Young played with a lighter tone, using smoother tonguing and less vibrato, and playing straighter (less swinging) eighth notes.

One consequence of the major contribution to jazz made by Hawkins, Young and other saxophonists of the swing era was that the role of the instrument was increasingly looked to as one in which innovative playing was expected. In the exceptionally innovative era of bebop, in the 1940s, this role was taken further by the alto playing of Charlie 'Bird' Parker in particular. Parker did not 'invent' bebop, but his contribution was a decisive one that took jazz saxophone playing into new areas. Not only were his musical ideas often expressed at much higher speed than had been typical of swing players, but they were more complex harmonically and rhythmically and, like his fellow innovator, trumpeter Dizzy Gillespie, his phrasing was highly unpredictable by earlier standards.

Sonny Rollins was an important tenor player who could turn his solos into concerto-like performances by developing melodic ideas. His playing often demonstrated not only ingenuity but also great humor.

After Parker, John Coltrane was the next figure to revolutionize jazz (saxophone) playing. He expanded conceptions of harmony by playing with the established chords for a tune, by playing against them, by exploring all the available colors and qualities of the different notes and scales over the chords. Coltrane's highly developed technique set a new standard for jazz saxophonists. His solos were powerful, urgent presentations described as 'sheets of sound.' He used thick lines of notes interacting with the chord structure of a song and often clashing with those chords. The later and larger part of Coltrane's work draws on elements of spirituality and non-Western music, and points toward 'free jazz.'

In the 1950s and 1960s, the light, airy sound of west-coast 'cool jazz' saxophonists Paul Desmond, Stan Getz, Gerry Mulligan and Lee Konitz contrasted with the intensity of hard bopper Joe Henderson and iconoclast Eric Dolphy. Julian 'Cannonball' Adderley, known for his work with Miles Davis, later formed his own soul-jazz group, which recorded the popular 'Mercy, Mercy, Mercy.'

Wayne Shorter has been a prominent saxophonist and composer in recent jazz movements, including modern jazz and jazz-rock fusion. Shorter's playing with Miles Davis and with the group Weather Report helped to popularize jazz-rock fusion. A movement that came to be known as 'free jazz' was based on an abandonment of conventional harmonic and rhythmic structures. Ornette Coleman's unconventional approach to saxophone playing influenced later 'free jazz' saxophonists such as Albert Ayler, Anthony Braxton and John Zorn. Zorn was known not only for his creative playing but also for his composing. He combined many different styles of playing, such as 'free jazz' and klezmer music. Influential jazz saxophonists of the 1980s and 1990s included Joe Lovano and Branford Marsalis. Norwegian saxophonist Jan Garbarek was well known for his work with Keith Jarrett, as well as with other international artists. The latter included Ustad Fateh Ali Khan, on whose CD *Ragas & Sagas* Garbarek performed.

As well as being a mainstay of jazz, the saxophone was able to cross over into other popular music genres, including 1940s rhythm and blues (R&B). Louis Jordan was a saxophone innovator in the 1940s within the smaller band or 'combo' style of R&B, which featured guitars, drums and small horn sections. Jordan's early compositions, such as the popular 'G.I. Jive,' 'Ain't Nobody Here But Us Chickens' and 'Choo Choo Ch'Boogie,' and his saxophone solos on such hits helped to establish a style that presaged rock 'n' roll saxophone playing. Curtis Ousley, better known as King Curtis, became popular through his soloing on tunes like the Coasters' 1958 hit 'Yakety Yak.' His career lasted well into the 1970s, as he played with Sam Cooke, the Isley Brothers, Aretha Franklin, Wilson Pickett, John Lennon and Eric Clapton.

One of the greatest R&B saxophone players of all time was Junior Walker. He became a star in the 1960s Motown era through his saxophone playing on a string of R&B hits like 'Shotgun' and 'Road Runner.' Saxophonist Maceo Parker introduced a new rhythmic style of playing in the mid-1960s with James Brown. Beyond his extensive funk playing, Maceo Parker worked with such diverse musicians as folk/alternative artist Ani DiFranco and Moroccan Gnaoua star Bachir Attar.

In the 1970s and 1980s, saxophonist David Sanborn's gutsy alto sound, employing extensive altissimo, was copied by many aspiring saxophonists in popular music. Other saxophonists working extensively in the popular music scene included Tom Scott, Michael Brecker, Grover Washington, Jr. and Kenny G.

In popular musical styles such as funk, blues, soul and rock, the saxophone is used both as a solo instrument and as part of a horn section. In these latter styles, the tenor saxophone has been used most often, due to its harder, more rasping sound. The saxophone's capacity for honking and screaming suits these genres, and each genre has drawn on similar saxophone licks (or melodic/rhythmic patterns) derived from the blues scale.

One of the improvisers of the 'Nashville sound' was a saxophone leader in the 'country style' called Boots Randolph, who became known through his solo playing on the 1960s hit 'Yakety Sax.'

The Saxophone in Popular Music Worldwide

In general, the saxophone is featured in popular music around the world just as it is in Anglo-American popular music, that is, as part of a vocalist's backup band. African examples include Ethiopian vocalist Aster Aweke and Sudanese vocalists Abdel Gadir Salim and Abdel Aziz el Mubarak, all of whom employ saxophones in their backup bands, the latter two artists both playing with saxophonist Hamid Osman. In addition to his work with Aweke, saxophonist Ray Carless has worked extensively with Indian popular vocalist Najma Akhtar, Polish pop-soul vocalist Basia, the Bhundu Boys, a 'jit' guitar band from Zimbabwe, and the UK acid jazz band Incognito. Other saxophonists active in non-Western popular music include Thierno Koite and Issa Cissocko (both of whom performed and recorded with Youssou N'Dour), Fekade Amdemsekel and Theodorus Meteku. In addition to their work in non-Western musical styles, saxophonists Philippe Herpin and Daniel Paboeuf were active in the popular music scene in France.

A further feature of popular music in countries around the world is the blending of folk music traditions with Western elements from the aforementioned genres to create a kind of fusion, or world music, that is still unique to each region. Often, Western instruments such as the saxophone are added to 'update' the folk or traditional music or to explore the fusion itself. In such cases, the fusion draws not only on the Western instruments but also on the energetic aesthetic of Western rock, pop, soul, funk and jazz.

Fusion music worldwide has incorporated the saxophone. Algerian *rai* musicians such as Bellemou Messaoud and Khaled included the saxophone, among other Western instruments, in their ensembles during the 1960s to 'update' their sound. In Spain, Jorge Pardo used the saxophone on his recording *In a Minute* to achieve a jazz/world/flamenco mix. The saxophone is also featured in the music of Egyptian Nubian and *shaabi* music stars Ali Hassan Kuban and Mohamed Mounir.

In the British Isles, Moving Hearts, an Irish rock group, has used an innovative mix of saxophones and *Uilleann* pipes to create a unique sound. The band UB40 from Birmingham has blended elements of Jamaican reggae with rock with the help of saxophonist Brian Travers. Steve Whitehead's soulful saxophone playing has helped the Welsh band Mabsant to achieve a blend of traditional and soul music. The Safri Boys, exponents of *bhangra* – dance music popular on the British/Asian scene since the 1970s – include the saxophone on their CD *Get Real*.

In the Scandinavian and Alpine regions of Europe, the saxophone has figured in popular bands that fuse folk music with jazz, rock and/or elements of both. Such bands were created in response to a folk music revival that emerged during the 1980s. The German group Die Interpreten fuses Bavarian folk with jazz; Piirpauke, a Finnish group, blends Finnish traditional music with Latin, Caribbean and Asian influences using the saxophone; and Sweden's Groupa features Jonas Simonson on bass saxophone in its lineup.

Other Eastern European/North American fusions include polka and klezmer music. It is common for polka bands such as Lenny Gomulka and Chicago Push, the Moms & Dads, and Jimmy Sturr and His Orchestra, and klezmer bands such as the Klezmatics, Brave Old World and the Klezmer Conservatory Band to include clarinets and saxophones in their lineups.

In the former Yugoslavia, brass bands such as the one led by clarinetist and saxophonist Jova Stojiljković have had a considerable following. Romania's Banat music has been described as modern, fast, intense and erotic – its freshness due, in part, to the inclusion of the saxophone. Traditional Macedonian bands that played for dancing and entertainment, as well as gypsy orchestras, were featuring the saxophone by the end of the twentieth century. Bulgarian saxophonist Yuri Yunakov collaborated with clarinetist Ivo Papasov in combining Bulgarian folk music and modal improvisation to produce lively, energetic wedding music. As well as appearing on Papasov's CDs *Balkanology* and *Orpheus Ascending*, Yunakov had begun a career in the United States, where he released two CDs under his own name – *Balada* and *New Colors in Bulgarian Wedding Music*.

Kadri Gopalnath, an Indian saxophonist popular in the 1990s, adapted the saxophone to Indian classical music. He has achieved fame by playing the music for a successful Tamil film, *Duet* (1994), as well as by performing at several international jazz festivals.

Perhaps the best-known Cuban saxophonist is Paquito D'Rivera who, from the 1970s to the early 2000s, played in many big bands as well as leading several bands and ensembles. Other saxophonists included in the lineups of popular Latin big bands are Mario Rivera, who has played in Tito Puente's band, and the much-recorded Jose Madera, who appears on many Afro-Cuban and Latin jazz recordings of big bands led by Machito, Tito Puente, Dizzy Gillespie, Chico O'Farrill and Paquito D'Rivera.

Reggae and ska are Jamaican styles of music that include the saxophone in their horn sections. The popular band the Skatalites included Roland Alphonso, Tommy McCook and Lester Sterling on saxophone. Alphonso was the founding member of the Skatalites and was much recorded from the 1960s onward. The saxophone appears in other styles of Caribbean music, such as merengue and calypso.

In Mexico, the saxophone figures prominently in both *tejano* (Tex-Mex) and *norteño* (regional) styles of music. In these types of music, the saxophone is featured either as a lead instrument, as part of a duet arrangement – often with accordion – and/or as part of the backing band of a *conjunto*. Other types of music that feature a saxophone and accordion combination include tango and merengue.

Conclusion

Perhaps the unique feature of the saxophone is its propensity for individual tone and sound and, ultimately, for individual expression, which makes it a very personal instrument. The flexibility that allows for individual expression of tone, rhythm and sound may also explain its popularity in so many different styles of music worldwide.

Bibliography

Cantonese Musical Instruments. http://www.members.aol.com/canopera/instruments.htm

Gridley, Mark C. 1997. *Jazz Styles: History & Analysis.* 6th ed. Upper Saddle River, NJ: Prentice Hall.

Sadie, Stanley, ed. 1984. *The New Grove Dictionary of Musical Instruments*, Vol. 3. London: Macmillan.

Tirro, Frank. 1993. *Jazz: A History.* 2nd ed. New York: Norton.

Discographical References

Cannonball Adderley Quintet, The. 'Mercy, Mercy, Mercy.' *Mercy, Mercy, Mercy!: Live at 'The Club'.* Capitol ST-2663. *1967*: USA.

Coasters, The. 'Yakety Yak.' Atco 6116. *1958*: USA.

Jordan, Louis. 'Ain't Nobody Here But Us Chickens'/'Let the Good Times Roll.' Decca 23741. 1946: USA.

Jordan, Louis. 'Choo Choo Ch'Boogie'/'That Chick's Too Young to Fry.' Decca 23610. 1946: USA.

Jordan, Louis. 'G.I. Jive'/'Is You Is or Is You Ain't My Baby?' Decca 8659. 1944: USA.

Papasov, Ivo, and His Orchestra. *Balkanology.* Hannibal HNCD-1363. *1991*: UK.

Papasov, Ivo, and His Orchestra. *Orpheus Ascending.* Hannibal 1346. *1989*: UK.

Pardo, Jorge. *In a Minute.* Milestone 9277. *1998*: USA.

Randolph, Boots. 'Yakety Sax.' Sony 44356. *1960*: USA.

Safri Boys, The. *Get Real.* Multitone Dmuta 1292. *1994*: UK.

Ustad Fateh Ali Khan. *Ragas & Sagas.* ECM 314-511263-2. *1990*: Germany.

Walker, Junior, and the All Stars. '(I'm a) Road Runner.' Soul 35015. *1966*: USA.

Walker, Junior, and the All Stars. 'Shotgun.' Soul 35008. *1965*: USA.

Yunakov, Yuri. *Balada – Bulgarian Wedding Music*. Traditional Crossroads 4291. *1999*: USA.

Yuri Yunakov Ensemble. *New Colors in Bulgarian Wedding Music*. Traditional Crossroads 4283. *1997*: USA.

Discography

Abdel Gadir Salim All-Stars, The. *The Merdoum Kings Play Songs of Love*. World Circuit 024. *1992*: UK.

Ahmed, Mahmoud. *Éthiopiques, Vol. 7: Erè Mèla Mèla – 1975*. Buda Musique BUD829802.2. *1999*: France.

Alphonso, Roland. *Something Special: Ska Hot Shots*. Heartbeat 617728. *2000*: USA.

Anthony Braxton Quartet, The. *Live at Yoshi's, Oakland, 1993*. Music and Arts 836. *1993*: USA.

Attar, Bachir. *The Next Dream*. CMP CMP-CD57. *1992*: USA.

Ayler, Albert. *Live in Greenwich Village: The Complete Impulse Recordings*. Impulse! 273. *1998*: USA.

Baker, Chet. *The Pacific Jazz Years*. Pacific Jazz 89292. *1994*: USA.

Bechet, Sidney. *The Fabulous Sidney Bechet*. Blue Note 30607. *2001*: USA.

Brave Old World. *Blood Oranges*. Red House 134. *1999*: USA.

Brecker, Michael. *Michael Brecker*. Impulse! MCAD-5980. *1987*: USA.

Coleman, Ornette. *The Shape of Jazz to Come*. Atlantic SD-1317-2. *1959*: USA.

Coltrane, John. *A Love Supreme*. Impulse! 155. 1964; *1995*: USA.

Coltrane, John. *Giant Steps*. Rhino 1311. *1960*: USA.

Coltrane, John. *My Favorite Things*. Rhino 1361. *1961*: USA.

Dave Brubeck Quartet, The. *Time Out*. Columbia/Legacy 65122. 1959; *1997*: USA.

Die Interpreten. *Nicht ganz sauber*. Trikont 0172-O. *1991*: Germany.

Dolphy, Eric. *Out to Lunch*. Blue Note 46524. *1998*: USA.

D'Rivera, Paquito. *Explosion*. Columbia 40156. *1985*: USA.

Ellington, Duke. *All Star Road Band, Vol. 1-2*. Signature 40012. *1964*: USA.

Ellington, Duke. *Highlights from the Duke Ellington Centennial Edition (1927–1973)*. RCA 63672. *2000*: USA.

Ellington, Duke. *The Far East Suite*. RCA SP-3782. *1967*: USA.

Getz, Stan, and Gilberto, Astrud. 'The Girl from Ipanema.' *The Girl from Ipanema*. Verve 10322. *1964*: USA.

Gomulka, Lenny, and Chicago Push. *Push It to the Limit*. Push CPE9504. *1998*: USA.

Groupa. *Fifteen Years*. Northside 6015. *1998*: USA.

Hawkins, Coleman. *Body & Soul*. RCA 5717. *1990*: USA.

Holiday, Billie, and Young, Lester. *A Fine Romance, Vol. 1*. Definitive 11101. *2000*: USA.

It's a Triple Earth. Triple Earth 114. *1996*: UK.

Kassav'. *Majestik Zouk*. Columbia 45353. *1989*: USA.

Keith Jarrett Quartet, The. *My Song*. ECM 821406. *1990*: Germany.

Kenny G. *Greatest Hits*. Arista 18991. *1997*: USA.

Khaled. *1, 2, 3 Soleils*. Caiman 86022. *2000*: USA.

King Curtis. *Live at Fillmore West*. Koch International 8024. 1971; *1999*: USA.

Klezmatics, The. *Jews with Horns*. Rounder 3183. *2002*: USA.

Klezmer Conservatory Band, The. *Dance Me to the End of Love*. Rounder 613169. *2000*: USA.

Kuban, Ali Hassan. *Walk Like a Nubian*. Piranha PIR43. *1994*: Germany.

Lovano, Joe. *Trio Fascination – Edition One*. Blue Note 33114. *1998*: USA.

Mabsant. *Trwy'r Weiar*. Sain 604-C. *1987*: Wales.

Machito and His Afro-Cuban Jazz Ensemble. *Latin Soul Plus Jazz*. Charly 149. 1957; *1993*: USA.

Marsalis, Branford. *Contemporary Jazz*. Columbia 12847. *2000*: USA.

Mellesse, Netsanet. *Spirit of Sheba*. Shanachie 64044. *1992*: USA.

Messaoud, Bellemou. *Le Père du Rai*. World Circuit 011. *1989*: UK.

Moms & Dads, The. *The Ranger's Waltz*. GNP Crescendo 2061. *1995*: USA.

Moving Hearts. *The Storm*. Tara 3014. *1985*: Ireland.

N'Dour, Youssou. *Best of the 80's*. Melodie 67003. *1998*: France.

N'Dour, Youssou. *Set*. Capitol 86195. *1996*: USA.

Orchestra Baobab. *Pirate's Choice: The Legendary 1982 Session*. Elektra/Asylum 79643. *2002*: USA.

Parker, Charlie, and Davis, Miles. *The Best of the Dial Years*. Stardust 913. *2000*: USA.

Parker, Maceo. *Life on Planet Groove*. Verve 314-517197-2. *1992*: USA.

Piirpauke. *Ave Maria*. Rockadillo ZENCD 2050. *1996*: Finland.

Puente, Tito. *Puente Caliente*. Concord Jazz 4953. *2001*: USA.

Rollini, Adrian. *Swing Low*. Affinity 1030. 1934–38; *1995*: USA.

Rollins, Sonny. *Saxophone Colossus*. Prestige/OJC 291. *1956*: USA.

Sanborn, David. *Voyeur*. Warner Brothers 2-3546. *1980*: USA.

Scott, Tom. *The Best of Tom Scott*. Columbia CK-36352. *1991*: USA.

Shorter, Wayne. *Speak No Evil*. Blue Note 46509. 1964; *1997*: USA.

Skatalites, The. *Foundation Ska*. Heartbeat 88. *1996*: USA.

Stojiljković, Jova. *Blow 'Besir' Blow!*. GlobeStyle 38. *1996*: UK.

Sturr, Jimmy, and His Orchestra. *Dance with Me*. Rounder 616087. *1998*: USA.

Trumbauer, Frank. *Tram! Vol. I: Frank Trumbauer's Legacy to American Jazz*. The Old Masters 107. *1997*: USA.

UB40. *The Very Best of UB40 1980–2000*. Virgin 50525. *2000*: USA.

Washington, Grover, Jr. *Winelight*. Elektra 305. *1980*: USA.

Webster, Ben. *Ben Webster Meets Oscar Peterson*. PolyGram 521448. 1959; *1997*: USA.

Young, Lester. *The Complete Lester Young Studio Sessions on Verve*. PolyGram 547087. *1999*: USA.

Zorn, John. *Naked City*. Elektra/Nonesuch 79238-2. *1992*: USA.

MEGAN JEROME with DAVID GIBSON, IAN BABB and PETR CANCURA

Part IV
Musical Form and Practise

16. Form

Blues Form

'Blues form' is a musical structure defined principally by particular lyric, melodic and harmonic patterns; it originated in the African-American song genre of blues, but was widely used in many spheres of twentieth-century popular music. Blues form is a type of chorus form: the structural unit carrying one stanza (which musically may be referred to as a verse or chorus) is repeated for subsequent stanzas. Most commonly, in 12-bar blues, this unit is divided into three four-bar phrases, the lyrics (and often the melodies) of which follow the pattern AAB; thus, the second phrase repeats the first (sometimes with variations), and the third acts as some sort of resolution. Harmonically, this phrase structure is articulated by a characteristic oscillation between tonic and subdominant, and tonic and dominant, chords (Ex. 1). Sometimes, the structure is contracted to eight bars (hence eight-bar blues), and occasionally it is expanded, most commonly to 16 bars. Dominant seventh-type chords are more usual than triads, and a variety of other harmonic substitutions and elaborations can appear. There is a range of specific musical techniques so closely identified with blues form that they are often regarded as defining features. These include a call-and-response pattern within the phrase between the voice and an answering instrument; a melodic tonality based on major-pentatonic or minor-pentatonic patterns; and blue notes and other melodic pitch inflections. But,

within the world of popular music as a whole, there is no doubt that the single most important defining feature of blues form is the normative 12-bar harmonic sequence.

It is generally accepted that many elements of blues form were present in African-American folk music genres well before 1900 – it has been suggested that some were derived ultimately from African sources – and in the 'common stock' songster and dance music repertoires, practised by both black and white musicians, of the late nineteenth and early twentieth centuries. They also appear in turn-of-the-century commercial sheet music (coon songs, cakewalks, ragtime): 'One o' Them Things,' for example, a 1904 rag by James Chapman and Leroy Smith, follows the harmonic structure of 12-bar blues (see Berlin 1980, 157). It has been argued too (Van der Merwe 1989) that some elements can be traced, via varied North American lineages, to Anglo-Celtic folk music practises. But the first hard evidence for the existence of a definite blues form, as it came to be understood, lies in the earliest publications of blues compositions: Hart Wand, 'Dallas Blues' (1912); W.C. Handy, 'Memphis Blues' (1913) and 'St. Louis Blues' (1914); Ferdinand 'Jelly Roll' Morton, 'Jelly Roll Blues' (1915). (Some of the songs collected a few years before this by Howard Odum – see Odum 1911; Odum and Johnson 1925 – suggest that the AAB lyric structure was in place earlier; but Odum gives no information about musical form except to indicate an inclination toward repetition.) Ironically, the rural practises on which the composers of such pieces drew were almost certainly much less standardized in form – at least, the evidence of the earliest recordings of country blues singers, from the second half of the 1920s, suggests as much. A Mississippi bluesman such as Charley Patton might drop an

Lyric and   A   A   B
Melody

Chords   / I / I / I / I // IV / IV / I / I // V / V(IV) / I / I //

Example 1

entire line, expand or contract a phrase by a few beats or bars, or use fewer chords than the 'norm,' perhaps in a different sequence, or even just a single drone chord. It was probably the widespread dissemination of records – especially records of city blues, in which the requirements of band (rather than solo) performance encouraged the coordination of structural formulae – that ensured the hegemony of the standard form. This hegemony was in place by the 1930s. Even so, important variants evolved. The most influential of these was the 'Tight Like That' model (named after the 1928 'hokum blues' hit by Tampa Red and Georgia Tom). In this model, the relationship between the lyric and the chord sequence is reorganized to incorporate a couplet-plus-refrain pattern (see Ex. 2).

```
VERSE: RHYMING        REFRAIN
COUPLET
/ I / I / I / I // IV / IV / I / I // V / V / I / I //
```

Example 2

Jazz musicians seem to have made use of blues form from the earliest days of their genre. The legendary New Orleans trumpeter, Buddy Bolden, was celebrated for his blues playing – though it is not clear if this meant that his pieces were in blues form. The 12-bar structure was certainly common in the jazz repertoire of the 1920s. From Louis Armstrong's 'West End Blues' (1928) through Duke Ellington's 'Ko-Ko' (1940) and Charlie Parker's 'Now's the Time' (1945) to Miles Davis's 'Freddie Freeloader' (1959) and beyond, this structure was at the core of the jazz repertoire, though often with elaborated harmonic patterns, including altered chords and chord substitutions (see Ex. 3). Piano players developing what would be called boogie-woogie also based their music on the blues form, while key elements influenced gospel music composers such as Thomas A. Dorsey. As documented on some of the earliest recordings (those of Jimmie Rodgers, for instance), white North American country musicians employed the 12-bar structure as well, and it has remained an important resource in that repertoire. In the hands of blues musicians themselves, blues form was adapted to a variety of contexts, ranging from the shouted swing blues, with riff underpinnings, originating in 1930s Kansas City, through the 'jump blues' of such 1940s stars as Louis Jordan, to the electrified Mississippi-style blues of postwar Chicago singers such as Muddy Waters.

While blues form had occasionally permeated mass

```
/ I / IV / I / ♭V⁷ // IV / VII⁷ / III⁷ / ♭III⁷ // II⁷ / ♭II⁷ / I / I //
```

Example 3

market popular music before the advent of rock 'n' roll (for example, Glenn Miller's 'In the Mood'), it was with rock 'n' roll that mainstream popular music, drawing variously on all the lineages mentioned above, placed 12-bar blues at its center. Many rock 'n' rollers (e.g., Elvis Presley) and 1960s rock bands (e.g., the Rolling Stones) covered older blues songs and recordings; many too, then and since, produced new songs using blues form (e.g., the Beatles, 'Can't Buy Me Love'; U2, 'I Still Haven't Found What I'm Looking For'). Even when blues form does not seem to be in the foreground, it is sometimes an important background structural influence: Cream's 'Sunshine of Your Love,' for example, is a riff song, but the riff is played over I then IV then I, and the chorus is completed by a passage focused around V harmony.

In the second half of the twentieth century, the influence of blues form on popular music was enormous. It operated on three levels: firstly, as a repository of songs and 'tune families' (Hatch and Millward 1987) available to African-American musicians and more widely; secondly, as a structural model that could be used, varied and elaborated across a variety of musical styles; and lastly, as an even more generally pervasive source of particular musical techniques – melodic phraseologies, call-and-response patterns, the 'feeling' associated with the I-IV-I-V-I sequence and derivatives (the last often important when not at first obviously present: see Brackett 1992 on James Brown's 'Superbad,' for example). This form would seem as central to Western music in the twentieth century as the principles of sonata form were in the eighteenth.

Bibliography

Berlin, Edward A. 1980. *Ragtime: A Musical and Cultural History*. Berkeley, Los Angeles and London: University of California Press.

Brackett, David. 1992. 'James Brown's "Superbad" and the Double-Voiced Utterance.' *Popular Music* 11(3): 309–24.

Brackett, David. 1995. *Interpreting Popular Music*. Cambridge: Cambridge University Press.

Hatch, David, and Millward, Stephen. 1987. *From Blues to Rock: An Analytical History of Pop Music*. Manchester: Manchester University Press.

Keil, Charles. 1966. *Urban Blues*. Chicago: University of Chicago Press.

Middleton, Richard. 1972. *Pop Music and the Blues*. London: Gollancz.

Odum, Howard W. 1911. 'Folk-song and Folk-poetry as Found in the Secular Songs of the Southern Negroes.' *Journal of American Folklore* 24: 255–94, 351–96.

Odum, Howard W., and Johnson, Guy B. 1925. *The

Negro and His Songs. Chapel Hill, NC: University of North Carolina Press.

Oliver, Paul. 1970. *Savannah Syncopators: African Retentions in the Blues.* London: Studio Vista.

Steedman, Mark. 1984. 'A Generative Grammar for Jazz Chord Sequences.' *Music Perception* 2(1): 52–77.

Titon, Jeff Todd. 1977. *Early Downhome Blues: A Musical and Cultural Analysis.* Urbana, IL: University of Illinois Press.

Van der Merwe, Peter. 1989. *Origins of the Popular Style: The Antecedents of Twentieth-Century Popular Music.* Oxford: Clarendon Press.

Sheet Music

Chapman, James, and Smith, Leroy. 1904. 'One o' Them Things.' St. Louis, MS: Jos. Placht & Son.

Handy, W.C., comp., and Norton, George A., lyr. 1913. 'Memphis Blues.' New York: Theron C. Bennett.

Handy, W.C., comp. and lyr. 1914. 'St. Louis Blues.' Memphis, TN: Pace & Handy.

Morton, Ferdinand 'Jelly Roll.' 1915. '(Original) Jelly Roll Blues.' New York: Edwin H. Morris. (Reissued in *Ferdinand 'Jelly Roll' Morton, The Collected Piano Music,* ed. James Dapogny. Washington, DC: Smithsonian Institution Press, 1982.)

Wand, Hart A., comp., and Garrett, Lloyd, lyr. 1912. 'Dallas Blues.' New York: Mayfair Music Corp.

Discographical References

Armstrong, Louis. 'West End Blues.' OKeh 8597. 1928: USA. Reissue: Armstrong, Louis. 'West End Blues.' *Original Jazz Performances.* Nimbus 2124. 1928–31; *1998*: USA.

Beatles, The. 'Can't Buy Me Love.' Parlophone R5114. *1964*: UK.

Brown, James. 'Superbad.' King K6329. *1970*: USA.

Cream. 'Sunshine of Your Love.' *Disraeli Gears.* Reaction 593 003. *1967*: UK.

Davis, Miles. 'Freddie Freeloader.' *Kind of Blue.* CBS BPG 62066. *1959*: USA.

Ellington, Duke. 'Ko-Ko.' Victor 26577. 1940: USA. Reissue: Ellington, Duke. 'Ko-Ko.' *Duke Ellington (1933–1941).* Jazz Roots 56012. *1991*: USA.

Miller, Glenn. 'In the Mood'/'I Want to Be Happy.' Bluebird 10416. 1939: USA.

Parker, Charlie. 'Now's the Time'/'Billie's Bounce.' Savoy 573. 1945: USA.

Tampa Red. 'It's Tight Like That.' Vocalion 1216. 1928: USA. Reissue: Tampa Red. 'It's Tight Like That.' *Tampa Red (1928–1942).* Story of the Blues 3505. *1994*: USA.

U2. 'I Still Haven't Found What I'm Looking For.' Island IS 328. *1987*: UK.

W.C. Handy Orchestra. 'St. Louis Blues'/'Memphis Blues.' OKeh 4896. 1923: USA.

RICHARD MIDDLETON

Bridge

A bridge is a subsidiary phrase or section in a song that contrasts with more predominant phrases or sections, and that is often heard as transitional between statements of the latter. The term probably originated during the period of, and in connection with, the early twentieth-century North American popular song, in which the structural function of the bridge can be defined fairly precisely. Subsequently, it has been widely used in connection with many popular song styles, although with a rather wider range of meaning.

In the Tin Pan Alley songs of ca. 1918–50, which usually consist of a short verse (frequently omitted in performance) and a more expansive chorus, a bridge often appears in the chorus. Most commonly, it is the third eight-bar section in a 32-bar AABA structure; hence, it is sometimes known as a 'middle 8.' Here, it provides melodic contrast with the A sections. Even where such contrast is slight, there is often a speed-up in harmonic rhythm and a shift in harmonic vocabulary; for example, chains of dominants (in circle-of-fifth progressions) and passing modulations are common, and chromatic chords may be introduced. At the extreme, the bridge may modulate to, or start off in, a different key. Johnny Green's 'Body and Soul' (1930) exemplifies all these techniques; its bridge begins in the key of the flat supertonic, and modulates chromatically back to the tonic.

The point of the bridge is, on the one hand, to provide a shift of perspective, offering temporary freedom from the orbit of the A material (hence, another term for this sort of bridge is a 'release') and, on the other, to make possible a satisfying homecoming (melodic, harmonic and, often, tonal) in the final restatement of A (the term 'channel,' sometimes used by jazz musicians, may reflect this latter role). In this sense – given that, in the 32-bar form, the A sections are as a rule tonally closed – the function of the bridge here is to offer the excursion in an overall home-away-home arch form that has deep roots in Western bourgeois musical tradition (see Maróthy 1974). Jazz improvisers and arrangers often make the most of this duality by giving the bridge a different treatment from the A sections, reordering the sections or giving them different numbers of repeats, or sometimes even omitting the bridge altogether.

The immediate sources of the Tin Pan Alley bridge can be found in the varied structures of nineteenth- and early twentieth-century North American and European popular songs. Though varied in detail, their normal mode of construction, by four- and eight-bar units, commonly utilizes the principle of a contrasting section. The AABA structure itself sometimes appears – for instance, in the verse of Charles K. Harris's 'After the Ball' (1892). Such songs can in turn be linked to the broader repertoire of eighteenth- and nineteenth-century European genres – lieder and other domestic songs, short piano pieces, dance music, marches – which often make use of the ternary (ABA) principle.

The Tin Pan Alley style of bridge can still be found in popular songs after rock 'n' roll, most commonly in ballads (for example, in Percy Sledge's recording of 'When a Man Loves a Woman,' written by C. Lewis and A. Wright) but sometimes too in songs that are more obviously in rock style – for instance, in the Beatles' 'I Saw Her Standing There' and 'I Want to Hold Your Hand' (written by Lennon and McCartney). More typical of this repertoire, however, is the use of a bridge within less predictable structures. Here, it generally functions as a sort of interlude, of variable length, between sequences of verses, choruses or verse and chorus pairs. With most rock music being less interested in chromatic harmony or modulation than was the case in the preceding period, rock song bridges are more likely to provide contrast in melodic material, rhythmic groove, timbre or overall style references than in tonal area. There are exceptions to this: for instance, Bryan Adams's rock ballad '(Everything I Do) I Do It For You' (written by B. Adams, R.J. Lange and M. Kamen) follows a 16-bar AABC verse with a bridge that starts by dropping the harmony a whole tone from the song's tonic, D♭, and then pursues a rising circle-of-fifths sequence all the way from C♭ to the dominant of the tonic, A♭, in preparation for a reprise of the verse. More typical, though, is to provide contrast in other spheres. At one extreme, a bridge might offer new material in the same style as the rest of the song, perhaps representing a slight shift within a succession of verses or choruses; Bruce Springsteen's 'Atlantic City' is an example of this. At the other extreme is a song like the Eurythmics' 'Sweet Dreams' (written by Annie Lennox and Dave Stewart), in which the two appearances of the bridge function within an intricate intertwining of sections (Ex. 1), bringing a distinctive stylistic configuration and apparently contributing to the overall narrative of the song.

Intro→ Chorus 1→ Verse 1→ Chorus 2→ Verse 2→ Chorus 3→

Bridge 1→ Interlude 1→ Verse 3→ Chorus 4→ Bridge 2→

Interlude 2→ Chorus 5→ Verse 4 (Playout)

Example 1

In the techno, house and other dance music of the 1980s and 1990s, with its tendency toward open-ended, iterative structures, bridges play little part, raising the possibility of a shift in the balance of formal principles in Western popular music. Such a shift would align this dance music repertoire more closely with much indigenous practise in other parts of the world. In African and South American popular music genres, for example – at least when not overly influenced by Western models – the bridge principle rarely plays a substantial role. In some African-American styles (R&B, funk, hip-hop), it has also been relatively unimportant.

Bibliography

Forte, Allan. 1995. *The American Popular Ballad of the Golden Era, 1924–1950*. Princeton, NJ: Princeton University Press.

Hamm, Charles. 1979. *Yesterdays: Popular Song in America*. New York: W.W. Norton.

Maróthy, János. 1974. *Music and the Bourgeois, Music and the Proletarian*. Budapest: Akademiai Kiado.

Moore, Allan. 1993. *Rock: The Primary Text. Developing a Musicology of Rock*. Buckingham: Open University Press.

Sheet Music

Green, Johnny, comp., and Heyman, Ed, Sauer, Robert, & Eyton, Frank, lyrs. 1930. 'Body and Soul.' New York: Harms.

Harris, Charles K., comp. and lyr. 1892. 'After the Ball.' Chicago: Charles K. Harris.

Discographical References

Adams, Bryan. '(Everything I Do) I Do It for You.' A&M AM 789. *1991*: USA.

Beatles, The. 'I Saw Her Standing There.' *Please Please Me*. Parlophone PMC 1202. *1963*: UK.

Beatles, The. 'I Want to Hold Your Hand.' Parlophone R5084. *1963*: UK.

Eurythmics, The. 'Sweet Dreams (Are Made of This).' RCA DA 2. *1983*: UK.

Holman, Libby. 'Body and Soul.' Brunswick 4910. 1930: USA.

Sledge, Percy. 'When a Man Loves a Woman.' Atlantic 2326. *1966*: USA.

Springsteen, Bruce. 'Atlantic City.' *Nebraska*. CBS 25100. *1982*: USA.

RICHARD MIDDLETON

Call-and-Response

Call-and-response is a structural device characterized by the integral relationship between two musical figures: an initial *call* followed by an answering *response*, produced by two distinct voices or instruments, or groups thereof. The term is most commonly applied to techniques of this kind occurring in African and Afro-diasporic musics, and in popular music styles influenced by these musics, but in a broader context it may be considered very close in meaning to 'antiphony' (from Greek *anti* = in return, and *phone* = sound), which occurs widely in many musics of the world.

The principle of dialog in call-and-response is a constant but, within this, several different types can be distinguished. The response may repeat the call (perhaps with variations), or it may be distinctive. Both call and response may stay the same from statement to statement, or both may change, or the call may change while the response stays constant. Sometimes, such relationships can take complex, permutational forms (ABCBABCB, ABCDABCD and so on). The response may be virtually, or wholly, continuous (i.e., a riff), a practise probably deriving from processes in which call and response overlap. Calls are usually delivered by a solo performer; responses may come from a solo instrumentalist (or less commonly, a singer) or from a group of singers or players, performing in unison, in octaves or in harmonies.

While the principle of call-and-response is widespread, the technique is generally regarded as being particularly characteristic of musical practise in Africa south of the Sahara; indeed, it remained a prominent feature of many twentieth-century popular music genres associated with that region. Throughout the Americas, it survived in a vast range of Afro-hybrid styles. For example, a variety of call-and-response techniques is well documented in the ring shout, work song and religious song repertoires of the southern United States. Interestingly, in the responsorial performance of psalms and hymns in that region, a congruence of two cultural traditions can be seen, for such performance may derive also from the procedure of 'lining out' derived from psalm-singing practise in early-modern Protestant Europe, which is itself an equivalent to the antiphonal singing of the Catholic liturgy. The idea of a vocal group responding to lead vocal calls remained a strong feature of the modern gospel music styles developed by African Americans in the twentieth century, and from there the technique entered soul music (the music of Ray Charles, for example, or of many of the Motown groups). Over the same period, call-and-response techniques were adapted to the needs of solo blues (responses from the singer's guitar), small group blues (responses from one or more instrumentalists) and big band blues (often riff responses). In jazz, too, both riff-oriented responsorial backings to solos and antiphonal exchanges between instrumental groupings became common. Post-rock 'n' roll pop music drew on all these techniques: vocal group responses, riff-based support patterns, solo instrument (especially guitar) comments.

Sociologically, call-and-response suggests dialogical, participatory, collectively oriented relationships rather than, say, the self-propelling individual point of view implied by tune-and-accompaniment, period-based structures. Floyd (1991, 1995) has suggested that it is a manifestation of a deeper principle – which he terms Call-Response – lying at the root of dialogical practise in African and Afro-diasporic musics, and generating both a range of quasi-conversational musical techniques and the operations of musical memory and tradition. Call-Response, he argues, is analogous to the African-American literary-theoretic concept of Signifyin(g) (Gates 1988), defined as constant revision of a 'changing same.' Even if such a principle is culturally more widespread, it is difficult to disagree that it is particularly prominent in African-derived lineages. (It is documented for pre-bellum African-American singing in Levine 1977, 24–30, where the author stresses both the link between Call-Response practise and the operation of cultural memory, and the interplay between individual and collective roles.) In the context of popular music practises, at least as interesting as the presence of the principle is the concrete form it takes, and the implications of this: for instance, call-and-response patterns often seem to be gendered (e.g., competitive rapping between male hip-hoppers; male solo singer answered by female vocal group, but rarely the reverse). At the same time, call-and-response techniques as such certainly offered a distinctive structural principle to twentieth-century popular music, one capable, at an extreme, of generating an open-ended musical process and minimizing the role of other large-scale formal inputs; and in some cases (parts of some funk recordings; the fade-outs of some R&B, soul and rock recordings), this condition has been achieved.

Bibliography

Courlander, Harold. 1963. *Negro Folk Music, U.S.A.* New York and London: Columbia University Press.

Floyd, Samuel A. 1991. 'Ring Shout! Literary Studies, Historical Studies, and Black Music Inquiry.' *Black Music Research Journal* 11(2): 265–87.

Floyd, Samuel A., Jr. 1995. *The Power of Black Music: Interpreting Its History from Africa to the United States.* New York: Oxford University Press.

Gates, Henry Louis, Jr. 1988. *The Signifying Monkey: A Theory of Afro-American Literary Criticism.* New York: Oxford University Press.

Levine, Lawrence. 1977. *Black Culture and Black Consciousness: Afro-American Folk Thought from Slavery to Freedom.* New York: Oxford University Press.

Roberts, John Storm. 1973. *Black Music of Two Worlds*. London: Allen Lane.

Southern, Eileen. 1971. *The Music of Black Americans: A History*. New York: Norton.

RICHARD MIDDLETON

Chorus

'Chorus' (from Greek *choros*, meaning 'dance') is a term often used in general musical discourse to refer to a group of singers (a choir) or the music sung by such a group. In popular song, however, it more often denotes a recurring structural unit, with unchanging words, which follows a verse or sequence of verses. In this context, it is synonymous with 'refrain.' Originally, a chorus in this sense was often performed by a group of singers, thus accounting for the derivation of this shift in meaning. In a further development, 'chorus' has sometimes come to refer to the repeating structural unit in iterative types of musical form (that is, forms that are built entirely out of repetition of a single structural unit: $AA^1A^2A^3$ and so on); this usage is common in blues and jazz, and in styles influenced by them.

The Greek etymological source of 'chorus' is of relevance since in the ancient Greek theater the *choros* was a group that danced and chanted interpolations commenting on the action. (In the twentieth-century US musical, the 'chorus line' did something not dissimilar.) Song repertoires from across Europe that used refrain forms with (most likely) choral performance of the refrain can be identified from the Middle Ages on; the medieval English carol is an example. Commercially produced songs with choruses for group performance (though often harmonized for several voice parts) were found in the nineteenth century, for instance in minstrel songs and subsequent nineteenth-century popular styles in the United States, and in British music hall (where the chorus would often be sung by the audience). With the early Tin Pan Alley song (ca. 1890), solo performance throughout became the norm, and the chorus tended to expand to something like the same length as the verse. This process continued in the Tin Pan Alley and Broadway repertoires of the first half of the twentieth century and their derivatives and analogs in Europe, with the chorus becoming much more prominent than the verse (which was sometimes omitted) and establishing itself as the site of the more musically distinctive and emotionally affecting material (including probably the song's hook).

When jazz musicians improvise on popular songs, it is the chorus (its melody and/or its chord sequence) that they use. Thus, the basic unit in a typical jazz performance, repeated with variations an indeterminate number of times, is called a chorus. For similar reasons, the repeating structural unit in a blues performance – the 12-bar blues or other framework – is generally known as a chorus. This terminology remains in use even when units contain a division (for instance, in some blues – those using the 'Tight Like That' 12-bar model, named after the 1928 hit by Tampa Red and Georgia Tom – each chorus ends with a recurring refrain) or, often, when they are components in newly composed, multisectional jazz pieces.

Post-rock 'n' roll pop musicians took over this usage for iterative structures (that is, when performing pieces in chorus form: blues, repeating 32-bar forms and so on). More commonly in this repertoire, though, choruses take their place in structures of variable design alongside verses and bridges. In this context, while the sequence and length of sections are now less standardized, choruses adopt a character familiar from earlier twentieth-century practise: unchanging words, the most memorable melodic idea, the song's hook, together with (in some styles) an anthemic quality reminiscent of the collective performance practises of still earlier traditions; indeed, it is noticeable that chorus sections are where band members are most likely to join in with the lead singer in vocal harmony, and where – especially in large-scale performance – audiences are most likely to sing along too. It is probably these characteristics that account for the appeal of refrain-like choruses across a wide range of popular song genres; their sing-along, collectively rousing qualities can be traced to an equally broad spectrum of precursors, including patriotic songs (for instance, those associated with the American Civil War) and evangelical hymns.

The changing meanings of the word 'chorus' in popular music discourses might, then, be said to map the tensions between sectional and iterative structural principles which were characteristic of the music's twentieth-century history.

Discographical Reference

Tampa Red. 'It's Tight Like That.' Vocalion 1216. 1928: USA. Reissue: Tampa Red. 'It's Tight Like That.' *Tampa Red (1928–1942)*. Story of the Blues 3505. *1994*: USA.

RICHARD MIDDLETON

Finale

A finale is the last movement in a multi-movement work. The term was originally applied in the eighteenth century to the last movement of an instrumental or orchestral work, and to the final section of an act in an opera. It was used in this sense with reference to operettas and other types of light opera in the nineteenth and early twentieth centuries, and this usage continued in the context of the twentieth-century US musical. In a less formal usage, it may be applied to the final number in any sort of musical show ('For our finale . . .'). Similarly, the finale principle – though perhaps not the term itself – can be found in operation in the context of the multi-sectional concept albums popular with progressive rock groups. From this perspective, the reprise of the title track on the Beatles' album *Sergeant Pepper's Lonely Hearts Club Band*, followed by 'A Day in the Life,' could be regarded as a sort of finale.

Discographical Reference

Beatles, The. *Sergeant Pepper's Lonely Hearts Club Band*. Parlophone PCS 7027. *1967*: UK.

RICHARD MIDDLETON

Form

In traditional aesthetic thought, 'form' is often distinguished from 'content.' 'Form' is taken to suggest the idea of a 'mold' into which the 'stuff' of 'content' is poured. Such a rigid dichotomy – increasingly under attack within aesthetic theory generally – seems to be of limited help for an understanding of popular music, where variable performance practise frequently blurs the sense of a fixed shape. As a noun, it is true, 'form' in music does suggest concepts of 'shape,' 'framework' or 'mold'; 'form' in the sense of a 'type' or even a 'formula' is also closely related. The verb 'to form,' however, carries connotations of process, of an active involvement with the shaping of temporal flow. In a consideration of form in popular music, it becomes evident that the idea of a stock of patterned artifacts on the one hand, and that of a set of shaping practises on the other, are two divergent but equally important and, indeed, interactive aspects of the term's usage.

Attempting to create a typology, some scholars have attached these two strands to 'Western' genres and 'non-Western' (or specifically African and Afro-diasporic) genres, respectively. Thus, Keil (1994) distinguishes between a tendency toward 'syntax' (and hence 'embodied meaning') in the former, and 'process' (hence 'engendered feeling') in the latter. Chester's (1990) distinction between 'extensional' and 'intensional' forms is similar. In both cases, a dichotomy is set up: overall pattern and structure on one side, moment-by-moment nuance and inflection on the other. As ideal types, these models have merit and, used to draw a contrast between, say, the relatively settled formal molds of nineteenth-century bourgeois domestic song or 1930s Broadway ballads and the iterative, potentially open-ended processes typical of blues and rock, their point is clear. Nevertheless, it should be remembered that both types are really *principles* and are variably active in *all* music; and that, at a deeper level, both originate in the interplay of repetition and difference that underlies all musical production.

Thinking about form in popular music is closely dependent on the specific theoretical perspective that is drawn on. Among the sets of distinctions that can be employed are:

(a) divergent tendencies toward sectionality or open-ended repetition ('iteration');

(b) divergent tendencies toward song (more inclined to lyrical closures) or dance (more inclined to open-ended continuity); however, one should bear in mind the many shapely, patterned dance genres, from waltz, Irish reel and ragtime to line dancing, as well as song genres organized around repetition of short units, perhaps with call-and-response sequences – from work song through riff-based numbers in rock to rap;

(c) divergent tendencies toward 'narrative' (linear) procedures (privileging verse functions in songs, for example), 'lyrical' shapes and units (privileging chorus functions) and 'circular' processes emphasizing iteration (Middleton 1990); and

(d) a dialog between overall shape or process on the one hand and individual moment (typified by the hook concept) on the other.

There is ample scope for theorizing on such distinctions sociologically. For instance, sectionality and narrative or lyrical patterns of closure have often been connected with the 'individualistic' ideological formations associated with the Western bourgeoisie, iterative and variative processes with social collectivities (Maróthy 1974). Historically, it seems clear that, overall, the balance in Western popular music over the twentieth century shifted away from the former and toward the latter, mostly because of the increasingly hegemonic status of African-American techniques grouped by Floyd (1995) under the principle of Call-Response. This assessment needs qualification, however; for example, pop since the mid-1950s (which, after all, has increasingly colonized and influenced popular music worldwide) has drawn not only on iterative African-American forms such as 12-bar blues, but also on the sectional patterns of Tin Pan Alley song.

Connecting the seeming predictabilities of such patterns to the pressures exerted by 'commodity form,' Adorno (among others) argued that standardized forms and processes are endemic to popular music in modern societies. He added that the apparently spontaneous inflections of 'intensional' forms provide no guarantee of escape, since in principle even the smallest nuance (for example, the choke in the voice that every country music singer can produce to order) can be formularized. From Tin Pan Alley, through the New York Brill Building and Motown production lines in the 1960s, to the Stock-Aitken-Waterman song factory in the 1980s, a certain tendency to standardized form grew directly out of the imperatives of a capitalist music industry. Yet the Adornian critique misses not only the *productivity* of formula, not to mention the *range* of formal types, but also the 'listener's share': in important ways, the listener, though admittedly not in conditions of his/her own making, actively produces the musical form by focusing attention in variable ways. Differences of context – is the music for background, dancing, listening and so on? – affect this too.

In its most acute forms, such variability raises the question of the level on which musical form is apprehended. Two developments, one in cultural theory, the other in musical practise, have added extra charge to this question. Theories of intertextuality (the idea that texts generate meaning through their connections with other, already existing texts) suggest that relationships between performances or pieces are of structural significance. Similarly, practises of sampling, 'versioning,' multiple mixes of the 'same' piece and live mixing bring into question the status of boundaries normally placed around a singular musical event. The issue raised here is just what the unit of form in popular music might now be thought to be – a repeating sound or moment, a hook, verse or chorus, a tune, a song, a performance or even a whole repertoire.

Bibliography

Adorno, Theodor W. 1990. 'On Popular Music.' In *On Record: Rock, Pop and the Written Word*, ed. Simon Frith and Andrew Goodwin. London: Routledge, 301–14. (First published in *Studies in Philosophy and Social Science* 9 (1941): 17–48.)

Chester, Andrew. 1990. 'Second Thoughts on a Rock Aesthetic: The Band.' In *On Record: Rock, Pop and the Written Word*, ed. Simon Frith and Andrew Goodwin. London: Routledge, 315–19. (First published in *New Left Review* 62 (1970): 75–82.)

Floyd, Samuel A., Jr. 1995. *The Power of Black Music: Interpreting Its History from Africa to the United States*. New York: Oxford University Press.

Gendron, Bernard. 1986. 'Theodor Adorno Meets the Cadillacs.' In *Studies in Entertainment: Critical Approaches to Mass Culture*, ed. Tania Modleski. Bloomington, IN: University of Indiana Press, 18–36.

Keil, Charles. 1994. 'Motion and Feeling Through Music.' In Charles Keil and Steven Feld, *Music Grooves: Essays and Dialogues*. Chicago and London: University of Chicago Press, 53–76. (First published in *Journal of Aesthetics and Art Criticism* 24 (Spring) (1966): 337–49.)

Maróthy, János. 1974. *Music and the Bourgeois, Music and the Proletarian*. Budapest: Akademiai Kiado.

Middleton, Richard. 1990. *Studying Popular Music*. Milton Keynes and Philadelphia: Open University Press.

RICHARD MIDDLETON

Interlude

An interlude (Latin *inter* = between, *ludus* = play) is a short passage of music that comes between parts of the main performance, contrasting with them in character, and generally having the function of interrupting the action and facilitating relaxation. Originating in medieval drama, the term has been applied to the passages sometimes played by church organists between verses of hymns, but its main musical use has been in the theater, for music performed between acts. By extension, it is sometimes used (along with 'intermission') for the recorded music often played between separate films in a cinema program or between different live acts in a concert; and it can be applied to passages with a similar function that divide sections or pieces on elaborately organized record albums (by progressive rock bands, for example).

RICHARD MIDDLETON

Introduction

'Introduction' denotes preliminary material designed to set the scene for, and lead into, the main substance of a piece. Generally instrumental, the introduction in most popular songs establishes tempo, mood and characteristic material, and directs attention to the opening of the vocal melody. In musical theater, an introduction might be quite lengthy (more like a prelude), but in popular songs it rarely exceeds a few bars. It is often based on material – a melodic phrase, a chord progression, a riff, a rhythmic groove – drawn from the body of the song. The exigencies of live performance have schooled musicians in the ability to fit the length of introductions to the needs of the moment, for example by vamping – repeating a figure 'til ready.'

Some introductions have become famous in their own right. This is perhaps most common in jazz – Louis Armstrong's unaccompanied trumpet introduction to 'West End Blues' is a celebrated example. Even in the sphere of popular song, however – where introductions are less likely to have a distinctive character of their own – they often bring a smile of recognition from the listener. For the popular music audience, it would seem, pleasure accompanies the announcement of what is to come as much as its satisfactory completion.

Discographical Reference

Armstrong, Louis. 'West End Blues.' OKeh 8597. 1928: USA. Reissue: Armstrong, Louis. 'West End Blues.' *Ori-*

ginal Jazz Performances. Nimbus 2124. 1928–31; *1998*: USA.

RICHARD MIDDLETON

Middle 8

The 'middle 8' is a type of bridge characteristic of the 'standard' Tin Pan Alley ballad form. In the typical 32-bar AABA structure, each section is eight bars long; hence, B is often called the 'middle 8.' This structure can be found in nineteenth-century music, but it became predominant in US popular song in the first half of the twentieth century; it survives as a subsidiary form in more recent styles. The middle 8 (which on occasion is less or more than eight bars long) has the function of providing contrast – melodic, harmonic and sometimes tonal – and so it is sometimes also known as the 'release': a temporary liberation from the 'home' area represented by the A sections.

Later pop musicians sometimes refer to a bridge as a 'middle 8,' even if it is situated in a different sort of structure from the 32-bar form (and even if it is nowhere near eight bars long). This usage seems to be an example of 'vernacular theory,' adapting an inherited terminology without too much concern for textbook niceties.

RICHARD MIDDLETON

Outro

'Outro' is a late twentieth-century neologism coined to create an analogy with the term 'intro(duction).' An outro is a (usually short) concluding section, designed to signal that the main part of a piece is over, to round off the piece and to produce a satisfying ending. Note, though, that in recordings an outro may fade out; this may be intended to represent a simulation of extended live performance. An outro is equivalent to what traditional musicology knows as a 'coda.' Like codas, outros often make use of material from the main part of the piece. Sometimes this is reworked to produce an emphatic conclusion. Sometimes, however, a characteristic figure (a riff, a call-and-response pattern, a harmonic 'loop') is repeated over and over and faded out. When a final chorus (the 'out chorus') is treated in this way, it may be regarded as taking on the function of an outro.

RICHARD MIDDLETON

Overture

An overture (French *ouverture*, meaning 'opening') is a piece of instrumental music (usually fairly extended) designed to introduce an opera or other work of musical theater. Overtures composed for nineteenth-century light operas (by Offenbach, Johann Strauss, Gilbert and Sullivan, and the like) were generally put together as a medley of tunes drawn from the opera itself, and this

practise continued in the twentieth-century musical (including the rock musical) and musical film. Music accompanying the opening credits of films, and even those of some television dramas, can work in a similar way, and may sometimes be regarded as a kind of overture. Occasionally, rock musicians have begun a large-scale concept album with an 'overture,' as, for example, the Who in *Tommy*. (*Tommy* also contains what Pete Townshend called an 'Underture.')

Discographical Reference

Who, The. *Tommy*. Track 61301314. *1969*: UK.

RICHARD MIDDLETON

Refrain

A refrain (from Latin *frangere*, meaning 'to break') is a short section (usually not more than one or two lines of text) that recurs at the end of every verse in a song; both words and music are repeated. This form of strophic construction can be found in several parts of the world, although it seems particularly common in Europe. Refrains appear to have often been sung by a group (in contrast to solo performance of the main body of the stanza); hence, 'refrain' is synonymous with one usage of the term 'chorus.' Short recurring sections in many nineteenth-century popular song genres (for example, British music hall) were called 'chorus' or 'refrain' interchangeably. In most twentieth-century popular song styles, sections with a refrain function tended to become more expansive, and 'chorus' was the preferred term. Older songs performed by folk revivalists, and new songs of a similar type (for instance, many of Bob Dylan's 1960s songs), recall earlier practise, however.

RICHARD MIDDLETON

Repetition

'Repetition' in music, as elsewhere, is a process that involves doing the same thing again. While it can take place on any scale, from repetition of a single sound to that of a complete piece, and on any musical parameter, the term is most commonly applied to the reiteration of recognized musical figures, melodic, rhythmic and/or harmonic, or of structural units (phrases, sections and so on). Processes of repetition are, of course, pervasive throughout human culture (and beyond), but they do seem often to have an especially high profile in music – and all the more so in popular music, where their prominence has attracted both censure and celebration.

The practise of repeating (often with variation) both short figures and entire units (for example, in stanzaic song forms) is widespread in vernacular musics throughout the world. In European art music from the late eighteenth century on, there is a tendency to reject or 'cover over' obvious repetition; nineteenth-century popular genres partly accede to this tendency on the micro-level, but resist it on the macro-level, generally retaining clear repetitions at the level of the phrase, the period and/or the entire section. During the same period, some African-American genres continued to pursue small-scale repetition techniques, often within call-and-response patterns and open-ended structures, and these techniques increasingly percolated into mainstream Western popular music during the twentieth century. In this repertoire, the AABA 32-bar form of the standard Tin Pan Alley ballad provides perhaps the clearest examples of repetition of structural units, including phrase repetition by sequence. Such techniques have continued to some extent in pop after rock 'n' roll, especially (but not exclusively) in ballads, and also in narrative and romantic song genres in other traditions (country music, French *chanson*, Italian *canzone*, and Latin American *balada*, bolero and tango, for instance). But small-scale repetition, derived from African-American exemplars, has become at least as important, operating most obviously through riffs, repeated short chord sequences and (particularly prominent in 1980s and 1990s studio-produced dance music) 'looped' rhythmic patterns.

Moore (1993, 47–53) discusses the relationship between these two types of repetition within rock music. Middleton (1990, 267–92) terms them *discursive* and *musematic* repetition, respectively, arguing that they tend to be associated with distinctive formal types (hierarchical and developmental on the one hand, one-leveled, open-ended, variative on the other) and socio-musical contexts (the 'individualism' of bourgeois song, the 'collectivism' of group and mass musical expression). Middleton's conception of musematic repetition is close to the theory of Signifyin(g) developed by African-American literary scholars (see Gates 1988) and to the similar perspective on African-American music associated with such writers as Baraka (1967), Gilroy (1991) and Floyd (1995). Baraka's delineation of the musical processes in terms of a 'changing same' (that is, constant variation of collectively known and permanently available materials) is particularly pertinent.

At the same time, processes of repetition pervade popular music practise (as they do many other musical repertoires throughout the world) at the level of the complete piece – or even the genre. Repeated performance (especially since mechanical reproduction technologies made this ubiquitous) is at the heart of the popular music culture. Moreover, many pieces lie so close to preexisting pieces – because they are 'covers,' they borrow material, they copy successful techniques, or they share a common compositional framework such as 12-bar blues or 32-bar ballad – that it is possible to think of genre as being constantly re-created through repetition and formula.

In terms of compositional technique, the use of repetition processes within a piece is often not completely distinct from the use of formula on a broader level to create repertoire. Both have been identified as especially characteristic of practise in orally/aurally oriented music cultures. Resisting the link between such long-established practises and the 'electronic orality' typical of twentieth-century popular music production, mass culture critics – most influentially, Theodor Adorno – relate formulaic repetition (both within a song and within a repertoire) to patterns of 'standardization' in late-capitalist societies and their allegedly deleterious social and psychological effects. By contrast, some poststructuralist thinkers have claimed repetition as an instrument of ecstatic self-loss, or *jouissance*. What is missed in both arguments (obscured, perhaps, by the stereotypical image of the hypnotically swaying crowd, which is often common to both) is the sheer range of repetition technique and the complexity of its effects. At the bottom of this complexity lies a key semiotic (indeed, philosophical) issue: what *is* repetition? At one extreme is the argument that nothing can repeat exactly – all is difference; at the other is the argument that, in a sense, nothing can be entirely new – so, on some level, all is repetition. Popular music deploys its own array of repetition practises on the terrain encompassed by these extremes, locating them, one might say, within the vernacular repetitions of everyday life.

Bibliography

Adorno, Theodor W. 1990. 'On Popular Music.' In *On Record: Rock, Pop and the Written Word*, ed. Simon Frith and Andrew Goodwin. London: Routledge, 301–14. (First published in *Studies in Philosophy and Social Science* 9 (1941): 17–48.)

Baraka, Amiri. 1967. *Black Music*. New York: Morrow.

Floyd, Samuel A., Jr. 1995. *The Power of Black Music: Interpreting Its History from Africa to the United States*. New York: Oxford University Press.

Gates, Henry Louis, Jr. 1988. *The Signifying Monkey: A Theory of Afro-American Literary Criticism*. New York: Oxford University Press.

Gendron, Bernard. 1986. 'Theodor Adorno Meets the Cadillacs.' In *Studies in Entertainment: Critical Approaches to Mass Culture*, ed. Tania Modleski. Bloomington, IN: Indiana University Press, 18–36.

Gilroy, Paul. 1991. 'Sounds Authentic: Black Music, Ethnicity, and the Challenge of a *Changing* Same.' *Black Music Research Journal* 11(2): 111–36.

Middleton, Richard. 1990. *Studying Popular Music*. Milton Keynes and Philadelphia: Open University Press.

Moore, Allan. 1993. *Rock: The Primary Text. Developing a Musicology of Rock*. Buckingham: Open University Press.

Snead, James. 1984. 'Repetition as a Figure of Black Culture.' In *Black Literature and Literary Theory*, ed. Henry Louis Gates, Jr. London: Routledge, 59–80.

RICHARD MIDDLETON

Song Form

Introduction

'Song form' is a composite term denoting those characteristics of musical form that are particular to song. The formal schemes and processes to be found in popular songs are multifarious. This entry covers the more important of these schemes and processes. It should be noted that the term 'song form' has also been used by some musicologists, especially in the nineteenth century, to refer specifically to *ternary* (ABA) form, in instrumental as well as in vocal pieces. This is of interest, both in relation to music history – in that some popular song genres in the nineteenth and twentieth centuries did indeed make use of ABA patterns – and in relation to ideological critique – for there is a suspicion that this usage is intended to signal the relative aesthetic lightness of songs compared to the allegedly more complex structural processes (e.g., *sonata form*) featured in more 'serious' instrumental movements.

General Considerations

It may be argued that in all music there is a tension, manifested to different degrees and in different ways, between *form-as-mold* and *form-as-process*. The former concerns the arrangement and interrelationship of component parts, the placing of punctuation points and the internal articulation of the overall time span. The latter concerns the specific shaping pressures exerted uniquely, moment by moment, by the material of a particular piece. In songs, however, there is an additional complication: namely, that imposed by the form taken by the words. The differing implications for musicians of the self-standing line, perhaps followed by a refrain or response, or a sequence (perhaps variable in length) of rhyming couplets, or a sequence of four- or eight-line stanzas, with a particular rhyme scheme and internal structure, are patent.

At the risk of oversimplification, two distinctive principles may be identified. The first is *additive*. A particular musical unit, setting a line, a couplet, a stanza or whatever, is repeated as many times as is necessary or desired. This is common in dance songs, work songs and ritual songs, but also in many narrative song genres, such as traditional ballads from many cultures. The second is *sectional*. A musical unit is divided up into clearly distinguished parts, usually organized so as to articulate an overall emotional or dramatic shape. This is most common, in its pure state, in operatic arias (including, sometimes, popular types of musical theater), in the European art song or lied (which has influenced some popular song genres), and in the multi-section, partly improvised forms that are common in the classical vocal genres of South Asia (influence from which can be found in some twentieth-century popular styles of that region). It should be added, however, that in practise aspects of the two principles frequently intermix, especially in popular songs.

It might be thought that, in additive structures, the words will tend to dominate the music, since they often change from stanza to stanza; certainly, in many traditional genres – the European folk ballad or the Mexican *corrido*, say – this would seem to be true, as the music is secondary to the story. Similarly, it could be argued that the more sectionally organized the form, the more likely musical appeal is to come to the fore; this probably is the case with many Tin Pan Alley songs, with their AABA forms, and the same appears to happen in other genres when there is a 'stand-out' chorus. Yet, a rigid distinction would be dangerous. In many dance songs with additive forms, the music (especially the rhythm) is clearly in charge, and the words may be felt to be almost incidental. Conversely, expert performance – by a Billie Holiday or a Frank Sinatra – of an AABA song may be achieved precisely by use of the sectionality of the musical form to trace the emotional drama represented in the lyrics. The 12-bar blues may stand as an example of a genre in which words and music intersect in a variety of ways, each additive unit often dividing up internally in a range of fashions reflecting a variable balance between the two elements.

It might be tentatively suggested that, in many popular song traditions, there was a shift in the balance of additive and sectional principles away from the former and toward the latter, which took place at the same time as broader processes of modernization and urbanization. These processes generally brought with them a spreading influence of bourgeois musical practises. Often, this shift can be observed around the late nineteenth and early twentieth centuries, when in many cases recognizably modern, mass-mediated popular song types first emerged. This seems to be the case with, for example, the Argentinian tango, the Cuban *son* and rumba, the Dominican merengue, the Portuguese fado and the Greek *rembétika*. In all these, the original strophic forms remained (often the verses are interspersed with refrains), but elements of sectionality (two-part forms, elaborate introductions, instrumental bridges and so on) crept in too. However, other genres – *mento*, calypso, samba – stayed resolutely strophic right into the twentieth century. In some regions, the shift, if it happened, took place later. In others – notably Europe and North America – it began earlier; partly for this reason, and partly because of the immense worldwide influence of the models developed in the 'North Atlantic' culture area, the historical shift that took place there can serve as an exemplary case for discussion.

Europe and North America: The Nineteenth Century

Most commercial popular songs produced in Europe and North America in the nineteenth century, for performance in the home, in the street or in music halls, cabarets, vaudeville theaters and the like, used a strophic form: that is, a sequence of stanzas was set so that each stanza was sung to the same tune. The roots of such forms went back to the eighteenth century (and even before), to popular theater and pleasure garden song, broadside ballad and *Gassenhauer*, romance and lied. In many cases, links can be observed to still older, non-commercial ('folk') strophic forms; and in the nineteenth century, this connection took a romanticizing turn in the huge production of 'folk-like' (*Volkstumlich*) songs. Commonly (though not universally), each stanza in these types of song ended with a short refrain. Sir Henry Bishop's 'Home, Sweet Home' (1823; readily accessible in Turner 1972, 140–42) illustrates the tendencies described.

As in 'Home, Sweet Home,' the phrase structure in these types of songs is generally made up of regular two-, four- and eight-bar units. Phrases are often repeated, either immediately or after a contrasting phrase, and there is an important role for open/closed (antecedent/consequent) relationships between adjacent phrase endings. Such relationships can be produced either melodically (in 'Home, Sweet Home,' for instance, phrases 1 and 3 end on the relatively open third of the scale, while phrases 2 and 4 end with closure on the tonic) or harmonically; often, for example, a phrase ending on the dominant chord or in the dominant key is 'answered' by a phrase ending in (and perhaps also on) the tonic. Here, infiltrating the additive strophic principle are elements of a more developed sectionalism, pointing toward the internally articulated 'shapeliness' characteristic of 'bourgeois song' (see Maróthy 1974). Perhaps under the influence of contemporary art song, some composers occasionally followed this move further, into through-composed songs (e.g., Henry Russell's 'The Maniac' (1846)), 'modified strophic' form (in which the music of a particular stanza was varied to suit its specific mood or narrative function (e.g., Sir Arthur Sulliv-

an's 'The Lost Chord' (1880); Felix McGlennon's 'Comrades' (1890)) or other more overtly sectional forms (e.g., rondo in Michael Balfe's 'Come into the Garden, Maud' (1857)).

From mid-century, North American songs often had a refrain intended to be sung by a group – hence the term 'chorus.' From about the same period, music hall songs in Britain followed the same principle, the chorus here often being sung by audience as well as performer. Eight- or 16-bar sections were the most common and, in both repertoires, a variety of phrase-structure relationships can be found, in both verse and chorus. 'Silver Threads Among the Gold' (H.P. Danks, 1873; see Jackson 1976, 195–97) has a 16-bar AABA verse, followed by an eight-bar chorus that repeats the second half of the verse. The music hall song 'Champagne Charlie' (Alfred Lee, 1868; see Waites and Hunter 1984, 92–94) has a more extended, musically distinct chorus, and both sections exhibit an ABAC design that is especially typical of this repertoire. Open/closed patterns pervade both songs, and the equally typical device of sequence is plentiful in 'Champagne Charlie.' The 'folding' of repetition into lyrical shape through sequence, and the 'rhyming' effects produced by permutations of phrase complementarity and contrast and by open/closed relationships, result in a sense of balance – of quasi-narrative movement balanced by degrees of closure – that is characteristic of popular song form in this period.

The Twentieth Century

The growth in the relative importance of the chorus, which is exemplified by 'Champagne Charlie' – it gets longer, and it becomes the site of the song's musical center of gravity – continued in the early Tin Pan Alley repertoire (ca. 1890–1914). At the same time, the verse shrank – in length and in numbers: by the 1920s, one verse was standard, and in a few cases the verse disappeared altogether; in any case, it was often omitted in performance. This would seem to mark the triumph of the sectional over the additive principle – and indeed, the overall song form typical of this period bears comparison with that of the operatic recitative-and-aria; but, while it is certainly true that the expansive, self-contained chorus could function as a unique compositional entity, at the same time the prevalence of iteration (repetition of sections, and of phrases within sections, sometimes with variation or through sequences) suggested a potential for a move in the direction of *process* rather than *mold* – a potential that rock music would later pursue. Similarly, jazz musicians improvising on the choruses of popular songs quickly discovered how one-off statement could be turned into open-ended jam. And *within* the phraseology of the chorus structure, the importation from ragtime and blues sources of the short repeated figure – on occasion not too far from the status of riffs – pointed in the same sort of direction. From Joe Howard's 'Hello Ma Baby' (1899) through Irving Berlin's 'Alexander's Ragtime Band' (1911) and Lewis F. Muir's 'Waiting for the Robert E. Lee' (1912) to W.C. Handy's blues compositions ('Memphis Blues' (1913) and 'St. Louis Blues' (1914), for example), the African-American roots of this musematic repetition technique are not in doubt. The technique was picked up strongly in dance songs of the 1920s 'jazz age' (Walter Donaldson, 'Yes Sir! That's My Baby' (1925); Roy Turk and Lou Handman, 'I'm Gonna Charleston Back to Charleston' (1925); George Gershwin, 'Fascinating Rhythm' (1924) and 'I Got Rhythm' (1930)), and in later jazz-influenced tunes (Joe Garland's 'In the Mood' (1939)).

At the beginning of the twentieth century, choruses of 16 or even, on occasion, eight bars were still to be found, but the norm was already 32 bars. While the four eight-bar sections may be related in a variety of ways, by the postwar period one particular pattern – AABA – was clearly predominant, to the extent that it is this pattern that is commonly understood by the terms '32-bar' or 'standard Tin Pan Alley ballad' form. By this point, 'ballad' had virtually lost the connotations it possessed within earlier vernacular traditions. It was now defined – and this continued for the rest of the century – partly in terms of its generic character as a slow love song, in a rather personal mode, but also partly by a propensity for this particular musical form. The repertoire produced by the best-known composers to employ this form – Irving Berlin, Jerome Kern, George Gershwin, Richard Rodgers, Cole Porter, Harold Arlen – has been studied in some detail (Wilder 1972; Hamm 1979; Forte 1995). The point generally made – that, despite the apparent rigidity of the form, these composers achieved an impressive variety and sophistication of melodic and harmonic design – is just. Nevertheless, if the repertoire is placed in the larger context of popular song in the interwar period, it becomes clear that 'subterranean' influences on structural process from other genres (especially I-IV thinking, pentatonic and 'blue' melodic shaping, and musematic repetition techniques, all from African-American musics) should be regarded as at least qualifying any claim that this should be considered an 'American *lied*,' with all the aesthetic aura that such claims entail (Middleton 1997).

Blues form itself, especially in its normative 12-bar version, should be seen as an alternative type of song form emerging in this period, historically of at least equal significance to the 32-bar pattern, if not yet so widespread. It should be remembered too that, in US country music

and in other folk-derived song traditions in Europe and elsewhere, forms that were more clearly additive – simple stanzaic and verse-and-refrain structures – remained common. After World War II, all of these forms would become more prominent.

As far as the mainstream of Western popular song is concerned, such simple stanzaic structures received their biggest boost from the US folk-protest movement of the early 1960s (Bob Dylan et al.). The influence of this formal principle, in its strongest manifestations, can then be traced through the history of singer-songwriter, folk-revival and neo-folk repertoires in many countries. For the commercially dominant repertoire after 1955, however, it was only one of the important sources (though after Dylan and US folk-rock, it *was* an important one); the others – if anything, more crucial – lay in the two major streams running through the first half of the century: the AABA pattern of the Tin Pan Alley ballad; and the 12-bar blues.

As is often observed, much mid-1950s rock 'n' roll grew directly out of the postwar lineages of R&B, and the 12-bar chorus form was at its center. Many songs used this form (e.g., Elvis Presley's 'Blue Suede Shoes' and 'Hound Dog' (both 1956); Little Richard's 'Long Tall Sally' (1956); Buddy Holly's 'Peggy Sue' (1957); Chuck Berry's 'Johnny B. Goode' (1958)). It is interesting that the 'Tight Like That' variant of the 12-bar form, named after the 1928 hit by Tampa Red and Georgia Tom, is often chosen; for examples, see Arthur Crudup's 'That's All Right,' recorded by Elvis Presley in 1954, and Bill Haley's 'Rock Around the Clock (1955); with its division of the 12-bar structure into an initial tension-building couplet followed by a 'release' into a more relaxed refrain, the emphasis is placed much more on the galvanizing effects of dance rhythm. It is interesting too that, right from the start of rock 'n' roll, the pattern of blues form was often modified in other ways. In Joe Turner's 'Shake, Rattle and Roll' (1954), the titular chorus functions *as* a 'chorus' (i.e., as a refrain, with other choruses interspersed as 'verses'). In 'Tutti-Frutti' (1956), Little Richard alternates 12-bar choruses with verses that modify the 12-bar pattern; and similarly, in 'Maybellene' (1955), Chuck Berry interpolates between blues choruses a series of narrative verses that are melodically and harmonically different. Elvis Presley's 'Heartbreak Hotel' (1956) is an *eight*-bar blues; so is Jerry Lee Lewis's 'Great Balls of Fire' (1957) – but with the addition of a bridge. Presley's 'All Shook Up' (1957) also has a bridge, but its main chorus has 16 bars and merely blues-*like* harmonies. In Buddy Holly's 'That'll Be the Day' (1957), also 16 bars, two different but closely related harmonic modifications to the 12-bar pattern are used in the alternating verses and choruses. Such modifications might be ascribed to the influence of rock 'n' roll's second main source: country music. Musicians in the country music tradition, as well as taking over the 12-bar form themselves, employed a wealth of other sequences of simple triadic chords, and also often favored the emotionally cathartic effect of a refrain. At the same time, the importance of African-American techniques for the micro-level of structure in rock 'n' roll is unquestionable. 'That'll Be the Day' has in both its sections an oscillating I-IV progression that almost has the status of a riff. Melodic riffs are pervasive throughout the repertoire, and stop-time effects are common. All these devices tend to focus the listener's attention on the processual moment, and similarly the construction of continuities of content across structurally distinct units (verses, choruses and so on) counterbalances the extra degree of sectionality that is being introduced, in some cases, into the 12-bar form.

During this period, the popularity of the 32-bar form continued as well – and not only with an older generation of musicians, but with rock 'n' roll and R&B performers as well (e.g., Elvis Presley, 'Love Me Tender' (1956); Clyde McPhatter, 'Long Lonely Nights' (1957); the Drifters, 'Save the Last Dance for Me' (1960)). And it was this form that was one of the key resources for the Beatles, many of whose early songs use or modify it. At the same time, they often used bluesy chord sequences in particular sections; and, more dramatically, the British R&B groups (the Rolling Stones, the Yardbirds, the Animals, Cream) reintroduced the 12-bar form itself. As the two traditions intersected, section lengths, sequences and interrelationships became more flexible – to the extent that it is difficult to generalize about formal patterns in the subsequent rock/pop repertoire, except for two loose observations:

(a) songs are generally constructed out of a sequence of sections of variable length, which, depending on their function and interrelationships, may be termed 'verses,' 'choruses' or 'bridges'; and

(b) continuities are often constructed across sections through the use of riffs, related musical figures or harmonically open chord progressions.

In the Beatles' 'She Said, She Said' (1966), for example, the sectionality (verse-verse-bridge-verse-bridge-verse-coda) is cloaked by the irregular lengths of sections and phrases, the changes of meter and the similarities of melodic and harmonic material across sections. In the Rolling Stones' 'Satisfaction' (1965), articulation points are even more obscure: really it is the prominent guitar riff that identifies some parts as having a 'chorus' function and its absence that suggests 'verses'; otherwise, the music (especially the pervasive I-IV chord oscillations) seems to flow continuously. At the same time, many songs are organized so that section breaks and interrelationships are absolutely clearcut.

The role of riffs and other repeated figures in tying songs together merits special comment. The Kinks' 'You Really Got Me' (1964), with its persistent I↓VII riff, is often described as 'the first riff song' (i.e., a song in which the overall form is governed by the repetitions of the riff). But Richard Berry's 'Louie Louie' (1957), not to mention 'Twist and Shout' (the Isley Brothers, 1962) and its model 'La Bamba' (Ritchie Valens, 1959), came earlier. The principle also goes back to R&B tunes such as 'The Hucklebuck' (1948), and even further to the 1930s swing bands. Mainstream popular songs organized solely around a riff are rare – usually it is played *through* a sectional form – but the riff structure is often sufficiently powerful to offer an alternative, more open formal process for the listener's attention. In particular, the use of repeated short chord sequences (from two to four chords, as a rule) is pervasive after the 1960s, even in many ballads and other songs clearly organized into sections. The divergent temporalities of harmonic cycle and larger sections can intertwine in powerful ways: in R.E.M.'s 'Losing My Religion' (1991), lyrics and musical content indicate an unorthodox sequence of verses, choruses and short bridges, but virtually all the music pivots around a two-chord riff (A minor-E minor), which, however, grows varied harmonic 'limbs' in the different sections of the song.

At the other extreme lies the move, especially within the 'progressive rock' of the 1960s and 1970s, toward more extended, freely invented forms, sometimes partly through-composed, sometimes partly improvised. Such pieces can be found on 'concept albums,' in the experimental compositions of such bands as Pink Floyd, and in classical-rock hybrids. Some are instrumental, and others push at the boundaries of the term 'song,' but many just extend the principle of sectionality (e.g., Queen, 'Bohemian Rhapsody' (1976)). While this strand may be subsidiary, it may be possible to detect its influence in the fluidities and irregularities often introduced into their songs by some of the more experimental singer-songwriters (e.g., Kate Bush, Björk, Jeff Buckley) and some 'indie' bands. Altogether, then, the breadth of practise within the fairly tight limits of the 'song' category is now quite considerable.

The shift back within the mainstream Western repertoire from what had previously seemed to be the 'natural' hegemony of Tin Pan Alley ballad sectionalism toward a more hybrid practise, containing a good deal of additive technique and open-ended process, needs to be put in a geographically wider context. The world dissemination of Western pop from the 1960s onward tended to pull many existing genres in other cultures into its orbit, in the sphere of musical form as in others. There were many variables and ambivalences, however. The case of Sub-Saharan Africa is particularly interesting, for here the impact of Western pop was accompanied by the direct influence of African-American genres, an influence that had a lengthy history – from ragtime and jazz through calypso and rumba to soul and reggae – and it encountered indigenous practises that were far more favorably inclined to additive than to sectional techniques. The result, broadly speaking, was that native African approaches – verse-and-refrain forms, call-and-response, overlapping choral antiphony, riff-like repeating pitch cycles and chord sequences – were easily adapted and rearranged in new contexts. This is what happened, in very varied ways, in Central African *soukous*, West African highlife and *jújù*, and South African *marabi*, *mbube* and *mbaqanga*. While the lengthy 'Afrobeat' pieces of Fela Kuti often divide into sections, this division is more like the seemingly arbitrary shift from one intrinsically open-ended groove to another that one hears in traditional West African percussion performances than it is like the sectionalism of the Western bourgeois tradition.

By contrast, in South and West Asia, what the Western pop influence encountered were popular song traditions that, though they had drawn previously on both indigenous folk and classical approaches, included a particular sort of sectionalism derived from the through-composed, semi-improvised vocal forms characteristic of their classical sources. In, for example, the Indian *ghazal* and the Egyptian *ughniyah* – both within and outside their film music contexts – such forms (though usually without much improvisation) are often given elaborate settings with lengthy instrumental introductions and interludes, and carefully composed contrasts between verses. Such an approach – deeply rooted in its specific cultural history – came under intense pressure, from the 1970s onward, from the global spread of disco and subsequent African-American dance music forms, where the triumph of musical process over sectional articulation is apparently consummated.

The Triumph of Process?

When, in the late 1970s, disco MCs started segueing records together into extended medleys; when hip-hop musicians such as Grandmaster Flash started creating collages, live and in the studio, out of looped rhythms and samples; when dance music producers followed up by developing a concept of form based on arbitrary 'cuts' between repetition-rich textures, each 'piece' (especially with live mixing) being potentially endless: at this point, the idea of song form as *mold* seems distinctly under threat. Admittedly, much of this music has little or no

vocal content and, even when it includes occasional sung phrases or vocal samples, it certainly pushes hard at one's understanding of what 'song' can be. But much of rap music, which is certainly a song genre, makes use of similar techniques. Sectionality as it has previously been understood in popular song virtually disappears in most rap. The vocal parts are generally organized in rhyming couplets, aggregated into sequences of seemingly arbitrary length; backings work through textural 'knots' of repeating figures. This is by no means to say that the pieces are 'formless,' but only that articulation points seem to be largely 'local' and attached to the rhetorical needs of the words; for example, refrain lines, rapped responses or, occasionally, sung phrases may divide up the couplets, and passages of 'break beats' or shifts in backing textures often sort the rapped lines into unschematized 'verses.' Overall, a processually apprehended dialog of *flow* and *breaks* governs the structure.

'Form' in Context

While the interplay between form as mold and form as moment-by-moment process is one useful principle in terms of which to understand song form in popular music, it is noticeable that the focus in analysis has been mostly on medium-level units and above. No doubt this results from the bias existing within analytical procedures; scholars have been slow to develop concepts and methods capable of grasping the structural significance of lower-level processes. Yet the evidence that popular song listeners give much attention to formal divisions is limited. Although it seems reasonable to assume that they respond on some level to distinctions between verses and choruses, to recurrences of melodic units, to the role of riffs, to melodic and harmonic closure, it is entirely possible that, in many cases, continuities of groove or the particularities of vocal timbre, pitching and dynamics at different moments may play a greater part in shaping temporal experience of a song. Without in the least downplaying the power of formal relationships (not to mention the categories of critical discourse) to channel response, it must be acknowledged that, in the end, perceptions of song form belong to the listener.

Bibliography

Forte, Allan. 1995. *The American Popular Ballad of the Golden Era, 1924–1950*. Princeton, NJ: Princeton University Press.

Hamm, Charles. 1979. *Yesterdays: Popular Song in America*. New York: W.W. Norton.

Jackson, Richard, ed. 1976. *Popular Songs of Nineteenth-Century America*. New York: Dover.

Manuel, Peter. 1988. *Popular Musics of the Non-Western World: An Introductory Survey*. New York: Oxford University Press.

Maróthy, János. 1974. *Music and the Bourgeois, Music and the Proletarian*. Budapest: Akademiai Kiado.

Middleton, Richard. 1990. *Studying Popular Music*. Milton Keynes and Philadelphia: Open University Press.

Middleton, Richard. 1997. 'Pop Goes Old Theory.' Review of Allan Forte, *The American Popular Ballad of the Golden Era, 1924–1950*. *Journal of the Royal Musical Association* 122(2): 303–20.

Moore, Allan. 1992. 'Patterns of Harmony.' *Popular Music* 11(1): 73–106.

Moore, Allan. 1993. *Rock: The Primary Text. Developing a Musicology of Rock*. Buckingham: Open University Press.

Turner, Michael R., ed. 1972. *The Parlour Songbook: A Casquet of Vocal Gems*. London: Michael Joseph.

Waites, Aline, and Hunter, Robin, eds. 1984. *The Illustrated Victorian Songbook*. London: Michael Joseph.

Wilder, Alec. 1972. *American Popular Song: The Great Innovators, 1900–1950*. New York: Oxford University Press.

Sheet Music

Balfe, Michael, comp. 1857. 'Come into the Garden, Maud.' London: Boosey & Sons.

Berlin, Irving, comp. and lyr. 1911. 'Alexander's Ragtime Band.' New York: Ted Snyder Co.

Bishop, Henry, comp., and Payne, John Howard, lyr. 1823. 'Home, Sweet Home.' London: Goulding, D'Almaine, Potter & Co.

Crudup, Arthur, comp. and lyr. 1947. 'That's All Right.' New York: St. Louis Music/Wabash Music.

Danks, H.P., comp., and Rexford, Eben E., lyr. 1873. 'Silver Threads Among the Gold.' New York: Charles W. Harris.

Donaldson, Walter, comp., and Kahn, Gus, lyr. 1925. 'Yes Sir! That's My Baby.' New York: Irving Berlin, Inc.

Garland, Joe, comp., and Razaf, Andy, lyr. 1939. 'In the Mood.' New York: Shapiro Music Publishers.

Gershwin, George, comp., and Gershwin, Ira, lyr. 1924. 'Fascinating Rhythm.' New York: New World Music.

Gershwin, George, comp., and Gershwin, Ira, lyr. 1930. 'I Got Rhythm.' New York: New World Music.

Gibson, Andy, comp., and Alfred, Roy, lyr. 1948. 'The Hucklebuck.' New York: Yellow Dog Music.

Handman, Lou, comp., and Turk, Roy, lyr. 1925. 'I'm Gonna Charleston Back to Charleston.' New York: Jerome H. Remick and Co.

Handy, W.C., comp., and Norton, George A., lyr. 1913. 'Memphis Blues.' New York: Theron C. Bennett.

Handy, W.C., comp. and lyr. 1914. 'St. Louis Blues.' Memphis, TN: Pace & Handy.

Howard, Joe, and Emerson, Ida, comps. and lyrs. 1899. 'Hello Ma Baby.' New York: T.B. Harms and Co.

Lee, Alfred, comp., and Cooper, George, lyr. 1868. 'Champagne Charlie.' New York: Wm. Hall and Son.

McGlennon, Felix, comp. and lyr. 1890. 'Comrades.' London: Francis Day & Hunter.

Muir, Lewis F., comp., and Gilbert, L. Wolfe, lyr. 1912. 'Waiting for the Robert E. Lee.' New York: F.A. Mills.

Russell, Henry, comp. and lyr. 1846. 'The Maniac.' Boston, MA: Ditson.

Sullivan, Arthur, comp., and Proctor, Adelaide A., lyr. 1880. 'The Lost Chord.' London: Boosey.

Discographical References

Beatles, The. 'She Said, She Said.' *Revolver*. Parlophone PMC 7009. *1966*: UK.

Berry, Chuck. 'Johnny B. Goode.' Chess 1691. *1958*: USA.

Berry, Chuck. 'Maybellene.' Chess 1604. 1955: USA.

Berry, Richard. 'Louie Louie.' Flip 321. *1957*: USA.

Drifters, The. 'Save the Last Dance for Me.' Atlantic 2071. *1960*: USA.

Haley, Bill, and His Comets. '(We're Gonna) Rock Around the Clock.' Decca 29124. 1955: USA.

Holly, Buddy. 'Peggy Sue.' Coral 61885. *1957*: USA.

Holly, Buddy. 'That'll Be the Day.' Brunswick 55009. *1957*: USA.

Isley Brothers, The. 'Twist and Shout.' Wand 124. *1962*: USA.

Kinks, The. 'You Really Got Me.' Pye 7N 15714. *1964*: UK.

Lewis, Jerry Lee. 'Great Balls of Fire.' Sun 281. *1957*: USA.

Little Richard. 'Long Tall Sally.' Specialty 572. *1956*: USA.

Little Richard. 'Tutti-Frutti.' Specialty 561. *1956*: USA.

McPhatter, Clyde. 'Long Lonely Nights.' Atlantic 1149. *1957*: USA.

Milton, Roy. 'The Hucklebuck.' Specialty 328. 1949: USA.

Presley, Elvis. 'All Shook Up.' RCA 47-6870. *1957*: USA.

Presley, Elvis. 'Blue Suede Shoes.' *Elvis Presley* (EP). RCA EPA-747. *1956*: USA.

Presley, Elvis. 'Heartbreak Hotel.' RCA 47-6420. *1956*: USA.

Presley, Elvis. 'Hound Dog.' RCA 47-6604. *1956*: USA.

Presley, Elvis. 'Love Me Tender.' RCA 47-6643. *1956*: USA.

Presley, Elvis. 'That's All Right.' Sun 209. 1954: USA.

Queen. 'Bohemian Rhapsody.' Elektra 45297. *1976*: USA.

R.E.M. 'Losing My Religion.' *Out of Time*. Warner 7599-26496-2. *1991*: USA.

Rolling Stones, The. '(I Can't Get No) Satisfaction.' Decca F 12220. *1965*: UK.

Tampa Red. 'It's Tight Like That.' Vocalion 1216. 1928:

USA. Reissue: Tampa Red. 'It's Tight Like That.' *Tampa Red (1928–1942)*. Story of the Blues 3505. *1994*: USA.

Turner, Joe. 'Shake, Rattle and Roll.' Atlantic 1026. 1954: USA.

Valens, Ritchie. 'La Bamba.' Del-Fi 4110. *1959*: USA.

RICHARD MIDDLETON

Standard

A standard is a song or tune widely regarded, by the public and by musicians, as having an assured place in the repertoire by virtue of its longevity and quality. 'Evergreen' is almost synonymous, but it does not always possess the same connotations of 'quality.'

For Silver and Bruce (1939), 'standards' were the best ballads and lieder of the nineteenth century and were to be contrasted with current popular songs, with their more formulaic patterns. Punning on this usage, Adorno (1990, 314) describes the structures of such non-standard songs as 'standardised.' And indeed there is some sense of ambivalence within the term, since 'stand-ards' are commonly thought to *typify* a musical category. Already, however, favored early twentieth-century com-positions were becoming standards, especially the most admired Tin Pan Alley and Broadway ballads – 'Stardust' (Hoagy Carmichael), 'All the Things You Are' (Jerome Kern), 'Body and Soul' (Johnny Green) and the like. In effect, the term now described those songs that formed the core repertoire of the most highly regarded US singers of the time – Bing Crosby, Billie Holiday, Ella Fitzgerald, Frank Sinatra – and that also comprised much of the source material used for improvisation by jazz musicians. In the early years of the rock era, 'standards' belonged to all that was to be stylistically superseded. It was not long, though, before selected songs by Lennon and McCartney, Bob Dylan and a few others were them-selves being described and treated as standards. The terms 'golden oldies' and 'rock classics' addressed the same process, but with rather less reverence and, per-haps, discrimination.

Clearly, then, the term 'standard' not only refers to a stock of available performance material, to a phenom-enon of popular memory, and to the availability of gen-eric, stylistic and critical models; it also broaches the question of canon formation.

Bibliography

Adorno, Theodor W. 1990. 'On Popular Music.' In *On Record: Rock, Pop and the Written Word*, ed. Simon Frith and Andrew Goodwin. London: Routledge, 301–14. (First published in *Studies in Philosophy and Social Science* 9 (1941): 17–48.)

Silver, Abner, and Bruce, Robert. 1939. *How to Write and Sell a Song Hit*. Englewood Cliffs, NJ: Prentice-Hall.

Sheet Music

Carmichael, Hoagy, comp., and Parish, Mitchell, lyr. 1929. 'Star Dust.' New York: Mills Music.

Green, Johnny, comp., and Heyman, Ed, Sauer, Robert, & Eyton, Frank, lyrs. 1930. 'Body and Soul.' New York: Harms.

Kern, Jerome, comp., and Hammerstein, Oscar, lyr. 1939. 'All the Things You Are.' New York: T.B. Harms.

RICHARD MIDDLETON

Stanza

A stanza is a group of lines of verse forming a definite pattern. Lyrics in popular songs are usually divided into stanzas, the most common patterns being formed through end-rhyme schemes that result most often in even-numbered groups of lines (though neither of these characteristics is universal). Stanzas usually correspond with musical sections (a verse, a chorus, a bridge and so forth).

The variety of stanza patterns used in popular songs is considerable. Traditional ballads usually have a regular scheme, unchanging from stanza to stanza. A short refrain may be incorporated or added. Similar patterns are common in nineteenth-century commercial popular songs. In the verse-refrain schemes typical of the later nineteenth and early twentieth centuries, the verse stanzas generally carry narrative, the refrain stanzas more reflective or affective content. Twelve-bar blues mostly have three-line stanzas, following an AAB pat-tern. Pop/rock songs may have a variety of stanza types and lengths, and arrange them in different orders. Under the influence, initially, of Bob Dylan, stanza patterns (rhyme schemes, line lengths, numbers of lines) often became much more varied, both within a song and between songs.

In some genres ('talking blues' and rap, for example), stanza length seems virtually arbitrary. Here especially – but also more widely, wherever songs are produced for performance and/or recording rather than publication – stanzaic divisions are best revealed, and sometimes only revealed, by musical punctuations.

RICHARD MIDDLETON

Verse

In popular songs, 'verse' is a term describing a complete unit (generally a stanza) in the lyrics, and the music used to set several such units. The same music is used for each verse, though perhaps with some variation, but not, usu-ally, the same lyrics. Refrains and choruses are distingu-ished from verses in that both lyrics and music are repeated.

The usage of the term 'verse' most likely derives in the first place from religious liturgy: verses in psalms and hymns are short, self-contained metrical units, each sung to the same tune. Much the same applies in many genres of traditional secular song. This usage was adopted in relation to commercially produced genres in the nineteenth century and earlier (for example, broadside ballads). In mainstream US popular song of the late nineteenth and early twentieth centuries, verses became fewer and less important in favor of the chorus, and by the 1920s they were sometimes not performed. In the more varied and fluid forms characteristic of Western popular song since the mid-1950s, the definition of verses has continued to be much the same as previously, although the narrative function that was usual before the twentieth century has become optional. In a significant vernacular usage, however, the term is sometimes applied to what musicologists might call a 'period' – that is, any self-contained musical statement – regardless of the relationship between words and music.

RICHARD MIDDLETON

17. Harmony

Antiphony

'Antiphony,' from the Greek *antifonía*, meaning 'opposing sound,' is an umbrella term denoting performance techniques in which one line of music is alternated with another contrasting or complementary musical line of roughly equal importance. Although no absolute limit of duration can be given, each antiphonal statement between different musicians, singers, instruments or recorded tracks is usually perceived as lasting at least the length of a musical phrase.

Most responsorial techniques – for example, African-American call-and-response, the *sawal-jawab* ('question and answer') of Indian *rāga* music, and the chanted dialog between precentor and congregation in many forms of Christian liturgy – are also antiphonal. Antiphony that is not necessarily responsorial occurs when one part of a vocal or instrumental ensemble exchanges alternate phrases or sections of music with another: for example, (a) the brass section playing one passage and the whole big band answering with another; (b) the jazz drummer or bass player performing two- or four-bar breaks and the rest of the band answering with passages of similar length, usually just before the final chorus; or (c) two sides of a choir or congregation singing alternate lines or verses from psalms or hymns. Stereo antiphony occurs either when the same sound is panned left (or right) for one phrase or passage and right (or left) for the subsequent one, or when two different sounds are assigned alternate phrases or passages at opposite panning positions.

PHILIP TAGG

Changes

'Changes' is used as a short form for 'chord changes.' It is a term used mainly by jazz musicians in the English-speaking world to denote (a) any harmonic progression; (b) any such harmonic/chord progression that forms the basis for improvisation; and (c) any progression of at least three chords, often many more, that recurs consecutively several times in the same number. Examples of its usage would include: (a) 'the "La Bamba" changes go one, four, five'; (b) 'which changes do you use in the middle eight of "Round About Midnight"?'; and (c) 'I was trying to work out the changes on that recording.'

Discographical References

Monk, Thelonious. 'Round About Midnight.' *Solo 1954*. Vogue 15022. *1993*: USA.

Valens, Ritchie. 'La Bamba.' Del-Fi 4110. *1959*: USA. Reissue: Valens, Ritchie. 'La Bamba.' RCA PB 41435. *1987*: UK.

PHILIP TAGG

Chord

A chord is the simultaneous sounding, by any polyphonic instrument or any combination of instrument(s) and/or voice(s), of two or more notes of different pitch. The simultaneous sounding of notes of the same name – that is, pitches separated by octave intervals – is not considered to be a chord. Derived from the Greek *chordē*, via the Latin *chorda* (meaning the string of a musical instrument), the term 'chord' came to denote, in sixteenth-century Europe, the sounding together of different notes played on several instruments of the same family, especially the strings.

Chords need not be heard as such by members of musical traditions in which polyphony emphasizes the interplay of independent melodic lines (counterpoint) much more strongly than music in the Western post-Renaissance tradition of melody and accompaniment. In

521

most types of popular music, chords are generally regarded as belonging to the accompaniment part of this melody/accompaniment dualism.

Owing to the global predominance of Western harmonic practises, it is useful to distinguish between two main categories of chords: tertial and non-tertial. Chords can be identified in both structural and phenomenological terms.

Structure and Terminology of Tertial Chords

Tertial Triads

Tertial chords are based on common triads (see below) and can be regarded as the fundamental harmonic building blocks in most forms of jazz, popular music and European classical music.

A 'triad' is any chord containing three notes (cf. German *Dreiklang*). The 'common triad' is constructed of two simultaneously sounding thirds, one superimposed upon the other. For example, the interval *c–e* (a major third) together with the interval *e–g* (a minor third) constitute a C major triad, while the interval *d–f* (a minor third) together with the interval *f–a* (a major third) constitute a D minor triad (Ex. 1).

There are four types of tertial triads: major, minor, diminished and augmented (see Table 1). The first three of these triad types can be generated from the seven key-specific notes of any standard major or melodic minor scale (the Ionian and Aeolian modes). As shown in Example 1, major triads derive from degrees 1, 4 and 5 of the major scale and degrees 3, 6 and 7 of the minor scale (for example, from C, F and G in C major/A minor), while minor triads are found at degrees 2, 3 and 6 of the

major scale and degrees 4, 5 and 1 of the minor scale (for example, at D, E and A in C major/A minor). Degree 7 of the major scale and degree 2 of the minor scale each produce a diminished triad. All four types of triad are set out, with C as their root, in Table 1.

Major triads are composed of a minor third on top of a major third (for example, *e–g* over *c–e* in C) and minor triads of a major third over a minor third (for example, *e♭–g* over *c–e♭* in C minor). Augmented triads are composed of two superimposed major thirds (for example, *e–g♯* over *c–e*) and diminished triads of two minor thirds (for example, *e♭–g♭* over *c–e♭*). All triadic chords contain the root (degree 1) and, with very few exceptions, both the third (degree 3) and the fifth (degree 5) of one of the triad types defined in Table 1.

Tertial Chord Symbols

Two types of shorthand that enable musicians to quickly identify tertial chords are in common use: (a) roman numerals (for example, I, vi, ii[7], V[7]) and (b) lead sheet chord symbols (for example, C, Am, Dm[7], G[7]).

Roman Numerals Roman numerals are used to denote chords and their relation to the tonic of any key. More specifically, roman numerals denote triads built on the scale degree they designate – the *root* – and, within any particular key, uppercase roman numerals denote major triads and lowercase roman numerals denote minor triads (see Ex. 1, in which the root notes of the triads are *c, d, e, f, g, a* and *b*). Bearing in mind that pitches extraneous to the triad, most frequently the seventh, are expressed as superscript arabic numerals, it is clear that I vi ii[7] V[7] designates the same chord progression in any

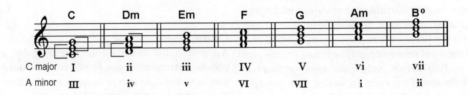

| C major | I | ii | iii | IV | V | vi | vii |
| A minor | III | iv | v | VI | VII | i | ii |

Example 1 Tertial triads on each degree of the C major / A minor scale.

Table 1 Definitions of tertial triad types (in C)

Type of Triad	Type of Third	Type of Fifth	Notes in Chord	Lead Symbol	Roman Num.
Major	Major	Perfect	*c e g*	C	I
Minor	Minor	Perfect	*c e♭ g*	Cm	i
Augmented	Major	Augmented	*c e g♯/a♭*	C[aug]/C[+]	I[+]
Diminished	Minor	Diminished	*c e♭ g♭/f♯*	C[dim]/C[o]	i[o]

Example 2 The sequence I vi ii⁷ V⁷ in C major and D major.

major key, whereas C Am Dm⁷ G⁷ and D Bm Em⁷ A⁷ designate the same sequence in two keys only (C major and D major, respectively; see Ex. 2). Similarly, a repeated I ♭VII IV progression (C B♭ F in C) is found as D C G (in D) throughout Lynyrd Skynyrd's 'Sweet Home Alabama' and as G F C at the end of the Beatles' 'Hey Jude' (in G). Note that triads built on pitches foreign to the standard major or minor key of the piece must be preceded by the requisite accidental – for example, ♭VII for a major triad built on b♭ in the key of C major, but just VII for the same chord in C minor. Similarly, notes within a triadic chord that are extraneous to the current key of the piece must also be preceded by the requisite accidental – for example, ii⁷♭5 for the second-degree chord in C major with d as the root and containing also f, a♭ and c.

Inversions In most popular music, the lowest note in a chord is also usually its root. However, in choral settings and in music influenced by the European classical tradition, triadic chords are frequently *inverted* – that is, the third, fifth or seventh is the lowest pitch. This is illustrated in Example 3, in which the first three chords are a standard triad of C major written, first, in its *root position* (with c in the bass), second, in its *first inversion* (with its third, e, in the bass) and, third, in its *second inversion* (with its fifth, g, in the bass). The final chord in Example 3 is a C major triad with the flat seventh (b♭) in the bass – that is, a C⁷ chord in its third inversion (with its seventh, b♭, as the lowest note).

European textbook harmony symbols, derived from figured bass techniques of the Baroque era (bottom line of symbols in Example 3), are largely incompatible with the way in which chords are understood by musicians in the popular field. Therefore, when inversions need to

be referred to, they are most commonly denoted in the absolute terms of lead sheet chord symbols (top line of symbols in Example 3), but can sometimes be referred to in the relative terms of roman numerals (as shown in the line of symbols between the two staves in Example 3) – that is, as 'I/3' for the tonic triad with its third as bass note, 'I/5' for the same chord with its fifth in the bass and so on.

Recognition of Tertial Chords

Individual chords can be identified and named according to their constituent notes and harmonic functions. They can also be recognized phenomenologically. Table 2 (pages 524–6) lists some of the most common chords in popular music, together with striking occurrences of those chords in well-known pieces of popular music. It also shows, where applicable, the musical styles or type of mood with which the chord is often associated.

Sheet Music

Addinsell, Richard, comp. 1942. 'Warsaw Concerto.' London: Keith Prowse.

Chopin, Frédéric François, comp. 1839. 'Marche funèbre' from 'Sonata, Op. 35.' Republished in *Motion Picture Moods for Pianists and Organists*, ed. Erno Rapee. New York: Schirmer, 1924; reprint New York: Arno Press, 1974.

Degeyter, Pierre, comp., 1888, and Pottier, Eugène, lyr. 1871. 'Internationale.' In *Chants révolutionnaires*. Paris, 1887.

Gershwin, George, comp., and Caesar, Irving, lyr. 1918. 'Swanee.' New York: Harms, Francis Day & Hunter.

Goldenberg, William, comp. 1973. *Kojak* (main theme, orchestral arrangement No. 1). Manuscript, Universal City Studios, Prod. No. 39000. Melville, NY: Duchess Music Corporation.

Hagen, E., comp. 1944. 'Harlem Nocturne for Eb Concert Sax and Orchestra.' New York: Shapiro & Bernstein.

Mendelssohn-Bartholdy, Felix, comp. 1843. 'Wedding March' from *A Midsummer Night's Dream* (arranged for organ by C.W. Pearce). London: Paxton.

Discographical References

ABBA. 'The Name of the Game.' Epic EPC 5750. *1977*: UK.

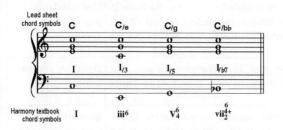

Example 3 Inversions of the C major chord.

Table 2 Familiar occurrences of triadic chords in popular music

Chord short-hand	Full chord description	Occurrences	Style
	Major triad	First and final chords of most national anthems, 'White Christmas' (Crosby), the 'Internationale' (Degeyter) and the Blue Danube waltz (Strauss); Beatles: 'Yellow Submarine,' all chords in the chorus	
m	Minor triad	Pink Floyd: 'Shine On You Crazy Diamond,' first long chord; Beatles: 'It Won't Be Long,' first chord; 'She Loves You,' first chord; 'I'll Be Back,' first chord; Chopin: Funeral March from 'Sonata, Op. 35,' first and final chords	
+	Augmented triad	Gershwin: 'Swanee,' at 'how I love you!'; Beatles: 'Being for the Benefit of Mr. Kite,' second chord; 'Fixing a Hole,' second chord	
6	Added sixth chord	Donaldson: 'My Blue Heaven,' first chord, at 'When whip-perwills call'; Weill: 'Mack the Knife,' first and final chords; 'Alabama Song,' first and final chords in the chorus, at 'Moon of Alabama'; Beatles: 'She Loves You,' at the final 'Yeah'	Jazz influences 1920s–40s
m6	Minor triad with added (major) sixth	Weill: 'Alabama Song,' first chord in the verse, at 'Show us the way to the next . . .'; Mendelssohn: Wedding March from *A Midsummer Night's Dream*, first chord after the fanfare	
7	(Dominant) seventh chord	Penultimate chord in most hymns and national anthems; Beatles: 'I Saw Her Standing There,' first chord; 'I Wanna Be Your Man,' first chord; 'She's a Woman,' first chord; 'Taxman,' first chord; 'Get Back,' first chord	
7+	Seventh chord with aug mented fifth	Miles Davis: 'Someday My Prince Will Come,' second chord, at 'day'; Mary Hopkin: 'Those Were the Days,' at 'were the' in upbeat to chorus; Beatles: 'Oh! Darling,' just after 'broke down and died,' as upbeat to the reprise of the hook	
7♭5	Seventh chord with dimin ished fifth	Jobim: 'The Girl from Ipanema,' penultimate chord; 'Samba de una nota só,' fourth chord; 'Desafinado,' second chord	Bossa nova, bebop, jazz fusion
maj7	Major seventh chord	Cole Porter: 'Night and Day,' first chord of chorus; Erroll Garner: 'Misty,' first downbeat chord of main tune; Beatles: 'This Boy,' first chord; Tom Jones: 'It's Not Unusual,' first chord; Burt Bacharach: 'This Guy's in Love with You,' first three chords; Beatles: 'Something,' second chord; Bacharach: 'Raindrops Keep Fallin' on My Head,' second chord	Jazz standards, pop 1960s–70s, bossa nova, Bacharach
m7	Minor seventh chord	Youmans: 'Tea for Two,' first chord (on 'tea'); Bacharach: 'Walk On By,' first chord; Beatles: 'Michelle,' second chord; 'Rocky Raccoon,' first chord of the hook; 'You Never Give Me Your Money,' first chord	Jazz standards, pop 1960s–70s
mmaj7/ mmaj9	Minor, major seventh/ninth	Hagen: 'Harlem Nocturne' (the *Mike Hammer* theme), first downbeat chord of tune; Norman (arr. Barry): 'The James Bond Theme,' final chord	Detective and spy music
m7♭5	Minor seven flat five or 'half-diminished'	Addinsell: Warsaw Concerto, second chord; Miles Davis: 'Stella by Starlight,' first chord; Nat 'King' Cole: 'Autumn Leaves,' first chord of middle eight	Romantic pop 'classics,' romantic ballads

Table 2 *Continued*

Chord short-hand	Full chord description	Occurrences	Style
dim	Diminished seventh chord	Beatles: 'Till There Was You,' second chord, at 'hill'; 'Strawberry Fields Forever,' at 'nothing is real'	The usual 'horror' chord in silent movies
9	(Dominant) ninth chord	Beatles: 'Things We Said Today,' at 'dreaming' ('some day when we're dreaming'); 'Because,' at 'round'/'high'/'blue'	Swing, bebop
+9	Plus nine chord	Jimi Hendrix Experience: 'Purple Haze,' first chord; Beatles: 'Come Together,' first chord; Blood, Sweat and Tears: 'Spinning Wheel,' first chord	Rock ca. 1970, jazz fusion
maj9	Ninth chord with major seventh	Jobim: 'The Girl from Ipanema,' first chord	Bossa nova, 1960s
m9	Minor ninth chord	Warren: 'Jeepers Creepers,' first chord of chorus; Weill: 'Speak Low,' first chord of chorus; Raksin: 'Laura,' first chord of chorus	Jazz standards
11	Chord of the eleventh	Righteous Brothers: 'You've Lost That Lovin' Feelin',' first chord; Beatles: 'She's Leaving Home,' at 'leaving the note,' 'standing alone,' 'quietly turning,' 'stepping outside' and 'meeting a man'; 'The Long and Winding Road,' at first occurrence of 'road'; Zawinul: 'Mercy, Mercy,' the 'Gospel' chord after unison run-up just before minor key section; ABBA: 'The Name of the Game,' at the repeated 'I want to know'	Gospel, soul, fusion, modal jazz
m11	Minor eleventh chord	Miles Davis: 'So What,' all chords; Goldenberg: 'Kojak Theme,' first two chords under melody	Modal jazz
13	Chord of the thirteenth	Degeyter: 'Internationale,' upbeat to chorus; Big Ben Banjo Band: 'The Luxembourg Waltz,' first chord (upbeat); Beatles: 'Because,' just before ecstatic 'Ah!' on D chord	Pre-jazz, swing, bebop
add9	Major triad with added ninth	Bacharach: '(They Long to Be) Close to You,' first chord, at 'why do birds suddenly appear?'; Nilsson: 'Intro: Without You,' first chord	Pop ballads
madd9	Minor triad with added ninth	Al Hirt: 'Music to Watch Girls By,' first chord; Lionel Richie: 'Hello,' first chord; Rota: 'Romeo and Juliet,' main theme, first chord	Wistful, sad or bittersweet ballads
/3	Major triad in first inversion	Beach Boys: 'God Only Knows,' hook line at 'knows what I'd be'; Foundations: 'Baby, Now That I've Found You,' at 'let you go' and 'even so'; Procol Harum: 'Homburg,' third and fourth chords in the introduction	'Classical'
/5	Major triad in second inversion	Beach Boys: 'God Only Knows,' first chord; Foundations: 'Baby, Now That I've Found You,' at 'love you so'; Procol Harum: 'Wreck of the Hesperus,' at start of major key section	'Classical'
m/5	Minor triad in second inversion	Simon and Garfunkel: 'Homeward Bound,' second chord; Sinatra: 'My Way,' second chord	Reflective ballads, 'classical'
7/7	Seventh chord in third inversion	Beach Boys: 'God Only Knows,' at 'are stars above you'; Foundations: 'Baby, Now That I've Found You,' at 'now that I've found you'; Procol Harum: 'Homburg,' second chord; ABBA: 'Waterloo,' second chord, on the 'oo' of 'At Waterloo' in verse one	'Classical'

Table 2 *Continued*

Chord short-hand	Full chord description	Occurrences	Style
maj7/7	Major triad with major seventh in bass	Procol Harum: 'A Whiter Shade of Pale,' second chord; Eric Clapton: 'Let It Grow,' second chord	'Classical,' reflective
sus4	Suspended fourth chord	Beatles: 'You've Got to Hide Your Love Away,' at 'away'; Rolling Stones: '(I Can't Get No) Satisfaction,' second of two chords in main riff	Pop 1960s–70s
	Quartal chord	Marvin Gaye: 'Ain't No Mountain High Enough,' first chord in the introduction	Pop 1960s–70s

ABBA. 'Waterloo.' Epic EPC 2240. *1974*: UK.

'Alabama Song.' *September Songs: The Music of Kurt Weill.* Sony CD 63046. *1997*: USA.

Alpert, Herb. 'This Guy's in Love with You.' A&M AMS 727. *1968*: UK.

Armstrong, Louis. 'Jeepers Creepers.' *Louis Armstrong Volume V '1938–39'*. Ambassador 1905. *1996*: Canada.

Astaire, Fred, and Reisman, Leo, and His Orchestra. 'Night and Day.' *Cole Porter Centennial Tribute.* Pearl Flapper 9751. *1993*: UK.

Beach Boys, The. 'God Only Knows.' *Pet Sounds.* Capitol DT 2458. *1966*: USA.

Beatles, The. 'Because.' *Abbey Road.* Apple PCS 7088. *1969*: UK.

Beatles, The. 'Being for the Benefit of Mr. Kite.' *Sergeant Pepper's Lonely Hearts Club Band.* Parlophone PCS 7027. *1967*: UK.

Beatles, The. 'Come Together.' *Abbey Road.* Apple PCS 7088. *1969*: UK.

Beatles, The. 'Fixing a Hole.' *Sergeant Pepper's Lonely Hearts Club Band.* Parlophone PCS 7027. *1967*: UK.

Beatles, The. 'Get Back.' Apple R 5777. *1969*: UK.

Beatles, The. 'Hey Jude.' Apple R 5722. *1968*: UK.

Beatles, The. 'I'll Be Back.' *A Hard Day's Night.* Parlophone PMC 1230. *1964*: UK.

Beatles, The. 'I Saw Her Standing There.' *Please Please Me.* Parlophone PMC 1202. *1963*: UK.

Beatles, The. 'It Won't Be Long.' *With the Beatles.* Parlophone PMC 1206. *1963*: UK.

Beatles, The. 'I Wanna Be Your Man.' *With the Beatles.* Parlophone PMC 1206. *1963*: UK.

Beatles, The. 'Michelle.' *Rubber Soul.* Parlophone PMC 1267. *1965*: UK.

Beatles, The. 'Oh! Darling.' *Abbey Road.* Apple PCS 7088. *1969*: UK.

Beatles, The. 'Rocky Raccoon.' *The Beatles [White Album].* Apple PCS 7067-8. *1968*: UK.

Beatles, The. 'She Loves You.' Parlophone R 5055. *1963*: UK.

Beatles, The. 'She's a Woman.' *Beatles '65.* Capitol 2228. *1964*: USA.

Beatles, The. 'She's Leaving Home.' *Sergeant Pepper's Lonely Hearts Club Band.* Parlophone PCS 7027. *1967*: UK.

Beatles, The. 'Something.' *Abbey Road.* Apple PCS 7088. *1969*: UK.

Beatles, The. 'Strawberry Fields Forever.' Parlophone R 5570. *1967*: UK.

Beatles, The. 'Taxman.' *Revolver.* Parlophone PMC 7009. *1966*: UK.

Beatles, The. 'The Long and Winding Road.' *Let It Be.* Apple PCS 7096. *1970*: UK.

Beatles, The. 'Things We Said Today.' *A Hard Day's Night.* Parlophone PMC 1230. *1964*: UK.

Beatles, The. 'This Boy.' Parlophone R 5084. *1963*: UK.

Beatles, The. 'Till There Was You.' *With the Beatles.* Parlophone PMC 1206. *1963*: UK.

Beatles, The. 'Yellow Submarine.' *Revolver.* Parlophone PMC 7009. *1966*: UK.

Beatles, The. 'You Never Give Me Your Money.' *Abbey Road.* Apple PCS 7088. *1969*: UK.

Beatles, The. 'You've Got to Hide Your Love Away.' *Help.* Parlophone PMC 1255. *1965*: UK.

Big Ben Banjo Band, The. 'The Luxembourg Waltz.' Columbia DB 4181. *1958*: USA.

Blood, Sweat and Tears. 'Spinning Wheel.' *Blood, Sweat & Tears.* CBS 63504. *1969*: UK.

Carpenters, The. '(They Long to Be) Close to You.' A&M AMS 800. *1970*: UK.

Clapton, Eric. 'Let It Grow.' *461 Ocean Boulevard.* RSO 2479 118. *1974*: USA.

Cole, Nat 'King.' 'Autumn Leaves.' Capitol CL 14364. *1955*: USA.

Crosby, Bing. 'White Christmas.' *Best of Bing Crosby*. Decca DXS-184. *1965*: UK.

Davis, Miles. 'Someday My Prince Will Come.' *Someday My Prince Will Come*. Columbia CS-8456. *1961*: USA.

Davis, Miles. 'So What.' *Kind of Blue*. CBS 62066. *1959*: UK.

Davis, Miles. 'Stella by Starlight.' *Basic Miles*. Columbia 32025. *1973*: USA.

Dietrich, Marlene. 'My Blue Heaven.' *Platinum Series*. D-3 Entertainment 33338. *2000*: USA.

Foundations, The. 'Baby, Now That I've Found You.' Pye 7N 17366. *1967*: UK.

Gaye, Marvin, and Terrell, Tammi. 'Ain't No Mountain High Enough.' Tamla Motown 54149. *1967*: USA.

Gentry, Bobbie. 'Raindrops Keep Fallin' on My Head.' Capitol CL 15626. *1970*: UK.

Gilberto, João. 'Samba de una nota só.' *Gilberto and Jobim*. Capitol 2160. *1960*: USA.

Goodman, Benny. 'Tea for Two.' *His Best Recordings*. Best of Jazz 4007. *1996*: USA.

Haymes, Dick. 'Laura.' Decca 18666. 1945: USA.

Hirt, Al. 'Music to Watch Girls By.' *Music to Watch Girls By*. RCA 3773. *1967*: USA.

Hopkin, Mary. 'Those Were the Days.' Apple 2. *1968*: UK.

Jimi Hendrix Experience, The. 'Purple Haze.' Track 604 001. *1967*: UK.

Jobim, Antonio Carlos. 'Desafinado.' *The Girl from Ipanema: The Antonio Carlos Jobim Songbook*. Verve 5472. *1996*: USA.

Jobim, Antonio Carlos. 'The Girl from Ipanema.' *The Girl from Ipanema: The Antonio Carlos Jobim Songbook*. Verve 5472. *1996*: USA.

John Barry Orchestra, The. 'The James Bond Theme.' Columbia DB 4898. *1962*: UK.

Jones, Tom. 'It's Not Unusual.' Decca F 12062. *1965*: UK.

Lynyrd Skynyrd. 'Sweet Home Alabama.' MCA 40258. *1974*: USA.

Mathis, Johnny. 'Misty.' Fontana H 219. *1960*: UK.

Nilsson, Harry. 'Intro: Without You.' *Son of Dracula*. Rapple ABL1-0220. *1974*: USA.

Ormandy, Eugene, and the Philadelphia Orchestra. 'An der schönen blauen Donau.' *Strauss Waltzes*. CBS Odyssey MBK 44892. *1979*: UK.

Pastorius, Jaco. 'Mercy, Mercy.' *Curtain Call*. Another Hit 2001. *1996*: USA.

Pink Floyd. 'Shine On You Crazy Diamond.' *Wish You Were Here*. Harvest SHVL 814. *1975*: UK.

Procol Harum. 'A Whiter Shade of Pale.' Deram DM 126. *1967*: UK.

Procol Harum. 'Homburg.' Regal-Zonophone RZ 3003. *1967*: UK.

Procol Harum. 'Wreck of the Hesperus.' *A Salty Dog*. Regal-Zonophone SLRZ 1009. *1969*: UK.

Richie, Lionel. 'Hello.' Motown 1722. *1984*: USA.

Righteous Brothers, The. 'You've Lost That Lovin' Feelin'.' London HLU 9943. *1965*: UK.

Rolling Stones, The. '(I Can't Get No) Satisfaction.' Decca F 12220. *1965*: UK.

Simon and Garfunkel. 'Homeward Bound.' CBS 202045. *1966*: UK.

Sinatra, Frank. 'My Way.' Reprise RS 20817. *1969*: UK.

'Speak Low.' *September Songs: The Music of Kurt Weill*. Sony CD 63046. *1997*: USA.

Tony Hatch Orchestra, The. 'Romeo and Juliet.' *Hit the Road to Themeland*. Pye NSPL 41029. *1974*: UK.

Valente, Caterina. 'Mack the Knife.' *The Collection*. Varèse Sarabande 5823. *1998*: USA.

Warwick, Dionne. 'Walk On By.' Pye International 7N 25241. *1964*: UK.

PHILIP TAGG

Circle of Fifths

Circle of fifths has been the central concept of tonality in Western music theory since the advent of equal-tone tuning (ca. 1700). Its main functions are (a) to visualize the system of keys and key signatures used in much of the music of the Western world; and (b) to facilitate understanding of the harmonic progressions found frequently in such music.

It has been known since ancient times that an interval of 12 fifths is, with a minimal margin of error (the Pythagorean comma or 0.24 percent of one semitone per octave), equal to an interval of eight octaves; that is, the frequencies of pitches one fifth apart are separated by a factor of 12:8 or 3:2 (×1.5) when ascending and 2:3 (×0.67) when descending. The concept also assumes that the interval of a fourth (4:3 or ×1.33 up and 3:4 or ×0.75 down) is complementary to that of the fifth within an octave, so that ascending a fourth and then descending an octave (for example, from c^3 to f^3 to f^2) will result in the same pitch as just descending a fifth (for example, from c^3 to f^2) and, conversely, that ascending a fifth and then descending an octave (for example, from c^3 to g^3 to g^2) will result in the same pitch as just descending a fourth (for example, from c^3 to g^2). Hence, a series of alternately falling fifths and rising fourths running anticlockwise around the complete circle of fifths (for example, $c^3 \searrow f^2 \nearrow b\flat^2 \searrow e\flat^2 \nearrow a\flat^2 \searrow d\flat^2 \nearrow g\flat^2/f\sharp^2 \searrow b^1 \nearrow e^2 \searrow a^1 \nearrow d^2 \searrow g^1 \nearrow c^2$; see Fig. 1) visits every note in the 12-tone chromatic scale within a relatively restricted range. The same applies to a series of alternately rising fifths and falling fourths running clockwise (for example, $c^2 \nearrow g^2 \searrow d^2 \nearrow a^2 \searrow e^2 \nearrow b^2 \searrow f\sharp^2/g\flat^2 \nearrow d\flat^3 \searrow a\flat^2 \nearrow e\flat^3 \searrow b\flat^2 \nearrow f^3 \searrow c^3$). The fact that the circle of fifths also constitutes a 'circle

527

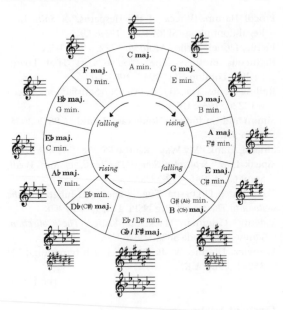

Figure 1 Circle of fifths.

the number of flats decreases (five for D♭ major at 25 to the hour, four for A♭ major at 20 to and so on). Since movement clockwise around the circle is by ascending fifths, and since an increase in sharps or a decrease in flats implies upward movement, this tonal direction 'sharpward' toward the dominant (from I to V – for example, C to G) can be referred to as rising, while anticlockwise tonal movement 'flatward' toward the subdominant (from V to I or from I to IV – for example, from G to C or from C to F) can be referred to as falling.

Harmonic progressions based on the circle of fifths are extremely common in popular music. Those running anticlockwise ('flatward' or falling; see Fig. 1) are particularly common in styles using the tertial harmonic practises of jazz or classical music. Two basic types of such progression exist: (a) the real or modulatory circle of fifths; and (b) the virtual or key-specific circle of fifths. Both these types of anticlockwise progression involve the same two-stage V→I cadence (for example, G⁷→C), because all unaltered notes in the dominant seventh chord (V⁷ – for example, G, B, D and F in G⁷) are contained in the major scale of the tonic (I – for example, C major, containing C, D, E, F, G, A and B). However, as soon as an anticlockwise circle-of-fifths progression contains more than two stages, it will become either real/modulatory – for example, VI⁷→II⁷→V⁷→I (A⁷→D⁷→G⁷→C in C; see Ex. 1), or virtual/key-specific – for example, vi⁷→ii⁷→V⁷→I (Am⁷→Dm⁷→G⁷→C in C). The former constitutes a real circle of fifths, because A⁷ (VI – the chord on the sixth degree) is the real dominant seventh of D (II – on the second degree) and D⁷ (II) is the real dominant seventh of G (V); this example can also be termed modulatory, because A⁷ and D⁷ both contain notes foreign to the tonic key of C major (C♯ and F♯, respectively). The virtual circle-of-fifths progression is key-specific, because all notes in all chords belong to the same tonic key (for example, C major; see Ex. 1); it can also be called virtual, because neither Am⁷ (on the sixth degree) nor Dm⁷ (on the second degree) is a real dominant seventh of a subsequent chord in the progression.

A certain predilection for 'real' circles of fifths in US popular songs of the first and second decades of the twentieth century was superseded by a preference for more 'virtual' variants in standards and evergreens of the

of fourths' but is never referred to as such probably stems from the European classical tradition within which the concept developed, where chords constructed on the fifth degree of any scale (V) are understood and referred to as 'dominant' and those on the fourth degree (IV) are considered to be 'subdominant.'

The circle of fifths is a tonal concept that is applied to harmony rather than melody, not least because chord progressions based on fourths and fifths are much more common than are melodic lines using these intervals. The concept is particularly useful in the theoretical and practical study of popular music, in most jazz idioms, as well as in other styles of music that have been influenced by European traditions of tertial harmony.

Keys and their signatures are arranged as the 12 figures of an analog clock, with C major and its relative A minor (no sharps and no flats) on the hour, and F♯/G♭ major with their relative D♯/E♭ minor (six sharps or six flats) on the half-hour. Moving clockwise, the number of sharps in each key signature increases (one for G major at five past the hour, two for D major at 10 past and so on) or

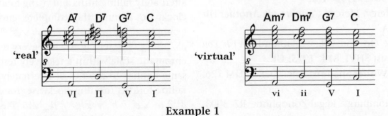

Example 1

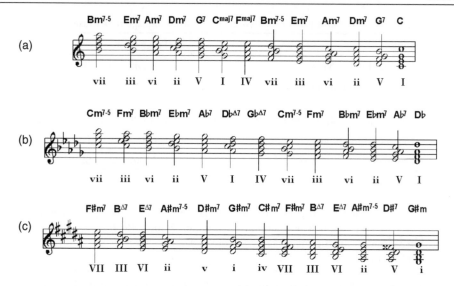

Example 2 Seventh chords in key-specific (virtual) sequence anticlockwise around the circle of fifths: (a) C major; (b) Db major; (c) g# minor.

1930s and 1940s (see Table 1). The virtual or key-specific circle of fifths is, moreover, a distinctive trait of the baroque style (as in works by Corelli, Vivaldi and J.S. Bach; see Ex. 2) and is also quite common in European popular songs that show classical influences (Table 1). Many well-known popular songs use a mixture of real and virtual circle-of-fifths progressions.

Anticlockwise circle-of-fifths progressions are, as shown in Example 1 and Table 1, frequently constructed as a chain of seventh chords (sometimes also of ninths, elevenths or thirteenths). Example 2 illustrates one common way of playing such chains as key-specific circles in C major (a), Db major (b) and G# minor (c). (This example assumes the presence of each chord's root

Table 1 Types of anticlockwise circle-of-fifths progressions in well-known English-language songs

Song	Type*	Chord progression
Sweet Georgia Brown	R	(B7)E^7 | E^7 | A^7 | A^7 | D^7 | D^7 | D^7 | G — (III)-VI-II-V-I in G
Charleston	R	[Bb] | D^7 | G^7 | G^7 | C^7 | F^7 | Bb G^7 | C^7 F^7 — III-VI-II-V-I in Bb
Has Anybody Seen My Gal	R	F | A^7 | D^7 | D^7 | G^7 | C^7 | F D^7 | G^7 C^7 — III-VI-II-V-I in F
All The Things You Are (start)	K	Fm^7 Bbm^7 | Eb^7 Ab^{Δ7} | Db^{Δ7} —vi-ii-V-I-IV in Ab
		Cm^7 Fm^7 | Bb^7 Eb^{Δ7} | Ab^{Δ7} — vi-ii-V-I-IV in Eb
Blue Moon	K	‖: Eb Cm^7 | Fm^7 Bb^7 :‖Eb | — (I)-vi-ii-V-I in Eb
Jeepers Creepers	K/M	(a) Gm^9 C^9 F^{Δ9} (b) Dm^7 C^9 F^6 | Gm^9 C^9 | ii V | (c) Am$^{7-5}$ D^9 Gm^7 C^9 F^6 — (a) ii V I (b) vi ii V I | ii V (c) iii VI ii V I, all in F
Moonlight Serenade	K/M	Bm$^{7-5}$ E^{-9} | Am^7 D^{-9} | Gm^7 C^{-9} ‖ F — +iv-VII-iii-VI-ii-V-I in F
Georgia on My Mind (end of bridge)	K/M	Bm$^{7-5}$ E^7 | Am^7 D^{-9} | Gm^7 C^7 ‖ F♯ — +iv-VII-iii-VI-ii-V-I in F
Autumn Leaves	K	Gm^7 C^7 | F^{Δ7} B^{Δ7} | E$^{7-5}$ A^7 | Dm — iv-VII-III-VI-ii-V-i in D min.
Windmills of Your Mind	K	E^7 Am D^7 G^{Δ7} C^{Δ7} F♯m$^{7-5}$ B^7 Em — I-iv-VII-III-VI-ii-V-I in E min.
Bluesette	K	[Bb] | Am^7 D^7 | Gm^7 C^7 | F^7 Bb^7 | Eb — vii-iii-vi-ii-V-I-IV in Bb
Yesterday	M	[F] | Em^7 A^7 | Dm | Bb(Gm^7) C^7 | F — vii-III-VI-IV(ii)-V-I in F†

* R=real; K=key-specific; M=mixed.

† IV (here Bb) can often appear as an alternative to ii (Gm7) at this point in a circle-of-fifths progression.

Table 2 Examples of clockwise circle-of-fifths progressions in English-language rock music

Artist	Song	Progression
Kinks	Dead End Street (verse)	C G Dm Am — III VII iv i in A minor
Rolling Stones	Brown Sugar (end of chorus)	A♭-D♭-A♭ E♭-B♭ F-C — (♭II-) ♭VI ♭III-♭VII IV-I in C
Rolling Stones	Jumpin' Jack Flash (the phrase 'It's alright')	D A E B — ♭III ♭VII IV I in B
Jimi Hendrix	Hey Joe (throughout)	C G D A E — ♭VI ♭III ♭VII IV I in E
Irene Cara	Flashdance (start of verse)	B♭ F Cm Gm — iii VII iv i in G minor

in the bass part.) To effectuate any complete key-specific circle of fifths, one step in the bass line will be a diminished fifth (between vii and IV in the major key and between ii and V in the minor key; for example, from $F^{\Delta 7}$ to $Bm^{7♭5}$ in C major or A minor), with each of the remaining seven steps either falling by a perfect fifth or rising by a perfect fourth.

Playing anticlockwise circle-of-fifths progressions demands a minimum of physical effort, because: (a) stringed bass instruments are tuned in fourths, facilitating leaps of the fourth, fifth and octave (see above); (b) fifths, fourths and octaves are easy to pitch on brass instruments playing a bass line; and (c) the constituent notes of any two contiguous seventh chords in a circle-of-fifths progression are, with the exception of the root, either immediately adjacent or the same (see Ex. 2), which renders them amenable to hand and finger positioning for keyboard players and guitarists.

Clockwise ('rising') circle-of-fifths progressions may be less common than their anticlockwise counterparts, but they do occur in pop and rock styles that use certain types of modal harmony. For example, the Mixolydian turnaround ♭VII IV I runs clockwise (e.g., B♭ F C), as do all progressions listed in Table 2.

Bibliography

Björnberg, Alf. 1995. 'Armonia eolia nella "popular music" contemporanea' [Aeolian Harmony in Contemporary Popular Music]. *Musica Realtà* 46: 41–50.

Ingelf, Sten. 1977. *Jazz-, pop- och bluesharmonik* [Jazz, Pop and Blues Harmony]. Malmö: Musikhögskolan.

Moore, Allan. 1992. 'Patterns of Harmony.' *Popular Music* 11(1): 73–106.

Discographical References

Armstrong, Louis. 'Jeepers Creepers.' *Fifty Years of Film Music*. Warner 3XX 2736. 1938; *1973*: USA.

Beatles, The. 'Yesterday.' *Help!*. Parlophone PCS 3071. *1965*: UK.

Cara, Irene. 'Flashdance . . . What a Feeling.' Casablanca 811440-7. *1983*: USA.

'Charleston.' *Great Gatsby – Original Soundtrack*. Paramount 2-3001. *1974*: USA.

Coleman, Bill. 'Georgia on My Mind.' *Bill Coleman 1936–1938*. Classics 764. *1994*: USA.

Dorsey Brothers, The. 'Charleston.' *Jazz of the Roaring Twenties*. Riverside RLP-1008. 1953: USA.

Dorsey Brothers, The. 'Five Foot Two, Eyes of Blue (Has Anybody Seen My Gal).' *Jazz of the Roaring Twenties*. Riverside RLP-1008. 1953: USA.

'Five Foot Two, Eyes of Blue (Has Anybody Seen My Gal).' *Great Gatsby – Original Soundtrack*. Paramount 2-3001. *1974*: USA.

Hirt, Al. 'Sweet Georgia Brown.' *Best of Dixieland*. Intersound 9329. *1996*: USA.

Jimi Hendrix Experience, The. 'Hey Joe.' Polydor 56139. *1966*: UK.

Kinks, The. 'Dead End Street.' Pye 7N 17222. *1966*: UK.

Miller, Glenn. 'Moonlight Serenade.' *The Glenn Miller Story [Original Soundtrack]*. MCA MCAD-1624. *1985*: USA.

Pettiford, Oscar. 'All the Things You Are.' *Original Jazz Masters Series*, Vol. 1 (1938–1980). DA Music 3701. 1938: Germany.

Piaf, Edith. 'Autumn Leaves (Les feuilles mortes).' *Edith Piaf – 30ᵉ Anniversaire*. Capitol 27097. *1994*: USA.

Rolling Stones, The. 'Brown Sugar/Bitch/Let It Rock.' Rolling Stones RS 19100. *1971*: UK.

Rolling Stones, The. 'Jumpin' Jack Flash.' Decca F 12782. *1968*: UK.

Sandpipers, The. 'Windmills of Your Mind.' *Movie Memories*. Music for Pleasure MFP 50438. *1973*: USA.

Thielemans, Toots. 'Bluesette.' *Do Not Leave Me*. Stash 1101. *1986*: USA.

Tormé, Mel. 'Blue Moon.' *The Rodgers and Hart Songbook*. Verve 183741. *1993*: USA.

Discography

Beatles, The. 'Hey Jude.' Apple R 5722. *1968*: UK.

The Envelope Please . . . Academy Award Winning Songs, Vol. 3 (1958–1969). Rhino 72278. *1996*: USA.

PHILIP TAGG

Counterpoint

Counterpoint (adj. contrapuntal), from the Latin *contrapunctus* (originally *punctus contra punctum*, meaning 'note against note'), is defined as: (a) a type of polyphony whose instrumental or vocal lines clearly differ in melodic profile; and (b) by analogy, the intentional contradiction in music of concurrent verbal or visual events.

Counterpoint is often understood as the horizontal aspect of polyphony, with harmony as its vertical aspect. The problem with this popular distinction is that, since chords, the building blocks of harmony, are usually sounded in sequence, and since each constituent note of each chord can often be heard as horizontally related to a note in the next chord, harmony frequently gives rise to internal melodies, some of which may 'clearly differ in melodic profile' – in other words, counterpoint; conversely, the simultaneous sounding of lines with differing melodic profiles (counterpoint) entails, by definition, consideration of the music's vertical aspect – harmony. Therefore, since melodic profile is as much a matter of distinct rhythm as of pitch, it is more accurate to consider homophony (music whose parts move in the same rhythm) as the polyphonic antithesis of counterpoint. Even so, polyphonic music can be considered contrapuntal or homophonic only by degree, never in absolute terms. For example, the final chorus in most trad jazz band performances (many instrumentalists improvising different rhythmic and tonal lines around the same tune and its chords, as illustrated by King Oliver's Creole Jazz Band's rendition of 'Dippermouth Blues' (1923)) is more contrapuntal than the preceding solos (one melodic line, a bass line and chordal rhythm), much more contrapuntal than conventional hymn singing (voices moving to different notes in the same rhythm) and infinitely more contrapuntal than doubling a vocal line at the third or sixth (following the same pitch profile in the same rhythm). In short, the more differences there are between concurrent parts in terms of melodic rhythm and pitch profile, the more contrapuntal the music.

Imitative counterpoint of the type taught to composition students is uncommon in popular music, even though a few well-known canons ('Frère Jacques,' 'Three Blind Mice' and 'London's Burning,' for example) must be among the most frequently sung songs in the world. Indeed, despite the fact that canonic singing is also widespread in some parts of Africa (for example, among the Ekonda of the Democratic Republic of Congo, the Shona of Zimbabwe and the Jabo of Liberia) (Nketia 1974, 144–45), the most common forms of counterpoint in popular music are the simultaneous occurrence of different melodies in the overlap between call-and-response (see Ex. 1) and the contrapuntal interplay between melodic line, accompanying or lead instrument, and bass line. An example of the latter can be heard in the Rolling Stones' song '(I Can't Get No) Satisfaction,' at the occurence of the famous riff in the lead guitar at the words 'but he can't be a man 'cause he doesn't smoke the same cigarettes as me.'

'Counterpoint' also denotes the technique whereby music is used to contradict or problematize the face value of concurrent actions or words. For example, to highlight essential aspects of the drama that are not visible or otherwise audible, Morricone, in the Bertolucci film *1900* (1976), uses music ('La Polenta') in the most delicate and noble vein of Viennese classicism to accompany two visual sequences showing peasants in abject poverty. Counterpointing can also be used ironically to provoke reflective distancing on the part of the audience. Kubrick's use of Vera Lynn's rendition of 'We'll Meet Again' (1942) to underscore the atomic holocaust at the end of *Dr. Strangelove* (1964) clearly illustrates this phenomenon. A noted exponent of counterpointing in the rock–pop sphere was Frank Zappa, who chose a cheerful sing-along ballad style to accompany the sociosexual self-degradation of 'Bobby Brown' (1979) and who, in 'You Are What You Is' (1981), set some of the most prosaic concepts in the English language – 'appropriate' and 'post office' – to ecstatic pentatonic melismas in the pop–gospel idiom.

Bibliography

Nketia, J.H. Kwabena. 1974. *The Music of Africa*. New York: Norton.

Example 1 Overlapping call-and-response parts in 'Please Mr. Postman' by the Marvelettes (1961).

Discographical References

King Oliver's Creole Jazz Band. 'Dippermouth Blues.' *Early Jazz*. Open University OU 42/CBS Special Products LSP 13223. *1923; 1978*: USA.

'La Polenta.' *1900*. RCA TBL 1-1221. *1977*: USA.

Lynn, Vera. 'We'll Meet Again.' *We'll Meet Again*. CD ASV/Living Era 5145. *1942; 1995*: UK.

Marvelettes, The. 'Please Mr. Postman.' Tamla 54046. *1961*: USA.

Rolling Stones, The. '(I Can't Get No) Satisfaction.' Decca F 12220. *1965*: UK.

Zappa, Frank. 'Bobby Brown.' *Sheik Yerbouti*. CBS 88339. *1979*: UK.

Zappa, Frank. 'You Are What You Is.' *You Are What You Is*. CBS 88560. *1981*: UK.

Filmography

Dr. Strangelove or How I Learned to Stop Worrying and Love the Bomb, dir. Stanley Kubrick. 1964. UK/USA. 93 mins. Black Comedy. Original music by Laurie Johnson.

1900 (*Novecento*), dir. Bernardo Bertolucci. 1976. France/West Germany/Italy. 320 mins. Political Drama. Original music by Ennio Morricone.

PHILIP TAGG

Drone

The term 'drone' (Fr. *bourdon*; Ger. *Bordun*; It. *bordone*) describes one or more sustained notes of identical pitch that, usually, accompany a melodic line often performed in a higher register. The note(s) can be sounded continuously (a 'continual drone') or be repeated at short intervals (a 'rhythmic drone'). Drones act as a tonal reference point and background for the changing pitch of other strands in the music. They are a common feature in many forms of popular music throughout the world and may be vocal or instrumental.

Vocal drones can be found in, for example, the antiphonal rhythms of traditional hymn singing from Tahiti (*himene*), as well as in backing vocal passages from some types of gospel singing in the United States (for example, in 'Trouble in My Way' by the Swan Silvertones (from 1:15 to 2 minutes)). Instrumental drones can be produced by the same (set of) instrument(s) used to perform the melody or by a separate (set of) instrument(s): bagpipes, hurdy-gurdy, *launeddas* (Sardinia) and jew's-harp belong to the former category, and didjeridu (Australia), *komuz* (Kirghizstan) and *tanpura* (India) to the latter. Some stringed instruments, such as the vina (South India) and other members of the lute family, are provided with one or more drone strings that can be plucked at appropriate junctures for purposes of tonal reference and rhythmic impetus. Rhythmic drone effects are also produced by fiddlers who make frequent, often percussive, use of open strings (for example, in 'Sally Goodin',' a field recording from 1922 by 'Fiddling' Eck Robertson, and *Spelmanslåtar från Dalarna* by Björn Ståbi, Ole Hjort and Nils Agenmark), and by guitarists plucking the low strings, often when adjusted to open-chord tuning (for example, in 'Whiskey and Women' by John Lee Hooker and 'Jesus on the Main Line' by Ry Cooder). Drone effects of a more continuous rhythmic character are often heard in the open-fifth guitar or banjo arpeggiations of artists steeped in European and North American folk traditions (for example, in 'Herr Olof och Havsfrun' by Folk och Rackare, 'Cold, Haily, Windy Night' and 'The Lark in the Morning' by Steeleye Span and 'The Cuckoo' by Doc Watson).

The connotative charge of drones varies according to cultural perspective and media context. In the heyday of Central European art music, drones were often used to evoke pastoral or bucolic settings (for example, in pastoral symphonies by Handel and Beethoven and 'Midsommarvaka' by Alfvén). In the latter part of the twentieth century, drones became increasingly common and were heard in, for example, folk-rock, ambient and 'Celtic mood' music (bygone rural days, broad stretches of time and space and so on), as well as in styles such as house and techno and in other types of 'modern dance music.' In the latter case, the drone's connotations, if any, have yet to be clearly established. However, the connotations of one latter-day drone are quite obvious: the 'doomsday mega-drone' that underscores ongoing threat scenarios in such popular television productions as *V* (alien reptiles occupy earth) and *Twin Peaks* (evil omnipresent in a small town). On the Indian subcontinent, the drone seems to have deeper connotations. For example, Coomaraswamy (1995, 77–80) describes the *tanpura*, the stringed instrument that produces the drone in much *rāga* music and that is heard before, during and after the melody, as 'the timeless and whole which was in the beginning, is now and ever shall be.' The account continues:

> The melody itself, on the other hand, is the shifting character of Nature which comes from the Source and returns to It . . . Harmony is an impossibility for us, for by changing the solid ground on which Nature's processes rely we would be creating another melody, another universe and destroying the peace on which Nature rests.

Bibliography

Bengtsson, Ingmar. 1975. 'Bordun' [Drone]. In *Sohlmans Musiklexikon* [Sohlmans Music Dictionary], Vol. 1. Stockholm: Sohlmans, 554.

Coomaraswamy, Ananda K. 1995. *The Dance of Śiva*. New York: Dover.

Malm, William P. 1967. *Music Cultures of the Pacific, the Near East and Asia*. Englewood Cliffs, NJ: Prentice-Hall.

Nettl, Bruno. 1965. *Folk and Traditional Music of the Western Continents*. Englewood Cliffs, NJ: Prentice-Hall.

Discographical References

Alfvén, Hugo. 'Midsommarvaka' (Swedish Rhapsody No. 1, Op. 19). Swedish Society Discofil SLT 33145. n.d.: Sweden.

Cooder, Ry. 'Jesus on the Main Line' (US trad.). *Paradise and Lunch*. Reprise 2179. *1974*: USA.

Folk och Rackare. 'Herr Olof och Havsfrun' (Swed. trad./ Värmland). *Folk och Rackare*. YTF 50240. *1976*: Sweden.

Hooker, John Lee. 'Whiskey and Women.' *Beale Street Blues*. King 474. ca. 1960; *1995*: USA.

Robertson, Eck. 'Sally Goodin'.' *Old-Time Texas Fiddler 1922–1929*. County 3515. 1922; *1999*: USA.

Ståbi, Björn, Hjort, Ole, and Agenmark, Nils. *Spelmanslåtar från Dalarna*. Sonet SLP 16. *1965*: Sweden.

Steeleye Span. 'Cold, Haily, Windy Night' (Eng. trad.). *Please to See the King*. Crest 8. *1971*: UK.

Steeleye Span. 'The Lark in the Morning' (Eng. trad.). *Please to See the King*. Crest 8. *1971*: UK.

Swan Silvertones, The. 'Trouble in My Way.' Specialty 853. 1952: USA.

'Twin Peaks Theme.' *Twin Peaks* (Original soundtrack). Warner Brothers 2-26316. *1990*: USA.

Watson, Doc. 'The Cuckoo' (US trad.). *Ballads from Deep Gap*. Vanguard VMD-6576. *1967*: USA.

Visual Recordings

'Twin Peaks.' 1990–91. Screen Entertainment VHS SE 9142 (video).

'V.' 1987. Warner Home Video WEV 11443-1 through 11443–5 (video).

PHILIP TAGG

Harmony

In a general sense, 'harmony' is defined as (a) tonal polyphony, that is, the simultaneous sounding of notes to produce chords and chord sequences. More specifically, it is (b) the chordal and accompanimental rather than the melodic or contrapuntal aspects of music. The term is also used to denote the theoretical systematization and study of (a) and (b).

Terminology

History

'Harmony' derives from the Greek *harmos*, meaning 'joint' or 'union' (hence, sonically, a concord), via the Latin *harmonia* ('agreement of sounds,' 'concord' or 'melody'). In medieval Europe, harmony initially meant the simultaneous sounding of two notes only (dyads), in much the same way that a backing vocalist in popular music may be described as 'singing harmonies' (even though 'harmony,' in the general sense of the term, is more likely to be provided by accompanying instruments). European theorists of the Renaissance extended the notion of harmony to include the simultaneous sounding of three notes, thus accommodating the 'common triad.' Since then, the concept of harmony has largely been associated with the chordal practises of music in the Central European tradition of the eighteenth and nineteenth centuries, that is, with European art music and styles of popular music relating to that tradition (see Classical Harmony: History, below). More recently, the notion of harmony has been popularly applied to any music that sounds in any way chordal to the Western ear, even, for example, to the vocal polyphony of certain African and Eastern European traditions or to the polyphonic instrumental practises of some Central and Southeast Asian music cultures. In short, whereas popular English-language parlance may classify as 'harmony' such phenomena as a melody plus drone or two voices singing in parallel homophony, conventional musicology would tend to reserve the term for chordal practises relating to the Central European classical tradition of tertial harmony (see Terminology: Definitions, and Classical Harmony, below). However, since popular music encompasses a wider range of tonal polyphonic practises than those conventionally covered by musicology, it is appropriate to classify any type of tonal polyphony as harmony. This wider meaning of the term makes it possible to speak of a variety of harmonic practises and, thus, to treat harmonic idiom as one important set of traits distinguishing one style of music from another.

Definitions

Two main types of harmonic practise are used in popular music: classical harmony and modal or nonclassical harmony, the latter type being divisible into the general sub-categories of tertial harmony and quartal harmony. Since most writing on harmony deals with procedure within only one of these categories or sub-categories at a time (for example, classical harmony, chorale harmony, bebop jazz harmony, modal harmony), cardinal problems arise when terms conventionally used for one category – usually classical harmony – are applied to a much wider range of practises. Two conceptual areas are in particular need of clarification: (a) classical harmony and (b) triads and tertial harmony.

Classical Harmony Classical harmony is so called because it denotes the most common practises of tonal polyphony found in the large and globally influential body of European classical music of the eighteenth and nineteenth centuries. Such harmony is also commonly referred to as 'triadic' (see below), 'diatonic,' 'functional,' 'tonal' (see Structural Traits, below) and so on, but these qualifiers are misleading, since they can each be applied to harmonic practises that diverge significantly from those of the European art music canon and its immediate precursors and successors. For example, all modal harmony using three-note chords is, by definition, triadic. It is also diatonic, if, as is often the case, its tonal material can be derived from a standard heptatonic scale containing two semitone intervals. Moreover, with the possible exception of 'atonal' film scores for horror scenes, all harmonic idioms in popular music are tonal, and none is without function. In short, although many popular styles of music throughout the world may follow the basic harmonic principles of the European art music tradition, 'classical harmony' is probably the least inadequate available descriptor of these principles.

Triads and Tertial Harmony Owing to the importance of harmonic narrative in European art music of the eighteenth and nineteenth centuries (see Voice Leading, the Ionian Mode and Modulation, below), harmonic theory has been overwhelmingly dominated by terms suited to the description of this particular type of polyphonic practise. (An example of incongruity arising from this domination is the use of 'suspended fourth' in reference to quartal harmony.) Similarly, terms applicable to any type of tonal polyphony (for example, 'triad') have become so identified with phenomena peculiar to classical harmony and to its direct successors that they require redefinition when other harmonic idioms are discussed. Moreover, terms from pre-classical music theory have had to be resurrected and redefined to denote modern modal practises, and a few new concepts have had to be added to the arsenal to denote phenomena for which harmonic theory previously had no name. One such term is 'quartal harmony' (see Quartal Harmony, below), so called because, from the point of view of European art music theory, its most distinctive trait appears to be chords built on fourths rather than thirds, this latter trait requiring no accurate descriptor as long as it is considered to be the norm from which all other practises are seen to diverge. Such a viewpoint is clearly untenable when discussing the variety of harmonic idioms used in popular music, and a general structural descriptor for harmony based on thirds becomes essential. Therefore, if harmony characterized by the use of fourths is called quartal harmony, harmony characterized by the use of thirds should be called tertial harmony.

The historical legacy of European classical music theory is so strong that a phenomenon as common as a triad, which occurs in several harmonic idioms, has been named as if no triads existed in modal or quartal harmony. The problem is that, if 'dyad' (from the Greek *dyo*, meaning 'two'), when applied to music, means any chord containing two different notes, then 'triad' (from the Greek *trias*) should mean any chord containing three different notes, 'tetrad' one containing four different notes, 'pentad' one containing five different notes and so on. However, as the expression 'common triad' indicates, triads built on the superimposition of two adjoining thirds are literally so common in classical harmony that 'triadic' has come to designate not so much chords that contain three different notes, as chords that are built on the superimposition of adjoining thirds. When discussing several harmonic idioms, including those associated with European art music of the classical period, it is necessary to use 'triad' and 'triadic' only in their original sense. Therefore, harmony based on superimposed thirds will be called 'tertial,' not 'triadic,' and 'triad' will mean any chord, tertial or not, that contains three different notes.

Classical Harmony

History

The tonal polyphony of European art music is generally regarded as having developed gradually into a form which, by the end of the seventeenth century, had crystallized into the set of practises that came to be known, in twentieth-century terms, as classical harmony. Its establishment is associated with the transition from contrapuntal to more homophonic types of tonal polyphony in late sixteenth- and early seventeenth-century Central Europe, and with the adoption of melody–accompaniment dualism, in which harmony is generally associated with instrumental or vocal accompaniment ('background harmony,' 'backing vocals,' 'underlying harmonies') as a basic compositional device. Practically all European art music of the seventeenth, eighteenth and nineteenth centuries uses harmonic practises that also form the basis of tonal polyphony in such common types of popular music as operetta, music hall, parlor songs, waltzes, marches, hymns, community songs, national anthems, romantic ballads, *schlager*, evergreens, jazz standards, swing, bebop and so on. This broad tradition of harmony also pervades much country and film music.

Structural Traits

Syntax, Narrative and 'Function' Classical harmony is generally thought to encompass the sequential (horizontal, linear) as well as the simultaneous (vertical) aspects of chords. It is, in other words, not just a matter of instantaneous sonority or of short repeated chord sequences. On the contrary, one of its most salient features is the implication of a tonal *direction* of notes within chords (shown as ↗, ↘ and → in Examples 1–8), such horizontal linearity being instrumental in the elemental processes of musical narrative (opening, continuation, change, return, closure and so on). The importance of these syntactic functions in the European art music tradition led influential musicologists like Hugo Riemann (see Mickelsen 1977) to classify the harmony of this tradition as 'functional' (*Funktionsharmonik*). Although this nomenclature is misleading in that it falsely assumes all other harmonic practises to be without function, its insistence on syntactic function underlines important differences of expression and narrative organization between European classical harmony and other types of tonal polyphony.

Voice Leading, the Ionian Mode and Modulation In classical harmony, in principle, dissonances are prepared as suspensions (notes held over from a previous chord) and resolved into consonances (for example, Csus4 → C or Cm; see Ex. 1b), while closure is generally assumed to be effectuated by perfect cadence (V-I, for example, G7 → C in C; see Ex. 1a and Ex. 1b). In such basic chord progressions, the concept of voice leading is paramount, in that the perfect fourth in relation to the keynote (for example, the *f* of G7 in relation to C; see Ex. 1a) usually descends to the third (*e* in relation to *c*), and the major seventh (for example, the *b♮* of the G or G7 chord in relation to C; see Ex. 1a and Ex. 1b) usually ascends to the keynote. These rules of voice leading are not arbitrary, but derive from the fact that, during the rise and hegemony of the bourgeoisie in Europe, the most popular array of notes within an octave was that of the Ionian mode (the standard major scale – for example, *c* to *c¹* on the white notes of the piano).

The Ionian is the only heptatonic diatonic mode to feature at the same time: (a) major triads on all perfect intervals of the scale (tonic, fourth and fifth – for example, C, F and G in C major; see Table 1); (b) a dominant seventh chord, containing a tritone, on the fifth degree (for example, G7, containing *f♮* and *b♮*, in C); (c) semitone intervals, one ascending and one descending, that adjoin two of the tonic triad's three constituent notes, that is, leading note to tonic (♯7 ↗ 8, or *b♮ ↗ c* in C) and subdominant to mediant (4 ↘ 3, or *f ↘ e* in C).

Table 1 Major triad positions in church modes

	I	♭II	II	♭III	IV	V	♭VI	♭VII
Ionian	✓				✓	✓		
Dorian				✓	✓			✓
Phrygian		✓		✓			✓	
Lydian	✓		✓			✓		
Mixolydian	✓				✓			✓
Aeolian				✓			✓	✓

In simple terms, in the Ionian mode the fourth is felt to be pulled down to the major third a semitone below, while the major seventh or leading note is so called because it is heard as leading up to the keynote one semitone above. This simple principle of voice leading endows the Ionian mode with its unique qualities of tonal directionality.

Although this directionality is that of the V-I cadence anticlockwise around the circle of fifths (for example, G7 → C), semitones in the Ionian mode can also exert a pull in the opposite direction (Ex. 2a and Ex. 2b), because the third degree can rise as leading note to the fourth (for example, *e ↗ f* in C; see Ex. 2a), while degree one (or eight) can descend to degree seven (for example, *c ↘ b♮*; see Ex. 2b), which also happens to be the major third in a simple triad on the dominant. In the first instance (degree 3 ↗ degree 4), harmonic direction remains subdominantal, in that the mediant of the tonic acts as leading note to the subdominant (*e ↗ f*; see Ex. 2a), but, in the second instance, the tonic acts as fourth descending to the mediant of the dominant (*c ↘ b♮*; see Ex. 2b).

Dominantal direction (clockwise around the circle of fifths – for example, from C to G) is usually enhanced by raising the tonic's fourth by one semitone (for example, from *f* to *f♯* in the D7 chord of Example 3a). Such alteration makes for a clearer direction toward the dominant by introducing a second rising semitone (*f♯ ↗ g*) to complement the falling semitone already mentioned (*c ↘ b♮*; see Ex. 2b and Ex. 3a). Raising the fourth by a semitone (for example, from *f* to *f♯*) moves the tonic of the Ionian mode to the dominant, that is, from I to V (for example, C → G), and constitutes a change of key or modulation, especially if a pivot chord is included in the progression (Ex. 3a). Conversely, lowering the leading note by half a tone (for example, from *b♮* to

Example 1

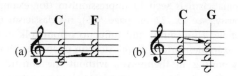

Example 2

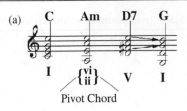

Pivot Chord

Example 3

$b\flat$ in the C7 chord of Example 3b) introduces a descending semitone ($b\flat \searrow a\natural$), and underlines the subdominantal direction of the semitone rising to the keynote of the new Ionian mode (for example, $e\natural \nearrow f$; see Ex. 2a and Ex. 3b). The introduction of accidentals to provide ascending or descending leading notes for V-I cadences in keys other than the tonic is an essential characteristic of classical Ionian-mode harmony, because such chromaticism is a precondition for the type of modulation without which the basic narrative of most European art music would be unthinkable.

Dissolution of Classical Harmony It is generally agreed that the harmonic idiom of influential European composers of art music in the late nineteenth and early twentieth centuries (for example, Wagner) became increasingly chromatic and modulatory, to the extent that tonality, in the sense of a home key for a particular piece of new music, was no longer considered to be a valid strategy for composition by figures like Schönberg (ca. 1910). The subsequent development of dodecaphonic and other types of 'atonal' music contributed to the widening of the gap between popular and art genres. Jazz harmony underwent a similar process of chromaticization in the 1940s, with the increasing use, in bebop, of chords containing two tritones: the rising augmented fourth ($\sharp 4$) or falling flat fifth ($\flat 5$) provided another leading note, in addition to the ascending major seventh and descending fourth of tertial harmony.

The response of 'tonal' art music to late Romantic chromaticism is seen in impressionism (for example, Debussy; see Ex. 22 on page 545), neoclassicism (for example, Hindemith) and influences from folk music (for example, Bartók). Impressionism often uses chords as sonorities in themselves, without the constituent notes of each chord requiring voice leading into those of the next. Music influenced by neoclassicism and

interest in folk music outside Central Europe shows clear traits of modality and often uses quartal harmony (see Quartal Harmony, below), which abandons the leading-note fixation of classical tertial harmony in favor of chords based on the fourth and fifth. Similar developments are found in jazz, with the change from bebop to modal and 'free' jazz forms. All these artistic movements have influenced postwar popular music styles.

Classical Harmony in Popular Music

Tertial harmony of the type used in operetta, parlor songs, marches, musicals, traditional church hymns and so on largely follows the voice-leading practises of European art music: flat sevenths descend, sharp sevenths rise and voices may move in parallel thirds or sixths but never in parallel octaves or fifths. Dominantal modulation (changing key by one step clockwise around the circle of fifths), V-I cadences and inversions of tertial triads and seventh chords are other common features found in these types of popular music.

Examples 4 and 5 are taken from two highly popular parlor songs. Each begins by establishing the home key (tonic, I) by means of an Ionian shuttle (I ↔ V; E♭ ↔ B♭ in bars 1–2 in Example 4 and F ↔ C in bars 1–4 in Example 5), whence they both modulate to the dominant: in Example 4 directly, using an F7 in second inversion (bar 4), and, in Example 5, via an initial V-I in D minor (bars 5–6), which then acts as pivot for the double dominant (G7) and a V-I cadence in C (bars 7–8). Note, also, the frequency of dominant seventh chords containing the Ionian mode's two leading notes a tritone apart, and how the major third in these chords ascends as leading note to the next chord's tonic ($\nearrow$ in Ex. 4 and Ex. 5), while the flat seventh descends to the next chord's third ($\searrow$ in Ex. 4 and Ex. 5). These traits, including, sometimes, the use of tertial chords in their inversions, form the harmonic core of a global idiom of popular music that flourished during the late nineteenth century and the first half of the twentieth century. They can be found, in varying proportions, in such popular tunes as 'Adeste Fideles,' 'Cocorocó,' 'La cucaracha,' 'The Blue Danube,' 'Le déserteur,' 'Giâi phóng mièn nam,' 'Jingle Bells,' 'L'hirondelle du faubourg,' the 'Internationale,' the 'Song of the International Brigade,' 'Liberty Bell,' 'Light Cavalry,' 'La Marseillaise,' Rubinstein's 'Melody in F,' 'Cielito Lindo,' 'Sous le ciel de Paris,' 'Sancta Lucia,' 'The Star-Spangled Banner,' 'Waltzing Matilda' (chorus), 'We Shall Overcome,' 'When the Saints Go Marchin' In,' 'Where Have All the Flowers Gone' and 'Workers of the World Awaken!'

Such traits as voice leading the dominant seventh chord's minor seventh and major third, dominantal modulation, subdominantal V-I directionality, the fre-

Example 4 Mendelssohn: 'Oh! For the Wings of a Dove.'

Example 5 James L Molloy: 'Love's Old Sweet Song' (1884).

quent occurrence of inversions and so on have, in fact, become so indicative of European art music that they can be inserted as genre synecdoches in the context of nonclassical harmony (for example, pop and rock) to connote, seriously or humorously, 'high art' rather than 'low-brow entertainment,' and 'deep feelings' and the 'transcendent' rather than the 'superficial' and the 'ephemeral' (Ex. 6, Ex. 7 and Ex. 8).

Together with dance styles like bossa nova, jazz has relied heavily on a sense of harmonic direction similar to that of the European classical tradition. Long and sometimes quite complex chord sequences, an increas-

Example 6 Tonic second inversion as second chord: a 'classical' move–outline keyboard arpeggiation structure. (a) J. S. Bach: Prelude in C major from 'Das Wohltemperiertes Klavier, Band I' (1722); (b) Elton John: 'Your Song' (1970, transposed to C).

Example 7 Inversions through a descending bass in a major key. (a) J. S. Bach: Air from 'Orchestral Suite in D Major' (ca. 1730; transposed to C); (b) Procol Harum: 'A Whiter Shade of Pale' (1967); (c) The bass line common to both (a) and (b).

ing amount of chromaticism and the use of modulation are all key factors in many types of jazz. The popularity of the 32-bar standard as the basis for improvisation bears witness to the essential role of harmonic narrative in jazz. Put simply, no jazz performance will work if musicians do not know or cannot follow the changes.

Jazz harmony can be divided into four main historical idioms: (a) trad jazz; (b) the swing era; (c) bebop; and (d) non-tertial jazz (see Quartal Harmony, below). With the exception of (d), all jazz harmony follows the same underlying principles as European art music: flat sevenths tend to fall, sharp sevenths rise, accidentals (alterations) are used for chromatic effect or for modulation, and there is fairly strict adherence to falling subdominantal (V-I) progressions anticlockwise around the circle of fifths. Trad jazz harmony tends to use real circle-

of-fifths progressions, adding sixths or sevenths to basic triads. Swing era harmony tends to favor virtual circle-of-fifths progressions, with sixths, sevenths and ninths added to basic triads. Bebop harmony can be regarded as a radical expansion of swing harmony. It is characterized by considerable chromatic alteration, typically through tritone substitution, which includes the flat fifth as an extra (voice) leading note, and by its use of chords of the eleventh and thirteenth. Basic differences between these jazz harmony idioms are illustrated in simplified form in Example 9, which shows various treatments of the (I-)VI-II-V-I vamp sequence.

Nonclassical Harmony

Nondirectional Tertial Harmony

Ionian Mode and Barré Although sequences of common triads in the Ionian mode form the essence of tonal polyphony in many postwar popular music styles, such harmonic practise – for example, that found in Latin American urban styles, such as *cúmbia* or *son*, or in urban African musics, like highlife and *kwela*, as well as in most pop, rock and soul music – cannot be categorized as classical, because it rarely conforms to European art music conventions of voice leading. Indeed, any barré chord progression involves a sequence of parallel fifths and octaves (forbidden in classical harmony), as can be seen, for example, between the triads on IV and V of the Ionian mode 'La Bamba' matrix (I-IV-V; see Table 2). Similarly, 'bottleneck' performance relies entirely on chords strung together in parallel motion. Moreover, it is clear that such matrices, rarely consisting of more than four chords, function in a way that is radically different from that of progressions in the idiom of classical harmony, not least because tertial matrices of this type con-

Example 8 Altered supertonic seventh chord in fourth inversion. (a) Mozart: 'Ave Verum Corpus,' K618 (1777); (b) Procol Harum: 'Homburg' (1967); (c) ABBA: 'Waterloo' (1974).

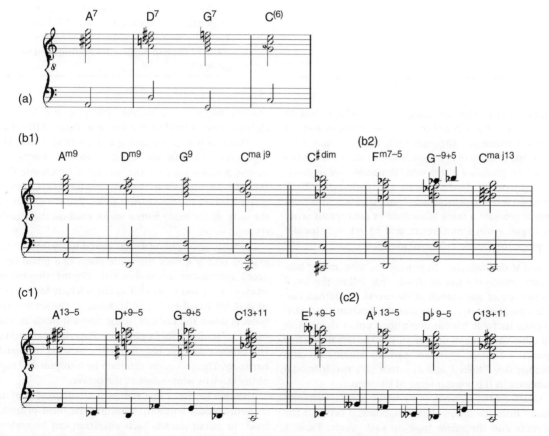

Example 9 Possible renditions in C of VI-II-V-I sequence in the main tertial idioms of jazz harmony. (a) Trad. jazz; (b) Swing era: (b1) standard and (b2) chromatic; (c) Bebop: (c1) standard and (c2) tritone substition.

Table 2 Major triads in tertial modal harmony

	Relative positions	On white notes	With four sharps	Examples
Ionian	I IV V	C F G	E A B	'La Bamba' (Valens) and 'Twist and Shout' (the Isley Brothers) (D-G-A in D); 'Guantanamera' (Martí) (F-B♭-C in F); 'Pata Pata' (Makeba) (F-B♭-F-C)
Dorian	(I) ♭III IV ♭VII	(D) F G C	(E) G A D	'Green Onions' (Booker T and the MGs) (E-G-A in E); 'Smoke on the Water' (Deep Purple) (E-G-A in E); Examples 10, 12 and 13
Phrygian	(I) ♭II ♭III ♭VII	(E) F C G	(E) F C G	Example 14; verse of 'E viva España' (Vrethammar); start of 'Concierto de Aranjuez' (Rodrigo); 'Misirlou'
Mixolydian	I IV ♭VII	G C F	E A D	'Sweet Home Alabama' (Lynyrd Skynyrd) (D-C-G in D); 'Hey Jude' (the Beatles) (G-F-C-G); theme from *The Magnificent Seven* (E♭-A♭-E♭-D♭ in E♭); Examples 15–21
Aeolian	(I) ♭III ♭VI ♭VII	(A) C F G	(E) G C D	'All Along the Watchtower' (Dylan, Jimi Hendrix Experience) (A-G-F-G in A); 'Flashdance' (Cara) (G-F-E♭-F in G); cadences in 'Lady Madonna' (the Beatles) (F-G-A), 'P.S. I Love You' (the Beatles) (B♭-C-D), 'S.O.S' (ABBA) (D♭-E♭-F), 'Brown Sugar' (the Rolling Stones) (A♭-B♭-C)

tain little or no chromaticism, do not modulate and do not contribute extensively to the construction of musical narrative. Although such matrices may vary from one (section of a) song to another, their main function is to provide a fitting tonal dimension for underlying patterns of rhythm, meter and periodicity. Their function is not to provide long-term harmonic direction, but to generate a more immediate or continuous sense of ongoing tonal movement, and to act as a tonally appropriate accompanimental motor.

Tertial Modal Harmony In general, the term 'modal harmony' means the use of chords that follow the tonal vocabulary of any church mode except the Ionian (see Classical Harmony, above) and the Locrian (excluded because its tonic triad is diminished rather than, as in all other cases, major or minor). It is the remaining five modes – Dorian, Phrygian, Lydian, Mixolydian and Aeolian (see Tables 1 and 2) – that give rise to modal harmony in the popular sense of the term.

Characteristic differences in tertial modal harmony derive from the unique tonal relationship between the keynote and the major triads of each mode. Table 1 shows that each mode contains three major triads (C, F and G on the white notes of the piano). It also shows

that the minor modes (Dorian, Phrygian and Aeolian) all have a major triad on the flat third degree (♭III), that the Phrygian is alone in having a major triad on the flat supertonic (♭II), that the Lydian mode is unique in having a major triad on the unaltered supertonic (II), that the Mixolydian is the only major mode with a major triad on the flat seventh (♭VII), that the Dorian is the only minor mode with a major triad on the fourth (IV) and so on.

The basic principles of tertial modal harmony can be grasped simply if only the white notes of a piano keyboard instrument are considered. Playing the major triads of F, G and C, as well as the relevant tonic triad (if it is not based on *f, g* or *c*), while at the same time holding down the keynote of the relevant mode in the bass (*c* for Ionian, *d* for Dorian, *e* for Phrygian and so on), will produce familiar but distinctive patterns of modal harmony. This procedure can then be transposed to any of the black or white notes of the octave.

It should be noted that the most common alteration in tertial modal harmony is raising the third of tonic triads in minor modes. Such alteration can be understood in terms of a *tierce de Picardie* that is used consistently throughout a piece of music as a substitute for the tonic minor triad and not just as an alteration of the final chord. This major triad substitution practise was commonly used in the modal harmony of Elizabethan popular song and dance (Ex. 10 and Ex. 12; see also 'Farnaby's Dreame,' 'The King of Denmark's Galiard' and so on).

Major third substitution in the tonic triad is widespread in much blues and in some country music where minor or blues thirds are sung or played to the accom-paniment of major triads (Ex. 11), or when barré techniques are used to progress between I, ♭III and IV, as in the well-known Dorian-mode riff in 'Green Onions' or 'Smoke on the Water.' In other words, Dorian harmonies are suited to the accompaniment of minor pentatonic melody (1 ♭3 4 5 ♭7) because, with alteration of the tonic, major triads occur on four of the five pitches (I, ♭III, IV and ♭VII).

During the ascendancy of the Ionian mode, the fifth degree triad of minor modes was also often altered to major in European polyphonic music, typically to intro-duce V-I cadences containing dominant sevenths and their double leading notes (see Voice Leading, the Ionian Mode and Modulation, above). Example 12 shows both Dorian (I IV ♭III; bars 1–2) and Mixolydian (I IV ♭VII; bars 4–5) progressions, each followed by the standard V7-I Ionian cadence of classical harmony.

Alteration of the minor dominant also occurs in blues-related styles, especially when barré, slide and bottle-neck techniques are used on the guitar. In these cases,

Example 10 Farnaby: 'Loth to Depart' (ca. 1610): Aeolian triads with major tonic triad (I iv ♭III iv (♭VI ♭VII)).

Example 11 'Darling Corey' (USA Trad.; Doc Watson 1963): major tonic triad for a minor mode tune

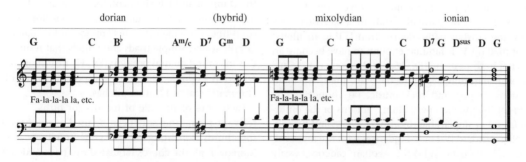

Example 12 Weelkes: 'Hark, All Ye Lovely Saints' (ca. 1610).

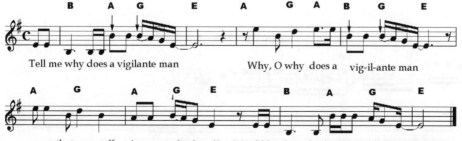

Example 13 Slide guitar chords (opening tuning E) for 'Vigilante Man' (Guthrie), adapted from Cooder (1971).

however, such alteration relates to tuning and playing practises, not to any predilection for the Ionian mode or perfect cadences, as is evident from the absence of V-I changes (B → E in Example 13; see previous page).

Table 2 shows the major triads, including, where applicable, the altered tonic (shown in parentheses) of each mode. (The Lydian and Locrian modes are excluded, because they are uncommon in most forms of popular music.) Table 2 also presents each mode's major triads as they would occur 'in C' (no sharps or flats (on the white notes)) and 'in E' (four sharps), along with references to examples of popular music in which each relevant modal tertial harmony can be heard.

The tertial harmony of each mode is often related to the frequency with which it is (assumed to be) used in particular types of music. Hence, Dorian harmony is a trait of some blues-based styles (Ex. 13), while Phrygian chord changes are often regarded, at least by non-Hispanics, as distinctive of Hispanic popular music styles (Ex. 14a and Ex. 14b). Tertial Phrygian harmony is also used extensively in popular music from Greece, Turkey, the Balkans and the Near East, mostly in accompaniment to melody in the *Hijaz* mode (for example, 'Misirlou,' aka the theme from *Pulp Fiction*).

Mixolydian harmonies are often linked with British and Irish or Anglo-American folk music (Ex. 21, page 545) and with some forms of rock and country music. They are found, as well, in music for westerns (Ex. 15a and Ex. 15b). One particular trait of Mixolydian harmony, the 'cowboy half cadence,' from ♭VII to an altered major triad on V, is familiar enough to have become an object of both pastiche (Ex. 16a) and parody (Ex. 16b).

Aeolian harmony seems to have acquired two main functions in pop and rock music: (a) connoting, by means of the 'Aeolian pendulum,' notions of the ominous, fateful or implacable (Björnberg 1995); and (b) substituting standard IV-I or V-I cadences with the more colorful and dramatic ♭VI♭VII-I Aeolian cadence, easily performed as barré chords on the guitar.

Quartal Harmony

Structural Definition Quartal harmony is so called because it is based on the fourth and on its octave complement, the fifth. Unlike its tertial counterpart, quartal harmony is not based on thirds, nor on the Ionian mode, nor do its basic chords contain tritones, the constituent notes of which demand voice leading by semitone steps. The structural elements of quartal harmony are set out in Example 17.

The first line of Example 17 shows: (a1) *c* at the center of a pile of fourths (*d g c f b♭*); (a2) the pentatonic scale resulting from that pile of fourths (1-2-4-5-♭7 or *c d f g b♭*); and (a3) *c* at the center of a pile of fifths that contains exactly the same tonal material as (a1) and (a2) – whether the notes are piled in fourths or fifths, they still constitute a run of five consecutive positions around the circle of fifths. The second (b1–b3) and third (c1–c3) lines of Example 17 show the pentatonic scales (b2 and c2) that result when *c* is shifted subdominantally, to position 2 (b1), or dominantally, to position 4 (c1), in the pile of fourths, and to positions 2 and 4 in the equivalent pile of fifths (b3 and c3, respectively). Note that the quartal notes of C in central position (Ex. 17, first line) coincide with the G minor or B♭ major anhemitonic pentatonic modes; that the quartal notes of C in dominantal position (Ex. 17, second line) coincide with the D minor and F major pentatonic scales; and that the quartal notes of C in subdominantal position (Ex. 17, third line) coincide with the C minor and E♭ major pentatonic scales. Simple triads and tetrads that result when C is in central quartal position (Ex. 17, first line) are presented in Example 18 and are transposable to any of the chromatic scale's 11 other pitches.

Each note of the pile of fourths (or fifths, or of the relevant pentatonic scale) can be used as the bass note for chords consisting of the same tonal vocabulary. Moreover, all the chords tabulated can be sounded with any pitch from the relevant pentatonic material as the

Example 14 Phrygian harmony. (a) A popular Malagueña figure. (b) Puebla: 'Hasta siempre.'

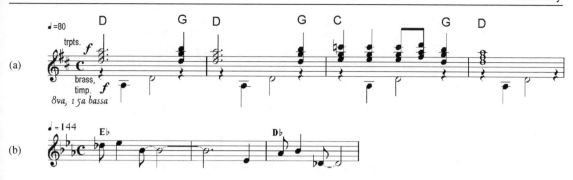

Example 15 Mixolydian shuttles. (a) Tiomkin: 'Duel in the Sun' (1947). (b) Mancini: 'Cade's County' (1971–72 television series).

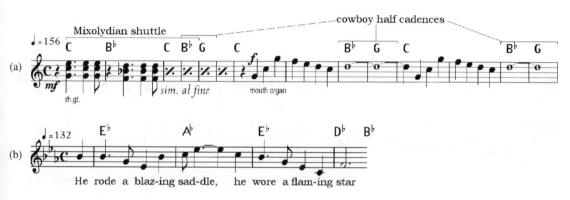

Example 16 Cowboy half cadences. (a) The Shadows: 'Dakota' (1964). (b) Brooks: Theme from *Blazing Saddles* (1974).

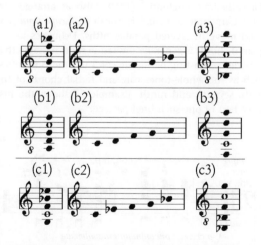

Example 17 The basis of quartal harmony in C.

a bass note foreign to the tertial chord in question. For example, with *c* in the bass, Gm(7) and B♭(6) produce variants of C11, a chord that, even in a tertial context, contains a fourth and is sounded without a third. Most of the chords in Example 18 are, however, unequivocally quartal.

In jazz and pop circles, quartal chords are sometimes referred to as suspensions. Chords C① and C② in Example 18 might, for example, be called Csus9 and Csus4, respectively. However, it is apparent from Examples 22–24 (pages 545–46) that quartal chords are consonances in their own right, not suspensions requiring resolution, as in Example 1b. Similarly, the chord marked C6/9 in the sheet music version of Sting's 'Seven Days' (Ex. 24) is neither a C6, a C9, a C9add6 nor a C6/9 chord, but a 1-2-5-6 quartal chord (C in dominantal position; see Ex. 17, b2) that constitutes the main keynote sonority of the whole song.

History and Usage Open fourths and fifths, as well as quartal chords, start to appear in modern urban Western

bass note. This procedure occasionally produces tertial chords (Gm and B♭, marked in black in Example 18) that, in a consistently quartal idiom, are usually supplied with

543

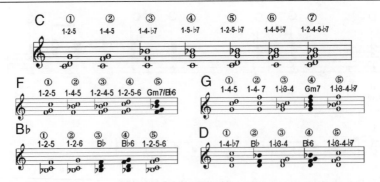

Example 18 Basic quartal triads and tetrads in C (central position).

(a) (b)

Example 19 Borodin: (a) 'Song of the Dark Forest' (1868) and (b) 'The Sleeping Princess' (1867).

music in the folk-influenced work of composers such as Mussorgsky and Borodin (Ex. 19a and Ex. 19b) living on the fringes of Europe. These were followed much later by composers of the Spanish school (Ex. 20, bar 2) but, for some time, tertial modal harmony was the most common approach to the problem of harmonizing music from outside it with the Central European classical idiom (for example, Dvořák, Grieg, Rimsky-Korsakov, Vaughan Williams).

However, the attitude of classically trained European musicians to music outside the canon did change during the nineteenth century. Whereas the Czech–German symphonist Carl Stamitz had, in 1798, deemed Irish tunes incapable of bearing any harmony (Hamm 1979, 50), Herbert Hughes, in his preface to *Irish Country Songs, Vol. 1* (1909), expressed the need for a radical and unacademic approach when dealing with such material, championing the work of 'M. Claude Debussy,' who, he claimed, had set the trend 'to break the bonds of this old slave-driver' (classical tonality and so on) 'and return to the freedom of primitive scales' (iv). Indeed, Hughes's accompaniment to the Mixolydian ballad 'She Moved Through the Fair' (popularized by Simple Minds as 'Belfast Child') resolves its chains of open fifths and tertial triads into a final quartal chord (Ex. 21).

Debussy was one of the first to use quartal harmony in modern Western music. Although whole sections of 'La cathédrale engloutie' (1910) (also as arranged by John Carpenter and Alan Howarth in *Escape from New York*) move in layered parallel fifths, Debussy's use of quartal chords is generally limited to short passages that provide contrasting harmonic color to other sonorities, such as the whole-tone scale and tertial chords of the sixth, seventh and ninth. Example 22 shows the first three bars of one such brief passage.

Example 20 De Falla: 'Farruca' from *El sombrero de tres picos* (1919).

Example 21 'She Moved Through The Fair' (Irish trad.; arr. Hughes; final chords in accompaniment).

The tertial aspects of Debussy's harmonic language were adopted by prewar US composers of popular song (for example, Gershwin and Kern). However, the type of quartal harmony just cited, and practised more widely by Bartók or Hindemith, first found its way into the popular mainstream through composers associated with film or the stage – for example, Aaron Copland (e.g., 'Billy the Kid Suite' (1938) and 'Fanfare for the Common Man' (1942; also used as title music for the Apollo–Soyuz broadcasts and in a General Motors commercial)), Miklos Rózsa (e.g., scores for *The Jungle Book* (1942) and *Quo Vadis?* (1951)), Leonard Bernstein (e.g., *On the Waterfront* (1954)) and Elmer Bernstein (e.g., *The Carpetbaggers* (1964)).

Quartal harmony was slower to enter the world of jazz. Miles Davis's album *Kind of Blue* (1959) is often seen as a turning point or defining moment when the tertial

constraints of bebop harmony were abandoned in favor of quartal chords as, for example, in 'So What'. Among the jazz musicians to follow in Davis's modal footsteps in the 1960s and 1970s were McCoy Tyner and Freddie Hubbard (Ex. 23).

Pentatonic improvisation and quartal chords became a cornerstone of jazz fusion harmony (for example, John McLaughlin and Chick Corea, not to mention Davis's *Bitches Brew* album (1970)), which was also heard as music for television (for example, Goldenberg's *Kojak* theme) and, later, in recordings by jazz-influenced pop artists such as King Crimson and Sting (Ex. 24).

In Anglo-US commercial music, the early use of bare fourths and fifths resembling quartal chords can be found in 'Nowhere to Run' (Martha and the Vandellas, 1965), 'Road to Nowhere' (Carole King, 1966) and 'I'm Your Kingpin' (Manfred Mann, 1964; Ex. 25). Although the first two are both modal tunes, their thirdless chords can be attributed to word-painting the emptiness of 'nowhere' rather than to the consistent use of a new harmonic idiom. Throughout 'I'm Your Kingpin,' on the other hand, Mann, a jazz pianist, uses quartal harmony in conjunction with minor blues pentatonicism in both melody and bass. Quartal harmony in pop is, in fact, most often found with tunes in

Example 22 Debussy: 'Sarabande' from *Pour le piano* (1901): start of a 5-bar quartal passage.

Example 23 Freddie Hubbard: 'Red Clay' (1970), cited in Ingelf (1977).

the Dorian, Aeolian or minor pentatonic mode, as, for example, in many a track by Steeleye Span or the Albion Country Band.

It is probable that the use of quartal harmony in pop and rock, including its occasional appearance in such hits as 'Jumpin' Jack Flash' and 'Gimme Shelter' by the Rolling Stones (1971), derives partly from old rural forms of polyphony (blues, folk song and so on). For example, Clarence Ashley's open-string banjo accompaniment to the minor pentatonic tune 'Coo-Coo Bird' is entirely quartal and described by the Folkways liner notes (1963) as archaic. Similarly, the third-less harmonies of minor-mode shape-note hymns like Hauser's 'Wondrous Love' (1835) bear more resemblance to the polyphony of Heinrich Isaac (d. 1517) than to their urbane contemporaries. Indeed, during tertial harmony's global hegemony (ca. 1650–ca. 1950), polyphony based on fourths or fifths was regarded as either archaic or primitive to such an extent that Hollywood stereotypes for almost any place or time felt to be distant enough from 'our own' were provided with a background score involving some kind of third-less polyphony. Ancient Egypt, Greece and Rome, pre-Renaissance Europe, the Chinese, the Arabs and Native Americans, however fundamentally different, were often indistinguishable harmonically.

From this perspective it might seem as if modal and quartal harmony constitute no more than a return to pre-classical polyphony. There is, however, little doubt that classical harmony will survive as just one polyphonic idiom among several. It has also left an indelible impression worldwide on practises of tonal polyphony. Its imprint on quartal harmony can be seen in the need to develop a means of 'changing key' inside a tonal idiom that, in earlier times, contained no modulation. Quartal key changes occur in Examples 22 (from $C^{\#4\text{-}5\flat7}$ to $E^{4\text{-}5\flat7}$) and 23 (a riff, the two poles of which are (1) Dm^{11} and $A^{4\text{-}5\flat7}$ and (2) Cm^{11}, $E\flat^{11}$, $G\flat_{7/}$). Moreover, the changes between Cm^{11} and $E\flat m^{11}$ in the *Kojak* theme and much of the dynamic in Bartók's harmonic language derive from tension between quartal chords a tritone apart (Lendvai 1971). In short, it is possible to change quartal key by introducing a chord in which the constituent notes are as different as possible from those in the previous one. The most usual key changes from a quartal sonority in central position (1-2-4-5♭7; see Ex. 17) are, therefore, those to a quartal chord situated on a minor third above or below, or to a quartal chord situated at a tritone's interval away, or to a quartal chord situated on either degree IV or V in relation to these three pitches – that is, to any note in the quartal tonic's diminished seventh chord or to either IV or V in relation to these three pitches. For example, a quartal key change from C can move to E♭, A♮ or F♯/G♭, or to A♭ (IV in relation to E♭), E (V in relation to A) or B or C♯/D♭ (IV or V in relation to F♯/G♭). Put simply, a 1-4-5 chord can only 'change key' to a 1-4-5 triad on a note at least three positions away in the circle of fifths (C to E♭, A♭, D♭, G♭/F♯, B, E or A). It cannot 'change key' to B♭, F, G or D, because these notes are already contained within its own tonal vocabulary (1-2-4-5♭7; see Ex. 17).

It is impossible to tell if developments in tonal polyphony during the twentieth century will survive as long as those of the classical tradition, or whether the tonal constraints of quartal and modal tonality will end up in the same sort of cul-de-sac as tertial chromaticism. It is more likely that harmony might be superseded, not least for technological reasons, by another compositional dynamic: sampling, MIDI-looping and the juxtaposition of preexistent musical and paramusical sounds. Whatever the future holds, it is clear that harmony, and whatever, if anything, supersedes it, is just as much an ideological as a technical or theoretical matter.

Example 24 Sting: 'Seven Days' (1993).

Example 25 Manfred Mann: 'I'm Your Kingpin' (1964): bass and piano riff.

Bibliography

Björnberg, Alf. 1995. 'Armonia eolia nella "popular music" contemporanea' [Aeolian Harmony in Contemporary Popular Music]. *Musica Realtà* 46: 41–50.

Burbat, Wolf. 1988. *Die Harmonik des Jazz* [The Harmony of Jazz]. Munich: Deutscher.

Dankworth, Avril. 1968. *Jazz: An Introduction to Its Musical Basis*. London: Oxford University Press.

Emsheimer, Ernst. 1964. 'Some Remarks on European Folk Polyphony.' *Journal of the International Folk Music Council* 16: 43–46. (Reissued in *Studia ethnomusicologica eurasiatica* 2 (1991): 277–80.)

Emsheimer, Ernst. 1979. 'Georgische Volksmusik' [Georgian Folk Music]. In *Die Musik in Geschichte und Gegenwart*, Vol. 16, ed. Friedrich Blume. Kassel: Bärenreiter, 447–55. (Reissued in *Studia ethnomusicologica eurasiatica* 2 (1991): 283–90.)

Hamm, Charles. 1979. *Yesterdays: Popular Song in America*. New York: Norton.

Harman, Alec, with Milner, Anthony, and Mellers, Wilfrid. 1962. *Man and His Music: The Story of Musical Experience in the West*. London: Barrie and Rockliff.

Hughes, Herbert, ed. 1909. *Irish Country Songs, Vol. 1*. London: Boosey & Hawkes.

Ingelf, Sten. 1977. *Jazz-, pop- och bluesharmonik* [Jazz, Pop and Blues Harmony]. Malmö: Musikhögskolan.

Lendvai, Ernö. 1971. *Béla Bartók: An Analysis of His Music*. London: Kahn and Averill.

Malm, William P. 1967. *Music Cultures of the Pacific, the Near East and Asia*. Englewood Cliffs, NJ: Prentice-Hall.

Manuel, Peter. 1989. 'Modal Harmony in Andalusian, Eastern European and Turkish Syncretic Musics.' *Yearbook for Traditional Music* 21: 70–94.

Mickelsen, William C. 1977. *Hugo Riemann's Theory of Harmony: A Study* and *History of Music Theory, Book III* by Hugo Riemann, trans. and ed. William C. Mickelsen. Lincoln, NE: University of Nebraska Press.

Moore, Allan. 1992. 'Patterns of Harmony.' *Popular Music* 11(1): 73–106.

Moore, Allan. 1995. 'The So-called "Flattened Seventh" in Rock.' *Popular Music* 14(2): 185–202.

Nketia, J.H. Kwabena. 1974. *The Music of Africa*. New York: Norton.

Norton, Richard. 1984. *Tonality in Western Culture*. London: University of Pennsylvania Press.

Rózsa, Miklos. 1982. *Double Life* (autobiography). Tunbridge Wells: Baton Press.

Tagg, Philip. 2000. *Kojak: 50 Seconds of Television Music*. 2nd ed. New York: Mass Media Music Scholars' Press. (First published Göteborg: Skrifter från Göteborgs universitet, Musikvetenskapliga institutionen, 1979.)

Winkler, Peter. 1978. 'Toward a Theory of Popular Harmony.' *Theory Only* 4(2): 3–26.

Sheet Music and Scores

'Adeste Fideles.' ca. 1933 (1751). *The Methodist Hymnbook*. London: Methodist Publishing House.

Bach, Johann S., comp. n.d. (1722). 'Das Wohltemperiertes Klavier, Band I.' Leipzig: Breitkopf und Härtel.

Bach, Johann S., comp. ca. 1973 (1730). 'Orchestral Suite in D Major.' BWV 1068, ed. Hans Grüß. Leipzig: VEB DVfM.

Benech, L., and Dumont, E. 1912. 'L'hirondelle du faubourg (valse musette).' Paris: Éditions Paul Beuscher.

Borodin, Aleksandr, comp. 1870 (1867). 'The Sleeping Princess.' Moscow.

Borodin, Aleksandr, comp. 1873 (1868). 'Song of the Dark Forest.' St. Petersburg.

Debussy, Claude, comp. 1901. *Pour le piano*. Paris: Jobert.

Debussy, Claude, comp. 1910. 'La cathédrale engloutie.' In *Préludes, I*. Paris: Durand.

De Falla, Manuel, comp. 1942 (1919). 'Farruca' from *El sombrero de tres picos*. London: Chester.

Degeyter, Pierre, comp., 1888, and Pottier, Eugène, lyr. 1871. 'Internationale.' In *Chants révolutionnaires*. Paris, 1887.

Farnaby, Giles, comp. 1957. 'Farnaby's Dreame.' In *Seventeen Pieces*, ed. T. Dart. London: Stainer and Bell.

Farnaby, Giles, comp. 1957 (ca. 1610). 'Loth to Depart.' In *Seventeen Pieces*, ed. T. Dart. London: Stainer and Bell.

Goldenberg, William, comp. 1973. *Kojak* (main theme, orchestral arrangement No. 1). Manuscript, Universal City Studios, Prod. No. 39000. Melville, NY: Duchess Music Corporation.

Hill, Joe, comp. 1973. 'Workers of the World Awaken!' In *Songs of the Workers*. 34th ed. Chicago: Industrial Workers of the World.

'La Marseillaise.' 1915. In *The Fellowship Song Book*, ed. H. Walford Davies. London: Curwen.

Mendelssohn-Bartholdy, Felix, comp. 1972. 'Oh! For the Wings of a Dove.' In *The Parlour Song Book*, ed. Michael R. Turner. London: Pan Books, 218.

Molinaire, Nicanor, comp. 1994. 'Cocorocó.' In *Clásicos de la musica popular chilena 1900–1960*, ed. J.-P. Gonzalez. Santiago: Ediciones Universidad Católica de Chile, 182.

Molloy, James L., comp. and lyr. 1973 (1884). 'Love's Old Sweet Song.' In *Favorite Songs of the Nineties*. New York: Dover.

Mozart, Wolfgang A., comp. 1900 (1777). 'Ave Verum Corpus.' *Sancta Maria*. Vienna: Universal.

Palacio, Espinosa, comp. 1981. 'Song of the International Brigade.' In *Sånger för socialismen*, ed. P. Ström. Stockholm: Arbetarkultur.

Pierpont, James, comp. and lyr. 1859. 'Jingle Bells (or The One Horse Open Sleigh).' Boston, MA: Oliver Ditson & Co.

Rubinstein, Anton G., comp. 1924. 'Melody in F.' In *Motion Picture Moods for Pianists and Organists*, ed. Erno Rapee. New York: Schirmer. (Reprinted New York: Arno Press, 1974.)

'Sancta Lucia' (Italian trad.). n.d. In *Songs That Will Live for Ever*, ed. M. Jacobson. London: Odhams.

Smith, John Stafford, comp., and Key, Francis Scott, lyr. 1856. 'The Star-Spangled Banner.' Boston, MA: Oliver Ditson & Co.

Vian, Boris, comp. 1970. 'Le déserteur.' In *Upp till kamp*, ed. Enn Kokk. Stockholm: Prisma.

Weelkes, Thomas, comp. 1945 (ca. 1610). 'Hark, All Ye Lovely Saints.' In *Historical Anthology of Music, Vol. 1*, ed. A.T. Davison and W. Apel. Cambridge, MA: Harvard University Press, 194.

Discographical References

ABBA. 'S.O.S.' Atlantic 3265. *1975*: USA.

ABBA. 'Waterloo.' Atlantic 3035. *1974*: USA.

Abdo, George, and the Flames of Araby Orchestra. 'Misirlou.' *The Art of Belly Dancing*. Monitor 61752. *1995*: USA.

Ashley, Clarence 'Tom.' 'Coo-Coo Bird.' *Old Time Music at Clarence Ashley's*. Folkways FA 2359. *1963*: USA.

Astronauts, The. 'Misirlou.' *Surfin' with the Astronauts*. RCA 2760. *1963*: USA.

Baez, Joan. 'We Shall Overcome.' Fontana H 428. *1963*: USA.

Barber, Chris, and His Jazz Band. 'When the Saints Go Marchin' In.' Storyville A 45006. 1954: USA.

Beatles, The. 'Hey Jude.' Apple R 5722. *1968*: UK.

Beatles, The. 'Lady Madonna.' Parlophone R 5675. *1968*: UK.

Beatles, The. 'P.S. I Love You.' *Please Please Me*. Parlophone R 4949. *1963*: UK.

Booker T and the MGs. 'Green Onions.' Stax 127. *1962*: USA.

Cara, Irene. 'Flashdance . . . What a Feeling.' Casablanca 811440. *1983*: USA.

Carpenter, John, and Howarth, Alan. *Escape from New York*. Milan 120137. *1981*: France.

Cooder, Ry. 'Vigilante Man.' *Into the Purple Valley*. Reprise 2052. *1971*: USA.

Davis, Miles. *Bitches Brew*. Columbia 26. *1970*: USA.

Davis, Miles. 'So What.' *Kind of Blue*. Columbia 8163. *1959*: USA.

Deep Purple. 'Smoke on the Water.' *Machine Head*. Warner Brothers 2607. *1972*: USA.

Dylan, Bob. 'All Along the Watchtower.' *John Wesley Harding*. Columbia 09604. *1968*: USA.

'Fanfare for the Common Man.' *BBC Space Themes*. BBC REH 324. *1978*: UK.

'Giâi phóng miên nam' (Vietnamese liberation song). *Freedom Singers 68*. Befria Södern BS 1 A-B. n.d.: Sweden.

Harris, Rolf. 'Waltzing Matilda.' *All Together Now*. EMI 701102. n.d.: UK.

Hubbard, Freddie. 'Red Clay.' *Red Clay*. Sony 85216. *2002*: USA.

Isley Brothers, The. 'Twist and Shout.' Wand 124. *1962*: USA.

Jimi Hendrix Experience, The. 'All Along the Watchtower.' *Electric Ladyland*. MCA MCAD-10895. *1968*: USA.

John, Elton. 'Your Song.' *Elton John*. DJM DJS 223. *1970*: UK.

King, Carole. 'Road to Nowhere.' London HLU 10036. *1966*: UK.

'La cucaracha,' as 'Lo struscio di Amarcord.' *Amarcord/Prova d'orchestra*. Cinematre/RCA NL 33211. *1974*: Italy.

Lynyrd Skynyrd. 'Sweet Home Alabama.' MCA 40258. *1974*: USA.

Makeba, Miriam. 'Pata Pata.' Reprise 20606. *1967*: USA.

Mancini, Henry. 'Cade's County.' *Golden Hour of TV Themes*. Pye Golden Hour GH 845. *1976*: UK.

Mann, Manfred. 'I'm Your Kingpin.' HMV 1282. *1964*: UK.

Mariachi Sol. 'Cielito Lindo.' *México Lindo*. ARC 1249. *1994*: USA.

Martha and the Vandellas. 'Nowhere to Run.' Tamla Motown TMG 502. *1965*: USA.

Martí, José. 'Guantanamera.' *Digno Garcia y sus Carios*. Pye 7N17172. *1966*: UK.

Mauriat, Paul, and His Orchestra. 'Sous le ciel de Paris.' *Best of France*. Verve 834 370. *1988*: USA.

New Zealand Symphony Orchestra, The. 'Billy the Kid: Orchestral Suite from the Ballet.' *Aaron Copland: Symphony No. 3; Billy the Kid (Suite)*. Naxos 8559106. *2000*: UK.

On the Waterfront (Original soundtrack). Varèse Sarabande 5638. *1995*: USA.

'Prelude and Legend from *Duel in the Sun*.' *The Western World of Dimitri Tiomkin*. Unicorn-Kanchana Digital DKP 9002. *1980*: UK.

Procol Harum. 'A Whiter Shade of Pale.' Deram DM 126. *1967*: UK.

Procol Harum. 'Homburg.' Regal-Zonophone RZ 3003. *1967*: UK.

Puebla, Carlos. 'Hasta Siempre.' *Hasta Siempre*. Egrem 83. *2002*: Cuba.

Pulp Fiction (Original soundtrack). MCA 11103. *1995*: USA.

Quo Vadis? (Original soundtrack). London 820200-2. n.d.: UK.

Reggiani, Serge. 'Le déserteur.' *Olympia 83*. Polydor 813 187. *1983*: UK.

Rodrigo, Joaquín. 'Concierto de Aranjuez.' *Guitar Music*. RCA LSC 2730-B. *1967*: USA.

Rolling Stones, The. 'Brown Sugar.' Rolling Stones RS 19100. *1971*: UK.

Rolling Stones, The. 'Gimme Shelter.' *Gimme Shelter [Live]*. Decca 5101. *1971*: UK.

Rolling Stones, The. 'Jumpin' Jack Flash.' Decca F 12782. *1968*: UK.

Seeger, Pete. 'Where Have All the Flowers Gone.' *World of Pete Seeger*. Columbia 31949. *1973*: USA.

Shadows, The. 'Dakota.' *Dance with the Shadows*. Columbia 1619. *1964*: USA.

Simple Minds. 'Belfast Child' ('She Moved Through the Fair'). *Street Fighting Years*. Virgin 1. *1989*: UK.

Sting. 'Seven Days.' *Ten Summoner's Tales*. A&M 89567. *1993*: USA.

'The Blue Danube' ('An der schönen blaue Donau'). *Strauss Waltzes*. CBS Odyssey MBK 44892. *1979*: USA.

'The King of Denmark's Galiard.' *Elizabethan Collection*. Boots Classical 143. *1988*: UK.

'Theme from Monty Python's Flying Circus' ('Liberty Bell,' comp. J.P. Sousa). *Top TV Themes*. Decca TAB 18. *1981*: UK.

'Theme from *The Magnificent Seven*.' *Magnificent Seven* (Original soundtrack). Rykodisc 10741. *1998*: USA.

USSR Defence Ministry Orchestra, The. 'Internationale.' Melodiya GOST 5289–68. *1968*: USSR.

Valens, Ritchie. 'La Bamba.' London HLU 8803. *1959*: UK.

Vrethammar, Sylvia. 'E viva España.' Recorded from Svensktoppen, Sveriges Radio P3. 1973: Sweden.

Watson, Doc, and Watson, Merle. 'Darling Corey.' *The Doc Watson Family*. Folkways FTS 31021. *1963*: USA.

'Wondrous Love.' *White Spirituals from 'The Sacred Harp'*. Notes by Alan Lomax. Atlantic SD-1349 (Southern Folk Heritage Series). *1960*: USA.

Discography

Albion Country Band, The. 'The Murder of Maria Marten.' *No Roses*. Crest 11. *1971*: USA.

Corea, Chick. *Light as a Feather*. Polydor 5525. *1972*: UK.

King Crimson. *Discipline*. Warner Brothers 3429. *1981*: USA.

McLaughlin, John, and the Mahavishnu Orchestra. *Birds of Fire*. Columbia CK-31996. *1972*: USA.

Music of Thailand. Folkways FE 4463. *1959*: USA.

Songs and Music of Tibet. Folkways FE 4486. *1962*: USA.

Steeleye Span. 'Cold, Haily, Windy Night.' *Please to See the King*. Crest 8. *1971*: USA.

Steeleye Span. 'Female Drummer.' *Please to See the King*. Crest 8. *1971*: USA.

Steeleye Span. 'Seven Hundred Elves.' *Now We Are Six*. Chrysalis CHR 1053. *1974*: USA.

Steeleye Span. 'The Lowlands of Holland.' *Hark! The Village Wait*. Crest 22. *1970*: USA.

Tyner, McCoy. *Expansions*. Blue Note 84338. *1967*: USA.

Visual Recordings

Brooks, Mel, Morris, John, and Laine, Frankie. 1974. 'Theme from *Blazing Saddles*.' Warner Home Video (video).

von Suppé, Franz, comp. n.d. 'Light Cavalry' (march). As used for 'The Mounties Musical Ride' in *The Granny of the Year Show: The Benny Hill Show, Vol. 2*. Thames video (video).

Filmography

Blazing Saddles, dir. Mel Brooks. 1974. USA. 105 mins. Comedy Western. Original music by John Morris.

Duel in the Sun, dir. King Vidor. 1946. USA/UK. 130 mins. Drama. Original music by Dimitri Tiomkin.

Escape from New York, dir. John Carpenter. 1981. USA. 99 mins. Adventure. Original music by John Carpenter.

On the Waterfront, dir. Elia Kazan. 1954. USA. 108 mins. Drama. Original music by Leonard Bernstein.

Pulp Fiction, dir. Quentin Tarantino. 1994. USA. 160 mins. Black Comedy.

Quo Vadis?, dir. Mervyn LeRoy. 1951. USA. 171 mins. Historical Epic. Original music by Miklos Rózsa.

The Carpetbaggers, dir. Edward Dmytryk. 1964. USA. 150 mins. Drama. Original music by Elmer Bernstein.

The Jungle Book, dir. Zoltan Korda. 1942. USA/UK. 109 mins. Adventure. Original music by Miklos Rózsa.

The Magnificent Seven, dir. John Sturges. 1960. USA. 128 mins. Western. Original music by Elmer Bernstein.

PHILIP TAGG

Heterophony

'Heterophony,' from the Greek *héteros* ('other') and *fóne* ('sound'), means the polyphony resulting from the differences of pitch that are produced when two or more people sing or play the same melodic line at the same time. 'Heterophony' can denote everything from the unintentional polyphonic effect of slightly unsynchronized unison singing to the intentional discrepancies between a vocal line and its instrumental embellishment that are characteristic of much of the music from Greece, Turkey and the Arab world (Ex. 1).

Heterophony is also at the heart of most forms of Indonesian gamelan music, in which several layers of heterophony can combine to produce a distinctly chordal effect (Ex. 2).

A different type of heterophony is found in traditional music from the Scottish Hebrides, in which each florid pentatonic improvisation on the same psalm tune is thought to present each individual's 'relation to God on a personal basis' (Knudsen 1968a, 10; see also Wicks 1989) (Ex. 3).

Bibliography

Chianis, Sotirios. 1967. *The Vocal and Instrumental Tsámiko of Roumeli and the Peloponnesus*. Ph.D. thesis, University of California, Los Angeles.

Knudsen, Torkel. 1968a. Liner notes to *Musique Celtique (Îles Hébrides)*. Ocora OCR 45.

Knudsen, Torkel. 1968b. 'Ornamental Hymn/Psalm Singing in Denmark, the Faroe Islands and the Hebrides.' *DFS Information* 68(2): 10.

Malm, William P. 1967. *Music Cultures of the Pacific, the Near East and Asia*. Englewood Cliffs, NJ: Prentice-Hall.

Ornstein, Ruby. 1980. 'Indonesia: Bali, Music.' In *The New Grove Dictionary of Music and Musicians*, Vol. 9, ed. Stanley Sadie. London: Macmillan, 179–87.

Wicks, Sammie Ann. 1989. 'A Belated Salute to the "Old Way" of "Snaking" the Voice on Its (ca) 345th Birthday.' *Popular Music* 8(1): 59–96.

Example 1 Heterophonic cadential formulae in Greek *tsámiko* music (transcribed in Chianis 1967).

Example 2 Gamelan *gong kebyar*: multiple heterophony (transcribed in Ornstein 1980).

Example 3 Hebridean home worship: 'Martyrdom' (*Musique Celtique (Îles Hébrides)*; transcribed in Knudsen 1968b).

Discographical Reference

'Martyrdom.' *Musique Celtique (Îles Hébrides)*. Ocora OCR 45. *1968*: France.

PHILIP TAGG

Homophony

'Homophony' (adj. homophonic), from the Greek *homófonos* (meaning 'sounding in unison or at the same time'), is defined as a type of polyphony in which the various instruments and/or voices move in the same rhythm at the same time; in other words, it is the polyphonic antithesis of counterpoint. In historical musicology, 'homophony' is sometimes opposed to 'polyphony,' the latter term being used in the restricted sense of imitative contrapuntal polyphony, and therefore it can also denote music in which one vocal or instrumental part leads melodically while others provide chordal accompaniment. However, since chordal accompaniment in many influential types of popular music is characterized by riffs (bass, lead guitar, backing vocals and so on), and thereby to a significant extent is contrapuntal, it is misleading to call such music homophonic.

Music can be considered homophonic (or contrapuntal) only in relative terms. This is illustrated by the excerpts shown in Examples 1 and 2. Here it can be seen that, although Example 1 (taken from one of the most popular hymn tunes in nonconformist Christianity) fulfills all the criteria of homophony, it is less homophonic than Example 2, because each voice has a clearly melodic character that sometimes proceeds in contrary motion to the tune (soprano), and the excerpt ends with a small contrapuntal intervention in the alto and bass parts. Example 3 illustrates

Example 1 'Cwm Rhondda' (refrain) (John Hughes, 1873–1932).

Example 2 'Old 100th' (French Psalter 1551).

Example 3 ABBA: 'Fernando' (1976).

both homophonic and contrapuntal characteristics: while lead singer and backing vocalists sing homophonically, their combined melodic gesture is counterpointed by bass line and *flauto dolce ostinato* doubled by strings.

Bibliography

Tagg, Philip. 1991. *Fernando the Flute*. Liverpool, UK: Institute of Popular Music.

Discographical Reference

ABBA. 'Fernando.' Epic 4036. *1976*: UK.

PHILIP TAGG

Modality

'*Modality*,' from Latin *modus* (meaning 'measure,' 'manner,' 'mode'), is a term used mainly to denote certain types of tonal vocabulary that diverge from that predominant within Central European art music (ca. 1730–1910) and tonally related forms of popular music (for example, popular hymns, marches, waltzes, polkas, evergreens).

General

The current usage of 'mode' and 'modality' derives from two main sources: (a) attempts by medieval European theorists to systematize the tonal vocabulary of liturgical music according to ancient Greek and Arab concepts – the 'church modes'; and (b) ethnomusicological classification of tonal vocabulary used in folk and non-European musics.

Modes are distinct from melody types, such as the Hindu *rāga* or Arab *maqam*, which contain not only modal templates, but also basic formulae for the improvised performance of melodic contour, mood and direction. Nor are modes mere scales; they are reductions of particular tonal practises to single occurrences of recurrent pitch used within those practises. Such sets of single occurrences are usually presented in scalar form spanning one octave (Ex. 1, overleaf).

Church Modes

Church modes presuppose: (a) the diatonic division of the octave into seven constituent pitches, five separated by a whole tone, two by a semitone; and (b) a tonal center or 'tonic,' which may sometimes be identified as a (real or potential) drone or as the final, or most frequently recurring, melodic note. The seven heptatonic church modes are presented in Example 1. The left column shows each mode, its tonic as numbers 1 and 8, using only the white notes of a keyboard instrument. The right column shows each mode transposed to E, highlighting each mode's configuration of intervals. Three interrelated factors determine each mode's unique sonic character: (a) the position of the two semitone steps (bracketed in the left column, shown as numbers in the right); (b) the one tritone interval (marked with a slur in the right column); and (c) the relation of these two phenomena to the tonic. Thus, only the Ionian mode has its tritone between perfect fourth and major seventh (4–♯7), only the Dorian between minor third and major sixth (♭3–♯6), only the Phrygian between minor second and perfect fifth (♭2–5) and so on. More general distinctions are often drawn (a) between major and minor modes (i.e., those containing a major or minor third in their tonic triad) and (b) between those including major and minor sevenths.

Non-Diatonic Modes

Many popular tonal practises cannot be categorized according to the diatonic framework of heptatonic church modes. For example, pentatonic modes are widespread throughout the world, the most common types being anhemitonic (without semitones) and qualifiable as either major – 'doh-pentatonic' (Ex. 2a) – or minor – 'la-pentatonic' (Ex. 2b). Popular melody from such widely flung areas as Eastern Asia, the Andes, Sub-Saharan Africa and the Celtic fringe of Europe makes extensive use of such anhemitonic pentatonicism, the latter two exerting a particularly strong influence on the development of popular music in North America. Other globally circulated non-diatonic

modes include: (a) the hexatonic whole-tone scale, used copiously by Hollywood as a mystery cue and by jazz musicians as improvisation material to fit chords containing an augmented fifth; and (b) variants of the *Hijaz* (or *Hejjaz*) mode (also known as *Hicaz* and *Bhairavi*), which is widespread throughout the Balkans, Greece, Turkey, southern Spain, the entire Arab world and parts of the Indian subcontinent.

Many non-diatonic modes enjoy considerable popularity on a less global scale: for example, the hemitonic Japanese penta-scale *zokugaku-sempô*, based on common koto tuning patterns (descends 8 ♭6 5 4 ♭2 1). Other well-known, non-diatonic modes, such as the heptatonic 'Gypsy' mode (ascends 1 2 ♭3 ♯4 5 ♭6 ♯7) and the related 'harmonic minor' (1 2 ♭3 4 5 ♭6 ♯7), recur frequently in popular melody from the Balkans, while much popular melody (for example, Javanese, Arabic) uses modes incompatible with the Western division of the octave into 12 equal semitones.

Modal Harmony

Harmonic practises derived from the use of church modes are as important as melodic vocabulary in determining modal character. For example, the melodies of both the Crystals' 'Da Doo Ron Ron' (1963) and Lynyrd Skynyrd's 'Sweet Home Alabama' (1974) are basically major tritonic (♯3 2 1) and thereby potentially Ionian, Mixolydian or major pentatonic. However, harmonization of the Crystals' song is unequivocally Ionian (I-IV-V-I), that of Lynyrd Skynyrd Mixolydian (I-♭VII-IV), this discrepancy contributing as much as timbre, rhythm or sound treatment to radical differences in character between the two recordings.

Perceived Characteristics of Modality

Mode nomenclature often reflects hegemonic identification of tonal vocabulary in ethnic terms – for example, the 'Gypsy' mode and the church modes named after areas of Greece, perceived as marginal from the power center of ancient Athens. Similarly, from a contemporary Northern European or North American viewpoint, the Phrygian mode is often thought to sound Spanish, while other modes, already mentioned, are heard as Arab, Balkan, Japanese and so on. US film music frequently uses such hegemonic perceptions of modality to transmit cultural stereotypes of place.

Different modes are also perceived as connoting different moods. ('Mood' and 'mode' are etymologically related.) Such connotations are culturally specific, the equation of minor modes with 'sad' and major with 'happy' being largely valid within the Central European tonal system of art music and related styles, but inapplicable to the music of most other cultures. Sim-

Example 1 'Church' modes.

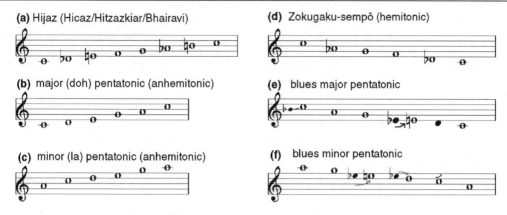

Example 2 Some common non-diatonic modes.

ilarly, rock and pop music using Aeolian harmony in a certain way has a tendency to be associated with alienation and the ominous, while Mixolydian rock and pop veers more toward a mood of wide open spaces. Within African-American music, descending minor pentatonic modes with 'blue' fifths are more likely to connect with blues, old times and oppression, while melismatic major pentatonic melodies link with the positive ecstasy of gospel music.

During the hegemony of Central European major–minor tonality, music from the continent's 'fringe areas' (Spain, Russia, Scandinavia, the Balkans and the British Isles) was often characterized by the musicological establishment as 'modal,' because, although much music produced in those areas conformed to the central (Ionian) norms of tonality, some – usually older forms of rural popular music – did not; it conformed to modes abandoned and regarded as archaic by the European bourgeoisie during the ascendancy of that class. Some of these modes, notably those containing a flat seventh (Dorian, Mixolydian, Aeolian), and the two anhemitonic pentatonic modes are regarded (rightly or wrongly) as typical of rural music from the British Isles. These modes blended with compatible tonal systems of West African origin to contribute to the establishment of North American popular styles, challenging the global hegemony of Central European major–minor tonality to the extent that the latter is now more likely than the former to own connotations of 'the old order.'

Bibliography

Björnberg, Alf. 1984. '"There's Something Going On" – om eolisk harmonik i nutida rockmusik' ['There's Something Going On': On Aeolian Harmony in Contemporary Rock Music]. In *Tvärspel: 31 artiklar om musik. Festskrift till Jan Ling* [Tvärspel: 31 Articles on Music. Festschrift for Jan Ling]. Göteborg: Skrifter från musikvetenskapliga institutionen 9, 371–86.

Burbat, Wolfgang. 1988. *Die Harmonik des Jazz* [The Harmonics of Jazz]. München: Deutscher Taschenbuch Verlag.

Malm, William P. 1977. *Music Cultures of the Pacific, the Near East and Asia.* 2nd ed. Englewood Cliffs, NJ: Prentice-Hall.

Manuel, Peter. 1989. 'Modal Harmony in Andalusian, Eastern European and Turkish Syncretic Musics.' *Yearbook for Traditional Music* 21: 70–94.

Nettl, Bruno, and Béhague, Gerard. 1990. *Folk and Traditional Music of the Western Continents.* 3rd ed. Englewood Cliffs, NJ: Prentice-Hall.

Power, Harold. 1992. 'Modality as a European Cultural Construct.' In *Secondo Convegno Europeo di Analisi Musicale* [Second European Convention on Musical Analysis], ed. Rossana Dalmonte and Mario Baroni. Trento: Università degli studi di Trento, 207–19.

Discographical References

Crystals, The. 'Da Doo Ron Ron.' Philles 112. *1963*: USA.

Lynyrd Skynyrd. 'Sweet Home Alabama.' MCA 40258. *1974*: USA.

Discography

Hellenic Music Archives Ensemble, The. *The Guardians of Hellenism, Vol. 3: Smyrna, Ionian Coast.* FM Records FM 803. *1996*: Greece.

PHILIP TAGG

Modulation

The term 'modulation' refers to a change from one key to another within a song, improvisation or composition. Conventionally, the term refers to a change of tonic pitch, but not to a change of mode with the same tonic pitch. Thus, a piece may modulate from D major to B minor, but a change from D major to D minor would not be considered modulation.

In many styles of popular music, modulation is an important resource in creating variety of sound. Usually, although not always, modulation brings a change in some pitches of the scale. For example, in a change from C major to E major, four new pitches (F♯, C♯, G♯, D♯) replace pitches of the C major scale (F, C, G, D). However, in a modulation from a tonic major to its relative minor, or a tonic minor to its relative major, there is a minimal change in pitches. The key signature remains the same, with some adjustment to the sixth and seventh degrees of the scale.

Modulation also brings a change in the meaning of any pitches that are common to the two keys. The three pitches shared by the keys of C major and E major take on different functions; for example, E becomes the tonic pitch, the most stable pitch of the new key, and B, previously the leading tone with a strong tendency to resolve up to C, now takes on a solid, stable sound as the upper fifth of the tonic. While most listeners do not consciously analyze such changes, modulation produces a vivid effect of reorientation and change of color that can be experienced without analysis.

The effect of a modulation depends partly on the number of pitches in common between the two keys. The major scales, the minor scales and church modes are particularly sensitive in the differentiation of contrast that they permit. For instance, C major has six pitches in common with G major or F major, five in common with D major or B♭ major, four in common with A major or E♭ major and so on. Some other scales, such as whole-tone or octotonic, are limited in this respect. In the theory of Western art music, one finds further generalizations about the character of modulations. For instance, tonics related by the interval of a third or a fifth are considered to be closely related; modulation that increases the number of sharps is considered 'bright,' while modulation that adds flats is considered 'dark.' Some of these generalizations seem to carry over to modulations in popular music, although more evidence about the perceptions of musicians and audiences is required before generalizing. Modulations may be relatively smooth or abrupt; one way to create a smooth modulation is through use of a pivot chord, made up of pitches belonging to both keys.

Modulation often helps to create musical structure, and frequently coincides with sectional boundaries, enhancing the contrast of sections. It also contributes, in many cases, to a structural pattern of departure and return, in which a return to the original key creates

closure. Many AABA song structures modulate for the bridge and return to the original key for the final A section. In arrangements of standards or in mid-twentieth-century musical comedy, a song may modulate upward for a final verse or chorus, using the fresh color and the increased tension of a higher pitch to offset the repetition of material. In recent popular music, such modulations can have a parodic character – as, for instance, in 'Stand' by R.E.M. or 'Go West' by the Pet Shop Boys.

Some music theorists differentiate between 'modulation' and 'tonicization,' the first term denoting a definite, long-lasting move to a new key, the second term a less emphatic key change. The two terms suggest a more definite distinction than musical experience can support. Other music theorists, particularly the early twentieth-century theorist Heinrich Schenker and promoters of his work, deny that modulation exists in eighteenth- and nineteenth-century Western art music, emphasizing unity of key in each movement of a composition. This extreme view is problematic and, for many musicians, counterintuitive; its pertinence to popular music is uncertain.

Notation sometimes shows modulation explicitly by a change of key signature, but notated music often introduces accidentals necessary to bring about the change of key without otherwise indicating a new tonic. It is necessary to rely on aural judgment in identifying modulations, in notated as well as in non-notated music.

Discographical References

Pet Shop Boys, The. 'Go West.' *Very*. Capitol 89721. *1993*: USA.

R.E.M. 'Stand.' *Green*. Warner Brothers 25795. *1988*: USA.

FRED E. MAUS

Parallel Interval

The term and concept of 'parallel interval' are used in understanding and defining: (a) parallel motion in the context of different kinds of melodic motion; (b) parallel chords; (c) parallel thirds and sixths; (d) doubling; and (e) parallel motion in popular music.

Parallel Motion

Music theorists classify ways in which simultaneously sounding melodic or other musical lines move in relation to one another. In oblique motion, one line keeps its pitch, while the other line moves to a different pitch. In contrary motion, both lines move to new pitches at the same time, but in opposite directions: one line up, the other line down. In similar motion, both lines move to new notes at the same time, going in the same direction: both lines up or both lines down.

Parallel motion is one kind of similar motion: both lines move up or both move down, keeping the same intervallic distance between them. In other words, the two lines form the same interval before and after they move. This means that the numerical portion of the interval name – for example, third or fifth – must be the same. However, the quality of the interval – for example, major, minor, augmented or diminished – may change. Thus, similar motion from a major third to a major third is parallel motion, and similar motion from a major third to a minor third is also parallel motion.

Descriptions of parallel motion refer to the intervals formed between simultaneously sounding notes in the two lines, not to the interval through which each line moves. If two lines form the interval of a fifth, and each line drops a third to a new note, the new notes also form a fifth. These are thus parallel fifths and not parallel thirds.

Parallel Chords

Parallel chords are formed when one chord follows another, with all parts moving up or down and with the same distance obtaining from each note of the first chord to the corresponding note of the second chord. For instance, a keyboard player might play a C major chord with the right hand (CEG), and move the hand down to play an A minor chord next (ACE). Each note of the first chord is followed by a note a third lower to make the second chord, creating parallel chords. Parallel triads and seventh chords are common in popular music.

Parallel Thirds and Sixths

It is common in vernacular and popular styles to accompany a melody with another melodic line moving in parallel thirds or sixths, shifting from one interval to the other when necessary to fit the harmony. Occasionally, the use of these parallel intervals, along with other stylistic markers, evokes particular vernacular or ethnic styles – for instance, German, Mediterranean or Latin American – sometimes with an implication of naiveté or primitivism. Parallel thirds and sixths are also a basic resource of vocal duets.

Doubling

Notes separated by the distance of one or more octaves count, for many purposes, as 'the same note.' If two melodic lines move in parallel octaves for more than a few notes, they form an octave doubling. Extended motion by parallel unisons is normally called unison doubling rather than parallel motion.

Parallel Motion in Popular Music

Theories of voice leading for Renaissance vocal polyphony and for Western art music through to the nineteenth century emphasize the independent motion of lines, recommending extensive use of contrary and oblique motion. Art music theorists discourage excessive reliance on similar motion and, in particular, prohibit parallel unisons, octaves and perfect fifths. Theorists distinguish doublings from parallel motion and allow doublings. The rules are complex (see Benjamin 1979; Aldwell and Schachter 2002).

These rules have little to do with popular music, especially blues and mainstream commercial music from rock 'n' roll onward. Parallel unisons, octaves and fifths are common in this music. Needless to say, complaints that popular music violates classical voice-leading rules are irrelevant, reflecting only the critic's lack of a sense of stylistic difference.

Because they categorize motion between any simultaneously sounding melodic or other musical lines, the kinds of motion described are ubiquitous in popular music. Any melody accompanied by a drone forms oblique motion with the drone. The beginning of Donna Summer's 'I Feel Love' uses a repeated bass note – a drone – along with a four-note ostinato. When the voice enters, it forms oblique motion against the bass, repeating the pattern at two other pitch levels before changing to note-against-note motion between voice and bass. The Orioles' 'Crying in the Chapel' accompanies its rising melody with a descending scale, creating contrary motion.

However, parallel intervals are particularly prevalent in popular music. For example, with few exceptions, Darude's 'Sandstorm' moves in parallel triads throughout. Performances of the carol 'Silent Night' typically accompany the melody with another line in parallel thirds and sixths. The introduction and verse of ABBA's 'Fernando' feature parallel thirds. Tagg (2000) discusses the ideological effects of the sense of exoticism thus evoked. The chorus of Bryan Adams' 'Heaven' moves in parallel fifths between bass and voice, with some elaboration in the vocal line. Nirvana's 'In Bloom' begins with power chords (parallel fifths), sometimes adding a third pitch (parallel chords, after 0:12 minutes). At 0:25 minutes, voice and bass form parallel fifths. Then, at 0:37 minutes, they move in contrary motion.

Bibliography

Aldwell, Edward, and Schachter, Carl. 2002. *Harmony and Voice Leading*. Belmont, CA: Wadsworth Publishing Company.

Benjamin, Thomas. 1979. *The Craft of Modal Counterpoint: A Practical Approach*. New York: Schirmer Books.

Tagg, Philip. 2000. *Kojak: 50 Seconds of Television Music*. 2nd ed. New York: Mass Media Music Scholars' Press. (First published Göteborg: Skrifter från Göteborgs universitet, Musikvetenskapliga institutionen, 1979.)

Discographical References

ABBA. 'Fernando.' Epic EPC 4036. *1976*: UK.

Adams, Bryan. 'Heaven.' *Reckless*. A&M 5013. *1984*: USA.

Chicago Symphony Brass. 'Silent Night.' *Christmas with the Symphony Brass of Chicago*. Vox 7501. *1995*: USA.

Darude. 'Sandstorm.' *Before the Storm*. Strictly Rhythm 35106. *2001*: USA.

Nirvana. 'In Bloom.' *Nevermind*. Geffen 24425. *1991*: USA.

Orioles, The. 'Crying in the Chapel.' *Best of Jubilee & C.P. Parker Years*. Collectables 81. *2000*: USA.

Summer, Donna. 'I Feel Love.' *Endless Summer*. Mercury 526178. *1995*: USA.

PHILIP TAGG

Pentatonicism

Pentatonicism is a type of modality based on five identifiable pitches within an octave. Pentatonic modes are widespread throughout the world. Particularly common in English-language popular music of the postwar period are the two anhemitonic pentatonic modes (that is, pentatonic modes without semitones), qualifiable as either major ('doh-pentatonic': for example, CDEGA) or minor ('la-pentatonic': for example, ACDEG).

PHILIP TAGG

Polyphony

'Polyphony,' from the Greek *poly* (meaning 'many') and *fonē* (meaning 'sound'), denotes: (a) music in which at least two sounds of clearly differing pitch, timbre or mode of articulation occur at the same time (general definition); (b) music in which at least two sounds of clearly differing fundamental pitch occur simultaneously (tonal definition); and (c) a particular type of contrapuntal tonal polyphony used by certain European composers between ca. 1400 and ca. 1600. Use of the term in the sense of definition (c), a practise widespread in historical musicology, is incongruous, since the polyphony alluded to is contrasted with homophony, itself another type of polyphony. Most popular music is, however, polyphonic according to definitions (a) and (b).

According to definition (a), music that features the simultaneous occurrence of sounds for which no fundamental pitch is discernible can be classified as polyphonic, especially when such 'unpitched' sounds are produced by different instruments or voices articulating different rhythmic patterns. The notion of a polyphonic synthesizer jibes well with this general definition, since such instruments allow for the simultaneous occurrence of several different 'unpitched,' as well as pitched, sounds, whereas monophonic synthesizers cater for only one pitch and/or timbre at a time. In short, a broad definition of the term permits such phenomena as drumkit patterns, single vocal line plus hand clap/foot stamp (as in Janis Joplin's 'Mercedes Benz' (1971)) or fife-and-drum music (for example, that of the Royal Welsh Fusiliers) all to be classified as polyphonic, while the tonal definition does not. According to the second (tonal) definition of polyphony, all unison playing or singing not accompanied by 'pitched' instruments is regarded as monophonic, while homophonic singing in parallel intervals is understood as polyphony. However, a single or unison melodic line accompanied by a drone (single-pitch or multi-pitch) is, at least strictly speaking, polyphonic according to both definitions (a) and (b), as are all forms of heterophony, homophony and counterpoint.

The degree to which music can be regarded as polyphonic is determined by the cultural habitat of that music's producers and users. For example, the *consecutively* articulated notes of guitar or piano accompaniment to popular songs are usually both intended and perceived to be harmony or chords (and thereby polyphonic), not least because the strings of the accompanying instruments are left to sound simultaneously, and/or because of reverberation created either within the instrument itself or by electroacoustic means (as in the introduction to the Animals' 'House of the Rising Sun' (1964) or in Elton John's 'Your Song' (1971)). On the other hand, the fast descending scalar pattern played on sitar or vina at the end of a raga performance (as heard, for example, in Ravi Shankar's *Sound of the Sitar* (1970)) may, for similar reasons of reverberation, sound like a chord to Western ears, but it is by no means certain that, in its original context, such a cascade of notes is intended to be heard as a chord or cluster.

Discographical References

Animals, The. 'House of the Rising Sun.' Columbia DB 7301. *1964*: UK.

John, Elton. 'Your Song.' DJM DJS 233. *1971*: UK.

Joplin, Janis. 'Mercedes Benz.' *Pearl*. CBS S 64188. *1971*: USA.

Shankar, Ravi. *Sound of the Sitar*. World Pacific/Liberty WPS-21434. *1970*: USA.

Discography

The Band and Drums 1st Battalion of Royal Welsh Fusiliers. Cassette RS/1 (Caernarfon Castle). *1995*: UK.

Transposition

The term 'transposition' can refer to: (a) the transposition of musical material; and (b) transposing instruments.

The Transposition of Musical Material

To transpose something – a song, a musical passage or a melody – is to move it up or down to a different pitch level. Transposition occurs as an aspect of performance. Instrumentalists or arrangers frequently transpose songs from an original key, as represented in sheet music or a recording, to allow a better performance by a solo vocalist. In mid-twentieth-century practise, it was common to transpose the final verse or chorus of a song up, often by a semitone, for an enhanced conclusion to a performance.

Transposition is relatively easy on some instruments and very difficult on others. The difficulty is greater on wind instruments or piano, where a change of key may require completely different fingerings. There is less change of fingering on stringed instruments, and a guitar capo makes transposition easy. Contemporary electronic keyboards transpose, so that the same fingerings create the musical sound in any key.

A song or other composition may be published in different transpositions to assist performers. Electronic notation programs can transpose material to any key. This renders simple what was previously a time-consuming, highly skilled task.

Transposition also occurs within a single composition or improvisation, where a musical idea may move to different pitch levels. For example, in George Gershwin's 'Fascinating Rhythm,' the basic musical idea is stated at an original pitch level, and is then transposed up by the interval of a fourth. In such cases, transposition may be exact and will involve a change of key, with the intervals remaining precisely the same, or it may remain within the same key by altering the qualities of intervals – for example, by replacing a minor second with a major second. In a sequence, transposed repetitions typically conform to the scale of the key; for example, the sequential repetitions in the chorus of Frederick Hollander's 'Falling in Love Again' use major or minor seconds and thirds as necessary. Exact transposition can create a sequence that modulates rapidly, something that is far more likely in Western art music than in popular styles.

Transposing Instruments

Many instruments play from notation with a uniform relation to pitch. If a piano, guitar, violin and flute play the note written as middle C (*c*), their pitches will match. For many other instruments, called transposing instruments, notation differs from actual sound. Sometimes, the name of the instrument identifies the transposition. When a B♭ clarinet plays notated C, it produces B♭; an A clarinet playing the same notation produces A. The standard modern French horn plays a fifth below notation. The double bass and bass guitar sound an octave below notation, while the soprano recorder sounds an octave above notation. Saxophones, despite their different registers, are notated uniformly in the treble clef. The chart shows the sounds produced by various instruments in the saxophone family in performing a notated middle C (*c*):

Instrument	Notation	Sound
E♭ soprano saxophone	middle C (*c*)	e♭ a third higher
E♭ alto Saxophone	middle C (*c*)	E♭ a sixth below
B♭ tenor saxophone	middle C (*c*)	B♭¹ an octave and a second below
E♭ baritone saxophone	middle C (*c*)	E♭¹ an octave and a sixth below

Notation for transposing instruments typically shows a different key signature from that for instruments at standard (or concert) pitch. Detailed information about transposing instruments appears in standard textbooks of arranging and orchestration.

Discographical References

Dietrich, Marlene. 'Falling in Love Again.' *A Portrait of Marlene Dietrich.* Gallerie 445. *2000*: UK.

Lanin, Sam. 'Fascinating Rhythm'/'Tell Her in the Springtime.' Columbia 279-D. 1924: USA.

18. Melody

Blue Note

The term 'blue note' has customarily referred to notes in blues – as well as in jazz, soul, rock and other related genres – whose perceived pitch center or fundamental is understood to be at variance with the pitches of the Western diatonic scale. The most common view is that blue notes in blues are constituted largely through a lowering of the third, seventh and, less often, fifth degrees of the diatonic scale. The lowering of the fifth degree is understood to be more common in jazz.

The view that these notes arose through the inability of African-American musicians to conform to the pitches of the Western diatonic scale has been dismissed as ethnocentric and invalid. The more common wisdom is that – as with oral-aural musics in general – the pitches of the African and African-derived musical traditions that may have contributed to the formation of blues were, in terms of Western musicological thinking, 'bent.' That is, although the pitches are perceived – perhaps by Euro-American, European and Western musicological ears – as having a recognizable tonal center or fundamental, they are also heard as being mobile, 'not fixed precisely,' moving 'through a tiny continuum of pitches,' and varying 'according to the performer's instinct and expression.' The blue note assumed to be constituted through a flattened third is heard, for example, as sliding 'from a lowered third up to proper third and then back again' (Robinson and Kernfeld 2002, 245).

The assumption here is that, rather than resulting from the inability of African-American musicians to conform to the relatively stable pitches of the Western diatonic scale, blue notes arise as a consequence of 'the blues African heritage' (Robinson and Kernfeld 2002, 245). Oliver (1970), for example, is on record as saying

that 'the "blue notes" themselves are found in Africa' (95). Allied to this view is the theory that the scales of many or some of the African and African-derived musical traditions that may have contributed to the formation of blues were pentatonic, that blues themselves are basically pentatonic – both melodically and harmonically – and that the concept of the 'blue note' therefore arises as a way of explaining the nonconformity of some pitches in blues and related genres to the Western diatonic scale and its related harmonic structures (see, for example, Wishart 1977).

Wishart (1977) argues that the pitch inflections characteristic of blues performances 'should be understood as part of a fundamentally different conception of correct intonation, rather than the result of an inability on the part of the blacks to accommodate Western diatonic skills' (169). Consistent with this view is the realization that not just certain degrees of the Western diatonic scale are 'bent' to give rise to 'blue notes,' but that, in fact, practically every degree of the scale – as well as the five notes extra to the scale, the 'chromatic' notes – can be 'bent.' Titon (1977), for example, notes that 'down-home accompanying instruments were set to the fixed Western division of the octave into twelve chromatic tones, but this did not prevent musicians from obtaining other tones.' Titon continues: 'Pianists, for example, by "crushing" notes (playing adjacent keys), made particular pitches ambiguous; guitarists slid a bottleneck on top of the strings to obtain infinite gradations of pitch; fiddlers had no frets to worry about; wind musicians "bent" notes in the Western twelve-tone scale by changing the force of their breath or manipulating the shape of the tongue, lips, and mouth' (1977, 154). This view has more recently been supported by Weisethaunet (2001), who asserts that 'every note of the twelve-tone chromatic scale may appear in a blues tune, possibly also as "blue notes," because microtonality, attack, and timbre variation are such essential parts of blues expression' (101).

Weisethaunet also supports the view that blue notes 'should be understood as part of a fundamentally different conception of correct intonation,' arguing, for example, that 'the harmonic foundation of blues, rock, and some jazz styles, in emic terms [the terms of practitioners rather than external analysts] and performance practice, in fact represents both a totally different conception of harmony to that of the Western functional (tonal) harmony and also represents a different comprehension of dissonance/consonance in music' (2001, 99). Importantly, this view has received support from blues performers themselves. Roberts (1973), for example, reports that 'Courlander was once told by an Alabama blues singer that he "played with notes" just as he "played with the beats," which suggests not vagueness about pitch, which some authors have attributed to black singers, but a high degree of tonal sophistication' (188–89). Again, 'Big' Bill Broonzy is on record as saying that 'to really sing the *old* blues that I learned in Mississippi I have to go back to my sound and not the right chords as the musicians have told me to make.' As Broonzy concludes, the 'right' chords 'don't work with the real blues . . . the blues didn't come out of no book and them real chords did' (quoted in Middleton 1972, 37).

The problem with the term and concept of the 'blue note' is that, as Weisethaunet asserts, they are 'derived from Western musicology.' As he concludes, 'the "blue note" may not even exist as an element of emic theory: its origin was surely invented to describe the structure of "Negro" music as opposed to that of European music' (2001, 100). The difficulty with the term is that it emerges from an understanding of music in which harmonic structure is seen – in a sense, quite literally, through the frozen artifact of the score – as fundamental to music, rather than from an understanding of music in which performance, and therefore process, is understood to be fundamental. Accordingly, Weisethaunet argues that '"blue notes" may obviously be seen as "participatory discrepancies" following Keil's definition which tries to capture the fundamental feature of participation, interaction and sociality of music performance' (2001, 103; see also Keil and Feld 1994, 96). B.B. King lends force to this understanding when he says, 'I think in terms of not just playing a note but making sure that every note I play means something.' As he concludes: 'You need to take time with these notes. If you just play notes and not put anything into it, you'll never have a distinctive style. You need to put yourself into what you are doing. It will set you apart from the person just playing the guitar. In other words, make music' (1973, 15).

Bibliography

Keil, Charles, and Feld, Steven. 1994. *Music Grooves: Essays and Dialogues.* Chicago: University of Chicago Press.

King, B.B. 1973. *Blues Guitar: A Method,* comp. and ed. Jerry Snyder. New York: C. Hansen.

Middleton, Richard. 1972. *Pop Music and the Blues: A Study of the Relationship and Its Significance.* London: Victor Gollancz.

Oliver, Paul. 1970. *Savannah Syncopators: African Retentions in the Blues.* New York: Stein and Day.

Roberts, John Storm. 1973. *Black Music of Two Worlds.* London: Allen Lane.

Robinson, J. Bradford, and Kernfeld, Barry. 2002. 'Blue Note.' In *The New Grove Dictionary of Jazz,* ed. Barry Kernfeld. London: Macmillan, 245–46.

Titon, Jeff Todd. 1977. *Early Downhome Blues: A Musical and Cultural Analysis.* Urbana, IL: University of Illinois Press.

Weisethaunet, Hans. 2001. 'Is There Such a Thing as the "Blue Note"?' *Popular Music* 20(1): 99–116.

Wishart, Trevor. 1977. 'Some Observations on the Social Stratification of Twentieth-Century Music.' In John Shepherd et al., *Whose Music?: A Sociology of Musical Languages.* London: Latimer New Dimensions, 166–77.

JOHN SHEPHERD

Break

The term 'break,' originally used in jazz, describes the practise whereby a single instrument briefly becomes the focal point of all musical activity. This usually takes the form of a short solo passage during which the other instruments in the ensemble are silent. In modern popular music, this term is used synonymously with 'solo,' where one part, often virtuosic in character, becomes the central point of attention for a passage or section.

In jazz, a break is a passage, usually lasting one or two bars and situated at the close of a section (for example, a 10- or 12-bar blues cycle), that forms a distinctive yet cohesive link between one section and the next. Typically, the jazz ensemble stops playing, leaving a solo instrument, such as the trumpet or saxophone, to play a short instrumental figure that commonly retains the harmonic and rhythmic characteristics of the preceding section. The point at which the ensemble rejoins the solo instrument marks the beginning of the ensuing passage. Occasionally, a break may occur within, rather than at the close of, a section; here, it can be employed as a hiatus to mark a deliberate contrast in arrangement, material and/or texture.

Although documentary evidence is lacking, it is likely that the break first appeared in African-American culture in the second half of the nineteenth century. By the middle of the second decade of the twentieth century, it was sufficiently widely recognized to be imitated, in stylized form, by popular concert bands such as the Victor Military Band (Schuller 1968, 249). In the early development of jazz, musicians from New Orleans subjected the idea to particularly imaginative treatment. The two-cornet breaks by Joe 'King' Oliver and Louis Armstrong in performances by Oliver's Creole Jazz Band at Chicago's Lincoln Gardens in 1922–24, and in studio recordings such as 'Snake Rag,' were eagerly anticipated by listeners. An improvised vocal break ('Oh, play that thing!') by banjoist Bill Johnson on the band's first recording of 'Dippermouth Blues' immediately became such an integral element that the piece could scarcely be performed subsequently, by any musicians anywhere in the world, without its inclusion (Lyttelton 1980, 50). Armstrong's individual prowess in the break was such that a book was published in 1927 containing transcriptions of 125 of his breaks. Most breaks were improvised, but in the piano music of 'Jelly Roll' Morton, which formed the basis of much of his band music, many breaks were written in, as part of a compositional framework (Schuller 1968, 147). In some instances – for example, 'Jelly Roll Blues' (originally written in 1905 and first published in 1915) – the pre-composed break was placed at the beginning of a section (Dapogny 1982, 293–302).

With time, the concept of the break has been expanded and confused with that of the solo. This has occurred to such an extent that, in popular music, the two are often used to denote the same practise. For example, in rock music the phrase 'guitar break' can be the term applied to a complete guitar solo lasting the full duration of a verse. In such cases, the accompaniment does not usually cease, as in jazz, but the position of the solo instrument is changed, most commonly taking the place of the lead vocal line (for example, in a recorded mix, moving from 'backing' to 'center stage').

Breaks, particularly those found in 1970s funk records, were also important in the development of the genre of hip-hop. DJs noticed that the break (usually a drum break) was the high point of the song for their audience, and they hit upon the idea of alternately playing two copies of the same record, cutting between them to extend the break indefinitely. This technique, or adaptations of it (such as sampling and looping a break), became the principle behind the production of hip-hop, particularly in the early years of the genre. Thus, 'break' also came to mean, at least with reference to hip-hop,

an extract of a piece of music used in a new musical context.

A form of break more akin to the term as it was originally used in jazz can be found in much late twentieth-century electronic dance music, such as drum 'n' bass or techno. Here, in a technique called a 'dropout,' the instrumentation is removed to leave a single part (for example, a rapid quarter-note-beat Roland TR808 bass drum) to sound alone for an indefinite period. The surrounding instrumentation is then reintroduced gradually, occasionally in a sporadic manner, to generate a sense of excitement for the listener as the return to full texture is anticipated.

Bibliography

Dapogny, James, ed. 1982. *The Collected Piano Music of Ferdinand 'Jelly Roll' Morton*. Washington, DC: Smithsonian Institution Press.

Kernfeld, Barry. 1986. 'Break.' In *The New Grove Dictionary of American Music*, Vol. 1, ed. H. Wiley Hitchcock and Stanley Sadie. London and New York: Macmillan, 289.

Lyttelton, Humphrey. 1980. *The Best of Jazz: Basin Street to Harlem – Jazz Masters and Masterpieces 1917–1930*. Harmondsworth: Penguin Books.

Schuller, Gunther. 1968. *Early Jazz: Its Roots and Musical Development*. New York: Oxford University Press.

Sheet Music

Armstrong, Louis. 1927. *125 Jazz Breaks for Cornet*. Chicago: Melrose Music Co.

Morton, 'Jelly Roll.' 1915. '(Original) Jelly Roll Blues.' Chicago: Will Rossiter.

Discographical References

Oliver, Joe 'King.' 'Dippermouth Blues.' Gennett 5132. 1923: USA.

Oliver, Joe 'King.' 'Snake Rag.' Gennett 5184. 1923: USA.

CHRIS SEDWELL with SIMON BOTTOM

Fill

The term 'fill' denotes a short musical episode in which an instrument executes a brief solo, either in response to a preceding musical event or to mark a specific point in the overall structure of a composition. Unlike a break, a fill is usually of very short duration, sometimes only a couple of beats, and does not necessarily require the same subordination of the accompaniment; as fills tend to occur as part of the constructed texture of a work, they generally do not require its significant reorganization.

One extremely common type of fill found in all types of popular music is the 'drum fill.' Typically, this is a short ornamentation of the basic rhythm pattern at a significant point of a musical section – for instance, at the end of a verse to denote the arrival of the chorus. An example can be heard in Alanis Morissette's 'Ironic,' where the final bar of the second verse sees the standard drum pattern interrupted by a brief one-and-a-half beat roll on snare and toms before returning to the original pattern for the first bar of the chorus. Fills of a similar nature, although not necessarily executed on the drums, occur in genres such as Dixieland jazz and ragtime, where an instrument such as the piano may provide a short decorative figure on the closing beats of a musical passage. Fills may also occur regularly throughout a section, particularly in guitar-based music such as blues and rock, when the guitar is used to provide short responses to the vocal melody. In such instances, a fill can take the form of an overlapping musical line, as in Dire Straits's 'Brothers in Arms,' where the electric guitar assumes an instrumental word-painting role.

Discographical References

Dire Straits. 'Brothers in Arms.' *Brothers in Arms*. Vertigo 824499 2. *1985*: USA.

Morissette, Alanis. 'Ironic.' *Jagged Little Pill*. Maverick 45901. *1995*: USA.

CHRIS SEDWELL

Hook

The term 'hook' is used to refer to that part of a song's musical and lyrical material through which the song remains in popular memory and is instantly recognizable in popular consciousness. The elements of a hook's musical material that tend to be foremost in popular memory and consciousness are the melody and also the timbre: the tone color of a singer's voice and of the song's instrumentation. In the majority of cases, the melodic and lyrical material of a hook come from the opening of a song's chorus, and may be constituted by the whole of the chorus. However, this is not incontrovertibly the case. As Kasha and Hirschhorn (1979) note, hooks may involve 'one note or a series of notes . . . a lyric phrase, full lines or an entire verse' (28). An important aspect of the hook is that it keeps recurring. This, indeed, is one of the hook's most important characteristics. In this, it differs from the verses of songs. Although the melodic, harmonic and timbral material of verses may recur, the lyrics invariably change.

In fulfilling this role in popular memory and consciousness, the hook reveals two important characteristics: the psychological and the commercial. In the words of Bennett (1983), the hook is an 'attention grabber' (30). According to Kuroff (1982), it is 'a memorable "catch" phrase or melody line which is repeated in a song' (397). In the thinking of Burns (1987), the term 'connotes being caught or trapped, as when a fish is hooked, and also addiction, as when one is hooked on

a drug' (1). And in the words of Shaw (1982), the hook is 'an appealing musical sequence or phrase, a bit of harmony or sound, or a rhythmic figure that grabs or hooks a listener . . . virtually no hit record is without a bit of music or words so compelling that it worms its way into memory and won't go away' (177). Therein lies the hook's commercial importance. According to Kasha and Hirschhorn, hooks are 'the foundation of commercial songwriting, particularly hit-single writing.' The hook is 'what you're selling' (1979, 28).

Effective hooks can be so powerful that they take on an existence independent of the song of which they are a part. Middleton (1990) identifies this possibility in invoking the work of Adorno: 'In popular music . . . the category of the "idea" (a relatively independent, memorable element within a totality . . .) lives on, and with it a sense of creative spontaneity . . . The music industry term for this is a "hook"' (51; see also Adorno 1976, 34–37). A good example of such 'independence' is provided by Tammy Wynette's song, 'Stand By Your Man.' The hook to this song seems to imply that women should be supportive of their male partners and, in so doing, fulfill a stereotypical role of female subservience to male dominance. However, as Shuker (1994) points out, placed in the context of the entire song, the hook conveys a very different message: 'The verse [presents] the hardships women face in their relationships with men . . . while the last line [of the verse] is a neatly condescending assertion of women's superior gender status . . . Wynette was using "Stand By Your Man" to make an ironic statement about the contradictory dimensions of women's experience of relationships' (139).

The powerful and independent status of hooks can be argued to rest largely, but also contradictorily, on their repetitive character. As Burns points out: 'While hooks in the form of repetition may, to an extent, be "the foundation of commercial songwriting" and record-making, repetition is meaningless without its opposite, change' (1987, 1). Hooks therefore form a vital aspect of the economies of desire present in popular music: the desire for that which is the same, familiar and safe in the context of an often subtly shifting background. It is this enticing opposition of sameness and difference grounded in the everyday that comes to be represented and encapsulated through the hook. As Middleton concludes: 'Popular music's investigation of "everyday life" . . . is apparent in lyric content and in the deliberately cultivated banalities, "hooks" and repetitions of the music' (1990, 98).

A systematic investigation and categorization of hooks is to be found in Burns (1987). In this article, Burns is concerned with 'the definition and classification of the structural elements of music as specifically exemplified in pop records, and with the analysis of how songwriters, performers and record producers manipulate these structural elements through use of repetition, variation and modulation [here defined as "a major change in any structural element (of music)"] to produce hooks' (1987, 2).

Bibliography

Adorno, Theodor W. 1976. *Introduction to the Sociology of Music,* trans. E.B. Ashton. New York: Seabury Press.

Bennett, Roy C. 1983. *The Songwriter's Guide to Writing and Selling Hit Songs.* Englewood Cliffs, NJ: Prentice-Hall.

Burns, Gary. 1987. 'A Typology of "Hooks" in Popular Records.' *Popular Music* 6(1): 1–20.

Kasha, Al, and Hirschhorn, Joel. 1979. *If They Ask You, You Can Write a Song.* New York: Simon and Schuster.

Kuroff, B.N., ed. 1982. *1983 Songwriter's Market: Where to Sell Your Songs.* Cincinnati, OH.

Middleton, Richard. 1990. *Studying Popular Music.* Milton Keynes: Open University Press.

Shaw, Arnold. 1982. *Dictionary of American Pop/Rock.* New York: Schirmer Books.

Shuker, Roy. 1994. *Understanding Popular Music.* London: Routledge.

Discographical Reference

Wynette, Tammy. 'Stand By Your Man.' Epic 10398. *1968*: USA.

JOHN SHEPHERD

Lick

The term 'lick,' ensconced in jazz parlance since the early 1930s, refers to a melodic fragment, gesture, phrase, formula, idea or motif used in improvisation. Most probably, the term is derived from the colloquial meaning of 'a blow,' which was adapted in jazz argot to mean 'play an instrument.' Jazz musicians often develop and rely on an arsenal of these personalized formulaic motifs during improvisation, and frequently employed licks can become clichés associated with their individual style. Part of jazz education, that of learning the jazz improvisatory language, includes copying the licks of other musicians and employing them in one's own improvisations. Since the late 1920s, published transcriptions of licks and solos have been commercially available to facilitate this process. The first such publication was a collection of Louis Armstrong's improvisations in two volumes, *50 Hot Choruses for Cornet* and *125 Jazz Breaks for Cornet*, published by the Melrose Brothers of Chicago in 1927.

The term 'lick' has been adopted in rock and other popular musics as well, where it is employed in a similar fashion. It can also refer to specific fingering patterns that can be carried out on any instrument. For instance, the term is used to describe (electric) guitar fingering and picking techniques that help create distinctive note patterns and sounds. As in jazz, during the first decades of rock licks were passed on aurally, that is, learned by ear; later, they became the subject of handbooks and training manuals, which helped to improve and standardize rock guitar techniques.

Discography

Louis Armstrong's '50 Hot Choruses for Cornet' (1927) as Recreated by Bent Persson, Vol. 1–2. Kenneth CKS 3411. *1996*: Sweden.

Louis Armstrong's '50 Hot Choruses for Cornet' (1927) as Recreated by Bent Persson, Vol. 2–3. Kenneth CKS 3412. *2002*: Sweden.

Louis Armstrong's '50 Hot Choruses for Cornet' (1927) as Recreated by Bent Persson, Vol. 3–4. Kenneth CKS 3413. *1986*: Sweden.

CHRIS WASHBURNE and FRANCO FABBRI

Melisma

The term 'melisma' refers to a string of several notes sung to one syllable. 'Melismatic' is usually opposed to 'syllabic,' the latter meaning that each note is sung to a different syllable. The words 'melismatic' and 'syllabic' are used relatively to indicate the general character of a vocal line in terms of notes per syllable, some lines being more melismatic, others more syllabic. A sequence of notes sung staccato (detached or cut up) to the same syllable – for instance, 'oh – oh – oh – oh – oh' in Buddy Holly's 'Peggy Sue' or Righeira's 'Vamos a la Playa' – does not constitute a melisma because each consecutive 'oh' is articulated as if it were a separate syllable. A melisma is therefore always executed legato, each constituent note joined seamlessly to the preceding and/or subsequent one. Since inhalation before the start of a new phrase constitutes a break in the melodic flow, no melisma can last longer than the duration of one vocal exhalation. Since several notes are sung to one syllable within the duration of one musical phrase, long note values are uncommon in melismas.

Melismatic singing differs more radically than syllabic singing from everyday speech in that it is uncommon to change pitch even once, let alone several times, within the duration of one spoken syllable. When such spoken pitch change does occur in English – for instance, a quick descending octave portamento on the word 'Why?' – it tends to signal heightened emotion. Together with the general tendency to regard melody as a form of heightened speech transcending the everyday use of words, it is perhaps natural that melismatic singing is often thought to constitute a particularly emotional type of vocal expression. Such connotations are further underlined by the fact that some of the most common words to be sung melismatically in English-language popular song are exclamations (for example, 'oh!,' 'ah!,' 'yeah!,' as in Luca Vitone's *Rock Suite in Y – Oh Yeah!*) or emotionally charged concepts (for example, 'love,' 'feel,' 'al*right*,' 'pain,' 'fly,' 'good*bye*,' 'why?').

Melismas occur in most musical cultures – for instance, in the muezzin's call to prayer, in RAJ music (for example, Cheb Khaled's 'El Ghatli'), in the *alap* sections of northern Indian *dhrupad* performances (for example, the Dagar Brothers' *Dhrupads – The Music of India, III*), in the Sámi *joik* (see Edström 1977), and in the Russian *bïlïnï*, the Ukrainian *dumy* and the Romanian *doina* (see Ling 1997, 84–89 and 106–107). They also occur in most plainchant settings of *Alleluia* and *Kyrie eleison*, as well as at particularly emotional points in arias from the European opera and oratorio repertoire. While Lutheran chorales are largely syllabic, a significant minority of low-church hymns do feature melismatic passages (see Ex. 1).

Particularly influential on the development of melisma in Anglo-American popular song are various florid, highly ornamented, often pentatonic vocal traditions originating in the British Isles (for example, Hebridean 'home worship,' as heard on *Musique Celtique (Îles Hébrides)*) – that is, the sort of vocal delivery found in Gaelic keening (*caoine*) and slow, solo ballad singing in the *sean-nós* style (for example, as in Mick Moloney's 'Seán A Duír A' Ghleanna'; see also Ex. 2). These 'old' ways of singing appear to have been the antecedents of the florid vocal lines produced by the Old Baptist and similar 'dissenting' congregations of the United States' mid-South (for example, Doc Watson's 'Amazing Grace'; see also Ex. 3 and Wicks 1989).

Such vocal techniques have strongly influenced the popular music of both white and black US Americans, the former through white gospel music into songs by country artists like Dolly Parton, Emmylou Harris, Bonnie Raitt and George Jones (see Wicks 1989), the latter through black gospel singers into the mainstream of the international pop music market. The protracted, proclamatory 'We – – – – – – – ll!' at the start of 'Shout' (in versions by both the Isley Brothers and Lulu) provides an early example of the black gospel melisma in Anglo-American hit recordings. Similar melismas were not uncommon in Motown vocal lines (for example, the Marvelettes' 'Mr. Po-o-o-o-stman' in 'Please Mr. Postman'), nor in Merseybeat influenced by gospel styles (for example, the Beatles' 'Please Mr. Postman'; see also Ex. 4 and Ex. 5).

Since the types of melisma mentioned here have, since World War II, been most widely disseminated through recordings made or influenced by African-American artists, it is often assumed that such melismatic techniques are of West African origin. However, since, for example, none of the 40 musical examples given in Nketia (1974, 147–74) in the chapters dealing with vocal lines in African music contain syllables set to more than two separate notes, the popular assumption that melismatic ornamentation is inherently 'black' must be challenged in the same way that the identification of the banjo (an instrument of African origin) with 'white' music must be regarded as historically inaccurate (Tagg 1989).

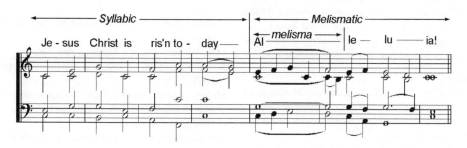

Example 1 *Jesus Christ is Ris'n Today* (Methodist Hymn Book, 1933, No. 204).

Example 2 Extract from *Cuil Duibh-Re*, as performed by Diarmuid O'Súillebháin (transcr. Tomás O'Canainn, reprinted in Ling 1997, 92).

Example 3 Extract from *Guide Me O Thou Great Jehovah*, Old Regular Baptist congregation; adapted from transcr. in Wicks (1989, 73).

Example 4 The Beatles: 'Not a Second Time' (1963).

Example 5 The Searchers: 'Goodbye My Love' (1965).

In recent decades, pentatonic melismas deriving from gospel traditions have become very common in recordings by such solo divas as Whitney Houston, who, for instance, on the word 'much' in the phrase 'I wish I didn't like it so much' from 'So Emotional,' launches into a florid pentatonic melisma consisting of at least six short separate notes each time the phrase occurs in the lead-up to the chorus. These virtuoso techniques had become such a mannerism of abandon by the 1980s that they were easily parodied – for example, by film composer Nile Rodgers in the 'Soul Glow' shampoo jingle from the Eddie Murphy movie *Coming to America* (1988), or by Frank Zappa who, in 'You Are What You Is,' set prosaic concepts like 'appropriate' and 'the post office' to ecstatically delivered pentatonic gospel melismas.

Bibliography

Edström, Karl-Olof. 1977. *Den samiska musikkulturen. En källkritisk översikt* [Sámi Music Culture: A Source-Critical Overview]. Göteborg: Skrifter från Musikvetenskapliga institutionen, 1.

Ling, Jan. 1997. *A History of European Folk Music*, trans. L. and R. Schenk. Rochester, NY: University of Rochester Press.

Nketia, J.H. Kwabena. 1974. *The Music of Africa*. New York: Norton.

Tagg, Philip. 1989. 'Open Letter: "Black Music," "Afro-American Music" and "European Music."' *Popular Music* 8(3): 285–98.

Wicks, Sammie Ann. 1989. 'A Belated Salute to the "Old Way" of "Snaking" the Voice on Its (ca) 345th Birthday.' *Popular Music* 8(1): 59–96.

Discographical References

Beatles, The. 'Not a Second Time.' *With the Beatles*. Parlophone PCS 3045. *1963*: UK.

Beatles, The. 'Please Mr. Postman.' *With the Beatles*. Parlophone PCS 3045. *1963*: UK.

Dagar Brothers, The. *Dhrupads – The Music of India, III*. Bärenreiter Musicaphon BM30 2018. n.d.: Germany.

Holly, Buddy. 'Peggy Sue.' Coral 61885. *1957*: USA.

Houston, Whitney. 'So Emotional.' Arista 9642. *1987*: USA.

Isley Brothers, The. 'Shout.' RCA-Victor 47-7588. *1959*: USA.

Khaled, Cheb. 'El Ghatli.' *Khaled*. Barclay 5118152. *1992*: France.

Lulu. 'Shout.' Decca F 11884. *1964*: UK.

Marvelettes, The. 'Please Mr. Postman.' Tamla 54046. *1961*: USA.

Moloney, Mick. 'Seán A Duír A' Ghleanna' (Irish trad.). As performed at Göteborg College of Music, September 1972 (private recording).

Musique Celtique (Îles Hébrides). Ocora OCR 45. *1968*: France.

Righeira. 'Vamos a la Playa.' A&M MAM 137. *1983*: USA.

Searchers, The. 'Goodbye My Love.' Pye 7N 15794. *1965*: UK.

Vitone, Luca. *Rock Suite in Y – Oh Yeah!*. AMF 1361. *1998*: Italy.

Watson, Doc. 'Amazing Grace' (lining-out version). *The Folk Box*. Elektra/Folkways Elektra EKL-9001. *1964*: USA.

Zappa, Frank. 'You Are What You Is.' *You Are What You Is*. CBS 88560. *1981*: USA.

Filmography

Coming to America, dir. John Landis. 1988. USA. 116 mins. Comedy. Original music by Nile Rodgers.

PHILIP TAGG

Melody

'Melody,' from the Greek *melos* (meaning a song or the music to which a song is set) and *ōdē* (meaning an ode, song or poem), is defined as (a) a monodic tonal sequence, accompanied or unaccompanied, that is perceived as a musical statement with a distinct rhythmic profile and pitch contour; (b) the monodic musical foreground to which accompaniment and harmony are, at least within most popular musical traditions of Europe and the Americas, understood to provide the background; and (c) all such monodic tonal sequences and/or aspects of musical foreground within one complete song (for example, '"Auld Lang Syne" is a popular Scottish melody').

It should be noted that *mélodie, Melodie, melodia* and *melodi* (French, German, Italian/Spanish and Scandinavian languages, respectively) can, in popular parlance, sometimes denote the entirety of any tune or song (including lyrics and accompaniment) in which melody, defined according to (a) and (b) above, is a prominent feature.

Defining Parameters

General Characteristics of Popular Melody

It is difficult to be precise about which characteristics constitute melody, since it relies, according to definitions (a) and (b), on cultural consensus to determine its nature. Nevertheless, the following parameters, most of them documented by Stefani and Marconi (1992, 13–24), seem to determine what is more likely to be popularly understood, at least within a mainstream European or North American context, as typically melodic about a monodic tonal sequence:

— easy to recognise, to appropriate and to reproduce vocally;

— perceptible as occupying periods of time resembling those of normal or extended exhalation (the 'extended present' – that is, consisting of melodic phrases lasting between about two and 10 seconds);

— delivered at a rate ranging from that of medium to very slow speech;

— articulated with rhythmic fluidity and unbroken delivery of tonal material within one sequence: legato rather than staccato;

— distinctly profiled in terms of pitch (melodic contour) and rhythm (accentuation, meter, relative duration of constituent events);

— delivered with relative regularity and metric articulation of breathing;

— relatively simple in terms of tonal vocabulary;

— exhibits a tendency to change pitch by intervallic step rather than by leap (conjunctive rather than disjunctive flow);

— rarely spans more than one octave.

In other words, a monodic tonal sequence is less likely to be considered melodic if it is not clearly tonal, if it is difficult to appropriate and reproduce, if it is too long or too short, if its constituent notes are delivered too fast, if it consists of no more than one or two very long notes, if it is broken up into very short units consisting of just one or two notes, if there is little or no metrical regularity between phrases, if it exhibits no clear tonal or rhythmic profile, or if it is too chromatic, contains too many large intervallic leaps or covers too large a pitch range. Indeed, it is for just such reasons that monodic sequences of the following types, even though they may exhibit some important melodic traits, are less likely than nursery rhymes, folk tunes or jazz standards to be considered melodic: rap or hip-hop declamation and *Sprechgesang*, because of unclear tonal articulation; recitative, because of irregular metricity; and riffs, because they are too short. Even so, some riffs are more singable than the melodic lines they 'accompany' (for example, 'Layla' (Ex. 1) and 'Hoochie Coochie Man' (Waters)), while some literally monotonous monodic sequences of tones are still considered to be melody (for example, the verse parts of 'Samba de una nota só' (Ex. 2), 'Un homme et une femme' (Lai) and 'Subterranean Homesick Blues' (Dylan)). Moreover, important sections of some well-known melodies are based on little more than repetitions or sequential variations of motifs almost too short to qualify as melodic phrases: for example, 'Volare' (Ex. 3) and 'Autumn Leaves (Les feuilles mortes)' (Ex. 4).

Metaphorical Nomenclature

The nature of melody can also be understood by an examination of words and expressions either commonly associated or partly synonymous with 'melody.' For example, 'melodic line' emphasizes the monodic and sequential (horizontal) aspects of melody, while 'melodic phrase' and 'melodic statement' draw attention to the relationship between melody and human speech or declamation. 'Motive' and 'motif' denote movement by definition, and melodies are thought of as proceeding in two-dimensional space – forward, upward, downward and so on – often with culturally specific patterns of implication (expected or unexpected continuation (see Meyer 1987)). Melodic 'profile,'

Example 1 Derek and the Dominoes: 'Layla.'

Example 2 A. C. Jobim: 'Samba de una nota só.'

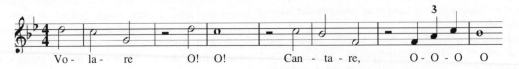

Example 3 D. Modugno: 'Volare.'

Example 4 'Autumn Leaves (Les feuilles mortes).'

'contour' and 'figure' refer to qualities of distinct linearity, shape and gesture. 'Strain,' meaning tune, evokes notions of distinct characteristics (cf. 'a genetic strain'), while 'lay,' an archaic synonym for melody, is defined as 'a song' or 'a short poem meant to be sung.'

'Tune' (a Middle English variant of 'tone') highlights melody's tonal nature, while 'air,' in the sense of tune, suggests speech, gesture and movement that have metaphorically taken off ('melody hath wings,' 'volare – cantare'; see Ex. 3), thereby emphasizing the notion of melody as heightened discourse transcending speech. These transcendent notions of melody can, in turn, be related to the connotations of monodic pitched declamation, which was necessitated, in the interests of comprehension and before the invention of microphones and public-address systems, by acoustic settings characterized by long reverberation times: for example, the chanting of prayers and biblical texts in cathedrals and large churches or the muezzin's call to prayer from the minaret across the town in the relative stillness of dawn or dusk. These notions are also related to the everyday observation that emotionally heightened speech exhibits greater variation in pitch and resembles melody more than does talking in a normal voice.

In short, melody is tonal monodic movement, both temporal and spatial, that is inextricably connected with human utterance – be it gestural or, in particular, vocal.

Typologies of Melody

Structurally, melodies resemble or differ from one another according to several factors: (a) pitch contour; (b) tonal vocabulary; (c) dynamics and mode of articulation (including phrasing); (d) rhythmic profile; and (e) metric and periodic organization. They can also be placed in 'experiential' (perceptual, semiotic) categories (Stefani and Marconi 1992, 111–229). Structural and experiential typologies are interrelated.

Structural Typologies

Pitch Contour   Figure 1 shows the basic types of pitch contour used by ethnomusicologists in the classification of melody (Skog and Bengtsson 1977). The con-

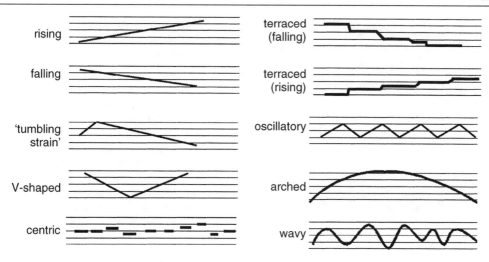

Figure 1 Melodic contour categories.

tour types are illustrated by the following examples: *rising* – Examples 5, 19a (phrase 1) and 19b (phrase 1); *falling* – Examples 6, 19a (phrase 2) and 19b (phrase 2); *tumbling* – Examples 7, 8, 9 and 18 (bars 1–2); *V-shaped* – Examples 10, 11 (bars 3–4) and 14 (bar 1); *centric* – Examples 12 and 13; *terraced* (*falling*) – Examples 11 (bars 1–2) and 14 (bars 3–4); *terraced* (*rising*) – Examples 14 (bars 2–3) and 18 (bars 4–9); *oscillatory* – Example 15 and the double-V shape of Example 10; *arched* – Example 16; and *wavy* – Example 17.

Boundaries between melodic contour types are fluid. For example, the double-V shape of Example 10 has an oscillating character, while parts of the oscillatory profile of Example 15 have the shape of a flat V. Similarly, many centric contours (Ex. 12 and Ex. 13) can also be heard as oscillating, while some 'wavy' phrases can be heard as short arcs (Ex. 17, bars 2–4 and 4–5). Moreover, a 'tumbling strain' is little more than an overriding melodic descent with an initial rising anacrusis or with intermediate subsidiary rises in pitch (hence 'tumbling'). It should also be noted that certain styles show a predilection for particular contours – for example, blues-related styles for the 'tumbling strain' (Ex. 7, Ex. 8 and Ex. 9). However, pitch contour alone is not enough to distinguish the style or character of one melody from that of another. Examples 19a and 19b illustrate how tonal vocabulary, rhythmic profile and metricity, not pitch contour, can be the operative distinguishing factors.

Tonal Vocabulary The popular device of putting major-key tunes into the minor and vice versa testifies to the fact that changing tonal vocabulary can radic-

ally alter the character of a melody. Example 20 shows the first six bars of the melody of the UK national anthem, first, as it actually is, in the major key (Ionian mode) (line 1) and, then, with the same melodic contour, rhythm, meter and so on, but in the following modes: Aeolian (or Dorian) (line 2), Phrygian (line 3), Hijjaz (line 4), major pentatonic (line 5) and minor pentatonic (line 6). All these variants would most probably be heard by members of the UK cultural mainstream as 'ethnic' or 'folksy': the second, fifth and sixth as, possibly, 'Celtic'; the fifth and sixth, conceivably also, as 'Chinese'; the third as vaguely 'Spanish'; and the fourth, most likely, as 'Arabic.' The same six bars could also be changed, without altering other factors, to create a dodecaphonic tone row that would produce an unsettling effect on most ears.

Dynamics and Mode of Articulation The structure and character of a melody are also determined by how loudly or softly it is presented in part or as a whole (yelling and crooning the same tune produce radically different effects); what timbre or instrument is used to articulate it – imagine Led Zeppelin's 'Whole Lotta Love' delivered bel canto, or a national anthem played on kazoo; in what tessitura it is executed (this influences whether it will sound growled or screeched, squeaky and strained); and, if lyrics are included, what kind of accent and diction are used – imagine Queen Elizabeth II delivering a Grandmaster Flash 'Message,' or a stirring union song being mumbled in the manner of Radiohead's Thom Yorke in 'Creep.' The characteristics of a melodic line are also determined by its phrasing and accentuation. Examples 21a and 21b are of identical length, melodic contour and tonal vocabu-

I get no   kick from champ - agne

Example 5 Cole Porter: 'I Get A Kick Out Of You' (1934).

Example 6 'The Raggle Taggle Gypsies' (English trad.) quoted from memory.

lary, but differ so radically in phrasing that Example 21b needs notating *alla breve*. Whereas the original version (Ex. 21a), with its staccato punch and syncopation, is well suited to the funky trickster character played by Eddie Murphy in *Beverly Hills Cop*, Example 21b bears more resemblance to some lyrical or pastoral

theme with an archaic flavor, and would be more appropriate played by strings than by a synthesizer of mid-1980s vintage.

Rhythmic Profile Just as they show the effect of differences in phrasing, Examples 21a and 21b also illustrate how a difference in rhythmic profile affects the character of melody. But rhythmic profile is related to bodily movement and posture as well as to patterns of language. The rhythmic profile of Example 21a – its staccato quality with short pauses, its lack of anacruses, its sudden disjunct leaps for agogic effect, and its anticipated downbeats (especially bar 4) – corresponds much more closely to a skipping or jumping movement than to the flowing, legato, constant type of movement inherent in the regularly measured downbeat dotted quarter notes, quarter notes and upbeat eighth notes of Example 21b.

Similar links between melodic rhythm and body movement can be found in work songs. For example, the slow, heavy task of hauling barges, with its repetitive to-and-fro of the arms, is better helped along by the kind of steady, measured rhythm and short phrases (as well as restricted oscillatory pitch contour) evident

(I'll) say it to you———   and I don't care if you get mad

you're 'bout the pret-tiest lit-tle girl———   That I ever——— had———

She's on-ly nine-teen ye-ar's old   She got ways   just like a ba-by child———

Noth-ing I can do to please   her

To make this your   wo-man feel—— sa-tis- fied

Example 7 Muddy Waters 'She's Nineteen Years Old' (cited by Miani 1992).

Example 8 Nashville Teens: Guitar introduction to 'Tobacco Road.'

I'll   buy   you a   dia-mond ring   my friend

Example 9 Beatles: 'Can't Buy Me Love' (1964).

Example 10 Ellington: 'Satin Doll' (1953, start of middle 8).

Example 11 'Warszawjanka' (Polish trad.).

Late   Saturday night   I saw a light   shine from your win-dow

Example 12 Billy J. Kramer and the Dakotas: 'From A Window' (1964).

Example 13 Mark Snow: 'The X-Files Theme' (1996).

O, the grand old Duke of York,   He had ten thousand men,   He marched them up to the top of the hill And he   marched them down again

Example 14 'The Grand Old Duke of York' (English trad.) quoted from memory.

Example 15 Beatles: 'If I Needed Someone' (1965).

Example 16 'Ack Värmeland du sköna' (Swedish trad.).

Example 17 P. DeRose: 'Deep Purple.'

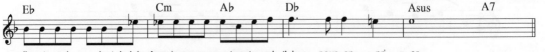

Example 18 Vigneault/Rochon: 'Je chante pour' (1973).

in Example 22, than by the brisk 2/4 or 6/8 call-and-response patterns of continuous melody spanning an octave that can be found in numerous British shanties. These evolved and are sung to help motivate nautical work involving quicker, more circular types of movement (for example, 'capstan' and 'windlass' songs, the latter sung when hoisting sails with a winch). 'A-

Roving,' 'Billy Boy' (Ex. 23), 'Bound for the Rio Grande,' 'What Shall We Do with the Drunken Sailor?,' 'Fire Down Below' and 'Johnny Come Down to Hilo' all belong to this category.

Clear links also exist between body and melodic rhythm in dance music. The mazurka, polka, schottische, jig, reel, slow waltz, Viennese waltz, samba,

Example 19 (a) 'Misirlou'; (b) E. Y. Harburg: 'Brother, Can You Spare A Dime?'

Example 20 'God Save the Queen': commutations of tonal vocabulary.

Example 21 Faltermeyer: 'Axel F' (1984) – (a) original; (b) as legato tune.

cueca, cha-cha, rumba, tango and so on exhibit unique and easily identifiable traits of melodic rhythm. Similar observations can be made about differences between the melodic rhythms of lullabies, marches, dirges, cattle calls, field hollers and so on, in each of which melodic rhythm tallies with the relevant type of bodily activity and/or acoustic conditions of the activity.

Since melody is so often a matter of singing words, melodic rhythm is also determined by the rhythm of the language in which those words are sung. For example, a melodic phrase ending ♪|♪ ♩., especially with a descending pitch contour (see Example 24 at *'negro,' 'rojo,' 'el día,' 'cantaría'*), is less likely to occur in a song in English than in one in a Latin language, as evidenced by the following trisyllabic words and phrases: *'volare,' 'cantare,' 'amore,' 'nel cuore'* (Italian), *'querida,' 'contigo,' 'belleza,' 'te quiero,' 'llorando,' 'tris-teza,' 'partido,' 'destino,' 'mi alma,' 'la noche,' 'y siento,'*

Example 22 'Song of the Volga Boat Men' (Russian trad.), as quoted by Ling (1997, 41).

Example 23 Capstan Shanty 'Billy Boy' (Northumbrian trad.).

Example 24 Ferlosio: 'El gallo negro.'

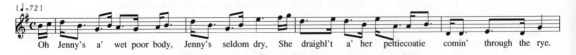

Example 25 'Comin' Thru The Rye' (Scottish trad.).

'tan solo,' 'en pena,' 'mi vida,' 'tus ojos,' 'tu pelo,' 'me mata' (Spanish, from tango lyrics; see Vilariño 1981a, 1981b). On the other hand, phrases starting with the onbeat 'Scotch snap' – |♪ ♩. or ♪ ♪. (inverted dotting) – especially with a rising pitch contour, are unlikely to appear in Germanic or Latin-language songs, simply because, except for Gaelic and Hungarian, English is the only European language to feature this trait (for example, 'mother,' 'brother,' 'do it,' 'hit it' or, in Example 25, at 'Jenny,' 'body,' 'pettie,' 'coatie' and 'coming').

Culturally Specific Melodic Formulae Melodies can also be recognized as belonging to particular cultures not only because of idiosyncracies of language rhythm, but also because particular turns of melodic phrase have

become, by convention, associated with these cultures. This observation applies not only to patterns of melodic ornamentation – for example, the onbeat ♫♫ ♩ figure often found in popular notions of Hispanic melody (Ex. 26a, Ex. 26b and Ex. 26c) or the one-note sixteenth-note triplets of Irish traditional music (Ex. 27) – but also to more substantial patterns of pitch contour and rhythmic profile.

Major key phrases descending to degree 6 (the final notes of Examples 28a, 28b and 28c) are typical of many traditional melodies from the British Isles, as are pentatonic melodic cadences of the types 8(1)-6-5 (Ex. 30, bar 3, first time) and 6-1 (Ex. 30, bar 3, second time) and those containing repeated final tonics (Ex. 29a, Ex. 29b and Ex. 29c) or final fifths (Ex. 29d).

Example 26 Hispanicisms in library music: (a) 'Cordigliera'; (b) Duncan: 'Wine Festival'; (c) Haider: 'Spanish Autumn.'

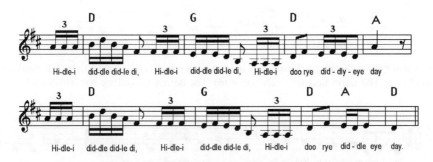

Hi-dle-i did-dle did-le di, Hi-dle-i did-dle did-le di, Hi-dle-i doo rye did-dly-eye day

Hi-dle-i did-dle did-le di, Hi-dle-i did-dle did-le di, Hi-dle-i doo rye did-dle eye day.

Example 27 'Poitín' (Irish trad.) – semiquaver triplets.

Strings of appoggiatura, on the other hand, which are highly unusual in popular melody from English-speaking and Celtic spheres, are very common in popular melody of the European classical tradition (Ex. 31) and its pastiches (Ex. 32) or of Arabic origin (Ex. 33 and Ex. 34). Finally, the (5)-4-1 cadence is typical of traditional Russian melody (Ex. 35a and Ex. 35b), while 8(1)-#7-5 patterns are an idiosyncratic trait of certain types of traditional Scandinavian melody (Ex. 36 and Ex. 37).

Patterns of Recurrence   Melody can also be categorized according to the manner in which constituent phrases or motifs are organized into a larger whole in patterns of variation and recurrence. Middleton (1983) suggests a sliding scale of musical syntaxes stretching from a *monadic* (circular, mythic, unchanging) to an *infinite set* (linear, narrative, teleological, 'nothing to be heard twice'), a scale along which any type of musical statement, including melody, can be placed.

Monadic melody is typical for song in which narrat-

Fare - well to friends of Dub - lin town, I bid ye all A - dieu.

We brave - ly fought and con - quered at Ross and Wex - ford town

O, sol - dier, sol - dier, won't you mar-ry me with your mus-ket, fife and drum?

Example 28 (a) 'Rossa's Farewell to Erin' (Irish trad.); (b) 'The Boys of Wexford' (Irish trad.); (c) 'Soldier, Soldier' (English. trad.), quoted from memory.

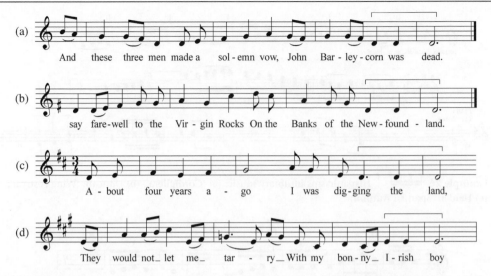

Example 29 Repeated final note cadence formulae: (a) 'John Barleycom' (English trad.); (b) 'The Banks of Newfound-land' (English trad.); (c) 'The Kerry Recruit' (Irish trad.); (d) 'The Bonny Labouring Boy' (Irish trad.).

Example 30 'Skye Boat Song' (Scottish trad., quoted from memory).

Example 31 Carissimi: Aria 'I Triumph!' (Vittoria!).

Example 32 ABBA: 'Fernando' (1975).

Example 33 Egyptian trad.

Example 34 'Mameluk,' aka 'Aya-Zehn' (Egyptian trad.).

Example 35 Russian 5-4-1 melodic cadences:
(a) 'Podmoskovskoye Vechera,' quoted from memory; (b) Aturov: 'Partisans' Song.'

Nu li - der det till Mi - ka - e - li-da- gen, då säl - bu-kullor - na tjänt ut sitt år.

Example 36 'Mikaelidagen' (Swedish trad.), as quoted in Ling (1964, 114).

Vår - vind - ar fris - ka le - ka och vis - ka lun - der - na kring likt äls - kan -de par

Example 37 'Vårvindar friska' (Swedish trad.).

ive interest resides in factors other than those mentioned so far, such as changing lyrics or varying meter (for example, chanted psalms and prayers), or harmonic progression (for example, 'Samba de una nota só' (Ex. 2)). At the other end of the scale are such phenomena as the dodecaphonic tone row, which is constrained by avant-garde imperatives of non-repetition and is absent from popular song. Instead, patterns of recurrence and difference vary from the relatively simple – single-layered (or 'immediate') – to the multilayered (or 'delayed'). Common processual devices in European and North American popular melody are reiteration, recapitulation, sequence, inversion, anaphora, epistrophe and 'ready-steady-go.' The ordering of melodic segments on a larger scale – for example, into the eight-bar sections of a 32-bar (AABA) jazz standard – is a question of song form rather than of melodic typology.

Reiteration – the consecutive occurrence(s) of identical motif or phrase – is found in Example 1 (both melodic line and riff), 22 (bars 1 and 2; bars 5–6 and 7–8), 26b (bar 1) and 34 (bars 1–2).

Recapitulation – the recurrence of a motif or phrase after different intervening material – is illustrated at the musematic level by Example 22, in which the motif of bars 1 and 2 recurs in bar 4 following the different material in bar 3 and, again, in the final bar of the song. Melodic recapitulation is, however, more commonly thought of on a larger scale.

Sequence – the reiteration of rhythm and relative pitch profile at a different absolute pitch – can be seen in 'Autumn Leaves (Les feuilles mortes)' (Ex. 4), 'El gallo negro' (Ex. 24), 'Poitín' (Ex. 27, bars 1–2 and 5–6), 'Vårvindar friska' (Ex. 37, bars 1–2) and Gershwin's 'A Foggy Day in London Town' (Ex. 38), in which 'B' (bars 1–4) is repeated a fourth higher (bars 5–8) and 'A1' (*d–db*, bar 3) can be regarded as a sequential variation of 'A' (*c–eb*, bar 1).

Inversion – repeating a rhythm profile but substituting up for down and down for up in the pitch profile – can be seen in Example 38, in which bars 9–12 are an upside-down variant of bars 1–4.

Anaphora – repeating the same element at the start of successive phrases – is inherent, in terms of rhyth-

Example 38 Gershwin: 'A Foggy Day in London Town' (1937), quoted by Middleton (1983, 251).

mic and relative-pitch profile, in any sequential repetition (see above). It can also recur at the same absolute pitch, as in the *d–c♯–d* ♩♩♩ figure of Example 39a or the ♪♩(♪) *c–d* figure of Example 39b. Even the single note *f* that recurs at the start of each short motif in 'Axel F' (Ex. 21) and rises in turn to different pitches (*a♭, b♭, c, d♭, f*) functions anaphorically.

Epistrophe – repeating the same or a similar element at the end of successive phrases – is seen at the words 'far away,' 'here to stay' and 'yesterday' of bars 3, 5 and 7 of the principal vocal melody of the Beatles' 'Yesterday.'

Ready-steady-go is a popular melodic device consisting of a motif, either simply reiterated or repeated by sequential transformation (usually once or twice), and followed by new rhythmic material or a new pitch

Example 39 Melodic anaphora – (a) Silvers: 'April Showers'; (b) Akst: 'Am I Blue?', as quoted by Middleton (1983, 250).

Example 40 Rossini: 'William Tell' Overture (1829), aka theme from 'The Lone Ranger' (1949).

Example 41 R. Schumann: 'Träumerei' (1838).

Example 42 Hoagy Carmichael: 'Star Dust' (1929).

pattern. For example, bars 1–2 and 3–4 of Akst's 'Am I Blue?' (Ex. 39b) are rhythmically identical ('ready' and 'steady') but, instead of leading to yet another long held note, the same anaphoric figure in bar 5 introduces the tonally and rhythmically different material of bars 6 and 7 ('go!'). The device can work on several levels, as shown in Example 40. The function of such repetition is propulsive, and is similar to circling on the spot to gain momentum before hurling a discus.

Experiential Typologies

Families of melody that can be defined according to the kind of structural parameters mentioned above are often grouped together in more perceptual or semiotic categories. Concepts such as the Arabic *maqam*, Iranian *dastgah* and Indian *rāga* bear witness to such connec-

tion, linking certain categories of tonal, rhythmic and motivic structure with certain regional locations or ethnic groups, as well as with specific moods, attitudes, activities, types of behavior, times of the day and so on.

Stefani and Marconi (1992, 111–229) expound several experiential categories of popular melody in Western culture. These include 'dream,' 'desire and tenderness,' 'supermusic' and 'meditation,' as well as 'recitation,' 'blues' and 'tango.' For example, structurally, the authors characterize 'dream' in such terms as slow movement, smooth articulation, arched or waved pitch profile spanning a large range, phrase length well in excess of normal breathing, continuous transformation of main motif(s), unexpected intervals, lack of hard scansion and accentuation and so on. More con-

Example 43 C. Williams: 'The Dream of Olwen' (1947).

Example 44 Ketèlby: 'In A Monastery Garden' (1915).

notatively, they note similarities to slow-motion camera work, soft focus, suspended animation, large spaces, fluid gestures (unpredictable flight, beauty, the unreal) and so on. This melodic category, including its connotations, is exemplified by Schumann's Träumerei (Ex. 41), 'Deep Purple' ('When the deep purple falls over sleepy garden walls,' Ex. 17), 'Stardust' (Ex. 42), 'The Dream of Olwen' (Ex. 43) and 'In a Monastery Garden' (Ex. 44).

'Supermusic,' on the other hand, exemplified by the main themes from *Superman, Star Wars, Dallas, Dynasty, Kojak, The FBI, Counterspy, Gunfight at the O.K. Corral, How the West Was Won, The Champions* and so on, uses staccato articulation at a brisk pace and favors rising leaps of the fourth, fifth and octave (see, also, Tagg 2000, 124–32).

'Recitation,' as an experiential rather than a formal category of melody in popular song, is usually articulated metrically rather than parlando rubato (recitative). Structurally, it is characterized by a reciting tone, to which most of the phrase's syllables are set, as well

as by a cadence formula and, sometimes, by an initial lead-in motif. Recitation tunes are generally of a declamatory character. For example, the italicized syllables in 'How many roads must a man walk down before they can call him a man?' from Dylan's 'Blowin' in the Wind' are all declaimed at the fifth (*a* in D major). The principle of lead-in motif (*initio*), reciting tone (*tuba* or *tenor*) and cadence formula (*terminatio*) is illustrated in Examples 45a, 45b and 45c. As Stefani and Marconi (1992, 132) observe, 'once the voice is activated (*initio*) ... it remains still in a manner of speaking, giving no further information about itself and drawing the listener's attention to the "message," that is, to the words.'

Bibliography

Barbrook, Richard. 1990. 'Melodies or Rhythms?: The Competition for the Greater London FM Radio Licence.' *Popular Music* 9(2): 203–19.

Baroni, Mario, and Jacobini, Carlo. 1978. *Proposal for a Grammar of Melody*. Montréal: Presses de l'Université de Montréal.

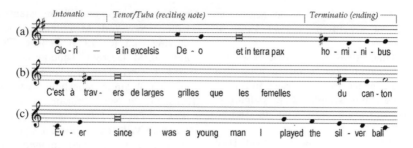

Example 45 'Recitation' melody – (a) Latin psalmody, tone 2 (plagal); (b) Brassens: 'Le gorille' (1952); (c) The Who: 'Pinball Wizard' (1969) as quoted by Stefani and Marconi (1992, 134).

Björnberg, Alf. 1987. *En liten sång som alla andra: Melodifestivalen 1959–1983* [A Little Song Like All the Others: The Eurovision Song Contest]. Göteborg: Skrifter från Musikvetenskapliga institutionen.

Bond, Carrie Jacobs. 1928. *The Roads of Melody.* New York: Appleton.

Borgersen, Terje. 1986. 'Melodi Grand Prix – Uten lyd og bilde – et pauseinnslag' [Eurovision Song Contest – Without Sound or Picture – an Intermission]. In *Eurovision Song Contest, 86: upretentiøse essays* [Eurovision Song Contest, 86: Unpretentious Essays]. Trondheim: Nordisk Institutt, Universitetet i Trondheim, AVH, 28–34.

Burns, Gary. 1987. 'A Typology of "Hooks" in Popular Records.' *Popular Music* 6(1): 1–20.

Connolly, Thomas H. 1980. 'Psalmody II.' In *The New Grove Dictionary of Music and Musicians*, Vol. 15, ed. Stanley Sadie. London: Macmillan, 322–32.

Cooke, Deryck. 1959. *The Language of Music.* London: Oxford University Press.

Dowling, W. Jay. 1985. 'Entwicklung von Melodie-Erkennen und Melodie-Produktion' [Development of Melodic Recognition and Production]. In *Musikpsychologie: ein Handbuch* [The Psychology of Music: A Handbook], ed. H. Bruhn, R. Oerter and Rolf H. Rösing. München: Urban & Schwarzenberg, 216–22.

Fiori, Umberto. 1996. '"In un supremo anelito": L'idea di poesia nella canzone italiana' ['In un supremo anelito': The Idea of Poetry in an Italian Song]. In *Analisi e canzoni* [Analyses and Songs], ed. R. Dalmonte. Trento: Editrice Università degli Studi di Trento, 145–60.

Freeman, Larry. 1951. *The Melodies Linger On: Fifty Years of Popular Song.* Watkins Glen, NY: Century House.

Johnson, Geir. 1986. *Norge i Melodi Grand Prix* [Norway in the Eurovision Song Contest]. Oslo: Forlaget Atheneum.

Kernfeld, Barry Dean. 1984. *Adderley, Coltrane and Davis at the Twilight of Bebop: The Search for Melodic Coherence (1958–59).* Ann Arbor, MI: University Microfilms.

Kwan, Kelina. 1992. 'Textual and Melodic Contour in Cantonese Popular Songs.' In *Secondo convegno europeo di analisi musicale* [Second European Conference on Musical Analysis], ed. R. Dalmonte and M. Baroni. Trento: Università degli studi, 179–88.

Lilliestam, Lars. 1984. 'Syntarnas intåg eller från melodi och harmonik till klang och rytm: 10 teser' [Entrance of the Synths, or from Melody and Harmony to Timbre and Rhythm: 10 Theses]. In *Tvärspel: 31 artiklar om musik. Festskrift till Jan Ling* [Tvärspel: 31 Articles on Music. Festschrift for Jan Ling]. Göteborg: Skrifter från Musikvetenskapliga institutionen, 352–70.

Lindblom, Paul, and Sundberg, Johan. 1970. 'Towards a Generative Theory of Melody.' *Svensk tidskrift för musikforskning* [Swedish Musicology Journal] 52: 71–88.

Ling, Jan. 1964. *Svensk folkmusik* [Swedish Folk Music]. Stockholm: Prisma.

Ling, Jan. 1997. *A History of European Folk Music.* Rochester and Woodbridge: Rochester University Press.

Mattheson, Johan. 1987 (1739). 'Concerning the Species of Melody and Their Special Characteristics' (paragraphs 80–98, 102–103 from *Der volkommene Kapellmeister* [The Complete *Kapellmeister*], Part II, Chapter XIII, Hamburg). In *Musik og betydningsinhold: kompendium i musikaestetik* [Music and Signification: A Compendium of Music Aesthetics], ed. P. Druud-Nielsen. Ålborg: Institut for musik og musikterapi, AUC, 16–18.

Meyer, Leonard B. 1987. 'Le "implicazioni" nella melodia tonale' ['Implications' in Tonal Melody]. In *Il senso in musica* [Meaning in Music], ed. Luca Marconi and Gino Stefani. Bologna: CLUEB, 187–96.

Miani, Guido. 1992. 'Gesti melodici del blues' [Melodic Gestures in Blues]. In *Dal blues al liscio* [From Blues to Ballo Liscio], ed. G. Nicotra and G. Bertoni. Verona: Edizioni Ianua, 11–48.

18. Melody

Middleton, Richard. 1983. "'Play It Again, Sam": On the Productivity of Repetition.' *Popular Music* 4: 235–71.

Postacchini, Pier Luigi. 1996. 'La melodia ossessiva: intense esperienze emotive con la musica' [Obsessive Melody: Extreme Experiences with Music]. In *Analisi e canzoni* [Analyses and Songs], ed. R. Dalmonte. Trento: Editrice Università degli Studi di Trento, 59–80.

Reimers, Lennart. 1979. 'Den svenska barnvisan' [The Swedish Nursery Rhyme]. In *Skriftfest: 19 uppsatser tillägnade Martin Tegen – 60 år* [Skriftfest: 19 Essays for Martin Tegen's 60th Birthday]. Stockholm: Institutionen för musikvetenskap, 150–60.

Rochon, Gaston. 1992. *Processus compositionnel – Genèse de chansons de Gilles Vigneault: un témoignage* [The Compositional Process – The Origins of Gilles Vigneault's Songs: A Testimony]. Göteborg: Skrifter från musikvetenskap nr. 28.

Sarosi, Bálint. 1985. 'An Instrumental Melody.' *Yearbook for Traditional Music* 17: 198–205.

Skog, Inge, and Bengtsson, Ingmar. 1977. 'Melodik' [Melody]. *Sohlmans musiklexikon* [Sohlmans Music Encyclopedia] 4: 489–92.

Stefani, Gino. 1987. 'Melody: A Popular Perspective.' *Popular Music* 6(1): 21–36.

Stefani, Gino, and Marconi, Luca. 1992. *La melodia* [Melody]. Milan: Bompiani.

Stefani, Gino, Marconi, Luca, and Ferrari, Franca. 1990. *Gli intervalli musicali* [Musical Intervals]. Milan: Bompiani.

Tagg, Philip. 1991. *Fernando the Flute*. Liverpool: Institute of Popular Music, University of Liverpool.

Tagg, Philip. 1994. 'From Refrain to Rave: The Decline of Figure and the Rise of Ground.' *Popular Music* 13(2): 209–22.

Tagg, Philip. 2000. *Kojak: 50 Seconds of Television Music*. 2nd ed. New York: Mass Media Music Scholars' Press. (First published Göteborg: Skrifter från Göteborgs universitet, Musikvetenskapliga institutionen, 1979.)

Vilariño, Idea. 1981a. *El Tango* (1) [The Tango (1)]. Chapter 117 of *La historia de la literatura Argentina* [The History of Argentinian Literature]. Buenos Aires: Centro Editor de América Latina, 409–32.

Vilariño, Idea. 1981b. *El Tango* (2) [The Tango (2)]. Chapter 121 of *La historia de la literatura Argentina* [The History of Argentinian Literature]. Buenos Aires: Centro Editor de América Latina, 529–52.

Williams, Martin T. 1966. *Where's the Melody?: A Listener's Introduction to Jazz*. New York: Minerva.

Sheet Music

'Ack Värmeland du sköna.' 1970. In *Vi gör musik*, ed. Bengt Olof Engström and Egil Cederlöf. Stockholm: Ehrlingförlagen, 74.

Akst, Harry, comp., and Clarke, Grant, lyr. 1929. 'Am I Blue?' New York: M. Witmark & Sons.

'A-Roving.' n.d. (ca. 1938). In *Songs That Will Live for Ever*, ed. M. Jacobson. London: Odhams Press, 158.

Aturov, T. 1981. 'Partisans' Song.' In *Sånger för socialismen*, ed. P. Ström. Stockholm: Arbetarkultur, 31.

'The Banks of Newfoundland.' 1959. In *The Penguin Book of English Folk Songs*, ed. A.L. Lloyd and R. Vaughan Williams. London: Penguin, 17.

'Billy Boy.' n.d. (ca. 1938). In *Songs That Will Live for Ever*, ed. M. Jacobson. London: Odhams Press, 160.

'The Bonny Labouring Boy.' 1939. In *Irish Street Ballads*, ed. Colm O'Lochlainn. Dublin: Three Candles, 18.

'Bound for the Rio Grande.' n.d. (ca. 1938). In *Songs That Will Live for Ever*, ed. M. Jacobson. London: Odhams Press, 161.

'The Boys of Wexford.' 1939. In *Irish Street Ballads*, ed. Colm O'Lochlainn. Dublin: Three Candles, 96.

Brassens, Georges, comp. 1977. 'Le gorille.' In *35 chansons, écrites, ou muse en musique, et chantées par Georges Brassens*. Mons: Marcom Music.

Carissimi, Giacomo, comp. 1903. 'I Triumph!' (Vittoria!). In *A Golden Treasury of Song, Vol. 1*. London: Boosey & Co., 44–47.

Carmichael, Hoagy, comp., and Parish, Mitchell, lyr. 1929. 'Star Dust.' New York: Mills Music.

'Comin' Thru' the Rye.' 1969. In *Robert Burns: Poems and Songs*, ed. James Kinsley. London: Oxford University Press.

DeRose, Peter, comp., and Parish, Mitchell, lyr. 1934. 'Deep Purple.' New York: Robbins Music Corporation.

Ferlosio, José Antonio Sánchez, comp. 1981. 'El gallo negro.' In *Sånger för socialismen*, ed. P. Ström. Stockholm: Arbetarkultur, 139.

'Fire Down Below.' n.d. (ca. 1938). In *Songs That Will Live for Ever*, ed. M. Jacobson. London: Odhams Press, 163.

Gershwin, George, comp., and Gershwin, Ira, lyr. 1937. 'A Foggy Day in London Town.' London: Chappell Music Ltd.

'God Save the Queen.' n.d. London: D'Almaine & Co.

Gorney, Jay, comp., and Harburg, E.Y., lyr. 1932. 'Brother, Can You Spare a Dime?' New York: T.B. Harms, Inc.

'John Barleycorn.' 1959. In *The Penguin Book of English Folk Songs*, ed. A.L. Lloyd and R. Vaughan Williams. London: Penguin, 56.

'Johnny Come Down to Hilo.' n.d. (ca. 1938). In *Songs That Will Live for Ever*, ed. M. Jacobson. London: Odhams Press, 167.

'The Kerry Recruit.' 1939. In *Irish Street Ballads*, ed. Colm O'Lochlainn. Dublin: Three Candles, 2.

'Mameluk.' 1970. In *Vi gör musik*, ed. Bengt Olof Engström and Egil Cederlöf. Stockholm: Ehrlingförlagen, 330.

Mercer, John H., Ellington, Duke, and Strayhorn, Billy, comps. and lyrs. 1992 (1953). 'Satin Doll.' In *The Complete Piano Player: Duke Ellington*. London: Wise Publications.

Porter, Cole, comp. and lyr. 1934. 'I Get a Kick Out of You.' New York: T.B. Harms, Inc.

'Rossa's Farewell to Erin' (Irish trad.). 1939. In *Irish Street Ballads*, ed. Colm O'Lochlainn. Dublin: Three Candles, 68.

Rossini, Gioacchino, comp. 1981 (1829). Overture to *William Tell*. London: Eulenburg.

Schumann, Robert, comp. 1997 (1838). 'Träumerei.' *Kinderscenen*, Op. 15. Vienna: Wiener Urtext Edition.

Silvers, Louis, comp., and DeSylva, Buddy, lyr. 1921. 'April Showers.' New York: Remick Music Corp.

'Vårvindar friska.' 1970. In *Vi gör musik*, ed. Bengt Olof Engström and Egil Cederlöf. Stockholm: Ehrlingförlagen, 72.

Vigneault, Gilles, comp. 1978 (1973). 'Je chante pour.' In *Gilles Vigneault, Vol. 1*. Montréal: Éditions Le Vent qui Vire.

'Warszawjanka.' 1981. In *Sånger för socialismen*, ed. P. Ström. Stockholm: Arbetarkultur, 43.

'What Shall We Do with the Drunken Sailor?' n.d. (ca. 1938). In *Songs That Will Live for Ever*, ed. M. Jacobson. London: Odhams Press, 162.

Discographical References

ABBA. 'Fernando.' Epic EPC 4036. *1975*: UK.

Abdo, George, and the Flames of Araby Orchestra. 'Misirlou.' *The Art of Belly Dancing*. Monitor 51752. *1995*: USA.

Achatz, Dag. 'Träumerei.' *Kinderszenen Op. 15*. Bis 144. *1979*: Sweden.

Astaire, Fred. 'A Foggy Day in London Town.' Brunswick 7982. 1937: USA.

Astronauts, The. 'Misirlou.' *Surfin' with the Astronauts*. RCA 2760. *1963*: USA.

'Auld Lang Syne.' *The Music and Song of Edinburgh*. Green Trax 090. *1995*: UK.

Beatles, The. 'Can't Buy Me Love.' *A Hard Day's Night*. Parlophone PCS 3058. *1964*: UK.

Beatles, The. 'If I Needed Someone.' *Rubber Soul*. Parlophone PCS 3075. *1965*: UK.

Beatles, The. 'Yesterday.' *Help!*. Parlophone PCS 3071. *1965*: UK.

Clinton, Larry. 'Deep Purple.' Victor 26141. 1939: USA.

'Cordigliera.' Creazioni artistiche musicale CAM 004. n.d.: Italy.

Crosby, Bing. 'Brother, Can You Spare a Dime?' Brunswick 6414. 1932: USA.

Culp, James. 'In a Monastery Garden.' *In a Monastery Garden*. Guild GMCD 7212. *1992*: Switzerland.

Derek and the Dominos. 'Layla.' Polydor 2058 130. *1970*: UK.

'The Dream of Olwen' (theme from *While I Live*). *Big Concerto Movie Themes*. Music for Pleasure MFP 4261. *1972*: USA.

Duncan, Trevor. 'Wine Festival.' *Boosey & Hawkes Recorded Library Music*. SBH 298. n.d.: UK.

Dylan, Bob. 'Blowin' in the Wind.' *The Freewheelin' Bob Dylan*. Columbia 98940. *1963*: USA.

Dylan, Bob. 'Subterranean Homesick Blues.' Columbia 43242. *1965*: USA.

Ellington, Duke. 'Satin Doll.' *Jazz Collection*. Sony International 488621. *2001*: USA.

Faltermeyer, Harold. 'Axel F.' *Beverly Hills Cop* (Original soundtrack). MCA MCAD-5553. *1984*: USA.

Gilberto, João. 'Samba de una nota só.' *Gilberto and Jobim*. Capitol 2160. *1960*: USA.

Grandmaster Flash. 'Message.' Sugar Hill 1007. *1982*: USA.

Haider, Hans. 'Spanish Autumn.' *Selected Sounds*. SL 556/9023. n.d.: Sweden.

Hare, Ernest. 'April Showers.' Brunswick 2188. 1921: USA.

Holman, Libby. 'Am I Blue?' Brunswick 4445. 1929: USA.

Jones, Isham. 'Star Dust.' Brunswick 4856. 1931: USA.

Jungle Brothers, The. 'I Get a Kick Out of You.' *Tribute to Cole Porter*. Chrysalis 1799. *1990*: UK.

Kramer, Billy J., and the Dakotas. 'From a Window.' Parlophone R 5156. *1964*: UK.

Led Zeppelin. 'Whole Lotta Love.' *Led Zeppelin II*. Atlantic 588-198. *1969*: USA.

Martin, Dean. 'Volare.' *Dean Martin: Greatest Hits*. Capitol 94961. *1998*: USA.

Milton, Roy, and His Solid Senders. 'Hucklebuck.' Specialty 328. 1949: USA.

Moloney, Mick. 'Poitín' (Irish trad.). Private recording at the Göteborg College of Music, 1972.

Nashville Teens. 'Tobacco Road.' Decca F 11930. *1964*: UK.

Overture to *William Tell*. *Rossini Overtures*. RCA Gold Seal AGL 1-5210. *1959*: USA.

Piaf, Edith. 'Autumn Leaves (Les feuilles mortes).' *Edith Piaf: 30ᵉ anniversaire*. Capitol C2-27097. *1994*: USA.

Radiohead. 'Creep.' *Pablo Honey*. Capitol 81409. *1993*: USA.

Rolling Stones, The. '(I Can't Get No) Satisfaction.' Decca F 12220. *1965*: UK.

'Theme from *The Lone Ranger*.' *Themes Like Old Times: 180 Original Radio Themes*. Viva 2572. *1969*: Sweden.

'Un homme et une femme.' *Movie Memories*. Music for Pleasure MFP 50438. *1976*: USA.

Vigneault, Gilles. 'Je chante pour.' *Pays du fond de moi*. Le Nordet GVN-1002. *1973*: Canada.

Waters, Muddy. 'Hoochie Coochie Man.' *Goin' Home: Live in Paris 1970*. New Rose 5099. *1970*: France.

Waters, Muddy. '19 Years Old.' *Newport Folk Festival 1959/65*. Vanguard VSD-25/26. n.d.: USA.

Who, The. 'Pinball Wizard.' *Tommy*. Decca DXW-7205. *1969*: USA.

'The X Files Theme' (aka 'Materia primoris'). *The Truth and the Light: Music from the X Files*. Warner Brothers 9362-46448-2. *1996*: USA.

Filmography

Beverly Hills Cop, dir. Martin Brest. 1984. USA. 105 mins. Action Comedy. Original music by Harold Faltermeyer.

Counterspy, dir. Vernon Sewell. 1953. UK. 68 mins. Drama. Original music by Eric Spear.

Gunfight at the O.K. Corral, dir. John Sturges. 1957. USA. 120 mins. Western. Original music by Frankie Laine, Dimitri Tiomkin, Ned Washington.

How the West Was Won, dir. John Ford, Henry Hathaway, George Marshall and Richard Thorpe. 1963. USA. 165 mins. Epic Western. Original music by Ken Darby, Dave Guard, Johnny Mercer, Alfred Newman, Whiskeyhill Singers.

Star Wars, dir. George Lucas. 1977. USA. 121 mins. Science Fiction. Original music by John Williams.

Superman – The Movie, dir. Richard Donner. 1978. USA/UK. 150 mins. Comic-Strip Superhero Film. Original music by Leslie Bricusse, John Williams.

Un homme et une femme [*A Man and a Woman*], dir. Claude Lelouch. 1966. France. 102 mins. Romantic Drama. Original music by Francis Lai.

While I Live, dir. John Harlow. 1947. UK. 85 mins. Thriller. Original music by Charles Williams.

PHILIP TAGG

Note

A note is defined as: (a) any single, discrete sound of finite duration within a musical continuum; (b) such a sound with easily discernible fundamental pitch; and (c) the duration, relative to the music's underlying pulse, of any such sound, pitched or unpitched.

Although 'note' originally referred to the scribal marking of these minimal elements of musical articulation, the word has come to denote a discrete sonic event on its own, without any reference to musical notation. This terminological practise is illustrated concisely by the notes of MIDI (musical instrument digital interface) sequencing, which are defined by such factors as: (a) the point at which a given sound will start; (b) the type of sound (timbre, volume, attack, envelope, decay) that will occur at that point; (c) (if pitched) the frequency at which the sound will be articulated; and (d) the point at which the sound will stop. According to this general meaning of the term, a note may be long, short, high, low, pitched, unpitched, loud, soft, sharp, rounded and so on. However, although a note may theoretically have any duration, it is virtually impossible to perceive as such, if it sounds for less than 0.1 or more than 12 seconds. Hence, certain types of ornamentation that, from a technical viewpoint, involve more than one note are perceived as single notes of a particular type (for example, drumrolls, *tremolandi* and fast trills), while extremely long notes are heard as pedals or drones.

'Note' is often used in a strictly tonal sense to refer to the specific pitch of a single sound event. A pitched-note name refers to either (a) an absolute pitch in any octave ('A,' 'F sharp' and so on), (b) the particular occurrence of such a sound (for example, 'high c,' 'a low b flat,' '*c*,' '*d³*') or (c) one pitch in relation to another (for example, 'a fifth below,' 'flat seventh,' 'leading note,' '*mi-do-so-la*'). Pitched notes are named in either absolute terms (A, B, C, D, E, F, G and so on) or relative terms (for example, *doh, re, mi, fa, so, la* and *ti*, or *sa, ri, ga, ma, pa, dha* and *ni*). In all instances, note names are identical from one octave to another. Absolute-note names are based on standard concert pitch (*a* at 440 Hz), while relative-note names presuppose the fixation of *doh, la* or *sa* to any one pitch for the duration of a musical continuum, the other names denoting intervallic relationship to that *doh* or *la*. Three main conventions for naming notes of absolute pitch are in everyday use in popular music throughout the world (see Fig. 1, facing page): (a) the English-language system; (b) the Latin convention (exemplified by French names), used in Russia and Poland as well as throughout the Latin world; and (c) the German convention, used in Scandinavia and German-speaking areas.

As shown by German and North American nomenclature, 'note' is often used when referring solely to the duration of a minimal musical sound event; for example, *ganze Note* (meaning 'whole note') and *Viertelnote* (meaning 'quarter note') (see Table 1, facing page).

PHILIP TAGG and GARRY TAMLYN

Octave

The term 'octave' refers to the interval between two pitches whose frequencies differ by a factor of two – for example, between A (220 Hz) (a_3 in the standard MIDI system of designating octaves, shown in Table 1, page 586) and a (440 Hz) (a_4), or between a (a_4) and a^1 (880 Hz) (a_5), or between c (c_4) and c^1 (c_5), or between $E\flat$ ($e\flat_3$) and $e\flat$ ($e\flat_4$) (see Fig. 1, page 586). With its simple frequency ratio of 2:1, the octave is also the interval

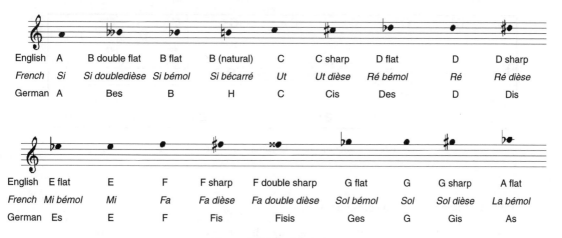

English	A	B double flat	B flat	B (natural)	C	C sharp	D flat	D	D sharp
French	*Si*	*Si doubledièse*	*Si bémol*	*Si bécarré*	*Ut*	*Ut dièse*	*Ré bémol*	*Ré*	*Ré dièse*
German	A	Bes	B	H	C	Cis	Des	D	Dis

English	E flat	E	F	F sharp	F double sharp	G flat	G	G sharp	A flat
French	*Mi bémol*	*Mi*	*Fa*	*Fa dièse*	*Fa double dièse*	*Sol bémol*	*Sol*	*Sol dièse*	*La bémol*
German	Es	E	F	Fis	Fisis	Ges	G	Gis	As

Figure 1 Pitched-note names

Table 1 Note-length names

Note	English (UK)	English (US)	German	French	Italian
𝄺	breve	double whole note	Brevis	carrée	breve
o	semibreve	whole note	gantz (Note)	ronde	semibreve
♩	minim	half note	Halbe	blanche	minima or bianca
♩.	dotted crotchet	dtotted quarter note	punktiert Viertel	noire pointée	nera con punto
♩	crotchet	quarter note	Viertel	noire	nera or semiminima
♪	quaver	eighth note	Achtel	croche	croma
♫	semiquaver	sixteenth note	Sechzehntel	double-croche	semicroma
♫	demisemiquaver	thirty-second note	Zweiunddreissigstel	triple-croche	biscroma
♫	hemidemi-semiquaver	sixty-four note	Vierundsechsigstel	quadruple-croche	semibriscroma

between a note's fundamental pitch and that of its first harmonic, which is, in turn, an intrinsic part of the timbre of every singing voice and acoustic instrument.

Octave as Unison

All known music traditions tend to treat two pitches an octave apart as 'the same note.' For example, men are understood to be singing the same tune as women and children if both parties follow the same pitch contour at the same time in parallel octaves. The octave's property of 'unison at another pitch' is also illustrated by the fact that: (a) a common chord consisting of the tonic, third, fifth and octave is treated as a triad because it contains three, not four, different notes (tonic/octave, third and fifth); (b) any single note sounded on instruments like the 12-string guitar, or using common types of organ registration, produces two pitches an octave apart; (c) parallel octaves are commonly used to enhance melodic timbre in jazz piano and guitar playing, and not as a harmonic device (for example, Erroll Garner and Wes Montgomery); (d) lower octave doubling of bass notes is used timbrally and dynamically in a huge variety of styles (for example, classical, jazz and rock) to boost the power of the bass line, and not as a harmonic device; and (e) the octave is closely associated with the concept of register.

Octave Pitch Designation

Music's range of fundamental pitches can be divided into octaves. A standard piano keyboard spans seven oct-

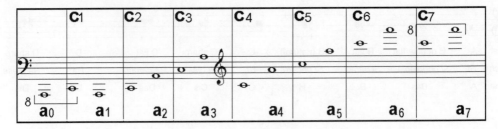

Figure 1 Range of Piano keyboard split into octaves.

Table 1 Octave designation conventions

MIDI	$c_0 - b_0$	$c_1 - b_1$	$c_2 - b_2$	$c_3 - b_3$	$c_4 - b_4$	$c_5 - b_5$	$c_6 - b_6$	etc.
older conven-tions	$C_2 - B_2$	$C_1 - B_1$	C–B	c–b	$c^1 - b^1$	$c^2 - b^2$	$c^3 - b^3$	
	$C_1 - B_1$	C–B	c–b	c'–b'	c''–b''	c'''–b'''	c''''–b''''	etc.
	CCC–BBB	CC–BB	C–B	c–b	c'–b'	c''–b''	c'''–b'''	
a = Hz*	27.5	55	110	220	440	880	1760	etc.

* i.e. the frequency, in Herz, of the note a within each octave.

aves from A^3 (27.5 Hz) (a_0 in Fig. 1) to a^3 (3,520 Hz) (a_7), a synthesizer keyboard four octaves from C^1 (c_2) to c^2 (c_6) (Table 1). The average human singing voice usually spans about two octaves.

Figure 1 shows the standard MIDI system of designating octaves, running from 0 to 10 and incrementing at every C. Such a system facilitates the absolute pitch specification of any note without resorting to the often complex numerical expressions of frequency designation in hertz (Hz). For example, the first note of the Rolling Stones' '(I Can't Get No) Satisfaction' riff (in E) is b_2, middle C is c_4, concert pitch is a_4 (440 Hz, a major sixth above c_4), and the first melodic note at the start of ABBA's 'Dancing Queen' (in A) is $c\sharp_5$. Although older octave designation conventions are still in operation (see Table 1), the MIDI convention is recommended because it is more consistent, is less confusing and is the industry standard.

Octave Leaps

Monophonic leaps (in a melodic line) up an octave to an accentuated note often have a proclamatory, sometimes even heroic, character and are found in prominent positions in the theme tunes to such television productions as *The FBI*, *Gunsmoke*, *Kojak* and *The Saint*, and to films such as *Superman* (Tagg 2000, 186–200).

Bibliography

Sirota, Warren. n.d. *Wes Montgomery – The King of Octaves*. http://www.slowgold.com/woodsheddin/Issue%208/Wes.htm

Tagg, Philip. 2000. *Kojak: 50 Seconds of Television Music*. 2nd ed. New York: Mass Media Music Scholars' Press. (First published Göteborg: Skrifter från Göteborgs universitet, Musikvetenskapliga institutionen, 1979.)

Discographical References

ABBA. 'Dancing Queen.' *Arrival*. Atlantic 18207. *1976*: USA.

Rolling Stones, The. '(I Can't Get No) Satisfaction.' Decca F 12220. *1965*: UK.

Discography

'Adventures of the Saint.' *Themes Like Old Times: 180 Original Radio Themes*. Viva 2572. *1969*: Sweden.

Erroll Garner Trio, The. *Misty*. Columbia 13-33180. 1954: USA.

'FBI Theme.' *100% Cotton: The Complete Jerry Cotton Edition*. Crippled Dick Hot Wax 4366. *1998*: Germany.

'Gunsmoke Theme.' *Themes Like Old Times: 180 Original Radio Themes*. Viva 2572. *1969*: Sweden.

Smith, Jimmy, and Montgomery, Wes. *Jimmy & Wes: The Dynamic Duo*. Verve V6-8678. *1966*: USA.

Superman: The Movie (Original soundtrack). Rhino 75874. *2000*: USA.

Filmography

Superman: The Movie, dir. Richard Donner. 1978. USA/UK. 150 mins. Comic-Strip Superhero Film. Original music by Leslie Bricusse, John Williams.

PHILIP TAGG

Pitch

The term 'pitch' refers to that aspect of a sound that is determined by the rate of vibrations producing it and that is denoted either in terms of absolute frequency or, more commonly, with reference to its perceived location on an axis from low to high frequency, usually within the range of human hearing from around 16 Hz (roughly equal to sub-contrabass C^3) to 20,000 Hz (roughly equal to the tenth harmonic of c^3).

According to this general definition, all sounds have pitch. However, although, for example, the hi-hat is heard as high-pitched and the kick drum as low, the ear is unable to detect a fundamental frequency in notes produced on those instruments, with the consequence that such sounds are heard as being of indefinite pitch or unpitched. Moreover, although the timbre of any pitched sound is determined by the relative strength and pitch of its overtones, the word 'pitch' is most frequently used to refer to the location of a note's perceived fundamental on the axis of low to high frequency.

Standard Pitch

Since 1939, there has been an internationally recognized pitch that sets a fixed frequency for a particular note – 440 Hz for *a*, the A above middle C (*c*) – from which the pitches of all other notes can be determined. This convention is referred to as 'philharmonic pitch' or, more commonly, 'concert' or 'standard' pitch. Until the nineteenth century, when the fixed pitch of *a* converged on a range between 410 Hz and 450 Hz, keyboard players would have to transpose, wind instrumentalists take extra lengths of tubing on their travels, and string players radically retune, all in accordance with the local norm. Thanks to standardized concert pitch, musicians can cross regional and national borders without having to perform the same music at different pitches (for exceptions, see below). Two other areas have benefited from the establishment of internationally recognized standard pitch: the mass production of instruments and the worldwide dissemination of music through the medium of recorded sound.

It should, however, be noted that concert pitch is of little relevance to musical traditions whose pitch names are relative rather than fixed, or in which no pitch names are used, or where participants have no need to interact with those following the concert pitch standard. While concert pitch is virtually essential to music featuring instruments whose overall tuning cannot be radically and quickly adjusted from one performance to another (such as the piano, organ, harmonica, accordion and, to some extent, most wind instruments), it is by no means a necessity for other pitched instruments such as the banjo, bass, *bouzoúki*, fiddle, guitar, mandolin, *sāz*, *'ūd* or even a synthesizer sporting the requisite detune options.

One recent divergence from standard pitch in popular music was caused by slight variations in the motor speeds of analog recording and playback equipment. Music recorded on one tape machine (reel-to-reel, audiocassette, videocassette) and played back on another, or heard on vinyl spinning too fast or too slow, meant that the entire recording would be heard at a pitch up to a semitone higher or lower than the original. Consequently, bands emulating an original recording would sometimes need to retune their instruments, or use a capo, or transpose wholesale in order to produce their cover in the key heard through their playback equipment. Similarly, transcriptions based on home taping could appear in an unintended key showing, for example, pitches consistently a semitone higher than those actually recorded or heard at the time of broadcasting (Tagg 2000, 133).

Although digital recording and playback cause none of the problems just mentioned, they have created other anomalies regarding standard pitch. While the quest for brighter sound seems to have provoked many concert ensembles to opt for a set pitch of *a* = 446 Hz or even higher (Corey 1996), modern sound postproduction allows for the creation of similar effects in several ways – for example, by using: (a) an equalizer/filter to boost the relative dynamics of higher pitches; (b) an Aphex exciter; (c) a harmonizer; or (d) a few clicks of the mouse and strokes on the computer keyboard to raise the pitch of an entire track or song.

Absolute Pitch

'Absolute pitch' refers to an individual's ability, based on acquired experience and long-term memory, to identify and/or reproduce a particular pitch, independent of musical context. This ability is useful in concert pitch situations because it allows the individual to quickly identify and/or produce the absolute pitch of particular notes, and thus facilitate processes of transcription and covering. However, it is a nuisance in non-standard pitch contexts; for example, if a guitar or fiddle playing patterns characteristic for a particular key (for instance, G, D, A or E) is heard a semitone higher or lower than concert pitch, a simple tune in, say, G major may then be heard, and its constituent notes seen, as if it were in G♭ (key signature of six flats) or G♯ (key signature of seven sharps, one of which is double) rather than in G (key signature of one sharp).

Range and Register

The terms 'range' and 'compass' both denote, in terms of pitch, the span of sounds that can be produced by a voice or instrument – for example, 'the range of a standard synthesizer keyboard is four octaves, from C^1 to c^2' (65.4–1,032 Hz). The terms 'range' and 'compass' can also denote the span of fundamental pitches covered in a piece of music, either in terms of its overall range from the lowest note in the lowest part to the highest note in the highest part, or within a particular voice or part. For example, although the melodic line of the Crystals' 'Da Doo Ron Ron (When He Walked Me Home)' (1963) is confined to the very restricted pitch range of a major third, the overall pitch range of all tracks on the whole recording is large. The term 'range' also applies to the span of pitches (re)produced through recording and playback equipment (for example, 'full frequency range recording'), and of those perceptible through human or other animal ears.

The term 'register' indicates a narrower concept that not only denotes a 'range within a range' – for example, the higher pitches of the head register within a singer's total range – but also connotes specific timbral qualities of that register. For example, pitches produced in falsetto or head register usually sound 'thinner' than those of the same singer's chest register. Players of stringed instruments tend to associate register either with the position of their hands on the fingerboard or with the timbral qualities of different strings, while wind players connect registral/timbral change with such phenomena as overblowing (flute), octave keys (saxophone) and lip tension (brass).

The historical musicological terms 'ambitus' and 'tessitura' have occasionally been applied to the description of pitch in popular music. 'Ambitus' refers to the pitch range or compass of a particular melodic passage, while 'tessitura' denotes the predominant register of a particular vocal or instrumental line.

Perceptual Aspects

The perceived 'high' or 'low' of a pitch relates not only to the high or low rate of vibrations intrinsic to the pitch, but also to where in the human body the pitch is most likely to resonate – head for high pitches, chest for middle pitches, stomach for low pitches. High pitch also relates to sharpness, as adjectives like 'agudo' (Spanish), and 'aigu' (French) suggest when qualifying pitch, not to mention 'sharp' (English) in the sense of raised pitch. Conversely, low pitch relates to depth or weight – 'grave'

(French), 'profundo' (Spanish), 'tief' (German). Consequently, music associated with bright, light and sharp phenomena is more likely to be high-pitched; dark, heavy and large phenomena are more likely to be represented by music pitched low (Tagg 2000, 150–80).

Some cultures, however, reverse notions of high and low. For example, the ancient Greeks called the cithara's highest-pitched string 'low' because it was, like the guitar's high E string, literally lowest, in the sense of nearest to the player's feet. Similarly, the instrument's lowest-pitched string, like low E on a guitar, was called 'high' because it was nearest to the player's head. Such conceptual reversal, deriving from the instrument's literal physical position in relation to the musician, does not, however, affect the perceived qualities of bright, sharp, light and small as against dark, deep, heavy and large.

Bibliography

Corey, Gerald E. 1976. 'The Standard Tuning Pitch: A = 440 Where Are You?' *To the World's Bassoonists* 6(3). http://idrs.colorado.edu/publications/TWBassoonist/TWB.V6.3/standard.html

Drabkin, William. 2001. 'Register.' In *The New Grove Dictionary of Music and Musicians*, Vol. 21, ed. Stanley Sadie. 2nd ed. London: Macmillan, 105.

Haynes, Bruce, and Cooke, Peter R. 2001. 'Pitch.' In *The New Grove Dictionary of Music and Musicians*, Vol. 19, ed. Stanley Sadie. 2nd ed. London: Macmillan, 793–804.

Ricard, Robin. n.d. *Greek Music*. http://www.pleasanthill.k12.or.us/Schools/High/Departments/Scholars%20Presentations/Pages/outline_robin.html

Tagg, Philip. 2000. *Kojak: 50 Seconds of Television Music*. 2nd ed. New York: Mass Media Music Scholars' Press. (First published Göteborg: Skrifter från Göteborgs universitet, Musikvetenskapliga institutionen, 1979.)

Discographical Reference

Crystals, The. 'Da Doo Ron Ron (When He Walked Me Home).' Philles 112. *1963*: USA.

PHILIP TAGG

Rāga

Rāga or *rāg* (from the Sanskrit *rāng* (meaning 'color,' 'mood,' 'atmosphere')) is an Indian melody type and form for modal composition and improvisation. The term '*rāga*' is central to the history of Indian music and appears in early Sanskrit treatises on music, such as the *Bṛhaddeśī* (ca. A.D. 800). The concept of *rāga* has continued to be the chief melodic structuring principle of Indian art music.

Several classificatory systems for *rāgas* have developed in India. In the main, these have been attempts to reduce all possible melodic configurations of *rāgas* to a number of identifiable scale-types. Common systems are the *mela* system of South Indian music, which consists of 72 scale-types, and the *that* system of North Indian music, which has 10. Whereas the former is derived from theoretical scalar possibilities of all *rāgs* calculated on a mathematical basis, the latter was developed in the early part of the twentieth century by the Indian musicologist V.N. Bhatkhande (1860–1936) from extensive observation of musical practise in North India (see Ex. 1).

Example 1

Each *rāga* has a number of specific musical features and aesthetic reference points. It has certain ascending and descending melodic orders; notes that have particular melodic weight and focus within the *rāga*; and a number of *pakars* and *chalans*, identifying melodic phrases and contours. Specific *rāgas* were also linked to the time of the day and season of the year, and were meant to be played only at those times. This practise is no longer observed by all contemporary Indian musicians.

Rāga in Popular Music

Although a *rāga* is explored in most detail in performances of Indian classical music, the idea has also influenced popular music in India, both in the type of modal material used and in certain formal aspects of its performance practises. *Rāga*-like structures are found in a variety of folk, regional and religious musics, such as *qawwālī*, *ghazal*, *bhajan* and *Rabindrasangīt*, which have in turn influenced popular musical forms. Since the inception of *filmī gīt* (film song), music directors have used *rāgas* as a basis for composing new songs. The melodic outlines of so-called 'light' North Indian *rāgas* such as *Pīlū*, *Kāfī*, *Khamāj* and *Bhairavī*, for example, are found in numerous songs. Formal aspects of *rāga* performance often appear in *filmī* songs. In particular, *ālāp*-like sections (free and unmetered preludes) giving way to a metered melody are a common feature.

During the fashion for Indian music in the West in the 1960s, the term 'raga-rock' briefly came into use. This term and the music it described had little to do with *rāga* structure at any detailed level, but rather was a general term for loosely modal improvisations with an Indian 'feel.' However, some pop and rock musicians, notably the Beatles' guitarist George Harrison, who studied the *sitār* with Ravi Shankar, integrated his knowledge of Indian music into several songs: for example, 'Within You, Without You' from *Sergeant Pepper's Lonely Hearts Club Band* (1967), which is based mainly on the *Khamāj thāt* of North Indian music. Jazz musicians have also used *rāga*-based material as a basis for improvisation: for example, John Mayer's Indo-Jazz Fusions and John McLaughlin with Shakti.

Bibliography

Jairazbhoy, Nazir Ali. 1995. *The Rags of North Indian Music*. Bombay: Popular Prakashan.

Kaufmann, Walter. 1984. *The Ragas of North India*. New York: Da Capo Press.

Kaufmann, Walter. 1991. *The Ragas of South India*. Sittingbourne: Asia Publishing House.

Manuel, Peter. 1988. 'Popular Music in India 1901–86.' *Popular Music* 7(2): 157–76.

Powers, Harold. 1980. 'India: Tonal Systems.' In *The New*

Grove Dictionary of Music and Musicians, Vol. 9, ed. Stanley Sadie. London: Macmillan, 91–104.

Discographical Reference

Beatles, The. 'Within You, Without You.' *Sergeant Pepper's Lonely Hearts Club Band*. Parlophone PCS 7027. *1967*: UK.

Discography

Indo-Jazz Fusions. *Indo-Jazz Suite*. EMI SX6025. *1966*: UK.

McLaughlin, John, and Shakti. *Shakti*. CBS 81388. *1975*: UK.

GERRY FARRELL

Range

In Western art music, the term 'range' is defined as (a) the pitch span of an instrument or voice from its lowest to its highest available pitch, often referred to as the 'compass'; (b) the pitch span of an instrumental or vocal part in a piece of music, usually used when describing a melody; and (c) the audio-frequency span or, in other words, the sonic and timbral spectrum of the music (particularly with reference to recorded music), where 'range' can be split into subsections, such as 'low range,' 'mid-range' and 'top range,' and thus help to verify, in an audiovisual context, the situation and character of separate sounds as part of a collective whole.

When used in the sense of compass, 'range' is primarily a technical issue that aids musicians in both compositional and performing capacities. When composing, it is vital to know the range of individual instruments, so that the separate parts will be not only physically manageable, but also complementary to one another. Furthermore, instrument and voice families are commonly distinguished and named in accordance with their range: for example, bass, baritone, tenor, contralto, mezzo-soprano and soprano are the designated names of the voice family.

In both popular and classical music, 'range' is applied to the span of notes covered by a musical part. This concept of range stems from the age of Gregorian chant, when the word '*ambitus*' was used to classify the ranges of the different chants. In this sense, 'range' has come to be associated most commonly with vocal parts, as it is largely interconnected with the characteristics and capabilities of an individual's voice. Thus, singers will often choose or adapt a melody (even if it means modifying the harmony by means of transposition) in accordance with their personal vocal range. In addition, the term 'tessitura' has been coined to describe that part of the range in which most of the melody is situated: for example, if a vocal line spends much of its time moving between e^2 and a^2, it would be adjudged to have a high tessitura.

The range of a part is often intrinsic to its character. Tunes with a small range that do not have too many large-interval leaps are easier for nonprofessionals to sing and, possibly, to remember, a factor that links many of the most memorable pop tunes with ubiquitous nursery rhymes. For example, the first half of the verse in Oasis's 'Wonderwall' is constructed around three adjacent notes. Typically, the ranges of male and female vocal lines in most pop songs tend to exceed little more than an octave. In contrast, pieces with large ranges tend to be less instantly memorable, but are often more dramatic.

Particularly when applied to the concept of sound production/reproduction in popular music, 'range' denotes the general pitch or audio-frequency span occupied by individual instruments/voices in a mix. A synthesizer set to 'Warm Pad' playing a g c^1 e^1 C major triad would be said to occupy the mid-range, whereas the high-frequency crash of hi-hat and cymbals would be said to fall in the top range. Consequently, any attempt to record an ensemble of instruments requires a comprehensive understanding of range, to ensure clarity and balance between all parts; too much activity in the mid-range or bass range can lead to a 'muddy' and indistinct mix of instrumentation. As a result, the range of particular instruments already present in a recording can influence the timbre and pitch of parts still to be added. In heavy metal, for example, the predominance of electric guitars in the mid-range leaves little room for a vocal part in the same acoustic space and is one reason why, in this style, male lead singers (for example, Brian Johnson of AC/DC and Steven Tyler of Aerosmith) commonly present their vocal lines at 'screaming' pitch, an octave higher than their counterparts in other styles.

Bibliography

Apel, Willi. 1972. 'Ambitus.' In *Harvard Dictionary of Music*. 2nd rev. ed. Cambridge, MA: The Belknap Press of Harvard University Press, 31.

Apel, Willi. 1972. 'Voices, Range of.' In *Harvard Dictionary of Music*. 2nd rev. ed. Cambridge, MA: The Belknap Press of Harvard University Press, 920.

Jander, Owen. 1980. 'Tessitura.' In *The New Grove Dictionary of Music and Musicians*, Vol. 18, ed. Stanley Sadie. London: Macmillan, 705.

Sadie, Stanley. 1980. 'Range.' In *The New Grove Dictionary of Music and Musicians*, Vol. 15, ed. Stanley Sadie. London: Macmillan, 583.

Discographical Reference

Oasis. 'Wonderwall.' *(What's the Story) Morning Glory?*. Epic 67351. *1995*: USA.

Discography

AC/DC. 'Shoot to Thrill.' *Back in Black*. Atlantic 270 735. *1980*: USA.

Aerosmith. 'Love in an Elevator.' *Pump*. Geffen 924 254-2. *1989*: USA.

CHRIS SEDWELL

Register

The term 'register' refers to the position and character of a select range of notes in relation to the overall compass or range of an instrument or voice. These positions are commonly described as upper, middle and lower registers, while the uppermost limits, practicable only to highly skilled performers, are called the extreme registers. Changes of octave placement are called changes of register.

The associated term 'tessitura' is used to refer to the common range of a part (usually vocal), according to how high or low this range is in terms of its average pitch. 'Tessitura' thus refers to something different from the actual range of a part in that – in referring to the general 'lie' of the part – it does not take into account isolated notes of an unusually high or low pitch. The term 'tessitura' thus refers to the pitch character of a particular kind of register, and in this way can also refer to a voice in relation to such a register.

The position of a note or range of notes within the compass of an instrument or voice influences the timbre, which serves to distinguish between registers. Indeed, the idea of register in music derives from the term's use in medieval organ construction, where it designated a particular configuration of pipes that could be brought into play by changing the stop. Changes in configurations of pipes thus effected resulted in distinct changes of timbre. Maintaining the idea of a level or plane characterized by a uniform timbre, 'register' in the modern sense concerns expressive regions generally.

Changes in timbre influence affective responses in the listener. For reasons partly due to the fact that the more extreme high registers are difficult to produce and to control, and partly due to their more piercing tone color, these regions are often associated with particular affective states such as strain, tension and excitement – as, for example, the extremely high-register trumpet style associated with Maynard Ferguson, or with the singing style of Robert Plant. On the other hand, middle and lower registers generally correlate to more comfortable or relaxed moods – such as the trumpet style of Herb Alpert or Chet Baker, for example, or the singing style of Bing Crosby or Karen Carpenter – although clearly there are other factors contributing to the overall impact of the music in these examples.

With reference to harmonics produced on stringed instruments and to falsetto vocal tones, register encompasses more than just tessitura. The sound quality of the harmonics is distinctly different from that of the normal modes of sounding, because the harmonics are constituted of upper partials only, without their fundamental frequencies. Variously described as 'glassy,' 'hollow' and 'ethereal,' among other things, harmonics, and their vocal analog, falsetto, represent a different kind of voice, the occurrence of which is usually very noticeable and arresting. The change of voice is again understood as a change of register.

With regard specifically to the voice, the question of register is more complex. Classical vocal technique differentiates between chest register and head register; however, within the field of popular music, where there is clearly no uniform vocal technique, these terms are of less significance. Of greater interest is the intersection of music and language or, more precisely, speech. Register in speech refers to types of vocalization appropriate to the particular circumstances of a given performance situation; these types of vocalization range from extremely intimate to extremely formal. Register further extends to matters of 'tone of voice,' such as, for example, 'sincere,' 'angry,' 'arrogant,' 'sarcastic' and so forth. Therefore, with popular music singing styles, register refers simultaneously to pitch-tessitura-timbre parameters on the music axis, and to the linguistic-semantic voice style on the language axis.

Each type of persona a singer reveals through vocal style and tone of voice thus involves matters of register. Moreover, 'tone of voice' clearly has two senses with regard to singing style: the first concerns the linguistic-semantic intention – such as confiding, mocking or boasting; the second involves the physical-acoustical tone of voice – as, for example, clear or rasping, whispering or shrieking, normal or falsetto, and so on. As an illustration, the huge contrast between Shelley Fabares' soft, almost bodiless vocal in 'Johnny Loves Me' and 'Big Mama' Thornton's heavy, growled and shouted 'Hound Dog' can be understood as differences of language register as well as of vocal register. The first sounds like the dreamy, half-whispered internal monolog of a teenager consumed by puppy love, the second a coruscating onslaught on a feckless lover, complete with mocking animal sounds; yet, hearers understand that both vocal performances result quite naturally from the singers/personas' relationship to the object of their attentions and the speech style appropriate to that relationship.

Whereas in classical music vocal style tends toward a normative 'ideal' vocal tone, especially with regard to maintaining tonal consistency through the registers (in the sense of tessitura), in popular music idiosyncratic vocal styles prevail. Thus, sudden changes of register are far more frequently exploited in popular music. These can be changes from normal voice to falsetto, as in the yodeling vocal style of Emmett Miller, or changes of types of vocal expression, as in the frequent interjections of whoops, hums or spoken passages in Robert Johnson's vocals. Therefore, register is not limited to considerations of octave placement: it is the parameter that delineates regions along the speech-song continuum, as well as along the intimacy-distance continuum, not to mention zones of other frequently encountered vocal modes, such as growling, humming, yodeling, scat-singing and whistling. All such expressive 'voices' are implicit in the concept of register. Register can therefore be conceptualized as the entire field of expressive possibility from which sonic events are drawn.

Bibliography

Backus, John. 1969. *The Acoustical Foundations of Music*. New York: W.W. Norton.

Bolinger, Dwight. 1975. *Aspects of Language*. 2nd ed. New York: Harcourt Brace Jovanovich.

Hoskyns, Barney. 1991. *From a Whisper to a Scream: The Great Voices of Popular Music*. London: Fontana.

Discographical References

Fabares, Shelley. 'Johnny Loves Me.' Colpix 636. *1962*: USA.

Thornton, Willie Mae 'Big Mama.' 'Hound Dog.' Peacock 1612. 1952: USA.

Discography

Johnson, Robert. *The Complete Recordings*. Columbia/Legacy C2K-46222. *1990*: USA.

Miller, Emmett. *The Minstrel Man from Georgia*. Columbia/Legacy 66999. *1996*: USA.

TIM WISE

Riff

A riff is a short repeated melodic fragment, phrase or theme, with a pronounced rhythmic character. Riffs can be played by any combination of instruments and can be spontaneously improvised or pre-composed. A riff may be repeated unchanged or it can be altered to fit the harmonic changes of a song. Riffs are derived from the ubiquitous call-and-response structures found in African and African-influenced music styles. The use of this systematic repetitive device can be traced back to the earliest African-American musics, such as work songs, ring shouts, field hollers, spirituals and early blues. According to Schuller (1968), the term 'riff' was first used by early New Orleans brass band musicians to describe the repeating refrain structures they adopted from blues forms (28).

Since the beginnings of jazz, riffs have played an essential role in soloing, composing and arranging. Early jazz musicians such as Joe 'King' Oliver and Louis Armstrong incorporated them as part of their improvised solos. For instance, one solo chorus in Armstrong's 1929 recording of 'Mahogany Hall Stomp' consists solely of a riff repeated six times. In the territory bands of the 1930s, especially those with strong ties to rural blues (i.e., Kansas City), riffs served as a definitive element in their arranging styles. Riffs functioned as a way of extending pieces for live performance, and they created excitement and rhythm propulsion that drove the music to new intensities. Bands led by Bennie Moten, Andy Kirk and Count Basie were known for their innovative 'riffing' abilities. Most often, riffs were played as accompaniment figures behind soloists and were spontaneously improvised and harmonized. The same riff might be played by the entire horn section, or a number of distinct riffs would be devised by the separate sections (trumpets, trombones and reeds, respectively) and stacked or played in counterpoint. Basie's recording of 'One O'clock Jump' (1937) is exemplary in its use of riffs as accompaniment and demonstrates the rhythmic drive and complexity that are achieved by having three distinct interlocking riffs played simultaneously. Throughout jazz's history, riffs have been fashioned into melodies, becoming what is known as 'riff tunes.' Bennie Moten's 'Elephant's Wobble' (1923) is one of the earliest recorded riff tunes, and Glenn Miller's 'In the Mood' (1939) is probably the best known. In later jazz styles, especially with the influence of Latin, funk and rock, bass riffs grew in prominence, and many compositions have been built around repeating bass figures. Examples include Dizzy Gillespie's 'Night in Tunisia' (1946) and Miles Davis's 'Bitches Brew' (1969).

The term 'riff' has been adopted from the jazz lexicon by other popular music styles, and it has continued to serve as an important compositional and soloing device in those respective styles as well. In rhythm and blues, rock and pop, examples show that many riffs are simple one- or two-bar ostinatos, with a distinctive, and thus memorable, melodic and rhythmic character, functioning both as a hook (attention catcher) and as counterpoint to the vocal line. Songs based on riffs, then, sound and 'work' differently, offering to memory and pleasure a distinctive dialectic scheme of interaction, which is added to (and may supersede) the formal pattern of verse-chorus or chorus-bridge.

Structural and functional characteristics of riffs vary considerably according to genre or individual style, and according to the way (which may or may not be style-related) in which they are placed in relation to the other structural elements of a piece. There are examples of very short and simple one-note riffs, based on unisons and octaves, as in the Spencer Davis

Group's 'Gimme Some Lovin'' (1967) or in the Knack's 'My Sharona' (1979), as well as of long and complex riffs that extend and develop over many bars, as in pieces by progressive rock groups such as King Crimson, Gentle Giant and Area. There are, in addition, riffs made up of chords or including chords (as in the Kinks' 'All Day and All of the Night,' 1964) and others consisting of catchy melodies taken over by the vocal line; guitar riffs doubled by the bass (the Beatles' 'Day Tripper,' 1965) or in counterpoint with it (the Rolling Stones' '(I Can't Get No) Satisfaction,' 1965); riffs accompanying a narrative verse (the Animals' 'We Gotta Get Out of This Place,' 1965) or the chorus of an AABA song (the Beatles' 'I Feel Fine,' 1964); riffs that adapt themselves to the harmonic context, changing as the chords change (as in most of the Beatles' riff-based songs), and riffs that remain the same, forming an ostinato harmonic pedal (Bo Diddley's 'I'm a Man,' 1955); riffs that appear in selected parts of a song and seem to have no influence on the basic materials of other parts; and riffs that are treated as motifs and generate melodic or rhythmic patterns used throughout a song.

To the extent that repetition plays a major role in the structure of popular songs and in the common-sense definitions and criticisms of popular music (Middleton 1983), riffs embody and, to some degree, clarify diverse functions and aspects of repetition: the way pleasure is sought through repeated actions, and the way repetition can freeze and expand the musical 'present' (as in the case of short, simple riffs), or create a sense of direction and movement (for an explanation of how this works in the case of longer, articulated riffs, see Fabbri 1996).

Bibliography

Fabbri, Franco. 1996. *Il suono in cui viviamo* [The Sound We Live In]. Milano: Feltrinelli.

Middleton, Richard. 1983. "'Play It Again, Sam'': Some Notes on the Productivity of Repetition in Popular Music.' *Popular Music* 3: 235–70.

Schuller, Gunther. 1968. *Early Jazz: Its Roots and Musical Development*. New York: Oxford University Press.

Discographical References

Animals, The. 'We Gotta Get Out of This Place.' Columbia DB 7639. *1965*: UK.

Armstrong, Louis. 'Mahogany Hall Stomp.' OKeh 8680. 1929: USA.

Basie, Count. 'One O'clock Jump'/'John's Idea.' Decca 1363. 1937: USA.

Beatles, The. 'Day Tripper'/'We Can Work It Out.' Parlophone R 5389. *1965*: UK.

Beatles, The. 'I Feel Fine.' Parlophone R 5200. *1964*: UK.

Davis, Miles. 'Bitches Brew.' *Bitches Brew*. Columbia 26. 1969; *1970*: USA.

Diddley, Bo. 'I'm a Man.' Checker 814. 1955: USA.

Gillespie, Dizzy. '52nd Street Theme'/'Night in Tunisia.' Victor 40-0130. 1946: USA.

Kinks, The. 'All Day and All of the Night.' Pye 7N 15714. *1964*: UK.

Knack, The. 'My Sharona.' Capitol 4731. *1979*: USA.

Miller, Glenn. 'In the Mood'/'I Want to Be Happy.' Bluebird 10416. 1939: USA.

Moten, Bennie. 'Elephant's Wobble'/'Crawdad Blues.' OKeh 8100. 1923: USA.

Rolling Stones, The. '(I Can't Get No) Satisfaction.' Decca F 12220. *1965*: UK.

Spencer Davis Group, The. 'Gimme Some Lovin'.' United Artists 50108. *1967*: USA.

CHRIS WASHBURNE and FRANCO FABBRI

Scale

The term 'scale' refers to a series of pitches, arranged in ascending or descending registral order, comprising the notes that are considered adjacent to each other in the motion of melodic or other musical lines.

Scales appear both as abstract theoretical formulations and as performed successions of notes. Specifically, scales are used: (a) in music theory, to summarize the interval and pitch material of a particular kind of music; (b) in training performers, where repeated practising of scales can increase technical fluency and familiarity with basic material; (c) as a 'surface' resource in composition or improvisation, where scales may appear as immediate note-to-note successions; and (d) as a 'structural' resource in composition or improvisation, where motion through a scale, elaborated by the addition of other notes, may shape an extended passage of music.

The Scale in Music Theory

The music theory of eighteenth- and nineteenth-century Western art music distinguishes between major and minor scales, and identifies three different kinds of minor scale. While these formulations are not adequate for understanding and analyzing scalar material in popular music, they are the origin and point of reference for subsequent accounts of popular music, and are useful for some repertoires, such as Tin Pan Alley songs or musical comedy.

Art music theorists normally represent a scale by giving an example with specific pitches: seven different pitches for major or minor scales, along with a repetition of the first pitch an octave higher or lower. For instance, a theorist might use a C major scale to illustrate major scales generally. Such examples depict a pattern of intervals that can be transposed to other pitches and therefore to other keys.

In art music and related popular styles, notes outside the basic scale are common. Theorists explain these as altered forms of scale degrees. Notes in a scale are diatonic ('through the notes'), while altered notes are chromatic ('colored'). Each scale degree in the major and minor modes has a name (Table 1).

Table 1

Scale degree	Name
1	tonic
2	supertonic
3	mediant
4	subdominant
5	dominant
6	submediant
7 in major	leading tone
altered 7 in minor	leading tone
unaltered 7 in minor	subtonic

The three minor scales summarize aspects of art music practise (Ex. 1). The pure minor or natural minor scale is a theoretical starting point, showing the relation of the minor scale to the major scale with the tonic a minor third higher (the relative major). Any notes not in the pure minor scale are considered altered notes, although the altered sixth and seventh degrees are ubiquitous in actual musical practise. The melodic minor scale encapsulates normal practise for stepwise motion within a melody or other musical line; stepwise motion from the

fifth degree up to the first degree normally uses altered sixth and seventh degrees, while stepwise descending motion uses the notes of the pure minor scale. The harmonic minor scale shows the notes of common harmonies in the minor mode – in particular, the dominant- and subdominant-function harmonies. (The harmonic minor scale does not reflect the normal mediant harmony in the minor mode, a major triad using the notes of the pure minor scale.)

Some aspects of this classical conceptualization are pertinent to popular music styles. However, the influence of blues and modal practises creates many differences. Melody and harmony derived from the Dorian, Mixolydian or Aeolian modes do not conform to the major or minor practises of eighteenth- and nineteenth-century art music. Popular music is especially likely to violate classical norms for treatment of minor. Major and minor scales do not adequately describe the melodic pitches of blues.

Other scales commonly discussed by theorists include: the chromatic scale, which includes all the available pitches in tempered systems and moves between successive notes by half step (a semitone); the whole-tone scale, which uses half the notes of the chromatic scale, moving by whole step (a whole tone); and the octotonic or 'diminished seventh' scale, which moves by alternating half step and whole step.

The Scale in Training Performers

Repetitive scale practise is a common requirement in the training of art music performers and in formalized

Pure minor

Melodic minor

Harmonic minor

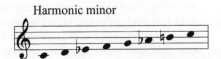

Example 1 C minor scales.

pedagogies of popular music, particularly where jazz is concerned. By practising different scales, musicians work toward control over evenness of duration, volume and timbre, and toward fluency in performing different successions of notes. Jazz pedagogy treats a knowledge of different scales as a basic resource for improvisation.

The Scale as a 'Surface' Resource

In composed and improvised music, scales occur frequently as note-to-note successions. Fast performances of scales display skill in art music, jazz and certain virtuosic popular styles such as heavy metal. Virtuosic performances – including scale passages – often contrast with more expressive performances of melodies. This opposition may structure an individual composition or improvisation. Melodies often use scale segments, and some melodies reproduce complete scales – as, for example, in Irving Berlin's 'There's No Business Like Show Business.'

Walking basses rely on scale motion. Normally, the bass notes that support important harmonies are related by skips. A walking bass fills in these skips with stepwise motion drawn from scales.

The Scale as a 'Structural' Resource

Apart from note-to-note stepwise motion, melodies may also move relatively slowly through the notes of a scale or scale segment, while adding additional notes that break up the immediate succession of scale degrees – as, for example, in Harold Arlen's 'Over the Rainbow' and Jerome Kern's 'The Way You Look Tonight.' The controversial theories of Heinrich Schenker – developed for art music but subsequently applied to popular music and jazz – emphasize elaborated motion through scale segments as a source of musical coherence and continuity. Schenkerian analyses can contribute to the understanding of the relations between scales and structure in some popular music (Forte 1995; Everett 1999, 2001).

Bibliography

Everett, Walter. 1999. *The Beatles as Musicians: Revolver Through the Anthology*. New York: Oxford University Press.

Everett, Walter. 2001. *The Beatles as Musicians: The Quarry Men Through Rubber Soul*. New York: Oxford University Press.

Forte, Allen. 1995. *The American Popular Ballad of the Golden Era, 1924–1950*. Princeton, NJ: Princeton University Press.

Discographical References

Astaire, Fred. 'The Way You Look Tonight.' Brunswick 7717. 1936: USA.

Berlin, Irving. 'There's No Business Like Show Business.' *The Irving Berlin Songbook*. Concord Jazz Special 4513. 1997: USA.

Garland, Judy. 'Over the Rainbow.' Decca 2672. 1939: USA.

Filmography

Swing Time, dir. George Stevens. 1936. USA. 103 mins. Musical. Original music by Jerome Kern.

The Wizard of Oz, dir. Victor Fleming. 1939. USA. 101 mins. Fantasy. Original music by Harold Arlen, Herbert Stothart.

FRED E. MAUS

Theme

The term 'theme' denotes a musical passage, typically characterized by a prominent melodic line, that, through the processes of repetition and/or variation, is established as the key musical idea by which a piece, a specific moment within a piece, or an event or subject associated with a piece is identified. A theme may be characterized by any musical parameter, be it rhythm, melodic shape or harmony, or any combination of such elements. The term originated in classical music, but it is also used in popular music and, particularly, in music for film and television.

The first use of the term 'theme' has been traced back to the Italian composer and theoretician Gioseffo Zarlino (1517–90), who described it as the melodic passage that is repeated and subjected to variation throughout a work. During the course of the seventeenth and eighteenth centuries, the term was employed synonymously with others, such as 'subject' and 'invention.' 'Subject' was commonly applied to the musical idea or theme that is delivered at the beginning of a fugue from which second subjects, countersubjects and so forth are spun contrapuntally, to both complement and contrast with one another. An extreme definition of theme arose when certain scholars restricted it to mean only the very opening four-bar phrase of a melodic passage, thus somewhat condensing the temporal duration of the concept as defined by Zarlino. However, by the mid-nineteenth century the meaning of 'theme' had stabilized as the notion of a complete musical idea, potentially consisting of a number of phrases, that could be situated anywhere within a piece (not just at the beginning) and that had a key structural role in the organization of a work. A common misconception exists that results in the terms 'theme' and 'motif' being used with the same intended meaning. However, the two terms are not synonymous. A motif is typically a significant, yet usually small, rhythmic and/or melodic aspect of a phrase or theme that is repeated to become a defining characteristic of a passage or piece. A good example of a motif can be heard at the very beginning of Beethoven's 5th Symphony, where the short phrase that is the key signature motif not only of the first theme, but of the entire work, is stated.

In popular music, the term 'theme' is generally understood in much the same way as it has been by classical music scholars since the mid-nineteenth century. However, the theme itself is not necessarily restricted to being just a single melodic line. It can be interpreted to mean a musical whole, the melody combined with the accompaniment, and, in certain instances, particularly in music for film and television, it may be not solely a passage of music, but a complete piece in itself. In film and television, 'theme' is used to describe a specific piece of music that is attributed to a particular person(s) or event(s) and is repeated intentionally at relevant moments in the visual narrative. For example, in *Leaving Las Vegas*, Mike Figgis uses a delicate, short Chopinesque piano piece entitled 'Ben and Sera' to underscore the rare moments of reciprocated love between the two main characters. Other examples of similarly 'personalized' leitmotifs are Maurice Jarre's 'Lara's Theme' from *Doctor Zhivago* and Ennio Morricone's 'Tema di Ada' from *1900*.

Recurrent radio and television programs, such as newscasts and serials, are usually heralded by what is known as a 'signature theme,' which is used to indicate aurally that a particular feature is about to commence. 'Title theme' is the term commonly applied to music accompanying either the initial ('main titles') or the final ('end titles') title and credit sequences of a film or one-off television production. However, title themes for films that are part of a series and that feature the same main character(s) and similar story lines function as signature themes in the same way as their television counterparts. Two well-known examples of this type of theme are Monty Norman's 'The James Bond Theme' and John Williams's 'Star Wars Theme.'

Discographical References

'Ben and Sera' (comp. Mike Figgis). *Leaving Las Vegas* (Original soundtrack). Pangaea Records 36071. *1995*: USA.

'Lara's Theme' (comp. Maurice Jarre). *Doctor Zhivago* (Original soundtrack). Rhino 71957. *1995*: USA.

'Tema di Ada' (comp. Ennio Morricone). *1900*. RCA TBL 1-1221. *1976*: USA.

'The James Bond Theme' (comp. Monty Norman, arr. John Barry). *The Best of Bond*. United Artists UAS 29021. *1975*: USA.

'Star Wars Theme' (comp. John Williams). *Star Wars*. Twentieth Century 6641.679. *1977*: USA.

Visual Recording

'The James Bond Theme.' 1992. MGM/UA Home Video PES 99210.

Filmography

Doctor Zhivago, dir. David Lean. 1965. USA/UK. 197 mins. Romantic Epic. Original music by Maurice Jarre.

Leaving Las Vegas, dir. Mike Figgis. 1995. USA. 112 mins. Romantic Drama. Original music by Mike Figgis.

1900 (*Novecento*), dir. Bernardo Bertolucci. 1976. France/West Germany/Italy. 320 mins. Political Drama. Original music by Ennio Morricone.

Star Wars, dir. George Lucas. 1977. USA. 121 mins. Science Fiction. Original music by John Williams.

CHRIS SEDWELL

Tuning

The term 'tuning' refers to: (a) the system or convention according to which pitches are determined; and (b) the manner or process of adjusting instruments to such a convention. There are two types of tuning convention: external, and internal or intra-octave.

External Tuning

External tuning is best exemplified by the concert pitch standard which establishes an agreed reference pitch for a named note: *a* at 440 Hz. External tuning conventions are used to ensure, for example: (a) that, before a performance or a recording session, musicians playing portable pitched instruments in the same ensemble will produce the same pitch (in unison or at octave intervals from that pitch) for the same designated note, or for its sounding equivalent on transposing instruments; (b) that the overall pitch of non-portable instruments (for example, the piano or the organ) matches that of a generally agreed overall standard, in order to facilitate tuning when such instruments are part of an ensemble; and (c) that unaccompanied vocalists start at a pitch that allows them to reach, with a minimum of difficulty, the highest and lowest notes of whatever they are about to sing.

Intra-Octave Tuning

Intra-octave tuning organizes pitches internally within the octave, dividing it into its constituent intervals. The functions of such tuning are: (a) to ensure that any designated pitch included in a performance or a recording session will be sounded in unison by all ensemble members; and (b) to facilitate the learning and application of tonal conventions.

Notes an octave apart are separated by a frequency factor of two (for example, A at 220, 440, 880 Hz) and are universally treated as unison – that is, as 'the same note' sounding higher or lower. The number and pitch of intervals within the octave are, however, subject to a wide variety of tuning.

The most common tuning system for popular music is equal temperament or equal-tone tuning. It divides the

Table 1 Just and Equal Temperament Intervals[1]

Interval	Unison/Tonic	Minor 2nd	Major 2nd	Minor 3rd	Major 3rd	Perfect 4th	Augmented 4th/ Diminished 5th	Perfect 5th	Minor 6th	Major 6th	Minor 7th	Major 7th	Octave/Tonic
Just	1:1	25:24	9:8	6:5	5:4	4:3	45:32	3:2	8:5	5:3	9:5	15:8	2:1
	1	1.042	1.125	1.2	1.25	1.333	1.406	1.5	1.6	1.667	1.8	1.875	2
Equal	1	1.060	1.123	1.189	1.260	1.335	1.414	1.498	1.587	1.682	1.782	1.888	2
'in' A	a	a♯/b♭	b	c	c♯/d♭	d	d♯/e♭	e	f	f♯/g♭	g	g♯/a♭	a

[1] Numerical expressions show the factor by which to multiply or divide the frequency of the unison pitch (1) to obtain the pitch of each interval within an octave of that unison.

octave into 12 equal intervals – semitones – and has been used in the West since the late eighteenth century. It was developed to solve problems caused by discrepancies between certain intervals as constituent parts of the octave and the same intervals in their 'pure' form – that is, as the simple frequency ratios of just tuning or just intonation (see Table 1). For example, the G♯ at the top of the three superimposed pure major thirds A♭-C, C-E, E-G♯ is one-fifth of a tone lower than the octave above the initial A♭, while the top A♭ in the four superimposed pure minor thirds G♯-B-D-F-A♭ is over one-quarter of a tone lower than the octave above the G♯. These natural discrepancies posed particular problems for keyboard players needing to produce both G♯ (as in an E7 chord) and A♭ (as in an F minor triad) in the same piece: one or the other would be seriously out of tune. Equal temperament tackled the problem by slightly detuning each of the octave's 12 constituent semitones so that the interval between each one became equal. Intervals smaller than an equal-temperament semitone ('microtones') are measured in cents (hundredth parts of a semitone).

While equal-tone tuning is essential in most genres using 'classical' harmony – for example, parlor song, operetta, musicals, brass band music, hymns, evergreens, most types of jazz, bossa nova, symphonic film scoring – it is unimportant in music requiring no enharmonic alignment (for example, between D♯ and E♭, or G♯ and A♭) for purposes of modulation or harmonic color. Equal temperament is unnecessary in, for example, most types of blues, bluegrass, blues-based rock and folk-rock, not to mention the traditional musics of Africa, the Arab world, the Balkans, the British Isles, the Indian subcontinent and Scandinavia. In fact, equal temperament is more likely to be the exception than the rule for musics whose tonality is modal and/or drone-based, because the constant sounding of tonic and fifth produces natural overtones inconsistent with equal-tuning intervals, and because the relationship of pitches within the octave to one unchanging tonic is essential to the expressive dynamic of such musics. In popular music of the traditions just mentioned, then, just tuning is far more likely to be used, unless instruments like the piano, the accordion or the non-detunable synthesizer are included in the ensemble.

Table 2 Octave division of four heptatonic modes (intervals in cents)

	100 →	100 →	100 →	100 →	100 →	100 →	100 →	100 →	100 →	100 →	100 →	100 →
Chromatic	a	b♭	b	c	c♯	d	e♭	e	f	f♯	g	g♯	a
Ionian	1	200 →	2	200 →	3		4	200 →	5	200 →	6	200 →	7	8
Rast	1	200 →	2	150 →	3	150 →	4	200 →	5	200 →	6	150 →	7	150 →	8
Bayati	1	150 →	2	150 →	3	200 →	4	200 →	5	150 →	6	150 →	7	200 →	8
Pelog	Nem 167 →		Pitu 245 →		Siji 125 →	Loro 146 →	Teilu 252 →		Papat 165 → (Pelog)	Lima 100 →	Nem

597

Within the general framework of just temperament, there is, however, a wide variety of tunings used in different popular music traditions. Despite a few exceptions, such as the various *pelog* and *slendro* systems of Java (Malm 1967, 45–47), most tunings include the natural fourth (4:3) and fifth (3:2) scale degrees (see Tables 1 and 2). However, Arab and Indian music theory divides the octave into 16 and 22 unequal steps, respectively, reflecting intra-octave tuning conventions that differ from those of the urbanized West. For example, the heptatonic Arab mode closest to the Ionian, *Rast*, features a 'neutral' third and seventh roughly halfway between Western major and minor pitches, while *Bayati* (similar to Dorian or Aeolian) contains a 'neutral' second and sixth.

Stringed Instrument Tunings

Unlike monophonic instruments, which merely need adjusting to a common reference pitch, polyphonic instruments (actual or potential) require further tuning. Piano and pipe organ tuning is carried out by experts, but portable stringed instruments are tuned by their players. The pitches to which open strings are tuned vary considerably from one instrument to another. Table 3 shows examples of standard tuning for some of popular music's most common stringed instruments. String note names are provided for clarification and do not necessarily indicate concert pitch. (In Scandinavian fiddling, for example, standard violin tuning is often raised by a whole tone.)

Several instruments listed in Table 3 have common alternative tunings. For example, a *sāz* can be tuned CFC, while other common *bouzoúki* tunings are CFAD or DAFC (2 × 4-string), and DAD (2 × 3-string, common in *rebetika*). *'Ūd* tunings vary considerably from region to region (for example, between Turkey and Armenia), and fiddle tunings are often adjusted to the character of the music to be played, typically to create tonic-and-fifth drone effects (for example, GDGD, G♯D♯G♯D♯, ADAD and AEAE). Some common alternative guitar tunings (aka *scordatura*) used in the Anglophone music traditions are set out in Table 4. All these tunings can be transposed using a capo. It should also be noted that several stringed instruments used in popular music of the Middle East, the Arab world and the Indian subcontinent (for example, the Turkish *sāz* or the *tanbur*) are provided with ligatures which function as movable frets allowing the musician to accommodate tunings based on a division of the octave into more than 12 intervals (see Table 2).

Tuning and Timbre

Many instruments are provided with double sets of strings – for example, the 12-string guitar (2 × 6 strings), the *rebetika bouzoúki* (3 × 2 strings) and different types of balalaika, each pair of strings being tuned in unison or

Table 3 Examples of standard open string tunings for common instruments

Instrument	Low string				High string			Instrument
Banjo		g	d/c	g	b	d		Banjo
Banjo-Tenor	c	g	d	a	c			Tenor Banjo
Bass	e	a	d	g				Bass
*Bouzouki			g	d	a	d		Bouzouki*
Charango		g	c	e	a	e		Charango
Fiddle			g	d	a	e		Fiddle
Guitar (see Table 4)	e	a	d	g	b	e		Guitar (see Table 4)
Mandolin			g	d	a	e		Mandolin
*Sāz			c/d	g	c			Sāz*
Sitār (e.g.)	sa-1 c-1	pa-1 g-1	sa c	ma e	pa g	sa+1 c+1	sa+2 c+2	
*'Ūd (Arabian)	d	g	a	d	g	c		'Ūd (Arabian)*
Ukelele				a	d	f♯	b	Ukelele

* Standard tunings vary widely for this instrument. Only one common tuning is given in the Table.

Table 4 Some alternative guitar tunings

Name	Low string					High string	Usage
STANDARD	e	a	d	g	b	e	general
Open E	e	b	e	g♯	b	e	slide, Delta blues, folk
Open D or Vestapol	d	a	d	f♯	a	d	
Drop D	d	a	d	g	b	e	folk
Drop double D	d	a	d	g	b	d	
D modal	d	a	d	d	a	d	
DADGAD	d	a	d	g	a	d	folk, esp. Irish etc.
Open G or Taropatch	d	g	d	g	b	d	slide, Delta blues
Dobro	g	b	d	g	b	d	Delta blues, Country
Open A or Hawaiian	e	a	e	a	c♯	e	Hawaiian, slide
C sixth	c	g	c	g	a	e	'New Age'

an octave apart. Each of the piano's upper keys is assigned its own triple set of strings. The point of such unison or octave doubling (tripling in the case of pianos) seems to be to create a brighter or fuller sound for each note. The 'bright' effect is due to doubling at the octave or higher, as in the case of 4′, 2′ and mixture stops, tabs or drawbars on the organ. The 'full' effect, however, more likely relates to unison doubling and works as follows. Two simultaneously sounding strings, pipes or reeds tuned to the same pitch rarely produce that pitch in perfect unison, with the result that a greater number of partials is created for each note than issues from just one of the two. Popular music exploits this timbral aspect of tuning in many ways, of which three can be summarized.

First, the characteristic 'rich' sound of the French accordion derives from each note being assigned two reeds which are slightly out of tune with each other. Second, recorded tracks are often doubled, sometimes several times, either digitally or 'live,' to create an effect of multiplicity. Not only can the copied or repeated tracks be offset from the original by a few milliseconds, but they can also be slightly detuned, either naturally or by digital manipulation. The effect of slightly detuning a copied track without simultaneous offsetting resembles the 'wider' sound produced by applying chorus or modest amounts of phasing to the same signal source (Lacasse 2000, 126–31). Third, digitally detuning a copied piano track and playing it back with the original produces a 'ragtime' or 'barrel piano' effect similar to that created by an out-of-tune piano or by one that has been intentionally 'soured.'

Bibliography

Asmar, Sami. n.d. *Maqamat: Commonly Used in Arab Music, with Ascending Intervals & Transpositions.* www.turath.org/Resources/MaqamTrans.htm

Definitions of Old Time Fiddle Styles. n.d. http://www.gpfn.sk.ca/culture/arts/fiddle/vfc/lessons/def_style.html

Godden, Brian. 2000. *Guitar Tunings.* http://www.silver-bushmusic.com/Tunings.html

Jeans, James. 1968. *Science and Music.* New York: Dover.

Just Tuning or Just Intonation. n.d. http://www.sfu.ca/sonic-studio/handbook/Just_Tuning.html

Lacasse, Serge. 2000. *'Listen to My Voice': The Evocative Power of Vocal Staging in Recorded Rock Music and Other Forms of Vocal Expression.* Ph.D. thesis, Institute of Popular Music, University of Liverpool.

Lindley, Mark. 2001. 'Temperaments.' In *The New Grove Dictionary of Music and Musicians*, Vol. 25, ed. Stanley Sadie. 2nd ed. London: Macmillan, 248–68.

Lloyd, L.S., and Boyle, Hugh. 1979. 'The History of Our Scale.' In L.S. Lloyd and Hugh Boyle, *Intervals, Scales, and Temperaments.* New York: St. Martin's Press, 34–51.

Malm, William P. 1967. *Music Cultures of the Pacific, the Near East, and Asia.* Englewood Cliffs, NJ: Prentice-Hall.

McGann, Cliff. 1996. *Celtic Guitar.* www.ceolas.org/instruments/celtic_guitar.html

Smyth, Bill. n.d. *Altered Tunings for the Intermediate Guitarist.* http://www.peak.org/~ritabill/Tunings/Web/Tunings.html

Weisstein, Eric. 2000. 'Scale.' *Eric Weisstein's Treasure*

Example 1 Typical turnaround figure for a slow blues in F.

Trove of Music. http://www.ericweisstein.com/encyclo-pedias/music/Scale.html

PHILIP TAGG

Turnaround

The original meaning of 'turnaround' denotes a short progression of chords played at the end of one section of a song or instrumental number, the purpose of which is to facilitate recapitulation of the complete harmonic sequence of the section. The transferred meaning of the term indicates any short sequence of chords, usually three or four, that recur consecutively inside the same section of a single piece of music.

Example 1 (above) shows a typical turnaround for a slow 12-bar blues in F in which the changes would run, for example, ‖:F|B♭|F|F⁷|B♭|B♭|F|F|C|B♭|F|F:‖. To avoid harmonic stasis, and in order to lead back into the initial F chord of bar 1, the final F chord of bars 11 and 12 can be replaced with a sequence such as the |F F⁷/ₐ B♭ Bdim|F/c D♭⁹ C⁷| progression shown in the example. This turnaround first increases the rate of harmonic change in motion toward the final C chord (bar 12), which, in its turn, leads back to the F of bar 1, creating in the process a highlighted V→I cadence and an effect of continuity over the join between the two passages.

The performance of jazz standards in AABA form features turnarounds before each recurrence of the A section. Table 1 shows the basic chord changes for the 10-bar 'A' section of the chorus of the World War II hit 'A Nightingale Sang in Berkeley Square' (Maschwitz). A harmonic rhythm of two chords to the bar is established in the first eight bars of this song. However, harmonic progression stops on E♭ in bars 9–10 and across the join to the reprise from bar 1. To avoid such harmonic stasis, the last two bars can be provided with a simple turnaround consisting of a standard I→vi→ii→V vamp figure – for example, ‖ E♭⁶ → Cm⁷ | Fm⁷ → B♭⁷ ‖ – or a tritone substitution of these changes (E♭⁶ → G♭¹³ → | Fm⁹ → E⁹♭⁵).

Since the purpose of a turnaround is, in the sense just described, to maintain harmonic rhythm and direction while at the same time effectuating a return to the first chord in a passage, it is by its very nature circular. In fact, one of the most common turnarounds in popular song is the I→vi/IV→ii→V progression (vamp) that is often used as a consecutively repeated two- or four-bar accompanying figure, to provide a sense of movement before the entry of a solo singer or instrumentalist between verses or passages or at the start of a song ('vamp until ready'). Moreover, the consecutively repeated I→vi→ii→V vamp and its variant I→vi→IV→V constitute either all or most of the chord changes found in much English-language popular song (see Table 2, row 2).

With vamps providing the majority of changes for large parts of many pop songs, it is hardly surprising that

Table 1 Basic changes for the 'A' section of 'A Nightingale Sang in Berkeley Square' (slow 4/4)

1		2		3		4		5	
E♭maj7	Cm7	Gm7	E♭9	A♭maj7	G7	Cm7	D♭9	E♭maj7	A♭maj7

6		7		8		9		10	
E♭maj7	A♭m7	E♭maj7	Cm7	F9	B♭-9	E♭6	E♭6	E♭6	E♭6
Vamp turnaround for reprise →						Cm7	Fm7	B♭7	
Tritone substitution of vamp turnaround for reprise 1 →						G♭13	Fm9	E9♭5	

Table 2 Some common pop turnarounds

Suggested name	Progression	Examples of songs containing a turnaround
'La bamba'	I→IV→V	Valens: 'La bamba'; B. Poole: 'Do You Love Me'; Marti: 'Guantanamera'; McCoys: 'Hang on Sloopy'; ABBA: chorus of 'The Name of the Game'; Isley Brothers, the Beatles, B. Poole: 'Twist and Shout'; the Troggs: 'Wild Thing'
'Vamp'	I→vii→ii/IV→V	Rodgers: 'Blue Moon'; Anka: 'Diana'; Valens: 'Donna'; Chacksfield: 'Ebb Tide'; Paul and Paula: 'Hey Paula'; Gerry and the Pacemakers: 'I Like It'; Twitty: 'It's Only Make Believe'; Capaldi: 'Love Hurts'; Sedaka: 'Oh Carol,' 'Happy Birthday, Sweet Sixteen,' 'Little Devil'; Tillotson: 'Poetry in Motion'; Presley: verse of 'Return to Sender'; Shannon: 'Runaway'; B. E. King: 'Stand By Me'; Maurice Williams and the Zodiacs, the Hollies: 'Stay'; Dion and the Belmonts: 'A Teenager in love'; Fields: 'These Foolish things'; the Beatles: 'This Boy'; Liberace: 'Unchained Melody'; Mann: 'Who Put the Bomp (in the Bomp, Bomp, Bomp)'; Frankie Lymon and the Teenagers: 'Why Do fools Fall in Love'
'Aeolian shuttle'	(I/i→) ♭VI→♭VII (→I/i)	Dylan, Hendrix: 'All Along the Watchtower'; Cara: chorus of 'Flashdance'; Collins: 'In the Air Tonight'; Aerosmith: 'run away' in 'Janie's Got a Gun'; Derek and the Dominos: 'Layla'; Led Zeppelin: end of 'Stairway to Heaven'; Dire Straits: 'Sultans of Swing'; 10cc: 'The Wall Street Shuffle'; the Pet Shop Boys: 'West End Girls'
'Mixolydian turnaround'	I→♭VII→IV→(V)	Creedence Clearwater Revival: 'Fortunate Son'; the Beatles: end of 'Hey Jude'; Darin, the Four Tops: 'If I Were a Carpenter'; the Bar-Kays: 'Soul Finger'; Lynyrd Skynyrd: 'Sweet Home Alabama'; the Kinks: 'Twentieth Century Man'

'turnaround' also came to denote, especially in pop and rock circles, *any* short consecutively repeated sequence of chords. In this transferred sense of the term, turnarounds usually consist of three or four chords covering a period of two or four bars. A sequence of only two chords constitutes a chord shuttle or pendulum, not a turnaround. Conversely, a harmonic progression occupying a complete passage (section) of eight or more bars cannot be a turnaround in itself, because a turnaround sequence must, in order to qualify as such, occur consecutively at least twice within one passage or section. Turnarounds are extremely common in pop and rock music, often contributing significantly to the particular character and style specificity of individual songs and instrumental numbers. For example, most of the vamp turnaround songs mentioned in row 2 of Table 2 were recorded in the United States around 1960. Similarly, most of the songs referred to in row 3 of Table 2 are in the rock vein, and sport lyrics that encompass 'a relatively uniform field of associations which might be characterised by

such concepts as "modernity," "uncertainty," "sadness," "stasis"' and so on (Björnberg 1984, 382).

Bibliography

Björnberg, Alf. 1984. '"There's Something Going On" – om eolisk harmonik i nutida rockmusik' ['There's Something Going On': On Aeolian Harmony in Contemporary Rock Music]. In *Tvärspel: 31 artiklar om musik. Festskrift till Jan Ling* [Tvärspel: 31 Articles on Music. Festschrift for Jan Ling]. Göteborg: Skrifter från musikvetenskapliga institutionen 9, 371–86.

Moore, Allan. 1992. 'Patterns of Harmony.' *Popular Music* 11(1): 73–106.

Tagg, Philip. 1993. '"Universal" Music and the Case of Death.' *Critical Quarterly* 35(2): 54–85.

Sheet Music

Rodgers, Richard, comp., and Hart, Lorenz, lyr. 1934. 'Blue Moon.' New York: Robbins Music Corp.

Sherwin, Manning, comp., and Maschwitz, Eric, lyr.

1940. 'A Nightingale Sang in Berkeley Square.' New York: Peter Maurice Music Co.

Discographical References

ABBA. 'The Name of the Game.' Epic EPC 5750. *1977*: UK.

Aerosmith. 'Janie's Got a Gun.' *Pump*. Geffen 924 254-2. *1989*: UK.

'A Nightingale Sang in Berkeley Square.' *We'll Meet Again: The Love Songs of World War II*. Smithsonian MSD2M-35384. *1994*: USA.

Anka, Paul. 'Diana.' Columbia DB 3980. *1957*: UK.

Bar-Kays, The. 'Soul Finger.' Stax 601014. *1967*: USA.

Beatles, The. 'Hey Jude.' Apple R 5722. *1968*: UK.

Beatles, The. 'This Boy.' Parlophone R 5084. *1963*: UK.

Beatles, The. 'Twist and Shout.' *Please Please Me*. Parlophone PMC 1202. *1963*: UK.

Capaldi, Jim. 'Love Hurts.' Island WIP 6246. *1975*: UK.

Cara, Irene. 'Flashdance . . . What a Feeling.' Casablanca 811440-7. *1983*: USA.

Chacksfield, Frank, and His Orchestra. 'Ebb Tide.' Decca F 10122. 1953: UK.

Collins, Phil. 'In the Air Tonight.' Atlantic 3824. *1981*: USA.

Creedence Clearwater Revival. 'Fortunate Son.' *Willy and the Poor Boys*. Liberty LBS 83338. *1970*: UK.

Darin, Bobby. 'If I Were a Carpenter.' Atlantic 2350. *1966*: USA.

Derek and the Dominos. 'Layla.' Polydor 2058 130. *1970*: UK.

Dion and the Belmonts. 'A Teenager in Love.' Laurie 3027. *1959*: USA.

Dire Straits. 'Sultans of Swing.' *Dire Straits*. Vertigo 9102 021. *1978*: UK.

Dylan, Bob. 'All Along the Watchtower.' *John Wesley Harding*. Columbia CL-2804. *1967*: USA.

Fields, Benny. 'These Foolish Things.' *Those Wonderful Thirties*. Decca DEA 7-1. 1936; *1974*: UK.

Four Tops, The. 'If I Were a Carpenter.' Tamla Motown 1124. *1968*: USA.

Gerry and the Pacemakers. 'I Like It.' Columbia DB 7041. *1963*: UK.

Hollies, The. 'Stay.' Parlophone R 5077. *1963*: UK.

Isley Brothers, The. 'Twist and Shout.' Wand 124. *1962*: USA.

Jimi Hendrix Experience, The. 'All Along the Watchtower.' *Electric Ladyland*. Track 613-008-9. *1968*: UK.

King, Ben E. 'Stand By Me.' London HLK 9358. *1961*: UK.

Kinks, The. 'Twentieth Century Man.' *Muswell Hillbillies*. RCA 4644. *1971*: UK.

Led Zeppelin. 'Stairway to Heaven.' *Led Zeppelin 4*. Atlantic SD 7208. *1971*: USA.

Liberace. 'Unchained Melody.' Philips PB 430. *1955*: UK.

Lymon, Frankie, and the Teenagers. 'Why Do Fools Fall in Love.' Columbia DB 3772. *1956*: UK.

Lynyrd Skynyrd. 'Sweet Home Alabama.' MCA 40258. *1974*: USA.

Mann, Barry. 'Who Put the Bomp (in the Bomp, Bomp, Bomp).' ABC-Paramount 10237. *1961*: USA.

Marcels, The. 'Blue Moon.' Colpix 186. *1961*: USA.

McCoys, The. 'Hang On Sloopy.' Immediate IM 001. *1965*: UK.

Paul and Paula. 'Hey Paula.' Philips 304012 BF. *1963*: UK.

Pet Shop Boys, The. 'West End Girls.' Parlophone R 6115. *1985*: UK.

Poole, Brian, and the Tremeloes. 'Do You Love Me.' Decca F 11739. *1963*: UK.

Poole, Brian, and the Tremeloes. 'Twist and Shout.' Decca F 11694. *1963*: UK.

Presley, Elvis. 'Return to Sender.' RCA 1320. *1962*: UK.

Sandpipers, The. 'Guantanamera.' Pye International 7N 25380. *1966*: UK.

Sedaka, Neil. 'Happy Birthday, Sweet Sixteen.' RCA 1266. *1961*: UK.

Sedaka, Neil. 'Little Devil.' RCA 1236. *1961*: UK.

Sedaka, Neil. 'Oh Carol.' RCA 1152. *1959*: UK.

Shannon, Del. 'Runaway.' London HLX 9317. *1961*: UK.

10cc. 'The Wall Street Shuffle.' UK Records UK 69. *1974*: UK.

Tillotson, Johnny. 'Poetry in Motion.' London HLA 9231. *1960*: UK.

Troggs, The. 'Wild Thing.' Fontana TF 689. *1966*: UK.

Twitty, Conway. 'It's Only Make Believe.' MGM 992. *1958*: UK.

Valens, Ritchie. 'Donna'/'La Bamba.' Del-Fi 4110. *1958*: UK.

Williams, Maurice, and the Zodiacs. 'Stay.' Herald 552. *1960*: USA.

PHILIP TAGG

Variation

Variation is a technique of modified repetition in which a basic idea or theme, usually stated initially in its original form, is subjected to a process of alteration, the extent and nature of which can vary considerably. European art music's concept of 'theme and variations' exemplifies this process: an original idea (often a simple tune taken from another composer) is presented first and forms the basis for a series of subsequent restatements, each illustrating a different modification of the initial theme. The technique involved can vary considerably. For instance, one variation may simply comprise ornamentation of the original melody. Others may retain the original melodic structure, but feature a different harmony; additionally, the melody may be retained, but the accompaniment be re-harmonized in a different key – from C major to its relative A minor, for example. In some cases, the structure of the theme may become so grossly distorted that it bears little, if any, resemblance to the original idea.

Variation is a feature of much jazz improvisation. An opening melody with a fixed accompanying chord sequence is often the platform from which a soloist will launch into improvisation. The resulting patterns of notes chosen can constitute melodic variation over a repeated chord progression. However, in such a case, the term 'variation' should be applied with care and be used only when a firm structural constant – such as a fixed chord progression over a specific number of bars – is present. As soon as this constant is discarded, the piece leaves the realm of variation and becomes purely improvisational. Consequently, in popular music, the instrumental verse of a song that features an electric guitar solo could be considered a variation in a case where, although the original vocal melody is not necessarily adhered to, the texture and structure of both the accompaniment and the solo passage remain substantially similar to their previous presence within the same piece.

CHRIS SEDWELL

19. Rhythm

Afterbeat

'Afterbeat' is a term used to denote the temporal location of a musical event in measured music that occurs 'after' a 'beat' but prior to the ensuing beat. In reference to fast-tempo quadruple-meter musics, where beats 1 and 3 are generally the main pulsing units or 'strong beats,' the terms 'afterbeat' and 'backbeat' are often used interchangeably to describe one and the same rhythmic phenomenon. At other times, afterbeat implies offbeat.

GARRY TAMLYN

Backbeat

'Backbeat' refers to a musical practise in which the primary accent is placed on the second and/or fourth beats of a nominal 4/4 bar. The term is commonly used to denote recurring, dynamically accented snare-drum performances on beats 2 and/or 4, noncontiguous with snare-drum performances on beats 1 and/or 3, occurring in quadruple-meter drumbeats (see Ex. 1). References to backbeat in relation to other accompaniments, such as those provided by bass or rhythm guitar, imply a similar performance practise, whereby beats 2 and 4 of accompanimental rhythms are emphasized, particularly by dynamic accent.

Early examples of snare backbeat are to be found in the recorded performances of Chicago jazz drummers, such as Gene Krupa and Paul Barbarin, who were recording during the 1930s. During that period, Chicago jazz drumming occasionally featured snare backbeat (or cymbal backbeat) in such formal-structural sections as final ('shout') choruses, loud tutti sections and/or instrumental solos. The characteristic presence of oom-pah rhythms in early jazz accompaniments provided Chicago jazz drummers with an opportunity to emphasize backbeats rather than 'strong' beats (beats 1 and 3) of a 4/4 bar; the 'strong' beats were highlighted by bass instruments, thereby creating a type of metrical 'punning.' It is possible that the occurrence of backbeat in 1930s Chicago jazz drumming was also inspired, at least in part, by sanctified gospel styles. For instance, the recorded output of 'Sister' Bessie Johnson, produced in Chicago during the late 1920s and early 1930s, displays the very considerable presence of emphatically performed backbeat, mostly in the form of handclaps.

Later jazz styles, including swing and bebop, typically featured comping snare rhythms or rhythms that emphasized all four beats of a 4/4 bar. Rhythm and blues (R&B) of the 1940s contained drumming similar to that found in contemporaneous jazz but, from the late 1940s, R&B produced in mid-US locations increasingly featured snare backbeat in loud, honking saxophone solos and/or shout choruses. Exceptionally, R&B recorded in Chicago between about 1946 and 1950 with Judge Riley drumming often included snare backbeat on beats 2 and/or 4 in most formal-structural sections of a song (for example, William McKinley 'Jazz' Gillum's 'Roll Dem Bones' (Chicago, 1946)). A consistent use of snare backbeat on beats 2 and 4 throughout all formal-structural sections of a song began to feature in recordings by R&B

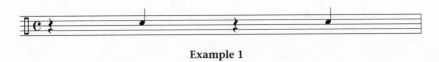

Example 1

musicians who were musically active in various mid-US locations from around 1949, most noticeably in the recordings of Fats Domino with Earl Palmer drumming. Apart from some instrumental performances, such as the extended saxophone solos of Big Jay McNeely (for example, 'Blow Big Jay' (Los Angeles, 1949)), R&B performed on the east and west coasts of the United States rarely included snare backbeat.

Early examples of backbeat can also be found in country and western musical styles. During the 1930s, the increasing use of country and western as dance music demanded a beat that could be clearly heard above the sounds of live performance situations. Country and western ensembles did not typically feature drums and, therefore, a percussive and dynamically highlighted backbeat was usually provided by rhythm guitar and double bass. Rhythm guitarists highlighted the backbeat by forceful and quickly executed strumming, which often produced a sound similar to that of a snare drum played with brushes; bassists, on the other hand, sometimes featured slap-bass executions on backbeat, particularly in live rather than recorded performances. Snare backbeat in country and western gradually evolved from such performance practises: early examples can be found in the recorded performances of drummer Smokey Dacus, who recorded with Bob Wills and His Texas Playboys throughout the late 1930s.

Country music produced in Hollywood during the late 1930s and early 1940s often contained accompaniments that emphasized all beats of a 4/4 bar. During the 1940s, however, a return to a rural honky-tonk country style was evident and, by the late 1940s, simpler accompanimental formats featuring percussive and dynamically emphasized backbeat dominated country music. For example, Hank Williams's late-1940s recordings – which reflect the stylistic trend toward a honky-tonk sound – commonly contained accompaniments similar to that notated in Example 2 (see 'Honky Tonkin'' (1947)).

Prototypical rock 'n' roll recordings, produced during

the early 1950s by such musicians as Bill Haley and Lloyd Price, for example, often featured snare backbeat throughout all formal-structural sections of a song. By the mid-1950s, a consistent use of snare backbeat throughout a song was firmly established in rock 'n' roll drumming style. This performance practise has constituted one of the defining characteristics of rock and rock-related musical styles.

Bibliography

Tamlyn, Garry. 1998. *The Big Beat: Origins and Development of Snare Backbeat and Other Accompanimental Rhythms in Rock 'n' Roll.* Ph.D. thesis, Institute of Popular Music, University of Liverpool.

Discographical References

Gillum, William McKinley 'Jazz.' 'Roll Dem Bones.' *Jazz Gillum: Complete Recorded Works 1936–1949 in Chronological Order, Vol. 4.* Document DOCD-5200. *1993*: Austria.

McNeely, Big Jay. 'Blow Big Jay.' *Big Jay McNeely: Road House Boogie.* Saxonograph BP-1300. *1986*: USA.

Williams, Hank. 'Honky Tonkin'.' *Hank Williams: The Original Singles Collection . . . Plus, Vol. 1.* PolyGram 847 195-2. *1990*: USA.

Discography

Haley, Bill. *Bill Haley and His Comets: Rock the Joint! The Original Essex Recordings, 1951–1954.* Schoolkids Records SKR 1529. *1994*: USA.

Johnson, 'Sister' Bessie. *Memphis Gospel, 1927–1929: The Complete Recorded Works of Sister Mary Nelson, Lonnie McIntorsh and Bessie Johnson in Chronological Order.* Document DOCD-5072. *1991*: Austria.

Price, Lloyd. *Lloyd Price: Lawdy!.* Ace Records CDCHD 360. *1991*: USA.

Williams, Hank. 'Fly Trouble.' *Hank Williams: The Original Singles Collection . . . Plus, Vol. 1.* PolyGram 847 195-2. *1990*: USA.

GARRY TAMLYN

Beat

The term 'beat' can have several meanings, all of which relate in some way to the organization of time in music. Beat can often suggest the idea of temporal units, such as those produced by the action of a metronome. In this context, beat denotes recurring isochronous, temporally equidistant reference points, not necessarily sounded, that evenly divide a musical continuum. Beat, therefore, serves as a temporal reference point for rhythm, beat rates being expressible in terms of tempo as evident from metronome markings (spoken of as so many 'beats per minute').

In musicological discussions of rhythm, beat (as previously defined) is sometimes referred to as 'pulse,'

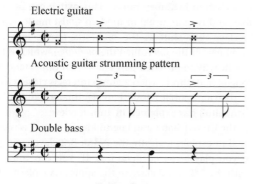

Electric guitar

Acoustic guitar strumming pattern

Double bass

Example 2

although the relationship between the two terms is generally not made clear. Further terminological confusion arises from discussions of beat and pulse in relation to metronomic and musical time. In order to account for variations in duration, as in rubato performance where one 'bends' rhythms for purposes of expressive nuance, beat and pulse are sometimes interchangeably used. For example, Lester (1986, 46) employs the term 'beat' in reference to 'functionally equivalent spans of time,' whereas Epstein (1995) prefers the term 'pulse' to account for temporal malleability associated with musical performance. In common parlance, 'beat' generally fulfills both of the aforementioned temporal characteristics; metronomic beat is often discussed as 'beats per minute,' whereas 'a good dance beat' suggests a level of rhythmic abstraction informed by interpretative aspects relating to musical performance.

'Beat' and 'rhythm' are also variously used, often interchangeably, in relation to the description of popular music. For instance, 'beat' can refer to a regularly recurring composite rhythm, such as a 'Bo Diddley beat' or a 'Latin beat.' In musicological accounts of popular music, temporal aspects of melodic material are more likely to be discussed in terms of 'rhythm' rather than 'beat.'

Finally, beat often implies a multi-part musical event consisting of simultaneously sounded accompanimental and often repetitive rhythms. It is possible, therefore, to isolate and then discuss bass or rhythm guitar, keyboard or drum performances in a rock accompaniment in terms of 'rhythm' and refer to any consistently repetitive accompanimental polyphony as 'beat.' Similarly, drumming can be discussed according to 'beat' or, alternately, can refer to the repetitive 'rhythms' produced on particular items of drumkit hardware. For instance, the drumming notated in Example 1 can be discussed in terms of its cymbal and snare and bass drum rhythms, the simultaneous sounding of which constitutes a 'drum beat.'

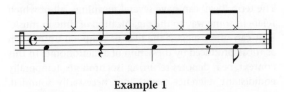

Example 1

Bibliography

Epstein, David. 1995. *Shaping Time: Music, the Brain, and Performance*. New York: Schirmer Books.

Lester, Joel. 1986. *The Rhythms of Tonal Music*. Carbond-

ale and Edwardsville: Southern Illinois University Press.

GARRY TAMLYN

Clave

The clave is a Cuban rhythmic pattern of 2/3 or 3/2 (used notably in the genre known as *son*) which always alternates weak and strong beats. It provides a time line for the music by keeping a constant five-beat measure, divided into 2-strike-pause-3-strike, or the reverse, i.e., 3-strike-pause-2-strike. This pattern may be played by a pair of claves or by another percussion instrument, or it may be subtly swopped around between instruments; in many cases, it may simply be playing inside the musicians' heads. As a time line, it enables many other rhythms to be played simultaneously by a whole orchestra and allows all the orchestra members to keep pace with each other rather than falling into the 'rhythmical anarchy' of crossed, or intersecting, clave rhythms or basically falling out of the groove.

However, the obligatory use of the clave may be more recent than imagined, due to a certain rationalization of Cuban oral traditions since the revolution and the dynamic between Cubans within and outside the island. According to musician Compay Segundo (Francisco Repilado), who participated in the original Buena Vista Social Club recording:

> In Havana, the *clave de son* is the most used and most classical. When we moved from the east to Havana, we were told that our music was 'out of clave' because we used a free style of singing, whereas in Havana we had to follow this pattern. Most of the Trio Matamoros songs were performed 'out of clave' because in the east the singing is free form and the rhythmic beat is not set, just played. (Ex. 1) (Segundo 1999)

In general, the 2/3 pattern is known as the rumba clave (Ex. 2), while the 3/2 pattern is known as the *son* clave (Ex. 3). However, in some pieces the reverse may occur for some parts due to the endemic nature of improvisation in Cuban music. This switch can be very subtle and is more usual in modern *timba* music, when the clave may shift as the orchestra moves into the second part of the *son* (called the *montuno*), which is the more heavily improvised part and which can extend for a long period; this is when a group interacts closely with the dancing public. José Luís Quintana (known as 'Changuito') has explained in an interview:

> In the United States and Puerto Rico, a system was created to explain logically the 2/3 or 3/2 clave concept. If you play a *son montuno* [Ex. 4], you can come in with the 2/3 or 3/2 clave in the appropriate place. The most important thing is that the percussion, bass,

Example 1 Clave used in Cuban *son* by Compay Segundo.

Example 2

Example 3

Example 4

piano and, most importantly, the bongo players come in at the same point of the clave. In Cuba, the 2/3 or 3/2 never existed; every time we created a musical orchestration, we came in together, without knowing if it was 2/3 or 3/2. What happens now in Puerto Rico or New York is an incorrect practise of this concept, and when listening to some recordings you can hear that the clave is crossed [Ex. 5], which is a mistake. This is the way it should be [Ex. 6]. Our musicians have understood the concept of being 'out of clave' since early on [Ex. 7]. Nonetheless, most musicians in the world who play Cuban music are aware of and know how to recognize the clave concept. ('Changuito' 1998)

Instrumentalists, musical groups and singers of salsa, boogaloo and a host of musics influenced by Caribbean rhythms have in different periods found using the clave to be a key inspiration. Among them are Oscar Valdés,

Pete 'El Conde' Rodríguez, and in Cuba practically every *son*, rumba, *charanga* and *vieja trova* ensemble, including Los Muñequitos de Matanzas, Los Papines, Adalberto Alvarez and Irakere. Notable recent innovators have been the orchestras Los Van Van, led by Juan Formell, and NG La Banda, led by José Luis Cortés, in developments in *son* called *songo* and, most recently, *timba*.

Bibliography

'Changuito' (José Luis Quintana). 1998. Interview with author, 6 June. Havana.

Segundo, Compay (Francisco Repilado). 1999. Interview with author, 9 April. São Paulo.

Discography

Buena Vista Social Club. *Buena Vista Social Club*. Elektra/Asylum 79478. *1997*: USA.

Los Van Van. *The Legendary Los Van Van: 30 Years of Cuba's Greatest Dance Band*. Ashe 2007. *1999*: USA.

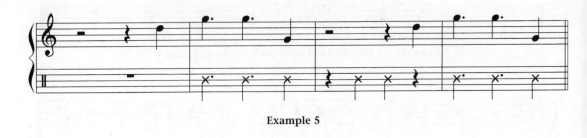

Example 5

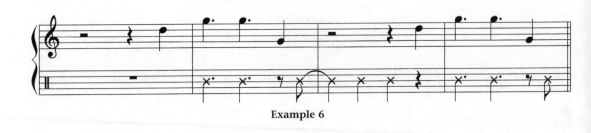

Example 6

Example 7

NG La Banda. *The Best of NG La Banda*. Blue Note 21391. *2000*: USA.

EDWIN RICARDO PITRE VÁSQUEZ (trans. ZUZANA PICK) and JAN FAIRLEY

Cross-Rhythm

'Cross-rhythm' is a term used to denote the conflicting durational, dynamic or pitch-based accents produced through the sounding of two or more seemingly metrically independent rhythms contained in a single-voice part or in simultaneously sounded multiple-voice parts. The interweaving, or crossing, of such dissimilar rhythms may obscure the location of the main beat and subsequently cloud metric perception. One resultant effect of cross-rhythm is a polyrhythmic texture that comprises multiple metric images. For example, the composite rhythm notated in Example 1, when performed with equally accented articulations on each note, might produce a two-level metric image, as notated in Example 2.

Multiple cross-rhythms are common to African and African-American music. In particular, cross-rhythms are most noticeable in ragtime, where the underlying meter exemplified in oom-pah accompaniment often competes with syncopated melodies of the right hand, creating two-level cross-rhythms. Example 3 displays a common 3/8 ragtime cross-rhythm that is largely informed by pitch-derived accents occurring on the first note of each three-note eighth-note group.

When cross-rhythms occur in popular music, the independent rhythms generally meet at a given metrical point (for example, George Gershwin's 'I Got Rhythm' or the Rolling Stones' 'Satisfaction'). Extended syncopation, however, can create continuous, albeit subtle, cross-rhythm, as in accented offbeats in boogie piano

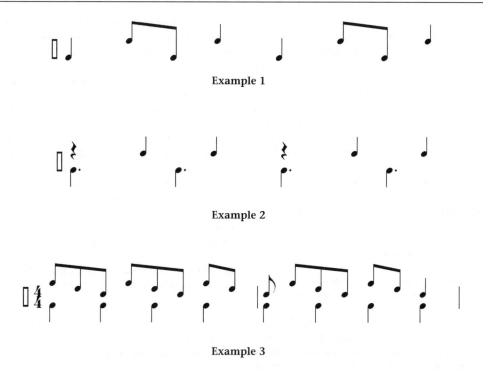

Example 1

Example 2

Example 3

accompaniments that create tension between the rhythms of the left and right hands.

Sheet Music

Gershwin, George, comp., and Gershwin, Ira, lyr. 1930. 'I Got Rhythm.' New York: New World Music Corp.

Discographical References

Gershwin, George. 'I Got Rhythm.' *Gershwin Performs Gershwin: Rare Recordings*. Music Masters 5062-2-C. *1991*: USA.

Rolling Stones, The. '(I Can't Get No) Satisfaction.' Decca F 12220. *1965*: UK.

GARRY TAMLYN

Downbeat

'Downbeat' is a term generally used to denote the first beat of a bar, as in beat '1' of a 4/4 bar. In this context, the term brings to mind the downward movement of a conductor's arm when directing measured music. At other times, downbeat can denote (a) every beat of a bar, as in beats 1, 2, 3 and 4 of a 4/4 bar (in this sense, downbeat is synonymous with onbeat); and (b) a temporal point in metrically free improvisations where musical structures converge in order to mark the beginning or end of a formal structural section (for example, the introductory section of the Allman Brothers' 'Les Brers in A Minor').

Discographical Reference

Allman Brothers Band, The. 'Les Brers in A Minor.' *Eat a Peach*. Polydor 823 654-2. *1972*: USA.

GARRY TAMLYN

Drive

The term 'drive' relates to the rhythmic character of a jazz, rock or rock-derived accompaniment where successively sounded pulse, metrical units or points of rhythmic interest in a beat are equally highlighted through timbral, dynamic or some other form of emphasis. A 'driving rhythm' can therefore eschew the accentual patterns contained in an established meter or beat and, through repetition, might be perceived in terms of rhythmic propulsion or directionality. In reference to the performance of a single melodic line, drive might also involve moments where a musician stretches, strains against or otherwise 'plays with' the beat. In jazz parlance, drive or vital drive is often associated with properties such as swing or groove and is often related to both musical and paramusical aspects. For instance, Hodeir (1956, 207–208) suggests that 'vital drive' is 'another element of swing' and a 'manifestation of personal magnetism, which is somehow expressed . . . in the domain of rhythm.'

Bibliography

Hodeir, André. 1956. *Jazz: Its Evolution and Essence*. New York: Grove.

GARRY TAMLYN

Groove

'Groove' or 'feel' generally denotes a perception of style – inclusive of experiential, phenomenological and musical-structural dimensions – that is largely informed by the inter-working of regularly recurring accompanimental rhythms contained in a beat. Groove emanates from musical performance (including recorded performance), not from a musical score, and is therefore best considered as a 'recognition of style in motion' (Feld 1994, 112). In this sense, the concept involves a degree of subjectivity and relies on the performer's or listener's understanding of the musical rules that shape a given musical performance. 'Getting into the groove' of a musical performance, for instance, suggests experiencing a sense of comfort resulting from the congruity of stylistic (and mostly rhythmic) elements and the interpretive or semiotic rules that are generally associated with a musical style.

At a syntactic level, groove comprises an accompanimental rhythmic matrix on which the rhythms of melodic lines and improvisations are based. Although accompaniments that consist of equal subdivisions of each beat (pulse) might be considered to constitute groove, the term more commonly describes rhythmic matrices that contain regularly recurring temporal discrepancies within a beat. Repeated accompanimental rhythms that push or pull against a beat might create points of rhythmic interest, and it is these that are likely to draw a participant's attention to groove. In music programming packages, 'groove' or 'feel' is effected by groove 'quantizing' functions that shift the placement of selected notes and rests along a rhythmic continuum according to a predetermined or preset rhythmic 'grid' or matrix.

Although located primarily within the rhythmic domain, other musical elements – including harmonic motion, melodic contour, timbre, and studio production effects in recorded performances – affect the individuality of a particular groove.

Bibliography

Feld, Steven. 1994. 'Aesthetics as Iconicity of Style (Uptown Title); or (Downtown Title) "Lift-Up-Over Sounding": Getting into the Kaluli Groove.' In Charles Keil and Steven Feld, *Music Grooves: Essays and Dialogues*. Chicago and London: University of Chicago Press, 109–50. (First published as 'Aesthetics as Iconicity of Style, or "Lift-Up-Over Sounding": Getting into the Kaluli Groove.' *Yearbook for Traditional Music* 20 (1988): 74–113.)

GARRY TAMLYN

Lead-In

A lead-in is a short, unidirectional musical line – commonly occurring at the very beginning of a musical performance – that points toward the introduction of new musical material. A lead-in occurring at the very beginning of a musical performance usually establishes the tempo and, in some instances, the meter of subsequent musical material. A lead-in that projects a different meter from that established in subsequent musical sections is best described as a 'false trail' (Van der Merwe 1989, 157).

In much popular music, a lead-in is about one or two bars in length and is often performed by a solo instrument or vocalist. A vocal lead-in commonly consists of a spoken or yelled '1 2 3 4' (for example, in the Ramones' 'Rockaway Beach' or the Beatles' 'Please Please Me') or '1, –, 2, –, 1, 2, 3, 4'; the latter signals to listeners the metrical orientation for subsequent musical material. In studio recordings, a vocal lead-in of the type previously mentioned gives an impression of a live performance (for example, the vocal lead-in in the Beatles' 'Sergeant Pepper's Lonely Hearts Club Band Reprise').

Bibliography

Van der Merwe, Peter. 1989. *Origins of the Popular Style: The Antecedents of Twentieth-Century Popular Music.* Oxford: Clarendon Press.

Discographical References

Beatles, The. 'Please Please Me.' *With the Beatles.* Parlophone PMC 1206. *1963*: UK.
Beatles, The. 'Sergeant Pepper's Lonely Hearts Club Band Reprise.' *Sergeant Pepper's Lonely Hearts Club Band.* Parlophone PCS 7027. *1967*: UK.
Ramones, The. 'Rockaway Beach.' *Rocket to Russia.* Sire SR-6042. *1977*: USA.

GARRY TAMLYN

Offbeat

'Offbeat' is a term commonly used to denote the location of a single note, chord or rest occurring between temporal points demarcated by successive beats (antonym: onbeat). An offbeat therefore occurs 'off' or away from a beat, but is often perceived as belonging to or associated with a prior or subsequent beat in terms of rhythmic gesturality. This is particularly so when an offbeat note or chord follows a sounded beat, as in the Scottish snap-type rhythms notated in Example 1. Sounded offbeats situated between unsounded beats (see Ex. 2) are likely to be discussed in terms of syncopation or cross-rhythm.

An offbeat might evenly divide a duration marked by two successive beats or occur prior to or after the temporal midpoint of such a duration. The latter temporal positioning of sounded offbeats creates 'laid-back' rhythms. Boogie piano accompaniments, for instance, typically feature bass notes that fall on the beat and

Example 1

Example 2

Example 3

chords (performed by the right hand) that are laid back on the offbeat, resulting in a 'long short' type of composite rhythm (see Ex. 3).

GARRY TAMLYN

Onbeat

'Onbeat' is a term commonly used to denote the temporal location of a single note, chord or rest on a beat (antonym: offbeat or afterbeat).

GARRY TAMLYN

Oom-pah

'Oom-pah' is an antipodal harmonic/rhythmic structure, occurring in either duple- or quadruple-meter accompaniments; it comprises low-register notes on 'strong' beats (beats 1 and 3 of a 4/4 bar), followed by treble-register chords on 'weak' beats (beats 2 and 4 of a 4/4 bar). With reference to drumming, the term denotes rhythmic activity between bass drum (which provides the 'oom') and snare drum (which follows with 'pah').

'Oom-pah' is generally associated with particular popular music styles of the late nineteenth and early twentieth centuries, such as concert band marches, in which an oom-pah accompaniment is often shared between low and high brass instruments, and early jazz. It also occurs in late nineteenth-century orchestral marches and in polkas. Oom-pah accompaniments occurring in early jazz are sometimes described as 'two-beat' (see, for example, Schuller 1989).

Bibliography

Schuller, Gunther. 1989 (1968). *The History of Jazz. Vol. 2: The Swing Era: The Development of Jazz, 1930–1945*. New York: Oxford University Press.

Tamlyn, Garry. 1998. *The Big Beat: Origins and Development of Snare Drum Backbeat and Other Accompanimental Rhythms in Rock 'n' Roll*. Unpublished Ph.D. thesis, University of Liverpool, UK.

GARRY TAMLYN

Phrasing

The term 'phrasing' generally denotes a performance practise that involves the demarcation of musical phrases according to silent or sounded points of musical rest. In this context, a 'musical phrase' is a sequence of notes and rests that conveys a complete musical idea, akin to a sentence in linguistic syntax. A musical phrase may comprise motifs, riffs, sub-phrases or themes; larger musical sections, such as verses or choruses, often contain many phrases.

Phrasing in much Western popular music commonly outlines a temporal span equal to the duration of an actual or nominal controlled human breath. Points of musical rest, or 'breathing spots,' are ordinarily indicated in music notation by signs such as slurs, breath marks and rests (silences), but these signs may also convey other meanings. In measured music, points of musical rest usually occur between hypermetrical temporal spans, which commonly consist of about four or eight bars. Phrasing therefore marks the recurrence of hypermetrical temporal spans and, like meter and beat (pulse), maps the flow of time in musical performance. Points of musical rest in non-metrical musics are often articulated by silence or a long note at the end of a durational process, the latter of which frequently signals rhythmic closure or 'cumulation' (Narmour 1977, 150) after successive shorter notes (for example, Robert Fripp's guitar

Example 1

soloing in 'The Heavenly Music Corporation'). Criteria for determining the articulation of phrases in non-metrical musics might include the regular recurrence of a melodic, harmonic or rhythmic idea.

At an interpretive level, phrasing serves to bind a set of musical sounds that have primarily affective and gestural content. Phrasing, in this sense, involves the connection or separation of notes or larger phrasing elements (such as motifs, riffs and themes) by balancing and blending musical sounds. It is impossible to define such phrasing in terms of definite balancing and blending elements, as diverse musical styles present varying musical realizations of elisions between notes and rests and between larger phrasing elements. In common parlance, however, the term 'phrasing' can refer to rhythmic fluidity in performance, as well as to the dynamic shaping of successive notes, and is commonly used as a synonym for 'articulation' (including, for example, staccato, legato and styles of bowing). The balancing and blending of musical sounds might therefore rely on modes of articulation, and rhythmic and dynamic control. In improvised popular musics, melodic contour, ornamentation and inflection might also be considered as central to such phrasing.

Phrasing in music performance is often based on musical understandings that arise from both familiarity with musical styles and personal perceptual reactions to the temporal unfolding of musical structures. Electronic means of balancing or reconstructing musical sounds to either highlight or form musical phrases is generally described by such terms as 'mixing,' 'remixing' and 'sound production.'

Bibliography

Narmour, Eugene. 1977. *Beyond Schenkerism: The Need for Alternatives in Music Analysis*. Chicago: University of Chicago Press.

Discographical Reference

Fripp, Robert, and Eno, Brian. 'The Heavenly Music Corporation.' *No Pussyfooting*. EG EEGCD-2. *1973*: USA.

GARRY TAMLYN

Polyrhythm

The term 'polyrhythm' denotes the rhythmic dissonance created by the simultaneous use of two or more dissim-

ilar rhythms in different voice parts. In a sense, most forms of polyphonic popular music contain contrasting rhythms and therefore might be considered as constituting an elementary polyrhythmic stage. However, the term refers particularly to levels of rhythmic organization that contain cross-rhythmic and other accentual rhythmic effects resulting from combinations of strikingly contrasted rhythms in which accentual patterns rarely coincide.

Extended syncopations of the type notated in Example 1 (above) may have a polyrhythmic effect. In this instance, a metric shift, achieved by a fixed duration, separates two rhythms of the same meter and tempo. The term 'polyrhythm' might also denote the simultaneous utilization of independent rhythms that proceed at different tempos, as in the combination of accompanimental rhythms and *musique concrète* musical lines contained in the Beatles' 'Tomorrow Never Knows.'

Discographical Reference

Beatles, The. 'Tomorrow Never Knows.' *Revolver*. EMI Records 7 46441 2. *1966*: UK.

GARRY TAMLYN

Rhythm

Definition

When applied to music, the term 'rhythm' refers to the relations that obtain in time between identifiable, individual sonic events having perceived durations. By definition, each sonic event or sound consists of a beginning (or initiation), a prolongation (or duration) and an ending (or cessation) of the sound. These sonic or musical events – customarily thought of as 'notes' – can also be constituted by silences within the context of sounds, in which case they are referred to as 'rests.' Rhythm occurs as a consequence of temporal relations between these musical events perceived and understood as being of significance within particular cultural communities.

Derived from the Greek word *rhythmos*, which is generally accepted as meaning 'flow,' rhythm is considered to be one of the four basic elements of music, along with melody, harmony and timbre. These elements are mutually dependent. Where rhythm is concerned, duration cannot be perceived without timbre, and melody and

Example 1 Bossa nova rhythm A.

Example 2 Bossa nova rhythm B.

harmonic progressions or 'changes' cannot occur without the rhythm made possible by durations.

Other common understandings of the term 'rhythm' include: (a) form in motion; (b) measured motion; (c) pull as opposed to flow; (d) movement in music marked by regular recurring strong and weak sounds or pulses; (e) a regularly recurring grouping of note values, as in bossa nova rhythm (Ex. 1 and Ex. 2), or as in a dotted eighth followed by a sixteenth-note rhythm (Ex. 3); (f) a regular grouping of recurring pulses into a specific meter, as in 3/4 rhythm (Ex. 4); and (g) movement that consists of regularly recurring characteristics, elements or events.

For rhythm to occur, a listener must be able to perceive a specific sound as having duration. For example, although each day is marked by a sunrise and a sunset, or a year by a change of seasons, the time span of an audible sound of this duration would be too great for perception and retention. Therefore, the individual sounds on which rhythmic relationships in music are based are generally thought of as lasting small periods of time, with 12 seconds as the most likely maximum length of perception.

Once a sound is of perceivable duration, and is heard in relation to the lengths of sounds that precede or follow it, the mind attempts to organize this series of sounds into relative proportions. These proportions are generally viewed as equal or unequal (having equal or unequal stress by virtue of length, dynamics or pitch) and as either recurring regularly or recurring irregularly. Music having a perceived, regularly recurring or estab-

Example 3 Dotted eighth/sixteenth rhythm.

Example 4 3/4 rhythm.

lished frequency of sound is said to have a pulse or beat. The rate of frequency – how fast or how slow the pulse or beat occurs – is known as tempo. When organized into a recognizable pattern of stressed and unstressed – or strong and weak – pulses, music is said to have meter or measure. Music without a regularly recurring pulse – such as free chant, a long melismatic passage or classical recitative – is said to be non-metered, in free rhythm or freely metered.

History

Detailed theories on rhythm as it relates to music, poetry and dance exist from antiquity and can be found in the writings of Xenocrates (fourth century B.C.), Plato and Aristotle. As music is often linked to spoken or sung verse, various systems of poetic constructs have been applied to musical rhythm throughout the ages. The most obvious of these is the application of poetic meter and feet based on stressed and unstressed syllables. When set to music, poetry warrants an appropriate meter in order to support correct diction and grammatical accuracy. This practise resulted in codified rhythmic relationships or patterns, as well as specified lengths of musical phrases. These metrical patterns include iamb (unstressed/stressed), anapest (unstressed/unstressed/ stressed), trochee (stressed/unstressed), dactyl (stressed/ unstressed/unstressed) and amphibrach (unstressed/ stressed/unstressed) (Cooper and Meyer 1960). In pre-fourteenth-century polyphony, these poetic feet were classified and applied to music as a set of rhythmic modes consisting of six patterns – the trochee, iamb, dactyl, anapest, spondee and tribrach (Ex. 5). By applying these modes, popular verse could easily be set to music, resulting in accurate declamation of the text.

Beginning in the fourteenth century, a method of organizing meter and rhythm proportionally was developed. This system allowed a specific unit of time or measure (a beat, grouping of beats or subdivision of a beat) to be proportioned into either two or three parts. The division into three parts held particular significance

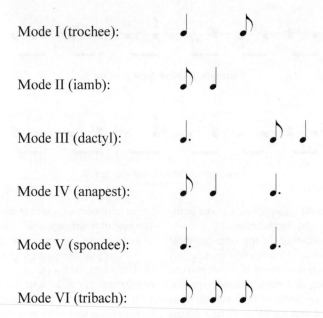

Mode I (trochee):

Mode II (iamb):

Mode III (dactyl):

Mode IV (anapest):

Mode V (spondee):

Mode VI (tribach):

Example 5 Rhythmic modes.

for sacred music due to its symbolic association with the Trinity. Division of any specific unit into three parts was termed 'perfect,' and division into two parts was termed 'imperfect.' These proportions were designated by circles and dots at the beginning of a piece of music, and have been passed down into modern notation as time signatures, first as symbols and then as fractional notations, such as C, 4/4 or 6/8.

Proportional notation eventually gave way to a more mathematical subdivision of regularly recurring beats following established metrical organization based on poetic meter, dance patterns or common practise among musical performers. Evolving over several centuries, examples of music rhythmically and metrically organized on dance patterns might include instrumental music of the Baroque period based on dances such as the sarabande, allemande or gigue, as well as more recent dances such as the waltz, bossa nova or bolero. Common musical practise might include the division of a beat into seven equal parts due to the performance of a major or minor scale between the two pulses.

Current Practise

Rhythm as used in popular music can generally be understood in terms of two methods of construction: additive and divisive. Additive rhythms are those rhythms that are built up from the smallest rhythmic unit (added together) until a cohesive, total phrase is

obtained (Ex. 6). Divisive rhythms are those rhythms that follow a predetermined metrical order, usually known as a measure, whereby the measure and then the beat are divided into parts based on a perceived pulse (Ex. 7). Additive rhythms can be constructed to any total number, including nonsymmetrical phrases (Ex. 8), whereas divisive rhythms presuppose that a unit, such as a beat or measure, must contain a specific quantitative total rhythmic value (Ex. 9).

When music is constructed using additive rhythms, there is often an absence of an ordered, metrical pulse; the music is without regularly stressed and unstressed beats aligning for all parts. Instead, there is an underlying faster unit, which may or may not allow points or

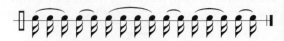

3 + 2 + 4 + 2 + 3 + 2 = 16 total counts
Phrased groupings result in the following accented rhythmic pattern:

Example 6 Additive rhythm.

Example 7 Divisive rhythm.

Example 8 Nonsymmetrical phrases based on additive rhythms.

Example 9 Symmetrical phrases based on divisive rhythms.

phrases to align among various instruments or singers. To make a note of a longer time value than the basic unit, two or more of the units are 'tied' together. A tie is a notational practise, using a curved line, which represents the process of joining two rhythmic values together. Additive rhythmic constructs are often found in African ceremonial music and drumming patterns, and also form a basis for understanding Indian tala.

Divisive rhythms generally pervade Western popular music in the form of standardized, patterned arrangements of strong and weak pulses resulting in what is known as meter. Metrical organization of music into current time signatures developed gradually, was codified over the last few centuries and continues to evolve. Generally speaking, meter organizes music into measures (bars) of recurring equal length where the first beat of the measure (the downbeat) is perceived as the strongest, with the remaining beats having relative strengths of importance, depending on the total number of beats per measure.

Standard meters for popular music usually have one, two, three, four or five beats per measure, and are classified as either simple or compound. Simple meter is defined as music in which each beat divides into two basic parts, whereas compound meter divides each beat into three equal parts. Generally speaking, this rule then allows the beat to be assigned to any known type of note value divisible by two (whole, half, quarter, eighth, sixteenth, etc.) as the designated pulse note value for simple meter, and those divisible by three (dotted whole, dotted half, dotted quarter, dotted eighth, dotted sixteenth, etc.) as the designated pulse note value for compound meter. Meters are labeled with a fractional or symbolic notation called a time signature at the beginning of a piece of music, and at any point within a piece

of music where the meter changes. Meters are also described as duple, triple, quadruple, quintuple and so on, based on the total number of pulses per measure (Ex. 10).

Common time, a meter notated as 4/4 or C and containing four quarter-note pulses per measure, was the most common meter for Western popular music of the twentieth century. *Alla breve*, also known as 'cut time,' a meter notated as 2/2 or ¢ and containing two half-note pulses per measure, was the more prevalent time signature for Western popular music of the early twentieth century. This shift from a 'two-beat' to a 'four-beat' measure was a gradual process, greatly influenced by the type of dances in vogue during the various time periods, as well as by the types of songs popular on the stage, radio and television and through various recorded media. Although 4/4 and 2/2 meters have dominated popular music in Western cultures for the last century, it should not be concluded that other meters are not also widely used, or that these two meters are prevalent in the popular music of other cultures.

Popular music, whether rhythmically structured additively or divisively, can be said to have various hierarchical levels of rhythmic organization. At the root of the additive process is a single rhythmic unit, whereas a metrical organization of strong and weak pulses forms the foundation for the divisive construct. Both types of construct lend themselves to larger rhythmic organization that can direct a listener toward a greater rhythmic goal, especially when coupled with melodic or harmonic elements. This larger construct – often in groups of two or three phrases – is known as periodicity. From the perspective of divisive rhythms, periodic cadences are constructed by having a series of measures that might regularly group into pairs of twos, fours or eights, in

(a)

Simple Duple	$\frac{2}{8}$	$\frac{2}{4}$	$\frac{2}{2}$
Simple Triple	$\frac{3}{8}$	$\frac{3}{4}$	$\frac{3}{2}$
Simple Quadruple	$\frac{4}{8}$	$\frac{4}{4}$	$\frac{4}{2}$

(b)

Compound Duple	$\frac{6}{16}$	$\frac{6}{8}$	$\frac{6}{4}$
Compound Triple	$\frac{9}{16}$	$\frac{9}{8}$	$\frac{9}{4}$
Compound Quadruple	$\frac{12}{16}$	$\frac{12}{8}$	$\frac{12}{4}$

Example 10 (a) Common simple and (b) compound meters.

Example 11 Two-phase periodicity.

rhythmic antecedent-consequent relationships, where the final phrase has a more conclusive cadence (Ex. 11). Periodicity in music leads toward larger formal structures often having points of rhythmic repose at cadences where the rhythm might stop, giving a stronger sense of rhythmic direction to the beginning of the next phrase. The common term for this is a rhythmic 'break.' Breaks are to be found in Louis Armstrong's 'Hotter Than That' and in Led Zeppelin's 'Good Times Bad Times.'

Rhythm, Meter and Tempo: Application and Interpretation

Rhythm and meter range from starkly simplistic patterns to highly complex, multilayered devices in the hands of skilled composers. Within this range of contexts, several terms warrant explanation as signaling devices common in the practise of popular music.

Among the most common devices used to change the perception of rhythm is accentuation, or the aural stress of a given sound. Accenting a musical sound can be accomplished by volume (dynamic accent), duration (agogic accent) or pitch (melodic or harmonic accent). A repetitive, patterned accentuation of a specific rhythm within music can, and often does, define a specific style. This can be illustrated by the use of a single rhythmic change and dynamic accent on the upbeat of count four in the first measure of a two-measure phrase in common time, which immediately identifies a tango dance rhythm to anyone familiar with that style (Ex. 12).

Augmentation is the process of elongating the duration of a rhythmic phrase or motif of music by increasing the duration of all notes by an equal value. For example, to make each original rhythmic value twice the length, one would take a rhythm consisting of two quarter notes and four eighth notes and write them as two half notes followed by four quarter notes. The relationship between the notes is perceived as the same by a listener, but over an extended period of time. The result is to 'slow down' the music to half the speed for dramatic effect. Examples of augmentation are to be found in 'Put on a Happy Face' and Thelonious Monk's 'Round Midnight' (which also contains examples of an interpretive, improvised diminution).

Example 12 Tango rhythm.

Diminution is the process of shortening the duration of a rhythmic phrase or motif of music by decreasing the duration of all notes by an equal value. For example, to make each original rhythmic value one-half the length, one would take a rhythm consisting of two quarter notes and four eighth notes and write them as two eighth notes followed by four sixteenth notes. The relationship between the notes is perceived as the same by a listener, but over a reduced period of time. The result is to 'speed up' the music by a factor of two for dramatic effect or musical contrast. Examples of diminution are to be found in the Drifters' 'Under the Boardwalk' and Yes's 'I've Seen All Good People.' Augmentation and diminution thus have the ability to impart stress and/or relaxation within a piece of music, and are often used at points of climax, at a cadence or when change of mood occurs.

Although meter is thought of as being simple (when the beat is divisible by two) or compound (when the beat is divisible by three), a compositional device exists that can facilitate the interchange of the two divisions on all hierarchical levels. Any rhythmic value that is normally divided into two parts can instead be divided into three parts by the introduction of the triplet. Conversely, any rhythmic value that is normally divided into three parts can be divided into just two by the introduction of the duplet. These devices allow for a mixing and matching of simple and compound divisions of the beat. They also allow for a mixing and matching at other hierarchical levels, giving rise to cross-rhythms, or rhythms derived from both duple and triple divisions occurring simultaneously. Examples of duple and triple cross-rhythms are to be found in the 'Theme from Peter Gunn,' 'Bluesette' by Toots Thielemans and Chicago's 'Make Me Smile.'

When a rhythmic pattern is repeated continuously, the technique is described as an ostinato. Rhythmic ostinatos were a common device for rhythm sections in

popular music of the latter half of the twentieth century. Examples are to be found in Queen's 'Another One Bites the Dust' and 'We Will Rock You,' and the 'Theme from Peter Gunn,' as well as – where electronic drum machines and techno dance styles are concerned – Madonna's 'Music' and 'Don't Tell Me.' Synthesized and computer-generated sound techniques – widely used for much popular dance music – are capable of rapidly generating series of monorhythms. These singular rhythmic patterns, usually one per measure, are then combined, resulting in a complex yet easily created polyrhythm.

Polyrhythm can be defined as the simultaneous use of two rhythms having divisors of the beat that are prime in relation to each other: for example, the use of rhythmic ratios between two or more musical lines that might incorporate two against three, three against four, three against five or four against five. A simpler definition might also include any music where two or more rhythmically contrasting, independently perceived rhythms occur simultaneously.

The use of polyrhythm results in what is known as rhythmic dissonance. Rhythmic dissonance occurs when in a set of two or more rhythmic levels the divisor for one does not divide the other(s) (for example, a level of half notes set against a level of dotted half notes) (Ex. 13). Conversely, rhythmic consonance occurs when in a set of two or more rhythmic levels the divisor for one is a factor of the divisor for the other(s) (for example, a level of half notes divided into a level of quarter notes) (Ex. 14) (Yeston 1976).

While most pieces of popular music are composed in one of the standard simple or compound meters throughout, many compositional devices exist to alter this. A piece may be written in what is known as an odd meter, as well as in a meter that contains regularly occurring pulses of differing lengths. Odd meters are charac-

Example 13 Rhythmic dissonance.

Example 14 Rhythmic consonance.

terized by a number not divisible by two or three as the top integer for the time signature (such as 5/4 or 7/8). However, by irregularly grouping standard meters, one can also obtain pulses of irregular length that result in odd metrical groupings. For example, 8/8 meter can be grouped in an arrangement of 3 + 3 + 2 eighth notes, which results in a felt pulse of two dotted quarter notes followed by a quarter note. These types of odd meters can be found in folk music of Eastern European nations as collected by Bartók during the early twentieth century.

Meters can also change, or be mixed, during a given piece, either regularly or irregularly, and can be either notated as changing meter or merely perceived as such. An excellent example of a recurring, regularly perceived changing meter occurs in Bernstein's 'America' from *West Side Story*. This piece features the regular alternation of two dotted quarter-note pulses with three following quarter-note pulses.

In addition to the process of changing meters, music is often composed in such a way that two or more meters exist simultaneously in a given piece. This is known as polymeter, and music composed using this process is described as polymetric. Polymeter is generally employed using one meter for one voice or instrument (or group of instruments) against a contrasting voice or instrument (or group of instruments). The meters may be of equal length, resulting in downbeats that coincide, or of unequal length, resulting in downbeats that do not coincide. Polymetric music is characteristic of the ceremonial music of Africa, especially when divisive rhythmic meters are mixed with additive rhythmic constructs.

Tempo is a defining characteristic of music that can alter perceptions of rhythm. When a tempo is constant, and the rhythmic pulse perceived to be a continuous non-changing one, the music is said to be 'motoric' or to have a motor rhythm. Examples are to be found in 'Land of 1000 Dances' and the Beach Boys' 'Fun, Fun, Fun.' Common devices used to alter tempo in music are

the accelerando and ritardando, which respectively gradually speed up or slow down the music. Examples of accelerando are to be found in Dexy's Midnight Runners' 'Come on Eileen' and – in particularly dramatic fashion – in Joe Cocker's live performances of 'With a Little Help from My Friends.' Slight tempo alterations, called rubato, can be an extremely effective means of musical nuance and expressiveness.

Several interpretive devices relate to rhythm in the performance of popular music. Among the most common is the perceived placement of individual notes in relation to the actual pulse. When notes are placed slightly ahead of the beat, the music seems to acquire a 'drive' (as with 'on top' jazz drummers and 'chunky' bass players), and when notes are placed slightly behind the beat it seems to acquire a 'dragging' feeling (as with 'layback' drummers and 'stringy' bass players). In jazz, as well as in other popular music styles, notated duple rhythms can be interpreted either in a 'straight rhythm' style – that is, in the exact notated duple feel (as in 'The Girl from Ipanema') – or in a 'swing rhythm' style (as in 'Take the "A" Train'), which lengthens the first of the two portions of the beat, resulting in a rhythm that typically matches the first and third notes of a triple division of the beat. Dizzy Gillespie makes effective use of both styles in his 'Night in Tunisia' and 'Manteca.'

The Influence of Rhythm in Popular Music

Tempos and standardized rhythms are sometimes used to define styles of music. These styles include, but are not limited to: Latin dances such as the bossa nova, samba (Ex. 15) and mambo (Ex. 16); rock music with its well-defined downbeat and backbeat (Ex. 17); formalized dances such as the tango, bolero, waltz, one-step, two-step and fox trot; odd-meter music by such notable figures as Don Ellis ('Indian Lady,' 'Pussy Wiggle Stomp' and 'The Great Divide') and Dave Brubeck ('Take Five'); the 12/8 feel of traditional blues or the jazz 'shuffle' (Ex. 18); and the unmistakable 'Scotch snap' (sixteenth fol-

Example 15 Samba rhythm.

Example 16 Mambo rhythm.

Example 17 Backbeat.

Example 18 Jazz 'shuffle' rhythm.

Example 19 Scotch snap.

Example 20 Irish jig rhythm.

lowed by a dotted eighth-note rhythm) (Ex. 19) or downbeat triplet figures used for traditional Irish or Gaelic folk songs, such as the jig (Ex. 20).

Many styles of music are constructed on clearly defined rhythmic principles which, at times, have either reflected the social status quo or served as a catalyst for societal change. Waltz rhythms of the nineteenth century reflected the stylized dances in vogue for upper-class functions, for example. The 'ragged' or broken rhythms of ragtime reflected the evolution of the two-beat march (as in 'Hungarian Rag'), first into energized interpretations of popular parlor songs (as in 'A Coon Band Contest'), then as a popular Tin Pan Alley style (for example, Scott Joplin's 'The Entertainer'). The syncopations (where beats not normally stressed are accented) found in ragtime as well as in jazz became controversial among classical and many, more conservative popular musicians, as well as in society in general. These rhythms – evidenced, for example, in Al Jolson's performance of George Gershwin's 'Swanee' and George Gershwin's 'I Got Rhythm' – became associated in the minds of many with 'immoral' dances and general 'moral decay.'

Bibliography

Bent, Ian D. 1980. 'Rhythmic Modes.' In *The New Grove Dictionary of Music and Musicians*, ed. Stanley Sadie. Washington, DC: Grove's Dictionaries of Music, 824–25.

Berry, Wallace. 1976. *Structural Functions in Music*. Englewood Cliffs, NJ: Prentice-Hall.

Berry, Wallace. 1985. 'Metric and Rhythmic Articulation in Music.' *Music Theory Spectrum* 7: 7–33.

Cone, Edward T. 1968. *Musical Form and Musical Performance*. New York: W.W. Norton.

Cooper, Grosvenor W., and Meyer, Leonard B. 1960. *The Rhythmic Structure of Music*. Chicago: University of Chicago Press.

Duckworth, William. 1995. *A Creative Approach to Music Fundamentals*. 5th ed. Belmont, CA: Wadsworth Publishing Company.

Dürr, W., Gerstenberg, W., and Harvey, J. 1980. 'Rhythm.' In *The New Grove Dictionary of Music and Musicians*, ed. Stanley Sadie. Washington, DC: Grove's Dictionaries of Music, 804–24.

Hall, Anne Carothers. 1998. *Studying Rhythm*. 2nd ed. Upper Saddle River, NJ: Prentice-Hall.

Kramer, Jonathan D. 1988. *The Time of Music: New Meanings, New Temporalities, New Listening Strategies*. New York: Schirmer Books.

Lester, Joel. 1986. *The Rhythms of Tonal Music*. Carbondale, IL: Southern Illinois University Press.

Lindeman, Carolynn A., and Hackett, Patricia. 1989. *MusicLab: An Introduction to the Fundamentals of Music*. Belmont, CA: Wadsworth Publishing Company.

Manoff, Tom. 1994. *The Music Kit, Rhythm Reader and Scorebook*. 3rd ed. New York: W.W. Norton.

Miller, Benjamin O. 1993. 'Time Perception in Musical Meter Perception.' *Psychomusicology* 12: 124–53.

Parncutt, Richard. 1987. 'The Perception of Pulse in Musical Rhythm.' In *Action and Perception in Rhythm and Music*, ed. Alf Gabrielsson. Stockholm: Royal Swedish Academy of Music, 127–38.

Rosenthal, David. 1989. 'A Model of the Process of Listening to Simple Rhythms.' *Music Perception* 6: 315–28.

Rothstein, William. 1989. *Phrase Rhythm in Tonal Music*. New York: Schirmer Books.

Westergaard, Peter. 1975. *An Introduction to Tonal Theory*. New York: W.W. Norton.

Willoughby, David. 1999. *The World of Music*. 4th ed. Boston, MA: McGraw-Hill.

Wold, Milo, and Cykler, Edmund. 1985. *An Outline History of Music*. 6th ed. Dubuque, IA: W.C. Brown.

Yeston, Maury. 1976. *The Stratification of Musical Rhythm*. New Haven, CT: Yale University Press.

Discographical References

'America.' *West Side Story* (Original cast recording). Columbia 32603. *1957*: USA.

Armstrong, Louis. 'Hotter Than That.' *Portrait of the Artist as a Young Man*. Sony 85670. 1927; *2001*: USA.

Beach Boys, The. 'Fun, Fun, Fun.' Capitol 5118. *1965*: USA.

Bennett, Tony. 'Put on a Happy Face.' *40 Years: The Artistry of Tony Bennett*. Columbia 46843. *1991*: USA.

Brubeck, Dave. 'Take Five.' *Take Five*. International Music 54005. *2001*: Germany.

Chicago. 'Make Me Smile.' Columbia 45127. *1970*: USA.

Cocker, Joe. 'With a Little Help from My Friends.' *Live in New York*. Mushroom 32178. *1999*: Australia.

Dexy's Midnight Runners. 'Come on Eileen.' *Too-Rye-Ay*. Mercury 4069. *1982*: USA.

Drifters, The. 'Under the Boardwalk.' Atlantic 2237. *1964*: USA.

Ellington, Duke. 'Take the "A" Train.' *The Best of Duke Ellington Centennial Edition*. RCA 63459. *1999*: USA.

Ellis, Don. 'Indian Lady.' *Electric Bath*. Columbia 9585. *1967*: USA.

Ellis, Don. 'Pussy Wiggle Stomp.' *Don Ellis at Fillmore*. Columbia 30243. *1970*: USA.

Ellis, Don. 'The Great Divide.' *Don Ellis at Fillmore*. Columbia 30243. *1970*: USA.

Gershwin, George. 'I Got Rhythm.' *Blue Gershwin*. Blue Note 99427. *1992*: USA.

Gillespie, Dizzy. 'Manteca.' *The Complete RCA Victor Recordings 1937–1949*. Bluebird/RCA 66528. *1995*: USA.

Gillespie, Dizzy. 'Night in Tunisia.' *The Complete RCA Victor Recordings 1937–1949*. Bluebird/RCA 66528. *1995*: USA.

Jobim, Antonio Carlos. 'The Girl from Ipanema.' *The Girl from Ipanema: The Antonio Carlos Jobim Songbook*. Verve 5472. *1996*: USA.

Jolson, Al. 'Swanee.' Decca 23470. 1945: USA.

Led Zeppelin. 'Good Times Bad Times.' *Led Zeppelin [I]*. Atlantic 8236. *1969*: USA.

Madonna. 'Don't Tell Me.' *Music*. Maverick 47598. *2000*: USA.

Madonna. 'Music.' *Music*. Maverick 47598. *2000*: USA.

Monk, Thelonious. 'Round Midnight.' *The Columbia Years (1962–1968)*. Sony 64887. 1968; *2001*: USA.

New York Military Band. 'Hungarian Rag.' *American Pop: An Audio History, Vol. 1*. West Hill 4017(9). 1913; *1998*: Canada.

Ossman, Vess. 'A Coon Band Contest.' *American Pop: An Audio History, Vol. 1*. West Hill 4017(9). 1900; *1998*: Canada.

Pickett, Wilson. 'Land of 1000 Dances.' *The Very Best of Wilson Pickett*. Atlantic 81283. *1967*: USA.

Queen. 'Another One Bites the Dust.' EMI 5102. *1980*: UK.

Queen. 'We Will Rock You.' *Live Killers*. Elektra 702. *1979*: USA.

Rifkin, Joshua. 'The Entertainer.' *Piano Rags by Scott Joplin, Vol. 1*. Nonesuch 71248. *1970*: USA.

'Theme from Peter Gunn.' *Peter Gunn* (Original soundtrack). Buddha 74465996102. *1999*: USA.

Thielemans, Toots. 'Bluesette.' *Do Not Leave Me*. Stash 1101. *1986*: USA.

Yes. 'I've Seen All Good People.' *The Yes Album*. Atlantic 19131. *1971*: USA.

JAMES A. STRAIN

Second Line

Second line rhythms are percussive patterns associated with African-American street processional music in New Orleans. In its primary sense, the term 'second line' refers to people who join or follow a parade or funeral march, but who are not officially part of the parading group. These participants, often contributing their own rhythms on sticks, bottles and shakers, provide vital interaction with the main parade group through shouting, singing and dancing.

In relation to musical practises, 'second line' is commonly used to describe the style of drumming used in the brass bands that supply music for the parades. In these bands, which date back to the years following the Civil War, the percussion duties are usually divided between two players: one provides the underlying beat on bass drum and cymbals and the other improvises marching cadences on snare.

The term 'second line' is also used more generally for march-like grooves performed on a drumset by one

Example 1 Bass drum patterns.

player that are evocative of these New Orleans street beats. As march-derived rhythmic matrices, second line grooves are typically in duple meter and are constructed from one-, two- and, occasionally, four-bar repetitive cells. The bass drum usually provides a syncopated, funkier version of the standard marching band oom-pah bass drum figure on beats 1 and 3. One distinctive feature of these grooves is the accented hit on the second half of beat 4 (or sometimes on '4' in a two-bar pattern). Several bass drum patterns are given in Example 1. Additionally, rhythms used in Mardi Gras Indian chants (such as the patterns in Example 2), played on drums, sticks or with bodily percussion, may contribute to second line grooves. These beats, which are also structurally similar to marching cadences, contrast on-the-beat playing on beats 1 and 2 with syncopated sixteenth notes around beats 3 and 4. As asymmetrical time cycles, they are suggestive of West African drumming and related Afro-Caribbean rhythms such as *tresillo* and *clave*.

Ultimately, second line grooves and other distinctive rhythms developed in New Orleans had a far-reaching impact on a wide variety of popular musics in the United States and beyond, from jazz to R&B, rock and funk.

Around the turn of the twentieth century, many drummers in New Orleans were active in both parade and dance bands, and second line rhythms were transferred to the drumset. Early jazz drummers from the city, such as Papa Jack Laine, Baby Dodds, Zutty Singleton and Paul Barbarin, had experience as parade drummers, and second line rhythms may have flavored New Orleans jazz styles more than recordings indicate. Because of the limitations of early recording studios, drummers were probably forced to tone down their playing. Also, as noted by Brown (1976, 245–46), the New Orleans style was short-lived, as drummers moved north to cities such as Chicago and assimilated the style of drummers there. Still, New Orleans jazz drummers seem to have incorporated and retained some of the rhythmic flexibility (even-eighths as well as swing rhythms) and interaction among performers (responsiveness to improvising soloists) characteristic of second line practises. These street beats continued to surface in jazz recordings featuring New Orleans drummers (for example, Vernell Fournier on Ahmad Jamal's recording of 'Poinciana').

New Orleans second line rhythms began to have their most widespread influence on popular music when they were incorporated into emergent styles of R&B in the early 1950s. As the rhythms in US popular music shifted away from shuffles and swing rhythms toward straight-eighths, march-flavored drumming patterns from New Orleans became an important resource for songwriters. One of the earliest R&B recordings exhibiting such

'Indian' marching pattern

'To-Wa-Bac-A-Way' (from Charters, Folkways Records FA 2461, recorded October 25, 1956)

'Red, White, and Blue Got the Golden Band' (from Charters, op. cit.)

Example 2 Rhythms used in Mardi Gras Indian Chants.

Example 3 Basic groove: 'Tipitian' (Professor Longhair, 1953).

rhythms is Professor Longhair's 'Tipitina,' featuring the drumming of Earl Palmer (Ex. 3). Palmer also used second line rhythms in his recordings with Fats Domino (for example, 'I'm Walkin'') and Little Richard ('Slippin' and Slidin').

Many musicians claim an important role for second line rhythms in the development of funk. According to James Brown's music director, Alfred 'Pee Wee' Ellis, Brown's change to a funkier, sixteenth-note-based style (most of his earlier songs were in 12/8 or shuffles) was a result of his adoption of 'a New Orleans beat'(Rose 1990, 47). Clayton Fillyau, the drummer on 'I've Got Money,' Brown's first recording in this new style, attributed his development of this beat to training in marching cadences and the influence of New Orleans drumming styles (Payne 1996, 21–22).

Second line rhythms continued to inform the New Orleans style that emerged in the late 1960s and the 1970s, in tunes such as Lee Dorsey's 'Working in the Coal Mine,' and in the music of Dr. John (Mac Rebennack) and of bands such as the Meters (featuring the drumming of Joseph 'Zigaboo' Modeliste) and the Neville Brothers (often with drummer Herman Ernest). By the end of the twentieth century, second line beats were no longer the exclusive domain of drummers from New Orleans and, like Latin grooves or reggae beats, had become standard in the repertoires of many drummers from outside the city. Recordings and instructional books and videos helped to make this groove accessible to many musicians.

Bibliography

Berry, Jason, Foose, Jonathan, and Jones, Tad. 1992 (1986). *Up from the Cradle of Jazz: New Orleans Music Since World War II*. New York: Da Capo Press.

Broven, John. 1995 (1974). *Rhythm and Blues in New Orleans*. Gretna, LA: Pelican.

Brown, T. Dennis. 1976. *A History and Analysis of Jazz Drumming to 1942*. Ph.D. thesis, University of Michigan.

Hannusch, Jeff. 1985. *I Hear You Knockin': The Sound of New Orleans Rhythm and Blues*. Ville Platte, LA: Swallow.

Lambert, Joe. 1981. '"Second Line" Drumming.' *Percussive Notes* 19: 26–28.

Payne, Jim. 1996. *Give the Drummers Some!: The Great Drummers of R&B, Funk and Soul*. Miami, FL: Warner Bros. Publications.

Rose, Cynthia. 1990. *Living in America: The Soul Saga of James Brown*. London: Serpent's Tail.

Schafer, William J. 1977. *Brass Bands and New Orleans Jazz*. Baton Rouge, LA: Louisiana State University Press.

Stewart, Alexander. 2000. '"Funky Drummer": New Orleans, James Brown and the Rhythmic Transformation of American Popular Music.' *Popular Music* 19(3): 293–317.

Thress, Dan, ed., with Riley, Herlin, and Vidacovich, Johnny. 1995. *New Orleans Jazz and Second Line Drumming*. Miami, FL: Manhattan Music.

Discographical References

Brown, James. 'I've Got Money.' King K5701. *1962*: USA. Reissue: Brown, James. 'I've Got Money.' *Star Time*. Polydor 849108. *1991*: USA.

Domino, Fats. 'I'm Walkin'.' Imperial 5428. *1957*: USA. Reissue: Domino, Fats. 'I'm Walkin'.' *Ten Best Greatest Hits*. Capitol 55905. *1997*: USA.

Dorsey, Lee. 'Working in the Coal Mine.' Amy 958. *1966*: USA. Reissue: Dorsey, Lee. 'Working in the Coal Mine.' *Wheelin' and Dealin'*. Arista 18980. *1997*: UK.

Jamal, Ahmad. 'Poinciana.' *Ahmad Jamal at the Pershing*. Argo 628. *1958*: USA. Reissue: Jamal, Ahmad. 'Poinciana.' *Cross Country Tour: 1958–1961*. GRP 813. *1998*: USA.

Little Richard. 'Slippin' and Slidin'.' Specialty 572. *1956*: USA. Reissue: Little Richard. 'Slippin' and Slidin'.' *Little Richard: Kings of Rock 'n' Roll Series*. Classic World 9918. *1999*: USA.

Professor Longhair. 'Tipitina.' Atlantic SD 7225. 1953: USA. Reissue: Professor Longhair. 'Tipitina.' *Fess' Gumbo*. Stony Plain 1214. *1996*: Canada.

Discography

Blanchard, Terence, and Harrison, Donald. 'New York Second Line.' *New York Second Line*. Concord GW-3002. *1983*: USA.

Charters, Samuel B. *The Music of New Orleans, Vol. 1: The Music of the Streets, the Music of Mardi Gras*. Folkways Records FA 2461. *1958*: USA.

Dr. John. *Gumbo.* Atco 7006. *1972*: USA.

Eureka Brass Band, The. *Jazz at Preservation Hall.* Atlantic 1408. *1962*: USA.

Meters, The. *Funkify Your Life: The Meters Anthology.* Rhino 71869. *1995*: USA.

Neville Brothers, The. *Fiyo on the Bayou.* A&M CD4866. *1981*: USA.

Professor Longhair. *Fess: The Professor Longhair Anthology.* Rhino Records R2 71502. *1993*: USA.

The Best of New Orleans Rhythm & Blues, Vols. 1 and 2: 1953–69. Rhino R218-75765; R218-75766. *1988*: USA.

Visual Recording

Thress, Dan. 1993. 'New Orleans Drumming: From R&B to Funk.' DCI music video.

ALEXANDER STEWART

Shuffle Rhythm

'Shuffle rhythm' is an accompanimental rhythm that comprises successive alternations of long onbeat notes and short offbeat notes (see Ex. 1). One 4/4 bar of shuffle rhythm contains eight notes and, consequently, shuffle rhythms are sometimes described as 'eight-to-the-bar,' a term that also encompasses eighth-note rhythms in which each of the eight beats receives an even stress. Shuffle rhythms occurring in drumbeats are usually performed on either cymbals (including hi-hat) or, less frequently, snare drum (as, for example, in Roy Brown's 'Good Rockin' Tonight' (1947)).

Early examples of shuffle rhythm can be found in boogie-woogie piano, a style that flourished in the United States during the 1920s and 1930s (see, for example, Pine Top Smith's 'Pine Top's Boogie Woogie' (1928)). From around the late 1930s, boogie-woogie piano accompaniments, comprising a composite shuffle rhythm of the type notated in Example 2, and shuffle rhythms performed on the drumset increasingly featured in swing era jazz and, later, in rhythm and blues. Examples of shuffle rhythm, particularly performed on the drumset, are also easily found in later genres of Western popular music.

Discographical References

Brown, Roy. 'Good Rockin' Tonight.' *Roy Brown: Good Rockin' Tonight: Legendary Recordings, Vol. 2, 1947–1954.* Route 66 KIX-6. *1978*: USA.

Smith, Pine Top. 'Pine Top's Boogie Woogie.' *Boogie*

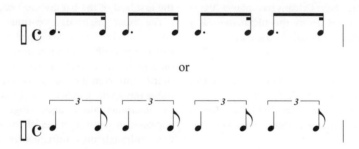

and long-short type rhythmic variations ranging between

Example 1

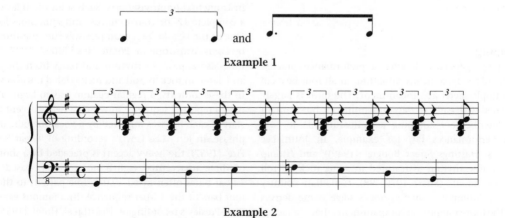

Example 2

Woogie and Barrelhouse Piano, Vol. 1, 1928–1932: The Complete Recorded Works of Pine Top Smith, Charles Avery, Freddie 'Redd' Nicholson, 'Jabo' Williams. Document DOCD 5102. *1992*: Austria.

GARRY TAMLYN

Slow Dragging

'Slow dragging' is a descriptor referring to a melodic line or accompaniment that consistently occurs slightly after each beat (pulse) and that contains equal accentuations of successive notes or chords, thus giving an impression of elongating or 'dragging out' the meter or beat of a musical performance.

The term 'slow drag' was first used as a dance reference and tempo indicator in early twentieth-century ragtime publications. For example, Scott Joplin's 'Palm Leaf Rag' is subtitled 'A Slow Drag' and includes the tempo instruction 'Play a little slow' (Blesh 1973, 100). The slow drag dance included 'Congo hip movements' (Stearns and Stearns 1994, 13), in which, according to New Orleans cornetist Charlie Love, 'couples would hang onto each other and just grind back and forth in one spot all night' (quoted in Stearns and Stearns 1994, 21). Performance practises of the type previously mentioned possibly reflected such 'grinding.' New Orleans bass player Alcide Pavageau (1888–1969) was given the nickname 'Slow Drag,' evidently because of his skill in the dance.

Bibliography

Blesh, Rudi, ed. 1973. *Classic Piano Rags: Complete Original Music for 81 Rags.* New York: Dover.

Stearns, Marshall, and Stearns, Jean. 1994. *Jazz Dance: The Story of American Vernacular Dance.* New York: Da Capo Press.

Sheet Music

Joplin, Scott, comp. 1903. 'Palm Leaf Rag.' New York: Victor Kremer Co.

GARRY TAMLYN

Stomping

'Stomping' generally denotes a performance practise that involves dynamic accentuation on all four beats of a quadruple-meter accompaniment. The term is largely associated with early jazz accompaniments, but it might also describe foot-stomping accompaniments to solo blues performances (as, for example, in John Lee Hooker's 'Hastings Street Boogie' (1949)) and 'stomp style' shuffle rhythm as featured in some rock 'n' roll accompaniments (Shaw 1970, 98). Canadian country musician Stompin' Tom Connors's stage name derives from the foot-stomping accompaniments that characterize his performances.

Bibliography

Shaw, Arnold. 1970. *The World of Soul: Black America's Contribution to the Pop Music Scene.* New York: Cowles Book Company.

Discographical Reference

Hooker, John Lee. 'Hastings Street Boogie.' *John Lee Hooker: 24 Vintage Sensation Recordings, 1948–1951.* Ace CDCHD 405. 1949; *1992*: UK.

Discography

Connors, Stompin' Tom. *Believe in Your Country.* EMI Canada 95596. *1999*: Canada.

Goodman, Benny. 'Stompin' at the Savoy.' Victor 25247. 1936: USA.

GARRY TAMLYN

Stop-Time

The term 'stop-time' derives from the practise of temporarily suspending a musical accompaniment in order to highlight a solo instrumentalist or voice. It typically involves a repeated pattern of accented chords and rests, during which all other accompaniment ceases. The accented chords can be in patterns of one, two or three, and their location can vary, although those placed on the first beat of the bar are most common.

The exact origin of stop-time is unknown, but it appears likely that it developed in accompaniment to dance, especially tap dance, in order to focus attention on a particular display of skill. It continued to be used in this context in the musical theater and film. The technique was applied, as Schuller (1968) says, 'by extension' to instrumentalists and singers (382). Stop-time appeared in ragtime pieces of the early twentieth century, although only infrequently (Berlin 1980, 14). It found a regular home in the performance practise of early jazz, where rhythm sections used the combinations of accents and suspended rhythms to highlight solo instrumental improvisations. Such solos often lasted for a complete 12- or 16-bar chorus, and sometimes longer. One of the best-known examples was the stop-time solo by Louis Armstrong in 'Potato Head Blues' (1927). Stop-time also appears in rhythm and blues from the 1940s and, later, in rock 'n' roll and rock-related musical styles. In these contexts, a regular custom was to begin a song with a repeated sequence in which a heavy accent at the start of each bar was followed by a vocal melodic line or phrase. In Jerry Lee Lewis's recording of 'Great Balls of Fire' (1957), the heavy accent is preceded by a short run of three unaccented eighth notes. Songs based on a 12-bar blues often fitted a stop-time pattern to the first four bars of the 12-bar sequence. In a famous example, Elvis Presley's recording of 'Heartbreak Hotel' (1956), the voice begins the song unaccompanied. It becomes apparent that this is stop-time only when two stop-time chords come in at the end of the first bar. The pattern is repeated for the second bar, but then the accented chords drop out.

Because stop-time involves both the suspension and the resumption of rhythm, it has the capacity to suggest combinations of contrasting or complementary meanings. In Armstrong's 'Potato Head Blues,' for example, the tensions and sense of challenge evident during the stop-time solo resolve into excited fulfillment at what was achieved.

Bibliography

Berlin, Edward A. 1980. *Ragtime: A Musical and Cultural History*. Berkeley, CA: University of California Press.

Schuller, Gunther. 1968. *Early Jazz: Its Roots and Musical Development*. New York: Oxford University Press.

Discographical References

Armstrong, Louis. 'Potato Head Blues.' OKeh 8503. 1927: USA.

Lewis, Jerry Lee. 'Great Balls of Fire.' Sun 281. *1957*: USA.

Presley, Elvis. 'Heartbreak Hotel.' RCA 47-6420. *1956*: USA.

DAVID HORN and GARRY TAMLYN

Swing

At a syntactic level, 'swing' denotes a repeated rhythm, occurring in quadruple-meter accompaniments, that comprises single notes on beats 1 and 3 followed by long–short types of rhythm on beats 2 and 4 (see Ex. 1). Swing rhythms performed on cymbals (including hi-hat) were a characteristic feature of swing era jazz, rhythm and blues, and bebop drumming. Used broadly, 'swing' also denotes a musical performance that features regularly recurring long onbeat and short offbeat notes, most commonly dividing a beat into triplet-based shuffle rhythms. Swing functions are to be found in many music programming packages. Utilizing such music programming techniques as 'quantizing' or 'track-shifting,' swing functions alter the rhythmic profile of a single programmed sequence or musical section by lengthening onbeat notes and rests and shortening offbeat ones, thus producing shuffle-type rhythms.

'Swing' takes on added meaning in relation to musical perception and description but, in this context, the term has resisted precise musical explication. Rhythmic fluidity, informed by performance practise conventions appropriate to the musical style, and the quality of note onsets appear to be central, but not exclusive, components of swing. In reference to jazz, with which the term is often associated, Schuller (1986), for instance, states that swing is 'a force in music that maintains the perfect equilibrium between the horizontal [melodic/linear] and vertical [chordal/rhythmic] relationships of musical sounds' (7). Elsewhere, Schuller notes that 'accentuation' and 'inflection' of notes are important to 'equilibrium,' but the former qualities involve 'an incredibly subtle process which . . . is analyzable only in the realm of microacoustics' (1989, 225). Musicological discussions of swing sometimes contain graphical illustrations that serve to depict the 'microacoustical' and temporal dimensions of note onsets. For example, Schuller (1989, 855–59) invites the reader to compare some graphical illustrations representing simple acoustical analyses of recorded phrases that swing to others that do not.

For swing to occur, it is generally considered necessary to have an unchanging, temporally equidistant sounded or unsounded beat (pulse), above which musical lines are defined by rhythms regularly recurring either before or after the beat. The placement of notes along the rhythmic continuum commonly involves constant repetition of asynchronizations to the underlying beat or meter, and these create varied and opposing metrical images in musical performance. Multiple asynchronous metrical images may also occur within ensemble performances between, for instance, a soloist and a rhythm section, or among members of the rhythm section, or among the rhythms contained in a drumbeat. Metrical opposition of the type discussed above is often described in terms of musical 'tension,' 'friction' or 'intensity.'

In common parlance, 'swing' often denotes a musician-centered, processual dimension of musical performance (see, for instance, Keil 1966; Prögler 1995). A 'swinging solo,' for example, might refer to stylistically successful performance effects achieved from the diverse

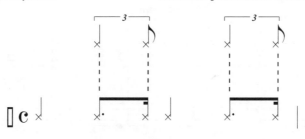

Example 1

array of musical, and primarily rhythmic, choices that arise through collective improvisation and ensemble performance. In this sense, the term might be considered synonymous with groove.

Bibliography

Keil, Charles. 1966. 'Motion and Feeling Through Music.' *Journal of Aesthetics and Art Criticism* 24(3): 337–49.

Prögler, J.A. 1995. 'Searching for Swing: Participatory Discrepancies in the Jazz Rhythm Section.' *Ethnomusicology* 39(1): 21–54.

Schuller, Gunther. 1986 (1968). *The History of Jazz. Vol. 1: Early Jazz, Its Roots and Musical Development.* New York: Oxford University Press.

Schuller, Gunther. 1989 (1968). *The History of Jazz. Vol. 2: The Swing Era: The Development of Jazz, 1930–1945.* New York: Oxford University Press.

GARRY TAMLYN

Syncopation

'Syncopation' is generally understood to be the stressing of notes, beats or pulses that are not normally stressed. Such stressing creates a disturbance in the normal arrangement of meters, accents and rhythms in a musical tradition. Syncopation has been judged to be important in popular music that has been subject to African-American influences in which such influences give rise to disturbances in the customary arrangement of meters, accents and rhythms derived from the tradition of Western art music. Syncopation in this kind of music frequently displays the added feature of 'inflection,' in which syncopated notes are performed slightly before or after the beat or pulse as customarily placed in European-influenced music. This kind of inflected syncopation creates a feeling of 'catchiness' for many individuals hearing such music. A good example of this kind of syncopation is provided by the 'right hand' or melody line of Scott Joplin piano ragtime pieces.

A more technically precise explanation is that 'syncopation' denotes a supplemental rhythmic image, collateral to the underlying beat or meter of a musical performance, created when a note or successive notes occurring either off the beat (pulse) or on metrically 'weak' beats (such as beats 2 and 4 of a 4/4 bar) are highlighted by dynamic accent, duration, timbre, pitch differentiation or some other means. Syncopation therefore 'shifts' or remaps the placement of established accentuations provided by the underlying beat or meter, and results in a type of displacement or irregularity to an otherwise rhythmically uniform flow of musical line. In order for syncopation to be perceived, it is necessary that established accentuations are heard or felt, either in the syncopated passage itself or in some other part. A rhythm consisting of extended syncopation, carried on without the type of rhythmic support previously mentioned, eschews metrical or onbeat accents altogether and therefore might no longer be felt as syncopated.

In simple, extended forms of syncopation, the highlighted notes are often spaced similarly to the underlying beat (pulse). Example 1, for instance, contains syncopation achieved by a fixed duration that separates two rhythms of the same meter and tempo. At a metric level, a form of syncopation occurs when accented notes do not agree with the highlighted sounded or unsounded beats (pulses) projected by a meter. In this context, backbeat – considered a remapping of the strong beats in a quadruple-meter bar – is often described in terms of syncopation. Similarly, the long notes contained in Example 2 might also be discussed in terms of syncopation. An upbeat is generally not considered in terms of syncopation unless it is tied over to the first beat of the subsequent bar or highlighted by some other means.

Example 1

Example 2

Although syncopation is rendered precisely in musical notation, the performance of syncopation in much popular music is often not mathematical in execution; syncopates are often performed slightly before or after their temporal location as rendered in musical notation. Further, notes occurring on the beat in musical notation might be either anticipated or delayed in popular music performance, thus resulting in a type of syncopation rubato in which the rhythm of the musical line is displaced, but the tempo remains constant.

Discography
Joplin, Scott. *Ragtime, Vol. 2 (1900–1910)*. Biograph BP-1008Q. *1971*: USA.

GARRY TAMLYN with JOHN SHEPHERD

Upbeat
'Upbeat' is a term generally used to denote the final beat or part thereof that precedes and anticipates the first beat of a subsequent bar, as in beat '4' or part thereof of a 4/4 bar. In this context, the term brings to mind the upward movement of a conductor's arm when directing measured music. The term is particularly used in reference to introductory musical passages, such as the beginning of a song or phrase.

GARRY TAMLYN

Walking Bass
'Walking bass' is a metaphor that denotes a technique used by performers on the double bass or electric bass involving a line of plucked notes that 'step' from one to the other. Occurring either in a solo or in an accompaniment, a walking bass line characteristically combines its stepwise melodic motion with steady quarter-note rhythms, and very few successive notes of the same pitch. Walking bass lines typically 'walk' through harmonic-structural sections.

The origin of walking bass is found in early jazz double bass accompaniments. During the 1920s, the main role of the bass instrument in an ensemble – the double bass or tuba – was to mark the first and third beats, but some bass players (for example, John Lindsay) began changing the character of the bass's rhythmic contribution by playing evenly on all four beats of a 4/4 bar (something the tuba player could not easily do, due to the need to take a breath). Some early jazz bassists also often employed 'slap-bass' technique, slapping or snapping the string against the fingerboard for extra percussive effect. George 'Pops' Foster, for instance, would often 'get to romping on a fast number' and 'slap out a good rhythm' on all four beats of a bar (Foster, quoted in Stoddard 1971, 76).

In the 1930s, as 'four-beat' technique became more standard, the bass took on a timekeeping role, slapping became less common, and most swing era bass players constructed their accompaniments on the basic harmonic requirements of the piece, changing notes as the harmonic changes demanded. It was at this time that players such as Walter Page (with the Count Basie Orchestra) and Jimmy Blanton (with Duke Ellington's Orchestra) began 'walking,' creating four-beat bass lines in stepping motion that were interesting in their own right. Blanton, in particular, in his short career with Ellington (1939–42), used walking bass lines as a key element in the development of a solo role for the instrument (see, for example, his duet with Ellington, 'Plucked Again' (1939), and his contribution to the band's recording 'Ko-Ko' (1940)). The technique was further developed by bebop bass players such as Ray Brown. Walking bass in both swing and early bebop was often performed without too many rhythmic ornamentations or pedal notes. As Owens (1995) notes, in the later 1950s bass playing 'pushed on to higher levels of virtuosity' (179) and players often avoided walking lines.

During the 1940s, walking bass increasingly featured in western swing (as in, for example, Bob Wills and His Texas Playboys' 'Twin Guitar Special' (1941)) and, later, in some rhythm and blues styles. Most notably, walking bass regularly appeared in double bass accompaniments to Chicago blues produced during the late 1940s; Muddy Waters' 'Mean Red Spider' (1946) is one early example.

A second use of the term 'walking bass' occurs in blues piano to describe bass patterns that rise and fall in broken octaves. Originally found in some ragtime pieces around the turn of the century, the technique was particularly characteristic of boogie-woogie from the late 1920s.

Bibliography
Kriss, Eric. 1974. *Barrelhouse and Boogie Piano*. New York: Oak Publications.

Owens, Thomas. 1995. *Bebop: The Music and Its Players*. New York: Oxford University Press.

Stoddard, Tom. 1971. *Pops Foster: The Autobiography of a New Orleans Jazzman as Told to Tom Stoddard*. Berkeley, CA: University of California Press.

Discographical References
Ellington, Duke, and Blanton, Jimmy. 'Plucked Again.' Columbia 35322. 1939: USA.

Ellington, Duke, and His Orchestra. 'Ko-Ko.' Victor 25677. 1940: USA.

Muddy Waters. 'Mean Red Spider.' *Muddy Waters: First Recording Sessions, 1941–1946, in Chronological Order*. Document DOCD 5146. *1992*: Austria.

Wills, Bob, and His Texas Playboys. 'Twin Guitar Special.' *Western Swing: Texas: 1928–1944*. Fremeaux CD FA 032. *1994*: France.

GARRY TAMLYN and DAVID HORN

20. The Piece

Accompaniment

In common parlance, the term 'accompaniment' is used to describe music that is heard as subordinate to a simultaneous aspect of performance, musical or otherwise: for example, a film score as an accompaniment to on-screen action and dialog, or a polyphonic choral piece sung with instrumental accompaniment as opposed to being sung a cappella. In musicological terms, 'accompaniment' refers to that part of a musical continuum generally regarded as providing support for, or the background to, a more prominent strand in the same music.

Accompaniment can only occur within a musical structure consisting of separate strands that exhibit different degrees of perceived importance. If a musical texture consists of several different strands of perceived equal importance, as in a round like 'Frère Jacques' or as in some forms of West African polyrhythm, there is neither accompaniment nor any particularly 'prominent strand.' Similarly, if the music consists of one strand only, as with Gregorian chant or a simple lullaby, there is no accompaniment. However, as soon as those performing monody tap their feet in time with the music, or members of an audience clap their hands in time with the tune, there is accompaniment.

Accompaniment can be provided by any number or type of instruments and/or voices, ranging from a simple foot stamp, as in Janis Joplin's 'Mercedes Benz,' to dramatic orchestral backing, as heard behind the Three Tenors' rendering of Puccini's 'Nessun' dorma.' The notion of the accompaniment's supporting role is echoed in the word 'backing,' used to qualify the voice(s) and/or instrument(s) heard as musical background to the lead vocal(s) or instrument(s) in the foreground.

Although, for example, rap backing tracks constitute accompaniment to the spoken word, accompaniment is most often used to support a melody. The dualism between melody and accompaniment is one of the most common basic devices of musical structuration. Its increasing popularity during and after the Renaissance in Europe was concurrent with the rise of central perspective in painting and of a visual dualism between figure and ground. Both dualisms – visual figure/ground and musical melody/accompaniment – also concurred historically with the gradual development of notions of the individual and of his/her relationship to his/her natural and social surroundings. In other words, accompaniment (including its aspects of texture, reverberation and so on) can be visualized, in general terms, as the acoustic background or environment against which melody stands out in relief as an individual foreground figure (Maróthy 1974; Tagg 1994). Such stylistically diverse types of music as Elizabethan dances, operatic arias, parlor ballads, jazz standards, Eurovision Song Contest entries and rock numbers all use the melody/accompaniment dualism as a basic structuring device. However, the accompaniment's degree of subordination to the melody can vary considerably. It can range, for example, from a solo singer-songwriter's guitar strum to the relative contrapuntality of the multilayered patterns of drumkit, bass and guitar riffs heard in many rock recordings; from the homophonically set alto, tenor and bass parts in the four-part harmony of traditional hymns to the cross-rhythms of many types of Latin American dance music (for example, *cumbia*, mambo, *murga* and salsa); and from the continuous drone note(s) accompanying the chanter melody on bagpipes to the hocket techniques of funk music.

The relative importance of melody and accompaniment can also be highlighted by assigning various degrees of prominence to one or the other at the mixing desk. For example, lead vocals on late twentieth-century recordings of pop songs from Italy, France and Spain tend to be mixed slightly louder, more 'up front,' than those on recordings from the English-speaking world. In addition to these general foregrounding practises, the melodic line is usually panned in the middle of the stereo array, while accompanying parts are more likely to be mixed within the acoustic semicircle behind and on either side of the melodic focal point (Lacasse 2000). Such acoustic positioning reflects the most common stage locations of lead vocalists and of the accompanying band members when in concert.

The general pattern of acoustic positioning just described is often subject to changes in focus during the course of the same piece. For example, a rock guitar can emerge from its accompanying role of providing support in the form of chords or riffs into a full-blown solo. As it does so, the main focus of listener attention turns from the vocal line to what now clearly becomes the *lead* guitar. This change of focus works because the guitar is played more melodically than before and because its volume is usually turned up (on the guitar itself and/or on the guitar amplifier and/or at the mixing desk) for the duration of the solo. Moreover, in concert, the guitarist will often go to the front of the stage at the start of the solo, be more visibly active during the solo, and retire to his/her previous position as accompanist after completing the solo. Similar changes of focus in the melody/accompaniment dualism occur in jazz, not only during the improvised solos that characterize gigs played by smaller combos and that usually span several choruses within the same number, but also in big-band performances when instrumentalists stand up to draw both visual and musical attention to much shorter passages considered to be of particular interest or importance, sitting down afterward to resume their accompanying role. When televised, these types of solo passages are usually marked by editing devices – for example, by switching the point of view from a general shot or closeup of the lead vocalist to one of the relevant soloist or by zooming in on the individual or instrument in question.

There are occasions when (parts of) the instrumental accompaniment to a popular song can be more memorable, sometimes more easily reproduced and, perhaps, even more important than its lead vocal line. This is certainly true of the verse part of such popular recordings as '(I Can't Get No) Satisfaction' and of the chorus in both 'Layla' and 'Samba de una nota só.' In '(I Can't Get No) Satisfaction' and 'Layla,' the accompanying guitar riffs are infinitely more singable than the lead vocals, while in 'Samba de una nota só' it is the chord progression of the accompanying guitar that provides the greater sense of profile and direction. Indeed, some of the most common functions of an accompaniment are to provide the melody with: (a) an ongoing kinetic and periodic framework (meter, patterns of accentuation, rhythmic figurations, episodic markers and so on); (b) tonal reference point(s); (c) a sense of harmonic direction and expectation; and (d) suitable background textures and timbres. Given these basic parameters, it is clear that accompaniment, despite notions of its supporting role, can be just as important as – sometimes more important than – melody in communicating the overall message of the music.

For example, imagine the first phrase of the title tune for the television detective series *Kojak* (Ex. 1), with its heroic unison horn calls and fanfare figures (Tagg 2000), accompanied not by the actual driving rhythms and woodwind stabs used when it was broadcast, but by a single hurdy-gurdy drone, or by a kazoo band, or by techno loops, or by a wordless cathedral choir or by massed mandolins. Such replacement of one type of accompaniment by another is similar to superimposing an identical visual foreground figure on different backgrounds – perhaps your favorite artist, first amidst industrial decay, and then in a village-school playground on a sunny spring day. The figures or melodies may be objectively identical, but such radical differences of background or accompaniment will alter not only the overall picture, but also the perception of the character of the foreground figure or melody. To illustrate this important function of accompaniment, Example 2 would probably put Kojak in the pastoral setting of a romantic soap opera, while Example 3 might place him among his African-American brothers and Example 4 would probably see him under a Martini parasol in Copacabana.

Bibliography

Lacasse, Serge. 2000. *'Listen to My Voice': The Evocative Power of Vocal Staging in Recorded Rock Music and Other Forms of Vocal Expression*. Ph.D. thesis, Institute of Popular Music, University of Liverpool.

Maróthy, János. 1974. *Music and the Bourgeois, Music and the Proletarian*. Budapest: Akadémiai Kiadó.

Tagg, Philip. 1994. 'From Refrain to Rave: The Decline of Figure and the Rise of Ground.' *Popular Music* 13(2): 209–22.

Tagg, Philip. 2000. *Kojak: 50 Seconds of Television Music*. 2nd ed. New York: Mass Media Music Scholars' Press. (First published Göteborg: Skrifter från Göteborgs universitet, Musikvetenskapliga institutionen, 1979.)

Sheet Music

Goldenberg, William, comp. 1973. *Kojak* (main theme, orchestral arrangement No. 1). Manuscript, Universal

Example 1 The first main melodic phrase of the theme from *Kojak* by William Goldenberg.

Example 2 The theme from *Kojak* as romantic pop ballad in French or Italian vein.

Example 3 The theme from *Kojak* as funk.

Example 4 The theme from *Kojak* as bossa nova.

City Studios, Prod. No. 39000. Melville, NY: Duchess Music Corporation.

Discographical References

Derek and the Dominos. 'Layla.' Polydor 2058 130. *1970*: UK.

Gilberto, João. 'Samba de una nota só.' *Gilberto and Jobim*. Capitol 2160. *1960*: USA.

Joplin, Janis. 'Mercedes Benz.' *Pearl*. Columbia 30322. *1971*: USA.

'Nessun' dorma' (from *Turandot* by G. Puccini, 1923). *The Three Tenors in Concert*. London 430 433. *1995*: UK.

Rolling Stones, The. '(I Can't Get No) Satisfaction.' Decca F 12220. *1965*: UK.

PHILIP TAGG

Arrangement

'Arrangement' denotes a version of a piece of music with specific reference to the instruments involved, the manner in which they are played, and the order of the sections of the piece. While every piece that is performed logically exists as an arrangement, the term nevertheless frequently denotes an adaptation of a preexisting piece of music for a different instrument or combination of instruments. An arrangement involves decisions about the choice of instruments and voices, the distribution of the pitches among the various instruments and voices, and the disposition of the diverse sections of the music, along with indications of dynamics, phrasing and so on. A person who creates an arrangement is an arranger.

'Arrangement' may imply a written score, but musicians who do not read music nevertheless make decisions about the shape of the music they play, such as whether to play an introduction, when to solo, where entries occur, how to end – in sum, all decisions concerning the disposition of the elements of a piece and the manner in which these are played. Memorized arrangements that are worked out in rehearsal are known as 'head arrangements.'

Commonly, so-called 'brass arrangements' or 'string arrangements' are worked out and added to, for example, a standard rock band ensemble. These parts are very often added at a later stage of production in the case of recording (such as the strings added to the Beatles' 'The Long and Winding Road'), or are sometimes added to supplement a band's head arrangement in a live performance.

While decisions about who will play what are certainly aspects of record production, 'arrangement' does not normally refer to studio adjustments to the sound, or to other forms of electronic manipulation and sampling, or to the relative dynamic levels of the channels in a recording mix. These kinds of changes to a piece of music are commonly designated in popular music by the generic terms 'mix' and 'remix.' Moreover, in the case of a cover of a rock song by another rock band, the resulting arrangement is much more likely to be called a 'version' – such as, for example, Jimi Hendrix's version of the Troggs' 'Wild Thing,' or Stevie Ray Vaughan's version of Hendrix's 'Voodoo Chile.' The use of the term 'version' instead of 'arrangement' in this context implies a head arrangement.

Publishers have found arrangements useful in the creation of new markets. In the nineteenth century, when published sheet music was the most important vehicle for the distribution of music, arrangements became very popular with publishers and consumers alike. Many pieces appeared not in a single arrangement, but in a variety of arrangements in order to serve the needs of professional, semiprofessional, amateur and domestic markets. John Philip Sousa's marches, for example, normally appeared in arrangements for piano (two

hands, four hands and six hands), orchestra, military band, zither solo, zither duet, mandolin solo, mandolin and guitar, two mandolins and piano, guitar duet, banjo solo, banjo duet and various other combinations. Likewise, popular arias and excerpts from opera were arranged for piano solo to cater to the large amateur and domestic market. The military bands of Sousa and Patrick Gilmore, among others, performed arrangements of ragtime, popular songs and symphonic works, introducing this repertoire to new audiences. Similarly, arrangements of all kinds were the lifeblood of the many small orchestras performing in music halls, vaudeville theaters and early cinemas everywhere. In the age prior to radio and recording, arrangements were the most important medium for the dissemination of music.

The idea of the arrangement is hugely significant in popular music. Through the creation and sale of new arrangements, a piece of music's commercial potential can be more fully exploited, and certainly the appearance of so many arrangements for sale indicates the desire of publishers to explore every market. But arrangements have a practical aspect as well: they serve the workaday requirements of theater orchestras, dance bands, variety shows, television shows and so on. In this respect, the popular music arrangement contrasts with the classical arrangement. Of course, classical composers create arrangements all the time – for example, Bach's Concerto for Four Harpsichords after Vivaldi or Webern's arrangement of Schoenberg's First Chamber Symphony for the ensemble used in *Pierrot Lunaire*. Often, classical piano pieces are orchestrated, such as Ravel's orchestration of Mussorgsky's *Pictures at an Exhibition*. The attitude toward the resultant text, however, reflects the different ideologies informing these two spheres of musical activity. In classical music, the text – that is, the score – is conceived to be a permanent artistic statement. Repeat performances of the same piece of music by different ensembles anywhere in the world will almost invariably use essentially the same text. Consequently, classical musicians are exceedingly reluctant to alter scores, and an arrangement tends to be justified as a homage. In popular music, the notion of the musical text is much more fluid, and a song will reappear in the repertoire of another performer in a different arrangement almost as a matter of course. With popular music performers, it is the reshaping of the material to suit their own performance styles or practical requirements that predominates.

Bibliography

Lanza, Joseph. 1995. *Elevator Music: A Surreal History of Muzak, Easy-Listening, and Other Moodsong*. New York: Picador.

Levy, Lester S., ed. 1975. *Sousa's Great Marches*. New York: Dover Publications.

Prendergast, Roy M. 1992. *Film Music – A Neglected Art: A Critical Study of Music in Films*. 2nd ed. New York: W.W. Norton.

Sargeant, Winthrop. 1959 (1946). *Jazz: Hot and Hybrid*. London: Jazz Book Club.

Discographical References

Beatles, The. 'The Long and Winding Road.' Apple 2832. *1970*: USA.

Jimi Hendrix Experience, The. 'Voodoo Chile (Slight Return).' *Electric Ladyland*. Reprise 6307. *1968*: USA.

Jimi Hendrix Experience, The. 'Wild Thing.' *The Jimi Hendrix Concerts*. CBS 88592. *1982*: UK.

Troggs, The. 'Wild Thing.' Fontana TF 689. *1966*: UK.

Vaughan, Stevie Ray. 'Voodoo Chile (Slight Return).' *Couldn't Stand the Weather*. Epic 39304. *1984*: USA.

TIM WISE

Backing

'Backing' denotes the practise of playing behind or supporting a front-line musician or group of musicians. The term first appeared in the United States around 1930 (Gold 1975, 7), mainly in a jazz and big band context, and is historically linked to the rise to prominence of both the solo instrumentalist and (perhaps especially) the solo vocalist. Its widespread usage in popular music by the 1940s ousted the previously dominant term 'accompaniment,' partly no doubt because of the latter's classical European connotations. Within jazz itself, the term 'comp' also emerged at about the same time, with the more specialized meaning of providing chordal accompaniment, usually on the piano. (Comping may also have carried its own extra sense, that of 'complementing.') In classical music, the term 'accompaniment' has persisted.

Since the 1940s, in both live and recorded form, popular music has exhibited a wide variety of backing styles, ranging from a single musician to an entire orchestra. The type of backing provided depends on both stylistic considerations and economic necessities. A rock band might have the backing of a number of extra guitarists, vocalists and/or drummers, some of whom might themselves be renowned as front-line musicians in their own right, while a ballad-singer is more likely to be backed by one or more orchestral sections, especially strings. Meanwhile, technological change has increasingly brought the sounds of a backing ensemble within the performance capabilities of musicians unable to afford the real thing (and of many who can).

Two more specialized usages of 'backing' have emerged since the 1950s. The term 'backing vocals' refers to the vocal parts accompanying the solo track. In recording, a backing vocal may or may not be recorded as a 'backing track,' a technical term referring to the supporting track (vocal or instrumental) accompanying the lead vocalist(s). A backing track may be recorded at the same time as, or independently of, the main track recording.

A high level of musicianship is regularly demanded of backing musicians, who are expected to sight-read and, not infrequently, to perform with minimum preparation. Nevertheless, in many popular music idioms the practise includes both an artistic and a professional/commercial sense of subsidiary status – something the word itself may be seen to reinforce. This is clearly linked to two hierarchical processes: an aesthetic one, which maps onto music a system of values in which foreground takes precedence over background; and an economic one, which needs to preserve categories of the lower paid. The spatial arrangements of the musicians at many live performances and the sound balance in both live and studio contexts tend to acknowledge the persistence of these ideas.

Where the term 'backing' is used indiscriminately to describe a range of sonic and spatial relationships, it risks restricting the ability to imply (as the more equivocal 'accompaniment' still can) that musicians are also present who are 'keeping company with' the musician(s) in the spotlight. At the same time, 'backing' retains a sense of 'actively supporting' which the more discreet 'accompaniment' lacks.

Bibliography

Gold, Robert S. 1975. *Jazz Talk*. Indianapolis, IN: Bobbs-Merrill.

DAVID HORN and STAN HAWKINS

Book (1)

'Book' is the name given to the script of a musical, excluding the lyrics of the songs.

The term 'book' was in occasional use in the late nineteenth century to refer to the words of a musico-dramatic work, such as an operetta. Its special attachment to the musical appears to have been associated with the phrase 'book musical,' which began to be used in the United States in the 1920s to distinguish a show with a sustained plot from a revue. As the musical grew in maturity and aspiration, the term 'libretto' began to be used interchangeably (if imprecisely), although the professional musical theater, in the United States at least, for a long time tended to prefer the term 'book' (as any survey of theatrical posters will show). In the 1960s, the phrase 'book musical' developed connotations of conventionalism.

Although several famous lyricists (such as Oscar Hammerstein II and Alan Jay Lerner) have also been book writers, the two tasks have more often been kept separate. Typically, the book writer works with both lyricist and composer at various points in what becomes a collective developmental process; however, the modus operandi is also frequently hierarchical, placing the book writer's influence and contribution high on the scale of functionality but low on the scale of artistic significance. As Gottfried (1979) has pointed out, although the book writers of successful shows have tended to be overshadowed by the composers and lyricists, the book writer is among the first to be singled out for blame if a show is unsuccessful. The book is also most likely to be cited as a reason why a show comes to be seen as 'dated.'

The book is generally the first part of a musical to be produced in some form. Sometimes entirely original in concept and execution, it is more usually an adaptation of a novel or play. The book provides the framework for the show and its basic ingredients: setting, characters, plot, themes, dialog. Because the time taken up by musical numbers limits the time available for each of these other elements, the book has to accomplish its task with the maximum economy of means. It also, crucially, provides the context – and, in many shows, the rationale – for the music. Musical numbers in book musicals regularly derive their dramaturgical purpose (for example, in characterization or in the exploration of a theme, such as ethnic gang warfare in New York in *West Side Story*) from ideas set in place by the book, however much the numbers may themselves add new perspectives, or indeed more impact, to those ideas.

But if the music can be said to extend the work of the book in this way, it may also add an element that exceeds the book's own capabilities. The book of a book musical typically belongs to a theatrical tradition in which the action takes place between the characters involved and within a space and time that they define, while the audience for its part, as it were, eavesdrops on that action in that setting. A musical number, however, may be – and quite often is – conceived as having two simultaneous functions: one, derived from the same theatrical tradition as the book, serves the show's internalized logic; the other, derived from music's role in the vaudeville family of entertainments, is directed at the audience. In these instances, there seem to be two spatio-temporal spheres – one involving the world created by the book and observed (often empathetically) by the audience, and the second forming around the singer and the audience, outside the context of the book. In Rodgers' and Hammerstein's *South Pacific*, for example, the book creates the context in which the female protagonist Nellie Forbush sings 'I'm Gonna Wash That Man Right Outa My Hair' as if to convince herself she is right to do so. The audience looks on and may or may not sympathize. But in making the song a show-stopping song-and-dance number, the composer and lyricist also allow singer and audience to create for themselves a different type of theatrical moment in the present, before the book intervenes to end the ambiguity by returning the singer to the dramatic fold and the audience to its eavesdropping. The role of the book at that point is to reestablish the conventions.

In some musicals from the mid-1960s on, the concept of the book began to change so that it too contributed to the ambiguity of the production, rather than being solely the bearer of the dramatic rationale. This is seen most clearly in musicals with a 'show-within-a-show' format (as in *Cabaret* or, perhaps especially, *A Chorus Line*). In other developments, the increase in the amount of music in many musicals from the late 1970s on left less and less time for the traditional functions of the book, which instead became more like a production script, while the rise of the 'through-composed' musical created a need for something closer to an operatic libretto.

Bibliography

Burrows, Abe. 1980. *Honest, Abe: Is There Really No Business Like Show Business?* Boston, MA: Little, Brown.

Engel, Lehman. 1972. *Words with Music.* New York: Macmillan.

Engel, Lehman. 1975. *The American Musical Theater: A Consideration.* Rev. ed. New York: Macmillan.

Frankel, Aaron. 1977. *Writing the Broadway Musical.* New York: Drama Book Specialists.

Gottfried, Martin. 1979. *Broadway Musicals.* New York: Abrams.

DAVID HORN

Book (2)

A 'book' is a collection of standard themes, either instrumental, vocal or both, which constitute the basic repertoire of a band or orchestra. These themes may take the form of band sheet music, with specially devised and written arrangements, or simply sequences of playing order. In early jazz, many of the entries in the 'book' were numbered (for example, No. 3, 'Tiger Rag'), the term 'number' for a tune or featured piece of music reputedly deriving from this practise. While some orchestras had small and manageable books, others accumulated extensive collections from which their repertoire could be drawn. Among those surviving are more than 7,000 items acquired by the violinist John Robichaux (1866–1939), leader in the 1920s of a New Orleans 'society' orchestra. This was drawn on by the reconstructed New Orleans Ragtime Orchestra led by the Swedish pianist Lars Ivar Edegran, with the drummer and vocalist John Robichaux, nephew of the former band leader. It is possible that the term 'book' was adopted by bands that had acquired published collections, such as the celebrated *Red Back Book of Rags*. The term was subsequently used to denote a repertoire even in cases where no book physically existed.

Bibliography

New Orleans Ragtime Orchestra, The. 1974. Notes to *Creole Belles*. Arhoolie CD 420.

Discography

Joseph Robichaux and His New Orleans Rhythm Boys: Complete Recorded Works (1933). Document DOCD-1016. *1999*: Austria.

PAUL OLIVER

Comping

The term 'comping,' derived from 'accompanying,' is used in jazz, where it refers to chordal accompaniment provided for soloists by the piano, guitar or vibes. Comping was pioneered in the big bands by pianists such as Count Basie and Duke Ellington, and became standard practise in the smaller groups of bebop (Owens 1995), where it was often both harmonically and rhythmically imaginative. Less usually, comping has been carried out in a more even four-to-the-bar, as in the technique of Count Basie's long-serving guitarist Freddie Green.

The term may also be used to denote an accompanimental rhythm provided by a snare drum, often countering the meter and providing a variegated rhythmic layer to a song's beat. In swing era jazz and some rhythm and blues styles, comping snare rhythms often punctuate or embellish horn section riffs.

Bibliography

Owens, Thomas. 1995. *Bebop: The Music and Its Players*. New York: Oxford University Press.

DAVID HORN and GARRY TAMLYN

Head Arrangement

'Head arrangement' is a term used in jazz to describe an arrangement that is worked out in rehearsal and learned by the musicians, who keep it 'in their heads.' It is only partially written down, if at all. Simple enough to be memorized, a head arrangement is also characterized by the collaborative effort that goes into it. Members of the band contribute suggestions ('from their own heads') relating to any aspect of the arrangement: an individual's role, improvisatory breaks, combinations of sound, even formal structure and overall 'feel.' Although the band leader may make final decisions, the resulting arrangement remains a collective idea, and this can manifest itself in performance in a greater sense of freedom. A significant number of the best-known pieces associated with bands such as those of Duke Ellington

and Count Basie were founded on the collective instructions and dynamics of head arrangements.

STAN HAWKINS and DAVID HORN

Lead Vocals

The term 'lead vocals' is used to refer to the vocal part or parts that make the most prominent contribution to a musical event in which a number of voices perform either individually or, more typically, as an ensemble. Lead vocals are peculiar to those genres and styles that feature combinations of multiple voices (they are rare in jazz, therefore) and that arrange them in such a way as to require a single voice or set of voices (for example, a vocal duet) to carry out either or both of two functions: to lead the vocal ensemble; and to be set against or emerge from the ensemble, by one or more means, as the dominant sound. 'Lead' itself therefore has two related senses: to act as a leader, and to be the leading sound striking the listener's ear. Of the two, the second is the more prominent.

The use of the word 'vocals' to mean vocal part or parts appears first in the language of North American popular entertainment in the early 1930s. (Short-story writer John O'Hara has his fictional New York nightclub singer, later turned into the leading character in the 1940 musical *Pal Joey*, speak of 'giving with the vocals.') Exactly when the term 'lead vocals' itself appeared is uncertain, but probably the phrase emerged around the late 1930s as mainstream North American popular music felt the increasing impact of vernacular performance idioms, which, unlike the solo-dominated vocals typical of dance music, featured rich vocal interplay in which one or more voices regularly stood out.

One place where the concept of a leading vocalist, if not the term itself, had already developed was in the style of some country music groups, such as the Carter Family, which showed a preference for arrangements in which a single voice took the melodic lead and was supported, discreetly but imaginatively, by other harmonizing voices. But it was in the more complex vocal idiom of African-American gospel groups (quartets and quintets) that the various alternatives around the relationships of the voices and the role of a 'leader' had been thoroughly explored. Within this style, it had become particularly common to arrange the voices so that one voice did not merely distinguish itself from the harmonizing group, but explored various types of relationship with it. The relationship could be hierarchical, with the lead tenor 'on top,' or – in a practise derived from older African-American call-and-response patterns – it could be more dialogical. Just how the role of lead vocalist had evolved in this context can be seen in the roles of tenor 'leads' Otto Tutson and Norman 'Crip' Harris in both the religious and the secular recordings of the Norfolk Jubilee Quartet/Norfolk Jazz Quartet between 1921 and 1940.

The period from the late 1930s to the mid-1950s was a key time for the development of lead vocals into a widely accepted and imitated concept. The main focus of this growth and transition involved two types of crossover: from religious to secular, and from an African-American to a white market. Important to both processes were the Ink Spots, whose late 1930s/early 1940s chart successes featured a sound organized around setting the impassioned, high-tenor lead of Bill Kenny against the deep bass of Orville Jones, the interplay of the two voices itself set against a middle layer of lower tenor and baritone.

As gospel further developed the roles given to its tenor (often falsetto) leads – as, for example, in the singing of Ira Tucker with the Dixie Hummingbirds, Archie Brownlee with the Five Blind Boys of Mississippi and Claude Jeter with the Swan Silvertones – the passionate high-tenor lead also became a central device in the recordings of influential 1950s rhythm and blues vocal groups such as the Drifters and the Coasters. The parallel idea of turning the spotlight on a bass or baritone lead was also developed in gospel. But despite being memorably transferred into a secular context by the Dominoes (for example, for their tongue-in-cheek celebration of sexual prowess, 'Sixty Minute Man'), the technique became associated with comedy and did not travel far outside an African-American context.

The arrangement of vocal parts to create some degree of interplay and dialog between the lead vocals and other vocalists became a regular feature in rock and pop music of the late 1950s and the 1960s, from the girl groups and Motown to British beat music. The relationship between the lead and the other vocal parts was often simply articulated but could nevertheless be subtle and expressive (as Bradby (1990), for example, shows in her analysis of recordings by girl groups such as the Shirelles and the Crystals). But as non-leading vocals became increasingly known as 'backing vocals,' and the terms 'lead' and 'backing' were consistently paired, usage of 'lead vocals' was stretched to cover any popular music context in which a foregrounded vocal part was accompanied – whether brashly or discreetly, consistently or intermittently – by other background voices. As a result, in much pop and rock, to 'take the lead vocals' is to take the main role in terms of delivering the lyrical and melodic content. Some variations on this broad but dominant concept may be noted – for example, in the Spice Girls' preference for regularly switching around the lead vocal roles in a single recording – but the main antithesis to lead-backing vocal dualism developed in the

area of dance music, which largely abandoned the idea of the foregrounded voice (Tagg 1994).

Although a significant part of its history, especially in the latter part of the twentieth century, suggests that the idea of 'lead vocals' is mainly linked to notions of a foregrounded individualism, its earlier applications point to a richer role in the expression of musical (and social) relationships. Lead vocals may be on top or alongside, they may open up dialog or close it down, they may provoke contradictions or invite affirmations.

Bibliography

Bradby, Barbara. 1990. 'Do-Talk and Don't-Talk: The Division of the Subject in Girl-Group Music.' In *On Record: Rock, Pop and the Written Word*, ed. Simon Frith and Andrew Goodwin. London: Routledge, 341–68.

Broughton, Viv. 1996. *Too Close to Heaven: The Illustrated History of Gospel Music*. London: Midnight Books.

Heilbut, Tony. 1985. *The Gospel Sound: Good News and Bad Times*. 2nd ed. New York: Limelight Editions.

Millar, Bill. 1971. *The Drifters: The Rise and Fall of a Black Vocal Group*. London: Studio Vista.

Millar, Bill. 1975. *The Coasters*. London: Allen.

Tagg, Philip. 1994. 'From Refrain to Rave: The Decline of the Figure and the Rise of Ground.' *Popular Music* 13(2): 209–22.

Discographical Reference

Ward, Billy, and the Dominoes. 'Sixty Minute Man.' Federal 12022. 1951: USA. Reissue: Ward, Billy, and the Dominoes. 'Sixty Minute Man.' *Sixty Minute Man*. See for Miles Records 6010. *1999*: UK.

Discography

Carter Family, The. *Country Music Hall of Fame*. MCA 10088. *1999*: USA.

Coasters, The. *The Very Best of the Coasters*. Rhino 32656. *1995*: USA.

Crystals, The. *The Best of the Crystals*. ABKCO 7214-2. *1992*: USA.

Dixie Hummingbirds, The. *Up in Heaven: The Very Best of the Dixie Hummingbirds & the Angelics*. Collectables 6103. *1998*: USA.

Drifters, The. *The Very Best of the Drifters*. Rhino R2-71211. *1993*: USA.

Five Blind Boys, The. *The Best of Five Blind Boys*. Capitol 74785. *1990*: USA.

Norfolk Jazz and Jubilee Quartets. *Complete Recorded Works (1923–1940)*. 6 vols. Document 5381–5386. *1995*: Austria.

Shirelles, The. *Anthology (1959–1964)*. Rhino R2-75897. *1986*: USA.

Spice Girls, The. *Spice*. Virgin 42174. *1997*: UK.

Swan Silvertones, The. *Hallelujah: Collection of Their Finest Recordings*. Music Club 50101. *1999*: USA.

Ward, Billy, and the Dominoes. *Sixty Minute Man*. See for Miles Records 6010. *1999*: UK.

DAVID HORN with STAN HAWKINS

Medley

A musical medley is a collection of recognizable features – chiefly the melodies – of other pieces of music grouped in sequence for performance as one continuous piece. The original, fourteenth-century meaning of the English word was 'hand-to-hand combat.' By the fifteenth century, it could also mean 'a mixture,' and was used particularly to refer to a cloth woven from different materials and using assorted colors. Hence, the word also acquired a sense of the bringing together of diverse, sometimes incongruous elements, often – though not invariably – for humorous effect. It was in this sense that 'medley' was first used in the early seventeenth century to refer to music.

Incongruity in popular music medleys – for example, a rap or punk song introduced into a medley of 1950s Broadway show tunes – can be a ready source of humor, but more often the issue is one of congruity. This takes two main forms: congruity of source, and congruity of performance style. Medleys typically consist of melodies that have something in common: they may have the same composer (a Burt Bacharach medley, for example); they may be associated with the same performer (such as a medley of songs made famous by Judy Garland); or they may be in basically the same idiom (a medley of music hall songs) or on the same theme (a medley of songs of the road). A particularly enduring form is the medley from a music theater show – from Gilbert and Sullivan's *HMS Pinafore* to *Les Misérables*. In each case, the medley is typically constructed as a single piece of continuous music.

Although many medleys are performed in a style associated with the original, this is not always the case. A stylistic shift can take place, caused by the performer's need (or desire) to transfer the chosen material into a style with which he/she is identified, or, as Hoggart observed of pianists in English working-men's clubs in the 1950s, the performer may recognize that the music must be 'transmuted into the received idiom' for the audience to accept it (1958, 124).

A medley is very versatile, and its performance can have one or more objectives. A medley of songs from a recently issued album can serve as a promotion for that album, by whetting the appetite. The overture to a musical may be constructed purely as a medley of songs from the show, thereby designed to give audiences a taste of what is to come. Alternatively, a performer concluding his/her act with a retrospective medley may do so in order to convey an idea of status and achievement (since a medley cannot be constructed from only one hit). By contrast, a medley can also be self-effacing. The club pianist and the cinema organist, both by tradition great purveyors of medleys, use the elements of familiarity and variety not to promote material or draw attention to themselves, but to ensure that their audiences are at ease, yet still modestly stimulated. A medley can also be ambiguous: it can be a genuine expression of homage to another artist and/or a way of attempting to associate one's name with that artist. A particularly rich kind of ambiguity was successfully exploited by the pianist Liberace, who used medleys (such as his 'Gershwin Medley') to pay homage, to link himself to another celebrity, to provide an opportunity to exhibit his particular skills in embellishment and in converting music to his own style, and to reinforce his role as a (mere) provider of measured entertainment.

Because they tend to consist of incomplete – yet familiar – fragments, medleys often provide audiences with opportunities for participation, in which individuals relate to each other through acknowledgment of a common musical taste and knowledge. At the same time, their fragmentary nature, coupled with their dependency on other music, has often led to medleys being denigrated (for example, in pop and rock circles) for evidently encouraging a short attention span. This did not prevent the medley becoming an avenue to chart success in 1981, when Dutch producer Jaap Eggermont, picking up on the interest of discothèques in edited medleys, created Stars on 45, a collection of session musicians brought together specifically to record a medley of extracts from earlier pop classics by the Beatles, the Archies and others. The manually mixed, multi-edit record topped the charts in Holland, the United Kingdom and the United States, and sold well in many countries around the world, creating something of a medley craze. Two more singles, a Beatles medley and a 'tribute' to Stevie Wonder, followed within the year.

As technology enabled medley creation to become more sophisticated, chart-designed medleys reached their zenith with Jive Bunny and the Mastermixers (from Rotherham, South Yorkshire), who achieved three consecutive UK Top 10 number one hits in quick succession in 1989.

Bibliography

Bronson, Fred. 1988. *The Billboard Book of USA Number One Hits*. New York: Billboard.

Hoggart, Richard. 1958. *The Uses of Literacy*. Harmondsworth: Penguin.

Discographical References

Jive Bunny and the Mastermixers. 'Let's Party.' Music Factory Dance MFD 003. *1989*: UK.

Jive Bunny and the Mastermixers. 'Swing the Mood.' Music Factory Dance MFD 001. *1989*: UK.

Jive Bunny and the Mastermixers. 'That's What I Like.' Music Factory Dance MFD 002. *1989*: UK.

Liberace. 'Gershwin Medley.' *Collection: Liberace.* Castle Collector Series CCSLP 201. *1988*: USA.

Stars on 45. 'Medley.' Radio 3810. *1981*: USA. (Issued in the United Kingdom as Starsound. 'Stars on 45.' CBS A 1102. *1981*: UK.)

Discography

Jive Bunny and the Mastermixers. *Jive Bunny: The Album.* Telstar PSTAR 2390. *1989*: UK.

DAVID HORN and STAN HAWKINS

Number

A 'number' is an item (song, dance, instrumental) in a program of musical entertainment, a musical compilation or the repertoire of one or more musicians. The term appears to derive from two related practises of numbering individual pieces of music: in a published score, where a number was employed to itemize either the separate parts of a single work such as an oratorio or opera, or the contents of a collection of shorter pieces; and in a band leader's or musical director's portfolio. In the latter case, during rehearsal or performance, the number of the piece often stands in place of a title, and this usage has spread to everyday parlance (for example, 'What did you think of the band's first number?'). The appeal of the term may lie in the fact that it permits imprecision while still preserving a sense of separate identity (more so than possible synonyms 'item' or 'piece'). Although 'number' as colloquially used has come to be associated uniquely with popular music – to the extent that any reference to a classical 'number' would be taken as ironic – this was not the case before the twentieth century.

DAVID HORN and STAN HAWKINS

Part

The term 'part' as it relates to the performance of music refers, quite literally, to the part played by an individual performer or group of performers in a musical ensemble of whatever size. In this sense, the term designates a musical division of labor. In common parlance, the term is often linked to a voice (contralto, tenor and so on) or instrument. Thus, reference is frequently made, for example, to the 'trumpet part' or the 'clarinet part' in a particular piece of music.

The term takes on another dimension of meaning when music is notated. Here, reference being made, for example, to 'the trumpet part' means that a material object is brought into play: the musical notation written out or printed specifically for one player or group of players in an ensemble. Thus, a piece of music as a whole may be notated – the score – and the individual parts for each instrument notated separately; these are then referred to as 'the parts.'

The notated representation of parts is intended as an aid to performance for a single performer or group of performers. The part can function as a cue card for informing the performer of the sequence of events that will occur during a performance. In jazz, the term 'chart' is often employed in the same way as 'part,' and in big bands and jazz orchestras most of the instructions occur in notated form. The extent to which the music is written out fully in the part varies considerably according to context and style. The part may be written out or printed fully using traditional five-line notation, for example, or be more perfunctory in character, using chord charts or even verbal notes scribbled on a piece of paper. Functioning mainly as a guide to the musician, a part serves as an important reminder to an individual player or group of players of their musical material within the context of a band or other kind of ensemble.

JOHN SHEPHERD and STAN HAWKINS

Repertoire (Repertory)

A repertoire or a repertory is a stock of pieces or songs that a soloist, band or orchestra selects, rehearses and ultimately is ready to present in a performance. For a soloist, band or orchestra to have a piece of music in its repertoire implies that the piece is ready for performance on very short notice. To refer to the repertoire of a soloist, band or orchestra is, as a consequence, to indicate a body of music with which the performer or performers have substantial familiarity.

The term has its origins in the classical music tradition, where it is commonplace to speak about the details of a symphony orchestra's repertoire. With classical music, repertoires are acquired overwhelmingly through scores, that is to say, printed music. With popular music, on the other hand, repertoires are acquired through a variety of means that include printed music, but also include learning from records, and through observation and demonstration. These other means of acquiring a repertoire are oral-aural rather than visual in character.

A repertoire usually aims to be varied and interesting, and presented in a way that shows off the performance and interpretative skills of the musician(s). In such cases, musicians are said approvingly to have a broad repertoire. A broad repertoire is usually contrasted with a narrow one, the implication being that the performer or performers with a narrow repertoire are lacking in skill or musicianship.

In pop and rock traditions, the terms 'repertoire' and 'repertory' are commonly replaced by terms such as 'set,' 'list,' 'group' or 'collection.' As a rule, all bands, orchestras and performing groups (including dance and theater companies) possess a repertoire or repertory list of their performance material.

STAN HAWKINS and JOHN SHEPHERD

Solo

A solo (Italian *solo*, meaning 'alone') is a piece or performance, or part of a piece or performance, for a single voice or instrument; while a soloist may perform completely alone, the term 'solo' is also used when he/she is accompanied – and indeed, when used as a verb, 'to solo' generally refers to such a context. The use of the term in musical discourse probably originated in the growing liking for solo genres and for solo spots within complex textures found in European art music from the seventeenth century onward. From there, it was taken into descriptions of popular music. In principle, solo *pieces* and the practise of soloing *within* pieces can be distinguished; in reality, however, the dividing line is often not clear: how would one describe a guitar break in a self-accompanied song, for example? This shifting quality in the term's usage – particularly clear in popular music, where most performance is for groups, but where the 'spotlit' individual is a common feature – is not surprising, since ultimately it is grounded in the variable social dynamics of performance events and musical textures.

Solo Pieces

Musical genres featuring a solo performer are widely distributed around the world, in both 'art' and 'vernacular' traditions. They include both vocal genres (epics, ballads, praise-songs, laments, lullabies and so on) and instrumental genres (for example, for fiddle or bagpipes in Europe, for the various musical bows, flutes, xylophones, lutes, harps and lyres of Africa, for the *'ud*, *sitār*, *sarangi* and *sarod* of the Middle East and India). Self-accompaniment by singers (on fiddle-type and lute-type instruments especially, but also on lamellophones such as the Zimbabwean *mbira*) is also widespread. Very often, it would seem (although the research is thin), such traditions are drawn upon in the evolution of proto- and early-'popular' genres. This was certainly the case in eighteenth- and nineteenth-century Europe, where street instrumentalists and singers (of broadside ballads, for instance), and performers in the various types of music hall, pleasure garden and popular theater and cabaret extended and built upon existing repertoires. (Accompaniment was assisted by the spread of the guitar and of free-reed instruments.) It seemed to apply also in

Africa, for example in the evolution of 'palm-wine' and early *jújù* styles (Waterman 1990), of the song styles of the *griots* and *jalis* of the Sahel region, and of Central and East African guitarists such as Mwenda Jean Bosco and Daniel Kachamba (Kubik 1981; Manuel 1988, ch. 3). Similar processes can be traced in the history of the numerous genres of *canción* in Latin America (Manuel 1988, ch. 2).

In the United States, solo instrumental performance (on fiddle, guitar or banjo, for dancing) and solo singing were common among white communities from an early date, and these traditions fed through into early commercial country music (Malone 1985); first to record, for example, was Fiddlin' John Carson. In the African-American repertoire, the solo holler is well documented (Courlander 1963); there is evidence for the development of a solo banjo repertoire (Winans and Kaufman 1994); guitarists, fiddlers and pianists played for dancing, and in the late nineteenth century ragtime pianists entertained those in search of a good time; blues singers were accompanying themselves on guitar at least as early as 1903, according to W.C. Handy (1961, 74); 'songsters' and 'musicianers' were performing many of these genres and more at tent shows and vaudevilles – and, a little later, recording them too (Oliver 1984). White and black repertoires interacted over a long period (Russell 1970). The result in due course fed into the rich folk revival, neo-folk and singer-songwriter strands in later twentieth-century North American popular music – from Leadbelly and Woody Guthrie to Joni Mitchell and Tracy Chapman; and similar trajectories can be observed in various other parts of the world.

But in what sense, exactly, may these earlier song types be described as solos? Without prejudging the answer to this question (which, without much more socio-musical research, would be rash), it may be suggested that they lacked a certain *charge* which attached to the presentation of some performers in more obviously commercialized settings in nineteenth-century Europe and North America. The establishment of the solo recital enabled violinist Nicolò Paganini and pianist Franz Liszt to construct themselves as 'personalities' for an impressionable mass audience. Using similar techniques, 'Swedish nightingale' Jenny Lind reached an even wider market, especially with the benefit of P.T. Barnum's publicity techniques for her US tour of 1850–51. With the leading British music hall singers – from the 'swells' of the 1860s and 1870s, such as George Leybourne, to turn-of-the-century celebrities such as Marie Lloyd – it is clear that audiences were in the presence of a star: even if the music involved a large band, the focus was unequivocally on the vocal soloist, who was expected to deliver a characteristic and individual performance.

From this time, the core of mainstream, mass-mediated popular music has been solo song. Increasingly, the characteristic texture has become tune-plus-backing; and to a seemingly ever-increasing extent, the history of the delivery of this texture can be told in terms of the collected biographies of singers. Even in parts of the world with rich traditions of collective music-making, such as most of Africa, the solo principle made sweeping advances in late twentieth-century popular music, with the emergence of internationally celebrated singers such as Youssou N'Dour and Salif Keita. There are, admittedly, many exceptions to this historical tendency – for example, the large amount of US and European inter-war dance band music with little or no vocal component. And the range of different textural relationships implies a considerable variety of social dynamics, just as the capacity in the multitrack recording process to mix voices 'up' or 'down' provides an even greater spectrum of possibilities. But even where several voices share the singing, the concept of *lead* singer points to the hegemony of soloistic form, and even where pieces are credited to a *group* – common in rock music after 1955 – the absence of a dominating solo presence in the performance is rare. The gradual shift through the twentieth century to associating music with its singer rather than its composer, or even the song itself – a shift that went hand in hand with the move from dissemination through sheet music to dissemination through recordings – marked the triumph of what would appear to be a new type of soloing.

In some late twentieth-century dance music styles, the entire piece could be assembled by one person, with the help of electronic technology, and this might seem to have eroded the old social dynamics within which a dominating solo vocal line could flourish (indeed, such vocalism was not a general feature in these styles). In a sense, however, the mantle of soloist was simply transferred, very often, from musical performer to producer/composer working in the studio, or to the DJ mixing live in the dance club. With an ancestry going back to Mike Oldfield's self-produced *Tubular Bells* (1973) on the one hand and the early hip-hop 'mixmasters' such as Grandmaster Flash on the other, this development implies that, in effect, the recording itself or its live rearticulation has become a solo piece.

Instrumental Solos

Within world music as a whole, the practise of setting aside a stretch of time within a group performance for one performer to produce a solo seems to be quite rare. Certainly there are cases where the listener's attention is meant to switch temporarily from one strand in the texture to another: this may happen in Indian art music, in Indonesian *gamelan* and in some kinds of African ensemble music (Nketia 1979, 124). In the call-and-response processes so common in Sub-Saharan Africa and in New World musics influenced by them, solo phrases generally alternate with group responses. Yet in all such cases, it seems fair to suggest that the technique is more like a slight refocusing of layout in what is essentially a collaborative schema than it is like the moment when, say, Wynton Marsalis 'takes a chorus' in a performance by his jazz orchestra. In the latter, a spotlight shines for a specified length of time (a chorus in this case), and the individual is given the chance to 'show what he can do.' This concept of soloing has some forebears in Western music history – in concertos; in European art music, however, the practise of composing unschematized instrumental solo phrases, of variable length and character, into complex orchestral textures is just as common, if not more so. The latter practise is of some significance for popular music: similar effects sometimes occur in relatively 'composed' jazz pieces (the large-scale works of Duke Ellington, for instance), and may be heard often in specially composed film and television soundtracks. In twentieth-century popular music as a whole, though, the 'jazz model' – set solo spots for a discrete structural unit (a chorus, a bridge, a turnaround break) – was much more important.

The earliest jazz recordings (the Original Dixieland Jazz Band, 1917; the New Orleans Rhythm Kings, 1922; Joe 'King' Oliver, 1923) demonstrate that solo breaks and choruses were a feature of performance by that stage. Breaks seem to have been more common, and historically were probably the first point of fracture in the prevalent texture of collective polyphony. Interestingly, 'King' Oliver's celebrated three-chorus cornet solo on 'Dippermouth Blues' (1923) is fully accompanied – the other front-line instruments just lower their dynamic level – suggesting that it too represented a transitional stage on the way to the startlingly virtuosic solos introduced in the second half of the 1920s by Louis Armstrong and others. By the early 1930s, Armstrong was fronting a large band, his personality and technique very definitely the major points of interest. From this point, the directions of development are clear: on the one hand, big bands 'arranged' spaces between ensemble sections, and often over riffed accompaniments, for their major soloists; on the other, there was a move in small band jazz toward conceiving a performance as primarily a sequence of solos, each player taking his turn – an approach perhaps originating in the 'jam session,' given a definitive format in bebop (where ensembles were often limited to thematic statements at the beginning and the end), and still, for modern jazz anyway, the basic structural format. When singers featured in this music, they often just took a chorus or two rather than dominating the performance; this approach pervaded the wider inter-war dance band practise too, with listeners generally having to wait until the last or penultimate chorus to hear a vocal presentation of the tune.

There is an issue in this culture (extending then into popular music practise more generally) to do with the relationship of 'solo' to 'improvisation': the right to solo is often connected with a capacity for inventiveness and spontaneous creativity, a perspective that reaches its apogee in the competitive individualism of 'cutting contests.' What is interesting in this context is the move in some avant-garde jazz, from the 1960s on, toward redefined forms of collective improvisation. When the solo format is refused, but when performance depends on relatively unplanned interaction between individual players, with a premium still on personal expression, what social dynamics are implied, and how might they relate to the principle of soloing?

While the jazz history from the 1920s on is fairly clear, what is less so is exactly when and how soloing began. It is not known if early, non-recorded jazz musicians such as Buddy Bolden ever soloed (although 'Jelly Roll' Morton implies that they may well have done: Lomax 1973, 61). It is not known if early twentieth-century ragtime/jazz pianists, when they appeared in a band, ever played a solo chorus – although, given their liking for improvised variation, it seems possible (Berlin 1980, 66–70, 76–78). Certainly Morton, one of the least modest of musicians, seems unlikely to have passed up the chance. It may be possible to think of a broad cultural shift at this time, encompassing blues and country music as well as ragtime and jazz, in which the ad hoc quality of performing groups, the fluid hybridity of musical styles and sheer practicality (in terms of lengthy sets for dancing and a consequent need for players to be able to take rests), together with incipient commercial pressures to single out individuals, contributed to the emergence of new social dynamics. With blues, it is easy to imagine how short responsorial phrases on guitar might grow into full-fledged solos; this happens in the early 1930s recordings of Leroy Carr and 'Scrapper' Blackwell, for instance, where guitarist Blackwell not only provides responses to pianist Carr's vocal phrases, but occasionally throws in a solo chorus as well. The jazz model was probably influential in this process, perhaps mediated by the band-accompanied recordings by 1920s women singers such as Bessie Smith, which often featured instrumental breaks by Louis Armstrong, Joe Smith and other well-known jazz players. During the same period, the occasional solo could be heard in records by white string

bands, but again this tendency solidified in the 1930s with the definite influence of jazz, especially clear in 'western swing,' which absorbed textural and structural patterns from contemporary jazz big bands. From this point on, instrumental solos – from fiddle, guitar, pedal steel guitar – were commonplace in almost all types of country music, appearing in their most virtuosic forms in bluegrass. In blues, the lineage of guitar soloists – from 'T-Bone' Walker through B.B. King and Elmore James to Buddy Guy and Stevie Ray Vaughan – was easily the strongest one, although in the big band blues and 'jump blues' of the 1930s and 1940s, and from time to time thereafter, saxophone and trumpet solos appeared as well. No doubt the guitar's predominance was partly ensured by the greater volume and flexibility offered by amplification.

Rock draws on the solo traditions of blues and country music, and occasionally jazz too, starting with the guitar and saxophone solos in many of the first rock 'n' roll recordings. However, instrumental solos are by no means normative in post-1955 pop, partly no doubt because of the degree of focus on the singer. The presence or absence, and the function, of a solo in this repertoire may relate to the ideological tensions between 'rock' and 'pop' tendencies. The 'rock' aesthetic favors 'musicianship' and 'truthful' individual expression, draws heavily on 'folk' roots, especially blues, tends toward simple iterative forms, and has developed from blues sources the focal figure of the 'guitar hero.' Solos here, then, are likely to be virtuosic, to occupy a whole chorus, to suggest improvisation. Jimi Hendrix, in particular, revolutionized the solo potential of the electric guitar; with him, one feels that much of the point of the performance is in waiting for his solo. Similarly, with his contemporaries Cream, the point seems to lie in anticipating and savoring the guitar solo from Eric Clapton, the drum solo from Ginger Baker. This approach continues throughout hard rock styles, especially heavy metal, and typically the extravagant performance style is clearly gendered with extreme machismo (Walser 1993). By contrast, the 'pop' aesthetic tends to privilege the voice, together with tightly organized arrangement and production, and to favor flexible forms. Solos, where they occur, are likely to be short, carefully planned, variable in placing, effect and instrumentation. Increasingly, in the 1980s and 1990s, solos would be produced on keyboards with or without sampled timbres. Progressive rock falls somewhere between these extremes in the typology, unschematic in its usage of solos and variable in instrumentation (with keyboard and wind joining guitar), but often virtuosic, with – sometimes – clear jazz influence.

With the growing hegemony of Western pop/rock across the world from the 1960s on, it is hardly surprising that its solo formats have affected all genres influenced by this new mainstream, from salsa to Fela Kuti's Afrobeat, from Irish and East European neo-traditional dance bands to South African *mbaqanga*. If an emergent socio-musical model is to be tentatively identified, it perhaps lies within the tension between, on the one hand, the principles of collective participation seemingly embodied in techniques of riff, iteration and call-and-response and, on the other hand, the social psychology of 'the solo' – both solo piece and instrumental solo.

Sociology of the Solo

It is tempting to connect the principle of the solo with the individualistic world-view so often identified as characteristic of Western culture, thought and science since the Renaissance. Given that solo music genres are widely distributed geographically and historically, this may, however, be premature. One possibility is that in the West, typically, solo performance as a socio-musical resource is mediated through certain culturally specific musical techniques: firstly, through a specific tune-and-backing type of texture (a 'figure and ground' duality: Tagg 1994), which 'backlights' the individual against his/her environment in a dramatic way; secondly, through sectional types of form, which, again, 'close off' personal experience in self-sufficient shapes, over against its background world (Maróthy 1974); and, thirdly, through a musical language (major-minor tonality) which, it has been argued, is homologous with the Cartesian structure of individual-point-of-view consciousness (Shepherd 1991). If all this were accepted, and if it could then be shown that, in typical solo performance in traditional genres outside Western art music, soloists act not so much as individual personalities, but more as sensitive mediators and refiners of collectively owned values, knowledge and material, the argument might be clinched. In any case, though, the dichotomy is not absolute. As pointed out above, in Western popular music the solo principle is in tension with other techniques suggesting groupiness.

At the same time, the argument that soloism takes on a new intensity, a new significance, in modern society – with a new kind of mass individualism fed by market economics, the pursuit of individual pleasures fed by social mobility, consumerism and advertising, and a new cult of the self fed by the collapse of religious belief and of social authority – is a strong one. And it meshes rather well with the historical rise of the spectacular star performer from the nineteenth century on. The study of stars – within a sociocultural nexus constituted by large-scale audiences on the one hand, and charismatic, mass-mediated personalities on the other – suggests that their role fits into broader mechanisms of identification and self-realization characteristic of social psychology in late modernity. Its implications may not always be welcome: this was the finding of the Frankfurt School's study of the 'authoritarian personality' and its relationship to processes of dictatorship and abjection. At any rate, the roles played by star performers in the formative processes of subjectivity in modern societies clearly set soloism in such societies aside from apparent progenitors elsewhere.

But anyway, as suggested previously, the social identifications transmitted by solos are not always straightforward. Who *exactly* is speaking in a solo? Who exactly, for that matter, is speaking through a riff or through a repeated, collectively played rhythmic groove? When dissemination of music through recorded forms first cut the link between 'voice' and 'person,' so that listeners no longer necessarily knew directly who or even what was the source of a given musical strand, this began to open up to reflection the fact that, in all musical performance, a musical voice and a social voice are, so to speak, forced together. A monophonic line can be performed by a group, as in soccer crowd chants (a situation sometimes mimicked at rock concerts). Why is this not a 'solo'? Conversely, a single performer can be responsible for the social dialog implied by a call-and-response process (on voice and guitar, for example), or the polyvocal complexities involved in many keyboard 'solos.' A solo singer's voice can be enhanced by double-tracking or 'chorus' effects. A single hip-hop or dance music producer can create, through sampling, sequencing and overdubbing, textures that, depending on one's point of view, sever all possibility of easy identification of musical voices with definite social actors, or alternatively open up the opportunity for a infinite range of such identifications.

Walter Benjamin (1973) suggested that mechanical reproduction offered the chance to destroy the 'aura' of unique artworks, democratizing their social ownership. T.W. Adorno swiftly replied (Bloch et al. 1977) that, in the actually existing society, what was likely was that the new media would be used to create new kinds of aura, focusing especially around the allure of the star. Adorno was surely correct. However, the question was not closed, and it is significantly refocused by the more recent changes in production technology. In music, the issue of aura is in part connected to the social dynamics of texture and performance – how textural relationships are mapped to social relationships and vice versa. Attempted closure – for example, reducing a texture to its 'lead' component and reducing this solo to an ideology of individualism, through techniques of production, tactics of listening or regimes of discourse – represents a monovocal perspective that is analogous to the 'monologic' strategies identified by Bakhtin (1981) as the linguistic instruments used to suppress the 'heteroglossia' characteristic of all actual language use.

Inside a solo-dominated texture, and even inside the solo voice itself, is a dialog. One question that developments of popular music in the twentieth century may have been putting to us, then, is whether we actually understand what 'a solo' is.

Bibliography

Bakhtin, Mikhail. 1981. *The Dialogical Imagination*, trans. Caryl Emerson and Michael Holquist. Austin, TX: University of Texas Press.

Benjamin, Walter. 1973. 'The Work of Art in the Age of Mechanical Reproduction.' In *Illuminations*, ed. Hannah Arendt, trans. Harry Zohn. London: Fontana, 219–53. (First published in *Zeitschrift für Sozialforschung* V(1) (1936).)

Berlin, Edward. 1980. *Ragtime: A Musical and Cultural History*. Berkeley and Los Angeles: University of California Press.

Bloch, Ernst, et al. 1977. *Aesthetics and Politics*. London: New Left Books.

Courlander, Harold. 1963. *Negro Folk Music, U.S.A.* New York and London: Columbia University Press.

Handy, W.C. 1961. *Father of the Blues: An Autobiography*. London: Sidgwick and Jackson. (First published New York: Macmillan, 1941.)

Kubik, Gerhard. 1981. 'Neo-traditional Popular Music in East Africa Since 1945.' *Popular Music* 1: 83–104.

Lomax, Alan. 1973 (1950). *Mister Jelly Roll: The Fortunes of Jelly Roll Morton, New Orleans Creole and 'Inventor of Jazz'*. 2nd ed. Berkeley and Los Angeles: University of California Press.

Malone, Bill C. 1985 (1968). *Country Music U.S.A.* Rev. ed. Austin, TX: University of Texas Press.

Manuel, Peter. 1988. *Popular Musics of the Non-Western World: An Introductory Survey*. New York: Oxford University Press.

Maróthy, János. 1974. *Music and the Bourgeois, Music and the Proletarian*. Budapest: Akademiai Kiado.

Nketia, J.H. Kwabena. 1979. *The Music of Africa*. London: Gollancz.

Oliver, Paul. 1984. *Songsters and Saints: Vocal Traditions on Race Records*. Cambridge: Cambridge University Press.

Russell, Tony. 1970. *Blacks, Whites and Blues*. London: Studio Vista.

Shepherd, John. 1991. *Music as Social Text*. Cambridge: Polity Press.

Tagg, Philip. 1994. 'From Refrain to Rave: The Decline of Figure and the Rise of Ground.' *Popular Music* 13(2): 209–22.

Walser, Robert. 1993. *Running with the Devil: Power, Gender and Madness in Heavy Metal Music*. Hanover and London: Wesleyan University Press.

Waterman, Christopher A. 1990. *Jùjú: A Social History and Ethnography of an African Popular Music*. Chicago: University of Chicago Press.

Winans, Robert B., and Kaufman, Elias J. 1994. 'Minstrel and Classic Banjo: American and English Connections.' *American Music* (Spring): 1–30.

Discographical References

Oldfield, Mike. *Tubular Bells*. Virgin V2001. *1973*: UK.

Oliver, Joe 'King.' 'Dippermouth Blues.' Gennett 5132. 1923: USA. Reissue: Oliver, Joe 'King.' 'Dippermouth Blues.' *King Oliver Vol. 1 1923–1929*. BBC RPCD 787. *1991*: UK.

RICHARD MIDDLETON

Song

Introduction

'Song' is a category of musical production characterized by the importance of vocalization. The vocal may stand alone or be accompanied by non-vocal (e.g., instrumental) sounds; it may be sung solo or by a group. Usually (although not absolutely always), it is made up of a series of clearly pitched sounds (i.e., a melody); usually (although, again, not absolutely always), it carries a meaningful series of words, often in verse. Throughout human history, songs have accounted for the bulk of musical activity; popular music is no exception: the overwhelming majority of popular music pieces are songs.

General Considerations

The possible origins of music in song, and their possible relationship with the origins of language, have been the subject of obsessive, if inconclusive, speculation. Whether the vocal productions of birds and some mammals can be classified as 'songs' is contentious. Nevertheless, the centrality of song to human culture is indisputable. Presumably this has to do with the ease with which people 'give voice,' from the baby's earliest cries onward, and with the rootedness of singing in basic bodily functions: vocal sounds are produced and projected by the 'breath of life.' Art musics often seem to distance themselves from this dimension through the development of instrumental genres (although this is far less true of Asia than it is of the West); but vernacular music cultures – even if instrumental dance pieces play an important role – rarely cede song's pride of place. While the evolution of art music in the West over the last two centuries, and its dissemination worldwide, pushed its vocal traditions very much into the background, the explosive growth in popular song production during the same period – especially with the development of the electronic media, carrying in particular the strong vocal emphasis of Afro-diasporic lineages around the world – has ensured that songs have continued to dominate the global musicscape.

Forms

In summary, the iterative and additive principles favored in most vernacular song traditions were modified, subsumed or threatened in eighteenth- and nineteenth-century song production in Europe and the United States by a greater emphasis on sectionalism. A similar tendency, though usually less strong, could be observed in some other parts of the world – for example, Latin America. With the explosive growth in influence of African-American techniques in the twentieth century, this trajectory was reversed. However, these principles always intersected, in complex and variable ways, and in the second half of the twentieth century this resulted in a wide range of structural types. Nevertheless, looking over the world popular music scene as a whole, open-ended processes of iteration finished the century in a strong position. It can be argued that sectional and iterative principles map sociologically onto 'individual' and 'collective' outlooks respectively, as these are refracted through the processes of song form – although the differences between, say, the sectionalism of many Indian *ghazals* and that of many Western ballads suggest that further research might be required in order to establish this.

Textures

Most popular songs feature a solo singer. The relationship between this singer and his/her instrumental accompaniment has been influentially theorized by Tagg (1994a, 1994b) as akin to that between figure and ground (or individual and environment) in the composition of pictorial space. The specifics of the relationship are highly variable, however. The singer may be self-accompanied, most commonly on guitar, sometimes on piano. He/she may be accompanied by a small band (the classic situation in country music, blues, rock, and many Latin American and African styles) or by a larger orchestra (the norm in musical theater, variety, show-biz and 'easy listening' or middle-of-the-road styles). A large-scale effect can be created by synthesizers. The backing may vary between complete homogeneity and more open, multi-stranded effects: a considerable conceptual and socio-musical distance lies between Phil Spector's 'wall of sound' (in, say, Ike and Tina Turner's 'River Deep, Mountain High') and James Brown's funk textures

(in, for example, 'Say It Loud – I'm Black and I'm Proud'); so too between a Sinatra (e.g., 'My Way') riding the big band sound, giving it its point of perspective, and some punk and post-punk recordings in which the solo vocal is mixed down so far as to subvert such hegemony. Moreover, the solo singer may not be alone. Sometimes there may be responses from other vocalists, perhaps in a developed call-and-response relationship, or supporting or background vocal harmonies; sometimes the musical material may be presented by the vocal group in harmonized form (all these may be heard, for instance, in the *iscathamiya* of Ladysmith Black Mambazo and similar South African groups). Tunes may be sung as duets (the Everly Brothers; the Beatles), or a soloist may be double-tracked (or his/her sound enhanced or modified through a variety of electronic devices). Needless to say, in all these relationships, vocal identities are always gendered, and these identities, together with the specificities of vocal range, tessitura and timbre, play crucial and also variable roles.

Words and Music

Again, it is difficult to generalize. In songs with a clear narrative or 'message,' it is presumably important that the words be heard and understood. In other types of songs, though, this often seems less critical, or the *sound* of the words seems more important than their meaning, or they are absorbed into the musical flow. The use of 'nonsense' words (Little Richard's 'Tutti-Frutti'), paralinguistic effects (e.g., James Brown's grunt) or scat singing (e.g., Louis Armstrong) takes this strategy of 'musicalizing' words to an extreme (and enables instruments to mimic the results, through vocalized tone). Working in the opposite direction, however, the rhythms and intonations of verbal phrases often seem to generate the musical figures that set them; and in many of the best hooks, it is the fusion of verbal and musical shapes that lodges the idea in the listener's memory. Moreover, the mode of address constructed in lyrics ('I' or 'we,' 'you' or 'they,' and so on) may be at least as important as the textural relationships of voices referred to above in locating a song's social connotations. It may be possible to think of three ideal types: modes dominated by *narrative* (the voice tends toward speech), by *musical gesture* (words as sound, the voice as instrument) and by *affect* (words and music fused in lyricism). But analytical care is essential. For example, rapping and toasting may initially seem to foreground verbal meaning; but, arguably, structured rhythm, vocal timbre and pitch shifts and inflections are at least as important.

Production

Talking about songs through references to their titles, their hooks, their tunes, and protecting them through copyright law both imply, on vernacular and legal levels, respectively, an ontological status as identifiable compositions or works. Ironically, however, while it was a growing division of labor in song production that, in the nineteenth century, first placed the spotlight on the distinction between composition and performance and prompted the demand for copyright protection, this same process went on to create a situation in which, underneath the legal framework of 'authorship,' actual production was increasingly collaborative. In the second half of the twentieth century, performers returned often to writing their own songs; yet, in many cases, the 'composition' hardly existed until other band members, producers and engineers got to work on it. Storage in recorded form in one sense hones the idea of the work's discreteness, but also, paradoxically, captures an apparently transitory event, eliding 'composition' and 'performance.' The ubiquity of covers and diverse mixes of a song and, at the same time, the centrality to song dissemination and identity of the 'star quality' of performers *qua* performers start to render porous the boundaries around the singular work. The radical changes to a song that can result from performance in different contexts – concert, club or disco mix, drive-time radio with DJ talkover, supermarket muzak – point in a similar direction. When a key song extract can migrate, in sampled form, around the repertoire, and when, in late twentieth-century dance music styles, vocal phrases have been placed 'in brackets' among the surrounding electronic loops, the common-sense understanding of the category 'song' seems to be placed in question. However, there seems little reason to doubt that the place of vocalization within popular music culture will remain secure.

Bibliography

Brackett, David. 1995. *Interpreting Popular Music*. Cambridge: Cambridge University Press.

Frith, Simon. 1988. 'Why Do Songs Have Words?' In *Music for Pleasure: Essays in the Sociology of Pop*. Cambridge: Polity Press, 105–28.

Frith, Simon. 1996. 'Songs as Texts' and 'The Voice.' In *Performing Rites: On the Value of Popular Music*. Oxford: Oxford University Press, 158–82, 183–202.

Laing, Dave. 1971. *Buddy Holly*. London: Vista.

Laing, Dave. 1985. *One Chord Wonders: Power and Meaning in Punk Rock*. Milton Keynes: Open University Press.

Tagg, Philip. 1994a. 'Subjectivity and Soundscape, Motorbikes and Music.' In *Soundscapes: Essays on Vroom and Moo*, ed. Helmi Järviluoma. Tampere: Department of Folk Tradition, 48–66.

Tagg, Philip. 1994b. 'From Refrain to Rave: The Decline

of Figure and the Rise of Ground.' *Popular Music* 13(2): 209–22.

Discographical References

Brown, James. 'Say It Loud – I'm Black and I'm Proud.' King 6187. *1968*: USA.

Little Richard. 'Tutti-Frutti.' Specialty 561. *1956*: USA.

Sinatra, Frank. 'My Way.' Reprise 0817. *1969*: USA.

Turner, Ike and Tina. 'River Deep, Mountain High.' London HLU 10046. *1966*: UK.

RICHARD MIDDLETON

Voice Leading

'Voice leading' refers to the linear movement, stasis or dissolution of tones during the progression from one chord to another. Tones can move in contrary motion (voices moving away from each other), oblique motion (one or more voices remaining constant while others move up and/or down), similar motion (down or up, not separated by an equal interval) and parallel motion (separated by a particular interval). Western music's voice leading techniques emerged from medieval and Renaissance part-writing traditions.

Voice leading can be divided into two nonexclusive categories, contrapuntal and harmonic. Contrapuntal voice leading involves an emphasis on contrary motion between the upper and lower voices, and imitation of phrases and motifs, whereas harmonic voice leading stresses the predominance of singular melodic interest in the foreground with stepwise oblique motion, and similar motion in the background, the lowest voice sometimes responding in contrary motion.

During the Renaissance and Baroque periods, contrapuntal voice leading dominated musical practise. During the Classical and Romantic eras, harmonic practise gained precedence. During the late nineteenth and early twentieth centuries, Debussy, Scriabin, Ravel and Bartók were among the most daring composers in exploring the possibilities of parallel motion. Debussy's music contains extended passages of parallel voice leading, at times reminiscent of the early medieval church practise of doubling at the fifths and octaves.

Harmonic voice leading has remained the most common form in popular music, although contrapuntal examples exist – as in early rock 'n' roll, where an ascending walking bass line is independent and, in some instances, contrapuntal to a descending guitar riff ('Johnny B. Goode'). The use of parallel voice leading is also common in various types of blues, jazz and rock music. Parallel octaves, fourths and fifths, for instance, can be heard in the guitar accompaniment to songs such as Bachman-Turner Overdrive's 'Takin' Care of Business' or Jimi Hendrix's version of Bob Dylan's 'All Along the Watchtower.' Jazz keyboardists, guitarists and arrangers sometimes use parallel chromatic, diatonic or modal voice leading to arrive at a particular chord, at times passing through a series of diatonic or chromatic parallel chords to the desired one.

Discographical References

Bachman-Turner Overdrive. 'Takin' Care of Business.' *Bachman-Turner Overdrive II.* Mercury SRM-1-696. *1973*: USA.

Berry, Chuck. 'Johnny B. Goode.' Chess 1691. *1958*: USA.

Jimi Hendrix Experience, The. 'All Along the Watchtower.' *Smash Hits.* Reprise MSK-2276. *1989*: USA.

BHESHAM SHARMA with STAN HAWKINS

Voicing

In its strictest sense, 'voicing' refers to the vertical arrangement of tones in a chord. In Western art music analysis, Roman numerals are sometimes used to indicate the type of chord. Numbers are used to indicate the lowest note and, in some instances, the resolution of the upper pitches, tones or notes. In the key of C major, for instance, I would be the C chord, IV the F, and V the G. Roman numerals under particular chords or passages suggest the voicing of the lowest note. I indicates that, in the chord C (comprised of C, E, G), the C tone or the tonic is the lowest note or at least the most important point in a bass line, depending on whether or not that tone is decorated. I^6 or the first inversion of the C chord means that the E is the lowest note. The '6' is used to denote the span between the E and the tonic C, and G in the bass of a C chord is classified as a I^6_4 because the span between the G and the E is a sixth, and the G and C a fourth. Seventh chords have similar ways of being classified in terms of vertical arrangement. For instance, the spelling of V^7 in C major, G^7, is G, B, D and F. V^6_5 indicates that the B is the lowest voice, V^4_3 that the D is the lowest, and V^4_2 that the F is the lowest.

In some popular sheet music and fake books, the vertical hierarchy of chords is often left to the discretion and inventiveness of performers, unless it is an arrangement or a transcription of a particular recording. Some charts indicate inversions of chords and passing tones through chord symbols. Jazz scores and folk guitar songbooks, for instance, sometimes specify the voicing of the lowest note to be played by using symbols such as Am^7 or D/A. In such instances, the chord is indicated before the solidus, and the lowest tone after it. The progression C, C/B, Am, Am^7/G, F, G, C tells the performer to play C, B, A, G, F, G, C in the bass. The result is an initial descending diatonic passage from C, B, A, G to F in the lowest voice, then to G, and then to C. In the example given above, Am^7/G in the key of C major could, for some, be classified as a VI^4_2.

Bibliography

Benward, Bruce, and Saker, Marilyn. 2002. *Music in Theory and Practice*, Vol. 1. 7th ed. Boston, MA: McGraw-Hill.

Leonard, Hal. 1994. *This Is the Ultimate Fake Book with Over 1200 Songs*. Milwaukee, WI: Hal Leonard Publishing Corporation.

BHESHAM SHARMA

21. Timbre

Sound

General

'Sound' (ME *soun*, OFr *son*, L *sonus*; akin to OE *swinn*, 'melody,' L *sonare*, 'to sound,' Skt *svanati*, 'it sounds') is the sensation produced in the organs of hearing when the surrounding air is set in vibration.

In the field of popular music, 'sound' may refer to the general sonic characteristics associated with a musician, or those of an instrumental or vocal technique ('dirty sound,' 'clean sound'); in this usage, it has much in common with the terms 'tone,' 'sonority' and 'timbre.' Differences in timbre and sound (in this usage) are due primarily to the number, strength and relationship of overtones or harmonics over a fundamental (which is identifiable by a musician as the 'pitch' of the sound), in combination with the 'envelope,' which consists of the characteristic attack, sustain, release and decay of the sound of an instrument or voice. An additional important component of 'sound' in popular music is the presence or absence of distortion or noise, which figures prominently in the production of 'dirty' or 'clean' sound. Distortion, in physical terms, results from the saturation of a region of sonic space by overtones or partials, similar to the effect known as 'noise,' which is most strongly associated with non-pitched percussion instruments, percussive attacks on pitched instruments, or electronic effects, such as white noise.

'Sound' may also refer to the unique 'timbre' and style of a musician or band (as in 'Hendrix's sound is instantly recognizable'), and has developed many specific meanings in the context of modern recording techniques (e.g., 'dry sound,' 'wet sound'). The emphasis on individualized or readily identifiable sounds in popular music is one of the most important features that distinguish it from Western art music, and forms one of the greatest analytical challenges for musicologists. For example, the 'sound' found on early Beatles' albums, such as *Please Please Me* and *With the Beatles*, is not reducible to the characteristics of the instruments used, the individual vocal and instrumental techniques employed, or the recording technology of the time, but, rather, results from a combination that includes all these factors (and more). Thus, the listener hears 'clean' electric guitar tones, a rather indistinct electric bass, a wash of cymbals, and clear snare drum and tom-toms, all recorded in a rather compressed way. These instrumental tracks are separated in the sonic space from the vocal tracks, which feature an occasionally double-tracked lead vocal along with background and harmonic vocals, all of which present the individualized vocal timbres of the singers in a variety of ways, and are themselves recorded in a compressed fashion (by contemporary standards). The sound of individual tracks on the albums is further individualized by the use of additional instruments, such as harmonica, piano and auxiliary percussion instruments.

It is these usages of the term 'sound' that comprise the subject of this entry.

Within popular music, the term 'sound' refers also to a characteristic style of a historical period, geographical region or recording company ('the Mersey sound,' 'the Nashville sound,' 'the Motown sound'), as well as to the audio element of film and television (probably derived from 'soundtrack'). These usages of the term are the subjects of separate entries.

Clean Sound

With its obsolete usage of 'clean' – 'clear in sound and tone' – dating from the eleventh century, the term comes close to describing contemporary usage. 'Clean sound' developed in opposition to 'dirty sound' (see below), and describes an instrumental or vocal sound that is relatively free of distortion and 'noise.' Examples of a clean sound in popular music include instruments and voices close in tone quality to those found in Western art music, such as Tin Pan Alley-era 'crooners,' studio orchestras and 'sweet' jazz bands; they can also include acoustic guitars, and electric guitars used with a minimum of distortion, as in West African pop music styles such as highlife and jújù, pre-1980 North American country music and most jazz.

Dirty Sound

This is a term that came into usage in the 1920s to describe the 'slurred' or 'raspy' tones of hot jazz musicians. Initially used in the sense of 'lowdown and dirty,' by the 1950s the term had shifted to refer to sonic manipulations of certain instruments, particularly the saxophone, which could produce raspy tones in response to increased pressure on the reed and a percussive attack. The term was transferred to the description of blues guitarists who produced a distorted sound through overdriving their amplifiers; this sense of the term has been used to describe recordings in which similar distorted effects are produced by overloading a recording device. 'Dirty sounds,' whether induced manually or electronically, include the saxophone tones of 'honkers' such as Illinois Jacquet, Earl Bostic and King Curtis, the amplified guitar and harmonica timbres of Chicago blues of the 1950s, and the expansion of this guitar sound in late sixties styles, such as blues rock, psychedelic rock and heavy metal, and their descendants, such as punk and 'grunge.' In many types of popular music outside the North American–United Kingdom axis prior to the early 1980s, distortion – and hence a kind of 'dirty' sound – figures prominently in recordings, as in, for example, Hindi film song.

Dry Sound

This is a term used mainly to describe the recording process or actual recordings in which the sound either has no added reverberation or echo or is otherwise lacking in warmth or resonance. The term 'dead' is used in a similar sense to describe a room or concert hall without reverberation, as opposed to a room with a great deal of reverberation, which is said to be 'live.'

Sonority

While, in discussions of twentieth-century Western art music, 'sonority' can refer to a simultaneous occurrence of pitches (in contradistinction to 'chord,' which is eschewed because of its stylistic affiliations), in popular music criticism the term most often refers to the quality

or type of tone produced by a performer on an instrument.

Tone

Sometimes used interchangeably with 'sonority,' 'tone' refers to the character of the sound achieved in performance on an instrument. It can also be used in a sense similar to 'timbre,' a term that is more properly analogous to 'tone color.'

Wet Sound

'Wet sound' denotes reverberant sounding. Used in opposition to 'dry,' the term has yet to achieve the same widespread usage, remaining confined to use by those technically involved in recording. 'Wet sound' has played an important role in popular music since the mid-1950s, and the ambiance of many distinctive recordings derives at least partially from their use of echo or reverb. Examples include the famous and much-imitated 'slapback' echo of the 1950s Sun recording studio (where the early recordings of Elvis Presley, Jerry Lee Lewis, Johnny Cash and Carl Perkins were made), surf music instrumentals (for example, the collected work of the Ventures, the Surfaris' 'Wipe Out' and the Chantay's 'Pipeline') and many of Phil Spector's 'wall of sound' productions.

Bibliography

Martin, George, ed. 1983. *Making Music: The Guide to Writing, Performing and Recording*. New York: W. Morrow.

Shaw, Arnold. 1978. *Honkers and Shouters: The Golden Years of Rhythm and Blues*. New York: Macmillan.

Discographical References

Beatles, The. *Please Please Me*. Parlophone PCS 3042. *1963*: UK.

Beatles, The. *With the Beatles*. Parlophone PCS 3045. *1963*: UK.

Chantay's, The. 'Pipeline.' Dot 16440. *1963*: USA.

Surfaris, The. 'Wipe Out.' Dot 16479. *1963*: USA.

DAVID BRACKETT

Timbre

'Timbre,' from Old French *timbre* (meaning 'bell,' 'small bell'), is the character or quality of sound that distinguishes one instrument or voice from another; it is also frequently referred to as 'tone color.' Differences in timbre and tone color (as in 'sound,' which is frequently used as a synonym for 'timbre' and 'tone color') are due primarily to the number, strength and relationship of overtones or harmonics over a fundamental (which is identifiable by a musician as the 'pitch' of the sound), in combination with the 'envelope,' which consists of the characteristic attack, sustain, release and decay of the sound of an instrument or voice. The attack, or onset of the sound, is especially important where timbre is concerned. The attack is directly related to the method of producing sound (with a guitar pick, single or double reed, brass mouthpiece or bow, for example) and varies drastically from one instrument type to another.

Timbre has a particularly vexed status in the study of popular music. On the one hand, musicologists who study popular music often assert that timbre is one of the characteristics that most strongly separate popular music from Western art music; on the other hand, the musicological modes of analysis designed to study Western art music, which form the starting point for any timbral analysis, are poorly developed. This very real difficulty presents an obstacle to an attempt to describe precisely what distinguishes the role of timbre in popular music from its role in art music.

To understand the difficulties involved in the analysis of timbre, one must comprehend not only the extent to which Western music analysis is bound up with the study of Western art music, but also the historical role of timbre within Western art music. Before the compositions of Gabrieli and Monteverdi in the early seventeenth century, most scores consisted of vocal parts that could be realized by a variety of different instrumental and vocal combinations. By 1750, most compositions specified instrumentation, without, however, detailing how the instruments should be played. The subsequent history of composition in Western art music from 1750 to the end of the twentieth century reveals an ever-increasing degree of refinement toward timbre. In Western art music, instrumental and vocal timbre are conceived in terms of standardization and consistency. Musicians are trained to produce as even and consistent a sound as possible, minimizing the sonic differences between registers. In ensemble playing, blending is of the utmost importance and, hence, individuality of timbre is not encouraged in the early stages of training, although it does become important at later stages within fairly limited parameters.

Timbre has been little analyzed primarily because of a lack of discrete representation within Western musical notation itself, which represents pitch most accurately, and other elements either proportionately (as in rhythm) or relatively (as in dynamics or articulation, for instance). Timbre is notated by indicating both when each instrument should play and how the instrument should be played. The fact that notation represents the instructions for an ideal performance means that it has difficulty transcribing the nuances of specific performances which have been so central to popular music since the advent of recording. Other notation systems have similar limitations, even when, as in the Chinese nota-

tion devised for the *chin* (a plucked zither-type instrument with seven strings), that system is far more detailed in terms of timbral specifications.

The timbral orientation of contemporary popular music (both Western and non-Western) differs from that of Western art music in much the same way as do those of 'folk' or 'traditional' musics. In contrast to the standardized timbres produced by performers, which are then combined with other standardized timbres in a way that the composer (who is usually not the performer) can predict, performers of the vast majority of popular musics (who are frequently also composers) strive to produce individualized timbres. Timbral differences between registers tend to be emphasized in these popular styles, rather than minimized as in Western art music. The texture produced by these individualized timbres, either singly or in combination, remains relatively constant throughout an individual song. This again contrasts with much post-1750 art music, in which the texture changes throughout a piece, corresponding to the emphasis placed on the formal process of organic development, a process not important in most contemporary popular music. Emphasis in analysis must correspondingly shift away from the study of timbre as it participates in the ever-shifting textures of an organically developing composition to an understanding of the singular timbre of a performer or an individual song. For example, in comparing the different recordings of 'Tutti-Frutti' by Little Richard and Pat Boone, an analyst could note the different overall timbre and texture of the two recordings, and the particularly important contribution made to this difference by the vocal timbres of the two singers. Individuality of timbre could also figure prominently in comparisons of instrumentalists, as in, for example, an analysis of the difference between late 1960s guitar icons such as Jimi Hendrix and Eric Clapton. Sensitivity to timbre could enhance a description of affective difference in the use of similar vocal techniques, as in a comparison of Frankie Valli's falsetto in the Four Seasons' 'Sherry' with Smokey Robinson's falsetto in the Miracles' 'Ooh Baby Baby.'

Two main approaches have been used in discussions of timbre in popular music: the first relies on descriptive adjectives such as 'dirty,' 'clean,' 'pure,' 'bright,' 'dark' and so on; the second relies on automatic transcription devices, such as a sound spectrum analyzer, to represent all sounding fundamentals and overtones in a performance in order to provide raw material for analysis. The approach that uses adjectival description is useful for contrasting and comparing timbres, as in the work of Shepherd (1982, 1987). For example, the 'raspy' vocal timbres of African-American soul music might be contrasted with the 'pure' timbres of Tin Pan Alley crooners or the 'nasal' timbres of Hindi film singers; or the 'bright,' 'clean' guitar tones of Nigerian *jùjú* might be compared with the 'dirty,' 'distorted' guitar sound of heavy metal. The disadvantage of this approach is that it depends greatly on a specific set of cultural associations that are likely to change drastically with changes in cultural context. It may even be difficult for two people who reside in a similar cultural location to agree on what is a 'bright' sound, for example. This cultural relativism could also be viewed as an advantage, as it might force analysts to consider the perceptions of listeners within specific listening contexts rather than assuming that there are objective criteria for the measurement of timbre that can transcend contexts. However, the lack of precision still presents obstacles to the kind of close textual study that would explicate the connection between technical means and sociocultural effects.

The advantages and disadvantages of using a sound spectrum analyzer to study timbre almost neatly invert those of adjectival description. Automatic transcription gives an impression of 'scientificity'; yet, curiously, science asserts that the psychophysics of the ear creates sounds, such as combination tones and difference tones (frequencies created in the inner ear as the result of two or more pitches), that are not physically present outside a listener's head. Thus, as Jairazbhoy pointed out in his critique (1977), automatic transcription does not reflect what a person actually hears. Most importantly, the sound spectrum analyzer does not incorporate the human mind's ability to adapt to new sounds, tuning systems, strange timbres and so on, and to make the unfamiliar familiar, soften loud sounds, amplify quiet sounds and tune out 'interference.' Musicologists such as Charles Seeger and Robert Cogan understood that the primary advantage of automatic transcription is that it allows analysts to study musical elements that they may not have heard initially, sounds that have been changed or distorted in the act of hearing. It has the potential to increase awareness of subtleties of sound that may otherwise go unnoticed, thereby acting as a kind of ear-training, sensitizing the listener to tone color transformations that are customarily neglected in musical training. Even if one accepts the representations produced by the sound spectrum analyzer, however, there is still the problem of what to do with the data, as the analyst must choose the examples and interpret the information. Work in phonology and linguistics has been suggestive, and comparisons of different performances of the same song may allow connections to be made between affective differences and timbral differences, as in Brackett's (1995) analysis of recordings by Billie Holiday and Bing Crosby of 'I'll Be Seeing You.'

The study of timbre also has ramifications for the understanding of 'authorship' – in other words, the relationship between the 'persona' projected in a piece of music and the biological human beings responsible for producing the music. On one level, the collaborative aspect of most genres of popular music confounds the search for a single author who can be linked to a given song's affect. In most popular music productions, singing, songwriting, instrumental playing, sound mixing, lighting, makeup and so on are all handled by different or, at the very least, several people. Yet, this multiplicity of origins for popular music has not dulled public curiosity about the lives of performers. This is probably due to the fact that most popular music consists of 'songs' that feature a single vocalist. This singer frequently becomes the focal point of the audience's search for meaning in the song; and it is because vocal timbre so strongly conveys a sense of the body of the performer that audiences frequently have such a strong sense of connection to that performer. Roland Barthes' comments (1977) have been most suggestive in this regard, using the concept of 'the grain of the voice' to discuss the way in which voices convey a sense of the performer's body; in the process, Barthes sketches a musical aesthetics organized not around issues of expression and communication, but rather around the pleasure of listening.

This introduces the equation of the personalized timbres so characteristic of popular music (in the global sense) with individual performers, be they singers or instrumentalists. Because value in popular music is commonly attached to the distinctiveness of a performer's timbre rather than to the complexity of pitch relations and form valued in Western art music, the study of popular music demands renewed interest in developing an analytical discourse for timbre.

Bibliography

Barthes, Roland. 1977 (1972). 'The Grain of the Voice.' In *Image-Music-Text*, trans. Stephen Heath. New York: Noonday Press, 179–89. (Reprinted in Simon Frith and Andrew Goodwin, eds. 1990. *On Record: Rock, Pop and the Written Word*. New York: Pantheon Books, 293–300.)

Brackett, David. 1995. *Interpreting Popular Music*. Cambridge: Cambridge University Press.

Chester, Andrew. 1970. 'Second Thoughts on a Rock Aesthetic: The Band.' *New Left Review* 62: 75–82. (Reprinted in Simon Frith and Andrew Goodwin, eds. 1990. *On Record: Rock, Pop and the Written Word*. New York: Pantheon Books, 315–19.)

Cogan, Robert. 1984. *New Images of Musical Sound*. Cambridge, MA: Harvard University Press.

Cogan, Robert, and Escot, Pozzi. 1976. *Sonic Design: The*

Nature of Sound and Music. Englewood Cliffs, NJ: Prentice-Hall.

Frith, Simon. 1996. *Performing Rites: On the Value of Popular Music.* Cambridge, MA: Harvard University Press.

Jairazbhoy, Nazir. 1977. 'The Objective and Subjective View in Music Transcription.' *Ethnomusicology* 21(2) (May): 263–73.

Randel, Don Michael. 1992. 'Canons in the Musicological Toolbox.' In *Disciplining Music*, ed. Katherine Bergeron and Philip Bohlman. Chicago: University of Chicago Press, 10–22.

Seeger, Charles. 1977. 'Prescriptive and Descriptive Music Writing.' In *Studies in Musicology 1935–1975.* Berkeley, CA: University of California Press, 168–81.

Shepherd, John. 1982. 'A Theoretical Model for the Sociomusicological Analysis of Popular Musics.' *Popular Music* 2: 145–77.

Shepherd, John. 1987. 'Music and Male Hegemony.' In *Music and Society: The Politics of Composition, Performance and Reception*, ed. Richard Leppert and Susan McClary. Cambridge: Cambridge University Press, 151–72.

Tagg, Philip. 1979. *Kojak: 50 Seconds of Television Music: Toward the Analysis of Affect in Popular Music.* Göteborg: Studies from the Department of Musicology.

Discographical References

Boone, Pat. 'Tutti-Frutti.' Dot 15443. *1956*: USA.

Crosby, Bing. 'I'll Be Seeing You.' *The Time-Life Bing Crosby.* SLGD-06. (Originally issued by Decca in 1944.) *1985*: USA.

Four Seasons, The. 'Sherry.' Vee-Jay 456. *1962*: USA.

Holiday, Billie. 'I'll Be Seeing You.' *I'll Be Seeing You.* Commodore XFL 15351. (Originally issued by Commodore in 1944.) *1980*: USA.

Little Richard. 'Tutti-Frutti.' Specialty 561. *1956*: USA.

Miracles, The. 'Ooh Baby Baby.' Tamla 54113. *1965*: USA.

DAVID BRACKETT

22. Words, Images and Movement

Dance

Dance may be broadly categorized as rhythmically patterned movement of the body and feet in time to music. Dance has been closely linked with the development of many popular music styles and indeed constitutes one of popular music's primary social uses. Throughout history and in all societies, dance and music have been an integral part of celebrations and ceremonies that mark important events for a variety of social groups. Accordingly, dance has featured in celebrations of religion, farming, the cycle of the seasons, rites of passage, courtship and marriage. With the demarcation between work and leisure time in developed industrial societies, the social practise of dance has become less tied to formal occasions, however, and has been incorporated into modern leisure activities. Thus, while dance continues to be performed as part of structured social occasions, its relationship with popular music has largely been founded on popular music's place as a form of entertainment. It has developed alongside popular music as part of entertainment practises that operate outside such seasonal or cyclical structures. Furthermore, dance has been central to performance practises within popular music – for example, the gestural or bodily movements of musicians and singers, the choreographed routines that are part of stage acts by professional performers, or the dancing done by dancers employed to accompany the playing of recorded music by DJs in contemporary dance club scenes. However, dance is mostly practised by non-professional dancers in settings as diverse as school halls and community centers, at house parties and festivals, and at dedicated venues such as ballrooms and clubs. This type of activity can be broadly categorized as social dance. Popular music thus shares a complex historical relationship with dance which encompasses most popular music genres and includes a variety of social practises.

Social and Vernacular Dance

Contemporary social dance practise ranges from informal and improvised movement to extremely stylized and prescribed dance styles that have strict formal rules and highly developed social etiquettes. The informal styles are often little more than what DeNora (2000, 44) terms 'mundane choreography' to describe 'micro-stylistic changes in comportment' as a reaction to music. Other, more prescribed styles have given rise to elaborate cultures in which the conventions of dance are highly formalized. Beyond this, social dance encompasses a number of different types of practise, from partnered dances, and solo and group dancing to 'challenge dancing,' in which individuals perform elaborate personalized moves in an informal but competitive context.

The development of social dance can be linked to vernacular dance traditions stretching back for a number of centuries. Indeed, many modern dance forms are often understood as expressive of certain cultural traditions or have developed through a process of cultural exchange. For instance, stylistic elements of contemporary dance practises in Central and South America are understood as a hybridization of traditions from Africa and the Iberian Peninsula, a process that Fryer (2000) terms the 'Atlantic dance tradition.' He points out that dances such as the Brazilian and Portuguese *ludu* (later evolving into samba), Chilean and Argentinian *cueca* and Haitian *chica* share formal characteristics and were derived from traditional courtship dances from these areas (2000, 109). By the early 1900s, the descendants of these traditions, such as the tango (Argentina) and the maxixe (Brazil), had become popular not only in South and

Central America but also in North American and European social dance contexts. These later forms were usually danced by couples (albeit in a variety of postures and degrees of closeness) and are often characterized by their syncopated steps which echo common rhythmic elements of Latin American music. The mambo is an example, having five steps to a 4/4 bar.

The African diaspora resulted in the evolution of dance forms throughout the Americas that subsequently went on to influence a multitude of dances associated with a variety of popular music genres. As Chasteen (1996) points out, dances that 'emphasised the lateral movements of the hips ... sinuous twists of the body below the torso ... imparting in the dancers movement's a sort of gyroscopic slide' had shared elements across a variety of dance forms 'expressed to some degree wherever enslaved Africans and their descendents formed a part of the population' (32–33). Van der Merwe (1989) points to evidence of African-derived steps being incorporated into European forms in North America as early as the mid-eighteenth century. More specifically, Stearns and Stearns (1994) trace a number of African-derived elements within dances associated with twentieth-century US popular musics, ranging from jazz to rock 'n' roll. They point out that popular dance crazes from the charleston to the twist have close similarities to antecedents found in African societies. These include elements such as improvisation, isolation, a centrifugal emanation of movement outward from the hips, and a propulsive rhythm that gives a swinging quality to the movement.

The African-derived nature of such dance forms is a cultural marker that holds continuing importance for contemporary populations with an African heritage. However, the cultural meaning of certain dances has also been subject to appropriation and contestation. For example, samba (a music and dance form whose name derives from an Angolan belly dance called *semba*) has been a contested form within (the racially and socially stratified) Brazilian society. Samba's adoption by the ruling class and its role in enhancing the country's national image abroad have been seen as at odds with its roots within poor black communities. As Fryer points out, while samba has become 'the universally recognised cultural symbol of Brazilian identity ... there is a certain irony in the fact that ... a creation of the poorest of the poor has become a tourist attraction' (2000, 157). Marre and Charlton (1985) quote a member of the Manguiera samba school as saying: 'Once the Samba school belonged only to black people. It was a black cultural place. But the dominating white class took it over. Today we make a distinction between black samba people who have sold out and those ... [who perform] committed

sambas' (218). Another instance of a shift in the cultural signification of a dance form is the case of *ingoma* dancing in South Africa. As Erlmann (1989) documents, between 1929 and 1939 the Zulu dance of *ingoma* went through a period of domestication, as it was transformed 'from a militant, oppositional and suppressed form of popular culture to a tourist attraction' (260).

Historical continuity and geographical dispersal can also be found in European dance forms. The waltz, for instance, emerged in the late eighteenth century from Germanic country dances before finding favor in Austrian dance halls of the early nineteenth century. With the international fame of Johann Strauss from the mid-nineteenth century onward, the waltz subsequently enjoyed widespread popularity across Europe, and by the time Strauss's 'Blue Danube' was written in 1867 the waltz as a musical form had become institutionalized within classical concert repertoire. However, both the dance and its musical rhythmic conventions lasted well into the twentieth century, when they were incorporated into various popular music cultures. Genres developing in the United States such as country and Cajun, for instance, had a tradition of triple-time pieces intended to accompany amended versions of the waltz. Likewise, square-dancing evolved in 1890s North America from French ballroom dances such as the quadrille. Both forms are danced by four couples, who begin by facing each other in a square before promenading and pairing off for bouts of couple dancing. This formation was also adopted within Irish 'set' dancing, where the tempo was raised and indigenous steps incorporated in order to fit in with musical conventions of traditional jigs and reels.

Many of these dance forms have been subject to a process of institutional codification whereby correct practise is governed and instruction takes place. This ranges from the publication of instructional books and pamphlets to formal dance classes, and has led to the establishment of national and international bodies that oversee teaching or competition in particular dance genres. Manuals giving detailed instructions on how to perform particular court dances started to appear as early as 1444 and they have continued to be used ever since (Jonas 1992, 74). As well as books giving detailed information about particular dances, there are publications that explain the etiquette and common phrases of dancing. For example, in the 1950s Jim Lees, a 'caller' of dances in Nottingham, England, produced a short 'manual' introducing readers to square-dancing. Lees describes the patter and dress codes of square-dancing, and gives instructions about the dance style: 'Worry about it and you will get nowhere. I prefer a short step in time to the music with the ball of the foot leading, hardly lifting the feet off the ground, almost like skating. Avoid skipping and jerking.

THIS IS NOT DANCING. A relaxed walk is good enough for a start' (ca. 1955, 4). Other publications and dance schools have actually attempted to change or shape the nature of particular dance forms for reasons related to wider social etiquette or ideology. For instance, in the early twentieth century Irene and Vernon Castle, the famous US ballroom dancing couple, opened a dance school and published instructional manuals that set out to adapt African-American dance forms for a white audience. Cook (1998) describes how their *Castle House Suggestions for Modern Dancing* (1914) 'presents a veritable description of how to dance "white"' through a homogenization of forms such as the turkey trot and cakewalk that involved cutting out certain movements regarded as improper or lascivious (142).

Dance forms that have enjoyed longevity or that have a perceived historical importance have often been subject to an even more severe process of institutional formalization. While Latin American–derived dances (particularly salsa) continue to be practised as part of semi-informal social dancing throughout the world, many individual dances (in a highly standardized and categorized form) have become a mainstay of competitive couple dancing in many places. Within modern ballroom dancing, the International DanceSport Federation (amateur) and the World Dance and Dance Sport Council (professional) both preside over member organizations from around 70 countries across Europe, Asia, Africa, Australasia and North America. These organizations govern the rules and aesthetic standards of competition and also prescribe the types of dance that are suitable for competitive practise.

In contrast with this institutionalization and strict regulation, social dancing associated with more contemporary forms of Western popular musics has undergone a process of informalization. The aftermath of rock 'n' roll, for instance, saw the rise to predominance of solo or partnerless dancing to accompany Western popular musical forms. One of the most popular and highly publicized of these was the twist, a craze of the early 1960s, in which solo dancers or groups performed rhythmic twists emanating from the hips while lowering the body into a crouch. The twist was one of many solo dance styles and moves that became popular at this time, such as the jerk, the monkey, the locomotion and, later, the pogo, the robot and the moonwalk. Despite the fact that solo and group dancing was found in earlier African-American forms and in many types of dance performance, it was only in this period that non-partnered styles became the predominant mode within social dancing.

The following 20 years saw a rapid erosion of strict rules for social dancing. Although fads for individual moves such as the roach (also known as the pigeon: a step-dance involving kicks of the leg) or the New York hustle (derived from swing styles) appeared during the disco boom of the 1970s, dance styles were open to much freer interpretation or were ignored completely in favor of highly individual, personalized reactions to music. Within some genres, strictly copied dances or moves were jettisoned altogether and replaced by less fixed patterns of movement (which often resembled roughly interpreted versions of earlier partnerless dancing) befitting the discourses of free expression that were common to youth cultures at this time. Indeed, since the 1970s such discourses of free expression have permeated the conventions of dance across many popular music genres, where learned or strictly defined moves have become largely outmoded. For instance, there tends to be no prescribed or correct way to dance to contemporary electronic dance music. Even though certain common moves may be discernible in this context, they are rarely named or demonstrated in the manner of earlier dance forms.

Social Institutions and Sociality

The development of dance as a large-scale entertainment practise has, of course, been accompanied by a parallel development of venues dedicated to social dancing. Such venues, from formal ballrooms of the early nineteenth century to discos and clubs of the late twentieth century, have provided a place where popular music has been consumed in a shared social context and where the social uses of dance and music have been played out.

These venues have also provided a space where cultural identity may be articulated through music and dance. Hazzard-Gordon (1990) outlines the way in which, from the late nineteenth century, US 'juke joints' and honky-tonks (in which dance was a central social practise) provided the primary secular arena for African Americans to share and express their culture. She points out that juke (or jook) joints served as 'a mixing ground for the remaining strains of African culture and those additional elements that developed during the slave experience' (82), and that many of the dancing styles later adopted by white Americans were developed in this context. Juke joints and other venues have supplied a location for more general aspects of community and fellowship. For example, during World War II the UK publication *Melody Maker* ran articles describing how dancing and music were raising the morale of the British people. On 31 August 1940, the front-page headline of *Melody Maker* proclaimed: 'Air Raids No Scare Raids – Thanks to Dance Bands.' The article went on to describe how dance bands entertained crowds during an air raid on London: 'Throughout the West End, dancers ignored the air raids and continued cheerfully hoofing to the strains of the bands. Musicians worked all-night sessions – but it was a great cause!' (reprinted in Johnstone 1999, 47).

The venues for social dancing figured prominently within dance's central relationship to courtship, as they provided a social space where men and women could meet and socialize. The vogue for couple dancing offered a socially permitted context in which couples could dance in close bodily contact. Nevertheless, various types of dance have repeatedly caused scares over perceived sexual immorality. Cook (1998), for instance, describes how the waltz was denounced in the early nineteenth century because of its close partnering hold and was still being attacked well after it had been incorporated as a respectable form of social dance. Pamphlets such as *From the Ballroom to Hell* from 1894 condemned the waltz as inducing a 'state of uncontrolled euphoria that made young women prey to male sexual demands' (quoted in Cook 1998, 134). It is interesting that, during the 1950s, people often differentiated between different dance halls, with some being marked out as places where people went to 'pick up' someone of the opposite sex. For example, Thomson (1989) describes how Burton House Ballroom in Greenock, Scotland developed a rather unsavory reputation as somewhere that married women would frequent while their husbands were awaiting demobilization after the end of World War II. As one of Thomson's interviewees comments, it was 'the only dance hall in the town with a cloakroom for wedding rings' (1989, 146).

It is not only dance forms and venues that have been the cause of moral panics. There are instances where the emergence of new dance musics and cultures has prompted disapproval and even restriction by local authorities and governments. During the 1920s, when jazz was gaining popularity in the United Kingdom, conservative voices within the British Establishment considered this new music to be dangerous and potentially corrupting. This concern about jazz was evidenced in 1927 when the dance license for a British venue called the Liberal Hall was renewed by magistrates on the condition that '"saxophones are not to be used by dancing bands." The magistrates explained that the instrument disrupted "the quiet of the neighbourhood"' (Johnstone 1999, 15). In extreme cases, condemnations of dance and dance cultures have led to institutional and governmental control or censorship. In Afghanistan during the 1990s, for instance, the Taliban government banned singing and dancing at weddings as, 'according to Education Minister Mullah Abdul Hanifi, the Taliban "oppose music because it creates a strain in the mind and hampers study of Islam"' (Rashid 2001, 115). The UK government's *Criminal Justice and Public Order Act* of

1994 was a direct response to the moral panic surrounding illegal raves. In an attempt to curb large dance gatherings in unlicensed open spaces, section 63 of the Act gave police the power to close down events where people congregated to listen to 'sounds wholly or predominantly characterised by the emission of a succession of repetitive beats.'

Different forms of dance have been initiated within and remain closely associated with particular scenes and subcultures. For example, within the 1970s northern soul scene in the north of England elaborate performative and acrobatic dance styles became part of a highly stratified form of subcultural practise. Here, status within the scene was achieved through both the collection of obscure US soul releases and technical and expressive ability on the dance floor. This example is perhaps indicative of the way in which dance styles associated with various subcultures are often a reflection of their ideological and behavioral practises as well as a reaction to particular forms of music. Thrash dancing or 'thrashing' as practised within hard-core punk scenes provides another example. As Lull (1987) comments, within this social practise the 'normal rules for social dancing are broken' (242). Thrashing takes place during a live performance and is restricted to participants directly in front of the stage area, often referred to as 'the pit.' People crowd into this area and move by flailing their arms in front of them and bumping and jostling with one another in response to the music. Such participation can be understood as echoing the intense, forthright style of the music being played through an enactment of what Lull describes as 'a parody of violence' (1987, 242).

Social institutions that have developed in response to dance have also provided a principal means of employment for musicians. The dance band era, for instance, provided regular work for thousands of musicians across North America and Europe between 1910 and 1950, and this period also saw a huge increase in the number of large dance halls being built. By the mid-1920s, hundreds of locally organized bands (usually consisting of around 15 musicians) playing US-style dance music were working in every Western European country as well as in Czechoslovakia and Poland (McCarthy 1971). Thomson (1989) provides an example of how dance halls afforded musicians regular work. He describes how demand for orchestra musicians in the Scottish town of Greenock between 1945 and 1955 was very high, and virtually all the musicians performing locally were members of the British Musicians Union (MU). These conditions allowed the MU to impose a regulation that every hall in the Greenock area that registered with it 'was obliged to employ a certain minimum number of players' (1989, 143). The number of players required was stipulated by the MU (according to the size of the venue and the cost of admission) and was clearly designed to assist musicians in finding work.

Accordingly, in many dance contexts the value of musicians has been judged according to their capacity to facilitate dance. For instance, following World War II there was a significant rise in dance hall blues in the United States. The large-scale migration of African Americans to urban industrial centers meant that dances were held on an unprecedented scale. Malcolm X has described the atmosphere in a big-band blues dance hall where emphasis was placed on the ability of the band to create excitement at the end of a dance. He recalls the close of an evening at the Roseland Ballroom in Boston, where he worked as a shoeshine boy: '"Showtime!" people would start hollering about the last hour of the dance. Then a couple of dozen really wild couples would stay on the floor, the girls changing to low white sneakers. The band would be really blasting, and all the other dancers would form a clapping, shouting circle to watch that wild competition as it began ... "wail man wail!" people would be shouting at the band' (Haley 1968, 134).

Throughout the second half of the twentieth century, there was a gradual shift away from live music as the primary accompaniment to dancing through the enculturation of recorded music within dance cultures. As Thornton (1995) argues, this move away from live music was echoed by the change in names of the institutions in which people danced for entertainment. In the 1950s, record hops, disc sessions and discothèques explicitly referred to the recorded nature of the entertainment. By the 1970s, the widespread use of the shortened term 'disco' perhaps signified how normalized recorded music had become in this context. By the 1980s, 'with clubs and raves, the enculturation is complete and it is "live" venues that must announce their difference' (1995, 29). The new predominance of recorded music in social dance contexts has clearly had implications for the day-to-day employment of musicians. However, this change has not taken place without resistance, and many musicians and musicians' organizations have actively lobbied against the perceived hegemony of disc cultures. During the 1970s and 1980s, the MU, for instance, mounted a concerted lobbying campaign to protect employment opportunities for its members under the slogan 'Keep Music Live.'

With the enculturation of recorded music came a change in both performance conventions and the structure of social dance events. Poschardt (1998) credits the 1970s New York disco DJ Francis Grosso with the invention of 'slip-cueing,' a technique in which beats from different records are perfectly matched to produce a seamless mix, resulting in an unbroken rhythm that provides an uninterrupted soundtrack for continuous dancing. Over the next two decades, this (and similar techniques) became normalized within various dance music cultures and led to DJs being judged and venerated for their technical prowess and their ability to keep an audience dancing. Focusing on house music, Rietveld (1998) discusses the skill with which DJs select tracks to play to the dancing crowd. She describes how DJs pick between records, gauging the 'mood' of the crowd, to create a soundscape that satisfies those present and keeps the crowd dancing: 'The crowd allows itself to be emotionally manipulated by the DJ, and if perhaps all the circumstances are right, after about six or seven hours s/he can make the crowd hold hands and jump for joy or weep and sit down on the floor' (112). The ubiquity of seamless beat mixing techniques also led to the emergence of entire genres and subgenres in which music was specifically written to be played as part of such a soundscape. The concurrent development of electronic synthesizer, drum machine and sampling technology allowed for the development of entire genres in which extended tracks with a predominant beat were the norm. Indeed, the beats-per-minute (BPM) rate of house music, drum and bass, and hardcore has often been a central defining feature of these genres.

Dancing to popular music has not, of course, been confined to dedicated venues. While dance can clearly take place in any social setting, a number of dances are particularly associated with outdoor locations. The United Kingdom in the 1980s and 1990s saw a rise in the popularity of 'raves' in unlicensed premises – in fields, in warehouses and under railway arches. Thousands of young people would drive to an arranged location to dance to various forms of house music. Certain dance forms have actually been established in urban locations other than designated dance venues. Perhaps the best-known example of this is break dancing, which is specifically tied into street culture. Developing on the US east coast in the late 1970s, break dancing and body popping developed into a competitive form of dance display in which rival 'crews' would dance to hip-hop and electro, trying to outdo one another in terms of the complexity and dexterity of individual moves. Ken Gabbert ('Prince Ken Swift') of the Rock Steady Crew has described the first time he saw his friend break dancing in the street in 1977: 'My friend Dante and I were walking past this record store on 96th and Broadway and its speakers out beside the doorway were playing some West Coast type of song. All of a sudden, Dante starts bopping his head, spins around, and then drops into a split, right in the middle of the sidewalk!' (quoted in Verán 1999, 55). This form of street display was echoed in Japan in the 1970s and 1980s when teenagers would congregate in Harajuku Park in central Tokyo to perform elaborate routines to 1950s rock 'n' roll. As Marre and Charlton point out, these outdoor gatherings constituted a very public display of nonconformity and social distinction in which these Japanese 'rockers' consciously rejected the behavioral norms of their peers (1985, 234).

Music of the Dance

While social dancing can be performed to the accompaniment of a range of music, many musical styles were first developed primarily for dancing. For instance, many of the generic names for dancing refer not only to patterns of physical movement or gesture, but also to the music written to accompany them. A polka, for example, denotes both a Bohemian dance with three steps and a hop and various types of double-time pieces common to musics such as Irish traditional and Finnish folk and pop forms. Likewise, a multitude of other generic dance names, such as 'waltz' and 'fox trot,' are also used to denote certain types of music that share formal and rhythmic conventions. Certain genres that began as music for dancing have been developed and transformed so that they are considered as distinct musical forms in their own right rather than as sounds to facilitate dance. As Johnson (2000, 65) notes, while 'jazz' is now clearly categorized as a musical form, in Australia during the 1920s the word was used interchangeably as both a musical form and a dance. Articles published in Australian papers of the era referred to 'the jazz' as a particular type of dance in the same way that they made reference to 'the waltz' or 'the tango.' This shift in the way in which jazz is understood reflects the changes in the social use of this music as well as marking its development.

Within certain jazz circles, jazz that is created and performed for dancing has been frowned upon as somewhat unsophisticated. Indeed, as the genre has developed, new forms of jazz have emerged that are understood primarily as art musics and that, incidentally or perhaps coincidentally, are almost impossible to dance to. In the 1950s and 1960s, prominent jazz musicians such as Thelonious Monk, John Coltrane and Don Cherry incorporated sonic and formal elements associated with contemporary composers, such as atonal passages, experimentation with meter and tone clusters. The use of such compositional devices illustrates how music for dancing has been held in low esteem in particular taste communities. Such value judgments emphasize the apparent split between the corporeal and the cerebral, where music for dancing is seen as uncomplicated, instinctive and basic, and music for listening is considered intellectually engaging, challenging and sophistic-ated. These distinctions are in evidence in the development and critical appraisal of contemporary dance music. Clearly, the development of musical forms such as house, techno and hardcore over the past 15 years cannot be separated from the rise of club culture and the demand for music for dancing. However, as contemporary dance musics have mutated and new forms have emerged, one can see how certain subgenres have been distinguished as more than transient dance-floor anthems. Labels such as 'intelligent house' and 'electronica' have served to elevate certain styles and to distinguish them as music to be appreciated by listeners rather than as music solely for dancing.

Performative Dance

Dance has been a feature of popular music performance throughout its history, through both the use of professional dancers as an element of stage acts and the dance displays of performers themselves. There has been a long tradition of dancers forming part of musical stage presentations. As Cunningham (1980) records, 'dancing of various kinds, clog and grotesque' was offered as part of the musical entertainment in English 'music saloons' of the Victorian era (167). In nineteenth-century North America, professional dancers such as Thomas Dartmouth 'Daddy' Rice and Master Juba (William Henry Lane) appeared alongside musicians in US minstrel shows. Stearns and Stearns (1994) point out that this performance tradition was a central site where African-American dance forms were blended with steps from Irish jigs and English clog dancing to create what would eventually become tap-dancing. Kouwenhoven (1998, 130) argues that many aspects of these performances, specifically their often improvised nature and their 'flights of fancy and fantasy held together by a rhythmic groundwork,' were deeply rooted in African-American traditions and foreshadowed many of the elements that would become central components of jazz.

Music and dance went on to share a close relationship in later jazz stage performance, especially in big bands. For instance, Cab Calloway's exuberant stage act featured the band leader dancing while his musicians engaged in synchronized movement and gesture. Likewise, throughout his career Duke Ellington featured dancers (such as Geoffrey Holder, Bunny Briggs and Buster Brown) as part of his stage act and preferred to employ musicians who could also dance. In this jazz context, tap-dancers sometimes formed an integral part of musical performance as participants in improvised call-and-response routines. Malone (1998), for example, cites the jazz drummer Max Roach recalling his stage act with the tap-dancer Baby Lawrence: 'I would play brushes on the snare and he would just dance and we'd exchange things . . . I would imitate him and then I would play time over it' (281–82). Professional dancers continue to play a part in stage performances across a variety of popular music genres (albeit generally as an accompanying spectacle rather than as an integral contributor to musical performance).

Singers and musicians have perhaps always used gestural movement of some kind to give rhythmic emphasis to live performance. A number of performers are celebrated because of their ability to entertain using both music and dance simultaneously. Vaudeville and burlesque featured 'song and dance' performers such as the singer, dancer and writer George M. Cohan, who went on to have considerable Broadway success in the first two decades of the twentieth century. For subsequent performers, dance has become an integral part of performance strategies and visual display. Singers such as Elvis Presley and James Brown are noted for introducing highly personalized and energetic dance moves into stage and screen performances. Presley's leg and hip movements were famously controversial in the mid-1950s, while Brown's reputation as a performer was based equally upon his prowess as a band leader/singer and his breakneck footwork, spins, star jumps and theatrical collapses. Although these singers clearly rehearsed such moves, their place in the stage show often gave the impression of improvised dancing expressive of the excitement of performance and reactive to the dynamics of the music.

There is, of course, a strong connection between performative dance by popular music artists and social dance practise. Numerous popular music performers have appropriated and customized older vernacular dances in their video and stage performances. Michael Jackson's use of the moonwalk (a mime-influenced move that gives the impression of seamless foot movements), for instance, was taken from the electric boogie street style (associated with early 1980s electro music) and became a trademark of the performer's dance routines. Likewise, Madonna appropriated and celebrated voguing (theatrical and highly stylized arm movements taken from the fan dances of drag performance mixed with elaborate floor moves) – a style that had developed as 'challenge dancing' in US black gay club scenes. The performances of both these artists are representative of the highly choreographed nature of pop stage shows for solo singers, which became increasingly common after the artists' international success in the 1980s; they contrast with rock performance conventions, which still largely rely upon gesture rather than dance.

In the case of popular music acts that feature a number of vocalists, the relationship between music and dance is perhaps even more formalized. In the 1950s, doo-wop vocal groups such as the Cadillacs and the Orioles developed well-honed stage acts involving synchronized dancing that echoed the closeness of their vocal harmonies. The Cadillacs in particular have often been credited with inventing the synchronized stage act in the United States. These finely tuned routines were adopted by many acts on the Motown label in the 1960s, such as Smokey Robinson and the Miracles, the Supremes, Gladys Knight and the Pips and, perhaps most famously, the Temptations. All of these acts were coached by the label's staff choreographer Cholly Atkins, who had been a notable performer himself before he moved into choreography for Broadway productions for the William Morris group. After this point, the use of choreography to create a visual spectacle for a band's stage show became commonplace within pop, soul and R&B, and it has now become integral to pop performance throughout the world. Indeed, many members of contemporary 'boy bands' and 'girl groups' have broad performing arts backgrounds (in that they are trained in both music and dance), and they are often selected for inclusion in such groups on the basis of their talent for dancing as much as for their singing ability.

The visual nature of dance means that, throughout the twentieth century, it has been recorded in the visual media. From the early days of sound-on-film technologies, dance has been a constant on-screen partner to popular music. The success of the first talking picture *The Jazz Singer*, featuring Al Jolson, in 1927 was an indicator of the commercial gain to be reaped when the film and music industries worked together. As Mundy (1999) comments, 'from now on the meaning of popular music would always to some extent be dependent on its visual economy' (51). In the 20 years following the release of *The Jazz Singer*, Hollywood cemented the connection between music and dance through its regular production of musicals. At first, these film musicals simply followed the structure of Broadway shows, such was the demand for 'all-talking, all-singing, all-dancing' movies (Mundy 1999, 54). However, the film musical soon took on developed plot lines, mixing straight acting and choreographed set pieces. The most celebrated of these films were those produced by ex-Broadway director Busby Berkeley, whose intricately choreographed, visually stunning set pieces using huge casts of dancers became highly popular in Depression-era North America. Joan Blondell, who starred in the 1934 film *Dames*, comments that, during the Depression years, 'People needed to laugh to be released from despair . . . they needed to sway, to hum, to gaze at the sort of things Berkeley did' (quoted in Kobal 1970, 119). The popularity of musical productions enabled performers who were principally dancers to carve out long careers in Hollywood. For instance, the renowned African-American tap-dancer Bill 'Bojangles' Robinson appeared in 18 movies from 1929 to 1943, while his pupil Sammy Davis Junior went on to find success as a singer and dancer from the 1950s onward. During the period from the 1930s to the 1950s, white US performers Fred Astaire, Ginger Rogers and Gene Kelly achieved international stardom and commanded huge fees for their film roles.

In the Hindi film industry (the world's largest and most prolific), music, dance and film are significantly more integrated than within its North American and European counterparts. Since the release of India's first sound picture, *Alam Ara*, in 1931, the conventions of Indian cinema have dictated that almost all productions include song and dance routines regardless of their subject matter. These highly stylized and often lavishly produced sequences may constitute the major attraction of an individual film. The introduction of the 'playback singer' system in the late 1940s – that is, the use of recorded music by star singers to which actors mimed – meant that directors no longer had to recruit talented singers to feature in films, but instead could select performers on the basis of acting and dancing skills alone. The centrality of dance means that Indian film generally forgoes the Hollywood conventions of dramatic realism. Song and dance sequences in these films are rarely framed as they would be in Western cinema, as 'slippage between registers does not need to be marked or rationalised' (Thomas 2000, 158). Instead, such film performances tend to echo Indian folk theater forms, where 'speech, song and dance are tightly integrated into a unified dramatic style' (Manuel 1988, 175). Accordingly, both music and dance within these films tend to be popularized versions of traditional forms, although, as Manuel points out, this is often in a highly amended form and 'often, the "folk dance" scenes in Indian cinema represent little more than the producers' naïve conceptions of rural styles' (1988, 180).

The connection between dance and music is also central in popular music's mediation in other forms of visual media. The predominance of television and the rise of the music video have provided new arenas for the performance of choreographed dance movements. The recorded nature of the music videoclip means that dance moves can be highly elaborate and perfectly synchronized. Indeed, one of the earliest MTV-sponsored international hits was 'Mickey' by singer and choreographer Toni Basil – a track that was originally intended to be released as the lead for an entirely choreographed video album. A classic illustration of the close relationship between music video and dance routines remains Michael Jackson's 1982 video for the song 'Thriller,' which in itself became a media event. In contemporary promotional strategies, dance is such a central part of music video within certain genres that a significant portion of a project's budget may be dedicated to choreography. Furthermore, individual choreographers often command large fees and are afforded high status within the music industry. The New York–based HiHat, for example, has coordinated dance routines for most of the major figures in contemporary R&B and hip-hop, including Puff Daddy, Destiny's Child, Missy Elliott, Mary J. Blige and Jay-Z, while pop choreographer Wade Robinson has been central to the international success of US acts such as Britney Spears, the Backstreet Boys and *NSYNC.

Dance on television has not only taken the form of singers or professional dancers performing choreographed routines, but has also had a tradition of members of the public dancing on-screen. Shots of a studio audience dancing are conventionally included in prerecorded television music shows such as *Top of the Pops* (UK/worldwide) and *The Pop Factory* (Wales). While a dancing studio audience is intended to offset the performance of the band onstage, there have been instances where the televised dancers have themselves become a focus of public attention. In 1957, *American Bandstand* was first broadcast nationally on television in the United States. It featured rock 'n' roll artists such as Fats Domino and Jerry Lee Lewis and a teenage studio audience that helped to add excitement to the screened performance. As Greig (1989) reports, *American Bandstand* audience members (particularly girls) who were featured regularly on the show quickly began to attract a fan following. Indeed, interest in these television 'regulars' was so great that they began to receive more fan mail than the featured stars. As Greig notes, 'their hairstyles, their dance partners, their clothes and of course, their dance routines' fascinated teenagers (1989, 28). This concept of dance instruction through youth music television can be noted in other instances. For example, the foremost 1960s UK pop show *Ready Steady Go!* featured full-time resident dancers who, in a designated weekly slot, would demonstrate new dance moves.

These examples illustrate how the depiction of dance within visual media is inherently bound up with the high turnover and mass dissemination of dance styles involved in a social dance context. Both film and television were central in popularizing new dance crazes throughout the twentieth century. For instance, Rust (1969, 112) points out that there was an 'intensive public campaign to popularise' the twist, with the release of several records named after the dance and its heavy exposure on television pop shows. This was, of course, nothing new, as, throughout the twentieth century, the music industry produced sheet music and numerous recordings to capitalize on popular dance crazes or to actively promote new ones. Thus, a complicated and intimately linked relationship is shared between dance and popular music. While contemporary dance forms have links with cultural practises stretching back centuries, they are also deeply entwined with and affected by relatively recent developments in the mass media.

Bibliography

Castle, Vernon, and Castle, Irene. 1914. *Modern Dancing*. New York: The World Syndicate Co.

Chasteen, John Charles. 1996. 'The Pre-History of Samba: Carnival Dancing in Rio De Janeiro, 1840–1917.' *Journal of Latin American Studies* 28(1): 29–478.

Cook, Susan C. 1998. 'Passionless Dancing and Passionate Reform.' In *The Passion of Music and Dance: Body, Gender, and Sexuality*, ed. William Washabaugh. Oxford: Berg, 133–50.

Crease, Robert P. 2002. 'Jazz and Dance.' In *The Cambridge Companion to Jazz*, ed. Mervyn Cooke and David Horn. Cambridge: Cambridge University Press, 69–80.

Cunningham, Hugh. 1980. *Leisure in the Industrial Revolution, c. 1780–c. 1880*. London: Croom Helm.

DeNora, Tia. 2000. *Music in Everyday Life*. Cambridge: Cambridge University Press.

Erlmann, Veit. 1989. '"Horses in the Race Course": The Domestication of Ingoma Dancing in South Africa, 1929–39.' *Popular Music* 8(3): 259–73.

Fryer, Peter. 2000. *Rhythms of Resistance: African Musical Heritage in Brazil*. London: Pluto.

Greig, Charlotte. 1989. *Will You Still Love Me Tomorrow?: Girl Groups from the 50s On*. London: Virago.

Haley, Alex. 1968. *The Autobiography of Malcolm X*. London: Penguin.

Hazzard-Gordon, Katrina. 1990. *Jookin': The Rise of Social Dance Formations in African-American Culture*. Philadelphia: Temple University Press.

Johnson, Bruce. 2000. *The Inaudible Music: Jazz, Gender and Australian Modernity*. Sydney: Currency Press.

Johnstone, Nick. 1999. *Melody Maker History of 20th Century Popular Music*. London: Bloomsbury.

Jonas, Gerald. 1992. *Dancing: The Power of Dance Around the World*. London: BBC Books.

Kobal, John. 1970. *Gotta Sing, Gotta Dance: A Pictorial History of Film Musicals*. London: Hamlyn.

Kouwenhoven, John. 1998. 'What's "American" About America?' In *The Jazz Cadence of American Culture*, ed. Robert G. O'Meally. New York: Columbia University Press, 214–36.

Lees, Jim. ca. 1955. *So You Want to Square Dance*. Nottingham: Nottingham District English Folk, Dance and Song Society.

Lull, James. 1987. 'Thrashing in the Pit: An Ethnography of San Francisco Punk Subculture.' In *Natural Audiences: Qualitative Research of Media Uses and Effects*, ed. Thomas R. Lindlof. Norwood, NJ: Ablex Publishing Corporation, 225–52.

Malone, Jacqui. 1998. 'Jazz Music in Motion: Dancers and Big Bands.' In *The Jazz Cadence of American Culture*, ed. Robert G. O'Meally. New York: Columbia University Press, 278–97.

Manuel, Peter. 1988. *Popular Musics of the Non-Western World: An Introductory Survey*. New York: Oxford University Press.

Marre, Jeremy, and Charlton, Hannah. 1985. *Beats of the Heart: Popular Music of the World*. London: Pluto.

McCarthy, Albert. 1971. *The Dance Band Era: The Dancing Decades from Ragtime to Swing, 1910–1950*. London: Studio Vista.

Mundy, John. 1999. *Popular Music on Screen: From the Hollywood Musical to Music Video*. Manchester: Manchester University Press.

Poschardt, Ulf. 1998. *DJ-Culture*, trans. Shaun Whiteside. London: Quartet.

Rashid, Ahmed. 2001. *Taliban: The Story of the Afghan Warlords*. London: Pan Books.

Rietveld, Hillegonda C. 1998. *This Is Our House: House Music, Cultural Spaces, and Technologies*. Aldershot: Ashgate.

Rust, Frances. 1969. *Dance in Society: An Analysis of the Relationship Between the Social Dance and Society in England from the Middle Ages to the Present Day*. London: Routledge & Kegan Paul.

Stearns, Marshall, and Stearns, Jean. 1994. *Jazz Dance: The Story of American Vernacular Dance*. New York: Da Capo Press.

Thomas, Rosie. 2000. 'Popular Hindi Cinema.' In *World Cinema: Critical Approaches*, ed. John Hill and Pamela Church Gibson. Oxford: Oxford University Press, 157–58.

Thomson, Raymond A. 1989. 'Dance Bands and Dance Halls in Greenock, 1945–55.' *Popular Music* 8(2): 143–55.

Thornton, Sarah. 1995. *Club Cultures: Music, Media, and Subcultural Capital*. Cambridge: Polity Press.

Van der Merwe, Peter. 1989. *Origins of the Popular Style: The Antecedents of Twentieth-Century Popular Music*. Oxford: Clarendon Press.

Verán, Christina. 1999. 'Breaking It All Down: The Rise and Fall of the B-Boy Kingdom.' In *The Vibe History of Hip Hop*, ed. Alan Light. London: Plexus, 53–59.

Discographical References

Basil, Toni. 'Mickey.' Chrysalis 2638. *1982*: USA.

Jackson, Michael. 'Thriller.' *Thriller*. Epic 38112. *1982*: USA.

Filmography

Dames, dir. Ray Enright. 1934. USA. 95 mins. Musical. Original music by Mort Dixon, Alexis Dubin, Irving Kahal, Harry Warren.

The Jazz Singer, dir. Alan Crosland. 1927. USA. 89 mins. Drama. Original music by Louis Silvers.

MARION LEONARD and ROBERT STRACHAN

Lyrics

Lyrics form the text of a song, and they are accompanied by music and are sung. The importance of lyrics within a song varies greatly between genres. Where lyrics exist in dance music of many kinds, they are less important than rhythm. In protest songs, religious songs or the praise-songs of West Africa, the lyrics are intended to have a primary signifying role. Indeed, such genres are defined in terms of the subject matter of songs rather than by musical style.

Structural Features of Lyrics

Like other aspects of many types of popular music, lyrics are frequently formulaic. They follow certain rules of song structure, such as the verse–chorus form of many genres or the AAB three-line verse form of blues in which the second line repeats the first and the line endings rhyme. Rhyme itself is the most widely used technique in lyrics written in languages of European origin. Relatively invariant rhyme schemes are conventionally found in seventeenth-century English broadside ballads, the Mexican immigrant *corridos* and *canciónes* of the nineteenth century discussed by Herrera-Sobek (1993), present-day rap (Perkins 1996) and numerous other genres. The importance of rhyme to the lyrics in many genres is emphasized by the publication of 'rhyming dictionaries' as an aid to songwriters. Other features, such as assonance, puns and double-entendres (Taylor 2000, 167), also link lyrics to poetry and verse, including comic or vulgar folk and demotic texts.

The thematic material of lyrics may also be formulaic. For instance, Simonett (2001) states that the Mexican ballads known as *corridos* 'are largely based on formulas: the opening statement of date and place; the introductory reference to the singing of the corrido; a reference to the singer, the audience or the song; dramatic speech events; journeys; certain words, exclamations, proverbial expressions, metaphors and allegories; the bird messenger; and the farewell and so forth' (224).

Successful lyric writers have sometimes offered advice to would-be songwriters. Charles K. Harris, author of the hit 'After the Ball' (1892), stated that 'many-syllabled words and those containing hard consonants, wherever possible, must be avoided. In writing lyrics, be concise; get to your point quickly and then make the point as strong as possible' (quoted in Hamm 1979, 290).

Motivation of Lyrics

Popular song lyrics have sometimes been associated with Romantic poetry in terms of their assumed origins in the free exercise of a writer's creativity. But it is equally the case that much, if not most, lyric writing is motivated by the demands or constraints of particular markets or commissions. Musical theater and the cinema present some of the most obvious examples of such motivation. The producers of the James Bond series of films, for instance, require authors to create lyrics for a song whose title is already decided. In much musical theater, the composition of lyrics is constrained by the demands of the story line or plot. Additionally, there have been numerous examples of songs being composed to order for a particular singer. Certain songwriters are renowned for their ability to contribute as coauthors to songs for well-known rock bands or pop groups. Equally, many writers gear their songs to the vocal style and range of leading recording artists, in the hope that the song will be selected to appear on a star's next CD.

Beyond these predominantly Western forms of popular music, the praise-song is found widely in Africa. In this genre, the lyrics must be composed in honor or praise of a political leader or the patron of the singer's band.

Words and Music

The most important constraint for the production of lyrics is, of course, their necessary combination with music and with the singing voice. The extent of this constraint varies according to the order in which the lyric and melody of a song are composed. While it has been commonplace in Western classical music for poems to become lyrics when a composer sets them to music, the opposite process has been found frequently in popular music. The majority of broadsides consisted of new lyrics written to be sung to existing tunes. Such lyrics were often satirical, political, sporting or obscene. Parodies of existing song lyrics can be traced to the nineteenth century, when songs from the famous ballad opera *The Bohemian Girl* were rewritten: 'I Dreamt I Dwelt in Marble Halls' became 'I Dreamt I Dwelt in Kitchen Halls' (Hamm 1979, 73).

Lyrics may also be set to music that already exists in instrumental form. Some pop songs have used classical music themes, while a certain type of jazz song associated with the lyricists and performers King Pleasure and Jon Hendricks is created by writing words to fit famous improvised solos on saxophone or trumpet.

Linguistic Factors

The lyric is the least transnationalized feature of a song and potentially the one marked most by cultural specificity. In an increasingly international market for popular music, lyric writers and their employers have responded to this situation in various ways. For many years, translation has been a thriving activity. In the 1960s, it was commonplace for Italian, French, North American or British hits to be exported with translated lyrics. In Mexico, Spanish-language versions of US rock songs were known as *refritos* ('refried'). More recently, the lyrics of many Anglophone songs performed by such artists as Madonna have been translated into Chinese and other Asian languages.

Another strategy has been to foreground the polyglot nature of communication in a globalized culture. 'The Italian rap group Frankie HI-NRG's song "Fight da faida" is built around the English refrain "you gotta fight" . . . the track uses standard Italian to give maximum comprehensibility to its message, although it includes a segment in which a woman's voice raps in Sicilian dialect' (Mitchell 2001, 195).

Analysis of Lyrics

Various types of analysis have been applied to popular music lyrics. As Frith (1987) points out, sociologists such as Horton (1957) and Mooney (1954) envisaged lyrics as evidence of popular attitudes toward courtship and used content analysis to support their findings. More recently, Cooper (1991) has categorized the ideological themes of US hit songs. More tactical uses of content analysis can be found in Laing (1985), who employs the methodology to distinguish punk songs from mainstream hits, and in von Schoenebeck (1998), who analyzes the principal themes of *volksmusik* in Germany.

Critical discussions of lyrics produced by specific writers sometimes attempt to analyze their work in terms of a unified set of themes or motifs, as if they are authors of poetry. For example, Weinstein (2002) claims that running through the lyrics of Roger Waters 'is a set of images, metaphors, allusions and metonyms that extend from his earliest lyrical forays through his later solo work' (101). The most substantial study of a single author's lyrics in the context of his music as a whole is Gray's work on Bob Dylan (2000).

A fruitful but underused methodology is discourse analysis. The placing of pronouns within lyrics can set up complex and frequently ambiguous relationships between the protagonists constructed in the lyric, the performer of the lyric and the listener. Bradby (1990, 2002) explores such relationships in 'girl group' songs and in certain texts sung by Buddy Holly. Hennion (1983) takes a different, linguistically derived approach in his distinction between denotative and connotative lyric features, where the latter 'are selected for the way they ring, for the expressive power that gives them their opacity' (179).

These various analyses of lyrics as such must, of course, be supplemented with further analysis that integrates lyrics into the song as a whole. Such an integration is increasingly found in the work of musicologists such as Brackett (2000) and the authors to be found in Middleton (2000). However, in reaction against perceived attempts to isolate lyrics as poetry in anthologies like Goldstein's *The Poetry of Rock* (1969) or through the publication of collections of song lyrics by authors from Ira Gershwin (1977) to Suzanne Vega (1990), many commentators on Western popular music have denied lyrics any efficacy in the impact of a song on listeners. For Frith (1983), 'the evaluation of pop singers depends not on words but on sounds – on the noises around the words' (35), while, referring to rock lyrics, Weinstein (2002) argues that they are 'ignored, misinterpreted or misheard. When words are grasped, it is fragmentarily through phrases or a chorus rather than as the full lyrical text. Fans and fan-pandering critics attempt interpretations but they tend to be superficial and naïve' (98).

These viewpoints are perhaps over-polemical in their relegation of the lyric to a supporting role in popular music. They tend to generalize from one (though dominant) genre of Anglo-American pop and rock. Lyrics continue to play an important role in the creation of musical meaning in many other genres, from French *chanson* to the *griot* music of West Africa and the protest or political song of many cultures and countries. Even in the Anglo-American tradition, the appreciation of the character, elegance or content of the lyrics of singer-songwriters has a primary role in the creation of pleasure in the audiences for such artists.

Bibliography

Brackett, David. 2000. *Interpreting Popular Music*. Berkeley, CA: University of California Press.

Bradby, Barbara. 1990. 'Do-Talk and Don't-Talk: The Division of the Subject in Girl-Group Music.' In *On Record: Rock, Pop, and the Written Word*, ed. Simon Frith and Andrew Goodwin. London: Routledge, 341–68.

Bradby, Barbara. 2002. 'Oh Boy! (Oh Boy!): Mutual Desirability and Musical Structure in the Buddy Group.' *Popular Music* 21(1): 63–92.

Cooper, B. Lee. 1991. *Popular Music Perspectives: Ideas, Themes, and Patterns in Contemporary Lyrics*. Bowling Green, OH: Bowling Green State University Popular Press.

Frith, Simon. 1983. *Sound Effects: Youth, Leisure and the Politics of Rock*. London: Constable.

Frith, Simon. 1987. 'Why Do Songs Have Words?' In *Lost in Music: Culture, Style, and the Musical Event*, ed. Avron Levine White. London: Routledge & Kegan Paul, 77–106.

Gershwin, Ira. 1977. *Lyrics on Several Occasions*. London: Elm Tree Books.

Goldstein, Richard, ed. 1969. *The Poetry of Rock*. New York and London: Bantam.

Gray, Michael. 2000. *Song & Dance Man III: The Art of Bob Dylan*. London and New York: Continuum.

Hamm, Charles. 1979. *Yesterdays: Popular Song in America*. New York: Norton.

Hennion, Antoine. 1983. 'The Production of Success: An Anti-Musicology of the Pop Song.' *Popular Music* 3: 159–93.

Herrera-Sobek, María. 1993. *Northward Bound: The Mexican Immigrant Experience in Ballad and Song*. Bloomington, IN: Indiana University Press.

Horton, Donald. 1957. 'The Dialogue of Courtship in Popular Songs.' *American Journal of Sociology* 62: 569–78. (Reprinted in *On Record: Rock, Pop, and the Written Word*, ed. Simon Frith and Andrew Goodwin. London: Routledge, 1990, 14–26.)

Laing, Dave. 1985. *One Chord Wonders: Power and Meaning in Punk Rock*. Milton Keynes: Open University Press.

Middleton, Richard, ed. 2000. *Reading Pop: Approaches to Textual Analysis in Popular Music*. Oxford and New York: Oxford University Press.

Mitchell, Tony. 2001. 'Fightin' da Faida: The Italian Posses and Hip-Hop in Italy.' In *Global Noise: Rap and Hip-Hop Outside the USA*, ed. Tony Mitchell. Middletown, CT: Wesleyan University Press, 194–221.

Mooney, H.F. 1954. 'Popular Music Since the 1920s.' *American Quarterly* 6: 250–66.

Perkins, William Eric, ed. 1996. *Droppin' Science: Critical Essays on Rap Music and Hip Hop Culture*. Philadelphia: Temple University Press.

Simonett, Helena. 2001. *Banda: Mexican Musical Life Across Borders*. Middletown, CT: Wesleyan University Press.

Taylor, Timothy D. 2000. 'His Name Was in Lights: Chuck Berry's "Johnny B. Goode."' In *Reading Pop: Approaches to Textual Analysis in Popular Music*, ed. Richard Middleton. Oxford and New York: Oxford University Press, 165–82.

Vega, Suzanne. 1990. *Bullet in Flight: Songs*. London: Omnibus Press.

von Schoenebeck, Mechthild. 1998. 'New German Folk-Like Song and Its Hidden Political Messages.' *Popular Music* 17(3): 279–92.

Weinstein, Deena. 2002. 'Progressive Rock as Text: The Lyrics of Roger Waters.' In *Progressive Rock Reconsidered*, ed. Kevin Holm-Hudson. New York: Routledge, 91–110.

Sheet Music

Harris, Charles K., comp. and lyr. 1892. 'After the Ball.' Milwaukee, WI: Charles K. Harris & Co.

Discographical Reference

Frankie HI-NRG. 'Fight da faida.' *Verba Manent*. RCA 74321 197842. *1994*: Italy.

DAVE LAING

Stage Act

A stage act is the means by which popular music performers present their music in concert and in other forms of performance to audiences. The key components of a stage act include the performers' costumes, stage movements and speech, plus stage design, lighting, amplification of sound and props such as dry ice.

In many genres of popular music, the clothing of a musician is an important signifier. In vaudeville and music hall, for instance, the 'cross-dressing' of women singers performing as men (for example, the English singer Vesta Tilley) or of males dressed as women alerted the audience to gender ambiguity. A different sort of cultural dissonance was set up by 'blackface' minstrelsy, where even African Americans would signify the artificiality of their performance as black singers and instrumentalists. In the twentieth century, one dichotomy in the stage clothing of bands was between uniformity and diversity. While members of many Western dance bands, and even the Beatles with their Cardin collared jackets, dressed in a uniform way, many other jazz and rock ensembles deliberately chose to appear onstage in casual dress.

The movement of performers on the stage has frequently been choreographed. The singers of the Tamla Motown company were coached by the dancer Cholly Atkins. Less sophisticated choreography was practised by seated members of brass sections in dance bands, who would rise to their feet in unison as they played emphatic sections. More dramatic movements were a compulsive and emotive element of the stage acts of singers such as Johnnie Ray and James Brown, who fell to their knees while singing into the microphone.

Stage acts frequently contain spoken passages in which singers or band leaders acknowledge applause or introduce the work about to be performed. The introductions may be perfunctory – simply announcing a title – or they may be lengthy, describing the source or genesis of the song or piece. Another function of spoken passages is to introduce by name all the members of an ensemble or those who have played, or are about to play, solos.

Some performers have included intricate or minimal decoration of the stage area, with backdrops or props onstage. These may vary from a simple logo design at the rear of the stage to back-projected film sequences or such large-scale features as the wall placed onstage during performances of the eponymous song cycle composed by former Pink Floyd member Roger Waters. Such stage decoration is given further impact by variations in the lighting of a stage act. Many touring groups take a lighting rig and engineer to each venue. During performances, the lighting engineer will vary the intensity, geography or color of the lighting to enhance the emotional character of the performance. Another feature of the stage acts of rock bands in the 1970s and later was the generation of dry ice, which drifted across the stage and combined with lighting to create dramatic effects.

But probably the most important single innovation to transform the stage act has been the amplification of sound. The introduction of the microphone enabled vocalists to create the impression of intimacy, first known as crooning. Before the microphone, singers needed to project their voices to fill a theater and necessarily sang in a declamatory mode. By the end of the twentieth century, the sound engineer was a ubiquitous figure in most popular music performances in concert halls and clubs. The engineer mixes the sound from the various vocal and instrumental sources onstage in a similar manner to a recording engineer in a studio. Amplification and PA (public-address) systems in larger halls also permit the presentation of previously recorded music as an overture to the stage entrance of a performer or ensemble.

As the component words of the term suggest, it is in their stage act that musical performers are closest to actors. But one key difference is that, in Western popular singing especially, audiences may take the stage act as the presentation of the true or authentic self of the performer.

Some performers use the elements of their stage act to construct a façade of honesty and ordinariness, while others project a flamboyance and otherworldliness in order to distance themselves from this normalcy. Nevertheless, all stage acts are constructed: even the most seemingly spontaneous of performances is still directed by the unwritten rules governing the way in which performers of a given genre are meant to behave.

For example, artists working within the soul and blues idiom have traditionally stressed authentic emotion through reciprocity (with fellow musicians or the audience). One of the key strategies is that of antiphony, or 'call-and-response,' a technique discussed in Charles Keil's book, *Urban Blues* (1966).

Keil establishes a homology between the secular and the nonsecular, and identifies the same patterns in blues performance as exist in the performances of the preacher in the pulpit. He compares the R&B stalwart B.B. King to the inspirational civil rights activist the Reverend Martin Luther King, and argues that they fulfilled similar roles within popular culture, and black consciousness in particular. In both performances, strong feeling, integrity, honesty and fidelity are vital. In a preacher–congregation relationship, the preacher's protestations customarily receive a corresponding response from the congregation. This, argues Keil, is indicative of a particular kind of individual–group relationship, common in African culture, which stresses dialog and thesis-antithesis patterns. This style of stage presentation (the pop spectacle as nonsecular revivalist meeting) forms the basis for soul artists such as James Brown, Aretha Franklin and Stevie Wonder. In the video for Talking Heads' 'Once in a Lifetime' (1981), David Byrne parodied the affectations of the preacher, thus making a direct comment on pop performance's debt to the nonsecular world.

Concerts by artists such as white soul Simply Red, pop-rockers Queen or acts such as the Rolling Stones are also overwhelmingly about reciprocity. Perhaps the prime exponent of the ideology of communion is Bruce Springsteen. His music is all broad gestures. Onstage, he has constructed the persona of the 'honest Joe.' Springsteen's concerts invite admiration for their musical prowess and for the artist's ability to power through a lengthy song set, sweat cascading onto the microphone stand, to give the audience demonstrable, 'authentic' value for money.

Much of what actually occurs at Springsteen's concerts is highly predictable, although essential to their success. A communication theory concept is of relevance here – that of 'redundancy' ('that which is predictable or conventional in a message') (Fiske 1990, 18). The opposite concept is 'entropy' – a message of low predictability. Like popular music itself, pop performance is bound by 'rules' and 'conventions' that are a major source of redundancy. To make performance work, to enable it to resonate or have any social or cultural significance, it must carry with it a degree of redundancy and predictability. As a popular art form, a pop concert, as opposed to an avant-garde theatrical presentation, must be able to connect. As Fiske states: 'If we wish to reach a larger, heterogeneous audience we will need to design a message with a high degree of redundancy' (1990, 12).

Redundant channels of information 'flesh out' performance and make it aesthetically pleasing, using the following strategies. Firstly, the 'gestural,' which includes the wave to the audience, shaking hands with the first row and a whole range of stock-in-trade movements from singers and musicians alike, from the caress of the microphone stand to the throwing of the drumsticks into the crowd at the end of the gig; secondly, the 'procedural,' which covers song introductions, band introductions, audience recognition (for example, 'Hello, London') and any encore or encores; and thirdly, technical devices, which, to an extent, have become hackneyed and clichéd: dry ice, backlit shots, the spotlight for slower, more emotive or 'serious' moments, and white light and audience illumination for the participatory rock numbers. On Sting's solo tour of 1993, the background of stars projected during the concert's finale, 'Fragile,' was the visual signal for the audience to hold their cigarette lighters aloft, a manipulative visual strategy to aid the process of communion in rock. All these devices (and there are many others) are recognized by both performer and audience as the currency of pop performance. In this context, antiphonal structures provide the musical and visual 'glue' that binds these disparate acts together.

A number of rock artists, however, deliberately set out to confuse or alienate the audience and to eschew the rock ideology of communion. One example would be the Velvet Underground's 1967 mixed-media presentation, the Exploding Plastic Inevitable, devised with Andy Warhol. This show incorporated film, stark, almost blinding lighting and images of sexual deviancy (dancers mimed sadomasochistic acts while the band played). Likewise, performance artists such as Laurie Anderson have used video, montage and various visual and vocal tricks to denude the rock spectacle of its visual clichés.

However, the musical signifiers that connote 'authenticity' change over time and are genre-specific. In the rock era, the lead guitar solo and technical virtuosity were synonymous with authenticity. However, when folk singer Bob Dylan converted to electric instrumentation at the Newport Folk Festival of 1965, he was ostracized by many purists in the folk community and dubbed a commercial faker as a result of distancing himself from the acoustic guitar, the totem of a certain homespun authenticity within the folk idiom.

A key element in the presentation of music in concert is the signification of sexuality. In discussions of rock music, this has frequently been seen mainly in connection with the guitar and its phallic connotations. A pioneer of this stage performance style was blues and jazz musician 'T-Bone' Walker. Walker 'developed a dazzling stage act that was reputed to have inspired Bo Diddley and Elvis Presley in its use of the guitar as a stage prop – sometimes for acrobatics, as the singer did the splits and held the instrument behind his head while he continued to play, and sometimes for sexual provocation, as he ground the guitar against his body or pointed it suggestively out at the audience' (Gillett 1983, 134–35). This stage act was an influence on the later flamboyance of guitar showmen such as Chuck Berry (with his trademark 'duckwalk'), Jimi Hendrix (whose stage act included playing his guitar behind his back or with his teeth, or even setting fire to it) and the Who's Pete Townshend (whose 'windmill,' a circular rotating chopping guitar style, often lacerated his hand).

In addition to its focus on the use of the guitar, Walker's stage act's emphasis on the bump-and-grind of the sexual act had a huge impact on white performers such as Elvis Presley. Before it was toned down in the 1960s, Presley's stage show was considered to be too risqué for television. On *The Ed Sullivan Show* in September 1956, Presley was famously shown from the waist up only.

However, later rock artists, notably the Doors' Jim Morrison and Iggy Pop, mined sexual outrage for their stage acts. Iggy Pop's psychotic stage act became the paradigm for punk in the 1970s. He moved around the stage with a contrived spastic gait, as if he was somehow trying to get out of his own body. He would deliberately lacerate himself onstage by throwing himself on shards of glass and mutilating himself. Iggy Pop's stage act was about catharsis. He also helped originate the 'stage-dive,' where a performer jumps into the audience and is helped back to the stage – a symbolic assertion of a desire by the pop performer to 'seek' or construct a direct connection with the audience through touch. The stage-dive became a stereotypical staple of many rock performers' stage acts.

Female performers have often found it very difficult to break free from male-constructed gender codes that determine how they should conduct themselves onstage. Overt expressions of carnality, for instance, have traditionally been vilified as transgressions of the mother-nurturer stereotype encoded within a male-dominated society. The result is that many female performers have been forced, sometimes unwittingly, to sell themselves as sexual commodities. This is nowhere better evidenced than in the 1970s and the work of soul and disco diva Tina Turner, as well as that of Donna Summer and Grace Jones. Jones's besuited androgyny (later an influence on the Eurythmics' Annie Lennox) did challenge the stereotypical view of the female body promulgated in the media. But her chest-revealing stage suits also pandered to the male gaze, playing on the white assumption of black women's sexual availability. Tina Turner's stage act played shamelessly to white men's fantasies about black prostitutes (see Herman 1994, 83). On one of her bestselling singles, 'Private Dancer,' Turner assumed the alter ego of a prostitute, although, predictably, the song itself was written by a man (Mark Knopfler). It took punk, and in particular punk artists such as Siouxsie Sioux and Poly Styrene in the United Kingdom and Patti Smith in the United States, to offer up more positive role models for women onstage – models that were not based primarily on a male-defined set of parameters for beauty and femininity.

Since the early 1970s, androgyny has been crucial to the way in which some pop stars have constructed their stage acts. David Bowie is a prime example. Throughout Bowie's career, his concerts have been conceived as theatrical experiences and have been variously influenced by extramusical ideas from Brechtian and Kabuki theater, mime and dance to the fine arts and film. He developed an outrageous stage act that subverted the rock spectacle. For example, the guitar, so often regarded as a heterosexual phallic symbol, was 'queered' during Bowie's Ziggy Stardust shows of 1972–73 when Bowie performed mock fellatio on his lead guitarist. Bowie also showed that being a pop performer was about presenting new versions of oneself for public consumption. He adopted a series of alter egos, such as Ziggy Stardust and the Thin White Duke, whom he would signify onstage, but not become. He thus confused the whole basis of the star–fan relationship by impersonating an inauthentic rocker. Bowie also plundered science fiction for visual imagery, visually encoding his own personal sense of alienation through reference to a fictive alien ancestry.

Bowie was the most successful and most radical totem of the tradition of artifice within pop performance. Mention should, however, also be made of Pink Floyd's 'Syd' Barrett, the first British male pop star to wear makeup onstage; Sun Ra, George Clinton and Lee 'Scratch' Perry, who used alien visual metaphors in their work to express their sexual and racial alienation; and, most obviously, Little Richard, whose flamboyant stage act and androgynous appearance bespoke an undeclared homosexuality in a climate hostile to both the gay and black causes. Some radical performers, such as Frank Zappa, also developed a neo-Dadaistic approach to pop performance that subverted audience expectations through the bizarre. Zappa's stage act incorporated such visual jokes as squirting the audience with whipped cream from the tail of a stuffed giraffe (Balfour 1986, 127). Other singers resurrected the idea of the blues' voodoo ancestry, and based their pop performances on ghoulishness. 'Screamin' Jay' Hawkins' act included macabre special effects and props such as a cape, a coffin and a skull. In the 1970s, progressive rock groups such as Peter Gabriel's Genesis and Jethro Tull produced an English variation of US vaudeville voodoo. Gabriel's theatrical stage act incorporated masks, elaborate costume changes and narrative sequences to link the rock show in a seamless narrative. Jethro Tull's Ian Anderson played a madcap country squire, his maniacal flute solos a direct challenge to the monopoly of the rock guitar as the solo instrument within rock.

However, it was punk, particularly British punk, that denatured pop performance. Whereas, prior to 1976, technical virtuosity onstage was a sine qua non, punk stressed the inarticulate and incompetent. It created an anti-communion in which mutual hatred between band and audience became the rationale of the event. Johnny Rotten from the Sex Pistols once ended a concert with the line: 'I bet you don't hate us as much as we hate you.' Dave Laing analyzes the punk paradigm in *One Chord Wonders* (1985). Punks substituted aggression for ingratiation: 'Just as the musicians launched a ritual assault, the audience responded appropriately. Unable to reply verbally (the power structure which put bands "on top" was literally based on electrical power) the fans responded physically, in three main ways: can throwing, invading the stage and "gobbing"' (1985, 84). Groups such as the Sex Pistols taunted their audience rather than displaying a contrived sincerity (a strategy pre-empted by Bowie's Ziggy Stardust when he mockingly sang, 'Give me your hands, cos you're wonderful' in 'Rock 'n' Roll Suicide' (1972)). Despite the rhetoric surrounding punk's 'honesty' and authenticity, theatricality lay as deeply ingrained as in the sort of overblown rock spectacle punk was seeking to replace. For example, the Sex Pistols' Johnny Rotten based his hunched, leering, sardonic onstage figure on Laurence Olivier's 1956 film portrayal of Richard III.

The 1980s and 1990s saw the development by 'top' performers of increasingly sophisticated and expensive stage acts and a return to grass-roots 'authenticity' from others. Madonna and Michael Jackson, for example, had shows that, with their strictly choreographed dance sequences, were more like Broadway musical productions than rock concerts. Madonna's stage act also dealt in the taboo. Some critics regarded the sequences involving simulated masturbation as a direct challenge to the machismo of the rock spectacle. On the other hand, both US grunge and UK Britpop tended on the whole to be untheatrical, keeping sartorial flamboyancy to a minimum.

Dance music largely simplified the stage act. As curator rather than originator of the sounds, the DJ, remixer or dance band member was not required to perform in any traditional sense or to have a stage act per se, except for an effective song sequence and lighting show. The members of the German group Kraftwerk took this strategy to its logical conclusion in 1991, when they had robot replicas of the group encore in their place, thereby undermining the traditional link between audience and performer. Unsurprisingly, perhaps, these simulacra got a more enthusiastic audience reaction than the human performers themselves.

Bibliography

Balfour, Victoria. 1986. *Rock Wives: The Hard Lives and Good Times of the Wives, Girlfriends, and Groupies of Rock and Roll*. London: Virgin.

Buckley, David. 1993. 'David Bowie: Still Pop's Faker?' In *The Bowie Companion*, ed. Elizabeth Thomson and David Gutman. London: Macmillan, 3–11.

Fiske, John. 1990. *Introduction to Communication Studies*. 2nd ed. London: Routledge.

Gillett, Charlie. 1983 (1970). *The Sound of the City: The Rise of Rock and Roll*. Rev. ed. London: Souvenir Press.

Herman, Gary. 1994. *Rock 'n' Roll Babylon*. 3rd rev. ed. London: Plexus.

Keil, Charles. 1966. *Urban Blues*. Chicago: University of Chicago Press.

Laing, Dave. 1985. *One Chord Wonders: Power and Meaning in Punk Rock*. Milton Keynes: Open University Press.

Taylor, Rogan P. 1985. *The Death and Resurrection Show: From Shaman to Superstar*. London: Anthony Blond.

Discographical References

Bowie, David. 'Rock 'n' Roll Suicide.' *The Rise and Fall of Ziggy Stardust and the Spiders from Mars*. RCA-Victor SF 8287. *1972*: UK.

Sting. 'King of Pain'/'Fragile'/'Purple Haze' (live). A&M 580302-2. *1993*: UK.

Talking Heads. 'Once in a Lifetime.' Sire SIR 4048. *1981*: UK.

Turner, Tina. 'Private Dancer.' Capitol CL 343. *1984*: UK.

DAVID BUCKLEY with DAVE LAING

Titles

A 'title,' from the Latin *titulus* ('notice,' 'inscription'), is the name given to a work. In his classic study *Seuils* (1987), Gérard Genette writes that titles have three fundamental functions: they identify a work; they designate its content; and they emphasize its value. Genette's examples are taken from literature, but titles apply to popular music in much the same way as they apply to novels and poems.

Identifying a Piece

The title is the name of a piece of music, or what it is called. Without a title, it could not be referred to (especially if it were instrumental) except through complicated and probably ineffective paraphrases ('the very slow ballad in C minor on the second track of the third record by John Smith'; 'the fast piece where the bass goes dum-de-dum, dum-de-dum . . .'). Identification, then, is the first and most obvious reason why pieces have titles, in popular as well as in classical music. In classical music, until recent times, instrumental compositions were usually given – by composers and/or by scholars – very technical, descriptive titles based on their form, tonality, number of parts, instruments involved and so on: for example, 'Concerto for Harpsichord and Strings in E Major,' or 'String Quartet in D Minor' (more evocative titles, like 'Death and the Maiden,' were occasionally added). Only vocal compositions (madrigals, cantatas, operas, lieder and so on) had 'real' (non-technical) titles, since they had a text. In popular music, even instrumental pieces have had in the past, and still have, real (not purely descriptive) titles: a piece written by Jerry Lordan and recorded by the Shadows is called 'Apache' rather than 'Piece in A Minor for Two Electric Guitars, Electric Bass and Drums.' Even in popular music, though, technical (or quasi-technical) titles can be found, referring – although generically, approximately and not exclusively – to the form of a piece, its style, the genre to which it belongs ('St. Louis Blues,' 'Chanson pour l'Auvergnat,' 'Serenata celeste,' 'Ballad of the Alamo') or the dance on which it is based ('The Champagne Waltz,' 'Blue Tango,' 'Samba de una nota só,' 'Jailhouse Rock'). The second type, especially, has slowly declined, as popular music has lost dance as a primary function, but, in general, 'descriptive,' 'cold' titles have tended to be superseded by more 'oblique' and 'warm' ones, with less or no reference to musical structure or form. Much more than a formal, technical description, a title, in fact, is supposed – in the context of popular music – to be a means of identifying a song in a more substantial way, being a synthetic representation of its originality, a surprise and a bait for audiences.

Popular music may also be identified by 'meta-titles': titles of collections of musical works or recordings. For example, the titles of albums of recorded music contain a number of pieces, each with its own title. On occasion, the album title may be identical to that of one of the tracks contained within the album. Additionally, operettas, musical shows and songbooks have such meta-titles.

Designating a Piece's Content

In theory, a title should provide, in a few words, as much information as possible about a piece's content. But what is a song's content? Is it its musical content or is it the content of its lyrics? Popular music titles tend to identify the verbal text as the (almost exclusive) carrier of content; if a piece has a verbal text, its title will usually refer – partially, at least – to the words, even when they are much less important than the music to which they are set (as in the case of dance music) or sometimes are totally irrelevant. This is one more instance of how lyrics typically seem to predominate in popular music, and how little music has appeared to free itself from verbal language in this context, compared to the 'classical' tradition.

In the case of instrumental pieces, the problem of referring to purely musical content is frequently solved by investing the undetermined, elusive suggestions of the music with a concrete object or concept. Titles like 'Moonlight Serenade' (Glenn Miller), 'Black Market' (Weather Report) or 'Ruins' (Henry Cow) help listeners to structure and focus their imagination, and give a more precise orientation to their spontaneous associations (the last example shows how a title can be, at the same time, 'evocative' and – metaphorically – 'descriptive' of the piece's form and style). Titles work, in such cases, as 'pre-interpretations' of a piece, and they have much the same function as the text, story or images on which program music is based and to which it alludes.

When a piece has words (as in the majority of popular music), the task may seem easier. This is the case if a title is conceived simply as a means of conveying information on what a given song is about. However, in practise, no song title says 'Song about two lovers parting; she cries, he promises to think about her all the time.' (Note that this sort of title, which sounds ridiculous today, was not unusual in poetry in past centuries.)

No title, in other words, does exactly and literally what it is supposed to do. A title can refer to a song's content in various ways, but the information that it gives about it is, most of the time, elliptical and oblique; its (relative) independence from the song's actual content allows it, sometimes, to be more effective. The relationship between a title and the text it refers to can be free, cryptic in some cases, even a pretext. A title is not strictly conditioned by the content of a song's lyrics any more than it is by its music; in some cases, it may overcome its 'servile' function and become the real text of a song: in pieces like 'L'elefante bianco' or 'Gioia e rivoluzione,' by the Italian progressive rock group Area, some time and explanation are needed to understand how a very weak handful of lines is connected to a very evocative title, until it becomes clear that the actual relationship is between the title and the group's image and ideology, and that the words were written afterward, as an appendix to the song's headline.

Common sense would suggest that authors give titles to their works when they are finished – that is, when they can see what it is that has to be named. However, this is not always the case. The title, which is, in theory, the culmination of a text, can in practise be its foundation, the matrix generating the song that it names. An example of this can be found in the form of 'catalog songs,' beginning with what lyricist Bob Hilliard called 'laundry-list titles' (Cole Porter's 'Let's Do It, Let's Fall

in Love,' Neil Sedaka's 'Calendar Girl,' John Lennon's 'Imagine' and so on).

Some titles simply give a résumé (sometimes metaphorically) of a song's content from 'outside' the text, as with Bob Dylan's 'My Back Pages' or the Rolling Stones' 'Sympathy for the Devil,' but these instances are rather rare; the prevalent model seems to be the one where a part of the text works as the song's title. It can be a single word or a whole line ('title line'), usually ones that are repeated, for example, as part of the 'hook' at the beginning of a chorus ('Douce France'), at the end of a verse ('Eve of Destruction,' 'The Times They Are A-Changin''), at its beginning ('Bus Stop') or even in the middle ('In the Midnight Hour,' 'Torna a Surriento,' 'Garôta de Ipanema').

Most frequently, song titles are made up of phrases: they can be statements, stock phrases, slogans or proverbs ('All You Need Is Love,' 'Ni Dieu ni maitre,' 'You Can't Always Get What You Want,' 'Everybody Needs Somebody to Love') or, more often, very ordinary fragments of everyday speech ('You Can't Do That,' 'Tu penses à quoi?,' '(I Can't Get No) Satisfaction,' 'Ne me quitte pas,' 'We Gotta Get Out of This Place'). In this type of title, what really counts is an antonym of originality. Sentences like 'Tu t'laisses aller' (which is the title of a famous song by Charles Aznavour) are not outstandingly creative, and yet they can act as powerful titles when they catch – in the sea of everyday speech – familiar words that have never before been artistically exploited. Within the context of the song they designate, ordinary phrases functioning as titles can spread an aura that comes from a mixed effect of the familiar and the unexpected. If it is true, as Frith (1987) has argued, that 'songs are more like plays than poems,' and that 'song words work as speech and speech acts' (97), then these kinds of titles, which are significantly rare in poetry and literature, seem to embody – more than any other type of title – a feature peculiar to popular music.

Emphasizing a Piece's Value

Centuries ago, when literature was not bought and sold on a wide scale, and the value of a text was supposedly based on its intrinsic artistic qualities (qualities that were, in theory, self-evident to competent readers), titles could be simply adequate descriptions of a work's subject. Since stories, poems and pieces of music have become commodities, and competition between books and between records has taken a commercial form, packaging has become increasingly important to the success of any kind of product. As a part of that, a product's name is expected to complement its appeal from a strategic standpoint. The title has always been the threshold of a work (*Seuils* is the name of Genette's study): if the door is closed (if the title is too austere), one may be repelled, or just too shy or too lazy to knock; if the door is wide open (if the title says too much about the work), one may lose all curiosity. In song titles, most of the time, the door is ajar: the name is like an invitation or, alternatively, an advertisement, emphasizing the value of a piece (Adorno (1941) once wrote that popular music is just self-advertising). Saying that the value titles emphasize is in fact a commercial value would be too easy, too general, inaccurate, and tantamount to succumbing to an ideological point of view. What most popular music titles really emphasize is the sentimental value of a piece, often presented in its most straightforward and elementary form. Perhaps more so than with titles invoking '*you*' ('You,' 'You and Me,' 'You and the Night and the Music,' 'You Are Beautiful,' 'You Are So Beautiful,' 'You Are Too Beautiful,' 'You Are Everything,' 'You Are Love,' 'You Are My Destiny,' 'You Are the Sunshine of My Life,' 'You Belong to Me,' 'You Keep Me Hangin' On' and so on), such a tendency can be epitomized by the use of women's names: 'Lucille,' 'Michelle,' 'Barbara,' 'Suzanne,' 'Angie.' Naming a song after a woman is not particularly original, and yet such titles have a strong rhetorical appeal: popular music listeners like to think that a song was inspired by real life, based on the author's personal experience, and dedicated to somebody ('Eleanor Rigby' or 'Nathan La Franeer,' 'Brigitte Bardot,' 'Bartali,' 'Biko' or 'Giulietta Masina' are possible variations on the same theme within different genres and in different ways).

Popular music titles may emphasize, in some cases, a piece's artistic (or cultural) value: 'A Whiter Shade of Pale' (Procol Harum) is a muted example, 'Mongoloid' (Devo) is a sharper one. The album title *We're Only in It for the Money* (Mothers of Invention) suggests how intertextuality can work, sometimes in connection with visual aspects, but phrase titles ('serious' ones) are probably the most attractive. While in 'plain,' 'non-spoken' titles ('The Sound of Silence,' 'Santa Lucia') the emphasis is on objects, in phrase titles ('I Can't Stop Loving You,' 'Don't Think Twice, It's All Right') the mark of subjectivity and personal relationships is stronger, and the urgency of the voice seems to pulsate in the words printed on a record's sleeve, promising something more than art.

Bibliography

Adorno, Theodor W., with Simpson, George. 1941. 'On Popular Music.' *Studies in Philosophy and Social Sciences* 9: 17–48.

Frith, Simon. 1987. 'Why Do Songs Have Words?' In *Lost in Music: Culture, Style, and the Musical Event*, ed. Avron Levine White. London: Routledge & Kegan Paul, 77–106.

Genette, Gérard. 1987. *Seuils* [Thresholds]. Paris: Editions du Seuil.

Discographical References

Alice Cooper. 'You and Me.' Warner Brothers 8349. *1977*: USA.

Animals, The. 'We Gotta Get Out of This Place.' Columbia DB 7639. *1965*: UK.

Anka, Paul. 'You Are My Destiny.' ABC-Paramount 9880. *1958*: USA.

Area. 'Gioia e rivoluzione.' *Crac!*. Barclay 940512. *1975*: Italy.

Area. 'L'elefante bianco.' *Crac!*. Barclay 940512. *1975*: Italy.

Aznavour, Charles. 'Tu t'laisses aller.' *Amours Toujours*. Barclay 810 782-2. *1984*: France.

Beatles, The. 'All You Need Is Love.' Parlophone R 5620. *1967*: UK.

Beatles, The. 'Eleanor Rigby.' Parlophone R 5493. *1966*: UK.

Beatles, The. 'Michelle.' *Rubber Soul*. Parlophone PMC 1267. *1965*: UK.

Beatles, The. 'You Can't Do That.' *A Hard Day's Night*. Parlophone PMC 1230. *1964*: UK.

Brassens, Georges. 'Chanson pour l'Auvergnat.' *Integrale Vol. 1: la mauvaise reputation*. Philips 836 2892. *1989*: France.

Brel, Jacques. 'Ne me quitte pas.' *Master Series: Jacques Brel*. Philips 816 458 2. *1988*: France.

Brubeck, Dave. 'St. Louis Blues.' *25th Anniversary Reunion Concert*. A&M CDA 0806. *1988*: USA.

Burke, Solomon. 'Everybody Needs Somebody to Love.' Atlantic AT 4004. *1964*: UK.

Cocker, Joe. 'You Are So Beautiful.' A&M 1641. *1975*: USA.

Cohen, Leonard. 'Suzanne.' *Songs of Leonard Cohen*. Columbia 9533. *1968*: USA.

Conte, Paolo. 'Bartali.' *The Best of Paolo Conte*. Nonesuch 79512. *1998*: USA.

Devo. 'Mongoloid.' *Booji Boy*. BOY1. *1978*: USA.

Dylan, Bob. 'Don't Think Twice, It's All Right.' Columbia 42856. *1963*: USA.

Dylan, Bob. 'My Back Pages.' *Another Side of Bob Dylan*. Columbia CL 2193. *1964*: USA.

Dylan, Bob. 'The Times They Are A-Changin'.' *The Times They Are A-Changin'*. Columbia CL 2105. *1964*: USA.

Ferré, Léo. 'Ni Dieu ni maitre.' *Ni Dieu ni maitre*. Barclay 70 788. *1965*: France.

Ferré, Léo. 'Tu penses à quoi?' *La Frime*. RCA 37668. *1976*: France.

Gabriel, Peter. 'Biko.' Charisma CB 370. *1980*: UK.

Gaye, Marvin. 'You.' *Anthology*. Motown WD 72534. *1989*: USA.

Gibson, Don. 'I Can't Stop Loving You.' RCA-Victor 7133. *1958*: USA.

Gilberto, Astrud. 'Garôta de Ipanema.' *Verve Jazz Masters 9*. Verve 519824. *1995*: USA.

Gilberto, Astrud, and Getz, Stan. 'Samba de una nota só.' *Gilberto-Getz*. Verve 810848-2. *1983*: USA.

Gray, Glen, and the Casa Loma Orchestra. 'The Champagne Waltz.' *Complete OKeh and Brunswick Hits*. Collectors Choice 184. *2001*: USA.

Henry Cow. 'Ruins.' *Concerts*. East Side Digital 80822. *1995*: USA.

Hollies, The. 'Bus Stop.' Parlophone R 5469. *1966*: UK.

Keel, Howard, and Grayson, Kathryn. 'You Are Love.' *Show Boat* (Original soundtrack). EMI/MGM CDP 793 306 2. *1990*: UK.

Lanza, Mario. 'Santa Lucia.' *A Portrait of Mario Lanza*. Stylus SMR 741. *1987*: UK.

Last, James. 'Blue Tango.' *Tango*. Polydor 800016-2. *1983*: UK.

Lennon, John. 'Imagine.' Apple R 6009. *1975*: UK.

Little Richard. 'Lucille.' Specialty 598. *1957*: USA.

London, Julie. 'You and the Night and the Music.' *Around Midnight/Julie At Home*. EMI CTMCD 100. *1996*: UK.

McGuire, Barry. 'Eve of Destruction.' Dunhill 4009. *1965*: USA.

Miller, Glenn. 'Moonlight Serenade.' HMV BD 5942. 1954: UK.

Mitchell, Joni. 'Nathan La Franeer.' *Joni Mitchell*. Reprise 6293. *1968*: USA.

Montand, Yves. 'Barbara.' *Montand chante Prévert*. Sony Columbia 488 903 2. *1990*: France.

Mothers of Invention. *We're Only in It for the Money*. Verve 5045. *1968*: USA.

Pavarotti, Luciano. 'Torna a Surriento.' *The Pavarotti Collection*. Stylus SMR 8617. *1986*: UK.

Pickett, Wilson. 'In the Midnight Hour.' Atlantic 2289. *1965*: USA.

Presley, Elvis. 'Jailhouse Rock.' RCA 47-7035. *1957*: USA.

Procol Harum. 'A Whiter Shade of Pale.' Deram DM 126. *1967*: UK.

Robbins, Marty. 'Ballad of the Alamo.' *Under Western Skies*. Bear Family 15646. *1998*: Germany.

Rolling Stones, The. 'Angie.' Rolling Stones RS 19105. *1973*: UK.

Rolling Stones, The. '(I Can't Get No) Satisfaction.' Decca F 12220. *1965*: UK.

Rolling Stones, The. 'Sympathy for the Devil.' *Beggars Banquet*. Decca SKL 4955. *1968*: UK.

Rolling Stones, The. 'You Can't Always Get What You Want.' *Let It Bleed*. Decca SKL 5025. *1969*: UK.

Sedaka, Neil. 'Calendar Girl.' RCA 7829. *1960*: USA.

Shadows, The. 'Apache.' Columbia DB 4484. *1960*: UK.

Simon, Carly. 'You Belong to Me.' Elektra 45477. *1978*: USA.

Simon and Garfunkel. 'The Sound of Silence.' Columbia 43396. *1965*: USA.

Sinatra, Frank. 'Let's Do It, Let's Fall in Love.' *Sinatra in Hollywood 1940–1964*. Warner Brothers 78285. *2002*: USA.

Sinatra, Frank. 'You Are Too Beautiful.' *Collection: Frank Sinatra – The Love Songs*. EMI CDP 748 616 2. *1987*: UK.

Stylistics, The. 'You Are Beautiful.' *All About Love*. Contour CN 2044. *1981*: UK.

Stylistics, The. 'You Are Everything.' Avco 4581. *1971*: USA.

Supremes, The. 'You Keep Me Hangin' On.' Motown 1101. *1966*: USA.

Trenet, Charles. 'Douce France.' *Le Fou Chantant, Vol. 3 (1945–50)*. EMI 790 633 2. *1990*: France.

Veloso, Caetano. 'Giulietta Masina.' *Caetano*. PolyGram 832938. *1990*: Brazil.

Villa, Claudio. 'Serenata celeste.' *I Successi*. Replay 2126597. *1991*: Italy.

Weather Report. 'Black Market.' *Black Market*. Columbia CK-34099. *1991*: USA.

Wonder, Stevie. 'You Are the Sunshine of My Life.' Tamla 54232. *1973*: USA.

Wynette, Tammy. 'You and Me.' Epic 50264. *1976*: USA.

Zé, Tom. 'Brigitte Bardot.' *Serie Dois Momentos, Vol. 1*. WEA International 84242. *2000*: Brazil.

UMBERTO FIORI with DAVE LAING

Index

Page numbers in bold indicate major headwords.
Page numbers in italic indicate musical examples and tables.

Index

Index

Index